OXFORD EU LAW LIBRARY

General Editors

DAVID ANDERSON QC

Barrister at Brick Court Chambers and
Visiting Professor of Law at King's College London

PIET EECKHOUT

Professor of Law at University College London

EU Justice and Home Affairs Law

Volume I: EU Immigration and Asylum Law

Fourth Edition

OXFORD EUROPEAN UNION LAW LIBRARY

The aim of this series is to publish important and original studies of the various branches of EC and EU law. Each work provides a clear, concise, and critical exposition of the law in its social, economic, and political context, at a level which will interest the advanced student, the practitioner, the academic, and government and community officials. Formerly the Oxford European Community Law Library.

The General Principles of EU Law
Second edition
Takis Tridimas

EU Securities and Financial Markets Regulation
Third edition
Niamh Moloney

EU Procedural Law
Koen Lenaerts, Ignace Maselis,
and Kathleen Gutman
Edited by Janek Tomasz Nowak

EU Anti-Discrimination Law
Second edition
Evelyn Ellis and Philippa Watson

The EU Common Security and Defence Policy
Panos Koutrakos

EU Employment Law
Fourth edition
Catherine Barnard

EU External Relations Law
Second edition
Piet Eeckhout

The EC Common Fisheries Policy
Robin Churchill and Daniel Owen

Goyder's EC Competition Law
Fifth edition
Joanna Goyder and Albertina Albors-Llorens

EC Customs Law
Second edition
Timothy Lyons QC

The European Union and its Court of Justice
Second edition
Anthony Arnull

Directives in EC Law
Second edition
Sacha Prechal

EC Company Law
Vanessa Edwards

EC Agricultural Law
Second edition
J.A. Usher

The Law of Money and Financial Services in the EC
Second edition
J.A. Usher

Workers, Establishment, and Services in the European Union
Robin C.A. White

EU Justice and Home Affairs Law

Volume I: EU Immigration and Asylum Law

Fourth Edition

STEVE PEERS

Professor of Law
University of Essex

OXFORD

UNIVERSITY PRESS

OXFORD

UNIVERSITY PRESS

Great Clarendon Street, Oxford, OX2 6DP,
United Kingdom

Oxford University Press is a department of the University of Oxford.
It furthers the University's objective of excellence in research, scholarship,
and education by publishing worldwide. Oxford is a registered trade mark of
Oxford University Press in the UK and in certain other countries

© S. Peers 2016

The moral rights of the author have been asserted

First Edition published in 1999
Second Edition published in 2006
Third Edition published in 2011
Fourth Edition published in 2016

Impression: 1

Published in the United States of America by Oxford University Press
198 Madison Avenue, New York, NY 10016, United States of America

British Library Cataloguing in Publication Data
Data available

Library of Congress Control Number: 2016934360

ISBN (Vol I) 978–0–19–877683–3
ISBN (Vol II) 978–0–19–877684–0
ISBN (Set) 978–0–19–877685–7

Printed and bound by
CPI Group (UK) Ltd, Croydon, CR0 4YY

To my mother Heather Bell, my wife Pamela Chatterjee, and my children Kiran, Isabella, Serena, and Sophia, with much love and thanks for your support

Preface to the Fourth Edition

In the six years since the entry into force of the Treaty of Lisbon, the European Union has developed its legal framework in the areas of immigration and asylum law, in particular adopting new rules on border controls, visa lists and legal migration, and setting up the second phase of the Common European Asylum System. There has also been important case law on all these issues, as well as on irregular migration. Most recently, the large increase in migration to the EU and asylum claims has raised great public controversy. The tension in this field between immigration control and protection of civil liberties and human rights grows ever-sharper.

In this light, the time was ripe for a fourth edition of this book, now divided into two volumes in light of the increase in case law and legislation. The focus of this book is the analysis of the developments since the Treaty of Lisbon entered into force and the previous third edition (completed in 2010).

As before, the book begins with an overview of the main themes of Justice and Home Affairs Law (in the immigration and asylum law fields) and then examines the institutional framework in these fields, followed by chapters on each of the substantive areas of law. As in previous editions, the focus is on the primary sources of EU JHA law, rather than the secondary literature; and the discussion of human rights in each chapter is not intended to be exhaustive, but to provide general background.

I am, as before, indebted to Tony Bunyan and Statewatch for continued advice and assistance. Thanks also to Ognjenka Manojlovic for help with the tables and indexes.

I have endeavoured to state the law as of 14 December 2015, with brief references to some major proposals made on 15 December 2015. Updates and analysis of later developments in this field, keyed to this book, are available on the 'EU Law Analysis' blog which I edit.

Summary Table of Contents

Table of Contents

Table of Cases

EUROPEAN COURT OF HUMAN RIGHTS

Table of Legislation

Recommendations

EU LEGISLATION (PRIOR TO TREATY OF LISBON)

Joint Actions

Joint Positions

Common Positions

Framework Decisions

Table of Proposed Legislation

EU MEASURES

Joint Actions

Conventions

Table of Abbreviations

ACP	African, Caribbean, and Pacific
ATV	Airport Transit Visas
CCI	Common Consular Instructions
CCP	Common Commercial Policy
CEAS	Common European Asylum System
CETS	Council of Europe Treaty Series
CFI	Court of First Instance
CFSP	Common Foreign and Security Policy
CIREA	Centre for Information, Discussion and Exchange on Asylum
CIREFI	Centre for Information, Discussion and Exchange on the Crossing of Frontiers and Immigration
CJEU	Court of Justice of the European Union
CMLRev	Common Market Law Review
CUP	Cambridge University Press
CYELS	Cambridge Yearbook of European Legal Studies
EASO	European Asylum Support Office
EC	European Community
ECHR	European Convention on Human Rights
ECR	European Court Reports
ECSC	European Coal and Steel Community
EDPS	European Data Protection Supervisor
EEA	European Economic Area
EEC	European Economic Community
EES	entry-exit system
EJML	European Journal of Migration and Law
ELJ	European Law Journal
ELRev	European Law Review
EP	European Parliament
EPC	European Political Cooperation
EU	European Union
Euratom	European Atomic Energy Community
FYROM	Former Yugoslav Republic of Macedonia
GATS	General Agreement on Trade in Services
GLJ	German Law Journal
HRQ	Human Rights Quarterly
ICAO	International Civil Aviation Organization
ICCPR	International Covenant on Civil and Political Rights
ICLQ	International and Comparative Law Quarterly
ICT	intra-corporate transferee
IHL	International humanitarian law
IIA	Inter-Institutional Agreement
IJRL	International Journal of Refugee Law
ILO	immigration liaison officers
JHA	Justice and Home Affairs

JSWFL	Journal of Social Welfare and Family Law
LIEI	Legal Issues of European/Economic Integration
LTR	long-term residents
LTV	Limited Territorial Validity
MEP	Member of the European Parliament
NGO	non-governmental organization
OJ	Official Journal
OUP	Oxford University Press
PCA	Partnership and Cooperation Agreement
QMV	Qualified majority vote
RSQ	Refugee Studies Quarterly
RTP	Registered Traveller Programme
SAA	Stabilization and Association Agreement
SCIFA	Strategic Committee on Immigration, Frontiers, and Asylum
SEA	Single European Act
SIS	Schengen Information System
TEU	Treaty on European Union
TFEU	Treaty on the Functioning of the European Union
UK	United Kingdom
UKHL	United Kingdom House of Lords
UKNCCL	United Kingdom National Committee on Comparative Law
UN	United Nations
UNHCR	United Nations High Commission for Refugees
USA	United States of America
VIS	Visa Information System
WTO	World Trade Organization
YEL	Yearbook of European Law

1

Introduction

Immigration and asylum are among the topics of greatest public concern. Given the sensitivity of such issues, and the initial perception that they were 'internal' issues with limited relevance, it was not surprising that they were among the last topics to be addressed in the European Union's integration project. But they have nevertheless moved up the EU's agenda.

This book sets out and analyses both the institutional arrangements for EU cooperation on immigration and asylum law and the substantive law which has been adopted in the various fields that make up this area of law. These fields are united by a series of four common and closely connected themes which are discussed in each chapter.

First and foremost, a central issue in EU immigration and asylum law is the balance between protection of human rights and civil liberties on the one hand and the State interests in public order, security, and migration control on the other. Although human rights issues arise in all areas of EU law, they have frequently been litigated in the field of immigration and asylum law. Therefore the relationship between EU immigration and asylum law and human rights obligations is analysed throughout this volume, in order to assess whether the EU is striking the right balance between the protection of rights and the interests of security and control.[1]

A second theme, now largely of historical importance following the entry into force of the Treaty of Lisbon, is the complex and often controversial interaction and overlap between the rules that apply to most areas of EU law (in particular, the free movement of EU citizens, and EU association agreements) and the specific issues of immigration and asylum law. This interaction and overlap still applies to the issues addressed in this book, because of the distinct institutional rules which applied to these areas in the past, and which were in force when much of the relevant legislation was adopted. So the relationship between immigration and asylum law and other areas of EU law is analysed throughout this book, in order to define the borderline between the two and to compare the relevant substantive law.[2]

The third theme is the continued dispute over the scope of the powers granted to the EU in the areas of immigration and asylum law, because the issues in question are considered to be central to the sovereignty of each State, and because there has often been a great reluctance to amend the details of particular national laws. This theme is connected with the other two, because Member States are in some cases reluctant to change their laws because they wish to maintain a particular approach to human rights protection. Therefore the extent of EU competence is analysed throughout this book,

---

[1] See s 3 of chs 2–7.   [2] See s 4 of chs 2–7.

in order to suggest a coherent interpretation of the scope of that competence in light of the text and context of the Treaties.[3]

Finally, the fourth theme is the convoluted territorial scope of EU immigration and asylum law, which has several elements. First of all, the underlying objections of some Member States to any EU obligations in these areas of law resulted in the creation of a complex series of 'opt-outs' for the UK, Ireland, and Denmark. Secondly, with the 2004, 2007, and 2013 enlargements of the EU, there was a lengthy delay before some areas of the law in this area applied to the new Member States (and some of those new Member States are still not covered by all of the EU laws in this area). A similar delay will apply to any future enlargements. Thirdly, Norway, Iceland, Switzerland, and Liechtenstein are very closely associated with parts of EU law in this area, but not at all associated with the other parts of that law. Therefore, the territorial scope of EU immigration and asylum law measures is explained throughout this book, so that readers can, if they wish, determine which rules apply to a particular State (or States).[4]

The entry into force of the Treaty of Amsterdam in 1999 created hopes that EU decision-making on JHA matters would be more open, that judicial control in this area would be improved, and that the substantive EU measures to be adopted would strike an acceptable balance between the protection of human rights and civil liberties and the interests of migration control and ensuring public security. Unfortunately, in practice, taken as a whole, there were widespread doubts about the adequacy of the substantive standards adopted by the EU from 1999 to 2009 in many areas of JHA law, and the democratic and judicial controls over the adoption, interpretation, and legality of EC and EU acts were by and large clearly deficient. Therefore there was a continued imbalance in both the substantive and institutional JHA law of the European Union, favouring repressive values and principles over other values and principles long established in European societies, and in particular over the human rights which the European Union claims to respect.

However, the entry into force of the Treaty of Lisbon brought the possibility of fundamental change in this area, in light of the improved rules on decision-making, judicial accountability, and human rights protection set out in the Treaty. Over six years have passed since then, and the record is mixed. Moreover, as this book went to press, tensions between human rights protection and immigration control flared up as a large increase in migration and asylum claims in the EU put great strains on the EU's Schengen system as well as its policies on asylum and irregular migration. This volume aims to assess the strengths and weaknesses of the law in this complex and controversial field.

---

[3] See s 2.3 of chs 2–7.   [4] See s 2.4 of chs 2–7.

2

Institutional Framework

2.1 Introduction

The central theme in the institutional development of EU Justice and Home Affairs (JHA) law has been the debate as to whether the law in this area should be adopted and applied on an 'intergovernmental' basis, reserving essentially all power to the national governments of the Member States, or instead on the basis of the supranational 'Community method', which gives much of the power instead to the more integration-minded EU institutions (the Commission, the European Parliament, and the EU's Court of Justice). Before the mid-2000s, the EU framework for the adoption of EU immigration and asylum law largely took an intergovernmental approach, allowing national executives to agree on measures without the usual level of control exercised by national parliaments and national courts, and without sufficient controls exercised by the European Parliament or the EU courts. The key reason for establishing an intergovernmental system was (some) Member States' view that these issues are so central to their sovereignty that the supranational Community method should not be applied. The intergovernmental approach impacted on the content of policy: unsurprisingly, the national ministries took this opportunity to focus on migration control objectives, arguably at the expense of a more balanced approach. But measures in this area also raise acute issues concerning human rights protection, legitimacy, and accountability, simply due to their subject-matter. Furthermore, the practical effectiveness of an intergovernmental approach was questioned.

The Treaty of Lisbon attempted to address a number of these concerns, by fully rolling out the EU decision-making process to those areas of immigration law where it did not yet apply, extending the jurisdiction of the EU courts, and increasing the level of human rights protection by means of making the EU's Charter of Fundamental Rights binding and planning EU accession to the European Convention on Human Rights (ECHR). This greater application of the traditional 'Community method' to this area was facilitated by retaining the existing opt-outs for those Member States (the UK, Ireland, and Denmark) which were reluctant to see this method applied to immigration and asylum law to stand aside and not participate fully in the EU's policies.

Because of continuing disputes between Member States on JHA institutional issues and the resulting renegotiations of the basic legal framework concerning JHA as set out in the Treaties establishing the EU, the institutional framework for EU JHA law is historically complex, in particular due to its use of different rules over time regarding decision-making, jurisdiction of the EU courts, legal instruments and their legal effect, and territorial scope. This chapter examines first of all the historical development of the institutional framework in this area, while fully examining the interpretation of the current rules as set out in the Treaty of Lisbon. It next looks at issues of EC and EU competence, the rules concerning the non-participation of some Member States from aspects of JHA cooperation, and the inclusion of some non-Member States (Norway, Iceland, Switzerland, Liechtenstein) in aspects of those rules. The chapter then provides an overview of: the rules concerning human rights protection in EU law; the division and overlap between the rules concerning JHA cooperation and other areas of EU law; the use of the EU budget to fund JHA cooperation; and the external relations aspects of JHA cooperation. Chapters 3–7 then follow the same structure, examining five particular topics from the same perspective, as well as analysing in detail the particular EU measures in each field. This chapter also provides a specific overview of the issues of transparency and legitimacy in EU Justice and Home Affairs Law.

Due to the division of the book into two volumes, the institutional chapter in this volume focuses on the general JHA institutional framework, as well as the institutional issues of particular relevance to immigration and asylum law. This includes the issues of particular relevance to civil law, since it has traditionally been bracketed with immigration and asylum issues. The parallel chapter in the second volume focuses on the issues specific to policing and criminal law.

2.2 Overview of the Institutional Framework

The European Communities were originally established in the form of three treaties: the Treaty establishing the European Coal and Steel Community (ECSC), in force in 1952, later joined by the Treaties establishing the European Economic Community (EEC) and the European Atomic Energy Community (Euratom), both in force in 1958. The ECSC Treaty expired in 2002, and the EEC Treaty (later renamed the European Community, or EC Treaty) has been the subject of five substantial amendments.

First of all, the Single European Act (SEA), which entered into force on 1 July 1987, focused on the completion of the internal market by the end of 1992. Secondly, the Treaty on European Union (TEU), or Maastricht Treaty, which entered into force on 1 November 1993, focused on the creation of economic and monetary union and set up special legal frameworks for the adoption of rules concerning a Common Foreign and Security Policy (CFSP) and Justice and Home Affairs in the new Treaty on European Union,[1] which stood alongside (but also amended) the three Community treaties.[2] Because of the different rules governing the adoption of measures concerning economic integration in the Community treaties, as compared to the rules concerning the CFSP and JHA, it was often suggested that the TEU created a sort of 'Greek temple' structure with 'three pillars', which comprised in turn the Community treaties (first pillar), CFSP (second pillar), and JHA (third pillar). This temple structure was held together by common core rules in the TEU concerning the foundations of the Union on the one hand,[3] and the final provisions of the TEU (addressing issues such as accession to the EU and amendment of the Treaties) on the other.[4]

---

[1] Respectively Arts J–J.11 TEU and K–K.9 TEU, as originally introduced by the Maastricht Treaty.
[2] Arts G, H, and I of the TEU, as originally introduced by the Maastricht Treaty, amended the three Community treaties.
[3] Arts A–F TEU, as originally introduced by the Maastricht Treaty.
[4] Arts L–S TEU, as originally introduced by the Maastricht Treaty.

Thirdly, the Treaty of Amsterdam, which entered into force 1 May 1999,[5] transferred part of the third pillar (dealing with immigration, asylum, and civil law) to the EC Treaty, subject to specific rules which differed considerably, at least initially, from the normal rules which applied to the first pillar. This Treaty also significantly amended the rules applicable to the issues which remained in the TEU's third pillar, namely police and criminal law cooperation.[6] Alongside these changes, this Treaty also integrated the substantive rules (the 'Schengen *acquis*') which had been developed by a core group of Member States outside the EU and EC legal framework, due to the absence of consensus among all Member States over whether all internal border checks between Member States should be abolished. The Schengen *acquis* comprised the 1985 Schengen Agreement to abolish border checks between Member States, the 1990 Convention implementing the Schengen Agreement ('Schengen Convention'), and the measures implementing the Schengen Convention,[7] into the EC and EU legal order.[8]

Next, the Treaty of Nice, which entered into force on 1 February 2003, made modest changes to issues relating to JHA cooperation, as it mainly focused on other amendments to the Treaties which were believed to be necessary to prepare the EU for substantial enlargement, which took place subsequently in 2004 and 2007.

Finally, the Treaty of Lisbon, which entered into force on 1 December 2009, transferred the remaining third pillar to the first pillar and made a number of changes to all aspects of JHA cooperation.[9] The European Community and the European Union, previously legally distinct entities, were merged into a single entity called the European Union. As a consequence, the EC Treaty was renamed the Treaty on the Functioning of the European Union (TFEU), and the TEU was revised considerably, so that it now contains the basic rules on the institutional foundations of the Union along with (as before) the detailed rules (as amended) on the Union's Common Foreign and Security Policy.

Since the Articles of the TEU have been amended significantly twice, this book refers throughout to the Maastricht Treaty version as the 'original TEU', the Treaty of Amsterdam version as the 'previous TEU', and the Treaty of Lisbon version as the 'revised TEU'. Although the Treaty of Lisbon transformed the institutional framework applicable to Justice and Home Affairs issues, it is still necessary to examine the previous institutional frameworks briefly, because many pre-Lisbon measures still remain in force.

There were four key distinctions between the Community method and the intergovernmental system for adoption of EU law. The first distinction was the role of the EU's political institutions. Within the first pillar, the Commission, made up of persons appointed by the Council or the European Council (see below) and approved by the directly elected European Parliament, had a monopoly over proposals for measures in the vast majority of cases. The Council, made up of ministers from Member States, acted to adopt measures by a qualified majority vote (QMV) in a sizable majority of cases. Although the job of implementing Community legislation was in principle left to the Member States, there are cases where implementing powers were conferred

---

[5] See further I:2.2.2 below.   [6] See generally II:2.2.2.
[7] For the text of the Schengen *acquis*, see [2000] OJ L 239.
[8] On the process of integrating the Schengen *acquis* into the EC and EU legal order, see I:2.2.2.2 below.
[9] See I:2.2.3 below.

on the Commission, or, in exceptional cases, upon the Council.[10] Also, the European Parliament had a substantial role in the adoption of legislation, in particular by means of the so-called 'co-decision' procedure, which gave it an equal role with the Council in the procedure for agreeing a large proportion of legislation.[11] However, in the 'intergovernmental' process, the Commission had no power of initiative or at least had to share its monopoly with Member States. The Council almost invariably had to vote unanimously, giving each Member State's representative a veto. The EP was at best consulted.

Secondly, there were distinctions as regards the EU's Court of Justice. Within EC law, the Court had extensive jurisdiction, particularly over: actions to enforce EC law, where the Commission sued the Member States for a declaration that they have breached their EC obligations;[12] references for a preliminary ruling on the interpretation or validity of EC law, which could be sent by any national court or tribunal;[13] and annulment actions against acts of the EC institutions.[14] There was also a special procedure applicable in advance of the EC's conclusion of an international treaty, to determine whether conclusion of that treaty would be compatible with EC law.[15] In contrast, the third pillar provided for special rules which significantly restricted the Court's jurisdiction.

Thirdly, there were distinctions as regards the legal instruments used. EC law applies via means of Directives, Regulations, and Decisions.[16] In contrast, EU third pillar law used different instruments, although those instruments changed with the adoption of the Treaty of Amsterdam.[17]

Finally, there was a distinction as regard the effect of the law. EC law measures had 'direct effect', meaning that they are applicable in national courts and could be directly invoked as part of national law if they were clear, precise, and unconditional (although Directives did not have direct effect against private parties). National law also had to be interpreted to be consistent with Directives 'as far as possible'. Furthermore, there were detailed rules on the remedies which had to be adopted to give effect to EC law, including, in certain conditions, a right of damages against a Member State which breached EC law. Finally, EC law was supreme over Member States' national law, requiring that conflicting national provisions be set aside.

In either the first or the third pillar, the EU institutions could only act where the relevant Treaties conferred a power upon them. Each legal base conferring power set out the limits of the relevant power and the applicable decision-making procedure. Finally, since the Treaty of Lisbon subsumed the Community into the Union, this book refers in most cases to 'EU' legislation and policy, except in special cases where it is necessary to distinguish between the Community and the Union for historical purposes.

---

[10] See Art 202 EC (now Art 291 TFEU after the Treaty of Lisbon). See further I:2.2.2.1 below.

[11] The rules of the co-decision procedure were set out in Art 251 EC (now the ordinary legislative procedure, as set out in Art 294 TFEU, after the Treaty of Lisbon).

[12] Art 226 EC; see also Art 227 EC (Member States suing Member States) and Art 228 EC (power to impose fines and penalties if Member States disobey an Art 226 ruling). See now Arts 258–60 TFEU after the Treaty of Lisbon, which also amended these provisions to some extent.

[13] Art 234 EC, now Art 267 TFEU after the Treaty of Lisbon.

[14] Art 230 EC. See also Art 232 EC (actions for failure to act) and Art 235 EC (actions for damages against the EC institutions). These provisions are respectively now Arts 263, 265, and 268 TFEU after the Treaty of Lisbon.

[15] Art 300 EC (now Art 218(11) TFEU after the Treaty of Lisbon).

[16] See Art 249 EC (now Art 288 TFEU after the Treaty of Lisbon).   [17] I:2.2.2.2 below.

2.2.1 Framework prior to the Treaty of Amsterdam

2.2.1.1 Framework prior to the Maastricht Treaty

Informal cooperation on JHA matters began in the 1960s and 1970s, when various drafts of a Convention addressing fraud against the EEC budget were considered, although not agreed.[18] Member States also signed Conventions beginning as far back as 1968 on civil law issues.

Prior to the Maastricht Treaty, the formal role of the EC institutions in JHA cooperation was nil. All negotiations were treated as discussions between the Member States, and any resulting acts were classified as public international law, not EC law. All agreements had to be reached unanimously. The Commission was an observer in these talks and the EP was occasionally asked for its opinion. Nor was there any role for the EC institutions in the 1985 Schengen Agreement or the 1990 Schengen Convention. As for the EU's Court of Justice, there was no interest in giving it jurisdiction to interpret intergovernmental measures, except for those dealing with civil cooperation.[19]

Furthermore, only a limited range of instruments were used during this 'informal' intergovernmental period. The only hard-law instruments adopted were Conventions, which are a standard form of international treaty. Although ten such Conventions were agreed before 1993 (excluding the Schengen Conventions, as they were not in principle agreed among all Member States), mostly within the framework of 'European Political Cooperation' (EPC), the original system for EU foreign policy cooperation, only the Rome and Dublin Conventions (dealing respectively with conflict of law in contractual disputes and allocation of responsibility over asylum applications) were ever ratified.[20] Otherwise there was occasional use of 'soft-law' Resolutions and Recommendations of interior ministers of the Member States.

Finally, the legal effect of the various measures adopted was up to national law to determine. So those Member States taking a 'dualist' view of the effect of public international law required changes to their national law before a Convention could take effect in their domestic legal order, and those taking a 'monist' view of public international law saw each Convention as an essential part of their legal system. Since the soft law measures were not binding, their effect in practice depended upon how many Member States wished to implement them.

2.2.1.2 Framework in the Maastricht Treaty

The intergovernmental approach was entrenched by the Maastricht Treaty, which effectively established a 'formal intergovernmental' system for JHA cooperation. While some Member States wished substantial amounts of this cooperation to take place within the framework of the supranational EC Treaty, other Member States wanted no application of the EC method whatsoever to JHA issues. In a compromise agreement, certain

---

[18]　For further detail, see p 9 of the first edition of this book.　　[19]　See II:2.2.1.2.
[20]　See ch 8 of volume 2 and ch 5 of this volume respectively; on the other Conventions see ch 3 of this volume.

aspects of visa policy were included within the EC Treaty, but all other measures remained subject to the intergovernmental system established by the Maastricht Treaty.

As noted above, the Maastricht Treaty consisted of a single Treaty—the Treaty on European Union—ostensibly governing all aspects of integration among the EC's Member States, but this Treaty contained three separate approaches to integration, commonly referred to as 'pillars'.[21] The rules governing the bulk of JHA cooperation constituted the third pillar. By way of exception, two provisions inserted into the EC Treaty addressed specific issues related to visas (the adoption of a visa blacklist, and a common visa format).[22]

The specific provisions of the original version of the third pillar rules began with the original Article K TEU, which formally established JHA cooperation as part of the European Union process. Article K.1 then listed nine items which the Member States regarded as matters of 'common interest', '[f]or the purposes of achieving the objectives of the Union, in particular for the free movement of persons, and without prejudice to the powers of the European Community', which included: asylum policy; rules on crossing of external borders; and immigration policy. In practice, very few measures on immigration or asylum issues were adopted pursuant to this framework, so it is discussed in detail only in the parallel chapter in the second volume of this book.

2.2.2 Treaty of Amsterdam

During negotiation of the Treaty of Amsterdam,[23] amendments to the JHA provisions of the TEU became a key issue, in particular on the grounds that: the objectives of JHA cooperation were not clear; the institutional roles were ill-defined and left in part for future negotiation; the legal effect of the new instruments was ambiguous; and aspects of the third pillar/first pillar borderline were controversial.

However, Member States were split on the issue of how decisively to introduce elements of the Community method to this area, and how much intergovernmentalism to retain. Also, the Member States participating in the Schengen Convention wanted to integrate the Convention and its associated implementing measures (the Schengen *acquis*) into the EU legal system. However, the UK and Ireland were not participants in the Schengen rules, and one Schengen participant (Denmark) had reservations about the legal effect of integrating portions of the Schengen *acquis* into EC law, consistent with its previous objections to the transfer of any third pillar matters to the first pillar.[24] Furthermore, most Member States wished to confirm that the EC Treaty required the abolition of all internal border controls,[25] but the UK and Ireland still resisted this interpretation.

---

[21] On the 'pillar structure', see R McMahon, 'Maastricht's Third Pillar: Load-Bearing or Purely Decorative?' (1995) 22 LIEI 1:51; P Muller-Graff, 'The Legal Bases of the Third Pillar and its Position in the Framework of the Union Treaty' (1994) 29 CMLRev 493; D Curtin, 'The Constitutional Structure of the Union: A Europe of Bits and Pieces' (1993) 30 CMLRev 17; and E Denza, *The Intergovernmental Pillars of the European Union* (OUP, 2002), ch 1.

[22] Art 100c and 100d EC, subsequently repealed by the Treaty of Amsterdam.

[23] [1997] OJ C 340; in force 1 May 1999.   [24] See I:2.2.5.2 below.

[25] Art 7a EC, subsequently Art 14 EC, and now Art 26 TFEU.

The result was a complex compromise, establishing two different forms of modified intergovernmentalism, establishing opt-outs for the UK, Ireland, and Denmark, and providing for specific rules for the integration of the Schengen *acquis* into the EU legal system. Most fundamentally, the framework for JHA was split up during this period between the rules governing the adoption of immigration, asylum, and civil law measures, on the one hand, and the rules on the adoption of policing and criminal law measures, on the other. The former issues were transferred to the first pillar, where they were addressed by new rules inserted as Title IV of Part Three of the EC Treaty ('Title IV');[26] these new rules also included the visa issues which were previously the subject of Article 100c and 100d EC.[27] The latter issues were still addressed within the framework of the third pillar, but the relevant rules were comprehensively amended.[28] The Treaty of Nice subsequently made limited amendments to each set of rules.[29]

One particular feature of JHA cooperation since the Treaty of Amsterdam is the role played by the European Council, the formal name for the regular summit meetings of EU leaders, which became an official EU institution with the entry into force of the Treaty of Lisbon.[30] The European Council had long had a role approving specific JHA measures and action plans in certain JHA areas (such as an immigration and asylum plan approved by the Maastricht European Council in 1991). In 1998, the European Council became further involved in the detail, approving an action plan for implementing the new JHA provisions of the Treaty of Amsterdam.[31] Subsequently, in autumn 1999, the European Council held a special summit devoted to JHA issues in Tampere (a town in Finland), adopting a further plan which largely set out broad political principles, in particular concerning asylum, migration, and criminal law (for instance, endorsing the principle of mutual recognition as the 'cornerstone' of EU criminal law measures), which are referred to further throughout Chapters 3–12 of this book. JHA issues played a greater or lesser role at a number of later summits, which included a special summit called in the wake of the terrorist attacks of 11 September 2001, a review of the implementation of the Tampere conclusions at the Laeken summit of December 2001, and a focus on immigration and asylum issues at the Seville summit of June 2002.

Following the end of the five-year transitional period set out in the Treaty of Amsterdam, it was considered that it was time to adopt a new policy plan, and so the Hague Programme, named after the location of the informal meeting of JHA ministers which agreed most of the text, was adopted by the European Council of

---

[26] Arts 61–9 EC.

[27] Art 100c and 100d EC were therefore repealed by the Treaty of Amsterdam.

[28] Previous Arts 29–42 TEU (previous Title VI of the TEU).

[29] [2001] OJ C 80; in force 1 Feb 2003. The Treaty added Art 67(5) EC to Title IV, as well as a Protocol relating to Art 66 EC. Within the third pillar, it amended Art 29 TEU, added a new Art 31(2) TEU, and revised the rules relating to enhanced cooperation (Arts 40, 40a, and 40b replaced Art 40 TEU).

[30] Art 15, revised TEU, and see also Art 68 TFEU, discussed further below (I:2.2.3.2). Before the Treaty of Lisbon, see the previous Art 4 TEU. It should be stressed that the European Council is a distinct body from the *Council*.

[31] [1999] OJ C 19. This became known as the 'Vienna' Action Plan, due to the location of the relevant European Council.

November 2004.[32] Subsequently, the European Council of June 2005 took note of an action plan to implement the Hague Programme, which had been adopted by the JHA Council, on the basis of a draft by the Commission.[33]

In general, the role of the 'supranational' EU institutions (the Commission, the EP, and the EU courts) increased with the entry into force of the Treaty of Amsterdam and increased further in practice after that, as evidenced in particular by the Commission's decision to create a Directorate-General for Justice and Home Affairs in 2000. Nevertheless, Member States still retained greater control over all aspects of JHA integration than they did over economic integration within the Community framework. The following analysis considers in turn the general rules relating to immigration and asylum law (which also applied to civil law) and the specific question of integrating the Schengen *acquis* into EU law.[34]

2.2.2.1 General rules

Although Community instruments (principally Directives and Regulations) were now used in this field, the decision-making rules in Title IV EC remained at first, from a political point of view, essentially intergovernmental, at least for an initial five-year transitional period, which ended on 1 May 2004 (coincidentally the same date as the enlargement of the EU from fifteen to twenty-five Member States).[35] During this transitional period, the Commission shared its usual right of initiative with any individual Member State. The Council still continued to act by unanimity, following consultation with the EP, except for the issues (visa list, visa format, emergency measures) which were already subject to QMV in the Council by the end of the Maastricht period. At the end of the transitional period, QMV in the Council and co-decision for the EP applied immediately to measures concerning the conditions and procedures for issuing visas, and the rules on a uniform visa, but any further change to decision-making in the Council and EP was subject to a further decision which the Council had to adopt unanimously.[36] Late in 2004, it was agreed as part of the Hague Programme that the Council would adopt a decision changing the rules to apply QMV and co-decision to all Title IV matters except legal migration and family law, which remained subject to unanimity in Council and consultation of the EP, and visa lists and visa formats, which remained subject to QMV in Council with consultation of the EP.[37] This Decision took effect from 1 January 2005.[38]

In the meantime, the Treaty of Nice had amended the decision-making rules so that from its entry into force, civil law measures (except family law) were already subject to QMV and co-decision, and the decision-making rules on asylum matters (except for burden-sharing between Member States) would shift to QMV and co-decision as soon

---

[32] [2005] OJ C 53.   [33] [2005] OJ C 198/1.

[34] The rules on the Amsterdam-era third pillar are considered in II:2.2.2.

[35] Art 67 EC, now repealed by the Treaty of Lisbon.   [36] See Art 67(2) EC.

[37] Emergency measures (Art 64(2) EC) remained subject to QMV in Council with no EP involvement.

[38] [2004] OJ L 396/45. For discussion, see S Peers, 'Transforming Decision-Making on EC Immigration and Asylum Law' (2005) 30 ELRev 283.

as the Council adopted EC measures 'defining the common rules and basic principles' on asylum issues.[39] The Treaty of Nice also added a Protocol to the EC Treaty which required the Council to act by QMV, consulting the EP, when adopting measures on administrative cooperation within the scope of Title IV.[40]

As for implementing measures, Title IV was covered by the standard rule in Article 202 EC (as it was then) that the Commission should in principle have power to adopt measures implementing EC legislation at Community level, assisted by various committees of Member States' representatives ('comitology committees'), but in special circumstances the power to adopt implementing measures can be conferred upon the Council.[41] The case law of the Court of Justice made clear that basic rules could not be the subject of implementing measures, but must be set out following the full legislative process, and that implementing measures could not be *ultra vires* the powers delegated by the parent measure.[42] There was a basic decision of the Council setting out the types of committee which assist the Commission (advisory, regulatory, and management committees),[43] and the EC legislative process was rife with disputes about the form of committee to be established; sometimes these disputes reached the Court of Justice.[44]

The Council sometimes departed from the normal rule in the area of immigration and asylum, and was challenged by the Commission. First, the Commission disputed the decision of the Council to confer power upon itself and the Member States to implement the Schengen visas and borders rules before the Court of Justice. Ultimately, the Commission lost this case, as the Court upheld the Council's decision, inter alia, because in 2001 the issues had until recently been dealt with pursuant to the third pillar, the transitional period for Title IV decision-making was still in force in 2001, the subject-matter being delegated was clearly circumscribed, and the Council had committed itself to review the delegation to itself by 2004.[45] Ultimately, when the Schengen measures were replaced by EU codes in 2005 and 2009, these special powers were replaced by the normal rule that the power to adopt implementing measures is conferred upon the Commission.[46]

Secondly, the EP successfully challenged before the Court of Justice the validity of the special powers which the Council had awarded itself to adopt common lists

---

[39] Art 67(5) EC. On the interpretation of this clause, see Case C-133/06 *EP v Council* [2008] ECR I-3189. The decision-making rules on asylum burden-sharing shifted separately to QMV and co-decision on 1 Jan 2005 (see Council decision, [2004] OJ L 396/45).

[40] Art 66 EC.

[41] From a large literature, see M Andenas and V Turk, eds., *Delegated Legislation and the Role of Committees in the EU* (Kluwer, 2000); C Joerges and E Vos, eds., *EU Committees: Social Regulation, Law and Politics* (Hart, 1999); and K Lenaerts and Verhoeven, 'Towards a Legal Framework for Executive Rule-Making in the EU? The Contribution of the new Comitology Decision' (2000) 37 CMLRev 645.

[42] See particularly Case 25/70 *Koster* [1970] ECR 1161 and Case C-93/00 *EP v Council* [2001] ECR I-10119.

[43] See initially Decision 87/393 ([1987] OJ L 197/33), replaced by Decision 1999/468 ([1999] OJ L 184/33) as amended in 2006 ([2006] OJ L 200/11).

[44] Cases C-378/00 *Commission v EP and Council* [2003] ECR I-937; C-122/04 *Commission v EP and Council* [2006] ECR I-2001; C-443/05 P *Common Market Fertilizers v Commission* [2007] ECR I-7209; and C-14/06 and C-295/06 *Parliament v Commission* [2008] ECR I-1649.

[45] Case C-257/01 *Commission v Council* [2005] ECR I-345.

[46] See Art 33 of the Borders Code, Reg 562/2006 ([2006] OJ L 105/1), and Art 52 of the Visa Code, Reg 810/2009 ([2009] OJ L 243/1).

implementing the asylum procedures Directive. The Court of Justice ruled in this case that EC law did not include a power to adopt secondary legislative acts (as distinct from implementing measures), which the Council had argued for.[47]

As for the Court of Justice, it was also subject to a distinct regime as compared to the rest of the first pillar (or 'EC law', as it was then). While the normal rules on the Court's jurisdiction as regards infringement actions and annulment actions were applicable to Title IV, its jurisdiction over references for a preliminary ruling from national courts were highly curtailed. Most importantly, the Court was only competent to receive references from the final courts of Member States, not from every court or tribunal.[48] Another special rule on the Court provided that it had no jurisdiction 'to rule on any measure or decision taken pursuant to Article 62(1) [concerning the abolition of internal border controls] relating to the maintenance of law and order and the safeguarding of internal security'.[49] Finally, the Treaty provided for the Council, the Commission, or a Member State to request an interpretation from the Court of either Title IV of the Treaty or the interpretation of any measure based on it.[50] In practice, the Court was never asked to interpret the exclusion relating to the abolition of border controls, or sent a request for interpretation pursuant to the final special rule.

Although the Treaty provided that the Council had to 'adapt' the rules relating to the Court's jurisdiction after the end of the initial five-year transition period in 2004, the Council failed to do so, even after the Commission proposed a Decision to this effect in 2006.[51] So the Court's jurisdiction over Title IV matters remained curtailed until the entry into force of the Treaty of Lisbon.

However, the Council was able to agree in December 2007 on the establishment of an emergency procedure to govern some JHA cases referred from national courts, known in practice as the 'PPU' procedure.[52] This special procedure was used particularly in child abduction cases and cases involving the legality of continued detention.[53]

In practice, despite the restrictions on the Court's jurisdiction regarding Title IV, final national courts sent an increasing number of references on EC civil law legislation, totalling fifty-three references by the time the Treaty of Lisbon entered into force.[54] On the other hand, there were significantly fewer references relating to immigration and asylum law, with a total of only eleven cases before the Treaty of Lisbon came into force.[55] It should also be noted that the Commission brought a number of infringement actions in this area, in particular to ensure that Member States implemented Title IV Directives,[56] and that a number of annulment actions were brought before the Court

[47] Case C-133/06, n 39 above. See further I:5.7 below.

[48] Art 68(1) EC, derogating from Art 234 EC (now Art 267 TFEU). However, the wording of Art 68(1) did suggest that there was an obligation to send references in such cases ('shall').

[49] Art 68(2) EC.   [50] Art 68(3) EC.   [51] See COM (2006) 346, 28 June 2006.

[52] Amendments to the Court's Statute and Rules of Procedure, and related statement [2008] OJ L 24/42, 39, and 44.

[53] See, for instance, Cases C-195/08 *Rinau* [2008] ECR I-5271 on child abduction; and C-357/09 PPU *Kadzoev* [2009] ECR I-11189 on immigration detention.

[54] On the substance of this case law, see ch 8 of volume 2.

[55] The judgments concerned: the EU Borders Code (I:3.6 below); transit rules (I:4.2.5 below); the freedom to travel (I:4.9 below); substantive asylum law and asylum responsibility (I:5.5 and I:5.8 below); family reunion (I:6.6 below); social security (I:6.8 below); and immigration detention (I:7.7.1 below).

[56] See chs 5–7 below.

concerning inter-institutional disputes and questions relating to the UK's opt-out from Title IV measures.[57] Due to the overlap between the special rules on Title IV cases and the rules applying to the Court's non-JHA jurisdiction, there was a possibility of 'mixed jurisdiction', ie cases which arguably fell within the scope of both rules. This issue is considered further below.[58]

2.2.2.2 *Integrating the Schengen* acquis

Article K.7 of the Maastricht version of the EU Treaty, later repealed by the Treaty of Amsterdam,[59] expressly permitted Member States to engage in bilateral or multilateral action as long as this did not 'conflict with, or impede' third pillar cooperation.[60] This was particularly relevant to the development of the Schengen *acquis*, in the form of the 1985 Agreement, the 1990 Convention, and the measures implementing the Convention.

The 1990 Convention came into force on 1 September 1993 in seven Member States (France, Germany, the Benelux States, Spain, and Portugal), but was not applied until 26 March 1995. Accession treaties were signed with Italy, then Greece, then Austria, then in December 1996 with Sweden, Denmark, and Finland. The latter accession was accompanied by an 'association agreement' with Norway and Iceland, because the Nordic EU Member States were not willing to abolish the border-free agreement that they shared with the non-EU Nordic states. The accession treaties with Italy and Austria entered gradually into force between 1996 and March 1998; but by the entry into force of the Treaty of Amsterdam, the accession treaty with Greece was only partly in force and the Scandinavian accession was still at least a year away.[61]

The ongoing 'widening' and 'deepening' of the Schengen rules, alongside developments in the EU, resulted in an increasing cross-over between Schengen and JHA cooperation.[62] In order to reconcile the overlap between the two processes, the Treaty of Amsterdam integrated the Schengen *acquis* into the framework of the EC and EU Treaties. This was accomplished by means of a Protocol on the Schengen *acquis*, attached to the EC and EU Treaties ('the Schengen Protocol'). This Protocol was subsequently amended by the Treaty of Lisbon, partly to update it because the Schengen *acquis* has already been integrated into the EC and EU legal orders.[63]

According to the Annex to this Protocol, the Schengen *acquis* consisted of the 1985 Schengen Agreement, the 1990 Convention implementing that Agreement, the measures implementing the Convention adopted by its Executive Committee, and the acts

---

[57] Cases: C-257/01 *Commission v Council* [2005] ECR I-345; C-540/03 *EP v Council* [2006] ECR I-5769; C-77/05 *UK v Council* [2007] ECR I-11459; C-137/05 *UK v Council* [2007] ECR I-11593; and C-133/06 *EP v Council*, n 39 above.

[58] I:2.4.2.   [59] On the relationship between the Schengen *acquis* and EU law, see ibid.

[60] See also the parallel Art 100c(7) EC, which was also repealed by the Treaty of Amsterdam.

[61] See annual report of the Schengen Central Group for 1997 (Sch/C (98) 60, 22 June 1998).

[62] See particularly s 2 of chs 3, 4, and 7 of this volume, and chs 3 and 7 of volume 2.

[63] The Treaty of Lisbon also made amendments to the Schengen Protocol relating to the specific position of the UK, Ireland, and Denmark. On these amendments, see I:2.2.5.1 and I:2.2.5.2 below. All references in this sub-section are to the Schengen Protocol, unless otherwise indicated.

of the other organs established by the Convention pursuant to implementing powers conferred by the Executive Committee.[64]

The core of the Protocol was initially the application of the Schengen *acquis*, from the date of entry into force of the Treaty of Amsterdam (1 May 1999) to the thirteen participating Member States, within the framework of the EU.[65] Following the entry into force of the Treaty of Lisbon, the core of the Protocol is now the application of the Schengen *acquis* to twenty-six Member States (again, all except the UK and Ireland).[66]

The Protocol initially gave the Council the power, with a unanimous vote of all Member States, to 'determine, in conformity with the relevant provisions of the Treaties, the legal basis for each of the provisions or decisions which constitute the Schengen *acquis*'.[67] Such a determination was necessary because the Schengen *acquis* included measures falling within the scope of the third pillar, Title VI EU (as amended by the Treaty of Amsterdam), Title IV EC (ie the rules on immigration), and even other parts of the EC Treaty. After that determination, the EU's Court of Justice had the jurisdiction over the *acquis* that it otherwise would have had under 'the relevant applicable provisions of the Treaties', but it had no jurisdiction on 'measures or decisions relating to the maintenance of law and order and the safeguarding of internal security'.[68]

To the extent that the Council had failed to allocate the *acquis*, the Protocol established a 'default' position: the entirety of the measures in the Schengen *acquis* would have been regarded as third pillar acts for as long as the Council had been unable to agree upon their allocation.[69] Also, the Protocol gave the Council the power, with the unanimous vote of the participating Schengen States, to 'take any measure necessary for the implementation of' the integration of the Schengen *acquis* into the EU legal order.[70]

Within three weeks of the entry into force of the Treaty of Amsterdam, the Council used the latter power to adopt a Decision determining which provisions of the Schengen *acquis* needed to be allocated to the EC or EU Treaties.[71] This Decision specified that certain parts of the *acquis* did not need to be allocated because, for example, they were redundant, had been overtaken by EC law (such as most of the firearms provisions of Schengen), or had been overtaken by Conventions concluded among all the Member States (such as the asylum provisions of Schengen, which had been overtaken by the Dublin Convention). The Decision also required the Council to publish all of the Schengen *acquis* which were being allocated to the EC and EU Treaties, except for those parts of the *acquis* which the Schengen Executive Committee had decided to keep

---

[64] The Annex was repealed by the Treaty of Lisbon.   [65] Original Arts 1 and 2(1).

[66] Revised Arts 1 and 2, which are 'without prejudice' to the specific rules regarding the phased application of the Schengen *acquis* to new Member States in the 2003, 2005, and 2011 Acts of Accession (on which, see I:2.2.5.3 below).

[67] Previous Art 2(1), second sub-paragraph. This provision was repealed when Art 2 was amended by the Treaty of Lisbon, presumably because the power was now spent.

[68] Previous Art 2(1), third sub-paragraph, also repealed by the Treaty of Lisbon amendments to Art 2.

[69] Previous Art 2(1), fourth sub-paragraph, also repealed by the Treaty of Lisbon amendments to Art 2.

[70] Previous Art 2(1), second sub-paragraph, also repealed by the Treaty of Lisbon amendments to Art 2.

[71] Decision 1999/435 ([1999] OJ L 176/1). This Decision was later corrected by Decision 2000/645 ([2000] OJ L 272/24), which corrected Schengen Executive Committee Decision SCH/Com-ex (94) 15 rev.

secret.[72] Simultaneously, the Council adopted a Decision allocating those provisions of the *acquis* to legal bases in the EC or EU Treaties, with the exception of the provisions relating to the Schengen Information System (SIS).[73] As a result, the SIS provisions of the *acquis* had to be regarded as based on the third pillar. The failure to allocate these provisions was due to disagreement over whether to allocate some of them to an EC Treaty legal base (because of the use of the SIS for immigration control) along with an EU Treaty legal base (because of the use of the SIS for police investigations and in relation to criminal proceedings), and if so, to what extent.[74] This issue is now moot, since the measures applying the second-generation SIS, which were adopted on proper EC and EU Treaty legal bases, became operational in April 2013.[75]

Next, the Council had the power to decide on when the Schengen provisions would be fully extended to the Schengen states which were not yet fully participating in the Schengen rules at the time of the entry into force of the Treaty of Amsterdam.[76] This power was used in 1999 to extend the Schengen rules fully to Greece as from March 2000,[77] and again in 2000 to extend the Schengen rules fully to Denmark, Sweden, and Finland as from March 2001.[78] At that point, this power was spent,[79] and this provision was duly repealed by the Treaty of Lisbon.[80] As for the staff of the Schengen secretariat, the Protocol provided for the Council to adopt arrangements for their integration into the Council's staff.[81]

The Council also decided to adopt further measures concerning the management and financing of contracts relating to the SIS,[82] and providing a Secretariat for the Schengen data supervisory authority.[83] The latter Decision was later repealed when a joint secretariat for different third pillar data supervisory authorities was established.[84]

---

[72] The *acquis* was finally published over a year later ([2000] OJ L 239). On the secret provisions of the *acquis*, including later declassification of some provisions, see further 2.5 below.

[73] Decision 1999/436 ([1999] OJ L 176/17).

[74] On the legal bases for the allocation of the SIS *acquis*, see further I:2.4.2 below.

[75] See I:3.7 below.

[76] Previous Art 2(2). The Council had to act with the unanimous vote of the Schengen states.

[77] Decision 1999/848 ([1999] OJ L 327/58); see Declaration, [1999] OJ C 369/1.

[78] Decision 2000/777 ([2000] OJ L 309/24); see Declaration, [2000] OJ L 309/28. Note that distinct rules apply to Denmark: see I:2.2.5.2 below.

[79] On the separate issue of the extension of the Schengen *acquis* to the Member States that joined the EU later, see I:2.2.5.3 below; on the later extension of the *acquis* to Switzerland and Liechtenstein, see I:2.2.5.4 below.

[80] It does not appear in the amended version of Art 2.

[81] Previous Art 7; this was the only provision of the Protocol which provided for the Council to act by QMV. This Art was repealed by the Treaty of Lisbon, presumably because this power was now spent. For the Council decision, see [1999] OJ L 119.

[82] One set of Decisions was applicable from 1999 to 2003 (Council Decisions 1999/322 and 1999/323, [1999] OJ L 123/49 and 51, repealed as of 27 Nov 2003 by Council Decisions 2003/835 and 2003/836, [2003] OJ L 318/22 and 23), while the other has been applicable since 1999 and 2000 (Council Decisions 1999/870 and 2000/265, [1999] OJ L 337/41 and [2000] OJ L 85/12; the latter has been amended by Decisions 2000/664/EC ([2000] OJ L 278/24), 2003/171 ([2003] OJ L 69/25), 2007/155 ([2007] OJ L 68/5), 2008/319 ([2008] OJ L 109/30), 2008/670 ([2008] OJ L 220/19), and 2009/915 ([2009] OJ L 323/9)). See also Decision 2007/149 ([2007] OJ L 66/19) and the amendments to the relevant Decision of the Schengen Executive Committee ([2000] OJ L 239/444) in [2007] OJ L 179/50, [2008] OJ L 113/21, and [2010] OJ L 14/9.

[83] Decision 1999/438 ([1999] OJ L 176/34).

[84] Decision 2000/641 ([2000] OJ L 271/1), which replaced Decision 1999/438 as from 1 Sept 2001 (Art 6, Decision 2000/641). On third pillar data protection, see further II:7.3 and II:7.6.

The Protocol also set out specific rules for measures, adopted after the entry into force of the Treaty of Amsterdam, which 'build upon' the Schengen *acquis*. Such measures shall be 'subject to the relevant provisions of the treaties'.[85] So after that point all Schengen-related measures have had to be regarded as 'regular' parts of EC law (until the Treaty of Lisbon entered into force) or EU law, with no special rules applying as regards their legal base (and therefore no special rules relating to decision-making or the Court of Justice, other than those rules applicable to any JHA measures adopted in the same area). However, there are still differences between measures building upon the Schengen *acquis* and other measures to be adopted under the EC or EU Treaties, as regards the territorial scope of the measures.[86]

In practice, nearly all EU measures concerning visas, border controls, and irregular immigration adopted or proposed since 1 May 1999 have built upon the Schengen *acquis*.[87] So have a handful of measures concerning legal migration,[88] and certain measures concerning criminal procedure and policing.[89] The result is that a substantial proportion of the Schengen Convention and a large number of the secondary Schengen measures integrated into the EU and EC legal orders in 1999 have been or would be amended, repealed, or supplemented by EC or EU acts.[90]

The Court of Justice has ruled on the provisions of the Schengen *acquis* on a number of occasions, in relation to the double jeopardy rules,[91] the adoption of subsequent implementing measures,[92] the operation of the SIS,[93] the freedom to travel rules,[94] the rules on external borders,[95] and on the scope of the rules concerning the British opt-in to the Schengen *acquis*.[96] A case concerning SIS contracts was settled.[97]

The Court has not yet determined the legal effect of the Schengen measures, or any provision of them, although it has ruled on the relationship between the Schengen *acquis* and EU free movement law.[98] Also, the Court has ruled that the integration of the Schengen *acquis* into the EC and EU legal order means that the *acquis* can no longer be interpreted according to the normal rules of public international law, but rather interpreted taking the EU framework into account.[99] On the other hand, the historical context of the pre-existence of the Schengen *acquis* was one factor justifying the

---

[85] Art 5(1), first sub-paragraph, which was *not* amended by the Treaty of Lisbon. This applied despite any failure to allocate the original *acquis* (see Art 5(2), repealed by the Treaty of Lisbon). Despite the repeal of Art 5(2), the general rule in the first sub-paragraph of Art 5(1) would still prevent the adoption of any measure relating to the SIS (ie the only parts of the *acquis* which were not allocated to a Treaty base) from being adopted using the 'wrong' legal base.

[86] See I:2.2.5 below.   [87] See 2.5 of chs 3, 4, and 7 of this volume.   [88] See I:6.2.5.

[89] See s 2.5 of chs 3 and 7 of volume 2.   [90] For details, see Appendix II.   [91] See II:6.8.

[92] Case C-257/01 *Commission v Council* [2005] ECR I-345.

[93] Case C-503/03 *Commission v Spain* [2006] ECR I-1097.

[94] Case C-241/05 *Bot* [2006] ECR I-9627. See I:4.9 below.

[95] Joined Cases C-261/08 *Zurita Garcia* and C-348/08 *Choque Cabrera* [2009] ECR I-10143. See I:3.6.1 below.

[96] Cases C-77/05 *UK v Council* [2007] ECR I-11459 and C-137/05 *UK v Council* [2007] ECR I-11593. See also C-482/08 *UK v Council* [2010] ECR I-10413. See I:2.2.5.1.3 below.

[97] Case T-447/04 R *Cap Gemini* [2005] ECR II-257.

[98] Case C-503/03 *Commission v Spain*, n 93 above; see further I:2.4.2 below.

[99] See Joined Cases C-187/01 and C-385/01 *Gozutok and Brugge* [2003] ECR I-1345. In particular, the double jeopardy rules aim to prevent multiple prosecutions as a consequence of exercise of free movement rights (see generally II:6.8).

Council's decision to apply unusual rules concerning the adoption of visas and borders implementing measures.[100] The CJEU has also accepted that the Schengen *acquis* can in principle be challenged for its compatibility with EU primary law (in particular, the EU Charter of Fundamental Rights).[101]

2.2.3 Treaty of Lisbon

2.2.3.1 Overview

The institutional framework governing EU JHA law again changed significantly with the entry into force of the Treaty of Lisbon on 1 December 2009.[102] First of all, the basic rules governing JHA cooperation were 'reunited' in one Title (Title V of Part Three) of the EC Treaty, which was in turn renamed the Treaty on the Functioning of the European Union (TFEU), because pursuant to the Treaty of Lisbon, the EU replaced and succeeded the European Community.[103] In effect, the previous third pillar was transferred into what was formerly known as the Community legal order, and the TEU no longer contains any detailed provisions on JHA matters. However, the TEU still specifies that the development of JHA law as a whole remains an objective of the EU:[104]

> The Union shall offer its citizens an area of freedom, security and justice without internal frontiers, in which the free movement of persons is ensured in conjunction with appropriate measures with respect to external border controls, asylum, immigration and the prevention and combating of crime.

Although the Treaty of Lisbon contains most of the provisions of the rejected Constitutional Treaty,[105] it is not identical to that Treaty, in particular as regards the opt-outs applicable to JHA law.

Title V contains in turn general provisions,[106] rules on immigration and asylum,[107] an Article on civil law,[108] five Articles on criminal law,[109] and three Articles on policing.[110] As for decision-making rules, the Treaty of Lisbon extended QMV in the Council and co-decision with the EP (now known as the 'ordinary legislative procedure')[111] to legal

---

[100] Case C-257/01, n 92 above; see further I:2.2.2.1 above.

[101] Case C-129/14 PPU *Spasic*, ECLI:EU:C:2014:586. See II:6.8.   [102] [2007] OJ C 306.

[103] Art 1, third paragraph, revised TEU.

[104] Art 3(2), revised TEU. This provision is identical to the prior Art 2, fourth indent TEU, except for the added words 'without internal frontiers' and the replacement of the obligation to 'maintain and develop' the area of freedom, security, and justice with the obligation to 'offer' it. But note that the 'objectives' clause of the EC Treaty (as it then was) was repealed by the Treaty of Lisbon, including Art 3(1)(d) EC, which had defined the objectives of the Community. This clause had been relevant in some cases concerning the interpretation of the powers of the EC; see, for instance, Case C-170/96 *Commission v Council* [1998] ECR I-2763.

[105] [2004] OJ C 310. On the JHA provisions of the Constitutional Treaty, see the second edition of this book, pp 85–90.

[106] Ch 1 of Title V (Arts 67–76 TFEU), discussed in I:2.2.3.2 below.

[107] Ch 2 of Title V (Arts 77–80 TFEU), discussed in chs 3–7 below.

[108] Ch 3 of Title V (Art 81 TFEU), discussed in ch 8 of volume 2.

[109] Ch 4 of Title V (Arts 82–6 TFEU), discussed in chs 3–6 of volume 2.

[110] Ch 5 of Title V (Arts 87–9 TFEU), discussed in ch 7 of volume 2.

[111] The details of this procedure are set out in Art 294 TFEU, which does not differ in substance from the previous Art 251 EC.

migration issues.[112] However, unanimity in the Council was retained for the adoption of measures relating to passports and similar documents.[113] In this case, the EP is only consulted; this is an example of a 'special legislative procedures' that differ from the ordinary procedure.[114]

The revised TEU also provides for a general power to alter decision-making rules (known as a '*passerelle*'), which applies to Title V as well as most of the rest of the Treaties. This permits a decision, without Treaty amendment, to move from unanimity to QMV or from a special legislative procedure to the ordinary legislative procedure.[115]

JHA law is also subject to the general changes which the Treaty of Lisbon made to EU law as regards legislative and non-legislative acts. The 'ordinary' and 'special' legislative procedures (as described above) are subject to particular rules concerning openness, transparency, and scrutiny by national parliaments.[116] The Treaty also now provides for the adoption of 'delegated' acts implementing legislative measures, as follows:[117]

> A legislative act may delegate to the Commission the power to adopt non-legislative acts of general application to supplement or amend certain non-essential elements of the legislative act.
>
> The objectives, content, scope and duration of the delegation of power shall be explicitly defined in the legislative acts. The essential elements of an area shall be reserved for the legislative act and accordingly shall not be the subject of a delegation of power.

The legislation in question must explicitly lay down the conditions for such delegations of power, which 'may' be either the revocation of the delegated power by the EP or the Council, and/or a power for the EP or the Council to block the entry into force of the delegated act by objecting to it within a specified period.[118] The general legal framework governing the adoption of implementing measures was also replaced shortly after the entry into force of the Treaty of Lisbon.[119] The CJEU has struck down one measure adopted as an implementing act, on the basis that, since it concerned human rights protection and the use of force, it should have been adopted in the form of legislation.[120]

Moving on to the jurisdiction of the Court of Justice over JHA matters, the restrictions previously imposed relating to immigration, asylum, and civil law were removed.[121] The special 'urgency' procedure for certain JHA cases before the Court of Justice, first created in 2008, remains in force.[122] In addition, the Treaty of Lisbon added a new

---

[112] See ch 6 of this volume.   [113] Art 77(3) TFEU (passports).

[114] On this concept, see Art 289(2) TFEU.

[115] Art 48(7), revised TEU. The *passerelle* procedure requires the unanimous support of the Member States and the consent of the EP, plus involvement by national parliaments. There are several specific provisions in the Treaties which are not subject to this procedure (Art 353 TFEU), but none of these exemptions concern JHA matters. It should also be noted that in the context of enhanced cooperation, the Member States participating in that cooperation can agree that the decision-making rules will change *for them*: see Art 333 TFEU and further I:2.2.5.5 below.

[116] See further I:2.5 below.   [117] Art 290(1) TFEU.   [118] Art 290(2) TFEU.

[119] Reg 182/2011 ([2011] OJ L 55/13).

[120] Case C-355/10 *EP v Council*, ECLI:EU:C:2012:516. On the substance of the measure, see I:3.10.1 below.

[121] For the basic rules on the Court's jurisdiction and functioning after the Treaty of Lisbon, see Art 19, revised TEU, and Arts 251–81 TFEU.

[122] See I:2.2.2 above.

paragraph to Article 267 TFEU (former Article 234 EC), concerning preliminary rulings from national courts to the Court of Justice, which provides that:

> If such a question [for a preliminary ruling] is raised in a case pending before a court or tribunal of a Member State with regard to a person in custody, the Court of Justice of the European Union shall act with the minimum of delay.

This provision has been applied several times as regards immigration detention and irregular crossing of internal borders.[123] It does not create a separate new procedure by itself, but rather requires the Court to invoke the procedures (the urgent JHA procedure or the more general accelerated procedures) already set out in the Court's Statute and Rules of Procedure.

In practice, the Court of Justice has received between ten and twenty references from national courts on immigration and asylum law every year since the Treaty of Lisbon entered into force.[124] It seems unlikely as things stand that this caseload will, by itself, overload the EU judicial system.

The Treaty of Lisbon also made some changes to the opt-outs on immigration and asylum law applicable to the UK, Ireland, and Denmark. These developments are considered further below.[125] Certain amendments were also made to the Protocol integrating the Schengen *acquis* into the EU legal order.[126]

Finally, a number of the more general amendments to the Treaties made by the Treaty of Lisbon have a particular impact on EU JHA law. The amendments relating to the legitimacy and accountability of the EU are discussed further separately,[127] as are the general amendments relating to the competence of the EU.[128] JHA provisions of the Treaties are included (as they were before) by the provision on Treaty amendment, including new provisions on simplified Treaty amendment.[129] There is still an obligation to ensure consistency between the various policies of the Union,[130] and the provisions concerning the relationship between the EU and its Member States, including the division of power between them, could be particularly relevant to JHA cooperation.[131] So could the revised rules on the protection of human rights within the EU legal order.[132]

2.2.3.2 *General provisions*

The general provisions of Title V of Part Three of the TFEU concern in turn: general objectives (Article 67 TFEU); the role of the European Council (Article 68 TFEU);

---

[123] See I:7.7.1 and I:3.5 below.　　[124] See generally chs 3–7 of this volume.　　[125] I:2.2.5.
[126] For details, see I:2.2.2.2 above.　　[127] I:2.5 below.　　[128] I:2.2.4 below.
[129] The possible use of the *passerelle* clause (revised Art 48(7) TEU) has been discussed above, but it should also be noted that the Treaty of Lisbon created the possibility for a slightly simplified system for amending the Treaty provisions concerning EU internal policies (revised Art 48(6) TEU), which applies, inter alia, to Title V TFEU. See generally G Barrett, 'Creation's Final Laws: The Impact of the Treaty of Lisbon on the "Final Provisions" of Earlier Treaties' (2008) 27 YEL 3.
[130] Art 7 TFEU, replacing the prior Art 3 TEU.
[131] Arts 4 and 5 TEU. See respectively II:2.2.3.2 and I:2.5 below. On the general rules on EU competence (Arts 2–6 TFEU), see I:2.2.4 below.
[132] Arts 6 and 7 TEU; see I:2.3 below.

the role of national parliaments (Article 69 TFEU); evaluation of JHA policies (Article 70 TFEU); the creation of a standing committee on operational security (Article 71 TFEU); a general security restriction (Article 72 TFEU); coordination of national security agencies (Article 73 TFEU); competence to adopt measures concerning administrative cooperation (Article 74 TFEU); competence over anti-terrorism measures (Article 75 TFEU); and a rule reserving power for Member States to propose policing and criminal law initiatives collectively (Article 76 TFEU). Some of these provisions (Articles 71, 72, 73, 75, and 76) are more relevant to policing and criminal law matters, and so are discussed in the parallel chapter in volume 2. The others (Articles 67, 68, 69, 70, and 74) will be considered in turn here.

First of all, Article 67 TFEU sets out objectives for the entire JHA Title, replacing the two separate provisions previously set out in Article 61 EC and Article 29 of the prior TEU:[133]

1. The Union shall constitute an area of freedom, security and justice with respect for fundamental rights and the different legal systems and traditions of the Member States.
2. It shall ensure the absence of internal border controls for persons and shall frame a common policy on asylum, immigration and external border control, based on solidarity between Member States, which is fair towards third-country nationals. For the purpose of this Title, stateless persons shall be treated as third-country nationals.
3. The Union shall endeavour to ensure a high level of security through measures to prevent and combat crime, racism and xenophobia, and through measures for coordination and cooperation between police and judicial authorities and other competent authorities, as well as through the mutual recognition of judgments in criminal matters and, if necessary, through the approximation of criminal laws.
4. The Union shall facilitate access to justice, in particular through the principle of mutual recognition of judicial and extrajudicial decisions in civil matters.

All of the principles set out in Article 67 could be relevant to the interpretation or even possibly the validity of JHA measures. The first paragraph places at the centre of JHA policy the twin obligation to respect both human rights and the divergences between national laws across the EU. While human rights obligations are referred to separately in the Treaty,[134] the repeated mention of this issue in the specific field of JHA should reinforce this obligation *a fortiori* in this field. The obligation to respect divergent national traditions could be regarded as a particular application of the principle of subsidiarity.[135]

The second to fourth paragraphs define in turn the concepts of 'freedom', 'security' and 'justice', although the word 'freedom' does not explicitly appear in paragraph 2. Article 67(2) is based on the prior Article 61(a) and (b) EC. As compared to the previous Article 61(a) EC, the revised provision does not use the words 'free movement' or

---

[133] It should be recalled that Art 3(2), revised TEU, sets out general JHA objectives as part of the EU's overall objectives: see I:2.2.3.1 above.

[134] Art 6 TEU; see I:2.3 below.   [135] On which, see I:2.5 below.

make reference to Article 14 EC (now Article 26 TFEU) any longer. However, it should be noted that a link between JHA measures as a whole and the free movement of persons and the abolition of internal frontiers is still made by the revised Article 3(2) TEU. The Union's other immigration-related policies are no longer described partly as 'flanking' the abolition of internal border controls, and the objectives clause in the JHA Title refers expressly now to the principles of fairness (toward third-country nationals) and solidarity (as between Member States).

Furthermore, unlike the previous Article 61(a) and (b) EC, all aspects of the Union's policy are described as 'common', stateless persons are expressly defined as third-country nationals, and there are new references to fairness and solidarity. The first of these changes reflects the 'common' policy on visas, asylum, and immigration referred to in Articles 77–9 TFEU, and makes clear that all aspects of that policy must be considered common. Next, while Article 79(1) refers to 'fair treatment' of legally resident third-country nationals, Article 67(2) requires that *all* EU JHA policies relating to third-country nationals must be 'fair', applying that principle therefore to irregular migrants and to asylum, visas, and borders policies. This principle in part derives from the 'Tampere programme' on JHA policy objectives adopted in 1999 (see the discussion of Article 68 TFEU below). Finally, the principle of solidarity is referred to in more detail in Article 80 TFEU, and EU legislation already frequently defined third-country nationals as implicitly including stateless persons.[136]

The first part of the third paragraph (up to the words, 'prevent and combat crime') is similar to the prior Article 61(e) EC, and the remainder of the paragraph is a succinct version of the prior Article 29 TEU, with the addition of a specific reference to mutual recognition in criminal matters but without a reference to any specific crimes other than racism and xenophobia. However, mutual recognition in criminal matters is in any event referred to as the basis of EU criminal law in Article 82(1) TFEU.

The fourth paragraph is more specific than the prior Article 61(c) EC, referring now expressly to the principle of 'access to justice' and to specific principles applicable to civil law. However, it should be noted that those principles are set out again (in the same words) in Article 81(1) TFEU, and an express power to adopt measures on 'effective access to [civil] justice' is set out in Article 82(1)(e) TFEU.[137] Moreover, the reference to civil law is not exhaustive ('in particular'), and so the reference to 'access to justice' should also be understood as applying to criminal law (as regards legal aid, for instance) and to administrative proceedings relating to immigration and asylum law.

Article 68 TFEU sets out a special role for the European Council in this area:

> The European Council shall define the strategic guidelines for legislative and operational planning within the area of freedom, security and justice.

This new provision largely reflects the role which the European Council (the EU institution made up of Member States' heads of state or government) was already playing as regards JHA law before the Treaty of Lisbon.[138] In particular, the European Council

---

[136] See, for instance, Art 2(a) of Dir 2003/86 on family reunion ([2003] OJ L 251/12).
[137] See ch 8 in volume 2.
[138] On the composition and functioning of the European Council, see the revised Art 15 TEU.

had already agreed multi-annual guidelines for JHA cooperation.[139] This provision was then applied to adopt the Stockholm Programme in December 2009.[140] Although the European Council is not a legislative body,[141] such guidelines are certainly politically highly significant since they are taken into account by other EU institutions.[142] They might also be legally relevant when interpreting JHA legislation, and as noted above, some aspects of the original JHA guidelines adopted by the European Council in Tampere in 1999 are reflected in the subsequent legislation. These guidelines are adopted by 'consensus' in the European Council, although the Treaty does not expressly define this concept.[143] There is no specific role in JHA matters for the President of the European Council.[144] Article 68 TFEU differs from the prior role of the European Council in that there is a specific reference to operational cooperation, but surely the European Council would not expect to play a major role in, for instance, the planning of operations by the relevant EU agencies (Europol, Eurojust, and Frontex, the EU border agency), since EU leaders obviously lack the specialist knowledge for this, and their involvement could compromise the agencies' operations.

Article 69 refers to a specific rule for national parliaments as regards scrutiny of JHA legislation:

> National Parliaments ensure that the proposals and legislative initiatives submitted under Chapters 4 and 5 comply with the principle of subsidiarity, in accordance with the arrangements laid down by the Protocol on the application of the principles of subsidiarity and proportionality.

It should be noted that this special role for national parliaments only relates to measures concerning policing and criminal law. Article 69 is considered further as part of the analysis of the legitimacy of EU JHA measures below.[145]

Next, Article 70 TFEU permits the Council to adopt evaluation measures:

> Without prejudice to Articles 258, 259 and 260, the Council may, on a proposal from the Commission, adopt measures laying down the arrangements whereby Member States, in collaboration with the Commission, conduct objective and impartial evaluation of the implementation of the Union policies referred to in this Title by Member States' authorities, in particular in order to facilitate full application of the principle of mutual recognition. The European Parliament and national Parliaments shall be informed of the content and results of the evaluation.

These evaluation measures are non-legislative acts to be adopted by QMV in Council on a proposal from the Commission, with no involvement of the EP.[146] This is a new provision in the Treaties inserted by the Treaty of Lisbon, although in fact a number of previous measures had been adopted concerning evaluation issues prior to the Treaty of Lisbon.

---

[139] See the 'Tampere programme', adopted in 1999, as well as the Hague Programme adopted in 2004 ([2005] OJ C 53/1).
[140] [2010] OJ C 115.   [141] Art 15(1), revised TEU.
[142] See the discussion of the implementation of the programmes in ss 2.2 and 2.3 of chs 3–7 of this volume.
[143] Art 15(4), revised TEU.   [144] Art 15(5), revised TEU.   [145] I:2.5.
[146] On the accountability of evaluation measures, see I:2.5 below.

In particular, a general system for evaluation was put in place, with one JHA issue selected in turn for each cycle of evaluation,[147] and there were also specific systems for evaluating candidate Member States, the application of the Schengen *acquis*, and the implementation of commitments concerning terrorism.[148] A suggestion by the Commission for a more elaborate system of evaluating JHA policies did not attract sufficient interest in the Council.[149] As for ensuring the correct implementation of Framework Decisions in national law, Member States agreed on a largely standard approach to assessing Member States' implementation of Framework Decisions. All but one Framework Decision specified that Member States should forward information on their implementation of each measure to the Commission and Council by or soon after the implementation deadline. Subsequently, the Commission and Council drew up reports on national implementation, and the Council was supposed to assess that implementation by a specified date.[150] Applying this procedure, there have been a large number of Commission reports and Council conclusions; the Council altered its procedure in 2005 to hold a full debate among ministers concerning the Commission's assertions about non-implementation of the Framework Decision on the European Arrest Warrant.[151] However, the Council stopped drawing up conclusions on national implementation of Framework Decisions after this point. The Commission has also produced reports concerning the national application of the Decision establishing Eurojust, and of the Convention on fraud against the EU's financial interests.[152] However, there was no ongoing evaluation of the application of most Decisions or Conventions, or of the Schengen Information System, or the Schengen rules on policing, criminal law, or border control, visas, and irregular immigration.

After the entry into force of the Treaty of Lisbon, the Commission proposed new rules on the Schengen evaluation system, on the basis of Article 70 TFEU. This led to controversy since the proposal was closely related to the substance of rules on border controls, as the evaluations would be used to trigger a process of re-instating border checks against a Member State which was failing to apply the rules on external borders correctly. Ultimately the controversy was resolved by including some basic rules on evaluations in the border controls legislation, while the main rules were still contained in a measure with the legal base of Article 70. This compromise is still legally dubious, given the very close link between the evaluation rules and the substantive law set out in the legislation.[153]

Indeed, in principle it is clear that evaluation measures may not concern the *substance* of EU JHA policy, in the absence of any wording conferring such competence. Otherwise the EP's participation in the legislative process as regards the substance of

---

[147] Joint Action ([1997] OJ L 344/7). The issues selected have been mutual assistance, drug trafficking, the supply of information to Europol, the European arrest warrant, financial crime, and Eurojust.

[148] Joint Action ([2000] OJ L 191/8); Schengen Executive Committee Decision SCH/Com-ex (98) 26 def ([2000] OJ L 239/138); and Decision ([2002] OJ L 349/1).

[149] COM (2006) 332, 28 June 2006.

[150] The exception is the second Framework Decision on counterfeiting currency, which makes no reference to a report or assessment ([2001] OJ L 329/3).

[151] For more detail, see II:3.5 below.   [152] See respectively II:6.9 and II:5.5 below.

[153] See further I:3.2.4 below.

policy would be circumvented entirely, as would the role of national parliaments.[154] Similarly, any rules on the evaluation of specific legislative measures should be included within the relevant legislation.

Finally, Article 74 TFEU provides for a power to adopt measures concerning administrative cooperation:

> The Council shall adopt measures to ensure administrative cooperation between the relevant departments of the Member States in the areas covered by this Title, as well as between those departments and the Commission. It shall act on a Commission proposal, subject to Article 76, and after consulting the European Parliament.

This power previously existed before the Treaty of Lisbon as regards immigration, asylum, and civil law (see the prior Article 66 TEC), but was expanded by that Treaty to cover policing and criminal law as well, subject to the possibility that one-quarter of Member States are able to propose a measure in this area in those fields.[155] These measures must be adopted by a qualified majority vote in the Council after consultation of the EP, and are not legislative. Because of the different decision-making procedure, it is important to distinguish this provision from the substantive legal bases in Title V which provide either for the ordinary legislative procedure or unanimous voting in the Council. Given the limited wording of Article 74 and the express provisions conferring competence as regards substantive law, Article 74 cannot be the legal base for any measure affecting substantive JHA law, for instance concerning border checks, the substance or procedure relating to applications for visas, asylum, or residence permits, or the substantive rules in the civil, criminal, or policing law fields. Instead, the Article is a legal base for measures concerning issues such as exchanges of personnel or exchanges of general information (as distinct from the exchange of information on individuals for specific purposes).

2.2.4 Competence issues

Historically, at least before the Treaty of Lisbon entered into force, the most intractable issue concerning the EC's or EU's competence over JHA matters has been the distinction between the various forms of JHA competence and the non-JHA competence of the Community. This issue is further dealt with below.[156] The remaining issues have concerned the scope and intensity of EC or EU competence over various JHA matters, and (where there are distinctions in decision-making rules) the distinctions between different JHA powers. Recurring issues in particular included the intensity of EC competence over asylum law, the scope of EC competence over access to employment by third-country nationals, and the distinction between legal and irregular migration. These issues remain relevant even though the Treaty of Lisbon has entered into force, in the event that the validity of measures adopted prior to the entry into force of that Treaty are challenged.

---

[154] On the latter point, see I:2.5 below.
[155] Art 76 TFEU, discussed further in II:2.2.3.   [156] I:2.4.

In fact, many of these issues remain relevant even after the entry into force of the Treaty of Lisbon. These issues are addressed in detail in various chapters of this book.[157] So far, there is no litigation concerning any of these issues, but the application of majority voting to most areas of JHA law obviously raises the prospect that outvoted Member States will raise competence issues in the Court of Justice, for those disgruntled Member States that do not have an opt-out.

It should be noted that the Treaty of Lisbon has introduced into the Treaties general horizontal rules concerning EU competence. JHA matters are described as a 'shared competence' between the EU and its Member States.[158] The Treaties define this concept as follows:[159]

> When the Treaties confer on the Union a competence shared with the Member States in a specific area, the Union and the Member States may legislate and adopt legally binding acts in that area. The Member States shall exercise their competence to the extent that the Union has not exercised its competence. The Member States shall again exercise their competence to the extent that the Union has decided to cease exercising its competence.

It follows from the second sentence that in areas of shared competence, the EU could in principle 'occupy the field' by fully harmonizing the issue concerned.[160] However, Article 2(6) TFEU also points out that the precise 'scope' of the competence concerned is set out in the specific Treaty provisions related to each area, and in Title V of the TFEU, competence related to certain aspects of economic migration is ruled out,[161] and harmonization of national law is ruled out as regards measures concerning integration of third-country nationals.[162] On the other hand, the EU has the power to 'frame a common policy on asylum, immigration and external border control',[163] which in principle suggests that the Union should be more ambitious as regards harmonization of such areas, without *requiring* the EU to harmonize the law in these areas fully.[164] But the reference to a common policy in these specific areas does not mean *a contrario* that full harmonization of the law is *excluded* in other areas, since the possibility of full harmonization in areas of shared competence still applies to those parts of Title V as well.

Finally, it should be noted that the exercise of the EU's JHA competences is subject to the principles of subsidiarity and proportionality, which are discussed further elsewhere in this chapter.[165]

---

[157] See s 2.4 of chs 3–7 of this volume.   [158] Art 4(2)(j) TFEU.   [159] Art 2(2) TFEU.

[160] On the question of external competence, see Art 3(2) TFEU and the discussion in I:2.7 below.

[161] Art 79(5) TFEU. See also Art 77(4), as regards Member States' competence to determine borders.

[162] Art 79(3) TFEU. The EU instead is limited to providing incentives, promoting, and supporting Member States' actions in this area. See Art 2(5) TFEU. Oddly, these areas of activity are not listed in Art 6 TFEU, which appears prima facie to be an exhaustive list of areas where the EU can only 'support, coordinate or supplement' Member States' action.

[163] Art 67(2) TFEU. See further Arts 77(2)(a), 78(1) and (2)(a) to (d), and 79(1) TFEU.

[164] Although the Treaty states that the Union 'shall' adopt 'uniform' and 'common' measures in these areas, this must be reconciled with the express allocation of JHA matters to the shared competence of the EU and the Member States.

[165] See Art 5, revised TEU, and I:2.5 below.

2.2.5 Territorial scope

Distinctions in the territorial scope of JHA measures have to some extent been created outside the EU legal framework, most prominently as regards the development of the Schengen *acquis* from 1985 onward.[166]

Since the normal EU rules on decision-making, legal instruments, and judicial control have applied to EU immigration and asylum law for a number of years, the question of the territorial scope of JHA measures remains the only issue that clearly differentiates JHA issues from most of the rest of EU law. The complexity of this issue results from the reluctance of several 'old' Member States to participate fully in EU integration in this area for various reasons, the unwillingness of all 'old' Member States to apply the full Schengen *acquis* immediately to new Member States, and the interest among several non-Member States in adopting the relevant EU measures. The following overview addresses in turn issues specific to: the UK and Ireland; to Denmark; to the Member States which joined the EU since 2004; and finally to Norway, Iceland, Switzerland, and Liechtenstein. Finally, it examines the general rules in the Treaties concerning 'enhanced cooperation', which in principle allow for the adoption of measures across most areas of EU law, including JHA law, without the full participation of all Member States. These latter rules also apply whenever the UK or Ireland (and possibly in future Denmark) wish to opt in to a JHA measure that they initially opted out of.

Also, it should be recalled that even though an opt-out means that the representatives of the UK, Ireland, or Denmark respectively do not participate in the Council as regards the relevant measure, the MEPs from those states nevertheless vote on the relevant measures during the EP's proceedings; the Commissioners and Court of Justice judges from those Member States also play their normal role.

2.2.5.1 United Kingdom and Ireland

The UK and Ireland are both covered by a specific protocol on border controls, a specific protocol on the possibility of opting in to any Title IV measure, and to specific rules as regards the Schengen *acquis*. These various opt-outs will be considered in turn.[167]

2.2.5.1.1 Border controls

A Protocol attached to the Treaties by the Treaty of Amsterdam entitles the UK and Ireland to maintain the 'Common Travel Area' in force between them and to check individuals coming from other Member States, no matter what other Member States do and no matter what interpretation the Court of Justice may give to Article 14 EC (now Article 26 TFEU) or to anything else. This Protocol also specifically exempts the UK and Ireland from any EC (now EU) legislation requiring the abolition of border controls, thus overlapping with their general exemption from Title IV of the EC Treaty (now Title V TFEU). The Treaty of Lisbon made no substantive amendments to this

---

[166] On Schengen integration, see I:2.2.2.2 above.
[167] There is also a specific criminal and policing law opt-out for the UK, discussed in II:2.2.5.1.

Protocol; the interpretation of the Protocol, as clarified by the CJEU, is discussed further in Chapter 3 of this volume.[168]

2.2.5.1.2 Title V TFEU

The UK and Ireland were granted an opt-out from all of the JHA issues transferred to Title IV of the EC Treaty (immigration, asylum, and civil law) under another Protocol attached to the EC Treaty by the Treaty of Amsterdam. This Protocol was amended by the Treaty of Lisbon as regards the procedure for opting-out of measures which amend acts which the UK and Ireland are already bound by (see discussion below).[169] It has become evident from the case law of the Court of Justice that this Protocol does not apply to measures which build upon the Schengen *acquis*, which are governed by different rules on participation by the UK and Ireland.[170]

Ireland (but not the UK) also has an option to denounce the Protocol altogether, which it has not invoked.[171] An Irish Declaration to the Final Act of the Treaty of Lisbon referred to its 'firm intention to exercise its right...to take part in the adoption of [JHA] measures...to the maximum extent it deems possible', and stated that 'Ireland will, in particular, participate to the maximum possible extent in measures in the field of police cooperation'.[172]

While the default position pursuant to the Title V Protocol is that the UK and Ireland opt-out of each individual JHA proposal,[173] the UK and Ireland can instead choose to 'opt-in' to each measure. To do this, they must tell the Council within a period of three months of receiving an initial proposal for a JHA act that they wish to take part in it. If one or both of these Member States opts in to a proposal, the Council then tries to agree the proposal with their participation. However, the Protocol provides that if it is not possible to obtain the agreement with the participation of the UK and Ireland after 'a reasonable period of time', the Council may go ahead and adopt the measure without them.[174] Even if they do not opt in to a proposed measure within the deadline (or if they opted in, but it was adopted without them), the UK and Ireland may then join in later under the general conditions applying to enhanced cooperation in the Treaties.[175]

In practice,[176] the UK and Irish governments have opted into: most or all of the *first-phase* measures establishing the Common European Asylum System, but only a few of

---

[168] I:3.2.5 below.

[169] The Treaty of Lisbon gave this Protocol a new name: the 'Protocol on the position of the United Kingdom and Ireland in respect of the area of freedom, security and justice'. This book refers to it more simply as the 'Title V Protocol' throughout. All references in this sub-section are to this Protocol, unless otherwise indicated.

[170] Cases C-77/05 *UK v Council* [2007] ECR I-11459 and C-137/05 *UK v Council* [2007] ECR I-11593. See I:2.2.5.1.3 below.

[171] Art 8 (not amended by the Treaty of Lisbon).

[172] Declaration 56 in the Final Act of the Treaty of Lisbon.

[173] Arts 1 and 2. The Treaty of Lisbon amended these Arts only to update the cross-reference to the Council voting rules which apply in the event of an opt-out (now Art 238(3) TFEU).

[174] Art 3. The Treaty of Lisbon amended this Art to (again) update the cross-reference to the Council voting rules which apply in the event of an opt-out (see Art 238(3) TFEU) and to provide for a special provision relating to JHA evaluations for the UK and Ireland (Art 70 TFEU, discussed in I:2.2.3.2 above).

[175] Art 4. The Treaty of Lisbon amended this Art to update the cross-reference to the general enhanced cooperation rules. On the substance of those rules, see I:2.2.5.5 below.

[176] For further detail, see s 2.5 of chs 3–7 of this volume.

the second-phase measures; and a small number of measures on irregular migration, visas, border controls, and legal migration. The approach of the two governments has been largely, but not entirely, consistent. There have been no cases where the Council went ahead and adopted JHA measures without either Member State's participation even though they had opted in to discussions. There have been several occasions in this area when Ireland initially did not participate in a proposal, but then opted in after its adoption,[177] in each case pursuant to the enhanced cooperation rules.[178]

A significant new provision in the Title V Protocol introduced by the Treaty of Lisbon concerns the position of the UK and Ireland when a proposal is made to amend a measure which they are already bound by.[179] This rule provides as follows:

1. The provisions of this Protocol apply for the United Kingdom and Ireland also to measures proposed or adopted pursuant to Title V of Part Three of the Treaty on the Functioning of the European Union amending an existing measure by which they are bound.

2. However, in cases where the Council, acting on a proposal from the Commission, determines that the non-participation of the United Kingdom or Ireland in the amended version of an existing measure makes the application of that measure inoperable for other Member States or the Union, it may urge them to make a notification under Article 3 or 4. For the purposes of Article 3, a further period of two months starts to run as from the date of such determination by the Council.

   If at the expiry of that period of two months from the Council's determination the United Kingdom or Ireland has not made a notification under Article 3 or Article 4, the existing measure shall no longer be binding upon or applicable to it, unless the Member State concerned has made a notification under Article 4 before the entry into force of the amending measure. This shall take effect from the date of entry into force of the amending measure or of expiry of the period of two months, whichever is the later.

   For the purpose of this paragraph, the Council shall, after a full discussion of the matter, act by a qualified majority of its members representing the Member States participating or having participated in the adoption of the amending measure. A qualified majority of the Council shall be defined in accordance with Article 238(3)(a) of the Treaty on the Functioning of the European Union.

3. The Council, acting by a qualified majority on a proposal from the Commission, may determine that the United Kingdom or Ireland shall bear the direct financial consequences, if any, necessarily and unavoidably incurred as a result of the cessation of its participation in the existing measure.

4. This Article shall be without prejudice to Article 4.

---

[177] Dir 2001/55 on temporary protection ([2001] OJ L 212/12); Reg 1030/2002 ([2002] OJ L 157/1); the Decision establishing a Migration Network ([2008] OJ L 131/7); and eleven readmission treaties (see I:7.2.5). The Commission approved Irish participation by means of Decisions, respectively: [2003] OJ L 251/23; Decision C(2007)4589/F of 11 Oct 2007 (not published in the OJ); [2009] OJ L 138/53; and [2014] OJ L 155/22. See also the Commission opinions on Irish participation in: SEC (2003) 907, 6 Aug 2003; COM (2007) 506, 7 Sep 2007; and [2009] OJ C 1/1. The UK opted in to some criminal law measures after adoption: see II:2.2.5.1 below.

[178] Art 11a EC (pre-Lisbon); Art 331(1) TFEU (post-Lisbon); see further I:2.2.5.5 below.

[179] Art 4a, as inserted by the Treaty of Lisbon.

It can be seen that in principle the Protocol applies as usual to such cases.[180] However, it is possible for the Council, acting by QMV on a Commission proposal,[181] to determine that the non-participation of the UK or Ireland in the proposed amended measure makes the application of the existing measure 'inoperable' for other Member States or the EU, to urge the UK or Ireland to notify its intention to opt in to the proposal while under discussion or after its adoption.[182] If the UK or Ireland fail to do so, the existing measure ceases to apply to them.[183] The Council, acting by QMV, may also impose financial sanctions on the UK or Ireland subject to certain conditions.[184] However, it is always open to the UK or Ireland to opt in to the original act and its amending measure after the latter is adopted.[185] These provisions have not yet been applied in practice, although the UK and Ireland have opted out of several measures which amended asylum legislation in which they already participated.[186]

The key question as regards these provisions is the definition of when the non-participation of the UK or Ireland in a measure should be considered to render that measure 'inoperable' as regards other Member States or the Union, for only in that case could the UK or Ireland be excluded from the existing measure or subjected to sanctions. Given that the EU has been able to tolerate prolonged periods when different versions of the same measure apply to most Member States on the one hand, and to Denmark or associated States on the other hand, the best interpretation of this rule is that it only applies where the non-participation of the UK or Ireland would make it genuinely and objectively *impossible* for the measure to apply in different forms in the UK or Ireland on the one hand and the other Member States on the other hand. It is not sufficient that it is *more difficult* to apply the two different sets of rules. Also, it should be noted that the high threshold is an entirely objective test, applying not only if the UK or Ireland are reluctant to be excluded from the relevant pre-existing measure but also if those Member States are enthusiastic about the prospect of releasing themselves from their pre-existing obligations. The separate question of whether the UK and Ireland remain bound by a measure which they originally participated in, but which is repealed by a later measure which they did not participate in, is considered further below.[187] The Protocol also specifies that non-participation in JHA measures exempts the UK and Ireland from the costs related to those specific measures.[188]

2.2.5.1.3 Schengen Protocol

The Protocol on the Schengen *acquis* (the 'Schengen Protocol') gave the UK and Ireland the possibility of applying to participate in only part of the Schengen *acquis*, subject

---

[180] Art 4a(1). The following analysis of these new rules draws upon S Peers, 'In a World of Their Own? Justice and Home Affairs opt-outs and the Treaty of Lisbon' (2008–09) 10 CYELS 383.

[181] The Council acts only with the votes of the participating Member States: Art 4a(3), third sub-paragraph. For the applicable voting rules, see Art 238(3) TFEU. There is no role for the EP.

[182] Art 4a(2), first sub-paragraph.   [183] Art 4a(2), second sub-paragraph.

[184] Art 4a(3). Note that in this case, the UK and Ireland will participate in the vote. Again there is no role for the EP.

[185] Art 4a(4).   [186] For details of the measures concerned, see I:5.2.5 below.

[187] I:2.2.5.1.4.

[188] Art 5, Title V Protocol. The Treaty of Lisbon amended this Art to provide that the Council could decide, acting with the unanimity of all Member States, to charge these costs to the UK or Ireland nonetheless. Obviously those Member States are unlikely to agree to this.

to a decision in favour by the Council, acting with the unanimous approval of the Schengen States.[189] The Council accepted the UK's application for partial participation in Schengen in 2000, and the parallel Irish application in 2002,[190] although the partial participation of these Member States in the Schengen rules only took effect (for the UK) or will take effect (for Ireland) when the Council approved or later approves it separately.[191] Both Member States participate (or will participate) in almost all of the criminal law and policing provisions of Schengen,[192] as well as the provisions on control of irregular migration.[193] However, they do not, or will not, participate in any of the rules relating to visas, border controls, or freedom to travel. Following this distinction, they will participate in the SIS to the extent that it applies to policing and judicial cooperation,[194] but not as it applies to immigration. The Decision on UK participation sets out a more limited list of Schengen rules that will apply to Gibraltar, and provides that the UK may request the partial participation of the Channel Islands and Isle of Man in some Schengen rules (subject to unanimous approval of the Schengen States).[195]

Both Decisions initially also purported to require UK and Irish participation in measures building on the Schengen *acquis* which were adopted after the integration of the Schengen *acquis* into the EC and EU legal order. This applies to certain measures concerning the SIS,[196] to three other adopted measures (for Ireland),[197] and to all proposals and initiatives which build upon those portions of the Schengen *acquis* which the UK and Ireland participate in (each State 'shall be deemed irrevocably' to have notified its intention to 'take part in' such measures).[198]

As regards measures building on the Schengen *acquis* which the UK and Ireland are not purportedly obliged to opt into, the Schengen Protocol states that '[p]roposals and initiatives to build upon the Schengen *acquis* shall be subject to the relevant provisions of the Treaties'.[199] The UK and Ireland took the view that the *Title IV Protocol* (as it then was) therefore applied if they wished to opt in to such measures—ie they did not need the Council's approval to opt in. Conversely, the Council and Commission took the view that the UK and Ireland could *not* opt in to Title IV proposals where these measures built upon those provisions of the *acquis* which the UK and Ireland had *not* opted into. This dispute was ultimately settled by the Court of Justice, when the UK challenged its exclusion from the EU legislation on security features for EU passports

---

[189] Art 4, Schengen Protocol. This provision has not been amended by the Treaty of Lisbon.

[190] Decisions 2000/365/EC ([2000] OJ L 131/43) and 2002/192/EC ([2002] OJ L 64/20).

[191] See Art 6 of Decision 2000/365/EC and Art 4 of Decision 2002/192/EC, n 190 above. The Council decided that the UK can participate in the Schengen *acquis* which it has opted into, except as regards the SIS (which was subject to a later decision), from 1 Jan 2005 ([2004] OJ L 395/70), but no such decision has yet been adopted as regards Ireland.

[192] Art 1 of each Decision. The exceptions are cross-border hot pursuit by police (for the UK) and cross-border police hot pursuit and surveillance (for Ireland).

[193] Arts 26 and 27 of the Convention; see further I:7.5.1 and I:7.5.3 below.

[194] This was put into effect for the UK in 2015: [2015] OJ L 36/8.

[195] Art 5, Decision on UK participation.

[196] Art 5(1), Decision on Irish participation; Art 7(1), Decision on UK participation.

[197] Art 2(2), Decision on Irish participation.

[198] Art 6(2), Decision on Irish participation; Art 8(2), Decision on UK participation. On the date of application of measures building on the Schengen *acquis*, see Art 6(3) and 8(3) of the respective Decisions. On the practical application of these provisions, see s 2.5 of chs 3–7.

[199] Art 5(1), Schengen Protocol, not amended by the Treaty of Lisbon.

and the creation of Frontex, the EU borders agency.[200] The UK also challenged (and lost) its exclusion from access to the Visa Information System by UK law enforcement officials.[201]

In the Court's view, the Commission and Council were correct: in order to preserve the 'effectiveness' of the rules on the UK and Ireland's participation in the Schengen *acquis*, there was a necessary link between the question of their participation in the original *acquis* and their participation in measures building upon it. Moreover, the Court adopted in these cases a broad interpretation of measures building upon the *acquis*, ruling that both measures *built* upon the *acquis* even though they did not actually *amend* it, because they were sufficiently linked to the control of external borders.[202] This broad approach was followed in the VIS case, where even a policing measure was held to build upon the Schengen *acquis* rules relating to visas.

The Treaty of Lisbon did not amend the provisions of the Schengen Protocol dealing with this issue, so presumably the Court's prior case law continues to apply. On the other hand, the Treaty of Lisbon *did* amend the rules governing the position if the UK and Ireland wish to opt out of a measure building upon a provision of the *acquis* which they are already bound by.[203] These rules now provide that the UK and Ireland can opt-out of a proposal measure which builds on the parts of the Schengen *acquis* in which they already participate, if they notify the Council of their position within three months. In that case, the UK and Ireland will not be bound by the proposal, but the procedure to adopt it will be suspended until that notification is withdrawn (ie the UK or Ireland decides that it wishes to opt in after all) or until the end of a separate procedure to remove the UK or Ireland from their participation in aspects of the Schengen *acquis*, 'to the extent considered necessary by the Council' by a qualified majority vote on a Commission proposal. The Council shall 'seek to retain the widest possible measure of participation of the Member State concerned without seriously affecting the practical operability of the various parts of the Schengen *acquis*, while respecting their coherence', and must 'act within four months of the Commission proposal'.

If the Council has not acted within that period, any Member State 'may' refer the matter to the European Council, which must then, at its next meeting, acting by QMV on a Commission proposal, take a decision pursuant to the same criteria which apply to the Council. If *that* process fails, the decision-making procedure concerning the original proposal resumes, but in the event that the proposed measure is adopted, then the *Commission* must decide to terminate the UK or Ireland's participation in the Schengen *acquis* by the time that measure is adopted, applying the same criteria, unless the UK and Ireland decide to opt in to the proposal after all.

---

[200] Cases C-77/05 *UK v Council* and C-137/05 *UK v Council*, n 170 above. The UK can, however, cooperate with other Member States as regards EU laws within the scope of the Schengen *acquis* to a limited extent: Case C-44/14 *Spain v Council and EP*, ECLI:EU:C:2015:554.

[201] Case C-482/08 *UK v Council* [2010] ECR I-10413.

[202] For criticism of the approach ultimately adopted by the Court, see the second edition of this book, at pp 58–9.

[203] Art 5(2) to (5), Schengen Protocol. The previous Art 5(2) of the Protocol was repealed by the Treaty of Lisbon.

It can be seen that these rules have effectively replaced the previous purported obligation to opt in to any measure building upon those provisions of the *acquis* which the UK and Ireland already participate in. These rules also apply to the policing and criminal law provisions of the Schengen *acquis*, which the UK and Ireland currently participate in widely. Unlike the revised provisions of the Title V Protocol, the process of excluding the UK and Ireland from the underlying measures is intended to be automatic, with the Council, the European Council, and the Commission called upon in turn to adopt the measure necessary to terminate part of the UK's or Ireland's participation in the Schengen *acquis*.

2.2.5.1.4 Opt-out by repeal?

The final issue as regards the JHA opt-outs of the UK and Ireland (which is potentially also relevant to Denmark) is the question of what happens when the UK or Ireland are bound by an existing JHA measure, but when that measure is repealed (not simply amended) by a later measure in which those Member States do *not* participate. Can it be argued that since the original JHA measure has been rescinded as regards most Member States, its repeal is also effective to those Member States which did not participate in its repeal? This has already happened in the case of the original measure establishing the EU's visa list,[204] as well as much of the EU's first-phase asylum legislation.[205]

There is no express provision of the relevant Protocols addressing this issue. However, it is strongly arguable that in this scenario, the measure concerned would *not* be repealed as regards the UK or Ireland. The drafters of the Treaty of Lisbon specifically considered the issue of the termination of the participation of the UK and Ireland in JHA measures in which they already participate, and provided for two routes for the EU institutions to terminate the participation of those Member States in existing JHA measures, and one route for the UK to terminate its participation in some JHA measures unilaterally. Moreover, since the termination of participation of a Member State in an EU measure in which it already participates is a profound departure from the uniform application of EU law, any possibility of terminating that participation must be expressly and unambiguously provided for. It will still remain open for the EU institutions to terminate the UK or Ireland's participation in a pre-existing measure which has been repealed pursuant to the specific provisions of the revised Schengen and Title V Protocols, where the relevant conditions are met, and the UK also terminated its participation in pre-existing third pillar measures as from 1 December 2014. But there is no additional unwritten rule allowing the UK or Ireland to end their participation in existing measures which have been repealed.

In one case, the Council has consistently repealed JHA measures only as regards the Member States which participate in the measure repealing it, leaving the existing

---

[204] Reg 539/2001 ([2001] OJ L 81/1).

[205] The UK and Ireland participated in the first-phase legislation concerning asylum procedures and the 'qualification' of refugees and persons needing subsidiary protection, and the UK participated in the first-phase legislation on reception conditions for asylum seekers, but they have opted out of the legislation which repealed those measures. For more detail, see I:5.2.5 below.

measure in force as regards the UK and/or Ireland.[206] If the interpretation above is correct, this is not the exercise of an option for the participating Member States, but merely a confirmation of their obligation, given that they presumably do not wish to terminate the UK's and/or Ireland's participation in the prior legislation on the grounds that the application of two different regimes is 'inoperable'.

It might be argued that it is not practical to leave one measure in force in only one or two Member States. But in fact the measure concerned will still be in force *as between* the UK or Ireland and *all of the other Member States*, since the latter can only repeal their obligations *to each other* when repealing the existing measure, unless they validly invoke the special rules in the Title V or the Schengen Protocol to terminate the UK's or Ireland's participation in the prior measure. Those special rules were designed precisely to deal with the practical issues that might result from the non-participation of the UK and Ireland in a JHA measure, in light of their previous participation in a measure.

2.2.5.2 Denmark

The non-participation of Denmark in JHA matters did *not* begin, as is often thought, when a Decision of the Heads of State and Government (known as the Edinburgh Decision) was adopted in 1992 to attempt to persuade Danish voters to support the Maastricht Treaty.[207] In fact, Section D of this Decision stated unambiguously and without exception that 'Denmark will participate fully in cooperation on justice and home affairs on the basis of the provisions of Title VI of the Treaty on European Union' (referring to the original third pillar, which was the basis for most JHA cooperation at the time of the Maastricht Treaty). Denmark did not object to JHA cooperation in principle, but rather to the idea that JHA cooperation should take place within the framework of supranational EC law (as it then was). This view was to have a substantial effect on the position of Denmark as regards JHA cooperation in the Treaty of Amsterdam, and subsequently the Treaty of Lisbon.

In order to exempt Denmark from JHA matters that were transferred to EC law by means of the Treaty of Amsterdam, a general 'Protocol on the position on Denmark' (the 'Danish Protocol') governed Denmark's status as regards measures concerning, inter alia, immigration, asylum, and civil law (the former Title IV EC),[208] while the Schengen Protocol originally set out special rules for Denmark as regards the integration of that *acquis* into the EU legal order.[209] However, following the Treaty of Lisbon, all of the special rules relating to Denmark as regards the Schengen *acquis* appear in the Danish Protocol.

---

[206] For example, see Reg 1231/2010 on social security for third-country nationals ([2010] OJ L 344/1), discussed in I:6.8 below.

[207] [1992] OJ C 348/1.

[208] The Danish Protocol also contains an opt-out relating to defence (originally Art 6 of the Protocol, renumbered Art 5 and amended by the Treaty of Lisbon), which is not further considered here. All further references in this sub-section are to the Danish Protocol unless otherwise indicated.

[209] Art 3, Schengen Protocol; see discussion below. The Treaty of Lisbon amended this Art to refer instead to the Danish Protocol as regards Danish participation in acts building upon the Schengen *acquis*.

According to the Danish Protocol in its original form, Denmark was exempted from *almost* all Title IV EC measures,[210] except for measures determining a list of third countries whose nationals require visas to cross the external borders of the Member States, or of measures determining a common visa format,[211] as both of these issues were already within EC competence prior to the Treaty of Amsterdam.[212] In conjunction with the termination of the third pillar by the Treaty of Lisbon, the Protocol was enlarged in scope by that Treaty to exempt Denmark from policing and criminal law measures adopted after the entry into force of that Treaty.[213]

There are special rules relating to Denmark's continued connection with the Schengen *acquis*. First of all, the Schengen Protocol originally provided that those provisions of the *acquis* that were allocated to Title IV of the EC Treaty following the Treaty of Amsterdam (ie immigration provisions of the Schengen *acquis*) still continued to have the effect of public international law, rather than EC law, in Denmark.[214] However, this rule was deleted by the Treaty of Lisbon. As for measures which build upon the Schengen *acquis* and also fall within the scope of Title V TFEU, Denmark has six months to decide whether to apply each such measure within its national law.[215] If it does so, this decision creates 'an obligation under international law' between Denmark and the other Member States participating in the measure. If Denmark fails to apply such a measure, the other Schengen States and Denmark 'will consider appropriate measures to be taken'.[216] In practice, Denmark has consistently opted into all such measures building upon the Schengen *acquis*.[217]

Otherwise, unlike the UK or Ireland, Denmark does not have the ability to opt in to specific JHA measures, either when they are initially adopted or at a later date. If Denmark wishes to change this position, initially, the Protocol only gave Denmark the possibility of denouncing 'all or part' of the Danish Protocol, in which case it has to immediately apply all measures adopted in the relevant field without any need for the Commission or Council to approve its intention to apply those measures.[218] The Treaty of Lisbon gave Denmark a further option: it may decide to replace the rules concerning its JHA opt-out with a different set of rules, which is almost identical to the Title V opt-outs for the UK and Ireland.[219] The only differences between the two

---

[210] Arts 1–3.

[211] Art 4, which was subsequently renumbered Art 6 (but not amended) by the Treaty of Lisbon.

[212] On the interpretation of this clause in practice, see I:4.2.5 below.

[213] Arts 1–3. The Treaty of Lisbon amended Arts 1 and 2 to this end, and updated the cross-reference to the Council voting rules which apply when Denmark does not participate in measures (see Art 238(3) TFEU).

[214] Previous Art 3, Schengen Protocol.

[215] Art 5(1), renumbered Art 4(1) and amended by the Treaty of Lisbon as regards its scope, to refer to all JHA measures which build on the Schengen *acquis*, not just measures within the scope of the previous Title IV EC.

[216] Art 5(2), renumbered Art 4(2) and amended by the Treaty of Lisbon to refer also to Denmark's participation in any such decision. There is no indication of the voting rule applicable or what the 'appropriate measures' might entail.

[217] See s 2.5 of Chs 3–4 and 6–7 of this volume.

[218] Art 7, not amended by the Treaty of Lisbon.

[219] Art 8(1), inserted by the Treaty of Lisbon, referring to an Annex inserted by the Treaty of Lisbon. This option is expressly 'without prejudice' to the possibility that Denmark can invoke Art 7 of the Protocol in order to relinquish any form of JHA opt-out entirely.

opt-out rules are that first, if Denmark chooses this option, the previous Schengen *acquis* and prior acts building upon the Schengen *acquis* will apply fully to Denmark as EU law, rather than international law, six months after the Danish decision takes effect.[220] Second, there is no special rule on evaluations relating to Denmark.[221] Also, the Annex to the Danish Protocol differs from the Protocol concerning the UK, Ireland and Schengen in that Denmark must make a decision on whether to apply measures building upon the Schengen *acquis* six months after their adoption; it if does not, the participating Member States and Denmark 'will consider appropriate measures to be taken'.[222] Furthermore, once Denmark opts in to a measure building on the Schengen *acquis*, it must opt in to any future measures that build upon that act to the extent that those future measures also build upon the Schengen *acquis*.[223] If Denmark decides to apply these rules, then obviously they should be interpreted consistently with the UK and Irish opt-out rules, *mutatis mutandis*.

In practice, Denmark held a referendum in December 2015 to decide on whether to apply the revised rules, but the Danish public voted against. However, Denmark had not planned to request participation in any immigration or asylum measures, beyond the changes as regards the Schengen *acquis* which have been discussed above. Rather, it was planning to opt in to a number of civil, criminal, and policing law measures, which are discussed further in the parallel chapter in volume 2.[224]

In any event, there is a declaration to the Treaty of Lisbon concerning the adoption of acts which are partly applicable to Denmark and partly not applicable to that country, because they have a legal base partly regarding JHA, pursuant to the Danish Protocol. In that case, 'Denmark declares that it will not use its voting right to prevent the adoption of the provisions' which are not applicable to Denmark.'[225]

One peculiarity of the Danish position is that in the absence of a possibility for Denmark to opt in to Title IV measures (now extended to all JHA measures), the EC (as it then was) and Denmark were nevertheless willing in certain cases to negotiate international treaties regarding Danish participation. These treaties concern participation in measures concerning responsibility for asylum applications, civil and commercial jurisdiction, and service of documents, which Denmark had applied or agreed to before the adoption of Community acts on these subjects. The treaties require Denmark to apply the Community acts, with minor amendments to the civil jurisdiction rules (but not to the other two measures); moreover the relevant jurisdiction of the Court of Justice is applicable to Denmark, and has therefore been expanded pursuant to the Treaty of Lisbon.[226] Denmark may refuse to apply subsequent measures amending or implementing the EC acts, but in such cases, the relevant treaty will be terminated.

---

[220] Art 8(2), inserted by the Treaty of Lisbon.

[221] Compare Art 3 of the Title V Protocol to Art 3 of the Annex to the Danish Protocol.

[222] Art 6(1) of the Annex.

[223] Art 6(2) of the Annex. Presumably the concept of 'building upon' such an act has the same meaning as 'building upon' the Schengen *acquis* (see I:2.2.5.1.3 above).

[224] II.2.2.5.2.   [225] Declaration 48 in the Final Act.

[226] For the text of the treaties, see [2006] OJ L 66/38 (asylum responsibility), [2005] OJ L 299/61 (jurisdiction rules), and [2005] OJ L 300/53 (service of documents). The asylum treaty entered into force on 1 Apr 2006 ([2006] OJ L 96/9), and the civil law treaties entered into force on 1 July 2007.

2.2.5.3 Accession states

The Schengen Protocol specifies that all future Member States were to be bound by the entire Schengen *acquis*.[227] This was implemented first of all by the 2003 Accession Treaty,[228] which specifies that the ten new Member States which joined the EU pursuant to that Treaty applied as from the date of accession (1 May 2004) the measures in the *acquis* as integrated into the EC and EU Treaties 'and acts building on it or otherwise related to it', as referred to in Article 3(1) of the Act of Accession and listed in Annex 1 to the Act, along with other such measures adopted between agreement of the Accession Treaty and the date of accession. However, there was a delay in applying the remaining provisions of the Schengen *acquis* (or measures building upon it).[229] Those measures were *binding* on the new Member States as from 1 May 2004, but did not *apply* until a unanimous Council decision by the representatives of the Member States fully applying the Schengen *acquis* at that time and the Member State(s) seeking to participate fully. The UK and Ireland participated in that decision to the extent that they had opted in to the *acquis*. The Act of Accession further provides that the agreements associating Norway and Iceland with the Schengen rules, as referred to in the Schengen Protocol, were binding on the new Member States as from the date of their accession to the EU.[230]

More precisely, the provisions of the Schengen *acquis* and the measures building upon it which applied as from 1 May 2004 in the new Member States are the rules on: external border controls (except for checks in the SIS); certain aspects of visas (particularly the visa list and visa format); irregular migration; policing (other than hot pursuit and surveillance); criminal law cooperation (except for references to the SIS); drugs; firearms; and data protection (to the extent that the other Schengen rules apply).

Conversely, the rules on abolition of internal border controls, other aspects of the common visa policy, freedom to travel, cross-border hot pursuit and surveillance by police officers, and the SIS did not apply in practice until the later Council decision. As for Schengen-related measures adopted after agreement on the Accession Treaty, and subsequently adopted after accession, each measure indicated whether it applied immediately or after a delay to the new Member States.

Next, the Act of accession provided that until the end of 2006, there were transitional funds to assist with the application of EU law including, inter alia, assistance to implement JHA obligations,[231] along with a specific facility to assist new Member States with external land borders to apply their Schengen obligations, by funding buildings, equipment, and training.[232]

Also, a Protocol relating to the UK's military base on the island of Cyprus contains specific rules on border control.[233] Finally, Annex II to the Act of Accession contains a list of technical amendments to existing measures made necessary by accession.[234] Point 18 of this Annex lists amendments to JHA civil law measures, the Common Consular Instructions (concerning Schengen visa applications), the Border Manual (for use by external border guards), and the EC's visa list Regulation.

---

[227] Art 8, Schengen Protocol, renumbered Art 7 by the Treaty of Lisbon.
[228] [2003] OJ L 236/33 (Act of Accession).   [229] Art 3(2), Act of Accession, ibid.
[230] Art 3(3), Act of Accession.   [231] Art 34, Act of Accession.
[232] Art 35, Act of Accession.   [233] Protocol 3 to the Act of Accession.
[234] See Art 20 of the Act of Accession, which gives effect to Annex II.

Ultimately nine of the ten Member States to join the EU in 2004 participated in the full Schengen system as from December 2007, and from March 2008 as regards air borders.[235] Only Cyprus was left out of the extension of the Schengen zone, because of the practical difficulties in controlling the borders as long as the country is divided. However, Cyprus has expressed an intention of applying the provisions of the Schengen *acquis* relating to visas; the Council has not yet acted on this request.[236]

The model set out in the 2003 Treaty of Accession was largely copied in the 2005 Treaty of Accession with Romania and Bulgaria, in force from 1 January 2007,[237] and again for the Accession Treaty with Croatia, in force 1 July 2013.[238]

2.2.5.4 *Norway, Iceland, Switzerland, and Liechtenstein*

As noted above, Norway and Iceland are in a distinct position as non-EU States whose participation in the Schengen rules was necessary if Sweden, Denmark, and Finland were to be able to participate in Schengen, because none of these States wished to relinquish the existing Nordic Passport Union. In fact, Norway and Iceland had already agreed to an association agreement with the Schengen States before the Treaty of Amsterdam was signed.[239] The Schengen Protocol therefore provided for conclusion of a replacement association agreement with Norway and Iceland, as well as for a separate agreement with those States concerning UK and Irish participation in the Schengen rules.[240] These treaties were agreed in 1999,[241] and the Schengen area was extended to Norway and Iceland in March 2001, at the same time it was extended to Nordic EU Member States.[242]

The Schengen association treaty requires Norway and Iceland to apply the Schengen *acquis*, including EC measures related to the *acquis*, as it existed in spring 1999. A Mixed Committee established by the treaty is a forum for discussions about implementation of the *acquis* and concerning measures building upon it.[243] If Norway or Iceland do not accept a measure building upon the *acquis*, the treaty is terminated regarding them, although the Mixed Committee may decide to retain it in force.[244] The parties must keep the judgments of the Court of Justice, and of Norwegian and Icelandic courts, under close review.[245] If a 'substantial difference' develops in judicial interpretation or national application of the agreement, and the Mixed Committee cannot agree a measure to ensure uniform interpretation or application of the treaty, or if a dispute relating to the agreement otherwise develops, then the Mixed Committee has a fixed period to settle the dispute, otherwise the agreement is terminated.[246]

---

[235] [2007] OJ L 323/34.   [236] See I:4.2.5 below.

[237] Art 3 and Annex I to Act of Accession ([2005] OJ L 157/203).   [238] [2012] OJ L 112.

[239] Council doc 11780/97, 28 Oct 1997.

[240] Art 6, Schengen Protocol. The Treaty of Lisbon made a minor amendment to this Art, to delete a reference to the pre-Amsterdam association treaty with Norway and Iceland (ibid).

[241] See respectively [1999] OJ L 176/35 and [2000] OJ L 15/1; both treaties entered into force on 26 June 2000 ([2000] OJ L 149/36). See also a Decision on implementation of the first treaty (Decision 1999/437/EC, [1999] OJ L 176/31).

[242] Decision 2000/777 ([2000] OJ L 309/24).

[243] Arts 2–5 of the treaty; and see Decision 1/99 of the Mixed Committee, adopting its rules of procedure ([1999] OJ C 211/9). These rules were later amended by Decision 1/2004 ([2004] OJ C 308/1).

[244] Art 8 of the treaty.   [245] Art 9 of the treaty.   [246] Arts 10 and 11 of the treaty.

It is striking that this treaty, in accordance with the Schengen Protocol, was negotiated by the Council, not the Commission, which normally negotiates treaties on behalf of the EC. Moreover, although the treaty was concluded by the Council, it is not clear whether the treaty also binds the European Union as such, although the treaty does state that it creates obligations for the Community and its Member States.[247] It is not clear whether the Court of Justice has jurisdiction to interpret the agreement as far as the Community, the Union, or both is concerned, although in one judgment the Court's jurisdiction as regards the third pillar provisions of the treaty was assumed.[248]

In practice, the treaty has entailed Norwegian and Icelandic acceptance of most measures concerning visas, border control, and irregular migration, and certain measures concerning policing and criminal law.[249] Also, Norway and Iceland agreed a similar treaty on asylum responsibility, paralleling the EU Member States' Dublin Convention, which entered into force in March 2001 at the same time that their Schengen association agreement was applied.[250] Furthermore, those States ultimately agreed to further treaties the borders agency (Frontex), the EU's borders funds legislation, and participation in comitology committees connected to the Schengen *acquis*.[251]

As for Switzerland, it agreed a treaty associating itself with the Schengen *acquis* in 2004, along with a parallel treaty on its application of the EU's asylum responsibility rules; these treaties entered into force on 1 March 2008,[252] and were applied as from 12 December 2008 (29 March 2009 as regards Schengen air borders).[253] These two agreements are essentially identical to the Schengen and asylum responsibility agreements with Norway and Iceland, except that: the Schengen treaty is expressly with the Community and Union (and creates obligations for the EC, the EU, and Member States); Liechtenstein may accede to either treaty; there is an obligation to negotiate parallel treaties with Denmark (as regards matters within the scope of the former Title IV of the EC Treaty),[254] Norway, and Iceland; and the Schengen and asylum responsibility treaties are linked (denunciation of one will terminate the application of the other one).[255] A Protocol concerning accession of Liechtenstein to these treaties was agreed in 2006, and came into force in 2011.[256] Also, Switzerland and Liechtenstein have agreed a treaty with the EC concerning their relationship with Frontex (paralleling the agreement with Norway and Iceland on this subject),[257] have signed treaties on links

---

[247] Arts 8(3) and 15(4) of the treaty. On the issue of EU legal personality, see I:2.7 below.

[248] Case C-436/04 *Van Esbroek* [2006] ECR I-2333.

[249] See s 2.5 of chs 3–4, 6–7 in this volume, and 3–7 in volume 2 below.

[250] [2001] OJ L 93/38. See I:5.2.5 below.   [251] See I:3.2.5 below.

[252] [2008] OJ L 53/13 and 52.

[253] [2008] OJ L 327/15. (Decision on full extension of Schengen *acquis*). For the rules of procedure of the Mixed Committee, see [2004] OJ C 308/2.

[254] As regards asylum responsibility, the EC (now EU) also had to be party to this parallel treaty alongside Switzerland and Liechtenstein. This treaty is in force as between the EU and Switzerland ([2009] OJ L 191/6).

[255] Arts 7(5) 13, 15, 16, and 18 of the Schengen treaty and Arts 11 and 14–16 of the asylum responsibility treaty. On the specific legislation which Switzerland applies, see s 2.5 of chs 3–7 of this volume and 3–7 of volume 2 below.

[256] [2011] OJ L 160. See also the amendment to the EU/Switzerland (Schengen) Mixed Committee rules of procedure ([2008] OJ L 83/37).

[257] [2010] OJ L 243. The treaty is in force between the EU and Switzerland.

with the European Asylum Support Office,[258] and are also parties to the treaties concerning association with the Borders Funds and comitology committees.[259]

2.2.5.5 *General rules on enhanced cooperation*

General provisions on 'enhanced cooperation', ie the process of some Member States participating in EU measures without some other Member States, were first introduced in the Treaty of Amsterdam, and these provisions were amended by the Treaty of Nice.[260] These rules were never in fact used, except in the context of the UK and Ireland opting in to immigration, asylum, and civil law measures after those measures had already been adopted.[261]

The Treaty of Lisbon subsequently amended the enhanced cooperation rules again, inter alia, in order to merge the separate rules governing the former first and third pillars.[262] The basic rule is that a group of Member States may establish enhanced cooperation among themselves, within the context of the EU's non-exclusive competences, by 'applying the relevant provisions of the Treaties'.[263] In other words, once enhanced cooperation has been approved, the normal rules on competence and decision-making (eg, unanimity as regards family law measures) will apply. Enhanced cooperation is authorized by the Council 'as a last resort, when it has established that the objectives of such cooperation cannot be attained within a reasonable period by the Union as a whole', and at least nine Member States must participate.[264] Furthermore, enhanced cooperation must: 'aim to further the objectives of the Union, protect its interests and reinforce its integration process'; 'comply with the Treaties and Union law'; not 'undermine' the internal market or 'distort' competition, et al.; and 'respect the competences, rights and obligations of those Member States which do not participate in it'. But in return, the non-participants 'shall not impede its implementation by the participating Member States'.[265] The Treaties are silent on the question of enhanced cooperation *outside* the EU legal framework, but of course there are prior examples of this taking place (the Schengen and Prum Conventions). It should follow from the division of competences between the EU and the Member States that enhanced cooperation outside the EU legal framework is permissible as regards all issues outside the scope of the EU's exclusive competences (ie all JHA matters), provided that the participating Member States comply with the relevant EU law.

Member States that wish to establish enhanced cooperation must address a request to the Commission, which 'may' then make a proposal for enhanced cooperation. If

---

[258] [2014] OJ L 102. The treaties are not yet in force.   [259] [2010] OJ L 169/22 and [2012] OJ L 103.

[260] See Arts 11 and 11a EC and Arts 43–45, previous TEU. There were specific rules for the third pillar in the prior Arts 40, 40a and 40b TEU.

[261] See I:2.2.5.1 and II:2.2.5.1.

[262] Art 20, revised TEU and Arts 326–334 TFEU. There remain some distinct rules for foreign policy enhanced cooperation, which are not considered further here (Arts 328(2), 329(2), and 331(2) TFEU).

[263] Art 20(1), revised TEU, first sub-paragraph. All JHA matters are shared competences, and so are therefore non-exclusive: see Art 4(2)(j) TFEU and the discussion in I:2.2.4 above.

[264] Art 20(2), revised TEU.

[265] Art 20(1), revised TEU, second sub-paragraph, and Arts 326 and 327 TFEU.

the Commission does not make a proposal, it must tell the requesting Member States why.[266] If the Commission proposes authorization of enhanced cooperation, it must then be approved by the Council (by QMV) and consent of the EP to go ahead.[267] This process is distinct from the process of adopting the substantive proposal concerned— which could entail the application of the ordinary legislative procedure or a special legislative procedure such as unanimity in Council with the consultation of the EP (ie as regards passports). A crucial point is that *all* Member States, whether they wish to participate in the substantive measure or have a relevant opt-out, participate in the vote to authorize enhanced cooperation.[268]

All Member States can participate in discussions on enhanced cooperation measures, but only those Member States which participate in the measure in question can vote.[269] Any acts adopted within the framework of enhanced cooperation only bind the participating Member States, and new Member States joining the EU after the adoption of those acts are not obliged to apply them.[270]

If Member States which did not participate in an enhanced cooperation measure originally wish to join in later, the Treaty provides that enhanced cooperation must 'be open at any time to all Member States'.[271] In particular, Member States joining enhanced cooperation after it is established must comply with the conditions of participation and any acts already adopted. The Commission and the participating Member States must 'promote participation by as many Member States as possible'.[272] A Member State wishing to join in must notify the Council and Commission. The Commission 'shall…confirm the participation of the Member State confirmed' within four months of this notification, and shall adopt 'any transitional measures necessary' to this end.[273] If the Commission rejects the application on the ground that the Member State concerned does not satisfy the conditions for participation, it shall indicate what further 'arrangements' must be adopted in order to fulfil those conditions, and set a deadline to re-examine the request. If the Commission at that point still rejects the application, the Member State concerned may appeal to the Council, which will decide on its participation by means of the vote of the participating Member States.[274]

Finally, the participants in enhanced cooperation can decide, acting unanimously, to change the decision-making rules governing the adoption of the substantive measures concerned from unanimity into QMV, or from a special legislative procedure into an ordinary legislative procedure. Unlike the general *passerelle* clause in the Treaties,[275] there is no requirement for consent of the EP or control by national parliaments. In the

---

[266] Art 329(1) TFEU, first sub-paragraph. There is no time limit set for the Commission's decision as to whether to propose enhanced cooperation or not.

[267] Art 329(1) TFEU, second sub-paragraph.

[268] See the distinction implicit in Art 20(2) and (3), revised TEU, and also *a contrario* the references to the voting rule in Art 330 TEU (as distinct from Art 329 TFEU) in Art 331(1) and 333(1) TFEU.

[269] Art 20(3), revised TEU and Art 330 TFEU, which refers to the rule recalculating Council voting weights to take account of non-participation of some Member States in adoption of measures, which is also applicable in the case of British, Danish, and Irish opt-outs (Art 238(3) TFEU).

[270] Art 20(4), revised TEU.   [271] Art 20(1), revised TEU, second sub-paragraph.

[272] Art 328 TFEU.   [273] Art 331(1) TFEU, first and second sub-paragraphs.

[274] Art 331(1) TFEU, third sub-paragraph.   [275] Art 48(7), revised TEU.

JHA area, this provision would permit a shift to QMV and/or the ordinary legislative procedure as regards passports et al.

Following the entry into force of the Treaty of Lisbon, the enhanced cooperation provisions have been used three times: as regards the Rome III Regulation on choice of law in divorce; patents; and the financial transaction tax.[276] In general, to date the use of enhanced cooperation has been modest, and it seems likely to remain confined to areas where unanimous voting applies—meaning that in the field of immigration and asylum law, it could only be applied in practice as regards passports.

2.3 Human Rights

The issue of whether EU JHA measures are consistent with human rights obligations and principles is a key theme of this book.[277] In section 3 of Chapters 3–7 of this volume and 3–8 of volume 2, the relevant human rights obligations are set out, and subsequently the compatibility of EU measures with those obligations is assessed in detail. But in order to lay the foundations for this analysis, it is necessary to set out the current framework for the protection of human rights in the EU legal order. This analysis examines in turn the overall legal framework, followed by the issues of the sources of EU human rights protection, the scope of EU human rights protection, the derogations and limitations upon human rights within the EU legal order, and the legal effect of EU human rights rules.

Since the entry into force of the Treaty of Lisbon, the basic legal framework on this issue is established by Article 6 TEU, as follows:

1. The Union recognises the rights, freedoms and principles set out in the Charter of Fundamental Rights of the European Union of 7 December 2000, as adapted at Strasbourg, on 12 December 2007, which shall have the same legal value as the Treaties.

   The provisions of the Charter shall not extend in any way the competences of the Union as defined in the Treaties.

   The rights, freedoms and principles in the Charter shall be interpreted in accordance with the general provisions in Title VII of the Charter governing its interpretation and application and with due regard to the explanations referred to in the Charter, that set out the sources of those provisions.

2. The Union shall accede to the European Convention for the Protection of Human Rights and Fundamental Freedoms. Such accession shall not affect the Union's competences as defined in the Treaties.

3. Fundamental rights, as guaranteed by the European Convention for the Protection of Human Rights and Fundamental Freedoms and as they result from the constitutional traditions common to the Member States, shall constitute general principles of the Union's law.

---

[276] On the substance of the Rome III Reg, see II:8.6.

[277] From a huge literature on human rights as general principles of EU law, see B de Witte, 'Past and Future Role of the European Court of Justice in the Protection of Human Rights' in P Alston, ed., *The EU and Human Rights* (OUP, 1999), 859, and T Tridimas, *The General Principles of EU Law*, 2nd edn (OUP, 2006), with further references. On the EU Charter of Rights, see S Peers, T Hervey, J Kenner, and A Ward, eds., *Commentary on the EU Charter of Fundamental Rights* (Hart, 2014).

There are therefore three basic sources of human rights protection in the EU legal order (the Charter, the ECHR, and the general principles of EU law), although these sources overlap considerably. These three basic sources will be examined in turn.

The first of the three basic sources to be established was the general principles of EU law. Although the initial EEC Treaty made no reference to human rights, the Court of Justice asserted from the late 1960s that the general principles of EC law (as they then were) included human rights protection. The sources of these human rights principles, according to the Court, were the national constitutions and international treaties upon which Member States have collaborated, with particular attention paid to the European Convention on Human Rights. This position was ultimately reaffirmed by the Treaties, in Article F(2) of the initial TEU, renumbered Article 6(2) by the Treaty of Amsterdam, which was in effect identical to the current wording of Article 6(3) TEU after the entry into force of the Treaty of Lisbon.

The TEU makes specific reference to the ECHR as a source of the general principles of EU law, confirming the long-standing case law of the Court of Justice which gives the ECHR a particular pre-eminence as a source of the general principles,[278] including the jurisprudence of the European Court of Human Rights and the (now-defunct) European Commission of Human Rights.[279] The Court of Justice has even stated that it 'must take account' of the judgments of the Strasbourg Court.[280] While many of the rights set out in the ECHR or its protocols have been recognized by the Court of Justice as forming part of the general principles of EU law, in particular the rights to private and family life, property, freedom of expression and association, the legality and non-retroactivity of criminal law, and to a fair trial, the Court of Justice has not had an opportunity to confirm that all the rights set out in the ECHR are protected as part of the EU general principles. But it is hard to imagine that the Court of Justice would deny that the EU general principles encompass any of the rights set out in the ECHR. Also, at least in one case, the protection conferred by the EU general principles is clearly wider in scope than that conferred by the ECHR: the right to a fair trial applies to any right set out in EU law, not just to trials in respect of civil obligations or criminal charges (as set out in Article 6 ECHR).[281] But on the other hand, it is not clear whether the rights set out in the Fourth and Seventh Protocols to the ECHR can all be regarded as recognized by the general principles of EU law, because not all Member States have ratified those Protocols. Then again, the rights in these Protocols are set out explicitly or implicitly in the International Covenant on Civil and Political Rights (ICCPR), which all Member States *have* ratified, and some of these rights have already been recognized by the Court of Justice as part of the general principles of EU law, and/or are set out in the EU's Charter of Fundamental Rights.[282]

As for national constitutional traditions as a source of the EU general principles, the Court of Justice has recognized the rights to carry on a business or profession and the

---

[278] Case law beginning with Case 222/84 *Johnston* [1986] ECR 1651.

[279] See S Peers, 'The European Court of Justice and the European Court of Human Rights: Comparative Approaches' in E Orucu, ed., *Judicial Comparativism in Human Rights Cases* (UKNCCL, 2003), 107.

[280] See cases discussed in ibid and subsequently Case C-105/03 *Pupino* [2005] ECR I-5285.

[281] Compare the Court of Justice judgment in Case C-327/02 *Panayotova* [2004] ECR I-11055 (para 27) to the ECHR judgment in *Maaouia v France* (Reports 2000-X); see further I:6.3.4 below.

[282] See s 3 of chs 3–5, and 7 of this volume, and chs 3 and 6 of volume 2.

right to human dignity.[283] EU law also recognizes a free-standing general principle of equality, which applies across the scope of EU law.[284] It may similarly be argued that the right to asylum must be recognized as a general principle, due to its recognition in several national constitutions.

Although there was no reference in Article 6(2) (and now Article 6(3)) TEU to human rights treaties other than the ECHR, the Court of Justice nevertheless still refers to such treaties occasionally. In particular, the Court refers occasionally to the ICCPR as a source of the general principles, although it took a dismissive view of the impact of the opinions of the Human Rights Committee set up to monitor the implementation and application of the Covenant.[285] The Court has also referred to the Convention on the Rights of the Child.[286] Moreover, Article 78 TFEU (previously Article 63 EC) expressly requires EC asylum policy to be 'in accordance with' the 1951 UN Geneva Convention on refugee status and 'other relevant treaties'. This suggests that the Geneva Convention and the other relevant treaties (the ECHR and ICCPR again, plus the UN Convention against Torture) should be considered to be sources of the general principles of EU law and/or that any breach of these measures in the asylum field would be a violation of the Treaties.[287] The Court of Justice has indeed confirmed that EU asylum legislation must be interpreted 'while respecting' the Geneva Convention and the other relevant treaties.[288]

The second basic source of human rights in EU law is the EU Charter of Fundamental Rights, which was originally drawn up by a special 'Convention' in 2000.[289] Initially, the Court of Justice was reluctant to refer to the Charter, until a landmark judgment in 2006, in which the Court ruled:[290]

> The Charter was solemnly proclaimed by the Parliament, the Council and the Commission in Nice on 7 December 2000. While the Charter is not a legally binding instrument, the Community legislature did, however, acknowledge its importance by stating, in the second recital in the preamble to the Directive, that the Directive observes the principles recognised not only by Article 8 of the ECHR but also in the Charter. Furthermore, the principal aim of the Charter, as is apparent from its preamble, is to reaffirm 'rights as they result, in particular, from the constitutional traditions and international obligations common to the Member States, the Treaty on European

---

[283] See respectively Joined Cases C-184/02 and C-223/02 *Spain and Finland v EP and Council* [2004] ECR I-7789 and C-36/02 *Omega* [2004] ECR I-9609.

[284] For example, see Case C-144/04 *Mangold* [2005] ECR I-9981.

[285] Case C-249/96 *Grant* [1998] ECR I-621 and Case C-540/03 *EP v Council* [2006] ECR I-5769. On the Court of Justice's references to international human rights treaties other than the ECHR, see further A Rosas, 'The European Union and International Human Rights Instruments' in V Kronenberger, ed., *The EU and the International Legal Order: Discord or Harmony?* (Asser Press, 2001). For the argument that this dismissive approach must be overturned or distinguished, see S Peers, 'Human Rights, Asylum and European Community Law' (2005) 24 RSQ 2:24.

[286] *EP v Council*, n 285 above, and Case C-244/06 *Dynamic Medien* [2008] ECR I-505.

[287] On the status of the Geneva Convention and associated 'soft law' within EU law, see Peers, n 285 above.

[288] Case law beginning with Joined Cases C-175/08, 176/08, 178/08, and 179/08 *Abdulla and others* [2010] ECR I-1493.

[289] [2000] OJ C 364.   [290] *EP v Council* (n 285 above), para 38.

Union, the Community Treaties, the [ECHR], the Social Charters adopted by the Community and by the Council of Europe and the case-law of the Court…and of the European Court of Human Rights'.

It can be seen that in this judgment, the Court confirms that the Charter was not legally binding, and had the 'principal' aim 'to reaffirm' rights which derive from the sources of the general principles of EU law. In a series of subsequent judgments before the Treaty of Lisbon entered into force, the Court of Justice referred to the Charter as having a subsidiary role 'reaffirming' the general principles.[291] The Court gave no further explanation of any role the Charter might have beyond its 'primary' role of 'reaffirming' existing rights, leaving open the question of whether the Charter might recognize further rights, or whether the Charter was different from the general principles as regards its scope or limitations on the rights. But obviously these questions had limited relevance anyway as long as the Charter was not legally binding.

However, the legal status of the Charter was transformed with the entry into force of the Treaty of Lisbon, which, as we have seen above, specifies that the Charter has the 'same legal value as the Treaties' (Article 6(1) TEU).[292] The Charter was subsequently amended in parallel with the signature of the Treaty, but continues to exist as a separate legal document.[293] It should be noted that the 2007 amendments did not alter the substantive rights recognized by the Charter, but rather the 'general' provisions concerning, inter alia, its scope and interpretation.[294] The explanations related to the Charter were also amended at the same time. It should be recalled that the revised Article 6(1) TEU places particular stress on the general provisions (emphasizing that the Charter does not extend the EU's competences) and on the explanations to the Charter.[295]

Since the entry into force of the Treaty of Lisbon, the CJEU has generally referred to the Charter in practice as the sole or main source of human rights rules in the EU legal order, with more limited references to the general principles of EU law than before.[296] Importantly, the Court has clarified that there are still some rights protected by the general principles which are not codified in the Charter, in particular the right to good administration as it applies to national administrations when they implement EU law.[297]

---

[291] See, as examples, Cases: C-432/05 *Unibet* [2007] ECR I-2271, para 37; C-303/05 *Advocaten voor de Wereld* [2007] ECR I-3633, para 46; C-438/05 *Viking Line* [2007] ECR I-10779, para 44; C-341/05 *Laval* [2007] ECR I-11767, para 91; and C-402/05 P and C-415/05 P *Kadi and Al Barakaat International Foundation v Council and Commission* [2008] ECR I-6351, para 335. But see the stronger reference in Case C-275/06 *Promusicae* [2008] ECR I-271, para 64.

[292] The revised text of the Charter (and the explanations concerning the Charter) is at [2007] OJ C 303.

[293] There is no specified procedure to amend the Charter again. But since Art 6(1), revised TEU, refers to the legal effect of the Charter *as adopted in 2000 and amended in 2007*, any further amendments to the Charter could *not* have the same legal value as the Treaties unless Art 6(1) TEU were amended to refer to them.

[294] Arts 1–50 of the Charter set out the substantive rights, while Arts 51–4 are the general provisions (Chapter VII).

[295] Both these specific points appear in the general provisions: Arts 51(2) and 52(7) of the Charter. The explanations to the Charter can be found in [2007] OJ C 303/17.

[296] See, for instance: *Abdulla*, n 288 above; Case C-578/08 *Chakroun* [2010] ECR I-1839; and Joined Cases C-411/10 and C-493/10 *NS and ME* [2011] ECR I-13493.

[297] See, for instance, Cases C-166/13 *Mukarubega*, ECLI:EU:C:2014:2336 and C-249/13 *Boudjlida*, ECLI:EU:C:2014:2431, discussed in I:7.7.1 below.

As for the sources of the rights in the Charter, as the Court of Justice pointed out (see above) the main sources are national constitutions, the ECHR, the EC/EU treaties, and other international treaties. The general provisions of the Charter address the relationship between the Charter and some of these sources,[298] and the CJEU has in particular been willing to refer to the link between the Charter and the ECHR, as set out in Article 52(3).[299] Furthermore, the Court has relied frequently upon the explanations relating to the Charter.[300] It should be noted that while the Charter includes most of the rights which appear in the ECHR and its Protocols, certain rights listed in the Fourth and Seventh Protocols to the ECHR are not mentioned in the Charter. In that case, at the very least Member States remain bound by their international commitments, and it is furthermore arguable that such rights must be recognized as part of the general principles of EU law, even though they are not referred to in the Charter.

Next, the third basic source of human rights protection in EU law is the ECHR itself. As we have seen, Article 6(2) TEU requires the EU to accede to the Convention. This provision of the Treaty was inserted by the Treaty of Lisbon; prior to that Treaty, despite the pre-eminent position of the ECHR and the case law of the Convention organs as a source of the human rights principles of EU law, the Court of Justice ruled that the EC (as it then was) lacked the competence to accede to the ECHR.[301] The question of accession to the ECHR by the EU (as then distinct from the EC) was not considered during this period.

Although the EC was not able to accede to the Convention, the Convention organs nevertheless declared themselves competent to exercise a form of 'indirect' review of acts of the EC bodies, to the extent that Member States implemented such acts. The extent of this jurisdiction was clarified in the *Bosphorus Airways* judgment of the Strasbourg Court.[302] According to this judgment, where Member States lack discretion over whether to implement EC rules, they are subject to only limited review by the Convention organs; otherwise there is no limit on the review by those organs. Furthermore, the limited review is only justified as long as the EC 'is considered to protect fundamental rights, as regards both the substantive guarantees offered and the mechanisms controlling their observance, in a manner which can be considered at least equivalent to that for which the Convention provides'. The Strasbourg Court makes it clear that 'equivalent' means 'comparable', not 'identical', but that any finding of equivalence 'could not be final and would be susceptible to review in the light of any relevant change in fundamental rights' protection'.[303]

The presumption of compliance could be rebutted if there were a manifest case of non-compliance with ECHR standards, but it seems from *Bosphorus Airways* that in practice the presumption extended to the EC (now the EU) will be well-nigh

---

[298] Art 52(2) to (4); see also Art 53 of the Charter.
[299] Case law starting with Case C-92/09 and C-93/09 *Volker and Schecke* [2010] ECR I-11063.
[300] See, for instance, Case C-617/10 *Fransson*, ECLI:EU:C:2013:105.
[301] *Opinion 2/94* [1996] ECR I-1759.
[302] *Bosphorus Airways v Ireland*, judgment of 30 June 2005 (Reports of Judgments and Decisions 2005-VI).
[303] Para 155 of the judgment.

irrebuttable,[304] due to the extent of human rights protection afforded by the EU legal order, in particular because of the substantive protection for ECHR rights guaranteed by that legal order and by the level of effective procedural protection for individuals offered by the EU judicial system in most cases. However, the Strasbourg Court did not comment on whether the level of procedural protection then applying to immigration and asylum cases, or policing and criminal law cases, was sufficient. It is arguable that it was not under the EU judicial system prior to the entry into force of the Treaty of Lisbon,[305] but that since that Treaty entered into force the procedural protection is sufficient as regards EU immigration, asylum, and civil law, and as regards any policing and criminal law measures adopted or amended after the entry into force of the Treaty of Lisbon and subsequently (following the end of the transitional period in 2014) the third pillar measures adopted before the Treaty of Lisbon as well.[306]

On the ECHR side, the ECHR provides for EU accession (as from the entry into force of the Fourteenth Protocol to the Convention, on 1 June 2010),[307] but this is dependent upon the negotiation of some form of accession treaty. On the EU side, the process of EU accession to the ECHR requires a negotiating mandate from the Council to the Commission, successful negotiations by the Commission, and then signature and conclusion of the accession treaty by the Council. The Council needs to act unanimously throughout the process, and the accession treaty will also require the consent of the EP and ratification by each Member State's national parliament before it enters into force.[308]

There are also substantive limits on EU accession set out in a special Protocol to the Treaties, which requires that the accession treaty 'shall make provision for preserving the specific characteristics of the Union and Union law, in particular' as regards: 'the specific arrangements for the Union's possible participation in' ECHR control bodies, and 'mechanisms necessary to ensure that proceedings by non-Member States and individual applications are correctly addressed to Member States and/or the Union as appropriate'.[309] Furthermore, the agreement concerned 'shall ensure that' EU accession to the ECHR 'shall not affect the competences of the Union or the powers of its institutions' and that nothing in that treaty 'affects the situation of Member States' as regards the ECHR, 'in particular' as regards Member States' position regarding Protocols to the ECHR, derogations from the ECHR made by Member States pursuant to Article 15 ECHR, and reservations to the ECHR made by Member States.[310] Finally, the Protocol provides that the accession treaty shall not affect Article 344 TFEU (formerly Article 292 EC), which awards exclusive jurisdiction to the Court of Justice to settle disputes between Member States as regards EU law.[311]

---

[304] Indeed, see the subsequent decisions in *Cooperative des Agriculteurs de Mayenne and Cooperative Laitière Maine-Anjou v France* (10 Oct 2006) and *Cooperatieve Producentenorganisatie van de Nederlandse Kokkelvisserij ua v Netherlands* (20 Jan 2009), neither yet reported, in which the presumption was not rebutted.

[305] See the critique in I:2.5 below.

[306] See previously the admissibility decision in *T.I. v UK*, discussed in I:5.3.1 below.

[307] See Art 59 ECHR, as revised by the Fourteenth Protocol.

[308] See Art 218(6)(a)(ii) and (8) TFEU.   [309] Art 1, Protocol 8.   [310] Art 2, Protocol 8.

[311] Art 3, Protocol 8. Since the Treaty of Lisbon, this provision also applies to policing and criminal law. For the application of this clause, see Case C-459/03 *Commission v Ireland* [2006] ECR I-4635.

In practice, the EU finished negotiations for a treaty on accession to the ECHR in 2013,[312] and the Commission asked the CJEU for its assessment of the compliance of that draft treaty with EU law. The Court's verdict, at the end of 2014, was resoundingly negative.[313] Among its objections was the way in which the draft treaty approached the issue of 'mutual trust' in the JHA area; for the CJEU, the draft treaty did not defer enough to the CJEU's conception of that issue. Due to the CJEU's ruling, the accession process has to be restarted, and due to the number and force of the Court's objections, it will likely be a long time, if ever, before the EU accedes to the ECHR. This is no bad thing: it is highly undesirable for the EU to undertake accession to the ECHR on the CJEU's terms, since this would lower the level of protection as regards JHA matters on asylum in particular.[314] In any event, it should follow that after the EU's accession to the ECHR, the particular doctrine of limited review of EU action set out in the *Bosphorus Airways* judgment will cease to apply, since it was designed to address the specific issues arising from the EU's status as a *non*-contracting party to the ECHR.

Moving on to the *scope* of the EU human rights rules, first of all, the general principles of EU law apply when assessing the interpretation and validity of EU measures, along with Member States' implementation of those acts and Member States' derogations from EU law.[315] On the other hand, the general principles of EU law do not apply unless an issue is linked to EU law: for example, the Court had no jurisdiction to rule on the human rights aspects of the family reunion of Turkish workers pursuant to the EU-Turkey Association agreement, because that agreement does not address the initial admission of workers' family members.[316] But the scope of EU law is of course subject to change; such a case now falls within the scope of the general principles of EU law, following the adoption of the EU's family reunion Directive.[317]

The issue of the scope of the Charter is addressed in Article 51 concerning the Charter's 'field of application', as amended in 2007, which reads:

1. The provisions of this Charter are addressed to the institutions, bodies, offices and agencies of the Union with due regard for the principle of subsidiarity and to the Member States only when they are implementing Union law. They shall therefore respect the rights, observe the principles and promote the application thereof in accordance with their respective powers and respecting the limits of the powers of the Union as conferred on it in the Treaties.
2. The Charter does not extend the field of application of Union law beyond the powers of the Union or establish any new power or task for the Union, or modify powers and tasks as defined in the Treaties.

---

[312] For the text of the draft treaty, see: http://www.coe.int/t/dghl/standardsetting/hrpolicy/accession/Meeting_reports/47_1(2013)008rev2_EN.pdf.

[313] *Opinion 2/13*, ECLI:EU:C:2014:2454.

[314] For an elaboration of this view, see S Peers, 'The EU's Accession to the ECHR: The Dream Becomes a Nightmare' (2015) 16 GLJ 213–22.

[315] See particularly Case 5/88 *Wachauf* [1989] ECR 2609 (national implementation) and Case C-260/89 *ERT* [1991] ECR I-2925 (derogations). As regards Member States' derogations from EU JHA law, see *EP v Council*, n 285 above.

[316] Case 12/86 *Demirel* [1987] ECR 3719. As regards criminal law, see Cases C-299/95 *Kremzow* [1997] ECR I-2629 and C-328/04 *Vajnai* [2005] ECR I-8577.

[317] On the substance of that Dir, see I:6.6 below.

To this end, the Court of Justice has dismissed cases in which the Charter was invoked for lack of a link with EU law, both implicitly and explicitly.[318] Moreover, the CJEU has confirmed that the Charter has the same scope as the general principles, applying wherever there is a link with EU law, not only where Member States are implementing EU law as such.[319] This includes cases where Member States are derogating from an internal market rule,[320] as well as cases where Member States are exercising an option within the scope of the Common European Asylum System.[321]

Next, the question of limitations on rights, as regards the general principles of law, has been addressed by the Court of Justice, ruling that 'restrictions may be imposed on the exercise of [human] rights, in particular in the context of a common organisation of the markets, provided that those restrictions in fact correspond to objectives of general interest pursued by the Community and do not constitute, with regard to the aim pursued, a disproportionate and intolerable interference, impairing the very substance of those rights'. The Court often also states that 'fundamental rights are not absolute rights but must be considered in relation to their social function'.[322] However, in some cases, the Court instead follows the limitations rules set out in the ECHR, including the relevant jurisprudence.[323]

As for the Charter, it contains a general rule on limitations of rights (Article 52(1)), which reads as follows:

> Any limitation on the exercise of the rights and freedoms recognised by this Charter must be provided for by law and respect the essence of those rights and freedoms. Subject to the principle of proportionality, limitations may be made only if they are necessary and genuinely meet objectives of general interest recognised by the Union or the need to protect the rights and freedoms of others.

However, the Charter also contains other provisions referring to consistency of interpretation with the rights set out already in the Treaties, the ECHR, and national constitutional rules, which should be understood as cross-references to the different rules on limitations of rights set out in those particular sources.[324] As for the ECHR, there are specific rules on limitations upon and derogations from the relevant rights expressly set out in the Convention, which the EU will obviously be bound by once it accedes to it.

Finally, as for the legal effect of the relevant measures, the practical impact of the general principles of EU law is that an act adopted by an EU body could be considered invalid, or interpreted in light of, the relevant human rights principle. The same is true

---

[318] For implicit dismissals of a sufficient link with EU law to invoke the Charter, see *Vajnai*, n 316 above and Case C-361/07 *Polier* [2008] ECR I-6*. For an explicit dismissal of a sufficient link, see Case C-217/08 *Mariano* [2009] ECR I-35*, para 29, which refers expressly to Art 51(2) of the Charter.

[319] *Fransson*, n 300 above.   [320] Case C-390/12 *Pfleger*, ECLI:EU:C:2014:281.

[321] *NS and ME*, n 296 above.

[322] Joined Cases C-20/00 and C-64/00 *Booker Aquaculture* [2003] ECR I-7411, para 68, quoting established case law.

[323] See the analysis of Art 52 of the Charter in Peers, Hervey, Kenner, and Ward, n 277 above.

[324] Art 52(2) to (4); see also Art 53. Furthermore, Art 52(6) states that '[f]ull account shall be taken of national laws and practices' referred to in the Charter; see the approach taken by the Court in *Laval* and *Viking Line* (n 291 above) as regards limitations on the right to strike, and the discussion of Protocol 30 below.

of the Charter.[325] This applies equally to national law, and the Court of Justice has in particular ruled that even in cases concerning the application of Directives between private parties, where Directives normally do not have direct effect, the principle of supremacy means that national law which infringes the rights in the Directive which give effect to the principle of equality must be set aside.[326] More generally, the Charter has primacy in relation to national laws.[327]

Protocol 30 to the Treaties concerns the legal effect of the Charter in the UK and Poland. According to the Protocol, the Charter 'does not extend the ability of the Court of Justice' or national courts to rule that national laws 'are inconsistent with the fundamental rights, freedoms and principles that it reaffirms'; '[i]n particular', nothing in Title IV of the Charter (setting out social rights) 'creates justiciable rights applicable to' those countries 'except in so far as' each of those countries 'has provided for such rights in its national law'. The Protocol also states that '[t]o the extent that a provision of the Charter refers to national laws and practices, it shall only apply to' those countries 'to the extent that the rights or principles that it contains are recognised in the law or practices of' those countries.

According to the CJEU, Protocol 30 does not constitute an 'opt-out' from the Charter, but rather restates its scope in a way which does not restrict its application in the UK and Poland in the same way as in any other Member State.[328] In any event, the Protocol does not limit the legal effect of the general principles, or of the ECHR once the EU accedes to it.[329]

As for the ECHR, once the EU accedes to it, it should be noted that many international treaties concluded by the EU are subject to the principles of direct effect and supremacy. The ECHR should easily meet the relevant criteria developed by the Court of Justice to this end.[330]

As regards JHA issues in particular, where acute and complex human rights issues are legion, the role of the Court of Justice in interpreting and ruling on the validity of EU acts in light of human rights, and ruling on national implementation and derogation from EU law, has already been significant,[331] and is discussed throughout this book.

Finally, while this section has focused on judicial mechanisms for protecting human rights in the European Union, there are also non-judicial mechanisms. The Commission has a procedure for checking the compatibility of its legislative proposals with the Charter.[332] Article 7 TEU, inserted into the EU Treaty by the Treaty of Amsterdam, provides for the Council to adopt sanctions, including suspension of the

---

[325] See the judgment in Joined Cases C-291/12 and C-594/12 *Digital Rights* and *Seitlinger*, ECLI:EU:C:2014:238, discussed in II:7.6.5.

[326] See the judgments in *Mangold* (n 284 above) and particularly C-555/07 *Kucukdeveci* [2010] ECR I-365.

[327] See *Fransson*, n 300 above.

[328] The Protocol expressly states that it 'is without prejudice to other obligations devolving upon Poland and the [UK] under the' TEU, the TFEU, 'and Union law generally' (twelfth recital in the preamble; see also the seventh recital).

[329] See *NS and ME*, n 296 above.   [330] See further I:2.7 below.

[331] See, for instance, *EP v Council* (n 285 above), and *Chakroun*, *Abdulla*, and *NS and ME* (all n 296 above).

[332] COM (2005) 172, 27 Apr 2005 and COM (2009) 205, 29 Apr 2009.

rights of the Member State concerned, against a Member State which commits a 'serious and persistent breach' of the values of the European Union, as defined in the revised Article 2 TEU, which asserts that:

> The Union is founded on the values of respect for human dignity, freedom, democracy, equality, the rule of law and respect for human rights, including the rights of persons belonging to minorities. These values are common to the Member States in a society in which pluralism, non-discrimination, tolerance, justice, solidarity and equality between women and men prevail.

To this end, Article 7 TEU provides for a special decision-making procedure, with limited jurisdiction for the Court of Justice.[333] Article 7 was amended by the Treaty of Nice, to provide for a 'yellow card' to warn a Member State which might commit a serious and persistent breach. None of the provisions of Article 7 have been used.[334] However, it should be noted that the Treaty of Lisbon broadened the grounds on which a Member State can be sanctioned, as previously Article 7 referred to a breach of the principles of human rights, democracy, and the rule of law.[335] These values (as revised by the Treaty of Lisbon) are also conditions for membership of the EU, according to Article 49 TEU.

Despite the lack of use of the sanctions procedure, the enshrinement of basic principles (now values) as the cornerstone of the EU legal system has a broader constitutional significance, as is clear from the Court of Justice ruling in *Kadi*, which established human rights protection as a core rule of EU law, prevailing over other primary rules set out in the Treaties as well as primordial international obligations of Member States. The subsequent entrenchment in the Treaties of the key 'values' of the Union has already affected the case law of the Court of Justice as regards substantive JHA matters: the Court has ruled that the 'assessment of the extent of the risk [of persecution as defined by the Geneva Convention on refugee status] must, in all cases, be carried out with vigilance and care, since what are at issue are issues relating to the integrity of the person and to individual liberties, issues which relate to the *fundamental values* of the Union'.[336]

Finally, in 2007 the EU created an Agency for Fundamental Rights, established in Vienna, which has the role of collecting data, carrying out studies, and formulating opinions and conclusions.[337] It does not have any powers of investigation or dispute settlement, and can only express its opinion on proposed legislation if requested. In order to establish the Agency as an effective actor in EU human rights protection, it should be given the right to express its opinion on any draft EU measure (without being requested) and any national implementation of EU measures, and should moreover

---

[333] See Art 269 TFEU.

[334] See the Commission communication on the application of Art 7 (COM (2003) 606, 15 Oct 2003).

[335] Previous Art 6(1) TEU.

[336] Para 90 of the *Abdulla* judgment, n 296 above (emphasis added).

[337] Reg 168/2007 ([2007] OJ L 53/1); see also the first multi-annual framework for the Agency's activities ([2008] OJ L 63/14). On the Agency's role in JHA matters, S Peers, 'Civil and Political Rights: the Role of an EU Human Rights Agency' in P Alston and O De Schutter, eds., *Monitoring Fundamental Rights in the EU: The Contribution of the Fundamental Rights Agency* (Hart, 2005). See also the decision on funding human rights policies ([2007] OJ L 110/33).

issue guidance as regards national implementation of EU measures. While the Agency's role was limited, before the entry into force of the Treaty of Lisbon, to Community matters only, the effect of merging the EC and the EU means that since that Treaty entered into force, the Agency has competence to address policing and criminal law matters as well.[338]

2.4 Impact of Other EU Law

It is obviously important in practice to distinguish between JHA rules (in their various forms) and the rules governing other areas of EU law ('non-JHA law'), because the latter, but not the former, usually entails full application of the law to all Member States.[339] Before the Treaty of Lisbon, there were also distinctions between JHA law and non-JHA law regarding the full jurisdiction of the Court of Justice, the legal effect of the legislation concerned, and the relevant decision-making rules. The following examines in turn the relationship of JHA law in general (and immigration and asylum law in particular) with non-JHA law during the 'Maastricht era', the Amsterdam era, and then following the entry into force of the Treaty of Lisbon. This is a horizontal overview; further more specific points are discussed in the remaining chapters of this book, including the broader relationship between JHA law and non-JHA law, particularly as regards EU free movement law and association agreements.[340]

2.4.1 Competence issues, 1993–99

A number of provisions of the original version of the EU Treaty addressed the relationship between the first and third pillars. First and foremost, Article M of the EU Treaty stated that nothing in the second or third pillars could affect the EC Treaty, and Article K.1 stated that the third pillar was without prejudice to the EC's powers. Furthermore, Article K.8(1) EU expressly made twenty two clauses of the EC Treaty applicable to the third pillar; these were the Articles dealing with the essential structure of the Council, Commission, and EP, as well as the rules on the EC's official languages. Article K.8(2) provided that administrative expenses related to the third pillar were to be charged to the EC budget, while operational expenses could be charged to that budget if the Council agreed following a unanimous vote of the Member States.[341] Otherwise, spending would be charged to the Member States on a scale to be determined.

Two JHA issues in fact fell within the EC's powers. The Maastricht Treaty inserted a new Article 100c into the EC Treaty, providing for the Council to adopt measures on a common visa format and on a common list of countries whose nationals would need visas to enter the EU. Article 100c included the 'standard' institutional rules of EC

---

[338] However, the Agency's second multi-annual framework Decision ([2013] OJ L 79/10) excludes criminal judicial cooperation from its scope.

[339] For the detailed rules governing the territorial scope of JHA measures, see I:2.2.5 above.

[340] See s 2.4 in each of chs 3–7 in this volume.

[341] In that case, EC rules relating to the budget were applicable: see Art 199 EC (later Art 268 EC). On funding of JHA measures, see I:2.6 below.

law: monopoly of initiative by the Commission, consultation of the EP, and QMV in the Council.[342]

Furthermore, Article K.9 of the original EU Treaty provided for a simplified system for potentially transferring the first six aspects of JHA cooperation to the first pillar. This would have required a unanimous vote of the Council and ratification by the Member States in accordance with their constitutional rules. However, Article K.9 was never applied in practice. So the scope of the JHA provisions remained unamended until the Treaty of Amsterdam entered into force. In the meantime, the Council, the EP, the Commission, and various Member States took different views on the first/third pillar borderline. The first relevant dispute concerned the validity of an EC development policy treaty with India. Portugal challenged the Council's conclusion of this treaty on the grounds, inter alia, that the provisions it contained on drug addiction had a legal base in the third pillar, not the first.[343] However, Portugal lost on the merits because the Court of Justice ruled that drugs cooperation as provided for in the treaty with India fell within the scope of the EC's development policy powers.

There were particularly intractable disputes over competence over visas and internal border controls. Ultimately, the Commission decided to sue the Council when the latter adopted a third pillar Joint Action setting out a list of countries whose nationals would have to carry airport transit visas,[344] although the Commission believed that this issue fell within the scope of EC powers to adopt a list of countries whose nationals would have to carry a visa to cross the EC Member States' external borders.[345] Although the UK challenged the admissibility of the action, on the grounds that the Court of Justice had no jurisdiction over Joint Actions, the Court of Justice ruled that Article L EU (subsequently Article 46 EU), defining the Court's jurisdiction over the EU Treaty) gave it jurisdiction to interpret Article M EU (later Article 47 EU), which, as noted above, provided that nothing in the EU Treaty amended the EC Treaty except those provisions expressly amending the latter. Therefore it was 'the task of the Court to ensure that acts which, according to the Council, fall within Article K.3(2) of the [TEU] do not encroach upon the powers conferred by' the EC Treaty 'upon the Community'. It thus had jurisdiction to rule whether the measure 'should have been adopted' pursuant to Article 100c EC (the legal base for adoption of visa list measures), rather than the third pillar. Implicitly, the Court also rejected the Danish argument that the scope of the 'pillars' was movable at the will of the EU/EC institutions,[346] and declined to analyse the issue by comparing the EU's third pillar powers with the EC's powers pursuant to Article 100c EC. Rather, the Court looked only at the scope of Article 100c EC and determined, by interpreting the Joint Action, whether it fell within the scope of the EC's power. So the Court did not offer a view on the powers conferred upon the Union at that time by the third pillar.[347]

---

[342] However, there was a transition period: before 1 Jan 1996, voting on the visa list had to be unanimous.
[343] Case C-268/94 *Portugal v Council* [1996] ECR I-6177.   [344] [1996] OJ L 63/8.
[345] Case C-170/96 *Commission v Council* [1998] ECR I-2763.
[346] See para 9 of the Advocate-General's Opinion, where this interpretation was explicitly rejected.
[347] To the same effect, see the earlier judgment in Case C-392/95 *EP v Council* [1997] ECR I-3213, particularly the Opinion of the Advocate-General.

Subsequently, the EU's Court of First Instance (CFI) expressly concluded that the Council's access to documents rules covered third pillar documents, and that the EU courts had jurisdiction to consider disputes concerning access to third pillar documents.[348] A parallel dispute arose over the competence of the EU's Ombudsman to hear disputes over the application of the Council's access to documents rules to third pillar documents. In March 1997, after Tony Bunyan, editor of Statewatch Bulletin, had complained to the Ombudsman about the Council's application of the Council rules to third pillar documents, the Council voted 9–6 to reject the Ombudsman's competence to examine the Council's administration of its rules as far as third pillar documents were concerned. But the Ombudsman maintained his position, and in June 1997 the Council reversed itself and maintained that it would consider the complaint as far as it related to the application of the Decision, not the substance of the documents.[349]

In one case, the EC and EU adopted parallel measures in the first and third pillar: a Convention concerning the third pillar aspects of the Customs Information System and a Regulation concerning the first pillar aspects.[350]

2.4.2 Treaty of Amsterdam

During the Amsterdam era (1 May 1999 to 1 December 2009), the dividing line between JHA measures and non-JHA measures remained important. Previously, there had been a single division between matters governed by EC law and matters governed by the third pillar. But for over ten years there were three categories of law: non-JHA measures; the provisions of the EC Treaty addressing asylum, immigration, and civil law; and the revised third pillar provisions. Additionally, the Schengen *acquis* was integrated into all three of these compartments, raising a number of further legal issues.

The disputes in the immigration and asylum field concerned the precise dividing line between Title IV of the EC Treaty and the non-JHA EC Treaty.[351] On this point, the Court of Justice confirmed that issues concerning the admission of third-country national family members of EU citizens to the territory of the EU fell within the scope of EU free movement law (not Title IV), whenever the EU citizen sponsor of the family member concerned was exercising free movement rights.[352] It should also be emphasized that many aspects of non-JHA Community law overlapped with the subject-matter of various JHA powers, in particular EU free movement law (as regards third-country national family members of EU citizens and posted third-country national workers) and EU association agreements.[353]

As for the Schengen *acquis*, the original Schengen Convention and the Protocol on the Schengen *acquis* both stated expressly, before the Treaty of Lisbon, that EC and EU law took priority over the *acquis* in the event of a conflict.[354] This

---

[348] Case T-174/95 *Svenska Journalistforbundet* [1998] ECR II-2289. See further I:2.5 below.
[349] See *Statewatch Bulletin*, Jan/Feb 1997 and May/June 1997.
[350] See further II:7.6.1.2 below.   [351] See s 4 of chs 3–7 of this volume.
[352] Case C-127/08 *Metock* [2008] ECR I-6241.   [353] See s 4 of each of chs 3–7 of this volume.
[354] Art 134 of the 1990 Convention ([2000] OJ L 239), and the preamble and (more ambiguously) Art 1 of the Protocol. On the position after the Treaty of Lisbon, see I:2.4.3 below.

position was confirmed and clarified in the 2006 judgment in *Commission v Spain*, which concerned the conflict between the Schengen rules on automatic refusal of visas and entry at the external border for persons listed on the SIS, and the provisions of EU free movement law, which require an individual assessment of the extent of the threat posed by third-country national family members of EU citizens, and set a higher threshold for refusing entry than the SIS sets out for listing persons to be refused entry.[355] The Court of Justice rejected the Spanish argument that, following the integration of the Schengen *acquis* into the EC and EU legal order, the provisions of the *acquis* 'cannot be contrary to Community law'.[356] Instead, the Court referred to the relevant provisions of the 1990 Convention and the Schengen Protocol,[357] and ruled that 'the compliance of an administrative practice with the provisions of the [Convention] may justify the conduct of the competent national authorities only in so far as the application of the relevant provisions is compatible with the Community rules governing freedom of movement for persons'.[358] Although, in the Court's view, the automatic nature of the Schengen blacklist was a necessary aspect of Schengen integration, the application of the Schengen rules in individual cases still had to be examined for conformity with EU free movement law. The Court did not address the question of the relationship between measures building on the *acquis* and other EU law, although it should be noted that most of these measures expressly give precedence to and/or do not affect other EU law.[359]

As for the allocation of the Schengen *acquis*, as noted above,[360] the provisions on the SIS were not allocated, and so fell by default into the third pillar. But subsequent measures concerning the management of the SIS II project, the update of the Sirene manual, the amendment of the SIS rules, and the migration from SIS to SIS II entailed the adoption of parallel first and third pillar measures, including also a measure within the scope of the EC's transport powers.[361] The legislation establishing SIS II followed the same approach. Given the application of the SIS to external border controls and the issue of visas in particular, this approach was surely correct.[362]

The overlap between the various areas of EU policy subject to different rules on decision-making, jurisdiction, legal effect, and territorial scope was reflected in the case law of the Court of Justice. One annulment action challenged a Commission decision

---

[355] Case C-503/03 *Commission v Spain* [2006] ECR I-1097. For more on the substance and implications of the judgment, see I:3.4.1, I:4.4.1, I:6.4.1, and I:7.4.1 below.

[356] Para 30 of the judgment, n 355 above.

[357] The previous Art 134 of the Convention gave priority to EU law before the entry into force of the Treaty of Amsterdam, while the third recital in the preamble to the Protocol gave priority to EU law afterward. It seemed that Art 1 of the Protocol also played a role (paras 33 and 34 of the judgment).

[358] Para 35 of the judgment, n 355 above.

[359] See, for instance, Art 3 of the Borders Code (Reg 562/2006, [2006] OJ L 105/1) and Art 1(2) of the Visa Code (Reg 810/2009, [2009] OJ L 243/1), and the more detailed comments in I:3.4.1, I:4.4.1, and I:7.4.1 below.

[360] I:2.2.2.2.   [361] See II:7.6.1.1.

[362] On the process of integrating the Schengen *acquis*, see D Thym, 'Schengen Law: A Challenge for Legal Accountability in the European Union' (2002) 8 ELJ 218 and S Peers, '*Caveat Emptor*? Integrating the Schengen *Acquis* into the European Union Legal Order' (2000) 2 CYELS 87.

applicable to both the third pillar and first pillar aspects of the SIS.[363] In other cases, Title IV issues arose in the context of non-JHA EU law, when the Court mentioned the EU's visa list Regulations and family reunion Directive when ruling on issues of EU free movement law.[364] Also, in several other cases, Advocates-General of the Court suggested an interpretation of Title IV or adopted or proposed measures based on Title IV in the context of cases concerning non-JHA EU law,[365] although some of these cases were not referred from final courts or were referred from Member States which had partly opted out of Title IV measures. Conversely, there have been cases where non-JHA EU law overlapped with JHA measures.[366]

The Court of Justice gave two rulings more specifically addressing the relationship between JHA measures and non-JHA rules, both concerning the EU's association agreement with Turkey. In *Payir*, the Court ruled that a Directive concerning third-country national students was 'not relevant' to the interpretation of the EU-Turkey rules as regards the status of students, because that Directive specifically permitted the EU and/ or its Member States to agree treaties with third States establishing more favourable rules.[367] In *Soysal*, there was a direct conflict between the EU visa list Regulation, which required visas to be imposed on Turkish nationals, and the 'standstill' rule in the EU-Turkey rules relating to service providers, which specified that the EU and its Member States could not make the provision of services in the EU by Turkish service providers more difficult than it was for them when those rules entered into force for the Member State concerned. The Court of Justice simply ruled that the priority of international agreements over EU secondary legislation meant that the latter had to be interpreted consistently with the former—overlooking the direct conflict between the two sources of law, which could not be solved by means of consistent interpretation.[368]

These 'overlap' cases raise questions about the appropriateness of interpreting a general EU rule applicable to all Member States in light of a rule applicable to only some Member States. What approach should be taken to these issues, which remain relevant after the entry into force of the Treaty of Lisbon due to the continued differences in the territorial scope of JHA measures?[369] There can be no objection to the Court of Justice interpreting general rules in light of specific rules applicable to some Member States only, as long as this does not have the effect of imposing the specific rules upon

---

[363] See interim measures ruling in Case T-447/04 R *Cap Gemini* [2005] ECR II-257; the case was later withdrawn.

[364] Cases C-459/99 *MRAX* [2002] ECR I-6591 and C-157/03 *Commission v Spain* [2005] ECR I-2911 (visa list) and C-127/08 *Metock* [2008] ECR I-6241 (family reunion). See also the Opinion in Case C-257/99 *Barkoci and Malik* [2001] ECR I-6557, which interprets an association agreement in light of the EU's 1999 visa list Regulation.

[365] Opinions in Cases C-416/96 *El-Yassini* [1999] ECR I-1209; C-387/97 *Wijsenbeek* [1999] ECR I-3207; C-70/99 *Commission v Portugal* [2001] ECR I-4845; C-109/01 *Akrich* [2003] ECR I-9607; C-467/02 *Cetinkaya* [2004] ECR I-10895; C-1/05 *Jia* [2007] ECR I-1; C-325/05 *Derin* [2007] ECR I-6495; C-16/05 *Tum and Dari* [2007] ECR I-7415; and C-337/07 *Altun* [2008] ECR I-10323. See earlier references to pre-Amsterdam JHA measures in the Opinions in *Barkoci and Malik* (n 364 above) and Case C-235/99 *Kondova* [2001] ECR I-6427. In Case C-237/02 *Panayatova* [2004] ECR I-11055, the Advocate-General asserted in a non-JHA case that in principle he had jurisdiction to interpret the Schengen *acquis*.

[366] See Case C-276/06 *El-Youssfi* [2007] ECR I-2851.

[367] Case C-294/06 [2008] ECR I-203, paras 47–8.

[368] Case C-228/06 [2009] ECR I-1031, paras 53–9.   [369] See I:2.2.5 above.

Member States which would otherwise not be covered by them. So it is unobjectionable for the Court to consider the EU's visa list legislation in the context of a judgment on EU free movement law, as long as the UK and Ireland are not thereby bound by the EC visa list. On the other hand, the Opinion in *Akrich* went too far in interpreting EU free movement law in light of Title IV EC and Title IV measures which were not binding on the UK (in addition to their irrelevance to the facts at hand).[370] In such cases, the Court must make clear when its interpretation of a general EU measure in light of a specific measure is relevant to all Member States. For example, the Court wisely made clear that the ban on discriminatory taxes on airline flights applies to *all* Member States due to its infringement of the free movement of services, and avoided leaving the impression that this rule only applied to Schengen States. And in the *Payir* case, the Court was right to point out simply that the Title IV legislation left it open for Member States and the EU to agree treaties that were more favourable to students.

2.4.3 Treaty of Lisbon

As noted already, the relationship between EU JHA and non-JHA law is less critical after the entry into force of the Treaty of Lisbon, since most of the institutional distinctions have been removed; but the distinction still remains relevant as regards the territorial scope of JHA measures as compared to most non-JHA measures. The approach to 'mixed jurisdiction' issues advocated above should apply *mutatis mutandis*.

As for the Schengen *acquis*, the amendments to the Schengen Protocol made by the Treaty of Lisbon include the deletion of the clause in the preamble to that Protocol which unambiguously stated that EU law took priority over the Schengen *acquis*. The issue of the relationship between that *acquis* (and measures building upon it) and other EU law is therefore governed since the Treaty of Lisbon by a more general provision in that Protocol, which states that Schengen cooperation 'shall be conducted within the institutional and legal framework of the European Union and with respect for the relevant provisions of the Treaties'.[371]

The case law decided on the distinction between the immigration law and non-JHA legal bases after the Treaty of Lisbon has clarified when social security matters fall within the scope of the EU's powers over association agreements, development policy, or social security, rather than its immigration law powers.[372]

2.5 Legitimacy and Accountability

An ongoing concern regarding the development of EU Justice and Home Affairs Law has been the legitimacy and accountability of the EU's activities in these areas of great public concern, considering the close link of these issues to national sovereignty, the

---

[370] With great respect, the Opinion also suffers from several factual errors and breached the procedural rights of the parties to the national proceeding by basing its reasoning on issues not raised by or before the national court or before the Court of Justice.

[371] Art 1 of the Schengen Protocol, as amended by the Treaty of Lisbon.

[372] See I:6.4.3 and I:7.9.1 below. See also I:4.4.1 below, on the relationship between the UK's borders opt-out and EU free movement law.

political sensitivity of the subject, and the perceived remoteness and lack of transparency of the EU. These concerns have applied *a fortiori* to the development of JHA law outside the EU framework (most notably the Schengen and Prum Conventions).

The legitimacy of EU measures should be considered from the perspective of two different aspects of legitimacy: the democratic legitimacy and legal legitimacy (or more broadly, the rule of law) of adopted measures. The accountability of those measures should be evaluated in light of the effectiveness of any measures to hold persons responsible for implementing EU measures in practice to account. Legitimacy and accountability are intrinsic elements of human rights standards, which require limits on rights to be prescribed by law and confer procedural rights on individuals to challenge restrictions on rights imposed by state authorities. Finally, it should also be kept in mind that given the extent of state powers of control and coercion involved, immigration, asylum, criminal law, and policing measures have traditionally (unlike foreign policy) been subject to extensive control by national parliaments and national courts.

The Treaty of Lisbon made an attempt to address these issues as regards the democratic and judicial accountability of EU action, by means of significantly increasing the powers of the European Parliament over legislation and treaty-making in this area, along with the application of the standard rules on the jurisdiction of the Court of Justice (except as regards the transitional period relating to pre-existing third pillar acts).[373] More general attempts to address the legitimacy issue include the enhancement of human rights protection within the EU legal order,[374] the clarification of EU competences,[375] and the development of rules on the powers of national parliaments and the level of openness and transparency within the European Union. These latter developments are considered further in this section.

First of all, openness and transparency assists public participation in, debate of, and awareness of activities of the public authorities, and contributes to the accountability of those who apply the policies in practice. Initially, the level of transparency during the Maastricht era (1993–99) was wholly inadequate, in particular as regards non-publication of many adopted measures and the negotiation of those measures; this applied in particular to the Schengen integration process (which was then separate from the EU process as a whole).[376] There was some improvement in access to documents after an NGO, Statewatch, brought successful complaints to the EU Ombudsman against the Council's practices of, inter alia, destroying copies of meeting agendas, not maintaining a register of documents, and refusing many requests for access to documents on dubious grounds.[377] As a result of these complaints, the Council began to conserve agendas and make more documents available, and established a register of documents on the Internet, which soon included access to the full text of many documents. Also, a 1998 judgment of the Court of First Instance confirmed that the Council's general access to document rules applied to third pillar matters and that the EU Courts had jurisdiction over the Council's application of the rules

---

[373] See generally I:2.2.3 above and (as regards treaties) I:2.7 below.   [374] See I:2.3 above.
[375] See I:2.4 above, and s 2.3 and 2.4 of each of chs 3–12 as regards specific areas of JHA law.
[376] For further detail, see the second edition of this book, at pp 19–20.
[377] See text of complaints in *The Statewatch Case* (Statewatch publication).

to JHA documents.[378] A series of Court judgments ruled against the Council's interpretation of the access to document rules as regards JHA documents: in *Carvel*, the
Council was wrongly automatically refusing requests for access to documents relating
to Council proceedings without considering the balance between the applicant's rights
and the Council's interests; in *Svenska*, the Council had wrongly applied the 'public
security' exception to the rules on access, in particular to deny access to a document
concerning Europol's office furniture requirements; in *Kuijer I*, the Council's reasons
for denying a number of asylum documents relating to conditions in the countries of
origin of asylum seekers on 'international relations' grounds were too sweeping; and in
Kuijer II, the Council had misapplied the 'international relations' exception relating to
the same documents, in particular by failing to consider the impact of releasing each
documents on the EU's relationship with each particular third State.[379]

Next, the Treaty of Amsterdam inserted into Article 1 of the previous EU Treaty a
requirement that the EU act 'as openly as possible', and a new Article 255 into the EC
Treaty that required the EU institutions to adopt legislation covering access to documents of the EP, Council, and Commission. A Regulation on this subject was duly
adopted in 2001.[380] Among other things, the Regulation retains exceptions for 'public
security', 'international relations', and institutional decision-making, but it does extend
the scope of the EU rules to include documents submitted from outside the institutions. In practice, the interpretation of the Regulation by the Court of Justice has been
mostly encouraging, with the Court limiting Member States' veto on the release of documents which they 'authored', and giving a strong priority to the requirement to release
access to documents as regards the EU's legislative activity.[381]

The Treaty of Lisbon gave a wider scope to the basic Treaty rule on access to documents, and required all Council and EP meetings to be held in public insofar as they
concern legislative discussions.[382] However, the legislation on access to documents has
not yet been amended, and a proposal to amend those rules released before the entry
into force of the Treaty of Lisbon would have made no positive improvement as regards
any aspect of transparency, and would even have lowered standards as regards some
important issues.[383] In practice, the Council now releases most draft texts under discussion, but only upon request (resulting in a delay of several weeks before release) and
usually with the names of Member States taking particular positions blacked out; these
restrictions still hinder public knowledge of Council discussions. A limited number
of texts are made available in connection with open meetings—sometimes after the

---

[378] Case T-174/95 *Svenska Journalistforbundet* [1998] ECR II-2289. See earlier Case T-194/94 *Carvel and
Guardian Newspapers* [1995] ECR II-2765, where it was simply assumed that the rules applied to third pillar
documents. The Council's initial access rules appeared in [1993] OJ L 340/43.

[379] *Svenska* and *Carvel* (n 378 above), and Cases T-188/98 *Kuijer I* [2000] ECR I-1959 and T-211/00
Kuijer II [2002] ECR I-485.

[380] Reg 1049/2001 ([2001] OJ L 145/43). For detailed comments, see S Peers, 'The New Regulation on
Access to Documents: A Critical Analysis' (2001–2002) 21 YEL 385, with further references.

[381] Respectively Case C-64/05 P *Sweden v Commission* [2007] ECR I-11389 and Joined Cases C-39/05 P
and C-52/05 P *Sweden and Turco v Council* [2008] ECR I-4723.

[382] Art 15 TFEU, which has replaced the prior Art 255 EC.

[383] COM (2008) 229, 30 Apr 2008. See the article-by-article commentary, online at: <http://www.state-
watch.org/foi/sw-analysis-docs-june-2008.pdf>.

meeting has taken place. The Council could also do more to hold discussions on non-legislative measures in public.[384]

As for the Commission, the main Commission register of documents is simply superficial, since it only lists documents which will be made public imminently anyway and only makes those documents available on the register after their official release; and the Commission's specialized comitology register is far from complete, as many JHA documents are not present.[385]

A particular transparency issue concerns the Schengen *acquis*, which included two Schengen Executive Committee Decisions on confidentiality, which designated certain Schengen acts as classified.[386] These measures were amended several times to declassify certain measures, and then repealed entirely, as classification of such documents is now determined entirely by the Council's security rules.[387]

As for the democratic legitimacy of EU Justice and Home Affairs measures, joint control by the EP, via means of the ordinary legislative procedure, applies now to almost all JHA measures. So if the EP is considered to be a sufficiently legitimate institution—and its legitimacy is an issue beyond the scope of this book—then the application of the ordinary legislative procedure now secures the democratic legitimacy of JHA measures in these areas (except for those matters subject to a special legislative procedure, if the EP is only consulted). But the ordinary legislative procedure is subject to significant defects in transparency, because it is largely subject to ad hoc negotiations between EP and Council staff which are not subject to any formal rules or any effective transparency.[388]

Democratic legitimacy can also be assured by giving national parliaments sufficient control over acts of the EU. Full national parliamentary control could only be ensured if every act had to be ratified by each national parliament, but this would obviously impose a high cost on efficiency, as evidenced by the lengthy delays before ratification of JHA Conventions (even though Conventions did not in fact require a full parliamentary approval process in the legal systems of all Member States).[389] An alternative solution, reconciling the objectives of both efficiency and democracy, would have been to provide for a reasonable fixed period for national parliaments to object to a text; an objection within would require a full ratification procedure to be followed, while an absence of objection would entail the immediate entry into force of the measure (with a further period allowed for adaptation of national legislation, if necessary).[390]

Instead, the Treaty of Amsterdam and the Treaty of Lisbon replaced national parliamentary control over Conventions with the adoption of secondary EU law, clearly

---

[384] See Art 8 of the Council's rules of procedure (current version in [2009] OJ L 325/35).

[385] The registers are at: <http://ec.europa.eu/transparency/regdoc/registre.cfm?CL=en>.

[386] [2000] OJ L 239/127 and 139.   [387] [2004] OJ L 5/78.

[388] The Joint Declaration on the co-decision procedure ([2007] OJ C 145/5) does not regulate these informal negotiations sufficiently. There is no information at all on *whether* informal negotiations are underway, never mind any information on the texts under discussion. See the detailed suggestions for reform in the Statewatch analysis, 'Proposals for greater openness, transparency and democracy in the EU', online at: <http://www.statewatch.org/analyses/proposals-for-greater-openness-peers-08.pdf>.

[389] See II:2.2.2.

[390] See the procedure set out in Art 48(7), revised TEU, as regards changes to EU decision-making.

fully binding on all Member States' organs but without a requirement of national parliamentary involvement besides the modest rules in the Protocols on national parliaments and subsidiarity (as amended by the Treaty of Lisbon), which provide for a very
short period of national parliamentary scrutiny and no adequate means of blocking
proposed measures entirely.[391] It still remains open for Member States individually to
provide for some additional degree of national parliamentary scrutiny or control of
executive decision-making in the JHA framework, but the degree of national parliamentary involvement is highly divergent and it is doubtful whether many national parliaments, or the general public, are fully satisfied with their degree of involvement,
given the traditionally pre-eminent role which national parliaments play in the adoption of legislation as regards justice and home affairs.

A further problem stems from the pre-eminent role of the European Council in
setting out the overall agenda for JHA matters. The European Council now applies
the Council's rules on access to documents,[392] but has not established any system of
public input; nor is it collectively accountable to national parliaments, the European
Parliament, or anyone else. It is doubtful whether the individual accountability of
Presidents and Prime Ministers to each individual national parliament (or national
public) can make up for this,[393] since the European Council is a separate body making
collective policy decisions.

Conversely, one positive development since the entry into force of the Treaty of
Amsterdam is the increased role of the Commission issuing Green Papers and similar
documents on JHA matters and holding wide public consultations before proposing
legislation, allowing for a degree of public input into the early stages of the decision-
making process. Previously, this was unknown, as the Council had no experience or
interest in arranging for public consultation or input when developing JHA policy, and
individual Council Presidencies could not claim any collective legitimacy outside their
own Member State.

As for the rule of law, the intrinsic lack of legal clarity due to the complexity of the
institutional framework of JHA law has been an issue in itself, as has the unjustified
restriction of the jurisdiction of the Court of Justice. These criticisms have largely been
answered by the entry into force of the Treaty of Lisbon, but the framework remains
unacceptably confusing as regards transitional rules and the rules on opt-outs. The
EU's secondary JHA measures remain highly complex, particularly where they are
connected to the Schengen *acquis*, and much more should be done to consolidate the
measures concerned, considering the impact of the legislation on individuals and the
need to ensure it is usable by practitioners.[394]

As for accountability, the key issue is the scrutiny of the implementation of JHA
measures at EU level (by the Council, Commission, or an EU agency) or at national
level. There is no formal system by which the public can assess the practical impact of

---

[391] See also Art 69 TFEU. For reform proposals, see n 388 above.
[392] Art 10(2) of the European Council's Rules of Procedure ([2009] OJ L 315/51).
[393] See Art 10(2), revised TEU.
[394] The situation would improved if the proposals to repeal some obsolete measures are adopted: COM (2014) 713, 714, and 715, 28 Nov 2014. But they do not go far enough; see the suggestions for further repeals in chs 3 and 4 of this volume.

many key JHA measures, in particular to consider whether they are justified in light of their cost and their effect upon human rights.

Finally, as regards implementing and delegated measures adopted by the Commission, the procedures for controlling the Commission's exercise of its implementing powers have often been criticized for their opaque nature and lack of sufficient democratic scrutiny;[395] the lack of transparency has been commented on above. It is too early to tell whether there will be greater transparency and accountability as regards the Commission's adoption of delegated acts. Finally, it is important in the area of JHA matters to have effective systems of accountability for the EU's agencies, in particular the EU Borders Agency; this issue is examined in more depth in separate chapters.[396]

2.6 EU Funding

Since the advent of formalized JHA cooperation in the Maastricht Treaty, JHA funding has come to take up an increased amount of the EC budget (now the EU budget).[397] In general, the budget is set annually by joint agreement of the EP and Council,[398] but the annual budgets are themselves agreed within the framework of a 'multi-annual financial framework', which was, until the entry into force of the Treaty of Lisbon, set out in the form of Inter-Institutional Agreements (IIAs) negotiated between the Commission, Council, and EP, but which is since then set out in the form of legislative acts.[399] Recent IIAs have governed spending for the period 1993–99, 2000–06, 2007–13, and now 2014–20.[400] Community (now Union) revenue is provided for in a series of 'own resources' decisions, adopted pursuant to Article 311 TFEU (previously Article 269 EC). All expenses must in principle be governed by EC (now EU) legislation adopted in accordance with the relevant provisions of the Treaties, although the Commission has a limited capacity to establish pilot or preparatory programmes.[401]

The EU Treaty, in the Maastricht period, initially provided that operational spending on JHA matters was left to be agreed between Member States, with the EC budget playing a role *only* if all Member States agreed.[402] Subsequently, the Treaty of Amsterdam brought spending on immigration, asylum, and civil law automatically within the EC budget framework as a consequence of the transfer of those issues to the first pillar.

During the Maastricht period, the Council initially adopted a Joint Action on JHA funding in 1995,[403] which was implemented by further Council Decisions as regards spending in 1995 and 1996.[404] Subsequently, the EU adopted Joint Actions on specific issues: a series of short-term asylum funding measures;[405] the 'Sherlock' programme

---

[395] See literature cited in I:2.2.2.1 above.   [396] See I:3.10.1 below.
[397] On the specifics of funding for policing, criminal, and civil law matters, see II:2.6.
[398] On the annual budget process, see Art 314 TFEU (previously Art 272 EC).
[399] Art 312 TFEU.   [400] Council Reg 1311/2013, [2013] OJ L 347/884.
[401] See Case C-106/96 *UK v Commission* [1998] ECR I-2729, and Art 54(2) of the Financial Regulation (Reg 966/2012, [2012] OJ L 298/1).
[402] Original Art K.8(2) EU.   [403] [1995] OJ L 238/1.
[404] [1995] OJ L 238/2 and [1996] OJ L 268/1.
[405] [1997] OJ L 205/3 and 5; [1998] OJ L 138/6 and 8; and [1999] OJ L 114/2.

on identity documents,[406] subsumed into the broader 'Odysseus' programme, which ran until 2002.[407]

The JHA funding programmes were provided for in the EC's annual budgets during this period. For example, the 1998 budget provided for €11.8 million for the named JHA funding programmes (including the planned Odysseus and Falcone programmes) and the ad hoc refugee programmes.[408] The 1999 budget provided for €21.9 million for the JHA funding programmes and a European refugee fund, while referring to possible additional funding for Eurodac and Europol.[409]

The Treaty of Amsterdam entered into force shortly before the application of the EU's new financial framework for 2000–06. During this period, the prior ad hoc measures on asylum funding were replaced by the European Refugee Fund, initially adopted for the years 2000–04,[410] then for 2005–10.[411] The Odysseus programme was replaced by the ARGO programme, which supported national spending on asylum, immigration, visas, and borders.[412]

The EC budget was also used to fund operational measures, in particular Eurodac, the development of the second version of the Schengen Information System (SIS II), and the Visa Information System.[413] As for EU agencies, the External Borders Agency (Frontex) had to be funded by the EC budget, since it was a Community agency.[414]

The annual EU budgets have kept pace with developments. Each annual budget includes as JHA spending several issues falling outside the scope of the EU/EC's JHA powers strictly speaking, but which fall within the competence of (initially) the Commission's Directorate-General (DG) for Justice, Liberty, and Security (ie Justice and Home Affairs), which was split up into two DGs from 2010. To this end, the 2000 JHA budget included: the 'Daphne' programme on combating domestic violence, a preparatory action concerning anti-discrimination measures, the EC's anti-racism and anti-drugs agencies, and action against harmful or illegal Internet content.[415] The budget also included funding for a preparatory action against drug trafficking. JHA funding commitments now amounted to €52 million, with further possible funding to be added.

The 2001 JHA budget jumped up again to €91.6 million,[416] including a pilot programme concerning child exploitation and committed funding for Eurodac. The 2002 JHA budget then topped the €100 million mark, allocating €103.5 million and for the first time committing funds for development of SIS II, supporting the European migration network (a preparatory programme) and human rights research and evaluation (a pilot programme), and referring to possible funding for Eurojust.[417] The 2003

---

[406] [1996] OJ L 287/7.   [407] [1998] OJ L 99/2.   [408] [1998] OJ L 44/1.
[409] [1999] OJ L 39/1.
[410] [2000] OJ L 252/12. The reference amount for spending was €216 million over five years.
[411] [2004] OJ L 381/52. The reference amount for spending was €114 million over the first two years, with the remaining funding to be decided later.
[412] [2002] OJ L 161/11. The reference amount for spending was €25 million over five years. The Decision was later amended ([2004] OJ L 371/48).
[413] See respectively Reg 2725/2000 ([2000] OJ L 316/1); Reg 2424/2001 and third pillar Decision ([2001] L 328/1 and 4; and [2004] OJ L 213/5).
[414] Reg 2007/2004 ([2004] OJ L 349/1).   [415] [2000] OJ L 40.   [416] [2001] OJ L 56.
[417] [2002] OJ L 29.

budget for the first time committed specific funds for Eurojust and for a pilot pro-gramme on the integration of third-country nationals, inter alia, raising JHA spending to €122.7 million.[418]

The 2004 budget saw a further jump to €161.7 million, with reference made to spending to assist application of the Schengen rules in the new Member States and for Lithuania to regulate movement from the Russian enclave of Kaliningrad, a huge increase in funding for the ARGO programme, the creation of pilot programmes for judicial exchange and support for victims of terrorism, a preparatory programme to support civil society in the new Member States, funding related to the development of crime statistics, a huge increase in funding for SIS II development, and reference to funding for the Visa Information System.[419] The 2005 budget, following adjust-ments for enlargement and the integration of the Schengen fund for new Member States, entailed a whopping increase in JHA spending to €570.6 million, with reference now made to a subsidy for the European Borders Agency, funding for a preparatory action on a 'European Return Fund', and commitments relating to the Visa Information System for the first time.[420] The 2006 budget increased spending to €590 million, pro-viding for a specific subsidy for the European Police College and setting aside funds for EU crisis management.[421]

Implementing the new financial framework, the EU institutions agreed during 2007 on a number of new programmes, to run until 2013. In the area of asylum and immigra-tion law, they comprised: a new Borders Fund, Integration Fund, and Return Fund,[422] and a revised Refugee Fund.[423] There were also programmes outside the scope of JHA law as such, concerning human rights protection and domestic violence.[424]

The 2007 budget duly integrated these new programmes, raising the spending on EU JHA programmes to €612 million, and introducing also a preparatory action for migration management.[425] The 2008 budget provided for a large increase in spending to €713 million for JHA programmes, including a huge increase in spend-ing on the EU's border agency, Frontex (from €21 million to €68 million), and new pilot or preparatory programmes on children's rights, an alert system for miss-ing children, and the development of European contract law.[426] The 2009 budget provided for an even bigger increase in JHA spending, to the level of €923 mil-lion, including a huge increase in the budget for the EU borders fund, significant increases for the other ongoing funding programmes, a new measure concerning harmonization of national law on violence against women and children.[427] The 2010 budget drove EU JHA spending above €1 billion, up to €1,060 million,[428] including new budget entries on Schengen evaluation and the European Asylum Support Office. JHA spending kept rising to €1,210 million (2011), €1,264 million (2012), and €1,296 million (2013).[429]

---

[418] [2003] OJ L 54. [419] [2004] OJ L 53. [420] [2005] OJ L 60. [421] [2006] OJ L 78.

[422] [2007] OJ L 144/22, [2007] OJ L 168/18, and [2007] OJ L 144/45. See I:3.11, I:6.10, and I:7.8 below.

[423] [2007] OJ L 144/1. See I:5.10.2 below.

[424] [2007] OJ L 110/33 and [2007] L 173/19. See I:2.3 above. [425] [2007] OJ L 77.

[426] [2008] OJ L 71. [427] [2009] OJ L 69. [428] [2010] OJ L 64.

[429] [2011] OJ L 68; [2012] OJ L 56; and [2013] OJ L 66.

Overall, the EU financial framework for 2007–13 provided for an annual 15% increase in JHA spending, from €600 million in 2007 to (in practice) nearly €1,300 million in 2013. But this remained a small proportion of the overall EU budget, and although the JHA budget more than doubled, this could be compared to the ten-fold increase in JHA spending from 2000–06. A modest increase in JHA spending also resulted from the accession of Croatia.[430]

The latest financial framework projects JHA spending rising from €2,053 million in 2014 to €2,469 million in 2020.[431] Alongside this, there was an overhaul of the EU funding legislation, which now consists of an Internal Security Fund, subdivided into specific funds for asylum and immigration, borders and visas, and police cooperation and crime prevention.[432]

The increase in JHA funding from the EU budget has entailed a growing role in JHA policy for the Commission, which implements EU funding programmes and other EU expenditure, and for the EP, which had (before the entry into force of the Treaty of Lisbon) a greater role in the annual budget process than it had adopting JHA legislation (until co-decision was extended to the latter). In particular, the EP often pushes for the indicative spending for various programmes to be altered and for the creation of pilot or preparatory programmes dealing with subjects which it considers to be political priorities.

2.7 External Relations

Since the entry into force of the Treaty of Amsterdam, external relations as regards immigration, asylum, and civil law were governed by Community law principles on external relations—now the general EU rules on external relations. [433] These general rules provide that the Union, which has legal personality enabling it to become party to treaties,[434] can enjoy external relations competence either expressly, by a provision such as Article 207 TFEU (ex-Article 133 EC), which grants express power for the EU to adopt treaties concerning trade policy, or implicitly, 'where the Treaties so provide or where the conclusion of an agreement is necessary in order to achieve, within the framework of the Union's policies, one of the objectives referred to in the Treaties, or is provided for in a legally binding Union act or is likely to affect common rules or alter their scope' (ie as a corollary of the exercise of its internal powers).[435] Title V of the TFEU is governed by the implied powers principle, except as regards readmission treaties, where there has been an express external power since the Treaty of Lisbon came into force.[436]

---

[430] See COM (2009) 595, 29 Oct 2009.   [431] Reg 1311/2013, n 400 above.
[432] See respectively Regs 516/2014 ([2014] OJ L 150/168), 515/2014 ([2014] OJ L 150/143), and 513/2014 ([2014] OJ L 150/93), alongside the general rules in Reg 514/2014 ([2014] OJ L 150/112).
[433] See generally B Martenczuk and S van Thiel, eds., *Justice, Liberty, Security: New Challenges for EU External Relations* (VUBPress, 2008).
[434] Art 47, revised TEU; before the Treaty of Lisbon, the EC had legal personality also (Art 210 EC).
[435] Art 216(1) TFEU.   [436] Art 79(3) TFEU. On readmission treaties, see further I:7.9.1 below.

Another question is the intensity of EU external relations power: it becomes *exclusive*, leaving no competence for Member States, when EU powers over an issue are inherently exclusive,[437] or also where its powers are in principle shared but 'when [a treaty's] conclusion is provided for in a legislative act of the Union or is necessary to enable the Union to exercise its internal competence, or in so far as its conclusion may affect common rules or alter their scope',[438] in particular where the EU has fully harmonized the issue internally.[439] This principle is relevant for JHA matters, which are in principle issues of shared competence,[440] but where in many respects the EU is either obliged to establish a 'common' policy or 'uniform' rules,[441] or in any event is not precluded from fully harmonizing the relevant area.[442] For example, the EU has exclusive external power over visa waiver treaties, due to the full harmonization of the visa list issue by internal EC (now EU) law.[443] A Protocol and several declarations attempt to clarify the issue of external competence as regards several aspects of JHA issues; these are considered elsewhere in this volume.[444]

However, even where the EU has exclusive competence, it may still empower the Member States to adopt legally binding acts, including treaties.[445] Arguably, an example of this is the legislation authorizing Member States to sign treaties on local border traffic, subject to a detailed EU framework.[446]

Otherwise, where the EU has only partially harmonized a field falling within the shared competence of the EU and its Member States, the EU's external competence is in principle shared with the Member States, and treaties within the field of shared competence are often 'mixed agreements', containing provisions falling with the scope of both EU and Member State power,[447] and which must therefore be ratified by both the EU and the Member States, thereby giving Member States a *de facto* veto over the negotiation of the agreement. However, it is striking that in the field of immigration and asylum law, Member States have not insisted to date on their participation, alongside the Community (now the EU), in treaties which they believe fall within the scope of shared competence.[448] In any case, even as regards areas of shared competence or in which there are already mixed agreements, Member States have some obligations to the Community (now the EU) in relation to treaty-making or other aspects of external competence, due to the 'loyalty' principle set out in Article 4(3) of the revised TEU (previously Article 10 EC).[449]

---

[437] See the list of exclusive EU powers in Art 3(1) TFEU.   [438] Art 3(2) TFEU.

[439] The possibility of full harmonization in areas of shared competence is implicitly provided for in the definition of shared competence in Art 2(2) TFEU.

[440] See Art 4(2)(j) TFEU.   [441] Arts 77(2)(a), 78(1), 78(2) and 2(a) to (d), and 79(1) TFEU.

[442] See also Art 79(5) TFEU, which entirely precludes EU measures affecting quotas on economic migration. On this provision, see I:6.2.4 below.

[443] By way of exception, Member States retain competence over issues such as waivers for transport or diplomatic staff, where the EC legislation does not fully harmonize the law: see I:4.5 below.

[444] See I:3.12 (Protocol on external borders) and I:6.2.4 (declaration on immigration competence).

[445] See the definition of exclusive EU competence in Art 2(1) TFEU.

[446] Reg 1931/2006 ([2006] OJ L 405/1). See further I:3.8 below.

[447] For a full analysis of these principles with detailed references, see P Eeckhout, *EU External Relations Law*, 2nd edn (OUP, 2011), chs 3 and 4.

[448] See in particular, as regards readmission treaties, I:7.9.1 below.

[449] See particularly Cases C-266/03 *Commission v Luxembourg* [2005] ECR I-4805, C-433/03 *Commission v Germany* [2005] ECR I-6905, and C-459/03 *Commission v Ireland* [2006] ECR I-4635, as well as Case

There is some protection for Member States' treaties in Article 351 TFEU (formerly Article 307 EC), which provides that Member States are entitled to retain in force pre-existing treaties which they ratified before their membership of the EC (now EU), but those treaties must ultimately be amended or denounced if they conflict with internal EC (now EU) obligations.[450]

The process for negotiating and concluding EU treaties starts with a Commission proposal for a mandate to negotiate.[451] This must be approved by the Council, and then the Commission begins negotiations on the EU's behalf.[452] When negotiations conclude, the Commission initials the completed text, and then proposes it to the Council for signature and ratification (called 'conclusion' by the Union). Throughout the procedure, the Council follows the same voting rule as applies to the adoption of internal EU legislation concerning the same subject-matter. So, for instance, immigration and asylum treaties are subject to QMV in the Council, following the general application of QMV to most of these issues starting between 2003 and 2005, and to legal migration since December 2009, with the entry into force of the Treaty of Lisbon.[453] The EP must consent to all treaties, inter alia, concerning issues which are subject to the ordinary legislative procedure as regards internal legislation;[454] this applies to the whole field of immigration and asylum law except as regards passports. It is possible, where EU involvement in particular treaty negotiations or ratification is impracticable, for the Council to authorize the Member States to act on the Union's behalf.[455]

Treaties concluded by the EC (now the EU) are binding on the Community (now the Union) institutions and the EU's Member States,[456] and take precedence over secondary EC (now EU) law; but the Treaties and the general principles of EC (now EU) law take precedence over treaties concluded by the Community (now the Union).[457]

To date, the EC (now the EU) has negotiated or concluded a considerable number of immigration and asylum law treaties.[458] There is also an important external relations aspect to these subjects, leaving aside the formal adoption of treaties.[459] It has been assumed in practice that the allocation of parts of the Schengen *acquis* to the EC Treaty gave the EC competence over such measures in the normal way; in particular, the EC (jointly with the EU) negotiated a treaty with Switzerland on association with

---

C-246/07 *Commission v Sweden* [2010] ECR I-3317. There are also obligations deriving from the 'loyalty' principle in the context of *exclusive* external competence: see Case C-45/07 *Commission v Greece* [2009] ECR I-701.

[450] See Cases C-62/98 *Commission v Portugal* [2000] ECR I-5171, C-84/98 *Commission v Portugal* [2000] ECR I-5215, C-475/98 *Commission v Austria* [2002] ECR I-9797, C-203/03 *Commission v Austria* [2005] ECR I-935, C-205/06 *Commission v Austria* [2009] ECR I-1301, C-249/06 *Commission v Sweden* [2009] ECR I-1335, and C-118/07 *Commission v Finland* [2009] ECR I-10889. See generally J Klabbers, *Treaty Conflict and the European Union* (CUP, 2009).

[451] On the EU's treaty conclusion procedure, see Art 218 TFEU (ex-Art 300 EC) and Eeckhout (n 447 above), ch 6.

[452] See Case C-425/13, *Commission v Council*, ECLI:EU:C:2015:483.

[453] See I:2.2.2 and I:2.2.3 above.   [454] Art 218(6)(a) TFEU.

[455] See the treaty on seafarers' visas, noted in I:4.11.3 below.

[456] Art 216(2) TFEU (ex Art 300(7) EC).   [457] See Eeckhout (n 447 above), ch 9.

[458] See: I:3.12, I:4.11, and I:7.9 below, and s 2.5 of each chapter in this volume.

[459] See I:5.11 and I:7.9 below.

the Schengen *acquis*, as well as a Protocol to that Treaty as regards Liechtenstein.[460] An earlier treaty with Norway and Iceland apparently also binds the Community (now the EU), although it was negotiated according to a *sui generis* procedure set out in the Schengen Protocol.[461]

The Court of Justice has jurisdiction to interpret and to rule on the legal effect of treaties concluded by the EC (now the EU), and measures implementing them, on preliminary rulings from national courts, and to enforce such treaties via infringement proceedings; it can also rule that the conclusion or termination of a treaty is invalid (as a matter of internal EU law) pursuant to an annulment action or an indirect challenge to validity through the national courts.[462] The Court also has a special jurisdiction as regards external relations, to give an opinion on whether a planned treaty would conflict with the Treaties, including the division of competence between the EU and its Member States.[463] So far, in the field of JHA, that special power has only been used as regards civil law and policing.[464]

It should be reiterated that, where not all Member States participate in particular internal EC (now EU) legislation, the non-participating Member States are not bound by the EC's (now EU's) external competence in the relevant field; this principle is obviously practically important to JHA issues. In fact, the EC took the unusual step of negotiating treaties with one of its Member States (Denmark), in order to associate that State with certain civil law and asylum legislation despite its opt-out from the relevant internal rules.[465]

2.8 Conclusions

In light of the issues addressed by JHA measures, JHA cooperation at EU level should be subject to parliamentary and judicial control, and effective human rights protection, at least equivalent to the principles established by the best national traditions in this area. Until the Treaty of Lisbon, it was clearly not. The institutional framework for JHA law was unduly complex, insufficiently open and transparent, lacked sufficient democratic and legal legitimacy and accountability, raised serious human rights concerns, had a convoluted relationship with other areas of EU law, and in some areas provided for insufficient financial control. The Treaty of Lisbon has addressed most of these problems sufficiently in theory. In practice, there are promising signs as regards human rights protection and democratic and judicial accountability, although the negotiation of legislation and other measures is still lacking in transparency and the web of legislation in this field is unduly complex. In any event, there has consistently been a fundamental trade-off as regards the institutional framework of JHA law between applying the 'normal' institutional rules of EU law and allowing ever-wider and more complex opt-outs for the UK, Ireland, and Denmark.

---

[460] See I:2.2.5.4 above.   [461] See ibid.
[462] This jurisdiction extends to mixed agreements, at least as regards those provisions that fall within EU competence or are linked to EU legislation, and treaties concluded by the EU can have 'direct effect', under conditions similar to EU legislation, depending on the nature and purpose of the treaty.
[463] Art 218(11) TFEU (ex-Art 300(6) EC).   [464] See II:2.7.   [465] See I:2.2.5.2 above.

3

Border Controls

3.1 Introduction

The abolition of internal border controls on persons is at the very heart of the European integration project. But the necessary corollary of this abolition, the shifting of controls to the external borders of the Member States, has become equally symbolic as a signal to the outside world that the EU Member States have a collective border which they aim (using the medium of the European Union) to defend and strengthen. As a consequence of the creation of a collective external border, the EU has become involved in the issues of identity, control, and security that are enmeshed with the concept of a border.

Yet in light of the individual rights and interests affected by border controls, such as the human right to seek asylum, to visit family members, and procedural rights related to borders, along with the effects of globalization, the issue of border control has become a pivotal battleground between, on the one hand, States' desire to retain discretion over control of their borders as a key aspect of their sovereignty, and on the other hand, the need to ensure effective protection of rights and liberties. Indeed, in light of the conflicts between the principles at stake in this field which flared up as a result of the refugee crisis beginning in 2015, the continued existence of the EU rules abolishing checks on internal borders was under threat.

A further complication in this field is that two Member States—the UK and Ireland—maintained for some time that the abolition of internal border controls was not part of the European integration process at all, leading to two divergent processes of integration first outside, and then inside, the EU legal framework.

The dispute over border controls initially led to disputes over EC competence, the boundaries between the first and third pillars, the substantive rules which the Union should adopt, and the territorial scope of Union measures. It also led to a massive experiment in 'black market' European integration in the form of the Schengen process, which the Treaty of Amsterdam later absorbed awkwardly into the 'official' EU legal system, while those aspects of integration that the UK could agree to during the Maastricht period led in large part to the expansion of 'official' EU JHA (Justice and Home Affairs) cooperation. Within Schengen, the core act of negative legal integration (abolition of internal border controls) led to considerable positive legal integration, particularly the strengthening of external barriers.

This chapter, like the others in this book, begins with a historical overview of the substance and institutional framework of the subject, including issues of legal competence and the territorial scope of the rules, followed by an analysis of the relevant rules of human rights law and other areas of EU law (ie non-JHA law). Then it examines in detail the Schengen and EC/EU rules applying to the abolition of internal border controls and the strengthening of external border controls, then the specific issues of the Schengen Information System, local border traffic, biometric passports, and operational cooperation on border controls, examining also the issues of administrative cooperation and external relations in this field.

The issues addressed in this chapter have close links with the issues discussed in other chapters in this volume, particularly Chapter 4 concerning visas and freedom to travel, which deals with issues intrinsically linked to border control matters but which forms a distinct chapter due to the separate details of visa rules. This chapter is also closely linked to Chapter 7, concerning irregular migration. Border controls are obviously aimed at preventing irregular or undesired entry into the territory of the Member States or intercepting irregular entry at the border. It follows that the definition of irregular migration is significantly influenced by the rules relating to external borders (where persons enter irregularly, or violate the conditions attached to the authorization to enter). More particularly, the creation of the Schengen Information System to list all persons who should be denied a visa or entry into the Member States' territories also, in practice, resulted in that system holding information for a wide array of criminal law and policing purposes, along with other immigration and asylum purposes. Furthermore, the EU's border agency has powers relating to expulsion, the network of immigration liaison officers established pursuant to EU powers over irregular migration assist border control in practice, and transfer of passenger data from carriers facilitates both control of irregular migration and external border control.

There are also important links between border control and asylum law (the subject of Chapter 5 of this volume), in particular because one of the principal effects of border controls is to prevent asylum seekers (whether their claim for asylum would likely be well-founded or not) from reaching the territory of the EU's Member States. More particularly, the EU's rules on responsibility for asylum applications in some cases assign responsibility for dealing with a claim based on the irregular or authorized entry of an asylum seeker at an external border, resulting in a close link between the responsibility rules and the EU's border policies. Finally, border controls are linked to longer-term migration (the subject of Chapter 6 of this volume) as well, in particular to the questions of whether longer-term migration can be authorized for persons who have only entered on a short-term basis without their return to their home country first, and to the denial or withdrawal of a residence permit or a long-stay visa due to inclusion of a person's name on the list of persons to be denied entry. This chapter (rather than Chapter 6) addresses certain other issues concerning long-stay visas that are indissolubly linked to the issue of external border control.

3.2 Institutional Framework and Overview

3.2.1 Framework prior to the Treaty of Amsterdam

3.2.1.1 *EEC Member States' cooperation pre-Maastricht*

The Single European Act (SEA), agreed late in 1985 and in force 1 July 1987, inserted an Article 8a into the EEC Treaty (as it then was), requiring the Community (as it then was) 'to adopt measures with the aim of progressively establishing the internal market over a period ending on 31 December 1992' by using certain specific legal bases in the EEC Treaty (without prejudice to any of the others).[1] Article 8a then defined the entity that had to be created: '[t]he internal market shall comprise an area without internal frontiers in which the free movement of goods, services, persons and capital is ensured in accordance with the provisions of this Treaty.'

Member States agreed that border controls on all goods, capitals, and services had to be abolished by the end of 1992, but the UK in particular took the view that border controls on persons need only be abolished as regards nationals of EEC Member States, because they were arguably the only, and certainly the principal, beneficiaries of the free movement of persons.[2] But in practice it was not possible to choose between checking no persons crossing an internal border and checking non-EEC nationals only. The only practical choice was between checking *no-one* and checking *everyone*, since it was not possible to know whether a person was a national of an EEC Member State without checking them. The UK argued that two Declarations attached to the SEA bolstered its view.[3]

Moreover, the abolition of internal border checks would necessarily mean that there had to be some harmonization of national law as regards external borders, immigration, and asylum, as otherwise with the abolition of internal borders, it would not be practical for Member States to retain completely distinct policies on these issues. In that case, it could be arguable that the EEC had competence to adopt measures on such issues using either Article 100 EEC (later Article 94 EC, and now Article 115 TFEU), giving the EC power to adopt measures harmonizing national law regarding the common market or Article 235 EEC (later Article 308 EC, and now Article 352 TFEU), giving the EC 'residual' power to adopt measures where no specific power was conferred by the rest of the Treaty. However, those Articles provided for unanimous voting of Member States in the Council, so this left the UK in a position to veto any proposal for EEC legislation which would have abolished internal border checks on persons. It was not possible to use Article 100a EC (later Article 95 EC, and now Art 114 TFEU), which permits qualified majority voting (QMV) in the Council to adopt measures harmonizing national law relating to the internal market, because Article 100a(2) excluded measures 'relating to the free movement of persons' from the scope of Article 100a.[4] Furthermore, the UK again pointed to the two relevant Declarations to the SEA on this issue, which also appeared to bolster its view that the EEC lacked competence on this matter. So although the Commission had announced in its White Paper on completion of the internal market that it would propose EEC immigration and asylum laws in the late 1980s,[5] it never did so.

---

[1] For a more detailed overview, see E Guild, *European Community Law from a Migrant's Perspective* (Kluwer, 2001), chs 7 and 8, and C Gortazar, 'Abolishing Border Controls: Individual Rights and Common Control of EU External Borders' in E Guild and C Harlow, eds., *Implementing Amsterdam* (Hart, 2001), 121.

[2] The UK has 'internal borders' with Member States other than Ireland, because the concept of 'internal borders' includes borders crossed by air, ferry, or tunnel.

[3] For more on the legal debate during this period, see C Timmermans, 'Free Movement of Persons and the Division of Powers between the Community and its Member States: Why Do it the Intergovernmental Way?' in H Schermers, et al., eds., *Free Movement of Persons in Europe: Legal Problems and Experiences* (Martinus Nijhoff, 1993), 352.

[4] Art 114(2) TFEU still contains the same exclusion.   [5] See White Paper (COM (85) 310).

The Commission was this reticent because it could see which way the wind was blowing. There was no prospect that EEC legislation on this issue would be adopted, and in the meantime a number of Member States had begun the Schengen process (discussed further below) and all had begun to adopt intergovernmental measures in this area. For example, all Member States had agreed to adopt the Schengen asylum responsibility rules in the form of the Dublin Convention.[6] So the Commission supported such measures as an interim solution, hoping that the time would one day come when Member States could agree to address these issues using Community law.

Some aspects of the treatment of third-country nationals definitely or arguably fell within the scope of Community law even prior to the adoption of the SEA.[7] While Article 52 EEC on freedom of establishment only referred to EEC nationals, Article 48 EEC on free movement of workers referred to 'workers of the Member States' and Article 59 EEC expressly gave the Council competence to extend the EEC rules on free movement of services to 'nationals of a third country who are established and provide services within the Community'.[8] But there was great opposition to the notion that Article 48 EEC could be used to further free movement of non-EEC nationals and the Commission did not present a proposal to extend services rights to third-country nationals until 1999.[9] The Commission did win a modest victory when the Court of Justice held that the Commission could adopt a Decision (even prior to the SEA) requiring Member States to supply information on their policies regarding third-country nationals under Article 118 EEC (later Article 140 EC and now Art 156 TFEU) to the extent that such policies affected the EEC employment situation.[10] This particularly applied to national policies on working conditions and access to employment of third-country nationals. However, this did not give the EC competence to adopt legislation concerning these issues under the social policy provisions of the Treaty, which were then quite limited. Eventually it became clearer that certain aspects of immigration law as regards association agreements and other aspects of the free movement of services fell within the scope of Community law even before the entry into force of the Treaty of Amsterdam,[11] but the majority of developments remained intergovernmental, including Resolutions of the Council and the Member States.[12]

3.2.1.2 Schengen integration

Outside the Community legal system, a group of Member States agreed first the 1985 Schengen Agreement and then the 1990 Convention implementing the Schengen Agreement (the 'Schengen Convention').[13] The former Agreement provided for the

---

[6] See I:5.8.1 below.   [7] On the current competence issues, see I:3.2.4 below.
[8] Now respectively Arts 45, 49, and 56 TFEU.   [9] See further I:6.4.4 below.
[10] Joined Cases 281–283, 285, and 287/85 *Germany and others v Commission* [1987] ECR 3203.
[11] See further I:6.4 below.
[12] Resolutions on simplified control at internal borders for nationals of Member States ([1984] OJ C 159/1) and on standard signs at the internal and external borders ([1986] OJ C 303/1).
[13] [2000] OJ L 239/13 and 19. On the initial Convention, see J Schutte, 'Schengen: Its Meaning for the Free Movement of Persons in Europe' (1991) 28 CMLRev 549; D O'Keeffe, 'The Schengen Convention: A Suitable Model for European Integration?' (1991) 11 YEL 185; and J Donner, 'Abolition of Border Controls' in *Free Movement of Persons in Europe* (n 3 above) 5.

principle of abolishing internal border checks among its signatories and set out a detailed list of measures to be agreed in order to implement this objective. The latter Convention in turn set out detailed rules on abolishing internal border checks, strengthening external border controls, harmonizing visa policy, and regulating movement of third-country nationals between its signatories,[14] in parallel with further rules restricting irregular immigration,[15] allocating responsibility for asylum requests,[16] addressing criminal judicial cooperation and police cooperation issues,[17] and creating a database (the Schengen Information System, or SIS).[18] The underlying logic of the Schengen rules was that there must be extensive 'compensatory' measures, including a common visa policy and a transfer of checks to the external borders of the signatories, in order to ensure that internal border checks could be abolished without a corresponding loss of security.

Although the UK and several other Member States would not accept the Schengen Convention's centrepiece obligation to abolish internal border controls, they could accept certain aspects of the Schengen rules, in particular the idea of strengthened border controls without the corresponding internal freedoms.[19] Therefore, they negotiated an External Frontiers Convention, largely based on the relevant provisions of the Schengen Convention, and nearly agreed this Convention in 1991 except only for the territorial scope, as Spain and the UK could not agree on whether the Convention would apply to Gibraltar.

3.2.1.3 Maastricht-era framework and overview

The negotiators of the TEU compromised on the issue of whether the EC was competent to address issues relating to visas and border controls, and did not settle the question of whether Article 8a EEC (which was renumbered Article 7a EC by the Maastricht Treaty) required the abolition of border checks on all persons. A new provision (Article 100c) was inserted into the EC Treaty (as it was then renamed), giving the Community certain powers relating to visas.[20] However, a number of other related issues were expressly part of the third pillar powers of the EU and listed in the original Article K.1 EU: asylum policy; rules on the crossing of external borders and related controls; and policy on immigration and third-country nationals, particularly 'conditions of entry and movement', 'conditions of residence...including family reunion and access to employment', and 'combatting unauthorized immigration, residence and work'. However, there was no explicit mention of internal borders in the third pillar provisions (although the reference to the 'movement' of third-country nationals could arguably have covered internal borders issues), and it will be recalled that the third

---

[14] Arts 1–25. See I:3.5, I:3.6, I:4.5, I:4.6, I:4.7, and I:4.9 below.
[15] Arts 26–7. See I:7.5.1 and I:7.5.3 below.   [16] Arts 28–38. See I:5.8.1 below.
[17] Arts 39–91. See generally ch 3 of volume 2 and II:7.6 and II:7.9.
[18] Arts 92–119. On the application of the SIS for border control purposes, see I:3.7 below. On the SIS generally, see II:7.6.1.1.
[19] They could also accept some other provisions: see further chs 5, 6 and 7 of this volume, and chs 3, 6, and 7 of volume 2.
[20] For details, see I:4.2.2 below.

pillar was without prejudice to and could not encroach upon Community law.[21] So the issue of whether the EC had competence over internal borders issues was still open.

Indeed, the Commission proposed three Directives on border controls issues in 1995,[22] following a legal challenge which the European Parliament (EP) brought against it for 'failure to act' because it had not proposed any measure to abolish border checks by the end of 1992.[23] As a result of the Commission's proposals, the EP's case was subsequently pulled. However, since the Commission's two key proposals were based on Article 100 EC,[24] and therefore still subject to unanimous voting requirements as discussed above, there was no prospect of the Council adopting them due to the UK's opposition.[25]

The EU's third pillar powers were also used to adopt a Recommendation on provision of forgery detection equipment at frontiers and a Joint Position on joint training of airline staff and joint assistance in third-country airports.[26] A number of other proposed EU measures, including a revived proposal for an external frontiers Convention, failed due to fundamental disputes about the scope of EC or EU powers, the desirability of extensive EU action, and the application of the proposed Frontiers Convention to Gibraltar.[27]

In the meantime, the Schengen Convention came into effect from March 1995. Its territorial scope was regularly expanded thereafter,[28] and a large number of measures implementing the Convention, many of which concern border controls, were adopted by the Executive Committee which it set up.[29] In practice, EC or EU measures on border controls adopted or discussed up to the entry into force of the Treaty of Amsterdam were clearly strongly influenced by developments among the Schengen States.

3.2.2 Treaty of Amsterdam

3.2.2.1 Institutional framework

The Treaty of Amsterdam renumbered Article 7a EC on the creation of the internal market EC as Article 14 EC, but did not otherwise amend that Article. Within Title IV of the EC Treaty, the special Title added by the Treaty of Amsterdam addressing

---

[21] See I:2.4 above.

[22] COM (95) 348, 347, and 346, 12 July 1995 ([1995] OJ C 289/16, C 306/5, and C 307/18), which concerned respectively the abolition of internal border controls, freedom to travel for third-country nationals within the EU for up to six months, and consequential amendments to EC free movement legislation. Amended versions of the former two proposals were presented in spring 1997 (COM (97) 102, 20 Mar 1997; [1997] OJ C 140/21). See S Peers, 'Border in Channel: Continent Cut Off' (1998) 19 JSWFL 108.

[23] Case C-445/93, *EP v Commission*. On the Court of Justice's jurisdiction over EU institutions' 'failure to act', see Art 265 TFEU.

[24] The proposal concerning consequential amendments to free movement legislation was based on Arts 49, 54(2), and 63(2) EC (now Arts 46, 50, and 59 TFEU).

[25] Indeed, following the entry into force of the Treaty of Amsterdam, the proposals were later officially withdrawn (COM (2001) 763, 21 Dec 2001).

[26] See respectively [1998] OJ C 189/19 and [1996] L 281/1.

[27] For more detail of the proposed measures, see the first edition of this book, pp 71–5. For the proposed Convention, see COM (93) 684, 10 Dec 1994 ([1994] OJ C 11/15).

[28] For details, see I:2.2.2.2 above.

[29] On some of these implementing measures, see I:3.5, I:3.6, and I:4.7.1 below.

immigration, asylum, and civil law, Article 61(a) EC specified that '[i]n order to establish progressively an area of freedom, security and justice, the Council shall adopt' within five years of the entry into force of that Treaty (so by 1 May 2004) 'measures aimed at ensuring the free movement of persons in accordance with Article 14, in conjunction with directly related flanking measures with respect to external border controls, asylum and immigration, in accordance with the provisions of Article 62(2) and (3) and Article 63(1)(a) and (2)(a), and measures to prevent and combat crime in accordance with the provisions of Article 31(e) of the Treaty on European Union.'[30] As regards border controls, the means of accomplishing this were set out in Article 62 EC, which required the Council to adopt the following within this five-year period:

(1) measures with a view to ensuring, in compliance with Article 14, the absence of any controls on persons, be they citizens of the Union or nationals of third countries, when crossing internal borders;

(2) measures on the crossing of the external borders of the Member States which shall establish:

(a) standards and procedures to be followed by Member States in carrying out checks on persons at such borders...[31]

The structure of these provisions closely followed the structure of Articles 1–25 of the Schengen Convention,[32] and furthermore closely paralleled EC or EU measures that had previously been proposed or adopted. The wording of Article 62(1) definitively settled the argument as to whether third-country nationals were covered by the abolition of internal border controls. However, the Court of Justice confirmed that the Treaty provisions merely conferred power on the EC institutions to adopt measures, and did not in themselves have the objective of granting rights to third-country nationals or obligations for Member States.[33]

Moreover, Article 64(1) EC provided that Title IV 'shall not affect the exercise of the responsibilities incumbent upon Member States with regard to the maintenance of law and order and the safeguarding of internal security'. Again, there was a relevant Declaration in the final Act of the Treaty of Amsterdam: '[t]he Conference agrees that Member States may take into account foreign policy considerations when exercising their responsibilities under Article [64(1)] of the [EC] Treaty.' Article 64(2) provided for an amended version of the 'emergency' power previously provided for in Article 100c EC, which was no longer concerned solely with visas:

In the event of one or more Member States being confronted with an emergency situation characterised by a sudden inflow of nationals of third countries and without prejudice to paragraph 1, the Council may, acting by qualified majority on a proposal from the Commission, adopt provisional measures of a duration not exceeding six months for the benefit of the Member States concerned.

---

[30] On the criminal law measures adopted, see ch 5 of volume 2.
[31] Art 62(2)(b) and 62(3) concerned visas and freedom to travel; see further I:4.2.2 below.
[32] See I:3.2.1.2 above.
[33] See Joined Cases C-261/08 *Zurita Garcia* and C-348/08 *Choque Cabrera* [2009] ECR I-10143, paragraph 43.

There was also a power to adopt measures on administrative cooperation between the Member States, or between the Member States and the Commission (Article 66 EC), which also applied to border control issues.[34]

As for decision-making,[35] Article 67(1) EC provided that the EC's border control powers were subject to unanimous voting in the Council, consultation of the EP, and shared initiative of the Commission and the Member States up until 1 May 2004. However, the powers over emergency measures in Article 64 were subject from the outset to QMV in the Council and the sole initiative of the Commission, but with no role for the EP.

From 1 May 2004, according to Article 67(2) EC, the Commission gained the sole right of initiative on all borders matters. The same provision obliged the Council to change decision-making rules as regards some aspects of Title IV, and it duly amended the rules concerning both internal border controls so that it acted by QMV and co-decision on these issues as from 1 January 2005.[36] Furthermore, a Protocol attached to the EC Treaty by the Treaty of Nice automatically changed the decision-making procedure applicable to Article 66 EC to QMV in Council with consultation of the EP from 1 May 2004.

In addition to the new provisions of the main EC Treaty concerning visas and border controls, the Treaty of Amsterdam added a Protocol to the EC Treaty, concerning external EC competence over external border control treaties.[37]

Finally, it should be recalled that in the area of visas and borders, the Court of Justice was subject during the Amsterdam era not only to restrictions on receiving references from lower national courts (as in the rest of Title IV EC), but also to a restriction on its jurisdiction as regards measures based on Article 62(1) EC.[38] Due to the general restriction on its jurisdiction, despite the extensive Schengen *acquis* which formed part of the EC legal order since 1 May 1999, the Court received only two references in this area from national courts during this period.[39]

3.2.2.2 *Overview of practice*

The entry into force of the Treaty of Amsterdam immediately entailed the integration of the Schengen *acquis* in this area into the EC legal order by means of the Protocol on the Schengen *acquis* and the Council Decisions defining and allocating the *acquis*,[40] with the exception of the immigration provisions of the Schengen Information System, which remained in the third pillar provisionally in the absence of any agreement within the Council on which legal base to allocate these provisions to.[41] At a stroke, the EC

---

[34] On administrative cooperation and EU funding in this area, see I:3.11 below.

[35] For an overview of all the decision-making rules applicable to Title IV EC, see I:2.2.2.1 above.

[36] [2004] OJ L 396/45. See further ibid.   [37] See I:3.12 below.

[38] On the Court's role during this period, see further I:2.2.2.1 above.

[39] Joined Cases C-261/08 *Zurita Garcia* and C-348/08 *Choque Cabrera* [2009] ECR I-10143. On the substance of these cases, see I:3.6.1 below.

[40] On the process on integrating the Schengen *acquis* generally, see I:2.2.2.2 above. For details of the borders provisions of the *acquis* integrated into EC law, see I:3.5 and I:3.6 below.

[41] See further I:2.2.2.2 above.

legal order contained an extensive set of rules concerning the abolition of internal border controls and the strengthening of external border controls.

Given the extent of this *acquis*, there was little immediate interest in further development of it. The issue of border controls was only briefly canvassed in the conclusions of the Tampere European Council of October 1999:

> .... The European Council calls for closer co-operation and mutual technical assistance between the Member States' border control services, such as exchange programmes and technology transfer, especially on maritime borders, and for the rapid inclusion of the applicant States in this co-operation.

There were no developments in this area until 2002, apart from a Regulation of April 2001, unsuccessfully contested by the Commission, conferring power upon the Council to amend key secondary Schengen borders rules,[42] which was applied several times subsequently.[43] From the end of 2001, the Council began to develop plans for an 'integrated border management system', culminating in a Council Action Plan on control of external borders, adopted in June 2002.[44] In the same month, the Seville European Council set a number of objectives for enhancing administrative cooperation between Member States and carrying out joint border control operations. Two other action plans adopted in 2002, both concerning irregular migration, also have some relevance to border controls.[45] Subsequently, the 2004 Hague Programme and its related implementation plan called for a number of detailed measures concerning border controls.[46]

To realize these objectives, a number of important legislative measures were adopted beginning in 2003, in particular concerning: the creation of an EU borders agency, known as 'Frontex' (amended in 2007); the stamping of travel documents at external borders; a harmonized border traffic regime; rules on passport security; a code comprising (and revising) all existing EU and Schengen rules on external (and internal) borders, known as the 'Schengen Borders Code'; and legislation to establish the new version of the Schengen Information System (SIS II).[47] Also, a Directive on transmission of passenger data by carriers was adopted in 2004, in part by using the EC's powers over external border control.[48] The Commission carried out a first review of the three Action Plans of 2002 in 2003,[49] and subsequently produced three 'annual' reports on the application of the Action Plans, in 2004, 2006, and 2009.[50] A 2006 communication on policy priorities as regards irregular immigration set out in part a future agenda

---

[42] The Commission disputed the Council's decision to confer implementing powers on itself, but the Court of Justice rejected its challenge (Case C-257/01 *Commission v Council* [2005] ECR I-345). For more on this issue, see I:2.2.2.1 above.

[43] On the implementing measures, see I:3.6 below.

[44] Council doc 10019/02, 14 June 2002. See earlier Commission communication (COM (2002) 233, 7 May 2002).

[45] Action Plans on illegal immigration and trafficking in human beings ([2002] OJ C 142/23) and on return (Council doc 14673/02, 25 Nov 2002). On the implementation of these plans, see ch 7 of this volume.

[46] [2005] OJ C 53/1 and [2005] OJ C 198/1.

[47] On the details of these measures, see I:3.5 to I:3.10 below.

[48] The Dir was also adopted by use of the EC's powers over irregular migration, and so is discussed separately in I:7.5.2 below.

[49] COM (2003) 323, 3 June 2003.

[50] SEC (2004) 1349, 25 Oct 2004; SEC (2006) 1010, 19 July 2006; and SEC (2009) 320, 8 Mar 2009.

relating to border controls;[51] this was followed up by three communications relating to the future development of border control policy in 2008.[52]

A fundamental development during the Amsterdam period was the continued extension of the Schengen free movement area, first (fully) to Greece in 1999, then to Nordic Member States (and associates Norway and Iceland) in 2001, then to nine newer Member States in 2007, and then to Switzerland in 2008.[53]

In the related area of administrative cooperation and Community funding, the Council, inter alia, established a funding programme which became focused in practice on border control projects, and was followed by a dedicated Borders Fund in 2007.[54] The special emergency powers conferred by Article 64 EC were never used. Finally, the EC's implied external relations powers over borders were used to agree treaties associating non-Member States with the relevant Schengen *acquis* and with the EU's borders agency.[55]

3.2.3 Treaty of Lisbon

The entry into force of the Treaty of Lisbon on 1 December 2009 amended the legal powers of the EC (now the EU) in this area, and also extended the normal jurisdiction of the Court of Justice to this field, in particular permitting all national courts and tribunals to send questions on EU immigration and asylum law to the Court of Justice.

The EC Treaty was renamed the Treaty on the Functioning of the European Union (TFEU) and the provisions relevant to border controls, now found in Article 77 TFEU, read as follows:

1. The Union shall develop a policy with a view to:
    (a) ensuring the absence of any controls on persons, whatever their nationality, when crossing internal borders;
    (b) carrying out checks on persons and efficient monitoring of the crossing of external borders;
    (c) the gradual introduction of an integrated management system for external borders.
2. For the purposes of paragraph 1, the European Parliament and the Council, acting in accordance with the ordinary legislative procedure, shall adopt measures concerning:
    ...(b) the checks to which persons crossing external borders are subject;
    ...(d) any measure necessary for the gradual establishment of an integrated management system for external borders;
    (e) the absence of any controls on persons, whatever their nationality, when crossing internal borders.

---

[51] COM (2006) 402, 19 July 2006.
[52] COM (2008) 67, 68, and 69, 13 Feb 2008, concerning respectively the future development of Frontex, the development of a European surveillance system (Eurosur), and the plans for an entry-exit system. See further I:3.10 and I:3.6.2 below.
[53] See I:3.2.5 below.   [54] See I:3.11 below.   [55] See I:3.2.5 and I:3.10 below.

3. If action by the Union should prove necessary to facilitate the exercise of the right referred to in Article 20(2)(a), and if the Treaties have not provided the necessary powers, the Council, acting in accordance with a special legislative procedure, may adopt provisions concerning passports, identity cards, residence permits or any other such document. The Council shall act unanimously after consulting the European Parliament.

4. This Article shall not affect the competence of the Member States concerning the geographical demarcation of their borders, in accordance with international law.

Comparing the revised Article to the previous text, the provision relating to internal borders no longer refers to Article 14 EC (now Article 26 TFEU), but is otherwise substantively unchanged.[56] As regards external borders, the Treaty no longer refers to 'standards' and 'procedures', but rather to 'efficient monitoring' of external border crossing. However, it is difficult to see what difference this slightly different wording makes.

A more substantial change is the addition of the objective of introducing gradually 'an integrated management system for external borders', along with an accompanying legal base. The full implications of this apparently new competence are considered further below,[57] but it should be noted that the relevant powers are subject, like the previous (and revised) powers on border controls, to QMV and the co-decision procedure, which was renamed the 'ordinary legislative procedure' by the Treaty of Lisbon.[58]

An even more significant change was the addition of a new express power relating to the adoption of measures concerning 'passports, identity cards, residence permits or any other such document', which are 'necessary to facilitate the exercise of the right referred to in Article 20(2)(a)' TFEU: the right in question is the right of EU citizens 'to move and reside freely within the territory of the Member States'. This compares to the equivalent provision in the citizenship Title of the Treaty before this amendment, which had provided that the power to adopt legislation facilitating EU citizens' free movement rights, which was subject to QMV and co-decision (as from the entry into force of the Treaty of Nice) 'shall not apply to provisions on passports, identity cards, residence permits or any other such document or to provisions on social security or social protection'.[59] While this provision apparently ruled out EC powers to adopt measures on these issues entirely, the TFEU now provides for these powers for the EU, subject to unanimous voting in the Council and consultation of the EP (known now as a form of 'special legislative procedure').[60] In fact, this is the only special legislative procedure now provided for in the immigration and asylum part of the Treaty. It is necessary therefore not only to define the scope of these new powers, but also to

---

[56] While the reference to non-Union nationals is slightly different, the revised Treaty provisions make clear that stateless persons are to be regarded as third-country nationals (Art 67(2) TFEU).
[57] I:3.2.4.   [58] See Arts 289(1) and 294 TFEU.   [59] Previous Art 18(3) EC.
[60] On the concept of a 'special legislative procedure', see Art 289(2) TFEU. It should be noted that while Art 77(3) TFEU does not mention the previously excluded power to adopt social security and social protection measures to facilitate EU citizens' free movement rights, there is now a power in the citizenship Title to adopt legislation on such issues, subject again to unanimity in Council and consultation of the EP (Art 21(3) TFEU). The real difference between the provisions on passports, etc. and social security/social protection is that the former, but not the latter, is subject to potential opt-outs by the UK, Ireland, and Denmark (on which see I:3.2.5 below).

distinguish them from the EU's powers relating to border control—an issue discussed further below.[61]

The new paragraph 4 reserves certain powers regarding the definition of their borders to Member States. It should be noted, however, that some EC legislation adopted before the entry into force of the Lisbon Treaty already provided for the same reservation of competence.[62]

As for the general provisions of the JHA Title of the revised Treaty,[63] Article 67(2) TFEU provides that the EU 'shall ensure the absence of internal border controls for persons and shall frame a common policy on asylum, immigration and external border control, based on solidarity between Member States, which is fair towards third-country nationals'. There are still separate references to 'free movement' and the abolition of internal frontiers within the definition of JHA policy set out in the revised Article 3(2) TEU.[64]

The other general provisions of the revised Title V of the TFEU include the European Council's power to adopt general guidelines relating to 'legislative and operational planning' (Article 68 TFEU), which is relevant to border control operations as well as legislation. The express provision relating to evaluation of JHA policies has been relevant to the process of evaluating Schengen states' application of the Schengen *acquis* ('Schengen evaluations').[65] Next, the standing committee on operational security has a role in border security.[66]

There is a general security restriction in Article 72 TFEU which simply repeats the previous Article 64(1) EC.[67] On the other hand, the previous Article 64(2) EC, concerning emergency measures, has been replaced by a provision relating only to asylum matters, so it no longer has any potential direct relevance to border control issues, although it is arguable that it has an indirect relevance (in the sense that the Article may be used to adopt measures relating to border control in order to satisfy an objective relating to asylum).[68] Finally, the power to adopt measures concerning cooperation between administrations remains in the Treaty, unchanged as regards borders (or other immigration-related) measures, and still subject to QMV in Council but consultation of the EP.[69] The protocol relating to external competence as regards external borders also remains unchanged,[70] although changes relating to the opt-outs for the UK, Ireland, and Denmark from JHA policies could be relevant for borders matters.[71]

As for the implementation of these provisions to date, the EU has: created a new agency to operate the second-generation Schengen Information System (SIS II); adopted new rules on maritime surveillance and a border surveillance system (Eurosur); and amended the existing laws on the Schengen Borders Code, local border traffic, EU funding, the EU's border control agency (Frontex), Schengen evaluations, and long-term visas.[72] Proposals for a new entry-exit system to keep precise track of the persons

---

[61] I:3.2.4.   [62] For instance, see the visa list legislation: Art 6 of Reg 539/2001 ([2001] OJ L 81/1).
[63] See further I:2.2.3.2 above.   [64] Ibid.   [65] Art 70 TFEU.
[66] Art 71 TFEU; see the Decision establishing this body ([2010] OJ L 52/50).
[67] On interpretation of this provision, see I:3.2.4 below.
[68] Art 78(3) TFEU. On the interpretation of this provision, see I:5.2.4 below.
[69] Art 74 TFEU, replacing Art 66 EC. The measures concerned are not legislative acts.
[70] See I:3.12 below.   [71] See I:3.2.5 below.   [72] See I:3.5 to I:3.8 and I:3.10 to I:3.11 below.

entering and leaving the Schengen area, alongside the development of a registered traveller programme and corresponding amendments to the Schengen Borders Code, are
still under discussion. So are proposals to check EU citizens more systematically when
they cross the external borders.[73]

Finally, the Treaty of Lisbon has had a modest impact on the number of cases reaching the Court of Justice in this area, resulting a number of questions referred from
national courts on various aspects of the EU's border code, the border traffic regime,
and the rules on biometric passports.[74]

3.2.4 Competence issues

To some extent, the argument over the existence and extent of EC competence over
borders issues is now purely historic. But even following the entry into force of the
Treaty of Amsterdam, and now the Treaty of Lisbon, there are some issues concerning
the division of competence between the borders' powers in Title V of the TFEU and the
rest of that Treaty, concerning the division of powers within Title V itself, and concerning the extent of competence conferred by these provisions.[75] The first of these three
issues is addressed further below,[76] while the other two are addressed in turn in the rest
of this sub-section.

The arguments concerning the distinctions between legal bases are practically relevant because of the different rules pursuant to different legal bases as regards decision-
making and the participation of Member States (where the comparison is between Title V
and the rest of the TFEU). As regards legal bases, the Court of Justice has held: that the
choice of the legal basis for an EU (previously EC) measure must rest on objective factors amenable to judicial review, which include in particular the aim and the content of
the measure; that in principle measures which pursue more than one purpose or component should be based on only one legal basis, corresponding to the main purpose
or component; that exceptionally, where there is more than one purpose or component that is inextricably linked, the institution must adopt the measure using multiple
legal bases; but that multiple legal bases are not possible if the various decision-making
procedures are incompatible with each other.[77] Such incompatibility exists where the
Council is obliged to vote unanimously throughout a procedure designed to give more
power to the EP, throughout which it would normally vote by QMV; in that case, a 'tie-
break' rule requires use of the procedure most favourable to the EP.[78] But incompatibility does not exist where the Council votes entirely by QMV while simultaneously
involving the EP both through the co-decision procedure and consultation.[79]

---

[73] See I:3.6 below.   [74] See I:3.5, I:3.6, I:3.8, and I:3.9 below.

[75] There are also issues regarding the EU's external competence; these are considered in I:3.12 below.

[76] I:3.4.

[77] See particularly Case C-300/89 *Commission v Council* [1991] ECR I-2867; Case C-211/01 *Commission v Council* [2003] ECR I-8913; Joined Cases C-164/97 and C-165/97 *Parliament v Council* [1999] ECR I-1139; and Case C-338/01 *Commission v Council* [2004] ECR I-4829.

[78] Case C-300/89, n 77 above. The CJEU does not always apply these principles in practice: see for instance, Case C-166/07 *EP v Council* [2009] ECR I-7135.

[79] Case C-491/01 *BAT* [2002] ECR I-11453, paras 101–11; see also Case C-178/03 *Commission v EP and Council* [2006] ECR I-107 and particularly Case C-155/07 *EP v Council* [2008] ECR I-8103.

As regards borders measures, originally all measures were subject to unanimity in Council and consultation of the EP. Following the changes to decision-making rules that entered into force on 1 May 2004 and 1 January 2005,[80] there was a different distinction between two categories of decision-making applicable to this area: measures subject to QMV and co-decision (rules on internal and external border controls) and measures subject to QMV and consultation of the EP (administrative cooperation). This essential distinction remains after the entry into force of the Treaty of Lisbon, which adds a further distinction between measures relating to passports (subject to unanimous voting and consultation of the EP) and the other two types of decision-making.

It is therefore necessary first of all to define the distinction between Articles 74 and 77 TFEU, in particular in relation to borders issues. This issue is relevant, for instance, to any decision-making concerning the databases (such as the SIS), for it will determine whether the legislation is subject to any effective parliamentary control.[81] The logical distinction between Articles 74 and 77 is that any measures which concern checks on individuals at the border, including the collection of or processing of personal data to those ends, clearly fall within the scope of the former Article, as such measures fall within the scope of its core subject-matter. Therefore, Article 74 must govern cooperation between administrations where the subject-matter does not relate to regulating the movement of persons across borders in concrete situations, governing instead issues such as exchanges of personnel or of general information. On the other hand, the exchange of information on individuals for specific purposes related to (for instance) border checks concerns the substantive law relating to border checks, and so falls within the scope of Article 77.[82]

A complex question relating to the EU's various border control powers has been posed by the addition of Article 77(3) TFEU, concerning passports and similar documents.[83] It is obviously necessary to distinguish this provision from the general external borders powers because, as noted above, it is subject to unanimity in Council and consultation of the EP, rather than the ordinary legislative procedure (ex-co-decision). Furthermore, surely the passports' legal base, and measures adopted pursuant to it, have to be interpreted in light of EU citizenship, not in light of the objectives of the borders powers or the general objectives of Title V of the Treaty.

In order to interpret the scope of this provision, it should be recalled, first of all, that the previous Article 18(3) EC, which was part of the Treaty Article concerning the free movement rights of EU citizens, ruled out the adoption of measures on such issues.[84] The Council nonetheless adopted in 2004 a Regulation on security features in passports issued by Member States, on the basis of the EC's external borders powers, on the grounds that such rules help to facilitate checks at external borders.[85] However,

---

[80] See I:3.2.2.1 above.

[81] The EP would ensure effective control to the extent that it has co-decision powers, while national parliaments could in principle exercise effective scrutiny over the provision concerning passports and similar documents, due to the unanimity requirement. Use of Art 74 would deny a significant role to parliaments at either level.

[82] On Art 74 generally, see I:2.2.3.2 above.

[83] See also I:3.2.5 below, on the territorial scope of measures to be adopted pursuant to this legal base.

[84] See I:3.2.3 above.

[85] On the substance of the Reg (which was subsequently amended in 2009), see I:3.9 below.

the common format of the EU passport has traditionally been set out in Resolutions of Member States, on the assumption that the EC lacked the competence to regulate such matters.[86] At first sight, this assumption was clearly correct in light of the previous Article 18(3) EC, for (by analogy with the case law relating to public health) the Community should not be able to circumvent restrictions on its competence set out in one legal base by employing another legal base instead.[87] Despite this, the CJEU ruled in *Schwarz* that the Regulation had the correct legal base, since the EC's powers on external borders could apply to EU citizens and could extend to ensuring the security of travel documents.[88]

The position after the Treaty of Lisbon came into force is that the Union has express competence to regulate not just passports, but also identity cards, residence permits, and similar documents. But this is subject to two provisos: such measures must be necessary for facilitating EU citizens' rights to 'move and reside freely'; and this power can only be applied if other provisions of the Treaty 'have not provided the necessary powers'. Taking the second proviso first, it is arguable that the general external borders legal base can still be used to adopt measures relating to passport *security*, because such measures will ensure more effective checks at the external borders by reducing the risk of document fraud.[89] As for identity cards, at first sight the external borders legal base cannot be used, since identity cards cannot be used for crossing external borders, unless they are considered to be travel documents or documents authorizing the person concerned to cross the border.[90] Next, as for residence permits or similar documents, the question is moot for EU citizens since they do not require such documents to cross the external borders.[91] The issue is not moot, however, for third-country national family members of EU citizens, since a 'residence card' (which could be considered an 'other such document') simplifies border checks for some of them.[92]

As for the proviso relating to facilitation of free movement rights, an EU citizen crossing the border between a Schengen State and a non-Schengen State is simultaneously crossing an internal border (from a free movement perspective) and a Schengen border (from the perspective of Title V), and passports and identity cards can be used to cross such a border.[93] The same is true of citizens' family members' residence

---

[86] See further I:3.4.1 below.

[87] For an elaboration of the following arguments concerning the passport security Reg, see the second edition of this book, pp 108–9, with further references. See in particular Case C-376/98 *Germany v EP and Council* (tobacco advertising) [2000] ECR I-8419.

[88] Case C-291/12, ECLI:EU:C:2013:670.

[89] See Art 7 of the Schengen Borders Code (Reg 562/2006, [2006] OJ L 105/1), discussed in I:3.6.1 below. It follows that a Resolution of Member States concerning passport security, adopted in 2000, could be adopted on the basis of the external borders powers ([2000] OJ C 310/1). Indeed, this measure fell within the scope of those powers even before the entry into force of the Treaty of Lisbon, in light of the Court's judgment in *UK v Council*.

[90] See Art 5 of the Borders Code (n 89 above), which moreover only sets out entry conditions for third-country nationals.

[91] N 89 above.   [92] See Art 10(2) of the Borders Code.

[93] Arts 4 and 5, Directive 2004/38 on EU citizens' movement rights ([2004] OJ L 158/77). It should also be noted that the preamble to the 1981 Resolution on a uniform passport format ([1981] OJ C 241/1) asserted that the uniform passport 'is likely to facilitate the movement of nationals of the Member States'.

cards.[94] Therefore the two provisos relating to the use of the power would overlap. Also, passports and identity cards can be used by EU citizens to exercise the right to reside in another Member State,[95] as can passports for third-country national family members.[96] But since EU citizens do not need residence permits to cross the internal borders or to reside in Member States, there is no link to facilitation of free movement rights there.

The best resolution of these conflicts is to accept that the EU's external borders competence is a valid legal base for the adoption of measures concerning the *security features* of EU citizens' passports, identity cards held by EU citizens, and residence cards held by EU citizens' family members, since such measures relate to checks at external borders, at least where such borders are also internal borders between Schengen and non-Schengen Member States. Moreover, the harmonization of such security features would not as such facilitate EU citizens' right to move and reside freely. On the other hand, harmonization of the format of such documents facilitates free movement of EU citizens and their family members (the latter free movement constituting a corollary of the former), because a common format ensures the immediate recognition of such documents by border guards when crossing internal EU borders—not just when entering and exiting the Schengen area, but also when entering and exiting non-Schengen EU Member States as well.

Also, it should be pointed out that the 'passports' legal base does not confer power on the EU to regulate the issue of identity cards, residence permits or any other such documents to *third-country nationals*, other than the family members of EU citizens, because the issue of such documents to such persons is unconnected with the free movement of EU citizens. So is the issue of passports to such persons, but of course in any event the issue of passports to third-country nationals (even those who are family members of EU citizens) is a matter for their home countries, not Member States or the EU. The external borders power is still a valid legal base regarding the issue of travel documents by Member States to third-country nationals, where there is a link to external border crossing but no link to facilitation of free movement.[97]

It is clear, though, that neither legal base has conferred competence upon the EU to require Member States to introduce identity cards or to harmonize national law on the *internal* use (ie within a Member State's national territory) of such cards. Such matters are not sufficiently connected to the crossing of external borders *or* the facilitation of EU citizens' free movement rights, considering that identity cards are only an *optional* method of proving nationality when crossing internal borders.

To what extent could either legal base govern the creation of databases and the exchange of information concerning such documents? Extrapolating from the previous analysis, the external borders power would be a sufficient legal basis for the adoption of such measures to the extent that storing, exchanging and accessing such data was linked to checks at the Member States' external borders. The applicable data protection rules would, however, have to be adopted on the basis of Article 16 TFEU, although these general rules could be supplemented by specific rules set out in the external

---

[94] Art 5(2), Dir 2004/38.   [95] Art 6(1), Dir 2004/38.   [96] Art 6(2), Dir 2004/38.
[97] See Art 1 of Reg 2252/2004 ([2004] OJ L 385/1).

borders legislation.[98] But the 'passports' legal base does not confer power to establish or regulate such databases or exchange of information, since the development of such policies would not facilitate EU citizens' rights to move and reside freely.

The next question is the extent of the EU's powers over borders. As for measures adopted during the Treaty of Amsterdam period, the Council correctly allocated the Schengen *acquis* concerning the regulation of border guards to the first pillar, not the third, since the measures concerned regulated border control, as distinct from other forms of law enforcement. For the same reasons, the EU border agency was rightly a creation of EC legislation, not a third pillar measure. A specific issue is the relationship between the power to regulate borders set out in Article 77 TFEU, and the adoption of rules on evaluations in Article 70; that issue is discussed elsewhere in this book.[99]

An interesting issue relating to both the borders and visas powers of the EU is their relationship with the foreign policy provisions of Title V of the TEU, where a number of measures have been adopted requiring Member States to refuse entry and transit to certain third-country nationals, in pursuit of foreign policy objectives, both before and after the entry into force of the Treaty of Lisbon.[100] These measures apply to all Member States, quite apart from the different decision-making procedures, jurisdictional rules, and legal effect involved.[101] It is submitted that the correct legal base for such measures is Title V TFEU, *not* the foreign policy provisions of Title V TEU. Although such measures have foreign policy objectives, their *content* is the regulation of entry of persons into the EU. There is extensive case law making it clear that measures fall within the scope of the EU's common commercial policy even if they have foreign policy objectives,[102] or other objectives besides commercial policy objectives,[103] if their essential *content* is the regulation of international trade.[104] Moreover, there were declarations to the Treaty of Amsterdam (set out above) accepting that the EC's visa powers, and Article 64(1) EC, (now Article 72 TFEU) are to be exercised with regard to foreign policy considerations. Furthermore, secondary EC (now EU) measures (and previously the Schengen *acquis*) refer to foreign policy issues,[105] It should be noted that, following the entry into force of the Treaty of Lisbon, the persons concerned now have the power to bring annulment actions against the relevant foreign policy measures (see Art 275 TFEU).

---

[98] See further II:7.2.4.   [99] I:2.2.3.2 above.

[100] For example, before the Treaty of Lisbon, see the Common Position banning the entry of persons whom the Council considers to be obstructing the work of the International Criminal Tribunal for the former Yugoslavia ([2004] OJ L 94/65). After the Treaty of Lisbon, see the amendment to the list of Burmese nationals banned from entry ([2009] OJ L 338/90).

[101] See Title V TEU, as revised by the Treaty of Lisbon.

[102] Cases C-83/94 and C-70/94 *Werner and Leifer* [1995] ECR I-3189 and Case C-124/95 *Centro-com* [1997] ECR I-81. See also the judgments concerning defence equipment and EU customs law, for instance Case C-284/05 *Commission v Finland* [2009] ECR I-11705.

[103] *Opinion 1/78* [1979] ECR 2871 and Case 45/86 *Commission v Council* (GSP) [1987] ECR 1493.

[104] On the analogy between the common commercial policy and Title IV (now Title V) powers, see S Peers, 'EU Borders and Globalisation' in E Guild, P Minderhoud, and K Groenendijk, eds., *In Search of Europe's Borders* (Kluwer, 2003), 45.

[105] See, for instance, Art 5(1)(e) of the Schengen Borders Code (Reg 562/2006, [2006] OJ L 105/1) and Art 21(3)(d) of the Visa Code (Reg 810/2009, [2009] OJ L 243/1). However, this is not decisive for interpretation of the Treaty: see *Opinion 1/94* [1994] ECR I-5273.

Similarly, the recent adoption of EU foreign policy (defence) measures intending to control the North African coast[106] is legally questionable—to say nothing of the risks of conflict and to refugees, given that an Advocate-General's Opinion previously argued that foreign policy acts closely related to JHA objectives on EU territory (obviously including immigration control) should have a JHA legal base.[107]

Next, what is the extent of the EU's competence to harmonize the law on borders? Logically, the powers conferred by Article 77 TFEU to harmonize rules on border checks must be extensive, given the obligation to abolish internal border checks, the corollary freedom to travel (which is moreover subject to a 'uniform application'),[108] the earlier Treaty reference to a 'uniform' visa (and now to a 'common policy on visas'), and comparison with the structure of the Treaty rules governing free movement of goods.[109] The Court of Justice's ruling in *Wijsenbeek*, emphasizing the link between the abolition of border controls pursuant to the previous Article 14 EC and the harmonization of the relevant law,[110] also bolsters this interpretation. Although that judgment concerned the legal position prior to the entry into force of the Treaty of Amsterdam, the subsequent Treaty amendments have maintained the link with the internal market (or more specifically, the free movement of persons, following the Treaty of Lisbon amendments) as the primary factor for interpreting the EU's borders powers, even though it is not the sole factor, as it was for the EC's visa list powers when the Court first ruled on their scope.[111]

Finally, does Article 72 TFEU, which refers to Member States' responsibilities as regards law, order, and security, limit the EU's competence? Since the Court of Justice has always interpreted derogations from the EC Treaty restrictively, and long ago rejected the idea that all immigration issues must be considered matters of public order,[112] the better view is that Article 72 simply confirms that implementation of measures adopted pursuant to Title V of Part Three of the TFEU is left to the Member States' authorities, particularly as regards coercive measures. Article 72 may also be relevant to interpreting the relevant EU legislation, suggesting a broad degree of national discretion when carrying out operations.[113] This interpretation is consistent with the specific limits placed upon EU police and criminal law bodies in the Treaties. Frontex, the EU's borders control agency, must therefore continue to be limited to supporting actions of national authorities. The December 2015 proposal to send EU border control forces to external borders without Member States' consent therefore breaches Article 72.[114]

---

[106] See the CFSP Decisions launching 'EUNAVFORMED' ([2015] OJ L 122/31 and L 157/51).

[107] Opinion in Case C-658/11 *EP v Council*, ECLI:EU:C:2014:41.

[108] See Case C-241/05 *Bot* [2006] ECR I-9627, para 41.

[109] On the competence issues, see S Peers, 'EU Immigration and Asylum Law: Internal Market Model or Human Rights Model?' in T Tridimas and P Nebbia, eds., *EU Law for the Twenty-First Century: Rethinking the New Legal Order*, vol 1 (Hart, 2004), 345 at 356. For a detailed comparison of the various rules on free movement and their external elements, see S Peers, 'EU Borders and Globalisation' (n 104 above).

[110] See discussion in I:3.4.1 below.

[111] Case C-170/96 *Commission v Council* [1998] ECR I-2763.

[112] See Joined Cases 281–3, 285, and 287/85 *Germany and others v Commission* [1987] ECR 3203.

[113] This appears to be the import of the brief reference to Art 72 in the CJEU ruling in Case C-278/12 PPU *Adil*, ECLI:EU:C:2012:508, discussed in I:3.5 below.

[114] On Frontex, see I:3.10.1 below. On Arts 72 and 73 generally, see I:2.2.3.2 above.

Finally, the revised Treaty, as noted above, contains now a power to adopt measures related to an 'integrated management system' for the external borders. A definition of this concept can be found in JHA Council conclusions adopted in December 2006, which specify that there are five 'dimensions' to the concept:

- Border control (checks and surveillance) as defined in the Schengen Borders Code, including relevant risk analysis and crime intelligence;

- Detection and investigation of cross border crime in coordination with all competent law enforcement authorities;

- The four-tier access control model (measures in third countries, cooperation with neighbouring countries, border control, control measures within the area of free movement, including return);

- Inter-agency cooperation for border management (border guards, customs, police, national security and other relevant authorities) and international cooperation;

- Coordination and coherence of the activities of Member States and Institutions and other bodies of the Community and the Union.

While it may be tempting to adopt the definition in these Council conclusions in order to define the scope of the powers conferred by the new legal base, this approach should be rejected. The basic problem with that analysis is that the TFEU contains specific legal bases relating to criminal law, policing, expulsion, and customs cooperation, as well as specific provisions on internal security,[115] which are subject to some extent to different rules as regards decision-making, the scope of EU competence, participation by Member States and non-Member States, and even (as regards operational police actions) the jurisdiction of the Court of Justice.[116] In the absence of anything in the Treaty to indicate such an all-encompassing notion of 'integrated border management', these various Treaty provisions should each be regarded as a *lex specialis*.

It is submitted therefore that while the Council may wish to develop of broad concept of integrated border management for political purposes, from a legal point of view the correct approach to interpreting the legal base concerning this issue is much narrower. However, it cannot be interpreted so narrowly as to add nothing to the powers relating to external border checks, considering that the Treaty drafters took the decision to add a new power for the Union on this issue. The best interpretation is therefore that the legal base should instead be understood to cover the regulation of the *link* between external border control and the activities regulated pursuant to other provisions of the Treaty. But in light of the variations in the different legal bases as regards opt-outs, the association of non-Member States, competence, and decision-making, a dividing line has to be drawn, for example, between the regulation of the movement of goods at the external borders per se (subject to the customs cooperation powers) and the regulation of the synergy between the different borders administrations (subject to the 'integrated management' powers).[117]

---

[115] See generally I:2.2.3.1 above.   [116] Art 275 TFEU: see II:2.2.2.
[117] The customs cooperation powers (formerly Art 135 EC), as amended by the Treaty of Lisbon, are now set out in the internal market provisions of the TFEU (Art 33). See further I:7.4.1 below.

3.2.5 Territorial scope

The small number of EU and EC measures[118] in this area agreed before the Treaty of Amsterdam are applicable to all Member States.[119] But most law in this area derives from the Schengen *acquis* or was adopted after the Treaty of Amsterdam, and therefore is subject to the complex opt-out rules set out in the Treaty of Amsterdam, as amended by the Treaty of Lisbon, which were agreed in order to settle the question of whether to abolish internal border checks between all Member States. To avoid convoluted repetitions of the territorial scope of the relevant rules, this chapter refers throughout to the position of 'Member States', on the understanding that most of the rules discussed are not applicable to all Member States, and are moreover applicable to some non-Member States. Readers who are concerned to know precisely which States are covered by which rules should refer to the following overview.

First of all, the position of the UK and Ireland as regards border controls is affected by no fewer than three Protocols attached to the EC Treaty (and now to the TEU and the TFEU) by the Treaty of Amsterdam: the Protocols concerning internal border controls, Schengen, and Title IV. The second and third of these Protocols were substantively amended by the Treaty of Lisbon, which also made purely technical amendments to the first Protocol.

The first of these Protocols, as amended by the Treaty of Lisbon, specifies that notwithstanding any Treaty Article or measure, or judgment of the Court of Justice, the UK 'shall be entitled...to exercise...such controls on persons seeking to enter' the UK across an EU internal border 'as it may consider necessary' to check that they do have the right to enter pursuant to the European Economic Area (EEA) agreement and other treaties,[120] and 'of determining whether or not to grant other persons permission to enter the United Kingdom'. In particular, '[n]othing in Articles 26 and 77' of the TFEU, or any other Treaty or secondary measure, 'shall prejudice the right of the United Kingdom to adopt or exercise any such controls'.[121] The UK and Ireland are entitled to maintain arrangements between themselves on simplified border crossing, and as long as they do, then Ireland is equally entitled to maintain checks on its internal borders with other Member States.[122] The other Member States are accordingly authorized to maintain controls on their internal borders with the UK and Ireland.[123]

It is clear from the wording of this Protocol that the UK and Ireland cannot in any circumstances be forced to drop their internal border controls with other Member States. However, the Protocol does not give those Member States full discretion to determine the *consequences* of irregular crossing of their internal borders. In particular, in light of the *Wijsenbeek* judgment, those Member States are limited in the extent and type of penalties they can apply to EU citizens who cross the border without authorization.[124] The scope of the discretion conferred by the Protocol is also limited to checks at the internal borders; it does not give any power to refuse entry to persons who have the

---

[118] For a general overview of the rules on the territorial scope of all JHA measures, see I:2.2.5 above.
[119] See I:3.2.1.3 above.   [120] On the EEA agreement, see I:3.4.2 below.
[121] Art 1 of the Protocol.   [122] Art 2 of the Protocol.   [123] Art 3 of the Protocol.
[124] See I:3.4.1 below.

right to enter pursuant to EU free movement law or certain other measures.[125] This interpretation was confirmed by the CJEU's *McCarthy* judgment, which made clear that the Protocol does not exempt the UK from complying with its specific obligations set out in EU free movement legislation.[126]

As for the Schengen Protocol,[127] the UK and Ireland have not as such opted in to any part of the Schengen *acquis* (as integrated into the EC legal order in 1999) in the area of border controls. However, this begs the question as to whether the Protocol applies to measures 'building on the Schengen acquis' adopted after May 1999, and the consequences if it does (see below).

Finally, the Title IV Protocol (now the Title V Protocol) has been invoked a few times as regards measures in this area,[128] with both Member States opting in to the passenger data Directive,[129] the UK (but not Ireland) opting in to the ARGO programme,[130] and the UK (but again, not Ireland) seeking to opt in to the Regulations on the EU border agency and the security features of EU passports.[131] The latter attempts by the UK to opt in were rebuffed by the Council, resulting in unsuccessful challenges by the UK to the Council's decisions before the Court of Justice, which held that before the UK could opt in to those measures, it had to opt in to the underlying measures set out in the original Schengen *acquis*, pursuant to the rules in the Schengen Protocol.[132] As argued previously, the Court's interpretation of the relevant Protocols is incorrect.[133] Be that as it may, the consequence of the judgments is that the UK and Ireland cannot opt in to any EU legislation relating to external or internal borders, as long as they do not opt in to any of the underlying rules regulating those issues (in particular, the Schengen Borders Code). It should be noted that the Treaty of Lisbon did not alter the legal position on this point.

Secondly, the position of Denmark as regards border controls was governed, before the entry into force of the Treaty of Lisbon, by both the Schengen Protocol and the Protocol on Denmark; both Protocols were subsequently amended by the Treaty of Lisbon.[134] The former Protocol provided originally that Denmark was bound by those provisions of the Schengen *acquis* allocated to the former Title IV EC, but only as public international law; the Treaty of Lisbon has repealed this provision.[135] The latter Protocol provides (both before and after the Treaty of Lisbon) that as regards all Title IV EC (now Title V TFEU) measures building on the Schengen *acquis*, Denmark can decide within six months of their adoption whether to apply them in its national law, in

---

[125] See I:3.4.1 and I:3.4.2 below.   [126] Case C-202/13, ECLI:EU:C:2014:2450.

[127] For detailed discussion of this Protocol, see I:2.2.5.1.3 above.

[128] For detailed discussion of this Protocol, see I:2.2.5.1.2 above.

[129] This Directive is discussed in I:7.5.2 below.   [130] See I:3.11 below.

[131] See I:3.9 below.

[132] Cases C-77/05 *UK v Council* [2007] ECR I-11459 and C-137/05 *UK v Council* [2007] ECR I-11593. See also by analogy Case C-482/08 *UK v Council* [2010] ECR I-10413, as regards an attempt of the UK to opt in fully to a measures governing law enforcement access to the Visa Information System. On the other hand, EU measures in this field can provide for a form of association for the UK and Ireland, subject to certain conditions: see the judgment in Case C-44/14 *Spain v EP and Council*, ECLI:EU:C:2015:554.

[133] See the second edition of this book, at pp 58–9.

[134] On the Danish position generally, see I:2.2.5.2 above.

[135] Previous Art 3, Schengen Protocol. See now Art 2, Schengen Protocol, which refers to the Protocol on Denmark for the legal position of Denmark as regards the Schengen *acquis*.

which case those measures bind Denmark and the other participating Member States as a matter of public international law.[136] Denmark has consistently applied this option to measures concerning border controls (and visas), although it was not able to use this power as regards two issues discussed in this chapter (the ARGO programme and international treaties),[137] as these measures did not build upon the Schengen *acquis*.

Thirdly, the Member States joining the EU in 2004, 2007, and 2013 (the 'newer Member States') were subject upon accession to only part of the Schengen *acquis* and measures building upon it in this area.[138] In particular, the rules on external border controls (except for checks in the SIS) applied immediately. Also, the ARGO programme also applied immediately upon accession, as it did not build upon the Schengen *acquis*.[139] Conversely, the abolition of internal border controls would not apply until the entire Schengen *acquis* (and subsequent measures building on it) was fully applied to the newer Member States. As for measures adopted following the agreement on the Treaty of Accession, each measure indicates whether it applied immediately to the newer Member States or only after the extension of the Schengen *acquis* to those States.[140] Moreover, the 2003 Accession Treaty made a number of technical amendments to secondary measures to refer to the rules in the newer Member States,[141] and special legislation was adopted to regulate transit via the newer Member States in the interim period before the Schengen *acquis* applied to them fully.[142]

The extension of the Schengen area to the newer Member States was delayed when it proved impossible to implement a new version of the Schengen Information System (SIS II) when initially planned, due to the delays in proposing and negotiating the legislation and to operational problems.[143] This issue was eventually tackled by adopting a proposal from Portugal for the development of an 'SIS One4All', which extended the existing SIS to the new Member States (a solution which had previously been thought to be technically impossible). The JHA Council agreed upon this proposal in December 2006, setting a new date for the enlargement of the Schengen zone between end-2007 and March 2008, and accepting the resulting delay in the development of SIS II.[144] The 'SIS One4All' proposal was then implemented successfully, and the Schengen area was duly fully extended to nine new Member States (all except Cyprus, Romania,

---

[136] Current Art 4, Protocol on Denmark; see, before the entry into force of the Treaty of Lisbon, the former Art 5 of that Protocol.

[137] See I:3.11 and I:3.12 below respectively.

[138] On the position of the newer Member States, see: Art 3 of the 2003 Treaty of Accession and Annex I to that Treaty ([2003] OJ L 236); Art 4 of the 2005 Treaty of Accession and Annex II to that Treaty ([2005] OJ L 157/203); and Art 4 of the 2011 Treaty of Accession and Annex II to that Treaty ([2011] OJ L 112/21). For a general discussion of the issue, see I:2.2.5.3 above.

[139] On the substance, see I:3.11 below.

[140] See, for instance, the Schengen Borders Code (Reg 562/2006, [2006] OJ L 105/1), which applied fully to all (Schengen) Member States immediately, except for the rules on internal border control abolition and the Schengen Information System, which did not (or will not) apply to newer Member States until the Schengen rules were (or will be) fully extended to them. On the substance of the Borders Code, see I:3.6.1 below.

[141] Annex II, part 18, to the 2003 Accession Treaty ([2003] OJ L 236). There were no such amendments in the 2005 or 2011 Accession Treaties, n 138 above.

[142] See I:4.2.5 below.

[143] See the 9th report of the House of Lords EU Select Committee (2006–07), para 23.

[144] See the conclusions of the JHA Council of 2–3 Dec 2006 on these various issues.

and Bulgaria) as from 21 December 2007, and as from 30 March 2008 as regards air borders.[145] None of those three Member States (or Croatia, which joined the EU in 2013) has yet fully joined the Schengen system, although Romania and Bulgaria have applied the SIS since 2010.[146]

Fourthly, as for the position of non-Member States,[147] the Schengen and EU rules discussed in this chapter are all fully applicable to Norway and Iceland as from March 2001 (or subsequently, for measures adopted later), following the Schengen association agreement with those States,[148] except for the ARGO programme, which did not build on the Schengen *acquis*.[149] Also, these States have agreed further treaties with the EU which set out specific arrangements for involvement in the EU borders agency and the Borders Fund,[150] along with their participation in committees which assist the Commission when it adopts implementing measures, in addition to those States' participation in the relevant Regulations.[151]

As for Switzerland, the Schengen association agreement signed with that country in 2004 entered into force on 1 March 2008,[152] and the Schengen *acquis* was then extended fully to Switzerland on 12 December 2008, except for the application of the *acquis* to air borders, which took place on 29 March 2009.[153] Switzerland and the EU have also agreed a treaty with the EU as regards Swiss participation in the EU's border agency,[154] and Switzerland participates besides Norway and Iceland in the treaties concerning the EU's border fund and participation in relevant Commission committees.[155]

Liechtenstein has participated in the Schengen *acquis* since 2011, pursuant to the relevant Protocol to the Schengen association agreement with Switzerland.[156] The EU-Swiss treaty on association with the EU borders agency also applies to Liechtenstein, as do the treaties concerning the EU's border fund and participation in relevant Commission committees.[157] Again, for Switzerland and Liechtenstein, special legislation was adopted to regulate transit via those States in the interim period before the Schengen *acquis* applied to them fully.[158]

Finally, as regards the EU's power after the Treaty of Lisbon to regulate issues relating to passports and similar documents, it should be noted that any measures adopted on

---

[145] [2007] OJ L 323/34. The *acquis* regarding the Schengen Information System in fact applied to these new Member States from 1 Sep 2007, except that before the full application of the Schengen rules to the new Member States, those States were not able to enter alerts banning entry to third-country nationals into the SIS and were not obliged to act on such alerts ([2007] OJ L 179/46).

[146] [2010] OJ L 166/17.   [147] See further I:2.2.5.4 above.   [148] [1999] OJ L 176/35.

[149] On the substance, see I:3.11 below.   [150] See I:3.11 below.

[151] Respectively [2007] OJ L 188/19; [2012] OJ L 103/4; and [2009] OJ L 169/24. The first treaty was signed in Feb 2007, but is not in force yet. The second and third treaties are in force between the EU and all of the Schengen associates.

[152] [2008] OJ L 53/18. For the treaty, see [2008] OJ L 53/52. On the parallel treaty on asylum applications, see I:5.2.5 below.

[153] [2008] OJ L 327/15. The SIS had previously been extended first to Switzerland, subject to certain restrictions until the full extension of the Schengen *acquis* to that country ([2008] OJ L 149/74; see nn 145 and 146 above on the equivalent restrictions for some newer Member States).

[154] [2010] OJ L 243/4.   [155] On those treaties, see n 153 above.

[156] For the Protocol and the decision on Schengen association, see [2011] OJ L 160.

[157] nn 153 and 154 above.   [158] See I:4.2.5 below.

the basis of this power will not build upon the Schengen *acquis*, because of their link to the free movement of all EU citizens.[159] This means that if these measures apply to associated States, this would take place, if at all, on the basis of association agreements. For the UK, Ireland, and Denmark, the general Title V opt-out rules, rather than the Schengen rules, will apply.

3.3 Human Rights

3.3.1 International human rights law

The starting point for any analysis of the application of human rights rules to migration issues is that as a general rule, there is no human right for anyone to enter or stay in a foreign country. However, human rights rules do entail a right to enter or stay in particular circumstances, although the precise scope of those circumstances is open to some dispute. To date, human rights rules have had more impact in practice on preventing the expulsion of persons who have a claim for asylum or some other need for international protection, or who have been resident for long periods.[160] The impact of human rights rules on entry is less clear. However, there are cases in which there is a right of entry for family reunion,[161] and arguably there is a right of entry in order to make a claim for international protection, since Article 33 of the Geneva Convention on refugee status (the non-refoulement clause) and Article 3 of the European Convention of Human Rights (ECHR) and other relevant ECHR Articles are applicable to persons who reach Member States' borders and make claims for protection. In particular, the European Court of Human Rights has made clear in the important 2012 judgment in *Hirsi Jamaa* that interception on the high seas needs to comply with the ECHR. An inadequate consideration of claims for protection and a return to an unsafe country in that case constituted a violation of Article 3 ECHR and the ban on collective expulsion of aliens set out in the Fourth Protocol to the ECHR.[162]

Since the latter category of entrants does not usually make a prior formal application for entry which can be examined by the host State's authorities and often attempts to cross the border irregularly, the rules governing entry control at the borders can be particularly important to their practical ability to enter and make a claim for protection. Also, Article 31 of the Geneva Convention exempts refugees who enter or stay without authorization from penalties, under certain circumstances.[163]

In which cases can persons claim the right to short-term entry? First of all, examining the rights set out in the ECHR, given their pre-eminence as a source of the general principles of EU law, their important role in connection with the EU Charter of Rights, and the EU's obligation to accede to the ECHR,[164] it is arguable that the 'right to respect

---

[159] In light of the Court of Justice's judgments in the *UK v Council* cases (n 132 above), it is hard to imagine a measure which falls within the scope of the external borders legal base but which does not build upon the Schengen *acquis*.

[160] See I:5.3 and I:6.3 below respectively.   [161] See I:6.3.1 below.

[162] For detailed comments and further references, see ch 3 of S Peers, V Moreno Lax, M Garlick and E Guild, *EU Immigration and Asylum Law: Text and Commentary*, 2nd edn, vol 3 (Brill, 2015).

[163] See I:7.3.2 below for details.   [164] See I:2.3 above.

for family life and private life' set out in Article 8 ECHR entails the right to short-term visits to family members, as broadly defined in light of the relationships between adult children and their parents and between adult siblings.[165] This principle could even apply to visits to friends, which would fall within the scope of 'private life'. To date, there is no judgment of the European Court of Human Rights to confirm whether such an argument would be successful or not.[166]

The rights to freedom of religion, expression, and association in Articles 9–11 ECHR could equally serve as a basis for a right for short-term admission, in order (for example) to participate in a religious event, to express a political, artistic, or other opinion, or to join with a group of like-minded protesters demonstrating at a particular event. In the case of *Piermont* the Human Rights Court ruled that an expulsion of a person along with the ban on re-entry into the territory, and a refusal of entry into another territory, merely for expressing her political opinions, violated the right to freedom of expression guaranteed by Article 10 ECHR.[167] The Court has subsequently confirmed the obvious implication that in some cases at least, there must be a right to initial entry (or re-entry) to a person at least for the purpose of expressing an opinion and for the purposes of freedom of religion (Article 9 ECHR);[168] this principle must logically also apply (given the similar wording of Articles 9–11 ECHR) to the freedom of association. In each case, of course, an interference with the right could still be justified on grounds of public order, if prescribed by law and necessary and proportionate in a democratic society.[169]

However, Article 16 ECHR provides that nothing in Articles 10, 11, or 14 of the Convention (Article 14 concerns non-discrimination) can prevent States 'from imposing restrictions on the political activity' of foreigners. The judgment in *Piermont* reasoned that Article 16 was not applicable since the applicant was both the national of another EU Member State and a Member of the European Parliament, leaving open the question of whether the subsequent creation of EU citizenship might afford even greater protection. Even the judges dissenting from the majority judgment accepted that '[a]ccount must be taken of the increased internationalisation of politics in modern circumstances', entailing limits on the application of Article 16; in their view, Article 16 merely accorded more discretion (but not absolute discretion) to a State when restricting foreigners' political expression than when restricting its own nationals' expression. In any event, Article 16 is not applicable to the freedom of religion pursuant to Article 9,

---

[165] As regards admission and stay for long periods, Art 8 appears to apply to a narrower scope of family members (see I:6.3.1 below), but such restrictions of scope should not be applicable to family *visits*, which constitute a normal part of family life as enjoyed by adults and which in principle do not entail immigration to the host State.

[166] See, however, the admissibility decision in *Bartik v Russia* (16 Sep 2004, unreported), which fails to consider the argument made in n 165.

[167] *Piermont v France* (A-314).

[168] See: *Nolan and K v Russia*, 12 Feb 2009; *Perry v Latvia*, 8 Nov 2007; and *Cox v Turkey*, 20 May 2010. See also, by analogy, *Women on Waves v Portugal*, 3 Feb 2009.

[169] In *Piermont*, the invocation of Art 10(2) failed because the opinions in question were non-violent, were spoken at a peaceful demonstration, and did not result in any disorder. In *Nolan*, the Art 9(2) defence failed because there was no evidence offered to prove the alleged risk to 'national security' of the person concerned; moreover, Art 9(2) ECHR does not list 'national security' as a possible ground to justify interference with the freedom of religion. In *Perry*, the national rules were not 'prescribed by law'. In *Cox*, the restrictions were disproportionate because although the applicant's opinions were controversial, she did not support violence.

or to the expression of *non*-political opinion. Moreover, the dissenting judges did not question the underlying principle that Article 10 entails rights in relation to immigration law. It should be emphasized that the applicant had *not* been exercising a free movement right under EU free movement law when she expressed her opinion, as the dispute concerned French territories where there is no right of free movement under EU law; so it follows that Article 10 curtails States' immigration law powers even in the absence of a free movement right.

Several other provisions of the Convention are relevant. Article 5 provides that a person can be deprived of liberty following a 'lawful arrest or detention...to prevent his [or her] effecting an unauthorized entry into the country', subject to obligations to inform that person about the grounds for detention, to permit judicial review, and to compensate persons in case of breaches of that Article.[170] Article 6 gives a right to a fair trial to 'everyone' to determine 'civil rights or obligations' or 'any criminal charge', but the Human Rights Court has held that this Article is not applicable to cases concerning immigration or asylum.[171] However, if an immigration or asylum case falls within the scope of another right protected by the Convention, there are in-built procedural protections connected with those rights.[172] Similarly, Articles 13 (the right to an effective remedy) and 14 (the right to non-discrimination) only apply where one of the ECHR rights has been violated. It should also be kept in mind that the right to respect for private life set out in Article 8 also comprises a right to protection of personal data, which is increasingly relevant as regards border controls.[173]

As for the Protocols to the ECHR, the ECHR organs have held that the right to property set out in the First Protocol does not entail a right to permanent residence for foreigners in order to enjoy access to their property, leaving open the argument that there is a right to short-term entry to that end.[174]

Next, the Fourth Protocol contains a number of important rights, although it has not been ratified by two Member States.[175] Article 2(1) of the Protocol states that '[e]veryone lawfully within the territory of a State shall, within that territory, have the right to liberty of movement and freedom to choose his [or her] residence'. Article 2(2) of that Protocol provides that '[e]veryone shall be free to leave any country, including his [or her] own'. However, States may set limitations on these rights similar to the limits they may place on Articles 8–11 ECHR, and they may set broader 'public interest' restrictions on the first of these rights.[176] Also, Article 3 of the Protocol gives nationals the right to enter the territory of their own State, and freedom from expulsion from their own State; this provision is considered in Chapter 7 of this volume.[177]

---

[170] These provisions of Art 5 ECHR apply equally to expulsion, and so are considered in I:7.3.2 below.

[171] *Maaouia v France* (Reports 2000-X). However, a State may be obliged to admit a person to take part in civil proceedings: see Commission decision in *Mangov v Greece* (18 Feb 1993, unreported).

[172] See the discussion in I:6.3.3 below, and in particular the judgment in *Nolan*, n 168 above.

[173] On the relevant ECtHR case law, see further II:7.3.1; on EU data protection legislation, see I:3.4.3 below. There is also a specific Convention of the Council of Europe concerning protection of personal data (CETS 108), which has been ratified by all Member States.

[174] Decision in *Ilic v Croatia* (Reports 2000-X).   [175] Greece and the UK.

[176] Art 2(3) and 2(4), Fourth Protocol.

[177] Also, the provisions prohibiting the collective expulsion of foreigners (Art 4, Fourth Protocol), and the procedural rights against expulsion for individual foreigners (Art 1, Seventh Protocol) are considered further in I:7.3 below.

The jurisprudence on Article 2 of the Fourth Protocol makes clear that Article 2(1) only applies to those lawfully within the country; it does not apply to persons following their expulsion or if they have not been legally admitted to the territory.[178] However, it appears clear from the *Piermont* judgment and the wording of Article 2(1) that both visitors and residents fall within the scope of the right.[179]

As for Article 2(2) of the Fourth Protocol, the Human Rights Court has held that in principle it prohibits States from seizing an individual's passport, unless this can be justified by significant grounds of public order.[180] Equally a refusal to issue a travel document in the first place breaches Article 2(2),[181] as does a ban on travel outside the country.[182] Moreover, the Court has found that a withdrawal of a passport and a denial of exit from a territory can in certain circumstances violate Article 8 of the Convention, thus applying equivalent obligations to States which have not ratified the Fourth Protocol.[183] It laid particular stress on the cross-border family and economic links which many individuals enjoy in the modern world.

Despite the non-ratification of the Fourth Protocol by two Member States, it should be noted that the rights set out in Article 2 of that Protocol are enshrined in nearly identical terms in Article 12(1) to (3) of the International Covenant on Civil and Political Rights (ICCPR), which all Member States have ratified.[184]

3.3.2 Application to EU law

To what extent do the most relevant rights set out in international human rights law form part of the general principles of EU law? The Court of Justice has not yet ruled on whether the rights set out in Article 2 of the Fourth ECHR Protocol are protected as part of the general principles of EU law, but it has referred to certain provisions of EU free movement law as specific manifestations of the provisions of Article 2,[185] and it

---

[178] *Piermont v France*, n 167 above. In the subsequent judgment of *Tatishvili v Russia* (22 Feb 2007), the Court found that a citizen of the former USSR fell within the scope of Art 2 of Protocol 4 in Russia, since at the relevant time such persons did not need a residence permit in Russia. In *Bolat v Russia* (2006 ECHR-XI), a violation of Art 2(1) was found as regards a foreigner, but in this case the Human Rights Court implicitly assumed that the person concerned was 'lawfully within' Russia for the purpose of Art 2.

[179] On other forms of restrictions on free movement, see, for example, the judgments in *Raimondo v Italy* (Series A-281), *Labita v Italy* (Reports 2000-IV), *Denizci and others v Cyprus* (Reports 2001-V), *Luordo v Italy* (Reports 2003-IX), *Antonenkov and others v Ukraine* (22 Nov 2005), and *Timishev v Russia* (12 Dec 2005).

[180] *Baumann v France* (Reports 2001-V); *Napijalo v Croatia* (13 Nov 2003); *Földes and Földesné Hajlik v Hungary* (31 Oct 2006).

[181] *Bartik v Russia* (21 Dec 2006). In this case the objective of protecting 'state secrets' was a legitimate ground for restriction pursuant to Art 2(3) of the Protocol, but nonetheless the restriction was disproportionate in all the circumstances.

[182] *Riener v Bulgaria* (23 May 2006). In this case the objective of ensuring payment of tax was a legitimate ground for restriction pursuant to Art 2(3) of the Protocol, but again the restriction was disproportionate in all the circumstances. See also *A.E. v Poland* (31 Mar 2009) and *Bessenyei v Hungary* (21 Oct 2008).

[183] *Iletmis v Turkey* (Reports 2005-XII).

[184] On the implications of this, see I:2.3 above. On the interpretation of the ICCPR provisions, see S Joseph, J Schultz, and M Castan, *The International Covenant on Civil and Political Rights: Cases, Materials and Commentary*, 2nd edn (OUP, 2004), at 348–64.

[185] Case 36/75 *Rutili* [1975] ECR 1219, para 28. See subsequently Case C-100/01 *Olazabal* [2002] ECR I-10981, where the Court failed to consider the human rights context. The Opinion in pending Joined Cases

does recognize the principles set out in Article 3 of the Fourth Protocol that states cannot expel and must admit their own nationals.[186] So it seems probable that the rights set out in Article 2 of the Fourth Protocol also form part of the general principles of EU law. In fact, several provisions of EU immigration and asylum legislation specifically set out the right to free movement within a Member State,[187] and EU law might also be relevant for determining whether a person is 'lawfully' within a Member State's territory. Moreover, it is arguable that within the scope of EU law, the relevant ECHR principles do not only apply within each individual Member State, but also have a *cross-border dimension*.

On the other hand, it is striking that the rights set out in Article 2 of the Fourth Protocol to the ECHR are not set out in the EU's Charter of Fundamental Rights. The Charter recognizes instead that EU citizens have the right to move and reside freely across the EU, while third-country nationals may be granted that right.[188] However, the CJEU has confirmed that even if a right is not listed in the EU Charter of Fundamental Rights, it might still be protected purely as part of the general principles of EU law.[189] In any case, Member States nonetheless have to uphold their obligations under international human rights treaties which they have ratified. It should be recalled that the EU itself is not planning to ratify the Fourth Protocol, as part of the process of acceding to the ECHR.[190]

As for Article 6 of the ECHR, even though the ECHR does not confer procedural rights in general relating to refusal of entry at the border, it should be recalled that rights to procedural protection (a fair trial and effective remedies) are recognized as forming part of the general principles of EU law and the EU Charter (which also draw upon national constitutional principles as a source of law), and that such rights have a *wider scope* within EU law than they do under the ECHR.[191] Arguably, therefore, there is a right to a fair trial and effective remedies in relation to refusals of entry at the border; but at the very least, such rights should be recognized as regards visits to family members and, since the general principles of EU law and the Charter recognize the right to carry on a business,[192] short-term admission for business visits. The general principles and the Charter also recognize the rights to freedom of religion, expression, and association.[193]

Finally, it should be noted that the EU's border control legislation makes express provision for human rights in several respects. The Schengen Borders Code has a

---

C-443/14 and C-444/14 *Alo and Osso* argues that freedom of movement within a Member State is indeed one of the general principles of EU law.

[186] See I:7.3.4 below.

[187] Art 7 of Dir 2013/33 on reception conditions for asylum seekers ([2013] OJ L 180/96) sets out permitted restrictions; Arts 11(1)(f) and 21(1) of Dir 2003/109 on long-term residents ([2003] OJ L 16/44) requires equal treatment with nationals, as does Art 14(1)(h) Dir 2009/50, the 'Blue Card' Directive on highly-skilled migration ([2009] OJ L 155/17); and Art 33 of Dir 2011/95 on refugee and subsidiary protection status ([2011] OJ L 337/9) requires equal treatment with third-country nationals. However, Dirs 2001/55 on temporary protection ([2001] OJ L 212/12), 2003/86 on family reunion ([2003] OJ L 251/12), 2004/81 on victims of trafficking ([2004] OJ L 261/19), 2004/114 on students and others ([2004] OJ L 375/12), and 2005/71 on researchers ([2005] L 289/15) make no express reference to the right. Neither does EU visas or borders legislation.

[188] Art 45 of the Charter ([2007] OJ C 303).   [189] See I:2.3 above.   [190] Ibid.

[191] See I:6.3.4 below.

[192] As regards the general principles, see, for example, Joined Cases C-184/02 and C-223/02 *Spain and Finland v Council and EP* [2004] ECR I-7789, paras 51 and 52. As for the Charter, see Art 16.

[193] See Arts 10–12 of the Charter and Case C-112/00 *Schmidberger* [2003] ECR I-5659.

general human rights exception, and more specifically provides that the obligation to impose penalties for unauthorized crossing of external borders is 'without prejudice to' Member States' international protection obligations,[194] and that the obligation to refuse entry to persons who do not meet the criteria for entry is 'without prejudice to the application of special provisions concerning the right of asylum and to international protection'.[195] The Borders Code also sets out procedural rights in the event of refusal of entry.[196] There are also rules on data protection safeguards and procedural rights in the concerning the Schengen Information System, biometric passports, and the EU's borders agency, Frontex;[197] and the latter furthermore includes a number of other human rights protections.[198]

3.4 Impact of Other EU Law

The debate over the extent to which 'other' (ie non-JHA) EU law applies to borders issues is not yet over.[199] Despite the powers now conferred by Article 77 TFEU (formerly Article 62 EC) regarding border controls and the special institutional rules applicable to them, other EU law rules still have an important impact on these issues, particularly in the area of free movement law, but association agreements and data protection law are also relevant. In case of any conflict between EC law (as it then was) and the initial Schengen *acquis* as integrated into the EC legal order in 1999, it should be kept in mind that EC law prevailed, according to the original version of the Schengen Protocol.[200] In the event of conflict between measures building on the *acquis* and EU free movement law, association agreements, the EU's general principles of law, or the EU Charter of Fundamental Rights (since the Treaty of Lisbon), the latter four sources of law are hierarchically superior to secondary EU law measures.[201] In any case, most measures building upon the Schengen *acquis* provide in some form expressly for priority for EU free movement law or human rights law.[202]

3.4.1 Free movement law

The starting point for any discussion of the effect of free movement law in this area is obviously Article 26 TFEU (previously Art 14 EC), concerning the abolition of internal border checks. The legal effect of Article 14 as regards checks on persons was finally clarified by the *Wijsenbeek* judgment of the Court of Justice in 1999.[203] Late in 1993, after the entry into force of the original TEU but before the application of the Schengen Convention, a Dutch MEP returning to the Netherlands had refused to present his documents to Dutch border guards, and had faced a criminal conviction imposing a

---

[194] See I:3.6.1 below.   [195] Art 13(1), Reg 562/2006 ([2006] OJ L 105/1).
[196] Art 13(2) and (3) and Annex V of the Code.   [197] See further I:3.7, I:3.9, and I:3.10 below.
[198] See further I:3.10 below.
[199] The question of the application of EC law to borders issues *prior* to the Treaty of Amsterdam is considered in I:3.2.1 above.
[200] See I:2.2.2.2 above.   [201] See further I:2.4.2 above.
[202] On the priority of human rights law, see I:3.3.2 above; on the priority of EU free movement law, see I:3.4.1 below.
[203] Case C-378/97 *Wijsenbeek* [1999] ECR I-6207.

small fine (or a day's imprisonment) as a result. The Court of Justice ruled that at the relevant time, Article 14 (then Article 7a) EC (now Article 26 TFEU) did not have the automatic effect of abolishing internal border checks between Member States. Such abolition could only result from the harmonization of national law on visas, external border checks, asylum, and immigration. It was not clear whether this harmonization of national law could be attained at the time by Schengen or third pillar measures, or only by means of Community legislation,[204] although given the subsequent development of EC (now EU) rules, the point is now moot.

Similarly, the right of EU citizens to 'move and reside freely' within the EU pursuant to Article 18 EC (Article 8a EC at the time of the dispute; now Art 21 TFEU) did not preclude Member States from checking whether persons were indeed citizens of the Union who could benefit from that right. As for the punishment imposed by the authorities, the Court reiterated the established principle of free movement law that '[i]n the absence of Community rules governing the matter, the Member States remain competent to impose penalties for breach of' obligations related to control of the movement and residence of persons, 'provided that the penalties applicable are comparable to those which apply to similar national infringements. However, Member States may not lay down a penalty so disproportionate as to create an obstacle to the free movement of persons, such as a term of imprisonment'. The Court then expressly stated that '[t]he same considerations apply as regards breach of the obligation to present an identity card or a passport upon entry into the territory of a Member State'.[205] There is no reason to doubt that the Court's ruling on the issue of limited penalties for breach of such obligations applies fully to the UK, Ireland, Denmark, and the new Member States, despite their particular positions as regards the abolition of internal borders.[206]

The Court's judgment in *Wijsenbeek* did not rule on the legal effects of the Declarations to the Single European Act, on whether the EU institutions were subject to an obligation imposed by Article 14 EC (now Article 26 TFEU), on whether that Article also applies to third-country nationals, on the effect of the Treaty of Amsterdam (or, obviously, the later Treaty of Lisbon), or on the effect of the Schengen *acquis*. These issues were all addressed in the Opinion of the Advocate-General, who concluded: that the declarations to the SEA could not affect the interpretation of the Treaty;[207] that Article 14 EC obliged the EC institutions to act in order to abolish internal border checks;[208] that the personal scope of that Article necessarily included third-country nationals;[209] that the direct effect of that Article was impossible before the EC gained the relevant powers to act in the Treaty of Amsterdam; that the five-year deadline set by that Treaty superseded the end-1992 deadline set by the previous Article 14 EC;[210] and that the validity of national measures restricting EU citizens' right to 'move and reside freely' should be assessed by national courts in light of the Schengen rules as they applied before the entry into force of the Treaty of Amsterdam.[211]

---

[204] Paras 40 and 43 of the judgment suggest the former interpretation, while para 42 suggests the latter. See also discussion of the Advocate-General's Opinion, below.

[205] On these established principles, see further below in this section.

[206] See I:3.2.5 above.   [207] See paras 48–56 of the Opinion.

[208] See paras 37–42 of the Opinion.   [209] See para 59 of the Opinion.

[210] See paras 63–73 of the Opinion.   [211] See paras 108–14 of the Opinion.

This judgment left much to be decided in future, particularly regarding the relation-ship between Article 14 EC (as it then was) and the Schengen rules abolishing internal border checks and harmonizing the other issues referred to by the Court, which were integrated into EC law (as it then was) by the Treaty of Amsterdam. Moreover, the Court did not address the question of whether Article 14 (as it then was) contained binding obligations for *EC institutions*, as distinct from directly effective rights. What can be discerned from the *Wijsenbeek* judgment is that the Court has expressly recog-nized that the negative legal integration resulting from the abolition of internal border controls was subject to the adoption of considerable positive legal integration meas-ures. There was an obligation to accompany free movement with security measures; but conversely it should not be forgotten that those security measures are subsidiary, according to the logic of the Court's analysis, to the abolition of internal borders pro-vided for in the previous Article 14 EC.

The CJEU has not ruled in any further cases on the any relevant issues concerning Article 26 TFEU. While the Court has been able to build up a considerable jurispru-dence on the previous Article 21 TFEU (previously Article 18 TFEU), none of that jurisprudence, aside from the *Wijsenbeek* judgment, concerns border controls. The Treaty has conferred powers to implement Article 26 TFEU by further legislation, but originally (when the provision was Article 18 EC) those powers did 'not apply to provi-sions on passports, identity cards, residence permits or any other such document'.[212] Of course, the position on this issue changed with the Treaty of Lisbon.[213] Instead, before the entry into force of that Treaty, Member States adopted a series of Resolutions on a uniform passport format for EU citizens,[214] and the Council adopted passport meas-ures pursuant to the EC's external border control powers.[215] The Council also adopted conclusions on identity cards.[216]

Even though Articles 26 and 21 TFEU (and the predecessor Articles of the EC Treaty) so far have not had much effect on the issue of border controls, there are other relevant provisions of EU free movement law which have frequently been the subject of judgments of the Court of Justice. These rules are set out in the free movement art-icles of the Treaties and secondary legislation, which was amended and consolidated in 2004 (see below). Prior to this point, Directive 68/360 set out the immigration law rules applicable to EU citizens who worked in another Member State and to their fam-ily members (regardless of nationality).[217] These rules also applied to EU citizens who moved for other reasons (along with their family members).[218] As regards exit,[219] this legislation provided that Member States had to allow EU citizens and their family the

---

[212] Previous Art 18(3) EC.   [213] See Art 77(3) TFEU, discussed in I:3.2.3 and I:3.2.4 above.

[214] [1981] OJ C 241/1; [1982] OJ C 179/1; [1986] OJ C 185/1; [1995] OJ C 200/1; [2000] OJ C 310/1; and [2004] OJ C 245/1.

[215] Reg 2252/2004 ([2004] OJ L 385/1). On EC competence to adopt this Reg, see I:3.2.4 above; on the substance, see I:3.9 below.

[216] See I:3.9 below.

[217] [1968] OJ Spec Ed L 257/13, p 485. On the definition of 'family members', see I:6.4.1 below.

[218] Dir 73/148 ([1973] OJ L 172/14) (self-employed persons and service providers and recipients). Art 2(2) of each of Dirs 90/364 ([1990] OJ L 180/26), 90/365 ([1990] OJ L 180/28), and 93/96 ([1993] OJ L 317/59) extended the relevant provisions of Dir 68/360 to other groups of EU citizens.

[219] Art 2 of Dirs 68/360 and 73/148.

right to leave the territory to enter another Member State, 'on production of a valid identity card or passport', and could not demand exit visas or any equivalent document from their citizens. Member States had to issue such documents to their nationals 'in accordance with their laws'; arguably this had to be read in light of their human rights obligations to issue passports to their citizens.[220] As for entry, Member States had to allow entry merely 'on production of a valid identity card or passport'.[221]

Interpreting these rules, the Court of Justice ruled that a policy of imposing an entry clearance stamp in an EU citizen's passport upon entry is an equivalent measure to requiring a visa, and was therefore banned.[222] It was not permissible for border guards to ask EU citizens questions about the intended purpose of their visit, or their financial means.[223] On the other hand, the Court ruled that unsystematic and sporadic checks on EU citizens, on occasion at the border, to see if they are carrying the correct permits, did not violate EC (now EU) law if similar checks are carried out on that State's own nationals, unless those checks were 'carried out in a systematic, arbitrary or unnecessarily restrictive manner'.[224] As for third-country national family members of EU citizens, the Court ruled that they could be turned back at the border if they lacked an identity card or passport, or (if necessary) a visa, but not if they were able to prove their identity and conjugal ties and if there is no evidence that they were a risk to public policy, public security, or public health.[225] Third-country national family members were covered by the legislation setting out substantive limits to Member States' power to expel or deny entry to citizens of other EU Member States on grounds of public policy, public security, and public health, as well as procedural protection for those affected.[226]

The codified and amended rules applying to most aspects of free movement of EU citizens and their family members are now set out in Directive 2004/38, which Member States had to apply by 30 April 2006 (the 'EU citizens' Directive').[227] The rules on border controls in this Directive are the same as the previous rules,[228] except that the right of entry and exit is 'without prejudice to the provisions on travel documents applicable to national border controls', passports of third-country national family members cannot be stamped if they present the aforementioned residence card, and EU citizens and family members without the required documents must be given the chance to obtain them or corroborate their identity before being turned back.

The 2004 Directive does not incorporate most of the prior relevant case law, except as regards the possibility to corroborate identity at the border.[229] However, presumably the prior case law continues to apply in the absence of any indication to the contrary, since the intention of the Directive is to 'simplify and strengthen' EU citizens' free movement

---

[220] See I:3.3.1 above.   [221] Art 3 of Dirs 68/360 and 73/148.

[222] Case 157/79 *Pieck* [1980] ECR 2171.

[223] Case C-68/89 *Commission v Netherlands* [1991] ECR I-2637.

[224] Case 321/87 *Commission v Belgium* [1989] ECR I-997, para 15.

[225] Case C-459/99 *MRAX* [2002] ECR I-6591, paras 53–62. On the further implications of this judgment, see I:4.4.1 and I:7.4.1 below.

[226] Dir 64/221 [1964] OJ Spec Ed 1964, No. 850/64, p 117. Art 1(2) of the Directive expressly extended its scope to family members.

[227] [2004] OJ L 229/35. For further implications of this Directive, see 4.4.1, 6.4.1, and 7.4.1 below.

[228] Arts 4 and 5, Directive 2004/38 (ibid).

[229] The Commission report on the application of the Dir stated that six Member States did not apply this provision (Art 5(4)) at all, and three of them applied it incorrectly (COM (2008) 840, 10 Dec 2008).

right, which 'should, if it is to be exercised under objective conditions of freedom and dignity, be also granted to their family members, irrespective of nationality'.[230] The only possible apparent reduction in standards in this area is the reference to national rules on travel documents. On the other hand, there are two improvements on the existing rules and case law: the ban on stamping passports of some third-country national family members, and the possibility of obtaining the necessary travel documents before being turned back. However, it is likely that the latter rule could have been derived from interpretation of the previous legislation.

In a key ruling on the EU citizens' Directive, the Court of Justice confirmed that third-country national family members of EU citizens who have moved to another Member State have a right of entry in order to stay on the territory of the host Member State with that EU citizen—even if those family members are entering directly from a non-Member State, and thereby crossing the EU's external border.[231] This judgment also confirms that the competence to address the issue of the entry across the external borders of the family members of EU citizens who have moved within the EU derives from EU free movement law, not the competences set out in Title IV of the EC Treaty, as it then was. There is no reason to doubt that this judgment is still good law following the entry into force of the Treaty of Lisbon.

Although there is no case law directly on this point, it is clear that EU citizens' right to move and reside freely encompasses also the right to visit another Member State to exercise human rights, such as the freedom of expression and of association or assembly.[232] The Court of Justice has confirmed that EU citizens have a right to leave their own Member State, which can only be restricted on grounds of public policy, public security, and public health.[233]

The relationship between EU free movement rules and the criteria for including a person on the Schengen Information System list of persons to be banned entry into the entire EU has been a matter of some controversy. On this point, the Commission took the view that in light of the Court of Justice's case law, a third-country national family member of an EU citizen cannot be listed in the SIS unless he or she is 'an actual, genuine and serious threat to public policy and public security in each Schengen State'.[234] The Court of Justice has upheld this interpretation,[235] ruling that the Spanish

---

[230] Recitals 3 and 5 in the preamble to Directive 2004/38. This interpretation has been confirmed by Case C-127/08 *Metock* [2008] ECR I-6241.

[231] *Metock*, ibid. For more on *Metock*, see I:4.4.1, I:5.4.1, I:6.4.1, and I:7.4.1 below.

[232] This can be derived from the broad scope of the freedom to receive services (see, for instance, Cases 186/87 *Cowan* [1989] ECR 195 and C-274/96 *Bickel and Franz* [1998] ECR I-7637), and by analogy from the political rights of EU citizens set out in Art 22 TFEU. In such cases, free movement law and human rights law will both support the legal position of the EU citizen: This would be analogous to the link between free movement law and the right to family life, which has been confirmed in a number of cases: see I:6.3.4 below.

[233] Cases: C-430/10 *Gaydarov* [2011] ECR I-11637; C-434/10 *Aladzhov* [2011] ECR I-11659; and C-249/11 *Byankov*, ECLI:EU:C:2012:608. In particular, a Member State cannot restrict its nationals from travel to another Member State due to a breach of immigration law in that Member State prior to the former Member State joining the EU: Case C-33/07 *Jipa* [2008] ECR I-5157.

[234] See Commission communication on the derogations from EC free movement law (COM (1999) 372, 19 July 1999), p 19. See also the Declaration of the Schengen Executive Committee on this issue (SCH/Comex (96) decl 5, [2000] OJ L 239/458).

[235] Case C-503/03 *Commission v Spain* [2006] ECR I-1097. For further discussion, see I:2.4.2 above (as regards the general issue of the relationship between Schengen rules and Community law).

government wrongly refused a visa and entry at the border to family members of EU citizens solely because their names were listed in the SIS by another Member State, without first using the mechanisms established (the Sirene system) to ensure that such persons actually were a sufficiently serious threat to a requirement of public policy affecting one of the fundamental interests of society—a far higher threshold than established by the Schengen Convention, as it then was.[236] The legislation establishing the second-generation Schengen Information System (SIS II) now provides expressly that a SIS II alert can only be issued in conformity with the EU citizens' Directive, and also requires use of the Sirene manual in accordance with the Court's judgment.[237] Equally, the Schengen Borders Code provides expressly for the primacy of EU free movement law.[238]

Next, the right of EU companies to send their third-country national employees to other Member States, as part of the corporate provision of services,[239] has implications for border controls. It must follow from the Court's case law that the employees have a right of entry to another Member State, otherwise their employers' right to provide services would be entirely nugatory.[240]

3.4.2 Association agreements

The European Economic Area (EEA) agreement with Norway, Iceland, and Liechtenstein,[241] and a further agreement with Switzerland on free movement of persons,[242] extend EU free movement law to these third States. The EU citizens' Directive applies as between EU Member States and EEA States,[243] while a distinct set of free movement rules, similar to the EU's previous legislation on free movement of persons, applies as between the EU and Switzerland.[244] To that extent, the rules concerning borders applicable to EU citizens and their family members are equally applicable to citizens of the EEA States and Switzerland and their family members.

However, the situation resulting from other association agreements is more complex. The Court of Justice has confirmed that the initial admission of Turkish workers and their family members, pursuant to the association agreement with Turkey,[245] is a matter for Member States,[246] although such admission has since become subject in

---

[236] Art 96 of the Convention; on the substance of these rules, see I:3.7 below.

[237] Art 25, Reg 1987/2006 ([2006] OJ L 381/4). On SIS II and border controls, see I:3.7 below.

[238] Art 3(a), Reg 562/2006 ([2006] OJ L 105/1). See also the definition of beneficiaries of free movement in Art 2(5) of the Code, and the specific rules in Arts 7(2) and 10(2). On the substance of these provisions, see I:3.6.1 below.

[239] Cases: C-43/93 *Van der Elst* [1994] ECR I-3803; C-445/03 *Commission v Luxembourg* [2004] ECR I-10191; C-244/04 *Commission v Germany* [2006] ECR I-885; C-168/04 *Commission v Austria* [2006] ECR I-9041; C-219/08 *Commission v Belgium* [2009] ECR I-9213; and C-91/13 *Essent*, ECLI:EU:C:2014:2206. For more on posted third-country national workers, see I:4.4.1, I:6.4.4, and I:7.4.1 below.

[240] In the *Commission v Austria* judgment (n 239 above) the Court confirmed that a refusal to issue an entry permit to a worker who had entered without prior authorization and lacked a required visa was a breach of Art 49 EC (now Art 56 TFEU). This suggests strongly that there is an underlying right of entry for such workers.

[241] [1994] OJ L 1/1.   [242] [2002] OJ L 114/6.

[243] Pursuant to EEA Joint Committee Decision 158/2007 ([2008] OJ L 124/20), Directive 2004/38 applied to EEA States as from 4 Dec 2007 (Art 4).

[244] See Annex I to the EC-Swiss treaty, n 242 above.   [245] [1977] OJ L 261/60.

[246] See I:6.4.3 below.

part also to the EU's internal law.[247] But it has also ruled that once such persons have acquired rights pursuant to the EU-Turkey association agreement and its implementing rules, they have a right to *return* to the Member State where they acquired those rights.[248] As for Turkish service providers and self-employed Turks, there is a directly effective standstill on national rules which make the provision of services or the exercise of establishment more restrictive.[249] The Court of Justice has confirmed that this standstill applies to rules on entry control.[250] So it follows that national rules on entry control for Turkish persons providing (or possibly also receiving) services or exercising establishment cannot become any more stringent than they were at the date when the relevant Protocol entered into force for the Member State concerned.[251] This equally applies to *EU* rules concerning border control.[252]

As for the freedom of establishment under the Europe Agreements with ten Central and East European States that have since joined the EU, the Court of Justice ruled that Member States could impose prior entry clearance requirements before nationals of the EU's associate members could enter and take up their right to establish themselves.[253] Presumably the same principles will govern the provisions on establishment in the Stabilization and Association Agreements (SAAs) with Western Balkan countries, once they are applied.[254]

3.4.3 Other issues

EU data protection legislation[255] applies to the area of immigration and asylum law, including border controls.[256] Although the EU data protection Directive excludes from its scope matters dealt with by Title VI EU (ie the former third pillar) and

---

[247] See the legislation on the admission of third-country nationals, and family reunion for third-country nationals (I:6.5 and I:6.6 below).

[248] See C-351/95 *Kadiman* [1997] ECR I-2133; C-329/97 *Ergat* [2000] ECR I-1487; and C-188/00 *Kurz* [2002] ECR I-10691.

[249] Case C-37/98 *Savas* [2000] ECR I-2927 (self-employed persons); Joined Cases C-317/01 and C-369/01 *Abatay and others* [2003] ECR I-12301 (services).

[250] See Case C-16/05 *Tum and Dari* [2007] ECR I-7415. See also I:4.4.2 below, as regards visas.

[251] For the first nine Member States, this date was 1 Jan 1973. For other Member States, the relevant date is the day of their accession to the EU: see Case C-256/11 *Dereci* [2011] ECR I-11315.

[252] By analogy with the case law applying the standstill to visas: Case C-228/06 *Soysal* [2009] ECR I-1031. See further the discussion in I:4.4.2 below.

[253] See judgments in Cases C-63/99 *Gloszczuk* [2001] ECR I-6369; C-235/99 *Kondova* [2001] ECR I-6427; C-257/99 *Barkoci and Malik* [2001] ECR I-6557; and C-268/99 *Jany* [2001] ECR I-8615. For further discussion, see I:6.4.3 and I:7.4.2 below.

[254] [2004] OJ L 84 (Former Yugoslav Republic of Macedonia (FYROM)), [2005] OJ L 26 (Croatia), [2009] OJ L 107 (Albania), [2010] OJ L 108 (Montenegro), [2013] OJ L 278 (Serbia), and [2015] OJ L 164 (Bosnia-Herzegovina). An SAA has also been agreed with Kosovo (COM (2015) 183, 30 Apr 2015), but it is not yet in force. The SAA with FYROM provides that a decision will be made five years after entry into force of the agreement 'whether' to extend the establishment rules to self-employed persons (Art 48(4), FYROM SAA), while the other SAAs state that after four or five years, the 'modalities' of extending the establishment rules to self-employed persons will be adopted (Art 49(4), Croatia SAA; Art 50(4), Albania SAA; Art 53(4), Montenegro SAA; Art 51(3), Bosnia SAA; and Art 53(4), Serbia SAA).

[255] Dir 95/46 ([1995] OJ L 281/31) applies to Member States' processing of data, while Reg 45/2001 ([2001] OJ L 8/1) applies to EU bodies' processing of data. For more on EU data protection law, see II:7.3.2.

[256] The Reg establishing Frontex, the EU border control agency, refers to Reg 45/2001 (Art 11a, Reg 2007/2004, [2004] OJ L 349/1, as inserted by Reg 1168/2011, [2011] OJ L 304/1). The Reg setting out security

matters relating to public security and related issues, the first exclusion ceased to apply in respect of immigration-related issues as from 1 May 1999, with the entry into force of the Treaty of Amsterdam, because the relevant issues no longer fell inside the scope of the third pillar.[257]

As for the exclusions related to security matters, it should be recalled that as far back as 1987, the Court of Justice ruled that the entire issue of migration could not simply be subsumed within the concept of public order.[258] Furthermore, the case law on the EC data protection legislation has made clear that it applies regardless of whether or not there is a direct link to the exchange of personal data between Member States, and that it applies to the public sector.[259] It must be concluded that the practice of the EU institutions is correct as regards the applicability of the EU data protection legislation to immigration and asylum issues.[260] The EU data protection Directive must be interpreted in accordance with the case law of the European Court of Human Rights regarding the protection of personal data pursuant to Article 8 ECHR.[261]

Finally, does the ban on discrimination on the basis of nationality set out in Article 18 TFEU (previously Article 12 EC) apply to third-country nationals?[262] The Court of Justice appeared to limit the application of this provision to citizens of EU Member States in its *Khalil and Addou* judgment, but that judgment was explicitly confined to the legal position as it stood in 1971.[263] Subsequently, the Court ruled out the application of this provision to third-country nationals generally;[264] there is no reason to doubt that this case is still good law after the entry into force of the Treaty of Lisbon. However, an Advocate-General has argued that the non-discrimination rule applies to third-country national family members of EU citizens,[265] and this approach was later confirmed by the EU citizens' Directive.[266] Furthermore, three of the EU's association agreements contain their own non-discrimination rule.[267] Also, even though Article 18

---

features for EU passports (Reg 2252/2004, [2004] OJ L 385/1) refers to Dir 95/46 in recital 8 in the preamble. However, see the problematic case law of the CJEU on related issues, discussed in I:3.9 below. The SIS II Reg (Reg 1987/2006, [2006] OJ L 381/4) states that Dir 95/46 is applicable, but is supplemented and clarified by the Reg (recital 15 in the preamble; see also Arts 40, 42(1), and 44; recital 16 in the preamble and Arts 45(1) and 47 refer to Reg 45/2001). The Dir also applies to a measure implementing the SIS II Reg (the Sirene manual: see the most recent version ([2015] OJ L 44/75, recital 9 in the preamble).

[257] See II:7.3.2.

[258] Joined Cases 281-283, 285, and 287/85 *Germany and others v Commission* [1987] ECR 3203.

[259] See Joined Cases C-465/00, C-138/01; and C-139/01 *Osterreichischer Rundfunk* [2003] ECR I-4989 and Case C-101/01 *Lindqvist* [2003] ECR I-12971.

[260] See also C-524/06 *Huber* [2008] ECR I-9705, which confirms the applicability of Dir 95/46 to EU free movement law, as well as the substantive analysis in that judgment.

[261] Paras 68–72 of the judgment in *Osterreichischer Rundfunk*, n 259 above. On that case law, see further II:7.3.1.

[262] For a more detailed analysis of this issue, see E Guild and S Peers, 'Out of the Ghetto? The Personal Scope of EU Law' in S Peers and N Rogers, *EU Immigration and Asylum Law: Text and Commentary*, 1st edn (Martinus Nijhoff, 2006).

[263] Joined Cases C-95/99 to C-98/99 and C-180/99 [2001] ECR I-7413. On the further implications of this judgment, see I:5.4.2 and I:6.4.2 below.

[264] Joined Cases C-22/08 and C-23/08 *Vatsouras and Koupatantze* [2009] ECR I-4585.

[265] Opinion in *MRAX* (Case C-459/99 [2002] ECR I-6591), para 59.

[266] Art 24(1) of Dir 2004/38 ([2004] OJ L 229/35).

[267] Art 4 of the EEA treaty ([1994] OJ L 1/1); Art 2 of the EU-Swiss treaty on free movement of persons ([2002] OJ L 114/6); and Art 9 of the EU-Turkey association agreement ([1977] OJ L 261/60). For more on these treaties, see I:6.4.3 below.

TFEU does not apply to third-country nationals generally, the general principle of equality which forms part of EU law arguably does.[268]

3.5 Internal Border Controls

3.5.1 EU rules

The EU rules on the abolition of internal border controls, including a power to reintroduce those controls, were initially set out, as mentioned above, in the Schengen Convention.[269] This provision of the Convention was also implemented by three Decisions adopted by the Schengen Executive Committee, which concerned the issues of: obstacles to traffic flows,[270] bringing the Convention into force,[271] and procedures for reintroducing border checks.[272] The relevant provision of the Schengen Convention and the three Executive Committee Decisions were then integrated into the legal order of the EC (as it then was) with the entry into force of the Treaty of Amsterdam; all were attributed the legal base of Article 62(1) EC (now Article 77(2)(e) TFEU).[273]

Research on the application of the Schengen Convention in two Member States indicated that following the abolition of internal controls, the size and powers of 'internal' border guard forces were increased considerably.[274] Also, the power to reintroduce controls was frequently invoked, in particular in the context of planned large-scale demonstrations at EU summit meetings.[275] The Council even adopted measures on this issue, which in particular provided for the exchange of information on alleged troublemakers, with the aim of lessening the effect of reimposed internal border controls by means of targeted policing.[276]

As from 13 October 2006, the basic rules regulating the abolition of internal border controls derive from the Regulation establishing the Schengen Borders Code, which also sets out common rules on external border control.[277] The Code replaced

---

[268] See E Guild and S Peers, n 262 above. Note that the equivalent provision of the EU Charter (Art 21(2)) must be interpreted consistently with Art 18 TFEU, according to the explanatory memorandum to the Charter ([2007] OJ C 303).

[269] Art 2 of the Convention ([2000] OJ L 239/1).

[270] SCH/Com-ex (94) 1 rev 2 ([2000] OJ L 239/157).

[271] SCH/Com-ex (94) 29 rev 2 ([2000] OJ L 239/130).

[272] SCH/Com-ex (95) 20 rev 2 ([2000] OJ L 239/133).

[273] Decision 1999/436 ([1999] OJ L 176/17). However, this Council Decision stated that Art 2(2) and (3) of the Convention were without prejudice to Art 64(1) EC (now Art 72 TFEU), which sets out Member States' responsibilities as regards law, order, and security. On the interpretation of this provision, see I:3.2.4 above. Furthermore, Art 2(4) of the Convention was not allocated any legal base, because it was believed to be obsolete (see Decision 1999/435, [1999] OJ L 176/1).

[274] See K Groenendijk, 'New Borders Behind Old Ones: Post Schengen Controls Behind the Internal Borders—Inside the Netherlands and Germany' in E Guild, P Minderhoud, and K Groenendijk, eds., *In Search of Europe's Borders* (Kluwer, 2003), 131.

[275] See K Groenendijk, 'Reinstatement of Controls at the Internal Borders of Europe: Why and Against Whom?' (2004) 10 ELJ 150, and generally the second edition of this book, p 133.

[276] See: JHA Council conclusions (Press Release of the July 2001 JHA Council); a security handbook for police use at such events (Council doc 12637/3/02, 12 Nov 2002); and a Resolution on security at European Councils ([2004] OJ C 116/18). See further II:7.7.

[277] Reg 562/2006 ([2006] OJ L 105/1), Art 40. On the external borders provisions, see I:3.6.1 below.

the relevant provision of the Schengen Convention and two of the three Executive Committee Decisions.[278] Following a Commission report on the application of the internal borders rules,[279] and concerns about the operation of those rules after the 'Arab Spring' of 2011, the internal borders rules in the Code were amended in 2013.[280] In 2015, the Commission proposed to codify the entire Code, but this proposal has not yet been adopted.[281]

Before the entry into force of the Treaty of Lisbon, the CJEU was effectively prevented from interpreting these rules, pursuant to the prior Article 68(2) EC, which stated that the Court did not have 'jurisdiction to rule on any measure or decision taken pursuant to Article 62(1) [which conferred powers to adopt measures concerning internal borders] relating to the maintenance of law and order and the safeguarding of internal security'. After this limit on its jurisdiction was lifted by the Treaty of Lisbon, the Court has twice been asked to interpret the rules on internal border controls.[282]

Title III of the Code concerns internal border controls,[283] and Chapter I of this Title concerns the abolition of such controls.[284] Furthermore, following the 2013 amendments, one provision of the external borders rules in fact concerns internal borders.[285] It provides that following a Schengen evaluation report which reveals that there are 'serious deficiencies in the carrying out of external border control' by a Member State, the Commission can recommend specific measures to that Member State (in particular the use of certain provisions of the Frontex Regulation),[286] by means of implementing measures. If a Schengen evaluation finds that a Member State is 'seriously neglecting its obligations' and must report on this within three months, and the Commission finds that the problem is still continuing after three months, it can then trigger the process of reintroducing internal border controls in 'exceptional circumstances', as discussed below.

The first provision of the internal borders Title repeats the basic rule at the core of the previous Schengen Convention: 'internal borders can be crossed at any point without any checks on persons being carried out'.[287] Despite this basic rule, four types of checks are still permitted:[288] the exercise of police powers, where there is no 'effect

---

[278] Art 39(1) and 2(b) of the Code. The Decision which was not repealed was SCH/Com-ex (94) 29 rev 2 (n 271 above), setting out rules concerning the initial application of the Convention. It has not subsequently been amended or repealed, although points 3 and 4 of this Decision are now clearly obsolete. Nor is it included in the list of obsolete Schengen measures which the Commission proposes to repeal (COM (2014) 713, 28 Nov 2014).

[279] COM (2010) 554, 13 Oct 2010, as provided for in Art 38 of the Code.

[280] Reg 1051/2013 ([2013] OJ L 295/1). All references in the rest of this section are to the Borders Code Reg as amended, unless otherwise indicated.

[281] COM (2015) 8, 20 Feb 2015. For the benefit of future readers, this section refers also to the Art numbers of the Code following the proposed codification.

[282] Joined Cases C-188/10 and C-189/10 *Melki and Abdeli* [2010] ECR I-5667 and Case C-278/12 PPU *Adil*, ECLI:EU:C:2012:508. The CJEU has also ruled on the external borders provisions of the Code: see I:3.6 below.

[283] Arts 20–31 (Arts 22–35, codified version).

[284] Arts 20–22 (Arts 22–24, codified version), which was not amended at all by Reg 1051/2013.

[285] Art 19a (Art 21, codified version), inserted by Reg 1051/2013.

[286] On Schengen evaluations and Frontex, see I:3.10 below.

[287] Art 20 (Art 22, codified version).

[288] Art 21 (Art 23, codified version). Member States must notify the national provisions relating to the third and fourth exceptions to the Commission: Art 37 (Art 42, codified version). For these

equivalent to border checks'; security checks at ports and airports (if such checks also apply to movement within a Member State); the possibility to impose an obligation to hold or carry documents; and the optional registration requirement set out in the free-dom to travel provisions of the Schengen Convention.[289] The 'police powers' excep-tion sets out four cases 'in particular' where the exercise of police powers shall not be considered equivalent to border checks:[290] the checks do not have border control as an objective; they are based on general police information and experience and aim 'in particular' at combating 'cross-border crime'; they are devised and executed differently from systematic checks at the external borders; and they do not entail spot-checks.

Interpreting these rules, the CJEU ruled in *Melki and Abdeli* that a French police check within a border zone, which had resulted in the apprehension of two unlaw-fully present Algerian citizens, was not carried out at the border, so was not prohibited by the Schengen Borders Code. The objective of the checks concerned was not border control (which would have been prohibited under the Code), but rather to check the national obligation to hold or carry papers or documents (which was permitted by the Code, as seen above). Moreover, next, the national rules did not breach the rules in the Schengen Borders Code merely because those rules only applied to border zones. However, those national rules contained 'neither further details nor limitations on the power thus conferred – in particular in relation to the intensity and frequency of the controls which may be carried out', for the purpose of preventing those checks from infringing the rules of the Code. A national rule which gave the police the power to carry out identity checks specifically in border regions, where those powers did 'not depend upon the behaviour of the person checked or on specific circumstances giving rise to a risk of breach of public order', had to 'provide the necessary framework for the power granted to those authorities in order, inter alia, to guide the discretion which those authorities enjoy in the practical application of that power', so that the exercise of that power in practice did not have an effect equivalent to border checks, and therefore breach Article 21(a) of the Code.

The Commission's 2010 report on the application of the rules in the Schengen Borders Code on reimposition of internal border controls took particular account of the *Melki and Abdeli* judgment.[291] In the report, the Commission called upon Member States to amend their laws granting specific competence on police in border zones to ensure that the Code was complied with correctly.

In the subsequent *Adil* judgment, the Court of Justice ruled on the compatibility with the Schengen Borders Code of a Dutch law which resulted in the apprehension of a purported Afghan national, following police checks on a bus in the border zone. Again, the Court of Justice started out by observing that the checks in question were not carried out at the internal border as such, and so were not prohibited by the basic rule in the Code. Rather, the checks were carried out on the territory, so fell within the

---

notifications, see: <http://ec.europa.eu/justice_home/doc_centre/freetravel/rights/doc_freetravel_rights_en.htm#notifications>.

[289] Art 22 of the Convention, as amended by Reg 610/2013 ([2013] OJ L 182/1); see I:4.9 below.
[290] Art 21(a) (Art 23(a), codified version).   [291] COM (2010) 554, n 279 above.

scope of the list of possible exceptions to the rule. Next, again the checks carried out in this case did not have border control as an objective, since they did not aim to regulate the authorization of *entry*, but rather sought 'to establish the identity, nationality and/or residence status of the person stopped in order, principally, to combat illegal *residence*,[292] even though there were special rules in national law as regards carrying out such checks in border zones as compared to the rest of the territory.

The absence of a reference to combating unauthorized residence in the Code was irrelevant, since the list of rules specifying when the exercise of police powers is not equivalent to border checks was not exhaustive ('in particular'). Moreover, both the Treaty and the Code still provided for Member States to retain powers 'with regard to the maintenance of law and order and the safeguarding of internal security.[293]

Also, the national rules did not breach the Schengen Borders Code just because they were limited in scope to border areas. The crucial question was whether there was a legal framework in place to ensure that the exercise of those controls in practice did not have an effect equivalent to border checks. Nor was it problematic that the national law did not require 'reasonable suspicion of illegal residence, in contrast to the identity checks for that purpose carried out in the remainder of the national territory.' It was sufficient that such checks were being carried out on the basis of 'general police information and experience', as referred to in the Code.

Having said that, the Court insisted that the greater the possibility of an 'equivalent effect' to internal border controls, evidenced by the objective of the checks in a border zone, the territorial scope of these checks and from the creation of a distinction between those checks and the checks carried out in the rest of national territory, 'the greater the need for strict detailed rules and limitations laying down the conditions for the exercise by the Member States of their police powers in a border area and for strict application of those detailed rules and limitations, in order not to imperil the attainment of the objective of the abolition of internal border controls'. Applying that principle to the Dutch law: the objective of the checks was distinct from border controls; the checks were based on 'general police information and experience regarding illegal residence after the crossing of a border'; the checks were clearly distinct from systematic checks at the external borders, since they were carried out only for a limited period and not on all vehicles; and they were carried out on the basis of spot-checks, since vehicles were stopped based on sampling or profiling.

The Court of Justice's judgments have provided contrary examples of police checks which were, in turn, incompatible and compatible with the rules of the Schengen Borders Code. It emerges from the case law that police checks can be applied uniformly throughout national territory (in which case the Code is unlikely to be breached), or that specific rules can apply to police checks at internal border zones. In the latter case, to avoid a breach of the Schengen Borders Code, the specific rules must be accompanied by detailed safeguards, in particular to ensure that any checks are selective and targeted. The checks can focus specifically on irregular residence, which in practice will often entail detecting those who have crossed an internal border without authorization,

---

[292] Emphasis added.   [293] Art 72 TFEU, as discussed in I:3.2.4 above.

given that such checks will take place in the border zone under specific rules. So the requirement that such checks must be selective and targeted is the only feature that distinguishes them in practice from checks at internal borders.

Unfortunately, there is no notification or transparency requirement which would assist in an assessment of whether the rules are being applied correctly. Furthermore, it should be noted that these police checks are not covered by the ban on discriminatory conduct set out elsewhere in the Borders Code, which only applies to checks at the external borders;[294] but surely it can be argued that a police check within the scope of this internal borders provision which is mainly aimed at non-white people falls nonetheless within the scope of the principle of equality, which is protected as a general principle of EU law.

Finally, Member States are obliged to remove road-traffic obstacles at the internal borders, including any unjustified special speed limits, but nonetheless they must be 'prepared to provide for facilities' to reintroduce internal border checks if necessary.[295]

In the Commission's view, according to the 2010 report on the application of the rules on internal border controls,[296] border zones might present 'a particular risk for cross-border crime', so police checks could validly be more intense and frequent in those zones than in other parts of national territory. However, the Commission argued that such checks had to be 'targeted and based on concrete and factual police information and experience' regarding public security threats, and could not be 'systematic'. Such information had to be reassessed constantly, and so checks had to be random and based on risk assessment.

Most Member States stated that their checks met such criteria, but it was difficult to check whether checks to enforce immigration law met them. The objective of checks (whether on goods or persons) was also important, but Member States were free to assign different responsibilities to different authorities. In the Commission's view, the *frequency* of police checks at or near internal borders, as compared to checks in the rest of a Member State's territory in a similar situation, was a crucial factor in determining whether the former checks breached the Schengen Borders Code. But most Member States do not keep data on such issues, and some consider that it is not possible to make such comparisons, because 'practice and priorities' are different in the two areas. Others state that the frequency of checks near the internal borders is the same as in the rest of the territory.

The Commission concluded that a 'strict definition of the appropriate frequency and regularity' of checks near the internal borders was not possible, since the decision in such issues has to take account of differing situations in each Member State. While a 'high frequency' of such checks could be an 'indication' of a breach of the rules in the Schengen Borders Code, it was still 'difficult to assess in individual cases' whether this had an effect equivalent to border checks. Having analysed the legal issues, the Commission took the view that it needed more information from Member States on

---

[294] Art 6(2) (Art 7(2), codified version).

[295] Art 22 (Art 24, codified version). This clause took over the gist of Schengen Executive Committee Decision 94(1) (n 270 above), which was repealed by the Code.

[296] COM (2010) 554, 13 Oct 2010.

the reasons for and frequency of police checks in border zones, in order to monitor the situation and address complaints that some travellers are automatically checked in some internal border zones. To that end, the Commission was planning to request statistics on police checks within national territory, particularly at the border.[297] It was also planning to provide for unannounced border visits in its then-upcoming revised proposal to amend the rules on Schengen evaluations,[298] to check whether Member States were applying the rules properly.

As regards the possibility of checks on persons, the Commission recommends that airport, port, or carrier personnel do not combine various checks on persons in order to verify their identity (although such a combination of checks is legal), in order to avoid the *perception* that such checks are obstacles to citizens' free movement rights. Furthermore, these checks should only identify the person concerned on the basis of a travel document, although carriers could identify persons on the basis of other documents, such as driving licences and bank cards. In the Commission's view, such checks could only be carried out for 'commercial or transport security reasons', so cannot be used to check whether a person holds a visa or a residence permit. Member States cannot request such checks and the carriers are not subject to liability if the persons concerned do not meet the criteria for entry or stay in another Member State, as the EU's carrier liability legislation does not apply.[299] Nor can carriers require third-country nationals to prove the legality of their stay, or include such a rule in the contract with travellers.

Next, as regards the rules on obstacles to traffic flows, the Commission first of all points out that Schengen associates may maintain infrastructure for checking *goods* at Schengen borders, since those States do not participate in the EU's customs union. Secondly, the Commission observes that some EU Member States have maintained obstacles to traffic flows, in part because they only joined the Schengen area relatively recently and such obstacles took time to remove. Some Member States intend to use the old infrastructure if border controls are reimposed temporarily, while others use, or plan to use, mobile equipment in that case. In the Commission's view, permanent infrastructure can be maintained at internal borders, in light of the possible reintroduction of internal border controls, as long as this is 'not an obstacle to fluid traffic flow and speed limits are not reduced'. But the Commission also emphasizes that mobile infrastructure could be used for this purpose.

The second key element of the rules on internal border controls are the provisions on the possible reintroduction of internal border controls by a Member State (Chapter II of Title III of the Borders Code).[300] On this point, the basic rule is that a Member State can 'exceptionally' reintroduce border controls for up to 30 days, or for a longer period if the duration of the relevant event is foreseeable, in the 'event of a serious threat to public policy or to internal security'; but the 'scope and duration' of the reintroduced checks 'shall not exceed what is strictly necessary to respond to the reintroduced

---

[297] There is no information as to whether the Commission has followed up on its intentions.
[298] See I:3.10 below.   [299] On carrier sanctions, see I:7.5.1 below.
[300] Arts 23–31 (Arts 25–35, codified version). These provisions were extensively amended by Reg 1051/2013.

checks'.[301] This must be a 'last resort', however.[302] The reintroduction of controls may be continued for further renewable periods of up to 30 days, 'taking into account any new elements'.[303] But the maximum time to reintroduce border controls is six months, or two years in 'exceptional circumstances' (see discussion below).[304] Furthermore, since the 2013 amendments, before they reintroduce or extend internal border controls, Member States are required to 'assess the extent to which' this will 'adequately remedy the threat to public policy or external security', as well as the 'proportionality' of that threat. The Member State must 'in particular' take into account the 'likely impact of any threats to its public policy or internal security', including terrorism and organized crime, alongside the 'likely impact' on the free movement of persons.[305] Compared to the previous Schengen Convention rules,[306] the threshold for reintroduction of checks is higher, the time period is more precisely specified and the necessity rule is stricter.

The basic rule is supplemented by more specific rules, depending on whether the reintroduction of border checks is foreseeable, urgent, or constitutes 'exceptional circumstances'. First of all, where the reintroduction of controls is foreseeable,[307] Member States must inform the Commission and other Member States four weeks beforehand of its plans to reintroduce controls, and provide information 'as soon as available' on the reasons for and the scope of the reintroduction of controls, the authorized crossing points, the date and duration of the introduction, and (if relevant) the measures to be taken by other Member States. The Commission or another Member State may issue an opinion on the planned reintroduction, and there shall be consultation on the planned controls between the Member States and the Commission in order to discuss the proportionality of the controls and possibly also 'mutual cooperation between the Member States'. These rules were a change from the original rules as regards the role of the Commission (which had no role at all in the initial version of the Schengen *acquis*), the date of the consultations (at least ten days before the reintroduction of controls), and the requirement to discuss the proportionality of the planned controls.[308]

Secondly, in the event that 'immediate action' is required, Member States may reintroduce controls without prior notification, provided that the relevant information is sent to the Commission and other Member States later.[309] Border controls can only be introduced for ten days, renewable for periods of twenty days up to a total of three months.[310]

Thirdly, the 2013 amendments introduced a new power to re-introduce border controls in 'exceptional circumstances when the overall functioning' of the Schengen

---

[301] Art 23(1) (Art 25(1), codified version).

[302] Art 23(2) (Art 25(2), codified version), inserted by Reg 1051/2013.

[303] Art 23(3) (previously Art 23(2) before Reg 1051/2013; Art 25(3), codified version).

[304] Art 23(4), inserted by Reg 1051/2013 (Art 25(4), codified version).

[305] Art 23a, inserted by Reg 1051/2013 (Art 26, codified version).

[306] Art 2(2) of the Convention, repealed by the Borders Code.

[307] Art 24, as amended by Reg 1051/2013 (Art 27, codified version).

[308] Compare to point 1 of SCH/Com-ex (95) 20 (n 272 above), which was repealed by the Code. The 2013 amendments added the four-week notification deadline, and cut the consultation period from 15 days to 10.

[309] Art 25 (Art 28, codified version). There is no change from the previous rules (point 2 of SCH/Com-ex (95) 20, ibid).

[310] The time limits were added by Reg 1051/2013.

system is 'put at risk' by 'serious persistent deficiencies' regarding external border control, which were revealed by Schengen evaluations (as described above), if this constitutes 'a serious threat to public policy or internal security'.[311] The border controls would last for up to six months, and could be renewed up to three times for the same period 'if the exceptional circumstances persist'. The re-introduction (or prolongation) would be based on a recommendation of the Council, based on a proposal from the Commission, that one or more Member States reintroduce internal border controls. Member States could request the Commission to table such a proposal. Member States would have to inform the Commission if they did not follow this recommendation, and the Commission would present a report assessing that Member State's decision. In urgent cases where there was less than ten days' notice of the exceptional circumstances, the Commission could adopt the recommendation to reintroduce border controls by means of an implementing act.

Before making its recommendation, the Council would have to assess whether this would 'adequately remedy the threat to public policy or internal security within the area without internal border controls', and also 'assess the proportionality of the measure in relation to that threat'.[312] This assessment would be based on information from the Commission and the Member State(s) concerned, and would have to take into account the availability of support at EU level, the impact of the 'serious deficiencies', and the impact on the free movement of people in the Schengen area. For its part, before making its recommendation, the Commission could request further information from EU bodies and Member States, and carry out on-site visits.[313]

Finally, Title III of the Code contains provisions on: informing and reporting to the EP as regards decisions on reintroduced controls; clarifying that the external borders rules will apply when internal border checks are reintroduced; requiring a report when internal border controls are lifted, outlining the operation of the internal checks and their effectiveness; requiring information to the public about reintroduced controls unless there are overriding security reasons to the contrary; and requiring the EU institutions and other Member States to respect the confidentiality of information submitted by a Member State at its request.[314]

In practice, according to the 2010 report on the application of the rules on internal border controls,[315] the Commission reported that since the Schengen Borders Code became applicable in 2006, twelve Member States had reintroduced border controls on twenty-two occasions (until the date of the report).[316] None of the Member States concerned had applied the rules on the prolongation of border controls, indicating that no specific long-term problems had arisen as regards the abolition of internal border

---

[311] Art 26 (Art 29, codified version), as revised by Reg 1051/2013.

[312] Art 26a(1) (Art 30(1), codified version), inserted by Reg 1051/2013.

[313] Art 26a(2) (Art 30(2), codified version), inserted by Reg 1051/2013.

[314] Arts 27–31 (Arts 31–5, codified version). Most of these provisions are new as compared to the previous rules. Reg 1051/2013 amended Arts 27, 29, and 30, mainly to strengthen the information and reporting requirements.

[315] COM (2010) 554, 13 Oct 2010.

[316] For more detail, see Annex I to the report. The 2010 report refers to the rules as they stood before the 2013 amendment.

controls. As for the substantive grounds for the reimposition of internal border controls, the Commission concluded that 'from the information available, Member States have not abused the possibility to reintroduce border controls'. However, the Commission was critical of Member States' application of the *procedural* rules applicable to the reimposition of such controls. In particular, the timeframe for the Commission to give a view on the planned reimposition of controls was too short for the Commission to give the formal opinion which the Schengen Borders Code provided for. Also, Member States often did not supply sufficient information in order for it to assess whether the reimposition of border controls was justified. Therefore the Commission had not yet issued any opinions on the issue. It argued that Member States need to supply more information, as well as updates to the information already submitted, and intended to suggest the use of a standard form to this end.[317]

In the Commission's view, Member States had difficulty allocating resources to apply reimposed internal border controls effectively. Usually cooperation with neighbouring States had been positive, due to early consultation, coordination of planned measures, regular contacts, and exchange of information. Operational cooperation between States had included joint risk assessments, joint checks, and liaison officers. As for the applicable law when internal border controls were reintroduced,[318] the Commission argued that the principle of proportionality applied, meaning that measures could only be taken if 'necessary for the public policy or internal security of the Member States'. It argued that not all persons need to be checked at the internal border if internal border controls are reintroduced, and checks must be targeted on the reasons for the reintroduction of internal border controls, carried out proportionately and 'based on risk analysis and available intelligence'. Persons can only be refused entry for reasons linked to the reintroduction of internal border controls, and in particular, EU free movement law still governs the entry of EU citizens. The Commission took the view that the Schengen rules on stamping of documents and carriers' liability do not become applicable, even when internal border controls are reintroduced, and that the EU's external borders agency, Frontex, does not have any role as regards reimposed internal border controls.

As regards information for the public, the Commission believed that the public has been 'sufficiently informed' about the reimposition of border controls in each case, and the provisions for confidentiality had only been used once. Overall, the Commission concluded that the then-current legal framework applicable to the temporary reimposition of internal border controls was 'sufficient', and called for Member States to give it more information on time, reiterating also the points made above about police checks and barriers to traffic flow. As we have seen, however, the Commission's view that there was no need to change the rules was soon overtaken by events.

Even the 2013 revision of the Code has subsequently proven inadequate to address public concern about the scale of migrant and refugee flows across the external and internal borders of the EU during 2015. A number of Member States therefore reintroduced internal border controls in the autumn of 2015 and were expressing interest in

---

[317] Note that the 2013 amendment of the rules does not provide for such a standard form.
[318] Art 28 of the Code (Art 32 of the codified version) provides that if border controls are reintroduced at internal borders, then the external border control rules apply to those borders.

invoking the possibility of a longer-term collective suspension of up to two years. The medium-term future of this key feature of the Schengen system is therefore uncertain.

3.5.2 Assessment

Ultimately, the procedures for Member States to reintroduce internal border controls on the *pre-existing* grounds of public policy were not changed very much by the 2013 revisions to the Schengen Borders Code. The most significant changes were: the requirement that such measures must be a 'last resort', which suggests a stronger application of the proportionality requirement; the requirement for the Commission to give its opinion on the planned reintroduction in some cases; and the more detailed rules on criteria and time limits.

What of the new 'serious deficiencies' ground for reimposing border controls? This is widely seen as a significant new power for Member States. Indeed, it has been argued that this new ground for reimposing border controls is in tension with the EU principles of solidarity, fair sharing of responsibility, and loyal cooperation.[319] However, there are important constraints on Member States. It appears that they cannot exercise this power without a prior recommendation from the Council, in light of the 'exceptional' nature of the reintroduction of internal border controls in such circumstances. In any event, the Council recommendation clearly has to be based on a prior recommendation from the Commission. It should not be forgotten that the Commission now has powers to issue recommendations beforehand to a Member State to 'fix' the deficiencies in question, and it might be argued that the 'last resort' clause requires the EU institutions to give the Member State whose border controls are deficient an effective opportunity to try and solve the problems,[320] particularly when the Commission has made recommendations to this end and there are signs that the 'deficient' Member State is acting or will shortly act upon those recommendations. Moreover, even where such recommendations have been issued, the reintroduction of controls will not be justified unless the Council and Commission have clearly demonstrated that there is no significant doubt that the criteria for such reintroduction are satisfied, and that all relevant procedural steps have been taken. Any Member State accepting such recommendations and reintroducing controls must also act in compliance with any national law which regulates the government's decision-making. An alleged failure to comply with these obligations could be the subject of a legal challenge to any Member State's decision to reintroduce internal border controls on this basis.

The 2013 amendments also enhance the accountability of Member States *after* they reintroduce border controls, in particular by the more detailed criteria that Member States' reports on such reintroduction have to satisfy, the possibility of a Commission

---

[319] D Vanheule, J van Selm, and C Boswell (2011), *The Implications of Article 80 TFEU on the principle of solidarity and fair sharing of responsibility, including its financial implications, between the Member States in the field of border checks, asylum and immigration*, Study for the European Parliament's Committee on Civil Liberties, Justice and Home Affairs.

[320] See by analogy the Court of Justice's interpretation of a 'last resort' requirement as regards the authorization of enhanced cooperation in Joined Cases C-274/11 and C-295/11 *Spain and Italy v Council*, ECLI:EU:C:2013:240.

opinion on those reports, and the requirement for the Commission to produce annual reports on the Schengen system, which will list such reintroductions of border controls. The Commission's suggestion (in its 2010 report) that there should be a standard form for supplying information about the planned reimposition of border controls should have been followed up, as this might have helped to fill the information gap that the Commission complained of in that report. Also, the Commission's guidelines on the reintroduction of internal border controls are a useful contribution to ensuring consistent practice.[321]

Possibly the greater emphasis on accountability will deter Member States from reintroducing border controls except where the criteria to reintroduce them are clearly satisfied, although it should not be forgotten that any views expressed by the Commission or European Parliament on whether those criteria are satisfied are not binding. The only way to obtain a binding decision on whether the rules have actually been broken is to obtain a ruling of the Court of Justice on that point, either pursuant to an infringement action brought by the Commission against the Member State concerned, or following a reference from a national court on this issue, by analogy with the case law on the definition of internal border controls discussed above. In any event, this case law leaves some leeway for Member States to control areas near the internal borders *without* this constituting a reimposition of internal border controls; and the legislation on this point has not been amended.

So overall, the 2013 amendments constituted neither a fundamental increase in the power of Member States to reimpose internal border controls (as some Member States had apparently desired), or a fundamental shift of power to the Commission to control the process of reimposing border controls (as the Commission had proposed). Rather, it was a compromise between these two extreme views, with a crucial issue that would determine whether the balance of power was shifting towards Member States or the Commission—namely whether Member States can reintroduce border controls in the absence of a Commission and Council recommendation on their own initiative, in the case of 'serious deficiencies'—not expressly clarified. Ultimately, if a Member State does attempt to judge for itself that there have been 'serious deficiencies' and impose border controls in the absence of a Commission and Council recommendation, it will likely face a legal challenge from the Commission and/or via the national courts which will resolve this issue.

The 2013 rules on reimposing border controls leave open the possibility that Member States could take a divergent approach on whether they wish to reintroduce border controls in response to another Member State's alleged 'serious deficiencies' as regards external border control. In other words, it is possible that some Member States may act upon a Council recommendation to reimpose border controls as regards the Member State concerned, whereas others will not. If this scenario transpires, the consequences could be chaotic, since it would be easy to circumvent the reimposed border controls by means of travelling to Member States which have not imposed them. There could be similarly difficult problems even if all Member States reintroduce such controls at the

---

[321] Recital 7 in the preamble to Reg 1051/2013 refers to this possibility.

same time, if those Member States subsequently decide to *end* those controls at different times. It is therefore regrettable that the 2013 rules did not ensure that all Member States would start and end the reimposition of border controls at the same time as regards a Member State which was responsible for 'serious deficiencies' as regards external border control.

Also, in light of the Commission's view on this issue, it would have been useful to take the opportunity to clarify whether reimposing internal border controls means that the borders concerned must be treated exactly the same as external borders for the time being—or whether only a more limited form of border control (and if so, what) is possible, as the Commission argued in its report. Again, in the absence of clarification of this issue, divergences among different Member States are likely on this issue, with the result that travellers and Member States' officials will be confused about the legal position, and the controls reimposed by the Member States with a stricter interpretation of the rules could be circumvented by travellers who cross the borders of Member States with a more liberal interpretation.

3.6 External Border Controls: Basic Rules

Like the rules on the abolition of internal border controls, the basic rules on harmonized external border controls were initially set out in the Schengen Convention,[322] along with measures adopted by the Schengen Executive Committee, particularly a Common Manual for use by border control authorities,[323] along with two other Decisions of the Schengen Executive Committee.[324]

Following the integration of the Schengen *acquis* into the EC and EU legal order, in accordance with the Treaty of Amsterdam,[325] these measures were supplemented by EC acts, in particular a Decision concerning border signs and a Regulation on the stamping of documents.[326] Furthermore, the Council adopted in 2001 a Regulation which conferred upon itself (and Member States) the power to amend the Common Manual.[327] A challenge to this measure by the Commission before the Court of Justice (on the grounds that the Council had not adequately explained why it conferred those

[322] Arts 3–8 of the Convention ([2000] OJ L 239/1). On the provisions of the Schengen *acquis* regarding internal borders, see I:3.5 above. For more detail on the measures concerning external border controls in force before the adoption of the Schengen Borders Code, see the second edition of this book, pp 135–9.

[323] The Manual (as consolidated in Schengen Executive Committee Decision Sch/Com-ex (99) 13) was initially classified, but was subsequently mostly declassified (see Decisions in [2000] OJ L 303/29 and [2002] OJ L 123/49). It was published in [2002] OJ C 313/97.

[324] These were Sch/Com-ex (94) 17 on introducing the Schengen system and Sch/Com-ex (98) 1 on the activities of a task force ([2000] OJ L 239/168 and 191).

[325] Arts 2–8 of the Convention and Schengen Executive Committee Decisions Sch/Com-ex (94) 17 and Sch/Com-ex (98) 1 were allocated to Art 62(2)(a) EC (now Art 77(2)(b) TFEU), except for Art 7 of the Convention, which was allocated to Art 66 EC (now Art 74 TFEU), and Art 4 of the Convention, which was not allocated at all due to obsolescence. The Common Manual was allocated to Art 62 and 63 EC (now Arts 77–9 TFEU). See the Council Decisions on the definition and allocation of the *acquis* (1999/435 and 1999/436, [1999] OJ L 176/1 and 17).

[326] See respectively [2004] OJ L 261/119 and Reg 2133/2004, [2004] OJ L 369/5. The Reg, inter alia, inserted two new provisions into the Schengen Convention (Arts 6a and 6b) and amended Art 6(2)(e) of the Convention, while the Decision, inter alia, amended Sch/Com-ex (94) 17, n 324 above.

[327] Reg 790/2001 ([2001] OJ L 116/5).

implementing powers upon itself, whereas the normal rule is to confer them on the Commission) was unsuccessful.[328] This Regulation was used to amend the Common Manual on several occasions, in particular to add a standard form for refusing entry at the border.[329] The Manual was also amended on several other occasions: by the EU's borders legislation,[330] by legislative acts concerning visas,[331] as well as incidentally when the Council amended the basic rules governing the procedure for visa applications (the Common Consular Instructions).[332]

In 2006, the various measures setting out the basic rules governing external border controls were all integrated and amended in the form of the Regulation establishing the Schengen Borders Code. The next major development in this area will be the development of an entry-exit system, ie a system which stores precise information on the movements of each third-country national (and possibly also each EU citizen) across the external borders. These two issues will be considered in turn. Of course, these measures should be seen in the broader context of the other measures discussed in this chapter, concerning passport security, the Schengen Information System, and the EU's border agency, Frontex.

3.6.1 Schengen Borders Code

The Schengen Borders Code,[333] which applied from 13 October 2006,[334] also integrated and amended all the previous rules concerning internal borders.[335] As regards external borders, the Code repealed the relevant provisions of the Schengen Convention, one Schengen Executive Committee Decision, the Common Manual (as amended by EC measures), and the legislation on border signs, the stamping of documents, and the power to amend the Common Manual.[336] Subsequently, the Code has been amended on six occasions.[337] In 2015, the Commission proposed to codify it, but this proposal

---

[328] Case C-257/01 *Commission v Council* [2005] ECR I-345.

[329] The first two amendments ([2002] OJ L 123/47 and [2002] OJ L 187/50) made 'housekeeping' changes; the third amendment increased checks on minors ([2004] OJ L 157/36); and the fourth amendment introduced a common form to be used when refusing entry at the border ([2004] OJ L 261/36).

[330] Art 3 of Reg 2133/2004, n 326 above.

[331] Art 7(2) of Reg 539/2001 ([2001] OJ L 81/3); Art 2 of Reg 334/2002 ([2002] OJ L 53/7); Art 5(2) and (3) of Reg 415/2003 ([2003] OJ L 64/1); and Art 11(2) of Reg 693/2003 ([2003] OJ L 99/8). On the substance of these measures, see I:4.5 to I:4.7 below.

[332] Art 1(2), 1(4), and 1(5) of Decision 2001/329 ([2001] OJ L 116/32); Art 3 of Decision 2001/420 ([2001] OJ L 150/47); Art 2 of Decision 2002/44 ([2002] OJ L 20/5); the Decision on fees for considering visa applications ([2003] OJ L 152/82); Decisions 2003/585 and 2003/586 on transit visa requirements ([2003] OJ L 198/13 and 15); Art 2 of Decision 2004/17 on travel medical insurance requirements ([2004] OJ L 5/79); and the June 2006 Decision on visa fees ([2006] OJ L 175/77). On the substance of these measures, see I:4.7 below.

[333] Reg 562/2006 ([2006] OJ L 105/1). All further references in this section are to the Borders Code Reg, unless otherwise indicated.

[334] Art 40.   [335] Arts 23–31 of the Code; see I:3.5 above.

[336] Art 39. More precisely, Sch/Com-ex (94) 17 was repealed, but Sch/Com-ex (98) 1 remained in force (for both, see n 324 above). The Commission has since proposed to repeal the latter Decision: COM (2014) 713, 28 Nov 2014. Some provisions relating to the abolition of internal border controls were also deleted: see I:3.5 above. Also, the Code deleted Annex 7 to the Common Consular Instructions (on which, see I:4.7 below).

[337] Firstly, Reg 296/2008 ([2008] OJ L 97/60) regarding 'comitology', amended Arts 12, 32, and 33. Secondly, Reg 81/2009, regarding the use of the Visa Information System at borders ([2009] OJ L 35/56),

has not yet been adopted.[338] The Commission has proposed three further amendments: (a) pursuant to planned legislation on an entry-exit system; (b) pursuant to the proposal for a touring visa; and (c) to allow for systematic security checks on EU citizens.[339]

The Code confers powers upon the Commission to adopt (initially) implementing measures as regards three of its eight attached Annexes; the Commission could also adopt implementing measures as regards border surveillance.[340] Since 2013, such measures have to take the form of 'delegated acts', as introduced by the Treaty of Lisbon.[341] To date, one implementing measure was adopted, regarding maritime surveillance.[342] However, it was annulled by the CJEU in 2012 because it should have taken the form of a legislative act,[343] and then replaced by a separate Regulation in 2014.[344] The CJEU has also interpreted the external borders provisions of the Code several times, following references from national courts.[345]

Certain decisions relating to external border crossing (such as the penalties for crossing at unauthorized points or times) have been left to the Member States' discretion, but there is nevertheless an obligation for Member States to inform the Commission of these decisions; the Commission must then inform the public.[346] The Commission has also drawn up a Recommendation containing practical information for border guards.[347]

Moving on to the content of the Schengen Borders Code, it comprises four Titles, with (as noted already) eight attached Annexes.[348] Title I sets out the purpose of the

---

amended Art 7(3). Thirdly, Art 55 of the Visa Code (Reg 810/2009, [2009] OJ L 234/1), amended Annex V. Fourthly, Reg 265/2010 ([2010] OJ L 85/1) amended Arts 5(1)(b) and 5(4)(a). Fifthly, Reg 610/2013 ([2013] OJ L 182/1) amended a large part of the Code. Finally, Reg 1051/2013 ([2013] OJ L 295/1) amended the provisions on internal borders, as discussed in I:3.5 above.

[338] COM (2015) 8, 20 Feb 2015. For the benefit of future readers, this section refers also to the Art numbers of the Code following the proposed codification (except for Arts 1–3, which would not be renumbered).

[339] See respectively COM (2013) 97, 27 Feb 2013, discussed in I:3.6.2 below; Art 13 of COM (2014) 163, 1 April 2014, discussed in I:4.7 below; and COM (2015) 678, 15 Dec 2015.

[340] Arts 12(5), 32, and 33, as amended by Regs 296/2008 and 610/2013. These powers concern Annexes III, IV, and VIII, which concern signs for separate lanes at border crossings, stamping of travel documents, and proof that the border has been crossed without travel documents being stamped.

[341] See I:2.2.2.1 and 2.2.3.1 above.   [342] [2010] OJ L 111/20.

[343] Case C-355/10 *European Parliament v Council*, ECLI:EU:C:2012:516. See I:2.2.3.1 above.

[344] Reg 656/2014, [2014] OJ L 189/93. See the detailed discussion of this Reg in I:3.10 below.

[345] Cases: C-261/08 and C-348/08 *Zurita Garcia and Choque Cabrera* [2009] ECR I-10143; C-430/10 *Gaydarov* [2011] ECR I-11637; C-606/10 *Association Nationale d'Assistance aux Frontières pour les Etrangers (ANAFE)*, ECLI:EU:C:2012:348; C-23/12 *Zakaria*, ECLI:EU:C:2013:24; and C-575/12 *Air Baltic*, ECLI:EU:C:2014:2155. The CJEU has also ruled on the internal borders provisions of the Code: see I:3.5 above.

[346] Arts 34 and 37 (Arts 39 and 42, codified version), as amended by Reg 610/2013; this information is also available online at: <http://ec.europa.eu/justice_home/doc_centre/freetravel/rights/doc_freetravel_rights_en.htm#notifications>.

[347] C(2006) 5186, reproduced in Council doc 15010/06, 9 Nov 2006, amended by: C(2008) 2976, reproduced in Council doc 11253/08, 30 June 2008; C(2009) 7376, online at: <http://ec.europa.eu/dgs/home-affairs/e-library/docs/pdf/subsequent_amendments_2009_en.pdf>; C(2010) 5186, reproduced in Council doc 13380/10, 8 Sep 2010; C(2012) 9330, reproduced in Council doc 18062/12, 20 Dec 2012; and C(2015) 3894, reproduced in Council doc 10087/15 add 1, 19 June 2015.

[348] Title III of the Code solely concerns the abolition of internal border controls, and was considered in I:3.5 above. Title IV solely sets out final provisions, and is not considered separately.

Regulation, along with rules on definitions and the scope of the Code.[349] First of all, the Code applies 'to any person crossing the internal or external borders of Member States'. Moreover, the Code does not address the issue of rules on local border traffic, which was the subject of separate legislation adopted some months later.[350]

The Code is 'without prejudice to' the rights of persons enjoying EU free movement rights or to 'the rights of refugees and persons requesting international protection, in particular as regards non-refoulement'.[351] The first of these categories follows from the priority of EU free movement law over Schengen rules,[352] while the latter arguably follows from the general principles of EU law and the EU Charter of Fundamental Rights.[353] More broadly, the Code specifies that when Member States apply it, they must act in full compliance with: EU law, including the Charter; 'relevant international law', including the Geneva Convention on Refugees; 'obligations related to access to international protection, in particular the principle of non-refoulement'; and fundamental rights. They must take all decisions under the Regulation on an individual basis.[354]

Title II of the Code, which contains five Chapters,[355] sets out the main rules concerning external borders. Chapter I comprises two Articles, which set out in turn out the rules concerning crossing external borders and the conditions for entry at the external borders.[356] Borders must be crossed at official points during official hours, and notice of opening hours must be provided. Derogations may be permitted where there is a 'requirement of a special nature' (subject to certain conditions), for individuals or groups in an unforeseen emergency, and for special categories of persons.[357] Penalties must be imposed by Member States for breach of the obligation to cross at official points; these penalties shall be 'effective, proportionate and dissuasive', and this obligation is 'without prejudice to ... [Member States'] international protection obligations'.[358] These two express provisions respectively reflect the underlying effective sanctions principles of EU law and the exemption of refugees from penalties for irregular entry as set out in Article 31 of the Geneva Convention on refugee status.[359] It should be noted that these provisions do not require Member States to criminalize irregular border

---

[349] Arts 1–3, as amended by Reg 610/2013. Note that the definition of 'residence permit' excludes temporary residence permits, as confirmed by *ANAFE*, n 345 above.

[350] Art 35 (Art 40, codified version); see Reg 1931/2006 ([2006] OJ L 405/1) as amended, discussed in I:3.8 below.

[351] Art 3. The former group is defined in Art 2(5).

[352] See the former Art 134 of the Schengen Convention, which was not integrated within the EU legal framework (Decision 1999/435, n 325 above); the Schengen Protocol; and Case C-503/03 [2006] ECR I-1097. See also I:3.4.1 above.

[353] Compare to the former Art 135 of the Schengen Convention, which was not integrated within the EU legal framework (see Decision 1999/435, n 325 above).

[354] Art 3a (Art 4, codified version), added by Reg 610/2013. See also I:3.3 above.

[355] Arts 4–19a (Arts 5–21, codified version). The fifth chapter (current Art 19a, codified Art 21) was added by Reg 1051/2013 and essentially concerns internal border controls; it was discussed in I:3.5 above.

[356] Arts 4 and 5 (Arts 5 and 6, codified version), as amended by Reg 610/2013 and (in the case of Art 5) Reg 265/2010.

[357] Art 4(2) (Art 5(2), codified version). For the first two exceptions, Member States can derogate from the rules on border checks (Art 7(8) (Art 8(8), codified version), as inserted by Reg 610/2013).

[358] Art 4(3) (Art 5(3), codified version).

[359] On the first point, see Case 68/88 *Commission v Greece* (Greek maize) [1989] ECR 2685. On the second point, see I:7.3.2 below.

crossing; more generally, EU law is silent on the criminal law aspects of irregular migration except for specific obligations to criminalize the smuggling, trafficking, and employment of irregular migrants, which do not require criminalization of the irregular migrants themselves,[360] and the limitations on imposing custodial penalties on irregular migrants which the CJEU has said are inherent in the Returns Directive.[361]

The key provision of the Schengen Borders Code sets out the conditions for entry for short-term stays (90 days within a 180-day period).[362] These conditions 'shall be the following':

a) possession of valid documents necessary to cross the border;[363]

b) possession of a visa if required by the EU visa list legislation,[364] although a residence permit or a long-stay visa is equivalent to a visa for this purpose;[365]

c) justification of the purpose and conditions of the stay, and possession of sufficient means of subsistence;

d) absence from the list of persons banned from entry set up within the Schengen Information System (SIS);[366] and

e) absence of a 'threat to public policy, national security or the international relations' of *any* of the Member States, 'in particular' where there is no alert in Member States' national databases refusing entry on such grounds.

The final provision could be interpreted as a requirement to check *all* Member States' national databases, but surely this is not practical on grounds of technical difficulties and cost. There are specific rules on how to calculate time periods.[367] A 'non-exhaustive' list of documents providing justification of the stay is set out in Annex I to the Code, which is a straightforward list of documents which can serve as evidence of travel for business, studies, tourism or private reasons, or for political, scientific, cultural, sports, religious, or other reasons.[368] The subsistence requirement 'shall be assessed in accordance with the duration and the purpose of the stay and by reference to average prices for board and lodging',[369] and Member States' reference amounts for subsistence are to be notified to the Commission.[370] The possession of sufficient subsistence 'may' be verified, 'for example', by 'the cash, travellers' cheques and credit cards in the third-country

---

[360] See I:7.5 below.   [361] See I:7.7.1 below.

[362] Art 5(1) (Art 6(1), codified version), as amended by Reg 610/2013.

[363] Art 5(1)(a) (Art 6(1)(a), codified version), as amended by Reg 610/2013. The relevant documents are listed in a Manual of travel documents, initially established by Schengen Executive Committee Decisions Sch/com-ex (98) 56 and (99) 14 ([2000] OJ L 239/207 and 298), but now pursuant to a 2011 Decision ([2011] OJ L 287/9).

[364] On the content of the visa list, see I:4.5 below.

[365] Art 2(15) (Art 2(16), codified version), as amended by Reg 610/2013, defines 'residence permit'. The exception for long-stay visas was added by Reg 265/2010.

[366] See further the definition in Art 2(7), which refers to Art 96 of the Schengen Convention, which concerns the grounds for issuing 'alerts' in the SIS for persons to be refused entry. This now refers to the SIS II Regulation (see I:3.7 below). There is also an express requirement to check the SIS upon entry (current Art 7 of the Code, discussed below).

[367] Art 5(1a) (Art 6(2), codified version), inserted by Reg 610/2013.

[368] Art 5(2) (Art 6(3), codified version).

[369] Art 5(3) (Art 6(4), codified version), first sub-paragraph.

[370] Art 34(1)(c) (Art 39(1)(c), codified version).

national's possession' as well as sponsorship declarations, where a Member State's law recognizes such declarations, and guarantees from hosts, as defined by national law.[371]

There are three exceptions to the rules concerning entry conditions:[372]

a) persons with a residence permit, (from 2010) a long-stay visa, or (until 2013) a re-entry visa from a Member State who wish to cross the external borders in transit back to the State which issued the permit shall be admitted across the border, unless they are listed on the watch-list of the Member State they wish to cross, along with instructions to refuse entry or transit;[373]

b) persons who do not meet the visa requirement, but who satisfy the criteria for obtaining a visa at the border set out in EU visa legislation, may be authorized to enter if a visa is issued at the border pursuant to those rules;[374] and

c) a person may be permitted to enter if a Member State 'considers it necessary' to derogate from the criteria for entry on humanitarian grounds, national interest or international obligations; but in such a case the permission to enter should be limited to the territory of that Member State, and other Member States must be informed of such decisions, if the person concerned is listed on the SIS.[375]

The first exception is mandatory ('shall be authorized to enter'); the residence permits concerned must be notified to the Commission.[376] The inevitable consequence of these rules is that persons who do not meet the criteria for entry must be denied entry, unless they fall into one of the three special categories listed above. However, the obligation to refuse entry is 'without prejudice to the application of special provisions concerning the right of asylum and to international protection or the issue of long-stay visas'.[377] The special provisions on the right to asylum and international protection are not further defined, and it could be argued that this is a reference to national law, to a uniform EU concept which could be defined by the Court of Justice, to a minimum EU standard which could again be defined by the Court, or to the asylum procedures Directive.[378] As for the special provisions on long-stay visas, this should now be understood as a reference to the provisions of the Borders Code itself.[379]

Interpreting the criteria for entry, the CJEU ruled in *Air Baltic* that in light of the inherent nature of the Schengen system, the list of permitted grounds for entry were exhaustive, with the result that Member States cannot refuse to let a third-country

---

[371] Art 5(3) (Art 6(4), codified version), second sub-paragraph.

[372] Art 5(4) (Art 6(5), codified version), amended by Reg 265/2010, which added the reference to long-stay visas, and by Reg 610/2013, which dropped the reference to 're-entry visas'. See previously Art 18 of the Schengen Convention, as amended by Reg 1091/2001 ([2001] OJ L 150/4). See also the transit decisions discussed in I:4.2.5 below.

[373] For interpretation of the rule on 're-entry' visas (now repealed), see *ANAFE*, n 345 above.

[374] This initially referred to Reg 415/2003, but Reg 610/2013 replaced this with an updated reference to Arts 35 and 36 of the Visa Code, which replaced Reg 415/2003.

[375] Cf the provisions for visas with 'limited territorial validity', set out in Art 25 of the Visa Code.

[376] Art 34(1)(a) (Art 39(1)(a), codified version), as amended by Reg 610/2013.

[377] Art 13(1) (Art 14(1), codified version).

[378] However, it should be recalled that the Schengen associates and Denmark do not apply the procedures Directive, and the UK and Ireland only apply the first-phase procedures Directive. On the substance of the Directive, see I:5.7 below.

[379] Art 5(4)(a) (Art 6(5)(a), codified version), as amended by Reg 265/2010.

national cross the external border if he or she meets the necessary criteria.[380] In the same judgment, the Court ruled that while a third-country national had to have both a valid visa and a valid passport, that visa did not have to be attached to that passport; it was sufficient that it was attached to a separate passport which had now expired.

Next, Chapter II of Title II of the Code concerns border checks and refusal of entry.[381] As regards the conduct of border checks, border guards must respect human dignity, act proportionately, and not discriminate on any listed grounds while carrying out border checks.[382] The CJEU has ruled that the EU Charter requires that Member States ensure effective remedies for breach of this provision.[383]

The Code then addresses the crucial issue of the checks that must be carried out at external borders on entry and on exit. In particular, the 'minimum checks' to be carried out on all persons at external borders must entail a 'rapid and straightforward verification' of the validity of the documents carried, including an examination for signs of counterfeiting or falsification, using technical devices, and consulting databases on lost or stolen documents 'where appropriate'.[384] Presumably it cannot seriously be intended that the documentation of every single traveller will be fully checked in all possible databases.

The Code specifies that while such checks are the 'rule' for persons exercising EU free movement rights, it is possible for border guards to check databases on a 'non-systematic basis' in order to determine that such persons 'do not represent a genuine, present and sufficiently serious threat to the internal security, public policy, international relations of the Member States or a threat to the public health'.[385] There is no cross-reference as regards these grounds to EU free movement law, and this proviso differs from EU free movement law because it refers to 'internal security' rather than 'public security' and also to 'international relations'.[386] However, it is specified that such checks 'shall not jeopardise' the right of entry set out in free movement legislation,[387] and further that checks on persons with free movement rights must be carried out 'in accordance with' EU free movement law.[388] Following the 'Charlie Hebdo' terrorist attacks of January 2015, Member States urged a revision of these provisions to allow more systematic checks on EU citizens who might be 'foreign fighters'. In December 2015, the Commission proposed to amend the Schengen Borders Code to this effect.[389]

---

[380] N 345 above. The Court had previously reached the same conclusion as regards the EU's Visa Code: see the discussion in I:4.5 below.

[381] Arts 6–13 (Arts 7–14, codified version).

[382] Art 6 (Art 7, codified version), as amended by Reg 610/2013 to refer to vulnerable persons in particular.

[383] *Zakaria*, n 345 above.   [384] Art 7(2) (Art 8(2), codified version), first sub-paragraph.

[385] Art 7(2) (Art 8(2), codified version), second sub-paragraph, as amended by Reg 610/2013.

[386] Moreover, compared to Art 28(2) of Directive 2004/38 on EU citizens' free movement rights ([2004] OJ L 229/35), there is no reference to 'personal conduct' or to threatening the 'fundamental interests of society'. But at least the definition of 'public health' is identical: Art 29(1) of the Directive and Art 2(19) of the Code (Art 2(21), codified version). For more on the free movement rules, see I:3.4.1 above.

[387] Art 7(2) (Art 8(2), codified version), third sub-paragraph.

[388] Art 7(6) (Art 8(6), codified version). It follows that disputes concerning EU citizens leaving their own Member State are regulated by free movement law, not the Borders Code: see *Gaydarov*, n 345 above.

[389] N 339 above.

Although these safeguards (and the general safeguard for free movement law set out in the Code),[390] in conjunction with the Treaty free movement rights, should be interpreted to prevent any restriction on free movement rights as a result of checking databases, it is possible in practice that a border guard might apply these conflicting provisions more restrictively. In particular, it is objectionable that the border checks provision of the Code does not fully reflect free movement rules and refers to more extensive grounds than free movement law provides for.

The Code then specifies the 'thorough checks' to be carried out on third-country nationals (other than those with EU free movement rights). On entry, such persons shall be checked as regards their documents, the purpose and period of stay including subsistence requirements, along with checks in national databases and the SIS.[391]

Furthermore, now that the Visa Information System (VIS) is operational, third-country nationals are also (if they hold a visa) checked in the VIS on entry for the purposes of verification (a 'one-to-one' search), using fingerprints and the visa sticker number.[392] Due to doubts about the practicality of this obligation, particularly as regards land borders,[393] it is subject to a derogation, concerning the checking of fingerprints, for a transitional period of three years, beginning three years after the VIS has started operations (so the derogation expires in autumn 2017).[394] The Commission must evaluate the application of the derogation and report on its implementation to the EP and the Council within two years of the start of the derogation. Either the EP or the Council may then suggest that the Commission table a proposal to amend the legislation.[395]

As for the substance of the derogation, it applies where intense traffic results in excessive delay at border crossing points, all resources have been exhausted as regards staff, facilities, and organization, and 'on the basis of an assessment there is no risk related to internal security and illegal immigration'.[396] The first two criteria match the criteria applicable to the decision to relax border controls in the Borders Code,[397] but the third criterion (risk assessment) does not. Also, as compared to the rules on the relaxation of border controls, a Member State will not have to show (as regards the derogation from the obligation to check fingerprints in the VIS) that there were 'exceptional and unforeseeable circumstances', which 'shall be deemed to be those where unforeseeable events'

---

[390] Art 3(a).   [391] Art 7(3)(a).

[392] Art 7(3)(aa), as inserted by Reg 81/2009. For the details of the VIS, see I:4.8 below. It should be noted that the VIS Reg (Reg 767/2008, [2008] OJ L 218/60) does not lay down a requirement for border guards to use the VIS; only an amendment to the Schengen Borders Code could do that.

[393] The practical difficulties at land borders have been ameliorated, however, by the extension of visa waivers to Western Balkan states, and will be further ameliorated if there are in future visa waivers for more ex-Soviet countries (see I:4.5 below).

[394] Art 7(3)(ae) (Art 8(3)(f), codified version), as inserted by Reg 81/2009. Presumably the transitional period did not begin for three years because of the three-year delay, after the VIS begins operations, before the VIS Regulation permitted the use of fingerprints to search the VIS at all borders (Art 18(2) of the VIS Reg).

[395] Art 7(3)(ae). See also Art 50(5) of the VIS Reg, which provides for evaluation of the provisions regarding fingerprint searches in the VIS by external border guards, one year and three years after the VIS starts operations.

[396] Art 7(3)(ab) (Art 8(3)(c), codified version), as inserted by Reg 81/2009.

[397] Art 8(1) (Art 9(1), codified version), discussed further below.

lead to the intense traffic in question. It follows that in principle, the decision to relax border controls and the derogation from full use of the VIS on entry will not always apply simultaneously, although in practice it is likely that this will often be the case.

If the derogation applies, the VIS must still be searched in all cases using the visa sticker, and in random cases using fingerprints as well.[398] The VIS will also have to be searched using visa sticker and fingerprints in 'all cases where there is doubt as to the identity of the holder of the visa and/or the authenticity of the visa'. Decisions to apply the derogation will have to be taken by the border guard in command at the border post or at a higher level, and notified immediately to the other Member States and to the Commission.[399] Member States must report annually on the use of the derogation to the Commission, including providing information on 'the number of third-country nationals who were checked in the VIS using the number of the visa sticker only and the length of the waiting time' which justified the derogation.[400]

A statement was adopted by the Council and Commission when the relevant Regulation amending the Borders Code was adopted, asserting that 'the Council and the Commission stress that the derogation...should not be applied for a total period of more than 5 days or 120 hours per year at any border crossing point'. Also, the statement provides that the 'evaluation carried out by the Commission...will consider the infrastructure of the border crossing points, including recent and planned developments, as well as any factor that may have an influence on passenger flows, and may contain suggestions for improvements accordingly'.[401] It should be recalled that according to the Court of Justice, 'such a declaration cannot be used for the purpose of interpreting a provision of secondary legislation where...no reference is made to the content of the declaration in the wording of the provision in question. The declaration therefore has no legal significance.'[402]

It should be noted that neither the obligation nor the option to check the VIS at external borders will apply to third-country national family members of EU citizens, since they are not subject to the relevant provisions of the Borders Code.[403] The point is important, because information on the persons concerned will nevertheless be stored in the VIS.[404]

These amendments to the Code will be relevant to the future establishment of an entry-exit system.[405] But it must be noted that an entry-exit system cannot function as long as a derogation applies at entry, and in the absence of an obligation to enter information on visa holders at exit points as well (on which, see below). The potential difficulties

---

[398] It should also be noted that passports also still have to be stamped, even where border controls are relaxed: see Art 8(3) (Art 9(1), codified version), discussed below.

[399] Art 7(3)(ac) of the Borders Code (Art 8(3)(d), codified version), inserted by Reg 81/2009. Note that the border guard on command at the border post also decides on whether to relax border controls in the first place: Art 8(2) (Art 9(2), codified version), discussed below. However, as compared to the VIS derogation, the Borders Code does not require the notification of each decision to relax border controls.

[400] Art 7(3)(ad) (Art 8(3)(e), codified version), inserted by Reg 81/2009. Note that Member States must also report annually on the relaxation of border checks generally (see discussion below).

[401] Council doc 15501/08 add 1, 20 Nov 2008.

[402] Case C-292/89 *Antonissen* [1991] ECR I-745, para 18.

[403] Art 7(2) and (3) (Art 8(2) and (3), codified version), along with the definitions in Art 2(5) and (6). See I:3.4.1 above.

[404] See I:4.4.1 below.   [405] See I:3.6.2 below.

in applying such a system would obviously be multiplied if it applies to non-visa nationals as well, as the Commission intends, although the Commission has suggested the parallel development of a 'trusted traveller' system in order to avoid bottlenecks.[406]

Moving on to controls on exit, checks must include a check on the validity and genuineness of travel documents and 'whenever possible' a verification that the person is not a threat to 'public policy, internal security, or the international relations of any of the Member States'.[407] Exit checks *may* also involve verification of a visa, checks as to whether a person overstayed, and checks in the SIS or national databases[408]—although of course the *required* check 'wherever possible' on whether the person is a threat to public policy would seem to entail a mandatory SIS check. Member States also have an option to check persons on exit in the VIS for the purposes of verification.[409] Again, these provisions are linked to the future development of an entry-exit system.[410]

Furthermore, Member States have an option to search the VIS, presumably either on entry or exit, to check persons in the VIS for the purposes of *identification* (a 'one-to-many' search).[411]

Through checks will take place, if possible, in a non-public area, at the request of the person concerned.[412] Persons must be given information about the purpose of the check and the procedures applicable, and may request the name or service number of the border guard(s) carrying out the check and the location and the date of crossing.[413] Both these provisions should contribute to the objective of ensuring fair treatment during border checks. Finally, the information which must be registered at the borders is listed in Annex II to the Code:[414] the names of the border guards; any relaxation of checks; the issuing of documents at the borders; persons apprehended and complaints; persons refused entry (grounds for refusal and nationalities); information on the security stamps used and the guards using them; complaints from persons subject to checks; police or judicial action; and particular occurrences. These amendments should make a useful contribution respectively to ensuring reasonable behaviour by border guards and to combating corruption or other criminal activity regarding falsified documents. It would be even more useful if this data were published.

Member States are obliged to provide for separate lanes at airports for EU and EEA citizens and their family members, on the one hand, and for all (other) third-country nationals, on the other hand. They have an option as to whether to provide for separate lanes at sea and land borders, and as to whether to provide for a separate lane for third-country nationals who do not need visas.[415]

As noted already, the Code provides for the possible relaxation of checks in limited circumstances, 'as a result of exceptional and unforeseen circumstances', which are 'deemed to be those where unforeseeable events lead to traffic of such intensity that the waiting time

---

[406] See ibid.   [407] Art 7(3)(b) (Art 8(3)(g), codified version).

[408] Art 7(3)(c) (Art 8(3)(h), codified version).

[409] Art 7(3)(c)(i) (Art 8(3)(h)(i), codified version), as amended by Reg 81/2009.

[410] See I:3.6.2 below.   [411] Art 7(3)(d) (Art 8(3)(i), codified version), inserted by Reg 81/2009.

[412] Art 7(4) (Art 8(4), codified version).

[413] Art 7(5) (Art 8(5), codified version); the right to information was strengthened by Reg 610/2013.

[414] See Art 7(7) (Art 8(7), codified version).

[415] Art 9 (Art 10, codified version), which took over the provisions of a 2004 Decision on this issue, n 326 above. The latter option was added by Reg 610/2013. See also Annex III.

at the border crossing point becomes excessive, and all resources have been exhausted as regards staff, facilities, and organisation'.[416] In that case, entry checks must take priority over exit checks, and there is anyway an obligation to stamp each travel document on entry and exit.[417] Member States must submit an annual report on the relaxation of border checks to the EP and Commission,[418] but there is no information available on these reports.

Next, travel documents (usually passports) must be stamped when all third-country nationals cross the border, both on entry and exit, regardless of whether the travellers are subject to a visa obligation or not.[419] There are exemptions for heads of state and dignitaries, certain transport workers, nationals of Andorra, San Marino, and Monaco, and third-country national family members of EU citizens if they hold residence cards, in accordance with EU free movement law.[420] The obligation might also '[e]xceptionally' be waived where stamping a travel document 'might cause serious difficulties' for an individual; in such cases, a separate sheet has to be stamped to record entry and exit.[421]

If a travel document is not stamped on entry, Member States may presume that the person concerned does not fulfil the conditions for the duration of stay in the Member State concerned.[422] This presumption can be rebutted by the traveller,[423] but if he or she cannot rebut it, they may be expelled.[424] The Court of Justice has confirmed that there is only an option, rather than an obligation, to expel the person concerned in this case,[425] although arguably the position has since been affected by the application of the Returns Directive.[426] These rules apply also if there is no exit stamp in a travel document.[427]

---

[416] Art 8(1) (Art 9(1), codified version). Arts 8, 10, and 11 (Arts 9, 11, and 12, codified version) took over the provisions of Reg 2133/2004, n 326 above.

[417] Art 8(2) and (3) respectively (Art 9(2) and (3), codified version); on stamping of documents, see below.

[418] Art 8(4) (Art 9(4), codified version).

[419] Art 10(1) (Art 11(4), codified version). The detailed arrangements for stamping are set out in Annex IV.

[420] Art 10(3) (Art 11(3), codified version), as amended by Reg 610/2013. On EU citizens' family members, see I:3.4.1 above.

[421] Ibid. Reg 610/2013 added an option to collect statistics on such cases.

[422] Art 11(1) (Art 12(1), codified version).

[423] Art 11(2) (Art 12(2), codified version) and Annex VIII.

[424] Art 11(3) (Art 12(3), codified version).

[425] *Zurita Garcia* and *Choque Cabrera*, n 345 above. Although the Spanish text of the Code states that the person 'must' be expelled, the Court gave priority to the wording in all of the other language versions, which indicate that there is an option to expel. With respect, it is not clear from the facts of these cases whether or not there was a failure to stamp the documents of the persons concerned; the Court (and Advocate-General) simply assumed that Art 11 of the Code was applicable. The judgment also interpreted Art 23 of the Convention, which was replaced by the Returns Directive (Dir 2008/115 ([2008] OJ L 348/98) as from 24 Dec 2010 (Arts 20 and 21 of the Dir). On this Art, see I:7.7 below.

[426] Dir 2008/115, n 425 above; see I:7.7.1 below. Reg 610/2013 amended Art 11(3) to refer to this Dir, but the Code provision still states that the person 'may' be expelled in accordance with the Dir. It is not clear how this prima facie optional expulsion relates to the mandatory expulsion set out in Art 6 of the Dir. However, the Dir does specify that it is 'without prejudice' to 'more favourable provisions' in 'the Community *acquis* relating to immigration and asylum' (Art 4(2) of the Dir). This must surely mean that the optional expulsion in the Code must take precedence over the mandatory expulsion in the Dir, where the two rules overlap. It should also be noted that Art 11(1) of the Code only provides for an option, not an obligation, to presume in the first place that the conditions for stay have been breached in the event that the documents in questions are not stamped. On the relationship between the Code and the Dir on this point, see also note 23 in the Opinion in *Zurita Garcia* (n 345 above), which, with respect, fails to take Art 4(2) of the Dir into account.

[427] Art 11(4), added by Reg 610/2013 (Art 12(4), codified version).

The Commission reported on the application of the provisions on stamping of documents and presumptions of irregular stay in 2009.[428] According to this report, there had been no problems applying the stamping obligations fully; in particular the obligations had not caused long waiting times at borders. Difficulties had arisen where a passport was full, where the stamping was confusing or illegible (due to stamping on top of a previous stamp), where children did not have a separate passport, and as regards whether the passport of a third-country national with a residence permit from a Schengen State should be stamped. In the latter case, the Commission took the view that the passport did not need to be stamped, because a risk of exceeding the authorized period of short stay did not arise. While this was a sensible argument, nevertheless there was no express exception to this end in the Code.[429] Equally the Commission did not see the need to create an exception to the stamping obligation for lorry drivers, who were the main group affected by stamps filling up a passport early, due to the risk of illegal immigration; it argued that an entry-exit system will eventually address their position.[430] On the other hand, the Commission did intend to propose an express exception from the stamping obligation for railway workers who regularly travel in and out of the EU; the 2013 amendments to the Code later put this into effect. Also, the Commission takes the view that a stamping obligation cannot be applied at internal borders, even where border checks are re-instated pursuant to the applicable provisions of the Code,[431] given that the re-introduction of those checks cannot alter the total length of authorized stay. This is again undoubtedly a sound argument, but not expressly set out in the wording of the Code.[432]

As for the presumption of illegality, most Member States did not collect statistics on the numbers of persons who were found on the territory or detected while exiting without an entry stamp, or who were able or not able to rebut any presumption of irregular stay, although in fact the Code does not require them to do so.[433] The Commission

---

[428] COM (2009) 489, 21 Sep 2009, pursuant to Art 10(6), which would be repealed by the codified version.

[429] The same point could be made where the person concerned holds a long-stay visa, but the Commission does not mention this. The Commission's argument raises the question whether the list of exceptions from the stamping obligation set out in Art 10(2) and (3) is exhaustive or non-exhaustive. The text of the Code does not make this clear, although the exclusion of third-country national family members of EU citizens with residence cards from the stamping obligation is not expressly set out—it follows from an *a contrario* reading of Art 10(2) along with Art 3(a). It might be possible to argue (although the Commission does not) that the stamping obligation does not apply to such persons because the Code only applies to persons admitted for a short stay in the first place (see Art 5(1)). But if that were the case, why does the Code contain references to persons with long-stay visas and residence permits in other provisions (Art 5(1)(b) and 5(4)(a), for instance)?

[430] See I:3.6.2 below. Note, however, that an entry-exit system is not forecast to be operational for many years to come, so this would not alleviate the position of the lorry drivers in the meantime. The Commission seems unwilling to consider any special solution for this category of persons (the creation of a special permit, a system of employers' liability, reciprocal agreements with states of origin on special travel documents, or the development of a *sui generis* entry-exit system for the meantime).

[431] See I:3.5 above.

[432] Art 28 (Art 32, codified version) provides that: '[w]here border control at internal borders is reintroduced, the relevant provisions of Title II shall apply *mutatis mutandis*.' It might be argued that Art 10(1) (Art 11(1), codified version) is not a 'relevant provision' for this purpose, but it would be better to specify exactly what these 'relevant provisions' are in the interests of legal certainty.

[433] This is a distinct issue from the obligation to provide statistics on *refusal of entry* decisions (Art 13(5); Art 14(5), codified version).

rightly points out that this information would obviously be useful in order to assess the effect of the provisions on stamping, but the fault here lies with the legislation, which failed to set out an obligation in this respect. Equally, most Member States have not informed the Commission about their practices on the presumption of illegal stay, although on this point the Code does set out an obligation.[434] It is not clear from the information supplied to the Commission whether or not Member States always presume that the absence of an entry stamp indicates an irregular stay. Ultimately, the Commission drew no conclusions about the rules in the Code on the presumption of an illegal stay, and did not mention the issue of the link between these rules and the Returns Directive (see the discussion above).

Next, the Code contains basic rules on border surveillance, addressing the purposes of surveillance, the types of units to be used, the numbers of border guards to be used and their methods, and the requirement to survey sensitive areas in particular.[435] As amended in 2013, the Code specifies that someone 'who has crossed a border illegally and who has no right to stay on the territory of the Member State concerned shall be apprehended and made subject to procedures respecting' the Returns Directive. This is awkward, since there is an optional exception in the Returns Directive for persons who have been apprehended in connection with crossing an external border.[436]

Further measures concerning surveillance may be adopted in accordance with (initially) a comitology procedure, or now (from 2013) delegated acts.[437] As noted above, an implementing measure relating to maritime border surveillance was adopted in 2010,[438] but then annulled because it was necessary to adopt a legislative measure on this issue instead.[439]

The Code then sets out rules concerning refusal of entry, which are obviously among its most important provisions. As noted above, the general rule is that persons who do not meet the criteria for admission must be denied entry, subject to certain exceptions;[440] more detailed rules on the procedure for refusing entry are set out in an Annex to the Code.[441] There are also procedural rights for persons denied entry. Entry may only be refused 'by a substantiated decision stating the precise reasons for the refusal', which is given by means of a standard form annexed to the Code. The decision must be taken by a legally empowered authority, must take effect immediately, and the decision form must be given to the person concerned, who 'shall acknowledge receipt'.[442]

Persons refused entry have 'the right to appeal'; the appeal 'shall be conducted in accordance with national law'. Member States must give the person concerned a written

---

[434] Art 11(2), final sub-paragraph (Art 12(2), codified version).

[435] Art 12(1) to (4) (Art 13(1) to (4), codified version).

[436] Art 12(1) (Art 13(1), codified version), as amended by Reg 610/2013. For a detailed discussion of the scope of the Returns Directive, see I:7.7.1 below.

[437] Art 12(5) (Art 13(5), codified version), as amended by Regs 296/2008 and 610/2013.

[438] N 342 above.   [439] For discussion of the later legislation, see I:3.10.1 below.

[440] Art 13(1) (Art 14(1), codified version); see the discussion of Art 5 (Art 6, codified version) above.

[441] Art 13(6) (Art 14(6), codified version), referring to Annex V, Part A, since amended by Art 55 of the Visa Code. Point 3 of this Annex refers to the Schengen and EU rules on carrier sanctions (see I:7.5.1 below).

[442] Art 13(2) (Art 14(6), codified version) and Annex V, Part B, as amended by Reg 610/2013.

list of contact points who could provide information on persons who could represent him or her. But appeals 'shall not have suspensive effect'. If successful, an appeal must entail that the cancelled entry stamp is corrected; this is '[w]ithout prejudice to any compensation granted in accordance with national law'.[443] Unsurprisingly, the Code specifies that border guards must ensure that persons refused entry shall not enter the territory of the Member States.[444] Member States must collect statistics on the numbers refused entry, their nationality, the grounds for refusal of entry, and the type of border where entry was refused. This information must be transmitted annually to the Commission, in accordance with EU statistics legislation.[445]

In some cases, these provisions overlap with the Returns Directive, which gives Member States an option (but not an obligation) to exclude persons refused entry in accordance with the Borders Code from the scope of that Directive, which contains its own specific rules on procedural rights and related issues such as detention. As noted above, Member States may also exclude from the scope of that Directive those persons 'who are apprehended or intercepted by the competent authorities in connection with the irregular crossing by land, sea or air of the external border of a Member State and who have not subsequently obtained an authorisation or a right to stay in that Member State'.[446] If Member States take up these options, the former category of persons will at least benefit from the procedural rights set out in the Borders Code.[447] But more problematically, the latter category of persons will not benefit from any procedural rights whatsoever as a matter of EU law; this position is impossible to defend. Arguably, due to the link with external border control, this category of persons still falls sufficiently within the scope of EU law to be covered by the general principles of EU law and the Charter, and can therefore derive procedural rights in that connection.[448] In any event, the Returns Directive requires that for both categories of persons, Member States must 'ensure that their treatment and level of protection are no less favourable than' the rules in that Directive regarding limitations on use of coercive measures, postponement of removal, emergency health care, the needs of vulnerable persons, and detention conditions, and must also 'respect the principle of non-refoulement'.[449]

Next, Chapter III of Title II of the Code concerns cooperation between national authorities, as well as staff and resources for border controls.[450] Member States must deploy 'appropriate staff and resources' in order to carry out border checks as provided for in Chapter II, 'to ensure an efficient, high and uniform level of control at their

---

[443] Art 13(3) (Art 14(3), codified version).   [444] Art 13(4) (Art 14(4), codified version).

[445] Art 13(5) (Art 14(5), codified version), as amended by Reg 610/2013. For more on this, see I:3.11 below.

[446] Art 2(2)(a) of Dir 2008/115, n 425 above.

[447] Conversely, of course, if a Member State does not invoke the exclusion, persons refused entry at the border will benefit from the provisions in both the Returns Directive and the Borders Code. Presumably, in the event of overlap, the rule setting the highest standards will apply.

[448] See by analogy the discussion of the *MM* judgment in I:5.7 below.

[449] Art 4(4), Dir 2008/115, n 425 above. The obligation to respect the principle of non-refoulement is not further defined (cf also Art 5 of the Dir), although note that there is some CJEU case law clarifying this concept, and in any event the Directive is subject to more favourable provisions in other EU immigration and asylum measures (Art 4(2) of the Dir). See further I:7.7.1 below.

[450] Arts 14–17 (Arts 15–18, codified version).

external borders'.[451] Checks must be carried out by border guards in conformity with national law; the guards must be sufficiently specialized and trained, and encouraged to learn relevant languages. Member States must ensure effective coordination of all relevant national services, and notify the Commission of the services responsible for border guard duties.[452]

As for cooperation between Member States, there is a general requirement of assistance and cooperation in accordance with other provisions of Code. They must also exchange relevant information. The code refers to the role of Frontex in coordinating border operations, as well as Member States' role as regards operational coordination, including the exchange of liaison officers, as long as this does not interfere with the work of the Agency. Member States must provide for training of border guards on border control and fundamental rights, taking account of the standards developed by the Agency.[453] Furthermore, there is a special rule concerning joint control of the common land borders of those Member States not yet fully applying the Schengen rules. Until the Schengen *acquis* is fully applicable to them, those States can jointly control their borders, without prejudice to Member States' individual responsibility. To this end, Member States may conclude bilateral agreements, which they must inform the Commission of.[454]

Finally, Chapter IV of Title II of the Code sets out specific rules for border checks in certain cases, concerning respectively different types of borders and different categories of persons.[455] For instance, as compared to the pre-2006 Schengen *acquis*, the rules on crossing by road in particular permit drivers usually to stay in their vehicles during checks; the rules for checking trains en route to or from third countries have been amended to allow for 'juxtaposed control' in third States; the rules on air travel contain entirely new provisions on private flights; and the rules on sea borders were amended in particular to strengthen the rules on control of cruise ships and pleasure boats and to tighten the definition of fishing vessels which will not generally be checked. To some extent, the rules were relaxed in 2013.

As for checks on particular categories of persons, there were initially six categories of persons subject to special treatment: heads of state; pilots and other aircraft crew; seamen; holders of diplomatic, official, or service passports and of documents issued by international organizations; cross-border workers; and minors. The 2013 amendments added two more such categories: rescue services, police and fire brigades and border guards; and offshore workers.

For example, the special rules for Heads of State and their delegation exempt them entirely from border checks; holders of diplomatic, official, or service passports and documents issued by international organizations are exempt from subsistence

---

[451] Art 14 (Art 15, codified version).

[452] Art 15 (Art 16, codified version), amended (as regards training) by Reg 610/2013; see Art 34(1)(d) (Art 39(1)(d), codified version) on notification.

[453] Art 16 (Art 17, codified version).

[454] Art 17 (Art 18, codified version); see Art 37 (Art 42, codified version) on notification.

[455] Arts 18–19 (Arts 19–20, codified version). The detailed rules appear in Annexes VI and VII. Reg 610/ 2013 amended all of these provisions.

requirements, must be given priority when crossing, and cannot be refused entry by border guards unless the guards first check with foreign ministries; cross-border workers need not be subject to a check every time they cross the border, if they are 'well known' to the border guards due to their 'frequent crossing' and they were not listed in the SIS when an initial check was carried out; and minors must be the subject of 'particular attention' from border guards, to ensure that accompanied minors are with persons entitled to exercise parental care and that unaccompanied minors are not leaving the territory against the wishes of the person with parental care of them.[456]

3.6.2 Entry-exit system

The next major step in the development of EU external border controls could be the creation of an 'entry-exit' system, which, as noted above, would keep track of the entry into and out of the Schengen zone of most categories of third-country nationals. Such a system was suggested by the Commission in a detailed communication in February 2008, which also addressed the related issues of a 'trusted traveller' programme and a system of electronic travel authorization.[457] Following a further communication on the options for implementing these plans,[458] the Commission proposed legislation to establish the entry-exit system and the registered traveller programme in February 2013, alongside consequential proposed amendments to the Schengen Borders Code.[459] However, due to objections over the details of the proposal, discussions in the Council have proceeded at a slow pace, and the Commission is planning to relaunch its proposals by suggesting a revised version in 2016. Member States have argued that the future proposal should also keep records on the entry and stay of EU citizens, for security purposes.[460]

First of all, the legislation to establish the entry-exit system (EES) would apply to all third-country nationals admitted for a short stay in accordance with the Schengen Borders Code, whether or not they were subject to a visa obligation, apart from: family members of EU citizens who hold a 'residence card'; those who have residence permits; and nationals of Andorra, Monaco and San Marino.[461] The purpose of the system would be to manage external borders and to fight against unauthorized immigration, by providing information on the time of entry and exit of migrants, in order to enhance external border checks, to calculate and monitor periods of stay, to identify third-country nationals who have 'overstayed' their period of permitted stay, and to assist the identification of anyone who might not, or no longer, fulfil the conditions for entry or stay on the territory.[462]

---

[456] See subsequently the action plan on unaccompanied minors (COM (2010) 213, 6 May 2010) and the Council conclusions on this issue (JHA Council press release, 3 June 2010), which refer to regular collection of data and risk assessments by Frontex on this issue. See also the follow-up to the plan: (COM (2012) 554, 28 Sep 2012).

[457] Communication on the next steps in border management (COM (2008) 69, 13 Feb 2008).

[458] COM (2011) 680, 25 Oct 2011.

[459] See respectively COM (2013) 95, COM (2013) 97, and COM (2013) 96, all 27 Feb 2013.

[460] See the EU Agenda for Migration (COM (2015) 240, 13 May 2015) and the conclusions of the Nov 2015 JHA Council.

[461] Art 3, proposed EES Regulation.   [462] Art 4, proposed EES Regulation.

The system will record data on the names, travel documents and visas of third-country nationals, as well as information on their participation in the registered traveller programme (see below), the time and place of entry and the length of authorized stay.[463] Where a person is not subject to a visa obligation, the authorities will also have to take his or her fingerprints, although this rule will not apply until three years after the EES starts operations.[464] Further data would be added if a period of stay is revoked or annulled.[465]

Access to the EES would be granted primarily to border guards for the purpose of carrying out border control tasks,[466] but also to authorities deciding on visa applications, applications for registered traveller status, and for verifying or identifying persons for other immigration control reasons.[467] Information in the EES will only be kept for six months, unless there is no record of exit, in which case it will be kept for five years.[468] The system will automatically generate a list of overstayers,[469] but a name must be taken off this list if the person concerned can provide evidence that he or she was forced to overstay due to an 'unforeseeable and serious event', has acquired a legal right to stay, or in the event of errors (ie he or she had left in time after all).[470]

As for data processing rules and data protection rights, in principle, EES data could not be given to third countries or international organizations, but as an exception, it could be necessary to prove identity, including for the purpose of return, if a number of further conditions are met.[471] Data subjects would have the right to information, and also rights to access the data, and to correct or delete the data in case of error.[472]

According to the second proposal, which would establish the registered traveller programme (RTP), that programme would be based on a system relying upon tokens held by travellers, on the one hand, and a central repository of the RTP data, on the other hand.[473] This Regulation would set out the process for applying for RTP status, which would entail filling in an application form, presenting a travel document, providing fingerprints and supporting documents, and paying a fee.[474] It should be noted that the RTP proposal is distinct from the idea of a 'trusted traveller' who will have special treatment for Schengen visa applications, which the Commission has proposed as part of its reform of the Visa Code.[475]

The grounds for admitting a person into the RTP would be: fulfilment of the entry conditions in the Schengen Borders Code; that the person's travel document and other documents were valid and not counterfeited; no prior record of overstaying and proof

---

[463] Art 11, proposed EES Regulation.   [464] Art 12, proposed EES Regulation.
[465] Art 14, proposed EES Regulation.   [466] Art 15, proposed EES Regulation.
[467] Arts 16–19, proposed EES Regulation.   [468] Art 20, proposed EES Regulation.
[469] Art 10(2), proposed EES Regulation.   [470] Art 21(2), proposed EES Regulation.
[471] Art 27, proposed EES Regulation.
[472] Arts 33 and 34, proposed EES Regulation. The remedies to this end are set out in Arts 36 and 37 of the proposal (respectively concerning individual remedies and the role of supervisory authorities).
[473] Art 2, proposed RTP Regulation.   [474] Arts 4–10, proposed RTP Regulation.
[475] See the discussion in I:4.7 below. However, it is possible that any definition of trusted visa applicants which may be agreed in the context of revising the Visa Code might later be reused or adapted in the future RTP Regulation. It is not necessary for the RTP system to be operational before a trusted traveller concept can be introduced into the Visa Code, since that concept is based on information in the Visa Information System.

of the applicant's 'integrity and reliability, in particular a genuine intention to leave the territory in due time'; justification of the intent and purpose of the intended stays; proof of the applicant's financial situation and subsistence; no alert in the Schengen Information System; absence of a threat to public policy; and the prior record of applications for the RTP which were refused or granted.[476]

National authorities would have to decide upon RTP applications within twenty-five days of submission.[477] A successful applicant would initially be granted access to the RTP for one year, which could be extended for two years upon request and a further two years automatically for travellers who have complied with Schengen rules.[478] There would be expedited access to the RTP for persons holding long-stay visas, residence permits, multiple-entry visas, and for family members of EU citizens.[479]

If the applicant did not satisfy the criteria for registration on the RTP, access to the programme would have to be refused. National authorities would have to give reasons for the refusal by means of a standard form, and the person concerned would have a right to a review of that decision. Information on the refusal would be added to the central repository of RTP data.

Finally, the Schengen Borders Code would be amended to take account of the two new measures. In addition to new definitions,[480] the Code would contain a new provision on data to be entered into the entry-exit system.[481] Data would be entered into that system except as regards groups of persons who benefit from the facilitation of border checks or who are exempt from such checks, pursuant to the Code: Heads of State and members of their delegation; specified transport crew members or passengers; and persons who are exempt from the obligation to cross at border crossing points during their opening hours. Information on the holders of border traffic permits 'may' be entered into the system, depending on whether border crossing has been facilitated for such persons. Where border checks are relaxed, information would still have to be entered into the entry-exit system.[482]

The rules on border checks would be amended,[483] in order to provide for an obligation to check the entry-exit system upon entry and exit, instead of an obligation to check the entry and exit stamps in the person's travel document, to ascertain whether the person concerned has overstayed. Checks on entry and exit would also have to include checks on the identity of a registered traveller and access to the registered traveller programme.

A new provision would set out specific rules on border checks of registered travellers, and the use of automated means for border checks.[484] Registered travellers would be exempted from most of the rules on entry checks, and checks on them on entry and exit 'may' be carried out in automated border gates. Persons whose fingerprints are

---

[476] Art 12, proposed RTP Regulation. However, Art 12(7) of the proposed Regulation specifies that applications by third-country national family members of EU citizens shall be subject to the same rules as their visa applications, ie the less stringent conditions of EU free movement law.

[477] Art 13, proposed RTP Regulation.   [478] Art 14(1), proposed RTP Regulation.

[479] Art 14(2), proposed RTP Regulation.   [480] Revised Art 2, Schengen Borders Code.

[481] New Art 5a, Schengen Borders Code.   [482] Revised Art 8(3), Schengen Borders Code.

[483] Revised Art 7, Schengen Borders Code.   [484] New Art 7a, Schengen Borders Code.

registered in the Visa Information System and also stored on their travel document 'may' also be checked on entry and exit in automated border gates. Both categories of persons could also use 'fast-track' lanes at border crossing points.[485]

The rules on stamping of travel documents would be deleted,[486] and the rules on presumption of fulfilment of the conditions of stay would be revised to refer to use of the entry-exit system, instead of the stamps in the travel document, to determine whether the person concerned can be presumed to have overstayed. If that presumption is rebutted, a new file in the entry-exit system would have to be created.[487]

Member States have expressed an interest in amending these proposals in order to collect data also on third-country nationals who reside in the Schengen area, and to make the information available to law-enforcement authorities.[488]

3.6.3 Assessment

Taken as a whole, the Borders Code is clearly vastly better drafted than the texts it replaced, although it has several flaws. There are significant improvements as regards procedural rights, fair treatment, accountability, and transparency, but several provisions are unclear (as regards the use of databases on EU citizens, exit checks and the exercise of police powers) or ill-considered (the rules on exit controls, which are arguably impractical). The CJEU has usefully confirmed that there is a right to entry if the relevant conditions are satisfied. While the additional provisions concerning asylum and (from 2013) human rights generally are welcome, the opportunity was missed to rethink the conditions for entry and to provide for detailed provisions ensuring that the right to asylum is respected at external borders; the latter issue is complicated by the application of the EU's asylum procedures Directive.[489]

The amendment to the Borders Code relating to the VIS may in particular prove to be impractical. It is striking that there was no impact assessment either of the proposal to amend the Code as regards VIS use or of the practical implications of this particular issue when the Commission assessed the impact of the original proposal for the VIS Regulation.[490] The derogation from use of the VIS upon entry set out in the Borders Code is drafted quite narrowly, and it may not prove feasible to spend time assessing the impact of granting a derogation when a quick decision has to be made to address traffic flows.[491] The proposed rules on systematic checks of EU citizens may run into the same problems.

---

[485] Revised Art 9, Schengen Borders Code.

[486] Current Art 10, Schengen Borders Code.   [487] Revised Art 11, Schengen Borders Code.

[488] See: <http://www.statewatch.org/news/2013/may/11eu-entry-exit-system.html>.

[489] See I:5.7 below.

[490] See SEC (2004) 1628, 28 Dec 2004. This impact assessment simply states (at p 17) that 'time will be lost at entry and exit points by providing and checking biometric data', without assessing the feasibility of checking such data in all cases of entry. On the same page, the Commission estimates the 'very significant' financial costs of the VIS at EU level and for national visa authorities, but this does 'not include the costs for the border crossing points as these costs cannot be estimated at the present time'.

[491] The absolute obligation in the Borders Code to stamp the passports of third-country nationals, even when border controls are relaxed, will already slow down any attempt to clear a backlog at the border crossing.

As for the stamping of documents, the rules in the Code have proved practical according to the Commission's assertions, although it does not follow that the use of VIS at the borders, especially the extra time taken to obtain fingerprints, would still be feasible. It would be useful to know more about how presumption regarding irregular stay is actually applied.

This brings us to the planned entry-exit system. In general, the proposals on this issue have generated significant controversy and their cost and necessity has frequently been doubted.[492] In particular, it has been suggested that in the absence of any facility to assist in determining the exact location of overstayers, the entry-exit system will amount to 'little more than an extremely expensive mechanism for gathering migration statistics'.[493]

On the details of the proposal, it should first of all be noted that in light of EU free movement law, it would not be legal to apply such a system to EU citizens and their family members, including citizens of non-Schengen States or Schengen associates, for the purposes of immigration control. It might be legal for the purposes of security, but it would arguably amount to disproportionate mass surveillance in light of the other measures which the EU already has at its disposal or will put into effect soon (passenger name records, SIS surveillance of terrorist suspects, systematic checking of EU citizens at external borders). Also, there is little point in applying this system to non-visa nationals, given the relatively limited risk of overstay which they pose in practice as compared to the extra costs and complications that would result from applying the system to them. If nationals of a particular country not subject to visa obligations in fact have a high rate of overstaying, the obvious solution is simply to impose a visa obligation on nationals of that country, not to impose an entry-exit system on all non-visa nationals. Similarly, there seems little point applying the system to legally resident third-country nationals as the Council desires, since their immigration status is checked when they apply for an initial or renewed residence permit or long-stay visa. If the entry-exit system is not applied to these groups, the cost and complications of the new system would presumably be significantly reduced.

While an entry-exit system, if it works as planned, will identify overstayers effectively, it will not assist authorities to find them if they have disappeared. It is assumed that an entry-exit system will either be integrated into the VIS or applied seamlessly in parallel with it. The costs and complications of the development of a completely separate system do not bear thinking about. In any event, any system will have to be subject to robust data protection rules to avoid the effect of erroneous identification, and the penalties for overstay will have to be proportionate and take account of legitimate grounds for overstay such as *force majeure*, applications for international protection, and humanitarian reasons. In particular, it should be ensured that overstayers are not removed if they have applied for asylum, in accordance with EU asylum legislation.[494]

---

[492] See the report by B Hayes and M Vermeulen, 'Borderline: Assessing the Costs and Fundamental Rights Implications of Eurosur and the Smart Borders' proposals, online at: <http://www.statewatch.org/news/2012/jun/borderline.pdf>.

[493] See the report by D Bigo, et al. (2012), 'Evaluating Current and Forthcoming Proposals on JHA Databases and a Smart Borders System at EU External Borders', Study for the European Parliament.

[494] See Bigo (ibid) and Hayes and Vermeulen, n 492 above.

The parallel proposal for an authorized traveller system would probably be essential if an entry-exit system is introduced, in order to ensure that delays at border crossings do not become intolerable. Again, such a system could not be used to store information on the movements of EU citizens, citizens of Schengen associates, and their family members. It will be essential to ensure that the rules for registration in this system are fair and transparent, and that data protection rights apply fully to the vetting process.

3.7 Schengen Information System

3.7.1 Legal framework

The Schengen Information System (SIS) [495] is a well-known and long-established element of the Schengen border control system, with the main purpose (in the immigration context) of making available to the relevant national officials a common list of names of persons who should not be allowed to enter the Schengen area. The first-generation SIS was replaced by a second-generation System (SIS II) in 2013.

The first-generation SIS was initially established by Articles 92–119 (Title IV) of the 1990 Schengen Convention,[496] as applied from March 1995. Further rules were set out in various decisions of the Schengen Executive Committee,[497] including the Decision establishing the SIRENE Manual, which governed subsequent exchanges of information following a 'hit' in the SIS.[498] Despite its dual application for immigration purposes on the one hand and criminal law and policing purposes on the other, the SIS remained almost entirely a third pillar measure due to the failure to allocate the relevant provisions of the Schengen *acquis* to the EC Treaty in 1999, when the Treaty of Amsterdam integrated the *acquis* into the EC and EU legal order.[499] However, the Schengen Convention SIS rules were amended in 2004 and 2005 to provide for certain changes to the System pending the application of SIS II—the so-called 'SIS I+'.[500] Furthermore, the procedure for updating the SIRENE Manual was set out in both first and third pillar legislation from 2004.[501]

The object of replacing the SIS with SIS II was initially twofold: to provide for more functions, including more categories of data (notably biometric data), and to permit the expansion of the SIS (and therefore the Schengen free movement zone) to include the Member States which joined the EU in 2004. To this end, the Council adopted a Regulation in 2006 which regulates the functioning of SIS II as regards immigration.[502] Parallel measures concern the use of SIS II by vehicle registration authorities[503] and a third pillar Decision concerning use of the system for policing and criminal law purposes.[504]

---

[495] On the general legal framework governing SIS and SIS II, see II:7.6.1.1.

[496] [2000] OJ L 239.   [497] Ibid.   [498] [2003] OJ L 38.   [499] [1999] OJ L 176/17.

[500] These amendments can be found in Council Reg 871/2004 ([2004] OJ L 162/29) and a third-pillar Decision of 2005 ([2005] OJ L 68/44).

[501] The first pillar measure is Reg 378/2004 ([2004] OJ L 64/5); for the text of the updated Manual, following the application of this legislation, see the Commission Decisions in [2006] OJ L 317.

[502] Reg 1987/2006 ([2006] OJ L 381/4). All references in this sub-section are to this Reg, except where otherwise noted.

[503] Reg 1985/2006 ([2006] OJ L 381/1).   [504] [2007] OJ L 205/63. See II:7.6.1.1 for details.

SIS II was put into operation as from 9 April 2013, when the Council decided, inter alia, that the relevant technical requirements had been satisfied.[505] In the meantime, the issue of enlargement of the Schengen area had been addressed by means of a different technical solution, allowing newer Member States and Switzerland to participate in the existing SIS and therefore to join the Schengen area in 2007 and 2008, without waiting for SIS II to become operational.[506] When SIS II became applicable, the previous provisions of the Schengen Convention concerning the SIS and the relevant Executive Committee Decisions, as well as the EC measures building upon this *acquis*, were repealed or replaced.[507]

The Commission has power to implement the SIS II Regulation by means of a 'comitology' committee which does not involve any extra control of the adoption of implementing measures by the EP.[508] It has already used this power several times, to adopt new versions of the Sirene manual governing action to be taken after a 'hit' in SIS II,[509] as well as a security plan.[510] SIS II is administered by an EU agency, 'EU-LISA', after an interim transitional period in which the Commission was nominally designated as the manager of SIS II, but in practice delegated this management to France and to Austria (where the backup site of the SIS II data is located), who were nonetheless held accountable for their management of the system in accordance with EU rules.[511] This agency also administers the Visa Information System and Eurodac.[512]

While the details of the SIS are considered elsewhere in the second volume of this book, this chapter focuses upon the issue of the criteria for placing the name of a third-country national on the joint list of persons who should in principle be banned from entry to the Member States.[513] More precisely, the consequence of an 'alert' for denial of entry being placed in the SIS is that the person must in principle be refused entry at the external border or refused a visa,[514] although exceptionally on humanitarian or other grounds a person listed in the SIS can be permitted to enter or receive a visa for a single Member State only.[515]

The first-generation SIS rules provided that a name had to be entered into the list following 'decisions taken by the competent administrative authorities or courts' in accordance with national law.[516] Such decisions 'may be based on a threat to public policy or public security or to national security' posed by a third-country national's

---

[505] [2013] OJ L 87/8 and 10: see Art 55(2) and (3).   [506] See I:3.2.5 above.

[507] Arts 52 and 53.   [508] Art 51. On the comitology process, see I:2.2.2.1 and I:2.2.3.1 above.

[509] Successive versions in: [2008] OJ L 123; [2011] OJ L 137/1; [2013] OJ L 71/1; and [2015] OJ L 44/75. The list of authorities with access to SIS II data is published in [2005] OJ C 208/1.

[510] [2010] OJ L 112/31.   [511] Art 15.

[512] Reg 1077/2011 ([2011] OJ L 286/1). See II:7.6.1.

[513] For the first-generation SIS, see Art 96 of the Convention. Art 17(3)(g) of the Convention conferred power on the Executive Committee to define principles governing the drawing up of the common list, but this power was never used. Art 17(3)(g) was repealed by Art 56(1) of the Visa Code ([2009] OJ L 243/1). The basic rule on immigration alerts now appears in Art 24 of the SIS II Reg.

[514] Arts 5(1)(d) and 15 of the Convention; the former Article was replaced by Art 5(1)(d) of the Schengen Borders Code (Reg 562/2006, [2006] OJ L 105/1) and the latter Art was replaced by Art 21(3)(c) of the Visa Code (Reg 810/2009, [2009] OJ L 234/1). See also Arts 18, 19(1), 20(1), and 25 of the Convention, discussed in I:4.9 below.

[515] Arts 5(2) and 16 of the Convention; the former Article was replaced by Art 5(4) of the Schengen Borders Code (n 514 above) and the latter Art was replaced by Art 25 of the Visa Code (see n 514 above).

[516] Art 96(1) of the Convention.

presence on national territory. This 'may arise in particular' where a person 'has been convicted of an offence carrying' a custodial sentence of at least one year, or where 'there are serious grounds for believing' that the person 'has committed serious criminal offences', including drugs offences as defined in the Convention, 'or in respect of whom there is clear evidence of an intention to commit such offences in the territory of a [Member State]'.[517] Furthermore, '[d]ecisions may also be based on the fact that the [person concerned] has been subject to measures involving deportation, refusal of entry or removal which have not been rescinded or suspended, including or accompanied by a prohibition on entry, or where applicable, a prohibition on residence, based on a failure to comply with national regulations on the entry or residence' of foreigners.[518] The Court of Justice confirmed that the EU free movement rules took priority over the SIS rules.[519]

The SIS II Regulation made only modest changes to the previous rules. It starts out by repeating the basic rule in the Schengen Convention that an alert is issued by a national body in accordance with national law, with the additional provisos that the decision must be taken 'on the basis of an individual assessment', and that '[a]ppeals against these decisions shall lie in accordance with national legislation'.[520] Next, an alert 'shall' (not 'may') be issued where there is a threat to public policy or public security or national security, which 'shall' (not 'may') be the case, 'in particular' in two cases: a conviction in a Member State for an offence carrying a deprivation of liberty for at least one year, or 'serious grounds' to believe that a person has committed a 'serious criminal offence' or 'clear indications' that the person intends to commit such offences.[521] This provision differs from the previous rule in the Convention in that: the issue of an alert on these grounds is mandatory (although it is not clear how the issue of a mandatory alert is compatible with the proportionality rule in the Regulation);[522] the threat could materialize in 'a Member State', rather than on national territory; a criminal conviction must have taken place in a Member State (although it should be recalled that the criteria remain non-exhaustive, so a Member State still has the option of issuing an alert on a person who was convicted of a crime in a non-Member State); and the previous threshold of 'clear *evidence*' of an intention to commit offences has been lowered to a 'clear *indications*' test. The SIS II Regulation retains the previous option of issuing an alert following a breach of immigration law, using wording essentially identical to the Convention.[523]

However, the general rules on issuing immigration alerts do not apply to a separate specific category of persons—individuals who have been barred from entry pursuant to an EU foreign policy measure.[524] Alerts relating to such persons 'shall' be entered into SIS II, and the rules concerning data which must be entered in respect of each alert, the obligation to carry out a specific assessment, and the requirement to

---

[517] Art 96(2) of the Convention.   [518] Art 96(3) of the Convention.
[519] Case C-503/03 *Commission v Spain* [2006] ECR I-1097; see I:3.4.1 above.
[520] Art 24(1).   [521] Art 24(2).
[522] Art 21 reads: '[b]efore issuing an alert, Member States shall determine whether the case is adequate, relevant and important enough to warrant entry of the alert in SIS II'.
[523] Art 24(3).   [524] Art 24(4).

permit appeals are not applicable.[525] However, this provision is '[w]ithout prejudice to' the second special category—third-country national family members of EU citizens. The SIS II Regulation expressly confirms the case law of the Court of Justice relating to the previous SIS rules as regards such persons, requiring conformity with the EU citizens' free movement Directive and providing for immediate use of the Sirene procedure after a 'hit' concerning such persons to contact the Member State issuing the alert to determine what action to be taken.[526]

The SIS II Regulation also requires the Commission to review the application of the basic rules on issuing alerts three years after SIS II starts operations (so by April 2016), and then to 'make the necessary proposals to modify the provisions of this Article to achieve a greater level of harmonization of the criteria for issuing alerts'.[527] However, entry bans are also regulated by the Returns Directive, which Member States had to apply by 24 December 2010.[528] This Directive sets out specific rules relating to entry bans; an 'entry ban' is defined as an 'act prohibiting entry into and stay on the territory of the *Member States*',[529] not merely an individual State. The link between these entry bans and the SIS II is recognized in the preamble to the Directive,[530] although there is not an express legal requirement to issue the entry bans as SIS II alerts; the Commission therefore stated when the Directive was adopted that the planned review of the SIS II rules would provide an 'opportunity to propose an obligation to register in the SIS entry bans issued under this Directive'.[531] Of course, in the meantime some or all Member States might well choose to register all entry bans issued pursuant to the Directive in SIS II, even in the absence of a legal obligation to do so. It should be recalled, though, that the Returns Directive binds those Member States which do not yet fully apply the Schengen *acquis*, whereas only full participants in Schengen use the SIS (or the future SIS II). In its anti-smuggling Action Plan, the Commission has recently reaffirmed its intention to propose legislation by 2016 to ensure that all entry bans are listed in the SIS.[532] Moreover, in principle the European Council has agreed with the Commission's suggestion in the same Action Plan that information on returns decisions should be included in the SIS.[533] It will take some time (and new legislation) to put this into effect.

As for the substance, the Returns Directive requires Member States to issue an entry ban in cases where a person has not been given a period for voluntary departure, or where an obligation to return has not been complied with,[534] although there is

---

[525] Art 26. However, the proportionality rule in Art 21 is still applicable. Note that following the entry into force of the Treaty of Lisbon, challenges to the underlying travel bans can be brought pursuant to Art 275 TFEU. On the question of the correct legal base for these travel bans, see I:3.2.4 above and I:4.2.4 below.

[526] Art 25. See Case C-503/03 *Commission v Spain* [2006] ECR I-1097 and I:3.4.1 above.

[527] Art 24(5).

[528] Dir 2008/115 ([2008] OJ L 348/98), Art 20(1). For more on the Dir, see I:7.7.1 below.

[529] Art 3(6), Dir 2008/115; and see more clearly recital 14 in the preamble to the Directive.

[530] Recital 18 in the preamble, which provides that 'Member States should have rapid access to information on entry bans issued by other Member States. This information sharing should take place in accordance with [the SIS II Reg]'.

[531] Summary of Council acts for Dec 2008 (Council doc 7478/08, 11 Mar 2009).

[532] COM (2015) 285, 27 May 2015.   [533] June 2015 conclusions of European Council.

[534] Art 11(1), first sub-paragraph, Dir 2008/115. On the voluntary departure rule, see the discussion in I:7.7.1 below.

considerable discretion to waive this obligation.[535] In other cases, Member States *may* issue an entry ban.[536] There are also rules on the time period of entry bans,[537] and rules on procedural rights (the form of return ban decisions and the remedy against them) which are more specific than the rules in the SIS II Regulation.[538] The preamble to the Directive states that an individual assessment is necessary before an entry ban is issued, but the main text appears to conflict with this.[539]

However, it must be pointed out that the Returns Directive is explicitly subject not only (like the SIS II Regulation) to EU free movement law,[540] but also (*unlike* the SIS II Regulation) to more favourable provisions in *other* EU immigration and asylum legislation.[541] More specifically, the entry ban rules in the Directive are expressly 'without prejudice' to EU asylum legislation.[542] So even if the Returns Directive is interpreted to mean that there is not a requirement to conduct an individual assessment before an entry ban is issued, the requirement in the SIS II Regulation to conduct an individual assessment before that ban is entered into the SIS must still apply.

Furthermore, to the extent that, following such an assessment, alerts are then issued in the SIS following entry ban decisions taken pursuant to the Returns Directive, the relevant EU immigration and asylum legislation must necessarily also take precedence *over the SIS II Regulation*, because the priority rule set out in the Directive would continue to govern those entry bans. Where the Directive is not applicable, it is arguable even in the absence of a specific rule in the current SIS provisions or the SIS II Regulations giving priority to other EU immigration and asylum legislation, that legislation still takes precedence over the SIS II rules to the extent that it gives effect to human rights obligations.[543] Anyway, to the extent that a check in the SIS II leads to a refusal of entry, it should be recalled that this refusal is governed by the Borders Code, which does contain express derogations in relation to asylum and human rights.[544]

It should be also be noted that that the Returns Directive potentially has a narrower personal scope than the SIS II Regulation, since Member States have the power to exclude from the scope of the Directive persons who are refused entry and persons intercepted in connection with irregular entry,[545] as well as persons who are subject to

---

[535] Art 11(3), Dir 2008/115. [536] Art 11(1), second sub-paragraph, Dir 2008/115.

[537] Art 11(2), Dir 2008/115. On these rules, see Case C-297/12 *Filev and Osmani*, ECLI:EU:C:2013:569 and the discussion of the entry ban more generally in I:7.7.1 below.

[538] Arts 12 and 13, Dir 2008/115.

[539] See recital 6 in the preamble to the Dir, which states that, as a general principle of EU law, entry bans and other decisions under the Dir 'should be adopted on a case-by-case basis'.

[540] Technically, the Dir does not apply to persons with free movement rights at all (Art 2(3), Dir 2008/115).

[541] Art 4(2), Dir 2008/115. The Dir is also subject to more favourable provisions of treaties concluded by the EC and/or the Member States (Art 4(1)), and by more favourable provisions of national law, provided they are 'compatible' with the Dir (Art 4(3)). It is not clear whether this provision gives Member States discretion to waive their obligations to issue entry bans above and beyond the discretion set out in Art 11(3) of the Dir. For a general discussion of such provisions in EU immigration and asylum law, see I:5.2.4 below; in the specific context of the Return Directive, see I:7.7.1 below.

[542] Art 11(5) of the Dir, referring to Dir 2004/83 ([2004] OJ L 304/12), the 'qualification Directive'.

[543] On the hierarchical effect of human rights rules in the EU legal order, see I:2.3 above. On Art 25 of the Schengen Convention in particular, see I:4.9 below.

[544] Arts 3(b), 3a, 4(3), and 13(1) of the Code (Reg 562/2006, [2006] OJ L 105/1), as amended; see I:3.6.1 above.

[545] Art 2(2)(a), Dir 2008/115; see further I:3.6.1 above. Aspects of the Dir apply to such persons (Art 4(4) of the Dir), but this does not include the entry ban rules.

return as part of a criminal law sanction or because of a criminal conviction, or who are subject to extradition procedures.[546] To the extent that these exceptions are applied,[547] the SIS II Regulation alone will govern any entry bans which are issued as alerts in SIS II. Conversely, if an entry ban issued pursuant to the Directive is not entered as an alert into SIS II, given the absence of a legal obligation to do so, only the Directive is applicable.

While the original SIS only provided for the collection of alpha-numeric data (letters and numbers), as noted above, the SIS II Regulation provides for the inclusion of photographs and fingerprints in the system.[548] This biometric data will only be entered following a 'special quality check' in order to ensure data quality.[549] The specifics of this quality check will be established by the Commission pursuant to a 'comitology' procedure. Initially, biometric data will only be used to 'confirm the identity' of a person whose name has been found in the SIS following an alphanumeric search, likely meaning in practice that his or her name matches a name in the SIS.[550] But later biometrics will be used to 'identify' persons 'as soon as technically possible'.[551] This will entail a 'one to many' search (comparing one set of biometric data to much or all of the biometric data in the database). There will be no further vote before this important functionality is put into practice.

The inclusion of this extra personal data means that the provisions of the SIS II Regulation relating to data protection gain added importance. These provisions include in particular a new right to information for persons who are the subject of an alert,[552] in accordance with the EU's data protection Directive.[553] The SIS II Regulation also bans the transfer of SIS II immigration data to third countries and international organizations.[554] As regards the right to information, it should also be noted that both the Borders Code and the Visa Code require a person who is refused entry or refused a visa to know the reason why—and that reason might be that the person concerned is the subject of an alert in SIS II.[555] It might be arguable that the right to appeal against the refusal or entry or a visa[556] also entails the right to challenge the underlying decision to issue the alert.

3.7.2 Assessment

The previous SIS rules were the subject of a great deal of commentary, much of it highly critical.[557] The main criticism of the rules concerned the extensive discretion

---

[546] Art 2(2)(b), Dir 2008/115. This exception could be relevant to many or all of the alerts issued pursuant to Art 24(2) of the SIS II Reg.

[547] The majority of Member States apply these exceptions. On their interpretation, see I:7.7.1 below.

[548] Art 20(2).   [549] Art 22(a).   [550] Art 22(b).   [551] Art 22(c).

[552] See generally II:7.6.4 below.

[553] Art 42(1), which refers to Arts 10 and 11 of the data protection Directive (Dir 95/46, [1995] OJ L 281/31).

[554] Art 39. This issue was not expressly addressed in the previous SIS rules.

[555] Art 13(2) and Annex V, Part B of the Borders Code (Reg 562/2006, [2006] OJ L 105/1); Art 32(2) and Annex VI of the Visa Code (Reg 810/2009, [2009] OJ L 243/1). In the latter case (but not the former), the person concerned must be informed *which* Member State issued the alert.

[556] Art 13(3) of the Borders Code and Art 32(3) of the Visa Code (see n 555 above).

[557] For detailed analyses, see R Cholewinski, 'No Right of Entry: The Legal Regime on Crossing the EU External Border' in E Guild, P Minderhoud, and K Groenendijk, eds., *In Search of Europe's Borders* (Kluwer, 2003), 105 at 115–27; T Eicke, 'Paradise Lost? Exclusion and Expulsion from the EU' in ibid, 147–68; R Cholewinski, *Borders and Discrimination in the European Union* (ILPA/MPG, 2002); J Steenbergen, 'Schengen and the Movement of Persons' in H Meijers, et al., *Schengen: Internationalisation of Central*

for Member States as to whether to list a person on the SIS; the problematic nature of mutual recognition of another Member State's decisions in this field; the consequential effects on human rights for those who claim a need to enter a Member State in order to seek protection or on other human rights grounds; the lack of procedural rights and remedies where there is a need to challenge an SIS entry made by another Member State; the risk of discrimination on racial or ethnic origin as regards the application of the rules; and the limited data protection rights in relation to immigration alerts issued pursuant to the previous SIS rules. The initial criticism of a lack of international judicial control was addressed by giving the Court of Justice jurisdiction following the entry into force of the Treaty of Amsterdam, but that control has not been exercised in practice, except as regards family members of EU citizens.

To what extent did the SIS II Regulation address these concerns? First of all, as for the grounds for a SIS II listing, the obligation to provide for an individual assessment and appeals is very welcome, assuming that the wording of the Regulation is interpreted to mean that there is a *right* to an appeal which is merely subject to more detailed regulation (as regards time limits and competent courts) by national law, rather than a discretion under national law to preclude a right to appeal altogether. It is submitted that the former interpretation is correct, in light of the general principles of EU law, which require an effective remedy for EU law rights, and that furthermore any national regulation of the right of appeal cannot render the right to appeal ineffective. It is unfortunate that a proposed express clause giving priority to other EU immigration and asylum legislation was dropped during negotiations, but as noted above, it is still arguable that such legislation takes priority over the SIS II legislation even in the absence of an express rule to that effect; and in any event the priority rules in the Returns Directive or the Borders Code may be applicable.

However, it is unfortunate that there was not some degree of greater harmonization of the grounds for issuing an alert, at the very least to provide that the rather vague grounds set out in the legislation are exhaustive grounds for issuing alerts. The Returns Directive has not subsequently ensured a sufficient degree of harmonization on this issue,[558] which should therefore be addressed in the near future in order to guarantee that alerts are only issued when they are genuinely objectively justified in light of the degree of criminality or seriousness of the breach of immigration law committed by a particular third-country national. There is also a fundamental problem in that there is no obligation to publish the national criteria for issuing alerts in the EU's *Official Journal*. Without that information it is clearly far more difficult for any person to know if the alert on him or her was correctly or lawfully added to SIS II, or for supervisory authorities to carry out their responsibilities to ensure correct application of the data protection rules more generally. A person refused entry at the border need not even be told which Member State issued a SIS II alert on him or her. The resulting lack of

---

Chapters of the Law on Aliens, Refugees, Privacy, Security and the Police, 2nd edn (Stichting NJCM-Boekerij, 1992); P Boeles, 'Schengen and the Rule of Law', also in Meijers, et al.; and Justice report, *The Schengen Information System: A Human Rights Audit* (Justice, 2000).

[558] See I:7.7.1 below.

foreseeability of the circumstances in which data will be collected and processed violates basic principles of data protection law.

In the case of persons subjected to a travel ban pursuant to EU sanction measures, the underlying problem is the inability to attack the 'pure' foreign policy acts of the EU directly in the EU courts, although, as noted above, the Treaty of Lisbon has remedied this problem.[559]

As for the use of biometric data, in certain cases it might have the positive effect of ensuring that individuals who are apparently listed in the SIS can 'clear their names', and certainly in many cases it will more quickly identify individuals who are genuinely the subject of an alert. But it remains to be seen in practice whether the risk of wrongful identification pointed to by data protection authorities in cases of 'one-to-many' searches has been sufficiently addressed.

Finally, since SIS immigration data was collected in the context of establishing joint border controls for the Schengen free movement zone, it would be inappropriate, in light of the 'purpose limitation' principle of data protection law, to share that data with non-EU countries or bodies which do not participate in Schengen. Therefore the absolute ban on the transmission of that data outside the EU can only be welcomed.

3.8 Local Border Traffic

The original Schengen Convention provided for the Executive Committee to adopt standardized rules concerning exceptions for local border traffic,[560] but this power was never used before the integration of the Schengen *acquis* into the EU legal order. In turn, as noted above, the Schengen Borders Code provides for the adoption of separate specific rules on local border traffic.[561] Those rules on this issue were duly adopted in late 2006,[562] in parallel with amendments to the EU's visa list legislation which provided for visa exemptions for persons benefiting from the new border traffic rules.[563] This Regulation was amended in 2011,[564] and has been the subject of one CJEU ruling.[565] The Commission has twice reported on its application in practice (see below).

The border traffic Regulation principally establishes standardized rules for local border traffic, in particular by introducing a standard local border traffic permit.[566] Member States are authorized to agree treaties with neighbouring third countries that are in accordance with the rules of the Regulation.[567] The Regulation does not affect EU or national law concerning long-term stays, access to economic activities, or customs and tax matters.[568] A 'border area' means an area within thirty kilometres of the border, but this may stretch to fifty kilometres in order to include entire districts adjoining the

---

[559] Art 275 TFEU.   [560] Art 3 of the Schengen Convention ([2000] OJ L 239).
[561] Art 35 of Reg 562/2006 ([2006] OJ L 105/1).
[562] Reg 1931/2006 ([2006] OJ L 405/1), which entered into force on 17 Jan 2007 (Art 21). All references in this section are to this Reg, unless otherwise indicated.
[563] See I:4.5 below.   [564] Reg 1342/2011 ([2011] OJ L 347/41).
[565] Case C-254/11 *Shomodi*, ECLI:EU:C:2013:182.   [566] Art 1(1).
[567] Art 1(2). On the broader context of EU external relations law, see I:3.12 below. See also the similar legislation conferring power on Member States to negotiate civil law treaties (II:8.9).
[568] Art 2.

border.[569] Pursuant to the 2011 amendment, the entire Russian enclave of Kaliningrad is considered to be a border area, regardless of the usual definition.[570] 'Local border traffic' is defined as a crossing for 'social, cultural or substantiated economic reasons, or for family reasons' by border residents,[571] who are defined as persons lawfully resident in the border area for more than one year, with a possibility of reducing this waiting period in 'exceptional' cases.[572]

Chapter II of the Regulation sets out the main features of an authorized local border traffic regime.[573] An external land border may be crossed by persons who hold a local border permit and possibly also travel documents (depending on agreements between Member States and non-Member States), who have been checked in the SIS, and who do not pose a threat to the public policy, public security, or public health of any Member State.[574] As compared to the normal rules for crossing borders, there is no requirement to hold a visa (a relevant point, when the Regulation was first adopted, for all bordering non-Member States except Croatia, leaving aside Schengen associates and micro-states),[575] no requirement to show subsistence or the purpose of the visit, and no absolute requirement to hold a travel document.[576] Border residents may stay up to three months in a border area, depending on bilateral agreements.[577] The CJEU has ruled that the border traffic rules have to receive an autonomous interpretation as compared where necessary, and in particular that the usual Schengen limit of 90 days' visit within a 180 day period does not apply to border traffic permits.[578] Although border residents are subject to entry and exit checks, their travel documents (when they require them) are not stamped, by way of derogation from the normal rules.[579] It remains to be seen how the development of an entry-exit system would affect the local border traffic rules.[580]

Chapter III of the Regulation sets out the basic rules governing the special border traffic permit.[581] The permit is limited in validity to the border area of the issuing Member State.[582] It must bear a photograph of the holder and other basic information as specified in the Regulation.[583] There is no standard EU-wide format for the permit, but its security features and technical specifications must comply with the EU legislation establishing a standard format for residence permits.[584] Since the subsequent amendment of that EU legislation, this means that the permit should have contained biometric information as from 2011 (photographs) and 2012 (fingerprints).[585]

---

[569] Art 3(2).   [570] Reg 1342/2011, which amended Art 3(2) and added an Annex to the Reg.
[571] Art 3(3).   [572] Art 3(6).   [573] Arts 4–6.   [574] Art 4.
[575] Note that due to amendments to the EU visa list legislation adopted in 2009 and 2010, most citizens of Western Balkans States are now exempt from a visa requirement. Also, citizens of Moldova have been exempt since 2014. See I:4.5 below.
[576] Compare to the entry conditions in Art 5 of the Schengen Borders Code (Reg 562/2006, [2006] OJ L 105/1).
[577] Art 5.   [578] Art 6; compare with Art 10 of the Schengen Borders Code, n 576 above.
[579] *Shomodi*, n 565 above; compare with the Borders Code rules discussed in I:3.6 above.
[580] See I:3.6.2 above.   [581] Arts 7–12.   [582] Art 7(2).   [583] Art 7(3).   [584] Art 8.
[585] Reg 1030/2002 ([2002] OJ L 157/1) was amended by Reg 380/2008 ([2008] OJ L 115/1) to provide for the introduction of biometric data (fingerprints and photographs) into residence permits. Biometric data had to be integrated into the permits two years (as regards photographs) and three years (as regards fingerprints) from the adoption of the relevant implementing measures (Art 9 of Reg 1030/2002, as amended by Reg 380/2008). These measures were adopted in May 2009. See further I:6.9 below.

A permit can only be issued if four conditions are met: possession of a valid travel document; proof of status as a border resident and of grounds to cross the external border frequently; a check in the SIS; and lack of any threat to the public policy, public security, or public health of any Member State.[586] The permits are valid for a period of between one and five years, and the fees charged cannot exceed those for issuing short-term visas; Member States may issue the permits free of charge.[587] The permits can be issued by national authorities or consulates, and Member States must keep a permanent record of them.[588] There are no other standardized conditions, so although the border traffic permit can be compared to a visa, the Visa Code (and previously the Common Consular Instructions) does not govern its issue, and the Visa Information System does not apply. On the other hand, there are no express provisions conferring procedural rights on persons applying for or holding a border traffic permit, although it is arguable that implied rights exist nonetheless pursuant to the general principles of EU law and the EU Charter of Fundamental Rights.

Chapter IV of the Regulation concerns the implementation of the local border traffic regime.[589] The only means to introduce or maintain a local border traffic regime is by means of bilateral agreements between Member States and neighbouring third countries. Any new bilateral agreement must be compatible with the Regulation, and any existing agreements must be amended to conform to it.[590] In either case, Member States must allow the Commission to screen draft agreements, and make any amendments required by the Commission.[591] Presumably, if a Member State disagrees with a Commission decision, it can sue to annul that decision in the EU courts; conversely, the Commission could bring an infringement action against a Member State which does not comply with a Commission decision. The relevant bilateral agreements must contain provisions on the readmission of persons abusing the border traffic regime, in the event that the EU or the Member State concerned has not concluded a readmission agreement with the relevant country.[592] Since the entry into force of EU readmission agreements with most neighbouring third countries, this provision is only relevant as regards Belarus.[593]

The bilateral agreements must confer reciprocal rights on EU citizens and legally-resident third-country nationals living in the border areas of Member States. Also, bilateral agreements can 'exceptionally' liberalize the normal requirements to cross the borders only at authorized crossing points on the condition that the Member States concerned still carry out surveillance and random checks along the borders, and ease the requirement that all third-country nationals must be subject to thorough checks at the external borders.[594]

---

[586] Art 9.

[587] Arts 10 and 11. Note that the Visa Code does not permit the issue of visas free of charge for persons in local border zones, so holding a local border traffic permit significantly simplifies the position (Art 16 of the Visa Code, Reg 810/2009, [2009] OJ L 243/1; see I:4.7 below). Then again, most of the third countries in question are either on the EU visa whitelist (see I:4.5 below), or have visa facilitation treaties with the EU, which reduce the fees for visa applications (see I:4.11.2 below).

[588] Art 12.   [589] Arts 13–15.   [590] Art 13(1).   [591] Art 13(2).   [592] Art 13(3).

[593] On the EU's readmission agreements, see I:7.9.1 below. An EU/Belarus readmission treaty seems likely to be agreed in the near future.

[594] Art 15; compare with Arts 4 and 7 of the Schengen Borders Code, n 576 above.

Lastly, Chapter V of the Regulation sets out final provisions.[595] The Regulation does not affect the specific rules concerning Spanish enclaves in Morocco.[596] Member States must establish penalties for abuse of a permit, and report regularly to the Commission on cases of abuse.[597] Member States have to notify all bilateral agreements to the Commission, which must make them public.[598] The Schengen Convention was amended to refer to this Regulation, rather than national border traffic treaties.[599]

Also, the Commission had to report on the application of the Regulation by January 2009.[600] This report (the 'first report') was submitted in July 2009,[601] and a second report was submitted in 2011.[602] According to the first report, a Hungary/Ukraine agreement entered into force in January 2008; a Poland/Ukraine treaty entered into force in July 2009; a Slovakia/Ukraine treaty applied from September 2008; and treaties were under discussion between Lithuania/Russia, Lithuania/Belarus, Latvia/Russia, Poland/Belarus, Bulgaria/Serbia, Bulgaria/FYROM, and Romania/Ukraine. The 2011 report refers also to a Romania/Moldova treaty, which applied from October 2010, and states that treaties between Poland/Belarus, Latvia/Belarus, Lithuania/Belarus, and Norway/Russia were expected to enter into force shortly.[603] Treaties between Latvia/Russia, Lithuania/Russia and Romania/Ukraine had been agreed, but not signed, while draft treaties between Bulgaria/Serbia and Bulgaria/Former Yugoslav Republic of Macedonia (FYROM) had not been taken forward since the 2009 report. One pre-existing agreement (Slovenia/Ukraine) was also examined in both reports. The reports do not mention any local border traffic treaties agreed or under negotiation in respect of several external borders: Greece/Albania, Greece/Turkey, Greece/FYROM, Bulgaria/Turkey, Estonia/Russia, Finland/Russia, Poland/Russia, Hungary/Serbia, Hungary/Croatia (now moot), and Romania/Serbia. Since Croatia joined the EU, there are two new external borders subject to the local border traffic Regulation (Croatia/Serbia and Croatia/Bosnia), but two previous external borders became internal borders instead (Hungary/Croatia and Slovenia/Croatia).

As regards the possible derogations from the general rules on external border control, all of the treaties concerned were in some way stricter. Also, there had been ambiguities in interpreting the Regulation. As regards the definition of the local border area, the Commission argued that this could be addressed by means of application of the EU's visa facilitation agreements.[604] Also, several Member States impose a health insurance requirement in their bilateral treaties. The Commission convincingly argues that such a requirement is implicitly ruled out by the Regulation, which sets out exhaustive criteria which may be applied for the issue of a local border traffic permit. While the Commission was initially willing to suggest amendments to the Regulation if it transpires that the

---

[595] Arts 16–21.   [596] Art 16.   [597] Art 17.

[598] Art 19. In practice, this information has not been made public, except in the context of the Commission's reports on the application of the Reg, on which see below.

[599] Art 20, amending Art 136(3) of the Convention ([2000] OJ L 239). However, this provision of the Convention has since been repealed. See further I:3.12 below.

[600] Art 18.   [601] COM (2009) 383, 24 July 2009.   [602] COM (2011) 47, 9 Feb 2011.

[603] Norway is subject to the Reg as a Schengen associate.

[604] On those agreements, see I:4.11.2 below. Note that many of these agreements contain declarations regarding local border traffic issues.

problems which result from this (ie the costs of providing emergency medical treatment for some persons with a local border traffic permit) could not be resolved by bilateral agreement between the health services of the States concerned, in 2011 it ruled out
amendments to this end, in particular because the Member States which did not impose
a health insurance requirement had in practice not suffered from 'medical tourism'.

As for the waiting period, in practice the 2009 and 2011 reports state that all of the
treaties concerned set waiting periods of more than one year, and indeed by 2011 all but
one of the treaties provides for a five-year period of validity. The applicable fees ranged
from €20 to €35. Member States had not always accepted the Commission's demands to
renegotiate agreements, although the Commission had not responded (as it could have
done) by bringing infringement actions against those States.[605] Presumably its reluctance to do so is due to a desire to avoid complicating the Member States' and the EU's
relations with the third countries concerned. Finally, on the abuse of the system, in the
2009 report the Commission noted that '[t]here were...no reports from the Member
States that there was a wide misuse by owners of [local border traffic] permits or that
the agreements raised some security risks for the Schengen area'. Similarly, the 2011
report refers to only about forty cases of reported abuse, out of over 110,000 permits
issued, and concludes that 'relatively few abuses occur in the practical implementation
of the' treaties and that 'there is no evidence that [permit] holders would systematically
travel to other Member States in violation of the rules'.

The border traffic rules addressed the need to simplify border crossing for the
many thousands of visa nationals who have been on the EU's external border following enlargement (although the numbers were reduced by the visa waivers for the
Western Balkan States in 2009 and 2010), and whose economic, cultural, and personal
links to the new Member States were sundered when visa obligations were applied to
these neighbouring countries and the other EU visa rules were extended when the full
Schengen *acquis* applied to most new Member States. So the border traffic legislation in
principle makes a useful contribution to enhancing both the EU's political relationship
with its neighbours—who are expected to take on many obligations to assist the EU
and who suffered substantial disadvantages following enlargement—and the daily life
of many individual residents of border regions, including those EU citizens who benefit
from maintaining economic, cultural, and personal links to the East.

3.9 Biometric Passports

In December 2004, the Council adopted a Regulation harmonizing the security features of EU citizens' passports as regards the inclusion of biometric information (fingerprints and digital photographs).[606] This Regulation was subsequently amended
in 2009,[607] partly in order to provide for exceptions from the obligation to include
biometrics in passports. The Regulation is intended to be consistent with other measures requiring the insertion of photos and fingerprints into residence permits and

---

[605] On the infringement procedure, see Art 258 TFEU.
[606] Reg 2252/2004, [2004] OJ L 385/1.
[607] Reg 444/2009, [2009] OJ L 144/1. The Reg has not been codified.

visas, although ultimately it proved technically impossible to insert biometric information into visas.[608] It should be recalled that there are also Resolutions of Member States which have established other features of the design of a uniform format for EU passports.[609]

There are several CJEU judgments on this Regulation. First of all, as noted above, the UK sued to annul the original 2004 Regulation because its attempt to opt in to the legislation was refused by the Council, but the UK's challenge was unsuccessful.[610] There have been three subsequent CJEU rulings on refererences from national courts on the interpretation of the Regulation,[611] and one Member State was condemned by the Court for not applying the legislation.[612] It should also be recalled that the EU now has a power, conferred by the Treaty of Lisbon, to adopt measures related to passports and similar documents in order to facilitate EU citizens' free movement rights.[613]

The Regulation, largely prompted by American demands for the inclusion of high-security features in the passports of countries subject to the American visa waiver programme,[614] provides for mandatory inclusion of digital photographs and fingerprints in EU passports, in accordance with the technical standards set out in an Annex to the Regulation, which refer to recommendations of the International Civil Aviation Organization (ICAO).[615] Passports must be issued as individual documents,[616] and the Commission had to report by 26 June 2012 on children travelling across the external borders in order to examine whether to adopt a common approach on the protection of children crossing the external borders.[617] Children under twelve years are exempt from the fingerprinting obligation, although Member States which already fingerprinted children between six and twelve years as of 26 June 2009 could continue to do so for a four-year period after that date (so until June 2013).[618] The Commission had to report by 26 June 2012 on whether to alter the age limit, based on an independent technical study of the accuracy of fingerprint data taken from children under twelve for 'identification and verification purposes' (ie checking the fingerprints on a one-to-one and one-to-many basis respectively).[619] Also, persons are exempt from the obligation if taking their fingerprints is physically impossible.[620]

---

[608] See I:4.6 and I:6.9.1 below as regards Schengen visas and residence permits respectively.

[609] [1981] OJ C 241/1; [1982] OJ C 179/1; [1986] OJ C 185/1; [1995] OJ C 200/1; [2000] OJ C 310/1; and [2004] OJ C 245/1.

[610] Case C-137/05 *UK v Council* [2007] ECR I-11593.

[611] Cases: C-291/13 *Schwarz*, ECLI:EU:C:2013:670; C-101/13 *U*, ECLI:EU:C:2014:2249; and C-446/12 to C-449/12 *Willems and others*, ECLI:EU:C:2015:238.

[612] Case C-139/13 *Commission v Belgium*, ECLI:EU:C:2014:80.

[613] Art 77(3) TFEU; see again I:3.2.4 above.

[614] See the explanatory memorandum to the proposal (COM (2004) 116, 18 Feb 2004), p 3.

[615] Art 1(1) and (2).

[616] Art 1(1), second sub-paragraph, as inserted by Reg 444/2009. This obligation had to be implemented by 26 June 2012 (see final sub-paragraph of Art 6, as inserted by Reg 444/2009).

[617] Art 1(1), third sub-paragraph, as inserted by Reg 444/2009. The Commission report (COM (2013) 567, 2 Aug 2013) indicated that there were no problems with the 'one person, one passport' principle, and did not make further proposals.

[618] Art 1(2a)(a), as inserted by Reg 444/2009.

[619] Art 5a, as inserted by Reg 444/2009. For that report, see: <https://ec.europa.eu/jrc/sites/default/files/fingerprint_recognition_for_children_final_report_(pdf).pdf>. The Commission did not make further proposals.

[620] Art 1(2a)(b), as inserted by Reg 444/2009. There is a special rule if this impossibility is only temporary: see Art 1(2b), as inserted by Reg 444/2009.

The Regulation applies to passports and travel documents issued by Member States, but not to identity cards at all, or to temporary passports or travel documents having a validity of under a year.[621] Biometric data must be collected by qualified national officials, who must act in accordance with international human rights law and ensure the dignity of the person concerned if the biometric information cannot be taken.[622] Further security standards can be adopted by the Commission, assisted by a 'comitology' committee of Member States' representatives.[623] There are basic data protection rules, and the Regulation specifies that checking the biometric information in the passport is without prejudice to the rules in the Schengen Borders Code concerning checks of EU citizens at the external borders.[624] Member States had to apply the Regulation eighteen months after the adoption of technical specifications as regards digital photographs, and thirty-six months after the adoption of technical specifications as regards fingerprints.[625] In practice, this obligation has applied as from 28 August 2007 as regards facial images, and 28 June 2009 as regards fingerprints.[626]

In the Commission's view, this is only a first step; that institution wishes to see the creation of '[a]t EU level, a centralised, biometrics-based, "EU passport register", which would contain the fingerprints of passport applicants' with the passport number 'and most probably some other, but limited, relevant data'.[627] However, the 2009 amendment to the Regulation states that the legislation is not a legal base regarding passport databases, which are 'strictly a matter of national law'.[628]

The Regulation was followed up by Council conclusions on the issue of national identity cards, adopted in December 2005.[629] While the conclusions are not legally binding, and do not require Member States either to adopt identity cards or to require biometric identifiers as part of the cards, they are likely to encourage this process. The conclusions state that the biometrics and security features of identity cards should be based on those applicable to passports, and set out guidelines for the process of issuing identity cards. A later Member States' resolution sets out agreed common technical standards for identity cards.[630] Again, it should be recalled that the EU now has a power, conferred by the Treaty of Lisbon, to adopt measures related to identity cards in order to facilitate EU citizens' free movement rights.[631]

According to the CJEU's judgment in *Schwarz*, the passports Regulation is not invalid for infringing fundamental rights,[632] because there are sound public interest

---

[621] Art 1(3), as clarified by the CJEU in *Willems*, n 611 above.

[622] Art 1a, as inserted by Reg 444/2009.

[623] Art 2, as amended by Reg 444/2009; see also Arts 3(1) and 5. For the English translations of two implementing measures, adopted by the Commission in 2005 and 2006, see: <http://ec.europa.eu/justice_home/doc_centre/freetravel/documents/doc_freetravel_documents_en.htm>.

[624] Art 4, as amended by Reg 444/2009, referring to Art 7(2) of the Borders Code (Reg 562/2006, [2006] OJ L 105/1); see I:3.6.1 above. It should be noted that the passports Reg does not amend the Borders Code, so there is no legal requirement to check passports going beyond the rules in the Borders Code.

[625] Art 6, as amended by Reg 444/2009.   [626] See SEC (2009) 320, 9 Mar 2009, p 10.

[627] See points 2 and 8 of its explanatory memorandum (COM (2004) 116, 18 Feb 2004).

[628] Recital 8 in the preamble, Reg 444/2009. See also the discussion of competence issues in I:3.2.4 above.

[629] Press Release of JHA Council, 1–2 Dec 2005.

[630] Press Release of JHA Council, 4–5 Dec 2006.

[631] Art 77(3) TFEU; see discussion in I:3.2.4 above.

[632] *Schwarz*, n 611 above. This judgment also considered the legal base of the Reg: see I:3.2.4 above.

reasons (preventing illegal entry) to interfere with the right to private life by taking fingerprints. That interference was proportionate, because biometric technology could reduce falsification, even if it was not 100% perfect. A false match with a stolen passport would not lead to refusal of entry, but rather extra checks by border guards. There were no alternatives which would better achieve the planned objectives.

The Court was less rigorous about applying human rights principles in the later judgment in *Willems*. Here it ruled that the collection of biometric passport data in national databases is outside the scope of the Regulation, as was the collection of biometric data for identity cards. Those findings are not objectionable, since the Regulation was clearly intended only to regulate the use of such data as regards the passports as such; but the Court went on to refuse to answer questions about the application of the EU's data protection Directive, even though the national court had asked about it and that Directive obviously does apply to this form of data collection.[633]

Finally, the *U* judgment concerned a German man who had changed his surname as compared to his birth name. The German authorities placed both names in his passport, indicating his birth name by 'GEB' (short for the German word for 'born'). The CJEU ruled that the Regulation requires all passports to apply the recommendations of the ICAO on document security. In the Court's view, Member States have flexibility to designate a person's birth name as part of his name on a passport, even though the ICAO rules refer to national law, and the relevant German law on fixing of names (as distinct from the law on passports) does not include birth names as part of a person's name. The rationale here was the interest of document security, which favoured the use of a fixed element (the name at birth). Next, the Court ruled that the birth name could not be included in the optional section of the passport. Finally, interpreting the Charter, it ruled that the right to a name, which forms part of the right to a private life set out in Article 7 of the Charter, means that any use of a birth name on a passport had to be clearly indicated. The abbreviation 'GEB' was not translated, so could not be comprehended by the authorities of other countries and was liable to lead to practical complications for the passport holder.

The Court's ruling partly addresses the practical problems faced by the passport holder, by requiring the German authorities to make it clear to non-German speakers that his birth name is just that, and that he now goes by a new name. But the Court did not acknowledge the great ambiguity in the ICAO rules, which the Advocate-General's Opinion had interpreted differently. If the Court had instead assessed whether the interference in the passport holder's right to his private life (ie the use of his current surname) was proportionate and necessary, the objective of ensuring passport security could still have been achieved by the alternative means of providing a precise record of Doktor U's *current* identity.

3.10 Operational Cooperation

Operational cooperation as regards border control within the EU has largely taken place within the context of the EU's border control agency, Frontex. Subsequently, the

---

[633] N 612 above. On the human rights issues, see I:3.3 above; for more on data protection, see II.7.3.

EU has established a surveillance system for southern frontiers (Eurosur). These two issues will be examined in turn.

3.10.1 Frontex

A perceived need to adopt EU measures to ensure more effective operational cooperation as regards borders control was first addressed by the Council's 2002 Action Plan on external borders, which addressed the issues of coordination of operations and cooperation, risk analysis, joint use of personnel and equipment, legislation, and burden-sharing.[634] Initially, the implementation of the Plan was coordinated by the heads of border guards meeting within the framework of the Strategic Committee on Immigration, Frontiers, and Asylum (SCIFA), who were dubbed 'SCIFA+'. By June 2003, a number of joint operations had been held, the creation of ad hoc centres on sea, land, and air borders was underway, and projects on a common risk analysis and a core curriculum for border guards were under development.[635] But it was soon decided that joint operations and cooperation between Member States needed a stronger institutional structure, and the principle of creating a EU Borders Agency was approved by the October 2003 European Council. The Agency (known in practice as Frontex) was established by Regulation 2007/2004, adopted in autumn 2004;[636] the legality of the Regulation was subsequently upheld by the Court of Justice, dismissing a legal challenge by the UK, which had objected to its exclusion from participation in the adoption of the Frontex legislation.[637] The Council decided that the agency's seat is in Warsaw, and it started operations on 1 May 2005.[638]

The Frontex Regulation has been substantially amended twice, in 2007 and 2011.[639] It has also been amended two other times: in 2013, when the EU adopted legislation establishing Eurosur,[640] to include tasks relating to Eurosur and to regulate the processing of personal data in the context of Eurosur; and in 2014, when the EU adopted detailed rules governing maritime surveillance operations coordinated by Frontex.[641] Frontex also has a formal role in the EU's network of immigration liaison officers, according to separate legislation.[642] In December 2015, the Commission proposed to amend the Frontex Regulation again, to transform it into a 'European Border Guard

---

[634] Council doc 10019/02, 14 June 2002.

[635] Council doc 10058/1/02, 11 June 2003. The creation of a network of immigration liaison officers was also linked to this process (see I:7.5.5 below). For more on the development of the operational aspects of the border plan, see ch 7 of S Peers and N Rogers, *EU Immigration and Asylum Law: Text and Commentary*, 1st edn (Martinus Nijhoff, 2006).

[636] [2004] OJ L 349/1. See the Frontex website: <http://www.frontex.europa.eu/>.

[637] Case C-77/05 *UK v Council* [2007] ECR I-11459. See further I:3.2.5 above.

[638] [2005] OJ L 114/15; see Art 34 of the Frontex Reg.

[639] Reg 863/2007 ([2007] OJ L 199/30) and Reg 1168/2011 ([2011] OJ L 304/1). The Frontex Reg has not been codified. All references in this sub-section are to Reg 2007/2004, as amended, unless otherwise indicated. Note that as well as amending Reg 2007/2004, Reg 863/2007 contains distinct provisions of its own (Arts 1–11, Reg 863/2007). For the background to the 2011 amendments, see the Commission communication on the future of Frontex (COM (2008) 67, 13 Feb 2008), and the independent evaluation, online at: <http://www.frontex.europa.eu/specific_documents/other/>.

[640] Reg 1052/2013 ([2013] OJ L 295/1). On Eurosur generally, see I:3.10.2 below.

[641] Reg 656/2014 ([2014] OJ L 189/93), discussed in more detail below.

[642] See further I:7.5.5 below.

and Coast Guard', to strengthen its role as regards expulsions and to give it the power to intervene at external borders without Member States' consent in emergencies.[643]

Frontex has not replaced national border guards: the Frontex Regulation states that 'the responsibility for the control and surveillance of external borders lies with the Member States'.[644] Rather, Frontex contributes to and coordinates national border guards' work. In particular, the main tasks of Frontex are the coordination of operational cooperation between Member States, assistance with training, risk assessment, participation in research on external borders, extra technical and operational assistance for Member States that need it, setting up and deploying European Border Guard Teams for joint operations, pilot projects and rapid interventions, the coordination or organization of expulsion, the development of information systems, and contribution to Eurosur, the border surveillance system.[645] However, the basic Regulation makes it clear that the powers of Frontex are not exclusive; Member States can continue with bilateral cooperation between each other or cooperation with third States outside the framework of the Agency.[646] Executive acts by 'guest officers' (the border guards of one Member State on the territory of another), are subject to the national law of the host Member State, in compliance with fundamental rights.[647]

More generally, Frontex must carry out its tasks 'in full compliance with' EU law, including the EU Charter of Fundamental Rights, the Geneva Convention on Refugee status, and 'obligations related to access to international protection, in particular the principle of non-refoulement', ie the obligation not to return a person to a country where their life or safety is threatened.[648] The Frontex Regulation also *specifies that* 'no-one shall be disembarked in, or otherwise handed over to the authorities of, a country in contravention of the principle of non-refoulement, or from which there is a risk of expulsion or return to another country in contravention of that principle'. Also, the 'special needs of children, victims of trafficking, persons in need of medical assistance, persons in need of international protection and other vulnerable persons shall be addressed in accordance with' EU and international law.[649]

To this end, Frontex had to draw up a Code of Conduct, to ensure that Frontex operations respect the 'principles of the rule of law and the respect of fundamental rights with particular focus on unaccompanied minors and vulnerable persons, as well as persons seeking international protection'.[650] As regards return, Frontex had to adopt a Code of Conduct on return proceedings, which must apply during all joint return operations coordinated by Frontex, and which describes 'common standardized procedures' to, inter alia, 'assure return in a humane manner and in full respect for fundamental rights, in particular the principles of human dignity, prohibition of torture

---

[643] COM (2015) 668, 15 Dec 2015. On expulsions generally, see I:7.7 below; on the legal problems with part of the proposal, see I:3.2.4 above.

[644] Art 1(2).

[645] Art 2; and see further details in Arts 3–11, as amended. For further details on Border Guard Teams, see also Arts 3–11, Reg 863/2007.

[646] Art 2(2).   [647] Art 10.

[648] Art 1(2), second sub-paragraph, Frontex Regulation, inserted by Reg 1168/2011. See further ch 5 of this volume.

[649] Art 2(1a), Frontex Regulation, inserted by Reg 1168/2011.

[650] Art 2a, Frontex Regulation, inserted by Reg 1168/2011.

and of inhuman or degrading treatment or punishment, right to liberty and security, the rights to the protection of personal data and non-discrimination.[651] This Code of Conduct 'in particular [had to] pay attention to the obligation' set out in the EU's Returns Directive 'to provide for an effective forced-return monitoring system', as well as the Fundamental Rights strategy which Frontex had to adopt (see below).[652]

Finally, Frontex had to 'draw up and further develop and implement' a Fundamental Rights Strategy, and 'put in place an effective mechanism to monitor the respect for fundamental rights in all the activities of the Agency'. It had to establish a 'Consultative Forum' to assist its senior staff as regards fundamental rights issues, and must invite the European Asylum Support Office, the EU's Fundamental Rights Agency, the United Nations High Commissioner for Refugees and other relevant organizations to participate in this Forum. In particular, the Consultative Forum has to be 'consulted on the further development and implementation of the Fundamental Rights Strategy, Code of conduct and Common Core Curriculum [for training of border guards]'. Frontex also had to designate a Fundamental Rights Officer, who must be 'independent in the performance of his/her duties as a Fundamental Rights Officer', reporting on a regular basis and contributing to the mechanism for monitoring fundamental rights.[653]

Frontex must cooperate with the UK and Ireland,[654] as well as a number of EU agencies and bodies and international organizations,[655] and third countries.[656]

As for the status of Frontex,[657] it is an independent EU 'body' with legal personality. The Regulation also provides for the possibility of establishing specialized centres.[658] EU law rules on staff, privileges and immunities, liability, access to documents, fraud control, and budgets apply. Overall strategic control is in the hands of a Management Board, meeting three times a year and consisting of one member per Member State and two Commission representatives, although the Regulation gives each Member State a veto over operations conducted on or near its territory. However, the day-to-day management is in the hands of an Executive Director and Deputy Executive Director, appointed by the Management Board on the basis of proposals from the Commission.

Maritime surveillance operations coordinated by Frontex are regulated in detail by a Regulation adopted in 2014.[659] This measure replaced a Decision implementing the Schengen Borders Code which was originally adopted in 2010,[660] but which was annulled by the CJEU in 2012 because it should have taken the form of legislation, not an implementing measure.[661]

The 2010 Decision contained binding rules on interception, and non-binding rules on search and rescue and disembarkation. However, the CJEU said that even the latter

---

[651] Art 9(2), Frontex Regulation, inserted by Reg 1168/2011.
[652] Art 9(3), Frontex Regulation, inserted by Reg 1168/2011. On the Returns Directive, see I:7.7 below.
[653] Art 26a, as inserted by Reg 1168/2011.   [654] Art 12.
[655] Art 13, as amended by Reg 1168/2011.
[656] Art 14, Frontex Regulation, as amended by Reg 1168/2011, inter alia, as regards the deployment of Frontex liaison officers in third countries.
[657] Arts 15–32.
[658] See the study on this issue: <http://www.frontex.europa.eu/specific_documents/other/>.
[659] Reg 656/2014 ([2014] OJ L 189/93).   [660] [2010] OJ L 111/20.
[661] Case C-355/10 *European Parliament v Council*, ECLI:EU:C:2012:516.

category of rules was binding. In the 2014 Regulation, both sets of rules are clearly binding. There are new rules on search and rescue, which include a detailed definition of whether vessels can be considered in a state of alert, uncertainty, or distress.[662] Provided that sinking vessels are detected in time and that these rules are properly applied, the Regulation should therefore ensure that migrants are rescued from drowning wherever possible.

On the other hand, the situation is more complex as regards the rules on protection of those migrants who are potentially at risk of persecution, torture or other forms of ill-treatment in their country of origin (or another country). The core of the 2014 Regulation is the protection against non-refoulement (removal to an unsafe country) and protection of fundamental rights.[663] According to the Regulation, no one can be 'disembarked in, forced to enter, conducted to or otherwise handed over to' an unsafe country as further defined in the Regulation. A country is unsafe if there is either: (a) a serious risk of subjection of the migrant to the death penalty, torture, persecution, or other inhuman or degrading treatment; or (b) the migrant's life or freedom would be threatened on the grounds set out in the Geneva Convention on Refugees (race, religion, nationality, political opinion, or membership of a social group), as well as sexual orientation. Also, a 'chain refoulement' is banned: a migrant cannot be handed over to a country which is safe in itself, but which would hand the migrant over to an unsafe country.

Compared to the criteria in EU asylum law,[664] the first category includes two of the grounds concerning the grant of 'subsidiary protection' (ie protection for those who do not qualify as refugees under the Geneva Convention): the death penalty and torture or other inhuman or degrading treatment. It does not include the third category, concerning ill-treatment in the event of armed conflict; however, it does include 'persecution', without further definition. The second category is identical to Article 33(1) of the Geneva Convention, except that it does not include the exception in Article 33(2) of that Convention for persons posing security threats, and it adds the grounds of 'sexual orientation' to those referred to in the Convention.[665]

Next, how must an unsafe country be determined? The 2014 Regulation states that when considering disembarking migrants in a third country, the host Member State must 'take into account the general situation in that third country', and cannot disembark or otherwise force to enter, conduct to or hand over if the host Member State or other participating Member States 'are aware or ought to be aware' that such a State presents such a risk.[666] A 'broad range' of sources of information must be taken into account, including other Member States, EU bodies, agencies and offices, and international bodies. The Member States 'may' take into account existing agreements and projects carried out using EU funds.

---

[662] Art 9, Reg 656/2014.   [663] Art 4, Reg 656/2014.   [664] See I:5.5 below.

[665] However, the CJEU's asylum case law has confirmed that homosexuals can form a 'particular social group' under the EU's Qualification Directive (see discussion in I:5.5 below).

[666] Art 4(2), Reg 656/2014. The 'host Member State' is the Member State from which an operation takes place or from which it is launched (Art 2(3)).

As for the migrants' procedural rights, the 2014 Regulation specifies that (in accordance with the *Hirsi* judgment of the European Court of Human Rights) before disembarking or otherwise conducting the migrants to a third State, taking into account the general situation in that State, the Member States' units shall 'use all means' to identify the migrants, assess their circumstances, inform them of their destination and give them an opportunity to object on grounds of the non-refoulement rule.[667] These obligations are subject to an override in the interests of the safety of all the persons involved.[668] The operational plan must 'where necessary' provide for medical staff, interpreters, legal advisers, and other relevant experts on shore. Also, the annual reports which Frontex must provide on the application of the Regulation must include 'further details' on cases of disembarkation in third States, as regards the application of the relevant criteria. There are also limits on the exchange of personal data with third countries, an obligation to respect human dignity, and rules on training of staff.[669]

The protection rules cannot be separated from the rules on disembarkation of migrants. There are three scenarios in the Regulation.[670] First, if migrants are intercepted in the territorial sea or contiguous zone of a Member State,[671] then they must be disembarked in the coastal Member State.[672] But this is subject to a crucial exception: it is possible under the Regulation that a vessel that has made it this close to a Member State could still be ordered to alter course towards another destination.

Secondly, if migrants are intercepted in the high seas, they may be disembarked in the country from which they are assumed to have departed, subject to the non-refoulement rules in the Regulation. If that is not possible, then disembarkation 'shall' take place in the host Member State. Thirdly, in the event of a search and rescue, the migrants shall be disembarked in a place of safety. If that is not possible, then they shall be disembarked in the host Member State.

These provisions raise many important questions. First of all, it should have been clearly specified that the general non-refoulement rule takes priority over any possibility of disembarkation in a third State. Secondly, as correctly noted in the preamble to the Regulation, the EU's asylum legislation applies to anyone in the territorial waters of the EU. This means that, in accordance with that legislation, once an asylum application is made in the territorial waters, the asylum applicant cannot be removed to a third State before there is a decision on the asylum application in accordance with that legislation, save for some limited exceptions not relevant here. The obvious corollary of this is that asylum seekers who make their application in the territorial waters must be disembarked on the territory of the Member State concerned, since it is unlikely that it will be practical to keep them on board a ship for the entire duration of a full asylum procedure. However, the main text of the Regulation does not reflect the wording of this legislation, since it provides for the possibility of persons intercepted or rescued in the territorial waters to be removed to third countries.

---

[667] Art 4(3), Reg 656/2014. On the *Hirsi* judgment, see further I:3.3 above.

[668] Art 3, Reg 656/2014.   [669] Art 4(4) to (8), Reg 656/2014.   [670] Art 10, Reg 656/2014.

[671] This means the waters adjacent to the territorial sea, according to international law: Art 2(13).

[672] This means the Member State in whose territorial waters or contiguous zone the operation takes place: Art 2(14).

Thirdly, when migrants are disembarked on the territory of a Member State, an awkward question could arise: is that *Member State* safe? While the specific non-refoulement rules in the Regulation refer to the safety of *third* countries,[673] the general rule refers to countries in general.[674] The European Court of Human Rights and the EU's Court of Justice have already both concluded that Greece in effect fails the standard set out in Article 4, and litigation in some Member States is also challenging the safety of Italy.[675] So there could be a clash between the non-refoulement rule and the obligation to disembark in a Member State which is the host State, coastal State, or place of safety, or in the territorial waters of which the applications were made.

Fourthly, as for those intercepted or rescued in the high seas or the contiguous zone (the Regulation does not contemplate the scenario of migrants being intercepted in the territorial waters of third States), the bulk of the EU's asylum legislation does not apply. However, the EU's qualification Directive (on the definition of refugee and subsidiary protection status) does—since there is nothing in the text of that Directive to limit its territorial scope.[676] But the wording of the Regulation is confusing in this regard, since it does not refer to the detailed text of that Directive but rather to general standards on non-refoulement, which are different from that Directive in some respects, as noted above (the omission of persons fleeing conflict, for instance).

Having said that, EU rules on asylum procedures and reception conditions do not apply to asylum seekers who are intercepted or rescued in the high seas or the contiguous zone,[677] and in that case the rules in the Regulation would apply. In effect, the rules summarized above provide for a highly simplified process—which might be dubbed the 'maritime asylum procedure'—for such cases. As noted above, though, the words 'where necessary' and 'use all means' arguably give Member States considerable flexibility not to apply these rules fully, and these rules are (understandably) subject to the requirement to give priority to the safety of all persons. This should mean that in the event of a risk to the safety of persons, if the application of the non-refoulement rule has not yet been assessed, the migrants must be taken to a (safe) Member State to avoid prejudicing the outcome of that assessment. Once the migrants enter a Member State's territorial waters, EU asylum law will apply fully (arguably it applies even if the application was made *before* the vessel entered those waters; if not, then there is nothing to stop the asylum seeker making a renewed application for asylum once the vessel is in those waters).

Since most EU asylum law does not apply to the high seas, the EU's Dublin rules on asylum responsibility do not apply either, and it is an open question whether they would apply where a person made an application on the high seas and was then brought to the territorial waters of a Member State while the application was being considered. If this is correct, in order to limit somewhat the huge impact of these Dublin rules on the coastal Mediterranean States, EU Member States could agree between themselves on new rules for responsibility for asylum seekers who make their application on the high seas. If necessary, this could take the form of an amendment to the Dublin rules.

As for the accountability of operations, Frontex must make annual reports on the application of the Regulation, including on Frontex's own procedures and information

---

[673] Art 4(2) and (3), Reg 656/2014.   [674] Art 4(1), Reg 656/2014.   [675] See I:5.8 below.
[676] See I:5.5 below.   [677] See I:5.7 and I:5.9 below.

on the application of the Regulation in practice, including 'detailed information on compliance with fundamental rights and the impact on those rights, and any incidents which may have taken place'. Presumably this means that these reports will have to include full information on where migrants were disembarked and the assessments that were made of the safety of any third countries (and Member States) in each particular case. It would have been better to clarify the extent of these obligations expressly, although any provision on accountability is better than none.[678]

3.10.2 Other operational cooperation

In 2006, the Commission suggested the creation of a permanent 'Coastal Patrol Network' for the southern maritime external borders and of a 'European Surveillance System for Borders', or 'Eurosur',[679] a system for information sharing to ensure enhanced surveillance of the external borders, in order to control Schengen external borders more effectively. The plans for its creation were initially outlined in a 'roadmap' presented by the Commission in 2008,[680] and the Commission subsequently reported on the practical development of the system in 2009 and 2011.[681] Ultimately, a Regulation establishing the Eurosur system was adopted in October 2013.[682] This Regulation applied from 1 December 2013 to the Member States on the EU's eastern or southern borders, and from 1 December 2014 to all other Member States.[683] Spain unsuccessfully challenged the provisions of the Regulation regarding cooperation with the UK before the CJEU.[684]

According to the Eurosur Regulation, its purpose is to establish 'a common framework for the exchange of information and cooperation between Member States and' Frontex, so as 'to improve the situational awareness and to increase the reaction capability at the external borders', applying to border surveillance with the purpose of 'detecting, preventing and combating illegal immigration and cross-border crime and contributing to ensuring the protection and saving the lives of migrants'.[685] It does not apply to actions taken following interception of the persons concerned.[686]

A general clause on human rights protection requires Member States and Frontex to observe 'fundamental rights, including the principles of non-refoulement and human dignity and data protection requirements, when applying' the Eurosur Regulation. They have to 'give priority to the special needs of children, unaccompanied minors, victims of trafficking, persons in need of urgent medical assistance, persons in need of international protection, persons in distress at sea and other persons in a particularly vulnerable situation'.[687]

---

[678] Art 13, Reg 656/2014.
[679] COM (2006) 733, 30 Nov 2006. See earlier the Commission communication on migration management (COM (2005) 621, 30 Nov 2005) and the Dec 2005 European Council conclusions, Annex I.
[680] COM (2008) 68, 13 Feb 2008.
[681] See SEC (2009) 1265, 24 Sep 2009 and SEC (2011) 145, 28 Jan 2011.
[682] Reg 1052/2013 ([2013] OJ L 295/1). See the Commission handbook on the application of the Eurosur system: C(2015) 9206, 15 Dec 2015.
[683] Art 21.
[684] Case C-44/14, *Spain v EP and Council*, ECLI:EU:C:2015:554. See further I:3.2.5 above.
[685] Arts 1 and 2(1).   [686] Art 2(2).   [687] Art 2(3).

The framework for Eurosur consists of:[688] national coordination centres;[689] national situation pictures;[690] a communication framework;[691] a European situational picture;[692] a common pre-frontier intelligence picture;[693] and common application of surveillance tools.[694] To apply the Eurosur Regulation, each Member State has had to divide its land and sea borders into sections, and inform Frontex.[695] In agreement with each Member State, Frontex has designated each section 'high-impact', 'medium-impact', or 'low-impact', as regards unauthorized migration and cross-border crime.[696] The Regulation then spells out the levels of surveillance which Member States should apply to each section, depending on the classification of risk. It also provides for possible requests for assistance from Frontex, and for coordination between neighbouring Member States.[697]

Within the framework of the Eurosur system, Frontex is obliged to cooperate with a number of relevant EU agencies, 'in particular': Europol, the EU Satellite Centre, the European Maritime Safety Agency, the European Fisheries Control Agency, the European Commission, the European External Action Service, and the European Asylum Support Office, as well as international organizations.[698] There are also special rules on cooperation with the UK and Ireland,[699] as well as non-EU countries.[700] The EU Commission will draw up a handbook on the operations of Eurosur.[701]

Finally, there must be regular monitoring of the functioning of Eurosur 'against the objectives of achieving an adequate situational awareness and reaction capability at the external borders and the respect for fundamental rights'.[702] Frontex has to report on the functioning of Eurosur every two years, while the Commission will evaluate it every four years.[703]

3.10.3 Schengen governance

A key feature of the Schengen system is the Schengen evaluation mechanism, which was revised after much controversy in 2013.[704] This mechanism applies both to evaluations of existing Schengen States and to evaluations to assess the readiness of non-Schengen States to join the Schengen system. Compared to the previous system which the Regulation replaced, the Commission has an enhanced role, responsible for 'overall coordination' as regards 'establishing annual and multiannual evaluation programmes,

---

[688] Art 4(1). On the relationship between these elements, see Art 4(2) to (4). See also Art 6, on the role of Frontex.
[689] On the role of the national coordination centres, see Art 5.
[690] On this concept, see Art 9. For the definitions of 'situational picture', see Arts 3(c) and 8.
[691] On the communication framework, see Art 7.   [692] On this concept, see Art 10.
[693] On this concept, see Art 11. For the definition of 'pre-frontier', see Art 3(f).
[694] On this concept, see Art 12.   [695] See Art 13.   [696] See Art 14.   [697] See Art 15.
[698] See Art 17.   [699] See Art 17a.   [700] See Art 18.   [701] See Art 19.
[702] See Art 20(1).   [703] See Art 20(2) and (3).
[704] Reg 1053/2013 ([2013] OJ L 295/27). This Reg replaced a Decision of the Schengen Executive Committee: SCH/Com-ex (98) 26 def ([2000] OJ L 239/138). The basic features of the system are set out also in the Schengen Borders Code: Art 37a of the Code (Reg 562/2006, [2006] OJ L 105/1), as inserted by Reg 1051/2013 ([2013] OJ L 295/1). For discussion of the controversy over the legal base of the Reg, see I:2.2.3.2 above.

drafting questionnaires and setting schedules of visits, conducting visits and drafting evaluation reports and recommendations', as well as ensuring 'the follow-up and monitoring of the evaluation reports and recommendations'.[705] Frontex also has a role producing risk analyses.[706] However, ultimately any recommendations to Member States will be adopted by the Council. Member States will have three months to reply to any recommendations to address deficiencies (or only one month, in cases of 'serious neglect'), and will also have to report regularly on the implementation of this action plan until the deficiencies have been addressed. The Commission will evaluate these reports, and ultimately has the power to recommend the possible reimposition of internal border controls pursuant to the criteria in the Borders Code if it deems that the relevant criteria (discussed above) are satisfied.[707]

As for the governance of the Schengen system more generally, a more systematic approach was launched by a Commission communication on this subject in September 2011,[708] which was a response to the concerns about the operation of the Schengen system that had arisen during the Arab Spring. This communication, which was released alongside the proposals (subsequently adopted) to permit further reintroduction of border controls and to reform the Schengen evaluation system,[709] confirmed the Commission's willingness to issue guidelines 'to ensure a coherent implementation of the Schengen rules', following the identification of 'shortcomings and areas where there might be need for further clarification on the Schengen *acquis*'. Along with these guidelines, and the reports that will follow from the revised rules on Schengen evaluations and border controls, the Commission committed itself to produce a bi-annual overview on the Schengen system, to 'provide the basis for a regular debate in the European Parliament and in the Council and contribute to the strengthening of political guidance and cooperation in the Schengen area'. Subsequent amendments to the Borders Code now require the Commission to produce an annual report on the entire Schengen system.[710]

Nevertheless, the Commission has continued to produce two reports a year on the Schengen system, and so far has issued a total of seven reports.[711] These reports set out information on developments regarding external borders, irregular migration, the reimposition of internal border controls, Commission complaints to Member States, Schengen evaluations, the SIS, visa issues (including the operation of the Visa Information System), along with guidelines on related issues.

Overall, the Commission's reports provide a useful summary of factual information relating to the operation of the Schengen system, which could be useful to inform

---

[705] Art 3, evaluation Regulation. For details of the programmes, see Arts 5 and 6; on questionnaires, see Art 9; on the visits and evaluations, see Arts 10–15.

[706] Art 7, evaluation Regulation. On other EU bodies, see Art 8.

[707] On the process of reimposing border controls, see I:3.5 above.

[708] COM (2011) 561, 16 Sep 2011.

[709] See also the compilation of measures which the EU could take to support Member States facing difficulties at the external borders (Annex I of the report).

[710] Art 29 of the Code, as inserted by Reg 1051/2013, n 704 above.

[711] COM (2012) 230, 16 May 2012; COM (2012) 686, 23 Nov 2012; COM (2013) 326, 31 May 2013; COM (2013) 832, 28 Nov 2013; COM (2014) 292, 26 May 2014; COM (2014) 711, 27 Nov 2014; and COM (2015) 236, 29 May 2015.

public debate about that system. So far the European Parliament and the Council have not responded directly to these reports. With the adoption of further new legislation on the Schengen system (concerning internal border controls, Schengen evaluation, Eurosur, maritime surveillance, and visa issues) since 2013, and the increased salience of the issues in light of surges in migration toward the EU, there will be an ever-greater need to develop this reporting system, in particular to link together the various reports that are or will be required under the different measures (ie the evaluations of individual Schengen States, the annual report on reimposition of internal border controls, the evaluation of the operations of Eurosur, the VIS and the SIS) and more general information about the Schengen system (such as the number of interceptions and apprehensions of unauthorized migrants). The Commission reports should also provide information as to whether prior breaches of human rights have been remedied.

3.10.4 Assessment

To what extent is Frontex accountable in practice? According to the own-initiative enquiry by the European Ombudsman into the human rights strategy of Frontex,[712] the Action Plan on human rights which Frontex drew up pursuant to the 2011 reforms of the Frontex Regulation was not sufficiently detailed, and did not clearly allocate responsibility as regards human rights breaches between Frontex and Member States. While Frontex intended that its general Code of Conduct, also drawn up as a response to those reforms, would be legally binding on all participants in Frontex operations, this was not made clear enough in all the relevant Frontex measures. The Ombudsman also believed that the rules on the use of force needed to be clarified, and observed that the Code of Conduct on returns operations had not yet been adopted.

Next, the Ombudsman examined the mechanisms to ensure protection for fundamental rights in Frontex activities. He believed that the precise circumstances which would require an operation to be terminated on human rights grounds ought to be specified in detail. Frontex also ought to reflect on when it should terminate returns operations on human rights grounds. Furthermore, the Ombudsman doubted whether the Fundamental Rights Officer was sufficiently independent, and criticized the lack of possibility of individual complaints to that Officer.

All of these concerns formed the basis of thirteen recommendations which the Ombudsman made to Frontex in April 2013. In November 2013, the new Ombudsman reported that Frontex had accepted many of the recommendations, except the recommendation to consider direct complaints by migrants. She therefore issued a special report to the European Parliament on this issue.[713]

While it would be preferable to ensure that individuals could raise complaints that Frontex had not complied with its obligations as regards human rights, it is also true to say that Frontex only coordinates Member States' authorities' actions. In any event, those authorities take actions that are not coordinated by Frontex. Given that (as the

---

[712] For the report and background documentation, see: <http://www.ombudsman.europa.eu/en/cases/draftrecommendation.faces/en/49794/html.bookmark>.
[713] See: <http://www.ombudsman.europa.eu/en/cases/specialreport.faces/en/52465/html.bookmark>.

2014 Regulation itself implicitly accepts) any control of the EU's external border, including by means of patrols outside a Member State's territorial waters, is linked to the application of the EU's own rules on external border controls, the EU Charter of Rights is applicable to Member States' control of those borders. And there have been allegations that Member States' authorities have on some occasions been responsible for push-backs and ill-treatment of migrants at the external borders.

In this context, it is possible that Frontex has been serving for too long as a 'lightning rod' for critics of the EU's external borders control policy, whereas attention should have focused more on Member States' authorities, whether they are being coordinated by Frontex or not. The 'right to life' in the European Convention of Human Rights entails, according to the European Court of Human Rights, an obligation to hold an independent investigation into losses of life that have arguably resulted from actions of the authorities. So arguably the EU is under an obligation pursuant to the EU Charter of Fundamental Rights to ensure that its Member States conduct such investigations into losses of life which are linked to the implementation of EU policies, in this case the EU external borders rules. Those authorities should also be held accountable for any alleged push-backs or other ill-treatment of migrants at the external borders. To that end, the EU should agree upon a general framework for independent investigations into such alleged abuses, with the results of these investigations reported and assessed by the Commission as part of its twice-yearly report on the Schengen system. Furthermore, it is long past time for the Commission to bring infringement proceedings against Member States where there is sufficient evidence that their authorities are responsible for push-backs or other ill-treatment.

3.11 Administrative Cooperation and EU Funding

During the Maastricht era, the Council first adopted a Joint Action establishing the 'Sherlock' programme, concerning cross-border cooperation between administrators checking identity documents.[714] This was later subsumed into a broader programme set up by a Joint Action establishing 'Odysseus', which funded cooperation on a wide variety of immigration, border control, and asylum issues, spending €12 million over four years.[715] By the time this programme expired, the Treaty of Amsterdam was in force, and so it was replaced from June 2002 by a Council Decision establishing a Community action programme called ARGO, which ran from 2002 to 2006.[716] Over that period, €25 million was initially devoted to assistance to national administrations to assist with the correct application of EC law and to ensure that account was taken of Community rules. Subsequently, the budget was enlarged to €14 million for 2004, and the Decision was amended in 2004, to relax the original requirement that projects must involve more than one Member State.[717]

---

[714] [1996] OJ L 287/7. For an overview of EU funding of JHA matters, see I:2.6 above.

[715] [1998] OJ L 99/2. For reports on the implementation of the programme, see: <http://ec.europa.eu/justice_home/funding/expired/odysseus/funding_odysseus_en.htm>.

[716] Decision 2002/463 ([2002] OJ L 161/11). For details of implementation of the programme, see <http://ec.europa.eu/justice_home/funding/intro/funding_2004_2007_en.htm#argo>.

[717] [2004] OJ L 371/48.

This programme was then replaced by the Decision establishing a European Borders Fund, which applied from 2007–13.[718] The objective of this Fund was to contribute to the control and management of external borders and the uniform application of EU law, particularly the Borders Code,[719] and the amount of money which was to be spent was €1.32 billion over 2007–13.[720] Most recently, legislation establishing an asylum and migration fund applies for 2014–20; the budgeted amount to be spent was €2.76 billion over that period.[721]

Furthermore, there is a secondary Schengen measure, which is still in force, concerning the exchange of statistical data as regards external borders.[722] This measure overlaps in part with the obligation to collect statistics pursuant to the Schengen Borders Code, concerning the numbers refused entry, the grounds for refusal, the nationality of the persons refused, and the type of border at which they were refused entry.[723] The latter obligation is in turn aligned with the 2007 Regulation on immigration statistics, as regards statistics on persons refused entry at the border,[724] which replaced the previous informal collection of statistics (in this case, through CIREFI, the EU's clearing house on immigration control), which concerned the numbers refused and their nationalities only.[725] The statistics produced pursuant to the statistics Regulation are available for the years beginning in 2008,[726] while the statistics produced prior to that point are assessed by the Commission in its reports on EU policy in this area.[727] However, so far these statistics have not been effectively integrated into public analysis and discussion of the relevant issues.

3.12 External Relations

As outlined elsewhere in this book,[728] the EU (and previously the EC) has implied external relations powers, in particular to conclude treaties, even in the absence of express external powers. The EU's external powers become exclusive if it has fully harmonized an issue in its internal law.

As regards external border controls, the EU's external competence is addressed by a special provision in the Treaties. This takes the form of a Protocol to the Treaties concerning this issue, attached originally by the Treaty of Amsterdam. According to this Protocol, as amended by the Treaty of Lisbon,[729] Article 77(2)(b) TFEU (previously

---

[718] [2007] OJ L 144/22. See also the treaty with Schengen associates regarding this fund (I:3.2.5 above).

[719] Art 3(1) of the Decision (ibid).

[720] Art 13(1) of the Decision, n 718 above.

[721] Reg 515/2014 on financial support for external borders and visa matters ([2014] OJ L 150/143).

[722] SCH/Com-ex (95) 21 ([2000] OJ L 239/176). The Commission has proposed to repeal this measure: COM (2014) 713, 28 Nov 2014.

[723] Art 13(5) of the Code (Reg 562/2006, [2006] OJ L 105/1), as amended by Reg 610/2013 ([2013] OJ L 182/1) to refer to the statistics legislation.

[724] Reg 862/2007 ([2007] OJ L 199/23), Art 5. See also Art 8(1)(c) of this Reg, on possible further disaggregations.

[725] See I:6.11 and I:7.8 below.

[726] See: <http://appsso.eurostat.ec.europa.eu/nui/show.do?dataset=migr_eirfs&lang=en>.

[727] See the annexes to SEC (2006) 1010, 19 July 2006 and SEC (2009) 320, 8 Mar 2009.

[728] On EU external competence and the procedure for negotiating and concluding treaties in EU law, see I:2.7 above.

[729] The Treaty of Lisbon amendments to the Protocol were technical, not substantive.

Article 62(2)(a) EC) is 'without prejudice to the competence of Member States to negotiate or conclude agreements with third countries as long as they respect Union law
and other relevant international agreements'. This Protocol could be interpreted to
mean either that the EU would fail to gain exclusive external power over this issue
even if it fully harmonized the internal law, or merely that Member States retain
external power as long as there is no internal legislation fully harmonizing the
issue—in other words, EU external power is not exclusive by *nature*, but can only
become exclusive by *exercise*. Given the obligation to respect EU law as specified in
the Protocol, the better interpretation is the latter one. This is confirmed by analogy
by the interpretation of an Advocate-General in a case concerning the non-exclusive
aspects of the Common Commercial Policy (before the entry into force of the Treaty
of Lisbon).[730]

Initially, there were provisions of the Schengen *acquis* concerning Member States'
competence to conclude external borders treaties.[731] According to these rules, Member
States which wished to conduct negotiations on external borders with third states had
to inform the other signatories of the Schengen Convention in good time.[732] Moreover,
Member States were banned from making agreements simplifying or abolishing border checks with third states, unless they had the consent of the other parties to the
Schengen Convention; this was subject to the right of Member States to conclude
treaties collectively.[733] Finally, a specific provision of the Convention addressed Member
States' power to conclude treaties on local border traffic:[734] Member States were allowed
to conclude such treaties on condition that they complied with the rules on such agreements to be adopted by the Schengen Executive Committee pursuant to Article 3 of
the Convention. But in fact, no such rules were agreed before the Schengen *acquis* was
integrated into the EC legal order, when the Treaty of Amsterdam entered into force
in 1999.[735]

Following the integration of the Schengen *acquis* into the EC legal order, the Schengen
Convention provisions have been replaced by EU rules. First of all, in 2006, the EU
adopted a Regulation setting out common rules to govern Member States' negotiation
of local border traffic treaties,[736] which, inter alia, amended the Schengen Convention
to refer back to that Regulation. This Regulation makes no reference to the external
borders Protocol, but this is not problematic as for the reasons set out above, that
Protocol does not preclude the adoption of EU rules which regulate Member States'
exercise of their external competence as regards border controls. The local border traffic Regulation could be regarded as an example of the rule that even where EU external
powers are exclusive, the EU can always choose to authorize the Member States to exercise some limited external powers.[737]

---

[730] Opinion of 26 Mar 2009 in Case C-13/07 *Commission v Council*, ECLI:EU:C:2009:190.
[731] Art 136 of the Schengen Convention ([2000] OJ L 239).
[732] Art 136(1) of the Convention.   [733] Art 136(2) of the Convention.
[734] Art 136(3) of the Convention.
[735] Art 136 of the Convention was allocated to Art 62(2)(b) EC, as it then was (Decision 1999/436, [1999]
OJ L 176/17).
[736] Art 20 of Reg 1931/2006 ([2006] OJ L 405/1); see I:3.8 above.   [737] Art 2(1) TFEU.

Secondly, in 2013, the entire provision of the Schengen Convention on external borders treaties was repealed.[738] In its place, the Schengen Borders Code now contains specific rules on Member States' bilateral agreements as regards border crossing, shared border crossing points, maritime traffic, and rescue services, etc.[739]

As for the EU's exercise of its external competence in this area, as well as the various Schengen association agreements (which obviously concern other issues as well as border controls), the EU has negotiated or concluded several treaties solely or largely on the issue of border controls, dealing with the Schengen associates' further participation in Frontex, the EU's border funds programme, and the Commission's committees.[740]

In the longer term, in the interests of 'tidying up' the primary law of the European Union, it would be desirable to repeal the Protocol on external competence as regards borders. If it is correct to interpret the Protocol as merely confirming that the EU's external competence on this issue is not a priori exclusive, but only exclusive by exercise, then the Protocol no longer serves any purpose, since this principle is now set out in the Treaty following the entry into force the Treaty of Lisbon.[741] If, on the other hand, the Protocol must be interpreted as precluding the EU from obtaining exclusive external competence on this issue even if it has fully harmonized the internal law relating to border controls, then the Protocol needs to be repealed because this would be incompatible with the objective of establishing common rules at the external borders, given the obvious impact which any unilateral treaty-making by individual Member States would have on the control of the common external border as a whole.

3.13 Conclusions

The EU's border controls rules must be seen in context. In recent years, the numbers of people trying to reach the EU via means of the Mediterranean has been increasing, with a corresponding increase in the death toll.[742] Leaving aside the question of how much responsibility Member States and the EU have for these deaths, this death toll should remain foremost in the minds of EU policy-makers when developing policy in this area. Certainly the concern about increasing numbers has driven the EU's actions in this field, in particular the expansion of Frontex's powers, the development of Eurosur, and the linked increases in the EU's budget.

In general, the second generation of EU legislation on these matters is a clear improvement as compared to the less ambitious Schengen rules, which were in many respects fragmented and lacked coherence, legal certainty, and accountability. However, internal border controls have still been repeatedly re-introduced since the adoption of the Schengen Borders Code. While there have also been improvements in the rules relating to external borders, most notably the right to appeal against a refusal of entry, improved procedural rights in relation to SIS II, the exclusion of younger children from

---

[738] Reg 610/2013 ([2013] OJ L 182/1), Art 2(5).

[739] Reg 562/2006 ([2006] OJ L 105/1), Arts 4 and 37 and Annexes VI and VII, as amended by Reg 610/2013. On the Code's external borders rules as a whole, see I:3.6 above.

[740] See I:3.2.5 above.   [741] Art 2(2) TFEU; see I:2.7 above.

[742] See: <http://www.borderdeaths.org/>.

passport fingerprinting obligations, the development of local border traffic rules, and the adoption of human rights obligations in relation to Frontex operations, there is still a lack of clear rules on the relationship between asylum issues and this field and on the accountability of Member States' and Frontex's actions. The rules on entry bans in SIS II and the Returns Directive still lack precision and give Member States too much leeway for disproportionate penalization of persons who commit relatively minor breaches of immigration law.

The plans to develop rules on an entry-exit system, together with a trusted traveller system and the use of the Visa Information System at the external borders, show signs of a disproportionate approach to these issues. Coupled with the planned further development of the Schengen Information System and biometric passports (taking into account the CJEU's evasion of important questions regarding data protection and passport databases), there is a risk that the development and interlinking of various EU and national information systems and databases will constitute further steps toward the creation of a European surveillance society.

4

Visas

4.1 Introduction

It was inherent in the process of abolishing internal border controls between (most) Member States and simultaneously constructing a collective external border that any persons who had been admitted for short-term stay or longer-term residence in one Member State would be entitled to the freedom to travel between Member States, once the prospect of checking their status at internal borders was removed. This, in turn, meant that Member States had to develop a common policy on short-term visas (authorizations for stay for a limited period), since a visa issued by one Member State would in effect allow travel to other Member States as well.

The initial source of rules on these issues was the 1990 Convention implementing the Schengen Agreement (the 'Schengen Convention'), providing for a uniform visa valid for the territory of all of the Schengen States (known in practice as a 'Schengen visa'). The rules on visas have since been developed much further by the European Community (and later the EU), in particular to harmonize fully the list of third States whose nationals do and do not require a visa, to adopt further rules governing visa applications, to establish a Visa Information System (a database of the information submitted by all visa applicants), and to develop an external policy in relation to visas.

The issues addressed in this chapter are inevitably inextricably linked with the issues of border control addressed in Chapter 3 of this volume. Like the border control issues, they are also very closely linked with the issue of irregular migration, examined in detail in Chapter 7 of this volume, since many irregular migrants have either entered the territory without a required visa, overstayed the period of authorization set out in the visa, or violated the conditions attached to the visa. Also, the freedom to travel within the EU for third-country nationals entails the possibility that some will violate the conditions for the exercise of that freedom, or travel without fulfilling them, and therefore be considered irregular.

Visa issues, like border control issues, are also linked to asylum issues (the subject of Chapter 5 of this volume), since visa obligations also serve to prevent entry to the territory for asylum seekers, and the issue of a visa is also a ground for assigning responsibility among Member States for processing asylum applications. The latter link has been strengthened by the Visa Information System (VIS), since it became operational. There is also a link between visa policy and the regulation of long-term legal migration (the subject of Chapter 6 of this volume), in particular the question of whether a person who is legally present on the basis of a short-term visa can make an application for a longer-term stay. Finally, there is a link between visa policy and policing, to the extent that the information in the VIS is also available to law enforcement agencies.[1]

This chapter addresses in turn: the adoption of a common list of States whose nationals do or do not require visas to enter the EU; the development of a common visa format; the adoption of common rules for processing visa applications; the creation of the Visa Information System; the rules governing freedom to travel between Member States (including related rules governing long-stay visas—ie visas for a stay longer than three months—and residence permits); and the EU's external visa policy.

4.2 Institutional Framework and Overview

4.2.1 Framework prior to the Treaty of Amsterdam

Due to the legal and political difficulties which stood in the way of developing EEC-wide integration on visa issues prior to the Maastricht Treaty [2] (the original Treaty on European Union, or TEU),[3] cooperation on those issues was first developed by a pioneer group of Member States within the framework of the 1985 Schengen Agreement and then the Schengen Convention.[4] The Convention contained detailed rules on short-term visa policy (Articles 9–17), supplemented by rules on freedom to travel (Articles 19–24).[5] These provisions of course formed part of an integrated whole, in particular in connection with the rules on abolishing internal border controls, harmonizing external border controls, and the establishment of the Schengen Information System (SIS).[6]

As for the EU as a whole, as part of the compromise in the original TEU on the issue of visas and border controls,[7] an Article 100c was inserted into the EC Treaty, giving the Community power to adopt 'a list of third countries whose nationals must be in possession of a visa when crossing the external borders of the Member States' and to 'adopt measures relating to a uniform format for visas'. The first power was subject to unanimous voting in the Council until 1 January 1996 and qualified majority voting (QMV) after that date, while the second power was subject to QMV from the outset. In both cases, the Council had to act on a proposal from the Commission, and consult the European Parliament (EP) before adopting the relevant measures; the Court of Justice had its normal EC law jurisdiction (ie it could receive references for a preliminary ruling on the interpretation or the validity of the legislation from all national court and tribunals). There was also a (never used) power in Article 100c EC to introduce a 'visa requirement for the nationals' of a country 'in an emergency situation' whose nationals were 'posing the threat of a sudden inflow...into the Community'. A corresponding amendment to Article 3 EC, which listed the activities of the Community, specified that

---

[1] See II:7.6.1.3.

[2] On this period, see in particular K Hailbronner, 'Visa Regulations and Third-Country Nationals in EC Law' (1994) 31 CMLRev 969–95.

[3] For details, see I:3.2.1.1 above.   [4] For further details, see I:3.2.1.2 above.

[5] Respectively Arts 9–17 and 19–24. See I:4.5 to I:4.9 below.

[6] See generally ch 3 of this volume.   [7] See generally I:3.2.1.3 above.

those activities included 'measures concerning the entry and movement of persons in the internal market as provided for in Article 100c'.[8]

The powers conferred by Article 100c EC were used to adopt a visa list Regulation and a visa format Regulation in 1995.[9] The visa list Regulation was annulled by the Court of Justice because the Council had failed to reconsult the EP despite the Council's legal obligation to do so, in the framework of the consultation procedure (as it was then), whenever the Council intends to adopt a measure that differs essentially from the Commission's original proposal.[10] However, the Court preserved the legal effect of the Regulation until the Council adopted a replacement. Following reconsultation of the EP, the Council duly adopted a replacement Regulation in the spring of 1999, which was essentially the same text as it had adopted in 1995.[11]

As for other issues related to visas, the third pillar powers of the EU as listed in Article K.1 of the original TEU included rules on the 'conditions of entry and movement' by third-country nationals (Article K.1(3)(c)); visas were not mentioned specifically. The question therefore repeatedly arose what legal base applied to the adoption of measures concerning visas. First of all, the Commission proposed legislation on third-country nationals' freedom to travel using the first pillar legal base of Article 100 EC (later Article 94 EC, now Article 115 TFEU). This was blocked by the UK's veto.[12]

Secondly, the Commission sued the Council in the Court of Justice regarding a particular dispute over the dividing line between the EC's first pillar visa powers and the EU's third pillar visa powers. After deleting provisions on airport transit visas (visas needed simply to change between planes in an airport) from the visa list Regulation in 1995, the Council then adopted in 1996 a third pillar 'Joint Action' comprising a list of ten non-EU states whose nationals would need airport transit visas in every Member State.[13] The Commission argued that the Joint Action should be annulled because its subject-matter fell within the scope of the EC's powers as set out in Article 100c EC. This time the Council was successful,[14] as the Court ruled that persons in an airport transit zone had not yet crossed the *legal* (as distinct from the *physical*) external borders of the Member States. The Court linked its interpretation of Article 100c EC to Article 3(d) EC, the 'Community activities' clause, and concluded that since persons within the airport transit zones could not be considered to be participating in the 'internal market' (as referred to in Article 3(d)), they had not crossed an external border for the purposes of Article 100c.

The EU's third pillar powers were also used to adopt: a Joint Action on schoolchildren's visas; a Recommendation on consular cooperation; a list of honorary consuls who could issue uniform visas; and a Recommendation on the detection of false documents by visa authorities.[15]

---

[8] Art 3(d) EC.   [9] See respectively I:4.5 and I:4.6 below.
[10] Case C-392/95 *EP v Council* [1997] ECR I-3213.   [11] See I:4.5 below.
[12] See I:3.2.1.3 above.   [13] For the details, see I:4.5 below.
[14] Case C-170/96 *Commission v Council* [1998] ECR I-2763.
[15] Respectively: [1994] OJ L 327/1; [1996] OJ C 80/1; [1996] OJ C 274/58; and [1999] OJ C 140/1. On the first measure, see I:4.9 below.

In the meantime, as in the case of border controls, the application of the Schengen Convention from March 1995 was both preceded and followed by the adoption of a number of measures implementing that Convention relating to visas, adopted by the Executive Committee established by that Convention, which clearly influenced the development of EU and EC visa measures before the entry into force of the Treaty of Amsterdam.

4.2.2 Treaty of Amsterdam

4.2.2.1 *Institutional framework*

Like the issue of border controls,[16] the issues of visas and freedom to travel were addressed by EC powers conferred by Article 62 EC, as inserted by the Treaty of Amsterdam. The relevant provisions were Article 62(2)(b) and 62(3) EC, which required the Council to adopt:

> (b) rules on visas for intended stays of no more than three months, including:
> > (i)   the list of third countries whose nationals must be in possession of visas when crossing the external borders and those whose nationals are exempt from that requirement;
> > (ii) the procedures and conditions for issuing visas by Member States;
> > (iii) a uniform format for visas;
> > (iv) rules on a uniform visa;
> (3) measures setting out the conditions under which nationals of third countries shall have the freedom to travel within the territory of the Member States during a period of no more than three months.

As noted in Chapter 3 of this volume, the structure of Article 62 as a whole closely followed the structure of Articles 1–25 of the Schengen Convention,[17] and furthermore closely paralleled EC or EU measures that had previously been proposed or adopted. It is clear that the powers conferred by Article 62(3) were strictly limited to a three-month maximum, while the powers concerning visas were slightly more flexible ('intended stays' of a three-month maximum). There was also a relevant declaration (number 16) in the Final Act of the Treaty of Amsterdam, stating that: '[t]he Conference agrees that foreign policy considerations of the Union and the Member States shall be taken into account in the application of Article [62(2)(b)] of the [EC] Treaty'. It should be noted that even 'uniform' visas are issued by Member States' authorities.

The EC's visa powers were also subject to the 'law and order' exception in Article 64(1) EC, the 'emergency powers' clause in Article 64(2) EC, and the power to adopt legislation on administrative cooperation in Article 66 EC.

As for decision-making, according to Article 67(1) EC, the powers concerning the procedures and conditions for issuing visas, rules on a uniform visa, and the freedom to travel (Article 62(2)(ii) and (iv) and (3)) were subject to unanimous voting in the Council, consultation of the EP, and shared initiative of the Commission and the

---

[16] See I:3.2.2 above.   [17] Ibid.

Member States up until 1 May 2004. However, Article 67(3) EC provided for a derogation: the powers concerning visa lists and visa formats were instead subject immediately upon entry into force of the Treaty of Amsterdam to qualified majority voting in
the Council, consultation of the EP and the sole initiative of the Commission. The latter
rule simply continued the position regarding the decision-making process applied to
these powers under the Maastricht version of the EC Treaty.[18]

Article 67(2) EC provided that from 1 May 2004, the Commission gained the sole
right of initiative on all visa issues, and Article 67(4) specified that at the same time,
the powers over visa conditions, procedures, and rules automatically became subject
to QMV in the Council and co-decision with the European Parliament. Furthermore,
Article 67(2) EC also obliged the Council, acting unanimously after consultation of the
EP, to change some or all of the decision-making rules applying to the rest of Title IV
after 1 May 2004, so that it used QMV and the co-decision procedure in further areas.
Applying this power, the Council decided that the rules on freedom to travel would be
adopted by QMV and co-decision as from 1 January 2005.[19] Finally, due to the relevant
Protocol attached to the EC Treaty by the Treaty of Nice, measures based on Article 66
were subject to QMV and consultation of the EP as from 1 May 2004. So from this date,
measures on administrative cooperation, the visa list, and visa formats were subject
to QMV and consultation, whereas other visa measures were subject to QMV and co-
decision. This gave rise to potential disputes between different legal bases, if those different legal bases involved different decision-making rules.[20]

As for the Court of Justice, in the area of visas, the Court of Justice was subject,
as in the rest of the former Title IV EC, to restrictions on receiving references from
lower national courts.[21] Due to the general restriction on its jurisdiction, despite the
extensive Schengen *acquis* which formed part of the EC legal order since 1 May 1999,
the Court received only four references in this area during this period from national
courts, and two of these were inadmissible.[22] The admissible cases concerned the freedom to travel and transit rules.[23]

4.2.2.2 Overview of practice

As with the issue of border controls, the entry into force of the Treaty of Amsterdam
immediately entailed the integration of the Schengen *acquis* in this area into the EC
legal order by means of the Protocol on the Schengen *acquis* and the Council Decisions
defining and allocating the *acquis*.[24] This meant that the EC legal order instantly

---

[18] See I:4.2.1 above.   [19] [2004] OJ L 396/45. See further I:2.2.2.1 above.
[20] See I:4.2.4 below.   [21] See further I:2.2.2.1 above.
[22] Cases C-51/03 *Georgescu* [2004] ECR I-3203 and C-45/03 *Dem'Yanenko*, judgment of 18 Mar 2004
(unpublished). Also, the *MRAX* reference on EU free movement law touched on the interpretation of the
first visa list Regulation (see further I:4.4.1 below), and the *Soysal* judgment concerning the EU-Turkey
association agreement touched on the subsequent visa list Regulation (see further I:4.4.2 below).
[23] Cases C-241/05 *Bot* [2006] ECR I-9627 and C-139/08 *Kqiku* [2009] ECR I-2887. On the substance, see
respectively I:4.9 and I:4.2.5 below.
[24] On the process on integrating the Schengen *acquis* generally, see I:2.2.2.2 above. For details of the visas
and freedom to travel provisions of the *acquis* integrated into EC law, see I:4.5, I:4.6, I:4.7, and I:4.9 below.

contained an extensive set of rules concerning short-stay visas and freedom to travel for third-country nationals.

Because of this, there was little immediate interest in further development of the visa rules, although the Tampere European Council of October 1999 did call for:

> ...[a] common active policy on visas and false documents...including closer co-operation between EU consulates in third countries and, where necessary, the establishment of common EU visa issuing offices.

However, the events of 11 September 2001 clearly changed the EU's priorities, with a perception that new visa measures could enhance the objectives of increased security and control, in particular the creation of a Visa Information System (VIS), which would comprise a database of information on all Schengen visa applicants.[25]

The EC also moved swiftly after the entry into force of the Treaty of Amsterdam to complete fully harmonized lists of countries whose nationals need (or do not need) visas to enter the Member States by March 2001; this legislation was amended several times later. In April 2001, as in the area of external borders, the Council gave itself powers, unsuccessfully contested by the Commission,[26] to amend many key secondary Schengen visa rules, and it used these powers subsequently to make a number of changes to these rules, aiming, inter alia, at further harmonization of visa policy. The Council amended the existing visa format Regulation, in particular to take account of security concerns. The special rules concerning the issue of visas at the border, in particular to seamen, were updated, and the Council adopted rules establishing special regimes for visas and border controls during the 2004 Summer Olympics and 2006 Winter Olympics and as regards travel across EC territory (after enlargement) to and from Kaliningrad from the rest of Russia. The Council also adopted principles and initial legislation to establish the VIS in 2004, with plans for further legislation later.[27]

On the other hand, the Council was unable to agree any amendment to the Schengen rules relating to freedom to travel for third-country nationals, despite considering several proposals, although it did agree to extend this freedom to persons holding a long-stay visa, in certain circumstances.[28] The EC's implied external relations powers over visas (along with borders) were used to authorize Member States to sign a relevant treaty on the admission of seafarers on behalf of the EC, and to agree treaties associating Switzerland with the Schengen *acquis*, providing for special rules for Chinese tourists, and the first treaty facilitating the issue of visas for a non-EU country (Russia).[29]

The EC's activity as regards visas stepped up after the adoption of the Hague Programme in 2004. This programme called for:[30] the eventual creation of common visa offices, starting with a proposal to establish common application centres (2005) and a broader review of the Schengen common consular instructions on visas (2006); the facilitation of visas to non-EU states prepared to assist the EU on readmission

---

[25] See the conclusions of the extraordinary JHA Council of 20 Sep 2001, point 26.
[26] Case C-257/01 *Commission v Council* [2005] ECR I-345.   [27] See I:4.8 below.
[28] See I:4.9 below.
[29] See I:4.2.5 and I:4.11 below. The Chinese treaty also had a legal base concerning irregular immigration.
[30] [2005] OJ C 53/1.

issues; and the development of the Visa Information System. Implementing this programme, the EC adopted more detailed legislation to govern the operations of the VIS in 2008,[31] and amendments to the common consular instructions in 2009, inter alia, concerning common visa application centres.[32] The EC also agreed a number of visa facilitation treaties with third states,[33] and amended the visa list legislation in 2006 and 2009, inter alia, to exempt some non-Member States from visa requirements.[34] More fundamentally, in 2009 the EC overhauled the complex web of existing Schengen and Community rules governing the conditions for issuing visas, replacing them with a modernized Visa Code.[35]

4.2.3 Treaty of Lisbon

As with the area of external borders, the issue of visas has been subject to Article 77 of the Treaty on the Functioning of the European Union (TFEU), since the entry into force of the Treaty of Lisbon on 1 December 2009. The relevant provisions of the Treaty provide as follows:

1. The Union shall develop a policy with a view to:
   (a) ensuring the absence of any controls on persons, whatever their nationality, when crossing internal borders;
   (b) carrying out checks on persons and efficient monitoring of the crossing of external borders;
   (c) the gradual introduction of an integrated management system for external borders.
2. For the purposes of paragraph 1, the European Parliament and the Council, acting in accordance with the ordinary legislative procedure, shall adopt measures concerning:
   (a) the common policy on visas and other short-stay residence permits;
   ...(c) the conditions under which nationals of third countries shall have the freedom to travel within the Union for a short period
   ...(e) the absence of any controls on persons, whatever their nationality, when crossing internal borders.

Although the abolition of internal border controls and the control of external borders was examined in detail in Chapter 3 of this volume,[36] it should be reiterated that these subjects remain closely linked to the issue of visas.

Comparing the previous version of the Treaty to the revised provisions, the power regarding a 'common policy on visas and other short-stay residence permits' is an *extension* of competence as compared to the previous competence concerning visas 'for an intended stay of no more than three months', as the later version of the Treaty dropped the time limit on the competence and added a new competence relating to 'other' forms of short-stay permit, which also form part of the 'common' policy. Indeed,

---

[31] See I:4.8 below.   [32] See I:4.7 below.   [33] See I:4.11.2 below.
[34] See I:4.5 below, and as regards connected visa waiver treaties, I:4.11.1 below.
[35] Reg 810/2009, [2009] OJ L 243/1. See I:4.7 below.   [36] I:3.2.3 above.

the Commission has proposed that the EU exercise these powers to provide for the existence of a 'touring visa' for periods of stay for more than three months.[37] Moreover, competence over visas is no longer broken down into four separate sub-areas. Another significant change is the extension of the co-decision process, now renamed the 'ordinary legislative procedure',[38] to cover the issues of visa lists and the visa format procedure.

Next, the EU now has the power to regulate the freedom to travel of third-country nationals within the EU 'for a short period', rather than (under the previous Article 62(3) TEC) 'for a period of no more than three months'.[39]

The revised provisions on visas and freedom to travel are also subject to the amended general provisions of the JHA Title of the revised Treaty,[40] including the more limited scope of the 'emergency powers' clause,[41] as well as the extended jurisdiction of the Court of Justice and the revised rules on opt-outs for the UK, Ireland, and Denmark.[42]

As for the impact of the Treaty of Lisbon, shortly after its entry into force the EU adopted a regulation which extended the freedom to travel for all long-stay visa holders.[43] The visa list rules have been amended several times,[44] and the Commission has proposed an amendment to the Visa Code, along with the parallel adoption of a 'touring visa'.[45] Furthermore, the Visa Information System has become operational, and was rolled out worldwide by the end of 2015.[46] The EU has continued to develop its networks of visa waiver and visa facilitation treaties.[47] The EU's plans to develop an entry-exit system and a registered traveller system will also have an impact on the visa issuing process.[48] Finally, despite the extended jurisdiction of the Court of Justice of the European Union (CJEU) in this field, it has received only a few cases concerning visas from national courts.[49]

4.2.4 Competence issues

As with the EC's powers concerning borders,[50] to some extent, the argument over the existence and extent of EC competence over visas is now purely historic. But even following the entry into force of the Treaty of Amsterdam, and now the Treaty of Lisbon, there are some issues concerning the division of competence between the visa powers of the EU in Title V of the TFEU (the JHA Title) and the rest of the Treaties, concerning the division of powers within Title V itself, and concerning the extent of competence conferred by these provisions.[51] The first of these three issues is addressed further below,[52] while the other two are addressed in turn in the rest of this sub-section.

---

[37] See I:4.7 below.   [38] See Arts 289(1) and 294 TFEU.
[39] On the competence issues arising from the previous wording, see I:4.2.4 below.
[40] See further I:2.2.5.2 and I:3.2.3 above.   [41] See I:5.2.3 and I:5.2.4 below.
[42] See I:4.2.5 below.
[43] Reg 265/2010, [2010] OJ L 85/1. For the substance of this measure as regards freedom to travel, see I:4.9 below.
[44] I:4.5 below.   [45] I:4.7 below.   [46] I:4.8 below.   [47] I:4.11 below.
[48] See I:3.6.2 above.
[49] These concern the Visa Code: see I:4.7 below. There has also been inter-institutional litigation (again) on visa lists: see I:4.5 below.
[50] See I:3.2.4 above.   [51] On the EU's external competence, see I:4.11 below.   [52] I:4.4.

Regarding visas, the arguments concerning the distinctions between legal bases are (or have been) practically relevant because of the different rules applied by different legal bases as regards decision-making[53] and the different rules on the participation of Member States.[54]

Within the former Title IV EC, there was initially (from the entry into force of the Treaty of Amsterdam) only one distinction between two categories of visa powers: visa list and visa format powers on the one hand (subject to QMV in Council, a Commission monopoly on proposals, and applicable as EC law to Denmark) and all other rules on visas and freedom to travel (subject to unanimity in Council, with shared competence over proposals, and not applicable as EC law to Denmark). After the changes to decision-making rules dating from 2004 and 2005, there were, during the Amsterdam period, two sets of decision-making rules: measures subject to QMV and co-decision, but not applicable to Denmark as EC law (rules on a uniform visa, conditions for the issue of visas, and freedom to travel) and measures subject to QMV and consultation of the EP (visa lists, visa format, and administrative cooperation).[55] Following the entry into force of the Treaty of Lisbon, the only remaining distinction as regards decision-making in this area concerns cooperation between administrations pursuant to Article 74 TFEU (still subject to QMV and only consultation of the EP) and other measures concerning visas, based on Article 77 TFEU. However, as regards the participation of Member States, there is still a distinction for Denmark concerning legislation on visa lists and visa format (fully binding on Denmark as part of EU law) and other measures concerning visas and freedom to travel, unless Denmark decides to abrogate its opt-out on most JHA issues.[56]

The distinction between Articles 77 and 74 TFEU has already been examined in Chapter 3 of this volume.[57] The argument there applies *mutatis mutandis* to the issue of visas, with the consequence that any measures regulating the consideration of visa applications or the conditions for freedom to travel fall within the scope of Article 77 (and the ordinary legislative procedure), rather than Article 74.

Next, the question which had arisen under the prior version of the Treaty as to which of the freedom to travel powers or the legal migration powers was the correct legal base for legislation concerning the freedom to travel for persons with long-stay visas, along with an extended travel authorization for longer periods, is no longer relevant following the entry into force of the Treaty of Lisbon, since the two subjects are subject to identical decision-making procedures.[58] Also on this point, given the flexibility conferred by Article 77(2)(c) TFEU, the EU is now free to adopt a measure extending freedom to travel for more than three months. This issue is connected with a complex situation arising from the application of pre-existing treaties between Member

---

[53] On the basic rules regarding the distinction between legal bases, see I:3.2.4 above.

[54] See I:4.2.5 below.

[55] The visa list and visa format rules were applicable as EC law to Denmark, whereas the administrative cooperation measures were not.

[56] See further I:4.2.5 below.   [57] I:3.2.4 above. See also I:2.2.3.2 above.

[58] It might be arguable that the distinction is still nonetheless relevant as regards Member States' (and non-Member States') participation in the relevant measures: see I:4.2.5 below. On this dispute, see pp 111–13 of the second edition of this book.

States and third countries dealing with the issue,[59] which has been reopened by the Commission's proposal to address this issue as part of its proposed Regulation establishing an EU touring visa.[60]

On the question of the issue of visas to persons for the purpose of carrying out economic activities, it should be noted that the limitation of EU competence regarding the admission of third-country nationals from third countries coming to the EU seeking work or self-employment, as set out in Article 79(5) TFEU, expressly only applies to that Article, and so cannot limit the EU's competence regarding visas for short-term economic migration. This distinction makes sense because persons admitted to the EU on the basis of short-term visas will obviously have less impact on the labour market than persons admitted to the labour market for a longer period.[61] Similarly, given the changes to the strict time limits on the EU's powers resulting from the Treaty of Lisbon, it must follow that Article 77 TFEU is a sufficient legal base for the proposal on touring visas, even though that proposal touches upon economic issues.[62]

As for other issues, the CJEU has ruled that giving police authorities and Europol access to the Visa Information System falls within the legal base for police cooperation, not visas. However, the issue is classified differently when assessing how it builds upon the Schengen *acquis*.[63] Also, again by analogy with the rules relating to borders, the question of whether a ban on issuing visas on foreign policy grounds should have a foreign policy legal base, or a visa legal base, remains an outstanding issue even after the entry into force of the Treaty of Lisbon.[64]

More broadly, what is the extent of the EU's competence to harmonize the law on visas? Following the entry into force of the Treaty of Lisbon, the question of whether the list of EC's visa powers was exhaustive or not became moot, given that Article 77 TFEU replaced the prior list of specific visa powers with a general power to adopt a 'common' short-term visa policy. Equally, for the same reasons, there are no longer any grounds to doubt the EU's competence to use its visa power to regulate the issue of airport transit visas.[65]

Logically, as with EU powers concerning borders, the powers conferred by Article 77 to harmonize rules on short-term visas must be extensive, given the connection with the core obligation to abolish internal border checks, the corollary freedom to travel, the Treaty reference to a 'common policy on visas', and comparison with the structure of the EC Treaty (now TFEU) rules governing free movement of goods.[66]

4.2.5 Territorial scope

The EC or EU measures relating to visas which were adopted before the entry into force of the Treaty of Amsterdam are (or were) applicable to all Member States.[67] In practice,

---

[59] See I:4.11.3 below.   [60] See I:4.7.3 and I:4.9 below.   [61] See further I:6.2.4 below.

[62] On that proposal, see I:4.7.3 below.

[63] Case C-482/08 *UK v Council* [2010] ECR I-10413. On the substance of the relevant Decision, see II:7.6.1.3. On the Schengen point, see I:4.2.5 below.

[64] See further I:3.2.4 above.

[65] On these issues, see pp 109–10 of the second edition of this book.

[66] See further the analysis of the comparable issue regarding borders in I:3.2.4 above.

[67] For a general overview of the rules on the territorial scope of all JHA measures, see I:2.2.5 above.

that means that the 1994 Joint Action on schoolchildren's freedom to travel is applicable to all Member States,[68] as was the 1996 Joint Action on airport transit visas,[69] which has subsequently been repealed by the EU's Visa Code.[70] Equally the 1995 Regulation on a visa list and the 1999 Regulation replacing it were applicable to all Member States, although the 1999 Regulation was subsequently repealed.[71] The repeal of the 1999 visa list Regulation and of the 1996 Joint Action on airport transit visas raise the question of whether the UK and Ireland, which did not participate in the measures repealing those acts, are still bound by those acts or not.[72] Also, the UK and Ireland are also bound by the original 1995 visa format Regulation; the UK opted in to the 2002 amendment to that Regulation, but Ireland did not. Neither the UK nor Ireland opted in to the 2008 or 2013 amendments to the Regulation.[73]

Following the integration of the Schengen *acquis* in this area into the EC legal order pursuant to the Treaty of Amsterdam, the UK and Ireland have not opted in to any measure of the 1999 *acquis* related to visas, and nor have they opted in to any measures adopted after that date, except for the UK's opt-in to the 2002 amendment to the visa format regulation. The UK did wish to participate in a third pillar Decision giving police authorities and Europol access to the Visa Information System, but the CJEU ruled that this Decision built upon the visa provisions of the Schengen *acquis* (which the UK has not opted in to), rather than the police cooperation provisions (which it has).[74] The Court reiterated its prior ruling, relating to border control measures, that the UK cannot opt in to a measure building upon the Schengen *acquis* as long as it has not opted in to the original Schengen *acquis* which that measure has built upon.[75]

Furthermore, it should be noted that the UK has opted in to a large majority of the EU's readmission treaties, but not in to the EU visa facilitation treaties agreed in parallel to those treaties.[76] However, there is a declaration to each of the visa facilitation treaties encouraging side agreements with the UK and Ireland.

As for Denmark, it is bound as a matter of EU law by all measures concerning visa lists and a common visa format,[77] since it has accepted EC (now EU) competence in those areas since the original TEU first entered into force.[78] Otherwise, its position is governed (after the entry into force of the Treaty of Lisbon) by the Protocol on Denmark, which provides that Denmark can decide, as regards measures which build upon the Schengen *acquis*, which of them bind Denmark as a matter of international law.[79]

---

[68] On the substance of this act, see I:4.9 below.   [69] [1996] OJ L 63/8.

[70] Art 56(2)(c) of Reg 810/2009 ([2009] OJ L 243/1).

[71] On the substance of these visa list measures, see I:4.5 below.

[72] On this general issue, see I:2.2.5.1.4 above.

[73] On the substance of these visa format measures, see I:4.6 below.

[74] Case C-482/08 *UK v Council* [2010] ECR I-10413. On the substance of the relevant Decision, see II:7.6.1.3.

[75] Cases C-77/05 *UK v Council* [2007] ECR I-11459 and C-137/05 *UK v Council* [2007] ECR I-11593. See further I:2.2.5.1.3 and I:3.2.5 above. This ruling applies equally to Ireland.

[76] See respectively I:7.9.2 and I:4.11.2 below.

[77] On these measures, see I:4.5 and I:4.6 below. On the position of Denmark generally, see I:2.2.5.2 above.

[78] See I:4.2.1 above. However, note that Denmark is not covered by Art 78(3) TFEU, which is the successor clause to the original 'emergency powers' provision in Art 100c EC, since that provision now refers only to asylum matters.

[79] Art 4, revised Protocol on Denmark.

Denmark has consistently opted for participation in visa measures on this basis.[80] The position is only different for measures which do not build upon the Schengen *acquis*, from which Denmark is excluded entirely. As regards visas, this only concerns the visa facilitation treaties concluded by the Community, and there is a declaration attached to each of these treaties urging Denmark and the third State concerned to negotiate a parallel treaty.[81] Denmark would have been fully covered (as a matter of EU law) by all Schengen visa measures, if the Danish public had approved a partial opt-in to JHA measures in a referendum held in December 2015; but the Danish public voted against that plan.[82]

There might be some question as to *which* measures bind Denmark as a matter of EU law, given the precise wording of the exceptions on this point.[83] This wording (referring to visa formats and the adoption of a list of countries whose nationals are subject to a visa requirement when crossing EU external borders) reflects the situation prior to the Treaty of Amsterdam, but the post-Amsterdam visa list power was worded slightly differently from the pre-Amsterdam power (in particular referring also to the adoption of a list of States whose nationals will *not* require visas), and the post-Lisbon power is worded differently again, referring broadly to a 'common policy on visas'. In practice it was assumed during the Amsterdam period (1999–2009) that Denmark is also fully covered by the post-Amsterdam legislation as part of EC law (as it then was), and presumably the same practice will apply following the entry into force of the Treaty of Lisbon.

Is this assumption correct? The former power to adopt a negative list did not expressly preclude the EC from fully harmonizing that list, and indeed the better interpretation is that full harmonization of the list was *required*.[84] The corollary of a fully harmonized negative list is obviously a fully harmonized positive list, so the revised visa list power (even following the Treaty of Lisbon, which has subsumed the visa list power into a general power to regulate visa policy) is therefore no different from the power which existed before the Treaty of Amsterdam. It should also be noted that the Danes have no opt-out from the general internal market clause (Article 26 TFEU), but in any event it appears that Article 26 by itself has limited legal effect.[85]

Thirdly, the Member States joining the EU in 2004, 2007, and 2013 (the 'newer Member States') were subject upon accession to only part of the Schengen *acquis* and measures building upon it in this area, namely the common visa list, the common visa format, and a small number of other provisions set out in the Schengen *acquis*.[86] Also,

---

[80] For detailed references, see I:3.2.5 above.

[81] On the substance of these treaties, see I:4.11.2 below. Note that Denmark is fully covered by the EU's visa *waiver* treaties (I:4.11.1 below).

[82] See I:2:2.5.2 above.

[83] See also the distinction between visa list and external borders measures made by the Court of Justice in Case C-139/08 *Kqiku* [2009] ECR I-2887.

[84] This follows from the link in the former Art 3(d) EC between the visa list and the internal market, from the obligation to harmonize visa matters implied by the previous Art 14 EC (now Art 26 TFEU, then Art 7a EEC), as established by the *Wijsenbeek* judgment (I:3.4.1 above), and from the application of the previous Art 14 to third-country nationals (as subsequently confirmed by the Treaty of Amsterdam).

[85] See I:3.4.1 above.

[86] On the position of the newer Member States, see Art 3 of the 2003 Treaty of Accession and Annex I to that Treaty ([2003] OJ L 236), and Art 4 of the 2005 Treaty of Accession and Annex II to that Treaty ([2005] OJ L 157). For a general discussion of the issue, see I:2.2.5.3 above.

the visa format and visa list Regulations, as well as (for the 2004 and 2007 enlargements) the Common Consular Instructions, were amended to add or remove technical references to newer Member States when they joined the EU.[87] The remaining visa rules, along with the rules on the freedom to travel, did not apply until the full extension of the Schengen *acquis* to nine of the newer Member States, as from December 2007.[88] There has been no such extension yet for Cyprus, Romania, Bulgaria, and Croatia, which therefore remain bound so far only by the more limited set of EU visa measures referred to in the accession treaties, until the full extension of the Schengen *acquis* to these Member States.

However, a particular issue has arisen concerning the position of Cyprus, a non-Schengen Member State that cannot fully join Schengen for practical reasons until there is a political settlement in Cyprus, due to the *de facto* external border within Cyprus and the Cypriot government's lack of *de facto* control over northern Cyprus. Because Cyprus expressed an interest in participating in the VIS, the Council adopted a statement when adopting the VIS Regulation taking note of Cyprus' intention to participate in the VIS before its full participation in Schengen.[89] This will therefore entail two separate Council decisions setting two separate dates—one date 'for the implementation of the common visa policy by Cyprus including the VIS and other relevant parts of the Schengen acquis' and the other date for full implementation of Schengen. The Council declared that the first of these decisions will require readiness by Cyprus to apply the 'common visa policy...in particular its integration in' the Schengen Information System, and a verification following a Schengen evaluation procedure that Cyprus has met 'the necessary conditions' to apply these rules. No decision has yet been taken to this end.

Next, as regards non-Member States, all of the Schengen and subsequent EC (now EU) visa measures are all fully applicable to Norway and Iceland as from March 2001 (or following the subsequent adoption of the EU measures), pursuant to the Schengen association agreement with those States,[90] except for the EU's various visa treaties, which do not build on the Schengen *acquis*.[91] In each case though, the relevant treaty contains a declaration encouraging the potential conclusion of side agreements between the non-EU State and the EU's associates.

The EC (now EU) visa rules, except for the visa treaties, are similarly applicable to Switzerland, as from its application of the Schengen *acquis* in 2008/2009, and subsequently Liechtenstein, as from its application of the Schengen *acquis* in 2011.[92] Again, there is an exception as regards the EU's visa treaties with third states, but the most recent treaties contain declarations on the conclusion of side agreements.[93]

---

[87] Annex II, part 18, to the 2003 Accession Treaty (n 86 above); Reg 1791/2006 ([2006] OJ L 363/1), part 11.B (Romania and Bulgaria); and Reg 517/2013 ([2013] OJ L 158/1) (Croatia).

[88] For instance, see Reg 1295/2003 on visas for participants in the 2004 Olympic Games ([2003] OJ L 183/1, recital 17 in the preamble).

[89] See the summary of Council acts for June 2008 (Council doc 12750/08, 8–9 Sep 2008).

[90] See further I:2.2.5.4 above.   [91] On the substance, see I:4.11 below.

[92] See I:2.2.5.4 above.

[93] See the visa waiver treaties with micro-States (I:4.11.1 below) and (for example) the EU/Georgia visa facilitation treaty (I:4.11.2 below).

Furthermore, in order to address the position of persons transiting though the newer Member States to the States fully applying Schengen rules, the EU adopted several transitional measures. First of all, as regards the ten Member States which joined the EU in 2004, a transitional Decision in 2006 permitted (but did not require) those newer Member States to recognize as equivalent to their national visas, for the purpose of transit, Schengen visas, long-stay visas, and residence permits issued by the Member States fully applying the Schengen rules.[94] Newer Member States were also permitted to recognize the various 'national short-term visas, long-term visas and resident permits' issued by other newer Member States for the purpose of transit.[95] Eight out of the ten newer Member States applied this transitional Decision.[96] Following the enlargement of the Schengen zone at the end of 2007, this Decision only applied to Cyprus.[97]

A similar Decision was adopted in June 2008, after Romania and Bulgaria had joined the EU in 2007.[98] These two Member States were given the same choice to recognize, for the purposes of transit, Schengen documents, documents issued by each other, and moreover documents issued by Cyprus; Cyprus in turn has the option to recognize documents issued by Romania and Bulgaria. All three States opted to apply this Decision.[99] Finally, following the accession of Croatia to the EU in 2013, both of the prior Decisions were repealed and replaced by a new Decision in 2014, applying the same rules to all four of the Member States which do not yet fully apply the Schengen *acquis*.[100]

A comparable approach was taken to the position of persons holding residence permits from Switzerland and Liechtenstein, before those States' full participation in the Schengen *acquis*. The EU adopted a separate transitional decision in 2006, which required full Schengen States to recognize residence permits issued by Switzerland and Liechtenstein as equivalent to a visa for the purposes of transit for a five-day period.[101] Member States which had joined the EU in 2004 had an option to apply this Decision, on condition that they also applied the transitional Decision relating to accession countries.[102] This Decision was then amended in 2008, to apply also to Romania and Bulgaria.[103] However, the Decision lapsed in 2011, after both Switzerland and Liechtenstein became full participants in Schengen.[104]

The Court of Justice was called upon to interpret the 2006 Decision relating to Switzerland and Liechtenstein, in the case of *Kqiku*.[105] In that case, a family holding passports of 'Serbia-Montenegro' (a country which has, of course, since split up) and residence

---

[94] Art 2, 2006 Decision ([2006] OJ L 167/8).

[95] Art 3, 2006 Decision (ibid). The types of documents covered by this rule are listed in an Annex to the Decision.

[96] [2006] OJ C 251/20. The exceptions were Estonia and Lithuania.   [97] Art 6, 2006 Decision.

[98] [2008] OJ L 161/30. Again, the national documents concerned were listed in an Annex to the Decision.

[99] [2008] OJ C 312/8.

[100] [2014] OJ L 157/23. All four of these Member States applied this Decision: [2014] OJ C 302/1.

[101] [2006] OJ L 167/8, Arts 1 and 3. The residence permits in question were listed in an Annex to the Decision.

[102] Art 3, 2006 Decision (ibid). Again, eight of ten of the newer Member States applied this Decision (see n 96 above).

[103] [2008] OJ L 162/27; the amended Decision was not codified. Romania and Bulgaria both decided to apply this Decision (n 99 above).

[104] Art 5, 2006 Decision (n 102 above).   [105] Case C-139/08, n 83 above.

permits from Switzerland visited Germany for several days in the summer of 2006 without obtaining a visa, but they were not transiting via Germany to or from any non-Schengen state. The Court of Justice ruled that, according to its wording, the Decision applied only to situations of transit. This ruling obviously applied also to the 2008 amendment to this Decision, and also, by analogy, to the various Decisions relating to newer Member States.

4.3 Human Rights

The application of human rights principles to the EU's visa rules parallels the application of those principles to EU border control legislation, an issue already addressed in Chapter 3.[106]

It should be noted that the EU's visa legislation makes implied provision for human rights in several respects. The Visa Code provides that a fee for a visa application can be waived or reduced in individual cases for humanitarian reasons.[107] Also, the Visa Code sets out procedural rights in the event of refusal of a visa application,[108] and there are parallel data protection safeguards in the legislation governing the Visa Information System.[109] According to the Visa Code, Member States 'shall' issue a visa with limited territorial validity (LTV visa) even if the usual criteria for obtaining one are not met, inter alia, for humanitarian reasons or because of international obligations.[110] This exception also applies where a person applies for a visa at the external borders,[111] thereby circumventing the rule that Member States can only issue visas at the border if, inter alia, there is certainty that the visa applicant will return to his or her country of origin or residence;[112] that criterion obviously cannot be applied to refugees. Arguably, the case law on the obligation to issue a general Schengen visa if the conditions in the Visa Code are met applies by analogy as regards applications for an LTV visa. If this is correct, effectively there is a right to a humanitarian visa.[113]

However, there is no express power for Member States to *waive* a visa obligation altogether on humanitarian grounds, although there are certain special rules relating to refugees in the visa list legislation.[114] If a person does enter a Member State in breach of a visa obligation (or enters with a visa, but overstays the permitted period of stay) and is subsequently detected, it should be recalled that the Geneva Convention on Refugees provides that, with certain conditions, irregular entry by refugees cannot be penalized.[115]

4.4 Impact of Other EU Law

4.4.1 Free movement law

As set out in the previous chapter,[116] the principal source of rules concerning the issues of visas and border controls in the context of EU free movement law is the secondary

---

[106] I:3.3 above.
[107] Art 16(6) of Reg 810/2009 ([2009] OJ L 243/1). For more on the Code, see I:4.7 below.
[108] Art 32(2) and (3) and Annex VI of the code.   [109] For detail, see I:4.8 below.
[110] Art 25(1)(a) of the code.   [111] Art 35(4) and (5) of the code.
[112] Art 35(1) of the code.   [113] See I:4.7 below.   [114] See I:4.5 below.
[115] See I:5.3 below.   [116] I:3.4.1 above.

legislation adopted to give effect to free movement rights. As regards visas, this legislation originally specified that Member States could not demand entry visas or an equivalent document, except for family members who were non-EU nationals. In that case, 'Member States [had to] afford to such persons every facility for obtaining any necessary visas'. These visas had to be free of charge.[117] The case law on these measures specified that in order to give the free movement Directives 'their full effect, a visa [where it is required] must be issued without delay and, as far as possible, on the place of entry into national territory'.[118]

These measures were replaced by Directive 2004/38 on the free movement of EU citizens, as from 30 April 2006 (the 'EU citizens' Directive').[119] This Directive incorporated the relevant provisions of the prior legislation, with several changes. First, there is an explicit reference to the EU visa list legislation 'or, where appropriate,... national law' as regards family members' visa requirements.[120] Secondly, third-country national family members are exempt from the visa requirement where they hold a residence card issued to third-country national family members of an EU citizen who resides in a different Member State. Finally, visas for non-EU family members of EU citizens must be issued 'as soon as possible and on the basis of an accelerated procedure'.[121]

As with the issue of border controls, Directive 2004/38 did not incorporate most of the prior relevant case law;[122] an exception is the express application of the EU's visa list legislation to determine which third-country national family members need a visa. On the other hand, there are two improvements on the previous rules and case law: the exemption of some third-country national family members from the visa requirement, and the obligation to issue visas 'as soon as possible and on the basis of an accelerated procedure'. However, it is arguable that the latter rule could have been derived from interpretation of the previous legislation.

The visa exemption applies to any third-country national family member of an EU citizen who has moved to another Member State, if that family member has obtained a 'residence card' there in accordance with the citizens' Directive. It is largely relevant only for movement to and from Schengen states on the one hand, to non-Schengen States on the other, and for movement between non-Schengen States, given that anyone resident in a Schengen state has the freedom to travel anyway to other Schengen states, if they have a residence permit or (as from April 2010) a long-stay visa.[123]

---

[117] Art 9(2) of Dir 68/360 ([1968] OJ Spec Ed L 257/13, p 485) and Art 7(2) of Dir 73/148 ([1973] OJ L 172/14). Art 2(2) of each of Dirs 90/364 ([1990] OJ L 180/26), 90/365 ([1990] OJ L 180/28), and 93/96 ([1993] OJ L 317/59) extended the relevant provisions of Dir 68/360 to other groups of EU citizens.

[118] Case C-459/99 *MRAX* [2002] ECR I-6591, para 60. The Court referred to the visa list legislation (I:4.5 below) as regards the list of third countries whose nationals require visas. On the further implications of this judgment, see I:7.4.1 below.

[119] [2004] OJ L 229/35. For further implications of this Directive, see I:3.4.1 above and I:6.4.1 and I:7.4.1 below.

[120] Presumably only the UK and Ireland apply national law, as they are the only Member States not bound to apply the EU visa list (see I:4.2.5 above).

[121] Art 5(2) of the Dir (n 119 above).

[122] The case law on the previous legislation continues to be valid, however: see C-127/08 *Metock* [2008] ECR I-6241.

[123] See I:4.9 below.

As for the case law on the EU citizens' Directive to date, the ruling in the *Metock* case that third-country national family members of EU citizens who have moved within the EU have a right of entry into the host Member State of the EU citizen, even when coming directly from non-EU States, has implications for the application of the EU's visa rules in such cases.[124] Also, this judgment confirms implicitly that the competence to address the issue of visas as regards the family members of EU citizens who have moved within the EU derived from EC free movement law (as it was then), not the competences set out in Title IV of the EC Treaty. There is no reason to think this legal position changed as a result of the Treaty of Lisbon.

Subsequently, in 2014 the CJEU confirmed that the visa exemption for holders of 'residence cards' pursuant to the citizens' Directive was absolute, and the UK could not impose an extra national law requirement to obtain a 'family permit' as a condition to obtain the exemption.[125] The power in the citizens' Directive to control abuses of free movement law was not relevant either, since that power could only be used in specific individual cases.

A Commission report on the application of Directive 2004/38 stated that only seven Member States set out legislative rules, as required by the Directive, to provide for accelerated access to a visa for third-country national family members of EU citizens who require one; two Member States comply with this obligation in practice.[126] Some (unnamed Member States) require those family members to comply with the entire visa process normally applicable to third-country nationals. Five Member States fail to exempt holders of residence cards from the visa obligation, and three Member States wrongly linked the right of residence for third-country national family members to the duration of their entry visa. Subsequently, the Commission's 2009 guidance on the implementation of the Directive argues for a four-week maximum for a response to a visa application from a third-country national family member of an EU citizen.[127] This clearly cannot be considered an 'accelerated' decision, given that the normal time for making a decision on a visa application for any third-country national is fifteen days;[128] the Commission has also forgotten about the case law which requires visas to be issued at the border to such family members.[129] However, the Commission is correct to point out that Member States cannot insist on documents other than a travel document and evidence of a family link in order to consider visa applications from such persons.

The Court of Justice also confirmed the supremacy of EC (now EU) free movement law over the rules governing the Schengen Information System (SIS) as regards the consideration of visa applications,[130] and the legislation establishing the second-generation

---

[124] N 122 above. Read in conjunction with *MRAX* (n 118 above), the failure to get a visa or the overstay of a visa in such cases can only be subject to limited sanctions, and a prior breach of visa rules can be 'cured' by becoming a family member of an EU citizen who has moved within the EU. For more on *Metock*, see I:3.4.1 above and I:5.4.2, I:6.4.1, and I:7.4.1 below.

[125] Case C-202/13 *McCarthy*, ECLI:EU:C:2014:2450.   [126] COM (2008) 840, 10 Dec 2008.

[127] COM (2009) 313, 2 July 2009.

[128] See Art 23 of the EU Visa Code (Reg 810/2009, [2009] OJ L 243/1). This can be extended to thirty days in individual cases and to sixty days in exceptional cases.

[129] *MRAX*, n 118 above.

[130] Case C-503/03 *Commission v Spain* [2006] ECR I-1097. See further I:2.4.2 above, as regards the general issue of the relationship between Schengen rules and EU free movement law.

Schengen Information System (SIS II) expressly confirms the application of the same free movement rules as regards SIS II, since it began operations in 2013.[131] Equally, the Visa Code is expressly 'without prejudice' to EU free movement law.[132] On the other hand, it is striking that the Regulation establishing the Visa Information System does not include any express special rule for the position of EU citizens' third-country national family members.[133] However, it must be presumed that in the event of any conflict, the EU free movement rules will take precedence over this Regulation as a higher rule of law, because the underlying substantive rules on visas are expressly subject to EU free movement law pursuant to the Visa Code. It should not be forgotten that many third-country national family members of EU citizens are exempt from visa requirements pursuant to the EU citizens' Directive, as discussed above. For those subject to the visa requirement, the amount of data which will be collected on them according to the VIS Regulation is legally dubious in light of the Court of Justice's judgment in *Huber*, which confirms that the personal data of EU citizens (and implicitly their family members) who move within the EU can only be kept in central databases if this is necessary pursuant to EU free movement legislation.[134]

The Commission's 2014 proposal to amend the Visa Code would clarify in more detail what facilitations must be applied to EU citizens' family members who apply for Schengen visas.[135] These rules would also apply to EU citizens in their own Member State whose third-country family members applied for a visa to visit them, and to EU citizens living outside the EU who wanted to visit the EU with their third-country family members. It remains to be seen if these proposals are agreed.

Next, the right of EU companies to send their third-country national employees to other Member States, as part of the corporate provision of services,[136] has implications for visas. In particular, the Court of Justice has ruled that a prior check in connection with a visa procedure breaches Article 49 EC (now Article 56 TFEU) in this context, because a prior declaration would be sufficient.[137] The Court has also ruled that an automatic expulsion and refusal to regularize the position of a posted worker who does not possess the required visa is a breach of Article 49 EC (now Article 56 TFEU).[138] It should follow by implication from the Court's case law that posted workers should not be subject to a visa requirement at all, or at the very least (by analogy with the family

---

[131] Art 24(1), Reg 1987/2006 ([2006] OJ L 381/4). On SIS II and border controls, see I:3.7 above.
[132] Art 1(2), Reg 810/2009 ([2009] OJ L 243/1). See also the specific rules in Arts 3(5)(d) and 24(2)(a), and Art 4 of Annex XI. On the substance of the Code, see I:4.7 below.
[133] Reg 767/2008 ([2008] OJ L 218/60).   [134] Case C-524/06 *Huber* [2008] ECR I-9705.
[135] COM (2004) 164, 1 April 2014. For more detail on this proposal, see I:4.7 below.
[136] Cases: C-43/93 *Van der Elst* [1994] ECR I-3803; C-445/03 *Commission v Luxembourg* [2004] ECR I-10191; C-244/04 *Commission v Germany* [2006] ECR I-885; C-168/04 *Commission v Austria* [2006] ECR I-9041; C-219/08 *Commission v Belgium* [2009] ECR I-9213; and C-91/13 *Essent*, ECLI:EU:C:2014:2206. The Opinions in *Commission v Germany* (para 16) and *Commission v Austria* (paras 112–14) cases also comment briefly on the relationship between the Schengen freedom to travel rules (see I:4.9 below) and the free movement of services, but it is clear that the exemption from a visa requirement that follows from the freedom to travel rules is not a complete answer to the breach of Art 49 EC (now Art 56 TFEU), because of the posting of workers from non-Schengen States and postings for periods of more than three months. For more on posted third-country national workers, see I:3.4.1 above, I:6.4.4 below, and I:7.4.1 below.
[137] *Commission v Germany*, n 136 above.   [138] *Commission v Austria*, n 136 above.

members of EU citizens) the visas must be issued automatically at the border, free of charge, following an accelerated procedure, and the failure to obtain a visa can only be punished by proportionate penalties (ie no expulsion or imprisonment) which would not impinge upon the basic right to provide services.[139]

4.4.2 Association agreements

EU free movement law applies essentially to Norway, Iceland, Liechtenstein, and Switzerland, so the rules on visas applicable to EU citizens and their family members are largely applicable to these non-Member States.[140]

Next, under an Additional Protocol to the EU's association agreement with Turkey,[141] there is a directly effective standstill on national rules which make the provision of services or the exercise of establishment more restrictive.[142] The Court of Justice has confirmed that this standstill applies to rules on the imposition of visas.[143] So no new visa requirements can be imposed on Turkish persons providing services or exercising establishment following the date when the relevant Protocol entered into force for the Member State concerned. It should be noted that the association agreement applies in principle to all EU Member States (ie, even those which do not (yet) participate fully in the Schengen *acquis*), but *not* to the non-Member States associated with Schengen. However, the CJEU has distinguished service *providers* from service *recipients*, such as Turkish tourists: the standstill does not apply to them, so they remain subject to the usual visa requirement for Turkish nationals.[144] The standstill applies as from the start of 1973, when the Additional Protocol first entered into force (for the first nine Member States), and from the date which each Member State joined the EU (as regards the other nineteen Member States).[145]

There is also an issue of territorial scope, since the precise date at which some Member States applied visa requirements to Turkey is not known either. The thirteen Member States which have joined the EU since 2004 have had an obligation to impose visa requirements on Turkish nationals as from the beginning of their membership,[146] so the standstill clause in the Additional Protocol cannot be invoked to object to their imposition of a visa requirement upon Turkish nationals. As for the other Member

---

[139] Note that visa requirements might apply not just to nationals of States on the EU's visa list (or the UK or Irish national lists), but also to nationals of States on the visa-free list, because Member States may require visas for such persons if they pursue economic activities (see I:4.5 below).

[140] See I:3.4.2 above. However, as regards Switzerland, there is no visa exemption for third-country national family members with a residence card (Art 1 of Annex I to the EU-Swiss agreement on free movement of persons, [2002] OJ L 114/6). Of course, due to Swiss participation in the Schengen area from Dec 2008 (see I:4.2.5 above), the visa requirement for third-country national family members now applies only for travel between Switzerland and EU Member States which do not (yet) apply the Schengen rules.

[141] [1977] OJ L 261/60.

[142] Case C-37/98 *Savas* [2000] ECR I-2927 (self-employed persons); Joined Cases C-317/01 and C-369/01 *Abatay and others* [2003] ECR I-12301 (services).

[143] Case C-228/06 *Soysal* [2009] ECR I-1031. The same rule applies to entry control: see Case C-16/05 *Tum and Dari* [2007] ECR I-7415 and I:3.4.2 above. The following discussion draws upon S Peers, 'EC Immigration Law and EC Association Agreements: Fragmentation or Integration?' (2009) 34 ELRev 628.

[144] Case C-221/11 *Demirkan*, ECLI:EU:C:2013:583.

[145] Case C-256/11 *Dereci* [2011] ECR I-11315.   [146] See I:4.2.5 above.

States, ten of them had ratified a Council of Europe treaty abolishing short-stay visa requirements for the other contracting parties, which includes Turkey.[147] However, this treaty allows for suspension of visa abolition as against other contracting parties.[148] Five of the first six Member States[149] suspended their visa abolition commitment regarding Turkey in 1980—but this was after the Additional Protocol came into force for those Member States. Italy never suspended the agreement as regards Turkey; nor did Spain, which joined the EU later. Portugal suspended the agreement as regards Turkey only from 1991, after its membership of the EU, while Greece never applied it to Turkey in the first place, and Austria suspended it as regards Turkey before it joined the EU.[150] But a further complication is the personal scope of the Council of Europe treaty, because it permits (but does not require) signatories to impose a visa requirement when a person enters the territory 'for the purpose of pursuing a gainful activity'.[151]

In the *Soysal* judgment, the Court of Justice expressly rejected the argument that (most) Member States were now exempt from compliance with the standstill clause as regards visas, because the visa obligation was now established by EU law, not national law. The Court could have rebutted this argument by pointing out that the Community (as it then was), along with its Member States, is a party to the association agreement, and moreover that most Member States have transferred competence over this issue to the Community, but it did not.[152] Instead, the Court looked solely at the question of whether service providers now faced more restrictions in each particular Member State than they did when the Additional Protocol entered into force for each Member State. This approach fragments the concept of a Schengen visa by requiring at least some Member States to revert to the different national rules which were applicable when the Additional Protocol entered into force for each of them.

Furthermore, it should also be pointed out that while the *Soysal* judgment concerned the core question of a visa obligation, various changes in the visa regimes of Member States, and subsequently also the EU, must also be covered by the standstill clause, to the extent that they make the provision of services and establishment from Turkey more difficult than it was when the Additional Protocol entered into force. So, for instance, increases in the visa fee, the requirement for visa applicants to pay a fee, and the requirement to attend at consulates in order to provide biometric information, are all prima facie breaches of the standstill clause.[153]

---

[147] European Agreement on Regulations governing the Movement of Persons between Member States of the Council of Europe (ETS 25, 1957). The Member States in question are Austria, Belgium, France, Germany, Greece, Italy, Luxembourg, the Netherlands, Portugal, and Spain. Also two of the newer Member States (Malta and Slovenia) have ratified this treaty.

[148] Art 7 of the Agreement (ibid).   [149] Germany, the Benelux countries, and France.

[150] So did Malta and Slovenia. As for Schengen associates, Switzerland suspended the agreement as against Turkey before its participation in the Schengen *acquis*, while Norway and Iceland never ratified it. Liechtenstein has ratified it, without any limitation as regards Turkey.

[151] Art 1(3) of the agreement. It is not known when each Member State imposed visa requirements on this category of Turkish visitors, although again the Member States joining since 2004 have had to impose visa requirements on this category of Turkish visitors as soon as they joined the EU. The *Soysal* judgment (n 143 above) provides some information on the German position.

[152] Of course, the temporal scope of the EU's obligations under the agreement might be an issue, because, as noted above, of the different dates at which the association agreement applied (if at all) for different Member States.

[153] See I:4.7 below. There is a 'public policy' defence to a breach of the standstill clause, however: see the discussion in I:6.4.3 below.

Finally, as regards the right to establishment set out in the Europe Agreements with ten Central and Eastern European states which later joined the EU, the Court of Justice ruled that nationals of associated States who had legally entered on a short-term visa or for a short period without being subject to a visa obligation did not have the right to make an in-country application for establishment.[154] Presumably the same will be true as regards Western Balkans states, once the provisions on the right to establishment in the Stabilization and Association Agreements with those states are activated.[155]

4.4.3 Other issues

It has been assumed in practice that the EU's data protection Directive[156] applies to the issue of visas.[157] For the reasons set out in the previous chapter, it is submitted that this practice is correct.[158] However, as argued above, the amount of data which will be kept in the Visa Information System on third-country national family members of EU citizens who have exercised free movement rights will amount to a violation of both free movement law and data protection law.[159]

4.5 Visa List

4.5.1 Overview

The EC (as it then was) first adopted a visa list Regulation, pursuant to the powers granted by Article 100c EC, in 1995.[160] This Regulation included a list of States whose nationals would require visas to visit any Member State (a 'blacklist'), but it left to Member States whether or not to impose visa requirements on the nationals of any State not on the list. However, the Regulation was annulled in 1997 for procedural reasons.[161] It was subsequently adopted again in 1999, without any substantive amendment.[162]

---

[154] Case C-327/02 *Panayotova* [2004] ECR I-11055.

[155] [2004] OJ L 84 (Former Yugoslav Republic of Macedonia (FYROM)); [2005] OJ L 26 (Croatia); [2009] OJ L 107 (Albania); [2010] OJ L 108 (Montenegro); [2013] OJ L 278 (Serbia); and [2015] OJ L 164 (Bosnia-Herzegovina). An SAA has also been agreed with Kosovo (COM (2015) 183, 30 Apr 2015), but it is not yet in force.

[156] Dir 95/46 ([1995] OJ L 281/31) applies to Member States' processing of data, while Reg 45/2001 ([2001] OJ L 8/1) applies to EU bodies' processing of data. For more on EU data protection law, see II:7.3.2 and II:7.6.4.

[157] The Reg establishing the Visa Code (Reg 810/2009, [2009] OJ L 243/1) refers to Dir 95/46 at several points (recital 12 to 14 in the preamble, Art 43(9), and point A(g) in Annex X). So does: Reg 333/2002, which concerns visa formats for unrecognized entities ([2002] OJ L 53/4, recital 8 in the preamble); Reg 390/2009, which concerns the taking of biometrics from visa applicants ([2009] OJ L 131/1, recitals 9 and 13 in the preamble) and the Reg establishing the Visa Information System (Reg 767/2008, [2008] OJ L 218/60), recital 17 in the preamble and Arts 31(2)(a), 37(4), and 38(1); also recital 19 in the preamble and Arts 39(2), 41(1), and 41(4) refer to Reg 45/2001. According to the latter Reg (recital 17 in the preamble), the Directive is clarified on several points as regards the VIS: responsibility for the processing of data; safeguarding the rights of the data subjects; and supervision on data protection.

[158] See I:3.4.3 above.   [159] See I:4.4.1 above.   [160] Reg 2317/95, [1995] OJ L 234/1.

[161] Case C-392/95 *Parliament v Council* [1997] ECR I-3213. See further I:4.2.1 above.

[162] Reg 574/99, [1999] OJ L 72/2. For Commission communications on implementation of the 1995 and 1999 visa list Regs, see: [1996] OJ C 379; [1997] OJ C 180; [1998] OJ C 101; [1999] OJ C 133; and [2000] OJ C 272.

In the meantime, the EU adopted a Joint Action in 1996 on the issue of airport transit visas, requiring all Member States to impose an obligation on the nationals of certain States to obtain an airport transit visa (ATV) merely for staying in an airport to switch between flights.[163] The Commission challenged the validity of this Joint Action, arguing that the issue of ATVs fell within the EC's powers at the time to establish a visa blacklist, but the Court of Justice ruled that the Joint Action was not within the scope of Article 100c EC.[164]

Furthermore, the Schengen states were proceeding during the 1990s to harmonize their visa lists more fully than the EC as a whole, pursuant to Article 9 of the Schengen Convention, which required a general harmonization to take place. To that end, the Schengen Executive Committee adopted decisions in 1997 and 1998, almost entirely harmonizing the visa lists of Schengen states.[165]

Following the entry into force of the Treaty of Amsterdam, the EC (now without the participation of the UK and Ireland) adopted a new visa list Regulation in 2001, which established a fully harmonized blacklist as well as a fully harmonized list of States whose nationals would *not* need a visa to cross the external borders of the Member States (a 'whitelist').[166] The 1999 EC Regulation and the two previous Schengen Executive Committee Decisions were repealed.[167] This Regulation was subsequently amended in 2001, 2003, 2005, 2006, 2009, 2010 (twice), 2013 (twice), and 2014 (twice),[168] as well as by (or in connection with) the Treaties of Accession in 2003, 2005, and 2011.[169] Finally, the list of States subject to an airport transit visa requirement is now set out in the Visa Code Regulation.[170]

In addition to the visa list legislation, the EU has also agreed treaties specifically providing for visa waivers, and more general association agreements which provide for visa waivers among other commitments.[171]

4.5.2 Visa lists

The original 1995 visa list Regulation, and its 1999 replacement,[172] obliged Member States to impose a visa obligation upon most States in Africa and Asia,[173] plus a number of

---

[163] [1996] OJ L 63/8.

[164] Case C-170/96 *Commission v Council* [1998] ECR I-2763. For the context, see I:4.2.1 above.

[165] Decisions SCH/Com-ex (97)32 and SCH/Com-ex (98)53 rev 2 ([2000] OJ L 239/186 and 206).

[166] Reg 539/2001 ([2001] OJ L 81/1).

[167] Art 7. On the question of whether the UK and Ireland are still bound by the 1999 EC Regulation, see I:2.2.5.1.4 above.

[168] Respectively Regs 2414/2001 ([2001] OJ L 327/1), 453/2003 ([2003] OJ L 69/10), 851/2005 ([2005] OJ L 141/3), 1932/2006 ([2006] OJ L 405/23), 1244/2009 ([2009] OJ L 336/1), 1091/2010 ([2010] OJ L 329/1), 1211/2010 ([2010] OJ L 339/6), 610/2013 ([2013] OJ L 182/1, Art 4), 1289/2013 ([2013] OJ L 347/74), 259/2014 ([2014] OJ L 105/9), and 509/2014 ([2014] OJ L 149/67). The CJEU has dismissed a legal challenge to parts of Reg 1289/2013: Case C-88/14 *Commission v EP and Council*, ECLI:EU:C:2015:499.

[169] Annex II, part 18.B.2, to the 2003 Accession Treaty (n 86 above); Reg 1791/2006, ([2006] OJ L 363/1), point 11.B.3; and Reg 517/2013 ([2013] OJ L 158/1). These amendments merely removed the names of the new Member States from the Regulation.

[170] See I:4.7 below.   [171] See respectively I:4.4.2 above and I:4.11.1 below.

[172] Regs 2317/95 and 574/99, nn 160 and 162 above.

[173] The exceptions were the Commonwealth States of southern Africa (except Zambia) and, in Asia, Israel, Japan, South Korea, Singapore, Malaysia, and Brunei.

States in Central and Eastern Europe,[174] and a small number of States in Latin America, the Caribbean, and the Indian and Pacific Oceans.[175] The priority criteria for inclusion on the list, according to the preamble to the Regulation, were 'risks relating to security and illegal immigration', although 'Member States' international relations with third countries also play a role'.[176] For its part, the 1996 Joint Action placed an airport transit visa obligation on ten States.[177] As noted above, both measures left it to Member States to decide whether other third countries would, or would not, be subject to visa obligations.

The Schengen countries had agreed by 1997 on a harmonized visa list in respect of almost all countries,[178] and then by 1998 on a harmonized list in respect of all but one country (Colombia).[179] These rules required Schengen States to impose visa requirements on all the States in Africa, the Caribbean, and the Indian Ocean, as well as most States in Asia and the Pacific,[180] and to waive visa requirements for most States in Europe and Latin America.[181] There was also a Schengen blacklist regarding ATVs, consisting of twelve States.[182]

The 2001 EC Regulation fully harmonized the visa list policy, by adding Colombia definitively to the blacklist.[183] It also set out revised criteria for defining which states would go on the blacklist or whitelist; this decision was based on:[184]

> ...a considered, case-by case assessment of a variety of criteria relating *inter alia* to illegal immigration, public policy and security, and to the European Union's external relations with third countries, consideration also being given to the implications of regional coherence and reciprocity.

To this end, the 2001 Regulation moved three states or other entities from the blacklist to the whitelist: Hong Kong, Macao, and Bulgaria, along with Romania (provisionally). Hong Kong and Macao received this benefit in return for agreeing readmission treaties with the EC (as it was then), which covered also the readmission of at least some persons who had merely transited through their territory (in practice, Chinese citizens).[185]

---

[174] Albania, Romania, Bulgaria, Turkey, the Federal Republic of Yugoslavia, the Former Yugoslav Republic of Macedonia, and all the former Soviet Union States except for the Baltic States.

[175] Peru, Guyana, Surinam, Cuba, the Dominican Republic, Haiti, Mauritius, the Maldives, and Fiji.

[176] Para 3 of the preamble.

[177] Afghanistan, Sri Lanka, Iran, Iraq, Ethiopia, Eritrea, Somalia, Nigeria, Ghana, and Congo.

[178] Decision SCH/Com-ex (97)32 (n 165 above), which placed thirteen States on the Schengen whitelist and four States on the Schengen blacklist.

[179] Decision SCH/Com-ex (98)53 rev 2 (n 165 above), which placed Bolivia, Ecuador, and the three Baltic states on the Schengen whitelist.

[180] The exceptions were Israel, Japan, South Korea, Singapore, Malaysia, Brunei, Australia, and New Zealand.

[181] The European exceptions were Albania, Romania, Bulgaria, Turkey, the Federal Republic of Yugoslavia, the Former Yugoslav Republic of Macedonia, Bosnia-Herzegovina, and all the former Soviet Union States except for the Baltic States. The Latin American exceptions were Peru, Guyana, Surinam, Cuba, the Dominican Republic, and Haiti.

[182] The list appeared in Annex 3, part of the Common Consular Instructions (Decision SCH/Com-ex (99)13, [2000] OJ L 239/317). These were the same States listed in the EU Joint Action (n 163 above), plus Pakistan and Bangladesh. This list of countries has now been incorporated in the Visa Code (see I:4.7.2 below).

[183] Reg 539/2001 (n 166 above).   [184] See para 5 of the preamble.

[185] See I:7.9.1 below. Note that this was the last time that third States or entities received a visa *waiver* in return for signing readmission treaties; the EU subsequently offered visa *facilitation* treaties in return for signing (some) readmission treaties, although in some cases the latter treaties served to start a process leading to full visa waiver later on. See I:4.11.2 below.

Bulgaria and Romania received this waiver partly in the interests of regional coherence, since those two States had just begun negotiations to join the EU, and all other countries which were then negotiating were already on the whitelist. But the Council also asked the Commission to prepare a prior report on Bulgaria's and Romania's attempts to prevent illegal residence of their nationals in the Member States and readiness to accept their readmission, as a *quid pro quo* for visa abolition.[186] The report, issued early in 2001,[187] satisfied the Council as regards Bulgaria, but Romania was placed in a 'waiting room', pending a further report on 'the undertakings it is prepared to enter into on illegal immigration and illegal residence, including repatriation of persons from that country who are illegally resident'.[188] This report was submitted in June 2001, and recommended abolition of the visa requirement for Romanians, in light of Romania's undertakings.[189] So following a further Commission proposal, the Council amended the visa list Regulation to place Romania definitively on the white list from 1 January 2002.[190]

The next amendment to the lists of countries dated from 2003, when the Council moved Ecuador from the whitelist to the blacklist due to concerns about illegal immigration, Switzerland was deleted from the lists altogether following the entry into force of its treaty with the EU on free movement of persons,[191] and East Timor was designated a State, rather than an entity only recognized by some Member States, after it had gained independence (although it remained on the blacklist).[192]

Next, in 2006 the Council moved Bolivia to the blacklist, on grounds of illegal immigration and crime, and moved six micro-States in the Pacific and Indian Ocean from the whitelist to the blacklist, on the grounds that there was limited migration pressure from those States and few or no Member States had consulates there.[193] However, the latter waiver was made subject to the conclusion of treaties establishing a reciprocal visa waiver between the EC (as it then was) and each of those countries; these treaties were not agreed until 2009.[194] The Council also decided in 2006 to adopt harmonized rules concerning various categories of quasi-British citizens. So a visa waiver applies to all 'British Nationals (Overseas)', while a visa requirement applied to four other such categories[195]—until a visa waiver was also applied to them in 2014 (see below).

In the meantime, in June 2003, the Council agreed criteria for potential abolition of the visa requirement for Western Balkan states,[196] comprising 'major reforms in areas

---

[186] See Press Release of JHA Council, 30 Nov and 1 Dec 2000.
[187] COM (2001) 61, 2 Feb 2001.   [188] Art 8(2), Reg 539/2001 (n 166 above).
[189] COM (2001) 361, 29 June 2001.
[190] Reg 2414/2001 ([2001] OJ L 327/1). On the legal questions resulting from the 'waiting period' for visa abolition for Romanians, see the order in Case C-51/03 *Georgescu* [2004] ECR I-3203.
[191] See I:4.4.2 above.   [192] Reg 453/2003 (n 168 above).
[193] The States concerned were Antigua and Barbuda, the Bahamas, Barbados, Mauritius, Saint Kitts and Nevis, and the Seychelles.
[194] See I:4.11.1 below.
[195] These categories are: 'British Overseas Territories Citizens who do not have the right of abode in the United Kingdom'; 'British Overseas Citizens'; 'British Subjects who do not have the right of abode in the United Kingdom'; and 'British Protected Persons'.
[196] Other than Croatia, which was always on the EU whitelist, and which subsequently joined the EU anyway.

such as' strengthening the rule of law, combating organized crime, corruption, and irregular migration, and strengthening administrative capacity regarding border control and document security.[197] This process encompassed visa facilitation treaties, in force from the start of 2008.[198] Subsequently, in light of the Commission's assessment that these States had sufficiently met the relevant criteria, Serbia, Montenegro, and the Former Yugoslav Republic of Macedonia (FYROM) were moved from the blacklist to the whitelist in 2009,[199] and Albania and Bosnia-Herzegovina were moved to the whitelist in 2010.[200] In each case, the visa waiver only applies to holders of biometric passports. Also, the holders of passports issued in Kosovo are not covered.[201] The EU has, however, opened a visa dialogue with Kosovo with a view to waiving visa requirements when the criteria are met.[202]

Subsequently, the EU dropped the visa requirement for Taiwan in 2010, on the grounds that it did not constitute a risk of illegal migration or threat to public policy.[203] It has also opened a visa dialogue with 'eastern partnership' countries (Ukraine, Belarus, Moldova, Armenia, Azerbaijan, and Georgia), expressing a willingness to remove visa requirements on the basis of a 'roadmap' addressing issues such as 'document security; fight against irregular migration, including readmission; public order issues; and external relations issues, including human rights of migrants and other vulnerable groups'.[204] This resulted in the waiver of the visa requirement for Moldova in 2014.[205] There was also a visa dialogue with Russia (currently suspended),[206] and more recently a dialogue has begun with Turkey.[207]

Most recently, the EU overhauled the visa list more generally in 2014.[208] The criteria for deciding on which States would be subject to a visa requirement were changed, to add a reference to 'economic benefit, in particular in terms of tourism and foreign trade', as well as human rights. Applying the revised criteria, the EU shifted nineteen States on to the whitelist, subject to agreeing visa exemption treaties with the EU: sixteen

---

[197] See the Press Release of the External Relations Council, 16 June 2003, and subsequently the Commission communication on the Western Balkans (COM (2006) 27, 27 Jan 2006). For detailed documentation of the visa liberalization process in the Western Balkans, see <www.esiweb.org>.

[198] See I:4.11.2 below.   [199] Reg 1244/2009, n 168 above.   [200] Reg 1091/2010, n 168 above.

[201] See recital 4 in the preamble to Reg 1244/2009, n 168 above.

[202] COM (2009) 534, 14 Oct 2009. For reports on this process, see: COM (2013) 66, 21 Feb 2013, and COM (2014) 488, 24 July 2014.

[203] Reg 1211/2010, n 168 above. The same Reg dropped 'Northern Mariana' from the lists, since all those living there have US passports.

[204] See COM (2008) 823, 2 Dec 2008 (eastern partnership). Note that the EU has—or plans to have—visa facilitation treaties with all of these countries: see I:4.11 below. On this dialogue, see: SEC (2011) 1076, 16 Sep 2011, SWD (2012) 10, 9 Feb 2012, COM (2013) 809, 15 Nov 2013, COM (2014) 336, 27 May 2014, and COM (2015) 200, 8 April 2015 (Ukraine); SEC (2011) 1075, 16 Sep 2011, SWD (2012) 12, 9 Feb 2012, COM (2012) 348, 22 Jun 2012, COM (2012) 443, 3 Aug 2012, COM (2013) 459, 21 Jun 2013, and COM (2013) 807, 15 Nov 2013 (Moldova); and COM (2013) 808, 18 Nov 2013, COM (2014) 681, 29 Oct 2014, and COM (2015) 199, 8 April 2015 (Georgia).

[205] Reg 259/2014 (n 168 above). The waiver applies only to the holders of biometric passports.

[206] See the St. Petersburg statement on EU/Russia relations: <http://www.delrus.ec.europa.eu/en/p_234.htm>. Note that the EU has a visa facilitation treaty with Russia (I:4.11 below). For the report on the process, see: COM (2013) 923, 18 Dec 2013.

[207] For the first report on the process, see: COM (2014) 646, 20 Oct 2014. The visa dialogue was linked to approval of a readmission treaty: see I:7.9.1 below.

[208] Reg 509/2014, which also added South Sudan (a newly formed State) to the blacklist.

tropical island states,[209] plus Peru and Colombia (reversing earlier decisions) and the United Arab Emirates. In each case, the visa waiver was again subject to concluding a visa waiver treaty with the EU.[210] The visa requirement was also waived for the remaining categories of British 'quasi-citizens'.

Finally, since 2013, it is possible to 'fast-track' a reimposition of the visa requirement in certain circumstances, as a 'last resort'.[211] This process is triggered if a Member State notifies that Commission that, over a six-month period, compared to the same period in the previous year or the last six months before the visa requirement was waived for the country concerned,[212] it faces 'an emergency situation which it is unable to remedy on its own' as a result of a 'substantial and sudden increase' in one of three things:[213] the number of irregularly staying nationals of a country; asylum applications from that country with a low recognition rate,[214] if that leads 'to specific pressures on the Member State's asylum system'; or rejected readmission applications of that country's nationals.

A Member State making such a notification must give its reasons, 'relevant data and statistics', and a detailed explanation of what it has done to solve the problem. The Commission must then examine the notification, considering: whether the triggers for fast-track reimposition of visas really are present; the number of Member States affected; the overall impact of the increased numbers 'on the migratory situation in the Union' (based on Member States' data); the reports by relevant EU agencies; and 'the overall question of public policy and internal security'. If the Commission believes, 'taking into account the consequences of' the reimposition of visas 'for the external relations of the Union and its Member States with the third country concerned, while working in close cooperation with that third country to find alternative long-term solutions', that it must reimpose the visa requirement temporarily for a six-month period, it must do so within three months of receipt of the notification, in the form of an implementing act.[215] Before that six-month period is up, the Commission must submit a report to the EP and the Council, which may propose an amendment to the main visa list Regulation to place the country concerned on the blacklist definitively. In that case, the Commission can adopt a further measure to keep the country on the visa blacklist for up to a further year. This whole process must be reviewed in a report from the Commission, which is due by 10 January 2018.

In practice, while the fast-track rules could apply to any State on the visa whitelist, it is generally understood that they are intended to apply principally to the Western

---

[209] Namely Dominica, Grenada, Kiribati, Marshall Islands, Micronesia, Nauru, Palau, Saint Lucia, Saint Vincent and the Grenadines, Samoa, Solomon Islands, Timor-Leste, Tonga, Trinidad and Tobago, Tuvalu, and Vanuatu.

[210] Only some of these States have concluded visa waiver treaties with the EU to date. For details, see I:4.11.1 below. The Commission also had to report on whether Peru and Colombia met criteria for a visa waiver; it reported positively (COM (2014) 663 and 665, 29 Oct 2014).

[211] Arts 1a and 1b, inserted by Reg 1289/2013.

[212] The latter comparison can only be made for a seven year period after the visa waiver, so cannot be applied after 2016–17 as regards Western Balkans states (the main target of the rules).

[213] Recital 5 in the preamble to Reg 1289/2013 states that this usually means an increase of over 50%, although the Commission can accept a lower figure as a trigger.

[214] Recital 6 in the preamble to Reg 1289/2013 states that this usually means a recognition rate below 3 or 4%, although the Commission can accept a higher figure as a trigger.

[215] For the procedure, see Art 4a, also inserted by Reg 1289/2013.

Balkans states. While the fast-track reimposition of the visa requirement has not been requested to date, the Commission has been reporting regularly on the position as regards Western Balkans countries since the EU took the decision to waive visa requirements for those States, having promised to do so as a condition of waiving visa requirements for Albania and Bosnia in 2010. According to the most recent report,[216] asylum applications from the Western Balkans States have been increasing considerably,[217] although the numbers who are staying irregularly have not. There is no reference to readmission statistics. The report mentions nationals of other countries who enter the EU via the Western Balkans, although that issue is irrelevant to the possible fast-track reimposition of a visa requirement.[218] Many Member States had responded by designating Western Balkan countries as 'safe countries of origin' in accordance with EU asylum law. Indeed, in July 2015, the Council urged all Member States to do so, and in September 2015, the Commission proposed legislation to this end.[219]

4.5.3 Exceptions

The 1995 and 1999 visa list Regulations permitted Member States to decide on the visa requirements for stateless persons and refugees, and to exempt various categories of persons from the visa requirement (transport and rescue workers, and holders of diplomatic or official passports).[220] The 2001 visa list Regulation, after amendment in 2006 and 2013, includes both mandatory and optional exceptions, which appear to be exhaustive.[221]

The mandatory exceptions require a waiver for people covered by the EU's local border traffic legislation, school pupils residing in a Member State which applies the EU Joint Action on liberalizing school trips, and recognized refugees and stateless persons who reside in a (Schengen) Member State and hold a travel document issued by that State.[222] The optional exceptions permit Member States to waive visa requirements for: school pupils taking part in a school trip from a non-Member State (including Switzerland and Liechtenstein) on the whitelist; refugees and stateless persons living in a whitelist country, or (from 2013) the UK and Ireland;[223] and members of the armed

---

[216] COM (2015) 58, 25 Feb 2015. See previous reports: SEC (2011) 695; SEC (2011) 1570, 7 Dec 2011; COM (2012) 472, 28 Aug 2012; and COM (2013) 836, 28 Nov 2013.

[217] For Albanians and Bosnians, the refugee recognition rate is above the 3–4% guideline referred to in the preamble to the Regulation. The recognition rate is below that level for other Western Balkan states. The report does not mention asylum applications by Kosovars, because Kosovo is not on the EU visa whitelist.

[218] For Albanians and Bosnians, the refugee recognition rate is above the 3–4% guideline referred to in the preamble to the Regulation. The recognition rate is below that level for other Western Balkan states. The report does not mention asylum applications by Kosovars, because Kosovo is not on the EU visa whitelist.

[219] Conclusions of the JHA Council, 20 July 2015 and COM (2015) 452, 9 Sep 2015. See further I:5.7 below.

[220] Arts 2 and 4 of the Regs.

[221] Arts 1 and 4 of Reg 539/2001, as amended by Regs 1932/2006 and 1289/2013 (n 168 above). On the implementation of these exceptions, see [2001] OJ C 363/21, [2003] OJ C 68/2, [2006] OJ C 311/16, and [2008] OJ C 74/40.

[222] On these categories, see further respectively I:3.8 above and I:4.9 and I:5.5 below.

[223] Member States are obliged to impose visa requirements on refugees and stateless persons living in *blacklist* countries, but the Reg is 'without prejudice to' the 1959 Council of Europe treaty on the abolition of visa requirements for refugees (CETS 31), which requires a visa exemption for lawfully resident refugees

forces of NATO members or of countries linked to NATO. Member States may *either* waive *or* impose a visa requirement on transport and rescue personnel, diplomats, and international officials; and they may impose a visa requirement on a person from a positive list State who seeks to carry out a paid activity. The 'paid activity' exception is not defined in the Regulation, but the EU's visa waiver treaties clarify the meaning of the concept, and there are some detailed rules in the EU Directive on seasonal workers.[224] There is no harmonization of visa policy in relation to workers posted from third countries pursuant to the General Agreement in Trade in Services.[225]

It should also be recalled that there are special rules, which have been amended over the years, concerning visa waiver for persons holding a long-stay visa,[226] and persons covered by EU rules on transit through Croatia, Cyprus, Romania, and Bulgaria.[227]

4.5.4 Visa reciprocity

In the years since the EU harmonized the visa list, it has increasingly ensured visa reciprocity (the waiver of the visa requirement for all EU citizens by every State on the EU visa whitelist) by signing visa waiver treaties with the third States concerned.[228] However, such treaties do not exist for every State on the whitelist, and so the EU's internal rules on this issue remain important.

There have been three versions of these rules. The first version dates from 2001.[229] It provided that if a third country not subject to any EU visa requirement imposed a visa requirement on one or more Member States, those Member States could notify this to the Commission and Council, with the effect that the EU would have imposed a visa requirement on that State automatically, unless the Council voted otherwise by a qualified majority or the non-Member State dropped its visa requirement. This procedure was never used.

The 2003 amendment to the visa list Regulation required the Commission to draw up a report on this issue, and this report documented that several countries benefiting from visa-free entry into the EU in fact imposed visa requirements on one or more of the first fifteen Member States; moreover, the large majority of such countries imposed visa requirements on one or more of the Member States which joined the EU in 2004.[230] There were also cases in which non-EU States arguably breached the reciprocity principle by imposing limitations on entry, such as limitations on the period of entry, that are not matched by the EU.

The Council subsequently amended the visa list Regulation in 2005 to institute the second version of the reciprocity rules.[231] This was a more diplomatic procedure. Instead of a semi-automatic imposition of an EU visa requirement against a third State

---

who hold travel documents issued by one of the Contracting Parties to that treaty. See Appendix I for ratification details.

[224] See respectively I:4.11.1 below and Dir 2014/36 ([2014] OJ L 94/375), discussed in I:6.5.2.2 below.
[225] On this issue, see I:6.4.6 below.   [226] See I:4.9 below.   [227] See I:4.2.5 above.
[228] See I:4.11.1 below.   [229] Art 1(4), Reg 539/2001 (before amendment).
[230] Document JAI-B-1 (2004) 1372, Rev, 18 Feb 2004.
[231] Reg 851/2005 (n 168 above), amending Art 1(4) and adding a new Art 1(5). See also Council and Commission statement ([2005] OJ C 172/1).

not applying reciprocity, the Commission had to enter into discussions with the third State with a view to ensuring visa-free travel. The Commission then had to report to the Council, possibly proposing reimposition of the visa requirement. In a series of reports on the application of these rules, the Commission described some success in encouraging third States to drop visa requirements for all EU Member States, with greater difficulties as regards Canada, Australia, and the United States.[232] In fact, Canada *reimposed* visa controls on Czech citizens in 2009, due to concerns about asylum applications by Czech Roma.[233]

The Canadian situation led to the third version of the reciprocity rules, adopted in 2013.[234] Since then, the rules combine the diplomatic and hard-line approaches. The overall diplomatic framework remains, but if a Member State requests the Commission to reimpose the visa requirement for a third State which has not waived visa requirements for all Member States, the Commission must reimpose that requirement temporarily within six months of the original imposition of the visa requirement, or explain why it has not done so (presumably because negotiations are underway). After forty-eight months, the Commission is obliged to reinstate the visa requirement against that State for a twelve-month period. The Commission acts by means of delegated acts,[235] and it is still possible to put that State on the blacklist definitively by means of a legislative amendment to the main Regulation. According to the Commission's initial reports on the application of the revised rules, there is some further progress extending visa reciprocity for EU citizens (notably Czech citizens in Canada), and no Member State has yet asked to trigger the revised rules on hardline retaliation.[236]

4.5.5 Analysis

The Schengen and EU visa lists were initially strongly criticized on a number of grounds,[237] in particular the imprecise criteria used to determine which States were subject to the visa requirement and the highly discretionary application of those criteria in practice, with (for example) the absence of any published evidence offered to justify placing Ecuador on the blacklist and the initial failure to institute a regular review to see whether States really should remain on the blacklist.[238] Also, the initial EU

---

[232] COM (2006) 3, 10 Jan 2006; COM (2006) 568, 3 Oct 2006; COM (2007) 533, 13 Sep 2007; COM (2008) 486, 23 July 2008; COM (2009) 560, 19 Oct 2009; COM (2010) 620, 5 Oct 2010; and COM (2012) 681, 26 Nov 2012.

[233] See the special report on this issue (COM (2009) 562, 19 Oct 2009). The Commission rejected Canada's suggestion of a Canada/EU treaty that would address asylum claims by EU citizens in Canada (see COM (2012) 681, n 232 above).

[234] Art 1(4), as revised by Reg 1289/2013. Art 1(5) was repealed.

[235] For the details, see Art 4b, as inserted by Reg 1289/2013.

[236] C(2014) 7218, 10 Oct 2014 and C(2015) 2575, 22 April 2015.

[237] See R Cholewinski, *Borders and Discrimination in the European Union* (ILPA/MPG, 2002), 20–37; E Guild, 'The Border Abroad—Visas and Border Controls' in E Guild, P Minderhoud, and K Groenendijk, eds., *In Search of Europe's Borders* (Kluwer, 2003), 87; E Jileva, 'Insiders and Outsiders in Central and Eastern Europe: the Case of Bulgaria' in ibid, 273; and P Boeles, 'Schengen and the Rule of Law' in H Meijers, et al., *Schengen: Internationalisation of Central Chapters of the Law on Aliens, Refugees, Privacy, Security and the Police*, 2nd edn (Stichting NJCM-Boekerij, 1992).

[238] R Cholewinski and E Guild, n 237 above.

visa blacklist arguably breached the principle of non-discrimination, given the application of the visa requirement to nearly all countries with a majority black or Muslim population; the airport transit visa list arguably similarly breaches the principle of non-discrimination.[239] Furthermore, the pressure placed on certain non-Member States to amend their immigration laws in order to secure visa abolition is disproportionate to the EU's legitimate interest in ensuring that citizens of those States do not abuse the abolition of the visa requirement; the EU's interests would be satisfied if readmission of *those States' nationals* was guaranteed and if passports issued by those States contained sufficient security features to ensure that passport-holders were genuine citizens. In particular, the EU's pressure has resulted in the application of national rules that arguably breach the human right to leave one's own country.[240]

Over the years, however, the EU's visa list has clearly developed in a more liberal direction, with the numbers of States moved to the whitelist far exceeding those moved to the blacklist. The criteria for applying a visa requirement have usefully been amended to include economic considerations, and there have been many removals from the blacklists on objective grounds. The EU has also been willing to stick with visa waivers for neighbouring countries despite clear pressure of irregular migration, in the interests of maintaining its strong relationship with the countries concerned. As discussed below,[241] this is consistent with a general trend to liberalize the conditions for obtaining a visa to visit the EU.

4.6 Visa Format

The Council first used the powers originally conferred by the former Article 100c EC to adopt an initial Regulation establishing a standard visa format in 1995.[242] Member States must issue visas for intended stays in that Member State or several Member States of no more than three months or transit through the territory or airport transit zone of that Member State or several Member States in the standard format set out in the Annex to the Regulation.[243] Further technical details making the visa difficult to counterfeit or falsify have been established in (secret) implementing measures adopted by the Commission, assisted by a committee of Member States' representatives (a 'comitology' committee).[244] Individuals to whom visas are issued have the right to verify the data on the visa and to ask for any corrections or deletions to be made, and only the data set out in the Annex to the Regulation or mentioned in that person's travel document can be included in machine-readable form on the visa.[245]

This Regulation was amended in 2002,[246] for two reasons. First of all, the amendment updated the 'comitology' rules in the Regulation concerning Member States' control of

---

[239] R Cholewinski, n 237 above.   [240] R Cholewinski, n 237 above.
[241] See I:4.7.   [242] Reg 1683/95 ([1995] OJ L 164/1).
[243] Arts 1 and 5 and Annex, Reg 1683/95.
[244] Arts 2, 3, and 6, Reg 1683/95. The secret implementing measures are set out in Commission Decisions 2/96, 7 Feb 1996 and COM (2000) 4332, 27 Dec 2000 (both unpublished; see COM (2001) 157, 23 Mar 2001, p 2). The standard visa format therefore became applicable on 7 Aug 1996 (see Art 8, Reg 1683/95).
[245] Art 4, Reg 1683/95.   [246] Reg 334/2002 ([2002] OJ L 53/7).

the Commission's use of implementing powers, since the general rules governing 'comitology' procedures had been amended in 1999.[247] Secondly, the amended Regulation requires Member States to include a photograph in visas in order to increase security and to pave the way for the introduction of the Visa Information System (VIS).[248] Member States have had an obligation to introduce photographs in visas from 3 June 2007.[249]

In 2003, the Commission proposed a further amendment to the Regulation,[250] in order to store further 'biometric' data (ie fingerprints) in relation to visas, in parallel with comparable changes then planned (and subsequently implemented) as regards residence permits and passports.[251] However, the proposed Regulation was not adopted due to technical difficulties, and the Commission withdrew the proposal early in 2006.[252] Instead of storing biometric data on visa applicants in a computer chip integrated into each visa sticker, this biometric data is instead stored in the central computer system of the VIS. The process of taking and storing biometric data was instead regulated by amendments to the Common Consular Instructions (CCI) adopted in 2009, which were later integrated into the EU's Visa Code.[253]

A second amendment to the original Regulation was nonetheless adopted in 2008,[254] in order to ensure that the standard format was consistent with the planned introduction of the VIS, so that visa sticker numbers could be searched easily via the VIS. The Regulation was amended again in 2013, to redefine the time period of the validity of visas consistently with other EU legislation.[255] In addition to these three substantive amendments, the visa format Regulation has also been amended three times following the accession of new Member States to the EU.[256] In 2015, the Commission proposed a further amendment, to fix a security breach as regards possible counterfeiting of visa stickers.[257]

A separate Regulation establishing a form of visa format where persons are travelling on a travel document issued by an entity which is not recognized by the Member State drawing up the form was adopted in March 2002.[258] It follows the structure of the main visa format Regulation.

Similarly, several other EU measures provide for a distinct form of visa format,[259] but on the other hand, a number of measures provide for the application of the standard

---

[247] On the issue of 'comitology', see I:2.2.2.1 above.

[248] On the VIS, which subsequently became operational in 2011, see further I:4.8 below.

[249] See Art 1(3), Reg 334/2002 and the secret implementing Commission Decision C (2002) 2002, 3 June 2002 (unpublished; see COM (2003) 558, 24 Sept 2003, p 2).

[250] COM (2003) 558, 24 Sept 2003.

[251] On the formats of residence permits, long-stay visas, and passports, see I:6.9 below and I:3.9 above.

[252] COM (2006) 110, 10 Mar 2006. On the technical difficulties, see Council doc 6492/05, 17 Feb 2005, online at: <http://www.statewatch.org/news/2005/feb/6492.05.pdf>; and see the Statewatch story with further documentation online at: <http://www.statewatch.org/news/2004/dec/07visas-residence-biometrics.htm>.

[253] See further I:4.7 below.

[254] Reg 856/2008 ([2008] OJ L 235/1), applicable at the latest on 1 May 2009 (Art 2).

[255] Reg 610/2013 ([2013] OJ L 182/1).

[256] See the 2003 Act of accession, Annex II, part 18.B ([2003] OJ L 236/1); Reg 1791/2006 ([2006] OJ L 363/1); and Reg 517/2013 ([2013] OJ L 158/1). See further I:4.2.5 above.

[257] COM (2015) 303, 24 June 2015.

[258] Reg 333/2002 ([2002] OJ L 53/4), applicable from 23 Feb 2002.

[259] The Regs regarding the Kaliningrad visa format (Reg 694/2003, [2003] OJ L 99/15) and the issue of collective visas to seamen (see originally Reg 415/2003, [2004] L 64/1, and now Art 36 and Annex IX to the Visa Code (Reg 810/2009, [2009] OJ L 243/1)). The Olympic visa regulations provide instead for insertion of numbers into the Olympic accreditation card as the format of the visa (Art 6, Reg 1295/2003, [2003] OJ L

visa format in other contexts.[260] In particular, a Regulation adopted in 2010 provides for the use of the common visa format for all long-stay visas also.[261] The proposed Regulation establishing a touring visa also provides for use of the common format.[262]

4.7 Conditions for Issuing Visas

4.7.1 Overview and background

The basic conditions governing the issue of Schengen visas were initially set out in Articles 9–17 of the 1990 Schengen Convention, as supplemented by a number of decisions of the Schengen Executive Committee, particularly establishing the Common Consular Instructions (CCI).[263] Following the integration of the Schengen *acquis* into the EC and EU legal order, the Council adopted a Regulation in 2001 which conferred powers to amend the CCI, along with a number of other Schengen measures concerning visas,[264] in part upon itself, and in part upon individual Member States.[265] The Commission brought a legal challenge to this Regulation, on the grounds that the Regulation did not adequately explain why implementing powers had not been conferred on the Commission (which is the normal legal rule), but the Court of Justice dismissed the challenge.[266]

This Regulation was used a number of times by the Council to amend the CCI up until January 2010,[267] in particular: to oblige applicants to pay a fee for a visa *application*, not just when the visa is issued;[268] to provide for a standard form for Schengen visa applications;[269] to set out harmonized rules on the use of travel agents in the visa process;[270] to establish a standard fee of €35 for Schengen visa applications;[271] to strengthen the normal obligation to interview visa applicants in consulates;[272] to liberalize the rules on the representation of one Member State by another, as regards visa

---

183/1 and Art 6, Reg 2046/2005, [2005] OJ L 334/1). The same rule will apply to any future Olympics held in the Schengen area (see Art 49 and Annex XI, Art 6 of the Visa Code). On these measures, see further I:4.7.3 below.

[260] The Joint Action on airport transit visas ([1996] OJ L 63/8) provided explicitly for use of the standard format (see Art 2(3)), although the Visa Code (n 259 above), which repealed this Joint Action, no longer contains an express rule to this effect; while the ADS treaty with China (see I:4.11.3 below) provides implicitly for the use of the standard visa format.

[261] Art 18 of the Schengen Convention, as amended by Reg 265/2010 ([2010] OJ L 85/1). See further I:6.9.2 below. Note that biometric data is *not* taken from long-stay visa applicants.

[262] Art 7(6) of the proposal (COM (2014) 164, 1 Apr 2014).

[263] [2000] OJ L 239/17 (Convention). The consolidated text of the CCI as of 1 May 1999, as integrated into the EC legal order, was set out in SCH/Com-ex (99) 13, [2000] OJ L 239/307. For a summary of the Schengen Convention and CCI visa rules, see the second edition of this book, pp 151–5.

[264] For details of those other measures, see the third edition of this book, p 258.

[265] Reg 789/2001 ([2001] OJ L 116/2). On the parallel Reg governing amendments to the Schengen Borders Manual, see I:3.6.1 above.

[266] Case C-257/01 *Commission v Council* [2005] ECR I-345. On the issue of implementing measures, see generally I:2.2.2.1 above.

[267] The amendments made by Member States to the CCI (see Art 2, Reg 789/2001) were not published in the OJ.

[268] Decision 2002/44 ([2002] OJ L 20/5).   [269] Decision 2002/354 ([2002] OJ L 123/50).

[270] [2002] OJ L 187/44.   [271] [2003] OJ L 152/82.   [272] [2004] OJ L 5/74.

applications;[273] to impose an obligation in principle for visa applicants to have medical insurance;[274] and to increase the standard fee for an application to €60 as from the start of 2007, in order to fund the Visa Information System (VIS).[275] The Council made a number of other more technical amendments,[276] and the CCI was also amended following enlargement of the EU.[277] It was also still possible to amend the CCI by means of legislation, and indeed several legislative acts amended the Instructions.[278] In particular, a major amendment to the CCI adopted in 2009 regulated the process of taking biometric data from visa applicants, pursuant to the planned operation of the Visa Information System.[279] Due to all these changes, the CCI were frequently codified informally.[280]

There were also a number of other Decisions of the Schengen Executive Committee relating to visas, besides the CCI.[281] Furthermore, the EC also adopted some separate measures setting out exceptions from the normal rules on issuing visas following the entry into force of the Treaty of Amsterdam. This highly fragmented legal framework was largely codified and significantly amended when the EU's Visa Code was adopted in 2009. However, a small number of separate measures on visa conditions remain in force alongside the Code, and the Commission has recently suggested the adoption of a major new Regulation on a 'touring visa'. These sundry measures and proposals are considered separately below.[282]

4.7.2 The Visa Code

The Visa Code Regulation was adopted in June 2009,[283] and has applied since 5 April 2010.[284] From that date, the Regulation repealed almost all of the prior Schengen and EC measures governing the conditions for the issue of Schengen visas.[285] It has been amended twice: once to alter the rules relating to the issue of transit visas,[286] and once to redefine the time period of the validity of visas consistently with other EU legislation.[287] In 2014, the Commission proposed to recast the code, making a number of major amendments;[288] this proposal is discussed further below. The CJEU has twice ruled on the interpretation of the code,[289] and the Commission has reported on its application in practice (the '2014 report').[290]

---

[273] [2004] OJ L 5/76.   [274] [2004] OJ L 5/79.   [275] [2006] OJ L 175/77.
[276] For details, see the third edition of this book, p 259.   [277] See ibid.
[278] Art 7(2) of Reg 539/2001 ([2001] OJ L 81/1); Art 2 of Reg 1091/2001 ([2001] OJ L 150/4); Art 2 of Reg 334/2002 ([2002] OJ L 53/7); Art 5(4) of Reg 415/2003 ([2003] OJ L 64/1); Art 11(1) of Reg 693/2003 ([2003] OJ L 99/8); and Art 39(2)(c) of the Schengen Borders code ([2006] OJ L 105/1).
[279] Reg 390/2009 ([2009] OJ L 131/1).
[280] [2002] OJ C 313/1, [2003] OJ C 310/1, and [2005] OJ C 326/1.
[281] For further details, see the third edition of this book, p 260.   [282] I:4.7.3.
[283] Reg 810/2009, [2009] OJ L 243/1. All the references in this section are to the code, unless otherwise indicated.
[284] Art 58(2). However, the rules concerning appeals (see discussion below) applied from 5 Apr 2011 (Art 58(5)).
[285] Art 56. Annex XIII to the Code sets out a correlation table comparing the Visa Code and the prior measures.
[286] Reg 154/2012, [2012] OJ L 58/3.   [287] Reg 610/2013, [2013] OJ L 182/1.
[288] COM (2014) 164, 1 April 2014.
[289] Cases: C-83/12 PPU *Vo*, ECLI:EU:C:2012:202; and C-84/12 *Koushkaki*, ECLI:EU:C:2013:862.
[290] SWD (2014) 101, 1 April 2014.

The Commission has the power to amend nine of the thirteen Annexes to the code, by means of the 'regulatory procedure with scrutiny' (involving a form of control by the EP), as well as the power to adopt operational instructions for consular authorities, by means of the 'regulatory procedure'.[291] The Commission has adopted two operational handbooks.[292] Member States must also notify a number of national decisions to the Commission, which is obliged to publish them.[293]

Title I of the Visa Code concerns respectively the objective and scope of the code, and the relevant definitions.[294] The code is 'without prejudice' to the position of third-country nationals as regards EU free movement law and agreements extending EU free movement law to non-EU states.[295]

Title II of the code concerns airport transit visas (ATVs).[296] There is a standard list of countries whose nationals require airport transit visas to cross through the international transit areas of airports, in place of the lists in previous EU laws which had addressed this issue.[297] Member States may decide that the nationals of additional States will require ATVs (ie a purely national list) in the event of 'urgent cases of massive inflow of illegal immigrants', subject to prior notification of the Commission before introducing or withdrawing such a national requirement.[298] These national lists are subject to annual review in the 'comitology committee' established by the Visa Code Regulation, in order to decide whether to add the countries concerned to the uniform EU list of states requiring ATVs.[299] If the countries concerned are not added to the uniform EU list, the Member State which listed them can either keep those countries on its national list (if the criteria for listing them are still met) or withdraw the ATV requirement.[300] There could presumably be a judicial review of whether the criteria are met for a national decision to place (or retain) a country on an ATV list in light of the criteria in the Visa Code. However, it should be noted that there are no express criteria governing the addition or removal of countries to the common EU list, other than a reference to combating 'illegal immigration'.[301] In practice, the 2014 report states that many countries were dropped from national ATV lists in 2011, and a few were dropped afterward.

In any event, neither the EU common list nor any national list can apply an ATV requirement to six categories of persons: those holding a Schengen visa, national long-stay visa, or residence permit issued by a Member State (even a non-Schengen State, following 2012 amendments); those holding a valid residence permit issued by the

[291] Arts 50–2. For a list of the Annexes, see below. On 'comitology', see I:2.2.2.1 above, and on delegated acts, see I:2.2.3.1 above.
[292] See: <http://ec.europa.eu/dgs/home-affairs/what-we-do/policies/borders-and-visas/visa-policy/index_en.htm>.
[293] Art 53.   [294] Arts 1 and 2.
[295] Art 1(2). On the relationship between EU free movement law and EU visa legislation in general, see I:4.4.1 above. See also Art 3(5)(d) of the Code, which exempts family members of EU citizens from any airport transit visa requirement, and also Art 24(2)(a) and Annex XI, Art 4.
[296] Art 3. For the definition of 'airport transit visa', see Art 2(5); see also Art 1(3) on the scope of the code.
[297] Art 3(1), referring to Annex IV. The Annex consists of the same twelve countries which were subject to a common ATV requirement under prior EU law.
[298] Art 3(2). These decisions have to be notified to the Commission: see Art 53(1)(b).
[299] Art 3(3).   [300] Art 3(4).   [301] Point 5 in the preamble.

USA, Japan, Canada, San Marino, or Andorra, if the permit is listed in Annex V to the Visa Code and guarantees unqualified readmission; those holding a visa issued by a Member State, an EEA State, or by the USA, Canada, or Japan, or when they return from those countries having used the visa; family members of EU citizens who have exercised free movement rights; holders of diplomatic passports; and flight crew members who are nationals of States which are party to the Chicago Convention on civil aviation.[302]

Title III of the Visa Code concerns the conditions and procedures for issuing visas. Chapter I defines the authorities taking part in the application procedure.[303] As a general rule, subject to limited exceptions, visa applications must be decided upon by consulates.[304] The Visa Code then specifies which Member State is responsible for considering applications for different types of visa;[305] Member States are obliged to cooperate to prevent situations in which an application cannot be processed because the Member State responsible does not have a consulate or representation from another Member State in the third State concerned.[306] There are also rules for visa applicants residing in Member States.[307] Member States are encouraged to represent other Member States, where the latter do not have a consulate, for the purpose of processing visa applications or for taking biometric information for applicants.[308] There is, however, no guarantee that a nearby consulate which is able to process applications will be available for all visa applications; the radical solution of a move toward common EU consulates, perhaps constituting part of the EU External Action Service which was established pursuant to the Treaty of Lisbon,[309] is not mentioned in the Visa Code.

Chapter II of Title III of the Visa Code concerns the application process.[310] Visa applications cannot be made more than three months before the date of travel, except as regards multiple-entry visas, where the application can be made up to six months before the date of travel.[311] If an appointment is required, it should 'as a rule' take place within two weeks of the application.[312] Applicants normally have to appear in person to apply for a visa, but this is subject to a number of exceptions.[313] Each applicant must fill out the standard application form, even children who are listed on their parent's passport.[314] Applicants must also present a valid travel document,[315] as well as biometric data (a photograph and ten fingerprints).[316] Fingerprints can be taken by honorary consuls or private service providers (see discussion below).[317] There are uniform

---

[302] Art 3(5). [303] Arts 4–8. [304] Art 4.

[305] Art 5(1) to (3). The 2014 report indicated that there are problems in practice applying these rules.

[306] Art 5(4). [307] Art 7.

[308] Art 8. These arrangements have to be notified to the Commission: see Art 53(1)(a).

[309] [2010] OJ L 201/30. [310] Arts 9–17.

[311] Art 9(1). According to the 2014 report, this time limit causes problems for seafarers, and those who would like to apply earlier to avoid peak times.

[312] Art 9(2). According to the 2014 report, this time limit was often breached in practice.

[313] Art 10. According to the 2014 report, a diminishing number of applicants apply in person, as more applications are processed by external bodies. The exception in Art 10(2) for persons known for their 'integrity and reliability' is very vague.

[314] Art 11. The standard application form is set out in Annex I to the Code. [315] Art 12.

[316] Art 13. However, fingerprints normally only need to be taken once every five years (Art 13(3)).

[317] Art 13(6), referring to Arts 42 and 43.

exemptions from the fingerprinting requirement: children under twelve; persons for whom fingerprinting is physically impossible; heads of state, senior politicians, and their spouses and delegations on official visits; and senior royal family members on official visits.[318]

The code then details the rules concerning supporting documents to be submitted by applicants,[319] the requirement of medical insurance,[320] the fee for visa applicants,[321] and the service fee for the use of private companies to collect biometric data (see further below).[322] The application fee remains €60, and the maximum service fee is half that amount.[323] However, the application fee must be reduced to €35 for children between six and twelve years old.[324] The fee must also be waived for: children under six years old; students, pupils, and teachers on study trips; researchers as defined by an EU recommendation; and representatives of non-profit organizations attending seminars and similar events.[325] Also, the fee *may* be waived for children between six and twelve, holders of diplomatic and service passports, and participants in non-profit seminars and similar events who are under twenty-five years old.[326] The fee may also be waived or reduced in individual cases, if this 'serves to promote cultural or sporting interests as well as interests in the field of foreign policy, development policy and other areas of vital public interest or for humanitarian reasons'.[327]

Chapter III of Title III of the Visa Code concerns the examination of and decisions taken upon applications.[328] This includes rules on verification of consular competence, admissibility of applications, and the stamping of applicants' travel documents.[329]

The key issue is of course the substantive grounds for deciding on the application for a visa. The Visa Code specifies that consulates are to apply the criteria for admission set out in the Schengen Borders Code.[330] In this context, 'particular consideration shall be given to assessing whether the applicant presents a risk of illegal immigration or a risk to the security of the Member States and whether the applicant intends to leave the territory of the Member States before the expiry of the visa applied for'.[331] According to the CJEU in *Koushkaki*, this is the main substantive rule governing decisions on applications for visas, and the code then goes on to set out the methods by which these substantive conditions are checked.[332]

What are those methods? First, the VIS must be checked for each application.[333] Next, consulates must also check for the veracity of documents, the intentions of the applicant, sufficient means of the applicant for subsistence, a listing for refusal of entry

---

[318] Art 13(7).   [319] Art 14 and Annex II.
[320] Art 15. The 2014 report argues that there are problems in practice applying the rules on medical insurance and supporting documents.
[321] Art 16.   [322] Art 17.   [323] Arts 16(1) and 17(4).   [324] Art 16(2).
[325] Art 16(4). The 2014 report indicates that the latter optional exception is rarely applied.
[326] Art 16(5).
[327] Art 16(6). The fee is also reduced or abolished by the EU's visa facilitation treaties: see I:4.11.2 below.
[328] Arts 18–23.   [329] Respectively Arts 18–20.
[330] Art 21(1) of the Visa Code, referring to Art 5 of the Borders Code (Reg 562/2006, [2006] OJ L 105/1). On the Borders Code, see further I:3.6.1 above.
[331] Art 21(1).   [332] N 289 above, para 28.
[333] Art 21(2). For details of the VIS, see I:4.8 below.

in the SIS, that the applicant is not 'a threat to public policy, internal security or public health' as defined in the Borders Code, and that the applicant has sufficient medical insurance.[334] The consulate must also assess whether the applicant has overstayed the permitted length of stay on the territory at present, or in the past.[335] There are separate criteria relating to applications for airport transit visas.[336] Decisions on the application have to be based on the 'authenticity and reliability' of the documents submitted, and the 'veracity and reliability' of the applicant.[337] If necessary, further documents or a personal interview can be requested.[338] Finally, the Visa Code specifies that a previous refusal of a visa application will not automatically mean a refusal of a new application; rather, a new application 'shall be assessed on the basis of all available information.'[339] However, it is possible that the introduction of the Visa Information System has in practice nonetheless led to an increased tendency to reject applications due to prior refusals, because information on prior refusals is now more readily available to consulates.[340]

The Visa Code then sets out rules for the controversial system of 'prior consultation', according to which one Member State may require the authorities of all other Member States to inform them of all visa applications from nationals of particular third countries or from particular categories of such nationals.[341] The consulted State's authorities must reply within seven days of the consultation, or they are deemed to have no objections to the application.[342] If they do have objections, this is not a ground as such for refusing a visa application, but obviously it is far more likely in practice that the application will be rejected. But in the event of an objection (or, in an emergency, pending the response to the consultation), the consulting Member State can still decide 'exceptionally' to issue a visa with limited territorial validity (an 'LTV visa').[343] The code does not specify expressly whether the applicant (or indeed the consulting Member State) must be told of the consulted Member State's reasons for objecting to an application. In practice, the consultation process is carried out in accordance with the 'Schengen Consultation Network' established by a previous Schengen Executive Committee Decision; this Network will be phased out as the VIS is rolled out, for the VIS has integrated its own system for such consultations.[344] Member States shall inform the Commission of any new consultation requirements, or any withdrawal of existing requirements; it shall inform other Member States and the public.[345] The requirement to inform the public of the consultation requirement is a major change from the position under the CCI, when such arrangements were kept secret.[346]

---

[334] Art 21(3). These are the same grounds set out in Art 5(1) of the Borders Code (n 330 above), with the addition of the medical insurance requirement. Art 21(5) sets out more rules relating to subsistence, including a further cross-reference to the Schengen Borders Code as regards subsistence criteria set by Member States.

[335] Art 21(4). This will obviously be facilitated if EU plans to establish an entry-exit system become operational: see I:3.6.2 above.

[336] Art 21(6).   [337] Art 21(7).   [338] Art 21(8).   [339] Art 21(9).

[340] On the VIS, see I:4.8 below.   [341] Art 22(1).   [342] Art 22(2).   [343] Art 25(1)(a).

[344] On the Decision, see I:4.7.3 below; on the relationship with the VIS, see Arts 16 and 46 of the VIS Reg (Reg 767/2008, [2008] OJ L 218/60), and the 2009 Commission Decision implementing the VIS Reg on this point ([2009] OJ L 117/3). The VIS was fully rolled out by November 2015 (see I:4.8 below).

[345] Art 22(3) and (4), and Art 53(1)(d) and (2).

[346] See Annex 5 to the consolidated CCI (n 280 above).

In practice, according to the 2014 report, there are consultation requirements for about 30 third countries, 15 of which are subject to a consultation requirement by a large number of Member States (the leaders were Iran, Iraq, Pakistan, and Afghanistan). About 10% of all visa applications are subject to the procedure.

Another change from the prior rules is the possibility to replace the consultation requirement with a less onerous information requirement, which is identical to the consultation requirement except for the lack of any facility for the informed Member State to comment on the visa application.[347] The 2014 report indicates that not many Member States switched from a consultation requirement to an information requirement.

A decision (whether positive or negative) on visa applications must be made within fifteen days, although extensions of this period to thirty or sixty days are permissible under certain conditions.[348] The 2014 report indicates that the fifteen-day deadline is 'generally' met.

Chapter IV of Title III of the Visa Code concerns issuing a visa.[349] It specifies that visas can be valid for one entry, two entries, or multiple entries, with (normally) a period of grace of fifteen days.[350] Multiple-entry visas, valid for between six months and five years, 'shall' be issued where there is both a proven need to travel frequently and the applicant has proven his or her 'integrity and reliability'.[351] The 2014 report indicates that the percentage of multiple-entry visas issued has been steadily growing, rising from 36% to 42% between 2010 and 2012. This was in large part due to the EU's visa facilitation agreements with countries like Russia, which have more precise rules on multiple-entry visas.[352] However, a large majority of multiple-entry visas were valid for less than one year, causing aggravation for seafarers and the tourist industry.

Next, there are rules on visas with limited territorial validity ('LTV' visas), ie visas which are valid only for one or possibly more, but less than all, of the Schengen States.[353] LTV visas 'shall' be issued 'exceptionally', either where a Member State 'considers it necessary on humanitarian grounds, for reasons of national interest or because of international obligations', to derogate from the criteria for entry set out in the Schengen Borders Code, to issue a visa despite the objections of a Member State which had to be consulted in accordance with the consultation procedure (see above); or to issue a visa 'for reasons of urgency' even though such a consultation has not been carried out;[354] or where a new visa is to be issued to a person who has already used a visa within the same six-month period.[355] There is also a special rule for cases where a travel document is not recognized by all Member States.[356] Arguably, by analogy with the case law on applications for general Schengen visas (see discussion below), there is an obligation to issue an LTV visa if the relevant conditions are satisfied. If correct, this would mean that the Schengen Visa Code can be used to obtain humanitarian visas in order to flee

---

[347] Art 31.   [348] Art 23.   [349] Arts 24–32.   [350] Art 24(1).

[351] Art 24(2).   [352] On these treaties, see further I:4.11 below.

[353] On the territorial scope of LTV visas, see Art 25(2).

[354] Art 25(1)(a). There is a requirement to inform other Member States in such cases: see Art 25(4).

[355] Art 25(1)(b). Compare to the general rules on extending visas, as set out in Art 33 of the code (see below).

[356] Art 25(3).

persecution. In practice, the 2014 report indicates that about 2% of all visas issued are LTV visas. The reasons for issuing them are not known, but they are frequently issued to citizens of countries for which prior consultation is required.

There are comparable specific rules on the issue of airport transit visas,[357] as well as detailed technical rules on filling in, invalidating, and fixing visa stickers.[358] The Visa Code confirms that simple possession of a visa 'shall not confer an automatic right of entry'.[359]

The Visa Code also contains key provisions on the grounds for refusing a visa and the procedural rights for visa applicants in the case of refusal.[360] An application 'shall' be refused: if the applicant does not meet the conditions for obtaining a visa;[361] if the applicant has already stayed for three of the last six months on the basis of a visa;[362] or if there are 'reasonable doubts' about the authenticity, veracity, or reliability of the applicant's documents or statements.[363] In its *Koushkaki* judgment, the CJEU confirmed that this is an exhaustive list of grounds on which a Member State can refuse a visa application. So in effect, a Member State *must* issue a visa if the conditions in the code are satisfied.[364] However, the Court accepted that assessing an individual visa application 'entails complex evaluations' of 'the personality of the applicant, his integration in the country where he resides, the political, social and economic situation of that country and the public policy', et al., of every Member State. This involves 'predicting the foreseeable conduct' of the applicant, 'based on ... an extensive knowledge of his country of residence' and analysis of the authenticity and veracity of various documents and the reliability of the applicant's statements. So national authorities have a 'wide discretion' when considering applications, and they cannot issue a visa as long as they have a 'reasonable doubt' about the applicant's intention to return (or presumably about any of the other substantive criteria for issue of a visa). The applicant must establish the credibility of his or her intention to return 'by means of relevant and reliable documents', if there are doubts about that intention 'which may arise as a result of, inter alia, the general situation in his [or her] country of residence or the existence of well-known migration flows between that country and the Member States'.

Following a refusal of an application, in a major change from the rules in the CCI, the applicant must be informed of the refusal and the grounds for it (by use of a standard form),[365] and applicants whose applicants are refused have the 'right to appeal' in accordance with the national law of the Member State which refused their application.[366]

---

[357] Art 26.   [358] Arts 27–9 and Annexes VII and VIII.   [359] Art 30.

[360] Art 32. These rules are 'without prejudice' to the possibility of issuing an LTV visa (see above).

[361] Art 32(1)(a)(i) to (iii) and (v) to (vi); these mirror the conditions for obtaining a visa set out in Art 21(3) (see above).

[362] Art 32(1)(a)(iv).   [363] Art 32(1)(b).

[364] N 289 above. The Court has reached similar conclusions as regards the Schengen Borders Code (I:3.6 above) and the students' Directive (I:6.5.3.2 below).

[365] Art 32(2). The standard form is set out in Annex VI.

[366] Art 32(3). The provisions on notification and appeal can be compared to the similar provisions in the Schengen Borders Code (see I:3.6.1 above) and to the right of access to information in the VIS (see I:4.8 below), considering that in the first case, the grounds for refusal of entry and refusal of a visa are nearly the same, and in the second case that information on refusals of visa applications, etc are inserted into the VIS (see Arts 32(5) and 34(8)) and therefore subject to the right of access to VIS data anyway.

The rules on notification and appeal also apply to visa applications at the border, and to decisions on annulment and revocation of visas.[367] According to the 2014 report, few refusals are appealed, and few appeals are successful. The report also indicates that some Member States take the view that there need not be judicial review of refusals. This interpretation is untenable in light of Article 47 of the EU Charter of Fundamental Rights, given that (according to the CJEU) there is an underlying obligation to issue visas if the conditions are satisfied.

Chapter V of Title III of the Visa Code concerns modification of an issued visa.[368] First, a visa 'shall' be extended (free of charge) where there is 'proof of *force majeure* or humanitarian reasons preventing [the visa holder] from leaving the territory of the Member States';[369] a visa *may* be extended (for a fee of €30) where there is 'proof of serious personal reasons' justifying this.[370] On the other hand, a visa shall be annulled (presumably with retroactive effect) 'where it becomes evident that the conditions for issuing it were not met at the time when it was issued, in particular if there are serious grounds for believing that the visa was fraudulently obtained', and a visa shall be revoked 'where it becomes evident that the conditions for issuing it are no longer met'.[371] The CJEU has clarified that the obligation to annul a visa applies to the State which issued it, whereas it is only an option for other Member States. However, even if the visas have not been annulled by another Member State, this does not as such preclude a prosecution for smuggling of migrants.[372] Moreover, the grounds for annulling (and presumably revoking) a visa are exhaustive, and do not allow for a visa to be annulled simply because a third country has withdrawn a travel document.[373]

Chapter VI of Title III of the Visa Code concerns issuing a visa at the border.[374] Visas can only be issued at the border in 'exceptional' cases, where the applicant meets the conditions for entry in the Schengen Borders Code, is certain to return to the country of origin or transit, and 'the applicant has not been in a position to apply for a visa in advance and submits, if required, supporting documents substantiating unforeseeable and imperative reasons for entry'.[375] The medical insurance requirement may be waived in certain cases for such visas,[376] but in these circumstances visas can only be issued for a maximum of fifteen days.[377] Where the conditions for entry at the border are not met, or the applicant is part of a category of persons whose application should be subject to prior consultation, an LTV visa can be issued.[378] There are special rules relating to the issue of visas to seafarers at the border.[379] According to the 2014 report, this possibility is rarely used, accounting for about 100,000 visa applications a year (out of thirteen million or so total).

Title IV of the Visa Code concerns the organization and management of visa sections.[380] It includes basic rules on the security and confidentiality at consulates, the resources of consulates, and the conduct of staff.[381] Member States are encouraged to cooperate

---

[367] Arts 34(6) and (7) and 35(7).   [368] Arts 33–4.   [369] Art 33(1).   [370] Art 33(2).
[371] Art 34.
[372] Judgment in *Vo*, n 289 above. On smuggling of migrants, see further I:7.5.3 below.
[373] Case C-575/12 *Air Baltic*, ECLI:EU:C:2014:2155.   [374] Arts 35–6.   [375] Art 35(1).
[376] Art 35(2).   [377] Art 35(3).   [378] Art 35(4) and (5).
[379] Art 36 and Annex IX.   [380] Arts 37–47.
[381] See respectively Arts 37–9. The rules on conduct of staff are identical to those initially set out in Art 6 of the Schengen Borders Code before its amendment in 2013 (see I:3.6.1 above), with the addition of a requirement to treat applicants courteously (Art 39(1)).

via various means, in particular as regards collection of biometric information, in the form either of representation (see further above), co-location, Joint Application Centres, honorary consuls, or, as a last resort, the use of external service providers (ie private companies) to collect biometric information.[382] The Visa Code also sets out detailed rules on the collection of statistics and the provision of information to the general public.[383]

Title V of the Visa Code concerns local consular cooperation.[384] Local consulates and the Commission must consult as to whether there should be harmonized rules on the local level, which would then be drawn up in accordance with a 'comitology' procedure, without any special involvement of the EP.[385] Local consular cooperation must also lead to the drawing up of common information sheets for applicants, the exchange of local information and statistics, and discussion of operational issues.[386] Local reports shall be drawn up, followed by an annual report by the Commission regarding each jurisdiction.[387] Interestingly, Member States not applying the Schengen *acquis*, or third States, may be invited to participate in local consular cooperation.[388]

Lastly, Title VI of the Visa Code sets out final provisions.[389] These concern: the standard special rules applicable to participants in the Olympic Games;[390] the procedures for amending most of the Annexes to the Regulation and for drawing up operational instructions regarding the code;[391] notifications to the Commission by Member States;[392] amendments to the VIS Regulation and the Schengen Borders Code;[393] repeal of prior measures;[394] monitoring and evaluation of the Visa Code;[395] and the entry into force of the Code.[396]

There are thirteen Annexes attached to the Code, concerning in turn:

a) the harmonized visa application form (Annex I);

b) a non-exhaustive list of documents supporting a visa application (Annex II);

c) a uniform format and use of the stamp indicating that an application is inadmissible (Annex III);

d) a list of the countries subject to a common EU ATV requirement (Annex IV);

e) a list of the non-Member State residence permits that, if held, will waive the ATV requirement (Annex V);

f) the standard form for notifying and giving reasons for refusing a visa application (Annex VI);

---

[382] Arts 40–5. For an explanation of the concepts of co-location and Common Application Centres, see Art 41(1) and (2). The 2014 report states that there are no fully-fledged Common Application Centres, only more limited forms of cooperation in two States (Congo and Cape Verde). Only five Member States used honorary consuls. In practice, outsourcing to private companies was very common, rather than a 'last resort'.

[383] Arts 46 and 47. The 2014 report indicates that many visa applicants were disappointed by the quality of information available to the public.

[384] Art 48. On the application of these rules in practice, see COM (2012) 648, 7 Nov 2012.

[385] Art 48(1), referring to Art 52(2).   [386] Art 48(2) to (4).   [387] Art 48(5).

[388] Art 48(6).   [389] Arts 49–58.   [390] Art 49, referring to Annex XI.

[391] Arts 50–2; see the discussion of these processes above. For a list of the Annexes, see below.

[392] Art 53.   [393] Arts 54 and 55.   [394] Art 56.   [395] Art 57.   [396] Art 58.

g) rules on filling in the visa sticker (Annex VII);

h) rules on affixing the visa sticker (Annex VIII);

i) rules on issuing visas to seafarers (Annex IX);

j) a list of minimum requirements to apply to external service providers (Annex X);

k) specific procedures relating to Olympic participants (Annex XI);

l) the requirements relating to annual statistics to be sent to the Commission (Annex XII); and

m) a correlation table comparing the code to the previous measures in force (Annex XIII).

Nine of the Annexes can be amended by the specific comitology process giving fuller powers to the EP (the 'regulatory procedure with scrutiny').[397] The exceptions are Annexes IX, X, XI, and XIII, which can only be amended by the full legislative process, although this point is moot for Annex XIII, since it consists only of a correlation table.

Finally, as noted above, in 2014 the Commission proposed a recast of the Visa Code, including some significant amendments to the existing rules.[398] The main aim of the proposal is to simplify the process of applying for a Schengen visa. So the obligation to appear in person to apply in a consulate would be dropped, except for when the applicant has to be fingerprinted for registration in the VIS database (once every five years). There would be revised rules determining which Member State consulate is responsible for each application, to make sure that each applicant will be able to apply for a visa without having to travel to a consulate in another country. Applicants could apply for a visa up to six months in advance (instead of three months at present).

Checks on whether applicants have accommodation, means of subsistence and an intention to return would be relaxed if they were regular travellers with a 'clean' immigration record (this could be checked in the VIS). Applicants would no longer have to obtain travel medical insurance, and Member States would have to make decisions more quickly. The rules on waiving the €60 visa application fee would become uniform, so that (for instance) there would be no fee for children under eighteen, researchers, or diplomats. Regular travellers with a clean record would have a right to a multiple-entry visa, with a three year validity rising to five years (instead of validity as short as six months, at present). There would also be more possibilities to apply for visas at borders, replacing the 'exceptional' nature of this rule at present.

4.7.3 Other rules governing the issue of visas

As noted already, the Visa Code repealed most EU and Schengen measures concerning visas. By way of exception, several separate measures remain in force. First of all, there were two Schengen Executive Committee Decisions concerning a manual of travel documents,[399] which were replaced by an EU Decision in 2011.[400] Secondly, another

---

[397] Art 50, referring to Art 52(3).   [398] COM (2014) 164, 1 April 2014.
[399] Executive Committee Decisions SCH/Com-ex (98) 56 and SCH/Com-ex (99) 14 ([2000] OJ L 239/207 and 298).
[400] [2011] OJ L 287/9.

Schengen Executive Committee Decision created a 'Schengen Consultation Network'; this Decision (as amended) will only apply until the Visa Information System is fully rolled out (this is scheduled for November 2015).[401] Next, six remaining Executive Committee Decisions relating to visas are still in force, concerning: harmonizing visa policy as regards Indonesia;[402] the principles for issuing Schengen visas as regards representation;[403] the stamping of passports of visa applicants;[404] an Action plan to combat illegal immigration;[405] the coordinated deployment of document advisers;[406] and the acquisition of common entry and exit stamps.[407] It may be questioned how much, if at all, these remnants of the Schengen *acquis* are still relevant in practice.[408] Indeed, the Commission has proposed that five of these six measures should be repealed for obsolescence,[409] and that the sixth and last measure be repealed when the EU entry-exit system is established.[410]

Other Schengen Executive Committee Decisions dealing with visas had previously been repealed by the EC's visa list Regulation in 2001, [411] and by EC legislation on the issue of visas to seamen, and the issue of visas at the border, adopted in 2003.[412]

Several other visa measures adopted by EC after the entry into force of the Treaty of Amsterdam also remain in force. First of all, to assuage Russian concerns about the transit of Russian citizens between the enclave of Kaliningrad, which became surrounded by EU Member States after enlargement of the EU, and the rest of Russia, the EU came to an arrangement with Russia and the Council adopted two special Regulations providing for facilitated transit between Kaliningrad and the rest of Russia.[413] The first

---

[401] Document SCH/II-Vision (99) 5 ('Schengen Consultation Network (Technical Specifications)'), referred to in Executive Committee Decision SCH/Com-ex (94) 15 rev ([2000] OJ L 239/165, as corrected by a later Council Decision ([2000] OJ L 272/24)), which concerns a computerized procedure for consulting the central authorities of other Member States on visa applications. The latter measure was initially confidential, but then was largely declassified by the Council (see Decision, [2003] OJ L 116/22). The Council has power to amend this Decision pursuant to Reg 789/2001 ([2001] OJ L 116/2), and the Visa Code retained the power to amend the Schengen Consultation Network pursuant to this Reg until the Network is fully replaced by the VIS (Arts 56(2)(d) and 58(4) of the code; see the following note). The amending Decisions adopted to date have been published in [2007] L 192/26, [2007] OJ L 340/92, [2008] OJ L 328/38, and [2009] OJ L 353/49.

[402] SCH/Com-ex (95) PV 1 Rev ([2000] OJ L 239/175).

[403] SCH/Com-ex (96) 13 Rev ([2000] OJ L 239/180).

[404] SCH/Com-ex (98) 21 ([2000] OJ L 239/200).

[405] SCH/Com-ex (98) 37 def 2 ([2000] OJ L 239/203).

[406] SCH/Com-ex (98) 59 Rev ([2000] OJ L 239/308).

[407] SCH/Com-ex (94) 16 Rev ([2000] OJ L 239/166).

[408] For instance, the issue of stamping the travel documents of visa applicants is addressed in detail in Art 20 and Annex III of the Visa Code—which conflicts in part with the Executive Committee Decision on this issue. Moreover, stamping the travel documents of visa applicants is a 'low-tech' method of preventing applicants from making multiple applications for Schengen visas from different Member States' consulates, and it is due to be phased out anyway when the VIS is fully operational (see Art 20(3), Visa Code). As for the Decision on representation, it is not clear how it relates to Art 8 of the Visa Code. On the other hand, the Decision on common entry and exit stamps is still referred to in Annex IV of the Schengen Borders Code (Reg 562/2006, [2006] OJ L 105/1).

[409] COM (2014) 713, 28 Nov 2014. The exception is the Decision on the acquisition of common entry and exit stamps (SCH/Com-ex (94) 16 Rev).

[410] COM (2013) 96, 28 Feb 2013: Art 2 would repeal the Decision on the acquisition of common entry and exit stamps (SCH/Com-ex (94) 16 Rev). On the entry-exit system, see further I:3.6 above.

[411] See I:4.5 above.   [412] That Reg was subsequently itself repealed by the Visa Code.

[413] Regs 693/2003 and 694/2003 ([2003] OJ L 99/8 and 15). See previously: COM (2001) 26, 18 Jan 2001; SEC (2002) 49, 15 Jan 2002; and COM (2002) 510, 18 Sept 2002.

Regulation provides for a special facilitated transit procedure, subject to fewer conditions and a lower fee than those applicable to Schengen visa applications, while the second Regulation provides for a standard format for the facilitated transit documents. Secondly, the EC adopted two Regulations governing the issue of visas to the 'Olympic family': firstly, for the summer 2004 Olympics, held in Greece, and secondly, for the Winter 2006 Olympics, held in Turin.[414] These Regulations exempted athletes, coaches, and others closely related to the running of the Olympics from any requirements for a visa, except for the requirement to hold travel documents and checks in national and EU databases, and waived the fee for visa applications entirely. This special legislation has now lapsed, but it has not been formally repealed. As noted above, there are now standard rules on this issue inserted into an Annex to the Visa Code in the event that the Olympics are held again in future in the Schengen zone.

Next, the EP and Council adopted a Recommendation on the issue of short-term visas to researchers in 2005, as one part of a three-part package designed to encourage third-country national researchers to visit or reside in the European Union.[415] According to the Recommendation, the Member States should: expedite the examination of visa applications from third countries subject to a visa obligation; promote international mobility by issuing multiple entry visas, taking account of the duration of the research programmes when determining the period of the visa's validity; attempt to harmonize their approach to supporting evidence regarding researchers' visa applications; encourage the issue of visas without fees to researchers, in accordance with the *acquis*; exchange best practice on the issue of visas to researchers within the framework of local consular cooperation; and inform the Commission by September 2006 about the best practices developed, to enable the Commission to evaluate the progress made. Depending on the evaluation, the EU should examine the possibility of making the Recommendation legally binding.[416]

The most significant 'sundry' EU measure on visa conditions would be the proposed Regulation on a touring visa, if adopted.[417] This legislation, if agreed, might ultimately be merged with the Visa Code, depending on the progress of negotiations. The starting point of the proposal is a replacement of various bilateral deals which a number of Member States have with third states such as the USA or New Zealand, allowing the nationals of those third States to add together a series of short stays in individual Schengen States. But this only applies to a fairly limited number of third countries. The Commission proposal would simplify this system, replacing it with a common Schengen-wide approach. It estimates that while only about 120,000 people would benefit from this proposal, they are relatively 'big spenders', and so the net benefit to the EU economy would be €1 billion.

A touring visa could be issued for up to one year, with a possible further extension to two years. It would also apply to the citizens of countries like the USA who did not

---

[414] See respectively Regs 1295/2003 ([2003] OJ L 183/1) and 2046/2005 ([2005] OJ L 334/1). The two Regs are essentially identical.

[415] [2005] OJ L 289/23. On the two other measures, see I:6.5.3.1 below.

[416] In practice, the Commission has not yet released any evaluation of the Recommendation.

[417] COM (2014) 163, 1 April 2014. The remaining footnotes in this section refer to this proposal.

normally need short-term visas, since their planned total stay in the Schengen area with a touring visa would exceed the normal limit which would usually apply (90 days in a 180-day period). The EU's Visa Information System database would apply, except that non-visa nationals like Americans would not have to give fingerprints. Also, the normal Visa Code rules (as amended by the separate proposals) would apply, with derogations. For instance, there would be no applications at borders; the first Member State the touring visa applicant would enter would be competent for the whole application; and sickness insurance would be required. There would be consequential amendments to the Schengen Borders Code, the Schengen Convention, and the VIS Regulation.[418] It remains to be seen if the Council and European Parliament agree to this proposal, especially given Member States' previous refusals to alter the terms of their bilateral agreements with third States in this area.[419]

4.7.4 Analysis

Before the adoption of the Visa Code, the EU rules on the conditions for issuing visas were vague, complex, and highly discretionary, and failed to ensure a sufficient level of procedural rights in the event of refusal.[420] However, the Visa Code clearly improved the position as regards procedural rights, and also contains *useful* provisions on inadmissible applications, which ensure that rejections of applications not based on the merits of the application are listed separately in the VIS and so should not be used against applicants when they make subsequent applications. The provisions on multiple-entry visas and the further provisions for reduction or waiver of visa fees (although limited) provide for further useful facilitation of the issue of visas, although as we have seen there are restraints on the use of these provisions in practice. The abolition of the secrecy relating to the rules on consultations was long overdue, and overall the code significantly simplified the legislative framework as compared to the prior rules, which can only be welcomed from the point of view of clarity, transparency, and legal certainty.

However, given that many applicants still face unnecessary practical difficulties in accessing the Schengen visa system, the Commission's proposals have much to recommend them. They would ease the hassle that many would-be visitors face when they apply to come to the EU: cutting the costs for families and researchers, ensuring that an application could be made more easily, and streamlining the process considerably for frequent visitors who have shown that they can be trusted.

The proposals would benefit the EU economy, too, if the Commission's estimates are correct. On top of the estimated €1 billion boost to the economy from the touring visa proposal, the accompanying Commission communication on visa policy suggests that the economic boost from the changes to the main Visa Code may be between €4 to €12

---

[418] Arts 12–14. See respectively I:3.6 above, I:4.9 below and I:4.8 below.
[419] See the discussion in I:4.9 below.
[420] See criticisms in R Cholewinski, *Borders and Discrimination in the European Union* (ILPA/MPG, 2002), 20–37 and P Boeles, 'Schengen and the Rule of Law' in H Meijers, et al., *Schengen: Internationalisation of Central Chapters of the Law on Aliens, Refugees, Privacy, Security and the Police*, 2nd edn (Stichting NJCM-Boekerij, 1992).

billion, with 80,000 jobs created.[421] It remains to be seen to what extent the Council and EP agree with the proposal.

4.8 Visa Information System

4.8.1 Legal framework

The Visa Information System (VIS), which began collecting extensive personal data on all applicants for Schengen visas as from 2011, was originally conceived as a reaction to the 2001 terrorist attacks on the United States. It was established by two measures. The first measure, adopted in 2004,[422] was a Council Decision which established the system in principle and authorized the Commission to manage the development of the VIS project, including the adoption of implementing measures,[423] with funding from the EU budget. But it was also necessary to adopt a second, more detailed, measure which sets out the precise functioning of the system. To that end, the second measure, Regulation 767/2008 (the 'VIS Regulation') was adopted in June 2008.[424]

The VIS was rolled out region by region, starting from October 2011. It was extended to a first set of regions (in North Africa and the Middle East) in 2011–12,[425] then to a second set of regions (the rest of Africa, South America, parts of Asia) in 2013.[426] Finally, it was extended to a third and final set of regions, and was fully rolled out by November 2015.[427]

---

[421] COM (2014) 165, 1 April 2014, on 'A Smarter Visa Policy for Economic Growth'. See also the prior communication on 'Implementation and Development of the Common Visa Policy to Spur Growth' (COM (2012) 649, 7 Nov 2012).

[422] [2004] OJ L 213/5.

[423] The Commission has adopted several implementing measures pursuant to the powers conferred by this Decision: see [2006] OJ L 267/41 (laying down technical specifications for standards for biometric features), [2006] OJ L 305/13 (establishing VIS sites during the development phase), and [2008] OJ L 194/3 (on interfaces with national systems).

[424] [2008] L 218/60. The Commission has adopted a number of measures implementing the VIS Reg. Apart from Decisions on rolling out VIS (see below), these concern: the consultation mechanism in the VIS (see below; Decision in [2009] OJ L 117/30); the specifications for the use of fingerprints in the VIS ([2009] OJ L 270/14); data processing ([2009] OJ L 315/30); the regional roll-out of the VIS ([2010] OJ L 23/62); security ([2010] OJ L 112/25); and data processing ([2010] OJ L 315/30).

[425] A Commission decision ([2010] OJ L 23/52) established the first set of three regions where the VIS would be applied, respectively North Africa, the Near East (except Palestine), and the Gulf. The VIS began operations in the first region (North Africa) on 11 Oct 2011 (Commission decision in [2011] OJ L 249/18), the second region on 10 May 2012 ([2012] OJ L 117/9) and the third region on 2 Oct 2012 ([2012] OJ L 256/21).

[426] Commission Decision on a second set of eight more regions where the VIS would be applied ([2012] OJ L 134/20), more precisely West Africa, Central Africa, East Africa, Southern Africa, South America, Central Asia, South East Asia, and Palestine. The VIS began operations in the fourth and fifth regions (West and Central Africa) on 14 March 2013 ([2013] OJ L 65/35); in the sixth and seventh regions (East and South Africa) on 6 June 2013 ([2013] OJ L 154/8); in the eighth region (South America) on 5 Sep 2013 ([2013] OJ L 223/15); and in the ninth to eleventh regions (Central Asia, South East Asia, Palestine) from 14 Nov 2013 ([2013] OJ L 299/52).

[427] Commission Decision on a third set of eleven more regions where the VIS would be applied ([2013] OJ L 268/13). The VIS began operations in the twelfth to fifteenth regions (Central America, North America, the Caribbean, and Pacific Islands) on 15 May 2014 ([2014] OJ L 136/51) and in the sixteenth region (Western Balkans and Turkey) on 25 Sep 2014 ([2014] OJ L 258/8). It was rolled out to: the seventeenth and eighteenth regions (Russia and Eastern Partnership countries) on 14 Sep 2015 ([2015] OJ L 116/20); the nineteenth region (East Asia, including China and Japan) on 12 Oct 2015 ([2015] OJ L 135/20);

As for the application of the Visa Information System in practice, the Commission released annual reports on the development and operation of the VIS from 2005 to 2013.[428] According to the 2011 report, many Schengen States were already using the VIS unilaterally in some parts of the world, even before the VIS was 'rolled out' to the consulates in the third States concerned for all Schengen states.[429] In the initial three months of operations of the VIS in the first region (North Africa), 468 cases of visa shopping had been detected. According to the 2012 report, as of 22 November 2012, the VIS had processed nearly 2 million visa applications, and the central system had dealt with almost 40 million operations received from consulates around the world and border crossing points. During the final three months of the reporting period in 2012, nearly 5,000 Schengen visas a day were being issued following the use of the VIS.

Later information on the operation of VIS in practice is available via the Commission's bi-annual reports on the Schengen system.[430] According to the May 2013 report, by 6 May 2013, the VIS had processed 2.9 million visa applications, with 2.4 million visas issued and 348,000 visa applications refused. There was still some concern about 'the mid to long-term effect of a non-optimal quality of data (both biometric and alpha-numeric) introduced by the consular authorities of Member States into the VIS.'[431] The November 2013 report stated that by 31 October 2013 the VIS had processed 5 million Schengen visa applications, with 4.2 million visas issued, but the concerns about data quality remained.[432] Those concerns were explained further in the May 2014 report, which stated that some VIS entries were incomplete (eg different visa applications for the same person or for family members travelling together were not linked) or were not filled in properly, and some fingerprints were of insufficient quality. This could lead to unreliable information when deciding on applications and complicate the prior con-sultation process.[433] By the end of July 2014, the VIS had processed (since its entry into operation) almost 9 million Schengen visa applications, with 7.5 million visas issued.[434]

It should be noted that the VIS does not apply to applicants for long-stay visas, but does apply to third-country national family members of EU citizens who apply for visas.[435] It will also apply to persons who apply for a touring visa, if the proposed Regulation on that topic is adopted.[436]

The VIS has also been the subject of a number of other EU and EC measures. First of all, at the same time as adopting the VIS Regulation, the Council also adopted a

---

the twentieth region (South Asia, including India) on 2 Nov 2015 ([2015] OJ L 148/30); and the final three regions (EU and Schengen States, along with European micro-States) from 20 Nov 2015 ([2015] OJ L 148/29). The VIS has been used at external borders since 31 Oct 2011. See also the list of authorities with access to the VIS ([2012] OJ C 79/5, updated in [2014] OJ C 106/4).

[428] SEC (2005) 439, 4 Mar 2005; SEC (2006) 610, 10 May 2006; SEC (2007) 833, 13 Jun 2007; COM (2008) 714, 10 Nov 2008; COM (2009) 473, 15 Sep 2009; COM (2010) 588, 22 Oct 2010; COM (2011) 346, 15 Jun 2011; COM (2012) 376, 11 July 2012 (the '2011 report'), and COM (2013) 232, 25 April 2013 (the '2012 report'). The two most recent reports detail developments since the VIS began operations.

[429] This is permitted: see Art 48(3), VIS Regulation.

[430] On the role of these reports in 'Schengen governance', see I:3.10.3 above.

[431] COM (2013) 326, 31 May 2013.   [432] COM (2013) 832, 28 Nov 2013.

[433] COM (2014) 292, 26 May 2014.

[434] Nov 2014 report on Schengen system (COM (2014) 711, 27 Nov 2014). See later the May 2015 report (COM (2015) 236, 29 May 2015).

[435] See the discussion in I:4.4.1 above.   [436] COM (2014) 163, 1 April 2014. See I:4.7.2 above.

third-pillar measure giving police access to the VIS (the 'third-pillar VIS Decision').[437] As noted above, the UK's challenge to the validity of this measure was unsuccessful.[438] This access was put into effect from 1 September 2013,[439] although the relevant decision was then annulled on procedural grounds.[440] The Council also subsequently adopted measures amending the visa format rules, the CCI, and the Schengen Borders Code in order to ensure consistency with the VIS.[441] Furthermore, the VIS Regulation itself has already been amended by the Regulation establishing the Visa Code, again in order to ensure consistency between the two measures.[442] In 2013, it was amended a second time, to clarify the rules on the period of validity of visas.[443] The proposed touring visa Regulation would amend the VIS Regulation a third time.[444] Interestingly, the very existence of the VIS has influenced the 2014 proposal to amend the Visa Code, which would streamline applications from those who have a 'clean' record in the VIS.[445] Finally, the VIS is managed by the 'EU-LISA' agency, which also manages the second-generation Schengen Information System (SIS II) and Eurodac.[446]

The VIS Regulation established that the VIS became operational following a decision adopted by the Commission, after the Commission had adopted all of the necessary implementing measures and tested the system successfully (along with Member States), and the Member States had notified the Commission that they were ready to transmit the necessary data from the first region in which the VIS became applicable.[447] This region was decided by the Commission by means of a comitology process, subject to the criteria of the risk of illegal immigration, threats to internal security, and the feasibility of collecting biometrics.[448] The roll-out to subsequent regions was decided by the same process and the same criteria, subject to the possibility of individual Member States applying the VIS to those further regions in advance, if they were capable of transmitting 'at least' the alphanumeric data and photograph data (so not necessarily the fingerprint data) connected to applications.[449]

Chapter I of the VIS Regulation sets out its general provisions.[450] These comprise a brief description of the subject-matter and scope of the VIS Regulation,[451] as well as a longer description of its purpose.[452] The VIS 'has the purpose of improving the implementation of the common visa policy, consular cooperation and consultation

---

[437] [2008] OJ L 218/129. This measure is discussed in more detail in II:7.6.1.3.

[438] Case C-482/08 *UK v Council* [2010] ECR I-10413. See also Art 3 of the VIS Regulation. On the broader issue of UK participation in visa measures, see I:4.2.5 above.

[439] Council Decision [2013] OJ L 198/45. For the list of agencies with access, see [2013] OJ C 236.

[440] Case C-540/13 *EP v Council*, ECLI:EU:C:2015:224. See discussion in II:2.2.3.3. The Council has adopted a replacement Decision: [2015] OJ L 284/146.

[441] See respectively Regs 856/2008 ([2008] OJ L 235/1), 390/2009 ([2009] OJ L 131/1), and 81/2009 ([2009] OJ L 35/56). Reg 390/2009 has since been subsumed into the Visa Code (Reg 810/2009 ([2009] OJ L 243/1).

[442] Art 54 of the Visa Code (ibid). The amended VIS Reg has not been codified. All references in this section are to the VIS Reg as thereby amended, unless otherwise indicated.

[443] Reg 610/2013 ([2013] OJ L 182/1), amending Art 12(2)(a).

[444] Art 14 of the proposal (COM (2014) 163, 1 April 2014).   [445] For details, see I:4.5 above.

[446] Reg 1077/2011 ([2011] OJ L 286/1). See II:7.6.1.

[447] Arts 51(2) and 48(1). On the details of the roll-out decisions, see above.

[448] Art 48(4).   [449] Art 48(3). As noted above, several Member States invoked this option.

[450] Arts 1–7.   [451] Art 1.   [452] Art 2.

between' Member States' visa authorities by facilitating the exchange of data in order to achieve seven purposes: to facilitate the application procedure; to avoid bypassing the rules concerning the responsible Member State for considering the application;[453] to facilitate the fight against fraud; to facilitate checks at external borders and within the territory; to assist in identifying irregular migrants; to facilitate application of the 'Dublin' rules on responsibility for asylum applications;[454] and to contribute to preventing 'threats to internal security' of any Member States.

Next, the VIS Regulation contains a 'bridging' clause linking it to the parallel third pillar VIS Decision, giving the police authorities access to VIS data.[455] Those authorities can access VIS data in individual cases following a specific request 'if there are reasonable grounds to consider that access to VIS data will substantially contribute to the prevention, detection or investigation of terrorist offences and of other serious criminal offences'. Europol, the EU's police agency, may also access VIS data 'within the limits of its mandate and when necessary for the performance of its tasks'.[456] Access by police authorities can only be obtained through central access points, which will check first whether the criteria for access are satisfied,[457] and VIS data accessed by this procedure cannot be made available to third countries or international organizations, other than in 'an exceptional case of urgency' as provided for in the third pillar VIS Decision.[458] The VIS Regulation is also 'without prejudice' to the obligation under national law for visa authorities to inform national police or prosecution authorities about suspected criminal offences.[459]

The VIS applies to the various forms of short-stay visas as defined in the Visa Code, but not to long-stay visas of any sort.[460] The only data which can be recorded in the VIS are:[461] alphanumeric data (eg letters and numbers) on the applicant and on visas requested, issued, refused, annulled, revoked, or extended;[462] photographs; fingerprints; and links to other visa applications by the applicant or persons who will be travelling with the applicant.[463] Only visa authorities can enter, delete, or amend data,[464] but other authorities (as well as visa authorities) can access the data for the purposes provided for in the VIS Regulation (see below).[465] A list of all authorities with powers to alter or access data must be published and regularly updated.[466] Member States must ensure that use of the VIS is 'necessary, appropriate and proportionate',[467] that there is no discrimination when using the VIS on grounds of 'sex, racial or ethnic origin, religion or belief, disability, age or sexual orientation', and that VIS use 'fully respects the human dignity and the integrity' of the applicant or visa holder.[468]

---

[453] For those rules, see Art 8 of the Visa Code Reg.   [454] On these rules, see I:5.8 below.
[455] Art 3; for the Decision, see n 437 above.   [456] Art 3(1). On Europol, see II:7.8 below.
[457] Art 3(2). In 'an exceptional case of urgency' the access can take place without a prior check.
[458] Art 3(3); on the position where VIS data is accessed by other authorities, see below.
[459] Art 3(4).
[460] Art 4(1), VIS Reg, as amended by Art 54(1) of the Visa Code. As noted above, however, the VIS may apply to 'touring visas' in future.
[461] Art 5(1).   [462] See the definition of 'alphanumeric data' in Art 4(11).
[463] See Art 8(3) and 8(4), which refer to group applications and applications by the applicant's spouse and children. A 'group' application is defined in Art 4(6) as a group of persons who are required for legal reasons to travel together.
[464] Art 6(1).   [465] Art 6(2).   [466] Art 6(3).   [467] Art 7(1).
[468] Art 7(2). The list of prohibited grounds for discrimination matches the list in Art 19 TFEU.

Chapter II of the VIS Regulation sets out rules on use of the VIS by visa authorities.[469] A national visa authority must create a file in the VIS without delay following an admissible visa application.[470] The authority has to check whether that applicant has made a previous visa application which is registered in the VIS,[471] and if so, to link the new application with the previous application(s).[472] Applications must also be linked to parallel applications by family members and members of a group.[473]

The following six Articles of the VIS Regulation then set out the data that must be entered in different circumstances: when a visa application is first lodged; if a visa is issued; if a visa application is discontinued; if a visa application is refused; if a visa is annulled or revoked, or has its validity shortened; or if a visa is extended.[474] For example, when a visa application is first lodged,[475] the data entered must comprise: the application number; the status information (the fact that a visa has been requested); the authority with which the application was lodged; thirteen items of data from the application form (concerning name, nationality,[476] travel document information, date of the application, information on the sponsor,[477] Member State(s) of destination and the duration of the intended stay or transit, the main purpose(s) of the journey, date of arrival and departure in the Schengen area, the Member State of first entry, applicant's home address, occupation and employer or educational establishment, and the names of minors' parents (with parental responsibility) or legal guardian; photographs; and fingerprints.[478]

Where a visa is refused, the authority concerned must enter data as to the reasons why, which match the grounds for refusal of a visa application set out in the Visa Code.[479] There is no provision for entering data into the VIS when a person overstays a visa or otherwise breaches immigration rules (eg by taking up employment without authorization). Instead, the Commission was invited to make proposals on this issue after the adoption of the Visa Code,[480] although it has not yet done so. However, this issue is linked to the proposed 'entry-exit' system for the EU, which would generate information automatically (assuming it works as planned) on any visa holder's failure to leave the territory of the Member States on time.[481] There is no ban on processing of 'sensitive' categories of personal data.[482]

---

[469] Arts 8–17.   [470] Art 8(1), as amended by Art 54(2) of the Visa Code.

[471] Art 8(2). Obviously visa applications made before the VIS became operational were not registered in the VIS.

[472] Art 8(3).   [473] Art 8(4).   [474] Respectively Arts 9–14.

[475] Art 9, as amended by Art 54(3) of the Visa Code.

[476] This includes both current nationality and nationality at birth.

[477] This is restricted to the name and address of natural persons, and to the name and address of legal persons, plus the name of a contact person at the legal person.

[478] The process of taking the fingerprints is set out in the Visa Code (see I:4.7 above). An implementing Decision sets out technical requirements for taking fingerprints (n 425 above).

[479] Art 12(2), as amended by Art 54(6)(b) of the Visa Code (for more on these grounds, see I:4.7 above). See also Art 13(2), as amended by Art 54(7) of the Visa Code, which requires the grounds for annulling or revoking a visa to be entered in the VIS.

[480] Joint Statement in the summary of Council acts for June 2008 (Council doc 12750/2/08, 13 Mar 2009). The Commission was also invited to make proposals three years after the VIS began operations (so by autumn 2014) on the issue of misuse by persons issuing invitations.

[481] See I:3.6.2 above.

[482] Compare with Art 40, SIS II Regulation, referring to Art 8(1) of the data protection Directive (Reg 1987/2006, [2006] OJ L 381/4).

As for the use of the VIS by visa authorities after information is entered, the VIS must be used when examining visa applications, including when taking decisions on whether to annul, revoke, or extend the validity of a visa.[483] Access to the VIS for this purpose must initially concern only specified data;[484] in the event of a 'hit', then the entire file of the applicant and all linked files can be examined for the purpose of deciding on the visa application.[485] The VIS shall also be used by visa authorities when applying the 'consultation' procedure discussed above,[486] and may also be used to transmit information and messages related to consular cooperation, to send requests for documents relating to visa applications, and to transmit such documents.[487] Finally, visa authorities can consult specified data in the VIS for the purposes of reporting and statistics, without identifying individual applicants.[488]

Chapter III of the VIS Regulation sets out rules on use of the VIS by other authorities, in five circumstances.[489] First of all, the VIS can be used by external border authorities, using the visa sticker number and fingerprints, for the purposes of checking the authenticity of the visa, verifying the identity of the visa holder (a 'one-to-one' search),[490] and confirming that the conditions for entry are satisfied.[491] However, fingerprints could not be used for these purposes for a three-year period after the VIS began operations; this meant that fingerprints have been checked at external borders since autumn 2014.[492] As noted above, a separate Regulation amending the Schengen Borders Code sets out more detail of how the VIS is used at external borders.[493]

Second, immigration authorities may have access to VIS data *within* the territory of a Member State, in order to verify the identity of a person, to check the authenticity of the visa, or to confirm that the conditions for entry are satisfied, either by using the visa sticker number in combination with fingerprints, or by using the visa sticker number alone.[494] Third, in order to *identify* a person (a 'one-to-many' search) who may be an irregular migrant, national immigration authorities or border guards may search the VIS using fingerprints.[495]

Fourth, in order to apply the rules on responsibility for asylum applications, a national asylum authority can search the VIS using fingerprint data.[496] Finally, national asylum authorities can search the VIS using fingerprint data in order to assist them with examining the merits of an asylum application.[497]

In each of these cases, in the event of a 'hit', the relevant national authorities are given access to more data from the VIS, for the specific purposes referred to in each case.[498]

---

[483] Art 15(1), as amended by Art 54(9) of the Visa Code.   [484] Art 15(2).   [485] Art 15(3).
[486] See I:4.7 above, and the relevant implementing decision, n 424 above.   [487] Art 16.
[488] Art 17, as amended by Art 54(1) of the Visa Code.   [489] Arts 18–22.
[490] On the definition of 'verification', see Art 4(9).   [491] Art 18(1).   [492] Art 18(2).
[493] Reg 81/2009, n 441 above. For details, see I:3.6.1 above.   [494] Art 19.
[495] Art 20. On the definition of 'identification', see Art 4(10). This Article also applies if an attempt to verify identity at the borders or on the territory by means of a one-to-one search has failed, or if there are otherwise doubts about, inter alia, the identity of the person concerned: see Arts 18(5) and 19(3).
[496] Art 21.   [497] Art 22.
[498] Arts 18(4), 19(2), 20(2), 21(2), and 22(2). In the event of a search regarding responsibility for asylum applications, further data can only be accessed if additional conditions are met, corresponding to the criteria for responsibility under the Dublin rules: see Art 21(2).

Chapter IV of the Regulation sets out rules on retention and amendment of VIS data.[499] Each file must be kept for a period of five years from a specified date, for example the expiry date of a visa, if one has been issued.[500] After that point, the file is deleted automatically. Only the Member State responsible for entering the data may delete or alter it, although another Member State may bring apparent errors to the attention of the responsible Member State.[501] Data shall be deleted in advance if a person gains the nationality of a Member State, or (as regards data on refusal of a visa) if the refusal is overturned.[502]

Chapter V of the Regulation sets out rules on the operation of the VIS and responsibilities for operation and use of the system.[503] In particular, as noted above, the VIS (like SIS II and Eurodac) is managed by a management authority (an EU agency),[504] after a transitional period in which it was managed by the Commission, which delegated its powers to Member States.[505] Those Member States were France and Austria, in light of the decision to locate the central VIS in France with a back-up system in Austria.[506]

Next, the VIS Regulation describes the relationship between the central VIS and the national systems,[507] and allocates responsibility as between the management authority and the national authorities.[508] It should be emphasized that the Member States, not the management authority, have the key responsibility of ensuring that data is collected, processed, and transmitted lawfully, and that the data are accurate and up-to-date when transmitted; the management authority is responsible for ensuring data security at its end as well as control of its staff.

VIS data can be kept in national files if necessary in specific cases, or where the data was entered by that Member State.[509] In principle, data from the VIS cannot be transferred to third countries or international organizations,[510] but 'by way of derogation',[511] certain data can be transferred to third countries or international organizations listed in the Annex to the Regulation,[512] 'if necessary in individual cases for the purpose of proving the identity of third-country nationals, including for the purpose of return', 'only' where a list of four conditions is fulfilled. First of all, one of the following three situations must exist: the Commission has decided on the adequacy of personal data protection in the relevant third state, in accordance with the data protection Directive;[513] or an EU readmission agreement is in place;[514] or the transfer of data 'is necessary or legally required on important public interest grounds, or for the establishment, exercise of defence of legal claims', again in accordance with the data protection Directive.[515] Secondly, the third country or international organization must have

---

[499] Arts 23–5.   [500] Art 23.   [501] Art 24.   [502] Art 25.
[503] Arts 26–36. Many of these rules are similar to those in the SIS II Reg (see I:3.7 above).
[504] On the agency concerned (EU-Lisa), see II:7.6.1.   [505] Art 26.
[506] Art 27; see the relevant implementing Decision ([2006] OJ L 305/13).   [507] Art 28.
[508] Art 29.   [509] Art 30.
[510] Art 31(1). The status of non-Schengen EU Member States is not clear.   [511] Art 31(2).
[512] These are UN organizations (such as the UNHCR), the International Organization for Migration, and the International Committee of the Red Cross.
[513] On data protection adequacy decisions, see generally II:7.3.2.
[514] For the list of states which have a readmission agreement with the EU, see I:7.9.1 below.
[515] Art 26(1)(d) of the data protection Dir ([1995] OJ L 281/31).

agreed only to use the data for the purpose for which they were transmitted. Thirdly, the data must have been transferred in accordance with the relevant provisions of EU and national law.[516] Finally, the Member State which entered the data in the VIS must have given its consent.

The VIS Regulation also provides that such transfers of data 'shall not prejudice the rights of refugees and persons requesting international protection, in particular as regards non-refoulement',[517] but it is not clear in concrete terms how this principle is observed in practice when data is transferred. It should be noted that only certain specific categories of alpha-numeric data can be transferred—not photographs, fingerprints, or any other category of alpha-numeric data.[518] Chapter V also contains rules on data security, liability for breach of the Regulation, the keeping of records, self-monitoring, and penalties for the misuse of data.[519]

Chapter VI of the Regulation sets out data protection rights and rules on data protection supervision of the VIS.[520] Applicants and sponsors have the right to information about the processing of their data.[521] They also have the right of access, correction, and deletion of their data;[522] Member States must cooperate as regards the enforcement of these rights.[523] There is a right of action before national courts to enforce the rights of access, correction, and deletion.[524] As for the collective enforcement of rights, the Regulation contains rules on supervision of national authorities by national supervisory bodies,[525] on supervision of the Management Authority by the European Data Protection Supervisor (EDPS),[526] on cooperation between national supervisory bodies and the EDPS,[527] and on data protection during the transitional period.[528]

Lastly, Chapter VII of the Regulation sets out final provisions, which concern: implementing powers for the Commission; the integration of the 'Schengen Consultation Network' into the VIS; notification of readiness to transmit data; the start of operations of the VIS (summarized above); the comitology process; rules on monitoring and evaluation; and the entry into force of the Regulation.[529]

4.8.2 Analysis

Now that it is fully rolled out, the VIS is perhaps the largest biometric database in the world. The VIS is problematic in several respects, to be considered in turn. But its existence will be even more problematic if it does not work accurately or if there is any human error in its application.

First of all,[530] the application of the VIS to the third-country national family members of EU citizens is objectionable in principle, for the reasons set out above.[531] The

---

[516] Art 26(1) of the data protection Dir gives Member States an option not to apply (inter alia) Art 26(1)(d) of the Dir if provided for by 'domestic law governing particular cases'.
[517] Art 31(3).
[518] The *chapeau* of Art 31(2) refers only to the data in Arts 9(4)(a), (b), (c), (k), and (m).
[519] Arts 32–6 respectively.   [520] Arts 37–44.   [521] Art 37.   [522] Art 38.
[523] Art 39.   [524] Art 40.   [525] Art 41.   [526] Art 42.   [527] Art 43.
[528] Art 44.   [529] Respectively Arts 45–51.
[530] See also the comments on police access to VIS, in II:7.6.1.3.   [531] See I:4.3.1 above.

absence of a sponsors' database and provisions on the 'misuse' of visas are welcome, given that there was no impact assessment which would have demonstrated the need and properly examined the practical implications of entering such data into the VIS.[532]

Next, the idea that VIS information might be used to determine the merits of asylum applications is highly questionable. A record of refused visa applications, even on prima facie serious grounds like the use of a forged passport, could arguably show that a person is intent on entering and staying in the EU in order to work without authorization—but it could equally arguably prove the genuineness of that person's desperation to flee persecution.[533] The risk is that an asylum authority that sees such a record in the VIS will assume the former, not the latter, and that procedural standards could be curtailed as a result, leaving it difficult for an asylum seeker to rebut the authority's conclusion effectively.

As compared to SIS II,[534] the VIS Regulation is certainly much clearer as regards the grounds for including data in the system, and as regards who can access the data for which purpose. There are also better provisions in the VIS Regulation as regards the right of information. But the SIS II Regulation has a provision regarding an information campaign for the public, and better provisions regarding the publication of annual statistics, the notification of inaccurate data in the system and remedies (as the SIS II rules apply also to compensation and the right to obtain information, and contain a mutual recognition obligation and a review clause). In fact, it is the VIS Regulation rules on remedies that need to be reviewed, not the SIS II rules.

On other points, it is unfortunate that data subjects are not informed when one Member State informs another that data in the VIS appears to be inaccurate. The rule that data on a visa refusal must be removed if that visa refusal is overturned is very welcome.

As for external transfers of VIS data, one of the conditions allows transfers on grounds of the general public interest; this could obviously be interpreted broadly by Member States. It is unfortunate that there is no general requirement of adequate data standards applicable to all external transfers of VIS data. And, as noted above, how exactly will the provision on non-refoulement work on this context? The one undeniably useful limit on the external transfer of VIS data in the Regulation is that only certain categories of data are covered.

Next, as regards data protection issues, the penalties clause in the Regulation could be better. It should also have applied to data security and to breaches of all data protection rules, and there should have been criminal penalties not only for serious infringements but also perhaps for serious stupidity—such as posting CD-Roms containing the VIS database or drunkenly leaving a computer containing a copy of the VIS on a train.[535] The data security rules in the VIS Regulation are good but can only work fully if we assume that the humans who use the VIS will be infallible. The rules on collective

---

[532] See the subsequent developments regarding an entry-exit system (I:3.6.2 above).

[533] Cf. the recognition in Art 31 of the Geneva Convention on refugee status that unauthorized or clandestine means of entry and stay might be necessary for genuine refugees. See further I:7.3 below. On asylum procedures generally, see I:5.7 below.

[534] See I:3.7.2 above.

[535] Both these examples are taken from the practice of the British civil service.

enforcement of the data protection rules are also good on paper, but in practice the resources of supervisory authorities are a crucial issue.

The monitoring provisions of the VIS Regulation have useful provisions as regards reviews on external transfers and the use of fingerprints, as well as data security. But it is unfortunate that there is no obligation to publish annual statistics or to review to what extent the VIS is being used lawfully.

In the absence of a full review of the VIS Regulation, it is not yet clear if, as planned, it is practically useful in identifying (or deterring) a significant number of persons who make multiple or fraudulent visa applications or who present a fraudulent visa at an external border. But if it is achieving these aims, it might have consequentially led to a greater use of irregular methods of entry across the external borders. Conversely the greater ease of identifying persons making fraudulent applications could likely lead in practice to facilitation of the visa applications of *bona fide* travellers, since author-ities will have available a full record of the 'clean sheets' maintained by such travellers. Indeed, the 2014 proposal to amend the Visa Code will entrench such a rule as a core feature of the Schengen visa system. The more problematic use of the VIS will be for the 'in-between' cases—where applications were refused on more questionable (or non-existent) grounds, or where circumstances have changed (ie an applicant was unem-ployed before, but now has a job), but the record of prior refusal or revocation in the VIS is used to justify subsequent refusals of applications indefinitely.

4.9 Freedom to Travel

The core rules on freedom to travel within the Schengen area for non-EU citizens were initially set out in Articles 19-24 of the Schengen Convention (Chapter IV of Title II of the Convention), which were integrated into the Community legal order (as it was then) by the Treaty of Amsterdam,[536] along with several related Decisions of the Schengen Executive Committee. These Decisions concerned: renegotiation of the treaties referred to in Article 20(2) of the Convention (see below);[537] principles and means of proof for readmission between Member States;[538] cooperation regarding returning third-country nationals by air;[539] measures to be taken regarding countries refusing readmission;[540] and treating residence permits issued by Monaco as if they were French residence permits.[541] There was also a declaration made by Portugal, when it acceded to the Schengen Convention, relating to the readmission of Brazilians.[542]

---

[536] The Council allocated all of these provisions to a legal base in the EC Treaty, except for Art 19(2), a clause concerning the transitional period before introduction of the Schengen visa, which had become redundant. See Decision 1999/435 ([1999] OJ L 176/1). It allocated the rest of Arts 19–22 and 23(1) of the Convention to Art 62(3) EC, the legal base concerning freedom to travel, but it gave Arts 23(2) to (5) and 24 of the Convention the 'dual' legal base of Arts 62(3) and 63(3) EC (immigration policy), presumably because they concerned expulsion as well as the freedom to travel (Decision 1999/436 ([1999] OJ L 176/17)).

[537] SCH/Com-ex(98) 24, 23 June 1998, not allocated to an EC Treaty legal base on the grounds that this Decision concerned an issue not covered by the EC or EU Treaty (Decision 1999/435, n 536 above).

[538] SCH/Com-ex(97) 39 Rev ([2000] OJ L 239/188), allocated to Arts 62(3) and 63(3) EC.

[539] SCH/Com-ex(98) 10 Rev ([2000] OJ L 239/193), allocated to Art 62(3) EC. See I:7.7.3.1 below.

[540] SCH/Com-ex(98) 18 Rev ([2000] OJ L 239/197), allocated to Arts 62(3) and 63(3) EC.

[541] SCH/Com-ex(98) 19 Rev ([2000] OJ L 239/199), allocated to Art 62(3) EC.

[542] [2000] OJ L 239/76, Part III, Declaration 1, of the Final Act, allocated to Art 62(3) EC.

Articles 23 and 24 of the Convention, which related to expulsion, were subsequently repealed and replaced by the more comprehensive Returns Directive,[543] as has one relevant Executive Committee Decision.[544] In 2014, the Commission proposed that two more of the Executive Committee measures be repealed.[545] The remaining provisions of the Schengen *acquis* in this area have been amended twice:[546] as regards the freedom to travel of long-stay visa holders (in 2010);[547] and as regards time limits and reporting requirements (in 2013).[548] This is the only area of the Schengen *acquis* regarding visas and borders which has not been entirely replaced by EU law.

As for the substantive rules, first of all, according to Article 19 of the Convention, persons with a Schengen visa who have legally entered a Member State may move freely throughout the Member States during the period of validity of their visas, as long as they meet the requirements for entry at the external borders (except the requirement to hold a visa, which they meet by definition).[549] However, persons whose visas are subject to limited territorial validity cannot exercise the right.[550]

Next, Article 20 of the Convention (as amended in 2013) provides that persons who do not need a visa to enter the Schengen area may move freely throughout the Member States for a maximum of 90 days in any 180-day period. Before the 2013 amendment, the rule was slightly different, allowing three months' travel in the six months after their 'first entry'. The freedom to travel is again dependent upon meeting the requirements for entry at the external borders (except the requirement to hold a visa, which they are exempt from by definition).[551]

Interpreting the previous version of this rule, the Court of Justice clarified that the 'date of first entry' for this purpose was the date of the initial entry of the person concerned, which then triggered a six-month period during which a person could travel to and within the Schengen area for either a single journey of three months or a number of journeys, which cannot cumulatively exceed three months in total during that six-month period. Following the end of that six-month period, the date of the next entry of the person concerned into the Schengen area triggered a further period of six months, during which the person concerned had the freedom to travel for a further period (or

---

[543] Art 21 of Directive 2008/115 ([2008] OJ L 348/98). On Arts 23 and 24 of the Convention, and that Directive, see I:7.7 below. On the interpretation of Art 23, see Joined Cases C-261/08 *Zurita Garcia* and C-348/08 *Choque Cabrera* [2009] ECR I-10143.

[544] SCH/Com-ex(98) 10 Rev (n 539 above), repealed by Art 11 of Directive 2003/110 on expulsion by air ([2003] OJ L 321/26). On that Directive, see I:7.7.3 below.

[545] COM (2014) 713, 28 Nov 2014, which proposes repealing SCH/Com-ex(97) 39 Rev and SCH/Com-ex(98) 18 Rev.

[546] A Commission proposal from 1995 to adopt an amended version of the Schengen freedom to travel rules as part of EC law (as it was then) was rejected: see I:4.2.1 above. A Portuguese initiative from 2000 and a Commission proposal from 2001 were also unsuccessful (see discussion below).

[547] Reg 265/2010 ([2010] OJ L 85/1), amending Art 21 of the Convention.

[548] Reg 610/2013 ([2013] OJ L 182/1), amending Arts 18, 20, 21, and 22 of the Convention.

[549] Art 19(1), Schengen Convention. This provision refers to Art 5 of the Convention, which has since been replaced by Art 5 of the Schengen Borders Code (Reg 562/2006, [2006] OJ L 105/1). It should be noted that the time limits concerned are enforced by an obligation to stamp documents at the external borders, and a presumption of irregular stay if the documents are not stamped (Arts 10 and 11 of the Code, idem). On the Borders Code, see further I:3.6.1 above.

[550] Art 19(3), Schengen Convention. On LTV visas, see I:4.7 above.

[551] Art 20(1), Schengen Convention. On the question of who needs a visa to enter, see I:4.5 above.

periods) of six months.[552] Obviously, Member States sought to change this approach with the 2013 amendment, which replaced the 'first entry' rule.

The Convention also specifies that Member States may permit a third-country national to stay for longer than three months in exceptional circumstances or on the basis of bilateral agreements with third States concluded prior to entry into force of the Convention.[553] Following the 2013 amendment, this clause now refers instead to extensions beyond ninety days. However, as noted above, a Schengen Executive Committee Decision, which was not allocated to the EC or EU Treaty (as they then were), requires Member States to denounce such pre-existing treaties, so that nationals of third states could enjoy only a maximum three-month stay in the entire Schengen zone, rather than three months in *each* Member State successively as they had been accustomed to. This issue would have been addressed by a Portuguese initiative for a Regulation which would have given the EC power to negotiate treaties with third States, permitting an extended period of freedom to travel over three months for those non-resident third-country nationals who do not need a visa to enter.[554] Alternatively, the Commission had proposed a Directive in 2001, which would have replaced most of the Schengen Convention rules on freedom to travel with an amended text that would, inter alia, have provided for a 'specific travel authorisation' to permit persons to stay in the Schengen area for up to six months (but no more than three months in each Member State),[555] in place of national treaties dealing with this issue. But due to legal disputes about the Community's competence to deal with stays of over six months, the Council was not able to agree on either measure. In any event, the Portuguese initiative lapsed on 1 May 2004 (the end of the Title IV transitional period),[556] and the Commission subsequently withdrew its proposal.[557] The legal issues arising from Article 20(2) of the Convention are considered elsewhere.[558] More recently, in 2014, the Commission tried again, proposing a Regulation establishing a touring visa, which would amend Article 20(2) to delete all references to Member States' bilateral agreements. It remains to be seen if this proposal is agreed.[559]

Thirdly, as regards persons with a residence permit issued by a Member State, Article 21 of the Convention provides that they may travel on the cover of that permit and a valid travel document for a period of up to three months (or ninety days, after the 2013 amendment), as long as they meet the requirements for entry at the external borders, excepting not only the requirement to hold a visa but also the requirement to be checked in the Schengen Information System (SIS), although they may be checked in national blacklists.[560] The freedom to travel also applies to persons who have a provisional residence permit from a Member State and a travel document issued by

---

[552] Case C-241/05 *Bot* [2006] ECR I-9627.   [553] Art 20(2), Schengen Convention.
[554] [2000] OJ C 164/6.
[555] COM (2001) 388, 10 July 2001. For further detail on this proposal and the Portuguese initiative, see the second edition of this book, pp 172–3.
[556] See I:2.2.1.1 above.   [557] COM (2005) 462, 27 Sept 2005 and [2006] OJ C 64/3.
[558] See I:4.11 below.
[559] Art 12 of the proposed Reg (COM (2014) 163, 1 April 2014). See further I:4.7 above.
[560] Art 21(1), Schengen Convention. On the implications of this for the free movement of services using posted third-country national employees, see I:4.4.1 above. Art 21(1) was also amended as from 5 Apr 2010 by Reg 265/2010 (n 547 above), purely to update the cross-references to other EU measures.

that State.[561] But Member States determine what constitutes valid travel documents, residence permits, and provisional residence permits for this purpose. These documents are notified by Member States pursuant to the Schengen Borders Code.[562]

A fourth category of persons enjoys freedom to travel rights: holders of long-stay visas. Initially, those rights were extended only to a small proportion of long-stay visa holders, pursuant to an amendment to Article 18 of the Schengen Convention set out in Council Regulation 1091/2001, adopted in May 2001.[563] Prior to the adoption of this Regulation, Article 18 of the Convention had specified only that persons who had a long-stay visa issued by a Member State could cross an external border without a short-stay visa, if they were in transit to the State which issued them the long-stay visa.[564] After the 2001 amendment, Article 18 provided that such persons also had the right to freedom to travel, for a period of up to three months following the initial date of validity of the long-stay permit, if their long-stay visas were issued in accordance with the rules on the issue of uniform visas and provided that they met the requirements for entry at external borders (except the requirement to hold a visa).[565] Such visas are issued as 'D+C visas'.[566] However, in practice few Member States issued D+C visas, because most Member States preferred to continue to issue ordinary long-stay visas which were *not* valid concurrently as short-stay visas;[567] some Member States did not even provide for the possibility of issuing D+C visas, and many consulates and visa applicants were not aware of the relevant rules.[568] Therefore, the EU Visa Code abolished D+C visas once the code became applicable in April 2010,[569] and at the same time a separate Regulation amended Article 21 of the Convention to provide that it applied to *all* holders of long-stay visas.[570]

Another category of persons who enjoy freedom to travel is established by a 1994 Joint Action on schoolchildren's visas, which provides that Member States shall exempt from a visa requirement a third-country national schoolchild who is resident in another Member State and travelling on a school trip, subject to certain formalities.[571] Since

---

[561] Art 21(2), Schengen Convention.

[562] Art 34(1)(a) of the Code (Reg 562/2006, [2006] OJ L 105/1), which replaced Annex 7 to the Common (Borders) Manual ([2002] OJ C 313/97), where this information was previously listed. The requirement to notify also previously appeared in Art 21(3) of Schengen Convention, but this was repealed by the 2013 amendments. Prior to the adoption of the Visa Code, this information was also listed in Annex 4 to the CCI ([2005] OJ C 326/1); the Visa Code repealed this Annex, along with the rest of the CCI (see I:4.7 above). For the notifications, see: <http://ec.europa.eu/justice_home/doc_centre/freetravel/rights/doc_freetravel_rights_en.htm>.

[563] [2001] OJ L 150/4; the Reg entered into force on 7 June 2001 (Art 3). On the competence issues deriving from this Reg, see I:4.2.4 above.

[564] See further I:3.6.1 above.   [565] Art 1 of the Reg.

[566] See the relevant amendments to the CCI ([2001] OJ L 150/47).

[567] Out of over 1 million D visas (long-stay visas) issued in 2004, only about 21,000 (2.1% of the total) were D+C visas (see COM (2006) 403, 19 July 2006, p 12).

[568] Ibid.

[569] Art 56(2)(e) of the Visa Code (Reg 810/2009, [2009] OJ L 243/1), repealing Reg 1091/2001. At the same time, Reg 265/2010 (n 547 above) amended the wording of Art 18 of the Schengen Convention again (see I:4.6 above and I:6.9 below).

[570] Reg 265/2010 (n 547 above), which inserted a new Art 21(2a) into the Schengen Convention. This Reg also made amendments to the Schengen Convention as regards visa formats (see I:4.6 above) and checks in the SIS (see below in this section), and to the Schengen Borders Code (see I:3.6.1 above). For an overview of the EU rules relating to residence permits and long-stay visas, see I:6.9 below.

[571] [1994] OJ L 327/1.

the pupils concerned would in any event be entitled to freedom to travel within the Schengen area, if they hold a designated residence permit or long stay-visa, the Joint Action is in practice relevant mainly for travel between the Schengen area and non-Schengen Member States, and between non-Schengen Member States.

Third-country nationals who exercise the freedom to travel in the Schengen may be required to declare entry to the authorities of the Member State they are visiting, in accordance with that Member State's conditions.[572] They must report either on entry or within three days of entry, at the discretion of the Member State they have entered. The Schengen Borders Code requires Member States to inform the Commission of the relevant national rules.[573] Prior to the 2013 amendments, the Convention in principle required Member States to establish such an obligation, but there was a wide variation between national practices, with some Member States not enforcing any reporting requirement and others enforcing it without exception.[574] In making the requirement optional, the 2013 amendments therefore simply confirmed Member States' practice.

Finally, a separate Chapter of Title II of the Schengen Convention, consisting of Article 25 of the Convention,[575] concerns the issue or renewal of residence permits and (from April 2010) long-stay visas. This issue is linked to the freedom to travel because, as we have seen, the issue of a residence permit or a long-stay visa by a Member State confers that freedom within all Member States. According to Article 25, when a Member State plans to issue a residence permit or long-stay visa, it must systematically check the SIS, and if it finds that the person concerned is listed on the SIS as a person to be denied entry, it must consult the Member State that issued the relevant 'alert' and take account of its interests; the permit shall then be issued 'for substantive grounds only, notably on humanitarian grounds or by reason of international commitments'.[576] Prior to issuing an alert in the SIS for refusal of entry, Member States must check their national records of residence permits and long-stay visas which have been issued.[577] If it transpires that such an alert has been issued regarding a person who already has a residence permit or long-stay visa, then the Member State issuing the alert shall consult the State which issued the permit or long-stay visa 'to determine whether there are sufficient reasons for withdrawing the residence permit' or long-stay visa.[578] In either case, if the residence

---

[572] Art 22, Schengen Convention, as amended in 2013. Compare with the rules on reporting requirements and EU free movement law, discussed in I:7.4.1 below.

[573] Arts 21(d) and 37 of the code (n 549 above), as amended by Reg 610/2013 (n 548 above).

[574] See the information reported in [2008] OJ C 18/25, [2008] OJ C 207/10, and [2009] OJ C 3/11, with online updates at: <http://ec.europa.eu/justice_home/doc_centre/freetravel/rights/doc_freetravel_rights_en.htm>.

[575] This provision was previously supplemented briefly by the CCI (point 3 of Annex 14, n 562 above), but that CCI provision was later repealed by the Visa Code (n 570 above) without replacement.

[576] Art 25(1), Schengen Convention. Reg 265/2010 (n 547 above) amended Art 25(1) to add the express requirement to check the SIS, and extended the rules to long-stay visa applications (inserting a new Art 25(3) into the Convention). As noted above (I:4.8), the *Visa* Information System does not apply to long-stay visa applicants. See also the conclusions of the Council and the Member States on information exchange as regards admission of persons held in the Guantanamo Bay detention centre by the USA (JHA Council press release, 4–5 June 2009).

[577] Art 25(1a), inserted by Reg 265/2010 (n 547 above).

[578] Art 25(2), first sub-paragraph, Schengen Convention, extended to long-stay visas from 5 Apr 2010 pursuant to Art 25(3) of the Convention, which was inserted by Reg 265/2010.

permit or long-stay visa is issued or withdrawn, the Member State which issued the alert must withdraw it from the SIS, but may keep the name on its national list of persons to be refused entry.[579] The legislation establishing SIS II, which applied from 2013, contains no express reference to Article 25 of the Convention, which will therefore remain in force (as amended in 2010) in the absence of any further amendment.[580]

The provisions on freedom to travel are one of the most valuable features of the Schengen system, and the full extension of the freedom in 2010 to persons holding long-stay visas was welcome. But there are nonetheless still several weaknesses. The freedom is limited to those holding only long-stay visas or specified permits, not to all those permitted to stay in a Member State. It is also unfortunate that the complex legal issues relating to the possible creation of an extended travel period for over three months have so far prevented the adoption of any useful Commission proposal on this issue.

In contrast to the freedom to travel rules, Article 25 of the Schengen Convention (as amended) is highly problematic,[581] as it constitutes the main application of the SIS to persons already resident on Member States' territory. There is therefore a particular risk that the use of this Article will breach EU free movement law (if national officials forget that EU free movement law takes precedence over the Schengen *acquis*) as well as human rights obligations of Member States, in particular where Article 8 ECHR or EU immigration or asylum legislation protects against expulsion.[582] The wording of the Article is particularly unfortunate, as it assumes that the question of granting or withdrawing a residence permit or long-stay visa is an issue to be agreed by interstate cooperation, without any requirement to give consideration to the substantive rights and interests of the person concerned or of any procedural rights of the individual (particularly rights in relation to the discussions between Member States' authorities). Again, however, the general principles of EU law and the EU Charter of Rights ensure remedies for the individuals concerned.[583]

4.10 Administrative Cooperation and EU Funding

In contrast to other areas of EU law, administrative cooperation and EU funding as regards visas has never been addressed as a separate issue. The cooperation and funding concerned has either formed a subset of measures relating to immigration issues in general or border controls in particular,[584] or been addressed by ancillary rules in legislation which concerns substantive issues relating to visas.[585]

---

[579] Art 25(2), second sub-paragraph, Schengen Convention.

[580] On the substance of the SIS II Reg, see I:3.7 above.

[581] See P Boeles, 'Schengen and the Rule of Law' in H Meijers, et al., *Schengen: Internationalisation of Central Chapters of the Law on Aliens, Refugees, Privacy, Security and the Police*, 2nd edn (Stichting NJCM-Boekerij, 1992), and the general criticisms of the SIS set out in I:3.7 above.

[582] See I:6.3.1 below on Art 8 ECHR, as well as the discussion of specific legislation in chs 5 and 6 of this volume.

[583] See also the procedural rights conferred by the ECHR and those forming part of the general principles in EU law and recognized in the EU Charter of Fundamental Rights (see I:6.3 below), as well as the SIS II Regulation (I:3.7 above).

[584] See, for instance, the programmes discussed in I:3.11 above.

[585] For example, see the provisions on statistics and consular cooperation in the Visa Code (Arts 46 and 48 of the code (Reg 810/2009, [2009] OJ L 243/1)). The EU-LISA agency which manages, inter alia, the VIS also plays a role in administrative cooperation (see II:7.6.1).

There are obligations to collect statistics on visas, deriving originally from Schengen Executive Committee Decisions,[586] and now incorporated into the Visa Code.[587] Unfortunately, there are no obligations to produce statistics as regards the operation of the VIS, although the Commission has published some in its bi-annual reports on the Schengen system.[588]

4.11 External Relations

The EU's visa rules have been developing in a broader external context.[589] Most obviously, the decision whether to impose or remove a visa requirement for third States is a significant political issue, as are (to a lesser degree) other aspects of the EU's visa rules: visa facilitation, including fees charged for visa applicants; exceptions for certain categories of persons from select third States; the possible re-imposition of visas for lack of reciprocity; the consultation procedure for certain third states; the gradual roll-out of the VIS; the imposition of airport transit visas; and the imposition of visa requirements on foreign policy grounds.[590] There are also some specific references to certain micro-states in EU visa legislation.[591]

At the same time, there are close and growing links between the EU's developing visa policy and its broader external policies, in particular the development of its neighbourhood policy and the accession process, but also there are links with its broader external migration policy, in the form of mobility partnerships.[592] Because of these developments, the EU's external visa policy has become highly nuanced and differentiated, like many of the EU's other highly developed external policies (notably its trade policy).

Unlike EU trade policy, the extent of EU external competence over visas has not been litigated, although there is a strong argument that given the degree of uniformity achieved by EU visa legislation, and the overall context of the visa rules (particularly freedom to travel between Member States), EU competence has become prima facie exclusive by exercise, except where EU legislation gives express competence to Member States—for example, as regards specific categories of persons who can be exempted from a visa obligation, or the (limited) discretion granted by the Visa Code for Member States to waive or reduce fees for visa applicants.[593] The same presumption arguably arises as regards the freedom to travel rules themselves. Indeed it is striking that there

---

[586] Decisions SCH/Com-ex (94) 25 and SCH/Com-ex (98) 12 ([2000] OJ L 239/173 and 196).

[587] Art 46 and Annex XII (Reg 810/2009, [2009] OJ L 243/1). The 2014 proposal to amend the code (see I:4.7 above) would amend these rules.

[588] See I:4.8 above.

[589] For an overview of the basic principles of EU external relations law, see I:2.7 above.

[590] See I:4.5 and I:4.7 above.

[591] For instance, see the Executive Committee decision relating to Monaco as regards freedom to travel: SCH/Com-ex(98) 19 Rev ([2000] OJ L 239/199).

[592] See I:7.9.2 below.

[593] See I:4.7 above, although note that the 2014 proposal to amend the Visa Code would alter the fee waiver rules. On the issue of external competence in this area, see B Martenczuk, 'Visa Policy and EU External Relations' in B Martenczuk and S van Thiel, eds., *Justice, Liberty, Security: New Challenges for EU External Relations* (VUBPress, 2008), 21.

are no 'mixed' agreements in the area of visas, only agreements concluded solely by the Community (now the Union).

Moving on to the specific treaties relating to visas which the EU has concluded, the most important of these are obviously the Schengen association treaties with Norway, Iceland, Switzerland, and Liechtenstein.[594] The EEA and EU-Turkey association agreements are also highly significant.[595]

As for the EU's treaties solely relating to visas, the Community (now the Union) has concluded a number of treaties concerning visa abolition and visa facilitation. The EU has also concluded, or authorized Member States to conclude, certain other treaties. Finally, the issue of freedom to travel is subject to particular complications relating to external competence. These issues are examined in turn.

4.11.1 Visa waiver treaties

First of all, visa waiver treaties were concluded between the Community (as it then was) and six micro-states (Barbados, Seychelles, Mauritius, the Bahamas, Antigua, and St. Kitts) in 2009,[596] following the decision to place those states on the EU's visa 'whitelist' in 2006, on the condition that those countries sign reciprocal agreements on visa abolition with the EU.[597] Subsequently, the visa waiver for a further sixteen countries in 2014 was again made conditional on signing reciprocal treaties with the EU. Nine of these countries agreed a visa waiver treaty with the EU in May 2015, and another five signed treaties in December that year.[598] Furthermore, Brazil agreed two visa waiver treaties with the EU, to ensure that it offered reciprocity to all EU Member States.[599]

The treaties concerned each provide that EU citizens and the nationals of each other party can travel visa-free to the other party for three months within a six-month period,[600] subject only to holding a 'valid ordinary, diplomatic or service/official passport'.[601] Within the EU, this means a three month stay in the Schengen area as a whole within a six month period, or three months' stay within six months in each Member State not yet applying

---

[594] I:4.2.5 above.   [595] I:4.4.2 above.

[596] [2009] OJ L 169 (text of treaties); [2009] OJ L 321/38 to 43 (Council decisions on conclusion). The treaties were provisionally in force as from their signature on 28 May 2009, and formally entered into force (see [2010] OJ L 56/1) on 1 Jan 2010 (Seychelles), 1 Mar 2010 (Barbados and Mauritius), 1 Apr 2010 (Bahamas), 1 May 2010 (Antigua), and 1 Aug 2015 (St Kitts).

[597] See I:4.5 above.

[598] Timor Leste, Vanuatu, Samoa, Saint Lucia, Dominica, Grenada, Saint Vincent and the Grenadines, Trinidad and Tobago, and the United Arab Emirates signed in May ([2015] OJ L 125 and L 173), and Peru, Colombia, Kiribati, Palau, and Tonga signed in December ([2015] OJ L 355, L 333, L 350, L 332, and L 317). These treaties applied provisionally from their signature. Treaties will also be negotiated with Marshall Islands, Micronesia, Nauru, Solomon Islands, and Tuvalu (see I:4.5 above).

[599] [2011] OJ L 66/2 (diplomatic visas), in force 1 April 2011, and [2012] OJ L 255/4 (ordinary visas), in force 1 Oct 2012.

[600] See, for instance, Arts 1 and 4, EU-Mauritius treaty (n 596 above). A Joint Declaration specifies that the three-month stay can constitute either a single visit or *multiple* visits totalling three months within a six-month period. This is not explicitly set out in the definition of 'visa' in the Visa Code (Art 2(2)(a) of Reg 810/2009 ([2009] OJ L 243/1), as amended by Reg 610/2013 ([2013] OJ L 182/1)), but reflects the previous Art 11(1)(a) of the Schengen Convention ([2000] OJ L 239).

[601] Art 3(1).

the Schengen *acquis* in full.[602] The agreements are without prejudice to the possibility of stays for longer periods in accordance with national law or EU law.[603]

However, the Member States and the other parties each reserve the right to require a visa if the person concerned wishes to carry out a 'paid activity'.[604] A joint declaration attached to each visa waiver treaty states the agreed interpretation that this means 'entering for the purpose of carrying out a gainful occupation/remunerated activity in the territory of the other Contracting Party as an employee or as a service provider'. But it does not include businesspersons who travel for business without being employed in the territory of another state; sportspersons and artists performing ad hoc activity; journalists sent by the media of their country of residence; and intra-corporate trainees.[605]

Moreover, the visa waiver is 'without prejudice to the laws of the Contracting Parties relating to the conditions of entry and short stay', and the possibility to deny entry and stay in accordance with those laws.[606] The visa waiver applies regardless of the mode of transport used for entry—although there will surely be few journeys by sea or land between the EU and the other parties.[607] Issues not addressed by the agreement are covered by the national law of the other parties or the Member States or by EU law.[608]

The agreements only apply to the European territory of France and the Netherlands;[609] there is a joint committee to manage each agreement;[610] and each agreement takes precedence over any bilateral agreements with Member States that cover the same issue.[611] Each party may suspend each treaty in whole or part 'in particular, for reasons of public policy, protection of national security or protection of public health, illegal immigration or the reintroduction of the visa requirement by either Contracting Party',[612] or each treaty may be terminated entirely.[613] Suspension and termination is only valid by, or as against, the entire EU.[614] A final joint declaration specifies that the parties will provide information to the public about the agreement and related issues, such as entry conditions.

4.11.2 Visa facilitation treaties

There are EU visa facilitation treaties in force with Russia, Ukraine, the Western Balkan states (except Kosovo), Moldova, Georgia, Armenia, Azerbaijan, and Cape Verde.[615]

---

[602] Art 4(2). The respective periods are to be calculated independently of each other. So it will be possible, for example, to spend three months in Romania and then three months in the Schengen area—until Romania joins the Schengen area in full.

[603] Art 4(3).

[604] Art 3(2). This is consistent with the possibility of each Member State to require a visa in such cases, according to the EU's visa list legislation: see I:4.5 above. The treaties refer to the *national law* of Member States and the micro-states, rather than the possibility to negotiate treaties to this effect.

[605] The various categories of persons are not further defined.

[606] Art 3(3). For the EU, this obviously refers principally to the Schengen Borders Code.

[607] Art 3(4). It is possible, however, that visitors from the micro-states might visit the UK or (say) Russia first and then travel to the Schengen area via ferry or rail.

[608] Art 3(5).   [609] Art 5.   [610] Art 6.   [611] Art 7.

[612] Art 8(4). There must be at least two months' prior notice.

[613] Art 8(5). There must be at least 90 days' prior notice.   [614] Art 8(6) and (7).

[615] EC-Russia treaty ([2007] OJ L 129/25), in force 1 June 2007; EC-Ukraine treaty ([2007] OJ L 332/68), in force 1 Jan 2008; treaties with Western Balkans and Moldova ([2007] OJ L 334), in force 1 Jan 2008;

Negotiations are underway with Belarus, Morocco, and Tunisia. In each case, a readmission agreement has also been negotiated or is under negotiation in parallel.[616] These agreements have less relevance now for Western Balkan States and Moldova given the visa waivers now applied for those countries, but are still relevant for those categories of persons who do not benefit from those waivers (for instance, because they do not have biometric passports).[617] It should also be recalled that even for third States whose nationals are generally still subject to visa requirements, certain categories of persons are exempt from that requirement.[618]

Taking the agreement with Ukraine as a typical example, the agreement applies to visas for a stay of three months within a six-month period, ie the standard period applicable to Schengen visas.[619] The agreement is in principle reciprocal, although this point is moot for the time being as Ukraine does not impose a visa obligation on EU citizens.[620] For a number of categories of persons, visas shall be issued according to a simplified procedure, subject only to the requirement to submit specified documents.[621] Multiple-entry visas with a term of validity of up to five years must be issued to: members of governments, parliaments and the highest courts; permanent members of official delegations who regularly participate in meetings, etc in the EU; specified close family members visiting Ukrainians who are legally resident in the EU;[622] business people; and journalists.[623] Multiple-entry visas with a term of validity of up to one year must be issued, subject to certain conditions, to: professional drivers; train crews; participants in 'scientific, cultural and artistic activities'; participants in sports events and professionals accompanying them; and participants in 'twin cities' exchange programmes.[624] Subsequently the latter category of persons can obtain a multiple-entry visa valid between two and five years.[625]

The fee for a visa application is fixed at €35, and is waived altogether for a long list of categories of persons.[626] The treaty requires visa decisions to be taken within ten days, with a reduction to two days in urgent cases and a possible extension to thirty days in individual cases, in particular if further scrutiny of the application is necessary.[627] In the event of lost or stolen travel documents, EU or Ukrainian citizens can leave the territory on the basis of valid replacement documents without the requirement to obtain a visa.[628] If a Ukrainian citizen cannot leave within the period of validity of the visa due

---

EU-Georgia treaty ([2011] OJ L 52/24), in force 1 Mar 2011; EU-Armenia treaty ([2013] OJ L 289/2), in force 1 Jan 2014; EU-Azerbaijan treaty ([2014] OJ L 128/48), in force 1 Sep 2014; and EU-Cape Verde treaty ([2007] OJ L 282/3), in force 1 Dec 2014.

[616] On those treaties, see I:7.9.1 below. In the specific case of Albania, the readmission agreement was negotiated several years before the visa facilitation agreement.

[617] See I:4.5 above.   [618] See ibid.

[619] Arts 1(1) and 3(d) of the EC-Ukraine treaty (n 615 above).

[620] See Art 1(2) of the treaty. Note that the treaty does not *oblige* Ukraine to waive the visa requirement. Of the states which have concluded visa facilitation agreements with the EU, only Russia imposes a visa requirement on EU citizens.

[621] Art 4 of the treaty.

[622] For the definition of legal residence, see Art 3(e) of the treaty.   [623] Art 5(1) of the treaty.

[624] Art 5(2) of the treaty.   [625] Art 5(3) of the treaty.

[626] Art 6 of the treaty. A higher fee of €70 applies to urgent applications, but that is either waived entirely or set at €35 only for the various special categories.

[627] Art 7 of the treaty. The consequence of a failure to decide within these time limits is not specified.

[628] Art 8 of the treaty.

to *force majeure*, the visa must be extended free of charge.[629] For persons with valid diplomatic passports, the visa requirement is waived altogether.[630] Ukrainians can travel within the territory of the Member States on an equal footing with EU citizens, subject to Member States' national rules on 'national security' and the EU rules on the limited territorial validity of visas.[631] There is a joint committee for the management of the agreement and the agreement takes precedence over any Member State's national treaties falling within the same scope.[632] Issues outside the scope of the treaty, such as 'the refusal to issue a visa, recognition of travel documents, proof of sufficient means of subsistence and the refusal of entry and expulsion measures', are addressed by the national law of Ukraine or the Member States, or by EU law.[633] Finally, there is a joint declaration on the issues of visits to burial grounds,[634] a Commission declaration on the reasons for refusing a visa,[635] a Community declaration on information for visa applicants,[636] and a declaration by four Member States on local border traffic.[637] There are also further joint declarations relating to the position of the UK, Ireland, Denmark, Schengen associates, and Member States not yet fully applying the Schengen *acquis*.[638]

As for the application of these agreements, a Commission assessment released in 2009[639] pointed out that the visa facilitation treaties applied to over half of visa applicants.[640] The report states that visa applications increased in some of the countries concerned, but decreased in others; it should be recalled that the application of most of these treaties broadly coincided with the extension of the Schengen zone. There were small drops in the refusal rate of applications, and there appeared to be a large increase in the numbers of visas issued free of charge and of multiple-entry visas. While the EU's neighbours continued to complain about a number of aspects of the visa-issuing process, the Commission argued that many of these complaints would be addressed by the (then) forthcoming application of the Visa Code. However, the Commission did suggest the renegotiation of the relevant treaties, to address the specific issues of the simplification of supporting documents, broader fee waivers, the possibility for external service providers to charge a service fee, and a ban on the discriminatory introduction of a visa obligation on citizens of only one EU Member State. Subsequently, the EU renegotiated the visa facilitation treaties with Ukraine and Moldova,[641] and opened

---

[629] Art 9 of the treaty.

[630] Art 10 of the treaty. This applies for the standard period of 90 days within a 180-day period.

[631] Art 11 of the treaty. [632] Arts 12 and 13 of the treaty. [633] Art 2(2) of the treaty.

[634] The standard period of validity for visas in this case will only be 'up to 14 days'.

[635] The declaration refers to the proposal for the EU Visa Code, then under discussion.

[636] Again, the declaration refers to the proposal for the EU Visa Code, but also states some elements of what an information policy should entail.

[637] These four states (Poland, Hungary, Slovakia, and Romania) each state a willingness to negotiate border traffic treaties with Ukraine in accordance with the EU's border traffic legislation (on which, see I:3.8 above).

[638] For more on this issue, see I:4.2.5 above. [639] SEC (2009) 1401, 15 Oct 2009.

[640] This percentage will have dropped since, due to the subsequent waiver of visa requirements for several States with visa facilitation agreements (see I:4.5.2 above).

[641] [2013] OJ L 168/3 (Moldova) and [2013] OJ L 168/11 (Ukraine). Both treaties entered into force on 1 July 2013.

talks to upgrade the treaty with Russia; but the latter talks were suspended after EU/Russia relations deteriorated in 2014.

4.11.3 Other EU measures

The EC (as it then was) concluded a treaty with China (the 'ADS treaty'), in force 1 May 2004,[642] which provides for procedures for China to designate the entire Schengen territory as an 'Approved Destination' for tourists, as a result of which Schengen visas are issued to designated tourists following a special procedure of certification of travel agencies. China is obliged to readmit any persons who do not comply with the scheme.[643]

Member States have also negotiated a treaty that falls within EC competence (as it then was) because it addresses the issue of seafarers' visas. But because it was too late to arrange for the EC to become a party to the treaty, the Council adopted a Decision authorizing the Member States to sign the treaty, effectively as trustees of the EC's external power.[644]

Finally, as regards the issue of freedom to travel, there are complex external relations issues, deriving from the existence of Member States' bilateral treaties with third states, which give nationals of those third States extra time to reside in the Member State in question, and therefore in the Schengen area as a whole.[645] Article 20(2) of the Schengen Convention specifies that Member States can retain such agreements, and Article 307 EC (now Article 351 TFEU) generally permits Member States to keep all pre-existing treaties in force, although in the latter case there could be an obligation to amend or denounce the relevant treaties eventually.[646] There is a Schengen Executive Committee Decision requiring amendment of such bilateral treaties, but this was not, as it should have been, defined by the Council in 1999 as forming part of the Schengen *acquis* for the purposes of allocation and then allocated to the EC Treaty (as it then was). The legal position on this issue therefore remains unclear,[647] although the Commission's proposal for a Regulation on a touring visa would remove Member States' power to sign such treaties.[648]

4.12 Conclusions

The basically unsatisfactory rules deriving from the Schengen *acquis* in this area have been significantly changed since 1999, in particular by means of the adoption of the Visa Code, which has ensured procedural rights for visa applicants and made some other useful changes to the rules. Other positive developments are the waiver of visa requirements for an increasing number of third States, a rethink of the requirements for

---

[642] [2004] OJ L 83/12.   [643] On the issue of readmission, see I:7.9.1 below.
[644] [2005] OJ L 136/1.   [645] For the background to this issue, see I:4.9 above.
[646] On Art 351 TFEU, see I:2.7 above. The Court of Justice has not addressed the question as to whether this Art, or at least the principle underlying the Art, also applies when a Member State concluded a treaty *after* joining the EU, but before the adoption of the relevant EU legislation, or before the Member States first conferred competence upon the EU in a particular area.
[647] See the discussion in the second edition of this book, pp 177–8.
[648] Art 12 of that proposal (COM (2014) 163, 1 April 2014; see further I:4.7.2 above), which would amend Art 20(2) of the Convention.

waiving the visa requirement, visa facilitation agreements with a number of countries, and the greater flexibility to waive visa requirements for certain categories of persons. The planned amendments to the Visa Code would go a long way to provide a fast-track visa with a long validity for visitors who can evidence that they can be trusted. Overall, the policy has becoming increasingly focused on the EU's economic interests rather than its security concerns, and has developed from a vague and incoherent system based on questionable and fragmented texts into a far more coherent system based more clearly on the rule of law, with enforceable individual rights. Clearly, the EU visa regime has been developing in the right direction.

5

Asylum

5.1 Introduction

Asylum law is one of the most complex areas of JHA cooperation, although one of the most high-profile and controversial. The complexity arises because of the number of different issues addressed by asylum law, in conjunction with the growing interconnection between national law, EU harmonization, and international human rights obligations. This chapter begins with an overview of the asylum process in the EU from an asylum seeker's point of view, and then examines specific issues in more detail. It will be seen that while the EU has the potential to ensure effective protection of the right to asylum in the Member States, in practice the results of conferring asylum powers on the Union have been rather modest to date. This gap between the potential of EU law and its application in practice became particularly manifest when the numbers applying for asylum increased sharply in 2015 (the so-called 'refugee crisis').

The journey through the labyrinth of EU asylum law begins in the territory of the asylum seeker's country of origin—usually the country of his or her nationality. At this point EU external relations law plays a large role. EU foreign policy affects developments relevant to asylum seekers, and the EU's development policy often addresses refugee issues explicitly through funding programmes and clauses in development policy agreements with third states.[1] The legality of including refugee assistance within development policy was indirectly addressed in *Portugal v Council*, in which the Court of Justice upheld the validity of a development policy agreement between the EC (as it then was) and India.[2] Refugee clauses were not specifically at issue in this case, but the Court of Justice's broad definition of 'development policy' in its judgment left little doubt that financial support to aid refugees in developing countries fell within it. Many persons fleeing persecution are able to find refuge in a neighbouring developing state or within the same state, in which case the EU's development funds are often spent on their behalf. Furthermore, the EU has elaborated a policy designed to assist neighbouring or transit States with large number of refugees on their territory, with a view to discouraging the refugees from contemplating travel onwards to the EU.

Those asylum seekers who do attempt entry into the EU will obviously be most directly affected by EU rules. They will likely have to obtain a visa as a first hurdle, as EU legislation requires visas for most or all countries generating significant numbers of asylum seekers, and there is no special procedure for persons requesting visas as asylum

---

[1] A detailed analysis is beyond the scope of this book. Development policy is governed by Arts 208–11 TFEU (previously Arts 177–81 EC). See I:7.9.2 below on external relations and irregular migration policy.
[2] Case C-268/94 [1996] ECR I-6177.

seekers.[3] The imposition of carrier sanctions will make it difficult for asylum seekers to get a plane ticket (or other legal transport) without a visa and other travel documents—but some asylum seekers do not have passports or other travel documents, because they have been denied them in their country of origin. If they attempt to enter the territory illegally, the EU rules enhancing border controls and criminalizing smugglers of persons, along with the EU's external policy on irregular migration (including readmission agreements) are intended to erect a significant barrier.

If asylum seekers do reach EU Member States' territory and attempt to make an asylum application, their claim could be dismissed without consideration of its merits by a Member State on the grounds that they should have applied for asylum in a country which they transited through (or perhaps even a country they did *not* transit through), on the grounds that that country is to be considered a 'safe third country'. Alternatively (or additionally), the Member State where the asylum seekers apply could enforce EU rules which allocate responsibility to another Member State for considering their applications.

If the asylum claim is considered on its merits, the Member State in question has a number of grounds on which it can conclude that the claim is 'unfounded' (or even 'manifestly unfounded') and thus subject the claim to a 'fast-track' procedure accompanied by limited procedural rights to appeal the Member State's decision. This can include a presumption that the asylum seeker comes from a 'safe country of origin'. If the application is deemed to have some substantive merit, it will be processed instead in a 'regular' procedure.

While the claim is being considered, the asylum seeker can enjoy certain minimum treatment as regards issues such as health, welfare, and accommodation ('reception conditions'). At the end of the determination procedure, the Member State's authorities decide whether the asylum seeker has a well-founded claim for refugee status, interpreting the 1951 Geneva Convention on refugees, as amended by the New York Protocol of 1967 and as interpreted by EU legislation. Alternatively, the asylum seeker might fall outside the definition of 'refugee' in the Geneva Convention, but still have a well-founded claim to international protection on some other basis. This is called a claim for 'subsidiary protection', and EU legislation also defines the circumstances in which such a claim can be made. If the claim for 'Convention refugee' status or subsidiary protection status is successful, the legal position of a successful claimant as regards issues such as access to employment, health, welfare, and (for refugees) family reunion is governed by EU law. Unsuccessful claimants have rights to appeal as defined in EU legislation, and if their appeals are unsuccessful, EU law on irregular migration, including the Returns Directive,[4] will facilitate their removal. Finally, in the event of a major crisis resulting in a mass influx into the EU or persons needing protection, the EU has established a framework for offering an ad hoc status, known as 'temporary protection', to large groups of persons. It can also adopt other emergency measures to deal with such an influx, such as the derogations for the asylum responsibility rules found in the 'relocation' decisions adopted in 2015.

---

[3] However, as discussed in I:4.7 above, it is arguable that the EU Visa Code must be interpreted to this effect.

[4] See I:7.7.1 below.

There is an obvious tension between the objective of ensuring full protection for the rights of refugees, asylum seekers, and other persons seeking international protection and the objectives of limiting irregular migration (and indeed, managing legal migration) and more effectively controlling the external borders of the EU's Member States, in particular because asylum seekers often have to resort to irregular means to enter or stay on the territory of the Member States. EU asylum law is therefore linked to EU visa policy (as regards particularly the list of States whose nationals need visas, the conditions for obtaining a visa, the Visa Information System (VIS) and the Schengen Information System (SIS), and the link between the issue of a visa and the grounds for deciding on responsibility for asylum applications) and EU rules on external border controls (as regards the entry of asylum seekers onto the territory and further grounds for deciding on responsibility for asylum applications).[5] The policy is also linked closely to EU law on irregular migration, as regards attempts to ensure that persons never reach EU Member States' territory, the criminalization of the smuggling of persons, and the EU's desire to 'externalize' its policies on irregular migration.[6] Finally, for those whose claim for international protection is successful, EU legislation on social security coordination, family reunion, and the status of long-term residents may apply.[7]

5.2 Institutional Framework and Overview

5.2.1 Cooperation prior to the Treaty of Amsterdam

Even before the Maastricht Treaty formalized Justice and Home Affairs cooperation between the EU Member States, those Member States had begun cooperating on asylum issues. The most visible sign of this was the agreement on the Dublin Convention on responsibility for asylum applications in 1990.[8] This Convention was followed by the three 'London Resolutions' of Member States' immigration ministers in 1992, on the important and controversial procedural issues of 'safe third countries', 'safe countries of origin', and 'manifestly unfounded applications'.[9] Also, a 'clearing-house' for asylum information, known as 'CIREA', was set up within the Council.[10]

Following the entry into force of the Maastricht Treaty, Member States began protracted negotiations on another Convention, to establish a system of taking and comparing asylum seekers' fingerprints, dubbed 'Eurodac'. They were able to agree this Convention, and a connected Protocol, just before the Treaty of Amsterdam entered into force.[11] During this period, the Council adopted a Resolution on asylum procedures,[12]

---

[5] See chs 3 and 4 of this volume. On the SIS, see II:7.6.1.1.   [6] See ch 7 of this volume.
[7] See ch 6 of this volume.   [8] See I:5.8.1 below.
[9] Unpublished in the OJ; see Bunyan, *Key Texts on Justice and Home Affairs in the European Union*, *Volume I* (1997), 64 and 66; E Guild and J Niessen, *The Emerging Immigration and Asylum Law of the European Union* (Kluwer, 1996), 141, 161, and 177.
[10] Centre for Information, Discussion, and Exchange on Asylum. See doc SN 2781/92 WGI 1107, 21 May 1992, published in Bunyan (n 9 above) 68 (setting up CIREA) and activity reports published at, 72; [1996] OJ C 274/55; [1997] OJ C 191/29 and 33. On the parallel CIREFI body, see I:7.8 below.
[11] On the draft Convention and Protocol, see the first edition of this book, pp 116–17.
[12] [1996] OJ C 274/13. See the first edition of this book, at 119.

a Joint Position on the definition of refugee,[13] and some very modest funding programmes.[14] However, it was not able to agree any measure dealing with subsidiary protection, reception conditions for asylum seekers, or the status of refugees,[15] and could agree only on very modest measures concerning the issue of temporary protection.[16] A Resolution on unaccompanied minors concerned asylum as well as migration issues.[17]

5.2.2 Treaty of Amsterdam

The Treaty of Amsterdam inserted Article 63(1) and 63(2) into the EC Treaty, conferring powers upon the Community (as it then was) to adopt measures concerning asylum and other forms of international protection:

> The Council, acting in accordance with the procedure referred to in Article 67, shall, within a period of five years after the entry into force of the Treaty of Amsterdam, adopt:
>
> (1) measures on asylum, in accordance with the Geneva Convention of 28 July 1951 and the Protocol of 31 January 1967 relating to the status of refugees and other relevant treaties, within the following areas:
>
> (a) criteria and mechanisms for determining which Member State is responsible for considering an application for asylum submitted by a national of a third country in one of the Member States,
>
> (b) minimum standards on the reception of asylum seekers in Member States,
>
> (c) minimum standards with respect to the qualification of nationals of third countries as refugees,
>
> (d) minimum standards on procedures in Member States for granting or withdrawing refugee status;
>
> (2) measures on refugees and displaced persons within the following areas:
>
> (a) minimum standards for giving temporary protection to displaced persons from third countries who cannot return to their country of origin and for persons who otherwise need international protection,
>
> (b) promoting a balance of effort between Member States in receiving and bearing the consequences of receiving refugees and displaced persons.

---

[13] [1996] OJ L 63/2. See the first edition of this book, at 119–20. There was also a Decision on monitoring implementation of EU asylum measures ([1997] OJ L 178/6).

[14] [1997] OJ L 205/3; [1998] OJ L 138/8; [1997] OJ L 205/5; [1998] OJ L 138/6; and [1999] OJ L 114/2. For more detail, see the first edition of this book, p 124.

[15] See the first edition of this book, at 120–2.

[16] The agreed measures comprised ministers' Resolutions in 1992 on the conflict in the former Yugoslavia (unpublished in the OJ; see Bunyan, n 9 above, pp 74 and 76), and a Council Resolution and Decision setting up a decision-making procedure to deal with potential crises ([1995] OJ C 262/1 and [1996] OJ C 63/10). Conversely, the Council failed in particular to agree an ambitious Joint Action proposed by the Commission. See the original version of this proposal in COM (97) 93, 5 Mar 1997 ([1997] OJ C 106/13) and the revised version in COM (1998) 372, 24 June 1998 ([1998] OJ C 268/13 and 22). For more detail, see the first edition of this book, pp 122–3.

[17] [1997] OJ C 221/23.

Another potentially relevant provision was Article 64(2) EC, which was never used in practice, but which provided as follows:

> In the event of one or more Member States being confronted with an emergency situation characterised by a sudden inflow of nationals of third countries and without prejudice to paragraph 1 [concerning national responsibilities for law and order and internal security], the Council may, acting by qualified majority on a proposal from the Commission, adopt provisional measures of a duration not exceeding six months for the benefit of the Member States concerned.

The asylum powers were subject initially to the standard rules applying to Title IV of Part Three of the EC Treaty, with unanimous voting in the Council and consultation of the European Parliament (EP), and a restricted jurisdiction of the Court of Justice. Also, the Treaty of Amsterdam attached a Protocol on asylum applications by EU citizens to the EC Treaty.[18]

As with other areas of JHA law, soon after the entry into force of the Treaty of Amsterdam, the priorities and principles for use of the new provisions were set out by the Tampere European Council in October 1999. The Tampere conclusions set out an ambitious agenda for developing a 'Common European Asylum System':

II. A Common European Asylum System

13. The European Council reaffirms the importance the Union and Member States attach to absolute respect of the right to seek asylum. It has agreed to work towards establishing a Common European Asylum System, based on the full and inclusive application of the Geneva Convention, thus ensuring that nobody is sent back to persecution, i.e. maintaining the principle of non-refoulement.

14. This System should include, in the short term, a clear and workable determination of the State responsible for the examination of an asylum application, common standards for a fair and efficient asylum procedure, common minimum conditions of reception of asylum seekers, and the approximation of rules on the recognition and content of the refugee status. It should also be completed with measures on subsidiary forms of protection offering an appropriate status to any person in need of such protection. To that end, the Council is urged to adopt, on the basis of Commission proposals, the necessary decisions....

15. In the longer term, Community rules should lead to a common asylum procedure and a uniform status for those who are granted asylum valid throughout the Union....

Following a initial discussion paper on the nature of the Common European Asylum System (CEAS),[19] the legislation to establish the first phase of the CEAS was proposed by the Commission in 2000 and 2001. All of the 'first-phase' measures were then adopted by December 2005.

Taking the EC's original asylum law powers in turn, first of all, Article 63(1)(a) EC was implemented by two first-phase measures: a Regulation establishing the 'Eurodac'

---

[18] See I:5.4.1 below.
[19] COM (2000) 755, 22 Nov 2000. See also later reports: COM (2001) 710, 28 Nov 2001 and COM (2003) 152, 26 Mar 2003.

system, adopted in December 2000, based on the agreement reached on the draft Eurodac Convention just prior to the entry into force of the Treaty of Amsterdam, and a Regulation setting out rules on responsibility for asylum applications, adopted in February 2003.[20] Both measures started to apply in 2003.

Secondly, the Council implemented Article 63(1)(b) EC with the adoption in January 2003 of Directive 2003/9, which set out first-phase minimum standards on reception conditions for asylum seekers.[21]

Thirdly, the Council adopted in April 2004 a first-phase Directive defining the meaning of 'refugee' and subsidiary protection (along with the content of the connected status).[22] This Directive implemented Article 63(1)(c) EC and the second line of Article 63(2)(a) EC, and also used the legal base for legal migration law (Article 63(3)(a) EC). It is generally known as the 'qualification Directive'.

Fourthly, in December 2005, the Council adopted a first-phase Directive on asylum procedures, implementing Article 63(1)(d) EC.[23] A portion of this Directive was annulled by the Court of Justice following a successful challenge by the European Parliament.[24]

Fifthly, in July 2001, the Council adopted a Directive setting out a model temporary protection system which the EU can take 'off the shelf' and use in the event of a future perceived crisis.[25] So far, it has not been considered necessary to use the model set out in the Directive.

The EC's sixth power concerned subsidiary protection, and as noted above, the Council adopted first-phase legislation concerning the definition and content of subsidiary protection status. However, the first-phase of the legislation establishing the Common European Asylum System did not include any rules concerning responsibility for considering applications for this status, reception conditions for applicants for this status, or procedures applicable to considering such applications.

Finally, the EC used its seventh power during the initial period of developing the CEAS by adopting a Decision establishing a 'European Refugee Fund' in September 2000. A subsequent Decision of December 2004 extended the application of the Fund (with some amendments) to 2005–10.[26]

By the time that the initial first-phase CEAS legislation was adopted, the institutional framework for decision-making concerning EC asylum law had been changed, as from the entry into force of the Treaty of Nice on 1 February 2003. This Treaty had inserted a new Article 67(5) into the EC Treaty, which provided that qualified majority voting (QMV) in the Council and co-decision with the European Parliament would apply once the Council adopted, by unanimity, Community rules which set out 'common rules and basic principles' on asylum. The Court of Justice subsequently confirmed that, as regards the asylum procedures Directive, sufficient common rules and

---

[20] Respectively Regs 2725/2000 ([2000] OJ L 316/1) and 343/2003 ([2003] OJ L 50/1). For detailed discussion, see I:5.8 below.
[21] Dir 2003/9 ([2003] OJ L 31/18); see further I:5.9 below.
[22] Dir 2004/83 ([2004] OJ L 304/12); see further I:5.5 below.
[23] Dir 2005/85 ([2005] OJ L 326/13); see further I:5.7 below.
[24] Case C-133/06 *EP v Council* [2008] ECR I-3189.
[25] Dir 2001/55 ([2001] OJ L 212/12). See further I:5.6 below.   [26] [2000] OJ L 252/12.

basic principles had been established to trigger the application of Article 67(5) as from the adoption of that Directive; no doubt the same was true as regards other areas of asylum law.[27] Although Article 67(5) did not apply to 'burden-sharing' measures adopted pursuant to the powers conferred upon the EC by Article 63(2)(b) EC, a separate Council decision shifted decision-making on those matters to QMV and co-decision as from 1 January 2005.[28]

The basis for the second-phase of the development of the Common European Asylum System was the Hague Programme on the development of JHA policy from 2005–09, adopted in November 2004. According to the Hague Programme, the second phase of the CEAS should be achieved by the end of 2010, following the adoption of legislative proposals made by the Commission following a review of the existing asylum measures in 2007.[29] To this end, the Commission issued a Green Paper on the review of the CEAS in 2007,[30] and followed this up with a policy plan on asylum in 2008.[31] In the meantime new legislation concerning the European Refugee Fund was adopted.[32]

A main feature of the policy plan was the review and update of existing legislation, with the twin objectives of increasing the degree and raising the level of harmonization. The rationale for this was the continued wide divergence in recognition rates (ie rates of successful asylum applications) as between Member States, both in general and in respect of particular nationalities, and also as regards the breakdown between the grant of refugee status and the grant of subsidiary protection status.[33] In fact, the wide divergence between national recognition rates was recognized by the 2008 Immigration and Asylum Pact adopted by EU leaders, which also set the aim of raising standards.[34]

To implement these objectives, first of all, in December 2008, the Commission proposed amendments to the Eurodac Regulation, the Dublin II Regulation, and the reception conditions Directive.[35] Secondly, the Commission proposed amendments to the qualification Directive and the asylum procedures Directive in October 2009.[36] However, there were great difficulties in the Council negotiating the proposed legislation, and the target date for completion of the second-phase of the CEAS was in any event moved from 2010 to 2012 by the Immigration and Asylum Pact adopted by the European Council in 2008.[37]

As for role of the Court of Justice, its role remained restricted before the entry into force of the Treaty of Lisbon, due to the restrictions on its jurisdiction imposed by Article 68 EC before that date.[38] However, the Court began to receive a number of requests for a preliminary ruling on asylum legislation as from 2007,[39] and it also

---

[27] Case C-133/06, n 24 above.   [28] [2004] OJ L 396/45.
[29] [2005] OJ C 53/1, points 1.3 and 1.6. See also the subsequent implementation plan: [2005] OJ C 198/1.
[30] COM (2007) 301, 6 June 2007.   [31] COM (2008) 360, 17 June 2008.
[32] [2007] OJ L 144/1.
[33] See Annex 6 to the impact assessment on the proposal to amend the asylum procedures Directive (SEC (2009) 1376, 21 Oct 2009, Part II).
[34] Council doc 13440/08, 24 Sep 2008.
[35] COM (2008) 815, 820, and 825, 3 Dec 2008. See further I:5.8 and I:5.9 below.
[36] COM (2009) 551 and 554, 21 Oct 2009. See further I:5.5 and I:5.7 below.   [37] N 34 above.
[38] See I:2.2.2.1 above.
[39] Cases: C-19/08 *Petrosian* [2009] ECR I-495; C-465/07 *Elgafaji and Elgafaji* [2009] ECR I-921; C-175/08, C-176/08, C-178/08, and C-179/08 *Abdulla and others* [2010] ECR I-1493; C-31/09 *Bolbol* [2010] ECR I-5539; and C-57/09 and C-101/09 *B and D* [2010] ECR I-10979. *Petrosian* concerned the Dublin II

received a number of infringement actions concerning EU asylum legislation, along with an annulment action concerning the asylum procedures Directive.[40]

5.2.3 Treaty of Lisbon

The issue of asylum is now addressed in Article 78 TFEU, as follows:

1. The Union shall develop a common policy on asylum, subsidiary protection and temporary protection with a view to offering appropriate status to any third-country national requiring international protection and ensuring compliance with the principle of *non-refoulement*. This policy must be in accordance with the Geneva Convention of 28 July 1951 and the Protocol of 31 January 1967 relating to the status of refugees, and other relevant treaties.
2. For the purposes of paragraph 1, the European Parliament and the Council, acting in accordance with the ordinary legislative procedure, shall adopt measures for a common European asylum system comprising:
   (a) a uniform status of asylum for nationals of third countries, valid throughout the Union;
   (b) a uniform status of subsidiary protection for nationals of third countries who, without obtaining European asylum, are in need of international protection;
   (c) a common system of temporary protection for displaced persons in the event of a massive inflow;
   (d) common procedures for the granting and withdrawing of uniform asylum or subsidiary protection status;
   (e) criteria and mechanisms for determining which Member State is responsible for considering an application for asylum or subsidiary protection;
   (f) standards concerning the conditions for the reception of applicants for asylum or subsidiary protection;
   (g) partnership and cooperation with third countries for the purpose of managing inflows of people applying for asylum or subsidiary or temporary protection.
3. In the event of one or more Member States being confronted by an emergency situation characterised by a sudden inflow of nationals of third countries, the Council, on a proposal from the Commission, may adopt provisional measures for the benefit of the Member State(s) concerned. It shall act after consulting the European Parliament.

Article 80 TFEU, concerning the principle of solidarity as regards EU immigration and asylum law, is also relevant:

The policies of the Union set out in this Chapter and their implementation shall be governed by the principle of solidarity and fair sharing of responsibility, including its financial implications, between the Member States. Whenever necessary, the Union acts adopted pursuant to this Chapter shall contain appropriate measures to give effect to this principle.

Regulation, while the other cases concerned the qualification Directive. On the substance of these cases, see I:5.5 and I:5.8 below.

[40] On the infringement actions, see I:5.5, I:5.6, I:5.8, and I:5.9 below; on the annulment action, see n 24 above.

Comparing Article 78 TFEU to the previous Article 63(1) and (2) EC, there was no change in the relevant decision-making rule, which remains the co-decision procedure (now known as the 'ordinary legislative procedure').[41] Article 78(3) TFEU replaced the previous Article 64(2) EC, and now includes a requirement to consult the EP before such measures are taken.[42] Unlike the previous rules, Article 78(1) states that the EU acts in this area 'with a view to offering appropriate status to any third-country national requiring international protection' and requires 'compliance with the principle of non-refoulement'. As with the previous Treaty Article, the policy has to be 'in accordance with' the Geneva Convention, the New York Protocol, and 'other relevant treaties'. The EU must therefore continue to ensure compliance with these treaties (and now also with the principle of non-refoulement and with a view to offering appropriate status) as an obligation deriving from the Treaty, not merely from Member States' treaty obligations, customary international law, or *jus cogens*. Moreover, this power now explicitly applies to all aspects of the EU's protection-related policies, not just (as previously) to the competences related to the Geneva Convention.

With the advent of the 'normal' jurisdiction of the Court of Justice in this area, there has been an increase in the number of cases concerning asylum reaching the Court. It has received between five and ten cases a year, concerning all the main first-phase legislation (and from 2015, the second-phase legislation).[43] The strengthened status of the EU Charter of Rights has also had an impact on EU asylum law in practice.[44]

Apart from these horizontal changes to JHA rules, the most significant change in this specific area was the amendment of the competence of the EU regarding asylum issues, in particular to include the objective of creating a 'common' policy, with the components of that policy taken from the Tampere conclusions and fully including subsidiary protection.[45]

An agenda for asylum measures after the Treaty of Lisbon entered into force was set out in the Stockholm Programme,[46] which stated that the Common European Asylum System 'should be based on high protection standards', with 'due regard' also for 'fair and effective procedures capable of preventing abuse'. It is 'crucial' that applicants are offered in each Member State an 'equivalent level of treatment as regards reception conditions, and the same level as regards procedural arrangements and status determination. The objective should be that similar cases should be treated alike and result in the same outcome'. Noting the 'significant differences' between national policies, the creation of the CEAS 'should remain a key policy objective for the EU', '[i]n order to achieve a higher degree of harmonisation'. The underlying principle is that '[c]ommon rules, as well as a better and more coherent application of them, should prevent or reduce secondary movements within the EU, and increase mutual trust between Member States'.

How was this agenda implemented in practice? The entry into force of the Treaty of Lisbon did not impact upon pending proposals for asylum legislation,[47] given that the

---

[41] For the details of that procedure, see Art 294 TFEU (ex-Art 251 EC).

[42] On Art 78(3), see further I:5.2.4 below. Like the previous Art 64(2) EC, this provision has never been used.

[43] See I:5.5, I:5.7, I:5.8, and I:5.9 below.   [44] For more on these issues, see I:5.3 below.

[45] For more on the issue of competence, see I:5.2.4 below.   [46] [2010] OJ C 115, s 6.2.

[47] See I:5.2.2 above.

decision-making process remained unchanged. Eventually, by June 2013, the Council and EP were able to agree upon all the proposals for a second-phase of the CEAS, concerning qualification for international protection, procedures for applications, reception conditions, the Dublin rules and Eurodac.[48] The EU also adopted legislation to create a European Asylum Support Office (EASO).[49] Furthermore, the EU adopted some immigration law measures relevant to asylum: a Regulation on social security for third-country nationals,[50] and a Directive on the extension of long-term residence status to refugees and persons with subsidiary protection.[51] EU funding in this area for 2014–20 is set out in the legislation establishing an Asylum, Migration, and Integration Fund.[52]

Subsequently, the Commission proposed an amendment to the Dublin rules dealing with the specific issue of unaccompanied minors,[53] and the EU reacted to the refugee and immigration crisis of 2015 by adopting two Decisions on the 'relocation' of asylum seekers within the EU and the resettlement of refugees from outside it.[54] As a further response to the refugee crisis, in September 2015 the Commission proposed a permanent system for relocating asylum seekers and a common list of safe third countries, and in December it proposed rules on resettlement. In 2016, it will propose legislation further revising the Dublin rules.[55]

5.2.4 Competence issues

Although the Treaty of Lisbon altered the rules on EU competence regarding asylum issues, in particular to remove the requirement that the EC (as it then was) could only set minimum standards as regards asylum, except as regards the rules on responsibility for applications, it is still necessary to examine first of all the prior rules on competence, since they affect the interpretation and possibly the validity of legislation adopted before the Treaty of Lisbon entered into force.

While the qualification Directive, the procedures directive, and the reception conditions directive all permit Member States to set higher standards,[56] they equally in turn require that any higher standards must nevertheless be 'compatible' with each Directive (the 'compatibility clauses'). The CJEU has made clear that this sets a

---

[48] See I:5.5.2, I:5.7.2, I:5.8.4, and I:5.9.2 below. For detailed analysis of all the asylum legislation, see S Peers, V Moreno Lax, M Garlick, and E Guild, *EU Immigration and Asylum Law: Text and Commentary*, 2nd edn, vol 3 (Brill, 2015).

[49] Reg 439/2010 ([2010] OJ L 132/11) and the accompanying amendment to the Refugee Fund ([2010] OJ L 129/1). See I:5.10.1 below.

[50] See I:6.8 below.

[51] See I:6.7 below. While this Directive gives refugees and beneficiaries of international protection the right to move to another Member State, it does not address the issue of transfer of protection to that other State. See the study on this issue, online at: <http://ec.europa.eu/justice_home/doc_centre/asylum/studies/doc_asylum_studies_en.htm>.

[52] Reg 516/2014 ([2014] OJ L 150/168).   [53] See I:5.8.4 below.

[54] See I:5.8.5 and I:5.11 below.

[55] See I:5.8.5 below (relocation), I:5.7 below (safe countries of origin), I:5.11 below (resettlement), and COM (2015) 240, 13 May 2015 (EU migration agenda).

[56] See, for instance, Art 3, Dir 2004/83 ([2004] OJ L 304/12). This applies to both the first-phase and second-phase legislation.

ceiling on Member States' extension of refugee or subsidiary protection status. First of all, in *B and D*,[57] the Court said that extending refugee status to persons who were excluded from that status by the Geneva Convention would exceed Member States' capacity to extend higher standards, since it would undercut the international refugee system. Secondly, in *M'Bodj*, the Court said that Member States could not give subsidiary protection status to an asylum seeker who faced a threat to his life from inadequate medical treatment in his country of origin, because the international protection system did not cover threats to individual well-being that did not stem directly from human action.[58] This did not mean that Member States had to expel the persons concerned, or even that they *could* expel them; rather that Member States could not award them refugee or subsidiary protection status.[59]

In light of these judgments, which more favourable standards *can* Member States apply? In the case of the qualification Directive, the Court says that higher standards must fall within the scope of international protection. It did not elaborate further, but this presumably refers back to the key concept of persecution or serious harm caused by a 'third party'. Higher standards can therefore apply only in relation to the Directive's definition of 'refugee' and 'subsidiary protection'. For instance, it should surely be open to Member States to grant subsidiary protection to persons fleeing indiscriminate violence even where the threat is not 'individual', or where the applicants are not civilians. As regards the other Directives, it is not clear what the implications are.

Following the entry into force of the Treaty of Lisbon, with the removal of the 'minimum standards' clause, the Union has the power to harmonize national asylum law as fully as it wishes, subject to the principles of subsidiary and proportionality. This is confirmed by the references to the creation of a 'common policy on asylum' and related issues[60] and to a 'common European asylum system', involving a 'uniform status' of asylum and subsidiary protection, a 'common system' of temporary protection, and 'common rules' on procedures for deciding applications,[61] along with the absence of any limitation on the scope of Article 78 TFEU. Three further powers are not be described as 'common' or 'uniform', but still fall within the scope of the general objective of developing a 'common' policy and system: the criteria and mechanisms for determining responsibility for applications; the reception standards for applicants; and relations with third countries. However, the EU does not have the *obligation* to harmonize asylum law fully, since competence regarding asylum law, along with the rest of JHA law, is shared between the EU and the Member States.[62] It is therefore possible (although no longer *obligatory*) for the EU to continue to set minimum standards only in its asylum legislation—which is indeed what it did in the second-phase asylum legislation.[63]

---

[57]   Joined Cases C-57/09 and C-101/09 *B and D* [2010] ECR I-10979.
[58]   Case C-542/13 *M'Bodj*, ECLI:EU:C:2014:2452. For more on both cases, see I:5.5 below.
[59]   In some cases, Member States may be obliged to let such persons stay, pursuant to the Returns Directive: see Case C-562/13 *Abdida*, ECLI:EU:C:2012:2453, discussed in I:7.7.1 below.
[60]   Arts 67(2) and 78(1).   [61]   Art 78(2).   [62]   Art 4(2)(j) TFEU.
[63]   See: Art 3, COM (2009) 551, 21 Oct 2009; Art 5, COM (2009) 554, 21 Oct 2009; and Art 4, COM (2008) 815, 3 Dec 2008.

Another important change brought about by the Treaty of Lisbon relates to the personal scope of EU asylum powers.[64] Before the entry into force of the Treaty of Lisbon, EC powers over asylum responsibility, the definition of 'refugee', and temporary protection were expressly limited to non-EU citizens, while the EC's powers over reception conditions, asylum procedures, subsidiary protection, and burden-sharing were not limited in personal scope. However, in practice EC asylum legislation adopted before the entry into force of the Treaty of Lisbon only addressed third-country nationals, presumably because the EC Treaty in principle ruled out asylum applications from EU citizens.[65] Following the entry into force of the Treaty of Lisbon, the EU's asylum powers only concern third-country nationals, and so therefore cannot be used to regulate asylum applications from EU citizens. The use of any alternative Treaty bases to regulate this issue would moreover be problematic in light of the relevant Protocol. So the impact of the Protocol can only be circumvented by making claims for subsidiary protection, or by arguing that the Protocol is in breach of the pre-existing Treaty commitments of the Member States (ie the Geneva Convention), and so must be disapplied pursuant to Article 351 TFEU.[66]

One specific amendment made by the Treaty of Lisbon worth considering further is the power to regulate the *status* of asylum (and subsidiary protection), instead of *qualification* as refugees. This wording reflects the full title of the Geneva Convention and could therefore be understood as encompassing the main content of that Convention—both the definition ('qualification') of refugees and their status on the territory (in terms of, for example, residence and access to employment and benefits). Within the previous legal framework, the latter issues were dealt with by using the EC's immigration powers,[67] but this should not be necessary after the entry into force of the Treaty of Lisbon.[68] It might also be argued that EU legislation regulating long-term residents' status and movement between Member States should, as regards at least refugees, have been adopted after the entry into force of the Treaty of Lisbon on the basis of the EU's asylum powers, since that legislation regulates the status of refugees and persons with subsidiary protection as regards immigration law (although not the distinct protection aspects of the status of such persons).[69] In any event, there is now no conflict between the decision-making rules applicable to asylum on the one hand and legal migration on the other. The most important point is to avoid regulating the immigration status of persons with international protection purely on the basis of their protection need, because then they would lose their status if that need ceased.

Furthermore, what is the scope of the provision concerning 'a status of asylum . . . valid throughout Union'? This should entail some degree of recognition by each Member State of other Member States' recognition of refugee status, but the full extent of that

---

[64] The remaining discussion in this section is largely adapted from S Peers, 'EU Immigration and Asylum Competence and Decision-Making in the Treaty of Lisbon' (2008) 10 EJML 219 at 235–8.

[65] See I:5.4.1 below.   [66] See further ibid.

[67] As noted above (I:5.2.2), Dir 2004/83 (n 56 above) was adopted on the basis of both asylum and immigration legal bases.

[68] Indeed, the second-phase qualification Directive is based on the EU's asylum law powers only (see I:5.5.2 below).

[69] That legislation was adopted on the basis of the EU's immigration law powers only: see I:6.7 below.

requirement is not clear. Could it be confined to recognition of the non-refoulement obligation, with the consequence that a refugee recognized by one Member State who is irregularly on the territory of another Member State must be returned to the Member State which first recognized that person's refugee status? Does it extend as far as to provide for a right of residence, valid in any Member State, entailing also all of the benefits (access to welfare, housing, and employment) accorded to legally resident Geneva Convention refugees, to the extent required by that Convention (and/or the qualification Directive)? Or would it entail something in between?

The best interpretation, in the absence of any clear indication in the Treaty, is that the EU institutions have a degree of discretion between different interpretations of this provision, and could choose to develop the Union-wide validity of that status gradually. It must always be kept in mind, however, that the Treaty does not refer expressly to a Union-wide validity of subsidiary protection status, so a distinction need always be made between the two types of status. However, it is arguable that even though the EU institutions are not *required* to provide for EU-wide validity of subsidiary protection status, they still have the *option* to provide for it, in the absence of a provision in the Treaty expressly limiting EU competence on this point.

As for temporary protection, the power following the entry into force of the Treaty of Lisbon not only constitutes a power to establish a 'common' policy, as noted above, but also it is limited, unlike the previous Treaty, to cases where there is a 'massive inflow'. However, it should be noted that the EU's previous temporary protection Directive is in any event limited to cases of a 'mass influx'.[70]

Next, the provision relating to 'partnership and cooperation' with third countries more clearly confers powers on the EU as regards this issue as compared to the previous Treaty, which expressly referred in most cases only to powers to regulate protection issues within or between Member States.[71] Furthermore, Article 78 TFEU is a *lex specialis* on this issue, which arguably therefore does not fall within the scope of the EU's development policy. The importance of this is that the EU has powers to harmonize asylum law fully, whereas EU development policy remains (as it was before the Treaty of Lisbon) a shared and parallel competence, meaning that the EU can never pre-empt national policy.[72]

The previous 'burden-sharing' power set out in the prior Article 63(2)(b) TEC was not retained as such. However, Article 80 TFEU refers to the principles of solidarity and fair sharing of responsibility, and specifies that EU immigration and asylum legislation 'shall contain appropriate measures to give effect to this principle' whenever this is 'necessary'. The objectives set out in Article 67(2) TFEU also provide that EU immigration and asylum policy shall be 'based on solidarity between Member States'. Article 80 is not a legal base in itself, but provides justification for the adoption of funding measures,[73] and possibly for non-financial measures concerning 'burden-sharing' as well.

---

[70] Art 1 of Dir 2001/55 ([2001] OJ L 212/12). For the definition of 'mass influx', see Art 2(d) of the Directive.

[71] See the previous Art 63(1)(a), (b), and (d), and 2(b). The exceptions were Art 63(1)(c) and 2(a), concerning the qualification of refugees and temporary protection.

[72] Art 4(4) TFEU.   [73] See I:5.10.2 below.

Finally, Article 78(3) TFEU, which confers power to address an 'emergency situation' constituting a 'sudden inflow' of third-country nationals, is identical to the previous Article 64(2) EC, except for the requirement to consult the EP, its placement in an Article dealing with asylum issues, the absence of a cross-reference to the general 'law and order' clause (which is now Article 72 TFEU), and the abolition of the requirement that measures should not exceed six months in duration.

What is the impact of these changes, as regards EU competence? First, the abolition of the cross-reference to the 'law and order' clause is immaterial, since this 'law and order' clause expressly applies in any event to the entire Title V. However, the placement of this emergency provision inside an Article solely concerned with asylum is new. Logically, this must mean that, after the Treaty of Lisbon entered into force, the 'sudden influx' clause is limited in its application to asylum-related issues, and moreover that its application is now governed by the general obligations set out in Article 78(1) TFEU as regards offering 'appropriate status' to persons needing international protection, along with compliance with the principle of non-refoulement, the Geneva Convention, and other relevant treaties. As for the abolition of the six-month limit, this can only mean that measures could, if necessary, last longer than six months; but the requirement that they be 'provisional' in nature obviously means that the measures could not apply indefinitely or for a very lengthy fixed period either. These criteria are satisfied by the first two measures based on Article 78(3), which the EU adopted in 2015. Furthermore, in the absence of a provision equivalent to Article 79(5), which limits EU powers to adopt rules on quotas for admission of economic migrants, EU legislation based on Article 78(3) can set out numbers of asylum seekers which Member States ought to admit. The interpretation of Article 78(3) will soon be clarified by the CJEU, since two Member States are challenging the second relocation Decision.[74]

5.2.5 Territorial scope

The UK opted in to all first-phase asylum measures, while Ireland opted in to all first-phase measures except the temporary protection Directive and the reception conditions Directive. It subsequently opted into the temporary protection Directive.[75] However, as regards second-phase measures, the UK and Ireland only opted in to the Dublin and Eurodac rules regarding asylum responsibility, the legislation creating the European Asylum Support Office, and the EU funding measures.[76] This means that the UK and Ireland are not covered by the key second-phase legislation on qualification, procedures, and reception conditions (or by the two relocation Decisions).[77] Since these measures not only *amended* the first-phase legislation but also *repealed* it, the question arises whether the UK and Ireland still remain bound by the first-phase

---

[74] Cases C-643/15 *Slovakia v Council* and C-647/15 *Hungary v Council*, both pending. On the substance of these Decisions, see I:5.8.5 below.

[75] See Commission Decision 2003/690 ([2003] OJ L 251/23). On the process of opting in after the adoption of a measure, see I:2.2.5.1.2 above.

[76] On the substance of these measures, see I:5.8.4, I:5.10.1, and I:5.11 below.

[77] On the substance of these measures, see I:5.5.2, I:5.7.2, and I:5.9.2 below.

legislation, considering that those Member States did not participate in the measure which repealed it. For the reasons set out in Chapter 2, the answer must be that they are still covered by the first-phase law.[78]

As for Denmark, it is automatically excluded from all EU asylum measures, although it remains a party to the 1990 Dublin Convention, which continued to govern the allocation of asylum applications between itself and all of the 'old' Member States, until the Community and Denmark concluded a treaty which extended the 'Eurodac' and 'Dublin II' Regulations to Denmark.[79] If Denmark does not agree to apply measures implementing or amending this legislation, the agreement will terminate unless the parties agree otherwise.[80] Pursuant to the revisions to the rules on Danish participation in JHA measures made by the Treaty of Lisbon, Denmark could in future decide to avail itself of an option to participate in EU asylum legislation on a case-by-case basis.[81]

Norway and Iceland are associated with the EU rules on responsibility for asylum applications (including Eurodac), due to a treaty between the EC (now the EU) and those States which has been in force since 1 April 2001.[82] This treaty requires Norway and Iceland to apply the Dublin Convention, the replacement EU rules (ie the Dublin II Regulation, and in future the proposals to amend that Regulation and the Eurodac Regulation, once adopted), and any measures implementing them.[83] Member States of the EU have reciprocal obligations,[84] except for Denmark, which was permitted to sign up to the treaty if it agreed a Protocol to that effect with the parties to the treaty.[85] Such a Protocol entered into force in 2006.[86]

The treaty can be suspended if Norway and Iceland fail to agree to new EU measures,[87] if major difficulties follow a substantial change in circumstances,[88] or if a divergence develops between the case law of the Norwegian and Icelandic courts and the Court of Justice's interpretation of the relevant rules, if the Joint Committee established by the treaty proves unable to agree a solution in either case.[89] To ensure future homogeneity of interpretation, Norway and Iceland have the right to comment on EU draft measures,[90] and to submit observations before the Court of Justice in relevant cases.[91] The practice of Norwegian and Icelandic courts and authorities should be kept under regular review.[92]

A treaty extending the responsibility rules (including Eurodac) to Switzerland entered into force on 1 March 2008, in parallel to the agreements on Swiss participation in the Schengen *acquis*.[93] This treaty is essentially identical to the EU treaty

---

[78] See I:2.2.5.1.4 above.
[79] [2006] OJ L 66/37, in force 1 Apr 2006 ([2006] OJ L 93/9). For discussion of the institutional features of the agreement, see I:2.2.5.2 above.
[80] Arts 3 and 4 of the agreement.
[81] See I:2.2.5.2 above. In that case, the 2006 agreement will terminate (see Art 10).
[82] Decision 2001/258 ([2001] OJ L 93/38). On the date of entry into force, see [2001] OJ L 112/16.
[83] On the substance of these measures, see I:5.8 below.   [84] Arts 1(2) and 1(5).
[85] Arts 12 and 13(3).
[86] [2006] OJ L 57/15, in force 1 May 2006. On the date of entry into force, see [2006] OJ L 112/12.
[87] Art 4(2) to (7).   [88] Art 5; compare with Art 17 of the Dublin Convention.
[89] Arts 7 and 8.   [90] Art 2; see also second and fourth Declarations to the treaty.
[91] Art 6(2).   [92] Art 7(1).
[93] [2008] OJ L 53/5; on the entry into force of the treaty, see [2008] OJ L 53/18. On Swiss participation in the Schengen rules, see I:2.2.5.4 above.

with Norway and Iceland, except that there was no need to associate Switzerland with the Dublin Convention (since it had already been replaced by an EU Regulation) and Switzerland has up to two years to implement its decision to apply new EU measures (in order to provide for a possible Swiss referendum). Additional protocols extend this treaty to Denmark and Liechtenstein.[94] Several of these countries also have treaties connecting them to the work of the European Asylum Support Office.[95]

The various treaties associating countries with the EU asylum responsibility rules are suspect because they set out conflict rules in the absence of harmonization of substantive asylum law, and because, like the internal EU responsibility rules, they force some families apart and ignore the 'applicants' choice' principle set out in United Nations High Commission for Refugees (UNHCR) Executive Committee conclusions, leading to an increase of destroyed documents (and therefore applications which are deemed to be 'unfounded' or 'manifestly unfounded').[96]

It should be noted that, notwithstanding the above rules on territorial scope, the special Protocol precluding EU citizens from applying for asylum in other Member States applies to all EU Member States, but not to any non-Member States.[97] In other words, this Protocol does not prevent an EU citizen from applying for asylum in Norway or Switzerland, or a citizen of one of the latter countries from applying for asylum in an EU Member State.

5.3 Human Rights

5.3.1 International human rights and refugee law

The starting point of international refugee law is the 1951 Geneva Convention on the status of refugees, together with the 1967 New York Protocol to that Convention.[98] The key provision of the Convention is Article 1.A(2), which defines a refugee (hereinafter a 'Convention refugee') as a person who:

> owing to a well-founded fear of being persecuted for reasons of race, religion, nationality, membership of a particular social group or political opinion, is outside the country of his [or her] nationality and is unable or, owing to such fear, is unwilling to avail himself [or herself] of the protection of that country, or who, not having a nationality and being outside of the country of his [or her] former habitual residence as a result of such events, is unable or, owing to such fear, unwilling to return to it.

Article 1.B of the Convention permits Contracting States to limit their obligations to events occurring within Europe, but no Member State now applies the geographical

---

[94] Arts 11 and 15 of the treaty. A Protocol regarding Danish participation in this treaty entered into force on 1 Dec 2008: see [2009] OJ L 161/6 and 8. A Protocol on Liechtenstein's participation came into force in 2011: [2011] OJ L 160.

[95] On that EU agency, see I:5.10.1 below. For the treaties, see: [2014] OJ L 109/1 (Norway); [2014] OJ L 102/1 (Switzerland); [2014] OJ L 102/3 (Liechtenstein); and [2014] OJ L 106/2 (Iceland).

[96] See criticisms in I:5.8 below.   [97] On the Protocol, see further I:5.4.1 below.

[98] All Member States are parties to both instruments. The Protocol removed the temporal limitation on the Convention, which was initially limited to persons fleeing developments which occurred before 1951. From a huge literature, see G Goodwin-Gill and J McAdam, *The Refugee in International Law*, 3rd edn (OUP, 2007) and E Feller, V Turk, and F Nicholson, eds., *Refugee Protection in International Law: UNHCR's Global Consultations on Refugee Protection* (CUP, 2003).

limitation and invoking it would be inconsistent with EC asylum legislation, which makes no provision for it. Article 1.C, the 'cessation' clause, sets out the grounds upon which persons cease to be Convention refugees, inter alia, where a person 'can no longer, because the circumstances in connexion with which he [or she] has been recognised as a refugee have ceased to exist, continue to refuse to avail himself [or herself] of the protection of the country of his [or her] nationality'.[99] The cessation clause does not apply to those categories of refugees who held status under prior international arrangements and who were 'able to invoke compelling reasons arising out of previous persecution' to object to the application of the cessation clause.[100]

Article 1.D specifies that:

> This Convention shall not apply to persons who are at present receiving from organs or agencies of the United Nations other than the United Nations High Commissioner for Refugees protection or assistance.
>
> When such protection or assistance has ceased for any reason, without the position of such persons being definitively settled in accordance with the relevant resolutions adopted by the General Assembly of the United Nations, these persons shall *ipso facto* be entitled to the benefits of this Convention.

Article 1.F states that a person is excluded from being a Convention refugee if 'there are serious reasons for considering that':[101]

> (a) he [or she] has committed a crime against peace, a war crime, or a crime against humanity, as defined in the international instruments drawn up to make provision in respect of such crimes;
>
> (b) he [or she] has committed a serious non-political crime outside the country of refuge prior to his [or her] admission to that country as a refugee;
>
> (c) he [or she] has been guilty of acts contrary to the purposes and principles of the United Nations.

The Convention is largely concerned with setting out the legal status of refugees, for example specifying the extent of their access to employment and welfare benefits in the state of refuge and providing for freedom of movement and the issue of travel documents to them.[102] Article 31 provides that in certain circumstances, refugees who enter or stay on a territory irregularly cannot be subject to penalties.[103] Article 32 specifies that a refugee who is 'lawfully in [the] territory' can only be expelled on 'grounds of national security or public order', and is furthermore entitled to procedural rights to contest the expulsion. Article 33, the non-refoulement clause, is regarded as the most important principle in the Convention, providing that:

> No Contracting State shall expel or return ('refouler') a refugee in any manner whatsoever to the frontiers of territories where his life or freedom would be threatened on account of his [or her] race, religion, nationality, membership of a particular social group or political opinion.

---

[99] Art 1(C)(5); Art 1(C)(6) applies the same principle to stateless persons.
[100] Art 1(C)(5) and (6).   [101] Art 1(E) also provides for an exclusion.
[102] Arts 12–30 of the Convention.   [103] On this principle, see I:7.3.2 below.

However, Article 33(2) of the Convention allows for an exception to this principle, where 'there are reasonable grounds for regarding [the refugee] as a danger to the security of the country in which he [or she] is, or' where, 'having been convicted by a final judgment of a particularly serious crime, [the refugee] constitutes a danger to the community of that country'.

Article 35 of the Convention requires Contracting States to cooperate with the UNHCR, which has the duty of 'supervising the application' of the Convention. However, the UNHCR is not a dispute settlement body; any disputes between Contracting Parties may be referred to the International Court of Justice for settlement (Article 38). There is no mechanism for individuals to bring a dispute about a State's application of the Convention before any international organ. In practice, the UNHCR has played a key role as regards the operational aspects of refugee protection (eg helping to establish refugee camps or resettlement programmes) and a role developing 'soft law' regarding the interpretation of the Geneva Convention and issues associated with it, in particular developing a Handbook on refugee protection and adopting Conclusions of its Executive Committee on refugee issues.[104]

The Convention does not expressly address the issues of the procedures for determining whether a claim to be recognized as a refugee is well-founded (asylum procedures), the conditions applicable to a person claiming recognition as a refugee (an asylum seeker) while a determination procedure is underway (reception conditions), or the issue of which State is responsible for the determination of a claim for recognition as a refugee. In fact, the Convention does not expressly state whether States can refuse to consider a claim for recognition as a refugee on the grounds that another State should be responsible for considering that claim. Nor does the Convention expressly deal with some key aspects of the legal status of refugee, in particular the right of residence of a person recognized to be a refugee and a refugee's right to family reunion. However, the non-refoulement clause gives rise to an implied right to remain on the territory if the conditions for application of that clause are met (unless another safe country is willing to accept the person concerned); and the conference which drew up the Convention agreed on a recommendation relating to family reunion.

The United Nations Convention against Torture, which has been ratified by all EU Member States, also deals with the question of the removal of people to face unsafe conditions. Article 3 of that Convention specifies that:

1. No State Party shall expel, return ('refouler') or extradite a person to another State where there are substantial grounds for believing that he [or she] would be in danger of being subjected to torture.
2. For the purpose of determining whether there are such grounds, the competent authorities shall take into account all relevant considerations including, where applicable, the existence in the State concerned of a consistent pattern of gross, flagrant or mass violations of human rights.

---

[104] See generally <http://www.unhcr.org>. For the Executive Committee conclusions, see: <http://www.unhcr.org/pages/49e6e6dd6.html>. For the Handbook, see <http://www.unhcr.org/3d58e13b4.html>.

A Committee against Torture, established to supervise the application of the Convention, can hear petitions from individuals, and has built up a considerable jurisprudence on the interpretation of Article 3.[105]

The International Covenant on Civil and Political Rights (ICCPR) contains no express provisions preventing persons from return to unsafe conditions, but the Human Rights Committee, which supervises the application of the Covenant, has ruled that the Covenant contains implicit protection against removal to face treatment which would amount to a breach of standards set out in the Covenant.[106] It is also arguable that protection against non-refoulement constitutes a rule of customary international law, or even a *jus cogens* rule that would trump any contrary international rule.[107] The right to asylum and related rights also appear in a number of national constitutions of Member States, in particular Germany and France.

As for the European Convention on Human Rights (ECHR), it does not contain any express provision relating to asylum or refugees, or limiting the substantive grounds upon which a person can be removed from a country. However, the jurisprudence of the European Court of Human Rights has addressed this issue in detail.[108] First of all, the Strasbourg Court has developed principles concerning the substance of international protection. Starting with its judgment in *Soering v UK*,[109] it established that a person could not be removed to a country where he or she faced a real risk of torture or inhuman or degrading treatment, in contravention of Article 3 ECHR. It did not matter whether the country of intended destination was a party to the ECHR or not, since the expelling State was liable to ensure that the removal did not breach Article 3. Although the *Soering* judgment concerned extradition, the Court soon confirmed that the principle applied equally to expulsions or other forms of removal, therefore including protected persons claiming refugee status or some other form of international protection.[110] However, it was clear from these and subsequent judgments that the threshold to show that a sufficiently high risk existed was not simple to meet.[111]

---

[105] On the Convention, see C Ingelse, *The UN Committee Against Torture: An Assessment* (Kluwer, 2001). For a critical view of the jurisprudence of the Committee, see J Doerfel, 'The Convention Against Torture and the Protection of Refugees' (2005) 24 RSQ 24:2 83.

[106] For an analysis of and excerpts from this jurisprudence, see J Schultz, S Joseph, and M Castan, *The International Covenant on Civil and Political Rights*, 2nd edn (OUP, 2004), 194–293.

[107] See E Lauterpacht and D Bethlehem, 'The Scope and Content of the Principle of *Non-Refoulement*: an Opinion' in Feller, Turk, and Nicholson (n 98 above), 87; N Coleman, '*Non-Refoulement* Revised. Renewed Review of the Status of *Non-Refoulement* as Customary International Law' (2003) 5 EJML 23; and J Allain, 'The *Jus Cogens* Nature of *Non-Refoulement*' (2002) 4 IJRL 533. The EU courts recognize customary international law and *jus cogens* as sources of law relevant to the interpretation and validity of Community measures: see respectively Cases C-162/96 *Racke* [1998] ECR I-3655, C-286/90 *Poulsen and Diva* [1992] ECR I-6019, and T-115/94 *Opel Austria* [1997] ECR II-39 (as regards customary international law), and Cases T-306/01 *Yusuf* [2005] ECR II-3533 and T-315/01 *Kadi* [2005] ECR II-3649 (as regards *jus cogens*).

[108] See H Lambert, 'Protection Against Refoulement from Europe: Human Rights Law Comes to the Rescue' (1999) 48 ICLQ 515 and 'The European Convention on Human Rights and the Protection of Refugees: Limits and Opportunities' (2005) 24:2 RSQ 39.

[109] A-161.

[110] See judgments in *Cruz Varas and Others v Sweden* (A-201) and *Vilvarajah and Others v UK* (A-215).

[111] See, for instance, the unsuccessful arguments in the cases of: *Venkadajalasarma v Netherlands* and *Thampibillai v Netherlands*, 17 Feb 2004; *Mamatkulov and Askarov v Turkey*, chamber judgment of 6 Feb 2003, and Grand Chamber judgment (ECHR 2005-I); *Muslim v Turkey*, 24 Apr 2005; *Aoulmi v France*, 17 Jan 2006; *FH v Sweden*, 20 Jan 2009; and *Puzan v Ukraine*, 18 Feb 2010. On the other hand, see, for

Subsequently, the Human Rights Court established the important principle that unlike Articles 32 and 33 of the Geneva Convention, Article 3 ECHR is absolute, precluding the application of limitations or derogations on the right not to be removed to face treatment in violation of Article 3, even in times of national emergency or where the person concerned was allegedly a terrorist.[112] This judgment was subsequently affirmed even after the terrorist attacks of 11 September 2001; moreover, the Human Rights Court has also consistently ruled that diplomatic assurances by the State of destination that torture will not be carried out are not in themselves sufficient to avoid the risk of it occurring, and equally the existence of domestic law safeguarding human rights and the ratification of international human rights treaties is not relevant if there is evidence of actual torture, etc. in the State concerned.[113]

Moreover, although some Member States traditionally limited the application of the Geneva Convention to cases where persecution emanated from the State, Article 3 ECHR covers cases where the person concerned fears violence from non-State actors, on the condition that the relevant State is unable to provide the person with protection.[114] While the ECHR case law does not generally accept that generalized violence in the country of origin gives rise per se to an Article 3 risk for any person returned there, it is possible in principle that an exceptional situation might exist where all persons returning there are at risk. Otherwise an applicant must show that there are special distinguishing features in his or her case, unless the applicant argues that he or she is 'a member of a group systematically exposed to a practice of ill-treatment', and 'there are serious reasons to believe the existence of that practice and his or her membership of the group concerned'. The need to show special distinguishing features is assessed in light of whether the situation of overall violence means that it is more likely that the group in question will be ill-treated.[115]

In 2011, the Human Rights Court ruled that, at least to some extent, the ECHR applies to a Member State's authorities operating on the high seas, when they intercept persons who object to their removal to a country which is unsafe on Article 3 grounds.[116] As for the position *within* the third State concerned, the Human Rights Court has ruled that while in principle an 'internal flight alternative' principle could apply (ie the asylum seeker might conceivably be safe in a *different* part of the country of origin that he or she fled from), there had to be guarantees that 'the person to be expelled must be able to travel to the area concerned, gain admittance and settle there'.[117]

---

instance, the successful arguments in the cases of: *Jabari v Turkey* (Reports 2000-VIII); *Hilal v UK* (Reports 2001-II); *Said v Netherlands*, 5 July 2005; *N v Finland*, 26 July 2005; *Klein v Russia*, 1 Apr 2010; and *SH v UK*, 15 June 2010.

[112] See particularly *Chahal v UK* (Reports 1996-V), followed by *Ahmed v Austria* (Reports 1996-VI) and *N v Finland*, n 111 above.

[113] *Saadi v Italy*, 28 Feb 2008. See subsequently *Ismoilov v Russia*, 24 Apr 2008; *Muminov v Russia*, 11 Dec 2008; *Ben Khemais v Italy*, 24 Feb 2009; *O and others v Italy*, 24 Mar 2009; *Abdolkhani and Karimnia v Turkey*, 22 Sep 2009; *Khodzhayev v Russia*, 12 May 2010; *Khaydarov v Russia*, 20 May 2010; and *Garayev v Azerbaijan*, 10 June 2010.

[114] *HLR v France* (Reports 1997-III); *N v Finland* (n 111 above); and *Salah Sheekh v Netherlands* (ECHR 2007-I).

[115] See *Saadi*, n 113 above, *NA v UK* (17 July 2008) and *Soldatenko v Ukraine* (23 Oct 2008).

[116] See *Hirsi Jamaa v Italy*, 23 Feb 2011.

[117] *Salah Sheekh* (n 114 above), para 141. On the facts of this case, the guarantees were not present, since the person concerned was from a minority group which could not expect 'clan protection' even in the 'safe' parts of Somalia.

Is there a 'Soering effect' to other provisions of the ECHR besides Article 3?[118] The *Soering* judgment itself also stated that a person could not be removed to face a manifest breach of the right to a fair trial as guaranteed by Article 6 ECHR in the destination State. However, to date the Strasbourg Court has not yet ruled in favour of an applicant who was arguing that such a risk exists. In *Bader*, the Court ruled that it would be a breach of Article 2 ECHR to send a person to a State of destination where he or she faced a death penalty imposed following an unfair trial,[119] and the Court has since confirmed that a *Soering* effect applies as regards expulsion to face the death penalty.[120] As for other ECHR articles, the Court hinted in its *Bankovic* decision that Article 5 ECHR conferred a *Soering* effect,[121] and the UK House of Lords has taken the view that any provision of the ECHR could in principle confer such an effect.[122]

A number of cases also concern procedural rights in relation to international protection, applying Article 3 in conjunction with Article 13 ECHR, which guarantees an 'effective remedy' in respect of the substantive rights set out in the Convention. Although the Court has repeatedly held that the standard system of judicial review applied in English law is adequate to meet the 'effective remedies' requirement,[123] except where the usual standard is substantially lower due to alleged security risks,[124] it has criticized particular procedural rules in other countries. In *Jabari v Turkey*,[125] it stated that the ECHR will be violated if there is no consideration of the merits of an asylum request for procedural reasons, where there is also no suspensive effect of an appeal or consideration of the merits on appeal. More broadly, States have obligations to ensure 'independent and rigorous scrutiny' of claims, entailing the 'possibility of suspending' a removal.

The Court returned to some of these issues in its judgment in *Conka v Belgium*, stating that Article 13 ECHR would be breached if national authorities carry out an expulsion before it is determined whether that expulsion is compatible with the ECHR, and ruling that the Belgian system denying suspensive effect (but permitting an application to a court which might grant it) was in particular a breach of Article 13, since only automatic suspensive effect will satisfy the requirements of the Convention; arguments about the overload of the courts and the 'risks of abuse of process' did not convince the Human Rights Court.[126] Although this judgment concerned collective expulsions, not Article 3 ECHR, the Court subsequently confirmed its applicability to Article 3 in the case of *Gebremedhin v France*, ruling that 'this finding obviously applies in a case where a State Party decides to remove an alien to a country where there are substantial grounds for believing that he or she would run [an Article 3] risk'.[127] Again, it was essential either that the asylum seeker be permitted to stay on the territory pending a

---

[118] See further the discussion in II:3.3.1.   [119] *Bader v Sweden* (2005 ECHR-XI).

[120] *Al-Saadoon and Mufdhi*, judgment of 2 Mar 2010.

[121] Decision in *Bankovic v UK and others* (Reports 2001-XII).

[122] *R. v Special Adjudicator ex parte Ullah and Do* [2004] UKHL 26. See also the analysis by R Piotrowicz and C van Eck, 'Subsidiary Protection and Primary Rights' (2004) 53 ICLQ 107.

[123] See *Soering, Vilvarajah, Hilal, and NA v UK*, nn 109 to 111 and 115 above.

[124] See *Chahal*, n 112 above.   [125] Paras 49 and 50, n 111 above.

[126] Paras 79–85 of the judgment (Reports 2002-I).

[127] Para 58 of the judgment, 26 Apr 2007. See subsequently *Muminov* and *Abdolkhani and Karimnia* (both n 113 above), and *Baysakov v Ukraine* (18 Feb 2010).

final decision, or that at least an application for an emergency ruling challenging an expulsion decision must have automatic suspensive effect.

Moreover, other procedural rights are conferred by the ECHR in asylum cases. It is clear from *Jabari* that an absolute and rigid time-limit for presenting applications is a procedural defect that violates Article 3 ECHR, although it might be remedied if the merits of a case were nonetheless considered in an appeal which entailed suspensive effect. In *Abdolkhani and Karimnia*, the Turkish government violated Article 13 ECHR due to failing to respond to an asylum application, failing to notify the reasons for not responding and for deporting the applicants, and failure to ensure legal assistance.[128] Other procedural issues were considered in a decision of the European Human Rights Commission in *Hatami v Sweden*,[129] a case subsequently settled. In this case, the government rejected an asylum application, inter alia, on the grounds that the applicant's story about his transit route was not convincing. The Commission concluded that a government refusal to recognize a refugee due to alleged inconsistencies resulting from a short interview conducted with inadequate interpretation facilities, resulting only in a short report lacking any detail and not explained to the applicant, led to a breach of Article 3 EHCR due to inadequate procedural safeguards in the State concerned. Moreover, the Commission explicitly placed great stress on the medical evidence presented by an applicant, where it is consistent with the applicant's statements concerning torture. It is also clear that, to avoid an Article 3 violation, instead of an obsessive focus by the authorities on alleged inconsistencies concerning an applicant's travel, the asylum determination process should focus on an applicant's assertions concerning the threat of torture, derived from an applicant's 'political affiliations…and his activities, his history of detention and ill-treatment'. Finally, the Commission made the important general observation that 'complete accuracy is seldom to be expected by victims of torture'. In later cases, the Human Rights Court ruled that lack of credibility in an applicant's story regarding his or her transit should be overlooked where there was nonetheless a sufficiently strong argument that an Article 3 risk would materialize upon return to the country of origin,[130] and that minor inconsistencies could not detract from the underlying credibility of the applicant, given the evidence that backed up his account of events.[131]

One decision of the Human Rights Court concerns the important issue of responsibility for asylum applications. An admissibility decision in the case of *T.I. v U.K.* concerned the application of the EU's Dublin Convention (as it then was), which in the relevant case provided that the responsible State to consider the asylum application would be Germany, not the UK.[132] The applicant argued that removal from the UK to Germany would breach Article 3 ECHR, on the grounds that Germany would in turn remove him to an unsafe country. In return, the UK argued that removal of an asylum seeker pursuant to the Dublin Convention should not engage its responsibility under Article 3 ECHR. The Human Rights Court decisively rejected that argument:

---

[128] *Abdolkhani and Karimnia*, n 113 above. See also *Baysakov*, n 127 above.
[129] Report, 23 Apr 1998 (unreported), paras 96 to 109. [130] *N v Finland*, n 111 above.
[131] *RC v Sweden*, 9 Mar 2010. [132] Reports 2000-III.

The Court finds that the indirect removal in this case to an intermediary country, which is also a Contracting State, does not affect the responsibility of the United Kingdom to ensure that the applicant is not, as a result of its decision to expel, exposed to treatment contrary to Article 3 of the Convention. Nor can the United Kingdom rely automatically in that context on the arrangements made in the Dublin Convention concerning the attribution of responsibility between European countries for deciding asylum claims. Where States establish international organisations, or *mutatis mutandis* international agreements, to pursue co-operation in certain fields of activities, there may be implications for the protection of fundamental rights. It would be incompatible with the purpose and object of the Convention if Contracting States were thereby absolved from their responsibility under the Convention in relation to the field of activity covered by such attribution.... The Court notes the comments of the UNHCR that, while the Dublin Convention may pursue laudable objectives, its effectiveness may be undermined in practice by the differing approaches adopted by Contracting States to the scope of protection offered.

The Human Rights Court has applied this judgment in the context of removals to other (non-European) transit countries, setting out a test as to the application of the rule: whether there is a legal framework providing adequate safeguards against removal to the country of origin from the third State concerned.[133] The Court has also applied the principle by analogy to removals to part of the country of origin (ie assessing whether the person concerned would be compelled to move from the 'safe' part of that country to the unsafe part).[134]

As regards removals to other EU States, the Human Rights Court has ruled that the *TI* decision 'must apply with equal force to the Dublin Regulation'. Ultimately, it ruled out any returns of asylum seekers to Greece, due to the evidence of the general collapse of the asylum system in that country, causing significant failures to apply ECHR and EU standards on reception conditions and procedural rights.[135] Subsequently, it applied a more limited version of this rule, holding in *Tarakhel v Switzerland* that a particular category of asylum seekers (families with children) could not be returned to Italy until it was clear that specific problems with their housing would be addressed.[136]

It should be stressed that protection against removal pursuant to Article 3 ECHR or other provisions of the ECHR does not necessarily guarantee that refugee status or any other formal legal status conferring rights such as social assistance or access to employment will be conferred. In the *Ahmed* case,[137] Austria in fact withdrew any form of government support from Mr Ahmed, with the result that he wandered penniless on the streets—and ultimately committed suicide.

Finally, the Human Rights Court has also addressed the issue of detention of asylum seekers pursuant to Article 5 ECHR, and the protection of private and family life

---

[133] *Abdolkhani and Karimnia* (n 113 above), para 89. This judgment was followed in *Tehrani v Turkey* and *Keshmiri v Turkey*, both 13 Apr 2010.

[134] *Salah Sheekh* (n 114 above), para 141.

[135] *MSS v Belgium and Greece*, 21 Jan 2011. For analysis of this judgment, see for instance V Moreno-Lax, 'Dismantling the Dublin System: *M.S.S. v Belgium and Greece*' (2012) 14 EJML 1. See earlier *KRS v UK*, decision of 2 Dec 2008.

[136] *Tarakhel v Switzerland*, 4 Nov 2014.   [137] N 112 above.

pursuant to Article 8 ECHR has implications for the admission of family members of persons in need of international protection, and for the expulsion of those persons or their family members.[138]

5.3.2 Application to EU law

The Court of Justice has ruled that the general principles of EU law include the rights guaranteed by Article 3 ECHR, including the relevant jurisprudence of the Strasbourg Court.[139] However, the Court of Justice has not yet ruled on whether the general principles incorporate a right to asylum or other form of protection from removal. Furthermore, in this area the primary law of the EU refers to the protection guaranteed by the Geneva Convention and other international treaties,[140] and the Court of Justice has duly ruled that these sources must be taken into account when interpreting EU legislation.[141]

As for the EU's Charter of Rights, it includes the right to asylum and a ban on expulsion to face torture, etc. or the death penalty.[142] The Court of Justice has in effect followed the *MSS* judgment of the European Court of Human Rights and held that returning asylum seekers to Greece pursuant to the Dublin rules would breach Article 4 of the Charter (which corresponds to Article 3 ECHR), although it has been resistant to any further limitation on the operation of the Dublin system.[143] The Court has also referred to the rights to privacy and dignity in the context of reception conditions and assessment of asylum applications,[144] along with the right to a fair trial in the context of asylum procedures.[145]

5.4 Impact of Other EU Law

5.4.1 Asylum and EU citizens

The Protocol on asylum applications by EU citizens was initially attached to the EC Treaty by the Treaty of Amsterdam, and the Treaty of Lisbon subsequently made technical amendments to the Protocol, inter alia, to refer to the EU Charter of Rights and the general principles of EU law, and to take account of the restructuring of the Treaties, by attaching the Protocol to both the revised TEU and to the TFEU. The Protocol begins with a lengthy preamble, referring to the protection of human rights guaranteed by the Treaties (and now the Charter), including the Court of Justice's jurisdiction to interpret these principles. It also refers to the obligation of Member States acceding to the EU to protect human rights and the possibility, introduced by the Treaty of Amsterdam, of suspending Member States which commit a 'serious and persistent' breach of human

---

[138] See respectively I:6.3.1 and I:7.3.2 below.
[139] Case C-465/07 *Elgafaji and Elgafaji* [2009] ECR I-921, referring to *NA v UK*, n 111 above.
[140] Art 78 TFEU (previously Art 63 EC).
[141] Case law beginning with Joined Cases C-175/08, 176/08, 178/08, and 179/08 *Abdulla and others* [2010] ECR I-1493 and C-31/09 *Bolbol* [2010] ECR I-5539.
[142] Arts 18 and 19 of the Charter ([2007] OJ C 303).   [143] See I:5.8 below.
[144] See I:5.5 and I:5.9 below.   [145] See I:5.7 below.

rights, democracy, and the rule of law.[146] Taking account of the 'special status and protection' which EU citizens have under the Treaties, and 'respect[ing] the finality and the objectives of the Geneva Convention', each Member State 'shall be regarded as' a safe country of origin by the others for 'all legal and practical purposes'.

However, an asylum application made by a national of one Member State in another 'may be taken into consideration or declared admissible for processing…only' if: the Member State of which the applicant is a citizen uses the 'national security' derogation of Article 15 of the ECHR after the entry into force of the Treaty of Amsterdam; or the Council or the European Council is considering punishing or has punished the applicant's Member State for human rights abuses pursuant to the procedure described in the preamble to the Protocol; or 'if a Member State should so decide unilaterally', in which case it must inform the Council and presume that this application is 'manifestly unfounded' (although this presumption cannot bind the national decision-making bodies).

The background to the Protocol indicates that it is an extradition measure in disguise. Its sole purpose was to prevent Belgium from considering asylum claims whom Spain wished to try for terrorist offences. However, the Protocol is couched in more general terms and it might have broader effect, particularly for a period after enlargement of the EU, when citizens of the newer Member States might still wish to make asylum claims in the old Member States because they will not have the right of free movement of workers for a transition period of up to seven years.[147] The Protocol is attached to the Treaties generally, not specifically to Title V of the TFEU, so it applies to all Member States.

In a unilateral Declaration to the Treaty of Amsterdam, Belgium declared that it would use the final option and 'carry out an individual examination of any asylum request made by a national of another Member State', while a Declaration to the Treaty of Amsterdam states that the Protocol does not prevent Member States from taking organizational measures which they deem necessary to apply the Geneva Convention. In light of these provisos, the Declaration was not likely to have much effect, although there is no information available on its implementation in order to test it. It should also be noted that the Protocol is not applicable to claims for subsidiary protection, so its effect is easy to avoid for any EU citizen who wishes to apply specifically for that form of protection, rather than for recognition of refugee status, in another Member State. But in light of the changes to extradition law brought about by the European Arrest Warrant (in particular the abolition of the protection against extradition traditionally enjoyed by a State's own nationals), the objectives of the Protocol may now have been achieved by other means.[148]

The validity of the Protocol may be doubted in light of the wording of the Geneva Convention, which expressly requires the Convention to be applied on a non-discriminatory basis.[149] Although the Court of Justice does not have the jurisdiction to rule on the validity of the founding Treaties (including Protocols to the Treaties),

---

[146] See Art 7 EU.
[147] For these limitations, see, for instance, Annex V to the 2003 Accession Treaty ([2003] OJ L 236).
[148] See II:3.5.2, and Case C-306/09 *I.B.*, [2010] ECR I-10341.   [149] Art 3 of the Convention.

Article 351 TFEU (previously Article 307 EC) does preserve the pre-existing obligations of Member States under prior treaties concluded with third countries, so it is still open to a national court to rule that the Protocol is inapplicable due to its incompatibility with Member States' obligations under the Convention. Although Article 351 requires Member States ultimately to amend or denounce their pre-existing treaty obligations to conform to EU rules,[150] it should be noted that the Court of Justice has ruled that the basic human rights rules in EU law prevail over Article 307 EC (now Article 351 TFEU).[151]

In any event, the dubious validity of the Protocol in light of the Geneva Convention entails a requirement to interpret it narrowly, with the consequence that a person holding the dual citizenship of a Member State and a non-Member State would not be prevented by the Protocol from relying on his or her non-Member State nationality to apply for asylum.[152] This derogation from the normal rule that a person with the dual nationality of a Member State and a non-Member State is not able to rely on his or her non-EU nationality is justified also by the broader human rights context.[153] Anyway, there can surely be no doubt that in the event that a person *loses* the nationality of a Member State (and does not retain or reacquire the nationality of another Member State),[154] then the Protocol no longer presents any bar to applying for asylum in a Member State.[155] Finally, there is nothing in the Protocol to question the validity of refugee status that was *already* granted to an EU citizen before the entry into force of the Treaty of Amsterdam, or (in respect of nationals of newer Member States) before the entry into force of the 2003, 2005, and 2011 Accession Treaties, or any future accession treaties. On the other hand, the position of a third-country national who obtains refugee status and then later acquires the citizenship of a Member State is addressed by a specific rule in the Geneva Convention.[156]

5.4.2 Other issues

The 1971 Regulation on social security for EU citizens and their family members who exercised free movement rights also expressly covered refugees and stateless persons (some of whom will be beneficiaries of subsidiary protection status in Member States).[157] In 2001, the Court of Justice ruled that this provision of the Regulation was

---

[150] See I:2.7 above.

[151] See Joined Cases C-402/05 P and C-415/05 P *Kadi and Al Barakaat* [2008] ECR I-6351, para 304. In that case, the Court was rejecting the argument that a pre-existing treaty obligation took preference over human rights obligations; but by analogy the judgment must also mean that an EU obligation to denounce pre-existing treaty obligations cannot apply where the EU obligation would breach human rights principles.

[152] He or she would surely still have to show, however, that the criteria for the refugee definition were not satisfied as regards *either* State of which he or she was a citizen.

[153] See Case C-179/98 *Mesbah* [1999] ECR I-7955 and the discussion in I:6.4.1 below.

[154] See Case C-135/08 *Rottmann* [2010] ECR I-1449, discussed ibid.

[155] Presumably, in such a case, the responsibility criteria could only take into account factors which post-dated the *de jure* loss of EU citizenship by the person concerned.

[156] See Art 1.C(3) of the Convention, which provides for refugee status to cease in the case that a person acquires the nationality of another country and enjoys the protection of that country. See also Art 11(1)(c) of the qualification Dir (Dir 2011/95, [2011] OJ L 337/9).

[157] Reg 1408/71 ([1971] OJ L 149/2). See further I:6.4.2 below.

valid, but stated that the Regulation only applied to refugees who had moved between Member States.[158] Subsequently, the 1971 Regulation was replaced as from 1 May 2010 by revised legislation, which also changed the rules as regards refugees and stateless persons.[159]

In the meantime, as from 1 June 2003, EU immigration legislation extended most of the 1971 Regulation on social security coordination for persons exercising free movement rights to third-country nationals other than refugees or stateless persons,[160] with the consequence that all persons with subsidiary protection or temporary protection have also been covered by the 1971 rules as from that date. These other categories of third-country nationals were covered by the free movement rules as from 1 January 2011, after the EU adopted legislation to that effect in 2010.[161]

The social security rules supplement the movement of refugees or persons with subsidiary protection between Member States, pursuant to legislation applicable since 2013.[162] Furthermore, EU employers have the right to post *any* third-country national employees to carry out a contract in another Member State,[163] regardless of any protection status they may have, as long as the employees are legally and habitually employed, so the application of the EU social security rules is also relevant to refugees and persons with subsidiary or temporary protection who are posted workers.

An important question is the overlap between refugee status (or other protection status) and status under EU free movement legislation (whether as an EU citizen or the family member of an EU citizen) or under an EU association agreement. The Court of Justice has confirmed that failed asylum seekers (and presumably also failed applicants for subsidiary protection, persons whose protection claims are pending, or persons whose protection claims have been successful) can benefit from EU free movement law if they become a family member of an EU citizen, even if their entry onto the territory was never authorized or became unauthorized following the failure of their asylum application.[164] Also, at least as regards the EU-Turkey association agreement, a refugee (and the refugee's family members) can rely on that agreement,[165] as can an asylum seeker whose asylum application was potentially subject to the rules in the Dublin Convention (and by analogy, the later Dublin Regulations) concerning responsibility for applications.[166] It is arguable by analogy that in the absence of anything to the contrary, there is nothing to preclude an individual relying on either protection status or

---

[158] Joined Cases C-95/99 to 98/99 *Khalil and others* and C-180/99 *Addou* [2001] ECR I-7413. See case note by S Peers, (2002) 39 CMLRev 1395.

[159] Reg 883/2004 ([2004] OJ L 166/1). This Reg only applied as from the date of effect of a subsequent implementing Reg, namely Reg 987/2009 ([2009] OJ L 284/1) (see Art 91 of Reg 883/2004, and subsequently Art 97 of Reg 987/2009 on the latter Reg's date of entry into effect).

[160] Reg 859/2003 ([2003] OJ L 124/1). See I:6.8 below.

[161] Reg 1231/2010 ([2010] OJ L 344/1). See Art 90(1)(a) of Reg 883/2004 and Art 96(1)(a) of Reg 987/2009 (both n 159 above).

[162] Dir 2011/51 ([2011] OJ L 132/1); see I:6.7 below.

[163] See Cases C-43/93 *Van der Elst* [1994] ECR I-3803, C-445/03 *Commission v Luxembourg* [2004] ECR I-10191, C-244/04 *Commission v Germany* [2006] ECR I-885, C-168/04 *Commission v Austria* [2006] ECR I-9041, C-219/08 *Commission v Belgium* [2009] ECR I-9213, and C-91/13 *Essent*, ECLI:EU:C:2014:2206. For further details of the principle, see I:6.4.4 below.

[164] Case C-127/08 *Metock* [2008] ECR I-6241.   [165] Case C-337/07 *Altun* [2008] ECR I-10323.

[166] Case C-16/05 *Tum and Dari* [2007] ECR I-7415.

the status under free movement law or an EU association agreement, depending on which status is more favourable.[167]

5.5 Uniform Status

The first-phase Directive 2004/83 on the definition of 'refugee' and subsidiary protection status and the content of that status was adopted in April 2004.[168] Member States had to implement the Directive by 10 October 2006.[169] The second-phase Directive, which was adopted in December 2011, had to be implemented by 21 December 2013.[170] The two Directives are discussed in turn.

5.5.1 First-phase Directive

The Commission had to bring cases against eight Member States for failure to implement the first-phase Directive on time. In four of these cases, the Court of Justice gave judgment against Member States,[171] while the Commission withdrew the other four complaints, presumably after tardy compliance by the Member States concerned.[172] Furthermore, there have been many references from national courts on the interpretation of the Directive.[173] The Commission reported on the implementation of the Directive (the 'implementation report'),[174] and furthermore the impact assessment accompanying its 2009 proposal

---

[167] The point was also relevant in *Khalil* and *Addou*, n 158 above, but was not referred by the national court.

[168] [2004] OJ L 304/12. All references in this sub-section are to the Dir unless otherwise indicated. On the Directive, see UNHCR, *Asylum in the European Union, A study on the implementation of the Qualification Directive*, Nov 2007 (<http://www.unhcr.org/cgi-bin/texis/vtx/refworld/rwmain?docid=4730 50632&page=search>); ELENA/ECRE, *The impact of the EU Qualification Directive on International protection*, Oct 2008 (<http://www.ecre.org/files/ECRE_QD_study_full.pdf>); K Zwaan, ed., *The Qualification Directive: Central Themes, Problem Issues, and Implementation in Selected Member States* (Wolf Legal Publishers, 2007); J McAdam, 'The European Union Qualification Directive: The Creation of a Subsidiary Protection Regime' (2005) 17 IJRL 461; MT Gil-Bazo, 'Refugee Status and Subsidiary Protection Under EC Law: The Qualification Directive and the Right to Be Granted Asylum' in A Baldaccini, E Guild and H Toner, eds., *Whose Freedom, Security and Justice? EU Immigration and Asylum Law and Policy* (Hart, 2007), 229; and H Battjes, *European Asylum Law and International Law* (Martinus Nijhoff, 2006), ch 5.

[169] Art 38(1). All references in I:5.5.1 are to Dir 2004/83 unless otherwise indicated.

[170] Art 39(1), Dir 2011/95 ([2011] OJ L 337/9). See the ECRE information note on the Directive: <http://www.ecre.org/topics/areas-of-work/introduction/92-qualification-directive.html>.

[171] Cases: C-256/08 *Commission v UK*, judgment of 30 Apr 2009; C-293/08 *Commission v Finland*, judgment of 5 Feb 2009; C-322/08 *Commission v Sweden*, judgment of 14 Jun 2009; and C-272/08 *Commission v Spain*, judgment of 9 July 2009 (all unreported).

[172] Cases: C-190/08 *Commission v Netherlands*; C-191/08 *Commission v Portugal*; C-220/08 *Commission v Greece*; and C-269/08 *Commission v Malta*.

[173] Cases: C-465/07 *Elgafaji and Elgafaji* [2009] ECR I-921; C-175/08, 176/08, 178/08, and 179/08 *Abdulla and others* [2010] ECR I-1493; C-31/09 *Bolbol* [2010] ECR I-5539; C-57/09 and C-101/09 *B and D* [2010] ECR I-10979; C-71/11 and C-99/11 *Y and Z*, ECLI:EU:C:2012:518; C-364/11 *El Kott*, ECLI:EU:C:2012:826; C-277/11 *MM I*, ECLI:EU:C:2012:2206; C-199/12 to 201/12 *X, Y and Z*, ECLI:EU:C:2013:720; C-285/12 *Diakite*, ECLI:EU:C:2014:39; C-148/13 to C-150/13 *A, B, and C*, ECLI:EU:C:2014:2406; C-542/13 *M'Bodj*, ECLI:EU:C:2014:2452; C-562/13 *Abdida*, ECLI:EU:C:2012:2453; C-472/13 *Shepherd*, ECLI:EU:C:2015:117; and C-373/13 *T*, ECLI:EU:C:2015:413. Pending cases: C-443/14 and C-444/14 *Alo and others*; C-573/14 *Lounani*; C-150/15 *N*; and C-429/15 *Danqua*. Another case essentially concerns procedural issues, and so is discussed in I:5.7 below: Case C-604/12 *HN*, ECLI:EU:C:2012:2206.

[174] COM (2010) 314, 16 June 2010.

for amendments to the Directive (the '2009 impact assessment') contained some additional information on the application of the Directive in practice, and so is also referred to below.[175] A key general point is that despite the adoption of the Directive, there remained significant divergences in recognition rates between Member States,[176] although neither the implementation report nor the impact assessment assess whether or not the differences in recognition rates have at least been *reduced* since the implementation of the Directive,[177] or whether recognition rates in general increased due to the Directive.

First of all, as a general point, the Court of Justice ruled that as regards refugee status, the Directive's preamble made clear 'that the Geneva Convention constitutes the cornerstone of the international legal regime for the protection of refugees' and the rules on refugee status in the Directive 'were adopted to guide the competent authorities of the Member States in the application of that convention on the basis of common concepts and criteria'.[178] So the Directive had to be interpreted 'while respecting the Geneva Convention and the other relevant treaties' referred to in Article 63(1) EC (now Article 78(1) TFEU), as well as the relevant provisions of the EU's Charter of Fundamental Rights in particular.[179] The Court also clarified the relationship between the two different systems of international protection provided for in the Directive.[180]

Moving on to the substance of the Directive, Chapter I set out general provisions, including definitions and permission for Member States to apply more favourable rules, provided that they are 'compatible' with the Directive.[181] The interpretation of that provision, an issue which is relevant generally to EU asylum legislation, is discussed further above.[182]

Chapter II then set out standard rules on assessment of applications,[183] which were applicable to claims for either refugee or subsidiary protection status. Member States could require the applicant to submit all the elements needed to substantiate the application, including the applicant's statements and all elements at the applicant's disposal, although it was the job of Member States (in cooperation with the applicant) to consider that application.[184] The Member State's assessment had to 'be carried out on an individual basis' and take account of the relevant facts in the country of origin, the statements and documentation submitted by the applicant, the position and circumstances of the applicant (including gender), whether the applicant's activities since leaving the country of origin were for the 'sole or main purpose of creating the conditions' for an application, and whether the applicant could 'reasonably be expected' to have sought protection in another country where he or she could obtain citizenship.[185] If the applicant had been subjected to prior persecution or serious harm as defined in the Directive, or 'direct threats' of such action, that would be a 'serious indication' that the claim was well-founded.[186] The implementation report was critical of Member States' divergences and errors when transposing this provision.

---

[175] SEC (2009) 1373, 21 Oct 2009.
[176] See Annex 13 to the 2009 impact assessment and the conclusions to the implementation report.
[177] The evidence in the 2009 impact assessment is that the rate of secondary movements of asylum seekers did not reduce following the implementation of the qualification Directive.
[178] Case law beginning with *Abdulla* (n 173 above), para 52.
[179] Case law beginning with *Abdulla*, paras 53 and 54.   [180] See I:5.7 below.   [181] Arts 1–3.
[182] I:5.2.4.   [183] Arts 4–8.   [184] Art 4(1) and (2).   [185] Art 4(3).   [186] Art 4(4).

In the *Abdulla* judgment, the Court of Justice clarified the application of this principle when refugee status ceased on the grounds of change of circumstance (on which, see further below), but where arguably there was now a different set of circumstances in the country of origin justifying the continuation of that status. If, in contrast, the refugee was arguing that the original circumstances had not changed enough for the cessation principle to apply, then the national authorities and courts concerned had to apply the cessation rules instead.[187]

Next, in the *MM* judgment,[188] the CJEU ruled that the general provisions on assessment of applications did not require authorities to send a draft of its reasons for its planned negative decision to an applicant and ask him or her for observations. If the EU legislature had wanted to impose such a rule, it would have said so expressly. The assessment rules mainly concerned the first stage of the process, concerning establishing the facts, while the second stage is a 'legal appraisal of the evidence'. A Member State's duty of cooperation mainly referred to an obligation to cooperate with the applicant in order assist with the elements of the application that may be incomplete, for instance by obtaining 'access to certain types of documents'. But a draft decision would only be produced at a later stage, when the general obligation to cooperate was no longer relevant.[189]

In its subsequent ruling in *A, B, and C*,[190] the CJEU examined the assessment process in more detail, in particular as regards lesbian or gay asylum seekers.[191] While authorities sometimes have problems establishing whether asylum seekers have actually been persecuted, the issue with asylum claims based on sexual orientation arises at an earlier point: authorities often do not even believe that the asylum seeker is gay or lesbian in the first place. According to the CJEU, although the Directive does not address the issue of the credibility of asylum seekers in much detail, the process of determining the credibility of an asylum seeker had to be consistent with the EU Charter of Fundamental Rights. In principle, the same rules on credibility assessment apply to all categories of asylum seekers, but they can be adapted to particular groups. A self-declaration by the asylum seeker was not sufficient, but was only the starting point of the assessment.

How should such claims be assessed? First of all, the CJEU stated that questions 'based on stereotypical notions may be useful' to national authorities. But they could not base their decisions purely on such notions, and the asylum seeker's inability to answer such questions could not mean that he or she had no credibility. Secondly, the CJEU ruled against detailed questioning about asylum seekers' sex life, on the grounds that this would breach Article 7 of the Charter (the right to privacy). Thirdly, the CJEU ruled that lesbian and gay asylum seekers should not perform sex acts, produce films of their sexual activities, or undergo medical testing to prove their orientation. This would breach Article 1 of the Charter (the right to human dignity) as well as Article 7. Finally,

---

[187] Paras 94–100 of the judgment (n 173 above).   [188] Ibid.

[189] The Court also made several points in this judgment about the procedural rules applicable to subsidiary protection claims, discussed in I:5.7 below.

[190] N 173 above.

[191] Earlier judgments had confirmed that homosexuals could claim a need for international protection if they faced persecution as a 'particular social group'. See discussion of Arts 9 and 10 below.

the CJEU ruled that Member States cannot assume that gay and lesbian asylum seekers lack credibility simply because they did not raise the issue of their sexuality as soon as possible, in light of the sensitivity of the topic.

Next, the Directive provided that a protection need may arise *sur place*, in other words following the applicant's departure from the country of origin, but Member States could provide that applicants who filed a subsequent application would not normally be granted refugee status if they had created the circumstances for that status themselves since they left the country of origin.[192] It also required a fundamental change to the traditional interpretation of the Geneva Convention applied in some Member States (in particular France and Germany) by stating the 'actors of persecution' need not be the State, but may also be private parties, if it can be 'demonstrated' that the State, or parties controlling the State, is 'unable or unwilling' to provide protection against non-state agents.[193] The implementation report criticized several Member States' restrictive application of this rule.

Next, the Directive addressed the issue of 'actors of protection', stating that parties, including international organizations, controlling all or part of a State could provide protection, if such bodies took 'reasonable steps to prevent the persecution or suffering of serious harm, inter alia, by operating an effective legal system for the detection, prosecution and punishment of acts constituting persecution or serious harm, and the applicant has access to such protection'; Council acts could give guidance as to whether effective protection was provided by such bodies.[194] The Commission's 2009 impact assessment indicated that there were wide divergences between the Member States as regards the application of this principle,[195] and the implementation report criticized those Member States which considered that clans, tribes, or NGOs could offer such protection, because 'in practice, protection provided by these actors proves to be ineffective or of short duration'.

In the *Abdulla* judgment, which concerned the situation in Iraq, the Court of Justice stated that 'the Directive does not preclude the protection from being guaranteed by international organisations, including protection ensured through the presence of a multinational force in the territory of the third country'. The adequacy of the protection provided must be verified on an individual basis, considering 'in particular, the conditions of operation of, on the one hand, the institutions, authorities and security forces and, on the other, all groups or bodies of the third country which may, by their action or inaction, be responsible for acts of persecution against the recipient of refugee status if he returns to that country', as well as the application of the law in practice in that country and the 'the extent to which basic human rights are guaranteed' there.[196]

There was also an optional 'internal protection alternative', which could apply where there was a risk-free part of the country of origin where the applicant could 'reasonably be expected to stay'.[197] Although Member States had to have regard to the general conditions in that country and to the applicant's personal circumstances, the principle could apply in spite of 'technical obstacles to return'. According to the 2009 impact assessment and the implementation report, there were again great differences in the

---

[192] Art 5.   [193] Art 6.   [194] Art 7.   [195] See Annex 5 to the 2009 impact assessment.
[196] Paras 70–75 of the judgment (n 173 above).   [197] Art 8.

national application of this principle, as well as some errors applying the conditions for the application of this rule. While only eight Member States applied the exception relating to technical obstacles to return, there are also differences in how they invoked that rule.[198]

The rules on qualification for refugee status were set out in Chapter III.[199] 'Acts of persecution' were defined by reference to the severity of the acts, and there was a non-exhaustive list of the forms such acts could take, along with an obligation to find a link between the acts and the grounds of persecution.[200] Member States took different approaches as to whether the Directive applied when private groups persecuted individuals for reasons *not* based on the Geneva Convention, but where States then *failed to protect* the persons concerned on 'Convention grounds'.[201]

To constitute persecution, the acts in question had to be 'sufficiently serious by their nature or repetition as to constitute a severe violation of basic human rights', particularly the non-derogable rights under Article 15 ECHR, or be 'an accumulation of various measures, including violations of human rights which [are] sufficiently severe' as to fall within the first criterion. Six examples were given: acts of violence; legal or similar measures which are discriminatory; disproportionate or discriminatory prosecution or punishment; denial of judicial redress resulting in the same outcome; prosecution or punishment for 'refusal to perform military service in a conflict' which would lead to acts falling within the scope of the exclusion clause; and 'acts of a gender-specific or child-specific nature'.[202]

As for the grounds of persecution set out in Article 1(A) of the Geneva Convention, the Directive set out detailed definitions of the concepts of 'race', 'religion', 'nationality', 'particular social group', and 'political opinion'.[203] For the 'particular social group' ground to apply, it had to be shown 'in particular' that the group members have an innate characteristic, common background, or characteristic that it would be unjust to force to change *and* that the group has a distinct identity; sexual orientation might be a common characteristic but this cannot apply where the acts would be criminal under the 'national law of the Member States'. The prospect of 'gender' as an example of social group was addressed by stating that 'gender-related aspects can be considered, without by themselves alone creating a presumption' of persecution. According to the 2009 impact assessment and the implementation report, Member States were split as to whether these criteria to define a 'particular social group' were alternative or cumulative, and took different approaches as regards gender-based persecution.[204] As for 'political opinion', it included any opinion related to the *persecutors*, not just the policy of a *state*.

The CJEU has ruled on some aspects of the grounds for persecution and the nature of persecution under the Directive. In the *Y and Z* judgment, concerning persecution

---

[198] See Annex 6 to the 2009 impact assessment, and point 5.1.5 of the implementation report. See also the ECHR jurisprudence discussed in I:5.3.1 above.

[199] Arts 9–12.

[200] Art 9(2) and (3). According to the implementation report, some Member States did not insist on a causal link; this is (rightly) regarded as an acceptable higher standard for the persons concerned.

[201] See Annex 18 to the 2009 impact assessment, point 1.1.   [202] Art 9(1) and (2).

[203] Art 10.   [204] See Annex 7 to the 2009 impact assessment.

on grounds of religion, it noted that freedom of religion was a right protected under the ECHR and the corresponding Article 10 of the Charter.[205] However, this did not mean that 'any interference with the right to religious freedom' amounted to persecution which required the grant of refugee status. Rather, as the qualification Directive stated, there had to be a 'severe violation' of religious freedom, having (in the Court's words) 'a significant effect on the person concerned'. A restriction on religious freedom which would be *justified* under the ECHR and the Charter certainly could not count as such a violation. Even *unjustified* restrictions of that right would not always amount to persecution, unless their 'gravity' was 'equivalent' to an infringement of non-derogable human rights, as the Directive prescribed.

But to determine the meaning of persecution, it was not necessary to distinguish between 'core areas' of religious belief (private worship) and non-core areas (public activities). That distinction would be 'incompatible with the broad definition of "religion"' in the Directive, 'which encompasses all its constituent components, be they public or private, collective or individual'. So persecution could also constitute 'serious acts which interfere with the applicant's freedom not only to practice his [or her] faith in private circles but also to live that faith publicly'. The focus should be solely upon the 'severity of the measures and sanctions adopted or liable to be adopted' as regards the applicant's expression of faith in either context. A ban on participation in formal worship in public could be sufficiently severe for the purposes of the Directive, if there was 'a genuine risk that the applicant will, inter alia, be prosecuted or subject to inhuman or degrading punishment by one of the actors referred to' in the Directive. When assessing this risk, the authorities had to examine the subjective importance of that religious practice in public for the applicant 'in order to preserve his [or her] religious identity', even if the observance of that practice is not 'a core element of faith' for that religious community.[206] Finally, the Court assessed whether the applicant could be expected to refrain from certain religious practices. In the Court's view, the possibility of abstaining from such practices could not be a factor in a refugee claim.

Some of these issues recurred in the Court's subsequent judgment in *X, Y, and Z*. First of all, the Court confirmed that a 'particular social group' could include homosexuals. Applying the relevant criteria, the Court ruled that an individual's sexual orientation is a characteristic so fundamental to his or her identity that he or she should not be forced to renounce it. Gays and lesbians also met the second criterion, because the existence of laws criminalizing them in the country of origin showed that they had a 'distinct identity' because the surrounding society believed that they were 'different'.

But does the existence of a criminal law targeting a certain group necessarily amount to *persecution*? As with religious freedom, the Court stated that 'not all violations of fundamental rights suffered by a homosexual asylum seeker will necessarily reach' the 'level of seriousness' necessary to constitute persecution. While sexual orientation was linked to the rights to private life and non-discrimination under the Charter and the ECHR, those rights were not non-derogable. So the mere existence of a law

---

[205] N 173 above. See also the *N* case, pending, also n 173 above.

[206] The Court also referred to 'objective' elements that had to be taken into account, but did not elaborate on this concept further.

'criminalizing homosexual acts' cannot be regarded as an act affecting the applicant in a manner so significant that it reaches the level of seriousness necessary for a finding that it constitutes persecution within the meaning of Article 9(1) of the Directive. But a term of imprisonment that results from such a law *can* 'in itself' constitute persecution, as long as it is 'actually applied' in practice in the country of origin, because it is not only an infringement of the ECHR and the Charter, but also a 'disproportionate or discriminatory' punishment or prosecution for the purposes of defining persecution.

Next, the Court returned to the question of whether there must be a distinction between different types of acts for the purposes of the Directive. In particular, could asylum seekers be expected to conceal their sexual orientation, or at least exercise some restraint in expressing it? The Court noted that, according to the Directive, a claim based on sexual orientation could not be based on acts which were criminal under a Member State's law. But other than that, the Directive did not suggest that the EU legislature wanted to exclude other forms of acts or expression from the protection from persecution on grounds of sexual orientation. There was no reference to their attitude or behaviour, and the idea of concealing sexual orientation was 'incompatible with the recognition of a characteristic so fundamental to a person's identity that the persons concerned cannot be required to renounce it'. Also, just like religious belief, the possibility of exercising greater restraint when expressing sexual orientation is irrelevant, as was any idea of a 'core area' of the expression of sexual orientation.

The Court's ruling was useful not only (obviously) for homosexual applicants— although it raised issues of credibility discussed already—but also to other asylum seekers too. Those who claim to be part of a 'particular social group' need only point to a law criminalizing them, to prove that they meet part of the test for being in such a group in the first place (the perception that they are different). If asylum seekers claiming persecution on any ground can show that a criminal law focused on them is actually enforced to the extent that it results in jail sentences, then that is sufficient to show persecution. And the absence of any obligation to conceal sexual orientation (or religious belief) must mean that there is no obligation to conceal other core facets of personal identity that might lead to persecution, such as language, political beliefs, ethnicity or nationality (manifested, perhaps, by dress or customs), or gender identity.

Most recently, the CJEU examined the concept of persecution again in *Shepherd*, a case concerning an American deserter from the Iraq war.[207] This judgment interprets the 'military service' ground of persecution, making four main points. First of all, the definition of 'military service' included support staff (like the soldier in this case), and the circumstances surrounding enlistment in the military were irrelevant. Implicitly it did not matter whether the soldier was conscripted or volunteered. However, the Court stated that being part of the military was a 'necessary but not sufficient' condition for the rule to apply.

Secondly, the Court elaborated upon the conditions for applying the provision, setting out four elements to be considered: there must be a relationship with an actual conflict; the rule can apply even to indirect participation in a conflict, if the soldier's

---

[207] N 173 above.

tasks could 'sufficiently directly and reasonably plausibly, lead them to participate in war crimes' (the possibility of prosecution before the International Criminal Court being irrelevant); there must be a likelihood of war crimes being committed in future (again, the possible role of the International Criminal Court was irrelevant); and the past conduct of the unit was not an automatic indicator that war crimes will be committed in future. Overall, the test is whether 'there is a body of evidence which alone is capable of establishing' whether it is 'credible' that war crimes will be committed.

Thirdly, the Court examined the context of the conflict in question, addressing three issues. If there was a Security Council resolution authorizing the conflict, there was 'in principle, every guarantee' that war crimes will not be committed, although this was not an absolute rule. This also applied to an 'operation which gives rise to an international consensus'. And if national law of the country of origin provided for the 'possibility' of prosecution of war crimes, then it was 'implausible' that such crimes would be committed. Overall, the asylum seeker had to show that there is 'sufficient plausibility' that his unit is 'highly likely' to commit war crimes.

Fourthly, the Court looked at the soldier's individual circumstances. Desertion had to be the only way in which he or she could avoid participation in war crimes, and the Court pointed out that Mr Shepherd had enlisted and then re-enlisted in the US armed forces.

Finally, the Court interpreted the clause on the 'disproportionate punishment' form of persecution. The starting point was that Member States are entitled to maintain an armed force, including by means of punishing soldiers who desert. A penalty of up to five years in prison was not disproportionate, in the CJEU's view. Nor was Mr Shepherd's punishment discriminatory, since there was no comparator for him. The social ostracism that might result from his desertion was legally irrelevant, since it was only a consequence of the punishment.

Refugee status, once obtained, is not necessarily permanent. It had to cease in particular where there has been a change of circumstances in the country of origin,[208] and in such cases, Member States 'shall have regard to whether the change of circumstances is of such a significant and non-temporary nature that the refugee's fear of persecution can no longer be regarded as well-founded'.[209] The implementation report stated that some Member States were less generous—or more generous—than the Directive provided for on this point. However, the Directive did not contain a reference to the provisions in Article 1(C)(5) and (6) of the Geneva Convention, which specifies that the cessation clause does not apply, for persons who were covered by prior international arrangements concerning refugees, where there are 'compelling reasons arising out of previous persecution' which justify a continuation of refugee status even though the criteria for cessation of status otherwise apply. The 2009 impact assessment was not able to examine whether this proviso was applied in practice or not, despite this omission in the Directive.[210]

The issue of cessation was addressed by the Court of Justice in the *Abdulla* judgment, which concerned Iraqi refugees who were potentially subject to cessation of refugee status due to the changed situation in Iraq after the removal of Saddam Hussein's

---

[208] Art 11(1). See Art 1(C) of the Geneva Convention (I:5.3.1 above).   [209] Art 11(2).
[210] See Annex 18 to the 2009 impact assessment, point 1.2.

regime.[211] According to the Court of Justice, the test for the application of the cessation principle was the same test as that applicable to the original determination of the well-foundedness of the claim for recognition as a refugee.[212] If the person concerned argued that, following the change in circumstances leading to the cessation of the *original* refugee status, there were now other factors indicating that a *separate* threat of persecution now exists in the country of origin, the substance of this claim had to be considered as far as possible in the same way that an initial application for recognition of refugee status had to be considered.[213] As for the question as to whether the change of circumstances was sufficiently significant and non-temporary, the Court ruled that this principle applied 'when the factors which formed the basis of the refugee's fear of persecution may be regarded as having been permanently eradicated'. Therefore, '[t]he assessment of the significant and non-temporary nature of the change of circumstances thus implies that there are no well-founded fears of being exposed to acts of persecution amounting to severe violations of basic human rights within the meaning of Article 9(1) of the Directive'.[214]

The Directive provided for exclusion from refugee status, first of all by explicit reference to Article 1.D of the Geneva Convention,[215] excluding persons receiving protection or assistance from UN organs other than the UNHCR, but also rephrasing the rule from Article 1.D of the Convention that '[w]hen such protection or assistance has ceased for any reason, without the position of such persons being definitely settled in accordance with the relevant resolutions adopted by the General Assembly of the United Nations, these persons shall ipso facto be entitled to the benefits of this Directive'. In practice, this exclusion relates only to Palestinian refugees, and a national court requested the Court of Justice to interpret it in the *Bolbol* and *El Kott* cases.[216]

First of all, according to the judgment in *Bolbol*, since this rule 'must…construed narrowly', a person is not covered by this provision unless he or she *actually* received protection or assistance from the relevant UN agency, rather than merely being *entitled* to receive it. However, the judgment confirmed that Article 1.D of the Geneva Convention would apply not just to persons displaced by the original 1948 conflict regarding Israel and Palestine, but also the 1967 conflict and any further conflict, and could apply not just to persons actually registered with the relevant UN body, but also to persons who were receiving benefits from that body *de facto*. An application for refugee status by a person *not* covered by this exclusion must be assessed in accordance with the normal rules in the Directive.

Subsequently, in *El Kott*, the Court ruled that the reference to protection or assistance ceasing 'for any reason' did not mean that 'mere absence or voluntary departure' from the UN agency's 'area of operations would be sufficient to end the exclusion from refugee status'. That interpretation would mean that any applicant on the territory of the EU would automatically escape the effect of the exclusion clause, so it would have no

---

[211] N 173 above.   [212] Paras 55–71 of the judgment, n 173 above.
[213] Paras 84–91 of the judgment, n 173 above.
[214] Para 73 of the judgment, n 173 above.
[215] Art 12(1)(a). On Art 1.D of the Convention, see I:5.3.1 above. The Dir also contains a provision corresponding to the exclusion clause in Art 1.E of the Convention (Art 12(1)(b)).
[216] Case C-31/09, n 173 above.

'practical effect'. So the exclusion applied not only to those currently receiving assistance but also to those who received it just before applying for asylum. In the Court's view, assistance ended (and so the exclusion clause was no longer applicable) either when the UN agency was abolished, or if 'it is impossible for that organ or agency to carry out its mission', ie the assistance itself had ceased. That could result from an event making it 'impossible' for the agency 'to carry out its mission', or from 'circumstances which have forced the person concerned to leave the [agency's] area of operations as they are beyond that person's control'.

In effect, then, this interpretation created an alternative test for protection for this category of persons. National authorities and courts must ask if the applicant's departure from the Palestinian area 'may be justified by reasons beyond his [or her] control and independent of his [or her] volition which force him [or her] to leave the area in question and thus prevent him [or her] from receiving [UN] assistance'. This could happen if the 'personal safety' of a Palestinian refugee 'is at serious risk and if it is impossible for that agency to guarantee that his [or her] living conditions in that area will be commensurate with the mission entrusted to that agency'. It is not clear if this test is alternative (ie *either* the risk to personal safety *or* the poor living conditions will suffice) or cumulative (ie the applicant must show *both* the risk to personal safety *and* the poor living conditions). There are also procedural rules: the authorities must carry out an individual assessment of such a claim, and the rules on assessment of refugee and subsidiary protection claims 'may be applicable by analogy'.[217]

What was the content of the status that such applicants received (if successful)? The Court went on to interpret the rule that they must 'ipso facto be entitled to the benefits of this Directive'. First of all, the Court clarified that this was a reference to refugee status in the Directive, not to subsidiary protection status. This also meant that the Palestinian exclusion regarding refugee status was not an exclusion from subsidiary protection status. Secondly, the Court confirmed that successful applicants did not simply obtain the right to *apply* for refugee status like any other applicant; they received the *refugee status itself*.[218] But this was not an 'unconditional right': applicants had to make an application for refugee status, to show that they sought assistance and that the assistance ceased, and that none of the *other* grounds for exclusion from refugee status are applicable. The cessation clause would apply if the circumstances that forced them to leave the Palestinian area no longer existed. Finally, this was not unjustified discrimination as compared to other refugees, because the signatories to the Geneva Convention deliberately chose to create a separate category of persons.

It could be added that Palestinian refugees are not really in a profoundly different position from others: according to the Court's reasoning, they still have to show that they were forced to migrate for reasons of personal safety. These reasons do not have to be linked to persecution, but in fact they have some broad similarities with the 'threat

---

[217] *El Kott*, para 64: the Court referred to Art 4(3).

[218] This must mean not only that they are entitled to the content of refugee status set out in the qualification Directive, but also that they are covered by the family reunion and long-term residents' Directives (I:6.6 and I:6.7 below).

from armed conflict' ground for subsidiary protection, discussed further below.[219] If the test for Palestinian refugee claims is cumulative, as explained above—ie, they must also show poor living conditions—then it contains an extra element that applicants for refugee or subsidiary protection status do not have to prove. The Court's judgment leaves open interesting questions, such as whether the concepts of sur place applications, agents of persecution,[220] sources of protection,[221] or internal flight alternatives apply to the Palestinians, and whether concepts from the procedures Directive can also apply.[222]

Another provision in the Directive corresponded broadly to the exclusion clauses of Article 1.F of the Geneva Convention,[223] but included several elements *not expressly found* in Article 1.F, in particular the exclusion of those who have committed 'particularly cruel' crimes with an allegedly political objective and of those who 'instigate or otherwise participate' in Article 1.F activities.[224] The CJEU interpreted this provision in the *B and D* judgment.[225] First of all, it ruled that terrorist acts could constitute a 'serious non-political crime', as they were characterized by 'violence towards civilians' despite their purportedly political objective. Secondly, terrorism was against the 'purposes and principles of the United Nations', in light of UN Security Council Resolutions on the issue.

But how should the exclusion clauses be applied in an actual case involving an alleged terrorist? The Court pointed out that (under the Geneva Convention and the Directive) there had to be 'serious reasons' for considering that the asylum seeker had committed the acts in question. This meant that national authorities had to make an individual assessment of each case to see whether the exclusion clauses applied.[226] So even if the person was a member of a group that committed terrorist acts, that was not sufficient in itself to exclude him or her from refugee status, even if that group had been designated as a terrorist group by a Council decision—although that was a factor in deciding whether the *group* was terrorist.[227] Equally, even if the asylum seeker's intentional participation in a terrorist group was a criminal act pursuant to EU criminal law on this issue,[228] it did not follow that the exclusion clause in the Directive applied, since asylum law was a different legal framework.

[219] In any event, as noted above, the CJEU observed that Palestinians are not excluded from subsidiary protection status as such.
[220] It makes little sense for the test for Palestinian refugees to have a 'sources of persecution or serious harm' element, when that test does not require them to show persecution or serious harm in the first place.
[221] Arguably the requirement to show that UN protection is deficient in practice amounts to a *lex specialis* 'sources of protection' test for Palestinian refugees.
[222] By analogy with the case law on subsidiary protection procedures, discussed in I:5.7.1 below, it should also follow that at least the general principles of EU law apply to the procedures for considering Palestinian claims.
[223] Art 12(2) and (3); on Art 1.F of the Convention, see I:5.3.1 above.
[224] Also, the scope of the exclusion for 'serious non-political crime' is more precisely defined by reference to acts committed prior to obtaining a residence permit based on refugee status; and the exclusion for acts contrary to UN principles is defined by reference to specific provisions of the UN Charter.
[225] N 173 above. See also Case C-573/14 *Lounani*, pending.
[226] This was true also of instigation or participation in terrorist acts, pursuant to Art 12(3) (para 94 of the judgment).
[227] On those rules, see II:7.4.5.   [228] On those rules, see II:5.5.

To determine whether the exclusion clause applied, then, it was necessary to find whether the asylum seeker had a share of the responsibility for the acts which the group committed when he or she was a member of it, applying both objective and subjective criteria. So the authority had to assess 'the true role played by the person concerned in the perpetration of the acts in question', the asylum seeker's 'position within the organisation', how much knowledge the asylum seeker had of its activities; any pressure to which the asylum seeker was exposed; or other factors which may have influenced the asylum seeker's conduct. If the asylum seeker had a prominent position in a group which used terrorist methods, a national authority could presume his or her 'individual responsibility', but still had to examine 'all the relevant circumstances' before excluding the asylum seeker from refugee status.

However, it was not necessary to assess whether the applicant was a present danger, since the exclusion clause concerned only acts committed in the past,[229] in order to exclude people who were 'undeserving' of refugee status and to avoid impunity from criminal liability for their crimes. Neither was there a proportionality test before the exclusion clause could be applied, because in effect one was built in to the application of the exclusion clause already, due to the need to assess the seriousness of the asylum seeker's acts and the degree of individual responsibility. Finally, the Court pointed out that exclusion from refugee status did not necessarily mean expulsion from the territory,[230] and ruled out the possibility that Member States could exercise their powers to apply 'more favourable provisions' to extend refugee status to those who were subject to the exclusion clause.[231]

Member States are obliged to grant refugee status to persons meeting the definition of 'refugee',[232] but are obliged to 'revoke, end or refuse to renew' the refugee status of any refugee whose refugee status has ceased, applicable to all applications filed after the Directive entered into force.[233] The Court of Justice has, however, ruled that it will still exercise jurisdiction as regards the cessation provision of the Directive even if a Member State decides to apply the cessation rules to persons who obtained refugee status before that date.[234]

Also, Member States had to revoke, end, or refuse to renew refugee status if it was 'established' that a person was subject to the exclusion clause or misrepresented or omitted key facts which were decisive for the grant of refugee status.[235] They *could* end refugee status if a person fell within the scope of the exceptions to the non-refoulement rule set out in Article 33(2) of the Geneva Convention, but in that case certain rights

---

[229] The Court noted that conversely Arts 14(4)(a) and 21 (discussed below) *did* in effect require an assessment of the present danger posed by a refugee.

[230] See the case law on the non-refoulement clause in the EU Returns Directive on irregular migrants, which has a broader scope than the qualification Directive and therefore prevents removal to an unsafe country for people who might not qualify for international protection (I:7.7.1 below). It is possible, however, that those excluded from refugee status might fall outside the scope of the Returns Directive if their expulsion is ordered on criminal law grounds.

[231] On this issue, see I:5.2.4 above.   [232] Art 13.

[233] Art 14(1). In accordance with Art 39, the Directive entered into force on 20 Oct 2004. The point had to be demonstrated on an individual basis (Art 14(2)), and was subject to procedural rights set out in the asylum procedures Directive (see I:5.7 below).

[234] Judgment in *Abdulla* (n 173 above), paras 45–50.   [235] Art 14(3).

'set out in or similar to' those in the Geneva Convention still applied, as regards non-discrimination, religion, court access, education, restrictions on expulsion, and non-refoulement.[236] This entailed the loss of Geneva Convention rights to protection of property, the right of association, access to employment, self-employment and the professions, housing, public assistance, social security, freedom of movement, and travel documents. The implementation report concluded that some Member States do not secure these rights in such cases.

Next, the definition of subsidiary protection provided that the risk of 'serious harm' necessary to establish a subsidiary protection claim was defined by reference to the death penalty or execution, or to torture or other inhuman or degrading treatment or punishment, or to a 'serious and individual threat to a civilian's life or person by reason of indiscriminate violence in situations of international or internal armed conflict'.[237] The latter provision was first interpreted by the Court of Justice in the *Elgafaji* judgment,[238] concerning the position of Iraqi nationals who feared violent retaliation due to their association with the American forces occupying Iraq. This judgment confirmed that this provision has a separate field of application from the other two aspects of the definition of subsidiary protection, given that its application was more general (as regards the types of violence and the circumstances in which the violence takes place) and also that the violence in question 'may extend to people irrespective of their personal circumstances'.[239] The Court defined the term 'individual' as meaning that it covered:[240]

harm to civilians irrespective of their identity, where the degree of indiscriminate violence characterising the armed conflict taking place – assessed by the competent national authorities before which an application for subsidiary protection is made, or by the courts of a Member State to which a decision refusing such an application is referred – reaches such a high level that substantial grounds are shown for believing that a civilian, returned to the relevant country or, as the case may be, to the relevant region, would, solely on account of his presence on the territory of that country or region, face a real risk of being subject to the serious threat referred in Article 15(c) of the Directive.

The Court went on to clarify that although risks to which the population of a country is exposed to do not *normally* constitute 'serious harm', this left open the 'possibility of an exceptional situation which would be characterized by such a high degree of risk that substantial grounds would be shown for believing that that person would be subject individually to the risk in question'.[241] However, this judgment did make clear that there had to be a degree of individual, rather than general risk, and concluded that 'the more the applicant is able to show that he is specifically affected by reason of factors particular to his personal circumstances, the lower the level of indiscriminate violence required for him to be eligible for subsidiary protection'.[242]

---

[236] Art 14(4) to (6).   [237] Art 15.   [238] N 173 above.   [239] Para 34 of the judgment.
[240] Para 35 of the judgment.   [241] Paras 36 and 37 of the judgment.
[242] Paras 38 and 39 of the judgment.

Next, in the *Diakite* judgment,[243] the CJEU interpreted the concept of 'international or internal armed conflict'. According to the Court, the EU legislature used that phrase instead of the concepts found in international humanitarian law (IHL), which refers (in the 1949 Geneva Conventions and their Protocol) to 'international armed conflict' and 'armed conflict not of an international character'. So it followed that the EU legislature wanted to grant protection based on a different concept, and it was 'not necessary for all the criteria' in the Geneva Conventions 'to be satisfied'. The IHL rules govern the conduct of conflicts and aim to protect civilian populations in a conflict zone, but does not (unlike the Directive) 'provide for international protection' for civilians 'who are outside both the conflict zone and the territory of the conflicting parties'. Therefore the IHL definition of 'armed conflict' was not designed to address the issue of subsidiary protection. Also, the IHL rules aimed to define individual criminal liability and were linked to international criminal law, while the qualification Directive was not.

Instead, the phrase 'internal armed conflict' in the Directive applied to a situation where 'a State's armed forces confront one or more armed groups or in which two or more armed groups confront each other', on condition that the other threshold in the Directive was met: the 'confrontations' must be 'exceptionally considered to create a serious and individual threat to the life or person of an applicant', as interpreted by the Court in *Elgafaji*. It was not necessary to 'carry out a specific assessment of the intensity' of such conflicts separate from the 'appraisal of the resulting level of violence', and the interpretation of 'armed conflict' was not 'conditional upon the armed forces involved having a certain level of organisation or upon the conflict lasting for a specific length of time'. Instead, it was 'sufficient if the confrontations in which those armed forces are involved give rise to the level of violence' required by *Elgafaji*. While the Court did not define 'international armed conflict', it seems clear that it is not defined by IHL either. Logically, it should be defined by analogy with 'internal armed conflict', with the Court's interpretation of that phrase applying *mutatis mutandis* to a conflict between the armed forces of two or more States.

Most recently, the CJEU examined the subsidiary protection concept again in the *Abdida* and *M'Bodj* judgments.[244] In *M'Bodj*, the Court stated that a non-EU citizen's state of health could not as such give rise to a claim for subsidiary protection, because it did not amount to inhuman or degrading treatment in the country of origin—unless it was the result of the intentional deprivation of health care. The list of actors of persecution suggested that 'serious harm' had to 'take the form of conduct on the part of a third party', rather than be 'the result of general shortcomings in the health system of the country of origin'. This interpretation was supported by the references in the preamble, indicating that the Directive did not apply to people granted leave to reside 'on a discretionary basis on compassionate or humanitarian grounds'. Even though individuals with very serious health conditions might be able to rely upon Article 3 ECHR to resist removal to a State that could not treat their condition, it did not follow that they were entitled to subsidiary protection under the Directive. Moreover, a grant of subsidiary protection to such persons would go beyond Member States' power to set

---

[243] N 173 above.   [244] N 173 above.

more favourable standards.[245] The Court repeated this conclusion in *Abdida*, but went on to explain that persons in this situation could receive a form of *de facto* protection pursuant to the EU's Returns Directive.[246] It follows from this judgment that fleeing environmental catastrophe as such does not give rise to a claim for subsidiary protection since there is no direct link with the conduct of a third party,[247] although fleeing a human conflict which might be exacerbated by such a catastrophe is another matter.

Subsidiary protection could cease in essentially the same circumstances as refugee status.[248] As for exclusion from subsidiary protection status, as the Court pointed out in *El Kott* (discussed above), there was no exclusion for Palestinian refugees. Otherwise, the Directive was wider in scope than Article 1.F of the Geneva Convention.[249] Along with the exclusions for war crimes and acts against the principles of the UN, persons had to be excluded where they had 'committed a serious crime' without geographical limitation, in place of exclusion for committing a 'serious non-political crime' prior to admission, or where they were considered 'a danger to the community or to the security' of that Member State. The rule on 'participation' or 'instigation' also applied. Moreover, Member States could also exclude persons who had committed *petty crimes*, if they would be punishable by imprisonment in that Member State and if the person in question fled to avoid imposition of sanctions.[250] There was no link made with the possibility of disproportionate or discriminatory punishment. Member States were obliged to revoke subsidiary protection status where the cessation or mandatory exclusion clauses applied, although revocation was only optional where the 'petty crime' ground applied.[251] Also, there was no 'fallback' in the Directive for persons with subsidiary protection status who lose that status.[252]

As for the content of status, Member States could reduce benefits to persons who created their refugee or subsidiary protection status by their actions after leaving the country of origin.[253] According to the Commission's 2009 impact assessment and the implementation report, only three Member States applied this provision.[254] Beneficiaries of refugee or subsidiary protection status had to be given information about their status.[255] Member States were obliged to apply the non-refoulement principle 'in accordance with their international obligations'; they could refoule a refugee, '[w]here not prohibited by [those] international obligations' on the grounds set out in Article 33(2) of the Geneva Convention. In such a case, Member States could revoke or refuse to renew the refugee's residence permit.[256] The CJEU case law on this issue is linked to the rules on residence permits, and so is discussed below.[257]

---

[245] See I:5.2.4 above.   [246] See I:7.7.1 below.

[247] There is arguably an *indirect* link, in that human action may have *contributed* to that catastrophe. But the same could be said of inadequate health systems; so the Court's ruling should be understood to insist upon a more direct link with human behaviour.

[248] Art 16. Presumably, therefore, the case law on Art 11 was relevant by analogy (see *Abdulla and others*, discussed above).

[249] Art 17. Presumably, the case law on Art 12(2) was relevant by analogy, to the extent that the two provisions correspond (see the *B and D* cases, discussed above).

[250] According to the implementation report, about half of the Member States applied this exception.

[251] Art 19.   [252] Compare Art 19 to Art 14(6).   [253] Art 20(6) and (7).

[254] Annex 18 to the impact assessment, point 1.3.   [255] Art 22.   [256] Art 21.

[257] *T*, note 173 above.

A key issue in the Directive was the possibility for Member States to distinguish between beneficiaries of subsidiary protection and persons with refugee status, as regards the content of the rights which Member States must guarantee.[258] Member States were obliged to ensure 'family unity', and family members could claim the content of refugee or subsidiary protection status as set out in the Directive,[259] although Member States could 'define the conditions' applicable to family members of persons with subsidiary protection status.[260] Residence permits for refugees had to be valid for at least three years and renewable, but permits for their family members could be valid for a lesser period. Persons with subsidiary protection had to get renewable residence permits with at least one year's validity. Residence permits could be refused where there were 'compelling reasons of national security or public order'.[261]

Refugees had the right to a Convention travel document, except again for 'compelling reasons of national security or public order'. Persons with subsidiary protection must be given, subject to the same proviso, 'documents which enable them to travel, at least when serious humanitarian reasons arise that require their presence in another State'.[262]

As for employment and self-employment, it had to be authorized subject to national rules for refugees or beneficiaries of subsidiary protection immediately. Member States had an option to apply priority labour-market rules for a limited (but undefined) period to persons with subsidiary protection.[263] Education for minors with status had to be offered on the same basis as nationals, but access to general education for adults could be offered only on the same basis as for legally-resident third-country nationals.[264] There were special rules for the protection of unaccompanied minors.[265] Access to social assistance and health care had to be offered on the same basis as nationals, with a possible limit to 'core benefits' for persons with subsidiary protection, but access to housing and freedom of movement in the host Member State had to be offered on the same basis as for other third-country nationals.[266] Member States had to admit

[258] On the approaches of Member States to this issue, see Annex 8 to the 2009 impact assessment.

[259] Art 22. 'Family members' were defined in Art 2(h). It should be recalled that the EU's family reunion Directive gives refugees a right to family reunion (see I:6.6 below). On the issue of family members of refugees, see H Lambert, 'The European Court of Human Rights and the Right of Refugees and Other Persons in Need of Protection to Family Reunion' (1999) 11 IJRL 427, and S Peers, 'EC Law on Family Members of Persons Seeking or Receiving International Protection' in P Shah, ed., *The Challenge of Asylum to Legal Systems* (Cavendish, 2005), 83.

[260] According to the 2009 impact assessment, only one Member State (Poland) applied this rule (Annex 18, point 1.4).

[261] Art 24.

[262] Art 25. According to the 2009 impact assessment, only three Member States made use of this proviso (Annex 18, point 1.4).

[263] Art 26. The draft Dir on third-country national workers would also confer equal treatment rights on family members of refugees and persons with subsidiary protection, in the latest version of that Dir (see I:6.5.1 below).

[264] Art 27.

[265] Art 30. See now the action plan on unaccompanied minors (COM (2010) 213, 6 May 2010) and the follow-up to that plan (COM (2012) 554, 28 Sep 2012).

[266] Arts 28, 29, 31, and 32. For the interpretation of the limit to 'core benefits', see by analogy C-571/10 *Kamberaj*, ECLI:EU:C:2012:233.

refugees to integration programmes, but this was optional for persons with subsidiary protection status.[267]

The only CJEU judgment to date on the content of status is *T*, which links the rules on residence permits to the *refoulement* clause, and concerns a recognized refugee who allegedly supported terrorism.[268] According to the Court, if the criteria to refoule a refugee (which the Court did not assess) are satisfied, a Member State can either (a) refoule the refugee; (b) expel the refugee to a safe country; or (c) allow the refugee to stay. In the event that Member States can refoule the refugee, then they can also revoke a residence permit. But conversely, if the criteria to refoule the refugee are not satisfied, then the Member State *cannot* withdraw a residence permit on this ground.

In that case, the Court ruled, the question arises whether the rules on granting residence permits apply. The Court ruled that it was implicitly possible to revoke a residence permit which had already been issued. It then interpreted the two sets of grounds for loss of a residence permit at issue in this case: the 'reasonable grounds' that the refugee is a security risk (pursuant to the refoulement clause), and the 'compelling reasons of national security or public order' (pursuant to the residence permit clause), in the overall context of the Directive—protecting human rights and developing a common policy. In the Court's view, refoulement of a refugee is a 'last resort' in the event that there is no other option to protect national security or the public. Since it could have a 'drastic' impact on the refugee, it was subject to 'rigorous conditions'.

In contrast, the mere loss of a residence permit did not lead to refoulement, and so the threshold for the application of the relevant rules was lower. The rules on loss of a residence permit 'only' applied where the refugee's actions 'cannot justify loss of refugee status, let alone the refoulement of that refugee', and so did not 'presuppose the existence of a particularly serious crime'. In the Court's view, the grounds for loss of a residence permit should be interpreted consistently with the public security exceptions in the EU's citizens' Directive, because 'the extent of protection a company (sic) intends to afford to its fundamental interests cannot vary according to the legal status of the person that undermines those interests'.[269] So terrorism is covered by that concept, and there must be a 'genuine, present and sufficiently serious threat affecting one of the fundamental interests of society'. Moreover, the EU had listed the group in question as a terrorist group, which is a 'strong indication' that had to be 'taken into account'. Since the CJEU had already ruled (in *B and D*, discussed above) that terrorist acts could lead to exclusion from refugee status, it must follow that they could equally justify revocation of a residence permit.

Furthermore, the national court also has to consider whether the specific actions of a refugee in fact constitute support for terrorism so as to justify revocation of a residence permit. Not all forms of support for an organization which the EU considers to be terrorist can lead to revocation of a refugee's residence permit. As with the exclusion

---

[267] Art 33.

[268] N 173 above. The judgment is relevant by analogy to the withdrawal of travel documents, to beneficiaries of subsidiary protection, and to family members. See now Joined Cases C-443/14 and C-444/14, *Alo and others*, pending, on the interpretation of the rules on free movement within a Member State.

[269] The judgment clearly assumes that the *refoulement* clause is subject to a higher threshold. On the threshold in the citizens' Directive, see I:6.4.1 below.

clause (see *B and D*), it was necessary to look at the individual's behaviour, examining 'in particular whether he himself has committed terrorist acts, whether and to what extent he was involved in planning, decision-making or directing other persons with a view to committing acts of that nature, and whether and to what extent he financed such acts or procured for other persons the means to commit them'. In this case, the refugee had participated in legal meetings, celebrated the Kurdish New Year and collected money for the PKK. The Court asserted that this 'does not necessarily mean that he supported the legitimacy of terrorist activities'. Indeed, such acts 'do not constitute, in themselves, terrorist acts'. The national court also had to consider the 'degree of seriousness of danger' the refugee posed. It could take into account his criminal conviction but also had to consider that he was only sentenced to a fine. Also, the principle of proportionality (which the Court stated was *not* relevant when applying the exclusion clause, in *B and D*) *was* relevant when it came to revoking residence permits: the national court had to consider if the refugee was still a threat to public security at the time the decision to revoke the permit was taken.[270]

Finally, the Court ruled on the consequences of the loss of a residence permit. The person concerned retained refugee status and so was still entitled to all of the rights granted to a refugee, including access to employment, education, welfare, healthcare, and housing. Although a clause in the preamble to the Directive stated that a residence permit could be made a condition of obtaining such benefits, the Court said that this clause was irrelevant since it was not reflected in the main text. Those rights could 'only' be restricted in accordance with the conditions in the Directive, and Member States 'are not entitled to add restrictions not already listed there'. On the other hand, it is arguable that the loss of a residence permit could still be relevant where it was a criterion for exercising rights *not* listed in the Directive—such as family reunion and freedom to travel.[271]

Overall, the Directive's provisions on the definition of status, as interpreted by the CJEU, constituted a relatively liberal approach to the definition of protection, in particular as regards the interpretation of political social group, the rejection of a concept of 'core' elements of freedom of religion or sexual orientation, and the clarification that jailing people on Convention grounds in practice usually constituted persecution. However, the Court's reasoning in *Shepherd* was, with respect, far less convincing: failing to clarify why a prison sentence was acceptable for a deserter, when it was not for others; implausibly asserting that a Security Council resolution is a 'guarantee' that war crimes will not be committed; inventing the idea that an 'international consensus' could justify a conflict (there was no such consensus in the Iraq war in any event); absurdly suggesting (in the face of all evidence, and ignoring the very rationale for international criminal tribunals) that the 'possibility' of national prosecution for war crimes is sufficient to avoid those crimes; and failing to consider that a soldier might change his or her mind about military action as the conduct of the war changes, or as facts about war crimes come to light.

---

[270] This implicitly requires the court to consider whether the refugee is a present danger—another element which does not apply to the exclusion clause, according to *B and D*.

[271] See respectively I:6.6 below and I:4.9 above.

Moreover, this overall liberal approach to the definition of protection status was at the expense of stronger cessation and exclusion clauses, the latter of which arguably contradicted the Geneva Convention, and the creation of a concept of 'revocation' of status. In particular, the 'revocation' clause arguably permitted Member States to circumvent the *Chahal* ruling of the European Court of Human Rights, which held that Article 3 ECHR may prevent the removal of a person within the scope of the exceptions to non-refoulement in Article 33(2) of the Geneva Convention.[272] According to the Directive, certain limited protection still applied to such persons, so while (in accordance with *Chahal*) they could stay in the country, Member States could eliminate their rights to move, earn an income, receive benefits, or obtain housing. The risk is that it would be effectively impossible for these persons to survive—as seen in the *Ahmed* case.[273]

As for the content of status, various vague provisions left some possibility for Member States to provide for a low level of protection, particularly for persons with subsidiary protection and to their family members. For refugees, the Directive was in accordance with the minimum standards in the Geneva Convention, but at least it made it easier to enforce those standards in the form of a Directive. For persons with subsidiary protection, any binding text was an improvement on the previous position at international or EU level, but the low standards in the Directive as regards the level of benefits for persons with subsidiary protection and their family members were disappointing, and arguably breached the ECHR ban on non-discrimination in regard to the rights protected by the Convention (taking Article 14 ECHR together with Article 3) as well as the principle of equality protected as one of the general principles of EU law. Furthermore, while there was no reference to procedural rights as regards access to benefits, the general principles of EU law and the EU Charter of Fundamental Rights conferred procedural rights in respect of any benefits which EU law provides for.[274]

5.5.2 Second-phase Directive

From December 2013, the definition and content of refugee and subsidiary protection status has been subject to the second-phase qualification Directive,[275] which made a number of amendments to the first-phase Directive. The following analysis (like the analyses of other second-phase legislation below)[276] examines what has changed in the second-phase rules. For those first-phase rules which were not amended (for instance, the exclusion clauses and the definition of subsidiary protection) the analysis above (including the relevant CJEU case law) remains valid.

First of all, the second-phase Directive widened the definition of 'family members' to include married minor children and parents of unaccompanied minors.[277] There were amendments to the concept of actors of protection, to confirm that the list of actors is exhaustive, to clarify that actors of protection must be 'willing and able to provide protection', and to confirm that such protection must be 'effective' and 'non-temporary'.[278]

---

[272] See I:5.3.1 above.   [273] I:5.3 above.

[274] See further ch 5 of S Peers and N Rogers, *EU Immigration and Asylum Law: Text and Commentary*, 1st edn (Martinus Nijhoff, 2006), ch 14.

[275] Dir 2011/95 ([2011] OJ L 337/9).   [276] I:5.7.2, I:5.8.2, and I:5.9.2.   [277] Revised Art 2(j).

[278] Revised Art 7.

The provisions on the internal protection alternative were amended to confirm that, for the exception to apply, the person concerned must have 'access to protection against persecution or serious harm' and 'can safely and legally travel to and gain admittance to' that part of the country, and be 'reasonably expected to settle' there; this reflects Strasbourg case law on this issue.[279] Also, there are new provisions on obtaining country-of-origin information in such cases, and the rule permitting the application of the internal alternative principle notwithstanding 'technical obstacles to return' was deleted.[280]

As for the substance of refugee status, the revised Directive clarified that the 'absence of protection' against private attacks for (Geneva) Convention reasons would constitute persecution.[281] The protection against gender-related persecution has been strengthened.[282] Furthermore, the cessation clause has been amended so that refugees can 'invoke compelling reasons arising out of previous persecution' to prevent the application of that rule.[283]

A number of changes have been made to the rules on the content of protection status. First, there are new references to additional categories of vulnerable persons (victims of trafficking and persons with mental health problems),[284] and Member States' power to reduce benefits for persons whose claims were supposedly manufactured was removed.[285] Second, the power to define special conditions for family members of persons with subsidiary protection was repealed.[286] Third, the possible distinctions between refugees and persons with subsidiary protection as regards travel documents,[287] employment,[288] health care,[289] and integration facilities were abolished.[290] However, there are still distinctions as regards residence permits (although the position of subsidiary protection beneficiaries was improved)[291] and social welfare.[292] Fourth, there were sundry other changes to the rules on content of status, as regards training and counselling for employment, grants and loans for employment-related education, recognition of professional qualifications, mental health care, tracing unaccompanied minors, access to accommodation, and integration programmes.[293]

---

[279] *Salah Sheekh v Netherlands* (ECHR 2007-I), discussed in I:5.3.1 above.   [280] Revised Art 8.

[281] Revised Art 9(3).

[282] Revised Art 10(1)(d). Gender-related issues 'shall be given due consideration' (in place of 'might be considered'), and now include gender identity. See also recital 30 in the preamble, which mentions 'genital mutilation, forced sterilisation and forced abortion'.

[283] New Art 11(3). A parallel amendment applies to cessation of subsidiary protection status (new Art 16(3)).

[284] Revised Art 20(3).   [285] The previous Art 20(6) and (7) were repealed.

[286] Revised Art 23(2).

[287] Revised Art 25(2) dropped the previous possible limitation to 'serious humanitarian reasons'. However, there is still a distinction between refugees and persons with subsidiary protection in that the Geneva Convention creates an obligation to recognize the travel documents held by the former, but not the latter.

[288] Compare the previous Art 26(3) and (4) to the second-phase Art 26(1) and (2).

[289] Compare the previous Art 29(2) to the second-phase Art 30.

[290] Compare the previous Art 33(2) to the second-phase Art 34.

[291] Revised Art 24(2): the permit is now renewable for two-year periods (not just one year) and family members of beneficiaries receive it also. But the period of validity for refugees is still three years (Art 24(1)).

[292] Art 29(2), which retains the optional 'core benefits' limitation without amendment. See I:5.5.1 above for interpretation of this clause.

[293] Revised Arts 26(2), 30(2), 31(5), 32, and 34, and new Arts 26(3) and 28.

The second-phase Directive addresses many of the key issues identified as failings by the Commission, although it is hard to assess whether it will reduce gaps in recognition rates given that the Commission did not assess to what extent those gaps had already been reduced as a result of the adoption of the original qualification Directive. Logically, the second-phase Directive ought to raise recognition rates above what they would otherwise be, given its clarification of the rules and tightening of the exclusions relating to both the general rules and the specific provisions on refugee definitions. The changes in the rules relating to the content of status, in particular the abolition of most distinctions between refugees and persons with subsidiary protection, are particularly welcome. However, it would have been preferable also to clarify the definition of 'particular social group' (ie whether it is cumulative or alternative), to address the incompatibilities between the exclusion clauses and the Geneva Convention, and to improve the revocation clauses. In any event, it is not yet known how well the national authorities and national courts are applying the revised rules.

5.6 Temporary Protection

Directive 2001/55 establishing a model EU-wide temporary protection scheme was adopted in July 2001,[294] and Member States had to implement the Directive by 31 December 2002. Three Member States were condemned by the Court of Justice for their failure to implement the Directive on time.[295] To date, the model temporary protection scheme set out in the Directive has never been used in practice, and the Commission has not suggested its amendment in the context of establishing the second phase of the Common European Asylum System. However, as discussed below, the power to adopt emergency measures in the event of a mass influx on the basis of Article 78(3) TFEU (former Article 64(2) EC) has been invoked separately.[296]

Chapter I of the Directive sets out its purpose, scope, and definitions.[297] The Directive applies to either a 'mass influx' or an 'imminent mass influx' of persons; it applies to persons who have been evacuated, as well as spontaneous arrivals; and it applies even where there is *no* risk that the asylum system will be unable to process the number of applications.[298] Temporary protection 'shall not prejudice' refugee recognition pursuant to the Geneva Convention.[299] Member States may adopt more favourable rules for persons covered by temporary protection.[300] The Directive does not apply to persons admitted on national temporary protection schemes before its entry into force;[301] it

---

[294] Dir 2001/55 ([2001] OJ L 212/12). All references in this section are to this Dir, unless otherwise indicated. On the Dir, see generally K Kerber, 'The Temporary Protection Directive' (2002) 4 EJML 193. Ireland, which opted in after the adoption of the Directive, had to apply it by 31 Dec 2003 (Commission Decision 2003/690, [2003] OJ L 251/23).

[295] Cases: C-454/04 *Commission v Luxembourg*, judgment of 2 Jun 2005; C-476/04 *Commission v Greece*, judgment of 17 Nov 2005; and C-455/04 *Commission v UK*, judgment of 23 Feb 2006 (all unreported). Three cases were withdrawn, presumably because the Member States concerned finally complied with the legislation: Cases C-461/04 *Commission v Netherlands*, C-515/04 *Commission v Belgium*, and C-451/04 *Commission v France*.

[296] I:5.8.5.   [297] Arts 1–3.   [298] Art 2(a), (c), and (d).   [299] Art 3(1) and (2).

[300] Art 3(5).   [301] Art 3(4). The date of entry into force was 7 Aug 2001 (see Art 33).

appears from the Directive and other provisions of EU asylum law that Member States are now precluded from establishing new national temporary protection schemes.[302]

Chapter II concerns the duration and implementation of temporary protection.[303] In principle, temporary protection is one year long, extended for further periods of six months to a two-year maximum, with a possible further extension for a third year.[304] A temporary protection regime can only be established if the Council, acting by a qualified majority on a proposal from the Commission and considering certain specified factors, agrees that there is a mass influx of displaced persons.[305] Such a decision will specify, inter alia, the groups of persons covered, although Member States can extend the regime to other groups displaced for the same reasons and from the same country or region of origin.[306] The regime would end at the time of the maximum duration or upon early termination by the Council adopted by qualified majority after a Commission proposal, if the Council has established that conditions in the country of origin have improved sufficiently so 'as to permit the safe and durable return' of the beneficiaries.[307]

Chapter III sets out obligations of the Member States regarding persons enjoying temporary protection.[308] Member States must issue residence permits and visas,[309] register personal data on beneficiaries and take back a person enjoying temporary protection if that person remains on or seeks to enter the territory of another Member State without authorization during the temporary protection period.[310]

As for access to employment or self-employment, Member States are required to permit temporary protection beneficiaries to take up employment or self-employment, but they may give priority to EU citizens and EEA nationals, as well as legally resident third-country nationals receiving unemployment benefit. The Directive provides that the 'general law' regarding remuneration, social security, and other conditions of employment in each Member State applies.[311] There are rules regarding housing and social assistance, along with education;[312] the Directive leaves Member States the option as to whether to allow adults access to the general education system. Also, there are detailed rules on the status of unaccompanied minors.[313] There are no provisions on detention in this Directive, so presumably the relevant provisions of other EU asylum legislation would apply, if the person concerned has the status of asylum seeker.[314] If he or she does not have that status, then the provisions in the Returns Directive would apply, if the person concerned otherwise fell within the scope of that Directive.[315]

---

[302] In particular, the asylum procedures Directive, the qualification Directive, and the reception conditions Directive make no allowance for such national schemes, and the EU's funding legislation (see I:5.10.2 below) refers only to the Directive, rather than national law, as regards temporary protection. The grounds for the possible extensions to time limits for deciding on asylum applications set out in the asylum procedures Directive (see I:5.7 below) address the issues which a national temporary protection regime would deal with.

[303] Arts 4–7.   [304] Art 4.   [305] Art 5(2).

[306] Art 7. However, the financial support provided for in the Directive will not apply to such groups (Art 7(2)).

[307] Art 6.   [308] Arts 8–15.   [309] Art 8.   [310] Arts 10 and 11.

[311] Art 12.   [312] Arts 13 and 14 respectively.

[313] Art 16. See now the action plan on unaccompanied minors (COM (2010) 213, 6 May 2010) and the follow-up to that plan (COM (2012) 554, 28 Sep 2012).

[314] See I:5.7 and I:5.9 below.

[315] See the judgment in Case C-357/09 PPU *Kadzoev* [2009] ECR I-11189; on the Returns Dir, see I:7.7.1 below.

Member States have to authorize entry of the 'core' family of the spouse and children; entry of other family members, comprising close relatives who lived with *and* were wholly or largely dependent on the sponsor, is discretionary.[316] Moreover, the *Member States* shall decide which Member State family members will enter,[317] and there are no provisions on the status of family members.[318]

Chapter IV concerns access to the asylum procedure.[319] Member States may delay consideration of an application for Convention refugee status until the temporary protection has ended;[320] the effect of such delay will be magnified by the possible application of the Directive to cases where the asylum system is *not* under pressure and by the possible lengthy period of temporary protection. Member States can also provide that a person cannot hold temporary protection status simultaneously with the status of asylum seeker, although if an application for asylum or other protection status fails, a Member State must continue to extend temporary protection status to the beneficiary.[321] The criteria for responsibility for asylum seekers apply, but '[i]n particular', a Member State shall be responsible for examining an asylum application if it has accepted that person's transfer onto its territory.[322] This clause is vague and appears to contradict both the Dublin Convention and the Dublin II Regulation, which do not expressly contain such a criterion for assigning responsibility.[323] Moreover, the Dublin II Regulation (and its subsequent replacement) do not take account of the Directive's rules on family members.

Chapter V concerns return.[324] Once the temporary protection regime ends, the 'general laws' on protection and on foreigners apply, 'without prejudice' to certain specific provisions in the Directive;[325] presumably the reference to the 'general laws' must now be understood as a reference not only to the relevant national legislation, but also to EU rules on asylum and the EU's Returns Directive.[326] The specific rules in the Directive concerning return first of all provide for rules on voluntary return.[327] There is an express possibility of enforced return of persons after the regime has ended, but such return must be 'conducted with due respect for human dignity',[328] and Member States 'shall consider any compelling humanitarian reasons which may make return impossible or unreasonable in specific cases'.[329] They must also 'take the necessary measures concerning' residence status of former beneficiaries of temporary protection 'who

---

[316] Art 15.

[317] It is not clear whether this applies only where the family have been scattered between Member States, or also when family members have been left outside the Union.

[318] If the family members are permitted to work, the Directive on third-country national workers also confers equal treatment rights on the family members of people with temporary protection, in the final version of that Dir (see I:6.5.1 below).

[319] Arts 17–19.   [320] Art 17.   [321] Art 19.   [322] Art 18.   [323] See I:5.8 below.

[324] Arts 20–3.   [325] Art 20, referring to Arts 21–3.

[326] For more on the Returns Dir (Dir 2008/115, [2008] OJ L 348/98), see further I:7.7.1 below. It should be noted that the Returns Dir is 'without prejudice to' more favourable rules in other EU immigration and asylum legislation (Art 4(3)), or in national law (Art 4(4)).

[327] Art 21; compare to Art 7 of the Returns Dir.

[328] Art 22(1); compare to Arts 8–10 of the Returns Dir.

[329] Art 22(2); see Art 9 of the Returns Dir.

cannot, in view of their state of health, reasonably be expected to travel; where for example they would suffer serious negative effects if their treatment was interrupted'. Specifically, those persons 'shall not be expelled so long as that situation continues'.[330] Finally on the issue of return, Member States have discretion over whether to let children complete their school year.[331]

Chapter VI concerns solidarity between Member States, and sets out rules concerning indication of reception capacity and transfer of beneficiaries (with their consent).[332] Finally, the Directive contains rules on administrative cooperation,[333] exclusion from the benefit of temporary protection (in parallel with the Geneva Convention exclusion clauses),[334] and final provisions, including the right to challenge exclusion from temporary protection or family reunion in the courts.[335]

This Directive represented a potential risk to the Geneva Convention, as its potentially wide scope of application could have been attractive to Member States who might have wished to grant considerable numbers of people the lower standards of protection in this Directive, which were weakened considerably during negotiations, instead of refugee status. However, the unwillingness to apply the Directive in practice, coupled with the apparent ban on Member States establishing national temporary protection regimes, is in fact quite a positive result for the system of international protection in the European Union.

5.7 Common Procedures

The first-phase Directive 2005/85 on asylum procedures was adopted in December 2005, after particularly difficult negotiations.[336] Member States had to implement the Directive by 1 December 2007, except as regards legal aid, where the deadline was 1 December 2008.[337] The second-phase Directive, which was adopted in June 2013, had to be implemented by 20 July 2015, except as regards the time limits for deciding on applications, which must be implemented by 20 July 2018.[338] The two Directives are discussed in turn.[339]

---

[330] Art 23(1); compare in particular to Art 9(2) of the Returns Dir, which provides only for an *option* to postpone the removal of persons in such circumstances.

[331] Art 23(2).   [332] Arts 24–6.   [333] Chapter VII (Art 27).

[334] Chapter VIII (Art 28). There is no mention of the relevance of Art 3 ECHR in such cases.

[335] Chapter IX (Arts 29–34), particularly Art 29. Compare with the exclusion clauses in the qualification Directive (Arts 12 and 17 of Dir 2004/83, [2004] OJ L 304/12; see discussion in I:5.5 above).

[336] Dir 2005/85 ([2005] OJ L 326/13). All further references in this section are to this Dir, unless otherwise noted. On the Dir, see: K Zwaan, ed., *The Asylum Procedures Directive: Central Themes, Problem Issues, and Implementation in Selected Member States* (Wolf Legal Publishers, 2008); C Costello, 'The Asylum Procedures Directive in Legal Context: Equivocal Standards Meet General Principles' in A Baldaccini, E Guild and H Toner, eds., *Whose Freedom, Security and Justice? EU Immigration and Asylum Law and Policy* (Hart, 2007), 151; H Battjes, *European Asylum Law and International Law* (Martinus Nijhoff, 2006), chs 6 and 7; and S Peers and N Rogers, *EU Immigration and Asylum Law: Text and Commentary*, 1st edn (Martinus Nijhoff, 2006), ch 14.

[337] Art 43.   [338] Art 51, Dir 2013/32 ([2013] OJ L 180/60).   [339] I:5.7.1 and I:5.7.2.

5.7.1 First-phase Directive

There have been several references from national courts to the Court of Justice on the Directive,[340] and there has been one infringement proceeding.[341] Also, the European Parliament brought a successful annulment action against certain provisions of the Directive;[342] the consequences of this judgment are discussed further below. In general terms, the CJEU has ruled that the Directive gives Member States 'in a number of respects, a margin of assessment' as regards asylum procedures.[343]

The Commission reported on the application of the Directive in 2010 (the '2010 report').[344] Further information on its application in practice is available in the Commission's impact assessment on the 2009 proposal to amend the Directive (the '2009 impact assessment'),[345] and in the UNHCR's report on the implementation of the Directive (the 'UNHCR report').[346] Both reports are referred to below.

The Directive's scope was limited to the minimum standards necessary for the granting and withdrawing of refugee status under the 1951 Geneva Convention on the status of refugees.[347] It included any application for asylum made at the border or on the territory of a Member State,[348] but it did not include determination of qualification under other international instruments or for persons otherwise in need of protection, in particular subsidiary protection or temporary protection. However, Member States were obliged to apply the Directive if they applied a single procedure for determining refugee claims and claims for subsidiary protection,[349] and they could opt to apply the Directive to applications for any other kind of international protection.[350] Member States were free to provide for more favourable standards on asylum procedures, provided that such standards were 'compatible' with the Directive.[351]

The Directive did not explicitly set out any hierarchy between applications for refugee status and applications for subsidiary or temporary protection status. On this point, in the *Abdulla* judgment, the Court of Justice noted that the qualification Directive 'governs two distinct systems of protection' (ie refugee and subsidiary protection status), noting that the qualification Directive defined subsidiary protection by opposition to refugee status, and stated that 'the cessation of refugee status cannot be made conditional on a finding that a person does not qualify for subsidiary protection status',

---

[340] Cases C-69/10 *Diouf* [2011] ECR I-7151 and C-175/11 *D and A*, ECLI:EU:C:2013:45. Pending: Case C-239/14 *Tall*. See also Cases C-277/11 *MM I*, ECLI:EU:C:2012:744, C-604/12 *HN*, ECLI:EU:C:2014:302, C-560/14 *MM II*, and C-429/15 *Danqua*, pending, which partly or wholly concern procedural rights, not substantive law on qualification for status.
[341] Case C-431/10 *Commission v Ireland* [2011] ECR-56*.
[342] Case C-133/06 *EP v Council* [2008] ECR I-3189.   [343] *Diouf* (n 340 above), para 29.
[344] COM (2010) 465, 8 Sep 2010.
[345] SEC (2009) 1376, 21 Oct 2009. On the second-phase Dir, see I:5.7.2 below.
[346] *Improving Asylum Procedures: Comparative Analysis and Recommendations for Law and Practice* (UNHCR, 2010). The key findings and recommendations are online at: <http://www.unhcr.org/4ba9d99d9.html>.
[347] Art 3.   [348] Art 3(2).
[349] Art 3(3). The 2010 report noted that every Member State except Ireland had a single procedure.
[350] Art 3(4).   [351] Art 5. On the issue of 'compatible' higher standards, see I:5.2.4 above.

for 'there would otherwise be a failure to have regard for the respective domains of the two systems of protection'. So 'the possible cessation of refugee status occurs without prejudice to the right of the person concerned to request the granting of subsidiary protection status'.[352]

Subsequently, in the *HN* case, the Court ruled that by its very nature subsidiary protection was ancillary to refugee status, and that Member States 'should not, in principle' decide on a subsidiary protection claim before deciding on refugee status.[353] Moreover, an application for subsidiary protection, since it relates to a right protected by the qualification Directive, was covered by the general principles of EU law. These principles preclude a requirement to make a separate application for subsidiary protection, and also require a decision on the subsidiary protection application within a reasonable period of time. They did not preclude sending a letter to the applicant threatening his expulsion.[354] In effect, Member States were required to deal with both forms of application in a single procedure—thereby triggering the application of the Directive to subsidiary protection claims. In any event, even before a Member State established such a single procedure, the procedure governing applications for subsidiary protection was covered by the general principles of EU law, even though it fell outside the scope of the Directive.

In the same vein, the Court had previously found that there was a 'right to be heard' as regards subsidiary protection claims, giving applicants for that status at least some guarantees comparable to those for applicants for refugee status under the first-phase procedures Directive.[355] This meant in particular: the right for an applicant to make his or her views known effectively during an administrative procedure before the adoption of a decision which could be adverse, and the obligation for the administration to pay attention to those arguments, examine all aspects of the case impartially, and to give detailed reasons for its decision. The CJEU has now been asked if this extends to a right to an oral hearing, and to call or cross-examine witnesses.[356]

Chapter II of the Directive set out basic procedural principles and guarantees for assessing asylum claims.[357] Access to the procedure had to be ensured.[358] Member States could not reject or exclude applications on the grounds that they had not been made as soon as possible, although this was 'without prejudice to' another rule which provided that Member States could consider an application 'unfounded' if an applicant had failed without reasonable cause to make an application earlier, where he or she had an opportunity to do so.[359]

There were specific rules on the position of family members of an asylum application during the determination process.[360] Applicants for asylum had to be allowed

---

[352] Paras 77–80 of the judgment (Joined Cases C-175/08, C-176/08, C-178/08, and C-179/08 [2010] ECR I-1493).

[353] *HN* (n 340 above), paras 30–5. The opposing point of view (expressed in note 24 of the Advocate-General's Opinion in *Abdulla*) is clearly incorrect.

[354] *HN* (n 340 above), paras 37-57.

[355] *MM I*, n 340 above. Compare to the right to be heard in expulsion proceedings (I:7.7.1 below).

[356] *MM II*, n 340 above.   [357] Arts 6–22.   [358] Art 6.

[359] Art 8(1), referring to Art 23(4)(i). The 2010 report indicated that several Member States had deadlines for making asylum claims; these may well have been incompatible with the Directive.

[360] Art 6(2) to (4).

to remain at the border or in the territory until such time as an initial decision was made, with the exception of 'subsequent applications' and cases where a person was surrendered or extradited to another Member State, a non-EU State, or an international criminal court or tribunal.[361] The CJEU confirmed that this provision covered asylum seekers subject to the Dublin rules on asylum responsibility up until the point when they were transferred from the territory.[362] The possibility that an asylum seeker might be subject to a European Arrest Warrant (EAW) is consistent with the Court's case law on the EAW, which noted that an application for asylum or subsidiary protection is not a ground for refusal to execute an EAW.[363] Also, the CJEU has ruled that asylum seekers cannot be regarded as 'illegally staying' as long as they have the right to remain on the territory pursuant to this provision.[364]

The requirements for the examination of applications included the need for precise and up-to-date country of origin information, the obligation to examine applications 'individually, objectively and impartially', and the necessity to ensure that decision makers had appropriate expertise.[365]

Guarantees for applicants included the right to have a decision on the asylum application in writing, the right to have reasons for a negative decision, the right to be informed of the procedure in a language that it is 'reasonably supposed' that they understood, a right to an interpreter, and a right to notification of decisions in a reasonable time.[366] There were detailed rules on the procedures and conditions for personal interviews, which specified that in principle, all applicants had to be given an interview, subject to a number of exceptions.[367] According to the 2009 impact assessment, many personal interviews were defective in practice, as 'factual mistakes or misunderstandings are common' since applicants are not allowed to comment on or provide clarification of the reports. The UNHCR report, after examining a selection of written decisions in actual cases, concluded that in a number of cases 'there was no evidence that these applications were examined and these decisions taken individually, objectively and impartially'.

There was a right to legal assistance, but with possible exceptions to the right to legal aid.[368] In particular, the right to legal aid arose only after a negative decision,[369] although Member States remained free to apply a higher standard of granting legal assistance from the very beginning of the application process. The 2009 impact assessment

---

[361] Art 7. According to the 2010 report, most Member States would not extradite to the country of origin until the asylum decision had been made.

[362] Case C-179/11 *Cimade and GISTI*, ECLI:EU:C:2012:594.

[363] Case C-306/09 *I.B.* [2010] ECR I-10341, para 43.

[364] Case C-534/11 *Arslan*, ECLI:EU:C:2013:343, para 48. The Court also stated that the exceptions to the right to remain were exhaustive and should be narrowly interpreted: 'Article 7(2)...allows an exception to the rule in Article 7(1) only under restrictive conditions' (para 46 of that judgment).

[365] Art 8. Note that the European Asylum Support Office has a role as regards country-of-origin information: see I:5.10.1 below.

[366] Arts 9 and 10. The 2010 report noted that there were deficiencies in the quality of reasoning of decisions in some cases.

[367] Arts 12 and 13. According to the 2009 impact assessment, ten Member States invoked a derogation. See Annex 9 to the impact assessment for details. The 2010 report stated that some Member States applied further derogations not mentioned in the Directive.

[368] Art 15.   [369] Art 15(2).

concluded that in general, Member States which grant legal assistance from the beginning of the process had a higher rate of positive decisions on asylum applications.[370] There were specific provisions on the rights of access to information that an asylum seeker's legal adviser should have, along with rules on the legal adviser's access to the applicant and to interviews.[371]

Unaccompanied minors enjoyed certain procedural guarantees, including the right to a representative.[372] As regards detention, Member States could not hold an applicant for asylum in detention for the sole reason that he or she was an applicant for asylum, and there had to be the possibility of 'speedy judicial review' in detention cases.[373] The Directive did not define the word 'detention'.

Next, the Directive set out a specific procedure in cases where an application for asylum is explicitly or implicitly withdrawn.[374] It also provided for the role of UNCHR in asylum proceedings, including the rights of access to detention facilities and to information on individual cases.[375] Disclosure of certain information relating to the asylum application to the authorities of the country of origin was prohibited.[376]

Chapter III was concerned with procedures at first instance for asylum applications, including accelerated and inadmissibility procedures.[377] There was no deadline to decide on an asylum application.[378] Member States were permitted to have special or accelerated procedures for a wide range of applications, including unfounded claims, *manifestly* unfounded claims, admissibility claims, and repeat applications, along with two types of special procedures for applications made at the borders.[379] There was a list of fifteen types of cases which Member States could prioritize for being unfounded, and the CJEU said that list was not exhaustive.[380]

According to the 2009 impact assessment report, all but one Member State had put in place some accelerated procedures, with at least one Member State applying grounds not referred to in the Directive,[381] and the use of such procedures in practice varying from 1% to 17% of all applications. The UNHCR report stated that in some Member States, accelerated procedures were 'the norm', and concluded that in some cases, the time limits applying to accelerated procedures made it 'extremely difficult' to ensure that basic procedural safeguards were upheld.

---

[370] For tables of recognition rates compared to the basic features of national asylum systems, see Annex 13 to the 2009 impact assessment.

[371] Art 16.

[372] Art 17. See the action plan on unaccompanied minors (COM (2010) 213, 6 May 2010) and the follow-up to that plan (COM (2012) 554, 28 Sep 2012). For details of the numbers of unaccompanied minor asylum seekers in practice, see Annex 27 to the 2009 impact assessment.

[373] Art 18. The second-phase reception conditions Directive contains more rules on detention of asylum seekers (see I:5.9 below). Note that the immigration detention rules in the Returns Directive do not apply to the detention of asylum seekers: see Case C-357/09 PPU *Kadzoev* [2009] ECR I-11189, *Arslan* (n 364 above), and I:7.7.1 below.

[374] Arts 19 and 20. The 2010 report states that the 'vast majority' of Member States used the rules on implicitly withdrawn applications.

[375] Art 21.   [376] Art 22.   [377] Arts 23–35.

[378] However, the CJEU's ruling that applications for subsidiary protection must be decided within a reasonable time (*HN*, n 340 above) surely applied by analogy to refugee claims.

[379] Arts 23, 24, and 28.   [380] *D and A*, n 340 above.

[381] For the details of the national variations, and the numbers and proportions of asylum seekers subject to them in practice, see Annex 22 to the 2009 impact assessment.

Next, the Directive set out circumstances in which a claim may be rejected as inadmissible,[382] including applications for which there is another country which can be considered as the first country of asylum to which applicant has been admitted,[383] or a 'safe third country'.[384] Member States are allowed to retain or introduce lists of designated 'safe third countries', subject to certain requirements.[385] The UNHCR reports noted that the principles of 'first country of asylum' and 'safe third country' are rarely if ever applied in the Member States studied, and argued that several Member States have not implemented these provisions correctly.[386]

The Directive originally set out the principle of a common EU list on 'safe countries of origin', along with a procedure for adopting such a list (a qualified majority vote of the Council on a proposal from the Commission after consulting the EP).[387] However, this provision was struck down by the Court of Justice, on application by the EP, because it amounted to a form of 'secondary legislative procedure' which was not provided for by the EC Treaty.[388] Member States could still however introduce or national laws regarding 'safe countries of origin'. These must prima facie be governed by a list of common principles,[389] but there was a derogation for existing national lists drawn up according to less stringent requirements (Article 30(2)).[390] According to the 2009 impact assessment, one group of six Member States did not apply this rule at all; three Member States applied it on a case-by-case basis; ten Member States applied national lists of 'safe countries of origin' pursuant to the criteria in the Directive; and three large Member States applied pre-existing national law which did not meet the usual criteria (Germany, France, and the UK).[391] Most Member States did not permit a challenge to the presumption of safety, and several designated such cases as manifestly unfounded or did not allow for the suspensive effect of appeals. The UNHCR report found a similar degree of divergence among Member States, including large variations in the actual rules applicable, some of which fell short of the Directive's requirements.

Member States could have specific procedures derogating from the rules in Chapter II to deal with fresh applications for asylum after a first application has been rejected or withdrawn, or where an applicant had failed to go to a reception centre or to appear before authorities.[392] Furthermore, Member States could also derogate from the normal procedural rules to put in place particular procedures for border applications, subject to certain safeguards.[393] According to the 2009 impact assessment, twelve Member States had such procedures in place; some of these procedures did not permit asylum seekers to present their views or to appeal against negative decisions with suspensive effect.

---

[382] Art 25.   [383] Art 26.   [384] Art 27.   [385] Ibid.

[386] The 2010 report also indicated that some Member States did not apply all of the safeguards applicable to the 'safe third country' rule.

[387] Art 29.

[388] Case C-133/06, n 342 above. The same principle must apply *a fortiori* after the subsequent entry into force of the Treaty of Lisbon, given its systemization of the legislative and non-legislative decision-making processes of the EU (see Arts 289–97 TFEU).

[389] Annex II.   [390] Art 30(2).

[391] For the content of the national lists of safe 'countries of origin', see Annex 12 to the 2009 impact assessment.

[392] Art 32.   [393] Art 35.

A further derogation was allowed from the basic procedural rights where persons sought irregular entry or had already entered irregularly from a State which had ratified and observes the Geneva Convention and the ECHR (this was known informally as the 'supersafe third countries' rule).[394] Again, the Court of Justice struck down the provisions which provided for a secondary legislative procedure to adopt a common EU list of such countries,[395] but Member States were free to apply this concept in their national law if they already did so on the day when the Directive was adopted.[396]

Chapter IV set out specific procedures concerning withdrawal of refugee status.[397] Chapter V set out rules on appeals,[398] confirming the principle that applicants for asylum were entitled to an effective remedy before a court or tribunal as regards 'a decision taken on their application for asylum'. According to the *Diouf* judgment of the CJEU, this rule did not apply to a decision to deal with an application in an accelerated procedure, but only to the actual decision on the merits (or admissibility) of an application that was subsequently made, provided that this later review could examine the merits of the earlier decision to fast-track the application in the first place.[399] Furthermore, in the Court's view, the right to an effective remedy in Article 47 of the EU Charter did not entitle an applicant to have two levels of judicial review, and the short time limit (fifteen days) to challenge a national decision in the national accelerated procedure was not so short as to render the remedy ineffective. Another case on similar issues is pending before the Court.[400] The CJEU also examined the Irish system of appeals in the *HID* judgment, and found that it was compatible with the Directive.[401]

The practical importance of appeals was confirmed by the 2009 impact assessment, which reported that 28% of appeals overturned a negative decision in asylum cases in 2008,[402] and that in 2007 77% of negative decisions were subject to appeal. The 2009 impact assessment also observed that five Member States granted a period to appeal of only one to three days, raising obvious questions as to whether the remedy was 'effective'.[403] The UNHCR report was critical of these time limits, and also of barriers to effective remedies due to limited access to legal aid and translation assistance.

Member States also had to set out rules 'where appropriate' dealing with the question of the suspensive effect of appeals, or the right to apply for protective measures in the absence of automatic suspensive effect of appeals; these rules 'must be in accordance with [Member States'] international obligations'.[404] According to the 2009 impact assessment, two Member States did not permit suspensive effect of some appeals, and three Member States did not allow, in their national law, applicants to stay on the territory pending a decision on a request for interim measures.

This Directive raised a large number of complex legal issues and moreover had led to great concern among non-governmental organizations and the UNHCR that the

---

[394] Art 36.   [395] Case C-133/06; see n 342 above.   [396] See in particular Art 36(7).
[397] Arts 37–8.   [398] Art 39.   [399] Case C-69/10, n 340 above.
[400] Case C-239/14, *Tall*.   [401] N 340 above.
[402] See Annex 25 to the 2009 impact assessment.
[403] Such deadlines are considerably shorter than the 15-day time limit which the CJEU approved in *Diouf* (n 340 above).
[404] Art 39(2).

Directive was not compatible with human rights obligations binding the Community and its Member States.[405]

First of all, the possible removal of an asylum seeker from the territory before an initial decision on the application when an extradition or similar request is accepted was particularly suspect where the extradition request came from the country of origin.[406] Since the grounds for resisting extradition overlap with the grounds for requesting recognition as a refugee,[407] it is arguably in breach of the Geneva Convention to accede to an extradition request before determining an asylum claim. In any case, extradition will be in violation of the ECHR where there is a sufficiently serious risk of violation of ECHR standards in the destination country.[408] In case an asylum seeker is extradited, there should be an implied obligation to readmit him or her and continue with the asylum determination process after the criminal trial is concluded or the relevant sentence is served (if imposed) following the extradition.

The exclusions and limitations on the right to a personal interview were questionable, particularly the possibility for a Member State not to hold a personal interview where the national authorities had already determined that the application is unfounded on certain grounds.[409] In the absence of other procedural protection in such cases, and given the stress laid by the Strasbourg organs on the importance of a full consideration of an asylum claim,[410] it is doubtful whether this provision was valid. Similarly, it was doubtful whether the possibility of not receiving a report of the personal interview until after the first-instance decision was valid,[411] again because of the absence of other procedural protection; coupled with the lack of suspensive effect of an appeal decision, this could mean that asylum seekers could be removed before seeing a report of their personal interview and being given an opportunity to dispute or clarify its content.

Although the Directive provided for legal aid and legal assistance, it allowed for questionable restrictions upon legal aid.[412] A right to legal aid exists surely exists as a corollary of the right not to be removed to face torture, etc or other breaches of the ECHR following removal to another state.[413] It must follows that the limitation of legal aid to appeals and the possible limitation of legal aid to cases considered likely to succeed (in the absence of any procedural rights or guarantees of competence and independence as regards legal aid applications) were arguably invalid.[414]

Moving on to the accelerated procedures provided for by the Directive, while the basic procedural guarantees in the Directive expressly applied (with certain exceptions) even where a case was accelerated or considered inadmissible, in the 'real world', truncated proceedings, which were likely often coupled with a lack of suspensive effect for appeals, often meant great difficulty for asylum applicants in obtaining a fair hearing for arguing their claim. As regards inadmissible applications,[415] the most important provisions concerned the 'first country of asylum', and 'safe third country' concepts.[416]

---

[405] For a full examination of all these issues, with further references, see Peers and Rogers (n 336 above), ch 14.
[406] See Art 7(2).   [407] See II:3.5.2.   [408] See I:5.3.1 above.   [409] Art 12(2)(c).
[410] See the case law discussed in I:5.3.1 above.   [411] Art 14(2).   [412] Art 15.
[413] See, by analogy, the judgments in *Airey v Ireland* (A-32) and *Steel and Morris v UK* 15 Feb 2005.
[414] Art 15(2) and 15(3)(d).   [415] Art 25.   [416] Respectively Arts 26 and 27.

Both concepts should have been interpreted in light of the principles of the relevant international treaties, which require: an agreement to readmit the person in the other State and to accord that person a fair refugee status determination or other 'effective protection'; no Convention fear of persecution for the person in the other State; no risk of refoulement from the other State; no risk of removal from the other State to face a violation of the other rights in the Geneva Convention; no risk of violation of any human rights protected by a treaty to which the removing State is a party; willingness and ability in the other State to provide effective protection for as long is the person is a refugee or can find another source of durable effective protection; no violation of the person's right to family unity; and an application of these principles on an individual basis, including suspensive effect of appeals.[417] To the extent that the Directive did not require Member States to consider the safety of individual applicants *and* the safety of particular third countries, and did not require Member States to consider the possible ECHR breaches other than those relating to Article 3 ECHR which might occur in the relevant 'safe third country', it should have been considered invalid for breach of human rights principles.[418]

The next controversial issue was the rule on 'safe countries of origin', which provided for the possible adoption of national lists of such countries and maintaining existing national lists of such countries (or parts of countries) using *different* criteria, entailing lower standards for judging the States concerned. The problem with all such rules was that they increased the standard of proof which the applicant had to discharge, and were either dangerous, because the list included countries that are still refugee producing, or meaningless, because if the country is no longer refugee producing then there are unlikely to be more than a handful of applicants from the country at any one time. Such lists are of dubious validity in light of the Geneva Convention. Moreover, the derogation for national lists to be maintained on the basis of criteria setting lower standards was arguably invalid, because: the absence of a criterion regarding the threat of indiscriminate violence in armed conflict directly contradicted one of the main grounds for considering whether a person is entitled to subsidiary protection status in accordance with the qualification Directive;[419] the absence of a requirement to consider the consistency of State practice as regards torture and persecution, which was obviously relevant to a consideration of the 'safety' of a country; and the absence of obligations to consider all of the factors of assessment set out in Annex II to the Directive and the existence of a democratic system, which were obviously good indicators as to whether persecution and/or torture or other inhuman or degrading treatment were generally carried out.

The provision for special procedures permitted at national borders was arguably invalid, because many key procedural safeguards were omitted (particularly access to

---

[417] S Legomsky, 'Secondary Refugee Movements and the Return of Asylum Seekers to Third Countries: the Meaning of Effective Protection' (2003) 15 IJRL 567 at 673–5. See also the analysis and critique by C Costello, 'The Asylum Procedures Directive and the Proliferation of Safe Third Countries Practices: Deterrence, Deflection and the Dismantling of International Protection?' (2005) 7 EJML 35.

[418] Arts 27(2)(b) and (c).

[419] See I:5.5 above, and the interpretation of this provision in Case C-465/07 *Elgafaji* [2009] ECR I-921.

the procedure, requirements for examinations and decisions, guarantees on appeal, legal aid, lawyers' access to the file, protection regarding detention, contact with the UNHCR, and confidentiality).[420]

This brings us to perhaps the worst provision of the Directive: the possibility to maintain national lists on 'European safe third countries'.[421] Fundamentally, this clause violated the Geneva Convention and the ECHR, by providing that 'no, or no full' examination need be carried out of an asylum application as regards applications from the countries meeting the criteria.

The special rules on withdrawal of refugee status are also questionable, to the extent that some key procedural safeguards in the Directive did not fully apply,[422] along with the full right to a personal interview, to the extent that withdrawal of status in practice led to removal from the territory. Finally, the possible lack of suspensive effect quite clearly seemed to breach the minimum safeguards developed by the Human Rights Court for asylum appeals, at least as regards appeals at first instance.[423]

The asylum procedures Directive was clearly at or below the lowest common denominator as regards most aspects of procedural rights of asylum seekers, as evidenced by the long list of provisions which could be considered invalid for breach of human rights law. It is doubtful that any piece of EU legislation was ever responsible for so many human rights breaches. The legitimacy of EU asylum law and of the EU's claims to support the Geneva Convention and fundamental human rights is therefore dependent on finding key provisions of the Directive invalid or radically reinterpreting or amending them, or adopting major amendments to the Directive as soon as possible.

Moreover, the position was exacerbated once the relevant national authorities gained access to certain information in the Visa Information System (VIS) in order to assist with determining the merits of asylum claims.[424] Without detailed rules on fuller subsequent exchange of information between national authorities and governing the relevance and use of such data in asylum proceedings, ensuring that the data are fully disclosed to asylum applicants before the authorities' decision, and requiring national authorities to explain the extent of the reliance which they placed upon such data, access to this data to determine refugee claims is highly objectionable.

5.7.2 Second-phase Directive

A large number of the concerns about the first-phase procedures Directive have in principle been addressed, at least partly, by the second-phase Directive.[425] First of

---

[420] Art 35.   [421] Art 36.   [422] In particular, Arts 7, 10, 15, 16, and 17.

[423] Art 39(3)(a) and (b); see discussion of the case law in I:5.3.1 above. On this issue, see also R Byrne, 'Remedies of Limited Effect: Appeals Under the Forthcoming Directive on EU Minimum Standards on Procedures' (2005) 7 EJML 71.

[424] Art 22 of Reg 767/2008 ([2008] OJ L 218/60). See also I:5.8 below, on access to the VIS to decide on responsibility for asylum claims. The VIS became operational in 2011.

[425] Directive 2013/32 ([2013] OJ L 180/60). All references in this sub-section are to this Directive, unless otherwise noted. See the ECRE information note on the Directive, and the booklet on applying the EU Charter of Rights to asylum procedural law: <http://www.ecre.org/topics/areas-of-work/introduction/37-asylum-procedures.html>.

all, however, this Directive only applies to applications made after 20 July 2015.[426] Secondly, as with the Dublin III Regulation on responsibility for asylum applications and the second-phase Directive on reception conditions,[427] the scope of the procedures Directive was extended to include applications for subsidiary protection status.[428] The territorial scope of the Directive now expressly includes Member States' territorial waters,[429] although arguably the 2005 Directive already covered such applications, since territorial waters form part of a Member State's territory. There are new provisions requiring Member States to ensure that they have sufficient numbers of staff to process asylum applications, along with relevant staff training.[430]

There are more precise rules on access to the asylum procedure,[431] including at border crossing points.[432] The Directive now contains a safeguard against direct or indirect *refoulement* by means of an extradition to a third country during the asylum process.[433] A new provision explicitly addresses the issue of hierarchy between claims for refugee status and subsidiary protection, requiring Member States' authorities to examine the former claim first.[434] This confirms the case law of the CJEU on this issue.[435] There are also new rules on translation of documents, obtaining information from the European Asylum Support Office, the use of expert advice, and disclosing information used to the applicant's lawyer.[436]

When deciding on applications, it is no longer possible to refuse to give reasons for rejecting a refugee claim in certain cases, and it is necessary to give a separate decision to dependants in certain cases.[437] Applicants have greater access to information, and must be informed about the consequences of withdrawing an application.[438] Member States are now obliged to require applicants to cooperate in establishing their identity and the key facts relating to a claim.[439] The rules on personal interviews have been improved by deleting the most problematic exceptions from the obligation to hold such interviews,[440] by improving the standards relating to personal interviews,[441] by adding detailed provisions on the content of interviews to the Directive,[442] and by amending the rules on transcripts and reports of the interviews.[443] There is a new provision on medical assessments.[444]

---

[426] Art 52, second sentence.   [427] See respectively I:5.8 and I:5.9 below.

[428] See in particular the revised Arts 1 and 2(b), (c), (h), (i), and (k).   [429] Revised Art 3(1).

[430] Revised Art 4(1) and (2).

[431] Revised Arts 6 and 7. This includes the definition of a lodged application, and a time limit to register an application (usually three days).

[432] New Art 8.   [433] New Art 9(3).

[434] New Art 10(2). See also the new Art 46(2), which permits a person granted subsidiary protection to appeal the decision to refuse refugee status.

[435] See the *HN* judgment (n 340 above), discussed in I:5.7.1 above. Recital 11 to the preamble states that there should be a single procedure for both types of status, as the Court also required in *HN*.

[436] Revised Art 10(3) and 9(5) (previous Art 8(2) and 8(4)).

[437] Revised Art 11(2) and (3) (previous Art 9(2) and (3)).

[438] Revised Art 12(1) (previous Art 10(1)).   [439] Revised Art 13(1) (previous Art 11(1)).

[440] Revised Art 14(2) (previous Art 12(2)), deleting the exceptions relating to unfounded applications and previous brief interviews of the applicant.

[441] Revised Art 15(3) (previous Art 13(3)). The interview must now take account of gender identity, gender, and sexual orientation, and interviewers and interpreters should normally be the same sex as the interviewee.

[442] New Art 16.   [443] New Art 17, replacing previous Art 14.   [444] New Art 18.

However, the general intention to raise the standards of first-instance decision-making stalled when it came to legal aid, where the new Directive does not make significant changes. Legal aid can therefore still be denied at the administrative stage.[445] There are new safeguards if the legal adviser is denied access to information, and legal advisers can also attend the personal interview, although this right has limited utility if the applicant cannot afford an adviser at this stage.[446] There is a new provision concerning applicants with special needs,[447] along with higher standards for unaccompanied minors.[448] For both categories of persons, there are complicated exceptions from certain special procedural rules in the Directive, considered further below.[449] The rules on implied withdrawal of applications have been amended to give applicants a better opportunity to restart their applications.[450]

As for procedures at first instance, Member States are required (as from July 2018) to conclude examinations of applications within six months, with various options for further extensions; but there is an absolute time limit of 21 months.[451] The list of circumstances in which Member States can apply accelerated procedures was cut from fifteen cases to ten,[452] but there are limitations on applying those procedures to unaccompanied minors and applicants with special needs.[453] Despite the Court's judgment on the previous Directive,[454] it might now be argued that this list is now exhaustive.[455]

There is no longer a possibility for general derogations from the basic rules on procedures as regards repeat applications, border procedures, and 'supersafe third countries'.[456] Member States must now hold a special interview before ruling a case inadmissible.[457] Applicants must be able to argue that a 'first country of asylum' was not safe in their particular circumstances.[458] The 'safe country of origin' rules have been amended to delete the possibility of treating only part of a country as safe and to repeal the option for Member States to retain pre-existing lower standards on this issue.[459] Although the idea of a common EU list of such countries (struck down by the Court in 2008) was not revived, Council conclusions adopted in July 2015 encourage all Member States to consider Western Balkans States as safe countries of origin, and in September 2015 the Commission proposed a Regulation which would designate those Western Balkans States and Turkey as 'safe countries of origin' for every Member

---

[445] Revised Arts 19–22 (previous Art 15).   [446] Revised Art 23 (previous Art 16).

[447] New Art 24.   [448] Revised Art 25 (current Art 17).

[449] Arts 24(3) and 25(6). See the comments on Arts 31(8), 33(2)(c), 43, and 46(6).

[450] Revised Art 28 (current Art 20).

[451] New Art 31(3) to (5). For the previous practice of Member States as regards the time required to make first-instance decisions, see Annex 23 to the 2009 impact assessment.

[452] Revised Art 31(8) (previous Art 23(4)).

[453] More precisely, Art 31(8) cannot be applied if Member States have been unable to support an applicant with special needs (Art 24(3)) or to unaccompanied minors, unless those minors have made a repeat application, come from a safe country of origin, or are a public danger, as further defined (Art 25(6)(a)).

[454] *D and A*, n 340 above.

[455] The Court's ruling turned in part upon recital 11 in the preamble to the prior Directive, but the 2013 Directive includes a new recital 20, referring to 'well-defined circumstances' for designating claims as unfounded. If this list is still not exhaustive, why else would the EU legislature take the trouble to shorten it? Moreover, an exhaustive list would reflect the move toward setting common standards which the second-phase Directive represents (see recital 12 in the preamble, besides many other references).

[456] The previous Art 24 has been repealed.   [457] New Art 34.

[458] Revised Art 35 (previous Art 26).   [459] Revised Art 36 (previous Art 30).

State.[460] Applicants can also now challenge the designation of a 'super-safe' third country in their particular circumstances, but Member States are no longer limited to applying this concept to third States which they had designated back in 2005.[461] Furthermore, the standards relating to repeat applications have been modestly raised,[462] and the derogations relating to border procedures were deleted.[463] Again, there are limits on applying the remaining special border procedures to unaccompanied minors and applicants with special needs.[464]

As for the 'safe third country' concept, it was revised to require Member States to assess the risk of 'serious harm' in the relevant third State and to allow the applicant to challenge both the presumption of safety and of the connection with the third State concerned.[465] Where the applicant is an unaccompanied minor, this exception can only be used if it is in the minor's best interests to use it.[466]

Finally, as regards the issue of remedies, the 2013 Directive requires Member States to let applicants stay on the territory as a general rule, and to provide for an appeal of the merits as well as the law, at least at first instance.[467] There are still exceptions from the right to stay during an appeal in certain cases; but even in those cases, the applicant has the right apply to a court for a stay of an expulsion order, and to remain on the territory in the meantime.[468] The CJEU's previous case law on remedies remains relevant despite these changes.

As noted already, the second-phase Directive addressed a number of the criticisms of the first-phase Directive, improving standards as regards territorial scope, access to procedures, extradition, personal interviews, time limits, accelerated procedures (if the relevant list is now exhaustive), first country of asylum, safe third countries, safe countries of origin, and remedies. On the other hand, the 'super-safe countries' rule is to some extent worse, since Member States can add new countries to it. Furthermore, the Directive could have gone further on many points, for instance abolishing the 'super-safe' rule entirely and ruling out extradition to the country of origin. While many of the new rules intend to improve standards of first-instance administrative decision-making, this intention may be undercut by the failure to ensure a right to legal aid at this stage. Also, while many national exceptions have been removed, leading in principle to a more common process across the EU, this simplification is undermined by the new rules which set higher standards for unaccompanied minors and vulnerable applicants, subject to highly complex conditions. Rather than negotiate an exception to an

---

[460] COM (2015) 452, 9 Sep 2015.

[461] Revised Art 39 (previous Art 36). Again, the idea of a common EU list was not revived.

[462] Revised Arts 40–2 (previous Arts 32 and 34); the previous Art 33 was repealed.

[463] Revised Art 43 (previous Art 35); the previous Art 35(2) and (3) were repealed.

[464] More precisely, Art 43 cannot be applied if Member States have been unable to support an applicant with special needs (Art 24(3)) or to unaccompanied minors, unless those minors have made a repeat application, come from a safe country of origin, are a public danger (as further defined), came from a safe third country, presented false documents, or destroyed documents in bad faith; there are extra conditions as regards the exceptions for false documents and destroyed documents (Art 25(6)(b)).

[465] New Art 38(1)(b) and revised Art 38(2)(c) (previous Art 27(3)(c)).   [466] Art 25(6)(c).

[467] Revised Art 46 (previous Art 39).

[468] Art 46(6) and (7); see also Art 41, on repeat applications.

exception to an exception to an exception,[469] it would surely have been easier to raise standards for everyone.

5.8 Responsibility for Applications

The rules on responsibility for asylum applications were first of all set out in the 1990 Schengen Convention and the Dublin Convention of the same year.[470] These rules were subsequently replaced by the Dublin II Regulation, as from September 2003,[471] as supplemented by the Eurodac Regulation, adopted in 2000 and applicable from January 2003.[472] The Commission released one report on the application of the 'Dublin system' (ie the 'Dublin II' Regulation along with the Eurodac Regulation) in practice.[473] Both Regulations were subsequently replaced as part of the development of the second phase of the Common European Asylum System.[474] But subsequently, due to serious problems with the Dublin system and the increased numbers of asylum seekers reaching the EU in 2015, the EU has adopted two emergency Decisions on 'relocation' of asylum seekers that derogate from the Dublin system.[475]

5.8.1 The Schengen Convention and the Dublin Convention

Articles 28–38 of the 1990 Schengen Convention set out rules on responsibility for asylum applications between the Schengen States, with effect from March 1995.[476] These rules were replaced by the essentially identical rules applicable to all Member States set in the Dublin Convention, in force from 1 September 1997.[477] The Dublin Convention was, like the Schengen Convention, explicitly related to the goal of abolishing internal borders within the EU, as set out in Article 14 EC (now Article 26 TFEU). But it is obvious that the Convention was agreed because Member States feared that loosening or abolishing internal border checks would lead to an increase in multiple asylum applications (ie applications by the same person in more than one Member State). However, without common rules on how to determine which Member State was responsible for an application, Member States would inevitably take different approaches to determining which other Member State was responsible, and many applications would likely fall within the jurisdiction of two (or possibly more) Member States. To solve this problem, the Convention set out a list of conflict rules for determining the Member State with jurisdiction over an application. These were to be applied in the following order:[478]

(a) the Member State where the applicant has a specified family member (spouse, parent or child) who already has been recognized as a Geneva Convention refugee;[479]

(b) the Member State which has issued the applicant a residence permit;[480]

---

[469] Art 25(6)(b), final sentence.
[470] I:5.8.1 below.   [471] I:5.8.2 below.   [472] I:5.8.3 below.
[473] COM (2007) 299, 6 June 2007.   [474] I:5.8.4 below.   [475] I:5.8.5 below.
[476] [2000] OJ L 239.   [477] [1997] OJ C 254/1.
[478] Art 3(2).   [479] Art 4.   [480] Art 5(1).

(c) the Member State which has issued the applicant a visa, with certain specified exceptions;[481]

(d) the Member State which the applicant first entered without authorization, unless the applicant has been living in the Member State where he/she has applied for over six months;[482]

(e) the Member State responsible for controlling entry of the applicant, unless the applicant is a non-visa national who does not require a visa to enter either the Member State of first entry or the Member State in which he or she subsequently applies;[483]

(f) the Member State in which an application is made in an airport transit zone;[484] or

(g) as a default, the Member State in which the application is made.[485]

It was also open to a Member State to decide that a non-EU country was responsible for the application,[486] or to either offer or accede to a request from another Member State to examine an application regardless of these conflict rules.[487] Detailed procedures on the transfer of asylum seekers and the exchange of information were set out.[488] The treaty was implemented by a body established by Article 18 of the Convention (the 'Article 18 Committee'), which adopted a number of measures in 1997, 1998, and 2000.[489]

The Convention was heavily criticized for forcing apart family members, for ignoring the differences in national interpretation of the Geneva Convention, and for inducing asylum seekers to destroy travel documents—thus avoiding the application of the conflict rules (due to an absence of proof about the countries they had previously entered) but raising a suspicion that their submissions about the persecution they faced would be disbelieved by authorities because of their lack of full disclosure of their prior travel details.[490] From the perspective of national authorities, the Convention was also disappointing, because only about 6% of asylum applications were identified as subject to it; since only two-thirds of those cases were accepted by the Member State identified as responsible and only 40% of the remaining cases actually resulted in the transfer of an asylum seekers, only 1.7% of all asylum applications made in the EU were ultimately subject to the transfer of an asylum seeker pursuant to the rules in the Convention.[491] In 2001, only 4.2% of asylum applications were subject to requests to take responsibility

---

[481] Art 5(2). If the applicant had multiple residence permits or visas, special rules in Art 5(3) and (4) applied.

[482] Art 6.

[483] Art 7(1). The responsible State for a non-visa national was the State in which he or she applied.

[484] Art 7(3).   [485] Art 8.   [486] Art 3(5).   [487] Respectively Arts 3(4) and 9.

[488] Respectively Arts 10–15.

[489] Decisions 1/97 and 2/97 ([1997] OJ L 281/1 and 26); Decision 1/98 ([1998] OJ L 196/49); and Decision 1/2000 ([2000] OJ L 281/1). On implementation of the Convention up to 1998, see the first edition of this book, pp 114–16.

[490] On the Convention, see C Marinho, ed., *The Dublin Convention on Asylum* (EIPA, 2000); K Hailbronner and C Thiery, 'Schengen II and Dublin: Responsibility for Asylum Applications in Europe' (1997) 34 CMLRev 957; A Hurwitz, 'The 1990 Dublin Convention: A Comprehensive Assessment' (1999) IJRL 646; and S Da Lomba, *The Right to Seek Refugee Status in the European Union* (Intersentia, 2004), 117–31.

[491] The statistics are for 1998–9, and were taken from the Commission evaluation of the Convention (SEC (2001) 756, 12 June 2001), p 2.

according to the Convention, and 71.4% of these requests were accepted (3.0% of the total asylum applications).[492]

5.8.2 The 'Dublin II' Regulation

The Dublin Convention was replaced as from 1 September 2003 by Regulation 343/2003, known in practice as the 'Dublin II' Regulation.[493] This Regulation set out certain additions and amendments to the hierarchy of criteria for responsibility in the Convention along with an acceleration of the procedure for transferring asylum seekers between states, and was implemented by a Commission Regulation.[494] It was amended once, in order to change the rules relating to the adoption of implementing measures.[495] As noted above, in 2007 the Commission released a report on the operation of the 'Dublin system',[496] which is considered also below.

The CJEU ruled on the Regulation a number of times following references from national courts.[497] Furthermore, the Commission brought one infringement action against a Member State (Greece) for incorrect application of the Regulation, because Greece refused to consider the merits of asylum applications brought by persons who had initially made applications there, made later applications in other Member States, and then were transferred back to Greece, on the grounds that the applications had been withdrawn.[498]

The most significant feature of the CJEU's case law on the Regulation is its ruling that it must be disapplied where there is a fundamental problem with the asylum system of the responsible Member State. In a line of case law beginning with *NS*,[499] the CJEU started from the assumption that mutual trust between Member States as regards the compliance of their asylum systems with human rights standards was justifiable in principle. However, it is 'not…inconceivable that that system may, in practice,

---

[492] There were 371,680 asylum applications, 15,776 outgoing requests under the Convention and 11,268 acceptances of those requests. The statistics do not indicate what percentage of asylum seekers were subsequently transferred. These statistics are taken from the Commission annual report on migration and asylum statistics: <http://ec.europa.eu/justice_home/doc_centre/asylum/statistics/doc_annual_report_2001_en.htm>.

[493] [2003] L 50/1; see Art 29 on the date of application. On the Reg, see: S Da Lomba, *The Right to Seek Refugee Status in the European Union* (Intersentia, 2004), 131–41; A Nicol, 'From Dublin Convention to Dublin Regulation: A Progressive Move?' in A Baldaccini, E Guild and H Toner, eds., *Whose Freedom, Security and Justice? EU Immigration and Asylum Law and Policy* (Hart, 2007), 265; and H Battjes, *European Asylum Law and International Law* (Martinus Nijhoff, 2006), ch 7.

[494] Reg 1560/2003, [2003] OJ L 222/3.

[495] Reg 1103/2008 ([2008] L 304/80), changing the rules to apply the 'regulatory procedure with scrutiny' for the adoption of implementing measures. See further I:2.2.2.1 above.

[496] COM (2007) 299, 6 June 2007.

[497] Cases: C-19/08 *Petrosian* [2009] ECR I-495; C-411/10 and C-493/10 *NS and ME* [2011] ECR I-13493; C-620/10 *Kastrati*, ECLI:EU:C:2012:265; C-245/11 *K*, ECLI:EU:C:2012:685; C-528/11 *Halaf*, ECLI:EU:C:2013:342; C-648/11 *MA*, ECLI:EU:C:2013:367; C-4/11 *Puid*, ECLI:EU:C:2013:740; C-394/12 *Abdullahi*, ECLI:EU:C:2013:813; and C-481/13 *Qurbani*, ECLI:EU:C:2014:2101. See also Case C-179/11 *CIMADE and GISTI*, ECLI:EU:C:2012:594, discussed further in I:5.9 below, which confirmed the application of the reception conditions Directive to asylum seekers subject to the Dublin rules.

[498] Case C-130/08 *Commission v Greece*. The Dublin III Reg now addresses this issue explicitly (I:5.8.4 below). On the concept of withdrawn applications, see also the asylum procedures Directive, discussed in I:5.7 above.

[499] N 497 above; see also *Puid* (n 497).

experience major operational problems in a given Member State, meaning that there is a substantial risk that asylum seekers may, when transferred to that Member State, be treated in a manner incompatible with their fundamental rights'. But this did not mean that 'any infringement of a fundamental right' could lead to the suspension of the Dublin rules. Rather, if the 'slightest infringement' of rights could have that effect, the objective of the Dublin rules (determining a responsible Member State quickly) would be compromised. To determine the existence of such a breach, the CJEU referred to the *MSS* judgment of the European Court of Human Rights, which had taken into account 'the regular and unanimous reports of international non-governmental organisations bearing witness to the practical difficulties in the implementation of the Common European Asylum System in Greece, the correspondence sent by the UNHCR to the Belgian minister responsible, and also the Commission reports on the evaluation of the Dublin system and the proposals for recasting' the Dublin II Regulation.[500]

Are these the *only* circumstances in which the application of the Regulation *must* be suspended on human rights grounds? The Court of Justice was not clear on this point in the *NS* judgment, but subsequently, in the case of *Abdullahi*,[501] it ruled that in a case where two Member States agreed among themselves that the 'irregular entry' criterion for responsibility (see discussion below) was applicable to the person concerned, it was only possible to challenge that decision on the grounds set out in the *NS* judgment. Its ruling was based on the broader context of the Dublin II Regulation, including the prospect of bilateral arrangements and conciliation between Member States, the bolstering of mutual trust by the second-phase CEAS legislation, and the existence of the sovereignty and humanitarian clauses. With respect, this judgment is dubious on its own terms, because: all of these factors existed also as regards the *NS* judgment (except for the adoption of the second-phase procedures Directive); the second-phase legislation was not applicable to the case concerned; conciliation has never been used; and in the *NS* judgment, the national discretion set out in the sovereignty clause was overridden by the Charter.

The Regulation still left Member States free to decide that a non-Member State should take responsibility, or to take responsibility even where the Regulation did not require it.[502] The first criterion for responsibility was a new criterion relating to unaccompanied minors; the Member State responsible for them was the Member State where a family member could take care of them, or failing that, as a default rule, the Member State where they lodged their application.[503] According to the CJEU ruling in *MA*,[504] where an unaccompanied minor has already made an application for asylum in one Member State, and then applies in another Member State, the default rule means that the Member State where the *most recent* application (rather than the *first* application) was made is responsible for the application. In the Court's view, this interpretation was necessary first of all for literal reasons, as the legislation does not

---

[500] See I:5.3.1 above.   [501] N 497 above.

[502] Arts 3(2) and 15 of the Reg. Art 3(2) was not subject to any particular condition, and there was no requirement to consult the UNHCR when determining the responsible Member State: *Halaf*, n 497 above.

[503] Art 6. See now the action plan on unaccompanied minors (COM (2010) 213, 6 May 2010) and the follow-up to that plan (COM (2012) 554, 28 Sep 2012).

[504] N 497 above.

refer to the first Member State where the application was made. Secondly, unaccompanied minors were vulnerable persons, so the procedure to apply the Dublin rules should be as short as possible. Finally, this interpretation was most consistent with the 'best interest of the child', as required by Article 24 of the EU Charter of Fundamental Rights.

The second criterion, family reunion with recognized refugees, was unchanged from the Dublin Convention.[505] The third criterion was new: a Member State was responsible for the family members of an asylum seeker if the latter was still waiting for a decision on the substance of the application in that Member State.[506]

The second criterion in the Convention rules (issue of a visa or a residence permit) became the fourth criterion in the Regulation, but it was not significantly changed in substance.[507] It should be noted that the Visa Information System, since it became operational in 2011, could be used in order to check more effectively whether a visa was issued to an asylum seeker.[508] The third criterion in the Convention (crossing the border irregularly) became the fifth criterion in the Regulation, but responsibility now terminated after twelve months.[509] In order to enforce this provision, the Eurodac Regulation required Member States to take fingerprints of persons who are stopped crossing the external borders irregularly.[510] Also, a further new provision specified that if a Member State could not or could no longer be held responsible on grounds of irregular border crossing, another Member State would become responsible if a person has resided there, having initially entered irregularly, for more than five months.[511] The political context of this provision was the settlement of a dispute between the UK and France concerning asylum seekers residing in France but who attracted little or no interest from the French authorities, who frequently attempted to enter the UK. Next, the sixth criterion (formerly the fourth) was the state responsible for controlling the entry of a non-visa national, with the wording of the Dublin Convention rules in effect retained.[512] The seventh criterion (formerly the fifth) was the Member State where the asylum seeker applied for asylum in the airport transit zone.[513] Finally, as before, the default criterion was the Member State where the asylum seeker submitted his or her application.[514]

There was a new 'tie-break' clause in the event of family members submitting an application in the same Member State close together,[515] but no such clause to govern the position where the family members submitted applications in *different* Member States. The old 'humanitarian' clause was retained and expanded, now focusing on family reunion alone.[516] According to the CJEU, it required a Member State to deal with the application of an asylum seeker's mother-in-law, upon whom the asylum seeker was dependent.[517]

The procedural rules and provisions on administrative cooperation were amended, in particular to accelerate the transfer of asylum seekers and to include some of the details of the previous implementing measures in the text of the Regulation (with the

---

[505] Art 7.   [506] Art 8.   [507] Art 9.
[508] Reg 767/2008 ([2008] OJ L 218/60), Art 21. See further I:4.8 above.   [509] Art 10(1).
[510] See I:5.8.3 below.   [511] Art 10(2).   [512] Art 11.   [513] Art 12.
[514] Art 13.   [515] Art 14.   [516] Art 15.   [517] *K*, n 497 above.

result that the Commission could not amend those provisions via means of a 'comi-tology' procedure).[518] The suspensive effect of an appeal against the application of the Regulation was permitted on a case-by-case basis, although it was only optional for Member States.[519] According to the Court of Justice, the time limit of six months to take an asylum seeker back following the agreement to do so by a Member State only started to run from the date of a final court decision on a challenge to a transfer deci-sion, not from the date on which a court or tribunal suspended that transfer pending its judgment.[520] The Court also ruled that the Regulation ceased to apply if an asy-lum seeker withdrew a claim for refugee status before the transfer was accepted by the requested Member State.[521]

As for the implementation of the Regulation,[522] the Commission's 2007 report indi-cates that over 2003–05, the number of asylum applications subject to requests to apply the Dublin II rules rose to 11.5%, as compared to 6% for the Dublin Convention. The acceptance rate of transfers was similar (72%) and the rate of transfers carried out rose to 52%, although the Commission still considered this disappointing. Overall 4.1% of asylum seekers were transferred under the rules, also a rise compared to the previous period, but still quite a modest percentage of the overall number of asylum seekers. The Commission did not suggest the reasons why such a low percentage of asylum seekers was still covered by the Dublin rules, given that the Eurodac system had started oper-ations and the EU had been enlarged in the meantime.

On the criteria in the Dublin rules, the Commission reported that: unaccompanied minors made up perhaps 1–2% of requests; the family members' provisions were 'rarely applied' due to evidence problems; the criteria regarding visas and residence permits were 'applied frequently', particularly as regards visas (about 6–20% of requests); the requests for the application of the irregular entry criterion 'far exceed transfers', because of the low rate of fingerprinting under the Eurodac system (see below) and the difficulty proving irregular entry without such data; the 'illegal stay' criterion was 'less often' used, again due to evidence problems; and the 'legal entry' criterion made up only a 'small proportion' of requests. The failure to carry out half of the agreed transfers was due to asylum seekers absconding (the evidence that detention was necessary to avoid this was mixed), the suspensive effect of an appeal (although few Member States allowed this), illness or humanitarian reasons, or voluntary return to the country of origin.

This evidence suggested that the Dublin rules remained an expensive waste of time, ultimately still applying to only a small percentage of asylum seekers and imposing an extra cost on top of the cost of considering each asylum application. The application of the Eurodac system and the increase in EU border controls had not altered the situ-ation profoundly. Yet, as we shall see, the subsequent Dublin III Regulation made only modest changes to the system.

From a human rights perspective, there was some improvement in the Regulation as regards the issue of family reunion, although with a narrow definition of 'family' in the Regulation and the limitation of reunion to certain categories (leaving out, for instance

---

[518] Arts 16–23.   [519] Art 20(1)(e).   [520] See the judgment in *Petrosian*, n 497 above.
[521] *Kastrati*, n 497 above.   [522] COM (2007) 299 and SEC (2007) 742, 6 June 2007.

reunion with an irregularly resident family member, a family member enjoying or applying for subsidiary protection, or a family member with legal residence on other grounds) many families were still separated by the revised rules. It is arguable that the fundamental objection to allocating responsibility for asylum claims in the absence of a common definition of the Geneva Convention should have been overcome after the qualification Directive took effect, from October 2006—although in practice there was still great divergence in Member States' asylum law, in spite of the latter Directive.[523] In any case, the negative impact of the Dublin Convention rules as regards the destruction of documents by asylum seekers was not reduced by the Regulation.

5.8.3 Eurodac

The first-phase Eurodac Regulation was adopted in December 2000,[524] and took effect on 15 January 2003, when Eurodac began operations following the satisfaction of complex technical requirements by the Commission and the Member States.[525] The Commission's operational management of Eurodac was transferred to an agency responsible for EU JHA database management in 2012.[526]

The Regulation required fingerprints of all asylum seekers over fourteen to be taken and transmitted to a 'Central Unit' which compared them with other fingerprints previously (and subsequently) transmitted to see whether the asylum seeker had made multiple applications in the EU.[527] Similarly, Member States had to take the fingerprints of all third-country nationals who crossed a border irregularly,[528] and transmit them to the Central Unit to check against fingerprints subsequently taken from asylum seekers.[529] Member States could also take fingerprints of third-country nationals 'found illegally present' and transmit them to the Central Unit to see whether such persons had previously applied for asylum in another Member State. There were provisions on data protection, data security, and rights of the data subject.[530] For a transitional period, the data on recognized refugees was blocked once the refugee status of a person is granted.[531] At the end of that period (January 2008), the EU institutions had to decide either to store the data and use it in the same way as data on asylum seekers, or to erase all data as soon as a person has been recognized as a refugee. No such decision was ever taken, although the second-phase version of the Regulation addresses this issue.[532]

The EU institutions disagreed as to which institution should have the power to adopt implementing measures. Ultimately, although Article 202 EC (now, after the Treaty of Lisbon, Article 291 TFEU) required implementing power to be delegated

---

[523] See I:5.5 above.

[524] Reg 2725/2000 ([2000] OJ L 316/1). On the Reg, see E Brouwer, 'Eurodac: Its Temptations and Limitations' (2002) 4 EJML 231.

[525] See Art 27(2) and the communication on start of operations ([2003] OJ C 5/2).

[526] Reg 1077/2011 ([2011] OJ L 286/1).   [527] Chapter II (Arts 4–7).

[528] Rather dubiously, this concept was extended in an unpublished statement in the Council minutes to include cases where a third-country national 'is apprehended beyond the external border, where he/she is still en route and there is no doubt that he/she crossed the external border irregularly' (Council doc 12314/00 Add 1, 15 Nov 2000).

[529] Chapter III of the Reg (Arts 8–10).   [530] Chapter VI (Arts 13–20).   [531] Art 12.

[532] See I:5.8.4 below.

to the Commission, with a limited possibility of delegating power to the Council, the Council decided that it would retain power to adopt the measures concerning the detailed operations of the Central Unit and concerning the 'blocking' of the fingerprints of recognized refugees, while leaving other measures to be adopted by the Commission following a form of 'comitology' procedure.[533] Applying this procedure, the Eurodac Regulation was subsequently implemented by Council Regulation 407/2002.[534] This Regulation sets out rules on transmission of data by Member States, carrying out comparisons by the Central Unit, communication between Member States and the Central Unit, and other tasks of the Central Unit, which concern the separation of data on different categories of fingerprints and gathering statistics on the number of recognized refugees who request asylum in other Member States.

The Commission was required to report annually on the operation of Eurodac and to evaluate Eurodac generally at regular periods, beginning in January 2006.[535] Neither the annual reports nor the general evaluation of the Dublin system (see above) were able to draw comprehensive conclusions about the link between Eurodac data and the application of the Dublin II Regulation, except to show that Member States rarely accepted responsibility for irregular border crossers in the absence of such data. But it is clear, as discussed above, that since Eurodac began operations, the percentage of asylum seekers covered by the Dublin rules increased only modestly. So it might be questioned whether Eurodac contributed to the operation of the Dublin rules sufficiently to justify the cost of the system for the EU and its Member States.

The operation of Eurodac was subject to the principles of data protection and the right to privacy, in particular requiring a link with the data collected and a legitimate aim and the application of the principle of proportionality (including the 'purpose limitation' principle of data protection law, ie giving access to the data only for the purposes it was originally collected for). In fact, the Eurodac system infringed this principle to the extent that data on irregular border crossers was kept for a longer period than the period during which a Member State could be held responsible under the Dublin II rules.

5.8.4 Second-phase Regulations

In 2013, the EU adopted recast versions of the Dublin and Eurodac rules; the former is known in practice as the 'Dublin III Regulation'.[536] The Commission has adopted a further measure implementing the Dublin III Regulation.[537]

---

[533] Art 23. On the issue of comitology, see I:2.2.2.1 above.   [534] [2002] OJ L 62/1.

[535] Art 24 of Reg 2725/2000. On the first general evaluation, see I:5.8.2 above.

[536] Regs 603/2013 and 604/2013 ([2013] OJ L 180/1 and 31), in force 20 July 2015 and 1 Jan 2014 respectively. Three CJEU cases on the Dublin III Reg are pending: C-63/15 *Ghezelbash*, C-155/15 *Karim*, and C-528/15 *Al Chodor*. See the ECRE guidance note: <http://www.ecre.org/topics/areas-of-work/introduction/10-dublin-regulation.html>.

[537] Reg 118/2014 ([2014] OJ L 39/1).

The Dublin III Regulation first of all extended the scope of that Regulation to persons who make applications for subsidiary protection.[538] Next, the scope of 'family members' was enlarged to include married minor children and the parents of married minor children.[539] The provision permitting Member States to determine that a third State is responsible for the application was amended to confirm expressly that such a State must be a 'safe third country' as defined in the asylum procedures legislation.[540] There are expanded procedural rights concerning the protection-seekers' right to information, the right to a personal interview, and special guarantees for minors.[541] A new clause entrenches the ruling in *NS* into the legislation. It is also arguable that the restrictive judgment in *Abdullahi* is no longer good law,[542] because the Dublin III Regulation alters the nature of the Regulation, by including new procedural rights for applicants (including at the decision-making and appeal stage: see below). It is implausible to suggest that the EU legislature, having made all these changes, also intended to restrict applicants to challenging the application of the Regulation on human rights grounds only in the cases referred to in this new provision.

The main criteria for responsibility were not amended, except to add a vague clause on timing of applications as regards the rules on family members and children,[543] and to amend the rules relating to dependent relatives.[544] There were some minor changes to the rules applicable to responsibility for unaccompanied minors;[545] the Commission later proposed a further amendment on this issue, which is still under discussion.[546] The procedural rules were amended in order to provide further information to the applicant, a stronger right to a remedy, and detailed rules regulating detention of applicants.[547]

As for the Eurodac Regulation, first of all its scope was also extended to cover persons who make applications for subsidiary protection.[548] Law enforcement agencies and Europol have been given access to Eurodac data.[549] As noted above, Eurodac is now managed by a specialist agency, rather than the Commission.[550] There is now a deadline to take the fingerprints within seventy-two hours after an application for international protection was made, or after apprehension in connection with irregular crossing of an external border.[551] The database includes additional information on the status of the data subject.[552] Data on irregular border crossers is now kept for eighteen months, instead of two years, but this is still inconsistent with the responsibility rules in

---

[538] See, for instance, the revised Arts 1 and 2(b). This also means that responsibility for applications lies with a Member State where a family member has received or applied for *international protection*, not merely refugee status (revised Arts 9 and 10). It also means that the Reg still applies if a person withdraws a claim for refugee status but maintains a claim for subsidiary protection status (compare to *Kastrati*, n 497 above).

[539] Revised Art 2(g).　　[540] Revised Art 3(3); on the procedures Directive, see I:5.7 above.

[541] New Arts 4–6.　　[542] On both judgments, see I:5.8.2 above.　　[543] New Art 7(3).

[544] Art 16. The new rules are less favourable to the persons concerned than the judgment in *K*, n 497 above.

[545] Revised Art 8.　　[546] COM (2014) 382, 26 June 2014.

[547] Arts 26–8; on the detention rules, see the pending case of *Al Chodor* (n 536 above). Further details on detention conditions set out in the reception conditions directive (see I:5.9 below) also apply.

[548] See, for instance, the revised Art 1(1).

[549] Arts 1(2) and 5–7. On the policing aspects of the Reg, see II:7.6.1.4.

[550] New Art 4; see n 526 above.　　[551] Revised Arts 9(1) and 14(2).　　[552] Arts 10–11.

the Dublin system.[553] However, data on persons who have received international protection status is now unblocked.[554] The rights of data subjects have been enhanced,[555] and there are new provisions on the role of the European Data Protection Supervisor (EDPS).[556] Finally, the provisions concerning the adoption of implementing measures by the Council or the Commission were repealed,[557] and the previous implementing measure was inserted into the text of the main Regulation.

The Dublin III Regulation usefully enlarges the possibility of family reunion, strengthens the procedural rights of asylum seekers who challenge transfers, and ensures that basic rights are secured during detention. Conversely, the Eurodac Regulation has, on balance, lowered standards as compared to the prior legislation, given that it gives access to Eurodac data for law enforcement purposes and unblocks the fingerprints of recognized refugees for no good reason. However, the failure to fix the underlying problems with the Dublin system has led the EU ultimately to agree a significant derogation from it, in the form of rules on relocation of asylum seekers.[558]

5.8.5 Relocation

In September 2015, the EU adopted two Decisions, based on the emergency powers set out in Article 78(3) TFEU, to derogate from the usual 'Dublin' rules as regards Italy and Greece, and distribute some of the asylum seekers which would normally be the responsibility of those Member States under the Dublin rules to other Member States. The second of these Decisions was challenged by two Member States in the CJEU. At the same time, the Commission proposed an amendment to the Dublin III Regulation to establish permanent rules on relocation.[559]

Under the first Decision, the relocated asylum seekers are split 60/40 between Italy and Greece, and are allocated to other Member States on the basis of optional commitments made by those other States. While the intention was to relocate 40,000 people, Member States could ultimately not agree to offer that many relocation spaces, falling several thousand short.[560] The second Decision relocates 120,000 asylum-seekers (50,400 from Greece; 15,600 from Italy; and 54,000 not yet designated), based on quotas allocated to other Member States (besides Hungary).

Relocation is selective, applying only to those nationalities whose applications have over a 75% success rate in applications for international protection. On the basis of the statistics for the second quarter of 2015, only Syrians, Iraqis, and Eritreans qualify in large numbers. The Member State of relocation is to be responsible for considering the application, and asylum seekers and refugees are not able to move between Member States, in accordance

---

[553] Revised Art 16(2).   [554] New Art 18.
[555] Revised Art 29. For a list of agencies with access to Eurodac data, see [2015] OJ C 237/1.
[556] New Arts 31 and 32. On the EDPS, see further II:7.3.2.   [557] Previous Arts 21 and 22.
[558] Permanent amendments to the Dublin system will be proposed in 2016: see the Commission's migration agenda (COM (2015) 240, 13 May 2015).
[559] [2015] OJ L 239/146 (first Decision); [2015] OJ L 248/80 (second Decision); Cases C-643/15 *Slovakia v Council* and C-647/15 *Hungary v Council* (legal challenges); COM (2015) 450, 9 Sep 2015 (proposal to amend Dublin III).
[560] For details, see the resolution of the Member States adopted at the July 2015 JHA Council.

with the normal Dublin rules (except for short visits by refugees on the basis of a residence permit, within the Schengen area). The selection of asylum seekers is made by Italy and Greece, who must give 'priority' to those who are considered 'vulnerable' as defined by the EU reception conditions Directive.[561] Furthermore, the preamble to the Decision states that 'specific account should be given to the specific qualifications and characteristics of the applicants concerned, such as their language skills and other individual indications based on demonstrated family, cultural or social ties which could facilitate their integration into the Member State of relocation'; the relocation States can express a preference to this end. But this preference is not binding: the main text of the Decision states that the relocation States must accept the asylum seekers nominated by Italy and Greece, except that they can refuse relocation 'only where there are reasonable grounds for regarding' an asylum seeker as a danger to their national security or public order or where there are serious reasons for applying the exclusion provisions in the qualification Directive.[562]

As for the asylum seekers themselves, there is no requirement that they consent to their relocation or have the power to request it. The Decisions only require Italy and Greece to inform and notify the asylum seekers about the relocation, and the preambles to the Decisions state that they could only appeal against the decision if there are major human rights problems in the country to which they would be relocated. So neither the relocation itself, nor the choice of Member State that a person will be relocated to, is voluntary. This is problematic, since compelling asylum seekers to move to a country that they do not wish to be in has already proved unworkable in the original Dublin context. It is possible, however, that the asylum seekers left behind in Italy or Greece will be disappointed that they are not picked. There is no specific remedy for them to challenge their non-selection, although arguably to the extent that Italy and Greece select people who are *not* vulnerable for relocation, vulnerable persons could challenge their non-inclusion, in light of the legal obligation to select vulnerable persons as a priority. Asylum seekers do have the right to insist that their core family members (spouse or partner, unmarried minor children, or parents of minors) who are already on EU territory come with them to the relocated Member State.

The numbers of asylum seekers grew while these Decisions were under discussion and after their adoption, and in light of this, the Decisions will have a fairly modest impact on the ability of Italy and Greece to manage their overloaded asylum systems. But it is the first time, after years of discussion about burden-sharing and significant reforms to the Dublin system, that the EU has agreed on either. It remains to be seen how effectively even this modest step is applied in practice.

5.9 Reception Conditions

The first-phase Directive 2003/9 on reception conditions for asylum seekers was adopted in January 2003, and had to be implemented by 6 February 2005.[563] The second-phase

---

[561] See I:5.9 below. However, in practice, as the preamble makes clear, prior consultation with the would-be States of relocation as to whom they wish to accept plays a large role.

[562] See I:5.5 above.

[563] Dir 2003/9 ([2003] OJ L 31/18). On the Dir, see S Da Lomba, *The Right to Seek Refugee Status in the European Union* (Intersentia, 2004), 219–62 and J Handoll, 'Directive 2003/9 on Reception Conditions of

Directive, which was adopted in June 2013, had to be implemented by 20 July 2015.[564] The two Directives are discussed in turn.[565]

5.9.1 First-phase Directive

Member States had to implement Directive 2003/9 by 6 February 2005,[566] but some of them missed this deadline.[567] The Commission issued a report on the application of the Directive, which is considered as part of the discussion of the Directive.[568] There have been two judgments of the CJEU interpreting the Directive.[569] According to the Court, the Directive had to be interpreted in light of the EU Charter of Fundamental Rights, and in light of its aim of promoting full respect for human dignity and facilitating the right to asylum.[570] This meant that asylum seekers should not be deprived even temporarily, of the rights set out in the Directive.[571]

The first-phase Directive applied to applications for Geneva Convention refugee status made at the border or on the territory of Member States, and to asylum seekers' family members if they were covered by the asylum seekers' applications according to national law.[572] Member States had an option to apply the Directive to persons claiming other forms of status.[573] The Directive applied to asylum seekers as long as a 'final decision' had not been taken on their application, 'as long as they are allowed to remain on the territory as asylum seekers'.[574] According to the Commission's report, some Member States failed to apply the Directive at all stages of the asylum procedure (not in transit zones, or during the admissibility stage, or during the determination of whether the Dublin rules apply), or applied the Directive only to certain categories of asylum seekers (holding a certain ID card, or who had already registered), and a significant number of Member States failed to apply the Directive in detention centres. The Court of Justice ruled that the Directive applied fully to those asylum seekers

---

Asylum Seekers: Ensuring "Mere Subsistence" or a "Dignified Standard of Living"?' in A Baldaccini, E Guild and H Toner, eds., *Whose Freedom, Security and Justice? EU Immigration and Asylum Law and Policy* (Hart, 2007), 195. All references in this section are to this Dir, unless otherwise indicated.

[564] Dir 2013/33 ([2013] OJ L 180/96).   [565] I:5.9.1 and I:5.9.2.   [566] Art 26(1).

[567] The Court of Justice ruled against two Member States that failed to meet the deadline: Cases C-72/06 *Commission v Greece*, judgment of 19 Apr 2007, and C-102/06 *Commission v Austria*, judgment of 26 Oct 2006 (both unreported).

[568] COM (2007) 745, 26 Nov 2007. See also ECRE, 'The EC Directive on the Reception of Asylum Seekers: Are Asylum Seekers in Europe Receiving Material Support and Access to Employment in Accordance with European Legislation?' November 2005, and A Baldaccini, *Asylum Support: A Practitioners' Guide to the EU Reception Directive* (Justice, 2005).

[569] Cases C-179/11 *Cimade and GISTI*, ECLI:EU:C:2012:594 and C-79/13 *Saciri*, ECLI:EU:C:2014:103.

[570] *Cimade and GISTI* (n 569 above) para 56.

[571] *Cimade and GISTI* (n 569 above) para 42, referring to the preamble to the Directive. See also *Saciri* (n 569 above) para 35.

[572] Art 3(1).

[573] According to the Commission report, the 'vast majority' of Member States chose to apply the Dir to persons applying for subsidiary protection status.

[574] Arts 2(c) and 3(1). The Directive did not define 'final decision'. On the issue of whether asylum seekers can remain on the territory, see the asylum procedures Dir (I:5.7 above). According to *Cimade and GISTI* (n 569 above) para 53, the decision to send a request to another Member State to take charge of an applicant according to the Dublin rules is not a 'final decision'.

who were the responsibility of another Member State pursuant to the Dublin rules, up until the point when the asylum seekers were actually transferred to that other State.[575] Since the Court stated that the Directive provided 'only for one category of asylum seekers', the other practices of Member States described by the Commission were clearly also in breach of the Directive.[576]

The reception conditions Directive did not apply when the EU's temporary protection Directive applied,[577] although this was never relevant in practice because the latter Directive was never invoked while the first-phase Directive was applicable. This suggested *a contrario* that the first-phase Directive *did* apply when a purely national temporary protection regime was in force—assuming that new national temporary protection regimes could still be established.[578] As with other first-phase asylum Directives, Member States could apply more favourable provisions as regards reception conditions, provided that they were 'compatible' with the Directive.[579]

Asylum seekers had to be informed within fifteen days of lodging their application of the rights and benefits to which they were entitled and the obligations placed upon them by Member States.[580] According to the Commission's report, the 'vast majority' of Member States complied with this obligation, but some Member States did not make sufficient information available, or did not make it available in many languages. Also, asylum seekers had to be given, within three days of their application, a document certifying their status or the legality of their presence on the territory (subject to certain exceptions), and Member States 'may' supply asylum seekers with a travel document permitting them to travel to another State.[581] The Commission's report indicates that while all Member States issued the required documentation, many did not issue it by the required deadline. However, in practice the form and content of the documents varied, and because the documents often did not certify identity,[582] this caused some problems for asylum seekers in daily life. The Commission suggested that a standard model document, which would certify identity, would address these problems.[583]

Next, asylum seekers were entitled to freedom of movement within a Member State, or at least within an assigned area, but Member States could decide on asylum seekers' residence on grounds of public order, public interest, or the necessity to decide on applications quickly; Member States could also 'confine' an asylum seeker 'to a particular place' where this 'proves necessary' in accordance with national law.[584] According to the Commission report, most Member States applied the Directive correctly to

---

[575] *Cimade and GISTI*, n 569 above. On the Dublin rules, see I:5.8 above. Presumably this ruling would also apply where the Dublin rules allocated the asylum seeker to a non-EU State associated with Dublin. The Court was not asked to rule on what happens if a Member State applies a 'safe third country' rule to the asylum seeker, pursuant to the procedures Directive (on such rules, see I:5.7 above).

[576] *Cimade and GISTI* (n 569 above) para 40.   [577] Art 3(3) and (4).

[578] See I:5.6 above.   [579] Art 4. On the issue of 'compatible' higher standards, see I:5.2.4 above.

[580] Art 5.   [581] Art 6.

[582] There was no requirement that the documents must do so: see Art 6(3).

[583] The second-phase Dir (see I:5.9.2 below) did not take up this suggestion.

[584] Art 7. It should again be recalled that the detention of asylum seekers falls outside the scope of the EU's Returns Directive (Dir 2008/115, [2008] OJ L 348/98): see Cases C-357/09 PPU *Kadzoev* [2009] ECR I-11189 and C-534/11 *Arslan*, ECLI:EU:C:2013:343. On the human rights rules relating to immigration detention, see I:7.3.2 below.

non-detained applicants, given the wide discretion that the Directive permitted them. However, the Commission convincingly argued that since detention of applicants was governed by a necessity requirement, detention without an individual evaluation was a breach of the Directive. The Commission also took the view that detention for an indefinite period, except for 'duly justified' reasons, was a breach of the Directive, since it prevented the applicants from enjoying the rights granted by it, and that detention of minors, including unaccompanied minors, had to take account of the special rules applicable to this group, including the best interests of the child.[585]

Member States had to maintain family unity 'as far as possible' if the asylum seeker is provided with housing by the Member State.[586] The Commission report questioned whether the additional procedural requirements in relation to family housing in two Member States were compatible with the Directive. In fact, in the *Saciri* judgment, the CJEU ignored the limitation of this provision to cases where the State provided housing, and concluded that Member States must also ensure that asylum seekers can obtain family housing on the private market.[587]

Asylum-seeking minors, and asylum seekers' minor children, had to be given access to education under 'similar' conditions as nationals of the host state until an expulsion order was actually enforced, although the access to education could be delayed or offered in accommodation centres.[588] According to the Commission report, access to primary schools was not an issue, but access to secondary school was complicated because access to school was only granted at certain times of the school year, or because access was dependent on places available or decisions by local authorities. Also, 'many Member States deny detained minors access to education or make it impossible or very limited in practice'; only 'a few' Member States gave effect to this right for such detainees.

Member States had to set out conditions on access to employment for asylum seekers whose application had been the subject of a first-instance decision within one year, but they could give priority to EU and EEA citizens and legally-resident third-country nationals; access to employment could not be withdrawn during an appeal against a negative decision if that appeal had suspensive effect.[589] Again, due to the flexibility of the Directive, the Commission did not find 'major' problems with the application of this rule by Member States, except that one Member State did not permit any labour market access at all for asylum seekers,[590] and the requirement to obtain a work permit and limits on labour market access and hours of work were questioned. Access to vocational training was at the discretion of Member States, although applicants had to have access to vocational training which was linked to an employment contract, to the extent that they had access to the labour market.[591]

---

[585] See Arts 18 and 19; Art 18(1) stated that '[t]he best interests of the child shall be a primary consideration' when applying the Dir to minors. See also by analogy the requirement to take account of the best interests of the child set out in the family reunion Directive (Dir 2003/86, [2003] OJ L 251/12), as interpreted by the Court of Justice in Case C-540/03 *EP v Council* [2006] ECR I-5769 (see further I:6.6 below).

[586] Art 8.   [587] N 569 above.   [588] Art 10.   [589] Art 11.

[590] Conversely, nine Member States gave asylum seekers access to labour markets less than one year after making their application.

[591] Art 12.

As for State assistance, Member States had to provide for 'material reception conditions' which were sufficient 'to ensure a standard of living adequate for the health of applicants and capable of ensuring their subsistence', although assistance could be reduced or eliminated for asylum seekers with means or who have been working.[592] Assistance could be provided in kind or in the form of money or vouchers.[593] Member States had similar flexibility as regards the forms of housing offered to asylum seekers: this could include border accommodation, accommodation centres, or private housing.[594] According to the Commission report, there were 'no major problems' where the assistance was provided in kind or in reception centres, although in some Member States there were still shortages of housing places, or problems regarding clothes for asylum seekers or the 'generally low level of reception conditions'. However, the 'main problems' were in 'Member States where asylum seekers are given financial allowances', since these allowances were 'often too low to cover subsistence', were 'only rarely commensurate with the minimum social support granted to nationals', and might be insufficient even where they matched social support for nationals. In its *Saciri* judgment, the CJEU ruled that allowances had to cover private housing or support via social assistance if the public sector accommodation for asylum seekers was overloaded.[595]

Health care provided to asylum seekers had to include as a minimum essential treatment of illness and emergency care.[596] The Commission reported that all Member States complied with this minimum requirement, and some Member States went beyond it.

Member States were allowed to reduce or withdraw reception conditions in certain cases, for example where rules on reporting or residence have been breached, or where 'an asylum seeker has failed to demonstrate that the asylum claim was made as soon as reasonably practicable after arrival in that Member State'.[597] According to the Commission report, 'only a few' Member States applied the latter exception, but '[s]ome Member States withdraw reception conditions in situations not authorised by the Directive'. Before reception conditions could be reduced or withdrawn, applicants had procedural rights, and in any case, access to emergency health care always had to be guaranteed.[598] The Court of Justice has stated that these were the 'only' grounds on which reception conditions could be withdrawn.[599]

There were special rules concerning groups with special needs, such as minors, in particular unaccompanied minors, the elderly, disabled persons, and victims of torture.[600] The Commission report on implementation of the Directive concluded that Member States were under an obligation to identify such persons (which many of them failed to do) and that some of the specific standards relating to vulnerable persons were not properly applied in some Member States (as regards health care, minors with special needs, and detention). The *Saciri* judgment referred generally to Member States' obligations to persons with specific needs, overlooking the requirement of an individual evaluation to establish such a need.[601] It also concluded that the 'best interests of the

---

[592] Art 13(2) to (4).   [593] Art 13(5).   [594] Art 14.   [595] N 569 above.
[596] Art 15.   [597] Art 16(1) and (2).   [598] Art 16(4) and (5).
[599] *Cimade and GISTI* (n 569 above) para 57.
[600] Arts 17–20. See now the action plan on unaccompanied minors (COM (2010) 213, 6 May 2010) and the follow-up to that plan (COM (2012) 554, 28 Sep 2012).
[601] N 569 above; see Art 17(2).

child' required Member States to ensure that families were housed together, if necessary on the private housing market.[602]

Finally, Member States had to allow an appeal or review, ultimately before a judicial body, of negative decisions on benefits and of decisions concerning freedom of movement; '[p]rocedures for legal assistance in such cases shall be laid down by national law'.[603] The Commission rightly argued that some Member States breached the Directive when they did not allow appeals against decisions regarding freedom of movement, or withdrawing or reducing reception conditions, or any other decision other than detention. In some cases, the Commission reported that there are poorly justified or orally notified withdrawal decisions,[604] and the provision of legal aid in some Member States was queried.

The Commission's general conclusion in its report on application of the Directive was that '[o]verall, the Directive has been transposed satisfactorily in the majority of Member States', with '[o]nly a few' issues of misapplication arising; the Commission promised to pursue these. Furthermore, the report asserted that contrary to predictions, 'it appears that Member States have not lowered their previous standards of assistance to asylum seekers'. Finally, the Commission considered that the wide discretion granted to Member States by the Directive in key areas of reception conditions 'undermines the objective of creating a level playing field' in this area, and could only be addressed by a revision of the Directive.

By and large the standards set out in the Directive were imprecisely worded, leaving considerable scope for argument as to their correct application. It was particularly regrettable that the Directive did not more precisely limit the detention of asylum seekers and provide for more extensive access to employment, education, and vocational training. The provisions on possible withdrawal or reduction of benefits were dubious on human rights grounds, in light of the case law of the UK courts.[605]

Some of the conclusions of the Commission's report on the application of the Directive were questionable. There was no evidence offered for the assertion that the Member States had not lowered their standards as regards reception conditions, and the report did not assess to what extent the Directive led to a rise in standards. The overall assessment that transposition was satisfactory overall was unconvincing, given the evidence that a number of Member States were not correctly applying the rules on making sufficient information available, issuing documentation in time, justification for detention, housing families together, ensuring access to education, giving sufficient access to employment and benefits, protecting vulnerable persons, withdrawing benefits, and providing effective remedies as regards alleged violations of the Directive. The Commission's promise to enforce the Directive was never followed up by further challenges before the Court of Justice, and there was no further report on the application of the Directive in order to assess whether

---

[602] N 569 above; see Art 18.   [603] Art 21; see also Art 16(4).

[604] A poorly justified withdrawal decision would probably have breached Art 16(4), but neither Art 16(4) nor Art 21 expressly required decisions to be in writing.

[605] *R (on the application of Adam and others) v Secretary of State for the Home Department* [2005] UKHL 66.

more Member States had applied the Directive correctly in light of the threat of Court action.

5.9.2 Second-phase Directive

As noted above, the second-phase reception conditions Directive, which 'recast' the first-phase Directive, was adopted in 2013. Member States had to implement it from 20 July 2015.[606] Directive 2013/33 modestly raised the previous standards, and introduced detailed rules on detention of asylum seekers. Since, unlike the asylum procedures and Dublin legislation it does not expressly apply only to asylum seekers who make an application after the implementation deadline, it must follow that it also applies to asylum seekers whose applications are pending as of that date, as well as (obviously) all those who apply for international protection later. This is particularly relevant for asylum seekers who were detained as of the implementation date.[607]

First of all, the 2013 Directive extended the reception rules to include applications for subsidiary protection, which confirmed the previous practice of almost all Member States.[608] The definition of 'family members' was widened to include the parents or guardians of unmarried minors, in common with the second-phase qualification Directive and the Dublin III Regulation.[609] As for the scope of the Directive, it now expressly includes transit zones, although arguably this was previously implicit in the first-phase Directive.[610] The Directive is still disapplied when the EU's temporary protection Directive is invoked—but conversely it will expressly apply to asylum seekers covered by the EU's new *relocation* rules, according to the preamble to the relocation Decision.[611] Furthermore, the separate Dublin III Regulation confirms the CJEU's prior case law that the reception conditions Directive applies to asylum applicants who are subject to the Dublin process.[612] To address problems with documentation issues, the 2013 Directive provides that Member States cannot 'impose unnecessary or disproportionate documentation or other administrative requirements' as a barrier to obtaining benefits.[613]

There are now detailed rules on detention, in particular setting out the circumstances in which asylum seekers can be detained, specifying guarantees for detained asylum seekers, regulating detention conditions, and establishing requirements relating to the detention of vulnerable persons.[614] While the Directive does not expressly set a time limit on detention,[615] the second-phase procedures Directive has set a time limit to

---

[606] Dir 2013/33 ([2013] OJ L 180/96), Art 31(1). All of the references in this sub-section are to this Directive, unless otherwise indicated. See the ECRE report on using the Charter to improve reception and detention standards, online at: <http://www.ecre.org/component/content/article/70-weekly-bulletin-articles/999>.

[607] See by analogy the judgment in Case C-357/09 PPU *Kadzoev* [2009] ECR I-11189.

[608] See, for instance, the new Art 2(a) and the revised Art 3(4).   [609] Revised Art 2(c).

[610] Revised Art 3(1).   [611] Art 3(3); on the relocation rules see I:5.8.5 above.

[612] Recital 11 in the preamble to Reg 604/2013 ([2013] OJ L 180/31); see *Cimade and GISTI*, discussed in I:5.9.1 above.

[613] New Art 6(6).

[614] New Arts 8–11; the previous Art 7(3) was repealed. In Case C-601/15 PPU *JN*, pending, the CJEU has been asked if one of the grounds for detention is invalid.

[615] Compare to the Returns Directive (I:7.7.1 below).

decide on the *application*.[616] It is arguable that an asylum seeker must be released from detention if that time limit is exceeded, or that (as the Commission argued in respect of the first-phase Directive) an asylum seeker will not be able to enjoy the benefits of the Directive if detained indefinitely.[617] These provisions are largely similar to the relevant provisions of the Returns Directive,[618] but generally set higher standards than that Directive (leaving aside the lack of a time limit for detention), and do not have the same rationale of ensuring removal from the territory.[619]

The rules on access to education were amended to set higher standards, in particular to eliminate the possible one-year waiting period for access to education, to require that Member States offer preparatory classes if necessary, and to require Member States to offer alternative forms to education if access to the regular education system is not possible.[620] Access to employment has also been enhanced, by reducing the maximum waiting period to nine months rather than one year (still subject to the condition that no first-instance decision has been taken), and by requiring that Member States ensure effective access to the labour market when applying national conditions.[621]

As for material reception conditions, the 2013 Directive specifies that financial support must be calculated by comparison with the level of social assistance for nationals, although it may be paid at a lower rate.[622] There is stronger protection for vulnerable persons and against gender-based violence, and fewer possibilities for exceptions from the normal modalities of providing support.[623] The obligation to provide health care has been extended to include mental health care.[624]

The possibility to withdraw reception conditions where an applicant has not made an application as soon as reasonably practicable has been deleted, although benefits could still be reduced in such cases. Any withdrawal or reduction of benefits must now still ensure a dignified standard of living.[625] The definition of persons with special needs has been expanded, and there is now an express obligation to identify such persons.[626] Also, the factors to take into account when considering the best interests of the child have been defined in further detail,[627] the rules concerning unaccompanied minors have been amended to strengthen the obligation to trace family members,[628] and the provisions on victims of torture have been amended, as regards access to rehabilitation services and training of persons who work with torture victims.[629] Finally, there is now a clearer obligation to grant legal aid, although many restrictions upon it are permitted.[630]

---

[616] See I:5.7.2.

[617] This could be seen as an application of the principle of effectiveness, which is frequently applied by the CJEU in immigration law cases: see particularly I:6.6, I:6.7, and I:7.7.1 below.

[618] Arts 15–18 of Dir 2008/115 ([2008] OJ L 348/98); see I:7.7.1 below.

[619] Nevertheless, some of the case law on the other Directive should apply by analogy, for instance as regards keeping immigration detainees out of prisons: Cases C-473/13 and C-514/13 *Bouzalmate* and *Bero*, ECLI:EU:C:2014:2095 and C-474/13 *Pham*, ECLI:EU:C:2014:2096.

[620] Revised Art 14.

[621] Revised Art 15. The nine-month waiting period is out of synch with the normal six-month deadline to take a first-instance decision in the second-phase procedures Directive (see I:5.7.2 above). See by analogy the CJEU judgment in C-15/11 *Sommer*, ECLI:EU:C:2012:371, concerning access to employment for non-EU students.

[622] New Art 17(5).   [623] Revised Art 18(2) to (5) and (9).   [624] Revised Art 19.

[625] Revised Art 20.   [626] Revised Arts 21 and 22.   [627] Revised Art 23.

[628] Revised Art 24.   [629] Revised Art 26.   [630] Revised Art 26(2) to (5).

Compared to the first-phase Directive, the second-phase Directive increased standards modestly as regards access to education, access to employment, the position of vulnerable persons, standards in the event of reduction of benefits, and the appeal process. The provisions on material reception conditions have remained relatively vague, however, and the absence of any provision setting time limits on detention is indefensible—particularly in light of the time limits on detention in the Returns Directive,[631] and the general time limit of six months to take a first-instance decision on an asylum application in the second-phase procedures Directive.[632] This is coupled with broad possibilities to detain asylum seekers, although Member States clearly have less discretion to detain them than previously. However, the experience with the first-phase Directive suggests that the Commission may be indifferent to any breaches of the second-phase Directive that happen in practice, so that even the modest improvements in asylum seekers' living conditions which should result from it will not always be realized in practice.

5.10 Administrative Cooperation and EU Funding

The most significant EU action to assist administrative cooperation in the field of asylum is the creation of a European Asylum Support Office. Furthermore, there is a long-established European Refugee Fund, and also EU measures on, inter alia, asylum statistics and information exchange.

5.10.1 European Asylum Support Office

In February 2006, the Commission released a communication on cooperation between national administrations as regards asylum,[633] followed by Council conclusions.[634] The next step was the creation of a European Asylum Support Office, by means of a Regulation adopted in 2010.[635] The seat of the Asylum Support Office is in Valetta, Malta.[636]

The Agency was established in order to 'improve the implementation of the Common European Asylum System..., to strengthen practical cooperation among Member States on asylum and to provide and/or coordinate the provision of operational support to Member States subject to particular pressure on their asylum and reception systems'.[637] Its main purposes are to 'provide effective operational support to Member States subject to particular pressure on their asylum and reception systems' and 'provide scientific and technical assistance in regard to [EU asylum] policy and legislation', in particular as 'an independent source of information'.[638] The Office's tasks are 'without prejudice' to those of the EU Fundamental Rights Agency, and it shall 'work closely' with that Agency and with the UNHCR.[639]

---

[631] The Directive also failed to address the question of whether detention of asylum seekers counts toward the maximum time limits in the Returns Directive (see I:7.7.1 below).

[632] See comments in I:5.7.2 above.

[633] COM (2006) 67 and SEC (2006) 189, both 17 Feb 2006.

[634] See press release of the JHA Council, 27–8 Apr 2006.

[635] Reg 439/2010 ([2010] OJ L 132/11). All further references in this sub-section are to this Reg unless otherwise noted. There was also a parallel amendment to the European Refugee Fund ([2010] OJ L 129/1). On the Fund, see I:5.10.2 below.

[636] [2010] OJ L 324/47.   [637] Art 1.   [638] Art 2(2) and (3).   [639] Arts 50 and 52.

As for the practical cooperation tasks, the Office must in particular 'organise, promote and coordinate' the exchange of information and identify and pool good practice; 'organise, promote and coordinate' activities relating to country-of-origin information (ie, information about conditions in asylum seekers' countries of origin), including gathering and analysis of that information and drafting reports on that information; assist with the voluntary transfer of persons granted international protection status within the EU; support training for national administrations and courts, including the development of an EU asylum curriculum; and coordinate and exchange information on the operation of EU external asylum measures.[640] For Member States under 'particular pressure', the Office must gather information concerning possible emergency measures, set up an early warning system to alert Member States to mass influxes of asylum seekers, help such Member States to analyse asylum applications and establish reception conditions, and set up 'asylum teams' (see further below).[641]

For its contribution to the implementation of the Common European Asylum System, the Office gathers information on national authorities' application of EU asylum law, as well as national legislation and case law on asylum issues. It also draws up an annual report on the situation regarding asylum in the EU. At the request of the Commission, the Office may draw up 'technical documents on the implementation of the asylum instruments of the Union, including guidelines and operating manuals'.[642]

The Office can also deploy 'asylum support teams' on the territory of a requesting Member State, in order to provide 'in particular expertise in relation to interpreting services, information on countries of origin and knowledge of the handling and management of asylum cases'.[643] The Regulation provides further detail on the process of deciding on the number of members and profiles of such teams, and on their deployment.[644]

As for the organization of the Office, it has a Management Board,[645] consisting of one member appointed by each Member State and two members appointed by the Commission, with the UNHCR as a non-voting Board member. The Board meets at least twice a year, or more if convened by its Chairman. It votes by an absolute majority, but Member States which did not participate in a particular EU asylum measure have to abstain from a vote relating solely to that measure. The main roles of the Board are to: appoint the Executive Director; adopt an annual report on the Office's activities; establish the staff policy of the Office; set up information systems; adopt an annual work programme; and take all (other) decisions necessary to fulfil the Office's terms of reference.

The Office's Executive Director is appointed by the Management Board for a five-year term from a list of candidates suggested by the Commission, after a hearing before the European Parliament. His or her term of office can be extended once for a three-year period. The job of the Executive Director is to manage the day-to-day running

---

[640] Arts 3–7.   [641] Arts 8–10.   [642] Arts 11 and 12.   [643] Arts 13 and 14.
[644] Arts 15–23. Compare with the rules on border support teams, as set out in the Frontex Regulation (I:3.10.1 above).
[645] Arts 24–9.

of the Office, including drafting reports on countries of origin.[646] Finally, there is a Consultative Forum which liaises between NGOs, civil society, and the Agency, and the Office can establish expert working parties.[647] There are also detailed provisions on the Office's budget, staff, legal status, languages, access to documents, security rules, liability, evaluation, and administrative control by the EU ombudsman.[648]

As for the Office's external relations, the Office is open to participation by countries which have agreements concerning the application of EU asylum legislation.[649] The Office also facilitates cooperation between the EU and third countries within the framework of EU external relations policy, and cooperates with other third countries as regards 'technical aspects' of policy, 'within the framework of working arrangements concluded with those countries'.[650] Furthermore, the Office has to collaborate with the UNHCR, Frontex, the EU's Fundamental Rights Agency, and other international organizations.[651]

5.10.2 Other measures

The most prominent form of 'burden-sharing' between the Member States is the European Refugee Fund, which was first established in September 2000,[652] replacing ad hoc agreements on modest short-term funding of asylum measures during the 'Maastricht era'.[653] This Fund expired in 2004, and a Decision establishing a second European Refugee Fund for 2005–10 was adopted in December 2004.[654] A third Fund Decision was adopted in 2007, to cover the years 2008–13.[655] This measure was amended in 2010, in parallel with the establishment of the European Asylum Office,[656] and again in 2012 as regards resettlement.[657] Most recently, funding is set out in the Asylum, Migration and Integration Fund (covering 2014–20).[658] The EU's ARGO funding programme also supported activities of Member States in areas falling within the scope of EU asylum policy.[659]

As for asylum statistics and information, a body known as CIREA, a clearing-house for asylum information, was initially established during the intergovernmental period of cooperation on immigration and asylum.[660] Subsequently, CIREA was terminated in 2002, and was replaced by the Commission's Immigration and Asylum Committee (a body for consulting Member States' experts), Eurasil (a body made up of asylum

---

[646] Arts 30–1.   [647] See respectively Arts 51 and 32.   [648] Arts 33–47.
[649] Art 49(1). For more on this association, see I:5.2.5 above.   [650] Art 49(2).
[651] Arts 50 and 52.
[652] Decision 2000/596/EC ([2000] OJ L 252/12). For more on the fund, see the second edition of this book, pp 345–8.
[653] [2000] OJ L 252/12. The first Fund made €216 million available over five years from 1 January 2000 to 31 December 2004 (or €43.2 million/year).
[654] [2004] OJ L 381/52. The second Fund made available €114 million to disburse over the first two years (€57 million/year): see Art 2(1), 2004 Decision.
[655] [2007] OJ L 144/1. The third Fund made available €628 million to disburse over six years (€104.7 million/year): see Art 12(1), 2007 Decision.
[656] [2010] OJ L 129/1. See I:5.10.1 above.   [657] [2012] OJ L 92/1. See I:5.11 below.
[658] Reg 516/2014, [2014] OJ L 150/168.
[659] [2002] OJ L 161/11 (Art 6) and [2004] OJ L 371/48; see further I:3.11 above.
[660] See I:5.2.1 above.

practitioners in national bodies), and Eurostat, the Commission's statistics body, which had taken over the role of drawing up immigration and asylum statistics in 1998.[661]

Eurostat's role was placed on a more formal footing when EU legislation concerning asylum and migration statistics was adopted in 2007.[662] This legislation requires Member States to provide statistics on: the numbers claiming international protection, the number of pending claims, and withdrawn applications; the first-instance or final decisions on the rejection, granting, or withdrawal of refugee, subsidiary protection, and temporary protection status, as well as the granting or withdrawal of humanitarian status under national law; the number of applicants who are unaccompanied minors or who have been admitted under a resettlement scheme; and (as regards the Dublin rules) the number of requests for transfer of an asylum seeker, the reasons for those requests, the response to those requests, the number of transfers, and the number of requests for information.[663] Except for the Dublin statistics, this information must be disaggregated by age, sex, and country of origin.

The role of official asylum statistics is absolutely crucial as regards public understanding of the nature of the asylum issue: in particular, there appears to be wide misunderstanding as to the numbers of persons claiming asylum in the EU and its Member States and the percentage of asylum seekers who are subsequently allowed to stay on one ground or another. It would also be useful to have data on the success rate of appeals and on the precise grounds why applications are unsuccessful (to evaluate, eg, how widely the 'safe third country' concept is applied to rule applications inadmissible), and to have further public data on issues such as detention of asylum seekers.

Finally, the EU measures on the exchange of information as regards asylum and immigration policy, the Migration Network, and the annual report on asylum and immigration also play a role in this field.[664]

5.11 External Relations

Following growing interest in the external aspects of asylum law, in particular the question of processing asylum applications outside the EU, the Commission released a series of communications on this controversial issue.[665] An initial communication of 2003 suggested that the EU should: develop a policy on an EU-wide 'protected entry' system and an EU resettlement scheme (ie a policy to admit persons staying in third States who had already been determined to have protection needs); develop burden-sharing within the EU and between the EU and third countries, in particular to place EU external migration funding on a formal legal basis, in order to support

---

[661] See COM (2003) 152, 26 Mar 2003, and, as regards statistics: JHA Council conclusions of Mar 1998 and May 2001; Communication (SEC (2001) 602, 9 Apr 2001); and Action Plan (COM (2003) 179, 15 Apr 2003). For the first annual EU report on asylum and migration statistics, see: <http://ec.europa.eu/justice_home/doc_centre/immigration/statistics/doc_immigration_statistics_en.htm>.

[662] Reg 862/2007 ([2007] OJ L 199/23).

[663] Art 4, Reg 862/2007 (ibid); for the definitions, which refer back to EU asylum legislation, see Art (2)(1)(j) to (o) of the Reg.

[664] For details, see I:6.11 below.

[665] For a detailed analysis of the issues, see G Noll, 'Visions of the Exceptional: Legal and Theoretical Issues Raised by Transit Processing Centers and Reception Zones' (2003) 5 EJML 303.

regions which housed a large number of asylum seekers who might wish to travel to EU Member States; and further speed up asylum procedures within the EU.[666] A seminar held by the Italian presidency found that Member States were more interested in a resettlement scheme than a protected entry scheme at EU level.[667] Subsequently, a Commission communication of 2004 endorsed the creation of an EU resettlement scheme, the possible future development of further support for non-EU states,[668] and the creation of Regional Protection Programmes to develop an integrated approach to asylum and migration issues in certain third countries or regions.[669]

In view of the initial lack of interest among Member States in an EU-wide resettlement scheme, the Commission proposed the creation of pilot Regional Protection Programmes, in East Africa and the Western ex-Soviet States.[670] Subsequently, the EU's Refugee Fund provided a source of finance for national resettlement schemes as from 2008,[671] and in 2009, the Commission proposed the creation of a European resettlement policy, along with corresponding changes to the legislation establishing the Refugee Fund.[672] The Commission aims in particular to encourage more Member States to take part in resettlement activities (which would remain voluntary); already more Member States have got involved in resettlement activities since the Refugee Fund started to provide funding.

With a large increase in the numbers of asylum seekers in 2015, and with increased numbers drowning in transit, the Commission adopted a Recommendation calling for an EU-wide initiative to resettle 20,000 likely refugees over two years.[673] Member States then made pledges to resettle just over that number, in the form of conclusions adopted at the July 2015 JHA Council. The priority regions are North Africa, the Middle East, and the Horn of Africa. While the Recommendation and the conclusions both refer to beneficiaries of resettlement receiving a status 'similar' to refugees and beneficiaries of subsidiary protection pursuant to the qualification Directive, there is nothing in the qualification Directive to exclude resettled persons from its scope. Indeed, unlike the EU's other asylum legislation, that Directive does not limit its geographical scope, other than the obvious limit (reflecting the Geneva Convention) that a refugee must be outside his or her country of origin.[674] So if a resettled person meets the criteria in that Directive for refugee or subsidiary protection status, he or she is still entitled to

---

[666] COM (2003) 315, 3 June 2003; see also the conclusions of the June 2003 Thessaloniki European Council. For studies on these issues, see: <http://ec.europa.eu/justice_home/doc_centre/asylum/studies/doc_asylum_studies_en.htm>.

[667] Council doc 14987/03, 18 Nov 2003.

[668] See also the development of the external aspects of migration policy, including the impact of readmission agreements on asylum seekers (I:7.9 below).

[669] COM (2004) 410, 4 June 2004; see also the conclusions of the Nov 2004 General Affairs/External Relations Council.

[670] COM (2005) 388, 1 Sep 2005; see the conclusions of the Nov 2005 General Affairs/External Relations Council.

[671] Arts 3(1)(d), 6(e), and 13(3), (4), and (6) of the 2007 Decision establishing the Fund ([2007] OJ L 144/1).

[672] COM (2009) 456 (proposed legislation) and COM (2009) 447 (communication), both 2 Sep 2009. The legislation was adopted in 2012: [2012] OJ L 92/1.

[673] Recommendation 2015/914, [2015] OJ L 148/32.

[674] The same requirement implicitly applies to persons claiming subsidiary protection: see Art 2(f), Dir 2011/95 ([2011] OJ L 337/9). The Geneva Convention does not exclude resettled persons from its scope either.

that status despite the means of his or her entry to EU territory. In December 2015, the Commission adopted a Recommendation on voluntary humanitarian admission, shortly after the EU and Turkey agreed on a controversial plan to assist Turkey with hosting large numbers of refugees.[675]

5.12 Conclusions

The development of EU competence on asylum initially promised much. It was an opportunity to break out of the cycle of competitive lowering of standards relating to asylum, by adopting EU-wide rules setting a high level of standards applicable and enforceable across the entire EU, taking into account also the involvement of the Commission and the European Parliament, traditionally supporters of high standards in this area.

The outcome has, so far, been more disappointing. As we have seen, minimum standards were initially set at rather low levels, and very low levels indeed in the case of asylum procedures, to the point where the first-phase Directive on this issue arguably seriously breached international human rights law in a number of respects. As a whole, the legislation establishing the first phase of the Common European Asylum System did not seem to result in major changes in national law or practice.

The second-phase legislation made modest improvements to most areas, with rather bigger improvements to the rules on asylum procedures—but then those rules were starting from a very low base. Overall, the CJEU has pushed the interpretation of the EU rules in a liberal direction, bar some aberrations such as the poorly reasoned judgments in *Shepherd* and *Abdullahi*. But it is not clear what effect those judgments, and the legislation itself, has at national level, taking into account the Commission's disinclination to enforce the law. Certainly the existence of the EU legislation did not stop the collapse of the Greek asylum system; indeed the Dublin rules surely exacerbated it.

The recognition in 2015 that the EU had to derogate from the Dublin rules on an emergency basis and move toward more resettlement of refugees is a big step forward compared to the history of EU action in this area, yet makes only a small contribution to the scale of the actual problem posed by the refugee crisis. It remains to be seen whether it constitutes the first step toward a more ambitious approach, or whether the EU's asylum system (along, perhaps, with the Schengen system) may prove unable to address the increased pressure.

---

[675] C(2015) 9490, 11 Jan 2016 (voluntary admission scheme); [2015] OJ C 407/8 (EU Refugee Facility fund for Turkey). See also the conclusions of the Nov 2015 EU/Turkey summit.

6

Legal Migration

6.1 Introduction

Migration poses fundamental issues for the economic, social, and cultural development of Europe. Certainly migrants have made substantial contributions of every kind to EU Member States throughout history, and continue to do so today, but migration still remains highly controversial, because of fears that significant migration flows would damage national economies, threaten social harmony, and challenge established national values. There are sharp differences within and between Member States on the issues related to migration, due not only to economic, social, and cultural divergences but also because Member States' different histories have resulted in diverse patterns of migration.

As a result, the EU's legal framework for legal migration issues has developed only gradually. The key issue of migration for economic purposes been addressed only partially, and legislation on other issues has in principle left considerable discretion to Member States, although the case law of the Court of Justice has significantly curtailed that discretion. As with other areas addressed in this book, legal migration raises some important human rights issues and intersects with important aspects of non-JHA EU law, in particular free movement law and external relations, as regards association agreements, commercial policy, and development policy (the latter issue is addressed further in Chapter 7 of this volume). The relationship between EU migration law and both human rights law and other areas of EU law has been the subject of continued controversy.

This chapter, like the others in this book, begins with a historical overview of the substance and institutional framework of the subject, including issues of legal competence and the territorial scope of the rules, followed by an analysis of the relevant rules of human rights law and other areas of EU law. Then it examines in detail the EU rules relating to admission of migrants, first of all primary admission and then secondary admission (for family reunion purposes), followed by the rules relating to long-term residence and integration, examining also the issue of administrative cooperation in this field.

The issues addressed in this chapter have close links with the issues discussed in other chapters in this volume, particularly Chapter 7 concerning irregular migration, since the definition of irregular migration is in part shaped by the rules relating to legal migration. There are also important links with asylum law (the subject of Chapter 5), in particular where a person has been granted refugee status and the EU's migration powers are used to regulate topics such as the issue of residence permits and access to employment. However, the issue of family reunion for refugees and the rules on long-term residence status for refugees and persons with subsidiary protection are addressed in this chapter. The grant of a residence permit or a long-stay visa or the admission of family members can also trigger the EU's rules on responsibility for asylum applications.[1] Finally, certain issues concerning long-stay visas and residence permits that are indissolubly linked to the issues of short-term visas and external border control are dealt with in Chapters 3 and 4, concerning border controls and visas respectively, due to their close link with the issues in those chapters.[2] It should also be recalled that some issues principally dealt with in this chapter, such as the provision of services by third-country nationals from either inside or outside the European Union and the movement of third-country national family members of EU citizens, are in part also affected by border control and visa rules, and so are partly dealt with in Chapters 3 and 4.[3]

6.2 Institutional Framework and Overview

As pointed out in Chapter 3,[4] several important aspects of the rules governing third-country nationals were part of Community law (as it then was) even before the entry into force of the Treaty of Amsterdam. These issues have remained within the framework of other EU law rules, rather than the specific rules for Justice and Home Affairs (JHA) set out (now) in Title V of the Treaty on the Functioning of the European Union (TFEU), or previously (before the Treaty of Lisbon entered into force) in Title IV of Part Three of the EC Treaty. However, this chapter considers those issues,[5] to the extent that they are connected to EU immigration law based on the specific JHA rules.

6.2.1 Cooperation prior to the Treaty of Amsterdam

Prior to the entry into force of the Maastricht Treaty, the Member States' interior ministries adopted a resolution on family reunion.[6] Subsequently, pursuant to the third pillar arrangements established by the Maastricht Treaty, the Council adopted a number of 'soft-law' measures on migration law. These measures concerned family reunion, admission of workers, admission of the self-employed, admission of students, the status of long-term residents, and marriages of convenience.[7] In order to convert these rules

---

[1] See I:5.8 above.

[2] As regards crossing external borders, see I:3.6.1 above; as regards freedom to travel and checks in the Schengen Information System, see I:4.9 above.

[3] See I:3.4.1 and I:4.4.1 above.   [4] I:3.2.1 above.   [5] I:6.4 below.

[6] SN 2828/1/93, not published in the Official Journal; see E Guild and J Niessen, *The Developing Immigration and Asylum Policies of the European Union: Adopted Conventions, Resolutions, Recommendations, Decisions and Conclusions* (Kluwer, 1996), 250–7; T Bunyan, ed., *Key Texts on Justice and Home Affairs in the European Union* (1997), 98.

[7] See respectively [1994] OJ C 274/7; [1996] OJ C 274/10; [1996] OJ C 80/2; and [1997] OJ C 382/1. There was a further Resolution on unaccompanied minors ([1997] OJ C 221/23) and a Decision on monitoring implementation ([1997] OJ C 11/1). These Resolutions, and the earlier Resolution on family reunion, are not covered further in this book; see the first edition of this book, 84–90; E Guild and J Niessen, n 6 above; S Peers, 'Building Fortress Europe: The Development of EU Migration Law' (1998) 35 CMLRev 1235; M Hedemann-Robinson, 'Third-Country Nationals, European Union Citizenship and Free Movement of Persons: A Time for Bridges Rather than Divisions?' (1996) 16 YEL 321; K Hailbronner, 'Migration Law and Policy Within the Third Pillar of the European Union' in R Bieber and J Monar, eds., *Justice and Home Affairs in the European Union* (European University Press, 1995); and P Boeles, et al., *A New Immigration Law for Europe: the 1992 London and 1993 Copenhagen Rules on Immigration* (Standing Committee of Experts on Immigration, 1994).

into 'hard law', the Commission proposed a migration law Convention in 1997, but this was not agreed by the Council.[8] Therefore the only 'hard law' on migration adopted before the entry into force of the Treaty of Amsterdam was a Joint Action on a uniform residence permit, adopted by the Council in 1996.[9]

6.2.2 Treaty of Amsterdam

The Treaty of Amsterdam conferred migration law competence upon the Community in Article 63(3) and 63(4) EC to adopt the following:

> (3) measures on immigration policy within the following areas:
>   (a) conditions of entry and residence, and standards on procedures for the issue by Member States of long term visas and residence permits, including those for the purpose of family reunion,
>   (b) illegal immigration and illegal residence, including repatriation of illegal residents;[10]
> (4) measures defining the rights and conditions under which nationals of third countries who are legally resident in a Member State may reside in other Member States.

However, the final provisions of Article 63 provided that:

> Measures adopted by the Council pursuant to points 3 and 4 shall not prevent any Member State from maintaining or introducing in the areas concerned national provisions which are compatible with this Treaty and with international agreements.

It was also specified, by implication, that there was no deadline to adopt measures pursuant to Article 63(3)(a) and 63(4) within the five-year deadline applicable to all of Article 62 (as regards visas and border controls) and almost all of the remaining provisions of Article 63 (as regards asylum and irregular migration). The immigration provisions were also subject to the 'emergency powers' derogation and the reserve of Member States' powers set out in Article 64 EC, and the possible adoption of measures to assist administrative cooperation in Article 66 EC.[11]

The Tampere European Council, held in October 1999, set out basic principles which EC migration law should uphold. In fact, the conclusions of the European Council contained an entire section on 'Fair treatment of third-country nationals':

> 18. The European Union must ensure fair treatment of third country nationals who reside legally on the territory of its Member States. A more vigorous integration policy should aim at granting them rights and obligations comparable to those of EU citizens. . . .

---

[8] COM (97) 387, 30 July 1997; [1997] OJ C 337/9. For more on the proposed Convention, see the first edition of this book, 90–2; M Hedemann-Robinson, 'From Object to Subject? Non-EC Nationals and the Draft Proposal of the Commission for a Council Act Establishing the Rules for Admission of Third-Country Nationals to the Member States' (1998) 18 YEL 289; and S Peers, 'Raising Minimum Standards or Racing to the Bottom? The Commission's Proposed Migration Convention' in E Guild, ed., *The Legal Framework and Social Consequences of Free Movement of Persons in the European Union* (Kluwer, 1999), 149.

[9] [1997] OJ L 7/1. See I:6.9 below.

[10] This sub-paragraph and measures based on it are considered separately in ch 7 of this volume.

[11] See further I:3.2.4 above on Art 64 (now Art 72 TFEU), and I:6.11 below on Art 66 and legal migration issues.

20. The European Council acknowledges the need for approximation of national legislations on the conditions for admission and residence of third country nationals, based on a shared assessment of the economic and demographic developments within the Union, as well as the situation in the countries of origin. It requests to this end rapid decisions by the Council, on the basis of proposals by the Commission. These decisions should take into account not only the reception capacity of each Member State, but also their historical and cultural links with the countries of origin.

21. The legal status of third country nationals should be approximated to that of Member States' nationals. A person, who has resided legally in a Member State for a period of time to be determined and who holds a long-term residence permit, should be granted in that Member State a set of uniform rights which are as near as possible to those enjoyed by EU citizens; e.g. the right to reside, receive education, and work as an employee or self-employed person, as well as the principle of non-discrimination vis-à-vis the citizens of the State of residence....

This ambitious programme led to a Commission proposal for a Directive on family reunion before the end of 1999,[12] followed by further proposals in 2001 on the status of long-term residents and admission for employment or self-employment,[13] a proposal in 2002 on the admission of students, school pupils, unremunerated trainees, and volunteers,[14] and a proposal early in 2004 for specific rules on admission of research workers.[15] It proved initially difficult to agree on most of these proposals, but eventually the Council finally adopted the Directives on family reunion and long-term residents in 2003,[16] on students, pupils, trainees, and volunteers in 2004,[17] and on researchers in 2005.[18] But the cost of reaching agreement on the various measures was a huge reduction in the standards proposed by the Commission, particularly in the family reunion Directive. The result was that the European Parliament (EP) sued to annul parts of the family reunion Directive for breach of the human rights principles forming part of EC law.[19] While the EP's challenge was unsuccessful, the Court of Justice's judgment clarified a number of important points as regards the interpretation of the Directive.

As for labour migration, the Council did not hold extensive discussions on the Commission's 2001 proposal concerning admission for migration for employment and self-employment, and it became clear that there was no prospect of the Council adopting it. A Directive on the legal status of victims of trafficking or smuggling of persons was adopted in 2004, but this is considered in detail in Chapter 7 of this volume, along with other EC measures concerning irregular migration.[20]

In the meantime, the Council adopted two Regulations on other aspects of migration law. First, it agreed in 2002 to 'communitarize' the Joint Action on residence permits.[21]

---

[12] COM (1999) 638, 1 Dec 1999.
[13] See respectively COM (2001) 127, 13 Mar 2001 and COM (2001) 386, 11 July 2001.
[14] COM (2002) 548, 7 Oct 2002.   [15] COM (2004) 178, 16 Mar 2004.
[16] Respectively Dirs 2003/86 ([2003] OJ L 251/12) and 2003/109 ([2004] OJ L 16/44). See I:6.6 and I:6.7 below.
[17] Dir 2004/114 ([2004] OJ L 375/12). See I:6.5.3.2 below.
[18] Dir 2005/71 ([2005] OJ L 289/15). See I:6.5.3.1 below.
[19] Case C-540/03 *EP v Council* [2006] ECR I-5769. For discussion of this judgment, see I:6.6 below.
[20] Directive 2004/81 ([2004] L 261/19); see I:7.6.2 below.
[21] Reg 1030/2002 ([2002] OJ L 157/1). See I:6.9 below.

Secondly, following a judgment of the Court of Justice in 2001 on the application of EC legislation on social security coordination to refugees and stateless persons,[22] the Council adopted in 2003 a Regulation extending these rules to other third-country nationals.[23]

The integration of the migration-related aspects of the Schengen *acquis* into EC law from 1 May 1999 had little impact on legal migration law. These provisions of the *acquis* consisted of Articles 18 and 25 of the Schengen Convention,[24] and a Decision of the Schengen Executive Committee relating to implementation of the EU's Joint Action on residence permits.[25]

The particular political difficulties agreeing measures on legal migration were underlined when the Hague Programme outlining future JHA policy was adopted in November 2004.[26] That Programme did not call for an immediate shift to a qualified majority vote (QMV) in the Council and co-decision with the European Parliament regarding legal migration, and as a result, from 1 January 2005, until the entry into force of the Treaty of Lisbon, legal migration remained the only immigration-related topic area still subject to unanimous voting in the Council and consultation of the EP. Furthermore, the Hague Programme, unlike the Tampere conclusions, failed to outline any substantial future programme of EC legislation concerning legal migration. It merely invited the Commission to draw up a policy plan on legal migration by the end of 2005, taking account of a Green Paper which the Commission was then planning, without any commitment to adopt legislation or invitation to the Commission to propose any.

However, the subsequent June 2005 implementation plan for the Hague Programme did refer to some further measures,[27] in particular a Directive to extend the scope of the long-term residents' Directive to refugees and persons with subsidiary protection status, measures on a European migration observatory, a mutual information system on national immigration law, a proposed integration fund, and a measure on migration and asylum statistics.

These plans were implemented by Commission proposals, subsequently adopted by the Council between 2006 and 2009, establishing an EU integration fund,[28] a Decision on exchange of information on immigration and asylum policy,[29] a Regulation on immigration and asylum statistics,[30] and a Decision formally establishing a European Migration Network.[31] The Council also adopted an amendment to the EU rules on harmonized residence permit formats, in order, inter alia, to insert biometric identifiers into residence permits.[32] On the other hand, the Council was not able to agree,

---

[22] Joined Cases C-95/99 to 98/99 *Khalil and others* and C-180/99 *Addou* [2001] ECR I-7413. See further I:5.4.2 above and I:6.4.2 below.

[23] Reg 859/2003 ([2003] OJ L 124/1). See further I:6.8 below.

[24] [2000] OJ L 239/1. On the original version of Art 18, see I:3.6.1 above; on the current version of Art 18, see I:6.9.2 below. On Art 25, as amended subsequently, see I:4.9 above and I:6.9 below.

[25] [2000] OJ L 239/187. See further I:6.9 below.   [26] [2005] OJ C 53/1.

[27] [2005] OJ C 198/1.   [28] [2007] OJ L 168/16; see I:6.10 below.

[29] [2006] OJ L 283/40; see I:6.11 below.

[30] Reg 862/2007 ([2007] OJ L 199/23); see I:6.11 below.

[31] [2008] OJ L 131/7. See I:6.11 below.

[32] Reg 330/2008 ([2008] OJ L 115/1), amending Reg 1030/2002 (n 21 above). See I:6.9.1 below.

before the entry into force of the Treaty of Lisbon, on a Directive applying the long-term residents' Directive to refugees and beneficiaries of subsidiary protection,[33] a Regulation to extend the revised social security rules for EU citizens to third-country nationals who move within the EU,[34] or a proposal concerning aspects of long-term visas.[35]

Again, labour migration proved a difficult issue. In light of the deadlock on its 2001 proposal for a Directive on economic migration,[36] the Commission released a Green Paper on this issue in January 2005, in order to launch a wide discussion on the topic, as a likely precursor to fresh proposals for legislation.[37] Subsequently, the Commission withdrew the 2001 proposal.[38] In December 2005, taking account of the response to the Green Paper on economic migration mentioned above, the Commission issued a policy plan on legal migration into the EU.[39] The legislative aspects of the policy plan comprised, first of all, proposals (issued in 2007) for legislation on highly skilled workers and on a single procedure for admission of third-country national workers.[40] The Council was able to agree on the first of these proposals (known generally as the 'Blue Card' Directive) in 2009,[41] but was not able to agree on the second proposal before the Treaty of Lisbon entered into force.

The 2008 immigration and asylum pact contained provisions on legal immigration,[42] making a commitment 'to organise legal immigration to take account of the priorities, needs and reception capacities determined by each Member State, and to encourage integration'. In particular, the Pact agreed: 'to increase the attractiveness' of the EU for highly qualified workers, and to take new measures regarding reception and movement of students and researchers; 'to regulate family migration more effectively by inviting each Member State, in compliance with' the European Convention on Human Rights (ECHR), 'to take into consideration in its national legislation, except for certain specific categories, its own reception capacities and families' capacity to integrate, as evaluated by their resources and accommodation in the country of destination and, for example, their knowledge of that country's language'; to strengthen existing systems for information exchange; and to develop integration policy further. There was no express reference to any EC legislation concerning any of these issues.

In addition to 'hard law', the EC developed a body of 'soft law' on the particular topic of integration of third-country nationals.[43] There were also a number of measures adopted relating to EU funding and to cooperation between administrations.[44] As in other areas of immigration and asylum law, there was an important external dimension to EC migration policy.[45]

---

[33] COM (2007) 298, 6 June 2007. See I:6.7 below.
[34] COM (2007) 439, 23 July 2007. See I:6.8 below.   [35] COM (2009) 90, 27 Feb 2010.
[36] COM (2001) 386, n 13 above.   [37] COM (2004) 811, 11 Jan 2005.
[38] [2006] OJ C 64/3.   [39] COM (2005) 669, 21 Dec 2005.
[40] COM (2007) 637 and 638, 23 Oct 2007.
[41] Dir 2009/50 ([2009] OJ L 155/17). See I:6.5.2 below.   [42] Council doc 13440/08, 24 Sep 2008.
[43] See further I:6.10 below.   [44] See further I:6.11 below.
[45] See further I:7.9.2 below; as regards association agreements and commercial policy, see I:6.4.3 and I:6.4.6 below.

As for the Court of Justice, the limitations on its jurisdiction prior to the entry into force of the Treaty of Lisbon meant that it only received one reference from national courts during this time concerning legal migration legislation.[46]

6.2.3 Treaty of Lisbon

Since the Treaty of Lisbon entered into force in 2009, the issue of migration, including legal migration, is regulated by Article 79 of the TFEU:[47]

1. The Union shall develop a common immigration policy aimed at ensuring, at all stages, the efficient management of migration flows, fair treatment of third-country nationals residing legally in Member States, and the prevention of, and enhanced measures to combat, illegal immigration and trafficking in human beings.

2. For the purposes of paragraph 1, the European Parliament and the Council, acting in accordance with the ordinary legislative procedure, shall adopt measures in the following areas:
   (a) the conditions of entry and residence, and standards on the issue by Member States of long-term visas and residence permits, including those for the purpose of family reunification;
   (b) the definition of the rights of third-country nationals residing legally in a Member State, including the conditions governing freedom of movement and of residence in other Member States....

4. The European Parliament and the Council, acting in accordance with the ordinary legislative procedure, may establish measures to provide incentives and support for the action of Member States with a view to promoting the integration of third-country nationals residing legally in their territories, excluding any harmonisation of the laws and regulations of the Member States.

5. This Article shall not affect the right of Member States to determine volumes of admission of third-country nationals coming from third countries to their territory in order to seek work, whether employed or self-employed.

It can be seen first of all that the EU's powers as regards migration were intensified by the Treaty of Lisbon, given the obligation to develop a 'common' policy and the abolition of the penultimate paragraph of the previous Article 63 EC, which had reserved to Member States the power to maintain or introduce national provisions alongside EC legislation. It is not clear what the previous proviso meant,[48] but arguably it remains relevant to any immigration measures adopted before the Treaty of Lisbon, until they are amended after the entry into force of that Treaty. Moreover, the obligation to establish a 'common' immigration policy is also referred to in the general provisions of Title V.[49]

Furthermore, Article 79(1) TFEU, unlike the previous Article 63 EC, sets out objectives specific to immigration policy: 'efficient' management, 'fair treatment' of legal

---

[46] Case C-578/08 *Chakroun* [2010] ECR I-1839, concerning interpretation of Dir 2003/86 on family reunion (n 16 above).

[47] Art 79(2)(c) and (d) and (3) TFEU concern irregular migration, and so are examined in I:7.2.3 below.

[48] See I:6.2.4 below.   [49] Art 67(2) TFEU; on the general provisions, see I:2.2.3.2 above.

residents, and prevention and combating of illegal immigration and human trafficking. Of these objectives, fairness is also mentioned in part of the general Title V objectives in Article 67(2) TFEU.

As for the specific provisions on legal migration, Article 79(2)(a) TFEU is identical to the previous Article 63(3)(a) EC, although since the overall legal framework of the EU's immigration powers has changed, as described above, there might be a case for a different interpretation of the same provision. On the other hand, Article 79(2)(b) TFEU sets out a wider express competence as regards the rights of third-country nationals legally resident in a Member State than the prior Treaty, and a different wording as regards third-country nationals' movement to other Member States (including an express reference to 'freedom of movement', which is obviously distinct from the 'freedom to travel for a short period' referred to in Article 77 TFEU).[50] However, it should be noted that the EC's previous powers were already used to define the rights of third-country nationals.[51] Furthermore, given that Article 77 TFEU is now less precise as regards the time limit for short-term entry of third-country nationals (as compared to the previous three-month limit), the dividing line between that Article and Article 79 TFEU is now less precise than the division between the previous Articles 62(3) and 63(3) and (4) EC.[52]

Article 79(4) constitutes an express 'legal base' providing for the adoption of EU measures 'to provide incentives and support' for Member States' action 'promoting the integration' of legally resident third-country nationals. Again, the EU was already active on this issue within the previous legal framework, in particular by establishing a 'European integration fund' which obviously falls within the scope of the EU's subsequent express competence to support Member States' integration policies.[53]

But the biggest change in this area was the extension of qualified majority voting in the Council to legislation, along with the extension of co-decision powers (redubbed the 'ordinary legislative procedure') for the EP. The impact of this change was that, shortly after the entry into force of the Treaty of Lisbon, the Council (now together with the EP) was soon able to adopt the previously proposed legislation on long-term visas,[54] the single permit for third-country national workers,[55] the extension of the revised social security rules to third-country nationals,[56] and the extension of the long-term residents' Directive to refugees and beneficiaries of subsidiary protection.[57]

The extension of qualified majority voting presumably also played a role in implementing the Stockholm Programme,[58] which called for the adoption of legislation on 'categories of workers currently not covered by Union legislation'. To this end, the Commission proposed new Directives on the seasonal workers and intra-corporate transferees, which were both adopted in 2014.[59] It subsequently proposed a major reform

---

[50] On Art 77, see I:4.2.4 above.

[51] See, for instance, Dir 2003/109 on long-term residents (n 16 above), although in this Directive, there is a link between the regulation of the status of long-term resident in a first Member State and the right to move to another Member State.

[52] See the discussion of the 'touring visa' proposal in I:4.2.4 above.   [53] See I:6.10 below.

[54] Reg 265/2010 ([2010] OJ L 85/1). See I:3.6.1 and I:4.9 above and I:6.9.2 below.

[55] See I:6.5.1 below.   [56] See I:6.8 below.   [57] See I:6.7 below.

[58] Council doc 17024/09, 2 Dec 2009, points 6.1.3 and 6.1.4.   [59] See I:6.5.2 below.

of the existing Directives on students and researchers, which was agreed in 2015.[60] However, there was no action to codify and extend the EU *acquis* on legal migration as a whole, which was also called for by the Stockholm Programme. Moreover, while there were defects with the implementation of EU legislation on legal migration, the Commission has made very few moves to ensure its correct implementation by means of court action.[61] At time of writing, the current Commission had plans to reform EU legislation on highly-skilled workers,[62] but had no plans regarding other areas.

The entry into force of the Treaty of Lisbon also meant an expansion in the jurisdiction of the Court of Justice of the European Union (CJEU) in this area. As a result, the number of cases on legal migration reaching the CJEU increased to about five per year, and the Court's rulings have had a significant impact clarifying the interpretation of the EU's legislation.[63] The Treaty of Lisbon has also amended the rules relating to opt-outs from this area of law.[64]

6.2.4 Competence issues

Prior to the entry into force of the Treaty of Lisbon, there were several disputes about the extent of the EC's competence over legal migration. These arguments remain potentially relevant as regards the validity of legislation adopted before the Treaty of Lisbon entered into force, at least until all of that legislation is amended by post-Lisbon measures—which is not yet the case.

First of all, as regards competence to regulate labour migration,[65] although the previous Article 63(3)(a) and 63(4) EC did not mention migration for employment as such, conversely those provisions did not exclude any form of legal migration from their scope. Furthermore, the prior Article 39 EC governed the movement of 'workers' of the Member States, without any restriction based on nationality, while the prior Article 137 EC granted competence to the Community to adopt measures concerning the 'conditions of employment' of third-country nationals. Between them, these provisions were sufficient to confer competence to regulate labour migration of third-country nationals, although complications could arise from their potential overlap.

Next, it was necessary to distinguish, after the change in Title IV decision-making rules which took effect on 1 January 2005,[66] between the legal base for the adoption of measures concerning legal migration and the legal base for the adoption of measures concerning irregular migration. The best interpretation is that the EC Treaty power over legal migration conferred competence to adopt rules concerning the acquisition and loss of legal migration status, while the power over irregular migration conferred

---

[60] See I:6.5.3 below.   [61] See particularly I:6.6 and I:6.7 below.

[62] COM (2015) 610, 27 Oct 2015 (2016 work programme). See further I:6.5.2 below.

[63] See particularly I:6.5.3 below (students' Directive), I:6.6 below (family reunion), and I:6.7 below (long-term residents).

[64] See I:6.2.5 below.

[65] For more detailed analysis, see the second edition of this book, pp 187–8; S Peers, 'The EU Institutions and Title IV' and E Guild and S Peers, 'Out of the Ghetto? The Personal Scope of EU Law', both in S Peers and N Rogers, eds., *EU Immigration and Asylum Law: Text and Commentary*, 1st edn (Martinus Nijhoff, 2006).

[66] See I:6.2.2 above.

power to adopt rules concerning persons who were not entitled to enter and stay or who had definitively lost their power to enter and stay. This particular dispute is clearly irrelevant to measures adopted after the entry into force of the Treaty of Lisbon, given the identical decision-making rules applicable to these issues.

Another argument concerned whether the EC had power to regulate limited stays of up to six months; this point is now also moot since the adoption of the Treaty of Lisbon.[67]

Finally, to what extent did the closing words of the prior Article 63 EC limit the scope of the EC's power to harmonize legal migration law? These words could possibly have been interpreted to mean that Member States could do whatever they wanted regardless of whether the EC had acted or not. But in order to give the EC's powers some practical effect, the best interpretation of those was that EC powers were not automatically exclusive, immediately precluding any national competence over immigration; but Member States were (and still are) obliged to comply with EC law to the extent that the EC has acted, and that it was open to the EC to harmonize national law fully in the field of immigration if it had desired, subject to the principle of subsidiarity.[68] This was also consistent with a declaration in the Treaty of Amsterdam, concerning the EC's external competence in this field. It should be noted that EU legislation on legal immigration adopted before the entry into force of the Treaty of Lisbon generally permits Member States to establish higher standards as regards most or all provisions of each measure, without requiring that such national measures be 'compatible' with the Directive in question.[69]

Following the entry into force of the Treaty of Lisbon, immigration remains a shared competence of the EU and its Member States.[70] However, the wording of the new provisions (in particular the references to a 'common immigration policy' and the removal of the final words of Article 63 EC) suggests that it is easier to justify more intensive EU action pursuant to the principles of proportionality and subsidiarity, and harder to argue that any particular area of immigration law is outside EU competence—apart from the express restriction on competence in Article 79(5) TFEU, which (as seen above) reserves competence of Member States over volumes of third-country nationals coming from third countries to seek work, including self-employed work. Arguably, this is a new restriction on competence as compared to the previous Article 63 EC, although this limit on competence had been incorporated into one relevant Directive adopted even before the Treaty of Lisbon entered into force.[71] In any event, in practice

---

[67] See I:4.2.4 above.

[68] See further: the Opinion in Case C-540/03 *EP v Council* [2006] ECR I-5769; G Brinkmann, 'Family Reunion, Third-Country Nationals and the Community's New Powers' in E Guild and C Harlow, eds., *Implementing Amsterdam: Immigration and Asylum Rights in EC Law* (Hart, 2001), 241 at 265; G Papagianni, *Institutional and Policy Dynamics of EU Migration Law* (Martinus Nijhoff, 2006), 49; and S Peers, 'EU Immigration and Asylum Law: Internal Market Model or Human Rights Model?' in Tridimas and Nebbia, eds., *EU Law for the Twenty-First Century: Rethinking the New Legal Order*, vol. 1 (Hart, 2004), 345 at 358–9.

[69] See the legislation discussed in I:6.5 to I:6.7 below. On the concept of the 'compatibility' of higher national standards, see I:5.2.4 above.

[70] See Art 4(2)(j) TFEU. On the concept of shared competence, see Art 2(2) TFEU and the discussion in I:2.2.4 above. The remainder of this sub-section is adapted from S Peers, 'EU Immigration and Asylum Competence and Decision-Making in the Treaty of Lisbon' (2008) 10 EJML 219 at 241–6.

[71] See Art 6 of Dir 2009/50 ([2009] OJ L 155/17), which reserves competence as regards volumes of all third-country nationals 'entering the territory' for highly-qualified employment, not just those entering from third countries.

no legislation was adopted prior to the Treaty of Lisbon which restricted Member States from adopting such measures.

First of all, as for the competence to regulate the economic migration of third-country nationals after the Treaty of Lisbon, the power to adopt measures regarding a 'common immigration policy' and the express restriction regarding economic migration in Article 79(5) TFEU both point to a power to regulate economic migration within the scope of Article 79(2) TFEU, as does the addition of the express power to regulate 'the rights of third-country nationals residing legally in a Member State'. Taking these provisions in turn, a 'common immigration policy' would obviously be incomplete without regulation of economic migration; a restriction relating to volumes of admission of economic migrants would be meaningless unless the EU had competence to regulate such migration in the first place; and the regulation of the 'rights' of resident third-country nationals would logically include the regulation of their access to employment, in the absence of any indication to the contrary.

It must therefore be concluded that Article 79 TFEU includes the power to regulate economic migration of third-country nationals, limited only by the express restriction on competence in Article 79(5) TFEU. As compared to other Treaty Articles, it could no longer be argued that any power to regulate this issue would be contained within Article 40 EC (now Article 46 TFEU), because Article 79 TFEU is now a *lex specialis*. On the other hand, Article 153 TFEU (previous Article 137 EC) is still a *lex specialis* as regards 'conditions of employment' of third-country nationals. The distinction between Articles 79 and 153 TFEU still matters because the social policy competence has remained subject to unanimous voting in the Council and consultation of the EP (ie, a 'special legislative procedure'),[72] with no facility for the UK, Ireland, or Denmark to opt out of legislation.

The best approach to the relationship between Articles 79 and 153 TFEU is that the former Article confers competence to regulate the conditions of employment of third-country nationals (or categories of third-country nationals),[73] if the regulation of this issue were ancillary to a measure regulating the rights of third-country nationals (or a category of them) generally, while the latter Article would be the correct legal base for a matter solely concerning the conditions of employment of third-country nationals.[74]

Three other provisions of the Treaties also need to be considered as regards the EU's competence to regulate economic migration. First, Article 56 TFEU (former Article 49 EC) explicitly gives (as it did before) the EU competence to regulate the provision of services in one Member State by third-country nationals who are legally resident in another Member State.[75] The Treaty of Lisbon changed the decision-making rules as

---

[72] See Art 289(2) TFEU.

[73] Except for persons seeking or obtaining protection status, who fall within the scope of Article 78 TFEU. On this point, see I:5.2.4 above.

[74] See by analogy *Opinion 1/94* [1994] ECR I-5273, as regards the relationship at the time between the commercial policy powers of the EC and the European Coal and Steel Community. See also the CJEU case law on the application of EU employment law to third-country nationals, discussed in I:6.4.5 below.

[75] On the substance of this issue, see further I:6.4.4 below.

regards this issue, but the competence itself was not altered.[76] So it must be concluded that Article 56 TFEU remains a *lex specialis* as regards this issue.

Next, Article 217 TFEU (previous Article 310 EC) continues to confer competence as regards the negotiation and conclusion of association agreements.[77] As the Court of Justice has confirmed, this Treaty Article confers competence upon the EC/EU to extend the entirety of the Treaty rules to non-member countries.[78] Indeed, the EC (as it then was) has used this power to extend the full free movement of persons to some non-EU States.[79] Since Article 217 TFEU has not significantly amended the previous Article 310 EC, the relationship between this provision and the EU's express immigration competence (by virtue of the extension of the internal market rules, inter alia, which association agreements may provide for) has presumably remained the same.[80] In fact, the CJEU has clarified some key points as regards the distinction between social security rules in association agreements and EU immigration law.[81]

Finally, the Treaty of Lisbon has revised the EC's (now the EU's) commercial policy powers (Article 207 TFEU; previous Article 133 EC) in order, inter alia, to extend the EU's powers to regulate the movement of services from *third states*.[82] Article 207 TFEU needs to be distinguished from the EU's powers over labour migration because the commercial policy power is fully exclusive and uniform, with no opt-outs for Member States. The definition of 'services' for the purpose of Article 207 TFEU includes the short-term movement of persons within the context of service provision,[83] so such movement falls within the concept of the EU's common commercial policy (CCP), not its immigration policy. However, the issue of transition to a long-term stay, and arguably also the specific regulation of visas for entry of service providers, would fall within the scope of the immigration and visa powers of the EU.

It remains to be determined to what extent Article 79(5) restricts the EU's competence. The starting point for the interpretation of the exclusion must be that as an exception from the EU's competence to establish a 'common' policy, it has to be narrowly interpreted.[84] Then the four specific aspects of the restriction have to be considered in turn. First of all, the provision only restricts competence in respect of '[t]his Article', ie Article 79 TFEU. So the competence regarding economic migration conferred by Articles 153, 207, and 217 TFEU is unaffected. Furthermore, from an external relations point of view, volumes of economic migrants coming to Member States from

---

[76] See ibid. On the scope of this competence, see Guild and Peers (n 65 above), 105–9.

[77] On the substance of this issue, see further I:6.4.3 below.

[78] See Case 12/86 *Demirel* [1987] ECR 3719.

[79] See the treaties establishing the European Economic Area ([1994] OJ L 1/1) and the EU-Swiss treaty concerning the free movement of persons ([2002] OJ L 114).

[80] On the scope of this competence, see Guild and Peers (n 65 above), 98–100.

[81] See I:6.4.3 below.   [82] For further detail, see I:6.4.6 below.

[83] See further ibid, and particularly *Opinion 1/2008* [2009] ECR I-11129. For a general explanation of the scope of the CCP as regards services since the Treaty of Lisbon, see Case C-137/12 *Commission v Council*, ECLI:EU:C:2013:675. See also *Opinion 2/15*, pending.

[84] See, by analogy, the judgments in Cases C-307/05 *Del Cerro Alonso* [2007] ECR I-7109 and C-268/06 *Impact* [2008] ECR I-2483 as regards the exclusions from competence in the previous Art 137(5) EC (now Art 153(2) TFEU) which, moreover, does not concern a limitation on competence to establish a 'common' policy. On the former Art 137(5) EC, see also Cases C-341/05 *Laval* [2007] ECR I-11767 and C-438/05 *Viking Line* [2007] ECR I-10779.

third countries could be regulated in mixed agreements, to which the EU together with the Member States is a party, presuming (in order to justify the EU's participation in the agreement concerned) that the treaty in question also concerned another issue within the EU's competence.

Secondly, the restriction only concerns *volumes* of admissions, rather than the question of access to employment for persons who have already been admitted or other aspects of the admission of economic migrants (such as the technical aspects of the admissions process or the grounds for admission, which could be separated from the question of permitted volumes per Member State).[85]

Thirdly, the restriction only applies to third-country nationals who come directly from third countries. Therefore, third-country nationals who are already resident, or at least legally resident, in a Member State (including presumably a Member State which has opted out of some EU immigration legislation) are not covered by the exclusion. So the EU is competent, for example, to abolish Member States' ability to restrict the movement of long-term residents between Member States by means of quotas.[86]

Fourthly, the limitation on competence only concerns people who *seek* employment or self-employment. It is possible to interpret this aspect of the limitation on competence very restrictively indeed, so that the EU competence is restricted only as regards the volumes of *work-seekers*, as distinct from the volumes of persons who already have work contracts or arrangements for self-employment. But such a highly restrictive interpretation would go too far, because it would leave Member States with a highly ineffective reserve of competence: the EU would be able to nullify that competence entirely by simply requiring any third-country nationals admitted for employment or self-employment in a Member State to have a contract of employment or to have made arrangements for self-employment beforehand.[87] On the other hand, the limitation on competence should not be construed so widely as to reserve to Member States a power to regulate the volumes of third-country nationals from third countries who might seek employment or self-employment on an ancillary basis, where the main reason for admission is for a non-economic purpose such as family reunion, study, or seeking international protection, but where EU legislation nevertheless regulates access to employment for the persons concerned.[88]

Finally, the Treaty of Lisbon did not expressly settle the question as to whether the EU's immigration powers extend to the regulation of social security for all third-country nationals who move between Member States.[89] Previously it was assumed by the EU institutions that the EC's migration powers applied to this issue, rather than its powers to regulate social security for EC workers pursuant to the previous Article 42 EC.[90]

---

[85] These two issues have been the subject of a number of Directives adopted since 2009 (see I:6.5.1 and I:6.5.2 below).

[86] See Art 14(4) of Dir 2003/109 ([2004] OJ L 16/44), discussed in I:6.7 below.

[87] For example, see Art 5(1)(a) of the 'Blue Card' Directive (Dir 2009/50, [2009] OJ L 155/17).

[88] See, for instance, Dirs 2003/86 and 2004/83 ([2003] OJ L 251/12 and [2004] OJ L 304/12). Indeed, as discussed in I:5.2.4 above, the employment status of persons seeking or obtaining protection falls within the scope of Art 78 TFEU, not Art 79 TFEU.

[89] On the substance of this issue, see I:6.4.2 below.

[90] For detailed comments, see ch 23 of Peers and Rogers (n 65 above).

However, a Declaration to the Treaty of Lisbon clearly assumes that the immigration powers (continue to) apply.[91] It should be noted that under the Treaty of Lisbon, the social security legal base (unlike any of the migration legal bases) is subject to an emergency brake which any Member State can pull in certain cases; but it is not subject to any opt-outs.[92] Given the Treaty power to develop a 'common' policy on migration and the absence of any exclusion for social security from that power, and by *a contrario* reasoning from the exclusion set out in Article 79(5) TFEU, it follows that Article 79 TFEU confers powers on the EU as regards social security for third-country nationals.[93]

6.2.5 Territorial scope

The UK has opted into:[94] the Regulation on the uniform residence permit and its 2008 amendment;[95] the 2003 Regulation on social security coordination, but not the 2010 Regulation on the same issue;[96] the 2006 Decision on exchange of information on migration policy;[97] the 2007 Decision adopting the Integration Fund;[98] the 2008 Decision on the European Migration Network;[99] and the 2014 legislation establishing the latest Asylum and Immigration Fund.[100]

Ireland has opted into: the 2003 and 2010 Regulations on social security coordination;[101] the 2006 Decision on exchange of information on migration policy;[102] the 2007 and 2014 legislation on immigration funds;[103] the Directive on researchers;[104] and the proposed Directive on economic migration (later withdrawn).[105] Also, Ireland opted in to the 2002 Regulation on the uniform residence permit after its adoption,[106] and then into the 2008 amendment to this Regulation in the ordinary way.[107] Ireland also opted into the Decision on the European Migration Network after its adoption.[108]

The main provisions of the Schengen *acquis* relating to legal migration are Articles 18 and 25 of the Schengen Convention. The substance and territorial scope of these measures is discussed in detail in Chapter 4 of this volume, as are measures building upon those provisions of the *acquis*,[109] except for the issue of the format and validity period of long-stay visas, which are discussed in this chapter.[110] Also, the EU measures concerning the uniform residence permit format (a Joint Action, replaced by a 2002 EC Regulation, as amended in 2008) fall within the scope of the Schengen *acquis*.[111]

---

[91] Declaration 22.   [92] Art 48 TFEU.
[93] This has also been the Council's practice: see the legislation discussed in I:6.8 below. See also the position as regards social security and association agreements, discussed in I:6.4.3 below.
[94] On the UK and Irish position, see I:2.2.5.1 above.
[95] Regs 1030/2002 ([2002] OJ L 157/1) and 380/2008 ([2008] OJ L 115/1). See I:6.9 below.
[96] Respectively Reg 859/2003 ([2003] OJ L 124/1) and Reg 1231/2010 ([2010] OJ L 344/1). On the substance, see I:6.8 below.
[97] [2006] OJ L 283/40. See I:6.11 below.   [98] [2007] OJ L 168/18. See I:6.10 below.
[99] [2008] OJ L 131/7. See I:6.11 below.
[100] Reg 516/2014 ([2014] OJ L 150/168). See I:6.10 below.   [101] See I:6.8 below.
[102] See I:6.11 below.   [103] See I:6.10 below.   [104] Dir 2005/71 ([2005] OJ L 289/15).
[105] COM (2001) 386, 11 July 2001.
[106] Commission Decision C(2007)4589/F of 11 Oct 2007, not published in the OJ.
[107] See I:6.9 below.   [108] See Commission Decision ([2009] OJ L 108/53).
[109] I:4.9 above.   [110] I:6.9 below.   [111] See ibid.

Applying the special provisions on the Schengen *acquis*, Denmark decided to apply the original residence permit Regulation in its national law,[112] and the Regulation and its amendment are also applicable to the Schengen associates (Norway, Iceland, Switzerland, and Liechtenstein).[113]

Finally, it should be recalled that the immigration provisions derived from other areas of EU law, as well as the legislation on immigration statistics, apply to all Member States (but not to any non-Member States).[114]

6.3 Human Rights

6.3.1 The right to family reunion, family life, and private life

The most important human rights protection offered to legal migrants in practice is the obligation to ensure the right to 'private and family life'. These rights are protected in a number of international human rights instruments, and furthermore several treaties recognize the family as a fundamental unit of society.[115] Of these, the European Convention on Human Rights (ECHR) is referred to expressly in the EU Charter of Rights, and is the best known and most influential source of human rights principles forming part of the general principles of EU law.[116] Article 8 ECHR guarantees the right to respect for private and family life, but Article 8(2) ECHR allows interference with that right, 'in accordance with the law' and if 'necessary in a democratic society', on a number of grounds, including public safety, national security, the economic well-being of the country, and the prevention of disorder or crime.[117]

The judgments of the European Court of Human Rights relevant to Article 8 and immigration can be broken down between those judgments concerning admission, those governing removal, and those governing status while in the country. A further distinction can be drawn in the 'expulsion' category between those persons to be expelled on public safety, public security, or similar grounds and those to be expelled in the economic interests of the host State.

First of all, the admission cases are relatively few; here the Strasbourg Court has consistently ruled that there is in principle no interference with the right to respect for family life if it is possible for the family to live elsewhere. This even applies in cases where the mother of the child has died and the father (after some years' residence abroad) wishes the child to

---

[112] See Danish letter of 9 Dec 2002 (Council doc 14807/03, 14 Nov 2003), and further I:2.2.5.2 above.

[113] See further I:2.2.5.4 above. [114] See respectively I:6.4 and I:6.11 below.

[115] See generally, R Cholewinski, *Migrant Workers in International Human Rights Law* (OUP, 1997), 68–70, 171–3, and 335–6; and R Cholewinski, 'The Protection of the Right of Economic Migrants to Family Reunion in Europe' (1994) 43 ICLQ 568. On the UN International Covenant on Civil and Political Rights, see S Joseph, J Schultz, and M Castan, *The International Covenant on Civil and Political Rights: Cases, Materials and Commentary*, 2nd edn (OUP, 2004), at 585–609.

[116] See I:2.3 above.

[117] For a detailed analysis, see J van Dijk, 'Protection of "Integrated" Aliens against Expulsion under the European Convention on Human Rights' in E Guild and P Minderhoud, eds., *Security of Residence and Expulsion: Protection of Aliens in Europe* (Kluwer, 2001), 23; C Harvey, 'Promoting Insecurity: Public Order, Expulsion and the European Convention on Human Rights' (ibid) 41; J Marin and J O'Connell, 'The European Convention and the Relative Rights of Resident Aliens' (1999) 5 ELJ 4 at 4–14; and H Storey, 'The Right to Family Life and Immigration Case Law at Strasbourg' (1990) 39 ICLQ 329.

join him, or where the parents have difficulty leaving a host state because of the illness of the mother.[118] However, the Convention can entail a right of admission in some cases: the Court has ruled that where some children are living in the host State with their parents and some have been left in the country of origin, the latter must be reunified in the host State of their parents if it is impractical for their siblings to leave school there.[119]

In recent years, the Court has developed a line of case law concerning persons who did not acquire a legal right to enter and stay, but who formed a family life during their period of residence on the territory. The factors to take into account in such cases are 'the extent to which family life is effectively ruptured, the extent of the ties in the Contracting State, whether there are insurmountable obstacles in the way of the family living in the country of origin of one or more of them and whether there are factors of immigration control (eg a history of breaches of immigration law) or considerations of public order weighing in favour of exclusion'. But if family life develops while a person was contesting or avoiding expulsion, and the family knew all along that the immigration status of one person was precarious, then Article 8 ECHR will benefit them only exceptionally.[120]

The exact scope of such exceptional situations was recently clarified by a Grand Chamber judgment in the case of *Jeunesse*. It was a breach of Article 8 to remove a third-country national from the Netherlands in that case, even though her status had been irregular for many years (after the expiry of here initial short-term visa), because: her spouse and children were all Dutch; her position had been tolerated for a long time; her family would face some hardship moving; and there would be a great impact on her young children.[121]

States are entitled to have a separate regime for persons with special links with that State that treats such persons more favourably as compared to other sponsors, but a distinction between men and women as regards family reunion is a breach of Articles 8 and 14 ECHR (the latter Article guarantees equality in respect of the rights set out in the Convention).[122]

As for expulsion, in principle there is an interference with family life where States seek to expel persons who have established family life in that State, and an interference with private life to the extent that even a person without a family life in a State has developed there a 'network of personal, social and economic relations' and property rental or ownership.[123] Where States simply wish to expel persons solely in their economic interest of the State, the Court is unwilling to accept an interference with family life, ruling that the State's interest was outweighed by the interest of an active father in continuing

---

[118] See *Ahmut v Netherlands* (Reports 1996-VI) and *Gul v Switzerland* (Reports 1996-I).

[119] *Sen v Netherlands*, 21 Dec 2001, and *Tuquabo-Tekle v Netherlands*, 1 Dec 2005.

[120] *Da Silva and Hoogkamer v Netherlands*, 31 Jan 2006, para 39. See subsequently *Konstantinov v Netherlands*, 26 Apr 2007; *Omoregie v Norway*, 31 July 2008, and *Y v Russia*, 4 Dec 2008. In the *Konstantinov* judgment (para 50), the Court acknowledges that a sufficient income requirement for family reunion is acceptable. Compare with the 'sufficient resources' rule in the EU family reunion Directive (discussed in I:6.6.1 below). See also *Kawala v Netherlands*, 1 June 2010, where the importance of legal residence is confirmed expressly.

[121] Judgment of 3 Oct 2014. It should be noted that there are parallels between this judgment and EU citizenship law, discussed in I:6.4.1 below.

[122] *Abdulaziz and others v UK* (Series A, no 94).

[123] See, for instance, *Slivenko v Latvia* (Reports 2003-X), para 96.

a relationship with his young daughter.[124] Also, where a father showed signs of wishing to develop a relationship with his child but faced difficulties due to the opposition of the child's mother, the State could not pre-empt the conclusion of the family law proceedings by expelling the father before those proceedings were properly completed.[125]

The position changes in cases where the State wishes to expel a person following a criminal conviction for a serious crime. In such cases, there must be a balancing test, which takes into account on the one hand the extent, timing, and seriousness of the criminal offences committed, and on the other hand, the difficulties that expulsion from that State would cause for the family life of the person concerned.[126] This aspect of the test entails assessing whether a family life could be maintained in the state of origin, taking into account such factors as the number of family members living in the State of origin as compared to the host State, along with the language skills and other connections with the State of origin which the expellee still maintains.

The principles derived from this case law were summarized in the *Boultif v Switzerland* judgment of 2001, which looked in particular at an extra factor: the difficulties which the family members with the nationality of the host State might have adjusting to life in the expellee's home State.[127] Those basic factors were restated and clarified in the Grand Chamber judgment of 2006 in *Uner v Netherlands*, as follows:[128]

- the nature and seriousness of the offence committed by the applicant;
- the length of the applicant's stay in the country from which he or she is to be expelled;
- the time elapsed since the offence was committed and the applicant's conduct during that period;
- the nationalities of the various persons concerned;
- the applicant's family situation, such as the length of the marriage, and other factors expressing the effectiveness of a couple's family life;
- whether the spouse knew about the offence at the time when he or she entered into a family relationship;
- whether there are children of the marriage, and if so, their age;
- the seriousness of the difficulties which the spouse is likely to encounter in the country to which the applicant is to be expelled;
- the best interests and well-being of the children, in particular the seriousness of the difficulties which any children of the applicant are likely to encounter in the country to which the applicant is to be expelled; and
- the solidity of social, cultural, and family ties with the host country and with the country of destination.

---

[124] *Berrehab v the Netherlands* (Series A, no 138).

[125] *Ciliz v the Netherlands* (Reports 2000-VIII). See subsequently *Da Silva and Hoogkamer v Netherlands* (n 120 above).

[126] Case law beginning with *Moustaquim v Belgium* (Series A, no 193). See further: *Beldjoudi v France* (Series A, no 234); *Nasri v France* (Series A, no 320); *C v Belgium* (Reports 1996-III); *Bouchelkia v France* (Reports 1997-I); *El-Boujaidi v France* (Reports 1997-VI); *Boujlifa v Belgium* (Reports 1997-VI); *Mehemi v France I* (Reports 1997-VI); *Dalia v France* (Reports 1998-I); *Baghli v France* (Reports 1999-VIII); *Ezzouhdi v France*, 13 Feb 2001; *Yildiz v Austria*, 31 Oct 2002; *Jakupovic v Austria*, 6 Feb 2003; and *Yilmaz v Germany*, 17 Apr 2003.

[127] Reports of Judgments and Decisions, 2001-IX. See subsequently: *Amrohalli v Denmark*, 11 July 2002; *Benhebba v France*, 10 July 2003; *Mokrani v France*, 15 July 2003; *Radovanovic v Austria*, 22 Apr 2004; *Keles v Germany*, 27 Oct 2005; *Aoulmi v France*, 17 Jan 2006; and *Sezen v Netherlands*, 31 Jan 2006.

[128] Judgment of 18 Oct 2006, paras 57–8.

These principles have been applied in a number of subsequent cases.[129] There seem to be special considerations for children, as it is not permissible to return them alone to a State of origin where they have no close family and there has been recent fighting when they have only committed a less serious crime.[130]

There have also been cases concerning expulsion on grounds of 'national security'; this concept can include the removal of foreign military and their family members, but it is nonetheless not 'necessary' to expel such persons where they have spent their entire lives in the country, have integrated to a sufficient degree into the civilian life of the host state, and do not represent an individual security threat.[131]

The concept of family member for the purposes of the ECHR initially appeared to be broad, encompassing not just the nuclear family but also co-habitees (at least in cases involving children), parents' relationship with children (and vice versa) after divorce or separation from the parent carer or adulthood of the children, and siblings, aunts, and uncles.[132] More recently, the Court has come to focus on 'core' family members, ruling that elderly non-dependent parents do not fall into this category, although relations with such persons still fall within the scope of 'private life';[133] it has also repeatedly emphasized that relations between adults do not normally fall within the scope of 'family life', except where there is a condition of dependence.[134]

Another aspect of the case law is the finding in several cases that while the offences committed by an applicant justified some period of expulsion, Article 8 ECHR was violated by the imposition of an unlimited period of expulsion, which violated the principle of proportionality in light of strength of the migrant's family links, weighed against the severity of his or her offences.[135]

Moreover, there are minimum procedural requirements for Member States where Article 8 rights may be involved; they cannot simply disrupt family life without considering objections by the individuals concerned, as 'the concepts of lawfulness and the rule of law in a democratic society require that measures affecting fundamental human rights must be subject to some form of adversarial proceedings before an independent body competent to review the reasons for the decision and relevant evidence, if need be with appropriate procedural limitations on the use of classified information'.[136] In conjunction with Article 13 ECHR, which guarantees effective remedies for breaches of

---

[129] Expulsions were justified in: *Kaya v Germany*, 28 June 2007; *Chair and JB v Germany*, 6 Dec 2007; *Grant v UK*, 8 Jan 2009; *Onur v UK*, 17 Feb 2009; and *Mutlag v Germany*, 25 Mar 2010. Expulsions were not justified in: *Emre v Switzerland*, 22 May 2008; *Maslov v Austria*, 23 June 2008; *Omojudi v UK*, 24 Nov 2009; and *Khan v UK*, 12 Jan 2010.

[130] *Jakupovic v Austria* (n 126 above). See also *Maslov v Austria* (n 129 above).

[131] See *Slivenko v Latvia* (n 123 above). A series of other 'national security' cases have been decided on the grounds that the restrictions were not 'prescribed by law': case law beginning with *Al-Nashif v Bulgaria* (10 June 2002), discussed further below. For a case where the national security argument justified expulsion, see *Cherif v Italy*, 7 Apr 2009.

[132] See, for example, *Abdulaziz* (n 122 above) and *Moustaquim* (n 126 above).

[133] See *Slivenko* (n 123 above), para 97.

[134] For instance, see *Uner* (n 128 above). The Court does not appear to be suggesting that relations between *spouses* fall outside the scope of 'core' family relationships. Relationships with an unmarried partner are covered, at least where there is a joint child—see, for instance, *Yildiz v Austria* (n 126 above).

[135] See, for instance, the judgments in *Yilmaz* (n 126 above), *Radovanovic*, and *Keles* (both n 127 above). Compare with EU legislation on the limited period of entry bans (I:7.7.1 below).

[136] *Al-Nashif v Bulgaria* (n 131 above), para 123.

rights guaranteed by the Convention, 'States must make available to the individual concerned the effective possibility of challenging the deportation or refusal-of-residence order and of having the relevant issues examined with sufficient procedural safeguards and thoroughness by an appropriate domestic forum offering adequate guarantees of independence and impartiality.'[137] Even in alleged 'national security' cases:

> ...the guarantee of an effective remedy requires as a minimum that the competent independent appeals authority must be informed of the reasons grounding the deportation decision, even if such reasons are not publicly available. The authority must be competent to reject the executive's assertion that there is a threat to national security where it finds it arbitrary or unreasonable. There must be some form of adversarial proceedings, if need be through a special representative after a security clearance. Furthermore, the question whether the impugned measure would interfere with the individual's right to respect for family life and, if so, whether a fair balance is struck between the public interest involved and the individual's rights must be examined.[138]

Even where judicial review exists, an interference with Article 8 rights will not be 'in accordance with the law' in such cases, if the extent of the judicial review is entirely inadequate.[139]

The consequence of a ruling that a person has been wrongly expelled in breach of Article 8 ECHR is that the State must ensure family reunion (or the right to a private life) by readmitting a person who has been expelled 'with special expedition'.[140] However, three-and-a-half months is not unduly long for this purpose, and States are not required to give a person any particular form of residence permit upon their return.[141]

This brings us to the third category of cases, concerning the legal status of migrants. Although the judgment just mentioned appeared to suggest that, in the absence of expulsion, the regulation of a person's migration status could not infringe Article 8, the Human Rights Court has ruled that a lengthy period of uncertain and precarious migration status could violate Article 8, with the consequence that States are obliged to regularize the position of the person concerned.[142] The Human Rights Court has applied this principle particularly strongly in the context of EU free movement law.[143]

Although it has been argued that foreign nationals should not be subject to expulsion when nationals are not, and that EU Member States should not subject nationals of non-EU states to discrimination as regards expulsion compared to nationals of

---

[137] *Al-Nashif* (n 131 above), para 133. For a simpler violation of the requirement that expulsions must be in accordance with the law in Art 8 cases, see *Estrikh v Latvia*, 18 Jan 2007.

[138] *Al-Nashif* (n 131 above), para 137. See subsequently: *Liu v Russia*, 6 Dec 2007; *Musa and Others v Bulgaria*, 11 Jan 2007; and *Bashir and Others v Bulgaria* and *Hasan v Bulgaria*, 14 June 2007.

[139] See *CG and others v Bulgaria*, judgment of 24 Apr 2008 and *Raza v Bulgaria*, judgment of 11 Feb 2010 (neither yet reported). A violation of Art 13 ECHR (the right to an effective remedy) was also found in these cases. See also *Kaya v Romania*, 12 Oct 2006, *Gulijev v Lithuania*, 16 Dec 2008, and *Nolan v Russia*, 12 Feb 2009.

[140] *Mehemi v France (II)*, 10 Apr 2003.   [141] Ibid.

[142] *Sisojeva v Latvia*, Grand Chamber judgment of 15 Jan 2007, along with *Kaftailova v Latvia* and *Shevanova v Latvia*, both Grand Chamber judgments of 7 Dec 2007. See also *Liu v Russia* (n 138 above) and *Zakayev and Sofanova v Russia*, 11 Feb 2010.

[143] *Mendizabal v France*, 17 Jan 2006; see further I:6.3.4 below.

EU states, the Strasbourg Court has rejected these arguments, on the grounds that in principle a State's nationals cannot be expelled at all, and that the EU has created a 'special legal order', so there is an 'objective and reasonable justification' for treating them better than persons from non-EU states.[144] A subsequent judgment updates this conclusion by referring to the subsequent creation of citizenship of the Union, failing to take account of the prospect that 'citizens' of the Union outside their Member State of nationality can be expelled from other Member States, unlike the citizens of the relevant Member State.[145] However, this is hard to reconcile with another line of case law from the Court, which rules that nationality discrimination as regards the rights set out in the Convention cannot easily be justified.

6.3.2 The right to non-discrimination

As observed above, Article 14 ECHR requires States to secure the rights set out in the Convention without discrimination on the grounds set out in that Article. The list of grounds set out is non-exhaustive, and Article 14 also applies to discrimination on grounds of nationality; indeed, 'very weighty reasons' must be given to justify discrimination on grounds of nationality.[146]

The Human Rights Court has ruled several times that emergency assistance benefits fall within the scope of Article 1 of Protocol 1 to the ECHR, which concerns the right to property. It follows that such benefits must be granted on the basis of non-discrimination on the grounds of nationality, whether the benefits are contributory or non-contributory, and so far the Court has not accepted justifications for discrimination based on the principle of reciprocity or States' desire to control their social benefits budgets.[147] The same principles apply to access to child benefits, where the benefit is linked to ECHR rights because child benefits aim to support family life, and where the discrimination is between the holders of different types of residence permits and therefore not on the grounds of nationality as such.[148] It is also a violation of Article 14 to refuse legal aid to persons on the ground that their residence is irregular, at least in certain circumstances.[149]

It should also be observed that Article 26 of the International Covenant on Civil and Political Rights (ICCPR) contains a non-discrimination clause, which also applies to non-discrimination on grounds of nationality and which secures equality as regards all rights (including particularly social and economic rights), not just the rights set out in the Covenant.[150]

---

[144] See *Moustaquim* (n 126 above) and earlier *Abdulaziz* (n 122 above).

[145] *C v Belgium* (n 126 above).

[146] *Gaygusuz v Austria* (Reports 1996-IV).

[147] See *Gaygusuz* (n 146 above), *Poirrez v France* (ECHR 2003-X), *Luczak v Poland* (ECHR 2007-XIII), and *Andrejeva v Latvia*, judgment of 18 Feb 2009, not yet reported. All EU Member States have ratified the First Protocol. The Court has definitively confirmed that non-contributory benefits fall within the scope of the right to property: decision in *Stec and others v UK* (Reports 2005-X).

[148] *Niedzwiecki v Germany* and *Okpisz v Germany*, judgments of 25 Oct 2005 (not yet reported).

[149] *Yula v Belgium*, judgment of 10 Mar 2009, not yet reported.

[150] See Joseph, et al. (n 115 above), 679–751.

6.3.3 Other human rights of migrant workers

Article 6 ECHR, which guarantees the right to a fair trial, does not cover immigration proceedings.[151] However, Article 6 *does* apply to disputes concerning foreigners' (or their would-be employers') applications for work permits,[152] and it should be recalled that if an immigration dispute can be brought within the other substantive provisions of the Convention, then procedural rights must nonetheless be guaranteed.[153] Specific procedural rights concerning expulsion are set out in the Seventh Protocol to the ECHR and in the ICCPR, but these are considered in detail in Chapter 7, along with the rules concerning detention in the context of immigration proceedings.[154] The rights to free movement within a State's territory and to enter and leave countries are considered in detail in Chapter 3.[155] There seems little doubt that, where no issues of nationality or immigration status are relevant, foreign nationals can generally assert the same human rights as nationals.[156] Migrant workers (or their children) may also apply to invoke the right to education (eg under the First Protocol to the ECHR), either alone or in conjunction with non-discrimination provisions of international treaties.

Specific rights for migrants, and particularly migrant workers, are guaranteed by a number of treaties, in particular the UN Convention on Migrant Workers, conventions adopted by the International Labour Organization, and certain Council of Europe conventions (regarding migrant workers, establishment, and social and medical assistance). However, these conventions have attracted little or no ratifications from EU Member States to date.[157] They are particularly concerned with regulating the legal status of migrant workers, including issues such as access to employment and equality as regards social and economic rights.

6.3.4 Application to EU law

The Strasbourg Court has ruled that the ECHR rules on the right to private life and family apply to cases within the scope of EU free movement law. In particular, a Member State that issues a series of short-term residence permits to the family member of a migrant EU citizen instead of the permits required by EU law is interfering with the right to family life, and the interference is not 'prescribed by law' if it does not comply with EU or national law.[158] Previously the Human Rights Court had examined in several judgments whether a non-EU national could move with an EU spouse to another EU country other than that wishing to expel the non-EU spouse,[159] but it never drew

---

[151] *Maaouia v France* (Reports 2000-X).
[152] *Jurisic and Collegium Mehrerau v Austria* and *Coorplan-Jenni GMBH and Hascic v Austria*, 27 July 2006, and *Koottummel v Austria*, 10 Dec 2009.
[153] See *Al-Nashif v Bulgaria* (n 131 above); as regards asylum proceedings, see I:5.3.1.
[154] I:7.3 below.   [155] I:3.3 above.
[156] For example, see *Djaid v France*, 29 Sep 1999, regarding the right to 'trial within a reasonable time' set out in Art 6 ECHR.
[157] For detailed analysis, see Cholewinski (n 115 above). The UN Convention entered into force on 1 July 2003 and has been ratified by over 40 States, but no EU Member States.
[158] *Mendizabal v France* (n 143 above).
[159] See particularly *Mehemi v France* (n 140 above), where the spouse of the expellee was actually a national of Italy, not France. In *Amrohalli v Denmark* (n 127 above), the Court rejected the possibility that

the obvious connection with EU free movement law in such cases. In fact, it might be questioned whether the crimes committed in these particular cases would be serious enough to permit another Member State to refuse the entry of such persons.[160] The Strasbourg Court instead focused in these cases on the extent of family life enjoyed by the expellee in the host Member State. In cases involving admission of a non-EU national to live with an EU national, free movement law could also be relevant.[161] The free movement of long-term resident third-country nationals in the EU could also be relevant to family reunion cases.

Also, there is one Strasbourg judgment involving application of an EU association agreement with a non-EU country, in which the Court of Human Rights left it to national courts to determine whether the association agreement with Turkey had been correctly applied.[162] Conversely, the Court of Justice has on a number of occasions referred to the right to family life when ruling on family reunion cases governed by EU free movement law and the EU's family reunion Directive, often referring to Article 8 ECHR and even, in several cases, to Strasbourg Court judgments.[163] However, the EU Charter right to family life does not apply if cases fall outside the scope of EU law.[164]

As for association agreements, the Court of Justice has ruled that it can only rule on human rights issues falling within the scope of EU law,[165] but it has nonetheless indicated that Member States must take account of the right to family life and the right to property of persons who do not meet the criteria for admission and stay pursuant to the Europe Agreements with Central and Eastern European countries.[166]

---

the expellee could live in Greece or Turkey on grounds of insufficient links there, not considering the prospect of the Danish spouse exercising free movement rights to live in Greece.

[160] See I:6.4.1 below.   [161] See ibid.

[162] *Yildiz* (n 126 above) concerning the EU-Turkey agreement; compare with the case law of the Court of Justice limiting expulsion of Turkish workers and their family members, discussed in I:6.4.3 below. The possible application of the EU-Turkey agreement was not referred to in the judgments in *Yilmaz, Uner, Keles, Kaya*, and *Onur* (nn 125 to 129 above).

[163] As regards EU free movement law, see: Cases 249/86 *Commission v Germany* [1989] ECR 1263; C-60/00 *Carpenter* [2002] ECR I-6279 (applying the *Boultif* judgment); C-459/99 *MRAX* [2002] ECR I-6591; C-413/99 *Baumbast and R* [2002] ECR I-7091; C-257/00 *Givane* [2003] ECR I-345; C-109/01 *Akrich* [2003] ECR I-9607 (referring to *Boultif* and *Amrohalli*); C-482/01 and C-493/01 *Orfanopolous and Olivieri* [2004] ECR I-5257 (referring to *Boultif*); C-157/03 *Commission v Spain* [2005] ECR I-2911; C-503/03 *Commission v Spain* [2006] ECR I-1097; Case C-441/02 *Commission v Germany* [2006] ECR I-3449 (referring to *Boultif*); Case C-127/08 *Metock* [2008] ECR I-6241; and Cases C-310/08 *Ibrahim* and C-480/08 *Teixeira* [2010] ECR I-1065. As regards the EU family reunion directive, see Cases C-540/03 *EP v Council* [2006] ECR I-5769 (referring to *Sen, Ahmut, Gul*, and *Rodrigues da Silva and Hoogkamer*); and C-578/08 *Chakroun* [2010] ECR I-1839; and Joined Cases C-356/11 and C-357/11, *O and S and L*, ECLI:EU:C:2012:776. On the links between the ECHR and EU free movement law, see also the Commission's report on the derogations from free movement law (COM (1999) 372, 19 July 1999), at 7–9 and 20–1.

[164] See Cases C-40/11 *Iida*, ECLI:EU:C:2012:691; C-256/11 *Dereci* [2011] ECR I-11315; and C-87/12 *Ymeraga*, ECLI:EU:C:2013:291.

[165] Case 12/86 *Demirel* [1987] ECR 3719. Conversely, see C-451/11 *Dulger*, ECLI:EU:C:2012:504, where the Court affirmed a link between the EU-Turkey association and the right to family life. See also the Opinion in Case C-65/98 *Eyup* [2000] ECR I-4747.

[166] Cases C-63/99 *Gloszczuk* [2001] ECR I-6369, para 85, and C-235/99 *Kondova* [2001] ECR I-6427, para 90.

Also, it has ruled that persons who wish to enter and stay pursuant to those agreements have a right to effective remedies stemming from the general principles of EU law:

> It follows in particular that the scheme applicable to…temporary residence permits [issued in order to exercise the rights conferred by the Europe Agreements] must be based on a procedural system which is easily accessible and capable of ensuring that the persons concerned will have their applications dealt with objectively and within a reasonable time, and refusals to grant a permit must be capable of being challenged in judicial or quasi-judicial proceedings.…It should be remembered, in this last respect, that Community law requires effective judicial scrutiny of the decisions of national authorities taken pursuant to the applicable provisions of Community law, and that this principle of effective judicial protection constitutes a general principle which stems from the constitutional traditions common to the Member States and is enshrined by the European Convention for the Protection of Human Rights and Fundamental Freedoms, signed at Rome on 4 November 1950, in Articles 6 and 13 of the Convention.…[167]

This general principle is also reflected in the EU Charter of Rights,[168] which has become binding in the meantime.[169] The ruling indicates indisputably that, at least as regards the right to a fair trial and effective remedies in immigration proceedings, the scope of the general principles of EU law (and now Article 47 of the Charter) is wider than the scope of the corresponding ECHR rights.[170] Rather the procedural rights apply whenever there is a link to a right conferred by EU law, with the consequence that all immigration and asylum proceedings linked to EU legislation are covered by the right to a fair trial and an effective remedy. Even where EU legislation sets out a minimum set of procedural rules, the general principles nevertheless (and now the Charter) require Member States to set a higher standard if necessary to ensure effective procedural protection.[171]

The EU Charter also includes the right to private and family life, plus equality in working conditions for third-country nationals, non-discrimination on grounds of nationality, and the possibility of free movement for third-country nationals.[172] So far, the Court of Justice has applied the Charter rules on private and family life (both before and after the Charter gained binding force with the Treaty of Lisbon),[173] but has not yet had the opportunity to rule on the other relevant Charter rights. Interestingly, though, it has ruled on the importance of the Charter provision on combating poverty and social exclusion, in the context of a long-term resident migrant's claim for housing

---

[167] Case C-327/02 *Panayotova* [2004] ECR I-11055, para 27.
[168] Art 47 of the Charter ([2007] OJ C 303). [169] See I:2.3 above.
[170] Compare with *Maaouia v France* (n 151 above).
[171] Case C-185/97 *Coote* [1998] ECR I-5199.
[172] Arts 7, 15(3), 21(2), and 45(2) of the Charter. On the status of the Charter, see I:2.3 above; on its impact on EU immigration and asylum law, see ch 3 of S Peers, V Moreno Lax, M Garlick, and E Guild, *EU Immigration and Asylum Law: Text and Commentary*, 2nd edn, vol 3 (Brill, 2015), which also discusses Art 18 TFEU (previously Art 12 EC), the Treaty provision on non-discrimination on grounds of nationality (identical to Art 21(2) of the Charter).
[173] See *EP v Council, Chakroun, O and S and L* (n 163 above), and *Dulger* (n 165 above).

benefit.[174] Finally, it should be recalled that if and when the EU becomes party to the ECHR, it will have the obligation to protect family and private life in that context.[175]

6.4 Impact of Other EU Law

The distinction between EU immigration law and other (ie, non-JHA) provisions of EU law remains important since the entry into force of the Treaty of Lisbon, for two reasons.[176] Firstly, several Member States have opt-outs from EU immigration law,[177] but not from the other relevant provisions of EU law. Secondly, the limitation on EU competence over volumes of admission of third-country national economic migrants coming from third countries, as set out in Article 79(5) TFEU, only applies, as noted above, to the immigration competence in Article 79 itself.[178] Put another way, the national competence reserved by Article 79(5) cannot be used to limit the numbers of third-country nationals admitted for economic purposes coming from third countries when another legal base in the Treaties is validly used to regulate the issue in question.

In any event, it is necessary to set out an overview of the other EU rules impacting upon immigration in order to get a fuller picture of the legal status of third-country nationals pursuant to EU law as a whole.[179]

6.4.1 EU citizenship and free movement law

The most important case of a non-JHA area of EU law applying to third-country nationals is EU free movement law—namely, where third-country nationals are family members of EU citizens. However, such family members can only claim status under EU free movement law if the EU citizen sponsor has exercised free movement rights; this will usually entail the EU citizen residing in an EU Member State other than that of his/her nationality.[180] However, there are several circumstances in which EU free movement law—or EU *citizenship* law—can be invoked as regards third-country national family members of an EU citizen, even where that EU citizen resides in his or her country of origin. The following discussion addresses in turn the general rules applying to EU citizens with non-EU family in another Member State, where EU free movement law always applies, followed by the exceptional cases where EU law applies to EU citizens with non-EU family in the citizens' own Member State.

---

[174] See I:2.3 above.

[175] See Case C-571/10 *Kamberaj*, ECLI:EU:C:2012:233, discussed in I:6.7 below.

[176] For a detailed analysis of the position of third-country nationals under other provisions of EC and EU law (before the Treaty of Lisbon), see Guild and Peers (n 65 above).

[177] For the details of these rules, see I:6.2.5 above.   [178] See further I:6.2.4 above.

[179] For the impact of non-JHA EU law in other related contexts, see further I:3.4, I:4.4, and I:5.4 above and I:7.4 below.

[180] See particularly Joined Cases 35 and 36/82 *Morson and Jhanjan* [1982] ECR 3723 and Joined Cases C-64/96 and 65/96 *Uecker and Jacquet* [1997] ECR I-3171. The position was confirmed in Case C-212/06 *Gouvernement de la Communauté française and Gouvernement wallon* [2008] ECR I-1683. The third-country national family members must reside in the same country as the EU family member: see Case C-40/11 *Iida*, ECLI:EU:C:2012:691.

6.4.1.1 General free movement rules

Although the rules governing the free movement of EU citizens and their family members used to be set out in the EC Treaty (as it then was),[181] and a number of different secondary legislative measures,[182] most of that legislation was consolidated and updated by Directive 2004/38, as of 30 April 2006.[183] The Court of Justice has confirmed that this Directive does not reduce the rights conferred by the prior legislation,[184] so it is therefore assumed in the following discussion that the Court's case law concerning the prior legislation is still relevant, *mutatis mutandis*, to the 2004 Directive. The analysis examines in turn the four central issues regarding family reunion, which are: the definition of sponsors; the definition of family members; the conditions attached to family reunion (eg waiting periods and financial requirements); and the treatment of family members after reunion (referred to as the issue of the 'status of family members'), concerning such issues as the grounds on which family members can be expelled, their access to education and employment, and their status in the event of family breakdown.[185]

As regards the definition of sponsors, it is first of all necessary to define EU citizenship. The Treaties specify that every national of a Member State is an EU citizen (Article 9 TFEU), but what about dual citizens? If a person is a dual citizen of two Member States, the CJEU has ruled that EU free movement law does not apply (as regards family reunion) unless that citizen has moved between Member States.[186] As for dual citizens of a Member State and a non-Member State,[187] the Court of Justice has made clear that there is an absolute obligation of other Member States to recognize and give effect to a person's acquisition of a Member State's nationality.[188] The complication arises where the person concerned instead seeks to rely, at least for some purposes, on his or her third-country nationality, rather than his or her EU citizenship. This would most likely occur where the person concerned has not exercised EU free movement rights, so could not rely on EU free movement law, and where the Member State where that

---

[181] The relevant TFEU Articles are Arts 45 (workers; ex-Art 39 EC), 49 (self-employed; ex-Art 42 EC), and 56 (service providers and recipients; ex-Art 49 EC). Also, Arts 18 and 166 (ex-Arts 12 and 150 EC), taken together, give free movement rights to students (Case C-357/89 *Raulin* [1992] ECR I-1027), and Art 21 TFEU (ex-Art 18 EC) on EU citizens' right to 'move and reside' freely can also confer free movement rights in certain cases (C-413/99 *Baumbast and R* [2002] ECR I-7091; Case C-200/02 *Chen and Zhu* [2004] ECR I-9925).

[182] The relevant legislation comprised Regs 1612/68 (OJ Spec Ed 1968, L 257/2, p 475) and 1251/70 (OJ Spec Ed 1970, L 142/24, p 402), along with Dirs 64/221 (OJ Spec Ed, 1963–64, 117), 68/360 (OJ Spec Ed 1968, L 257/13, p 485), 72/194 ([1972] OJ L 121/32), 73/148 ([1973] OJ L 172/14), 75/34 ([1975] OJ L 14/10), 75/35 ([1975] OJ L 14/14), 90/364 ([1990] OJ L 180/26), 90/365 ([1990] OJ L 180/28), and 93/96 ([1993] OJ L 317/59).

[183] [2004] OJ L 229/35. Arts 1–9 and 12 of Reg 1612/68 (n 182 above) remain in force (see Art 38 of the Directive). Also, the relevant TFEU (ex-EC Treaty) Articles remain in force.

[184] Case law starting with Case C-127/08 *Metock* [2008] ECR I-6241.

[185] See S Peers, 'Family Reunion and Community Law' in N Walker, ed., *Towards an Area of Freedom, Security and Justice* (OUP, 2004), 143.

[186] Case C-434/09 *McCarthy* [2011] ECR I-3375. EU free movement law can, however, be invoked as regards dual citizens of non-Member States who have not moved, but claim that national rules on the use of their names affect their free movement: see Case C-148/02 *Avello* [2003] ECR I-11613.

[187] On this issue as regards criminal law, see II:3.5.2 below; as regards civil law, see Case C-168/08 *Hadadi* [2009] ECR I-6871.

[188] Case C-369/90 *Micheletti and Others* [1992] ECR I-4239.

person is a national treats its nationals worse than third-country nationals, at least for some purposes. This is the case, for instance, in some Member States as regards family reunion.[189] In that scenario the person concerned would likely find it easier in practice simply to 'stay put' in his or her 'own' Member State and invoke his or her third-country nationality in order to fall within the scope of the relevant rules, rather than trigger EU free movement law by moving to another Member State (if only for a limited period).

For these cases, the Court of Justice initially ruled in the *Mesbah* judgment, concerning the EU's cooperation agreement with Morocco, that a person with the nationality of a Member State and of a non-Member State can *only* rely on his or her EU citizenship, not on his or her third-country nationality, in particular because a free movement right is not being invoked.[190] However, the CJEU subsequently ruled in *Kahveci and Inan* that the family members of Turkish citizens who were also nationals of a Member State could rely on such Turkish citizenship only if they wanted, on the grounds that the EU/Turkey rules aimed to extend free movement to Turkey eventually, and aimed to facilitate family reunion.[191] This judgment was in turn qualified in *Demirci*, where the CJEU limited the ability of dual citizens of Turkey and a Member State to invoke their Turkish citizenship to invoke the rules relating to social security.[192]

Logically, the *Kahveci and Inan* judgment applies by analogy to the European Economic Area (EEA) treaty (extending EU free movement law to Norway, Iceland and Liechtenstein) and to the EU/Swiss free movement treaty, given that EU free movement law as such applies to these treaties. For other cases of EU/non-EU dual citizenship, it is arguable that the position in the *Mesbah* case should be reconsidered in light of the subsequent development of EU immigration and asylum law, and/or particularly where there is a link with a human right such as family reunion or asylum, given the central role of human rights within the EU legal order.[193]

What if an EU citizen loses the nationality of a Member State and either retains (or automatically reacquires) the nationality of a third State, or thereby becomes stateless? In this scenario, assuming that the withdrawal of the Member State nationality is valid,[194] the person concerned would obviously be entitled to rely, as from the loss of his or her EU citizenship,[195] on any rights that derived from the third-country nationality which he or she retained or reacquired, or failing that, from the status of statelessness, which is a form of third-country nationality as far as EU immigration law is concerned.[196] The more challenging question is whether, in light of the loss of EU

---

[189] See I:6.6 below.
[190] Case C-179/98 *Mesbah* [1999] ECR I-7955. Although technically this judgment only considered the position of third-country national family members of such persons, the principle developed in this case must logically also apply to the dual citizens themselves.
[191] Joined Cases C-7/10 and 9/10, ECLI:EU:C:2012:180.
[192] Case C-171/13, ECLI:EU:C:2015:8. For more on association agreements, see I:6.4.3 below.
[193] See generally I:2.3 above. On the position of persons with the dual nationality of a Member State and a non-Member State as regards asylum, including cases in which the EU citizenship is lost, see I:5.4.1 above.
[194] On the limits to withdrawal of a Member State's nationality deriving from EU law, see Case C-135/08 *Rottmann* [2010] ECR I-1449.
[195] If the loss of EU citizenship was retroactive, reliance on third-country citizenship or statelessness status would take effect from the date on which citizenship was lost *de jure*.
[196] See Art 67(2) TFEU.

citizenship, the person concerned could rely on his or her third-country nationality retroactively, even before the date of losing their EU citizenship status, in particular in order to qualify themselves for (or toward) long-term residence status or status as a Turkish worker or Turkish worker's family member.[197] The answer to that question is arguably dependent on whether it had been possible to rely on third-country nationality while also an EU citizen. If so, then obviously reliance on the third-country nationality can simply continue after the loss of EU citizenship. If not, then arguably reliance on the third-country nationality (or statelessness status) can only start once the EU citizenship was lost.

No Member State has yet withdrawn from the EU, and so EU law has not yet had to address the question of whether that Member State's nationals lose their EU citizenship. The logical consequence of such a withdrawal is that the nationals of the ex-Member State lose their EU citizenship status, unless of course they also have the nationality of a remaining Member State. If such persons also have the nationality of (another) non-EU State, they can invoke that, on the basis set out above. Most obviously, they can also invoke their nationality of a newly non-Member State on the same basis. Having said that, it is possible that in practice, the details of the relationship between the EU and an ex-Member State would be regulated by a new treaty setting out *lex specialis* rules.

As for the position of family members of EU citizens whose lose their EU citizenship, if the family members are third-country nationals,[198] arguably, following the loss of EU citizenship by their sponsor, the family members would still retain any status which they had already acquired under EU free movement law, by analogy with the case law on the EU/Turkey association agreement and the free movement law rules governing other circumstances in which the link between EU citizens and family members is broken.[199] As to whether the family members could rely on their third-country nationality, the question is whether the principles in the *Mesbah* and *Kahveci and Inan* case law would apply to determine whether or not they, like EU citizens, can rely on their third-country nationality as such to obtain rights;[200] these rules might even apply where the family members retain rights as family members of EU citizens which they had obtained before the EU citizen's loss of nationality. If these principles do apply, the family members would nevertheless at least be able to rely on their third-country nationality once their sponsor had lost his or her EU citizenship, if those family members were not able to claim acquired rights under EU free movement law.[201]

---

[197] See respectively I:6.7 and I:6.4.3 below.

[198] If the family members are EU citizens, then they can continue to claim EU citizenship status in their own name, and the person who has lost EU citizenship moreover then has the right to be treated as the family member of an EU citizen. If the family members of the EU citizen who has lost his or her citizenship lose *their* EU citizenship in turn, as a direct result of the sponsor's loss of EU citizenship (ie because the family members only acquired their citizenship because of the sponsor's citizenship), then the principles set out above apply *mutatis mutandis*.

[199] On the former point, see Case C-337/07 *Altun* [2008] ECR I-10323; on the latter point, see discussion further below in this section.

[200] Although these cases concern third-country national family members of dual citizens as regards the non-EU citizenship of the *sponsor*, arguably this can be distinguished from the question of whether those family members can rely on *their own* (single) third-country nationality in its own right.

[201] Note that in either case, there might be practical complications, if the person who lost EU citizenship was the 'breadwinner', while his or her family members are not economically active.

Moving on to the details of EU free movement legislation, the EU citizen sponsor of a third-country national family member in another Member State could be *any* EU citizen, for an initial three-month period.[202] After that period, sponsors can be workers, self-employed persons, students, or others with sufficient resources and sickness insurance,[203] as defined relatively broadly by the Court of Justice's interpretation of the Treaty free movement rights and the prior secondary legislation.

Secondly, the family members who can 'accompany or join'[204] an EU citizen in another Member State are: a spouse; a registered partner (in accordance with a Member State's law) if the national law of the host State treats registered partnerships equally to marriage and in accordance with the national conditions in the host State;[205] direct descendants under twenty-one or dependents of the sponsor and of the spouse or partner; and dependent ascending relatives of the sponsor and of the spouse or partner.[206] Member States are also obliged to facilitate, in accordance with national law, the entry and residence of extended family members: persons who are dependants or members of the household in the country of origin, who require medical care from an EU citizen, or who are the partner of an EU citizen with a durable relationship which is duly attested.[207]

According to the CJEU's case law, a 'spouse' refers only to a relationship of marriage, although Member States must extend to citizens of other EU Member States the same treatment that they extend to their own citizens as regards admission of unmarried partners.[208] Spouses retain their status during marital separation and in the different stages of divorce proceedings falling short of the final legal termination of the marriage, as long as they reside in the same EU Member State as the sponsor.[209] Children also include step-children of the sponsor.[210] It should be noted that a child can invoke EU free movement law if he or she is a citizen of another Member State, even if his or her parent is a third-country national. This could even entail corollary rights for the third-country national parent of that child to stay in the country, as long as the family is not a financial burden on the host State.[211]

As for extended family members, the legal position was clarified in the *Rahman* judgment of the CJEU.[212] According to the Court, they have no right of entry and residence, but Member States are obliged to confer upon them a 'certain advantage' as

---

[202] Art 6, Dir 2004/38.

[203] Art 7(1) to (3), Dir 2004/38. The 'sufficient resources' could be supplied by a third-country family member: Case C-218/14 *Singh*, ECLI:EU:C:2015:476.

[204] Art 3(1), Dir 2004/38; see also Art 7(1)(d) and (2).

[205] On such national conditions, see by analogy Cases C-267/06 *Maruko* [2008] ECR I-1757 and C-267/12 *Hay*, ECLI:EU:C:2013:823.

[206] Art 2(2). Students still lack the right to bring in ascending relatives (Art 7(3)).

[207] Art 3(2).

[208] Case 59/85 *Reed* [1987] ECR 1283. This interpretation of the prior legislation is arguably confirmed by the explicit distinction between spouses and partners in Dir 2004/38.

[209] As regards the prior legislation, see Case 267/83 *Diatta* [1985] ECR 5671 and Case C-370/90 *Surinder Singh* [1992] ECR I-4265. The CJEU has confirmed this position as regards Directive 2004/38: see *Iida* (n 180 above) and Case C-244/13 *Ogierakhi*, ECLI:EU:C:2014:268.

[210] See *Baumbast* (n 181 above).

[211] *Chen and Zhu* (n 181 above), confirmed in Case C-86/12 *Alokpa and Others*, ECLI:EU:C:2013:645. It is not clear if the parent has the right to work in that case.

[212] Case C-83/11, ECLI:EU:C:2012:519.

compared to other third-country nationals. National authorities must undertake an 'extensive examination' of their individual circumstances, and justify their reasons for refusing entry. They must consider factors such as the degree of economic and physical dependence of the family member and the degree of relationship. Although Member States have a wide degree of discretion developing their national rules, and can impose conditions concerning the nature and duration of dependence, those rules must comply with the ordinary meaning of 'facilitate' and 'dependence', and the rules themselves and their application must be subject to judicial review. The dependence itself must exist in the country which the family member comes from, at the time when he or she applies to join the EU citizen.

Thirdly, EU free movement rules do not set waiting periods or other conditions of admission of family members above and beyond the restrictions inherent in the definitions of sponsors and family members, except for a 'dependence' requirement as regards certain (not all) family members,[213] and some limited possibilities to require a short-term visa.[214] Directive 2004/38 repealed the accommodation requirement which had previously applied to workers' family members.[215] The Directive does not permit Member States to require that third-country national family members must have been previously lawfully resident in a Member State, so those family members can invoke EU free movement law even if they were unauthorized migrants before forming a family relationship with EU citizens.[216]

As for the status of family members after admission, Directive 2004/38 grants permanent residence for EU citizens and family members after five years' legal residence.[217] Time spent in prison does not count towards this period, for either EU citizens or their third-country family members.[218] A special rule governs the acquisition of permanent residence in the event of retirement or disability of the sponsor who is a worker or self-employed, or the death of such a sponsor during his or her working life.[219] Before that point, there is one set of rules regarding the position of family members in the event of the death or departure of the EU citizen sponsor,[220] and a second set of rules governing the position after divorce, marriage annulment, or termination of a registered partnership.[221] The CJEU has clarified that if an EU citizen departs from a family

---

[213] On the definition of dependency, see: Case 316/85 *Lebon* [1987] ECR 2811; *Chen and Zhu* (n 181 above); Case C-1/05 *Jia* [2007] ECR I-1; and C-423/12 *Reyes*, ECLI:EU:C:2014:16.

[214] For details, see I:4.4.1 above. Member States cannot impose a long-term visa requirement for EU citizens' family members: see C-157/03 *Commission v Spain* [2005] ECR I-2911. For the position as regards border controls, see I:3.4.1 above.

[215] On that prior requirement, see Case 249/86 *Commission v Germany* [1989] ECR 1263.

[216] See particularly Case C-127/08 *Metock* (n 184 above), followed in Case C-551/07 *Sahin* [2008] ECR I-10453, overturning Case C-109/01 *Akrich* [2003] ECR I-9607. See earlier Case C-60/00 *Carpenter* [2002] ECR I-6279 and Case C-459/99 *MRAX* [2002] ECR I-6591; and see also *Jia* (n 213 above). See further I:7.4.1 below.

[217] Arts 16–21, Dir 2004/38. On the acquisition of that status by EU citizens, see particularly Cases C-162/09 *Lassal* [2010] ECR I-9217; C-325/09 *Dias* [2011] ECR I-6387; and C-424/10 and C-425/10 *Ziolkowski and Szeja* [2011] ECR I-14035.

[218] Respectively Cases C-400/12 *G*, ECLI:EU:C:2014:9 and C-378/12 *Onuekwere*, ECLI:EU:C:2014:13.

[219] Art 17. See Case C-257/00 *Givane* [2003] ECR I-345.   [220] Art 12, Dir 2004/38.

[221] Art 13, Dir 2004/38. The CJEU has ruled that Art 13 does not apply to unregistered partnerships: Case C-45/12 *Hadj Ahmed*, ECLI:EU:C:2013:390. On the acquisition of permanent residence by third-country nationals covered by either set of rules, see Art 18, Dir 2004/38.

member before divorce proceedings begin against a third-country national spouse, in principle EU free movement law no longer protects that spouse.[222] However, it should be noted that some family members can rely in such cases on the more favourable rules set out in other EU free movement legislation, which confers upon migrant workers' children a right to reside in order to obtain education even where the parent who is an EU citizen has left or divorced the other parent, along with a corollary right for the parent caring for that child to stay on the territory.[223] Despite this, those who only have a right to stay pursuant to the other legislation cannot claim a right to permanent residence on the basis of the 2004 Directive.[224] But the separation of the EU citizen from his or her third-country national spouse does not prevent accrual of the five years of legal residence, provided that they both continue to reside in that Member State.[225]

Family members have the right to take up employment or self-employment in all cases where an EU citizen is a resident or permanent resident,[226] along with a general right to equal treatment, including as regards social assistance, with derogations concerning social assistance and student support.[227] Member States may refuse admission to EU citizens' family members, or expel them, on grounds of public policy, public security, or public health, but such decisions are subject to strict substantive thresholds and procedural requirements identical to those applicable to EU citizens.[228]

According to the Commission report on the application of Directive 2004/38,[229] Member States' transposition of the definition of core family members in the Directive was 'satisfactory'. However, the transposition of the requirement to 'facilitate' entry of extended family members was 'less satisfactory', with thirteen Member States applying the law incorrectly (although ten Member States go further than required, and admit all such family members). Thirteen Member States admit same-sex registered partners.

---

[222] *Singh* (n 203 above).

[223] See Cases C-310/08 *Ibrahim* and C-480/08 *Teixeira* [2010] ECR I-1065, decided on the basis of Art 12 of Reg 1612/68, which was not repealed by Dir 2004/38, as interpreted previously in the judgment in *Baumbast* (n 181 above). This rule now appears as Art 10 of Reg 492/2011 ([2011] OJ L 141/1). Moreover, the child must have entered the educational system, and the child of a non-EU citizen who cohabited with (but did not marry) an EU citizen is not within the scope of these rules (*Hadj Ahmed*, n 221 above). It is not sufficient that a parent was *self*-employed (Joined Cases C-147/11 and C-148/11 *Czop and Punakova*, ECLI:EU:C:2012:538). See earlier Joined Cases 389/87 and 390/87 *Echternach and Moritz* [1989] ECR 723, on the position of older children remaining to complete their education after their parents leave the country. On the scope of the right to education, see Case 9/74 *Casagrande* [1974] ECR 773.

[224] Case C-529/11 *Alarape and Tijani*, ECLI:EU:C:2013:290.

[225] Case C-244/13 *Ogierakhi*, ECLI:EU:C:2014:268.

[226] Art 23. See in particular Cases 131/85 *Gul* [1986] ECR 1573 and C-165/05 *Commission v Luxembourg*, judgment of 27 Oct 2005, unreported. Third-country national family members only have access to employment in the Member State where the EU citizen is resident: see Case C-10/05 *Mattern and Cikotic* [2006] ECR I-3145.

[227] Art 24. See Case 32/75 *Christini* [1975] ECR 1085 (social benefits), applied to third-country national family members in Case 94/84 *Deak* [1985] ECR 1873. Equal treatment does not appear to extend to independent residence status: Cases C-356/98 *Kaba I* [2000] ECR I-2625 and C-466/00 *Kaba II* [2003] ECR I-2219, although it might be arguable that this issue could be revisited pursuant to Dir 2004/38.

[228] Arts 26–33. See further *MRAX* (n 216 above), Case C-503/03 *Commission v Spain* [2006] ECR I-1097, and the further discussion in I:3.4.1 above and I:7.4.1 below. By way of exception, the special protection for ten years' residence in Art 28(3) only applies to EU citizens.

[229] COM (2008) 840, 10 Dec 2008.

Residence rights for family members were restricted by the eleven Member States which required prior lawful entry in another Member State (following the Court's case law, later overturned), and by one Member State which imposed an accommodation requirement regarding family members. Twelve Member States did not opt to restrict the admission of students' family members beyond spouses and children, but eight of the other fifteen Member States applied the obligation to facilitate the admission of students' other family members incorrectly. In some Member States, the 'residence card' for family members had a different title, which could cause complications, and six Member States did not apply the rules on the position of third-country national family members after death, divorce, etc. correctly.

In its subsequent guidance on the correct application of the Directive,[230] the Commission asserts that in principle Member States must recognize marriages to EU citizens contracted anywhere in the world, with an exception for forced marriages (as distinct from arranged marriages). As to the definition of a 'durable partnership', a Member State could examine the length of time that the partnership had lasted, but had to consider other factors as well. The concept of 'family' includes adoptive relationships, guardians with custody of children, and possibly even foster children. Finally, while Member States may offer integration courses for EU citizens and their family members, no consequence could be attached to a refusal to attend these courses.[231]

6.4.1.2 'Static' EU citizens

The first category of EU citizens who can claim the application of EU free movement law against their own Member State as regards third-country national family members are those who have moved to another Member State, and then returned to their home Member State.[232] CJEU case law has clarified that: this right can be invoked by all EU citizens, not just those who are employed or self-employed; the 2004 citizens' Directive applies by analogy to their position on return to the home Member State;[233] some period of longer-term residence (more than three months) on the territory of the host State is necessary to trigger application of the right; and the family members must live with the EU citizen in the host State.[234]

Secondly, another category of EU citizens who can invoke free movement rules against their own Member States are those who exercise some economic activity in another Member State, while still resident in the Member State of their nationality.[235] Again, the CJEU has clarified the position of this category of persons,[236] ruling that the principle applies not just to those providing services in another Member State, but also those whose work was linked to another Member State; it must follow that the principle applies by analogy to self-employed persons, and arguably students, too. The Court

---

[230] COM (2009) 313, 2 July 2009.

[231] Compare with the position under EU immigration law (I:6.6 and I:6.7 below).

[232] *Surinder Singh* (n 209 above); see also Case C-291/05 *Eind* [2007] ECR I-10719.

[233] Although note that the EU citizen does not have to take up employment or be self-sufficient in his or her home Member State for the rules to apply (*Eind*, n 232 above).

[234] Case C-456/12 *O and B*, ECLI:EU:C:2014:135.   [235] *Carpenter* (n 216 above).

[236] Case C-457/12 *S and G*, ECLI:EU:C:2014:136.

ruled that there was an obligation to admit the third-country family member when that was necessary to guarantee the effective exercise of the EU citizen's free movement rights. One factor to be taken into account was whether the third-country national was looking after the EU citizen's child. However, the Court drew a distinction between admitting a spouse on this basis, and admitting a mother-in-law; the absence of the latter was not dissuasive to exercising free movement rights, in the Court's view.

Finally, EU citizenship law (as distinct from free movement law) can be invoked by those EU citizens who have never left their country of origin, but who would be forced to leave it if a third-country national family member is expelled (or conceivably, not admitted). This principle was first established in the well-known *Ruiz Zambrano* judgment,[237] and the CJEU has clarified its application in a number of later cases (see below). The starting point (*Ruiz Zambrano*) is that a Member State breaches the citizenship provisions of the Treaty if it deprives EU citizens of genuine enjoyment of the substance of citizenship rights, in particular by removing the third-country family member of an EU citizen to a non-EU State and thus *de facto* requiring the EU citizen to leave the territory of the Union. Equally, the Court ruled that the third-country national family member concerned also had a right to a work permit, otherwise he would not have had sufficient resources and might have been forced to leave the EU in practice, with his EU citizen child(ren) in tow.

However, in *Dereci* the Court qualified its position,[238] holding that the *Ruiz Zambrano* ruling only applied 'exceptionally', and that EU citizens could not argue that they would be deprived of substance of their EU citizenship rights merely because it was economically or personally desirable for their family members to reside with them. While *Ruiz Zambrano* concerned the third-country national parent of an EU citizen child who was dependent on that parent, *Dereci* concerned EU citizens who were not dependent upon the third-country national adult family members who wished to stay or enter Austria. The CJEU has also refused to apply *Ruiz Zambrano* where the EU citizen child of a non-EU parent was living in another Member State.[239] Where the non-EU mothers of EU children wished to be joined by their non-EU spouses, the CJEU confirmed that the *Ruiz Zambrano* case law did not only apply to blood relatives. But the permanent residence status of the non-EU mothers in the host Member State was also relevant, and the absence of any dependence of the EU citizens upon their non-EU step-fathers was decisive.[240] On the same grounds, the Court also rejected application of *Ruiz Zambrano* to a case where an EU citizen wished to be joined by his non-EU parents and brother.[241] Finally, *Ruiz Zambrano* could not apply in a case involving the non-EU parents of EU citizen children who were nationals of *another* Member State, since it would always be possible to live in that other State, rather than leave the EU altogether.[242]

---

[237] Case C-34/09 *Ruiz Zambrano* [2011] ECR I-1177.

[238] Case C-256/11 *Dereci* [2011] ECR I-11315.

[239] *Iida* (n 180 above). The CJEU also mentioned that the non-EU parent had a secure position under national law and the EU long-term residents' Directive (on which, see I:6.7 below)

[240] Joined Cases C-356/11 and C-357/11, *O and S and L*, ECLI:EU:C:2012:776. The Court's judgment also discusses whether the EU's family reunion Directive might apply instead: see I:6.6.1 below.

[241] Case C-87/12 *Ymeraga*, ECLI:EU:C:2013:291.   [242] *Alokpa and Others* (n 211 above).

Overall, the *Ruiz Zambrano* judgment seems to be limited primarily to cases where a non-EU parent looks after an EU citizen child who is a national of that Member State,[243] although it is conceivable that it applies also where there is an adult dependent relative who is an EU citizen. This situation is likely to arise either where the Member State in question takes a generous approach to conferring its nationality (ie to all children born on the territory, even if their parents are irregular migrants), or where an EU citizen and non-EU citizen have had a common child, but their relationship has ended. It is presumably not relevant that the EU citizen child could be taken into care in order to remain on the territory (otherwise the CJEU would surely have mentioned that in *Ruiz Zambrano*). Such a forced removal of a child from its parents, which would be wholly unnecessary on child welfare grounds, could hardly be described as the 'genuine enjoyment' of EU citizenship. It remains to be seen if a criminal conviction of the non-EU parent might be relevant,[244] and whether *Ruiz Zambrano* still applies if an EU citizen parent could take responsibility for the child if the non-EU parent were removed.[245]

6.4.2 Social security coordination

The second case where non-JHA EU law applies to third-country nationals in part in the context of immigration is EU law on coordination of social security. This subject is closely connected to free movement law, but a separate Regulation (dating previously from 1971, then replaced by a Regulation adopted in 2004) sets out detailed rules on social security coordination for all EU citizens who exercise rights of free movement within the EU, and all of their family members.[246] Family members of EU citizens, including third-country national family members, used to be covered by a rule—known as the 'derived rights' rule—that restricted their ability to rely on the legislation in their own name. However, in 1996 the Court of Justice largely scrapped that rule, and thus enhanced the application of the legislation to family members of EU citizens.[247]

Both the 1971 Regulation and the 2004 Regulation also apply to stateless persons and refugees, and in 2001 the Court of Justice delivered its *Khalil and Addou* judgment on the scope and validity of the application of the 1971 Regulation to these groups.[248] In this judgment, the Court concluded that the Council had validly included such categories of persons within the scope of the EC's then-existing social security Regulation by using what was originally Article 51 EEC (later Article 42 EC, and now Article 48 TFEU) as a 'legal base' for adoption of the legislation. But the Court also ruled that the legislation only governed the position of refugees and stateless persons when they

---

[243] Compare with the position under human rights law, cf the *Jeunesse v Netherlands* case discussed in I:6.3.1 above.

[244] See the pending Cases C-165/14 *Rendon Marin* and C-304/14 *CS*.

[245] See the pending Cases C-115/15 *NA* and C-133/15 *Chavez-Vilchez*.

[246] Until 1 May 2010, the applicable law was Reg 1408/71 [1971] OJ L 149/2. This Reg was replaced from that date by Reg 883/2004 ([2004] OJ L 166/1), when Reg 987/2009 ([2009] OJ L 284/1) implementing Reg 883/2004 entered into force (see Art 91, Reg 883/2004, and Art 97, Reg 987/2009).

[247] Case C-308/93 *Cabanis-Issarte* [1996] ECR I-2097. See comments by S Peers, 'Equality, Free Movement and Social Security' (1997) 22 ELRev 342. The 'derived rights' rule still applies to unemployment benefits: see Case C-189/00 *Ruhr* [2001] ECR I-8225.

[248] Joined Cases C-95/99 to 98/99 *Khalil and others* and C-180/99 *Addou* [2001] ECR I-7413.

moved within the Community (now the Union). It followed that refugees and stateless persons did not have the right to equal treatment in a single Member State. At the time, this meant that the legislation had little impact, since refugees and stateless persons did not then have the right to move between Member States—although it was relevant if they were posted to another Member State by their employer to carry out services.[249] Subsequently, it has become more relevant, since refugees and persons with subsidiary protection (some of whom may be stateless) have the right to move between Member States following an amendment of the EU's long-term residence Directive in 2011.[250]

Apart from the categories of family members of EU citizens exercising free movement rights, and stateless persons and refugees, there are also social security rules for some categories of persons covered by association agreements and 'immigration law' legislation applying to third-country nationals in general.[251] Arguably the latter rules were initially adopted using the wrong 'legal base' (the immigration provisions of the EC Treaty, as they then were), but the later version of these rules adopted after the Treaty of Lisbon, correctly used the immigration law powers of the EU.[252] It is not clear whether persons with refugee status can rely on the association agreements as regards social security, if they have the relevant nationality other than the agreement with Turkey.[253] However, it seems clear that persons with dual nationality of an EU Member State and a non-EU country cannot rely on the association agreements as regards social security, except arguably where the relevant agreement creates or is linked to free movement rights (ie, the EEA and the treaties with Switzerland).[254]

6.4.3 Association agreements

The third category of cases where non-JHA EU law applies to third-country nationals is the case of association agreements concluded by the EU (previously the Community) and (usually) its Member States with non-EU countries. The Court of Justice has ruled that such agreements form an integral part of EU law;[255] that it can interpret their provisions, even those relating to immigration;[256] that provisions in these agreements can have 'direct effect' allowing individuals to rely on them in their national courts, where those provisions are clear, precise, and unconditional;[257] and that where the agreements have similar or identical wording to EU free movement rules, the agreements

---

[249] See I:6.4.4 below.   [250] See I:6.7 below.   [251] See respectively I:6.4.3 and I:6.8 below.

[252] On the legal base issue, see I:6.2.4 above.

[253] This point was relevant in *Khalil and Addou* (n 248 above), but was not referred by the national court, which assumed that refugees could not rely on the EU-Morocco agreement. For the argument that refugees *can* rely on such agreements, see S Peers, case note on *Khalil and Addou* (2002) 39 CMLRev 1395. The Court of Justice has since confirmed, in Case C-337/07 *Altun* [2008] ECR I-10323, that the family members of a Turkish worker with refugee status are covered by the relevant rules in the EU-Turkey agreement. This judgment obviously strengthens the general argument that persons governed by association agreements can rely on the rules in the agreements even if they have refugee status.

[254] See Case C-179/98 *Mesbah* [1999] ECR I-7955 and the discussion in I:6.4.1 above. There are particular issues as to whether dual citizens of Turkey and a Member State can rely upon the relevant rules: see I:6.4.3 below.

[255] Case 181/73 *Hagemann* [1974] ECR 449.   [256] Case 12/86 *Demirel* [1987] ECR 3719.

[257] *Demirel* (n 256 above); see also Case 104/81 *Kupferberg* [1982] ECR 3641.

will not *necessarily* be interpreted the same way.[258] A number of these agreements contain provisions on immigration, or at least some aspects of the status of migrants, but these specific clauses vary widely in scope. It is therefore necessary to consider the relevant migration provisions of each agreement in turn.

First of all, the European Economic Area (EEA) agreement with Norway, Iceland, and Liechtenstein essentially fully extends the EU rules on free movement of persons, including rules on mutual recognition of qualifications and social security, to these States.[259] Secondly, most of the EU free movement rules (except for the imposition of transitional periods and certain limitations on the right to provide services) also apply to Switzerland, pursuant to a bilateral treaty on free movement of persons which entered into force on 1 June 2002.[260] The Court of Justice has ruled on the provisions of this treaty as regards self-employed frontier workers, but has also confirmed that legal persons cannot derive rights from it, and that services providers do not have a non-discrimination right.[261] As regards social security, these treaties mean that nationals of Norway, Iceland, Liechtenstein, and Switzerland are covered both by the right to equal social security treatment in one EU Member State and by the coordination rules if they move to another EU Member State.

Thirdly, the position of Turkish citizens is particularly complex. Their status in EU law is governed by several instruments: the original 1963 Association Agreement with Turkey; a 1970 Protocol to that Agreement; Decisions 2/76 and 1/80 of the Association Council established by that Agreement concerning the access to employment of Turkish workers and their family members; and Decision 3/80 of the Association Council, concerning Turkish workers' social security.[262] First of all, the original association agreement sets out a goal of full free movement of workers, services, and self-employed persons. The Court of Justice has ruled that these provisions set out only a goal to be achieved and therefore do not confer 'directly effective' rights on individuals which can be enforced in the national courts.[263] Next, the 1970 Protocol sets a deadline to achieve the goal of free movement of workers and sets a standstill barring any new national rules which make establishment of the provision of services between the parties more difficult than it was before that Protocol entered into force. The Court of Justice has ruled that the 'workers' provisions in the Protocol are not directly effective, but that the two standstill clauses are.[264]

---

[258] Case 270/80 *Polydor* [1982] ECR 329.

[259] [1994] OJ L 1/1. See Case C-92/02 *Kristiansen* [2003] ECR I-14597, para 24.

[260] [2002] OJ L 114. See S Peers, 'The EC-Switzerland Agreement on Free Movement of Persons: Overview and Analysis' (2000) 2 EJML 127.

[261] Cases: C-13/08 *Stamm* [2008] ECR I-11087; C-351/08 *Grimme* [2009] ECR I-10777; C-541/08 *Fokus Invest* [2010] ECR I-1025; C-70/09 *Hengartner and Gasser* [2011] ECR I-7233; C-257/10 *Bergstrom* [2011] ECR I-13227; C-506/10 *Graf and Engel* [2011] ECR I-9345; C-425/11 *Ettwein*, ECLI:EU:C:2013:121; C-241/14, *Bukovansky*, ECLI:EU:C:2015:766; and the discussion of the Court's jurisdiction over and legal effect of the agreement in the Opinion in the withdrawal case of *Zentralbetriebsrat der Landeskrankenhäuser Tirols and Land Tirol* (Case C-339/05 [2006] ECR I-7097).

[262] The Agreement is published in [1977] OJ L 261/60; the Protocol is published [1972] JO L 293/1; Decision 3/80 is published at [1983] OJ C 110/60; the other Decisions are unpublished in the OJ.

[263] *Demirel*, n 256 above (workers), Case C-37/98 *Savas* [2000] ECR I-2927 (self-employed persons). The same is undoubtedly true as regards services.

[264] *Demirel*, n 256 above (workers), *Savas*, n 263 above (self-employed persons); Joined Cases C-317/01 and C-369/01 *Abatay and others* [2003] ECR I-12301 (services).

Next, Decisions 2/76 and 1/80 (which replaced Decision 2/76) set out detailed rules regarding Turkish workers and their family members, falling short of full free movement rights. The Court of Justice has delivered over forty judgments on these provisions.[265] For Turkish workers, the key provision in Decision 1/80 is Article 6(1), which provides that '...a Turkish worker duly registered as belonging to the labour force of a Member State:' is entitled to a renewed work permit after one year's 'legal employment' in order 'to work for the same employer, if a job is available'. That worker is then entitled to respond to another job offer 'in the same occupation' after three years' legal employment, subject to priority for EU workers. Finally, the Turkish worker has free access to any paid employment after four years' legal employment. Article 6(2) provides that annual holidays, maternity absences, work accidents, and short sicknesses count as 'legal employment', and that involuntary unemployment duly certified and long absences due to sickness 'shall not affect rights acquired as the result of the preceding period of employment'. For family members, Article 7(1) of Decision 1/80 provides that '[t]he members of the family of a Turkish worker duly registered as belonging to the labour force of a Member State, who have been authorized to join him' are entitled to respond to offer of employment after three years legal residence, subject to EU nationals' priority, and then have free access to any paid employment after five years' residence. Article 7(2) provides that '[c]hildren of Turkish workers who have completed a course of vocational training in the host country may respond to any offer of employment there, irrespective of the length of time they have been resident in that Member State, provided one of their parents has been legally employed in the Member State concerned for at least three years'. Article 9 states that Turkish children resident with parents who are or have been legally employed in a Member State have equal treatment in access to education in that State (compared to that State's nationals) as regards their qualifications, and 'may' be able to take advantage of the relevant benefits. Article 10 provides for a right to equal treatment in working conditions; Article 13 provides for a standstill on any new restrictions on access to employment for legally resident Turkish workers and their family members; and Article 14(1) specifies that

---

[265] Cases: C-192/89 *Sevince* [1990] ECR I-3461; C-237/91 *Kus* [1992] ECR I-6781; C-355/93 *Eroglu* [1994] ECR I-5113; C-434/93 *Bozkurt* [1995] ECR I-1475; C-171/95 *Tetik* [1997] ECR I-329; C-351/95 *Kadiman* [1997] ECR I-2133; C-386/95 *Eker* [1997] ECR I-2697; C-285/95 *Kol* [1997] ECR I-3095; C-36/96 *Günaydin* [1997] ECR I-5143; C-98/96 *Ertanir* [1997] ECR I-5179; C-210/97 *Akman* [1998] ECR I-7519; C-1/97 *Birden* [1998] ECR I-7747; C-340/97 *Nazli* [2000] ECR I-957; C-329/97 *Ergat* [2000] ECR I-1487; C-65/98 *Eyup* (n 165 above); C-188/00 *Kurz* [2002] ECR I-10691; C-171/01 *Birklite* [2003] ECR I-1487; *Abatay and others*, n 264 above; C-275/02 *Ayaz* [2004] ECR I-8765; C-467/02 *Cetinkaya* [2004] ECR I-10895; C-136/03 *Dorr and Unal* [2005] ECR I-4759; C-373/03 *Aydinli* [2005] ECR I-6181; C-374/03 *Gurol* [2005] ECR I-6199; C-383/03 *Dogan* [2005] ECR I-6237; C-230/03 *Sedef* [2006] ECR I-157; Case C-502/04 *Torun* [2006] ECR I-1563; C-4/05 *Guzeli* [2006] ECR I-10279; C-325/05 *Derin* [2007] ECR I-6495; C-349/06 *Polat* [2007] ECR I-8167; C-294/06 *Payir and others* [2008] ECR I-203; C-152/08 *Kahveci* [2008] ECR I-6291; C-453/07 *Er* [2008] ECR I-7299; C-337/07 *Altun* [2008] ECR I-10323; C-242/06 *Sahin* [2009] ECR I-8465; C-462/08 *Bekleyen* [2010] ECR I-563; C-14/09 *Genc* [2010] ECR I-931; C-92/07 *Commission v Netherlands* [2010] ECR I-3683; C-484/07 *Pehlivan* [2011] ECR I-5203; C-303/08 *Bozkurt* [2010] ECR I-13445; C-371/08 *Ziebell* [2011] ECR I-12735; C-300/09 and C-301/09 *Toprak and Oguz* [2010] ECR I-12845; C-7/10 and 9/10 *Kahveci and Inan*, ECLI:EU:C:2012:180; C-187/10 *Unal* [2011] ECR I-9045; C-268/11 *Gulbahce*, ECLI:EU:C:2012:695; C-451/11 *Dulger*, ECLI:EU:C:2012:504; and C-225/12 *Demir*, EU:C:2013:725. See also Case C-465/01 *Commission v Austria* [2004] ECR I-8291. There is one pending case: C-561/14 *Genc*.

the provisions of the Decision are 'subject to limitations justified on grounds of public policy, public security or public health'.

The key points established in the jurisprudence are that the Court of Justice has the competence to interpret Decision 1/80;[266] that Articles 6, 7, 9, 10, and 13 of the Decision are directly effective;[267] and that the right to employment brings with it a right to residence.[268] However, the Court has constantly made clear that the Decision does not affect national control over initial entry and employment of Turkish workers or family members,[269] and does not grant right to free movement between Member States.[270] Also, the Decision should be interpreted consistently with EU free movement case law 'as far as possible'.[271]

The standstill on establishment and services should also be interpreted consistently with EU free movement law as far as possible.[272] It has a significant impact on EU law on borders and visas,[273] and limits the application of rules on irregular migration.[274] As regards legal migration, it restrains the increases in fees for residence permits,[275] and prevents Member States from making the rules on family reunion more restrictive, as regards either self-employed Turkish citizens who want to join a family member,[276] or self-employed Turks who want their family member to join them.[277] However, in the latter case the Court ruled that an exception to a standstill could be 'justified by an over-riding reason in the public interest', if it was 'suitable to achieve the legitimate objective pursued and does not go beyond what is necessary in order to attain it'. However, even if a new restriction on family reunion was justified, it could only be applied on a case-by-case basis.[278]

As for the rules on Turkish workers, the case law has made clear that the definition of a 'Turkish worker' follows the same broad definition applicable in EU free movement law.[279] The concept of registration in the labour force simply means that Turkish workers must comply with rules on entry to the Member States' territory and initial

---

[266] *Sevince* (n 265 above).
[267] See *Sevince and Kus* (Arts 6 and 13); *Kadiman* (Art 7(1)); *Eroglu* (Art 7(2)); *Gurol* (Art 9); and *Birklite* (Art 10) (all n 265 above).
[268] See *Sevince and Kus* (Art 6); *Kadiman* (Art 7(1)); and *Eroglu* (Art 7(2)).
[269] The case law in recent years has failed to point out that EU legislation now impacts upon national competence in these areas: see the legislation discussed in I:6.5 and I:6.6 below.
[270] See particularly *Tetik*, n 265 above. Again, the EU's long-term residence Directive (I:6.7 below) now addresses this issue, as does the legislation on researchers, students, intra-corporate transferees, and Blue Card holders (I:6.5 below).
[271] Case law starting with *Bozkurt*, n 265 above. Dual nationals of a Member State and Turkey can benefit from the rules: see *Kahveci and Inan* (n 265 above) and the broader discussion in I:6.4.1 above.
[272] See the judgment in *Abatay*, n 264 above, paras 101 and 110.
[273] See Cases: C-16/05 *Tum and Dari* [2007] ECR I-7415; C-228/06 *Soysal* [2009] ECR I-1031; and C-221/11 *Demirkan*, ECLI:EU:C:2013:583, discussed in I:3.4.2 and I:4.4.2 above.
[274] Case C-186/10 *Oguz* [2011] ECR I-6957, discussed in I:7.4.2 below.
[275] *Commission v Netherlands* (n 265 above).   [276] Case C-256/11 *Dereci* [2011] ECR I-11315.
[277] Case C-138/13 *Dogan*, ECLI:EU:C:2014:2066.
[278] It is not clear how much the position under the standstill substantively differs from the position under the family reunion Directive (see I:6.6.1 below). However, the limitations on the scope of that Directive as regards the sponsor (holding a residence permit of one year's duration with a prospect of permanent residence; exclusion of EU citizens' family members and persons with subsidiary protection) do not apply to the EU/Turkey standstill, as is evident from *Dereci* (which concerned the family member of an EU citizen).
[279] See particularly *Ertanir, Gunaydin, Birden, Kurz, Payir,* and *Genc* (n 265 above).

access to employment,[280] plus maintain a territorial link with a Member State;[281] it does not permit Member States to establish distinct labour markets on which Turkish workers cannot participate.[282] Next, the requirement of 'legal employment' means that the Turkish worker must have a 'stable and secure situation on the labour force', or in other words authorized residence.[283] However, it is clear that Turkish workers can obtain rights under Article 6 of Decision 1/80 even if their entry and employment was authorized on grounds other than entry for employment, such as to marry a host state national,[284] where the worker was permitted to enter for a limited period only,[285] as a refugee,[286] or as a student.[287]

Regarding the time periods set out in Article 6, the Court has established that Turkish workers cannot claim rights under the first indent of that Article if they changed their employers during the first year,[288] and similarly cannot claim rights after three or four years if they changed employers before that point.[289] However, after four years, their access to employment must be fully equal to that of EU citizens.[290] Turkish workers lose status under Article 6 once they have completely retired or become permanently disabled,[291] but they do not lose status immediately upon voluntary unemployment, but have a 'reasonable period' to find work.[292] Moreover, they do not lose status under Article 6 just because they have been in prison for any reason.[293] The list of circumstances set out in Article 6(2) where the clock either 'keeps ticking' for the acquisition of a Turkish worker's rights under Article 6 or where the clock is 'stopped' is non-exhaustive; rights can also be acquired or frozen where comparable legitimate reasons for interruption of employment exist.[294]

As for Article 7(1),[295] during the first three years of the family member's residence in the host Member State, it only confers rights to stay if that family member stays with the Turkish worker that he or she was 'authorized to join', unless there is an objective reason to live apart such as work or education.[296] However, after that point, the family member has independent rights to seek employment, with the corollary right to reside, even if he or she spends some time in prison and/or ceases employment or does not actually take up employment, or becomes independent of his or her parents, or the sponsor's residence right is called into question retroactively, and even if the worker which the family member joined is no longer employed in the host Member State.[297]

---

[280] See *Birden*, n 265 above.   [281] *Bozkurt*, n 265 above.   [282] *Birden*, n 265 above.
[283] See *Sevince and Kus* (n 265 above) in which the Court made clear that a Turkish worker cannot gain the status of legal employment just because national law allowed the worker to work while contesting a deportation order, and *Kol* (n 265 above), in which the Court established that Turkish workers could not obtain rights under the Decision if it was proven that they entered on the basis of fraud (all cases n 265 above).
[284] *Kus*, n 265 above. On the impact of separation from a partner or divorce, see also *Unal* and *Gulbahce*, n 265 above.
[285] *Ertanir*, n 265 above.   [286] *Altun*, n 265 above. See I:5.4.2 above.
[287] *Payir*, n 265 above.   [288] *Eker*, n 265 above.   [289] *Eroglu* and *Sedef*, both n 265 above.
[290] *Tetik*, n 265 above.   [291] *Bozkurt*, n 265 above.   [292] *Tetik*, n 265 above.
[293] *Nazli* and *Dogan*, n 265 above.   [294] *Sedef*, n 265 above.
[295] On the relationship between Arts 6 and 7, see *Aydinli*, n 265 above.
[296] *Kadiman*, n 265 above. A child of a worker retains Art 7 status if she gets married during this period, as long as she continues to live with that worker (*Pehlivan*).
[297] *Ergat*, *Cetinkaya*, *Aydinli*, *Derin*, *Altun*, and *Er*, n 265 above. See also *Bozkurt*: if the spouse of the Turkish worker gets divorced from that worker after the three year period, that spouse retains rights gained

A 'family member' includes a spouse and child,[298] comprising also step-children and children born on the territory of the relevant Member State;[299] it can even include an unmarried partner, at least where a married couple divorced, stayed together, and then remarried.[300] It can also include a third-country national (in this context, a citizen of neither the EU nor Turkey).[301]

Article 7(2) applies independently of Article 7(1), so can confer rights on Turkish graduates even if they entered a Member State as a student, not as a family member of a Turkish worker.[302] The Court has also established that the condition of three years' residence for one of the graduate's parents set out in Article 7(2) can be fulfilled before the graduate's entry into the workforce; Article 7(2) will even benefit the graduate if the parent has returned to Turkey, it the graduate has become independent of his or her parents or began education after the parent left the country, or if the graduate does not in fact take up employment.[303] Following five years' residence pursuant to Article 7(1) of the Decision, or upon graduation pursuant to Article 7(2) of the Decision, family members must be treated equally to EU citizens as regards access to employment.[304]

Article 9 applies even if the children are no longer residing with their parents due to attendance at an educational institution, and gives a right to equal treatment as regards educational grants, even when pursuing higher education in Turkey. Also, by analogy with the case law on Articles 6 and 7 of the Decision, it seems likely that children falling within the scope of Article 9 have a right of residence corollary to their right to equal treatment to education.[305]

Next, the Court has ruled that Article 10 of the Decision, which sets out the right to equal treatment in working conditions, is directly effective and has a similar meaning to the equivalent right which EU free movement law extends to EU citizens and their family members. In particular, it gives a right to equal treatment as regards elections to works councils, access to professional sports matches, and further rights of residence.[306]

As for the standstill on new restrictions on access to employment for legally employed workers and their family members in Article 13, this rule is not restricted in scope to those Turkish workers and family members who were resident when Decision 1/80 entered into force, but also covers persons who have entered the host Member State since then. However, it does not cover Turkish workers unless they have an intention to integrate into the host Member State.[307] The persons concerned must be lawfully resident, but status under Article 10 of the Decision is not lost just, for example, because of technical difficulties renewing residence permits, where the person's underlying residence status remains legal.[308] To benefit from the standstill, the persons concerned

---

pursuant to Art 7, even in the event of domestic violence against the worker. The criminal offences are addressed by Art 14 of Decision 1/80.

[298] *Kadiman* and *Ergat*, n 265 above.   [299] See respectively *Ayaz* and *Cetinkaya*, n 265 above.

[300] *Eyup*, n 265 above.   [301] *Dulger*, n 265 above.   [302] *Eroglu* and *Bekleyen*, n 265 above.

[303] See *Akman, Torun, Derin*, and *Bekleyen* (all n 265 above).

[304] *Ergat* and *Akman* (both n 265 above).

[305] See the reasoning of the Court of Justice as regards EU citizens' residence rights derived from the rights of access to education in *Raulin* (n 181 above).

[306] *Birklite, Kahveci*, and *Guzeli* (all n 265 above).   [307] *Abatay and others* (n 264 above).

[308] See *Sahin*, n 265 above, applying case law concerning Art 7 of the Decision (*Ergat*, n 265 above). On the meaning of lawful residence, see *Demir*, n 265 above. The same judgment clarifies that the standstill applies to any new rules extending the concept of unlawful residence.

need not have qualified for status under Article 6 of Decision 1/80; indeed the Court has apparently suggested that only persons *not* covered by Article 6 of the Decision are covered by Article 13.[309] With respect, it is submitted that the Court of Justice should rethink this case law, since the wording of Article 13 of the Decision does not restrict its scope either to persons with an intention to integrate into the host Member State or to persons who are not covered by Article 6 of the Decision.[310] Excluding the latter category of persons from the scope of Article 13 of the Decision could prevent a significant number of people from relying on that Article, and either exclusion frustrates the underlying objective of interpreting the Turkish rules in the same way as the EU free movement rules as far as possible.[311]

Furthermore, the case law establishes that the standstill cannot result in Turkish nationals being treated better than EU citizens, although any difference between the two categories must be proportionate.[312] The Court of Justice has also confirmed that the standstill applies where the national rules in question became more favourable after the standstill date, but then the Member State purported to make those national rules more restrictive again.[313] In such cases, the standstill freezes the later more favourable national rules.

Finally, the Court has ruled that Article 14(1) of the Decision must be interpreted consistently with the former Article 39(3) EC (now Article 45(3) TFEU), meaning that Turkish workers and their family members cannot be expelled as part of a policy of treating foreigners harshly for commission of crimes as a deterrent or imposing automatic expulsions; they can only be expelled where their personal conduct is a serious present threat to one of the fundamental interests of society.[314] The CJEU has ruled that the higher standards established by Directive 2004/38 to limit expulsion of long-settled EU citizens and their family members do not also apply to Turkish workers and their family members.[315]

As for the social security rights of Turkish workers and their family members, the Court of Justice has ruled that while the equal treatment provisions of Decision 3/80

---

[309] *Sahin, Commission v Netherlands*, and *Toprak and Oguz*, n 265 above. The same principle should *not* apply by analogy to family members, since they are covered by Art 7 of the Decision from the outset (see *Kadiman*, n 265 above).

[310] This means that the standstill should apply also to pre-existing rules which benefited persons who had already obtained some status pursuant to Art 6 of Decision 1/80. For example, Art 13 should cover a national rule which applied when Decision 1/80 entered into force in the Member State concerned, and which allowed access to the entire labour market after *two* years' work with the same employer.

[311] See the example in the previous footnote. If Art 13 of Decision 1/80 did not apply to such a rule, all persons who have worked between two and four years for the same employer would be unable to rely on the continued application of such a rule. There might even be paradoxical cases where persons who had worked for less than one year with the same employer would be better off than people who had worked for the same employer for longer periods. Moreover, unlike Art 7 of the Decision (see *Aydinli*, n 265 above) Art 13 is not 'subject to' Art 6.

[312] See *Sahin* and *Commission v Netherlands* (both n 265 above).

[313] *Toprak* and *Oguz*, n 265 above.

[314] Case law beginning with *Nazli*, n 265 above. See further I:7.4.2 below.

[315] *Ziebell* (n 265 above), which also linked the EU/Turkey level of protection with the EU legislation on long-term residents (see I:6.7.1 below). An earlier reference on this issue pre-dated the application of Directive 2004/38 (*Polat*, n 265 above). On the substance of these higher levels of protection, see I:7.4.1 below.

are directly effective, the coordination rules in that Decision cannot apply until the EU adopts internal legislation to apply them.[316] Arguably, in light of the adoption of internal EU legislation coordinating the social security rights of all third-country nationals who move within the EU,[317] such a measure is now unnecessary, although a Decision to this end will likely be adopted soon (see below).

A general point arises as regards the potential cross-over between rules in EU immigration legislation and the rights derived from the association agreement. Since treaties concluded by the EU take precedence over secondary EU legislation, the latter cannot set standards lower than the former.[318] But conversely, where the legislation sets higher standards than the association agreement, it would not conflict with the agreement to apply those higher standards to Turkish workers and their family members, since applying such higher standards would be consistent with the objective of enhancing the position of Turkish workers and their family members as much as possible with a view to applying the full internal market rules in future.[319]

These first three association agreements have each led to case law on the correct legal base for social security measures.[320] In each case, the UK challenged the 'legal base' of Council Decisions which established the EU's position as regards the extension of revised EU rules on social security coordination to particular third countries. In each case, the Council decided that the correct legal base was Article 48 TFEU, concerning the coordination of social security for employed and self-employed workers within the EU, which does not provide for an opt-out. But the UK argued that Article 79 TFEU, the immigration legal base which does provide for an opt-out, applied.

In the first judgment (on the EEA), the CJEU ruled that Article 48 TFEU had to be used because: the EEA was a particularly close association between the EU and the countries concerned; the decision aimed to extend the whole EU internal market to those countries; the relevant provisions of the TFEU and EEA treaty were the same; the EEA has particular rules on the legal effect of EEA law; the decision also applied to EU citizens in the third countries concerned; the decision merely updated prior commitments; and it would be difficult to ensure free movement in the event of parallel regimes. Article 79 TFEU could not be used, because it was 'manifestly irreconcilable' with the context and objectives of the EEA.

---

[316] Respectively, Cases C-262/96 *Surul* [1999] ECR I-2685 and C-277/94 *Taflan-Met* [1996] ECR I-4085. See further Joined Cases C-102/98 *Kocak* and C-211/98 *Ors* [2000] ECR I-1287; Case C-485/07 *Akdas* [2011] ECR I-4499; Case C-171/13 *Demirci*, ECLI:EU:C:2015:8; and on the distinction between equal treatment rules and coordination rules, Case C-373/02 *Ozturk* [2004] ECR I-3605. See S Peers, 'Equality, Free Movement and Social Security' (1997) 22 EL Rev 342 and 'Social Security Equality for Turkish Nationals' (1999) 24 EL Rev 627.

[317] See I:6.8 below.

[318] The Court of Justice has confirmed this point: see the judgments in *Payir* and *Soysal* (nn 265 and 273 above). Moreover, the principle is expressly set out in the relevant EU immigration legislation (see I:6.5 to I:6.7 below), although not in EU asylum legislation, which might also interact with the EU/Turkey rules in practice (see *Altun*, n 265 above).

[319] See S Peers, 'EU Migration Law and Association Agreements' in B Martenczuk and S van Thiel, eds., *Justice, Liberty, Security: New Challenges for EU External Relations* (VUBPress, 2008), 53.

[320] Cases: C-431/11, *UK v Council* (EEA), ECLI:EU:C:2013:589; C-656/11, *UK v Council* (Swiss), ECLI:EU:C:2014:97; and C-81/13, *UK v Council* (Turkey), ECLI:EU:C:2014:2449.

Most of those points were unique to the EEA, but in its second judgment, the CJEU extended this case law to cover the EU/Swiss decision as well. It reasons were that: Switzerland has a 'vast' number of treaties with the EU which aim to strengthen the EU/Swiss economic relationship, even though the Swiss had voted not to participate in the EU internal market, via means of the EEA; the EU/Swiss treaty has the same wording as Article 48 TFEU; and the decision simply extends the revised EU rules to the third country concerned. The CJEU also ruled that Article 48 TFEU can apply to third-country nationals where an association agreement (which was the basis for the approval for the 'package' of seven EU agreements with Switzerland, in 1999) has already extended EU social security rules to the country concerned, and the decision in question merely aims to update the references concerned. Finally, the CJEU rejected the UK's argument that Article 48 could not apply to the rules on social security for those Swiss citizens not exercising economic activities (who are outside the scope of Article 48), on the grounds that this aspect of the new decision was purely ancillary to the rules on employed and self-employed persons.

Thirdly, the Court ruled against the UK's challenge on the amendment of social security rules concerning Turkey, on somewhat different grounds. In the Court's view, in this case the correct legal base was Article 48 *as well as* Article 217 TFEU, the legal base for the adoption of measures implementing association agreements (so again, there was no opt out). This was because the draft Decision was not an immigration measure, but constituted a further stage securing freedom of movement of workers between the EU and Turkey, in accordance with the association agreement. But since free movement of workers had not yet been established (unlike the cases of the EEA and Switzerland), Article 48 TFEU alone was the wrong legal base too, since it could only be used for external relations 'as a rule' where third States 'can be placed on the same footing' as an EU Member State. But Articles 48 and 217 combined were the correct legal bases because the latter provision allowed the EU to adopt measures 'in the framework of an association agreement', alongside the legal base corresponding to a particular area (in this case, social security). Furthermore, although Article 217 required a unanimous vote to conclude an association agreement or to supplement or amend its institutional framework, it only required a qualified majority vote where (as in this case) it was used only to implement an association agreement.

In fact, the Council has taken a number of other decisions regarding social security rules for associated countries, based on Article 79 TFEU as the UK has advocated (see further below). On the basis of the prior case law, it could be argued that these measures should have been based on Articles 48 and 217 TFEU in conjunction—with no opt-out. However, it is uncertain how much the objective of future free movement of workers between the EU and Turkey (an objective absent from other association agreements) was crucial to the Court's latest judgment. The Commission has also argued for a broader strategy toward social security and third countries, in a communication adopted in 2012.[321] If social security treaties were adopted *outside* the framework of an association agreement, as the Commission suggests, then there is a stronger argument

---

[321] COM (2012) 153, 30 Mar 2012.

for using Article 79 TFEU. However, the Council does not seem interested in agreeing such treaties.

Next, the Europe Agreements with Central and Eastern European countries are no longer in force, but contained four key provisions on migration: the right of establishment; the right to equal treatment in working conditions; the right of specified legally resident family members of a worker to take up employment in a Member State; and the right of corporations to send certain key employees to an establishment in a Member State.[322] These provisions could be relevant by analogy to the interpretation of the Stabilization and Association Agreements (SAAs) in force with the Western Balkans states.[323] These agreements are similar to the Europe Agreements, except that rules on the self-employed will not be discussed or adopted until five years after the agreements entered into force.[324] The Association Councils have adopted decisions to implement the social security rules as regards Croatia, the former Yugoslav Republic of Macedonia, Albania, and Montenegro.[325]

The case law on the Europe Agreements held that the right to establishment was directly effective and carried with it a corollary right of entry and residence; it precluded the imposition of 'economic needs' tests upon nationals of Central and Eastern Europe who wished to enter the EU to create a company or work as a self-employed person. The concept of 'establishment' had the same broad meaning as it does under EU free movement law as regards the types of activities covered (even potentially prostitution), but since the Europe Agreements permitted EU Member States to maintain immigration law restrictions, checks could be imposed in advance of taking up self-employment to ensure that the planned activity did not constitute disguised employment, and Member States could oblige persons without existing residence rights to submit an application from outside the territory.[326] As regards equality in working conditions, the Court of Justice held that this was a directly effective right and should be interpreted the same way as the equivalent right guaranteed by EU free movement law; therefore it precluded indirect discrimination in state-sector employment contracts and rules of private associations which restricted the number of Eastern European nationals who can play at any given time for a professional sports team.[327] There was never any case law on the other two migration rights guaranteed by the Europe Agreements, and the powers to adopt social security rules provided for in each Europe Agreement were not exercised.[328]

---

[322] Europe Agreements with Poland, Hungary, the Slovak and Czech Republics, Latvia, Lithuania, Estonia, Slovenia, Romania, and Bulgaria (respectively [1993] OJ L 347 and 348; [1994] OJ L 359 and 360; [1998] OJ L 26, 51, and 68; [1999] OJ L 51; and [1994] OJ L 357 and 358).

[323] [2004] OJ L 84 (Former Yugoslav Republic of Macedonia); [2005] OJ L 26 (Croatia); [2009] OJ L 107 (Albania); [2010] OJ L 108 (Montenegro); [2013] OJ L 278 (Serbia); and [2015] OJ L 164 (Bosnia-Herzegovina). An SAA has also been agreed with Kosovo (COM (2015) 183, 30 Apr 2015), but it is not yet in force.

[324] See further I:3.4.1 above.   [325] [2010] OJ L 306 and [2012] OJ L 340.

[326] See Cases: C-63/99 *Gloszczuk* [2001] ECR I-6369; C-235/99 *Kondova* [2001] ECR I-6427; C-257/99 *Barkoci and Malik* [2001] ECR I-6557; C-268/99 *Jany* [2001] ECR I-8615; C-327/02 *Panayotova* [2004] ECR I-11055; and C-101/10 *Pavlov and Famira* [2011] ECR I-5951. For more on the border control and visas aspects of the Europe Agreements, see I:3.4.2 and I:4.4.2 above.

[327] See Cases C-162/00 *Pokrzeptowicz-Meyer* [2002] ECR I-1049 and C-438/00 *Calpak* [2003] ECR I-4135.

[328] Commission proposals to use these powers (COM (1999) 675 to 684, 20 Dec 1999) were not agreed. The Commission withdrew the proposals ([2006] OJ C 64/3 and COM (2007) 640, 23 Oct 2007).

Also, there are Partnership and Cooperation Agreements (PCAs) in force with Russia and all other ex-Soviet states except Belarus and Turkmenistan.[329] These agreements provide for the right to equal treatment in working conditions, and the Court of Justice has ruled that at least in the agreement with Russia, this right has direct effect and has the same meaning as the Europe Agreement treaties.[330]

Next, treaties with the three Maghreb States (Algeria, Morocco, and Tunisia) provide for equal treatment in social security for workers and family members and equality in working conditions.[331] The case law of the Court of Justice makes clear that both of these rights are directly effective. However, the right to equal treatment in 'working conditions' does not entail a continuing right to reside in order to work, although it does prevent Member States from terminating legal residence as long as a Maghreb worker is legally employed, except on grounds of public security, public policy, or public health.[332] The extensive case law of the Court of Justice on the right to equal treatment in social security makes clear that 'workers' can claim the benefit of the equal treatment rule even after retirement, disability, or unemployment; that the definition of 'family members' of workers has a wide scope, including even parents and mothers-in-law residing with the worker; that family members can claim benefits independently, even after the worker has ended employment or died; and that the definition of 'social security' is the same as that in the EU free movement rules.[333] The Association Councils have adopted decisions to implement the social security rules.[334]

As for the EU's agreements with Latin American States, the association agreement with Chile contains provisions on free trade in services, including rules on the admission of employees of service providers,[335] and on the establishment of companies (although not establishment by self-employed persons).[336] The EU's free trade agreements with Colombia and Peru and with Central America have also liberalized the

---

[329] See [1997] OJ L 327 (Russia); [1998] OJ L 49 (Ukraine); [1998] OJ L 181 (Moldova); [1999] OJ L 196 (Kazahkstan); [1999] OJ L 196 (Kyrgyz Republic); [1999] OJ L 205 (Georgia); [1999] OJ L 229 (Uzbekistan); [1999] OJ L 239 (Armenia); [1999] OJ L 246 (Azerbaijan); and [2009] OJ L 350 (Tajikistan). An agreement with Turkmenistan (COM (97) 693, 6 Feb 1998) has been signed, but not yet ratified.

[330] Case C-265/03 *Simutkenov* [2005] ECR I-2579, regarding limits on the fielding of foreign football players during professional matches.

[331] Agreements with these States initially entered into force in 1978 ([1978] OJ L 263, 264, and 265). Replacement treaties were agreed between 1995 and 2002. They have all now entered into force (Tunisia: [1998] OJ L 97; Morocco: [2000] OJ L 70; Algeria: [2005] OJ L 265). However, the migration provisions in these treaties are not different in substance to the 1978 rules.

[332] C-416/96 *El-Yassini* [1999] ECR I-1209. A subsequent judgment appears to suggest that this rule has the same meaning as in EU free movement law (Case C-97/05 *Gattoussi* [2006] ECR I-11917).

[333] Cases: C-18/90 *Kziber* [1991] ECR I-119; C-58/93 *Yousfi* [1994] ECR I-1353; C-103/94 *Krid* [1995] ECR I-719; C-126/95 *Hallouzi-Choho* [1996] ECR I-4807; C-113/97 *Babahenini* [1998] ECR I-183; C-314/96 *Djabali* [1998] ECR I-1149; C-179/98 *Mesbah* (n 254 above); C-33/99 *Fahmi and Cerdeiro-Pinedo Amadao* [2001] ECR I-2415; C-23/02 *Alami* [2003] ECR I-1399; C-336/05 *Echouikh* [2006] ECR I-5223; and C-276/06 *El-Youssfi* [2007] ECR I-2851.

[334] [2010] OJ L 306, which also includes a Decision regarding Israel.

[335] See Arts 95–115, particularly 95(1)(d) and 101, and Annex VII to the Agreement, and the special rules for financial services in Arts 116–29 and Annex VIII to the Agreement ([2002] OJ L 352/3). The services provisions entered into force on 1 Mar 2005 ([2005] OJ L 84/21). For the context, see the discussion of World Trade Organization commitments in I:6.4.6 below. The agreement with Chile goes further establishing free trade in services than the EU's WTO commitments.

[336] See Arts 130–35 and Annex X to the Agreement (n 335 above).

movement of businesspersons.[337] In Asia, the EU has a free trade treaty with Korea, including provisions on trade in services.[338]

Finally, the EU's relations with the African, Caribbean, and Pacific (ACP) States were governed from 1976 to 2003 by the Lomé Convention, which has now been replaced by the Cotonou Convention. Annexes to the Lomé Conventions (starting with Lomé II) referred to equal treatment in social security and working conditions for ACP nationals.[339] However, the legal effect of these Annexes was not clear, as the Court of Justice never ruled on their legal effect,[340] although the Court did rule that at least some provisions of the Lomé Conventions could be directly effective.[341] The Cotonou Convention now contains a right to equal treatment in working conditions in the main text of the Convention.[342] By analogy with the case law on the Lomé Convention and the EU's other association agreements, this provision is directly effective and comprises at least the right to be treated equally as regards public-sector employment contracts, rules of private associations on the nationality of persons who can play at any given time for a professional sports team, and rules about elections to chambers of workers.[343] Other types of discrimination as regards working conditions falling within the scope of the ban could also be imagined. However, again by analogy from the case law on other agreements, there are also limits on the right: the equal treatment rule does not entail a continuing right to reside in order to work, although it does prevent Member States from terminating legal residence as long as an ACP worker is legally employed, except on grounds of public security, public policy, or public health.[344] Also the right to equal treatment in working conditions should be distinguished from initial access to the territory and the rules on access to employment,[345] which remain (to the extent that there is no EU legislation on the issue) within the competence of Member States.[346]

The EU plans to agree full Economic Partnership Agreements with ACP states, which would include provisions on services, addressing, inter alia, the movement of natural persons. So far, the EU has agreed such a treaty with Caribbean States.[347]

6.4.4 Posting of workers

Article 56 TFEU (formerly Article 49 EC) provides that EU citizens established in a Member State have the right to provide services to persons in another Member State.[348]

---

[337] Arts 122–26 of the treaty with Colombia and Peru ([2012] OJ L 354); Arts 173–76 of the treaty with Central American states ([2012] OJ L 346).

[338] Chapter 7 of the Agreement ([2011] OJ L 127).

[339] See Lomé II ([1980] OJ L 347); Lomé III ([1986] OJ L 86); Lomé IV ([1991] OJ L 229); and revision of Lomé IV ([1998] OJ L 156).

[340] But see Case C-206/91 *Poirrez* [1992] ECR I-6685, where the facts fell just outside the scope of both the Convention rules and EU free movement law. On the human rights aspects of the *Poirrez* case, see 6.3.2 above. On the right to non-discrimination in establishment in Lomé I, see Case 65/77 *Razanatsimba* [1977] ECR 2229. This right was removed from later Lomé Conventions.

[341] Case C-469/93 *Chiquita Italia* [1995] ECR I-4533. See further Cases C-280/93 *Germany v Council* [1994] ECR I-4973 and C-369/95 *Somalfruit* [1997] ECR I-6619.

[342] Art 13 of Cotonou Convention ([2000] OJ L 317), in force 1 Apr 2003.

[343] *Pokrzeptowicz-Meyer* and *Calpak* (both n 327 above); *Birklite* (n 265 above).

[344] *El-Yassini*, n 332 above.   [345] *Calpak*, n 327 above.

[346] On the relevant EU legislation, see I:6.5 below.

[347] [2008] OJ L 289; see Arts 80–4 of the agreement.

[348] The issue should be distinguished from that of persons posted from *outside* the EU to provide services: see I:6.4.6 below.

This right affects third-country nationals in two ways. First of all, the Court of Justice has ruled that EU employers have the right under Article 56 TFEU to send all of their 'legal and habitual' employees, regardless of those employees' nationality, to another Member State in order to enable the employer to provide services there (eg by carrying out a construction or demolition contract).[349] The host Member State cannot require work permits for these workers. In subsequent judgments, the Court of Justice ruled that a Member State may not insist on a prior authorization of such postings (even if such decisions are subject to judicial review), or a requirement that the employee be hired on an indefinite contract at least six months or a year earlier, or any particular period of work or residence in the host Member State, or the furnishing of a bank guarantee, or the automatic refusal to issue an entry and residence permit if a worker has entered without a visa.[350] The Court has not yet delivered a judgment on whether Article 56 could also preclude other restrictions imposed by the host State on such employees (eg a long-stay visa or residence permit requirement).[351] However, it is arguable that for the right to provide services to be effective, the workers concerned must be allowed to reside on the territory, and therefore any such documents would be purely declaratory. They must be issued by the Member State concerned and any failure to obtain them by the workers concerned cannot be punished by disproportionate penalties such as exclusion for the territory or imprisonment, which would negate the freedom to provide services.

Second, Article 56 TFEU expressly provides that the Council, by means of the ordinary legislative procedure,[352] can extend the freedom to provide services to third-country nationals established in the EU. In 1999, the Commission proposed legislation (based on Articles 57 and 66 EC, later Articles 47 and 55 EC, now Articles 53 and 62 TFEU) to facilitate the exercise of the right of EU service providers to send third-country national employees to other Member States, and (based on Article 49 EC, now Article 56 TFEU) to extend free movement of services to established third-country nationals.[353] The Council did not adopt these proposals, and they were withdrawn in 2004.[354]

However, the EU's general Directive on services permits Member States to impose visa and residence permit requirements on third-country nationals who move to another Member State in the context of service provision,[355] if they are not covered by the Schengen rules on freedom to travel,[356] along with reporting requirements on such persons.[357] It must be noted that as secondary legislation, the Services Directive cannot

---

[349] Case C-43/93 *Van der Elst* [1994] ECR I-3803. See similarly, as regards the nationality of directors of companies exercising the right to establishment, Case C-299/02 *Commission v Netherlands* [2004] ECR I-9761.

[350] Cases C-445/03 *Commission v Luxembourg* [2004] ECR I-10191, C-244/04 *Commission v Germany* [2006] ECR I-885, C-168/04 *Commission v Austria* [2006] ECR I-9041, C-219/08 *Commission v Belgium* [2009] ECR I-9213, and C-91/13 *Essent*, ECLI:EU:C:2014:2206.

[351] For further implications of the case law, see I:3.4.1, I:4.4.1, and I:5.4.2 above, and I:7.4.1 below.

[352] Before the entry into force of the Treaty of Lisbon, the relevant voting procedure was a qualified majority vote in Council on a proposal from the Commission (with no involvement of the EP).

[353] For the text of the proposals, see COM (1999) 3, 26 Feb 1999, amended in 2000 (COM (2000) 271, 8 May 2000). For discussion of the legal base of the proposals, see E Guild and S Peers, 'Out of the Ghetto? The Personal Scope of EU Law' in S Peers and N Rogers, eds., *EU Immigration and Asylum Law: Text and Commentary*, 1st edn (Martinus Nijhoff, 2006).

[354] COM (2004) 542, 6 Aug 2004.

[355] This appears to cover both self-employed persons and posted workers.

[356] See I:4.9 above.   [357] Art 17(9), Dir 2006/123 ([2006] OJ L 376/36).

restrict rights which the employers of posted workers derive directly from Article 56 TFEU, and so the application of any such requirements imposed by Member States on posted workers must respect the underlying Treaty right, as discussed above.[358]

6.4.5 Social policy

Article 153(1)(g) TFEU (previously Article 137(1)(g) EC) expressly provides that the Council can adopt legislation on the 'conditions of employment for third-country nationals legally residing in Union territory'.[359] According to Article 153(2) TFEU (previously Article 137(2) EC), this power can only be exercised following a 'special legislative procedure', namely a unanimous vote in the Council, acting on a proposal from the Commission and after consulting the EP.[360] Although this power has existed since the entry into force of the Maastricht Treaty in November 1993,[361] the Commission has never proposed legislation to implement this power and therefore the Council has never adopted any such legislation. It should also be recalled that the EU Charter of Fundamental Rights states that third-country nationals who are authorized to work on Member States' territories 'are entitled to working conditions equivalent to citizens of the Union';[362] this differs from a mere *power* to adopt *some* rules on this issue (which might not necessarily guarantee equality), as set out in Article 153 TFEU. It is also not clear whether the Treaty powers over 'conditions of employment' are wider than rules relating to 'working conditions', and in particular whether these powers extend to issues of access to employment for third-country nationals.[363]

The CJEU confirmed that EU social policy legislation in general applies to third-country nationals, in the 2014 judgment in *Tumer*.[364] First of all, it stated that the EU's employment law powers were not limited to EU citizens, 'to the exclusion of third-country nationals', referring to the Advocate-General's observation that the Treaty social policy rules did not exclude non-EU citizens, and that excluding them from EU employment law could lead to 'social dumping'. Therefore, the specific power to adopt rules on non-EU citizens' working conditions does not have an *a contrario* effect. The existence of a particular directive giving equal treatment rights to long-term resident third-country nationals did not preclude other EU legislation from applying to third-country nationals more generally.[365] Although the legislation in question (on insolvent

---

[358] Note that the services Dir does not expressly permit Member States to require visas or residence permits *as a condition of* entry, residence, or service provision.

[359] See previously Joined Cases 281-283, 285, and 287/85 *Germany and others v Commission* [1987] ECR 3203, discussed in I:3.2.4 above.

[360] The same provision also permits the Council, acting by the same procedure, to extend QMV and the 'co-decision' procedure to adoption of such measures. No such change in the decision-making procedure has been adopted or proposed.

[361] Initially, this power was contained in the Agreement on Social Policy attached to a Protocol to the EC Treaty. This Agreement did not apply to the UK. However, the Treaty of Amsterdam integrated the Protocol into the EC Treaty (as it then was) and since then these provisions are applicable to all Member States.

[362] Art 15(3) of the Charter ([2007] OJ C 303). See further I:6.3.4 above.

[363] For a discussion of the legal base issue, see I:6.2.4 above.

[364] Case C-311/13, ECLI:EU:C:2014:2337.

[365] On that Directive, see I:6.7 below. There are also equal treatment rules in some other EU immigration legislation: see I:6.5, I:6.6, and I:6.8 below, as well as I:5.7 above (asylum).

employers) left it open to national law to define 'employee', Member States' discretion to do so was not unlimited. The legislation did not exclude third-country nationals from its scope, or expressly permit Member States to do so. Their discretion was 'circumscribed by the social objective' of the law, which aimed to protect employees who had claims for back pay against insolvent employers.

The impact of the Court's ruling is clearly not confined to the insolvent employers' Directive only. It refers very generally to the prospect of adopting 'other EU acts, *such as*' this Directive, which apply to third-country nationals. Having said that, the Court clearly states that EU legislation could subject its application to third-country nationals to 'different conditions'. What conditions are those? Based on *Tumer*, third-country nationals will fall within the scope of EU legislation if the legislation in question does not exclude third-country nationals, or expressly permit Member States to do so. Even if it leaves a key definition (like 'employee', in this case) up to national law, third-country nationals will still be covered, if excluding them would undercut the 'social objectives' of the EU rules. This will always be the case for EU employment legislation, since excluding them could lead to social dumping. However, there are limits to the ruling: it does not mean that third-country nationals can invoke the application of purely *national* employment law in areas which are not subject to EU law; and it does not alter the immigration status of the third-country nationals concerned. Finally, it should be noted that the Court's ruling is consistent with the 2009 Directive on employment of irregular migrants, which provides that irregular migrants are entitled to the normal rates of pay from their employer, with effective means in place to enforce this, in order to avoid employers gaining a benefit from their exploitation of irregular migrants.[366]

6.4.6 Common commercial policy

The World Trade Organization (WTO) agreements, in force since January 1995, contain a General Agreement on Trade in Services (GATS).[367] Under this agreement, the EC (as it was then) and its Member States made commitments to allow temporary entry of intra-company transferees (managers or specialists being transferred within a company), business visitors (persons entering temporarily in order to sell services or to establish a commercial presence for a services company), and contractual service suppliers (companies providing services by sending their employees to perform the service in the host State).[368] The latter is, in effect, the external equivalent of EU companies' free movement right to post such employees within the EU.[369] Member States' legal obligations to accept such employees under the WTO rules are much more limited than under the EU free movement rules, as the obligations are limited to certain services sectors and to a limit of three months within any year. However, the EU, along with a number of other WTO Members, is seeking to widen the scope of the WTO obligations in this area.[370] The EU's GATS offer includes particularly: the addition of graduate trainees to the

---

[366] See I:7.6.1 below.   [367] [1994] OJ L 336/191.
[368] This form of service provision is known as 'Mode 4' of service supply pursuant to the GATS.
[369] See I:6.4.4 above.
[370] On the EU's current commitments and its proposed offer, see the EC's GATS offer of 1 Apr 2005, online at: <http://trade.ec.europa.eu/doclib/docs/2008/september/tradoc_140501.pdf>.

category of intra-corporate transferees; setting standard rules on admission of intra-corporate transferees (three years, or one year for graduate trainees) and business visitors (three months a year) to the EU; an increase in the services sectors covered and the time limit applicable to admission of contractual service supplies; and the admission of independent self-employed service suppliers in a small number of sectors. Also, it is open to WTO Members to conclude services liberalization or labour market liberalization agreements with each other, subject to certain conditions;[371] the EU's services agreement with various countries are an example of this.[372]

The framework governing international trade in services within the EU legal order has been evolving for a number of years. First of all, before amendments were made to the rules governing the EC's CCP,[373] the Court of Justice ruled in 1994 that competence to conclude GATS initially was shared between the Community (as it then was) and the Member States, inter alia, because the EC had not fully harmonized the rules relating to entry of service providers' employees.[374] However, the Court of Justice nevertheless ruled later that it had jurisdiction to give a ruling on any dispute concerning provisions of the GATS, even if that dispute involved issues within Member States' competence, as long as the provision in question could also apply to an issue within the EC's competence.[375] This means that, during this period, the Court likely had jurisdiction to rule on most or all disputes involving admission of service providers' employees pursuant to GATS. But, during this period, WTO rules lacked direct effect in EC law and could not be used to attack the validity of EC acts, except where the EC act aimed to implement WTO obligations or referred to WTO obligations.[376] On the other hand, the Court also ruled that EC legislation (and national law within the scope of EC legislation) had to be interpreted consistently with WTO rules,[377] but if the EC had not yet adopted legislation within the scope of a particular WTO obligation, it was up to Member States to determine what legal effect their WTO obligations had.[378]

Following amendments to the EC's commercial policy powers brought about by the Treaty of Nice,[379] the CCP included all issues related to services (and trade-related intellectual property), as defined in the GATS.[380] Although the EC's power over the 'classic' CCP issues (goods and limited aspects of services and intellectual

---

[371] See Arts V and Vbis of GATS.

[372] See I:6.4.3 above. In particular, as noted above, these agreements liberalize the posting of workers considerably as compared to the EU's GATS commitments to other WTO members.

[373] See Art 113 EC, before the Treaty of Amsterdam.   [374] *Opinion 1/94* [1994] ECR I-5273.

[375] See Cases: C-53/96 *Hermes* [1998] ECR I-3603; C-300/98 and 392/98 *Christian Dior and Layher* [2000] ECR I-11307; and C-245/02 *Anheuser-Busch* [2004] ECR I-10989. For the limits of this approach, see Case C-431/05 *Merck* [2007] ECR I-7001. These cases concerned the WTO's intellectual property agreement, but there was no reason to doubt their applicability to the GATS.

[376] Case C-149/96 *Portugal v Council* [1999] ECR I- 8395 and *Dior*, n 375 above. But see the more flexible approach in Case C-377/98 *Netherlands v Council* [2001] ECR I-7079, para 55: the Court can review the validity of an EC act if it arguably requires Member States to breach their WTO obligations, while expressly claiming not to do so. This judgment was subsequently interpreted narrowly in the judgment in Case T-19/01 *Chiquita Italia* [2005] ECR II-315.

[377] See Case T-256/97 *BEUC* [2000] ECR II-101, paras 66 and 67 and Case C-76/00 P *Petrotub* [2003] ECR I-79, para 57.

[378] *Dior* (n 375 above).   [379] Revised Art 133 EC.

[380] For a full analysis of the position, see *Opinion 1/2008* [2009] ECR I-11129; see also the Opinion in Case C-13/07 *Commission v Council*, ECLI:EU:C:2009:190.

property) was exclusive, in these new areas, Member States remained free to maintain and conclude agreements as long as they 'compl[ied] with Community law and
other relevant international agreements'. Moreover, where a treaty related to 'trade
in cultural and audiovisual services, educational services, and social and human
health services', it fell within the shared competence of the EC and its Member States
and had to be concluded by both of them.[381] Arguably this covered any agreement
concerning the posted workers of companies providing services in these fields. In
any event, the Council had to act unanimously regarding treaties in these fields
where the EC had not yet acted internally or had to act unanimously to adopt
internal rules.

The position changed again with the entry into force of the Treaty of Lisbon.[382]
Since then, the entirety of the area of the CCP, including all aspects of services and
intellectual property, is an exclusive competence of the EU, although the EU can
delegate some of this competence to Member States,[383] much as the Community (as
it then was) for many years delegated aspects of its 'classic' commercial policy competence to the Member States, subject to conditions which the Court of Justice had
attached to such delegation.[384] This competence includes not only treaty-making,
in the context of the WTO or bilaterally, but also internal legislation, which is now
adopted by means of the ordinary legislative procedure.[385] But for treaty-making,
the Council is still obliged to act unanimously 'where such agreements include provisions for which unanimity is required for the adoption of internal rules', or 'in
the field of trade in cultural and audiovisual services, where these agreements risk
prejudicing the Union's cultural and linguistic diversity', or 'in the field of trade in
social, education and health services, where these agreements risk seriously disturbing the national organisation of such services and prejudicing the responsibility of
Member States to deliver them'.[386] Also, transport services treaties are still subject
to the transport Title of the Treaty, which is a shared competence, not an exclusive
one.[387] While the first of the general exceptions would not require the use of unanimous voting as regards the movement of service providers—since QMV applies to
this area internally—it might be possible to argue that, depending on the extent of
the liberalization, the movement of persons in the fields of cultural and audiovisual
services, and social, education, and health services, will require unanimous voting.
It is also possible that unanimous voting will be required as regards the movement

---

[381] For interpretation of these provisos, see *Opinion 1/2008* and the Opinion in *Commission v Council*
(n 380 above).
[382] On the distinction between commercial policy competence and immigration competence after the
Treaty of Lisbon, see I:6.2.4 above.
[383] Arts 2(1) and 3(1)(e) TFEU. The EU has not yet delegated any competence to Member States as
regards services.
[384] See M Cremona, 'The Completion of the Internal Market and the Incomplete Commercial Policy
of the European Community' (1990) 15 ELRev 283 and the further references in S Peers, 'EU Borders and
Globalisation' in Groenendijk, Guild and Minderhoud, eds., *In Search of Europe's Borders* (Kluwer, 2003),
45 at 48, note 29.
[385] See Art 207 TFEU.   [386] Art 207(4) TFEU.
[387] Art 207(5) TFEU; see Art 4(2)(g) TFEU. Presumably this exception must be interpreted the same
way as the previous very similar provision (Art 133(7) EC): see *Opinion 1/2008* and Case C-13/07 (n 380
above). In any case the EP has the power of consent over such treaties: see Art 218(6)(a)(v) TFEU, read with
Art 207(2).

of service providers in the field of transport, depending on the adoption of legislation on that area.[388]

To date there is no internal EU legislation which generally governs the provision of services from outside the EU into the EU. The immigration law aspects of these issues have partly been harmonized by the 2014 Directive on intra-corporate transferees,[389] and in 2015 the Commission suggested that the EU should adopt legislation on the trade aspects of this issue—which would apply to all Member States.[390]

6.5 Primary Migration

As noted in the overview,[391] for a long time the European Union found it difficult to agree on rules governing the initial admission of migrants to enter and reside on the territory of Member States. In particular, it found it difficult to agree on the key issue of labour migration, in light of its significant social and economic impact. So the Council was not able to agree on the Commission's 2001 proposal for a Directive on migration for employment and self-employment,[392] and was not interested in a parallel communication on applying an 'open method of coordination' to labour migration policy.[393]

However, subsequently, as noted above, the Commission attempted to restart discussion on the issue by means of a Green Paper released in early 2005,[394] announced in September 2005 that it would withdraw the 2001 proposal for a Directive,[395] and issued a 'policy plan' on legal migration in December 2005.[396] The legislative aspects of the 'policy plan' included a number of Directives which were proposed between 2007 and 2010, and adopted between 2009 and 2014, concerning: the admission of highly-skilled workers; a general framework on the status of all persons admitted for employment (known as the 'single permit' Directive); seasonal workers; and intra-corporate transferees.[397]

In addition to the rules on labour migration, the EU has adopted legislation concerning the admission of researchers and of students, which will also apply (after amendment) to trainees and some volunteers, and potentially to others seeking admission for non-economic purposes.

The following section examines in turn: the general rules governing admission of workers on to the territory; the specific rules governing admission of other workers; and the rules concerning admission of researchers and non-economic migrants.

6.5.1 General rules on labour migration

General rules on labour migration are set out in Directive 2011/98, the 'single permit' Directive, which Member States had to apply from Christmas Day 2013.[398] The

---

[388] On the exclusive treaty-making competence of the EU derived from the adoption of internal legislation, see Art 3(2) TFEU. On the scope of the EU's CCP powers over services following the Treaty of Lisbon, see further Case C-137/12 *Commission v Council* ECLR:EU:C:2013:675 and *Opinion 2/15*, pending.

[389] See I:6.5.2.3 below.   [390] Agenda on Migration (COM (2015) 240, 13 May 2015).

[391] I:6.2.2 above.   [392] COM (2001) 386, 11 July 2001.

[393] COM (2001) 387, 11 July 2001.   [394] COM (2004) 811, 11 Jan 2005.

[395] COM (2005) 462, 27 Sep 2005. For confirmation of withdrawal, see [2006] OJ C 64/3.

[396] COM (2005) 669, 21 Dec 2005.

[397] See I:6.5.1 (single permit Directive) and I:6.5.2 (other Directives).

[398] [2011] OJ L 343/1, Art 16(1). All references in this sub-section are to this Directive, unless otherwise indicated.

Directive has the twin goals of regulating procedural aspects of admission for employment and of setting out rules concerning equal treatment of third-country national workers generally, whether those workers were admitted for employment as such or whether they were admitted for another purpose and nevertheless permitted to take up employment.[399] It does not alter the rules on the substantive grounds of admission of third-country nationals to national labour markets.[400]

Moreover, the Directive does not apply to persons who: have free movement rights as family members of EU citizens or pursuant to association agreements which extend EU free movement rights;[401] were posted from inside or outside the EU, or who are intra-corporate transferees;[402] have applied for or received some form of protection status under national or EU law;[403] have status as a long-term resident of the EU;[404] are subject to expulsion, if that process has been suspended for reasons of fact and law;[405] have applied for or been accepted for admission as a self-employed person;[406] or work in certain sectors of the labour market (as au pairs, seafarers, or seasonal workers).[407] Also, the rules on the single permit process do not apply to persons admitted on the basis of a visa,[408] and Member States may *opt* to exclude persons who have been authorized to work for less than six months, and who have been admitted for the purpose of study, from the rules on the single permit process.[409] The Directive is without prejudice to more favourable rules in national or EU law, or in treaties concluded by the EU and/ or the Member States.[410]

As to the procedure of applying for work in the Member States, applications have to be made for a single permit (ie a combined work and residence permit) on the basis of a single procedure.[411] The single permit also has to be issued when pre-existing permits are renewed or modified after the Directive is implemented by Member States.[412] It is up to Member States to decide whether applicants have to be outside their territory when

---

[399] Arts 1 and 3(1). On the definition of the latter category, see Arts 2(b) and 3(1)(b). On the specific employment rights of various categories of persons within the scope of the Dir, see I:6.5.2 (Blue Card holders), I:6.5.3 (researchers and students), and I:6.6 (family reunion) below, as well as I:6.4.3 above (association agreements, particularly with Turkey).

[400] Art 1, second sub-paragraph.

[401] Art 3(2)(a) and (b). On these categories of persons, see I:6.4.1 and I:6.4.3 above.

[402] Art 3(2)(c) and (d). On these categories of persons, see I:6.4.4 above and I:6.5.2.3 below.

[403] Art 3(2)(f) to (h). On these categories of persons, see I:5.5, I:5.6, and I:5.9 above.

[404] Art 3(2)(i), referring to Dir 2003/109 ([2004] OJ L 16/44), on which, see I:6.7 below.

[405] Art 3(2)(j). The Dir on sanctions against employers of irregular migrants (Art 2(3) of Dir 2009/ 52, [2009] OJ L 168/24) leaves it to Member States to decide whether such persons are permitted to be employed; on this Dir, see I:7.6.1 below. For the rules on suspension of removals, see the Returns Directive, discussed in I:7.7.1 below.

[406] Art 3(2)(k). The EU's GATS commitments do not (yet) extend to self-employed persons, so this category of persons is currently entirely regulated by national law, except for certain association agreements (see I:6.4.3 above).

[407] Art 3(2)(e) and (1). On the specific legislation on seasonal workers, see I:6.5.2.2 below. The Commission has proposed to regulate au pairs (I:6.5.3.3 below).

[408] Art 3(4), referring to Arts 4–10.

[409] Art 3(3), referring to Arts 4–10. On persons admitted as students, see Dir 2004/114 ([2004] OJ L 375/ 12, discussed in I:6.5.3 below.

[410] Art 13. On the more favourable rules in the Blue Card Dir (Dir 2009/50, [2009] OJ L 155/17), see discussion in I:6.5.2.1 below.

[411] Art 4.   [412] Art 4(4).

applying for a permit, and whether the application has to be made by the employer and/or the worker.[413] The national authority has to decide on the application for a single permit within four months, but is allowed to delay its decision past this date if the application is particularly complex.[414] The single permit has to be issued in the EU's standard residence permit format, and both the single permits and any residence permits issued for other purposes have to indicate the extent of the person's permitted labour market access.[415] Member States have to grant procedural rights if the single permit is not issued or renewed, or is withdrawn, including the right to bring a 'legal challenge' against such a decision,[416] but it is open to Member States to declare an application inadmissible on the grounds that a quota has already been filled.[417] The Directive does not set out substantive grounds for refusing, withdrawing, or not renewing a permit. There are no common rules on the validity of single permits, but there are rules on the information to be made available to applicants and employers and on the fees to be charged.[418] The single permit entitles the holder to enter and stay on the territory of the Member State issuing it, to have free access to the territory of that Member State,[419] to exercise the authorized employment activity, and to be informed about his or her rights linked to the single permit and/or national law.[420]

The remaining provisions of the Directive apply both to single permit holders and to persons who were admitted for other purposes, but who were permitted to work (if they are not excluded from the scope of the Directive).[421] These rules concern equal treatment,[422] the power to set more favourable standards,[423] and the obligation to make information on labour migration conditions available to the general public.[424] The equal treatment clause entitles both single permit holders and other persons permitted to work to equal treatment with nationals in seven areas: 'working conditions', which includes pay, dismissal, and health and safety rules in the workplace; 'freedom of association' as regards bodies such as trade unions, 'without prejudice to the national provisions on public policy and public security'; 'education and vocational training'; recognition of diplomas, etc. in accordance with national procedures; access to social security as defined EU free movement rules;[425] tax benefits; access to goods and services including procedures for obtaining housing; and counselling services offered by national employment offices. There is also a separate provision requiring equal

---

[413] Art 4(1).   [414] Art 5.

[415] Arts 6 and 7. On the standard format for residence permits, see further I:6.9.1 below.

[416] In light of the ECHR judgments relating to work permit applications (see I:6.3.3 above) and the case law on the similar provision in the family reunion Directive (see Case C-540/03 *EP v Council* [2006] ECR I-5769), this entails a right of access to court.

[417] Art 8(3).   [418] Arts 9 and 10.

[419] On the human rights context of this provision, see I:3.3 above.

[420] Art 11. Note that this Art, unlike Arts 4–10, applies to those admitted as students, allowed to work on the basis of a visa, or admitted as students (see Art 3(3) and (4)).

[421] These rules therefore also apply to persons admitted to work before the implementation of the Dir, and who have not yet obtained a single permit because their prior permit has not yet been renewed or modified after the Dir was implemented (see Art 4(4)).

[422] Art 12.   [423] Art 13, referred to above.

[424] Art 14. In fact, the wording of this provision only covers persons admitted for the purpose of work.

[425] On the EU free movement rules applicable to social security and their scope, see I:6.4.2 above. See also the general social security rules applicable to third country nationals who move within the EU (discussed in I:6.8 below).

treatment as regards the payment of pensions for workers or their survivors who move to a third country.[426]

The equal treatment right is without prejudice to a Member State's right to refuse to renew or withdraw any residence permit or authorization to work.[427] Furthermore, Member States are permitted to set several limitations on equal treatment rights.[428] In particular, Member States may also restrict equal treatment as regards grants and loans for 'secondary and higher education and vocational training'; more generally Member States may either restrict equal treatment in this area for persons admitted as students, and/or restrict equal treatment in this area (along with equal treatment as regards all goods and services) to persons who are in employment only. Access to education and vocational training may also be subject to proof of language proficiency or other 'specific prerequisites', including payment of fees. Social security rights may be restricted, except where the worker is either in employment or is unemployed after working in that Member State for at least six months. Member States may also deny equal treatment in family benefits to: students; persons who have been admitted to work for less than six months; or persons who were admitted on the basis of a visa. Tax benefits might be subject to residence conditions. Finally, Member States have a general power to restrict equal treatment regarding housing, and can restrict equal treatment as regards goods and services to third-country workers who are in employment.

While there is no information on the application of the Directive in practice yet,[429] overall it should have made a useful contribution towards ensuring equal treatment for migrant workers and streamlining Member States' processes relating to admission. However, it does not go far enough to ensure their fair treatment as regards issues such as access to employment and grounds for the non-renewal of permits. It can only be hoped that further EU measures will address these issues for all workers, not just specific categories of them.

6.5.2 Specific categories of workers

6.5.2.1 Highly-skilled workers

Directive 2009/50 was adopted by Council in May 2009,[430] and had to be implemented by Member States by 19 June 2011.[431] Although the purpose of the Directive is to regulate 'highly-qualified employment' by third-country nationals in the Member States, it is widely known as the 'Blue Card' Directive, because it creates an EU 'Blue Card' to compete with the well-known American 'Green Card' for labour migrants.[432] In order to enhance the attractiveness of the EU for highly-qualified workers, the Directive contains derogations from the family reunion Directive and the long-term residents

---

[426] Art 12(4).
[427] Art 12(3). It should be recalled that several association agreements limit Member States' right to withdraw residence permits for persons with work permits: see I:6.4.3 above.
[428] Art 12(2).   [429] The first such report is due by Christmas Day 2016 (Art 15(1)).
[430] [2009] OJ L 155/17. All further references in this sub-section are to this Dir unless otherwise indicated.
[431] Art 23(1).   [432] See Art 2(c).

Directive, which are examined separately below.[433] The Commission reported on the application of the Directive in 2014,[434] and plans to propose amendments to it in the near future.[435]

The core of the Directive is the definition of 'highly qualified employment', since it applies only to admission for such employment.[436] This definition has three parts.[437] First, the person concerned must be 'protected as an employee under national employment law and/or' practice, 'irrespective of the legal relationship, for the purpose of exercising genuine and effective work for, or under the direction of, someone else'. This definition is similar to the definition of 'worker' under EU free movement law.[438] Second, this employee must be 'paid' (with no further definition).[439] Third, the person concerned must have 'the required adequate and specific competence, as proven by higher professional qualifications'. In turn, 'higher professional qualifications' are defined either as 'qualifications attested by evidence of higher education qualifications' or alternatively, 'by way of derogation, when provided for by national law, attested by at least five years of professional experience of a level comparable to higher education qualifications and which is relevant in the profession or sector specified in the work contract or binding job offer'.[440] Such 'professional experience' is defined simply as 'the actual and lawful pursuit of the profession concerned'.[441]

Next, the Directive defines a 'higher education qualification' as 'any diploma, certificate or other evidence of formal qualifications issued by a competent authority attesting the successful completion of a post-secondary higher education programme, namely a set of courses provided by an educational establishment recognised as a higher education institution by the State in which it is situated'; the course concerned must last at least three years to be covered by the definition in the Directive.[442]

As for its scope,[443] the Directive does not apply to persons who have obtained or who are seeking temporary protection, 'international protection' under EU legislation, or who are 'beneficiaries of protection in accordance with national law, international obligations or practice of the Member State' or who are seeking such status.[444] Also, it does not apply to the family members of EU citizens who have free movement rights, or to the citizens of countries (or the family members of those citizens) who have a free movement agreement with the EU.[445] Furthermore, the Directive does not apply to persons covered by the researchers' Directive, the Directive on long-term residents (if

---

[433] See respectively Arts 15 and 19, examined in I:6.6.2 below, and Arts 16 and 17, examined in I:6.7.2 below.

[434] COM (2014) 287, 22 May 2014 ('the 2014 report').

[435] See the 2016 work programme (COM (2015) 610, 27 Oct 2015). The public consultation was launched in May 2015: <http://ec.europa.eu/dgs/home-affairs/what-is-new/public-consultation/2015/consulting_0029_en.htm>.

[436] Art 3(1).   [437] Art 2(b).

[438] See, for instance, Case 66/85 *Lawrie-Blum* [1986] ECR 2121.

[439] On this point, as regards EU free movement law, see for instance Case C-3/87 *Agegate* [1989] ECR I-4459.

[440] Art 2(g). The 2014 report indicates that twelve Member States apply this derogation.

[441] Art 2(i).   [442] Art 2(h).

[443] The relevant exclusions are nearly identical to the single permit Dir (Art 3(2), Dir 2011/98, [2011] OJ L 343/1); see further I:6.5.1 above.

[444] Art 3(2)(a) to (c).   [445] Art 3(2)(e) and 3(2), second sub-paragraph.

they have moved to another Member State), or the EU Directive on posted workers,[446] who enter pursuant to 'an international agreement facilitating the entry and temporary stay of certain categories of trade and investment-related natural persons' (most obviously the GATS), who have been admitted as seasonal workers, or whose expulsion has been suspended for reasons of fact or law.[447]

The EU and/or the Member States can also exempt certain professions from the Directive by means of international agreement, 'in order to assure ethical recruitment, in sectors suffering from a lack of personnel, by protecting human resources in the developing countries which are signatories to these agreements'.[448] Member States may also reject an application on similar grounds on the basis of their domestic law.[449]

Most significantly, the Directive is without prejudice to the right of Member States to issue permits *other than* in the form of a Blue Card for 'any purpose of employment'.[450] Such national permits do not confer the right of residence in other Member States. According to the 2014 report, fifteen Member States have exercised this option, and in many (but not all) of them, such national permits are issued in a large majority of cases instead of Blue Cards.

Implicitly, such national rules can either set higher standards or lower standards than the Directive, or some combination of *both* higher and lower standards.[451] The Directive does not address the question of the relationship between such purely national rules on admission and the EU rules. For example, if a Member State has a quota on admission of labour migrants, or on certain categories of labour migrants within the scope of the Directive, how will the quota be divided between the national rules and the Blue Card rules? Will employees and employers, whichever is applicable,[452] have a choice as to whether to apply under the national rules or under the Blue Card rules? Logically, they must have a choice,[453] and any national quotas must be open to both Blue Card and applicants applying pursuant to different rules established by national law, otherwise the effectiveness of the Directive would be seriously undermined.

In any event, Member States retain a general power to control the overall volumes of admission of third-country nationals entering the territory for the purpose of highly-qualified employment.[454] This explicitly applies regardless of whether the third-country

---

[446] Art 3(2)(d), (f), and (j). The posted workers Dir is Dir 96/71 ([1997] OJ L 18/1); see I:6.4.4 above. On the researchers' Dir (Dir 2005/71, [2005] OJ L 289/15) and its agreed replacement, see I:6.5.3 below. On long-term residents, see I:6.7 below.

[447] Art 3(2)(g), (h), and (i). On these categories, see respectively I:6.4.6 above, I:6.5.2.2 below, and I:7.7.1 below.

[448] Art 3(3). The EU has not concluded any such agreements. According to the 2014 report, no Member State has either.

[449] Art 8(4) gives Member States an option to refuse applications 'in order to ensure ethical recruitment in sectors suffering from a lack of qualified workers in the countries of origin'. The 2014 report states that six Member States have exercised this option, but none have used it in practice. However, it indicates that some Member States use alternative means to the same end.

[450] Art 3(4).   [451] This is an interpretation of Art 3(4) *a contrario* Art 4(2).

[452] See Art 10(1).

[453] This is confirmed (as regards employees) by recital 7 in the preamble to the Directive.

[454] Art 6. An application for a Blue Card may be considered inadmissible on such grounds (Art 8(3)). According to the 2014 report, eight Member States have used this option; one of them (Cyprus) has a quota of zero.

nationals concerned come from outside the EU or within it,[455] and so is broader in scope than the national reserve of competence which was subsequently inserted into the Treaties.[456]

Furthermore, even within the scope of the Directive, Member States retain power to establish 'more favourable provisions' in bilateral or multilateral treaties, as does the EU, either by itself or with the Member States.[457] Member States may also retain or adopt more favourable provisions in their national law, as regards particular issues: the salary criteria for admission, as regards admission to a second Member State; procedural safeguards; the option to grant equal treatment with nationals as regards employment access after two years; changes of employer within the first two years; the consequences of temporary unemployment; equal treatment with nationals; the admission of family members; and the possible extension of the period of absence from the EU allowed before long-term resident status will lapse.[458] In either case, there is no requirement that the more favourable rules must be 'compatible' with the rules in the Directive.[459] Also, there are other specific derogations permitted in the Directive.[460]

The next key issue in the Directive is the criteria for admission. Member States decide whether applications can be made by the employer and/or the employee.[461] The mandatory conditions for Blue Card applications are:[462] a 'valid work contract' or, if specified under national law, a 'binding job offer', for 'highly qualified employment' for at least one year;[463] proof that the applicant meets the conditions set out by national law as regards EU citizens' exercise of a 'regulated profession';[464] as regards unregulated professions, proof that the applicant has 'the relevant higher professional qualifications in the occupation or sector'; a valid travel document and possibly a short-term or long-term visa or residence permit (or application for one) as determined by national law; evidence of having, or having applied for, sickness insurance, if such sickness insurance would not be a benefit pursuant to the employment contract; and the absence of a threat to public policy, public security, or public health. Each Member State may also opt to require the applicant to provide his or her address on the territory of the Member

---

[455] Art 18(7).

[456] Art 79(5) TFEU, discussed in I:6.2.4 above. On the similarly broad clause in the long-term residents' Directive (Art 14(4) of Dir 2003/109, [2003] OJ L 16/44), see I:6.7 below.

[457] Art 4(1).

[458] Art 4(2), referring to: Art 5(3) in conjunction with Art 18; Art 11; Art 12(1), second sentence; Art 12(2); Arts 13–15; and Art 16(4). There is an unlimited power for other EU legislation to set higher standards (Art 4(1)(a)).

[459] See I:6.2.4 above.

[460] Arts 2(g), 5(1)(a), (d) and (e) (to an extent), 5(2), 5(5), 6, 8(3), 8(4), 8(5), 10(3), 10(4), 14(2), 14(4), 15(7), 16(5), 18(2), 18(5), 18(7), 19(3), and 19(4). Furthermore, various provisions provide for options for Member States (Arts 5(3), 7(2), 8(2), 9(3), 10(1), and 12(1), (3), and (4)), and Arts 2(b), 2(g), 3(2)(c), 5(1) (b), (c), and (d), 8(2), 11(1), 11(3), 12(2), 14(1)(e), (f), and (h), 14(4), 18(2), 18(4)(b), 18(5), and 19(2) refer to 'national law' as regards some issues.

[461] Art 10(1). The 2014 report indicates that a majority of Member States require the migrant to apply; five require the employer to apply; two require a joint application; and four allow either to apply.

[462] Art 5(1).

[463] According to the 2014 report, two Member States do not provide for the one-year minimum time limit.

[464] See the definition of 'regulated profession' in Art 2(j).

State.[465] A further mandatory condition is a requirement to set a salary threshold of *at least* 1.5 times the average gross annual salary in the Member State concerned.[466]

However, the threshold set by the latter mandatory condition may be reduced to 1.2 times the average gross annual salary by way of derogation, for 'professions which are in particular need of third-country national workers' and which fall within one of two groups of jobs classified internationally.[467] This derogation refers to managers and professionals.[468] On the other hand, Member States may insist that meeting the salary threshold must also entail ensuring that 'all conditions in the applicable laws, collective agreements or practices in the relevant occupational branches for highly qualified employment are met'.[469] Presumably this means that any applicable legally required minimum salaries for certain jobs could not be circumvented. More generally the rules on admissions criteria are 'without prejudice to the applicable collective agreements or practices in the relevant occupational branches for highly qualified employment'.[470]

If an applicant meets the criteria for obtaining a Blue Card, and the national authorities have taken a positive decision on the application, an EU Blue Card shall be issued.[471] The Directive does not expressly address the question of whether or not the authorities are *obliged* to issue a Blue Card if the conditions are satisfied,[472] although the person concerned must be granted 'every facility to obtain the requisite visas'.[473] A Blue Card shall be valid for a 'standard' period, which must be between one and four years; if the work contract is for a shorter period, the Blue Card shall be valid for that period plus four months.[474] The Blue Card shall be issued in the EU's standard residence permit format,[475] and shall entitle the holder to 'enter, re-enter and stay in the territory of the Member State issuing the EU Blue Card',[476] and to enjoy the rights recognized by the Directive.[477]

Next, the Directive sets out grounds for refusal of a Blue Card application. Member States are obliged to reject an application if the criteria for obtaining a Blue Card are not satisfied, or if 'the documents presented have been fraudulently acquired, or falsified or tampered with'.[478] Member States have an option, as regards the initial application

---

[465] Art 5(2). Only four Member States did not invoke this option (2014 report).

[466] This is to be calculated in accordance with EU statistical data and national data 'where appropriate': see Art 20(3). The 2014 report is very critical of Member States' methods of calculating the threshold. Two Member States set a threshold higher than this.

[467] Art 5(5). For the calculation rule, see n 466 above. Nine Member States have invoked this derogation, but only four make use of it in practice (2014 report).

[468] More precisely, group 1 consists of: chief executives, senior officials, and legislators; administrative and commercial managers; production and specialized services managers; and hospitality, retail, and other services managers. Group 2 consists of science and engineering professionals; health professionals; teaching professionals; business and administration professionals; information and communications technology professionals; and legal, social, and cultural professionals. See: <http://www.ilo.org/public/english/bureau/stat/isco/docs/resol08.pdf>.

[469] Art 5(4).　　　[470] Art 5(6).　　　[471] Art 7(1), first sub-paragraph.

[472] The CJEU has confirmed that such an obligation arises regarding the admission of students (see I:6.5.3.2 below).

[473] Art 7(1), second sub-paragraph. On long-stay visas and EU law, see generally I:6.9.2 below.

[474] Art 7(2). On residence permits and EU law, see generally I:6.9.1 below. A large majority of Member States provide for a one-year or two-year validity for the Blue Card (2014 report).

[475] Art 7(3). On this standard format, see further I:6.9.1.　　　[476] Art 7(4)(a).

[477] Art 7(4)(b). Chapter IV of the Directive (Arts 12–17) is entitled 'Rights'.　　　[478] Art 8(1).

or during the first two years of legal employment of the Blue Card holder, to apply national rules giving priority to their own citizens, other EU citizens, legally resident third-country nationals already part of its labour market, or long-term residents moving from another Member State.[479] As noted above, applications can also be rejected because of a quota on labour migration, a ban on hiring to protect against a 'brain drain' from third states, or because the relevant employer has breached the rules on undeclared work or illegal employment.[480] The Directive does not expressly state whether these grounds for refusal of a Blue Card, taken together with the criteria for grant of a Blue Card,[481] are the only criteria relating to the grant or refusal of a Blue Card, but given Member States' express powers to apply different rules as regards certain provisions of the Directive, or the Directive in general,[482] it should follow that they are, by *a contrario* reasoning. By reducing the number of options to refuse applications and criteria for grant of a Blue Card, this interpretation would also best reflect the Directive's objective of encouraging highly-skilled workers to come to the EU.[483]

Member States are obliged to withdraw or to refuse to renew the Blue Card when: the Blue Card 'has been fraudulently acquired, or has been falsified or tampered with'; if the holder did not meet or no longer meets the criteria for a Blue Card or is residing for purposes other than the grounds for authorization to reside; or where the holder has breached the rules on the Directive concerning changing employment or becoming unemployed (discussed further below).[484] A lack of communication concerning unemployment or changes in employer shall not be a reason for withdrawal or non-renewal of the Blue Card, if the Blue Card holder can prove that the Card was not received for reasons other than his or her will.[485] Member States *may* withdraw or refuse to renew the Blue Card: for 'reasons of public policy, public security or public health'; where the Blue Card holder lacks 'sufficient resources' to maintain himself or family members without recourse to social assistance; for failure to communicate an address; or because of an application for social assistance.[486] As with the rules on the criteria for applications and refusals of applications, the Directive does not expressly state whether or not these are the only grounds for withdrawal or non-renewal of a permit, but it should follow that they are, for the reasons set out above.

The latter issue raises the question as to whether the Directive *implicitly requires* Member States to renew Blue Card permits, by way of necessary corollary from the

---

[479] Art 8(2). Twelve Member States provide for a labour market test (2014 report).

[480] Art 8(3) to (5). As regards the latter rule, see the employer sanctions Directive (Dir 2009/52, [2009] OJ L 168/24; see I:7.6.1 below); but note that 'undeclared work or illegal employment' has a wider scope than the prohibition on employment of irregular migrants.

[481] Art 5, discussed above.   [482] In particular, in Arts 3(4) and 4(2).

[483] See by analogy the CJEU's reasoning as regards the EU criteria for admission of students, discussed in I:6.5.3.2 below.

[484] Art 9(1).   [485] Art 9(2).

[486] Art 9(3). All but two Member States apply the option regarding public policy; a majority apply the sufficient resources condition; eight apply the non-communication of address condition; and seven apply the social assistance condition (2014 report). The 'sufficient resources' condition is similar to one of the conditions for admission of family members in the family reunion Directive (Art 7(1)(c) of Dir 2003/86, [2003] OJ L 251/12), and arguably the case law on the interpretation of that provision is relevant by analogy (Case C-578/08 *Chakroun* [2010] ECR I-1839). However, note that the Blue Card Directive, unlike the family reunion Dir, does not require that these resources be 'stable and regular', and that this requirement cannot be imposed during the period of unemployment permitted by Art 13 (on which, see below).

exhaustive nature of the list of grounds for non-renewal of the permit. While the Directive does not *expressly require* Member States to renew Blue Card permits,[487] neither is such an obligation expressly ruled out.[488] The Directive obviously contemplates that permits should be renewed, given a number of references to their renewal,[489] and the (facilitated) possibility of obtaining long-term residence status necessarily assumes that permits can be renewed.[490] An obligation to renew permits would obviously also facilitate the attainment of the Directive's objectives, since highly-skilled workers would hardly be attracted to the EU if there were no guarantee of renewal of their initial Blue Card. This interpretation also follows from the absence of wording to the contrary, given the large number of derogations that Member States expressly inserted in the Directive. Therefore Blue Card permits *must* be renewed unless one of the express grounds for non-renewal apply; it follows that Member States cannot refuse to renew Blue Card permits, inter alia, on grounds of labour market admission quotas, EU preference, or brain drain.[491]

The 2014 report confirms the interpretation that the Directive obliges Blue Cards to be renewed when the relevant conditions are met. In fact, every Member State allows for the renewal of Blue Cards, although some of them provide for different periods of validity as compared to the initial issue of the Blue Card. The Commission rightly criticizes this, since the Directive refers to a 'standard' period of validity. One Member State (Sweden) provides for a total length of renewals of the Blue Card of four years; this is a breach of the Directive, which does not provide for any possibility of limiting the total number of renewals.

As regards the application process, the applicant must either be outside the territory of the Member State concerned, or legally resident on that territory as the holder of a long-stay visa or residence permit.[492] However, Member States can derogate either to set a more favourable rule (admitting applications from any applicant who is otherwise legally present),[493] or a less favourable rule (requiring all applicants to be abroad when the application is made).[494]

Procedurally, national authorities must adopt a decision in writing on the application and inform the applicant no more than ninety days after the application is made.

---

[487] See, for instance, Art 8 of the researchers' Directive.

[488] There is certainly no obligation to *refuse* to renew permits.

[489] As well as Art 9(1), (2), and (3), see Arts 7(2), 8(2), 11(2), 14(3), and 20(2).

[490] The five-year qualification period for long-term residence status exceeds the four-year maximum validity of a Blue Card. It would also be bizarre for the Directive to provide for the possibility of movement to another Member State even before obtaining long-term residence status, if there was no possibility of renewal of a residence permit in the *first* Member State during the same time period.

[491] Art 9 *a contrario* Art 8.

[492] Art 10(2). As a matter of EU immigration law, students, researchers, family members, seasonal workers, intra-corporate transferees, and single permit holders all hold such permits (see I:6.5.1, I:6.5.3, and I:6.6).

[493] Art 10(3). This would obviously cover the situation where either the applicant holds a valid short-term visa, or where the applicant has legally entered for a short-term stay and is not subject to a visa obligation because his or her country of origin is on the EU visa 'whitelist' (see I:4.5 above). All except eight Member States apply this derogation (2014 report).

[494] Art 10(4). This option is only valid where this restriction (for all third-country nationals or for certain categories of them) existed already at the time of adoption of the Directive (25 May 2009). Only one Member State (Bulgaria) applies this rule (2014 report).

The consequences of missing the deadline are laid down in national law.[495] If further documents are needed, the national authorities shall inform the applicant and set a reasonable deadline to receive the further documents; the ninety-day deadline to reply to the application will then be suspended. If the applicant does not send the further documents within the time required, the application may be rejected.[496] A refusal of an application, a refusal to renew a Blue Card, or a withdrawal of a Blue Card must be notified in writing to the holder or applicant and, where relevant, the employer. This decision must be open to legal challenge in accordance with national law, and the notification must 'specify the reasons for the decision, the possible redress procedures available and the time limit for taking action'.[497] As with other EU immigration legislation, the right to a legal challenge should be understood as a right of access to court.[498] All of the rules relating to procedural standards are 'minimum standards' provisions.[499]

Chapter IV of the Directive sets out provisions concerning access to employment, unemployment, equal treatment, family reunion, and long-term residents' status.[500] First, for the first two years of their legal employment as a Blue Card holder, Blue Card holders are restricted to employment that meets the criteria of their initial admission.[501] They may not change employers without prior authorization of the national authorities, and any changes 'that affect the conditions for admission shall be subject to prior communication or, if provided for by national law, prior authorisation'.[502]

After the first two years, Member States *may* grant equal treatment with nationals as regards to access to highly qualified employment.[503] If a Member State does not take up this option, the Blue Card holder must communicate any changes affecting the conditions for admission to national authorities.[504] In any event, Member States may retain restrictions on access to employment (presumably after the two year period), where 'such employment activities entail occasional involvement in the exercise of public authority and the responsibility for safeguarding the general interest of the State', *and* such activities were restricted to nationals in accordance with 'existing' law;[505] or more generally, where in accordance with existing law, any category of employment activities is 'reserved to nationals, Union citizens or EEA citizens'.[506]

---

[495] Art 11(1). This compares with a four-month deadline as regards applications for single permits (see I:6.5.1 above). Nearly half of the Member States have shorter deadlines (2014 report).

[496] Art 11(2).   [497] Art 11(3).

[498] See the relevant ECHR case law (I:6.3.3 above), the relevant CJEU case law (I:6.3.4 above); and, by analogy, Case C-540/03 *EP v Council* [2006] ECR I-5769.

[499] Art 4(2)(b).

[500] Arts 12–17. As noted above, the latter two issues are examined further below (I:6.6.2 and I:6.7.2).

[501] Art 12(1), first sentence. Member States do *not* have the power to set higher standards on this point (see Art 4(2)(b) *a contrario*).

[502] Art 12(2). In accordance with Art 4(2)(b), this clause is a 'minimum standards' rule. National authorities must reply to applications to change employer within 90 days. All except two Member States require prior authorization (2014 report).

[503] Art 12(1), second sentence. In accordance with Art 4(2)(b), this is a 'minimum standards' rule. Nine Member States did not apply the option (2014 report).

[504] Art 12(2). Again, in accordance with Art 4(2)(b), this is a 'minimum standards' rule.

[505] Art 12(3). It is not clear when such rules had or have to be 'existing'. By *a contrario* comparison with Art 12(4), these two conditions are cumulative, not alternative.

[506] Art 12(4). Again, it is not clear when such rules had or have to be 'existing'.

Unemployment will not lead instantly to the withdrawal of the Blue Card, unless it lasts longer than three consecutive months or occurs more than once during each period of validity.[507] During this three-month period, the Blue Card holder may search for other work, subject to the general rules on access to employment.[508] The Blue Card holder may remain on the territory while waiting for authorization. Alternatively, where a Member State requires prior communication of change of employment, that communication shall end the period of unemployment of the Blue Card holder.[509] A Blue Card holder must in any event communicate the start of the unemployment period to the national authorities.[510] All of the rules relating to unemployment are 'minimum standards' provisions.[511]

The Blue Card Directive also contains important provisions concerning equal treatment. Blue Card holders are entitled to equal treatment with nationals in eight areas: 'working conditions', which includes pay, dismissal, and health and safety rules in the workplace; 'freedom of association' as regards bodies such as trade unions, 'without prejudice to the national provisions on public policy and public security'; 'education and vocational training'; recognition of diplomas, etc. in accordance with national procedures;[512] access to social security in accordance with EU free movement rules, subject to the special rules applicable to most third-country nationals;[513] payment of pensions when moving to a third country; access to goods and services including procedures for obtaining housing; and free access to national territory, 'within the limits provided for by national law'.[514]

Limitations are permitted, however.[515] Member States may limit equal treatment regarding grants or loans as concerns housing and 'secondary and higher education and vocational training'.[516] Access to education and vocational training may also be subject to 'specific prerequisites in accordance with national law',[517] and Member States may restrict equal treatment to cases where the Blue Card holder or family member has his or her 'registered or usual place of residence' on national territory. The right to equal treatment to goods and services is without prejudice to the freedom to contract. Moreover, the right to equal treatment does not prejudice Member States' power to withdraw or refuse to renew a Blue Card under the applicable conditions.[518] There is also a specific rule concerning the limitation of equal treatment after a Blue Card holder moves to another Member State.[519] Compared to the general rules set out in the

---

[507] Art 13(1). As noted above, the period of validity of the Blue Card will be between one and four years, depending on the Member State (Art 7(2)).

[508] Art 13(2), referring to Art 12, discussed above.   [509] Art 13(3).   [510] Art 13(4).

[511] Art 4(2)(b). Indeed, some Member States apply more favourable rules, or only apply Art 13 in cases of involuntary unemployment (2014 report).

[512] The Directive does not expressly address recognition of qualifications in the context of an *application* for a Blue Card.

[513] On the applicable social security rules, see I:6.4.2 above and I:6.8 below.

[514] On the human rights context of access to the territory, see I:3.3 above.   [515] Art 14(2).

[516] Nine Member States applied this exception (2014 report).

[517] Thirteen Member States applied this exception (2014 report). It is not clear whether the 'specific requisites' can amount to an infringement of the equality rule.

[518] Art 14(3).

[519] Art 14(4), discussed further below. Only five Member States applied this exception (2014 report).

single permit Directive, the right to equal treatment is the same but the possible derogations are less far-reaching.[520] On the other hand, the rules are less generous than for long-term residents, who (subject to certain exceptions) have a right of equal treatment to employment or self-employment, as well as social assistance and social protection.[521]

There are provisions on the possibility of Blue Card holders moving between Member States, even before they have the status of long-term residents.[522] The basic rule is that after eighteen months of legal residence in the first Member State as a Blue Card holder, a Blue Card holder can move with his or her family members to take up highly-qualified employment in another Member State.[523] To exercise this possibility, the Blue Card holder and/or his or her employer must make an application within one month of moving to the second Member State; that State may decide that the Blue Card holder cannot work until its authorities take a decision on the application.[524] The application could also be submitted to the second Member State while the Blue Card holder still resides in the first Member State.[525] In accordance with the general procedural safeguards, the second Member State shall either accept the application or refuse to issue the Blue Card; in the latter case the first Member State must readmit the applicant and family members, and the rules on temporary unemployment apply.[526] It is not clear whether the second Member State *must* accept the application if the criteria for admission as a Blue Card holder are satisfied, but the Directive does preserve Member States' power to control volumes of admission during this process.[527] If the Blue Card expires during the application process, Member States *may* issue a temporary residence permit or equivalent authorization to stay.[528] There are also provisions on the movement of family members with the Blue Card holder who has not yet obtained long-term residence status, discussed further below.[529]

Finally, the Blue Card Directive requires Member States to report to other Member States and the Commission if they make use of certain options set out in the Directive,[530] and to communicate statistics concerning Blue Card applications and renewals.[531]

There are some interesting points of interaction between the rules in the Directive and the rules in the EU-Turkey association agreement. In particular, the obligation to renew the original Blue Card is stronger as regards Turkish workers,[532] due to the obligation to renew their work permit (and therefore their residence permit)

---

[520] Art 12 of the single permit Dir; see I:6.5.1 above.

[521] Art 11 of Dir 2003/109 ([2004] OJ L 16/44); see I:6.7 below.

[522] Compare to the provisions of Dir 2003/109, discussed above. The 2014 report concludes simply that there are wide variations among Member States as regards application of these provisions.

[523] Art 18(1).

[524] Art 18(2). If a Member State permits work, then the equal treatment rules are applicable, otherwise most of the equal treatment rules can be disapplied (Art 14(4)).

[525] Art 18(3).   [526] Art 18(4).   [527] Art 18(7).   [528] Art 18(5).   [529] I:6.6.2.

[530] Art 20(1). The 2014 report complains that this obligation is often not complied with.

[531] Art 20(2); see further I:6.11 below.

[532] See the discussion of Art 9 of the Directive above. The analysis there as to whether there is an obligation to renew Blue Cards is also entirely moot as regards Turkish workers who hold one. On the interaction between the EU-Turkey rules and EU immigration law in general, see Case C-294/06 *Payir and others* [2008] ECR I-203 and the discussion in S Peers, 'EU Migration Law and Association Agreements' in B Martenczuk and S van Thiel, eds., *Justice, Liberty, Security: New Challenges for EU External Relations* (VUBPress, 2008), 53. For more on the substance of the EU-Turkey rules, see I:6.4.3 above.

with the same employer after one year's employment; also any restrictions on labour market access which Member States apply pursuant to the Directive cannot apply to Turkish workers (as regards the same occupation) after three years with the same employer, and after four years overall. Presumably if Turkish Blue Card holders move to another Member State, whether before or after gaining long-term residence status, they will obtain a second 'Turkish worker' status under the Ankara Agreement from scratch.

Since the purpose of the Blue Card Directive, according to its preamble, is to 'attract and retain highly qualified third-country workers' in the context of enhancing the relative competitiveness of the EU economy, it should be assessed in that light.[533] The broader context of the Directive is the evidence that the EU is less likely than other advanced economies to attract highly-skilled workers from third countries,[534] coupled with the argument that 'the immigration regime is a significant factor in attracting such persons, in particular as regards routes to permanent residence'.[535] Furthermore, it was also argued that geographic mobility for such persons needed to be improved within the EU in order to attract highly-skilled workers,[536] and that the collective development of an EU policy on this issue would have a sort of collective 'publicity effect'.[537]

To this end, the preferred option set out in the impact assessment, reflected in the original proposal for the Blue Card directive, included: decision-making on applications within 30/60 days; a special derogation for the scheme for young workers (ie a lower salary threshold); validity of residence permits for over one year; in-country applications; and internal job mobility after two years.[538] It is remarkable that all of these features of the proposal were either removed in the final text (as regards the young workers' derogation) or watered down by permitting national derogations (as regards the valid period of permits, in-country applications, and job mobility) or less favourable standards (as regards the period for processing applications). Due to the legitimate concern that the Directive might contribute to a 'brain drain' from developing countries, the impact assessment report also referred to the possibility of '*obliging* Member States to pursue ethical recruitment policies by not actively recruiting in countries suffering from recognised situations of brain drain',[539] but neither the proposal nor the final Directive contains an obligation to this effect. There was no examination of the alternative or parallel possibilities of using the existing EU third-country national workforce more intensively, by means

---

[533] Recital 3 in the preamble. See also recital 7 in the preamble. It should also be noted that the impact assessment prepared by the Commission when it originally proposed the Dir (SEC (2007) 1403, 23 Oct 2007) also justified it by reference to the demographic issue, ie the effect of an expected decline in the EU working age population on the sustainability of economic growth and the welfare state. There is no reference to these demographic justifications as such in the preamble to the final text of the Directive, which contains purely economic explanations.

[534] See pp 14 and 113 of the impact assessment report.

[535] pp 14–15 of the impact assessment report.   [536] pp 12–15 of the impact assessment report.

[537] pp 18, 56, and 69 of the impact assessment report.

[538] p 55 of the impact assessment report. For the original proposal, see COM (2007) 637, 23 Oct 2007.

[539] p 65 of the impact assessment report, ibid.

of removing the restrictions which still remain on the employment of legal residents, or of facilitating labour migration from Turkey, in light of its negotiations for EU accession.

The 2014 report gives an initial indication of the impact of the Directive, although the information available is only partial because the only year for which full statistics were available was 2012, and the majority of Member States had not yet applied the Directive from the start of that year (all have applied it since). About 3,700 Blue Cards were issued to migrants in 2012; and about 1,107 family members of Blue Card holders were admitted. The Directive was extensively used in Germany, Spain, and Luxembourg, but a number of Member States barely used it at all. For 2013, only partial statistics are available, but at least 15,000 Blue Cards were issued, mainly in Germany, Luxembourg, and France.

The provisional statistics for 2013 indicate that the Blue Card Directive did not by itself accomplish its objective of increasing the numbers of highly-skilled migrants who come to the EU, at least initially, because Member States had issued more national permits for the purpose of highly-skilled employment in previous years.[540] Certainly it is clear that in some Member States, the maintenance of parallel national immigration regimes has hugely reduced the numbers of migrants using the Blue Card system. There has not been a 'brain drain' issue, due to the modest numbers of highly-skilled migrants.

How should the Blue Card Directive be reformed?[541] To increase the publicity effect of the Blue Card system, competing national systems could be curtailed or even prohibited. Based on the initial impact assessment and the 2014 report, the system would be more attractive if it provided for: in-country applications for all those legally resident; shorter decision-making deadlines; a ceiling on the salary threshold; a derogation from that salary threshold for younger workers; stronger rules on equal treatment as regards access to education and employment; longer periods of validity of initial permits; clearer rules on renewal of permits; and the flexibility to switch into self-employment, especially for migrants who want to establish a job-creating business. There could be a link between the period of stay after research or study, provided for in the proposed revision of the students' and researchers' Directive,[542] and the Blue Card system. Furthermore, the continued possible application of national quotas to Blue Card holders who *move between* Member States, even after they obtain long-term residence status, goes beyond the wording of the Treaty of Lisbon,[543] and likely deters such mobility. And if the EU wants to attract highly-skilled individuals to the EU, why focus only on employees, and not also establish a parallel EU system for the initial admission of self-employed persons who meet requirements comparable to those set out in the Blue Card directive?

---

[540] See Table 3 in the 2014 report. This conclusion has to be tentative, because the 2013 statistics for admission of highly-skilled migrants under national schemes were not available.

[541] See also the comments on the provisions on family reunion and long-term residents (I:6.6.2 and I:6.7.2 below).

[542] See I:6.5.3.3 below.   [543] See I:6.2.4 above.

6.5.2.2 *Seasonal workers*

After a long negotiation, the Council and EP adopted in 2014 a second Directive dealing with a specific category of labour migrants: seasonal workers.[544] Member States
have to apply this Directive by 30 September 2016.[545]

This Directive is limited in scope to those who normally reside outside the territory
of the EU, and who apply to be admitted as seasonal workers, or who have already been
admitted under the terms of the Directive.[546] The Directive applies to those admitted for less than three months as well as those admitted for a longer period. For the
former group, Directive specifies that the Borders Code, Visa Code, and visa list legislation continues to apply,[547] and makes a number of cross-references to those measures. Furthermore, the Directive does not apply to those workers who are usually
employed in other Member States, and who are 'posted' by their employers to work in a
second Member State, to non-EU family members of EU citizens, and to non-EU citizens covered by an agreement which extends free movement rights (the EEA or EU/
Swiss treaties).[548]

Consistently with the scope of the Directive, a 'seasonal worker' is a worker who
normally resides outside the EU, and who lives temporarily in the EU to 'carry out an
activity dependent on the passing of the seasons', pursuant to a fixed-term contract
concluded directly with an employer established in a Member State.[549] The concept
of a seasonal activity is in turn defined as an 'activity that is tied to a certain time of
the year by a recurring event or pattern of events linked to seasonal conditions during
which required labour levels are significantly above those necessary for usually ongoing operations'.[550]

The Directive leaves the EU free to set higher standards in other legislation, and
the EU and/or the Member States free to set higher standards by means of treaty
commitments.[551] However, while the Member States will be free to set higher standards as regards procedural safeguards, accommodation, workers' rights, and facilitation

---

[544] Directive 2014/36 ([2014] OJ L 94/375). All references in this sub-section are to this Directive, unless
otherwise noted.

[545] Art 28(1).

[546] Art 2(1). The Directive does not expressly ban Member States from considering seasonal worker
applications from people who are already present, but such applications would fall outside the scope of the
Directive. Recital 15 in the preamble says that applications should 'only' be made from outside the EU, but
recital 18 then states that the Directive does not affect the right of legally-resident third-country nationals
to work.

[547] Art 1(2). On these measures, see respectively I:3.6, I:4.7, and I:4.5 above. It should be recalled that
according to the visa list Reg, Member States are free to require a visa for those who would otherwise be
exempt from one, if the person concerned intends to take up work.

[548] Art 2(3). On these categories of persons, see I:6.4.4, I:6.4.1, and I:6.4.3 above.

[549] Art 3(b). The reference to a contract concluded directly with the employer means that employees of
temporary work agencies fall outside the scope of the Directive, although recital 12 suggests that in some
cases they would be covered by it. Also, the requirement that the employer be established in a Member
State implicitly excludes persons posted by employers established in third countries from the scope of the
Directive.

[550] Art 3(c). Art 2(2) requires Member States to define exactly what the relevant sectors are. Recital 13
in the preamble refers to the labour market sectors where seasonal work is common: tourism, agriculture,
and horticulture.

[551] Art 4(1).

of complaints, they will not be free otherwise to set higher standards.[552] Neither will they be free to maintain or establish a separate national system regarding seasonal workers.[553] So Member States will not be able to alter the substantive grounds for admission or the rules on duration of stay and re-entry.

The key criteria for admission in the Directive are fully mandatory. Member States will have to ensure that an application to enter as a seasonal worker is accompanied by: a valid work contract or binding job offer, setting out all of the details of the job; a valid travel document (possibly valid for the entire duration of the seasonal work); evidence of having, or having applied for, sickness insurance (unless such coverage comes with the work contract); and evidence of having accommodation, as defined in the Directive (see below).[554] Member States will have to check that the seasonal worker will have sufficient resources not to have to use the social assistance system,[555] cannot admit persons considered to pose a threat to public policy, public security, or public health, and must check that the applicant does not pose a risk of illegal immigration and intends to leave the Member States' territory when the authorization for seasonal work expires. It is implicit from the context of the Directive, in particular the development of a 'common immigration policy' in accordance with the Treaty, that this list of grounds for admission is exhaustive, in the absence of any express wording to the contrary.[556]

Member States will be obliged to reject applications whenever these conditions are not met, or where the documents presented with an application are 'fraudulently acquired, or falsified, or tampered with'.[557] They will also have to reject applications, 'if appropriate', where there has been a prior sanction against the employer for 'undeclared work and/or illegal employment', the employer is being wound up or has no economic activity, or the employer has been sanctioned for breach of the Directive.[558] However, otherwise the grounds for refusal of an application will be optional: a labour market preference test for home State citizens, other EU citizens, or third-country nationals lawfully residing and forming part of the labour market;[559] the application of Member States' rules on volumes of admission of third-country nationals;[560] or breaches of employment law by the employer, the use of seasonal work to replace a full-time job, or a prior breach of immigration law by the would-be worker.[561] There are similar provisions on withdrawal of the authorization to work as a seasonal worker,[562] although it should be noted that Member States can withdraw authorization if the worker applies for international protection.[563] Again, it is implicit that these lists of grounds for refusal

---

[552] Art 4(2). There is no requirement that any higher national standards will have to be 'compatible' with the Directive.

[553] Compare to the Blue Card Directive (see I:6.5.2.1 above).

[554] Arts 5 and 6. For workers who intend to stay 90 days or less, the Member States applying the Schengen rules will use the Schengen border and visa rules to check some of these requirements.

[555] Arts 5(3) and 6(3). These provisions are similar to Art 7(1)(c) of the family reunion Directive ([2003] OJ L 251/12), so it is arguable that the Court of Justice's interpretation of the latter provision would be relevant by analogy: Case C-578/08 *Chakroun* [2010] ECR I-1839, discussed in I:6.6.1 below.

[556] See by analogy the case law on admission of students, discussed in I:6.5.3.2 below.

[557] Art 8(1).

[558] Art 8(2). This includes, but is wider than, the EU Directive on sanctioning employers of irregular migrants (see I:7.6.1 below). Member States will have the power to require employers to cooperate (Art 10).

[559] Art 8(3).   [560] Art 7.   [561] Art 8(4).   [562] Art 9.   [563] Art 15(8).

or withdrawal are exhaustive, in the absence of any express wording to the contrary. It should follow that there is an obligation to issue a permit where the grounds for admission are satisfied, but none of the grounds for refusal exist.

As for the admission procedure, Member States will first of all have an obligation to make information available on the conditions of entry and residence and rights, as well as the admission process.[564] It will be up to Member States to decide whether the applicant or the employer makes the application.[565] Member States will have to designate the relevant national authority,[566] and the application process takes the form of a single application procedure for a combined work/residence status.[567] Member States must grant the person concerned every facility to obtain the necessary visa.[568] Those workers who fulfil the admission criteria and who do not fall foul of the grounds for refusal must be granted a permit or visa,[569] in the format of the EU standard visa or residence permit.[570]

The Directive will set a total maximum limit of between five and nine months per calendar year of residence for a seasonal worker; workers must then return to a third country.[571] Since the Directive will only regulate admission and stay of seasonal workers, it should follow that Member States will retain discretion to permit the worker to stay for longer on some other ground. Member States may also set a limited time period each year when employers can hire seasonal workers.[572]

Within the maximum time limit, seasonal workers will be able, on one occasion, to change employers or to obtain an extension of their stay with their employer, if they still meet the criteria for admission, although the grounds for refusal will still apply.[573] Member States will have an option to allow further extensions or changes of employer,[574] and can refuse to extend the stay if the worker applies for international protection.[575] Next, the Directive will facilitate the re-entry of seasonal workers who were admitted at least once within the previous five years, if they complied with immigration law during their stay. This could include a simplified application process, an accelerated procedure, priority for previous seasonal workers, or the issue of several seasonal worker permits at the same time.[576]

Member States will have to impose sanctions against those who have breached their obligations under the Directive, including a possible ban on employing seasonal workers.[577] If seasonal workers' permit to work is withdrawn because of the employer's illegal behaviour, the employer must compensate the employees for all the work they have done or would have done.[578] There are specific rules on the liability of sub-contractors.[579]

Moving on to procedural safeguards, the Directive provides for: a notified decision in writing within ninety days of the application; special rules on the renewal of authorization; a chance to provide additional necessary information within a reasonable

---

[564] Art 11(1). Information will also have to be provided to those whose are authorized to work as seasonal workers (Art 11(2)).
[565] Art 12(3).   [566] Art 13(1).   [567] Art 13(2).   [568] Art 12(7).
[569] Art 12(1) and (2).   [570] Art 12(4) and (5).   [571] Art 14(1).   [572] Art 14(2).
[573] Art 15(1) and (3). Recital 31 in the preamble explains that this provision will help to avoid abuse because the worker will no longer be exclusively tied to a single employer. Art 15(6) gives Member States the option of applying a labour market test again.
[574] Art 15(2) and (4).   [575] Art 15(8).   [576] Art 16.   [577] Art 17(1).
[578] Art 17(2).   [579] Art 17(3).

deadline; and a requirement that a rejection (or withdrawal or non-renewal of a permit) be issued in writing and open to a legal challenge, with information on the reasons for the decision, the redress available, and the relevant time-limits.[580] Member States may charge fees for applications, if they are not disproportionate or excessive, and may require employers to pay the costs of workers' travel and sickness insurance.[581] Workers' accommodation must ensure an 'adequate' standard of living, rents cannot be excessive, a contract for housing must be issued, and employers must ensure that accommodation meets health and safety standards.[582] Member States may insist that seasonal workers can only be placed by public employment services.[583]

As for the rights of seasonal workers, Chapter IV of the Directive first of all states that they will have the right to enter and stay on the territory of the relevant Member State, free access to the territory of that Member State, and the right to carry out the economic activity which they have been authorized to take up.[584] Furthermore, seasonal workers are entitled to equal treatment with nationals as regards terms of employment (including working conditions), freedom of association, back payments, social security, the transfer of pensions, access to goods and services available to the public (except housing), employment advice (on seasonal work), education, and recognition of diplomas, and tax benefits.[585] However, equal treatment can be restricted as regards family benefits, unemployment benefits, education, and tax benefits, and Member States are still free to withdraw or to refuse to renew the permit in accordance with the Directive.[586] Finally, Member States must ensure monitoring, assessment, and inspections, and facilitate complaints workers or by third parties supporting or acting on their behalf.[587]

The intention of this Directive is to regulate the admission of seasonal workers with a view to enhancing the EU's economic competitiveness, optimizing the link between migration and development, while guaranteeing decent working and living conditions for the workers, alongside incentives and safeguards to prevent overstaying or permanent stay.[588] In principle it has achieved some of these goals, in particular by including a number of provisions to ensure equal treatment and decent accommodation for seasonal workers, to punish employers who mistreat workers or who breach immigration law, and to guarantee that the rules in question are enforced. But it remains to be seen how much resources Member States are actually willing to expend on enforcement. Furthermore, since the Directive is limited in scope to those who are not yet on the territory, it can do nothing to alleviate the position of those who are present without authorization but who cannot be returned in practice,[589] and it gives Member States express *carte blanche* to deprive asylum seekers of even the modest income which they would earn as seasonal workers.[590] Seen in light of the EU's immigration policy as a

---

[580] Art 18.
[581] Art 19. On the issue of fees, the case law on the long-term residents Directive is presumably applicable by analogy (see I:6.7 below).
[582] Art 20.   [583] Art 21.   [584] Art 22.   [585] Art 23(1).
[586] Art 23(2) and (3).   [587] Arts 24 and 25.
[588] Recitals 6 and 7 in the preamble to the Directive.
[589] See the discussion of the Returns Directive in I:7.7.1 below.
[590] On the access to employment for asylum seekers generally, see the discussion of the reception conditions Directive in I:5.9 above.

whole, it constitutes a classic example of fixing one hole in a dam while ignoring the many leaks springing up elsewhere.

6.5.2.3 *Intra-corporate transferees*

After another long negotiation, the Council and EP adopted a Directive regulating a third specific category of labour migration in 2014: intra-corporate transferees ('ICTs').[591] Member States have to apply this Directive by 29 November 2016.[592]

The Directive defines an 'intra-corporate transferee' as a person who is outside the territory of the Member States, who applies for an ICT permit due to an intra-corporate transfer, which is essentially a secondment within a company or group of companies.[593] There are three categories of ICTs: managers, specialists, and trainees.[594] However, several categories of persons are excluded from the scope of the Directive: researchers, as defined in other EU legislation;[595] persons governed by treaties between the EU and third States which extend free movement rights;[596] persons who are posted within the EU;[597] self-employed persons; agency workers; and students or those who are undergoing training as part of their studies.[598]

Member States retain the power to issue residence permits which fall outside the scope of the Directive.[599] Furthermore, Member States and/or the EU can grant more favourable conditions for ICTs by means of treaties with third States, and Member States can grant more favourable conditions for them in their national law as regard the definition and admission of family members, procedural rights, and equal treatment.[600]

Most of the criteria for admission of ICTs are fully mandatory. Member States will have to ensure that an application for an ICT permit was accompanied by: evidence that the host entity in the EU and the parent company outside it are part of the same undertaking, or group of undertakings;[601] evidence of employment within the same group of undertakings (for three months to a year, or three months to six months as regards trainees);[602] an assignment letter with details of the duration of the transfer, the location of the host entity (or host entities), the pay and working conditions which the worker will receive during the transfer, evidence that the person concerned has a post as either a manager, specialist, or graduate trainee, and evidence that the worker will be transferred back to the same group, within a third country, at the end of the assignment;[603] evidence of professional qualifications and experience or (for graduate trainees) the relevant university degree;[604] documents certifying that the worker fufils the conditions applicable to EU citizens to exercise the regulated profession that the worker will work in;[605]

---

[591] Directive 2014/66 ([2014] OJ L 157/1). All references in this sub-section are to this Directive, unless otherwise noted.

[592] Art 27(1).

[593] Arts 2(1) and 3(b) and (c). See also the definition of 'host entity' and 'group of undertakings' in Art 3(d) and (l).

[594] Art 2(e) to (g).   [595] Art 2(2)(a). See I:6.5.3.1 below.

[596] Art 2(2)(b). See I:6.4.3 above.   [597] Art 2(2)(c). See I:6.4.4 above.

[598] Art 2(2)(d) to (f). There is no cross-reference to the EU legislation on admission of students (on which, see I:6.5.3.2 below).

[599] Art 2(3).   [600] Art 4.   [601] Art 5(1)(a).   [602] Art 5(1)(b).   [603] Art 5(1)(c).

[604] Art 5(1)(d).   [605] Art 5(1)(e). A 'regulated profession' is defined in Art 3(o).

presentation of a valid travel document, and a visa if required;[606] and evidence of having, or having applied for, sickness insurance (unless such coverage comes with the work contract).[607] There is also a mandatory requirement that the ICT would not pose a threat to public policy, public security, or public health.[608] ICTs must receive the same pay as national workers, and other work conditions equivalent to 'posted workers'.[609] Member States have an option to impose a 'sufficient resources' requirement, to require a training agreement in the case of an application to admit a trainee, or to apply a quota within the meaning of Article 79(5) TFEU.[610] However, it is not possible to apply an economic needs test, except to the extent required by accession agreements.[611] It is implicit from the context of the Directive, in particular the development of a 'common immigration policy' in accordance with the Treaty, that this list of grounds for admission is exhaustive, in the absence of any express wording to the contrary. Therefore any applicant who meets the criteria for an ICT permit has the right to receive one.[612]

Member States will be obliged to reject applications whenever these conditions are not met, where the documents presented with an application were 'fraudulently acquired, or falsified, or tampered with', where the employer was established to circumvent national rules, or where the maximum period of stay has been exceeded.[613] They will have an option to reject applications where the employer or host entity has previously been sanctioned for 'undeclared work and/or illegal employment'.[614] There are further options to reject applications where: the employer or host entity has breached its employment law, social security law, or tax obligations; the employer or host entity is being wound up under national insolvency law; the ICTs are being brought in as 'scabs' during a labour dispute; or less than six months have passed since the ICT finished a previous period in the EU.[615] The optional exceptions can only be applied on a case-by-case basis, respecting the principle of proportionality.[616] Very similar rules apply to the withdrawal or refusal to renew ICT permits.[617] Again, it is implicit that this list of grounds for refusal, non-renewal, or withdrawal is exhaustive. It should follow that there is an obligation to renew a permit where none of the grounds for non-renewal exist.

Member States may also hold the host entity liable for failure to comply with the conditions of admission, and must in that case provide for effective sanctions.[618] This option co-exists awkwardly with an obligation to 'prevent possible abuses and to sanction infringements' of the Directive, including 'monitoring, assessment and, where appropriate, inspection'.[619]

---

[606] Art 5(1)(f).   [607] Art 5(1)(g).   [608] Art 5(8).

[609] Art 5(4). There is no definition here of 'posted workers'. See also the discussion of the equal treatment clause below.

[610] Arts 5(5) and (6) and 6. On Art 79(5) TFEU, see I:6.2.4 above.

[611] Recital 21 in the preamble. Currently, the only relevant accession treaty is with Croatia.

[612] See also the case law on the students' Directive (I:6.5.3.2 below).   [613] Art 7(1).

[614] Art 7(2). This includes, but is wider than, the EU Directive on sanctioning employers of irregular migrants (see I:7.6.1 below), since it could presumably include non-payment of social security contributions for EU citizen employees.

[615] Art 7(3) and (4).   [616] Art 7(5).   [617] Art 8.   [618] Art 9(1) and (2).

[619] Art 9(3).

As for the admission procedure, Member States first of all have an obligation to make information available on entry, residence, and rights, as well as the evidence to be submitted for an application.[620] It is up to Member States to decide whether the applicant or the employer makes the application,[621] but the applicant has to be outside the territory when the application is made.[622] The application must be made to the authorities of the Member State where the longest stay will take place.[623] Member States have to designate the relevant national authority,[624] and the application process takes the form of a single application procedure for a combined work/residence status.[625] They may provide for a 'fast-track' application process for some companies.[626]

An ICT permit can only be valid for a maximum limit of three years for a manager or specialist, or one year for a graduate trainee, although Member States retain discretion to permit the worker to stay for longer on some other ground.[627] It is implicit that ICTs could not change employers within this period. An ICT can apply to come back on the same basis afterward, although there must be at least a six-month gap before the application can be considered.[628]

Those workers who fulfil the admission criteria and who have received a positive decision must receive an ICT permit.[629] This document must use the same format as the EU's uniform residence permit,[630] and Member States cannot issue any other documents as proof of access to the labour market.[631] Member States must grant the person concerned every facility to obtain the necessary visa.[632]

Next, the Directive provides for procedural safeguards: a notified decision in writing within ninety days of the application;[633] a chance to provide additional necessary information within a reasonable deadline;[634] and a requirement that a rejection (or withdrawal or non-renewal of a permit) be issued in writing and open to a legal challenge, with information on the reasons for the decision, the redress available and the relevant time-limits.[635] Member States may charge fees for ICT applications.[636]

As for the rights of ICTs, Chapter IV of the Directive first of all states that they will have the right to enter and stay on the territory of the relevant Member State, free access to the territory of that Member State, and the right to carry out the economic activity which they have been authorized to take up.[637] Furthermore, ICTs will be entitled to the same working conditions as posted workers (as defined by EU law on cross-border services in the internal market), although this is 'without prejudice' to the rule that in the admission procedure, Member States should ensure that ICTs get the same pay as the host State's *nationals*.[638] Also, there will be a right to equal treatment as regards

---

[620] Art 10(1).   [621] Art 11(1).

[622] Art 11(2); this bolsters the rule that the Directive does not apply to in-country applicants.

[623] Art 11(3).   [624] Art 11(4).   [625] Art 11(5), in conjunction with Art 2(k).

[626] Art 11(6) to (9).

[627] Art 12(1). The permit must be valid for at least one year or the duration of the transfer to the first State, whichever is shorter: Art 13(2).

[628] Art 12(2).   [629] Art 13(1).   [630] Art 13(3) and (4).   [631] Art 13(5).

[632] Art 13(7).   [633] Art 15(1).   [634] Art 15(2).   [635] Art 15(3) and (4).

[636] Art 16. Presumably the fees are limited, by analogy with the case law on the long-term residents' Directive: see I:6.7 below.

[637] Art 17.

[638] Art 18(1), referring to Art 5(4)(a). On the posted workers' legislation, see I:6.4.4 above.

freedom of association, recognition of diplomas, social security, the transfer of pensions, and access to goods and services available to the public—but not housing or employment placement services.[639] Member States will still be free to withdraw or to refuse to renew the permit in accordance with the Directive.[640] There are also special rules for family members of ICTs, which derogate from the family reunion Directive in order to encourage the admission of ICTs; they are discussed further below.[641]

Like several other groups of third-country nationals, ICTs will have the right to mobility between Member States, although the rules governing this issue are particularly complex.[642] The final provisions of the Directive require Member States to draw up precise statistics on the admission of ICTs.[643] Member States will also have to appoint contact points to share information on the mobility of ICTs.[644]

Assessing this Directive, first of all it raises 'legal base' issues, which were discussed above.[645] As for the merits of the Directive, the starting point is the rationale of the Commission for its proposal, which (according to the explanatory memorandum) was the ongoing globalization of international business, entailing the frequent seconding of staff within a business, which was frustrated by obstacles arising from the current legal framework: the absence of specific schemes in many Member States, complex rules, delays and costs in obtaining visas and work permits, and the uncertainty and diversity of national rules, including limits on family reunion. This argument was further substantiated in the Commission's impact assessment, which referred to evidence that enhancing the movement of ICTs contributed to attracting and retaining productive foreign investment,[646] and gathered a list of complaints from stakeholders about the barriers they faced in this area, which included also restrictions on mobility between Member States and restrictions on the employment of ICTs' family members.[647]

The ICT Directive addresses all of these barriers, but how well does it do it? While family members of ICTs will be able to take up employment pursuant to the rules in the family reunion Directive, this will be of limited use to them, since they will be limited to the same employment access as the sponsor. As for mobility, at first sight the rules in the Directive on this issue are possibly too complex to address this particular barrier effectively, although perhaps they can be made to work in practice. Also, all of the objectives of the Directive would have been strengthened by including within its scope those who are already legally on the territory of a Member State.

There is an understandable concern that the admission of ICTs could undercut social standards in the EU. While the Commission argues that highly-qualified and highly-paid staff are unlikely to have such an effect, it is hard to see why the Directive does not simply entitle ICTs to equal treatment with nationals as regards all working

---

[639] Art 18(2). Member States can also derogate from equal treatment for family benefits, if the ICT stays for less than nine months (Art 18(3)).

[640] Art 18(4).   [641] Art 19; see I:6.6.2 below.

[642] Arts 20–3. The Commission's report on the application of the Directive, due in Nov 2019 (see Art 25), will have to focus on the application of these provisions.

[643] Art 24.   [644] Art 26.   [645] I:6.2.4 above.

[646] SEC (2010) 884, 13 July 2010, pp 14–15.

[647] Ibid, Annex 5. For details on previous national laws (where they existed), see ibid, Annex 2. The Commission estimated that there were then 17,500 ICTs a year entering the EU—or 15,500 a year, not including the UK and Ireland.

conditions, instead of equal treatment with posted workers. Relying on equal treatment with posted workers is not sufficient, since the posted workers' Directive does not fully guarantee their equal treatment with nationals, in light of the case law of the CJEU, which limits the extent to which Member States can insist on their national employment legislation applying to workers posted from other Member States.[648] Admittedly, the Directive does provide that *Member States* must ensure equal pay for ICTs as a criterion for admission, but it does not specify the same rule as an equal treatment right. At best, this is poor drafting technique; at worst, it is a cynical attempt to prevent ICTs from enforcing a condition of their admission. The absence of an equal treatment right on this issue, without any clear justification for it, is incompatible with the EU's Charter of Fundamental Rights, which refers to equal treatment in working conditions for third-country national workers.

6.5.3 Other primary migration

6.5.3.1 *Researchers*

In 2005, in order to increase the number of research workers in the EU with a view to meeting the 'Lisbon agenda' objective of making the EU the world's most competitive and dynamic knowledge economy by 2010, the Council adopted Directive 2005/71 on admission of third-country national researchers,[649] alongside Recommendations on the longer-term admission and the issue of short-term visas to third-country national researchers.[650] Member States had to apply the Directive by 12 October 2007,[651] and one Member State was condemned by the Court of Justice for failure to meet this deadline.[652] The Commission reported on the application of this Directive in 2011,[653] and proposed amendments to it in 2013, which were agreed in 2015.[654]

Directive 2005/71 applies to admission as a researcher for periods of more than three months.[655] It contains definitions of 'researcher', 'research', 'research organisation', and 'residence permit', with a special 'researcher' residence permit to be issued to beneficiaries of the Directive.[656] 'Research' is broadly defined to mean 'creative work undertaken on a systematic basis in order to increase the stock of knowledge'. The definition incorporates the social sciences, not just the physical sciences, as it includes 'knowledge of man, culture and society'; and the definition also includes applied research ('and the use of the stock of knowledge to devise new applications'). A 'research organisation' could include not just a public organization, but also a private organization.

---

[648] See Cases: C-341/05 *Laval* [2007] ECR I-11767; C-346/06 *Rüffert* [2008] ECR I-1989; and C-319/06 *Commission v Luxembourg* [2008] ECR I-4323. From a large literature, see the contributions in (2007–08) 10 CYELS.

[649] [2005] OJ L 289/15. All references in this sub-section are to this Directive, unless otherwise noted.

[650] [2005] OJ L 289/26 (long-term admission); [2005] OJ L 289/23 (visas). The latter Recommendation is discussed in I:4.7.1 above.

[651] Art 17(1).   [652] Case C-523/08 *Commission v Spain*, judgment of 11 Feb 2010, unreported.

[653] COM (2011) 901, 20 Dec 2011.   [654] See I:6.5.3.3 below.   [655] Art 1.

[656] Art 2. According to the Commission report, a number of Member States do not apply the definition of 'researcher' correctly.

As for the scope, the Directive applies to persons applying for admission to carry out a research project.[657] But the Directive does not apply to: applicants for international protection; persons on a temporary protection scheme; persons applying for admission as students under Directive 2004/114 on the admission of students and other categories of persons to take up doctoral studies;[658] persons whose expulsion is suspended for reasons of fact or law; or researchers seconded by a research organization to another research organization in a different Member State.[659] The Directive is without prejudice to more favourable provisions in treaties concluded by the Member States, the EU, or both together; and it leaves Member States the power to adopt more favourable provisions of national law, without a requirement that such measures be 'compatible' with the Directive.[660]

The core of the Directive is a special procedure for admitting researchers, which entails a significant delegation of power from national immigration authorities to research institutions as regards the admission of researchers. First of all, there are detailed rules on the process of Member States' approval of the research institutions.[661] Then, the Directive sets out rules concerning the 'hosting agreement' to be agreed between the institution and the researcher.[662] These agreements provide for the institution to host the researcher while the researcher works on a research project for the institution, subject to the issue of a residence permit to the researcher. An agreement can only be signed if: the research project has been accepted by the institution, in light of the purpose and duration of the research and financial resources to fund it, and of the researchers' qualifications, and if the researcher can meet resources and sickness insurance conditions. The institution then issues a statement to the researcher that it assumes responsibility for his or her health, residence, and return costs. Member States may require the institution to assume responsibility for the researcher's stay and return costs if he or she becomes an irregular resident. Also, the agreement will lapse if the legal relationship between the researcher and the institution is terminated, or if the researcher is not admitted.

As for the immigration process, Member States are obliged to admit researchers following the mandatory conclusion of checks to ensure that the conditions for admission are met.[663] The conditions are fourfold: possession of a valid travel document, as determined by national law; a hosting agreement; a statement of financial responsibility from the host institution; and a lack of threat to public policy, public security, or public health.[664] Member States must issue residence permits for at least one year, unless the period of project is less than one year's duration, and the permit must be renewed if the conditions for its renewal are still met.[665] A provision on family members specifies that their residence permit shall have the same validity as that of the researcher, if

---

[657] Art 3(1).   [658] [2004] OJ L 375/12. On this Directive, see I:6.5.3.2 below.

[659] Art 3(3).   [660] Art 4.   [661] Art 5.   [662] Art 6.

[663] Art 7(3). This interpretation is confirmed by the CJEU's interpretation of Directive 2004/114 as regards the admission of students (see I:6.5.3.2 below). According to the Commission report, some Member States breach the Directive because admission is only discretionary.

[664] Art 7(1).

[665] Art 8. For more on residence permits generally, see I:6.9.1 below. The Commission report indicates that some Member States do not provide for obligatory renewal; this is a breach of the Directive.

the validity of their travel documents allows it; but Member States may shorten such permits' validity in 'duly justified' cases.[666] Moreover, the period of residence of family members shall not be made dependent on a minimum period of residence of the researcher. However, there is no explicit right of family reunion, although a recital to the preamble encourages family members' admission. Member States may withdraw or refuse to renew a permit if it was acquired by fraud, if the holder no longer meets the conditions of the permit or is residing for other purposes, or on grounds of public policy or public security.[667]

Chapter III of the Directive concerns researchers' rights. Researchers admitted under the Directive may teach in accordance with national law, although Member States may set a maximum number of teaching hours per year.[668] They have the right to equal treatment as regards recognition of diplomas, certificates and qualifications, working conditions (including pay and dismissal), social security as defined under EU free movement legislation, subject to the limitations allowed by the Regulation extending those rules to third-country nationals, tax benefits, and access to goods and services made available to the public.[669] Finally, a researcher has the right of mobility to other Member States to conduct part of his or her research project there.[670] If the period of mobility is less than three months, the second Member State cannot insist on a new hosting agreement, although the mobility is subject to meeting a sufficient resources test and requirements of public policy, etc. in the second Member State. After three months, the second Member State may insist on the negotiation of a new hosting agreement. Any necessary visas or residence permits must be issued 'in a timely manner' and Member States cannot require the researcher to leave their territory while the application is processed.

The procedural rules in Chapter IV of the Directive comprise first of all an option for Member States to determine whether the researcher or the research organization submits the application. An application must be submitted while the researcher is outside the Member States which he or she wishes to enter, although Member States have an option to consider applications made by persons who are already present.[671] If an application is successful, Member States must grant the person concerned 'every facility' to obtain the necessary visas.[672] Member States must respond to applications 'as soon as

---

[666] Art 9. There is no definition of 'family members'.   [667] Art 10.

[668] Art 11. The Commission report expresses some doubt that all Member States are fully compliant with this provision of the Directive.

[669] Art 12. On the social security legislation applicable to third-country nationals, see I:6.4.2 above and I:6.8 below (and, as regards association agreements, I:6.4.3 above). Note also that the subsequent Dir on single permits furthermore confers equal treatment rights on researchers in the context of employment; see I:6.5.1 above. To some extent, the researchers' Directive is more favourable to the persons concerned, since it lacks the exceptions to the equal treatment rules found in the single permit Dir; but the latter Dir expressly allows for other EU immigration legislation to set higher standards.

[670] Art 13. The Commission report states that some Member States have not transposed these rules in their national law, causing legal uncertainty.

[671] Art 14. A clause in the preamble states that holders of residence permits 'should' be able to make an application for researcher status without leaving the territory. The Commission report states that six Member States allow in-country applications only; eight Member States allow out-of-country applications only; and twelve Member States allow both.

[672] Art 14(4). On long-stay visas generally, see I:6.9.2 below.

possible', but with no deadline set.[673] Persons must be notified of negative decisions and have a right to 'mount a legal challenge before the authorities' of the relevant Member State in the event of a dispute.[674]

The Commission's 2011 report on the application of this Directive indicated that it had little success accomplishing its intended objective, with only 7,000 researchers admitted in 2010. As a result, as noted already, the Commission soon suggested significant amendments to the Directive, which were subsequently agreed and are discussed further below. Why was it not successful? Even though several provisions of the Directive are sufficiently clear, precise, and unconditional to confer directly effective rights,[675] resulting in a right of entry and residence for researchers once the criteria for admission are met initially, and a right of continued residence if the conditions for admission are still met, there are some significant gaps.

In particular, the Directive is missing rules on: speedy responses to applications; the right to submit in-country applications; and a right to family reunion (or any status for family members after entry, such as the right to work).[676] Although the researchers' Directive clearly at least precludes banning entry of family members based solely on the time period of the researchers' entry, overall its miserly attitude to the issue of family reunion compares unfavourably with the provisions of the Blue Card Directive and the intra-corporate transferees Directive, which both made a point of waiving a number of restrictions in the family reunion Directive.[677]

The next question to consider is the application of the long-term residents' Directive to researchers. There is no provision in the researchers' Directive on its relationship with Directive 2003/109. However, it can be assumed that in the absence of any explicit derogation in either Directive that researchers will ultimately be able to qualify for long-term residence status, particularly because their residence permits under the researchers' Directive are expressly renewable as long as the conditions for their issue are still met, and therefore should not be considered as 'limited' permits taking them outside the scope of the long-term residents' Directive.[678] Indeed, conversely, it will be possible for long-term residents settled in one Member State to become researchers covered by this Directive in another Member State; this could be appealing where the second Member State is applying restrictions on movement of long-term residents permitted by Directive 2003/109. Eventual long-term resident status for researchers would offer the added attraction of enhanced long-term movement between Member States, expanded equality rights (except as regards social security in the first Member State, where the researchers' Directive is more beneficial), and the ability to switch status. For example, researchers might wish to take up a relevant job in a university or private industry that falls outside the scope of the 'researcher' category defined by this Directive, or to establish a company that makes use of their expertise. Also, as argued

---

[673] Art 15(1).   [674] Art 15.   [675] Arts 7(3), 8, 9(1) (first sentence), 11, 12, 13, and 15.

[676] Researchers will not necessarily be able to claim the application of the family reunion Directive 2003/86 ([2003] OJ L 251/12; see I:6.6 below) since they will not always have the prospect of permanent residence (see Art 3(1), Dir 2003/86). In any event, the standards in that Directive are quite low.

[677] Art 15 of Dir 2009/50 ([2009] OJ L 155/17); see I:6.6.2 below.

[678] Art 3(2)(e), Dir 2003/109 ([2004] OJ L 16/44). See further I:6.7 below.

below, the acquisition or prospect of long-term resident status would be sufficient to trigger application of the family reunion Directive,[679] and indeed it could be argued that the right to a renewable permit under the researchers' Directive offers researchers a strong argument that they have a 'reasonable prospect' of permanent residence, as required for the family reunion Directive to apply, not long after their initial entry.

Like the Blue Card Directive, Directive 2005/71 could also interact with the association agreement with Turkey. Since the latter Directive is 'without prejudice to more favourable provisions' of such agreements,[680] it should follow that the two sets of rules both apply to Turkish workers, with the highest standard of protection applying in the event of overlap, as any Turkish nationals admitted as researchers pursuant to the researchers' Directive will be considered 'workers' under the EU-Turkey agreement if they have an employment relationship as defined by EU free movement law.[681]

As for the clause on family members, it is hard to see when it would be 'duly justified' to limit the duration of residence of family members. In the absence of a reference to national law, the concept should be considered a concept of EU law. The obligation for due justification implies a duty to give objective reasons to the person concerned and since the potential limitation would amount to an exception to a rule in the Directive, it should be interpreted narrowly.

While the Directive appears equivocal about another right for researchers, the right to teach, it is arguable that the reference to national law allows Member States to place reasonable and proportionate limits on the right to teach, but that a complete or nearly-complete ban on teaching would violate the Directive. As a purely practical matter, it may not be realistic for research institutions to sign non-EU citizens to research agreements unless the researchers can take up some of the teaching load of the institution (if the institution has students); and any deterrent to signing such agreements will make the objectives of the Directive harder to achieve.

Finally, as in other EU immigration law measures, the weak procedural standards are objectionable in principle. But given that the Directive appears to create a right to entry and stay, and in light of the rights to fair administration inherent in the general principles of EU law and the right to a fair trial set out in the EU Charter of Rights,[682] Member States' authorities nevertheless have a duty to give reasons for negative decisions, and Member States must allow challenges to such decisions in the courts. The latter part of this interpretation is confirmed, by analogy, by the Court of Justice ruling in the EP challenge to the family reunion Directive.[683]

6.5.3.2 Students and other non-economic migrants

In December 2004, the Council adopted Directive 2004/114 on admission of students, pupils, trainees, and volunteers.[684] Member States had to comply with the Directive by

---

[679] See I:6.6 below.   [680] Art 4(1)(a).
[681] See the relevant case law discussed in I:6.4.3 above. In particular the case law concerning students (Case C-294/06 *Payir* [2008] ECR I-203) should be relevant by analogy.
[682] See I:6.3.4 above.   [683] Case C-540/03 *EP v Council* [2006] ECR I-5769.
[684] [2004] OJ L 375/12. All references in this sub-section are to this Dir, unless otherwise indicated.

12 January 2007.[685] The CJEU has ruled on the interpretation of this Directive several times.[686] For its part, the Commission reported on the application of the Directive in 2011 (the '2011 report'),[687] and proposed major amendments to the Directive in 2013, which were agreed in 2015.[688]

Chapter I of the Directive sets out general provisions, comprising the purpose of the Directive, definitions, and scope.[689] The Directive only covers stays of over three months.[690] As for the scope, Member States are only obliged to apply the Directive to students; application of the rules in the Directive to the other three categories of persons remains optional.[691] Member States are free to provide for more favourable rules in national law or by international treaties; the EU (alone or with the Member States) is also empowered to adopt more favourable rules by means of treaties. Employed or self-employed persons, asylum seekers, persons on temporary protection or subsidiary protection schemes, persons whose expulsion is suspended, long-term residents within the scope of the long-term residents' Directive, and third-country nationals who are the family members of EU citizens who have moved within the EU are all excluded from the scope of the Directive.[692]

Chapter II sets out conditions of entry and residence.[693] A person can only enter if he or she meets the specific conditions set out for various categories of persons set out in the Directive. In *Ben Alaya*, the CJEU confirmed that an applicant who met the criteria for admission as a student had to be admitted, since Member States did not have any power to require that additional conditions for admission had to be complied with.[694] There are general rules applying to all four categories of migrant: presentation of a travel document; parental authorization if the migrant is a minor; sickness insurance; requirements of public policy, public security, or public health; and proof of fee payment. Next, there are specific conditions and specific limits on residence status for each of the four groups;[695] it is not possible for anyone to obtain an indefinite residence status pursuant to the Directive. Member States must facilitate admission for persons participating in EU education schemes,[696] and permit mobility between Member States for students.[697]

Residence permits may be terminated on grounds of public policy or fraud,[698] and students are entitled to work, subject to certain limits.[699] In particular, students have the right to employment outside term time for at least ten hours a week, and may be authorized to take up self-employment.[700] Member States can take account of their

---

[685] Art 22.

[686] Cases: C-294/06 *Payir* [2008] ECR I-203; C-15/11 *Sommer*, ECLI:EU:C:2012:371; and C-491/13 *Ben Alaya*, ECLI:EU:C:2014:2187. Pending case: C-544/15 *Fahimian*.

[687] COM (2011) 587, 28 Sep 2011.   [688] See I:6.5.3.3 below.   [689] Arts 1–3.

[690] Art 1(a).

[691] According to the 2011 report, ten Member States extended the Directive to all three extra groups of persons, while five Member States extended the Directive to one or two of these groups.

[692] Most of these categories of persons are also excluded from other EU immigration legislation: see I:6.5.1 above.

[693] Arts 5–11.   [694] N 686 above.   [695] Chapter III (Arts 12–16).

[696] Art 6(2). The 2011 report concludes that these rules are not clear or satisfactory.

[697] Art 8.   [698] Art 16. On the public policy exception, see *Fahimian* (n 686 above), pending.

[699] Art 17. The single permit Directive furthermore confers equal treatment rights on students in the context of employment; see discussion in I:6.5.1 above.

[700] The 2011 report states that twelve Member States permit students to be self-employed.

labour markets, require prior authorization, and ban students' employment for the first year.[701] According to the CJEU, the application of a labour market test can only take place in exceptional circumstances, and must be justified and proportionate. It cannot entail the application of further conditions, such as an overall quota.[702] Finally, there are limited procedural rights regarding time limits for taking decisions and appeals against negative decisions, and Member States are allowed to set up fast-track procedures and to charge fees.[703]

Assessing the Directive,[704] its extended scope as compared to the prior Resolution on students is welcome,[705] but it would have been preferable to include all persons not covered by other EU migration legislation. Such an approach would have guaranteed that minimum standards on entry and residence apply to all persons who have been legally authorized to reside by a Member State.

The result is that, in at least those Member States that opt out of this Directive's rules on the three additional categories, the EU has not fundamentally achieved any more harmonization of the rules on admission of 'other' categories than it had following its failed attempts to agree soft law on such admission in 1995.[706] Also, it is disappointing that family members, at least of students, are not included within the scope of the Directive, as the presence of family members could facilitate students' integration into the life of the host state and provide them with financial and emotional support; some of the best students might be deterred from entry if they cannot bring their family members with them.

The CJEU case law has answered some important questions about the implementation of the Directive, confirming that Member States do not have the power to set conditions for entry other than those specified within the Directive as regards students (*Ben Alaya*) and limiting Member States' ability to exclude students from access to employment (*Sommer*). More generally, the Court has referred to the provisions in the preamble, according to which the Directive aims to promote the mobility of students to Europe as a world centre of educational excellence. Taking account of this case law, it is clear from the wording of the Directive that Member States must permit mobility of students if the relevant conditions are met,[707] and must also renew students' residence permits if the conditions set out in the Directive are still met.[708]

As for expulsion or refusal to admit on grounds of public policy, it would have been preferable to include limits on the use of such criteria in order to provide for 'fair' treatment of third-country nationals 'comparable' to that of EU citizens, in line with the Tampere conclusions. Nevertheless, in the absence of a reference to national law for interpreting such concepts, it could still be argued that the restrictions for public policy

---

[701] The 2011 report states that six Member States apply a labour market test, thirteen require prior authorization, and four apply a waiting period of up to one year before any employment is allowed.

[702] Judgment in *Sommer* (n 686 above).

[703] Arts 18–20. Presumably the level of fees is limited, by analogy with the case law on the long-term residents' Directive (see I:6.7.1 below). The 2011 report criticizes the level of fees in one Member State.

[704] For more detailed comments on the Directive, see ch 7 of S Peers et al., *EU Immigration and Asylum Law: Text and Commentary*, 2nd edn (Brill, 2012).

[705] I:6.2.1 above.   [706] On this, see Peers, n 704 above.

[707] Arts 8 and 12.   [708] Arts 6 and 7; see Art 12(1).

have an EU-wide meaning, possibly even a meaning identical or comparable to that applicable to EU citizens. In any event, it could be argued that the EU law principle of proportionality would limit a Member State's expulsion. For example, if a Member State refuses to renew a residence permit where the student is not making sufficient progress in studies, the decision could be disproportionate if the student's lack of progress is due to extenuating circumstances, or a change in course; and it should in any event be sufficient to meet the criterion that the student is passing his or her studies, or at least willing to switch to another course if having difficulty with the original course of studies.

For Turkish students, the rules on access to employment are linked with the EU-Turkey agreement, where the Court of Justice has ruled that since the Directive is without prejudice to higher standards set out in treaties concluded by the EU, 'Directive 2004/114 cannot justify a narrow construction of Article 6(1) of Decision No 1/80 and no interpretation of that provision can be inferred from it.'[709] The Court did not expressly rule on whether Turkish students authorized to work pursuant to the Directive could benefit from the EU-Turkey agreement, but this is unsurprising since the student concerned in this case was outside the temporal and geographic scope of the Directive.[710]

Finally, the weak provisions on procedural rights in the Directive are objectionable, given the basic principles of the rule of law and judicial protection underlying EU law, the basic procedural standards of international human rights law regarding expulsion of lawful migrants, and the effects of expulsion upon the individuals concerned. As with the procedural rules in other immigration Directives, it is arguable that notwithstanding the wording of the Directive, persons who wish to contest decisions taken in the context of this Directive have a right to a sufficiently reasoned and objective decision and the right to contest the merits of that decision in the courts of the Member State concerned.[711] This should also apply to disputes over the access to employment of students and unremunerated trainees, and disputes with private bodies when they are able to take decisions affecting entry and residence under a fast-track procedure or send progress reports on students to the State authorities.

6.5.3.3 New rules

In 2013, in light of its concerns about the application of the students and researchers' Directives, the Commission proposed a new Directive, subsequently agreed in 2015,[712] which will merge the two Directives, making major changes to them both. In order to attract more researchers and students to EU territory, there will be stronger rules on their equal treatment and their movement ('mobility') between Member States for the

---

[709] Para 48 of the *Payir* judgment, n 686 above.

[710] See generally the discussion of the interaction between the two sources in S Peers, 'EU Migration Law and Association Agreements' in B Martenczuk and S van Thiel, eds., *Justice, Liberty, Security: New Challenges for EU External Relations* (VUBPress, 2008), 53

[711] See the comments on the comparable provisions in I:6.5.1, I:6.5.2, and I:6.5.3.1 above, and I:6.6 and I:6.7 below, and in particular Case C-540/03 *EP v Council* [2006] ECR I-5769, as regards access to a court.

[712] COM (2013) 151, 25 Mar 2013 (proposal); Council doc 13974/15, 20 Nov 2015 (agreed text). Member States will have to apply the Directive two years after its adoption (likely in spring 2016).

purpose of their studies and research. They will be able to stay after their research or study for a period of nine months to look for work or self-employment, although after three months Member States will be able to ask the migrant to prove that he or she has real prospects. Students will be able to work for fifteen hours a week (instead of ten hours), and the option to ban students from working during their first year of studies will be dropped.

Also, the new Directive will replace the weak rules on family reunion in the current researchers' Directive with a fully-fledged right to family reunion, which will moreover waive some of the restrictions in the EU's Directive on family reunion for third-country citizens.[713] There will be a new ninety-day deadline to decide on applications for admission, shortened to sixty days where there are fast-track admission schemes in place. The new Directive will require Member States to apply the rules relating to trainees (now including paid trainees) and volunteers participating in European Voluntary Service; Member States will retain an option to apply the rules concerning school pupils, other volunteers, and au pairs (the latter group is not covered by the current legislation). Finally, the new law will also limit Member States' current power to apply more favourable rules for students and researchers, confining that power to only a few provisions relating to the rights of migrants, while harmonizing the rules on admission.

In principle the new Directive will address a lot of the reasons why students and researchers are not sufficiently attracted to the EU: family reunion, delays in processing applications, limited access to employment, and the absence of a right to stay afterward and look for work. It remains to be seen how fully Member States apply this new Directive in practice.

6.6 Family Reunion

The issue of family reunion is important for a large number of third-country nationals and EU citizens alike, and is closely linked to the right to family life,[714] but remains controversial as regards third-country national family members, largely due to the broader economic, social, and cultural concerns about immigration into the EU.[715] The legal rules governing this issue in part derive from EU free movement law and association agreements,[716] but are largely set out in the EU's family reunion Directive, adopted in 2003, which governs the admission of family members of third-country nationals residing in the EU.[717] In addition, there are several special regimes in EU law for family reunion with special categories of third-country nationals, which derogate from the family reunion Directive, namely those for refugees, intra-corporate transferees, and Blue Card holders, including Blue Card holders who move to another Member State before obtaining long-term residence status. These special regimes are discussed

---

[713] See I:6.6 below.   [714] See I:6.3.1 and I:6.3.4 above.

[715] See S Peers, 'Family Reunion and Community Law' in N Walker, ed., *Towards an Area of Freedom, Security and Justice* (OUP, 2004), 143.

[716] For details, see I:6.4.1 and I:6.4.3 above. Note that only the EEA and the EU/Swiss agreement on free movement of persons fully extend EU free movement rules to third States; other association agreements, such as the EU/Turkey agreement, only touch on aspects of family reunion.

[717] Dir 2003/86, [2003] OJ L 251/12, discussed in I:6.6.1 below.

separately in this section.[718] The equal treatment rules in the single permit Directive also apply to family members.[719] Finally, there is also some reference to family reunion in the EU legislation on long-term residence status, researchers, and international protection,[720] but these measures do not derogate from the family reunion directive as such. There will be special rules on researchers' families in future, since the proposal to update the Directive on this issue was agreed in 2015.[721]

6.6.1 General rules

Directive 2003/86 on family reunion for third-country nationals was adopted by the Council in September 2003.[722] Member States had to comply with the Directive by 3 October 2005,[723] but several Member States failed to implement the Directive on time.[724] As noted several times already, the European Parliament challenged parts of this Directive for breach of the human rights principles of EU law,[725] and the Court of Justice has also ruled on three references from national courts concerning the Directive.[726] A further case is pending.[727] Moreover, the Commission released a report in 2008 on national implementation of the Directive (the 'Commission report', discussed below),[728] followed by a Green Paper on family reunion in 2011.[729] The Green Paper asked if the Directive should be amended, in particular as regards the conditions and restrictions attached to sponsors and family members, the special rules for refugees' family members (whether to relax the conditions attached to those rules, and extend them to persons with subsidiary protection), and the procedures attached to family reunion. Ultimately, the Commission decided not to propose any amendments to the Directive, but instead issued guidance (the 'guidance document') on its interpretation in 2014.[730]

As regards the Directive in general, the Court of Justice has ruled that:[731]

> Since authorisation of family reunification is the general rule, the faculty provided for in Article 7(1)(c) of the Directive [ie, the condition relating to social assistance] must

---

[718] I:6.6.2 below.

[719] See Directive 2011/98, discussed in I:6.5.1 above, particularly point 20 in the preamble.

[720] See respectively I:6.7 below and I:6.5.3, I:5.5 and I:5.6 above. On the latter category of rules, see also S Peers, 'EC Law on Family Members of Persons Seeking or Receiving International Protection' in P Shah, ed., *The Challenge of Asylum to Legal Systems* (Cavendish, 2005).

[721] On that new Directive generally, see I:6.5.3 above.

[722] [2003] OJ L 251/12. All references in this section are to this Dir unless otherwise indicated.

[723] Art 20.

[724] The Court of Justice gave one judgment against a Member State for failure to apply this Directive on time: C-57/07 *Commission v Luxembourg* (judgment of 6 Dec 2007, unreported). Three cases were withdrawn following tardy implementation—Cases: C-87/07 *Commission v Malta*; C-91/07 *Commission v Italy*; and C-192/07 *Commission v Germany*.

[725] Case C-540/03 [2006] ECR I-5769. The EP had challenged the validity of Arts 4(1), last sub-paragraph, 4(6), and 8(2). See discussion below.

[726] Cases: C-578/08 *Chakroun* [2010] ECR I-1839; C-338/13 *Noorzia*, ECLI:EU:C:2014:2092; and C-153/14 *K & A*, ECLI:EU:C:2015:453. See also the Advocate-General's Opinion in Case C-138/13 *Dogan*, ECLI:EU:C:2014:287 (the CJEU's ruling in this case did not interpret the Directive) and Joined Cases C-356/11 and C-357/11, *O and S and L*, ECLI:EU:C:2012:776, para 74, where the CJEU interpreted the Directive without any request from the national court.

[727] Case C-558/14 *Khachab*. [728] COM (2008) 610, 8 Oct 2008.

[729] COM (2011) 735, 15 Nov 2011. [730] COM (2014) 210, 3 Apr 2014.

[731] Judgment in *Chakroun*, para 43. The Court has repeated this statement in *K and A*, at para 50 and in *O and S and L*, para 74 (n 726 above).

be interpreted strictly. Furthermore, the margin for manoeuvre which the Member States are recognised as having must not be used by them in a manner which would undermine the objective of the Directive, which is to promote family reunification, and the effectiveness thereof.

It should follow by analogy that all exceptions and derogations from the general rule of authorization of family reunion should be interpreted strictly, including the rules relating to the scope of the Directive and the definition of family members.[732] In particular, this approach to interpretation must mean that the lists of the exceptions, derogations, and conditions in the Directive which might restrict family reunion must all be regarded as exhaustive. Furthermore, the Court has consistently ruled that the Directive 'imposes precise positive obligations, with corresponding clearly defined individual rights, on the Member States, since it requires them, in the cases determined by the Directive, to authorise family reunification of certain members of the sponsor's family.'[733]

Chapter I of the Directive concerns its purpose, definitions, and scope.[734] The scope of the Directive is limited to those third-country national sponsors who have 'reasonable prospects of obtaining the right of permanent residence', and who hold a residence permit issued by a Member State and valid for one year or more.[735] This definition of sponsors excludes EU citizens (whether they have moved within the EU or not),[736] although in a family containing an EU citizen child with a third-country national parent, the latter is within the scope of the Directive even though the former is not.[737] The CJEU has not yet clarified whether a dual citizen of an EU and non-EU Member State might be able to rely upon the Directive.[738]

According to the Commission report, most Member States allow for family reunion with a temporary residence permit, but subject to a minimum period of residence on the territory. In light of the obligation to interpret derogations from the scope of the Directive strictly, this approach is objectionable if sponsors are not given any opportunity to prove that they have in fact a reasonable prospect of becoming a permanent resident even if they have not had spent that minimum period on the territory. Another group of Member States require the sponsor to *have* a permanent residence permit; this is a clear breach of the Directive, unless (and to the extent that) those Member States issue a permanent residence permit upon entry. A third group of Member States simply transpose the Directive literally, which is not problematic as such, although the Commission objects to one Member State (Cyprus) which in principle does not renew residence permits for longer than

---

[732] See para 50 of the Opinion in *Dogan* (n 726 above).
[733] Case law beginning with *EP v Council*, para 60 (n 725 above).   [734] Arts 1–3.
[735] Art 3(1).
[736] Art 3(3). The CJEU confirmed this in Cases C-256/11 *Dereci* [2011] ECR I-11315, paras 44–9 and C-87/12 *Ymeraga*, ECLI:EU:C:2013:291, paras 24–7. Of course, this is only relevant for EU citizens who are resident in their own Member State, and who therefore cannot usually rely on the family reunion rules in EU free movement or citizenship law. See further I:6.4.1 above. Note that the family members of EU citizens who do not move have rights to equal treatment pursuant to Art 12 of the single permit Dir (n 567 above), and can qualify for long-term residence status (see I:6.7 below).
[737] *O and S and L*, para 74 (n 726 above).   [738] See the discussion in I:6.4.1 above.

four years (except for employees of an international company). While this should not be considered a breach of the family reunion Directive, since this Directive does not regulate the issue of the renewal of the sponsor's residence permit, it is a breach of the obligations in other EU legislation to renew residence permits for refugees, researchers, and Blue Card holders.[739] A refusal to renew a residence permit after several years' residence might also amount to a breach of the ECHR in some cases,[740] although (in the absence of EU regulation of this issue) this would fall outside the scope of EU law. For Turkish workers, depending on the circumstances, it would in some cases also amount to a breach of the EU-Turkey association agreement,[741] although in practice of course there are few if any Turkish nationals resident in the southern part of Cyprus.[742]

According to the guidance document, the 'reasonable prospect' of long-term residence should be based on the nature and type of residence permit, taking account also of the administrative practice and circumstances of individual cases. Even if the sponsor does not currently meet the criteria for permanent residence, it is sufficient if there is a reasonable prognosis that he or she will do so. Member States have a wide margin of appreciation applying this test. Sponsors whose residence permit was issued for limited purposes and is not renewable would not qualify.

The last of these points is convincing, but not the others, because the guidance document fails to mention the relevance of other EU law rules. Surely the prospect of obtaining permanent residence must, where relevant, be assessed pursuant to potential status under the EU long-term residents' Directive or to the EU's association agreement with Turkey.[743] Renewal of residence permits is not simply an administrative practice, but an obligation under EU legislation on researchers, refugees, and Blue Cards, and the EU/Turkey association, if the criteria are still met. In the absence of any reference to national law, the concept of a reasonable prospect of permanent residence is surely an autonomous concept of EU law, by analogy with other CJEU judgments on the Directive.[744]

Sponsors applying for or receiving protection status are excluded from the scope of the Directive, except for recognized refugees.[745] It is open to the EU, with or without the Member States, to sign more favourable bilateral treaties with third countries;[746] three specified multilateral treaties signed by Member States can also set higher standards.[747]

---

[739] See respectively: Art 24(1) of Dir 2011/95 ([2011] OJ L 337/9; see further I:5.5 above); Art 8 of Dir 2005/71 ([2005] OJ L 289/15; see I:6.5.3.1 above); and Art 9 of Dir 2009/50 ([2009] OJ L 155/17), discussed in I:6.5.2 above.

[740] See I:6.3.1 above.   [741] See I:6.4.3 above.

[742] If EU law is extended to the northern part of Cyprus (see I:2.2.5.3 above), the position would obviously be different.

[743] See I:6.7 below and I:6.4.3 above.   [744] *Chakroun* (n 726 above), para 45.

[745] Art 3(2). As noted above, some EU asylum legislation governs the position of family members of persons seeking or receiving international protection. According to the Commission report, nine Member States have decided anyway to apply the Dir to sponsors who have subsidiary protection.

[746] Art 3(4)(a). See the Opinion in *K & A*, suggesting that this would justify Member States exempting nationals of some countries but not others from integration tests.

[747] Art 3(4)(b). Note that it is implicitly not permissible for the Member States to set higher standards via any *other* international treaties, unless the EU concludes those treaties alongside the Member States.

Member States can also set higher standards unilaterally in domestic law,[748] and there is no requirement that such standards be 'compatible' with the Directive.[749] However, there is no general 'standstill' requirement applicable to national law falling within the scope of the Directive.

'Family reunification' is defined as 'the entry into and residence in a Member State by family members of a third country national residing lawfully in that Member State in order to preserve the family unit, whether the family relationship arose before or after the resident's entry'.[750] The Court of Justice has ruled that this includes the concept of 'family formation' (ie where the family was only formed after the sponsor was admitted to the territory).[751]

Chapter II of the Directive specifies the family members who must or may be admitted to join a sponsor.[752] The spouse and minor unmarried children must be admitted,[753] subject to certain qualifications regarding adopted children and children whose custody is shared. Member States also have an option, subject to certain conditions, to admit dependent parents of the sponsor or the spouse if those family members 'do not enjoy proper family support in the country of origin', adult children of the sponsor or the spouse who cannot support their own needs for health reasons, or unmarried partners of the sponsor, along with relevant children.[754]

However, there are a number of derogations from these rules. First of all, Member States have an option to retain legislation which existed on the date of implementation of the Directive which imposes a special 'integration requirement' for children over twelve years old, if they arrive separately from the rest of their family.[755] Arguably Member States which liberalize their law cannot later revert back to the original more restrictive provision.[756] Next, in the event of polygamy, Member States cannot admit additional spouses once one spouse is resident within the EU, but have the option to admit (or not admit) the children of the additional spouse(s).[757] It is presumably up to the sponsor to determine which of his wives will have the honour of joining him, although arguably the sponsor has the right to rotate the spouses which do so.[758] Thirdly, '[i]n order to ensure better integration and to prevent forced marriages', Member States can set a minimum age (up to twenty-one) for the sponsor and/or the spouse, 'before the spouse is able to join the sponsor'.[759] Finally, a Member State can optionally require that applications concerning children must be made before the children turn fifteen, if provided for by its existing law on the date of implementation of the Directive; Member States applying this derogation 'shall

---

[748] Art 3(5).   [749] On this issue, see I:6.2.4 above.   [750] Art 2(d).
[751] Paras 59–62 of the *Chakroun* judgment, n 726 above.   [752] Art 4.   [753] Art 4(1).
[754] Art 4(2) and (3). The guidance document suggests that 'dependency' be interpreted consistently with EU free movement law: see I:6.4.1 above. It also suggests that 'proper family support' means that no other family member in the country of origin is obliged by law to support the parent, or *de facto* supports them.
[755] Art 4(1), final sub-paragraph.
[756] See by analogy Joined Cases C-300/09 and C-301/09 *Toprak and Oguz* [2010] ECR I-12845.
[757] Art 4(4).
[758] The Dir only prohibits admission of further spouses when the first spouse 'has a spouse *living with him* in the territory of a Member State' (emphasis added). If that spouse *ceases* to live with him, the sponsor could then invoke the right to family reunion with another spouse.
[759] Art 4(5).

authorise the entry and residence of such children on grounds other than family reunification'.[760]

The Court of Justice has ruled twice on these exceptions.[761] First of all, the Court has ruled although the ECHR, the Convention on the Rights of the Child, and the EU's Charter of Fundamental Rights 'stress the importance to a child of family life and recommend that States have regard to the child's interests...they do not create for the members of a family an individual right to be allowed to enter the territory of a State and cannot be interpreted as denying States a certain margin of appreciation when they examine applications for family reunification'.[762] With respect, this assessment understates the effect of the line of case law of the European Court of Human Rights beginning with *Sen v the Netherlands*, according to which there are certain circumstances in which a State must admit children;[763] it also makes no references to the other circumstances in which a State should be obliged to admit family members because the 'elsewhere' test is not applicable, for instance because the State of one family member refuses to admit the other family members, or because of reasons connected to international protection. On the other hand, as noted above, the Court has stressed that the Directive '[goes] beyond those provisions', requiring the admission of some family members 'without being left a margin of appreciation'.[764]

As for the exceptions to the rules challenged by the EP, the CJEU ruled that the optional integration requirement for children over 12 simply 'partially preserv[es] the margin of appreciation of the Member States' in 'strictly defined circumstances'.[765] Indeed, that margin of appreciation 'is no different from that accorded to [Member States] by the European Court of Human Rights, in its case-law relating to that right, for weighing, in each factual situation, the competing interests' and so 'cannot be regarded as running counter to the right to respect for family life'.[766] Moreover, when applying this provision, Member States had to take account of other provisions of the Directive regarding the best interests of the child and setting out factors to take into account when refusing applications for admission;[767] permitting Member States to impose an integration requirement does not as such violate human rights principles.[768] According to the Commission report, only Cyprus and Germany have invoked this derogation, and the Cypriot derogation was adopted after the date of implementation of the Directive. It is therefore invalid.

Similarly, the Court of Justice upheld the other challenged derogation, concerning a requirement to apply for reunion with children before they turn fifteen, on the grounds that this provision 'cannot...be interpreted as prohibiting the Member States from taking account of an application relating to a child over 15 years of age or as authorising them not to do so', and that like the first derogation challenged by the EP, this rule must

---

[760] Art 4(6).   [761] *EP v Council* (n 725 above) and *Noorzia* (n 726 above).
[762] Para 59 of *EP v Council* judgment (n 725 above).
[763] See further I:6.3.1 above.   [764] Para 60 of *EP v Council* judgment (n 725 above).
[765] Para 61, ibid.   [766] Para 62, ibid.
[767] Paras 63 and 64, ibid, referring to Arts 5(5) and 17, set out below. The Court also links Art 17 to the case-law of the European Court of Human Rights on admission of family members, and refers to Strasbourg case law taking account of the child's age and independent entry when considering a possible obligation to admit the child (para 65, ibid).
[768] Paras 66–76, ibid.

be applied in conjunction with the Directive's provisions regarding the best interests of the child and setting out factors to take into account when refusing applications for admission.[769] However, the Commission report states that no Member State has invoked this derogation, and since this derogation could only be validly invoked prior to the implementation date, any attempt to invoke it in future would be invalid.

As for the other derogations from the obligation to admit family members, the Commission report states that most Member States set a minimum age for spouses, five of them setting it at the highest possible age of twenty-one. The CJEU interpreted this exception in *Noorzia*, ruling that if a Member State applies this option, it could insist that the sponsor and/or spouse had to be (up to) twenty-one before *applying* for family reunion. According to the Court, this interpretation was justified on the grounds that the Directive did not specify when national authorities had to assess the age limit, therefore leaving to Member States 'a margin of discretion',[770] as long as they did not impair the effectiveness of EU law. The minimum age represented the point when, according to each Member State, the young spouse was presumed to be mature enough not only to refuse a forced marriage, but to choose to move to another country to take up family life and integrate there. Moreover, the national measure did 'not prevent the exercise of the right to family reunification nor render it excessively difficult', and did not 'undermine the purpose of preventing forced marriages', since it presumed that it would be harder to influence a young person to contract a forced marriage and family reunion if they had to be twenty-one by the time the application was lodged. The rule was also consistent with the principles of equal treatment and legal certainty, since all applicants who were the same age would be treated the same way.

With great respect, this judgment is inconsistent with the Court's other rulings which interpret the conditions for family reunion strictly. Moreover, the Court is simply wrong to say that the Directive does not specify when national authorities had to assess the age limit: the words 'before the spouse is able to join' quite clearly refer to the date of admission. An approach based on the age as of entry into the territory would equally respect the principles of equal treatment and legal certainty, since everyone affected could enter as they each turned twenty-one, and it is easy to determine that date. The Austrian approach certainly does make family reunion excessively difficult, given that a further long waiting period (discussed below) might be added on once the sponsor or spouse has turned twenty-one and can then apply for admission. It should be noted that the Court did not address the argument (in the guidance document) that this provision can only apply on a case-by-case basis, being only one factor to take into account, outweighed (for instance) by the existence of a common child.

Cyprus also requires that the marriage took place a year before admission; the Commission report rightly doubts the validity of this provision, since (as argued above) it follows from the requirement to interpret the exceptions from the Directive strictly that the list of derogations from the obligations to admit family members is exhaustive.

---

[769] Paras 84–90, ibid.

[770] Presumably this means that those Member States applying this exception are not *obliged* to take this approach, given that this is an optional clause, and in light of Member States' general power to set higher standards.

Furthermore, the Commission report indicates that seven Member States permit entry of unmarried partners, while over half admit parents of the sponsor and/or the spouse.

Chapter III sets out procedural rules on the submission and consideration of applications.[771] This includes a proviso that applications should normally be submitted when the family member is outside the territory of the Member State in which the sponsor resides, although as a 'derogation', Member States can accept an in-country application 'in appropriate circumstances'.[772] This particular derogation should *not* be interpreted strictly, since it facilitates family reunion, rather than hinders it. So it must follow that it is entirely up to Member States to determine how often they will consider in-country applications. Although this provision of the Directive could, on its face, be interpreted to rule out the possibility of *always* permitting in-country applications, Member States must be regarded as retaining the power to provide for this pursuant to their power to set higher standards as regards family reunion, given that the power to set higher standards is not constrained by a requirement that such standards must be 'compatible' with the Directive. The Commission report is therefore wrong to complain that 'five Member States...impede this provision as they do not even enact the primary rule of family members having to reside outside their territory'. According to the report, all Member States except one (Cyprus) permit some in-country applications, subject to differing rules.

Next, the Directive establishes a time limit of nine months to make a decision on an application, although this deadline can be exceeded in 'exceptional' cases, due to the complexity of the application. There is an obligation to issue a written decision on an application, and to give reasons for the rejection of an application.[773] There is no provision on fees for family reunion applications, but the Commission guidance document is surely correct when arguing that, in light of the CJEU ruling on fees for long-term residence applications, any such fees cannot be so high as to make the right to family reunion excessively difficult.[774] This interpretation is confirmed by the CJEU's subsequent ruling on fees for taking integration tests as a condition of family reunion (see discussion below). Finally, 'Member States shall have due regard to the best interests of minor children' when examining applications.[775] As noted already, as interpreted by the Court of Justice, this provision is not merely an empty gesture, but is an obligation which pervades the interpretation of all of the derogations and conditions in the Directive which were challenged by the EP; it must follow that the obligation to consider the best interests of the child equally applies to the interpretation of *any* provisions of the Directive.

Chapter IV sets out additional conditions which *may* be imposed by Member States before entry of family members is authorized.[776] These concern requirements of 'public policy, public security or public health', as clarified by the preamble; accommodation, sickness insurance, and resources requirements; an integration requirement; and a

---

[771] Art 5.   [772] Art 5(3).

[773] Art 5(4). According to the Commission report, all Member States comply with the latter rules. The guidance document rightly points out that limited administrative capacity is not a legitimate reason for exceeding the nine-month threshold.

[774] See I:7.7.1 below.   [775] Art 5(5).   [776] Arts 6–8.

waiting period. As regards the resources requirement, the Directive states that Member States may require the sponsor to have 'stable and regular resources which are sufficient to maintain himself/herself and the members of his/her family, without recourse to the social assistance system of the Member State concerned'. Also, 'Member States shall evaluate these resources by reference to their nature and regularity and may take into account the level of minimum national wages and pensions as well as the number of family members'.[777]

On this condition, the Court of Justice ruled in its *Chakroun* judgment that 'the concept of "social assistance system of the Member State" is a concept which has its own independent meaning in European Union law and cannot be defined by reference to concepts of national law'. The concept has to be 'understood as referring to social assistance granted by the public authorities, whether at national, regional or local level'.[778] Because the Directive contrasts the concept of 'social assistance' with that of 'stable and regular resources', the former concept 'refers to assistance granted by the public authorities, whether at national, regional or local level, which can be claimed by an individual, in this case the sponsor, who does not have stable and regular resources which are sufficient to maintain himself and the members of his family and who, by reason of that fact, is likely to become a burden on the social assistance system of the host Member State during his period of residence'.[779] Member States are entitled to 'indicate a certain sum as a reference amount', but this does not mean that Member States 'may impose a minimum income level below which all family reunifications will be refused, irrespective of an actual examination of the situation of each applicant'.[780] In this case Dutch law, which applied a reference amount of 120% of the minimum income of a worker aged twenty-three in cases of family formation, breached the Directive because the concept of social assistance could only refer to cases of *ongoing* need for State support, not the level of support 'which enables exceptional or unforeseen needs to be addressed'.[781] Furthermore, there was a breach of the Directive because the income threshold applied in cases of family formation was higher than the threshold applied where the family had already been established prior to the admission of the sponsor.[782]

According to the Commission report, all except one Member State (Sweden) applies this condition, and some (rightly) could be criticized, either due to the high increases in the reference amounts due to additional family members or due to *de facto* discrimination on grounds of age (cf. the Dutch rules). The guidance document convincingly argues that Member States should accept that the sufficient resources condition is satisfied in the case of fixed-term contracts, if they are renewable. Finally, the CJEU has stated that 'in principle' only the sponsor's income is relevant for applying the 'sufficient resources' test, rather than the resources which the spouse might provide.[783] As

---

[777] Art 7(1)(c).

[778] Para 45 of the judgment, n 726 above. The Court has been asked further questions about this condition, in the pending case of *Khachab*.

[779] Para 46, n 726 above.

[780] Para 48, n 726 above, referring again to Art 17. Presumably, where relevant, Member States must also consider the best interests of the child when applying this condition (the *Chakroun* case only concerned a spouse).

[781] Para 49, n 726 above.   [782] Paras 51 and 64, n 726 above.

[783] *O and S* judgment (n 726 above), para 72.

the guidance document states, this suggests some flexibility on this point (an exception in individual circumstances), and in any event Member States are free to consider the spouse's potential resources too if they wish to.

As regards the other conditions, the Commission report indicates that most Member States (all except four) apply an accommodation requirement, and rightly criticized the two Member States which required the sponsor to satisfy the accommodation requirements before entry of the family members. The guidance document argues that this provision should be applied on a non-discriminatory basis and that authorities are limited to assessing the *prognosis* of the sponsor obtaining a property to house a bigger family once family reunion is granted, not whether the sponsor owns or rents such a property already. Furthermore, the report states that about half of the Member States apply a sickness insurance requirement; the Commission criticism of one Member State which requires applicants to have either sickness insurance *or* sufficient resources is not convincing, since that rule facilitates family reunion by refraining from requiring applicants to satisfy both conditions.

In practice, a key issue for family reunion is the option to require family members to undergo integration measures. According to the Commission report, three Member States insist upon an integration requirement before entry, and four others impose that requirement after entry. The integration condition has been interpreted by the CJEU,[784] which began by confirming that Member States can indeed impose an integration requirement on applicants for family reunion *before* entry, unless they are joining a refugee.[785] Next, the Court invoked the principle of proportionality, insisting that any integration measures must be linked to the actual purpose of facilitating family members' integration. In this case, the Court accepted that a test on the host State's language and society is a legitimate way of ensuring integration, but emphasized that the conditions relating to this requirement cannot exceed its aims. This would 'in particular' happen if the requirement 'were systematically to prevent' family reunion even though, 'despite having failed the integration examination, [family members] have demonstrated their willingness to pass' it and 'have made every effort' to do so. The integration tests cannot be aimed at 'filtering' family members, but instead must actually help them integrate.

The Court went on to require Member States to consider 'specific individual circumstances, such as the age, illiteracy, level of education, economic situation or health' of a family member, 'in order to dispense' them from the integration test where those circumstances make the family member 'unable to take or pass that examination'. Otherwise the test would create a 'difficult obstacle' to the family reunion right, and circumvent the requirement to make a 'case-by-case' decision on applications. Overall, then, in this case Dutch law on integration measures went beyond the limits imposed by EU law (as interpreted by the Court), since the hardship clause in the Dutch law set

---

[784] *K & A* (n 726 above). See also the Opinion in Case C-138/13 *Dogan*, ECLI:EU:C:2014:287. The CJEU judgment in the latter case does not interpret the Directive, but instead clarifies when a newly introduced integration requirement conflicts with the 'standstill' rule forming part of the EU-Turkey association (see further I:6.4.3 above). See also the comparable requirement in the long-term residents' Directive (I:6.7 below).

[785] On the special rules on refugees, see I:6.6.2 below.

out fewer exceptions from the integration requirement than EU law allowed. Finally, the Court ruled that the Dutch fees were too high, also forming an obstacle to the effective exercise of family reunion, in conjunction with travel costs, considering that they had to be paid also when the test was retaken.[786]

Overall, the Court's judgment strikes a good balance between concerns that migrants integrate into the host society and the effectiveness of the principle of family reunion. The list of cases when the proportionality principle applies is non-exhaustive ('in particular'), and so is the list of individual circumstances which Member States must consider ('such as'). It is clear that an integration test cannot simply be a method of filtering out family members, and the Court even hints that family members ought to be admitted even if they have failed it. The cap on high fees will be important for lower-income sponsors. By analogy from the Court's judgment, the proportionality test would be relevant also to issues of accessibility of integration tests, as the Commission report argues.[787]

The Commission also rightly criticizes some Member States which impose conditions outside the scope of the condition of public policy or which permit non-renewal or withdrawal of a residence permit on public health grounds after admission, which is a breach of the express provisions of the Directive.[788] Although the limitation of entry and possible expulsion of family members on grounds of 'public policy, public security and public health' makes no reference to the substantive rules applied to migrant EU citizens and their family members pursuant to EU free movement law,[789] it is nonetheless arguable that equal treatment is required, by analogy with the Court's rulings on similar provisions in other EU immigration legislation.[790]

Next, as regards the waiting period, the Directive specifies that the maximum period possible is two years' lawful stay by the sponsor, subject to a derogation permitting Member States to retain an existing three-year waiting period following submission of the application, if legislation in force on the date of adoption of the Directive took account of that Member State's reception capacity.[791] This provision was the third clause challenged by the EP, and again the Court of Justice upheld its validity,[792] ruling that this provision does not prevent family reunion, but merely permits Member States to delay it, in accordance with the 'margin of appreciation' granted to them by the case law of the European Court of Human Rights, in the interests of ensuring better integration by family members. Moreover, Member States could not simply reject an application due to a waiting period, but still had to consider the best interests of the child and all of the other factors referred to in the Directive when imposing such a requirement.[793] In particular, the Directive could not be interpreted as authorizing a quota system.

---

[786] This followed prior judgments on the fees charged for long-term residents: see I:6.7 below.

[787] See also the Opinion in *Dogan* (n 726 above), para 59: Member States must make study materials available, and provide some form of support and instruction, for integration tests. As the guidance document points out, the tests themselves should not be excessively difficult.

[788] See Art 6(3).   [789] See I:6.4.1 above.

[790] See the case law interpreting the Returns Directive voluntary departure clause (I:7.7.1 below) and the qualification Directive (I:6.5 above).

[791] Art 8.   [792] *EP v Council* judgment (n 725 above), paras 97–103.

[793] Again the Court referred to Arts 5(5) and 17.

The Commission report does not give much information on the specific waiting periods applied by Member States, but rightly criticizes four Member States that calculate the two-year waiting period from the date of *application*, given that the literal wording of the Directive (never mind the requirement to interpret the conditions strictly) makes clear that the two-year waiting period (as distinct from the three-year derogation) can be calculated only as regards the period of the sponsor's *lawful stay* on the territory, not from the date of the application.[794] There is no reason why the judgment in *Noorzia* should affect this analysis, since the different wording of the two paragraphs of the Directive on waiting periods inescapably suggests an *a contrario* interpretation, and there is no special factor (the need to prevent forced marriages) like that which the Court relied partly upon in that judgment.[795] As the guidance document points out, the concept of 'lawful stay' includes any period of legal presence on the territory of the host State, and short periods of interruption of stay should not mean that the clock has to be reset from scratch.

According to the Commission report, only Austria applied the derogation permitting a three-year waiting period, and in light of the Court's judgment in *EP v Council*, Austria eliminated a quota system that applied to applications for family reunion. The report also rightly states that this provision of the Directive 'precludes the introduction of the notion of reception capacity as a condition in national law'.

Specific rules for refugees are set out in Chapter V, and are addressed further below.[796] Chapter VI then deals with the entry and residence of family members, including the status of family members after entry.[797] They must be given the 'facility' to obtain the necessary visas,[798] and a renewable residence permit of at least one year's validity to start with.[799] The Commission report rightly criticizes the Netherlands for double-checking an application again later (when a residence permit is applied for) and for limiting the locations where an entry visa can be applied for.

Next, the Directive gives family members the right of access to education, employment, self-employment, and training on the same footing as the sponsor,[800] although access to employment and self-employment can be restricted for non-nuclear family members,[801] or subjected to a waiting period of up to a year for all family members, during which the Member State concerned 'may examine the situation of [its] labour market before authorising' the exercise of an activity.[802] According to the Commission report, five Member States impose no restrictions on labour market access, seven apply a labour market test, and three breach the Directive by imposing a blanket ban on employment for one year. Some Member States breach the Directive by requiring

---

[794] Note also that the special rules which disapply this provision (Art 12(2) of Dir 2003/86, Art 15(2) of the Blue Card Dir, and Art 19(2) of the ICT Directive) refer to '*residence*' of the sponsor (emphasis added).

[795] Moreover, it is not specifically required that the sponsor must already have met the criteria for family reunion at the time when the application is submitted. Arguably, this is not necessary.

[796] Arts 9–12; see I:6.6.2 below.   [797] Arts 13–15.

[798] Art 13(1). On long-stay visas, see generally I:6.9.2 below.

[799] Art 13(2). These take the form of the EU's standard residence permit format: see Art 2(e) and further I:6.9.1 below.

[800] Art 14(1). As noted above, a broader right to equal treatment is conferred by the single permit Directive (see I:6.5.1).

[801] Art 14(3).   [802] Art 14(2).

family members to have a work permit even if the sponsor does not need one. It should be recalled that the EU-Turkey association agreements with Turkey and the Western Balkans contain rules on employment of family members, which prevail to the extent that they set higher standards or interact with the rules in the Directive.[803] These rights might also interact with other EU legislation which defines, inter alia, the labour market access of the sponsor.[804]

After five years' residence at the latest, the spouse or partner, and a child who has reached majority, must be given an autonomous residence permit.[805] Such permits *may* be granted earlier in the event of 'widowhood, divorce, separation, or death', and *must* be granted earlier in the event of 'particularly difficult circumstances'.[806] They may also be granted to other family members.[807] The conditions concerning the granting and duration of the permit are laid down in national law.[808] Note that if the sponsor's residence comes to an end and the family members do not (yet) have an autonomous right of residence, Member States may withdraw or refuse to renew the family member's residence permit.[809]

According to the Commission report, most Member States do not issue an autonomous permit before five years' residence, although four Member States offer autonomous permits after three years. In one Member State the five year period is counted from the issue of a residence permit, which is a breach of the Directive if the person concerned held a visa beforehand,[810] since the Directive only refers to five years' *residence*. Other Member States breached the Directive by defining the beneficiaries of the autonomous permit too narrowly, or by not making issue of the permit obligatory. Eleven Member States limit the grant of the permit in cases of family breakdown. As for the early grant of a permit, sixteen Member States grant the permit early in the event of widowhood, etc.; the Commission report does not refer to the provision which requiring issue of a permit early in 'particularly difficult circumstances'. Seven Member States either do not lay down the conditions for granting the permit or do so by giving too much leeway to the authorities. On this point, it should be recalled that EU measures which refer to Member States' competence to establish 'conditions' cannot be applied in such a way as to limit the underlying substantive rights which are granted by the provision in question.[811]

In particular, the Directive does not regulate how to take account of absences from national territory as regards calculating the five-year period,[812] but the principle of

---

[803] For example, the family members of Turkish workers must be entitled to the same labour market access as the Turkish worker as defined in the EU-Turkey rules as interpreted by the Court of Justice; this is a dynamic concept since the rules permit progressively greater labour market access for the worker (see I:6.4.3 above).

[804] For instance, the long-term residents' Directive (see I:6.7 below).

[805] Art 15(1), although Member States may limit this obligation 'to the spouse or unmarried partner in cases of breakdown of the family relationship'.

[806] Art 15(2).　　　　[807] Art 15(3).　　　　[808] Art 15(4).

[809] Art 16(3). This provision refers to a 'right of residence' rather than a 'residence permit'; the implication is that a person who is *entitled* to an autonomous residence permit but who does not yet hold one is also protected from removal on this ground.

[810] According to other EU legislation, a long-stay visa can be valid for up to one year before it is replaced by a residence permit: see I:6.9.2 below.

[811] See, for instance, the case law on Art 6 of EU-Turkey Association Council Decision 1/80, referred to in I:6.4.3 above.

[812] For comparison, see the rules on the calculation of: the waiting period for permanent residence for EU citizens and their family members (I:6.4.1 above); the waiting period for long-term residence status (I:6.7 below); and the various time periods applicable to Turkish workers and their family members (I:6.4.3 above).

proportionality (applied to the Directive by the CJEU in the *K and A* judgment on integration conditions) must mean that short absence periods which occur in the ordinary course of life (ie for annual holidays) must still count toward the five-year period, and that longer periods of absence which are essentially unavoidable (ie due to obligatory military service or the serious illness of a parent in the country of origin) must at least mean that the family members do not have to start accruing the right to an autonomous residence permit from scratch.[813] It should also be kept in mind that family members might be eligible to obtain long-term residence status under EU or national law, and that the family members of Turkish workers benefit from special rules in this regard.[814]

Chapter VII of the Directive concerns penalties and redress.[815] Status may be removed in the event of, inter alia, changed circumstances or fraud.[816] However, there are substantive limits, clearly based on ECHR jurisprudence, regarding both the admission of family members and the termination of their residence, including removal of the sponsor:[817]

> Member States shall take due account of the nature and solidity of the person's family relationships and the duration of his residence in the Member State and of the existence of family, cultural and social ties with his/her country of origin where they reject an application, withdraw or refuse to renew a residence permit or decide to order the removal of the sponsor or members of his family.

As noted already, the Court of Justice has ruled that this principle applies as regards the application of the three derogations and conditions challenged by the EP, as well as the 'sufficient resources' condition.[818] It must follow that this principle applies to all other derogations and conditions, and furthermore (in accordance with its wording and the ECHR case law) to any removal from the territory. The Commission report has rightly pointed out that those Member States which strictly apply the national rules relating to family reunion are violating this principle.

There is also a parallel procedural right, namely the 'right to mount a legal challenge' for the sponsor and/or the family members if an application for family reunion is rejected, removal is ordered, or a residence permit is withdrawn or not renewed.[819] While there is no explicit requirement that such legal challenges must be brought before the *courts*, such a principle follows from the human rights protection forming part of EU law,[820] and has been implicitly conformed by the Court of Justice, which has ruled,

---

[813] See by analogy the guidance document comments on Art 8.

[814] See respectively I:6.7 below and I:6.4.3 above.   [815] Arts 16–18.

[816] Art 16. The Commission report only examines implementation of Art 16(4), arguing rightly that Member States which systematically suspect all applicants of fraud, et al. breach the Dir, which refers only to '*reason* to suspect' such activity (emphasis added). As regards change of circumstances, there are again particular rules deriving from the EU-Turkey agreement: see, for instance, Case C-337/07 *Altun* [2008] ECR I-10323. The guidance document indicates that the separate Commission guidance on marriages of convenience (see I:7.4.1 below) applies equally to this Directive.

[817] Art 17.   [818] *EP v Council* (n 725 above) and *Chakroun* (n 726 above).

[819] Art 18. The 'procedure and competence' for such challenges are established by each Member State. As noted already, national competence over procedure cannot be used to empty rights guaranteed by EU law of their substance.

[820] See I:6.3.1 and I:6.3.4 above.

interpreting the relevant provision, that '[i]mplementation of the Directive is subject to review by the national courts....'[821] Also, while the Directive does not specify that there must be a right to bring legal challenges as regards other aspects of the Directive (such as a refusal to permit employment, to issue an autonomous residence permit, or to challenge the refusal of a visa),[822] such a right must also follow from the general principles of EU law and the EU Charter of Fundamental Rights.[823] It is also arguable that the general principles and the Charter, along with the principle of effectiveness,[824] guarantee other procedural rights, for example judicial review of the *merits* of decisions and effective time limits to challenge decisions, as well as legal aid.[825]

The first point to consider regarding the Directive is its temporal scope, a point of broader relevance to EU immigration and asylum law.[826] Does the Directive only apply to persons who submitted applications for family reunion after 5 October 2005, or did it also apply to applications pending on that date, and to persons already admitted prior to that date? The latter group might have an interest in relying, for instance, on the Directive's provisions on protection against expulsion or access to employment. The answer, according to the case law of the Court of Justice, is that in the absence of explicit provisions to the contrary, EU legislation applies to the future effects of past situations, including to proceedings that are already underway when the new rules come into force.[827] This has been explicitly confirmed as regards the calculation of detention conditions in the Returns Directive,[828] and so this principle should obviously apply by analogy as regards other provisions of EU immigration and asylum legislation.

Moving on to an assessment of the Directive, its scope is severely restricted as compared to the original proposal, which had included family members of EU citizens, of persons with subsidiary protection, and of any other third-country nationals who had been admitted for more than one year.[829] Moreover, there is no plan to propose amendments to the Directive. The limitation to sponsors with a prospect of 'permanent residence' is very similar to the threshold in the 1993 Ministers' resolution on family reunion, and violates principles of clear and precise drafting.

---

[821] *EP v Council* (n 725 above), para 106.

[822] According to the Commission report, four Member States do not permit a challenge to the refusal to issue a visa. Since such a refusal entirely prevents family reunion from taking place, this is a particularly blatant breach of procedural rights. See further I:6.9.2 below.

[823] The Commission's guidance is correct on both points.

[824] The principle of effectiveness as regards the Dir is expressly referred to in the *Chakroun* and *K and A* judgments.

[825] According to the Commission report, five Member States deny or restrict judicial review of the merits of decisions, and seven deny legal aid.

[826] See also I:5.5 above.

[827] See in particular: Cases C-122/96 *Saldanha and MTS* [1997] ECR I-5325; C-60/98 *Butterfly Music* [1999] ECR I-3939; C-195/98 *Österreichischer Gewerkschaftsbund* [2000] ECR I-10497; C-464/98 *Stefan* [2001] ECR I-173; C-162/00 *Pokrzeptowicz-Meyer* (n 327 above); C-28/00 *Kauer* [2002] ECR I-1343; C-290/00 *Duchon* [2002] ECR I-3567; C-224/98 *D'Hoop* [2002] ECR I-6191; C-512/99 *Germany v Commission* [2003] ECR I-845; and C-519/03 *Commission v Luxembourg* [2005] ECR I-3067.

[828] Case C-357/09 PPU *Kadzoev* [2009] ECR I-11189; see also Case C-297/12 *Filev and Osmani*, ECLI:EU:C:2013:569. On the substance of these judgments, see I:7.7.1 below.

[829] For the original proposal, see COM (1999) 638, 1 Dec 1999; later versions can be found in COM (2000) 624, 10 Oct 2000 and COM (2002) 225, 3 May 2002. For a detailed history of negotiations, see ch 19 of S Peers and N Rogers, eds., *EU Immigration and Asylum Law: Text and Commentary*, 1st edn (Martinus Nijhoff, 2006).

As for the scope of family members, the absence of a requirement to admit extended family and unmarried partners has obviously limited the numbers of family members who will be able to enter, discriminating on grounds of culture and sexual orientation against those groups who traditionally live with extended family and those with same-sex partners. The 'knock-on' effect on the long-term residents' Directive (which, as discussed below, permits Member States to prevent movement of third-country nationals' family members other than spouses and children between Member States)[830] will in turn hinder movement of third-country nationals within the EU. The various possible age limits are contradictory, assuming that teenagers are too mature to integrate into the host State but too immature to decide on marriage. As noted above, the CJEU has exacerbated the effects of the latter rule.

Next, the conditions attached to entry could mean an indefinite delay in receiving a reply to an application and a lengthy wait for entry, with discrimination permitted as regards accommodation, resources, and sickness insurance requirements.[831] The absence of any final absolute date to reply to applications appears incompatible with Article 13 ECHR, which requires effective remedies in respect of all of the rights guaranteed by that Convention. Checks on family members after entry are permitted potentially indefinitely, raising the prospect that particularly intrusive checks could constitute an unjustified interference in private and family life.

As regards the possible conditions of accommodation, sickness insurance, and stable and sufficient resources, the Directive could be interpreted to mean that failure to satisfy any of these conditions after entry could justify removal.[832] While avoidance of an additional cost to the public could be considered justified on economic grounds under Article 8(2) ECHR, the Strasbourg case law makes clear that removals on purely economic grounds in the absence of criminal activity by the family member are very difficult to justify.[833] If family members' housing is considered inadequate after entry, but *without* a demand for public funds, it is hard to see how expulsion could be justified.[834] The Court's justification of the waiting period requirement on integration grounds is, with respect, unconvincing, given that the Directive contains a separate specific provision on integration.

While the jurisprudence of the Court of Justice on the Directive to date is broadly encouraging, it is clear from the Commission report that a number of Member States are not even correctly applying many of fairly low standards set out in the Directive. Although the Commission report promised to bring infringement proceedings against Member States in 2009, it has not yet done so years later. It remains to be seen whether the 2014 guidance document will have any positive effect; to ensure that it did so, the Commission should have made a firm commitment to bring infringement proceedings against Member States which did not apply the Directive consistently with these guidelines.

The 2008 report concluded (without evidence) that due to the Directive, national standards have been raised as regards access to the labour market by family members,

---

[830] See I:6.7 below.
[831] On this issue, see particularly R Cholewinski, 'Family Reunification and Conditions Placed on Family Members: Dismantling a Fundamental Human Right' (2002) 4 EJML 271.
[832] Art 16(1)(a).   [833] See I:6.3.1 above, in particular the *Ciliz* and *Berrehab* judgments.
[834] See Case 249/86 *Commission v Germany* [1989] ECR 1263.

but in practice standards have also been lowered (although the Directive does not *require* this) as regards waiting periods, sponsors' minimum ages, the income requirement, and integration requirements. It is of course possible that standards would anyway have fallen, and indeed below the minimum set by the Directive, in at least some respect in some Member States, if the Directive had not been adopted; we can never know what would have happened if the Directive had never existed. But we can be certain that standards would not have dropped as far, and would have risen more in some Member States, if the Directive had established better standards from the outset. It is unfortunate that the idea of revising this Directive has been rejected indefinitely. The least the Commission could do is attempt to enforce it properly in the meantime.

6.6.2 Special rules

EU legislation has established several sets of special (favourable) rules regarding family reunion. Firstly, there are some specific rules regarding refugees in the main family reunion Directive, requiring Member States to waive some of the restrictive rules in that Directive as regards family reunion with refugees. Secondly, with the objective of encouraging the migration of highly-skilled persons, the Blue Card Directive and intra-corporate transferees Directive also waive some of the restrictive rules in the family reunion Directive,[835] and the Blue Card Directive moreover includes a second set of rules relating to family members who move with a Blue Card holder who has not yet obtained long-term residence status to another Member State.[836] The EP and Council have agreed that researchers' family members will in future be covered by rules nearly identical to those for Blue Card holders.[837]

Starting with the special rules for refugees, the family reunion Directive defines a 'refugee' by reference to the Geneva Convention on refugee status,[838] not by reference to the definition of that term in EU legislation (known as the 'qualification Directive')[839]—for the obvious reason that the latter Directive was adopted after the former one. In light of the case law of the Court of Justice, which provides that the family reunion Directive should not be interpreted strictly, it is arguable that the definition of 'refugee' in that Directive should incorporate not just refugees as defined in the qualification Directive, but also any other person considered to be a refugee pursuant to national law.[840] The Directive does not preclude the possibility of family members obtaining refugee status in their own right.[841]

---

[835] Art 15 of Dir 2009/50 ([2009] OJ L 155/17) and Art 19 of Dir 2014/66 ([2014] OJ L 157/1). For more on these Dirs, see I:6.5.2 above.

[836] Art 19 of Dir 2009/50 (n 835 above).

[837] Arts 25 and 26C of agreed text of Dir (Council doc 13974/15, 20 Nov 2015). On the main text of the agreed Dir, see I:6.5.3.3 above.

[838] Art 2(b), Dir 2003/86 ([2003] OJ L 251/12); see generally I:6.6.1 above.

[839] Dir 2004/83 ([2004] OJ L 304/12), replaced by Dir 2011/95 ([2011] OJ L 337/9). This Dir also includes some specific rules on the status of family members of refugees: see I:5.5.1 above.

[840] Note that Art 3 of the qualification Dir (n 839 above) permits Member States to have higher standards. Also, the Blue Card Dir (Art 3(2)(b) and (c)) refers to qualification for international protection *either* under the qualification Dir *or* pursuant to national law.

[841] Art 9(3), Dir 2003/86. On this point, see the asylum procedures Directive (Art 7, Directive 2013/32, [2013] OJ L 180/60), discussed in I:5.7 above. The 'Dublin' rules on asylum responsibility also contain provisions on family reunion in that context (see I:5.8 above).

The specific rules relating to refugees are mostly set out in Chapter V of the general family reunion Directive.[842] It should be noted at the outset that Member States can confine the scope of these rules to refugees whose family relationships predated their entry to the territory.[843] These rules are more generous than the main regime in the Directive, in that: the possible special limits on children over twelve cannot apply;[844] admission of additional dependent family members may be authorized;[845] there are special rules on admission of the family or guardians of unaccompanied minors who are refugees;[846] the rules on proving a family relationship are more liberal;[847] the integration requirement cannot be applied until the persons concerned have entered the country;[848] and the waiting period[849] and accommodation, sickness insurance, and resources requirements are waived.[850] The guidance document rightly points out that like the main rules in the Directive, these specific rules for refugees create a right of admission for family members if the conditions for family reunion are satisfied.

There are certain exceptions to these rules, however. The waiver of the accommodation, sickness insurance, integration, and resources requirements can be refused either if 'family reunification is possible in a third country with which the sponsor and/or family member has special links', or where the application for family reunion was not submitted within three months of granting refugee status.[851] According to the guidance document, the 'special links' rule cannot be applied unless the third country in

---

[842] Arts 9–12, Dir 2003/86l see also Art 7(2). According to the Commission report on implementation of the Dir (the 'Commission report': COM (2008) 610, 8 Oct 2008), two Member States (Cyprus and Malta) do not implement these special rules at all.

[843] Art 9(2), Dir 2003/86. As the Commission guidance document on the Directive (COM (2014) 210, 3 Apr 2014) points out, this limitation does not apply to the special rule on the integration requirement in Art 7(2), since that special rule falls outside the scope of Chapter V.

[844] Art 10(1) of Dir 2003/86, disapplying Art 4(1), third sub-paragraph. On the application of this provision in practice, and its interpretation by the Court of Justice, see I:6.6.1 above.

[845] Art 10(2), Dir 2003/86.

[846] Art 10(3), Dir 2003/86; 'unaccompanied minor' is defined in Art 2(f). For other rules on unaccompanied minor refugees (or asylum seekers), see I:5.5 to I:5.9 above. See the action plan on unaccompanied minors (COM (2010) 213, 6 May 2010) and the follow-up to that plan (COM (2012) 554, 28 Sep 2012). According to the Commission report, this provision is not implemented in Bulgaria.

[847] Art 11, Dir 2003/86. The Commission report questions whether two Member States comply with this rule. The guidance document points out that any fees for DNA testing cannot be excessive (compare with the case law on integration tests, discussed in I:6.6.1 above, and long-term residents, discussed in I:6.7 below). On the process for admitting family members of refugees, see also the judgments of 10 July 2014 of the European Court of Human Rights in *Mugenzi v France*, *Tanda-Muzinga v France*, and *Senigo Longue and Others v France*.

[848] Art 7(2), second sub-paragraph, Dir 2003/86. According to the Commission report, the Netherlands imposes an integration condition in cases of family formation. However, it should be noted that Art 9(2) permits Member States to disapply all the special rules for refugees in such cases; a Member State is surely therefore permitted to disapply only *some* of these special rules to such cases if it chooses.

[849] Art 12(2), Dir 2003/86, waiving Art 8. On the application of this provision in practice, and its interpretation by the Court of Justice, see I:6.6.1 above.

[850] Art 12(1), first sub-paragraph, Dir 2003/86, waiving Art 7. According to the Commission report, Poland requires refugees to satisfy the accommodation requirement. This is an obvious breach of the Dir, except as regards those cases where the Dir still permits Member States to refuse to waive that requirement (see below). It should be noted that the qualification Directive contains provisions on refugees' and their family members' access to integration programmes, accommodation, health care, housing, welfare, and employment: Arts 22, 26, 29, 30, 32, and 34, Dir 2011/95 (n 839 above).

[851] Art 12(1), second and third sub-paragraphs, Dir 2003/86. The waiver of the integration requirement cannot, however, be refused in the latter case. The guidance document states that most Member States do not apply the latter exception, and urges others to follow them.

question: is 'a realistic alternative and, thus, a safe country for the sponsor and family members'; 'does not pose a risk of persecution or of refoulement for the refugee and/ or his [or her] family members'; and provides an opportunity for the refugee to receive protection there in accordance with the Geneva Convention on Refugees.[852] Moreover, the rule implies that the refugee and/or family member have 'family, cultural and social ties with the third country', and Member States have the burden of proof to show that such special links exist.[853]

It should be noted that any refugee sponsors admitted pursuant to the qualification Directive will necessarily have a residence permit valid for over one year,[854] although refugee sponsors are not exempt from the requirement to show a prospect of permanent residence.[855] Also, it must be recalled that the family members of Turkish workers who are refugees are entitled to retain that status after a certain point even if the worker's refugee status is questioned.[856] Like other family members admitted pursuant to the family reunion Directive, the family members of refugees, once authorized to work, have additional rights pursuant to the EU's single permit Directive.[857] Finally, pursuant to the application of the family reunion Directive to persons who were already present before implementation of the Directive,[858] the rules also apply where the sponsors concerned obtained refugee status before the Directive was implemented.

Secondly, the main Blue Card regime for family members contains six derogations from the family reunion Directive, which otherwise applies to family reunion with Blue Card holders.[859] The Directive on intra-corporate transferees ('ICTs') contains nearly identical derogations,[860] so the two sets of rules should be considered together.

First of all, the two Directives waive the waiting period of up to two or three years before family reunion is authorized, and also the requirement that the sponsor show

---

[852] Surely the alternative State is not 'realistic' unless it is willing to admit the refugee and family member(s).

[853] This interpretation, if correct, largely aligns the rule with the 'safe third country' rule in the asylum procedures Directive (Art 38, Dir 2013/32, n 841 above), except the family reunion Directive appears to require a stronger link between the refugee and the country concerned before the waiver can be refused. Therefore if the refugee has already been granted status in a Member State without this safe third country rule being applied, it is hard to see how Member States' authorities could justifiably refuse to waive the conditions in the family reunion Directive on the basis of the refugee's links with that third country. However, it might be arguable that the *family member's* links are a different matter; but still, if the third country will not admit the refugee, the refusal to waive the conditions represents an excessive restriction on family reunion rights.

[854] Art 3(1), 2003/86; Art 24(1) of Dirs 2004/83 and 2011/95 requires a residence permit for refugees to be valid for at least three years.

[855] This may be easier to satisfy now that the EU's long-term residence Directive applies to refugees, as from May 2013 (see I:6.7 below). It is also still open to Member States to extend national long-term residence regimes to refugees (Art 13, Directive 2003/109 on long-term residents).

[856] Case C-337/07 *Altun* [2008] ECR I-10323.

[857] See Art 12, Dir 2011/98, and the discussion in I:6.5.1 above. Although that Dir excludes refugees from its scope, it does not exclude their family members from it. The same is true of family members of persons with subsidiary or temporary protection.

[858] See further I:6.6.1 above.

[859] Art 15(1), Dir 2009/50. Pursuant to Art 4(2)(b) of this Dir, these rules are minimum standards rules. The Commission's report on the application of this Directive states that over 1000 family members of Blue Card holders were admitted in 2012, and over 2000 were admitted in 2013, but it does not comment further on national implementation of these rules (COM (2014) 287, 22 May 2014).

[860] Art 19, Dir 2014/66. Pursuant to Art 4(2) of this Dir, these rules are minimum standards rules. Art 19(1) of the Directive makes clear that apart from the derogations, the family reunion Directive otherwise applies to ICTs' family members.

that he or she has a reasonable prospect of obtaining permanent residence.[861] The waiver of these rules is crucial to ICTs, who might otherwise not enjoy family reunion at all due to the limited period of their stay on the territory.[862] As for Blue Card holders, although it is likely in practice that they can argue that they have a reasonable prospect of permanent residence,[863] waiving this requirement is likely to be useful in at least some cases. It should be noted that the requirement in the family reunion Directive to have a residence permit of at least one year's validity will almost always be met by Blue Card holders and ICTs.[864]

Next, the integration requirements permitted by the family reunion Directive can only be imposed after the family members have been admitted to the territory.[865] Thirdly, permits must be granted at the latest six months after application by a Blue Card holder, and ninety days after application by an ICT.[866] Fourthly, family members' residence permits shall be valid for the same period as the Blue Card holder or ICT, if those family members' travel documents are valid for long enough.[867] Fifthly, the possible waiting period for family members' access to the labour market is waived.[868] Finally, as regards the Blue Card Directive only, Member States have the *option* to cumulate the time periods the family member of the Blue Card holder has spent in different Member States, when calculating the time period for the acquisition of an autonomous residence permit for that family member.[869]

---

[861] Art 15(2), Dir 2009/50 and Art 19(2), Dir 2014/66, referring to Arts 3(1) and 8 of Dir 2003/86. It should be recalled that the latter provision was one of the clauses challenged by the EP before the Court of Justice.

[862] See Art 12, Dir 2014/66.

[863] The Blue Card residence permit is implicitly renewable, and all Member States provide for renewal in practice. Only one Member State has wrongly set a time limit on the total period of validity of a renewed Blue Card. See the discussion in I:6.5.2.1 above.

[864] Art 7(2), Dir 2009/50 requires that the residence permit be valid for a period of between one and four years, except where the work contract is for a shorter duration. Art 13(2), Dir 2014/66 requires an ICT permit to be valid for at least one year, unless the duration of the transfer is shorter.

[865] Art 15(3), Dir 2009/50 and Art 19(3), Dir 2014/66. This applies to both the general possibility of integration measures, provided for in Art 7(2) of Dir 2003/86, as well as the possible particular requirements for older children who arrive separately, as set out in Art 4(1) of the latter Directive. It should again be recalled that the latter provision was one of the clauses challenged by the EP before the Court of Justice.

[866] Art 15(4), Dir 2009/50 and Art 19(4), Dir 2014/66, referring to the first sub-paragraph of Art 5(4), Dir 2003/86, which sets a normal period of nine months for a decision. It should be noted that the *second* sub-paragraph of Art 5(4) of Dir 2003/86, which exceptionally permits a longer period to decide on a complex application, will still apply to Blue Card holders and ICTs. However, in practice this provision should not apply to them often, since their applications will not be as complex due to the relevant waivers from the normal rules and the greater ease which Blue Card holders and ICTs should have meeting the accommodation, resources, and insurance requirements. The ICT Directive also provides that applications by ICTs and their family members should be processed simultaneously, and expressly extends the procedural safeguards in that Directive to family reunion applications.

[867] Art 15(5), Dir 2009/50 and Art 19(5), Dir 2014/66, referring to Art 13(2), Dir 2003/86. The latter provision requires that family members' residence permits should be valid for at least one year, whereas the Blue Card must normally be valid for a period between one and four years (Art 7(2), Dir 2009/50), and the ICT permit will be valid for at least one year (Art 13(2), Dir 2014/66). The ICT Directive provides that this is the 'general rule'; there is no equivalent provision in the Blue Card Directive.

[868] Art 15(6), Dir 2009/50 and Art 19(6), Dir 2014/66, referring to Art 14(2), Dir 2003/86. Note that Art 14(1) of Dir 2003/86, requiring that the family member have the same level of access to employment as the sponsor, will continue to apply. On the issue of the Blue Card holder's access to employment before obtaining long-term residents' status, see Art 12 of Dir 2009/50, discussed in I:6.5.2 above. Presumably this rule is dynamic, ie the family member will get enhanced labour market access at the same time as the sponsor.

[869] Art 15(7) of Dir 2009/50, referring to Art 15(1), Dir 2003/86. Art 15(8) of Dir 2009/50 provides that in this case, the special rules on calculating the qualification for long-term residence status for the Blue Card holder in Art 16(2) of that Dir (see I:6.7.2 below) will apply *mutatis mutandis*.

The second set of special rules in the Blue Card Directive applies to family members of Blue Card holders who move between Member States pursuant to that Directive even before they obtain long-term resident status.[870] These rules provide that where a family was already constituted in the first Member State, the family members in question shall be authorized to join the Blue Card holder in the second Member State.[871] They (or the Blue Card holder) must apply for residence permits in the second Member State within one month;[872] Member States *must* issue the family members with temporary authorizations if their residence permit from the first Member State has expired or no longer allows them to stay in the second Member State.[873] Member States may require the family members to present evidence of: their prior stay in the first Member State as the family member of a Blue Card holder; travel documents, visas, and residence permits; and sickness insurance in the second Member State.[874] They may also require the Blue Card holder to meet accommodation and minimum income requirements before his or her family members can be admitted[875]—but the latter criterion, in the form of the salary threshold requirement, would have had to be met anyway before the Blue Card holder was admitted into the second Member State.[876] It should be noted that the provisions on accommodation and minimum income are identical to the equivalent provisions in the family reunion Directive, and so should logically therefore be interpreted the same way.[877] Next, the derogations from the family reunion Directive that applied to the admission of family members in the first Member State shall continue to apply in the second Member State.[878] Finally, if the family members were not admitted already into the first Member State, than the specific rules on family reunion in the Blue Card directive will apply in the second Member State.[879]

The special provisions for refugees should make it easier in practice for refugees to be reunited with family members, although the requirement of a prospect of permanent residence for the sponsors might in practice still prove a difficulty, and the possible requirement to make an application within three months of the grant of refugee status in order to benefit from some of the waivers from the general rules could prove a

---

[870] Art 19, Dir 2009/50. On the underlying rules allowing Blue Card holders to move between Member States, see Art 18 of that Dir, discussed in I:6.5.2.1 above. It should be noted that Art 19 does *not* set minimum standards only (see Art 4(2) of the Dir, *a contrario*). The special family reunion rules in the ICT Directive apply equally to cases where the ICT exercises mobility between Member States in that Directive (Art 19(1), Dir 2014/66). On those mobility rules, see I:6.5.2.2 above.

[871] Art 19(1), Dir 2009/50.   [872] Art 19(2), first sub-paragraph.

[873] Art 19(2), second sub-paragraph.

[874] Art 19(3). Logically a visa requirement should not apply where the Blue Card holders move between Member States which fully apply the Schengen *acquis* (see I:4.9 above).

[875] Art 19(4).

[876] See Art 18(2), referring to the conditions in Art 5. In practice, due to the higher than average salary which must be earned by the Blue Card holder, it should not be difficult to afford the cost of meeting the accommodation and sickness insurance requirements.

[877] Compare Art 19(4), Dir 2009/50, to Art 7(1)(a) and (c) of Dir 2003/86. This would mean that the judgment in Case C-578/08 *Chakroun* [2010] ECR I-1839, concerning the sufficient resources exception, would also apply. As for sickness insurance, Art 19(3)(c) of Dir 2009/50 is slightly different from Art 7(1)(b) of Dir 2003/86 (the latter refers to 'all risks normally covered for' the host State's own nationals, while the former refers to 'all risks' more generally).

[878] Art 19(5).   [879] Art 19(6).

problem for refugees who need a longer period in practice to save up in order to afford the cost of travel, et al. for their family members.

As for the special Blue Card and ICT rules, the underlying question (as with the Blue Card and ICT regimes as a whole) is whether these rules will contribute to the objective of the two Directives—making the EU more attractive for highly-skilled workers? On this point, the changes to the family reunion regime of the EU (waiting periods and permanent residence requirements abolished, longer period of validity of residence permits, immediate access to employment by family members, waiver of advance integration requirements, and shorter time limits for decision-making) may prove rather more attractive. In fact, it is even conceivable that the family reunion rules in the Blue Card or ICT Directives will induce some persons to apply for Blue Card or ICT status purely to take advantage of them, even if the applicant has few reasons to apply for Blue Card or ICT status otherwise, in particular in Member States which have a restrictive regime for family reunion for other third-country nationals. The special family reunion regime for Blue Card holders who move between Member States before they obtain long-term residence status will also facilitate that movement, although in practice these rules are likely to have an impact on much fewer people than the general Blue Card rules.

6.7 Long-Term Residents

The status of long-term resident (LTR) third-country nationals of the European Union, including their right to move between EU Member States, is regulated first of all by Council Directive 2003/109, which sets out the basic rules on this issue.[880] This Directive was amended in 2011, to extend it to refugees and persons who have subsidiary protection status, who were initially excluded from its scope.[881] Moreover, as with the issue of family reunion,[882] there are special rules set out in the Blue Card Directive, which are discussed separately below.[883] It should also be noted that EU legislation on researchers and students, as well as the Blue Card and ICT Directives, contains separate rules on the movement of third-country nationals and their family members between Member States, even before such persons have attained long-term residence status.[884]

6.7.1 General rules

Member States had to implement Directive 2003/109 by 23 January 2006.[885] The Court of Justice gave three judgments against Member States for failure to apply this Directive on time.[886] Another three infringement cases were withdrawn following delayed

---

[880] [2004] OJ L 16/44.

[881] Directive 2011/51 ([2011] OJ L 132/1). All references in this section are to the Directive as amended, unless otherwise indicated. The Directive has not been codified.

[882] See I:6.6 above.   [883] Arts 16 and 17 of Dir 2009/50 ([2009] OJ L 155/17). See I:6.7.2 below.

[884] See I:6.5.2 and I:6.5.3 above.   [885] Art 26.

[886] Cases: C-5/07 *Commission v Portugal* (judgment against Portugal, 27 Sep 2007); C-59/07 *Commission v Spain* (judgment against Spain, 15 Nov 2007); and C-34/07 *Commission v Luxembourg* (judgment against Luxembourg, 29 Nov 2007).

implementation of legislation by Member States.[887] There have also been several references to the Court of Justice on the interpretation of the Directive.[888] Directive 2011/51, which extended the scope of the original Directive, had to be applied by 20 May 2013.[889] Finally, the Commission presented a report on the implementation of the Directive in 2011 (the '2011 report').[890]

The principal purpose of the Directive, according to its preamble and CJEU case law, is to integrate third-country nationals who are long-term residents.[891] It also aims to approximate their legal status to EU citizens.[892] Furthermore, the provisions on movement between Member States aim 'to contribute to the effective attainment of an internal market as an area in which the free movement of persons is ensured'.[893] Like the family reunion Directive, the LTR Directive creates enforceable rights: third-country nationals who satisfy the conditions 'have the right to obtain long-term resident status as well as the other rights which stem from the grant of that status'.[894] According to the Court, the equal treatment rules in the Directive are the general rule, and exceptions from that rule must be interpreted strictly.[895] In light of the objective of the Directive, the same approach should apply to all of the conditions and derogations from the Directive, along with exclusions from its scope.[896]

Chapter I of the Directive sets out its purpose, definitions, and scope.[897] It applies to all lawful residents of a Member State who are third-country nationals,[898] except for: diplomats;[899] persons who are seeking refugee, temporary protection, or subsidiary protection status, or who have received temporary protection;[900] students;[901] and those who 'reside solely on temporary grounds such as' au pairs, seasonal workers, cross-border service providers, workers posted by cross-border service providers, or

---

[887] Cases: C-30/07 *Commission v Hungary*; C-37/07 *Commission v France*; and C-104/07 *Commission v Italy*.

[888] Cases: C-571/10 *Kamberaj*, ECLI:EU:C:2012:233; C-508/10 *Commission v Netherlands*, ECLI:EU: C:2012:243; C-502/10 *Singh*, ECLI:EU:C:2012:636; C-469/13 *Tahir*, ECLI:EU:C:2014:2094; C-579/13 *P and S*, ECLI:EU:C:2015:369; and C-309/14 *CGIL and IMCA*, ECLI:EU:C:2015:523. The Court also discussed the Directive in Case C-40/11 *Iida*, ECLI:EU:C:2012:691 and Case C-371/08 *Ziebell* [2011] ECR I-12735.

[889] [2011] OJ L 132/1, Art 2(1).   [890] COM (2011) 585, 28 Sep 2011.

[891] *Kamberaj*, para 90; *Commission v Netherlands*, para 66; *Singh*, para 45; *Tahir*, para 32. See also *P and S*, para 32, where the Court linked this objective to economic and social cohesion.

[892] *Singh*, para 45.   [893] *Commission v Netherlands*, para 66.

[894] *Commission v Netherlands*, para 68.   [895] *Kamberaj*, para 86.

[896] The Opinion in *Commission v Netherlands*, para 61, argues that the conditions for obtaining LTR status must be interpreted strictly. See by analogy the case law on the family reunion Directive, discussed in I:6.6.1 above.

[897] Arts 1–3.

[898] Art 3(1). According to the *Singh* judgment, para 39 and the *Iida* judgment, para 36, the Directive does not define 'legal residence', and so that concept is left to the Member States to define. With respect, the Court usually concludes rather that in the absence of a reference to national law, concepts in EU legislation must have an autonomous interpretation. Furthermore, the Court ignores the possibility that legal residence might be governed by EU law, for instance as regards family members of third-country nationals or of EU citizens who have moved within the EU, the EU/Turkey association agreement, or the Blue Card or researchers' Directives.

[899] Art 3(2)(f), referring to specific relevant treaties.

[900] Art 3(2)(b) to (d), as amended by Directive 2011/51. Art 2(f) makes clear that 'refugee' and 'subsidiary protection' have the same definition as EU asylum law; on this legislation, see I:5.5 above. There is no cross-reference to EU law on temporary protection (on which, see I:5.6 above).

[901] Art 3(2)(a). On this category, see I:6.5.3.2 above. There is no cross-reference to the EU students' Directive (since it was adopted the following year).

persons whose 'residence permit has been formally limited'.[902] In light of the objective of the Directive, the list of exclusions from its scope is surely exhaustive. It therefore applies, for instance, to third-country nationals whose status has been regularized, family members of third-country nationals, and third-country national family members of EU citizens, whether those persons have moved within the EU with their sponsors (and are therefore covered by EU free movement law) or not.[903]

According to the CJEU, the category of those whose 'residence permit has been formally limited' is distinct from the category of those who 'reside solely on temporary grounds'.[904] Defining the former concept, the Court ruled that a formal limitation of a residence permit according to national law was not decisive, since the definition did not refer to national law and so should receive a uniform and autonomous interpretation throughout the EU. Since the main purpose of the Directive was the integration of those staying for a long period, it excluded those whose residence was 'lawful' and 'possibly continuous', but which did not '*prima facie* reflect any intention to settle on a long-term basis'. The Court confirmed that the list of 'temporary grounds' exceptions was not an exhaustive list of activities which are 'per se of a temporary nature'. In contrast, it was not self-evident whether a person with a formally limited permit 'might settle on a long-term basis', despite that restriction. So if a permit was formally limited under national law, but did not prevent long-term residence in practice, it could not be considered 'formally limited' for the purposes of the exclusion from the Directive, since otherwise the Directive would be deprived of its effectiveness. It is irrelevant that the formal limitation concerns only a 'specific group of persons'. Conversely if the validity of a residence permit can be extended successively, past a five-year period and possibly even indefinitely, that is a 'strong indication' that the exception does not apply.

The Court's judgment starts out by saying that a 'formally limited' residence permit was distinct from a residence permit issued on 'temporary grounds', but ultimately that is a distinction without a difference. For the judgment essentially concludes that a 'formally limited' permit is one that cannot lead in practice to long-term residence—in other words, a *temporary* form of stay on the territory. The 2011 report indicates that five Member States are in breach of this provision (as subsequently interpreted by the CJEU), excluding migrants from LTR status 'even though their residence permit may be renewed for a potentially indefinite period, without any definite time limit'. This affects, for instance, 'artists, athletes, ministers of religion, social workers, researchers, family members of permanent third-country nationals, and low skilled migrant workers'.

The Directive is without prejudice to more favourable provisions of EU or mixed agreements with third states, pre-existing treaties of Member States, and certain

---

[902] Art 3(2)(e). On service providers, see I:6.4.4 and I:6.4.6 above. On seasonal workers, see I:6.5.2.2 above; there is no reference to the EU's seasonal workers' Directive, since it was adopted over a decade later. The 'temporary grounds' exception would also apply to volunteers, trainees, and school pupils (if Member States opt to apply the EU rules on these groups: see I:6.5.3.2 above), as well as ICTs and seasonal workers (see I.6.5.2 above), in light of the limits on the validity and renewability of residence permits set by EU law for these categories of persons.

[903] The Directive notably lacks the usual exclusion of free movement cases found in much other EU immigration legislation. An interesting question is whether it would apply to *Ruiz Zambrano* cases (see discussion in I:6.4.1 above), on the basis that their immigration status must be considered 'lawful'.

[904] *Singh*, n 888 above.

Council of Europe migration treaties and treaties relating to refugees.[905] In the absence of wording to the contrary, the Directive should apply to persons who were already resident in the Member States at the time of its adoption (as well as, obviously, those who entered later).[906]

Chapter II sets out rules concerning long-term resident status in one Member State.[907] The basic rule is that third-country nationals are entitled to such status after residing 'legally and continuously for five years in the territory of the Member State concerned' before their application for status.[908] This definition does not limit itself to lawful stays on the basis of a residence permit, and so the 2011 report is right to criticize five Member States for not counting stays on the basis of (for instance) long-stay visas.

Absences from the host Member State of up to six months at a time, totalling no more than ten months during the five-year period, must be taken into account in calculating that period.[909] Member States may permit longer periods of absence for 'specific or exceptional reasons of a temporary nature and in accordance with their national law', but such absences will not count toward the qualifying period (in other words, the clock will be stopped).[910] But Member States may allow the clock to keep ticking if a person is detached for employment purposes.[911] Prior residence as a diplomat or on a temporary permit does not count at all, while prior residence as a student must be discounted 50%.[912] Member States may also discount time spent as an asylum seeker before a person obtains international protection, by up to 50%.[913]

Long-term resident status shall be denied on grounds of insufficient resources, or lack of sickness insurance.[914] Member States may require applicants to fulfil integration conditions,[915] or refuse to grant status on grounds of public policy or public

---

[905] Art 3(3); the reference to refugee treaties was added by Directive 2011/51. On the first category of treaties, see I:6.4.3 above.

[906] On the temporal scope of EU immigration and asylum law, see I:5.5 above and Case C-357/09 PPU *Kadzoev* [2009] ECR I-11189; see also Case C-297/12 *Filev and Osmani*, ECLI:EU:C:2013:569. See also, by analogy, Joined Cases C-424/10 and C-425/10 *Ziolkowski and Szeja* [2011] ECR I-14035.

[907] Arts 4–13.

[908] Art 4(1). The Blue Card Directive provides for a derogation from this rule: see I:6.7.2 below. Being the family member of a long-term resident does not exempt a migrant from this rule (*Tahir*, n 888 above).

[909] Art 4(3), first sub-paragraph. Again, the Blue Card Directive provides for a derogation from this rule, see n 908 above.

[910] Art 4(3), second sub-paragraph. The 2011 report states that 13 Member States apply this option.

[911] Art 4(3), third sub-paragraph.

[912] Art 4(2). The 2011 report states that all except six Member States use these optional rules.

[913] Art 4(2), third sub-paragraph; but if the waiting period before obtaining a residence permit is more than 18 months, the whole period must be counted. On the time limits for asylum procedures, see I:5.7 above. Art 4(1a) states that a person whose protection status was revoked, ended, or not renewed cannot obtain LTR status; on these concepts, see the qualification Directive, discussed in I:5.5 above. Both of these provisions were added by Dir 2011/51.

[914] Art 5(1). Logically these conditions must be interpreted consistently with the same conditions in the family reunion Directive; see the discussion of the *Chakroun* judgment in I:6.6.1 above, except that in light of the time already spent on the territory, it makes sense to consider also the income of family members, not just the applicant's own income. The 2011 report rightly criticizes one country which requires applicants to have a work contract lasting at least eighteen months; it should be sufficient to show that the contract is renewable.

[915] Art 5(2). This provision is worded slightly differently than its equivalent in the family reunion Directive, which refers to 'measures', not 'conditions'. See the *K and A* judgment on the equivalent clause in the family reunion Directive, in I:6.6.1 above. The CJEU has ruled on the imposition of integration measures *after* obtaining LTR status: see the discussion of the *P and S* judgment below.

security.[916] In light of the objectives of the Directive, the list of conditions to obtain LTR status should be regarded as exhaustive.[917] Although the Directive, unlike some other EU migration Directives, does not expressly regulate the issue of fees for applications, the CJEU has ruled that excessively high fees for LTR applications can diminish the effectiveness of the Directive, and so amount to a breach of Member States' obligations.[918]

The Directive also sets out detailed rules on the procedure for acquisition and withdrawal of long-term residence status.[919] According to the CJEU, a third-country national does not obtain LTR status automatically, but has to apply for it.[920] There is a right to 'mount a legal challenge' if LTR status is rejected or withdrawn; it is again arguable that given Strasbourg jurisprudence, the general principles of EU law, and the EU Charter of Fundamental Rights, this must, inter alia, include the right to argue the merits of any issue falling within the scope of the Directive before a court or tribunal.[921]

LTR status 'shall' be lost due to its fraudulent acquisition, the adoption of an expulsion measure, or following absence from the *EU* (not just the particular Member State which granted the status) 'for a period of 12 consecutive months', although Member States *may* provide that absences for longer periods *or* for 'specific and exceptional reasons' will not lead to loss of the status.[922] Where status is lost due to departure from the EU or a lengthy stay in another Member State, Member States must establish a procedure to 'facilitate' re-acquisition of the status.[923] As the 2011 report rightly points out, the list of grounds for loss or withdrawal of LTR status is exhaustive.

Substantively, long-term residence status entitles its holders to equal treatment with nationals in a number of areas: employment and self-employment; education and vocational training; recognition of diplomas; social security, social assistance, and social protection 'as defined in national law'; tax benefits; access to goods and services; freedom of association; and free access to the territory.[924] However, there are exceptions: Member States can impose residence requirements in most cases,

---

[916] Art 6. The CJEU has ruled that such provisions must be interpreted consistently with the same exception in EU free movement law: see the case law discussed in I:7.7.1 below and I:5.5 above.

[917] See the Opinion in *Commission v Netherlands*, para 60. In particular, as the 2011 report points out, the Directive does not provide for adequate housing as a condition of obtaining LTR status. Also, the report rightly criticizes one State for requiring that an LTR applicant first obtain a 'settlement permit' (itself based on a quota and points system).

[918] *Commission v Netherlands* and *CGIL and INCA*.

[919] Arts 7–10. Art 7 requires compliance with the five-year waiting period in Art 4 (*Tahir*, n 888 above).

[920] The CJEU helpfully pointed out in its *Iida* judgment that the person concerned met the criteria to obtain LTR status, if he chose to apply for it. Subsequently, in Cases C-312/12 *Ajdini*, ECLI:EU:C:2013:103 and C-257/13 *Mlamali*, ECLI:EU:C:2013:763, the Court refused to discuss LTR status since the person concerned had not applied for it.

[921] See again the judgment on the analogous provision in the family reunion Dir (Case C-540/03 *EP v Council* [2006] ECR I-5769) and I:6.3.1 and I:6.3.4 above.

[922] Art 9(1) and (2). The Blue Card Directive provides for a derogation from the rule regarding the period of departure from the EU (Art 9(1)(c)): see I:6.7.2 below.

[923] Art 9(4) and (5).

[924] Art 11(1). This is stronger protection as regards access to employment and self-employment, along with social assistance and social protection, as compared to the equal treatment rules in other Directives (see, for instance, Arts 12(1) and 14 of the Blue Card Dir and Art 12 of the single permit directive (Dir 2011/98, [2011] OJ L 343/1)). The 2011 report suggests that some Member States are applying unjustified restrictions as regards university fees, equal treatment, and movement on the territory.

limit access to employment and education, and 'limit equal treatment in respect of social assistance and social protection to core benefits'.[925] The CJEU clarified the latter provision in *Kamberaj*, ruling that housing benefit restrictions in the Italian province of Bolzano breached the equal treatment rule because they were calculated on a different basis for third-country nationals.[926] While the reference to national law in principle meant that it was up to each Member State to define the meaning of 'social assistance and social protection', the national court also had to take account of Article 34 of the Charter, which referred to a right to 'social and housing assistance' as regards combating poverty and social exclusion.[927] As to whether housing assistance was a 'core benefit', the CJEU ruled that this exception had to be interpreted strictly, and that the list of such benefits in the preamble to the Directive (which does not mention housing benefit) was non-exhaustive. There was an implied procedural obligation to announce that a Member State was invoking the derogation (which Italy had not done), and the Court, again taking account of the Charter, defined core benefits as those 'which enable individuals to meet their basic needs such as food, accommodation and health'.[928] While it was up to the national court to apply the Court's reasoning to the case, on the whole the Court strongly supported equal treatment rights in this case.

In contrast, it seemed less concerned by the equal treatment of long-term residents in the *P and S* judgment. This case concerned third-country nationals who had already obtained long-term resident status, but were still subjected to an integration requirement. The Court ruled that this obligation did not fall within the scope of the equal treatment rule because Dutch citizens could be presumed to have knowledge of Dutch society and the Dutch language, whereas non-EU citizens could not. But it went on to assess whether the requirement compromised the effectiveness of the Directive. In principle it did not, because the main objective of the Directive is the integration of long-term residents, and learning the national language and about the host State could facilitate communication with Dutch citizens. Acquiring a knowledge of Dutch also 'makes it less difficult' to find work and take up training courses. The integration requirement therefore contributed to the aims of the Directive. However, the Court did place some limits upon what Member States can do, as regards 'the level of knowledge required to pass the civic integration examination', 'accessibility of the courses and the material necessary to prepare' for the exams, the level of registration fees, and 'specific individual circumstances, such as age, illiteracy or level of education'. In particular, the Court ruled that the fines for failing the exam were too high and were imposed too often (for every failure, or even where the long-term resident had not sat the exam within the required time), on top of the high fees to sit the exam.

---

[925] Art 11(2) to (4); although the exceptions in Art 11(3) and (4) are 'without prejudice' to the higher protection for refugees and persons with subsidiary protection in the qualification Directive (Art 11(4a), inserted by Dir 2011/51; on the substance of those rules, see I:5.5 above). According to the 2011 report, 12 Member States apply the residence condition.

[926] *Kamberaj*, paras 70 to 75.   [927] *Kamberaj*, paras 76 to 81.

[928] *Kamberaj*, paras 82 to 93. The Court also noted that there is no possibility to restrict equality to 'core benefits' as regards social security.

Next, long-term residents are also entitled to enhanced, although not absolute, protection against expulsion, which is clearly based on ECHR jurisprudence.[929] The CJEU has linked this protection to the safeguards accorded to EU citizens before the advent of the EU citizens' Directive.[930]

The EU rules on LTR status co-exist with national rules dealing with the same issue. The Directive states that Member States may create or maintain national systems that are more favourable than the rules in Chapter II, but acquisition of status under such more favourable rules will not confer the right of residence in other Member States pursuant to Chapter III.[931] According to the CJEU, it follows that a residence permit obtained on the basis of such more favourable rules cannot constitute an EU LTR permit at all.[932] According to the 2011 report, 13 Member States have maintained national rules, and 14 of them force a choice between a national permit and an EU permit. As the report rightly points out, this is a breach of the Directive, since it does not provide for Member States to impose such a condition.[933]

Chapter III concerns the exercise of the right of residence for periods above three months in other Member States,[934] other than as a posted worker or provider of services.[935] Member States can impose labour market tests limiting movement on economic grounds, or an overall quota on the numbers of third-country nationals (if that quota existed at the time of adoption of the Directive), along with special rules restricting movement of seasonal workers or cross-border workers.[936] The right of residence can be exercised if the long-term resident is pursuing an economic activity or a non-economic activity, but the 'second' Member State can insist that the long-term resident has sufficient resources and sickness insurance and comply with integration measures, provided that such measures were not already complied with in the first Member State.[937] Long-term residents can bring with them their 'core' family members as defined by the family reunion Directive,[938] but the second Member State retains the option to decide whether to admit other family members.[939] Again, sickness insurance and sufficient resources tests can apply. Admission of long-term residents and their family members can also be refused not just on grounds of public policy and public security, but also public health.[940] Moving to another Member State could be less

---

[929] Art 12.

[930] *Ziebell*, which also applied these rules to the protection of Turkish citizens against expulsion (see I:6.4.3 above). Also, as noted above (as regards Art 6), other CJEU case law reinforces the view that 'public policy etc' exceptions in EU immigration law must be interpreted consistently with the free movement exceptions.

[931] Art 13.

[932] See the judgment in *Tahir*, which concerns an Italian law giving early access to national long-term residence schemes for family members.

[933] Equally they cannot force a choice between international protection status and LTR status, since Arts 8(4) to (6), 9(3a), and 12(3a) to (3c) and (6), inserted by Dir 2011/51, explicitly contemplate holding both statuses at the same time. But as noted below, an LTR who moves to *another* Member State may not be able to transfer protection status there.

[934] Arts 14–22.

[935] Art 14(5), first sub-paragraph. On this category of persons, see I:6.4.4 above.

[936] Art 14(3), (4), and (5), second sub-paragraph. Compare the two former exceptions to Art 79(5) TFEU, discussed in I:6.2.4 above.

[937] Art 15.   [938] See I:6.6 above.   [939] Art 16.   [940] Arts 17–18.

attractive to refugees and persons with subsidiary protection, since the Directive does not provide for the transfer of protection to the second State.[941]

The potential 'second' Member State must process the application within four months, with a potential three-month extension. The CJEU has ruled that the fees for the LTR's application to move, along with his or her family members to join them, cannot be excessive.[942] If the various conditions are met, the second Member State must issue the long-term resident and his/her family members with a renewable residence permit.[943] Reasons must be given if the application is rejected, and there is a 'right to mount a legal challenge' where an application is rejected or a permit is withdrawn or not renewed.[944] Once they have received their residence permit, long-term residents have the right to equal treatment in the second Member State,[945] 'with the exception of social assistance and study grants', and subject to a possible one-year delay in full labour market access.[946] Family members have the same status as family members under the family reunion Directive as regards access to employment and education, once they have received their long-term residence permit.[947]

Before the long-term resident gains long-term resident status in the second Member State, that Member State can remove or withdraw his or her residence permit and expel the long-term resident and family in accordance with national procedures on grounds of public policy or public security, where the conditions for admission are no longer met and where the third-country national 'is not lawfully residing' there.[948] The first Member State must readmit such persons, although if there are 'serious grounds of public policy or public security', the person concerned can be expelled outside the EU. Once the conditions for obtaining long-term resident status are satisfied in the second Member State, the long-term resident can apply for long-term resident status there, subject to the same procedural rules that apply to initial applications for long-term resident status.[949] According to the 2011 report, there were a number of legal and practical problems applying the various rules on movement to a second Member State.

On the whole, this Directive is an accomplishment simply because it facilitates the security of residence, equal treatment, and free movement of third-country nationals more than EU law previously provided for.[950] Nevertheless, the 2011 report indicates that only about half a million third-country nationals had qualified as LTRs, despite a far higher eligibility. The numbers are lower than they would otherwise be in large part because of breaches in national implementation of the Directive (notably the forced choice between the national and EU LTR systems). The defective implementation of the

---

[941] See recital 9 in the preamble of Directive 2011/51. There are other frameworks for the transfer of protection status, but many Member States do not apply them. For a detailed analysis of this issue, see S Peers, 'Transfer of International Protection and European Union Law' (2012) 24 IJRL 527.

[942] *Commission v Netherlands.*   [943] Art 19.   [944] Art 20.   [945] As defined in Art 11.

[946] Art 21.

[947] The family members are also entitled to equal treatment under Art 12 of the single permit Dir: see I:6.5.1 above.

[948] Art 22.   [949] Art 23.

[950] For more detailed comments, see K Groenendijk in S Peers et al., *EU Immigration and Asylum Law: Text and Commentary*, 3rd edn (Brill, 2011), ch 10, and D Acosta, *The Long-Term Residence Status as a Subsidiary Form of EU Citizenship* (Brill, 2011).

conditions for obtaining LTR status (notably as regards housing) is also problematic. Unfortunately the Commission has not brought any further infringement proceedings besides its earlier challenge to the fees charged to LTR applicants by the Netherlands.

As for movement to a second Member State, since there are many express possibilities for Member States to limit movement of long-term residents, it should follow that unless one of these express exceptions applies, long-term residents enjoy equal treatment as regards the initial take-up of employment, self-employment, or non-economic activities in the second Member State. Also, it appears that the Directive can be used where a long-term resident wishes to move between Member States to join a sponsoring family member in another Member State. This means that such persons will only have to satisfy the criteria for obtaining long-term residents' status, and may therefore avoid the limitations and conditions set out in the family reunion Directive or EU free movement law. For example, an American national with long-term resident status in France could rely on that status to move to Austria to join his unmarried partner (of either sex).

6.7.2 Special rules

As noted above, the only set of special rules adopted to date regarding long-term residents appears in the Blue Card Directive.[951] These special rules provide that the long-term residents' Directive applies to Blue Card holders, with three derogations provided for in the Blue Card Directive.[952] All of the special rules presumably apply to persons who have already spent some period of legal residence in a Member State (taking account of the calculation rules in the long-term residents' Directive) before they obtain a Blue Card.[953]

First of all, in order to obtain long-term residence status in the first place, Blue Card holders do not need to show five years' continuous residence in the *single* Member State where they make their application for a long-term residence permit, but can cumulate residence in *different* Member States, as long as they have *two* years' residence in that Member State just prior to their application for long-term resident status there, and have five years' 'legal and continuous' residence *within the EU* as a Blue Card holder, having made use of the possibility in the Blue Card Directive of moving between Member States even before obtaining long-term resident status.[954]

Secondly, when calculating the five-year residence period for Blue Card holders, Member States must moreover include absences from *EU* territory of up to *twelve*

---

[951] Arts 16 and 17 of Dir 2009/50 ([2009] OJ L 155/17), applicable since 19 June 2011. All references in this sub-section are to the Blue Card Dir unless otherwise indicated.

[952] Art 16(1).

[953] This includes periods before the Blue Card Directive applied. On the temporal scope of EU immigration and asylum law, see I:5.5 and I:6.6 above.

[954] Art 16(2); this is an express derogation from Art 4(1) of Dir 2003/109 ([2003] OJ L 16/44). The specific rule in Art 4(2) of Dir 2003/109 continues to apply (see Art 16(1)). Point 20 in the preamble explains the purpose of this derogation: it exists 'in order not to penalise geographically mobile highly qualified third-country workers who have not yet acquired' EU long-term resident status, and 'in order to encourage geographical and circular migration'.

months, adding up to *eighteen* months' absence in total.[955] This rule applies regardless of whether the Blue Card holder has moved within the EU or not, and derogates from the rule in the long-term residents' Directive which requires Member States to include in the calculation only absences from *national* territory of up to *six* months, adding up to *ten* months in total.[956]

Thirdly, a Blue Card holder who has obtained long-term residence status (and his or her family members with long-term residence status) is entitled to a period of two years' absence from the EU, not just one year, before Member States are entitled to withdraw his or her long-term residence permit.[957] However, Member States *may* limit the second and third derogations from the long-term residence Directive to cases in which the person concerned 'can present evidence that he [or she] has been absent from the territory of the [EU] to exercise an economic activity in an employed or self-employed capacity, or to perform a voluntary service, or to study in his [or her] own country of origin'.[958] Finally, the favourable rules in the Blue Card Directive on family reunion and on the transfer of pensions to third countries continue to apply to former Blue Card holders who have obtained long-term residence status.[959] Once Blue Card holders qualify for long-term residence status, they must receive a long-term residence permit in the standard format, marked 'former Blue Card holder'.[960]

It should be noted that the Council dropped an important part of the Commission's original proposal, which would have disapplied any national quotas on the total number of resident third-country nationals as regards any Blue Card holders who obtained long-term resident status, and would also have required Member States who applied priority employment rules against long-term residents who moved to their Member State to give long-term residents who held Blue Card preference as compared to all other third-country nationals applying to reside there for the same reasons.[961]

As with the parallel derogations from the family reunion Directive, the key question is to what extent these particular provisions has contributed to the objective of the Blue Card Directive—making the EU more attractive for highly-skilled workers? The Commission's first report on the Blue Card Directive does not assess this issue, and says little about the implementation of these provisions.[962] Presumably the removal of some restrictions on obtaining and retaining long-term resident status

---

[955] Art 16(3).

[956] More specifically, the derogation is from the rule in the first sub-paragraph in Art 4(3) of Dir 2003/109. On the purpose of this derogation, see again point 20 in the preamble. It follows from Art 16(1) that the rules in the second and third sub-paragraphs of Art 4(3) of Dir 2003/109 continue to apply to Blue Card holders.

[957] Art 16(4), derogating from Art 9(1)(c) of Dir 2003/109. On the purpose of this derogation, see point 21 in the preamble. It follows from Art 16(1) that the other rules on the loss or withdrawal of long-term residence status in Art 9 of Dir 2003/109 continue to apply, including the discretion to permit longer periods of absence for 'specific or exceptional reasons' (Art 9(2)) and the requirement to facilitate the re-acquisition of long-term residence status after losing it on this basis (Art 9(5)).

[958] Art 16(5). According to the Commission's report on the Blue Card Directive (COM (2014) 287, 22 May 2014), twelve Member States chose this option.

[959] Art 16(6). On these rules, see respectively I:6.6.2 and I:6.5.1 above.

[960] Art 17. On the residence permit format, see I:6.9.1 below.

[961] Art 20 of the original proposal (COM (2007) 637, 23 Oct 2007), referring to Art 14(3) and 14(4) of Dir 2003/109 (on which, see I:6.7.1 above).

[962] N 958 above.

might have had a modest impact on the attractiveness of the Blue Card system to would-be applicants. The Commission's proposals to lift quotas and weaken the local preference rule for Blue Card holders who obtained long-term status would have been more significant, but the Council rejected them entirely. The most obvious step to attract highly-skilled workers to the EU would have been to shorten the period needed to obtain long-term residence status for Blue Card holders—but this idea was not even considered.[963]

6.8 Social Security Coordination

It should first of all be recalled, as set out above, that certain third-country nationals (refugees, stateless persons, and family members of EU citizens exercising free movement rights) are covered by EU free movement legislation governing social security coordination[964], and certain others are governed by the EU's association agreements.[965] The social security position of other third-country nationals was governed initially by Regulation 859/2003, which took effect from 1 June 2003.[966] This Regulation extended the 1971 free movement legislation on social security to all third-country nationals and members of their families who were not already covered by that Regulation, on two conditions: they had to be 'legally resident' and, following the *Khalil and Addou* judgment,[967] there had to be a cross-border dimension within the EU.[968] Third-country nationals had to apply for equal treatment within two years (so by 1 June 2005), otherwise they were limited to equal treatment from the time of their application.[969] Finally, an Annex provided that in Germany, only persons in possession of a particular permit qualified for certain family benefits, while Austria was permitted to set out special additional conditions for access to family allowances. The Court of Justice has interpreted the Regulation several times.[970]

This Regulation was replaced in 2010,[971] in order to ensure that the EU rules on third-country nationals were consistent with updated basic rules on social security coordination for EU citizens and their family members, along with refugees and stateless persons, which took effect from 1 May 2010.[972] The new Regulation also removed

---

[963] Note that Member States do retain the power to set more favourable standards (including a shorter waiting period) for highly-skilled workers as regards national long-term residence regimes (Art 13, Dir 2003/109).

[964] For detailed comments on the background to this issue, see ch 23 of S Peers and N Rogers, eds., *EU Immigration and Asylum Law: Text and Commentary*, 1st edn (Martinus Nijhoff, 2006).

[965] See I:6.4.1, I:6.4.2, and I:6.4.3 above.   [966] [2003] OJ L 124/1.

[967] Joined Cases C-95/99 to 98/99 *Khalil and others* and C-180/99 *Addou* [2001] ECR I-7413.

[968] On this requirement, see C-276/06 *El-Youssfi* [2007] ECR I-2851.   [969] Art 2.

[970] The Reg does not apply to third-country nationals who live in an EU Member State but work in Switzerland (Case C-247/09 *Xymshiti* [2010] ECR I-11845). In its judgment in Case C-45/12 *Hadj Ahmed*, ECLI:EU:C:2013:390, the CJEU confirmed that the Reg only applied to cross-border situations. The CJEU has also been asked about the temporal scope of the Reg, as regards a third-country national whose State of nationality later joined the EU: Case C-465/14 *Weiland and Rothwangi*, pending.

[971] Reg 1231/2010 ([2010] OJ L 344/1), applicable from 1 Jan 2011 (Art 3).

[972] Reg 883/2004 ([2004] OJ L 166/1). This Reg only applied as from the date of effect of a subsequent implementing Reg, namely Reg 987/2009, [2009] OJ L 284/1 (see Art 91 of Reg 883/2004, and subsequently Art 97 of Reg 987/2009 on the latter Reg's date of entry into effect).

the derogations regarding Austria and Germany which had been set out in the 2003 Regulation, since they were questionable in light of the Strasbourg jurisprudence.[973]

Those third-country nationals who have *not* moved within the EU must look to another source of EU law if they wish to claim equal treatment as regards social security. In addition to association agreements and free movement law,[974] several JHA Directives address access to social security benefits, as regards temporary protection, refugee and subsidiary protection status, long-term residents, workers, and researchers.[975]

The legislation on this issue is a useful contribution towards ensuring the effective application of free movement of third-country nationals, and is of practical use to long-term residents, posted workers, researchers, students, Blue Card holders, intra-corporate transferees, and any other third-country nationals who are allowed in practice to move between Member States.[976] It also helps to ensure equality in respect of social security, as required by human rights law.

6.9 Residence Permits and Long-Stay Visas

EU legislation sets out obligations to issue residence permits and long-stay visas in many contexts, and also regulates the validity of the permits and visas, their formats, and procedural rules related to applications for their issue and renewal. The two forms of document are considered in turn. It should be noted that in the context of EU free movement law, residence permits are not issued. Instead, Member States issue 'registration certificates' to EU citizens, if they oblige them to register their presence on the territory after three months' stay,[977] and a 'residence card' to third-country national family members of EU citizens.[978] It should also be recalled that, following the entry into force of the Treaty of Lisbon, the Council has the power (not yet used), in order to facilitate free movement rights, to adopt measures concerning 'passports, identity cards, residence permits or any other such document'.[979]

---

[973] See I:6.3.2 above, particularly the judgments of 25 Oct 2005 in *Niedzwiecki v Germany* and *Okpisz v Germany* (not yet reported), and H Verschueren, 'EC Social Security Coordination Excluding Third-Country Nationals: Still in Line with Fundamental rights After the *Gaygusuz* judgment?' (1997) 24 CMLRev 991.

[974] See further I:6.4.2 and I:6.4.3 above, and in particular *El-Youssfi* (n 968 above), where the Court pointed out that a Moroccan woman who had not moved within the EU could not claim benefits on the basis of Reg 859/2003, but could potentially rely on the EU-Morocco treaty instead.

[975] See respectively: Art 12 of Dir 2001/55 ([2001] L 212/12); Art 26(4) of Dir 2011/95 on refugee and subsidiary protection status ([2011] L 337/9); Art 11(1)(d) of Directive 2003/109 ([2004] OJ L 16/44); Art 14(1)(e) of Dir 2009/50 ([2009] OJ L 155/17); Art 12(1)(e) of the single permit Dir (Dir 2011/98, [2011] OJ L 343/1); Art 18(2)(c) of Dir 2014/66 ([2014] OJ L 157/1); Art 23(1)(d) of Dir 2014/36 ([2014] OJ L 94/375); and Art 12(c) of Dir 2005/71 ([2005] OJ L 289/15).

[976] On these categories of persons, see respectively I:6.7, I:6.4.4, and I:6.5 above.

[977] Art 8 of Dir 2004/38 ([2004] OJ L 229/35). Note that Member States cannot insist on production of these documents as a condition for exercise of a right (Art 25, Dir 2004/38).

[978] Arts 9–11, Dir 2004/38 (ibid). Note that Member States may not require a long-term visa for third-country national family members of EU citizens: Case C-157/03 *Commission v Spain* [2005] ECR I-2911. According to the Commission guidance on the Dir, Member States can define the format of the residence card as they see fit, but it must be a free-standing document, not a stamp in a passport (COM (2009) 313, 2 July 2009). On the residence card, see further Case C-202/13 *McCarthy*, ECLI:EU:C:2014:2450, discussed in I:4.4.1 above.

[979] Art 77(3) TFEU, discussed in I:3.2.4 above.

6.9.1 Residence permits

Member States are obliged to issue residence permits to beneficiaries of refugee or subsidiary protection status, beneficiaries of EU temporary protection status, victims of trafficking or smuggling, single permit holders, Blue Card holders, intra-corporate transferees, researchers, students and other non-economic migrants, persons admitted for family reunion, and long-term residents.[980]

There are specific rules concerning the validity of the relevant permits. Permits for refugees must be valid for at least three years and renewable, but can have a shorter period of validity for refugees' family members.[981] Permits for persons with subsidiary protection status and their family members must be valid for at least one year initially and renewable for two years afterward.[982] The permits for persons admitted under an EU temporary protection scheme must be valid for the entire duration of the temporary protection.[983] For victims of trafficking, the permits shall be valid for at least six months and renewable.[984]

As for immigration legislation, there are no rules on the period of validity of single permits.[985] For Blue Card holders, the permits shall be issued for a standard period of between one and four years, or for less if the work contract covers a shorter period.[986] Intra-corporate transferees' permits can be valid for no longer than three years for managers or specialists, or one year for trainees.[987] Researchers' permits must be issued for periods of at least one year, renewable if the conditions for admission are still met.[988] For non-economic migrants, students' permits must be valid for at least one year and renewable; school pupils' permits must be valid for a maximum period of one year; unpaid trainees' permits must be valid for a one-year maximum, and renewed only in exceptional cases; and volunteers' permits must also be valid only for a maximum period of one year, with an exceptional possibility of a longer period.[989] Persons admitted for family reunion must receive a permit valid for at least one year (renewable), and an autonomous permit, subject to certain conditions and exceptions, after five years.[990]

---

[980] According to EU asylum procedures legislation, the issue of residence permits to asylum seekers is only an option for Member States, but nonetheless asylum seekers have the right to stay until a first-instance decision on their application: Art 7 of Dir 2005/85, [2005] OJ L 326/13 (see now Art 9 of Dir 2013/32, [2013] OJ L 180/60), confirmed by the CJEU ruling in Case C-534/11 *Arslan*, ECLI:EU:C:2013:343. Note that Member States have an obligation to issue documents to all asylum seekers, subject to certain exceptions, which must be valid as long as the asylum seekers are authorized to remain on the territory (Art 6 of Dir 2013/33, [2013] OJ L 180/96).

[981] Art 24(1), Dir 2004/83 ([2004] OJ L 304/12), replaced by Art 24(1), Dir 2011/95 ([2004] OJ L 337/9). On the residence permit for refugees et al., see further Case C-373/13 *T*, ECLI:EU:C:2015:413, discussed in I:5.5 above.

[982] Art 24(2), Dir 2011/95 (n 981 above). Previously, according to Art 24(2) of Dir 2004/83 (n 981 above), there was no specific reference to family members and no two-year renewal period. See further I:5.5 above.

[983] Art 8, Dir 2001/55 ([2001] OJ L 212/12). See further I:5.6 above.

[984] Art 8(3), Dir 2004/81 ([2004] OJ L 261/19). See further I:7.6.2 below.

[985] Note, however, that the issue of a residence permit in the EU standard format (see below) determines the *scope* of Dir 2011/98 ([2011] OJ L 343/1) in some respects (Art 3(1)(b)). See further I:6.5.1 above.

[986] Art 7(2), Dir 2009/50 ([2009] OJ L 155/17). See further I:6.5.2.1 above.

[987] Art 13(2), Dir 2014/66 ([2014] OJ L 157/1) See further I:6.5.2.2 above.

[988] Art 8, Dir 2005/71 ([2005] OJ L 289/15); see also the special rule for researchers' family members (Art 9(1), Dir 2005/71). See further I:6.5.3.1 above.

[989] Respectively Arts 12–15, Dir 2004/114 ([2004] OJ L 375/12); see further I:6.5.3.2 above.

[990] Arts 13(2) and (3) and 15, Dir 2003/86 ([2003] OJ L 251/12); see further I:6.6 above.

Finally, for long-term residents, the permit must be valid for at least five years (renewable automatically),[991] with a special rule for cases where the long-term resident has moved to a second Member State without yet transferring his or her long-term residence status there.[992]

States fully participating in the Schengen *acquis* have procedural obligations to check the Schengen Information System (SIS) before issuing *any* residence permit; if the person concerned is already listed on the SIS, the State planning to issue the permit must consult with the State which issued the alert.[993] The holders of such permits, if they are issued, then benefit from the freedom to travel within the EU,[994] as well as a simplified process to cross the external borders.[995] Applicants for, or holders of, residence permits also have procedural rights relating to the issue or withdrawal of the permits, pursuant to much EU legislation.[996]

EU legislation has for some time established a uniform format for residence permits for third-country nationals. First of all, a 'Joint Action' was adopted in 1996,[997] during the initial third pillar period, in order to increase the level of security applicable to such documents.[998] This Joint Action was subsequently replaced by a Regulation adopted in 2002,[999] which was in turn amended in 2008.[1000] The later measures had the particular objectives of enhancing document security by inserting photographs (2002)[1001] and subsequently fingerprints (2008) into the permit.

The Regulation applies to *all* residence permits authorizing a legal stay on the territory (ie regardless of any link to EU legislation which regulates substantive immigration

---

[991] Arts 8(2) and 23(2), Dir 2003/109 ([2004] OJ L 16/44). See further I:6.7 above.

[992] Art 19(2) and (3), Dir 2003/109 (ibid).

[993] Art 25(1) of the Schengen Convention ([2000] OJ L 239), as amended by Reg 265/2010 ([2010] OJ L 85/1); see further I:4.9 above. A 'residence permit' for these purposes is defined as 'an authorisation of whatever type issued by a Contracting Party which grants right of residence within its territory. This definition shall not include temporary permission to reside in the territory of a Contracting Party for the purposes of processing an application for asylum or a residence permit' (Art 1, Schengen Convention).

[994] Art 21 of the Schengen Convention, as amended by Reg 265/2010 (n 993 above) and Reg 610/2013 ([2013] OJ L 182/1); see further I:4.9 above.

[995] Art 5 of the Schengen Borders Code (Reg 562/2006, [2006] OJ L 105/1), as amended by Regs 265/2010 and 610/2013, n 994 above. On the substance of this rule, see I:3.6.1 above.

[996] See: Art 8, Dir 2011/98 (single permit); Art 11, Dir 2009/50 (Blue Card holders); Art 5, Dir 2014/66 (intra-corporate transferees); Art 15, Dir 2005/71 (researchers); Art 18, Dir 2004/114 (non-economic migrants); Art 18, Dir 2003/86 (family reunion); and Arts 10, 20, and 23(2), Dir 2003/109 (long-term residents). On the interpretation of these provisions, see Case C-540/03 *EP v Council* [2006] ECR I-5769, concerning the family reunion Directive, which presumably applies by analogy to the other legislation. Note also the judgment in Case C-327/02 *Panayotova* [2004] ECR I-11055, discussed in I:6.3.4 above, which refers to procedural rights in connection with all immigration proceedings linked to EU law.

[997] [1997] OJ L 7/1. See communication on technical specifications ([1998] OJ C 193/1) and Decisions on sharing costs of preparing film masters and on common standards for filling in the permit ([1998] OJ L 99/1 and 333/8). A Schengen Executive Committee Decision (which has not been repealed) required Schengen States to use the standard format early if possible (Sch/Com-ex (97) 34 rev ([2000] OJ L 239/187)). This is not included in the list of obsolete Schengen measures which the Commission proposes to repeal (COM (2014) 713, 28 Nov 2014).

[998] For more detail on the background, see pp 92–3 of the first edition of this book.

[999] Reg 1030/2002 ([2002] L 157/1), which entered into force 15 June 2002 (Art 10).

[1000] Reg 330/2008 ([2008] L 115/1), which entered into force on 19 May 2008 (Art 2). The legislation has not been codified. All further references in this sub-section are to the 2002 Regulation as amended, unless otherwise indicated.

[1001] Point 14 of the Annex to Reg 1030/2002. The Joint Action had required inclusion of a photograph only where the permit was produced as a stand-alone document.

law), with the exception of: visas; permits issued pending examination of an application for asylum or a residence permit or for a residence permit's extension; permits issued exceptionally allowing for a further stay of one month; and (for Member States not applying the Schengen *acquis* fully) permits for an initial stay for a period defined by national law (but no longer than six months).[1002] However, it does not apply to permits issued to family members of EU citizens exercising their right to free movement, nationals of EEA states, or to any non-visa nationals who are permitted to stay in a Member State for less than three months.[1003] Permits must be issued in the form of a stand-alone document.[1004] Member States are allowed to use the format for other purposes, as long as they avoid confusion between those purposes and the residence permit as defined in the Regulation.[1005] The Regulation specifies that Member States' powers over recognition of States, territorial entities, and documents are not affected by it.[1006]

Individuals to whom the permits are issued have the right to verify the data on the permit and to ask for any corrections or deletions to be made, and only the data set out in the Annex to the Regulation or mentioned in that person's travel document can be included in machine-readable form on the permit, although Member States may store additional data on government services in the chip inserted into the residence permit.[1007]

The biometric data to be stored in residence permits must consist of a photograph and two fingerprints; fingerprinting is compulsory from six years of age.[1008] The Commission has powers to implement the Regulation, assisted by a 'comitology' committee of Member States' representatives, in line with the standard approach to implementing EU law.[1009] It should be noted that the rules in the residence permit legislation are based on those applicable to the common EU visa format,[1010] although an important difference between the two issues is that the biometric data included in the uniform residence permit is not linked to any EU-wide information systems.

In order to allow Member States to adjust to their new obligations, the original Joint Action did not apply for a period of up to five years after the implementing measures were adopted.[1011] Member States then had to implement the 2002 Regulation by August 2003, and had to include (non-biometric) photos in all permits by 14 August

---

[1002] Art 1(2). Note that this definition differs to some extent from that in Art 1 of the Schengen Convention, which applies to residence permits as regards checks in the SIS and freedom to travel. When the 2008 Reg was published in the OJ, a Council statement was also published asking the Commission to consider 'the most appropriate and proportionate way of introducing harmonised security features of the residence permits' covered by the second and third categories of excluded documents.

[1003] Art 5. Again, note the differences with Art 1 of the Schengen Convention (n 1002 above). It should also be noted that EU citizens' family members and EEA citizens no longer need residence permits (see I:6.4.1 and I:6.4.3 above). Separate legislation determines which third-country nationals do not need visas to enter Member States (apart from the UK and Ireland): see I:4.5 above.

[1004] Art 1(1); prior to the 2008 Reg, Member States had the choice whether to issue permits in the form of a stand-alone document or a sticker. The obligation to use a stand-alone document applies from May 2011 (see Art 9, discussed below), although Member States may choose to provide that previously issued permits are still valid.

[1005] Art 5a.   [1006] Art 8.   [1007] Art 4.   [1008] Arts 4a and 4b.

[1009] Arts 2, 6, and 7. See also the possibility of secrecy (Art 3). On 'comitology', see further I:2.2.2.1 above.

[1010] See I:4.6 above; and see also the subsequent adoption of a Reg on security features in EU passports, as later amended (I:3.9 above).

[1011] Art 7 of the Joint Action.

2007.[1012] As for the 2008 Regulation, Member States had to include photographs as biometric identifiers two years after adoption of the relevant implementing measures, and fingerprints three years after the adoption of those measures;[1013] these obligations therefore applied from May 2011 and May 2012 respectively.[1014]

Although, as described above, much EU immigration and asylum legislation requires the issue of residence permits, that legislation does not always refer expressly to the 2002 Regulation as amended (or its precursor Joint Action). All the immigration legislation refers expressly to the Regulation,[1015] but EU asylum law and EU legislation on trafficking victims refers to national law for the definition of 'residence permit'.[1016] Nonetheless, given the wording of the Regulation, the uniform permit format has to be used for the various permits issued pursuant to other EU legislation.

6.9.2 Long-stay visas

Member States have the obligation to 'facilitate' the issue of long-stay visas pursuant to EU legislation concerning temporary protection, Blue Cards, intra-corporate transferee, researchers, and family reunion.[1017] This specific legislation has no rules on the validity of long-stay visas, but there is a general rule in the Schengen Convention, as amended in 2010: *any* long-stay visa (ie regardless of any link to substantive EU law) shall have a period of validity of a maximum of one year.[1018] If a Member State allows a person to stay after that period, then it must issue a residence permit before the end of that period. This rule is without prejudice to the EU legislation which requires the issue of a residence permit, instead of a long-stay visa.[1019] It should be noted that the

---

[1012] See Art 9, Reg 1030/2002 and the secret implementing Commission Decision C (2002) 3069, 14 Aug 2002 (unpublished; see COM (2003) 558, 24 Sep 2003, p 2).

[1013] Art 9.

[1014] The secret implementing decision (C(2009)3770/F) was adopted on 26 May 2009.

[1015] See: Art 6, Dir 2011/98 (n 985 above); Art 7(5) of Dir 2009/50 (n 986 above); Art 13(3), Dir 2014/66 (n 987 above); Art 2(e) of Dir 2005/71 (n 988 above); Art 2(g) of Dir 2004/114 (n 989 above); Art 2(e) of Dir 2003/86 (n 990 above); and Arts 2(g), 8(3), and 23(2) of Dir 2003/109 (n 991 above). The Blue Card Directive requires an express reference to 'Blue Card' status, and the conditions of permitted labour market access, to be indicated on the permit. In the case of Dir 2003/109, the reference only concerns the long-term residents' permit, not the other permits within the scope of the Directive (see Art 19); also, the Directive requires an express reference to the long-term residence status to be entered onto the permit (Art 8(3)). The Annex to Reg 1030/2002, as amended, requires Member States to indicate 'family member' status in the permit for family members of EU citizens who have *not* moved within the EU, and permits Member States to indicate a specific status for the non-core family members covered by EU free movement law (Art 3(2) of Dir 2004/38, n 977 above). Dir 2003/109 refers to issue of the permit in either sticker or stand-alone format; this is now obsolete in light of the 2008 amendments to the residence permit Reg (see discussion above).

[1016] Art 2(m) of Dir 2011/95 (n 981 above); Art 2(g) of Dir 2001/55 (n 983 above); and Art 2(e) of Dir 2004/81 (n 984 above).

[1017] Art 8(3), Dir 2001/55 (n 983 above); Art 7(1), Dir 2009/50 (n 986 above); Art 13(7), Dir 2014/66 (n 987 above); Art 14(4), Dir 2005/71 (n 988 above); and Art 13(1), Dir 2003/86 (n 990 above). Although this legislation refers to 'visas' generally, not to long-stay visas in particular, it follows from the immigration law legal bases of the legislation concerned, and the intention that the persons concerned stay *longer* than three months, that the legislation envisages the issue of long-stay visas.

[1018] Art 18(2) of the Convention, as amended by Reg 265/2010 (n 993 above). A 'long-stay visa' is not defined, other than by reference to national and EU law and a validity period of more than three months (see Art 18(1) of the Convention, as amended by Reg 265/2010).

[1019] Art 3, Reg 265/2010, n 993 above. Note that Dirs 2005/71 and 2004/114 gave Member States a further two years (now expired) before they had to issue permits pursuant to those Dirs in the form of a residence permit (Art 18 of Dir 2005/71, n 988 above, and Art 23 of Dir 2004/114, n 989 above).

seasonal workers' Directive contains special rules: if the stay is longer than three months, Member States can issue a long-stay visa, a seasonal worker's permit, or both.[1020]

The process of issuing *any* long-stay visa involves, as for residence permits, an obligatory prior check in the Schengen Information System in States which fully apply the Schengen rules, followed by consultation between Member States in the event that the person concerned has already been the subject of an alert for the refusal of entry.[1021] Equally, the issue of any long-stay visa gives rise to the freedom to travel between the Schengen States,[1022] as well as a simplified process to cross the external borders.[1023] However, in the case of long-stay visas, there are no express procedural rights in any EU legislation. But since the denial of the long-stay visa would mean that the relevant rights could not be invoked in practice, it must follow from the general principles of EU law and the EU Charter of Fundamental Rights that there are procedural rights for individuals whose application for a long-stay visa is refused, if there is any link with EU legislation.[1024]

Finally, as from 2010 there has been a common format for long-stay visas, namely the same format as for *short-term* visas.[1025] It should be noted, however, that in the case of long-stay visas, there is no obligation to take biometric information, and therefore no obligation to store such information in the Visa Information System.[1026]

6.10 Integration Policy

The integration of migrants is to a large degree facilitated by EU immigration and asylum legislation, in particular to the extent that this legislation sets out rights to equal treatment and secure residence status. As set out above, the family reunion and long-term residents' Directives, as interpreted by the CJEU, also allow Member States to apply an integration test as a condition for obtaining status (or subsequently), and the latter Directive has the purpose of facilitating integration.[1027] Integration is also facilitated by EU measures in other areas, for example the EU's equality Directives, which aim to eliminate, inter alia, discrimination on grounds of race and religion for EU citizens and third-country nationals alike.[1028]

[1020] Art 12(2), Dir 2014/36 ([2014] OJ L 94/375). For short-term entries, a short-term visa should be issued (Art 12(1), Dir 2014/36). If a seasonal worker permit is issued, it must have the same format as a residence permit (Art 3(d), Dir 2014/36).

[1021] Art 25(3) of the Schengen Convention, as inserted by Reg 265/2010 (n 993 above). On the substance of this process, see I:4.9 above.

[1022] Art 21(2a) of the Schengen Convention, as inserted by Reg 265/2010 (n 993 above). On the substance of this freedom, see I:4.9 above.

[1023] Art 5 of the Schengen Borders Code (n 995 above), as amended by Reg 265/2010 (n 993 above). On the substance of this rule, see I:3.6.1 above.

[1024] See Case C-327/02 *Panayotova* [2004] ECR I-11055, discussed in I:6.3.4 above.

[1025] Art 18(1) of the Schengen Convention, as amended by Reg 265/2010 (n 993 above). On the legislation setting out the short-term visa format, see I:4.6 above. As noted in the preamble to Reg 265/2010 (point 5), this obligation reflects the prior practice of Member States.

[1026] For the relevant rules on short-stay visas, see I:4.6 to I:4.8 above.

[1027] I:6.6 and I:6.7 above.

[1028] Dirs 2000/34 ([2000] OJ L 180/22) and 2000/78 ([2000] OJ L 303/16). For further details of relevant EU policies, see the Commission's communication on employment, migration, and integration (COM (2003) 336, 3 June 2003).

But an EU integration *policy* has also developed, in particular following the conclusions of the Thessaloniki European Council of June 2003,[1029] which called for 'the elaboration of a comprehensive and multidimensional policy on the integration of legally residing third country nationals', which would 'cover factors such as employment, economic participation, education and language training, health and social services, housing and urban issues, as well as culture and participation in social life'. This policy is to contribute to 'the new demographic and economic challenges which the EU is now facing, taking into account' certain groups such as women, children, the elderly, and persons with international protection status. Furthermore, 'integration policies should be understood as a continuous, two-way process based on mutual rights and corresponding obligations' of third-country nationals and host States; although Member States had 'primary responsibility' for integration policies, 'such policies should be developed within a coherent European Union framework, taking into account the legal, political, economic, social and cultural diversity of Member States'. In particular, 'common basic principles' on integration should be defined. The European Council therefore welcomed the creation of contact points on integration, which had just been established, in order to develop cooperation, exchange information, and strengthen coordination on this issue.

A subsequent Commission communication urged a focus upon introduction programmes, language training, and participation in civic, political, and cultural life, and announced a pilot funding programme on integration policy.[1030] In 2004, the Hague Programme called again for development of common basic principles on integration and set out some basic elements of the principles.[1031] Next, the JHA Council of November 2004 adopted conclusions on integration,[1032] elaborating the basic principles of integration policy, comprising: integration as a two-way process; the importance of employment; the knowledge of a host State's society, language, history, and institutions; education; access to institutions, goods, and services; interaction between immigrants and host State citizens; guaranteeing the practice of diverse cultures and religions *unless* that practice conflicts with national law or European rights; participation of immigrants in the democratic process; mainstreaming integration policies; and developing goals and benchmarks regarding integration policy. At this time, the Commission also published an integration handbook for policy-makers and practitioners.[1033]

In 2005, the Commission issued a communication on integration, which suggested a list of concrete actions at national and EU level to implement those principles.[1034] As for the institutional framework, the communication suggested that the national contact points should focus their work on the common basic principles, and their results should be presented in other fora on some occasions. A second edition of the Handbook would be established, a website was planned,[1035] an integration forum

---

[1029] Points 28–32 of the conclusions.
[1030] Communication on employment, migration, and integration (COM (2003) 336, 3 June 2003).
[1031] [2005] OJ C 53/1, point 1.6.   [1032] Press release of JHA Council, 19 Nov 2004.
[1033] The handbook was subsequently updated in 2007 and 2010. See: <http://ec.europa.eu/justice_home/doc_centre/immigration/integration/doc_immigration_integration_en.htm>
[1034] COM (2005) 389, 1 Sep 2005.   [1035] See: <http://ec.europa.eu/ewsi/en/index.cfm>.

involving 'stakeholders' would be established, and national ministers should hold an annual debate on the integration issue. The JHA Council subsequently adopted conclusions supporting the Commission's suggestions for developing the framework.[1036]

The next step was the Council's adoption, in 2007, of a Decision establishing a formal Integration Fund, in order to facilitate the practical application of the common basic principles.[1037] The main objectives of the Integration Fund were: to assist the development and implementation of admission procedures linked to the integration process, and of the integration process itself; to increase Member States' capacity to develop and implement integration policies; and to exchange information and best practices in and between Member States in this area.[1038]

Since the Treaty of Lisbon, this issue now falls within the scope of Article 79(4) TFEU, inserted by the Treaty of Lisbon, which provides for the adoption of measures, pursuant to the ordinary legislative procedure, 'to provide incentives and support for the action of Member States with a view to promoting the integration of third-country nationals residing legally in their territories, excluding any harmonisation of the laws and regulations of the Member States'. This power has been invoked to merge the previous integration fund into the Asylum, Migration and integration Fund (covering 2014–20).[1039] The focus of this policy in recent years has been issues relating to employment, education, and the evaluation of integration policy.[1040]

Most recently, the Commission's latest communication on integration policy (released in 2011) addresses issues of migrants' low employment and rising unemployment rates, social exclusion, gaps in education, and lack of integration. It examines the issue from three main angles: integration through participation, more local level action, and involvement of countries of origin.[1041]

6.11 Administrative Cooperation and EU Funding

The main development as regards EU funding and legal migration has been the pilot programme and subsequent adopted Decision establishing an integration fund (later consolidated with the Asylum and Immigration Fund), already mentioned above.[1042] The EU's ARGO funding programme also supported activities of Member States in areas falling within the scope of EU immigration policy.[1043]

As for administrative cooperation, the principal focus of EU activity has been information exchange and analysis. The first step in this area is gathering information, where the Commission's statistics body, Eurostat, took over the role of drawing up immigration and asylum statistics in 1998.[1044] Eurostat's role was then formalized in 2007 when

---

[1036] Press release of JHA Council, 1–2 Dec 2005.   [1037] [2007] OJ L 168/24.

[1038] Art 3 of the Decision.   [1039] Reg 516/2014 ([2014] OJ L 150/168).

[1040] Council doc 8771/10, 20 Apr 2010, and the Council conclusions on the education of migrant children, [2009] OJ C 301/5.

[1041] COM (2011) 455, 20 July 2011.   [1042] See I:6.10 above.

[1043] [2002] OJ L 161/11 (Art 6) and [2004] OJ L 371/48; see further I:3.11 above.

[1044] See: JHA Council conclusions of Mar 1998 and May 2001; Communication (SEC (2001) 602, 9 Apr 2001); and Action Plan (COM (2003) 179, 15 Apr 2003). For the first annual EU report on asylum and migration statistics, see: <http://ec.europa.eu/justice_home/doc_centre/immigration/statistics/doc_immigration_statistics_en.htm>.

EU legislation concerning asylum and migration statistics was adopted.[1045] This legislation requires Eurostat to produce, starting in 2008, annual data on immigration, emigration, and population breakdown by, inter alia, citizenship, as well as annual statistics on the issue of residence permits for specific reasons and on the numbers of long-term residents (as defined by Directive 2003/109).[1046] A subsequent Commission implementing measure requires Member States to disaggregate the data on residence permits by reference to admission for the purposes of family reunion, education, remunerated activities, and other reasons, referring specifically to EU legislation on students and researchers.[1047] Subsequently, the EU's Blue Card Directive requires Member States to send information to Eurostat annually on the issue, renewal, or withdrawal of Blue Cards, broken down by nationality and occupation, as well as statistics on the family members of Blue Card holders and the movement of Blue Card holders between Member States.[1048] Member States have similar obligations as regards single permits, seasonal workers, and intra-corporate transferees.[1049] The statistics produced pursuant to this legislation are available on the Eurostat website.[1050]

In order to use the statistical data to assess the impact of EU policy and legislation, and its relevance for the further development of policy and legislation, there needs to be further analysis of the statistics and collection and analysis of broader information on immigration policy—and it is not Eurostat's job to provide either function. To perform these functions, first of all a European Migration Network has been gradually established in recent years. Originally, from 2002, the Commission has used preparatory funds to establish the network, which was later formally established pursuant to a Council Decision.[1051] The main tasks of the Network are, inter alia, to collect and analyse data and information relating to immigration and asylum.[1052] It consists of national contact points designated by Member States and of the Commission, and is guided by a Steering Board made up of members appointed by Member States and the Commission.[1053] In practice, the Network has produced very useful and detailed annual reports on both statistics and policy from each Member State.[1054] The Network has also produced a number of interesting reports on specific issues.

Next, information on national immigration *policy* is exchanged between Member States pursuant to a Decision adopted in 2006,[1055] which the Council had requested the Commission to propose following a dispute between Spain and other Member States over a Spanish decision to regularize large numbers of irregular migrants.[1056] This Decision requires the exchange of information on national measures 'that are

---

[1045]   Reg 862/2007 ([2007] OJ L 199/23).
[1046]   See Arts 3 and 6, Reg 862/2007, along with the definition of 'long-term residents' (Art 2(1)(h)).
[1047]   Commission Reg 216/2010 ([2010] OJ L 66/1).
[1048]   Art 20(2), Dir 2009/50 ([2009] OJ L 155/17).   [1049]   See I:6.5.1 and I:6.5.2 above.
[1050]   <http://epp.eurostat.ec.europa.eu/portal/page/portal/population/data/database>. For reports on the application of the Reg, see COM (2012) 528, 20 Sep 2012 and COM (2015) 374, 30 July 2015.
[1051]   [2008] OJ L 131/7. See the earlier Green Paper on the development of the Network (COM (2005) 606, 28 Nov 2005), and the communication on the operation of the Network (COM (2012) 427, 1 Aug 2012).
[1052]   Art 2, Council Decision.   [1053]   Arts 3 and 4, Council Decision.
[1054]   See the Network website: <http://emn.sarenet.es/html/index.html>.
[1055]   [2006] OJ L 283/40.   [1056]   See Press release of JHA Council, 14 Apr 2005.

likely to have a significant impact on several Member States or on the European Union as a whole', for the purpose of preparing 'exchanges of views and debates on such measures'.[1057] Member States decide which (publicly available) measures are likely to have such a significant impact, and it is possible for other Member States or the Commission to request further information (except as regards final court judgments).[1058] The Commission must prepare an annual report summarizing this information, which serves as the basis for a debate at ministerial level.[1059] According to the Commission's report on the implementation of this Decision,[1060] over a two and a half year period, sixteen Member States communicated information on forty-five measures, half of which were legislation (usually adopted already), much of it concerning the implementation of EU law. The other measures communicated were policy plans or general administrative decisions or circulars. In the Commission's view, the implementation of the Decision was disappointing due to the modest number of communications, in particular as regards draft measures.

As regards the later development of the 2006 Decision, the Commission has merged its reports pursuant to the Decision with the reports which the European Council has requested in the meantime, on the application of the EU's Immigration and Asylum Pact, as adopted in 2008, and subsequently the Stockholm Programme, which are intended to prepare the ground for an annual debate on immigration and asylum issues at European Council level.[1061] The Commission's communication on the 'tracking mechanism' for gathering information to prepare this report included a draft list of questions to Member States about national policy developments.[1062] This communication indicated that the Commission wanted to subsume Member States' reporting obligations under the 2006 Decision within the new process. Presumably the new process will also replace the annual reports on immigration and integration which the Thessaloniki European Council in 2003 invited the Commission to present.[1063] The Commission also intends to use information provided by the European Migration Network and the statistics provided by Eurostat to prepare each report.

These annual reports have been released regularly since May 2010, and comprise a useful summary of developments at EU level and in the Member States.[1064] It is hard to see that they have had much influence on policy development, however.

Given the intensity of concerns about immigration policy, it is important to ensure that objective, accurate, and timely information and analysis is available to inform the debate. The EU has made important steps in that direction with the development of the European Migration Network and statistics legislation, but the statistics legislation needs to be much more focused (along the lines of the provisions in the Blue Card Directive) in order for the statistics to be more useful, and the operation of the European Migration Network needs to be much more timely. At the level of the Commission and

---

[1057] Art 1 of the Decision.   [1058] Art 2 of the Decision.   [1059] Art 4 of the Decision.

[1060] COM (2009) 687, 17 Dec 2009.   [1061] Council doc 13440/08, 24 Sep 2008.

[1062] COM (2009) 266, 10 June 2009.

[1063] There have been three reports: COM (2004) 408, 16 July 2004; SEC (2006) 892, 30 June 2006; and COM (2007) 512, 12 Sep 2007.

[1064] COM (2010) 214, 6 May 2010; COM (2011) 291, 24 May 2011; COM (2012) 250, 30 May 2012; COM (2013) 422, 17 June 2013; and COM (2014) 288, 22 May 2014.

the European Council, the initiatives taken in this field have been spasmodic and unco-ordinated, with an unfortunate detour (by way of the 2006 Decision) to make a political gesture. The annual assessment of policy in this area should also be more incisive.

6.12 Conclusions

At least until the Treaty of Lisbon entered into force, it was difficult to agree rules on migration at EU level, resulting initially in only modest steps towards achieving the Tampere objectives of fair treatment for third-country nationals and equal treatment for long-term residents, which were moreover understandably criticized on human rights grounds. Nevertheless, the later agreement on the Blue Card Directive, which actually aims to attract immigration, proved an exception.

Since the entry into force of the Treaty of Lisbon, the resulting changes in decision-making have led to new legislation on migrant workers, as well as important rulings of the CJEU which take a generally liberal view as regards legal migrants. However, there is still a gap between the law on the books and the law on the ground, exacerbated by the Commission's unwillingness to bring infringement proceedings to ensure the correct application of the law in Member States. In principle, the EU is moving steadily towards developing a fair and comprehensive policy on legal immigration, but this implementation gap remains a significant limit on achieving such a policy in practice.

7

Irregular Migration

7.1 Introduction

States' desire to control access to and stay on their territory manifests itself particularly in a desire to prevent irregular migration, to detect irregular migrants, and to remove any irregular migrants once they are detected.[1] But the exercise of this policy raises obvious questions about the human rights of the persons affected by such a policy, most obviously if they have a claim for asylum or another form of international protection. But irregular migrants' rights are also impacted as regards detention (the permissibility of detention, procedural rights concerning detention, and detention conditions), the general rules governing persons subject to expulsion (procedural rights to challenge expulsion orders, living conditions), and the conduct of expulsion operations (the health and human dignity of the persons being expelled).

This chapter, like the others in this book, begins with a historical overview, including issues of legal competence and the territorial scope of the rules, followed by an analysis of the relevant rules of human rights law and relevant rules deriving from other areas of EU law (ie areas of law other than Justice and Home Affairs law). Then it examines in detail the Schengen and EU rules concerning the prevention of irregular migration, the treatment of irregular migrants inside the territory, and expulsion (including the controversial Returns Directive), along with the rules on cooperation between Member States' administrations and on the external relations aspects of irregular migration.

These issues obviously close links with the issues discussed in other chapters, particularly Chapters 3 and 4 of this volume, concerning visas and border controls. Such measures are obviously also aimed at preventing irregular entry into the territory of the Member States, and regulate in detail the interception of irregular entrants at the border, along with the planned development of an 'entry-exit' system to identify 'overstayers' (ie those who enter the territory legally but remain after their permission to stay expires). EU law defines an irregular migrant as 'a third-country national present on the territory of a Member State, who does not fulfil, or no longer fulfils, the conditions for stay or residence in that Member State';[2] those 'conditions for stay or residence' are largely shaped by the rules relating to visas, external borders, and freedom to travel, along with the rules relating to asylum (discussed in Chapter 5 of this volume) and legal migration

---

[1] Since unauthorized migrants have not generally committed any criminal offences besides breaches of migration law, which is in any event sometimes punishable by administrative sanctions, rather than criminal penalties, this chapter refers throughout to 'irregular', rather than 'illegal', migration.

[2] See, for instance, Art 2(b) of Dir 2009/52, on sanctions against irregular migrants ([2009] OJ L 168/24) and similarly Art 79(3) TFEU. Further on the issue of defining irregular migration, see E Guild, 'Who is an Irregular Migrant?' in B Bogusz, R Cholewinski, A Cygan, and E Szyszczak, eds., *Irregular Migration and Human Rights* (Martinus Nijhoff, 2004), 3.

(discussed in Chapter 6 of this volume). Irregular migration may also result in a listing in the Schengen Information System (SIS) blacklist for denial of further entry, an issue considered further in Chapter 3 of this volume.[3] Furthermore, the EU's border agency, Frontex (also discussed in that Chapter), has powers relating to expulsion.[4]

There are further links between the rules on irregular migration and on asylum law, in particular because of the impact of rules concerning irregular migration on asylum seekers' ability to reach refuge and on the treatment and procedural rights of rejected asylum seekers, including persons who are appealing a rejection of their asylum applications but who are nonetheless subject to expulsion because their appeal does not have suspensive effect.[5] Also, the EU's rules on responsibility for asylum applications in some cases assign responsibility for dealing with a claim based on the irregular stay of an asylum seeker on a Member State's territory,[6] and EU policy concerning external control of irregular migration impacts upon external aspects of asylum.

Finally, there are links between irregular migration and criminal law and policing, in particular as regards: the application of criminal law to aspects of irregular migration (discussed in detail in this chapter, but on the general relationship between EU law and criminal law, see Chapter 5 of volume 2); expedited criminal procedural rules relating to irregular migration (see Chapter 3 of volume 2); and the application of cross-border policing rules and the competence of EU-wide policing bodies to address irregular migration issues (see Chapter 7 of volume 2).

7.2 Institutional Framework and Overview

7.2.1 Framework prior to the Treaty of Amsterdam

Prior to the Maastricht Treaty, there was loose intergovernmental cooperation on the issue of irregular migration, as Member States did not accept the Commission's argument that the effect of irregular migration on the EEC's common market (as it was then) was sufficient to adopt a proposed Directive on the issue.[7] Starting in the period just before the Maastricht Treaty entered into force, the Member States' immigration ministers (and subsequently the Council) began to adopt a number of Recommendations on the subject of irregular immigration.[8] An initial Recommendation of 1992 set out general principles governing control of irregular migration, which were supplemented in later measures.[9] A series of three later Recommendations concerned particularly in-country detection of irregular migration and irregular employment.[10] Other

---

[3] I:3.7 above. On the SIS generally, see II:7.6.1.1. Another database, the Visa Information System, is also used to control irregular migration (see I:4.8 above).

[4] See I:3.10.1 above.   [5] See I:5.7 above, on the asylum procedures Directive.

[6] See I:5.8 above.

[7] See the proposed Directive in [1976] OJ C 277/2, revised in [1978] OJ C 97/9.

[8] These measures are not discussed in this edition of this book. For details, see the first edition, pp 94–9.

[9] Recommendation of Immigration Ministers on 30 Nov/1 Dec 2002 (SN 4678/92, WGI 1266, 16 Nov 1992), published in E Guild and J Niessen, *The Developing Immigration and Asylum Policies of the European Union: Adopted Conventions, Resolutions, Recommendations, Decisions and Conclusions* (Kluwer, 1996), and in T Bunyan, ed., *Key Texts on Justice and Home Affairs in the European Union* (Statewatch: 1997).

[10] Recommendation of Immigration Ministers on 1–2 June 2003 (SN 3017/93, WGI 1516, 25 May 1993), published in Guild and Niessen and in Bunyan, n 9 above; [1996] OJ C 5/1; [1996] OJ C 304/1.

Recommendations addressed operational aspects of expulsion,[11] and three further Recommendations concerned readmission,[12] setting out a standard travel document (or laissez-passer) for use in individual expulsions, a standard bilateral readmission agreement, and principles to be included in protocols to readmission agreements. The Council also adopted a Decision on monitoring the implementation of the post-Maastricht measures.[13] Finally, the EU's immigration ministers established CIREFI (the Centre for Information, Discussion, and Exchange on the Crossing of Borders and Immigration), to exchange information between national administrations on irregular migration.[14]

Within the scope of the Schengen *acquis*, Articles 23 and 24 of the Schengen Convention addressed the legal status of persons who were not lawfully on the territory; Article 26 set out rules concerning carrier sanctions to prevent irregular entry; and Article 27 concerned penalties to be imposed on persons who facilitate such entry.[15] There were also further Executive Committee decisions in the area of irregular migration.[16]

7.2.2 The Treaty of Amsterdam

7.2.2.1 Institutional framework

Following amendment of the EC Treaty by the Treaty of Amsterdam, the EC gained express powers to address the issue of irregular migration, as set out in Article 63(3)(b) EC, which gave the EC powers over 'illegal immigration and illegal residence, including repatriation of illegal residents'. During a transitional period, this power was initially subject to the general decision-making rules governing Title IV of the EC Treaty: a shared initiative of the Commission and Member States, unanimous voting in the Council, consultation of the European Parliament (EP), and restricted jurisdiction of the Court of Justice.[17] Following the end of that transitional period on 1 May 2004, the Commission gained its usual monopoly of initiative in this area; and following the agreement as part of the Hague Programme to alter most of the Title IV decision-making rules, measures in this area were subject to qualified majority voting (QMV) in the Council and co-decision of the EP starting on 1 January 2005.[18] Also, the EU adopted a number of third pillar criminal law measures which are relevant to irregular immigration, and so are considered in some detail in this chapter; such measures were subject to unanimous voting in the Council, shared competence among the Commission and Member States to make proposals, consultation of the European Parliament, and a different regime of jurisdiction of the Court of Justice, until the entry into force of the Treaty of Lisbon.[19] But even before the entry into force of that Treaty, the Community adopted measures setting out criminal law obligations for Member States in this area.

---

[11] [1996] OJ C 5/3, 5, and 7.   [12] [1996] OJ C 274/20, 21, and 25.   [13] [1996] OJ L 342/5.
[14] See I:7.8 below.   [15] [2000] OJ L 239; see further I:7.7, I:7.5.1, and I:7.5.3 below.
[16] See I:7.7 below.   [17] See I:2.2.2.1 above.   [18] Ibid.   [19] See I:2.2.2 above.

The issue of irregular migration also fell within the scope of Article 66 EC, which conferred powers relating to cooperation between national administrations, or between national administrations and the Commission.[20] Also, the topic was subject to the national sovereignty safeguard and emergency powers clause set out in Article 64 EC.[21]

7.2.2.2 Overview of practice

The Council allocated Articles 26 and 27(1) of the Schengen Convention to Article 63(3)(b) of the EC Treaty, along with Article 17(3)(g) of the Convention, concerning the powers to define further the criteria for inclusion in the Schengen 'blacklist'.[22] Article 18 of the Convention, on the status of persons with long-stay visas,[23] was allocated jointly to Articles 62(2) and 63(3). Articles 23(2) to (5), 24, and 25 of the Convention, on expulsion of persons and checks in the SIS in connection with residence permits, were allocated jointly to Articles 62(3) and 63(3), while Article 23(1) was allocated only to Article 62(3).[24] Executive Committee Decisions concerning means of proof in readmission agreements and transit for expulsion were allocated jointly to Articles 62(3) and 63(3),[25] and three other Decisions were allocated jointly to Article 63(3) and other 'legal bases': an action plan on irregular migration, a measure on the coordinated deployment of document advisers, and the Common Manual (on border controls) and Common Consular Instructions (on short-term visas).

The Tampere European Council in 1999 set out specific objectives relating to irregular migration, in particular calling for the adoption of legislation concerning trafficking in persons by the end of 2000, assistance to countries of origin and transit, an invitation to the Council to conclude readmission agreements between the EC and third States or 'standard clauses' on this issue in broader agreements with third States, and the possible adoption of rules on internal readmission (ie between Member States).

The trafficking proposal referred to was released by the Commission at the end of 2000, although not adopted until 2002.[26] Also, the Community adopted an active policy of attempting to conclude readmission agreements, including standard clauses concerning readmission in its association or cooperation agreements, and developed further the other external relations aspects of its irregular migration policy.[27]

As for other measures, a first set of Directives concerning irregular migration (carrier sanctions, facilitation of irregular entry and residence, and mutual recognition of expulsion decisions) were all adopted by the Council in 2001–02.[28]

In an attempt to develop an overall strategy for EU measures concerning irregular migration, the Commission released a communication on irregular migration in 2001;[29] the Council duly adopted a detailed action plan early in 2002.[30] Soon afterward,

---

[20] See I:7.8 below on substantive measures in this area. On the scope of Art 66 compared to Art 63(3)(b), see (*mutatis mutandis*) I:3.2.4 above (as regards Art 74 TFEU as compared to Art 77 TFEU).

[21] See I:3.2.4 above (as regards Art 72 TFEU). [22] See [1999] OJ L 176/17.

[23] On Art 18, see I:3.6.1 and I:4.9 above. It is assumed that the Article was only allocated to Art 63(3) EC due to its relevance to *legal* migration.

[24] On these provisions, see I:4.9 above and I:7.7 below. Again, it is assumed that Art 25 was only allocated to Art 63(3) EC as regards its impact on legal migration.

[25] On the latter issue, see further I:7.7.3 below. [26] I:7.5.4 below. [27] I:7.9 below.

[28] I:7.5.1, I:7.5.3, and I:7.7.2 below. [29] COM (2001) 672, 15 Nov 2001.

[30] [2002] OJ C 142/23.

the Commission issued a Green Paper on expulsion ('return') policy;[31] this too was followed by a detailed Council action plan.[32] The parallel action plan on external border control was also relevant to irregular immigration issues.[33]

A series of further measures were adopted afterwards, consisting of: a Directive on assistance for expulsions via air transit;[34] conclusions on assistance for expulsions via land and sea;[35] a Regulation on a network of immigration liaison officers;[36] a Decision on financing expulsion measures;[37] a Directive on the exchange of passenger data;[38] a Decision on joint expulsion flights;[39] a Directive on the legal status of victims of trafficking in persons;[40] and a Decision establishing an information and coordination network for Member States' migration management services.[41] Measures concerning the SIS were adopted in 2001 and 2004, and in 2006, legislation to establish a new system (SIS II) was adopted.[42] The Commission also released a discussion paper on the link between legal and irregular migration,[43] along with several updates on the implementation of EC policy on irregular migration (as well as visas and border control).[44] In addition to the negotiation of readmission treaties and the broader external agenda concerning irregular migration, the EC concluded Protocols to the UN Convention on organized crime, concerning smuggling and trafficking in persons.[45]

The Hague Programme on the Justice and Home Affairs (JHA) agenda for 2004–09 called for negotiations to start on a proposal on expulsion standards, along with further readmission agreements, the creation of a European Return Fund, and the adoption of a policy plan on trafficking in persons.[46] Implementing the Hague Programme, the EU eventually adopted in 2008 a Directive touching on many key aspects of expulsions (known as the 'Returns Directive'), after three years of difficult negotiations.[47] In the meantime, the EU had agreed on legislation to establish European Return Fund in 2007,[48] and a number of further readmission treaties were also agreed with third States.[49] Also, the Council agreed an action plan on trafficking in persons in December 2005.[50] There were also developments as regards the external aspects of migration control.[51] Finally, the Commission issued a communication on policy priorities as regards irregular migration in 2006,[52] in particular addressing the question of deterring the employment of irregular migrants. This ultimately led to legislation on this subject—a Directive adopted in 2009, which was the first EC immigration legislation (as distinct from a third pillar measure) to establish criminal law offences.[53]

---

[31] COM (2002) 175, 10 Apr 2002; see later communication on the same topic (COM (2002) 564, 14 Oct 2002).

[32] Council doc 14673/02, 25 Nov 2002.   [33] See I:3.2.2.2 above.   [34] I:7.7.3.1 below.

[35] I:7.7.3.2 below.   [36] I:7.5.5 below.   [37] I:7.7.2 below.   [38] I:7.5.2 below.

[39] I:7.7.4 below.   [40] I:7.6.2 below.   [41] I:7.8 below.   [42] See I:3.7 above.

[43] COM (2004) 412, 4 June 2004.

[44] COM (2003) 323, 3 June 2003; SEC (2004) 1349, 25 Oct 2004; SEC (2006) 1010, 19 July 2006; and SEC (2009) 320, 9 Mar 2009.

[45] See I:7.5.2 and I:7.5.4 below.

[46] [2005] OJ C 53, points 1.6.4 and 1.7.1. See also the later implementation plan: [2005] OJ C 198, point 2.6.

[47] Dir 2008/115 ([2008] OJ L 348/98); see I:7.7.1 below.   [48] [2007] OJ L 144/45; see I:7.8 below.

[49] See I:7.9 below.   [50] See I:7.5.4 below.   [51] See I:7.9.2 below.

[52] COM (2006) 402, 19 July 2006.   [53] Dir 2009/52 ([2009] OJ L 168/24). See I:7.6.1 below.

Alongside the Hague Programme, the decision-making rules relating to irregular migration were altered, as from 1 January 2005, so that qualified majority voting in the Council applied in this area, along with co-decision with the European Parliament.[54] As regards the Court of Justice, due to the limitations on its jurisdiction before the Treaty of Lisbon entered into force, it received only one case referred from national courts during this period, concerning the interpretation of the rules on immigration detention set out in the Returns Directive.[55] On the other hand, the Commission brought before the Court a number of infringement actions in order to ensure that Member States complied with the legislation adopted in this area.[56]

7.2.3 The Treaty of Lisbon

The former Article 63(3) and (4) EC, concerning migration, became Article 79 of the Treaty on the Functioning of the European Union (TFEU), as amended by the Treaty of Lisbon with effect from the entry into force of the latter Treaty on 1 December 2009.[57] Article 79 TFEU provides (in part) as follows:

(1) The Union shall develop a common immigration policy aimed at ensuring, at all stages, the efficient management of migration flows, fair treatment of third country nationals residing legally in Member States, and the prevention of, and enhanced measures to combat, illegal immigration and trafficking in human beings.

(2) For the purposes of paragraph 1, the European Parliament and the Council, acting in accordance with the ordinary legislative procedure, shall adopt measures in the following areas: …

    (c) illegal immigration and unauthorised residence, including removal and repatriation of persons residing without authorisation;

    (d) combating trafficking in persons, in particular women and children.

(3) The Union may conclude agreements with third countries for the readmission to their countries of origin or provenance of third-country nationals who do not or who no longer fulfil the conditions for entry, presence or residence in the territory of one of the Member States.

Paragraphs 4 and 5 and sub-paragraphs 2(a) and 2(b) of this Article concern only legal migration, and so were considered instead in Chapter 6.[58] As for the provisions concerning irregular migration, there was no change in the decision-making rules, which as noted above, were subject to QMV in Council and co-decision already from 1 January 2005. There was, however, an extension of the jurisdiction of the Court of Justice, with the result that a large number of disputes concerning the rules on irregular migration set out in the Returns Directive have reached the Court of Justice.[59]

As with legal migration, the EU's powers as regards irregular migration are now part of an obligation to develop a 'common' policy,[60] and the penultimate paragraph of the

---

[54] [2004] OJ L 396/45.
[55] Case C-357/09 PPU *Kadzoev* [2009] ECR I-11189. See I:7.7.1 below.
[56] See I:7.5.1, I:7.5.3, I:7.7.2, and I:7.7.3.1 below.
[57] [2007] OJ C 306. The consolidated TFEU is in [2008] OJ C 115.
[58] See I:6.2.3 and I:6.2.4 above.   [59] See I:7.7.1 below.
[60] See also Art 67(2) TFEU.

previous Article 63 EC has now been removed.[61] Article 79(1) TFEU, unlike the previous Article 63 EC, also sets out, inter alia, the objective of the prevention and combating of illegal immigration and human trafficking. The general provisions of Title V of Part Three of the TFEU also specify that the common immigration policy includes fairness towards *all* third-country nationals, that is including irregular migrants as well as legal residents.[62]

The revised Treaty text refers now to 'unauthorised', rather than 'illegal' presence, and also refers expressly to 'removal'. There is a definition of irregular migration in the context of readmission treaties (Article 79(3)), which reflects EU legislation in this area.[63]

Article 79(2)(d) confers an express competence as regards trafficking in persons, although it should be noted that there is also an explicit reference to this issue in the criminal law provisions of the Treaty.[64] As regards other criminal law aspects of migration policy, the general power to adopt criminal law measures linked to harmonization in other areas is obviously relevant.[65]

The external power over readmission agreements became explicit, and the EP gained powers of consent over the conclusion of readmission agreements.[66]

The EU has not adopted a lot of legislation in this area since the Treaty of Lisbon entered into force. In fact, the only legislation relying on Article 79(2)(c) as a legal base was an amendment to the legislation on immigration liaison officers.[67] The only significant measure adopted in this field since 2009 is the criminal law Directive on trafficking in persons.[68]

The Stockholm Programme of 2009 largely reiterated established EU policy in this area, without calling for further legislation,[69] except for a more general call for the consolidation and amendment of all legislation in the area of migration—although this was never followed up.[70] The programme also called for an evaluation of EU readmission policy in 2010, and the conclusion of readmission agreements with a number of countries.[71] Most recently, the 2015 Migration Agenda and Action Plan against smuggling called for: revision of EU anti-smuggling legislation; possible changes to EU laws on immigration liaison officers, the SIS, and Frontex as regards expulsions, as well as agreement on more readmission treaties and greater efforts to enforce the Directives on irregular migration and prohibition of employment of irregular migrants.[72] It should also be noted again that the EU's plan to establish an entry-exit system will impact upon regulation of irregular migration.[73]

7.2.4 Competence issues

There were a number of historic disputes, before the entry into force of the Treaty of Lisbon, over the extent of the EC's competence over irregular migration issues

---

[61] See further the discussion of competence issues below (I:7.2.4).
[62] Compare Art 67(2) TFEU with Art 79(1) TFEU, which refers only to fairness as regards legal residents.
[63] See n 2 above.   [64] Art 83(1) TFEU. See further I:7.2.4 below.
[65] Art 83(2) TFEU. See further I:7.2.4 below.
[66] On external competence in JHA matters, see generally I:2.7 above.   [67] See I:7.5.5 below.
[68] See I:7.5.4 below. On the issue of the correct 'legal bases' for this Directive, see I:7.2.4 below.
[69] [2010] OJ C 115, point 6.1.6.   [70] Ibid, point 6.1.4.   [71] Ibid, points 6.1.6 and 7.5.
[72] COM (2015) 240, 13 May 2015 and COM (2015) 285, 27 May 2015.   [73] See I:3.6.2 above.

pursuant to the previous Article 63(3)(b) EC. These issues remain relevant if the validity of any EU measures adopted before the entry into force of the Treaty of Lisbon is challenged. In fact, in light of the similar wording of the Treaty provisions in this area after the entry into force of the Treaty of Lisbon, the historic disputes might even still be relevant to measures adopted after that Treaty's entry into force.

The boundary between the irregular migration powers and EU free movement law and association agreements is explored further below, as is the practice and scope of the EU's external relations powers in this field.[74]

Since the Treaty of Lisbon has unified the decision-making rules applicable to the adoption of legislation on legal migration and irregular migration, it is no longer necessary to distinguish between the powers over legal migration and the powers over irregular migration.[75] This means, for instance, that there would not be an awkward problem if the EU wanted to amend the existing Directive concerning the legal status of victims of trafficking.[76] However, it remains necessary to distinguish between the legal base concerning irregular migration and the legal basis for cooperation between national administrations,[77] as the latter provision entails a different rule on involvement of the European Parliament (consultation only). The most logical distinction is that the former provision governs the adoption of rules which directly regulate the issue, while the latter provision is confined to regulating issues such as the exchange of personnel.[78]

As for the intensity of the EC's powers to regulate irregular migration, despite the final words of Article 63, Member States did not have *carte blanche* to adopt measures in this field regardless of EC legislation. Member States were still obliged to comply with EC law to the extent that the EC has acted, and the EC could harmonize national law fully in this field if it wished, subject to the principle of subsidiarity; but EC powers were not prima facie exclusive.[79] This position was confirmed by the Treaty of Lisbon, which removed the final provisions of Article 63 EC, and instead subjected the entire JHA Title explicitly to the rule of shared competence.[80] This leaves Member States free to act to the extent that the EU has not acted, but it is open to the EU to harmonize the field as much as it wishes.[81]

According to Court of Justice of the European Union (CJEU) case law, where the legislation in this area permits Member States to set higher standards if they are 'compatible' with the legislation concerned, it is necessary to assess whether the higher standards which Member States wish to set are consistent with the underlying objective of that particular legislation.[82]

---

[74] Respectively I:7.4 and I:7.9.1 below. See also the discussion of the division between EU foreign policy powers and border control powers in I:3.2.4 above, which applies equally to the division between foreign policy and anti-smuggling powers.

[75] On this issue, see further I:6.2.4 above.

[76] Dir 2004/81 ([2004] OJ L 261/19); see I:7.6.2 below.

[77] Now Art 74 TFEU, previously Art 66 EC.   [78] See the analysis in I:2.2.3.2 and I:3.2.4 above.

[79] See I:6.2.4 above.   [80] Art 4(2)(j) TFEU; see I:2.2.4 above.   [81] Art 2(2) TFEU; see ibid.

[82] See the case law on the Returns Directive, discussed in I:7.7.1 below.

As to the material content of the EU's powers regarding irregular migration, does it extend to issues such as deportation, expulsion, and interior enforcement measures? The EP expressed doubts over the EC's powers in this area,[83] as did academics.[84] But surely powers over 'repatriation of illegal residents' logically had to include deportation and deportation measures, since the Treaty did not refer only to *voluntary* repatriation. Equally, mutual recognition of expulsion measures was not excluded from the scope of the EC's powers, and surely competence over 'illegal immigration and illegal residence' had to include internal enforcement measures against common breaches of immigration law such as overstays and clandestine entry. It is doubtful whether the changes made by the Treaty of Lisbon to the legal base in this area (to refer to 'unauthorised' residence, and add a reference to 'removal') added to the EU's competence, because persons who are not authorized to reside would likely be considered 'illegal' anyway, and the previous powers over irregular migration, which were expressly non-exhaustive ('including…') were obviously apt to include competence concerning removals, which presumably differ from 'repatriation' in that a 'removal' could take place other than to the country of origin. Indeed, several measures adopted before the entry into force of the Treaty of Lisbon address this issue.[85]

However, even after the entry into force of the Treaty of Lisbon, the EU still lacks the power to regulate irregular *employment* as such, as it is not mentioned in Article 79 TFEU (or in the prior Article 63(3)(b) EC), or in the social policy provisions of the TFEU (previously the EC Treaty). However, the EU (and the EC before it) can regulate this issue indirectly where it is ancillary to one of the powers which clearly has been conferred upon the EU. This allowed the EC to use the powers conferred by the prior Article 63(3)(b) EC to prohibit the employment of irregular migrants.[86] The EU could also (using the same legal base) regulate the position of persons who definitively lose their legal status because of irregular employment, or use its legal migration powers (as it did) to set out the circumstances in which employment may or must be authorized (thus indirectly regulating irregular employment), and/or in which unauthorized employment will terminate legal migration status.[87] The Treaty of Lisbon has now conferred these powers on the European Union, pursuant to Article 79 TFEU.

As for the distinction between EU competence over criminal law as compared to immigration law,[88] first of all, the EU's express power to regulate trafficking in persons in Article 79 only extends to the regulation of immigration-related issues, as the *criminal* law response to trafficking in persons falls within the scope of the *lex specialis* set out in Article 83(1) TFEU. The distinction between Articles 79(2) and 83(1) TFEU is important because an emergency brake applies to the adoption of legislation under the

---

[83] See, for instance, the Nassauer report on the proposed Directive on mutual recognition of expulsion orders (A5-0394/2000, 11 Dec 2000).

[84] See K Hailbronner, 'European Immigration and Asylum Law after the Amsterdam Treaty' (1998) 35 CMLRev 1047 and J Monar, 'Justice and Home Affairs in the Treaty of Amsterdam: Reform at the Price of Fragmentation' (1998) 23 ELRev 320.

[85] See generally I:7.7 below.   [86] Dir 2009/52 ([2009] OJ L 168/24).

[87] On this issue, see the more detailed argument in S Peers and N Rogers, *EU Immigration and Asylum Law: Text and Commentary*, 1st edn (Martinus Nijhoff, 2006), ch 3. See also the Council resolution on irregular employment, adopted as an employment policy measure ([2003] OJ C 260/1).

[88] See further II:5.2.4 and II:5.4.1 below.

latter provision, but not the former.[89] So the Directive on the criminal law aspects of trafficking in persons correctly uses legal bases concerning criminal law only.[90]

The criminal law aspects of facilitation of irregular migration, or of sanctioning employers of irregular migrants,[91] now fall within the scope of Article 83(2) TFEU, which provides for EU competence over criminal law measures if such measures are necessary to ensure the effective implementation of a Union policy, once harmonization measures have been adopted. The same decision-making procedure applies to the adoption of such measures as applied to the original Union policy, except that the emergency brake is again applicable.[92] However, it should also be noted that the EU's Returns Directive, an immigration law measure discussed in this chapter, has a significant indirect impact on national laws criminalizing irregular migration.[93]

7.2.5 Territorial scope

All of the measures discussed in this chapter build upon the Schengen *acquis*, with the exception of the readmission treaties, the Directives on trafficking victims and criminal measures against trafficking, the funding measures, and the Directive on sanctioning employers of irregular migrants.[94] Several measures build on the Schengen *acquis* in part, to the extent that they apply to persons who no longer meet the criteria for short stays within the Schengen area: the Decision on the system for exchange of operational information, the Decision on financing of expulsion decisions, the Directive on transit for expulsion, and the Returns Directive.[95] The specific rules on participating in Schengen measures (see further below) therefore applied to such measures.

Several measures discussed in this chapter do not fall within the scope of the immigration provisions of the TFEU (previously Title IV of Part Three of the EC Treaty): the Regulation on migration management funding (which fell within the scope of EU development policy and policy on cooperation with non-developing countries) and the legislation on trafficking in persons (which fall either within the scope of the previous third pillar or of the post-Lisbon EU criminal law powers). So those measures apply to all Member States (except that Denmark does not apply the Directive on trafficking in persons), and to no non-Member States. Furthermore, to the extent that measures related to irregular migration fall within the scope of the EU's foreign policy powers or development policy powers, they apply to all Member States.[96]

The UK and Ireland are covered by all of the measures considered in this Chapter, except for: the Directive on trafficking victims; the Decision on financing expulsions (the UK is covered in part, while Ireland is not covered at all); the 2003 Directive on transit for expulsion; the Returns Directive; the Directive on sanctions for employers of irregular migrants; the Decision on the system for exchange of operational information (which covers the UK fully, but Ireland only to the extent that it builds on the

---

[89] On the emergency brake, see II:2.2.3.4.   [90] On the substance, see I:7.5.4 below.
[91] See I:7.5.3 and I:7.5.4 below.   [92] See further II:5.4.1.2.   [93] See further I:7.7.1 below.
[94] See I:7.5.4, I:7.6, I:7.8, and I:7.9 below.   [95] See I:7.7 and I:7.8 below.
[96] See respectively I:3.2.5 above and I:7.9 below.

Schengen *acquis*); and some EU readmission treaties.[97] However, the UK has opted out of its prior participation in the Framework Decision on smuggling as from December 2014.[98]

As for Denmark, its position regarding measures adopted before the entry into force of the Treaty of Lisbon follows the scope of the previous Title IV EC and the Schengen *acquis*. So it is covered by the Framework Decisions on trafficking in persons and facilitation of irregular entry (which fell outside the scope of Title IV). It decided to apply in full or in part the Decision on the system for exchange of operational information, the Decision on financing of expulsion decisions, and the Directives on mutual recognition of expulsion measures and transit for expulsion, to the extent that they built on the Schengen *acquis* (ie as regards persons who no longer meet the conditions for entry as set out in the Schengen Borders Code, or who never met those conditions).[99] It could not participate in the readmission treaties, the Directive on trafficking victims or the Return Fund, although a Joint Declaration to each readmission treaty encourages the EU's contracting partner to negotiate a readmission treaty separately with Denmark. As for measures adopted since the entry into force of the Treaty of Lisbon, Denmark is not bound by the Directive on trafficking in persons, and remains subject to the Framework Decision on this subject instead. It would have opted in to that Directive if the Danish public had approved a partial opt in to JHA measures in a referendum held in December 2015.[100]

The newer Member States are covered by the measures in this chapter immediately as from their accession (or, if those measures first applied after their accession, at the same date as the other Member States), except for the Directive on mutual recognition of expulsion orders and the connected Decision on funding expulsions, which only applied (or will apply) fully when the Schengen rules were (or will be) fully applied for each of the newer Member States in turn.

Pursuant to their association with the Schengen *acquis*,[101] Norway, Iceland, Switzerland, and Liechtenstein are not covered by the measures outside the scope of that *acquis*: the readmission treaties (although each treaty contains a Joint Declaration urging the negotiation of parallel agreements with Schengen associates); the Directive on trafficking victims; the return fund Decision; the Directive on sanctioning employers of irregular migrants; the Framework Decision (and subsequent Directive) on trafficking in persons; and the measures on immigration statistics. Like Denmark, they

---

[97] See the Decisions on the UK participation in the Schengen *acquis* ([2000] OJ L 141/43, applicable from 1 Jan 2005: [2004] OJ L 395/70) and on Irish participation in the Schengen *acquis* ([2002] OJ L 64/20, not yet applied), as well as the preambles to the relevant legislation and treaties. On readmission, for a list of the seventeen EU readmission treaties, see I:7.9 below. Neither the UK nor Ireland applies the treaties with Turkey, Azerbaijan, Armenia, or Cape Verde. Ireland has opted in to eleven of the remaining thirteen treaties: all except the treaties with Hong Kong and Ukraine (see Commission decision authorizing Irish participation: [2014] OJ L 155/22).

[98] For the background, see the discussion of the UK 'block opt out' from pre-Lisbon EU criminal law in II:2.2.5.1.

[99] Council docs 14261/01, 23 Nov 2001; 9963/02, 20 June 2002; 10661/04, 18 Jun 2004; 12195/04, 10 Sep 2004; and 12907/04, 29 Sep 2004.

[100] Denmark would also have been fully covered by Schengen measures as ordinary EU law. On the Danish position generally, see I:2:2.5.2 above.

[101] See further I:2.2.5.4 above.

are covered in part by those measures which build on the Schengen *acquis* in part (as regards persons who no longer meet the criteria for short stays within the Schengen area): the Decision on the system for exchange of operational information, the Decision on financing of expulsion decisions, the Directive on transit for expulsion, and the Returns Directive. They are fully covered by everything else which builds upon the Schengen *acquis*.

7.3 Human Rights

7.3.1 European Convention on Human Rights

The starting point for the consideration of the human rights aspects of irregular migration is the European Convention on Human Rights (ECHR). Examining the relevant ECHR rights in turn, Articles 2 and 3 ECHR (and possibly other ECHR provisions as well) prevent persons from being expelled to a country where they would face the death penalty or a sufficient risk of torture or other inhuman or degrading treatment.[102] Article 5(1)(f) ECHR permits deprivation of liberty either following a 'lawful arrest or detention of a person to prevent his [or her] effecting an unauthorized entry into the country' or 'of a person against who action is being taken with a view to deportation . . .'. This is considered further below.

As regards trafficking in persons, Article 4(1) ECHR prohibits holding people in slavery or servitude,[103] and Article 4(2) proscribes any requirement to perform forced or compulsory labour.[104] According to the Human Rights Court, Article 4 creates positive obligations for States, to criminalize actions by private persons; 'forced or compulsory labour' covers cases where an underage migrant who had not been authorized to reside feared police arrest and expulsion and was induced by promises of regularized status; 'slavery' means a case of actual ownership of a person; and 'servitude' is 'an obligation to provide one's services that is imposed by the use of coercion'.[105] Moreover, trafficking in persons, as defined in UN and Council of Europe instruments, falls within the scope of Article 4, and there is a positive obligation on States to take operational measures to protect persons from trafficking if their authorities 'were aware, or ought to have been aware, of circumstances giving rise to a credible suspicion that an identified individual had been, or was at real and immediate risk of being, trafficked'.[106]

Next, the right to a fair trial set out in Article 6 of the ECHR does not apply to immigration disputes,[107] although as discussed below, the principles of a fair trial and effective remedies have a wider scope within the context of EU law.[108]

Article 8 ECHR, which protects against expulsion where family or private life is established in a State,[109] can apply to irregular migrants. It appears that if the migrant

---

[102] See further I:5.3.1 above.
[103] It is not possible to derogate from this provision in times of emergency: see Art 15(2) ECHR.
[104] This provision *is* subject to possible derogation pursuant to Art 15 ECHR; moreover, Art 4(3) ECHR lists forms of labour which are not covered by this proscription.
[105] *Siliadin v France* (Reports of Judgments and Decisions 2005-VII).
[106] *Rantsev v Cyprus and Russia*, 7 Jan 2010. On these international instruments, see I:7.5.4 below.
[107] *Maaouia v France* (2000-X).　　[108] I:7.3.4.　　[109] See generally I:6.3.1 above.

has been convicted of serious crimes, his or her irregular status is a further aggravating factor supporting expulsion; but conversely, if the State's interest in expulsion is purely economic and the migrant has established a strong family life with his or her small children, the irregular migration status must be disregarded.[110] In certain circumstances, States must regularize the status of irregular migrants.[111] Article 8 is also relevant to data protection, an issue which arises in the context of irregular migration.[112]

Next, the Fourth Protocol to the ECHR contains a number of important rights, although it has not been ratified by two Member States.[113] Article 3 of the Protocol gives nationals the right to enter the territory of their own State, and freedom from expulsion from their own State. Article 4 of the Protocol prohibits the collective expulsion of foreigners, implicitly regardless of their immigration status. These rights are not subject to any limitations, although they are subject to the 'public emergency' derotation set out in Article 15 ECHR.

The rights set out in Article 3 of the Fourth Protocol have not yet been the subject of a judgment by the Human Rights Court,[114] although admissibility decisions have made clear that Article 3 leaves intact a State's power to determine who are its own nationals.[115] Article 3 of the Fourth Protocol can be compared to Article 12(4) of the International Covenant on Civil and Political Rights (ICCPR), which all Member States have ratified. This provision states that '[n]o-one may be arbitrarily deprived of the right to enter his [or her] own country'.[116] Unlike the ECHR clause, the provision does not expressly set out a ban on expulsion (although this is surely a necessary corollary of the right to enter); the right extends beyond nationals of the country; and it sets out a possible justification for State action (it must merely be non-'arbitrary'), rather than an apparently absolute ban.

As for Article 4 of the Fourth Protocol, the Human Rights Court has issued only two judgments, defining collective expulsion as 'any measure compelling aliens, as a group, to leave a country, except where such a measure is taken on the basis of a reasonable and objective examination of the particular case of each individual alien of the group'.[117] In the *Conka* judgment, the Court ruled that even where individual decisions had been taken, it could examine the background to them; in this particular case, the stated political intention of removing a particular group of people from the territory and the standardized procedure followed to that end amounted to a collective expulsion. Furthermore, there were extensive procedural rights which had to be observed before the expulsion could be carried out, in particular the suspensive effect of any

---

[110] See respectively the cases of *Dalia v France* (Reports 1998-I) and *Da Silva and Hoogkamer v Netherlands*, 31 Jan 2006.

[111] See I:6.3.1 above.   [112] See II:7.3.2.

[113] Greece and the UK. See also Art 2 of the Protocol, which grants free movement within a territory and the freedom to leave any country, discussed further in I:3.3 above.

[114] See *Denizci and others v Cyprus* (Reports 2001-V), where the Court declined to rule on an allegation that Art 3 had been breached.

[115] *Slivenko v Latvia* (23 Jan 2002) and *Nagula v Estonia* (25 Oct 2005),

[116] On the interpretation of the ICCPR provisions, S Joseph, J Schultz, and M Castan, *The International Covenant on Civil and Political Rights: Cases, Materials and Commentary*, 2nd edn (OUP, 2004), at 364–76.

[117] *Conka v Belgium* (Reports 2002-I). See also *Hirsi Jamaa v Italy*, discussed in I:3.3 above in the context of border controls (ban on collective expulsion from international waters).

challenges to enforcement of the expulsion decisions. On the other hand, where an asylum seeker's application had been the subject of an individual assessment of its merits, a State did not violate Article 4 simply because it expelled him on a 'joint flight' together with other expellees.[118] Article 4 has no equivalent in the ICCPR, but then the procedural rights in cases of individual expulsion decisions set out in Article 13 ICCPR (on which, see below) should necessarily prevent collective expulsions.

Finally, the Seventh Protocol to the ECHR, which three Member States have not ratified,[119] sets out procedural rights applicable to individual cases of expulsion (Article 1 of the Protocol). A lawfully resident foreigner may only be expelled following a 'decision reached in accordance with law' and has the right to submit reasons against expulsion, have the case reviewed, and be represented for this purpose before a 'competent authority'. A State may insist that these rights can be exercised only after expulsion, 'when expulsion is necessary in the interests of public order or is grounded on reasons of national security'. These procedural rights are nearly identical to those set out in Article 13 of the ICCPR,[120] and (as regards refugees lawfully on the territory) very similar to Article 32(2) of the Geneva Convention on the status of refugees.[121]

First of all, as for the personal scope of the ECHR provision, the Human Rights Court has ruled that a failed asylum seeker can no longer be regarded as lawfully in the territory.[122] As distinct from persons whose visas had expired and who had no reasonable expectation of being permitted to stay once an asylum application was turned down, Article 1 of the Seventh Protocol applied to persons who had been lawfully admitted for residence, issued a residence permit, and were eligible for and had applied for extensions of that permit,[123] as well as persons issued a valid long-stay visa who were not subject to a deportation order.[124] The application of the Protocol could not cease simply because a person who was previously legally resident had become subject to an expulsion order, and status of 'resident' is not lost simply because a person who has not established any residence in another State takes a short trip abroad from his normal State of residence.[125] An 'expulsion' has an autonomous meaning, and applies to any act other than extradition which compels a person to depart from the territory, in particular to removal of a person from his home and placing him on a flight to another country,[126] and to banning re-entry to the State of residence after his next trip abroad.[127]

Secondly, as to the specific procedural rights established by Article 1 of the Seventh Protocol, the European Court of Human Rights has ruled that the right to a decision 'in accordance with the law' was violated where the relevant national law lacked sufficient basic safeguards and the national court did not examine the merits of the

---

[118] *Sultani v France*, 20 Sep 2007.   [119] Germany, the Netherlands, and the UK.
[120] The difference is that there is no 'public order' exception in Art 13 ICCPR. On the interpretation of this clause, see Joseph et al. (n 116 above) at 377–87.
[121] Art 32(1) of this Convention also sets out substantive limitations on the expulsion of such refugees, and of course Art 33 of the Convention further sets out a rule of non-refoulement. Art 32(3) also provides that expelled refugees must be given a 'reasonable period of time' in which to seek admission to another State. On Art 32, see J Hathaway, *The Rights of Refugees under International Law* (CUP, 2005), 659–95.
[122] *Sultani v France*, n 118 above.   [123] *Bolat v Russia* (ECHR 2006-XI).
[124] *Nolan v Russia*, 12 Feb 2009.   [125] Ibid.   [126] *Bolat*, n 123 above.
[127] *Nolan*, n 124 above.

administration's decisions.[128] It is also not in accordance with the 'law' to expel a foreign national without a judicial order, where national law requires such an order to be issued as a condition for expulsion.[129] Furthermore, even where there was an alleged breach of 'national security', the specific rights to submit reasons against expulsion and to have the case reviewed were violated where the person concerned was not informed of the offence of which he was suspected, he did not have a copy of the order against him until the (only) day of his hearing, and the national court refused a request for adjournment.[130] The right to a review of the case was violated where a national court refused to gather evidence regarding the allegations to the expulsion decision, or to review the merits of the national decision,[131] and where there was a three-month delay in the communication of the decision on expulsion, there was no possibility to submit reasons against the expulsion and to have the case reviewed with the assistance of counsel.[132] There was no justification for preventing in-country exercise of the procedural rights where the 'national security' arguments were not genuine (the deprivation of in-country procedural rights could in any event in that case still only be justified if this were necessary and proportionate), and where there was no convincing argument for the 'public order' exception to apply.[133]

Finally, it should be recalled that Articles 2 and 3 ECHR (as regards asylum) and Article 8 ECHR (as regards family reunion and long-term residents) also contain implied procedural rights.[134]

7.3.2 Geneva Convention and detention issues

The other main source of international legal rules governing the rights of irregular migrants is the Geneva Convention on the status of refugees. Article 31(1) of this Convention specifies that States 'shall not impose penalties, on account of their illegal entry or presence, on refugees who, coming directly from a country where their life or freedom was threatened in the sense of Article 1 [of the Convention], enter or are present in their territory without authorization, provided they present themselves without delay to the authorities and show good cause for their illegal entry or presence'. Article 31(2) then provides that States shall only restrict the movement of such refugees if 'necessary' and only until 'their status in the country is regularized or they obtain admission to another country'. Although it is considered in this chapter because of its relevance to irregular migration, Article 31 is obviously also relevant to EU rules on external borders, visas, and asylum, which were discussed in detail in Chapters 3, 4, and 5 of this volume.

---

[128] *Lupsa v Romania* (Reports of Judgments and Decisions 2006-VII); *Kaya v Romania*, 12 Oct 2006; and *CG v Bulgaria*, 24 Apr 2008. In the latter case, the Court confirmed that the 'in accordance with the law' requirement must be intepreted in the same way as other similar provisions in the ECHR, for example in Art 8(2).

[129] *Bolat*, n 123 above.   [130] *Lupsa* and *Kaya*, n 128 above.   [131] *CG*, n 128 above.

[132] *Nolan*, n 124 above.

[133] *CG* and *Nolan* (nn 128 and 124 above, respectively). The Court also stated in *CG* that any use of the 'public order' exception would be subject to the principle of proportionality.

[134] See I:5.3 and I:6.3.1 above.

A detailed analysis of Article 31(1) suggests convincingly that:[135] the provision applies to asylum seekers as well as recognized refugees; it does not apply to removal from the territory, in effect because Articles 32 and 33 of the Convention are *lex specialis* rules concerning removal (the latter applying regardless of the migration status of the refugee);[136] the refugees can present themselves to any authorities, although they cannot rely on the provision after their apprehension unless there was no reasonable possibility to contact the authorities beforehand; the 'without delay' criterion must be applied on a case-by-case basis, without the application of any inflexible deadline; the 'coming directly' criterion means that persons who have obtained refuge in another State cannot enjoy the benefit of Article 31, but that persons who have transited through other States and who feared persecution in other States can still benefit from it; and a 'good cause' explanation can be invoked by persons fleeing persecution and who needed to avoid rejection at the border. While Article 31(1) cannot be invoked by bodies that or persons who assist refugees to avoid immigration rules, it was recognized that States should refrain from initiating prosecutions in such cases. The definition of 'penalties' encompasses criminal and civil/administrative penalties, plus arguably different (lower) standards of procedural rules applicable to the consideration of the refugee claims and the denial of benefits.[137]

As for Article 31(2), the possibility of detention on grounds of irregular entry per se is only possible until an initial assessment has been made and the person concerned is admitted to the asylum determination process. The necessity test imposed by this provision also entails a proportionality requirement, so refugees must be released from detention if bail is provided or if they agree to reside in accommodation centres, and can only be detained if there are specific reasons, such as a risk of absconding.

This brings us to the more general issue of the detention of irregular migrants. As noted above, Article 5(1)(f) ECHR permits detention of persons in accordance with the law in order to prevent unauthorized entry or against whom action is being taken as regards deportation; this is subject to safeguards to inform that person about the grounds for detention (Article 5(2)), to permit judicial review (Article 5(4)), and to compensate persons in case of breaches of this Article (Article 5(5)). Article 5 applies to detention within immigration transit zones,[138] as well as to detention following the interception of a vessel on the high seas.[139] While the detention of children pursuant to Article 5(1)(f) is not prohibited, any immigration detention of children must be adapted to their particular vulnerability in order to be lawful.[140]

Most of the cases concern detention with a view to deportation: the Human Rights Court has ruled that in such cases, it is sufficient that expulsion proceedings

---

[135] Hathaway, n 121 above, 370–439. See also G Goodwin-Gill, 'Article 31 of the 1951 Convention Relating to the Status of Refugees: Non-Penalization, Detention and Protection' in E Feller, V Turk, and F Nicholson, eds., *Refugee Protection in International Law: UNHCR's Global Consultations on Refugee Protection* (CUP, 2003), 185.

[136] On those provisions, see I:5.3 above.   [137] On these issues, see I:5.7 and I:5.9 above.

[138] See *Amuur v France* (Reports 1996-III), *Shamsa v Poland* (27 Nov 2003), *Riad and Idiab v Belgium* (24 Jan 2008), and *Nolan* (n 124 above).

[139] *Medvedyev v France*, 29 Mar 2010.

[140] *Mayeka and Mitunga v Belgium* (Reports of Judgments and Decisions [2006] ECR-XI) and *Muskhadzhiyeva v Belgium* (19 Jan 2010).

are underway and are being pursued with 'due diligence' in order to justify continued detention pursuant to Article 5; there is not a separate 'necessity' requirement, even though such a requirement applies to other grounds of permissible detention.[141] Detention is therefore no longer justified if the removal is unfeasible, and if an alternative measure to prevent absconding can be applied in practice.[142]

Also, Article 5(1) is violated where authorities mislead asylum seekers and render remedies inaccessible,[143] where national law does not set out sufficiently precise details of the basis for detention,[144] or where the national law in question is breached.[145] As for detention in order to prevent unauthorized entry, the leading case is *Saadi v UK*,[146] in which the Human Rights Court ruled that: the provision can apply to asylum seekers; entry can be regarded as 'unauthorised' if it has not yet been authorized, and even if the persons concerned are trying to effect an authorized entry for asylum purposes; and the principles for justifying detention are the same as those applicable to detention cases. The key test is:

> ...such detention must be carried out in good faith; it must be closely connected to the purpose of preventing unauthorised entry of the person to the country; the place and conditions of detention should be appropriate, bearing in mind that 'the measure is applicable not to those who have committed criminal offences but to aliens who, often fearing for their lives, have fled from their own country'; and the length of the detention should not exceed that reasonably required for the purpose pursued.[147]

On the facts of this case, detention for the purpose of fast-track processing was in good faith and was related to the prevention of unauthorized entry; the detention centre was adapted to asylum seekers and had relevant facilities, notably legal assistance; and the length of detention (seven days) was not unreasonable.

Next, the right to information about detention set out in Article 5(2) ECHR has been violated in a number of immigration detention cases, or analogous extradition cases.[148] Article 5(4) is violated where, inter alia, national security considerations preclude any

---

[141] *Chahal v UK* (Reports 1996-V), *Slivenko* (n 115 above), *Singh v Czech Republic* (25 Jan 2005), and *Raza v Bulgaria* (11 Feb 2010); the 'due diligence' requirement was violated in the *Singh* and *Raza* cases. On the ECHR and ICCPR jurisprudence, see D Wilsher, 'Detention of Asylum-Seekers and Refugees and International Human Rights Law' in P Shah, ed., *The Challenge of Asylum to Legal Systems* (Cavendish, 2005), 145. On this issue, see J Hughes and F Liebaut, eds., *Detention of Asylum-Seekers in Europe: Analysis and Perspectives* (Martinus Nijhoff, 1998).

[142] *Mikolenko v Estonia*, 8 Oct 2009.   [143] *Conka* (n 117 above).

[144] Case law beginning with *Soldatenko v Ukraine*, 23 Oct 2008; see also *Sadaykov v Bulgaria*, 22 May 2008, *Khudyakova v Russia*, 8 Jan 2009 and *Abdolkhani and Karimnia v Turkey*, 22 Sep 2009. On the specific situation of cases where the European Court of Human Rights has blocked the expulsion pending its decision on the merits of an application, see *Gebremedhin v France*, 26 Apr 2007.

[145] See: *Khudyakova* (n 144 above); *Riad and Idiab*, n 138 above (detention continuing despite court orders for release); *Eminbeyli v Russia*, 26 Feb 2009 (no extradition of refugees permitted under national law); *S.D. v Greece*, 11 June 2009 (no detention of asylum seekers permitted under national law); *Hokic v Italy*, 1 Dec 2009 (where detention continued after the deportation order had been set aside); *Shchebet v Russia*, 12 June 2008; *Dzhurayev v Russia*, 17 Dec 2009; *Rusu v Austria*, 2 Oct 2008 (where a 'necessity' requirement was part of national law); and *Khaydarov v Russia*, 20 May 2010. For an example of lawful detention, see *Liu v Russia*, 6 Dec 2007.

[146] Grand Chamber judgment, 29 Jan 2008.

[147] Para 74 of the judgment (n 146 above), case-law reference omitted.

[148] See, for instance, *Saadi v UK* (n 146 above); *Abdolkhani and Karimnia* (n 144 above); *Rusu* (n 145 above); as regards detention at the border; *Kaboulov v Ukraine*, 19 Nov 2009; and *Khodzhayev v Russia*, 12 May 2010.

judicial review of detention in expulsion cases,[149] and in a number of other immigration and/or extradition cases.[150] Finally, Article 5(5) has also been violated in some immigration and/or extradition detention cases.[151] Article 3 ECHR also protects migrants against mistreatment during detention (or during removal operations) which is sufficiently severe to amount to torture or other inhuman or degrading treatment.[152]

The position under the ECHR can be contrasted with the ICCPR, Article 9 of which protects individuals against arbitrary detention, and Article 10 of which sets standards for detention conditions.[153] Article 9 has been interpreted by the Human Rights Committee to require a necessity test for detention of asylum seekers who entered irregularly, for example requiring the State to give specific reasons for the detention of individuals and to demonstrate why alternative forms of control of movement are not sufficient.

7.3.3 Other rights

Rights for irregular migrants are specifically guaranteed by the UN Convention on Migrant Workers and certain conventions adopted by the International Labour Organization. However, these conventions have attracted little or no ratifications from EU Member States to date, in particular because of their provisions concerning irregular migrants, and so they are not considered in detail here.[154]

7.3.4 Application to EU law

To what extent do the relevant rules discussed above form part of the general principles of EU law, and/or the EU Charter of Fundamental Rights? [155] The Court of Justice has ruled many times that the right to family life (as manifested in family reunion) and the right to a fair trial and effective remedies for protection of rights form part of the general principles.[156] These rights are also set out in the Charter.[157] A crucial point is that, in the context of both the general principles and the Charter, the right to a fair trial and to effective remedies have a wider scope where there is a link to EU law, applying in particular to immigration proceedings, raising the prospect that procedural rights equivalent to those guaranteed by Articles 6 and 13 ECHR apply regardless of

---

[149] See *Chahal* (n 141 above) and *Al-Nashif v Bulgaria* (10 June 2002).

[150] See, for instance, *Conka* (n 117 above); *Singh* (n 141 above); *Soldatenko* (n 144 above); *SD v Greece* (n 145 above); *Eminbeyli* (n 145 above); *Shchebet* (n 145 above); *Nolan* (n 124 above); *Dzhurayev* (n 145 above); *Raza* (n 141 above); *Abdolkhani and Karimnia* (n 144 above); and *Khaydarov* (n 145 above).

[151] See *Nolan* (n 124 above) and *Kaboulov* (n 148 above).

[152] For instance, see *Mogos v Romania* (17 Oct 2005), concerning treatment in a transit centre, and similarly *Riad and Idiab* (n 138 above); see also: *Dougoz v Greece* (2001 ECHR-II); *Tabesh v Greece* (26 Nov 2009); *Shchebet* (n 145 above); and *SD v Greece* (n 145 above). There are special considerations as regards the detention conditions of children: see *Mayeka and Mitunga* and *Muskhadzhiyeva* (n 140 above).

[153] On these ICCPR provisions, see Joseph et al. (n 116 above), at 303–47 and 274–93.

[154] See I:6.3.3 above.

[155] On human rights in EU law, see generally I:2.3 above. On human rights in this area of EU law, see R Cholewinski, 'European Union Policy on Irregular Migration: Human Rights Lost?' in B Bogusz, et al., eds., *Irregular Migration and Human Rights* (Martinus Nijhoff, 2004), 159.

[156] See I:6.3.4 above.   [157] Arts 7 and 47 ([2007] OJ C 303).

the limitations of the Seventh Protocol to the ECHR (non-application to some Member States, limited list of rights, restriction to lawful residents). The Court has not yet had an opportunity to rule on whether the right to life, the freedom from torture, the prohibition of slavery, and the ECHR restrictions on detention are a recognized part of the general principles of EU law, but it would be astounding if they were not; and in any event, there are relevant provisions in the Charter.[158]

In the case of restrictions on detention, the CJEU has interpreted Article 6 of the Charter consistently with the case law of the European Court of Human Rights on Article 5 ECHR.[159] In light of the more favourable rules applied by the Human Rights Committee when interpreting the ICCPR, it may be necessary to revisit the issue of whether the Court of Justice can accept that the rulings of that Committee can be considered a source of the general principles of EU law,[160] although in any event the EU's Returns Directive incorporates the ICCPR jurisprudence on the 'necessity' of immigration detention.[161]

As for the ECHR Protocols, EU law also recognizes the principle set out in Article 3 of the Fourth Protocol that 'Member States have no authority to expel [their nationals] from the territory or deny them access thereto',[162] although the Court of Justice has only referred to the source of this principle as human rights law on two occasions,[163] and has not formally recognized this principle as a human right forming part of the general principles of EU law. Moreover, there is no express provision in the Charter on this point. In fact, the Court has made use of the principle only to distinguish between a Member State's own citizens and nationals of other Member States (or non-Member States) in order to legitimize the greater protection which Member States may afford to the former in certain circumstances. The reason for the limited recognition of the source of the rule in human rights law may be that EU free movement law does not grant rights to EU citizens in their 'own' Member State, unless they have previously exercised free movement rights,[164] and that EU law does not generally impinge upon Member States' rights to determine who their own citizens are.[165] Nonetheless, if a

---

[158] Arts 2, 4, 5, and 6 (ibid).

[159] Case C-237/15 PPU *Lanigan*, ECLI:EU:C:2015:474, regarding detention pursuant to a European Arrest Warrant. See further II:3.3.

[160] See I:2.3 above.   [161] See I:7.7.1 below.

[162] Cases 41/74 *Van Duyn* [1974] ECR 1337, para 22; 115/81 and 116/81 *Adoui and Cornuaille* [1982] ECR 1665, para 7; C-370/90 *Singh* [1992] ECR I-4265, para 22; C-65/65 and 111/95 *Shingara and Radiom* [1997] ECR I-3343, para 28; C-171/96 *Roque* [1998] ECR I-4607, para 37; C-348/96 *Calfa* [1999] ECR I-11, para 20; C-235/99 *Kondova* [2001] ECR I-6557, para 83; C-257/99 *Barkoci and Malik* [2001] ECR I-6427, para 80; C-63/99 *Gloszczuk* [2001] ECR I-6369, para 78; and C-100/01 *Olazabal* [2002] ECR I-10981, para 40.

[163] In the *Singh* judgment, n 162 above, para 22, it referred to the Fourth Protocol to the ECHR, although not to the ICCPR, and also stated that the right was derived from national citizenship, not EU law. In Case C-434/09 *McCarthy* [2011] ECR I-3375, para 29, it referred again to the Protocol. In *Van Duyn*, *Roque* (para 38), *Kondova* (para 84), *Barkoci and Malik* (para 81), and *Gloszczuk* (para 79), all n 162 above, it referred to the principle as a 'principle of international law, which the [EC] Treaty cannot be assumed to disregard in relations between Member States'. In Case C-456/12 *O and B*, ECLI:EU:C:2014:135, para 42, the Court referred to it simply as a principle of international law.

[164] See generally I:4.4.1 above; and in this field, see particularly the Opinion in Case C-192/99 *Kaur* [2001] ECR I-1237, which argued on this ground against the claim of a 'second-class' UK citizen pursuant to EU free movement law to enter the UK from outside the EU, even though she had referred to the Fourth Protocol to the ECHR.

[165] Compare the judgment in *Kaur*, n 164 above, to the judgment in Case C-135/08 *Rottmann* [2010] ECR I-4449.

Member State tried to prevent its own citizens (as it defines them) from entering its territory from another Member State, the issue would fall within the scope of EU free movement law, and so the Court of Justice would presumably officially recognize the right as forming part of the general principles of EU law; it should be recalled that this right appears in the ICCPR, which all Member States have ratified.[166]

On the other hand, the Court of Justice has not yet ruled on whether the rights set out in Article 4 of the Fourth ECHR Protocol, or Article 1 of the Seventh Protocol, are protected as part of the general principles of EU law,[167] although the EU Charter refers expressly to the ban on collective expulsion in Art 4 of the Fourth Protocol.[168] Nor has the Court ruled on the status within the general principles or the Charter of Article 31 of the Geneva Convention, and indeed has ruled that it cannot interpret Article 31 of the Convention unless EU legislation makes a reference to it.[169] However, Article 31 is expressly referred to in the preambles to the second-phase legislation on responsibility for asylum seekers and asylum seekers' reception conditions and in the main text of EU anti-smuggling law, and is reflected implicitly in the provisions of the Schengen Borders Code, as regards external border control.[170]

As always, it should be recalled that the Court of Justice has also recognized the existence of other rights as part of the EU general principles, in particular the rights to dignity and integrity,[171] which may be relevant to detention conditions or the conditions of removal, or as a substantive ground to resist expulsion (ie because of the treatment the person concerned might suffer in the country of destination). These rights are also protected in the EU Charter, and in CJEU case law.[172]

Finally, to the extent that some of the rights in the ICCPR and the ECHR Protocols do not appear in the EU Charter of Fundamental Rights, there is still an argument that they can be recognized as part of the general principles of EU law regardless. In any event, Member States must uphold their obligations under international human rights treaties which they have ratified.[173]

7.4 Impact of Other EU Law

As with other areas of immigration and asylum law, EU free movement law and EU association agreements have a considerable impact on the issue of irregular migration. EU development policy measures, EU statistics legislation, and EU data protection law are also relevant.[174] Also, as discussed further in Chapter 6 of this volume,

---

[166] On the rule of the ICCPR as a source of the general principles, see for instance Case C-540/03 *EP v Council* [2006] ECR I-5769.

[167] The rule in Art 2 of the Fourth Protocol has been referred to: see I:3.3.1 above.

[168] Art 19(1) of the Charter.

[169] Case C-481/13 *Qurbani*, ECLI:EU:C:2014:2101. On the Convention and EU law generally, see I:5.3.2 above.

[170] See respectively I:5.8, I:5.9 above, I:7.5.3 below, and I:3.6.1 above.

[171] See Cases C-36/02 *Omega* [2004] ECR I-9609 and C-377/98 *Netherlands v Council and EP* [2001] ECR I-7079.

[172] Arts 1 and 3. See also I:5.3 above.   [173] See generally I:2.3 above.

[174] See respectively I:7.9.2, I:7.8, and II:7.3.2.

EU employment law generally applies to third-country nationals—including irregular migrants.

7.4.1 Free movement law

EU free movement law applies both to EU citizens and to their family members, as long as they have exercised free movement rights within the EU. They have the right to move and reside in another Member State pursuant to the Treaty on the Functioning of the European Union (previously the EC Treaty) and/or secondary legislation if they meet the relevant conditions. Since these rights are quite extensive, it is very difficult for EU citizens or their family members to be considered to be irregular migrants in another Member State. A number of specific issues are addressed by the case law and relevant legislation; the latter was codified and recast in Directive 2004/38, which Member States had to apply by 30 April 2006.[175]

The case law of the Court of Justice makes clear that EU citizens and their family members cannot be expelled from another Member State or imprisoned there simply for breaching formal administrative requirements, such as the obligation to hold a residence permit or to report to the authorities, if they satisfy the underlying conditions for the exercise of free movement rights.[176] In particular, third-country national family members who satisfy the underlying conditions cannot be expelled because they entered illegally or because their visa has expired.[177] Directive 2004/38, essentially codifying the prior case law, expressly states that while Member States may impose reporting obligations, sanctions for failure to breach those obligations must be 'proportionate and non-discriminatory'.[178] Also, EU citizens and their family members are entitled to stay in another Member State for up to three months on the basis only of a passport or (for EU citizens) an identity card.[179] After that point, the host Member State may require the EU citizen or family member to register with the authorities, subject again to the proviso that a failure to register can only be punished by 'proportionate and non-discriminatory' sanctions.[180] The Directive expressly states that breaches of the various administrative requirements cannot result in expulsion, and provides for procedural safeguards for persons whose free movement is restricted on grounds other than public policy, public security and public health.[181] Again codifying the case law, the Directive specifies that possession of the various forms of residence documents mentioned in the Directive may 'under no circumstances' be a condition for exercising a right.[182]

---

[175] Dir 2004/38 ([2004] OJ L 229/35). For further details, see 3.4.1, 4.4.1, and 6.4.1 above.

[176] Cases: 48/75 *Royer* [1976] ECR 497; 118/75 *Watson and Bellman* [1976] ECR 1185; 8/77 *Sagulo and Others* [1977] ECR 1495; 157/79 *Pieck* [1980] ECR 2171; C-265/88 *Messner* [1989] ECR 4209; C-363/89 *Roux* [1991] ECR I-273; C-376/89 *Giagounidis* [1991] ECR I-1069; C-215/03 *Oulane* [2005] ECR I-1215; and C-408/03 *Commission v Belgium* [2006] ECR I-2647. See E Guild, 'Who is an Irregular Migrant?' in B Bogusz, et al., eds., *Irregular Migration and Human Rights* (Martinus Nijhoff, 2004), 3. See also Art 3(3) of Directive 64/221 (OJ Spec Ed, 1963–4, 117), which provided expressly that expulsion could not be ordered due to expiry of a passport or identity card.

[177] Case C-459/99 *MRAX* [2002] ECR I-6591.   [178] Art 5(5) of the Directive. See also Art 26.

[179] Art 6 of the Directive; this reproduces provisions in the prior legislation.

[180] Arts 8 and 9 of the Directive. See also Art 26.

[181] Art 15 of the Directive.   [182] Art 25(1) of the Directive.

Furthermore, the Court of Justice has ruled in several cases on the link between irregular migration status and access to social benefits, indicating that there are circumstances in which EU citizenship confers a right of access to benefits, with the result that the conditions for continued residence are satisfied and expulsion cannot be carried out.[183] The Court has also ruled on whether third-country family members with irregular migration status can nonetheless rely on EU free movement law once they become part of the family of an EU citizen. At one point this case law was unclear,[184] but the Court has now overturned prior case law and clearly established that family members can rely on their connection with the sponsor regardless of their irregular immigration status, even if they were irregular migrants before they even met the sponsor and formed a family relationship.[185]

The 2004 Directive has substantially changed the rules concerning expulsion on grounds of public policy, public security, or public health.[186] Previously, these rules were set out in Directive 64/221.[187] The substantive provisions of the 1964 Directive, supplemented by extensive jurisprudence of the Court of Justice,[188] specified that it applied even where a person was not legally resident.[189] An expulsion could not be used to 'service economic ends'.[190] Also, expulsions on grounds of public security or public policy must be based 'exclusively' on the 'personal conduct' of the individual, and 'previous criminal convictions' must not 'in themselves' constitute grounds for expulsion,[191] although a host Member State may request another Member State to furnish the police records of a particular individual.[192] 'Personal conduct' may entail association with an organization; the organization need not necessarily be banned, although it must be subject to repressive measures by the State, and the definition of 'public policy' may differ between Member States, subject to supervision by the Court of Justice.[193] Moreover, the 'personal conduct' criterion means that Member States cannot expel persons as a general deterrent to other foreigners who might commit criminal activities, but only

---

[183] See particularly Cases: C-85/96 *Martinez Sala* [1998] ECR I-2691; C-184/99 *Grzelczyk* [2001] ECR I-6193; C-138/02 *Collins* [2004] ECR I-2703; C-456/02 *Trojani* [2004] ECR I-7572; C-209/03 *Bidar* [2005] ECR I-2119; C-258/04 *Ionnidis* [2005] ECR I-8275; and C-406/04 *De Cuyper* [2006] I-6947. See also C-22/08 and C-23/08 *Vatsouras and Koupatantze* [2009] ECR I-4585, and E Szyszczak, 'Regularising Migration in the European Union' in Bogusz, et al. (n 176 above), 407.

[184] See in particular Case C-109/01 *Akrich* [2003] ECR I-9607.

[185] Case C-127/08 *Metock* [2008] ECR I-6241; see further Case C-60/00 *Carpenter* [2002] ECR I-6279 and *MRAX* (n 177 above). In the interim see also Cases C-1/05 *Jia* [2007] ECR I-1 and C-291/05 *Eind* [2007] ECR I-10719.

[186] Arts 27–33 of the Directive. On these provisions, see E Guild, S Peers, and J Tomkin, *The EU Citizenship Directive: A Commentary* (OUP, 2014), ch 6.

[187] N 176 above. See also the Commission's report on the derogations from free movement law (COM (1999) 372, 19 July 1999).

[188] See in particular *Van Duyn* (n 162 above), and Cases: 67/74 *Bonsignore* [1975] ECR 297; 36/75 *Rutili* [1975] ECR 1219; 30/77 *Bouchereau* [1977] ECR 1999; *Adoui and Cornuaille* (n 162 above); C-348/96 *Calfa* [1999] ECR I-11; C-100/01 *Olazabal* [2002] ECR I-10981; C-482/01 and C-493/01 *Orfanopolous and Olivieri* [2004] ECR I-5257; and C-441/02 *Commission v Germany* [2006] ECR I-3449.

[189] Case C-50/06 *Commission v Netherlands* [2007] ECR I-4383. Similarly, there are specific safeguards in the Directive (Arts 14 and 15) applicable to those who might be expelled because they do not (or arguably do not) meet the economic conditions for free movement, for example as in Case C-333/13 *Dano*, ECLI:EU:C:2014:2358.

[190] Art 2(2) of the Directive.   [191] Art 3(1) and 3(2) of the Directive.

[192] Art 5(2) of the Directive. On criminal records, see further II:3.6.1.4.

[193] *Van Duyn* and *Adoui and Cornuaille*, n 162 above.

following a consideration of the personal circumstances of the particular individual.[194] Expulsion of non-nationals does not infringe the principle of non-discrimination, since it is generally not possible for a State to expel its own nationals.[195] A Member State may limit an individual to part of its territory only in certain circumstances, in particular where such a measure would be comparable to measures which could be imposed against its own nationals.[196] The concept of 'public policy' entails a requirement that the person concerned is a genuine and sufficiently serious threat affecting a fundamental interest of society; as the person concerned must be a 'present' threat, his or her past conduct is only·decisive where it indicates a propensity to repeat the same actions in future.[197] An automatic expulsion for life following a conviction for specific crimes is therefore a breach of the EU rules.[198] As for public health, expulsion on such grounds can only take place in relation to specified illnesses and only before the issue of the first residence permit.[199]

The 1964 Directive also included procedural rights, in particular specifying that a decision to grant or refuse an initial residence permit had to be taken within six months; the individual could remain on the territory in the meantime.[200] Individuals had to be informed of the grounds of their expulsion, unless this was contrary to State security interests, and informed officially of the decision expelling them, with a period of a least fifteen days or (if they already had a residence permit) one month to leave the territory.[201] The Directive required that an expellee had remedies equal to those of a national challenging administrative acts,[202] and at the very least, where there were limited or non-existent rights of appeal, an expulsion decision could not be taken until the opinion of an independent competent authority had been obtained, except in cases of urgency.[203] These procedural rules also were also interpreted in extensive jurisprudence of the Court of Justice.[204]

The 2004 Directive amended the substantive criteria in the 1964 Directive by adding, as derived from the Court's jurisprudence, an express reference to the principle of proportionality and the requirement that the person concerned constitute a sufficiently serious individual threat to public policy.[205] Also, the later Directive expressly specifies that factors such as length of residence and degree of integration must be taken into account when deciding on an expulsion.[206] A new point is that there is a more precise

---

[194] *Bouchereau*, n 188 above; see also Case C-50/06, n 189 above.   [195] See I:7.3 above.

[196] *Rutili* and *Olazabal*, n 188 above.   [197] *Bonsignore*, n 188 above.

[198] *Calfa*, n 188 above.   [199] Art 4 and Annex to the Directive.

[200] Art 5(1) of the Directive. For a breach of this provision, see Case C-157/03 *Commission v Spain* [2005] ECR I-2911.

[201] Arts 6 and 7 of the Directive.   [202] Art 8 of the Directive.

[203] Art 9(1) of the Directive, concerning expulsion following the issue of a first residence permit. Where a permit had not yet been issued, Art 9(2) gave the person concerned the right to request the opinion of this competent authority.

[204] See: *Rutili* (n 188 above); *Royer* (n 176 above); Case 98/79 *Pecastaing* [1980] ECR 691; Case 131/79 *Santillo* [1980] ECR 1585; *Adoui and Cornuaille* (n 162 above); Joined Cases C-297/88 and C-197/89 *Dzodzi* [1990] ECR I-3763; Case C-175/94 *Gallagher* [1995] ECR I-4253; *Shingara and Radiom* (n 162 above); Case C-357/98 *Yiadom* [2000] ECR I-9265; *MRAX* (n 177 above); *Orfanopolous and Olivieri* (n 188 above); Case C-136/03 *Dorr and Unal* [2005] ECR I-4759; and the judgment in Case C-441/02 (n 188 above).

[205] Art 27(2) of the Directive. On proportionality, see para 99 of the judgment in *Orfanopolous and Olivieri* (n 188 above).

[206] Art 28(1) of the Directive. Again, see para 99 of the judgment in *Orfanopolous and Olivieri* (n 188 above).

degree of protection for EU citizens and their family members who have resided for a longer period: permanent residents can only be expelled 'on serious grounds of public policy or public security' and EU citizens who are minors or resident for over ten years can only be expelled on 'imperative grounds of public security'.[207] Expulsion on grounds of public health is now only possible within three months of arrival, although the substantive public health grounds have been amended and medical checks during the first three months are now expressly permitted.[208]

As for procedural rules, the notification requirements have been clarified and all persons now have one month to leave the territory (except in urgent cases) if expelled.[209] Individuals are entitled to judicial (and possibly also administrative review) of the merits and legality of any expulsion decision, and subject to certain exceptions, the expulsion cannot be carried out if the expellee applies for an interim suspension of the order pending a decision on the appeal.[210] Expulsion orders have to be reviewed after three years to determine if the grounds motivating them are still valid.[211] Finally, if there is a delay in enforcement of the expulsion order of over two years, Member States must re-examine its validity before executing it.[212]

Interpreting the rules on expulsion in the Directive,[213] the CJEU has ruled that 'public policy' may encompass repayment of tax debts, but not private debts (given the existence of an EU legal framework dealing with the latter issue), and that a criminal conviction in a third State was not sufficient in itself to justify restricting free movement of persons.[214] The Court has taken account of the length of stay on the territory generally, noting that there would have to be very good reasons to expel someone who has spent his childhood and youth in the host State.[215] As for the specific rules on enhanced protection against expulsion, the CJEU has ruled that a drug dealing offence is a 'serious ground of public policy or public security' which might justify expulsion of a permanent resident, and the further additional protection for EU citizens who have resided in the host State might be lost due to departure; the national court has to make an overall assessment of the continuing degree of links to the host State.[216] In the latter case, the ground for expulsion on the basis of an 'imperative threat to public security'

---

[207] Art 28(2) and (3) of the Directive. On the concept of 'permanent residence', which was introduced by the Directive, see I:6.4.1 above.

[208] Art 29 of the Directive.   [209] Art 30 of the Directive.   [210] Art 31 of the Directive.

[211] Art 32 of the Directive. See _Adoui and Cornuaille_, para 12, and _Shingara and Radiom_, paras 38–44 (both n 162 above).

[212] Art 33 of the Directive. See _Orfanopolous and Olivieri_ (n 188 above), paras 77–82.

[213] Note that questions also arise where a third-country national parent of a child who is a national of the host Member State has the right to stay in that State due to the judgment in _Ruiz Zambrano_ (Case C-34/09 [2011] ECR I-1177; see further I:6.4.1 above). Can such parents be expelled for criminal offences, and if so, in what circumstances? See Cases C-165/14 _Rendon Marin_ and C-304/14 _CS_, both pending.

[214] Cases: C-430/10 _Gaydarov_ [2011] ECR I-11637; C-434/10 _Aladzhov_ [2011] ECR I-11659; and C-249/11 _Byankov_, ECLI:EU:C:2012:608. Nor can free movement be restricted due to a breach of immigration law committed prior to the EU citizen's host State joining the EU (Case C-33/07 _Jipa_ [2008] ECR I-5157). All of these cases concern restrictions on _exit_, but would apply equally to expulsion. For details of the EU rules on cross-border private debt collection, see ch 8 of volume 2.

[215] Case C-145/09 _Tsakouridis_ [2010] ECR I-11979.

[216] Case C-145/09 _Tsakouridis_, ibid. Note also that periods of imprisonment do not count for the acquisition of permanent residence status, or for the enhanced protection after ten years' residence: Cases C-400/12 _G_, ECLI:EU:C:2014:9 and C-378/12 _Onuekwere_, ECLI:EU:C:2014:13.

could be satisfied where the EU citizen was involved in drug dealing or sexual offences against a child; it is relevant that the offences in question are listed as serious crimes in Article 83 TFEU.[217] As for the procedural rules, the CJEU has clarified in detail the balance that must be struck between public security concerns and the EU citizen's right to an effective challenge to an expulsion decision.[218]

A Commission report on the application of Directive 2004/38 stated that all Member States except Ireland have set up a registration system applicable to EU citizens and their family members.[219] Thirteen Member States do not comply with the provision of the Directive which rules out expulsion as the automatic consequence of an application for social assistance, and four Member States make the right of residence conditional upon lawful entry. Implementation of the rules concerning expulsions is 'often insufficient or incomplete'; in particular, two Member States provide for automatic expulsion for certain crimes, and Italy increases the length of detention for irregular migrants who commit crimes. The Commission's guidance on the application of the Directive claims that 'persistent petty criminality' could in some cases provide a ground for expulsion.[220]

As for the provision of the Directive that permits expulsion on grounds of 'abuse' or 'fraud',[221] the Commission guidance argues that 'fraud' constitutes a conviction for the use of forged documents or false representation of material facts, while an 'abuse' constitutes artificial conduct for the sole purpose of obtaining a right, while not complying with the purpose of EU law. A 'marriage of convenience' (also ruled out by the Directive) is a marriage agreed for the sole purpose of obtaining free movement rights, but a marriage cannot be regarded as such purely because it confers an immigration advantage. There can be no systematic checks on all third-country nationals, or all members of a particular ethnic group, but Member States' authorities can still link their checks to 'certain characteristics'. The communication offers 'indicative' lists of behaviour which suggests that a marriage is genuine on the one hand, or a marriage of convenience on the other, and of behaviour which suggests whether or not a move to another Member State has the sole purpose of evading national law. The burden of proof in asserting fraud or abuse is on national authorities. Subsequently, the Commission released a Handbook providing more detailed guidance on the concept of a 'marriage of convenience'.[222] Time will tell whether the Court of Justice agrees with the Commission's analysis. In the meantime, the CJEU has ruled that the 'abuse' clause can only be used in specific cases, not against those categories of people whose behaviour is presumed to be abusive.[223]

It should also be recalled that the Court of Justice has ruled that the Schengen *acquis*, and in particular the Schengen Information System, is subject to the application of Community law (as it was then), inter alia, free movement law.[224] While the Court's

---

[217] *Tsakouridis*, n 215 above, and Case C-348/09 *I*, ECLI:EU:C:2012:300. On Article 83 TFEU, see ch 5 of volume 2.

[218] Case C-300/11 *ZZ*, ECLI:EU:C:2013:363.   [219] COM (2008) 840, 10 Dec 2008.

[220] COM (2009) 313, 2 July 2009.   [221] Art 35, Dir 2004/38.

[222] SWD (2014) 284, 26 Sep 2014; see also COM (2014) 604, 26 Sep 2014.

[223] Case C-202/13 *McCarthy*, ECLI:EU:C:2014:2450.

[224] Case C-503/03 *Commission v Spain* [2006] ECR I-1097. See further I:2.4.2, I:3.4.1, and I:3.6.1 above. This judgment has now been integrated into the legislation establishing the second-generation SIS, which began operations in 2013: see I:3.7 above.

ruling concerned the specific issue of visas and borders, the judgment would also be applicable by analogy to expulsion proceedings carried out on the basis of an SIS listing.

Finally, EU free movement law (Article 56 TFEU, formerly Article 49 EC) also grants to EU employers the right to post their third-country national employees to another Member State within the framework of the provision of services.[225] The Court has not yet delivered a judgment on whether Article 56 entails the right to post workers without the need to obtain visas or residence permits (thus preventing such workers from being considered irregular migrants in such circumstances), or whether expulsion of such workers on grounds of public policy, public security, or public health pursuant to Articles 52 and 62 TFEU (formerly Articles 46 and 55 EC) is subject to substantive and procedural rules identical to those applicable to free movement of EU citizens and their family members. However, the Court has ruled that an automatic refusal of entry and residence permits for a posted worker who has not obtained a visa is a breach of the Treaty rights.[226] By analogy, it is arguable that since entry and residence onto the territory is inherent in the freedom to provide services, any penalties imposed due to any failure to obtain any necessary permits must be proportionate, and in particular cannot entail expulsion or imprisonment. Logically, since the freedom to post workers derives directly from the Treaty, individual posted workers could only be expelled pursuant to substantive and procedural rules equivalent to those applying to EU citizens and their family members.

7.4.2 Association agreements

The EU's association agreements have implications for the definition of irregular migration.[227] To start with, the European Economic Area (EEA) agreement with Norway, Iceland, and Liechtenstein and the EU-Switzerland agreement on free movement of persons both essentially extend the EU rules on free movement of persons to these States.[228] It should follow that all of the relevant principles derived from EU free movement law, as discussed above, apply to these agreements.

Next, the status of Turkish nationals in the EU is governed by the initial EU-Turkey association agreement (the Ankara Agreement), a Protocol to that agreement dating from 1970, and Decision 1/80 of the EU-Turkey Association Council.[229] Although the Protocol establishes a standstill on national measures which make more restrictive the establishment of Turkish nationals or the supply of services from Turkey, the Court of Justice has ruled that this standstill cannot benefit those who have entered or stayed without

---

[225] Cases: C-43/93 *Van der Elst* [1994] ECR I-3803; C-445/03 *Commission v Luxembourg* [2004] ECR I-10191; C-244/04 *Commission v Germany* [2006] ECR I-885; C-168/04 *Commission v Austria* [2006] ECR I-9041; C-219/08 *Commission v Belgium* [2009] ECR I-9213; and C-91/13 *Essent*, ECLI:EU:C:2014:2206. Also, the EU's services Directive in part addresses this issue. On this Dir and other related issues, see I:6.4.4 above; for further implications of the case law, see I:3.4.1, I:4.4.1, and I:5.4.2 above.

[226] See *Commission v Austria*, n 225 above.

[227] For an overview of the migration provisions of these agreements, see I:6.4.3 above.

[228] Respectively [1994] OJ L 1/1 and [2002] OJ L 114.

[229] The Agreement is published in [1977] OJ L 261/60; the Protocol is published in [1972] JO L 293/1; Decision 1/80 is unpublished in the OJ.

authorization.[230] As for Turkish workers and their family members, they have rights to work and/or reside pursuant to Decision 1/80 following periods of employment or residence in a Member State, but that employment or residence must be authorized by the Member State in question; periods accrued solely during purely provisional residence pending expulsion or a decision on the grant of a residence permit do not qualify.[231] Furthermore, these rights cannot be acquired if the worker is convicted of fraud in relation to his or her immigration status.[232] On the other hand, if the entry and residence status of the worker or family member is fundamentally legal, that person cannot be expelled merely for technical breaches of immigration law such as the failure to renew a residence permit on time;[233] the position of Turkish workers and family members on this point is therefore comparable to that of EU citizens.[234] As for the loss of residence on grounds of public policy, public security, and public health, Turkish workers and their family members within the scope of the Decision enjoy substantive and procedural protection at least equivalent to that enjoyed by EU citizens *before* the application of Directive 2004/38,[235] but not the *enhanced* protection in this regard offered by Directive 2004/38.[236]

The Europe Agreements with Central and Eastern European countries, which, inter alia, included provisions on the right of establishment of the self-employed,[237] have since been superseded by membership of the countries concerned, but the case law on these agreements could still be relevant to the establishment provisions of the Stabilization and Association Agreements (SAAs) with Western Balkan States, once those provisions are applied.[238] The Europe Agreements case law specified that since those treaties allowed EU Member States to maintain immigration law restrictions, the right of establishment did not entail the right to enter and begin self-employment without prior authorization.[239] However, the Court of Justice made clear that a later application to exercise freedom of establishment pursuant to the Agreements always had to be considered, regardless of any prior irregular entry or residence.[240]

---

[230] Cases C-37/98 *Savas* [2000] ECR I-2927 (self-employed persons) and Joined Cases C-317/01 and C-369/01 *Abatay and others* [2003] ECR I-12301 (services). On the limits of this exception, see however Case C-16/05 *Tum and Dari* [2007] ECR I-7415 and C-186/10 *Oguz* [2011] ECR I-6957.

[231] Cases C-192/89 *Sevince* [1990] ECR I-3461 and C-237/91 *Kus* [1992] ECR I-6781.

[232] Case C-285/95 *Kol* [1997] ECR I-3095. However, note that the link between the behaviour of the worker and the status of his or her family member is broken after a certain period: see Case C-337/07 *Altun* [2008] ECR I-10323.

[233] Cases C-434/93 *Bozkurt* [1995] ECR I-1475; C-351/95 *Kadiman* [1997] ECR I-2133; C-36/96 *Günaydin* [1997] ECR I-5143; C-98/96 *Ertanir* [1997] ECR I-5179; C-1/97 *Birden* [1998] ECR I-7747; and C-329/97 *Ergat* [2000] ECR I-1487.

[234] See I:7.4.1 above.

[235] Cases C-340/97 *Nazli* [2000] ECR I-957, C-467/02 *Cetinkaya* [2004] ECR I-10895, and *Dorr and Unal* (n 204 above). See also Cases C-373/03 *Aydinli* [2005] ECR I-6181, C-383/03 *Dogan* [2005] ECR I-6237, C-502/04 *Torun* [2006] ECR I-1563, C-325/05 *Derin* [2007] ECR I-6495, and C-349/06 *Polat* [2007] ECR I-8167.

[236] Case C-371/08 *Ziebell* [2011] ECR I-12735.   [237] See further I:6.4.3 above.

[238] [2004] OJ L 84 (Former Yugoslav Republic of Macedonia (FYROM)), [2005] OJ L 26 (Croatia), [2009] OJ L 107 (Albania), [2010] OJ L 108 (Montenegro), [2013] OJ L 278 (Serbia), and [2015] OJ L 164 (Bosnia-Herzegovina). An SAA has also been agreed with Kosovo (COM (2015) 183, 30 Apr 2015), but it is not yet in force. For further detail, see I:3.4.1 above.

[239] See Cases C-235/99 *Kondova* [2001] ECR I-6557, C-257/99 *Barkoci and Malik* [2001] ECR I-6427, C-63/99 *Gloszczuk* [2001] ECR I-6369, C-268/99 *Jany* [2001] ECR I-8615, and C-327/02 *Panayotova* [2004] ECR I-11055.

[240] *Gloszczuk* judgment, para 85; *Kondova* judgment, para 90 (both n 239 above). It is not clear whether the prior breach of immigration law could be taken into account or not when reviewing the fresh application.

If names had been placed in the Schengen Information System as a result of those prior offences, resulting in a refusal of entry to exercise the right of establishment on that ground alone, the Europe Agreements would arguably have been breached.[241] Furthermore, the right of establishment under the Agreements could be restricted on grounds of public policy, public security, or public health; the Court of Justice ruled that this has the same substantive meaning as the restrictions permitted by EU free movement law.[242]

Finally, the Euro-Mediterranean treaties with the three Maghreb States (Algeria, Morocco, and Tunisia) provide, inter alia, for equality in working conditions,[243] and the Court of Justice has ruled that this right prevents Member States from terminating legal residence as long as a Maghreb worker is legally employed, except on grounds of public security, public policy, or public health, and that this apparently confers substantive and procedural protection equivalent to EU free movement law, at least before the application of Directive 2004/38.[244] This raises the question of whether all association agreements which give a right to equal treatment in working conditions must be interpreted the same way. This would mean that equivalent protection is granted pursuant to the Stabilization and Association Agreements, the EU-Turkey Agreement, the Partnership and Cooperation Agreements with ex-Soviet States, and the Cotonou Convention with African, Caribbean, and Pacific States.[245]

7.5 Prevention of Irregular Migration

Prevention of irregular migration is obviously more attractive to States than detecting and expelling persons once they have already arrived, provided that it can be accomplished at a reasonable cost. One method of reducing costs for the State is to transfer the liability for controlling entry to the private sector, in particular passenger transport companies, as regards the requirement to carry visas and valid travel documents.[246] But this strategy, if effective in practice, is likely to lead to an increase in entry via unofficial means of transport, in particular by means of smuggling. Smuggling of persons may in turn be connected to trafficking in persons, where there is a lack of valid consent. In order to deter the perceived increase in both smuggling and trafficking, the EU has resorted to measures setting out criminal sanctions.

It should be noted that, apart from the specific issues of smuggling and trafficking in migrants and the separate issue of sanctioning employers for hiring irregular migrants,[247] no provisions of EU law lay down express rules on criminalization *or* decriminalization in relation to immigration law; in particular there is no EU requirement to criminalize

---

[241] See by analogy Case C-503/03 (n 224 above).

[242] *Jany* judgment, paras 58–62 (n 239 above). Arguably, following the case law on the EU-Turkey agreement, it must also follow that the same procedural protection applies.

[243] Tunisia: [1998] OJ L 97; Morocco: [2000] OJ L 70; Algeria: [2005] OJ L 265. Previous agreements with these states with similar clauses applied from 1978.

[244] Cases C-416/96 *El-Yassini* [1999] ECR I-1209 and C-97/05 *Gattoussi* [2006] ECR I-11917 .

[245] The Court has apparently confirmed that the principle applies to the EU-Turkey agreement: Case C-4/05 *Guzeli* [2006] ECR I-10279.

[246] On visa and border control rules, see chs 3 and 4 of this volume.   [247] See I:7.6.1 below.

(or to decriminalize) migrants who have breached immigration law as such. However, the case law on the EU's Returns Directive (discussed below) sets out some limits on the penalties that can be imposed for irregular migration.[248] Furthermore, it should not be forgotten that Article 31 of the Geneva Convention on refugee status exempts refugees who have entered or stayed irregularly from penalties under certain circumstances.[249] Moreover, irregular migration (of whatever type) through a number of Member States consecutively falls within the scope of the EU's double jeopardy rules, which preclude in principle prosecution by more than one Member State for the same act.[250]

7.5.1 Carrier sanctions

The issue of carrier sanctions was initially addressed by Article 26(1)(a) of the Schengen Convention,[251] which requires carriers to 'take responsibility for' third-country nationals whom the carriers have brought to the external borders of the Community by air, sea, or land, but who are then refused entry. The carriers, at the border authorities' request, must return such persons to a third state as specified in the Convention, comprising either the state from which that person came, the state issuing that person a travel document, or any other state willing to guarantee entry of that person. Article 26(1)(b) of the Convention requires sea or air carriers to ensure that third-country nationals have the travel documents required for entry. To enforce this obligation, Article 26(2) of the Convention requires Member States to impose (unspecified) penalties on carriers which transport, by air or sea, third-country nationals who do not possess the necessary travel documents from a third state to their territories. Article 26(3) extends the provisions of Article 26(1)(b) and (3) to transport by coach, but not to other forms of land transport. Also, Article 26(1) and (2) are both 'subject to' the Geneva Convention on the status of refugees and its Protocol; Article 26(2) furthermore applies 'in accordance with [Member States'] constitutional law'.

Article 26 of the Convention was later supplemented by Directive 2001/51, which Member States had to implement by 11 February 2003.[252] Luxembourg was condemned by the Court of Justice for failure to implement this Directive on time,[253] and the Commission withdrew cases brought against the Netherlands and Belgium following late implementation.[254]

First of all, the Directive extends the personal scope of carriers' obligations as compared to the Schengen Convention. Carriers must also take responsibility for and return persons to *persons in transit to another State*, if that State refuses to admit them and sends them back, or if a carrier refused to transport them onward to that State.[255] Secondly, the Directive then extends the material scope of carriers' obligations: if they cannot effect return of persons immediately, they must find means of returning them

---

[248] See I:7.7.1 below.   [249] See I:7.3 above.   [250] See II:6.8.   [251] [2000] OJ L 239.
[252] Art 7(1) of the Directive ([2001] OJ L 187/45). The Dir and the Convention provision have not been codified. There is no obligation to review implementation of the Dir (or the Convention provision) by Member States, and the Commission has not in fact conducted such a review.
[253] Case C-449/04 *Commission v Luxembourg*, judgment of 21 July 2005 (unreported).
[254] Cases C-460/04 *Commission v Netherlands* and C-516/04 *Commission v Belgium*.
[255] Art 2.

with another carrier.[256] Failing that, they must pay for the costs of the stay and return of that person. Thirdly, the Directive harmonizes, although to a limited degree, the level of the penalties applying to carriers: Member States can opt for a maximum amount of at least €5,000 per person; or a minimum amount of €3,000 per person; or a lump sum with a maximum amount of at least €500,000.[257] A declaration in the Council minutes attempts to define carriers' obligations further; it asserts that for the purpose of applying the Directive, 'the Council has agreed that using an obvious forgery or obvious usurpation is equivalent to the absence of a travel document', although it is up to each Member State to determine whether such forgeries or usurpations are detectable.[258] But it should be recalled that for the purposes of EU law, the legal effect of statements in the minutes of Council meetings is very limited.[259]

The original French initiative had proposed an exemption from carrier sanctions for cases where a third-country national is 'admitted to the territory for asylum purposes'.[260] However, the final text provides only that the obligation to impose penalties is 'without prejudice to Member States' obligations in cases where a third-country national seeks international protection'.[261] The Directive does provide that Member States must grant 'effective rights of defence and appeal' against proceedings which may give rise to penalties,[262] but this does not apply to the other obligations imposed on carriers by the Directive and there is no obligation to ensure that procedures are in place for passengers to bring disputes against the carriers, or against the Member State.

This replacement of an enforceable asylum exception with fuzzy ambiguity is the biggest disappointment in this Directive. Although Article 26 of the Schengen Convention (and therefore presumably the 2001 Directive, which supplements it) is still expressly subject to the Geneva Convention and the New York Protocol, it remains unclear what this reference to the Geneva Convention means in practice. Furthermore, the Directive has likely led to increased difficulties for persons who wish to challenge the private enforcement of immigration law, because the extension of personal and material scope of carriers' obligations has increased the complications involved. It is possible for Carrier A to bring a person to a Member State, Carrier B to deny him or her entry into another state, and then Carrier C to remove that person to another country. Also, the potential for increased costs under the Directive, without any accompanying clarity regarding asylum cases, likely further discouraged carriers from transporting likely asylum seekers and thus increased the likelihood that such persons will use illegal means to enter the Union. In fact, at least one delegation expressly admitted that its goal was to deter asylum seekers, arguing that the exemption in the initial proposal 'could make penalties for carriers ineffective and *increase asylum applications*'.[263]

---

[256] Art 3. This appears to apply both to persons refused entry to a Member State pursuant to Art 26(1) of the Convention, and to persons refused entry in transit pursuant to Art 2 of the Directive.

[257] Art 4(1).

[258] See Statement 75/01, in the monthly summary of Council Acts for June 2001 (Council doc 11450/01, 27 Aug 2001).

[259] See, for example, Case C-292/89 *Antonissen* [1991] ECR I-745.

[260] Art 4(3) of initial proposal ([2000] OJ C 269/8).   [261] Art 4(2).   [262] Art 6.

[263] Comments of the German delegation (Council doc 12361/00, 16 Oct 2000).

7.5.2 Passenger data

Directive 2004/82 on passenger data transmission,[264] which further increases the role of passenger transport companies in the enforcement of immigration law, was adopted in April 2004.[265] Member States had to implement the Directive by 5 September 2006.[266]

The objective of this Directive is to improve border controls and to combat irregular immigration by means of transmission of passenger data by carriers in advance to the relevant national authorities.[267] Its core obligation is for carriers (defined as persons or companies providing passenger air transport services) to transmit specified information on passengers who will be crossing an external border (a border between the Member States and non-EU countries), at the request of external border control authorities, at the latest before the end of check-in of passengers.[268] This obligation comprises nine categories of information: the number and types of travel documents; nationality; full names; date of birth; border crossing point to be used; transport codes; departure and arrival time; total number of passengers carried; and the initial point of embarkation.[269] But compliance with the obligation to transmit information will not exempt carriers from compliance with the carrier sanctions rules in the Schengen Convention and Directive 2001/55.[270] It should be stressed that the obligation to transmit information apparently applies to information on all passengers, not just to information on non-EU nationals.

If carriers fail in their obligations and, due to fault, do not transmit data or transmit incorrect or false data, Member States must impose penalties upon them. The penalties must comprise either a maximum of at least €5,000 per journey or a minimum of €3,000 per journey.[271] Member States are free to impose further sanctions, such as a withdrawal of an operating licence, for very serious infringements.[272] But Member States must ensure that carriers have effective rights of defence and appeal.[273] These rules can be compared to the carrier sanctions Directive, which (as outlined above) provides for a third sanctions option for Member States, requires the sanctions to be applied per individual (rather than per journey), has a lower threshold for applying further sanctions, and provides for a vague safeguard where a person seeks international protection.

As for data protection,[274] the information must be transmitted to external border control authorities for the purpose of facilitating checks with the objective of combating illegal immigration. These authorities shall save the data in a temporary file and shall delete it within twenty-four hours, unless the data are needed later for fulfilling the statutory functions of those authorities in accordance with national law and subject to the EU's data protection Directive.[275] Member States must oblige carriers to delete the information within twenty-four hours, and to inform the passengers on the

---

[264] For further information on the issue of passenger data transmission within the EU, see the Statewatch observatory on the issue: <http://www.statewatch.org/eu-pnrobservatory.htm>.
[265] [2004] OJ L 261/24. [266] Art 7(1). All further references in this sub-section are to this Dir.
[267] Art 1. [268] Art 3(1). For the definitions, see Art 2(a) and (b). [269] Art 3(2).
[270] Art 3(3). [271] Art 4(1). [272] Art 4(2). [273] Art 5. [274] Art 6.
[275] Dir 95/46 ([1995] OJ L 281/31). On this Dir (and the planned replacement Reg), see further II:7.3.2.

information being transmitted. Furthermore, Member States may also use the data for law enforcement purposes, in accordance with national law and subject to the data protection Directive. It should be noted that the EU will soon adopt legislation on the law enforcement use of passenger name records.[276]

This Directive is highly questionable for several reasons. It is not necessary or proportionate to require transmission of information on EU citizens or their family members, and to permit continued storage of their data for 'law enforcement' purposes. In fact, this is probably not valid pursuant to EU free movement law, given the very limited grounds upon which EU citizens or their family members can be refused entry or expelled.[277] The continued storage of data on any individual should not be permitted for 'law enforcement' purposes in general, without a specific limitation to cases where it is necessary to keep the information for an ongoing or imminent criminal investigation or prosecution. Such a general exception, depending on the interpretation of the data protection Directive, could be interpreted to permit the compilation of a database on all travellers' movements across the EU external borders. Moreover, vague references to the collection of data for such general purposes are not permissible in light of the case law of the European Court of Human Rights on Article 8 ECHR, requiring that accessible legislation must set out the specific cases when data is going to be collected and the uses to which the data is to be put.[278]

Finally, it should be noted that Directive 2004/82 is a separate measure from another controversial issue, an EC-US agreement on the transfer of passenger data to the United States. The EP had referred this planned treaty to the Court of Justice,[279] but the Council went ahead and concluded it anyway;[280] the EP then decided to bring an annulment action against both the conclusion of the treaty and the Commission's decision that the United States provided adequate protection for this transfer of personal data, but the Court of Justice rejected this argument.[281] Also, the EU has agreed subsequent treaties on this issue with the USA, Australia, and Canada; the last of these treaties is being reviewed by the CJEU.[282] Because these treaties concern the use of data for the purposes of law enforcement, not immigration control, they are discussed further in Chapter 7 of the second volume of this book.[283]

7.5.3 Facilitation of unauthorized entry and residence

In order to address the issue of smuggling of persons, Article 27(1) of the Schengen Convention provided that Member States 'undertake to impose appropriate penalties

---

[276] Proposed Directive on passenger name records (COM (2011) 32, 2 Feb 2011), agreed in Dec 2015. See further II:7.6.3.
[277] See I:7.4.1 above and further I:3.4.1 and I:4.4.1 above.   [278] See further II:7.3.1.
[279] *Opinion 1/2004*, withdrawn.
[280] See [2004] OJ L 183/83 and [2004] OJ L 235/11. For more information on the EU/US agreement, see the Statewatch observatory on this issue, online at: <http://www.statewatch.org/pnrobservatory.htm>.
[281] Joined Cases C-317/04 and C-318/04, *EP v Council and Commission* [2006] ECR I-4721.
[282] Respectively [2007] OJ L 204/18, [2008] OJ L 213/47, and COM (2013) 528, 18 July 2013. See *Opinion 1/15*, pending. A previous EC/Canada agreement ([2006] OJ L 82/14) has expired.
[283] II:7.6.3.

on any person who, for financial gain, assists or tries to assist an alien to enter or reside within the territory of one of the Contracting Parties in breach of that Contracting Party's laws on the entry and residence of aliens'. Article 27(2) and 27(3) were supplementary measures. According to Article 27(2), a Member State which was informed of actions as defined in Article 27(1) which are in breach of the law of another Member State had to inform that Member State. Article 27(3) provided that if one Member State asked another to prosecute actions referred to in Article 27(1) on the grounds that its laws had been breached, it had to specify by official means which provisions of its law was concerned.

Article 27 of the Schengen Convention was subsequently repealed by Directive 2002/90 and a related third-pillar Framework Decision as from 5 December 2004,[284] when Member States had to implement both measures.[285] The Commission brought infringement proceedings against Member States which missed the deadline to implement the Directive.[286] It should be noted that the EU's mutual recognition measures have generally required Member States to relinquish the dual criminality principle as regards the crime of the facilitation of illegal entry or residence.[287]

Reflecting the allocation of Article 27 of the Schengen Convention between the previous first and third pillars, the Directive defines facilitation of illegal entry, residence, or movement, while the Framework Decision sets out the criminal penalties that must apply, along with rules on jurisdiction. However, in light of subsequent judgments of the Court of Justice on the Community's competence to adopt criminal law measures, it might be argued that aspects of the Framework Decision, as regards the definition of criminal offences, fell at the time within Community competence.[288] Following the entry into force of the Treaty of Lisbon, the entire Framework Decision is now within the scope of Article 83(2) TFEU.[289]

The Directive requires Member States to impose sanctions upon any person who intentionally assists a third-country national 'to enter or transit across' a Member State 'in breach of the laws of the State concerned on the entry or transit' of foreigners,[290] and any person 'who, for financial gain, intentionally assists' a third-country national to 'reside within' a Member State in breach of its national laws on residence.[291] Identical sanctions must also be applied to instigators or accomplices and those who attempt to commit the activities in question.[292] There is a 'humanitarian' exemption, applying 'where the aim of the behaviour is to provide humanitarian assistance to the person concerned'. But this exception is *optional*, and only applies to the first category of offence.[293] However, the subsequent Directive concerning sanctions against employers

---

[284] Directive 2002/90 ([2002] OJ L 328/17) and Framework Decision 2002/946 ([2002] OJ L 328/1). On the repeal of Art 27 of the Convention, see Art 5 of the Directive and Art 10 of the Framework Decision.

[285] Art 4(1) of the Directive and Art 9(1) of the Framework Decision.

[286] Cases C-48/06 *Commission v Luxembourg* (judgment of 7 Dec 2006, unreported) and C-485/06 *Commission v Germany* (withdrawn).

[287] See volume 2, ch 3.

[288] Cases C-176/03 *Commission v Council* [2005] ECR I-7879 and C-440/05 *Commission v Council* [2007] ECR I-9097; see II:5.4.1.

[289] See further I:7.2.4 above and II:5.4.1.

[290] Art 1(1)(a) of the Directive.   [291] Art 1(1)(b) of the Directive.   [292] Art 2 of the Directive.

[293] Art 1(2) of the Directive.

for hiring irregular migrants specifies that assistance to those migrants in order to lodge complaints against their employers must *not* be considered to be facilitation of unauthorized residence for the purpose of the 2002 Directive.[294] Furthermore, the 2014 Regulation on maritime surveillance states in its preamble that a shipmaster and crew should not face criminal sanctions for rescuing migrants and bringing them to a place of safety.[295]

The Framework Decision requires Member States to punish all the conduct defined in the Directive by 'effective, proportionate and dissuasive criminal penalties, which may entail extradition',[296] accompanied if appropriate by confiscation of transport, prohibition of practice of an occupation, or deportation.[297] According to the CJEU, Member States are entitled to prosecute for smuggling where third-country nationals have been assisted to obtain visas fraudulently, even if those visas have not been annulled by another Member State.[298] In cases of unauthorized entry or transit, there must be a maximum sentence of at least eight years if the activity was committed by a criminal organization as defined in another EU measure or if committed while endangering a would-be migrant's life.[299] Member States can reduce the maximum sentence to at least six years if necessary to preserve the coherence of national penalty systems.[300]

There are also standard provisions on liability of legal persons and jurisdiction;[301] the latter rules require Member States to take jurisdiction where an act is carried out on its territory, by one of its nationals, or for the benefit of a legal person established in its territory.[302] Member States can derogate from the second and third jurisdictional rules if they inform the Council.[303] In any event, each Member State must either prosecute or extradite when the relevant conduct has been committed by its own nationals outside its territory.[304] The provisions of Articles 27(2) and 27(3) of the Convention were reproduced in the Framework Decision without any amendment.[305] The entire Framework Decision is 'without prejudice to the protection afforded refugees and asylum seekers in accordance with international law on refugees or other international instruments relating to human rights', in particular Articles 31 and 33 of the Geneva Convention on the status of refugees.[306]

Compared to Article 27 of the Schengen Convention, the Directive broadened the scope of the obligation to impose penalties on facilitators of irregular entry or residence. Most importantly, it requires Member States to impose penalties even where

---

[294] Art 13(3) of Dir 2009/52 ([2009] OJ L 168/24); see further I:7.6.1 below.
[295] Recital 7, Reg 656/2014 ([2014] OJ L 189/93); see further I:3.10.1 above.
[296] Art 1(1), Framework Decision.   [297] Art 1(2), Framework Decision.
[298] Case C-82/12 PPU *Vo*, ECLI:EU:C:2012:202. On the visa legislation relevant to this case, see I:4.7 above.
[299] Art 1(3), Framework Decision, referring to a 1998 Joint Action ([1998] OJ L 351/1) on organized crime, which has since been replaced by a Framework Decision ([2008] OJ L 300/42).
[300] Art 1(4), Framework Decision.
[301] Arts 2 to 5, Framework Decision. For an analysis of such standard provisions in this and other EC and EU criminal law measures, see II:5.5.2.
[302] Art 4(1), Framework Decision.   [303] Art 4(2) and (3), Framework Decision.
[304] Art 5; this provision is largely irrelevant in light of the Framework Decision on the European Arrest Warrant; see further II:3.5.
[305] Art 7 of the Framework Decision.
[306] Art 6 of the Framework Decision. See I:5.3 and I:7.3 on these provisions.

the facilitators do *not* facilitate irregular entry for financial gain. It also extends the penalty obligation to irregular transit alongside irregular entry or residence. Moreover, Member States' obligation extends beyond persons attempting to commit the infringement, to include also instigators and accomplices.[307] On top of this, the Framework Decision now defines more precisely the minimum level of sanctions which Member States must impose. But as we have seen, there is an optional exception from liability in the Directive as regards the 'entry or transit' infringement, and a general safeguard clause in the Framework Decision.

According to the Commission's report on the application of the Framework Decision,[308] Member States were broadly in compliance with the measure, although some had not clearly distinguished between trafficking and smuggling in persons. However, the range of penalties imposed by Member States was wide, and the Commission therefore thought there was scope for considering a greater degree of harmonization. The Commission was not aware that any Member States had made notifications regarding derogations from the jurisdiction rules.[309] As for the safeguard clause, the Commission had no information on the application of this clause, but there was 'no indication that the international law on refugees has been violated as a result of the implementation of this Framework Decision'. Of course, if Member States were responsible for such violations, one would hardly expect them to inform the Commission. Overall, the Commission found it difficult to assess national implementation of the Framework Decision in practice in the absence of relevant statistics.[310]

Do these measures strike the right balance between a justifiable attempt to ensure the effective application of immigration control, and the need to ensure that persons needing international protection are still able to seek it effectively? An optional humanitarian exception is obviously not worth much and clearly shows some contempt for the very humanitarian principle which supposedly inspires it. Moreover, the vague 'saving clause' referring to the Geneva Convention would only assist refugees and asylum seekers, while leaving intact the effect of the two measures on the persons who facilitate the entry of those persons into the Member States. Should persons who assist persons in need of international protection be subject to criminal sanctions, in particular when they do not do so for financial gain? Without a clear exemption for all cases in which a person claims asylum, there is a high risk that these two measures will impact negatively upon refugees and asylum seekers.

The Directive and Framework Decision can be compared to the Protocol on smuggling of persons attached to the UN Convention on organized crime, which has been ratified by every Member State except Ireland, and also concluded by the EU.[311] The

---

[307] On these extended forms of liability, see the analysis in II:5.5.2.

[308] COM (2006) 770, 6 Dec 2006, adopted pursuant to Art 9(2) of the Framework Decision. There is no obligation to review implementation of the Dir by Member States, and the Commission has not in fact conducted such a review.

[309] In fact, two declarations are publicly available, from Denmark (Council doc 14401/05, 22 Nov 2005) and Hungary (Council doc 13754/05, 26 Oct 2005).

[310] On the statistics issue generally, see I:7.8 below.

[311] [2001] OJ L 30/44 (signature of Protocol); [2006] OJ L 262/24 and 34 (conclusion of Protocol). The Protocol entered into force on 28 Jan 2004. On the details of ratification by the Member States, see Appendix I. The EU also concluded the main UN Convention on organized crime ([2004] OJ L 261/69).

Protocol differs from the EC/EU measures in particular in that the obligation to criminalize acts only applies where those acts are committed for financial gain, and that aggravating circumstances include the inhuman or degrading treatment, including exploitation, of migrants, rather than acts carried out within the framework of a criminal organization. Also, there is no requirement to provide for specific potential sentences when the aggravating circumstances apply, States must also criminalize the creation of false documents for the purpose of smuggling, migrants cannot be criminalized for the fact of being subject to conduct to be criminalized pursuant to the Protocol, and the Protocol sets out detailed rules concerning the smuggling of migrants by sea.[312]

EU policy in this field will be developed in line with an Action Plan on migrant smuggling adopted in 2015.[313] In light of the huge increase in smuggling in recent years, this Plan foresees a revision of the legislation in 2016, to address criminal penalties and exemptions for humanitarian assistance, and the adoption of a Handbook on migrant smuggling in 2017. The EU also launched a military mission which ultimately aims (subject to consent of the Security Council or the Libyan government) to destroy smugglers' boats.[314]

7.5.4 Trafficking in persons

The parallel concern to address the issue of trafficking in persons, which also reflects obligations pursuant to international human rights law to combat slavery and forced labour,[315] led initially to the adoption of a Joint Action in 1997, which also addressed the issue of pornography and prostitution.[316] This was replaced by a Framework Decision, which Member States had to implement by 1 August 2004.[317] That Framework Decision in turn was replaced by Directive 2011/36,[318] which Member States had to apply by 6 April 2013.[319] It should be noted at the outset that neither the 2002 Framework Decision nor the 2011 Directive limit themselves to the issue of persons trafficked for the purposes of prostitution.

The EU has also addressed this issue by adopting a Directive on the status of trafficking victims who assist in prosecutions,[320] as well as a number of soft-law measures,[321]

---

[312] Those rules are reflected in the EU legislation on maritime surveillance, discussed in I:3.10.1 above.

[313] COM (2015) 285, 27 May 2015.

[314] See the CFSP Decisions launching 'EUNAVFORMED' ([2015] OJ L 122/31 and L 157/51).

[315] See I:7.3.1 above.   [316] [1997] OJ L 63/2.

[317] [2004] OJ L 203/1. The other provisions of the Joint Action were replaced by a Framework Decision on sexual exploitation and child pornography ([2004] OJ L 13/44; see further II:5.5 below).

[318] [2011] OJ L 101/1. The Framework Decision on sexual exploitation and child pornography was also replaced by a Directive in 2011 (see II:5.5).

[319] Art 22(1), Directive 2011/36. On the competence to adopt this measure, see I:7.2.4 above.

[320] Dir 2004/81 ([2004] OJ L 261/19); see further I:7.6.2 below.

[321] For instance: Council conclusions on trafficking in persons ([2003] OJ C 137/1); Council resolution on the law enforcement response ([2003] OJ C 260/4); a Commission decision establishing an expert group of advisors ([2003] OJ L 79/25, replaced by [2007] OJ L 277/79); an Action Plan against human trafficking ([2005] OJ C 311/1); Council conclusions of Apr 2006 (press release of JHA Council, 27–8 Apr 2006); reports to the Council as regards trafficking for prostitution and the 2006 World Cup (Council docs 5008/07 and 5006/1/07, 3 Jan and 19 Jan 2007); Council conclusions of Nov 2007 (press release of JHA Council, 8–9 Nov 2007); Council conclusions of June 2009 on an informal network of national rapporteurs (press release

and by concluding the relevant Protocol to the UN Convention on organized crime.[322] In parallel, the Council of Europe agreed a Convention on the issue in 2005; all but one of the Member States have ratified.[323] Moreover, the EU's mutual recognition measures have generally required Member States to relinquish the dual criminality principle as regards the crime of trafficking in human beings,[324] and the Framework Decision (and soon the Directive) on confiscation of criminal proceeds requires Member States to take measures against the proceeds of this crime in certain circumstances.[325] There are also some relevant provisions in the EU's general Framework Decision on the status of victims in criminal proceedings, which was replaced by a Directive from autumn 2015.[326] The EU Commission has also appointed an anti-trafficking coordinator,[327] and published guidelines on the identification of trafficking victims and a guide to victims' rights.[328]

Directive 2011/36 requires Member States to adopt criminal sanctions to combat trafficking in human beings, a concept with a three-part definition.[329] There must be the 'recruitment, transportation, transfer, harbouring, or reception' of a person; there must be a use of force by the person involved (in other words, the use of 'threat or use of force or other forms of coercion, of abduction, of fraud, of the abuse of power or of a position of vulnerability', or payment in return for the consent to transfer control of a person); and the trafficking must be for the purpose of 'exploitation', defined as prostitution or other sexual exploitation, or forced labour, including begging, servitude, slavery, the removal or organs, or the exploitation of criminal activities.[330]

---

of JHA Council, 4 Jun 2009). See also the Commission's communications on human trafficking (COM (2005) 514, 18 Oct 2005 and COM (2008) 657, 17 Oct 2008) and the reports and opinions of the expert group, online at: <http://ec.europa.eu/justice_home/doc_centre/crime/trafficking/doc_crime_human_trafficking_en.htm#Experts%20Group%20on%20Trafficking%20in%20Human%20Beings>. See also the recommendations drawn up by the Commission for the 2007 Anti-Trafficking Day: <http://ec.europa.eu/justice_home/news/information_dossiers/anti_trafficking_day_07/documents_en.htm>. Most recently see the Commission communication on the EU Strategy towards the Eradication of Trafficking in Human Beings 2012–2016 (COM(2012) 286, 19 June 2012), and the mid-term report on the application of that Strategy (SWD (2014) 318, 17 Oct 2014).

[322] [2001] OJ L 30/44 (signature); [2006] OJ L 262/44 and 51 (conclusion). All Member States have also ratified the Protocol, which entered into force on 25 Dec 2003. The EU has also concluded the main UN Convention on organized crime ([2004] OJ L 261/69).

[323] ETS 197, in force 1 Feb 2008. The exception is the Czech Republic.

[324] See ch 3 of volume 2.

[325] Art 3 of Framework Decision ([2005] OJ L 68/49), which was replaced by Directive 2014/42 ([2014] OJ L 127/39; see Art 3(i)) from 4 Oct 2015 (Art 12(1)). See further II:3.7.4.

[326] [2001] OJ L 82/1 (Framework Decision), which was replaced by Directive 2012/29 on crime victims' rights ([2012] L 315/57) from 16 Nov 2015. See II:4.7.

[327] See: <http://ec.europa.eu/anti-trafficking/eu-anti-trafficking-coordinator>.

[328] Respectively <http://ec.europa.eu/dgs/home-affairs/e-library/docs/thb-victims-identification/thb_identification_en.pdf> and <http://ec.europa.eu/dgs/home-affairs/e-library/docs/thb_victims_rights/thb_victims_rights_en.pdf>.

[329] Art 2(1) and (3). All remaining references in this sub-section are to the Directive, unless otherwise noted. For more detailed comments, in particular a comparison between the Directive and international instruments, see chapter 14 of Peers, et al., *EU Immigration and Asylum Law: Text and Commentary*, 2nd edn, vol 2 (Brill, 2012).

[330] The Directive added the references to 'begging', criminal activities, and the removal of organs (compare to Art 1(1), Framework Decision).

Where the specified types of force are applied, the consent of the victim is irrelevant,[331] and where a child is involved, there is no requirement that force was used.[332] There is no requirement of a cross-border element to the offence, or that the victim must be the national of another State. However, the issue is nevertheless considered in this chapter because a cross-border element to human trafficking is often present in practice.

The acts in question have to be intentional.[333] Also, the Directive requires Member States to consider criminalizing the use of services of a victim, if there is knowledge that the person concerned was the victim of trafficking.[334] On this point, it should also be noted that the employer sanctions Directive requires Member States to criminalize employers who use 'work or services exacted from an illegally staying third-country national with the knowledge that he or she is a victim of trafficking in human beings', where the employer has not been charged or convicted of an offence pursuant to the Framework Decision on trafficking in persons.[335] In light of this, the trafficking Directive will only be relevant on this point where a person who is *not* an employer uses the services of trafficking victims—for example a prostitute's client.[336]

Directive 2011/36 (like the prior Framework Decision) also requires Member States to criminalize aiding and abetting trafficking offences, as well as attempts to commit such offences or to instigate them.[337] Member States are obliged to provide for a possible maximum sentence of at least five years in duration for trafficking offences,[338] whereas the prior Framework Decision only set out a basic obligation to impose 'effective, proportionate and dissuasive' criminal penalties for commission of the relevant offences.[339]

Furthermore, under the Framework Decision, Member States had to ensure that a maximum sentence of at least eight years for trafficking in persons was possible, in four particularly serious circumstances: endangering the life of the victim deliberately or by gross negligence;[340] committing the offence against a 'particularly vulnerable' victim, including at least children below the age of sexual majority trafficked for the purpose of sexual exploitation;[341] using serious violence in order to commit the offence or causing 'particularly serious harm to the victim';[342] or committing the crime within

---

[331] Art 2(4).

[332] Art 2(5); a 'child' is defined as any person under eighteen years of age (Art 2(6)).

[333] Art 2(1).   [334] Art 18(4).

[335] Art 9(1)(d) of Directive 2009/52 on sanctions for employment of irregular migrants ([2009] OJ L 168/24); see I:7.6.2 below. The references in Directive 2009/52 to the Framework Decision on trafficking in persons now have to be understood as references to Directive 2011/36, as regards the Member States participating in the latter: see Art 21 of Directive 2011/36. Member States must also criminalize inciting and aiding or abetting such offences: Art 9(2), Directive 2009/52. There is no provision on jurisdiction in Directive 2009/52.

[336] Art 18(4) of the trafficking Directive has, however, a broader scope in Ireland and the UK, since those Member States are not bound by Directive 2009/52 (n 335 above).

[337] Art 3 of the Directive; Art 2 of the Framework Decision.

[338] Art 4(1). There is a basic obligation to provide for 'effective' penalties (rather than specific possible sentences) as regards inchoate offences (Art 4(4)). There is no reference in the Directive to the penalties which might be applicable if a Member State criminalizes the use of services of trafficking victims.

[339] Art 3(1) of the Framework Decision.   [340] Art 3(2)(a) of the Framework Decision.

[341] Art 3(2)(b) of the Framework Decision.   [342] Art 3(2)(c) of the Framework Decision.

the framework of a 'criminal organisation' as defined by an EU measure on organized crime, but without the threshold for criminal liability set out in that measure.[343]

Directive 2011/36 raised the maximum possible sentence in these cases to ten years from eight, and the definition of a 'particularly vulnerable' victim was extended to include *all* child victims.[344] The Directive also requires Member States to treat cases where a public official committed the offence in the performance of his or her duties as an aggravated circumstance, although it does not specify a minimum increased penalty in this case.[345] There are also standard provisions on the liability of legal persons.[346] Although there is no direct cross-over or conflict between the EU legislation on facilitation (smuggling) and trafficking, there are likely still circumstances where the two measures cross over, since the offences covered by the Framework Decision on smuggling will also fall within the Directive on trafficking if the additional elements set out in the latter measure are also present. This will be particularly true in the case of children, given the absence of the 'force' element in the trafficking offence where children are involved.

As for previous convictions for trafficking, the EU has more general legislation on this issue, which requires all prior convictions handed down by other Member States to be taken into account as regards all aspects of criminal procedure in a Member State.[347] The Directive also requires Member States to confiscate the proceeds and instrumentalities related to trafficking offences.[348]

Next, the Directive requires Member States to provide that national authorities are entitled not to prosecute or impose penalties on the victims of trafficking offences, where they were compelled to commit criminal activities as a direct consequence of being victims of trafficking.[349] As for jurisdiction over trafficking offences, the Framework Decision required each Member State to take jurisdiction where an act was carried out on its territory, by one of its nationals or for the benefit of a legal person established in its territory.[350] Member States could derogate from the second and third jurisdictional rules if they inform the Council.[351] In any event, each Member State had to either prosecute or extradite when the relevant conduct was committed by its own nationals outside its territory.[352] Directive 2011/36 extended jurisdiction over human trafficking offences to any offences committed by nationals of a Member State, without any possibility of derogation by Member States.[353] As regards offences committed by their citizens outside their territory, Member States are not allowed to make prosecution dependent upon the act being an offence in the territory where it was committed, upon a report by the victim, or upon a denunciation by the State where the act was committed.[354]

---

[343] Art 3(2)(d) of the Framework Decision, referring to a 1998 Joint Action ([1998] OJ L 351/1) on organized crime, which has since been replaced by a Framework Decision ([2008] OJ L 300/42).
[344] Art 4(2).   [345] Art 4(3).   [346] Arts 5-6; compare to Arts 4-5, Framework Decision.
[347] See the Framework Decision on this issue ([2008] L 220/32), discussed in II:3.7.2, and the EU legislation on the exchange of information on criminal convictions in general, discussed in II:3.6.1.4.
[348] Art 7.   [349] Art 8. There was no such clause in the Framework Decision.
[350] Art 6(1), Framework Decision.   [351] Art 6(2) and (4), Framework Decision.
[352] Art 6(3), Framework Decision.
[353] Art 10(1). The previous 'extradite or prosecute' rule was dropped. See generally II:6.5.
[354] Art 10(3).

The Framework Decision required Member States to permit investigations or prosecutions to begin in the absence of a complaint by a victim, at least in cases where the acts took place on national territory.[355] Directive 2011/36 went further, by removing the territorial limitation on this point, and by requiring Member States to ensure that 'criminal proceedings may continue even if the victim has withdrawn his or her statement'.[356] The Directive also provides for Member States to permit prosecutions for trafficking for 'a sufficient period of time after the victim has reached the age of majority', and requires that Member States ensure that the relevant persons receive training and that there must be 'effective investigative tools' available to investigators and prosecutors.[357]

There are specific provisions on the role of victims, supplementing the general rules in EU crime victims' legislation,[358] as well as general rules on the prevention of trafficking.[359] Finally, Member States are obliged to establish national rapporteurs on trafficking,[360] and work with the EU's anti-trafficking coordinator.[361]

According to the Commission's report on the national application of the Framework Decision,[362] most Member States implemented the definition of trafficking sufficiently in national law, including as regards inchoate offences. Equally Member States had applied the rules on penalties, although there was a wide variation in penalties in practice. The large majority of Member States applied the rules concerning extra-territorial jurisdiction,[363] but it was difficult for the Commission to assess whether the specific provisions on victims were complied with.

Further information on the practical application of the Framework Decision was set out in the Commission's 2008 communication on the issue of trafficking in persons,[364] which stated that there had been a steady increase in the number of prosecutions for trafficking related to sexual exploitation to 1,500 a year by 2006, although this fell short of estimates of 500,000 persons trafficked each year into the EU.[365] Most countries offered police protection and compensation to very few victims in practice. A subsequent Eurostat study in 2013 estimated that nearly two-thirds of victims were trafficked for the purpose of sexual exploitation, and overall women and girls made up 80% of the victims.[366] The most recent study (from 2014) indicated that there were 30,000 victims over three years, of which two-thirds were EU citizens.[367]

In the absence of the report on the implementation of Directive 2011/36,[368] it is too early to tell if the Directive has, in and of itself, reduced trafficking in persons.

---

[355] Art 7(1), Framework Decision.   [356] Art 9(1).

[357] Art 9(2) to (4).   [358] On those general rules, see II:4.7.   [359] Art 18.

[360] Art 19.   [361] Art 20.   [362] COM (2006) 187, 2 May 2006.

[363] The only relevant declaration available in the Council's register of documents concerns Hungary (Council doc 13756/05, 26 Oct 2005).

[364] COM (2008) 657, 17 Oct 2008.

[365] For further statistics, see the impact assessment of the 2009 proposal for a new Framework Decision on this issue (SEC (2009) 358, 25 Mar 2009), pp 7–12 and Annex I.

[366] See:<https://ec.europa.eu/anti-trafficking/sites/antitrafficking/files/trafficking_in_human_beings_-_dghome-eurostat_en_1.pdf>.

[367] <http://ec.europa.eu/anti-trafficking/sites/antitrafficking/files/trafficking_in_human_beings_-_eurostat_-_2014_edition.pdf>.

[368] The report was due by 6 April 2015 (Art 23(1)). A further report is due by 6 April 2016 on the criminalization of the use of services of trafficking victims (Art 23(2)).

Compared to the international measures on this issue, the Directive now corresponds to or goes further than the Council of Europe and UN measures as regards the definition of trafficking, prevention of the offence, jurisdiction, and rules concerning victim protection and assistance in the context of criminal law. The EU rules also go further in that they set specific possible sentences for the offences concerned. Furthermore, the EU measures are more easily enforceable in the national courts and the Court of Justice than any international measures.

However, there are a number of key provisions of the Council of Europe Convention in particular that are not reflected in EU law (as regards prevention, broader victim assistance, discouraging demand, identification of victims, and international cooperation). Also, as discussed further below, the Directive on the immigration status of victims of trafficking still suffers from significant defects and gaps in its implementation by Member States. It should soon become clear whether Directive 2011/36 also needs to be revised and/or more effectively implemented before it can play a decisive role in reducing human trafficking in practice.

7.5.5 Immigration liaison officers

An important practical role in preventing irregular migration is played by Member States' immigration liaison officers (ILOs) posted in third countries. The creation of a framework to coordinate the activities of these national officers started with the JHA Council conclusions of 2000 on irregular immigration networks, which suggested that Member States 'improve cooperation between liaison officers operating in the same immigration source country or in the same region of the world, which could lead to mutual and reciprocal assistance or even complementarity in carrying out tasks'.[369] Next, the JHA Council of May 2001 adopted conclusions on the creation of an ILO network in the Western Balkans,[370] which set out detailed guidelines on the establishment of such a network.

In the event, the funding to establish this network was not available, but the Council's Action Plan on external borders policy, adopted in 2002, nevertheless called for the creation of a general ILO network. A report on the creation of the network indicated that common training, a common handbook, and the improvement of cooperation and information sharing were necessary.[371] This resulted in the adoption of further Council conclusions adopting most of the report's recommendations (except as regards training).[372]

The next step was the formalization of the ILO network by means of a Council Regulation adopted early in 2004.[373] Regulation 377/2004 establishes the ILO network, defines the concept of ILOs and sets out their powers, and sets out the scope of the

---

[369] See the press release of the JHA Council, 30 Nov/1 Dec 2000.
[370] See the press release of the JHA Council, 28/29 May 2001.
[371] Council doc 13406/02, 28 Oct 2002.
[372] See the press release of the JHA Council, 28/29 Nov 2002.
[373] Regulation 377/2004, [2004] OJ L 64/1, in force 5 Jan 2004. All references in this sub-section are to this Reg unless otherwise indicated.

ILO network, which includes the Member States as well as non-EU countries.[374] The ILOs collect information of use to the prevention of irregular immigration and may also assist with establishing the identity of third-country nationals and facilitating their return to their country of origin. Member States must ensure that their ILOs act in accordance with national law (particularly regarding data protection) and international agreements with the host States.[375] They must also keep each other, the Council, and the Commission informed of ILO postings.[376] The tasks of ILO networks include: regular meetings; exchange of information; coordinated positions as regards commercial carriers; organization of information and training sessions for diplomatic and consular staff, when appropriate; adoption of common approaches to collecting and reporting strategic information; contribution to bi-annual reports on common activities; and establishing contacts with networks in neighbouring countries.[377] Commission staff are entitled to attend network meetings and the Member State holding the Council Presidency is to take the lead in holding those meetings.[378] Member States may agree that ILOs can look after the interests of other Member States, or share tasks among each other.[379] Each Council Presidency must draw up a report, in accordance with a model and format drawn up by the Commission, on the activity of ILO networks in each country where it has a representative.[380] The Presidency must then prepare an overall evaluation report, drafted by the Commission, and a factual summary on the basis of these reports is to be included in the annual Commission report on the development of EU policy on illegal immigration, external border controls, and expulsion.[381] Finally, the entire Regulation is without prejudice to the rules on consular cooperation.[382]

According to the Commission's 2009 report on EU policy on irregular migration, visas, and border control, the ILO network had in 2006 identified four key migration routes from Africa to Europe, and four Member States started work to develop cooperation among ILOs on these routes. Links had also been created between the ILO network and Europol and Frontex. The ILO system had also received money from the EU borders fund, to promote the establishment and development of ILO networks in Africa and in eastern and south-eastern Europe.[383]

In order to develop the ILO network further, the ILO Regulation was amended in 2011.[384] This amendment: added references to the use of the 'Iconet' system for transferring information and to the possible exchange of information on persons seeking protection;[385] entitled Frontex, the EU border agency, to send representatives to all network meetings;[386] permitted Member States other than those holding the Council Presidency to call network meetings;[387] and reduced the reporting burden on the Council Presidency and Commission, since the requirements in the 2004 Regulation

---

[374] Art 1.   [375] Art 2.   [376] Art 3.   [377] Art 4(1).   [378] Art 4(2) and 4(3).
[379] Art 5.
[380] Art 6(1) and (2). The Commission adopted a Decision setting out the standard model in Sep 2005: [2005] OJ L 264/8.
[381] Art 6(3) and (4).   [382] Art 7. On those rules, see I:4.7 above.
[383] SEC (2009) 320, 9 Mar 2009, pp 18 and 25.   [384] Reg 493/2011 ([2011] OJ L 141/13).
[385] Amended Arts 3 and 4(1). On Iconet, see I:7.8 below.
[386] Amended Art 4(2). On Frontex, see I:3.10.1 above.   [387] Amended Art 4(3).

had proved impossible to satisfy.[388] Subsequently, the legislation establishing the EU border agency, Frontex, was amended to allow Frontex to send liaison officers to non-EU States, with such officers forming part of the overall ILO network.[389]

7.6 Treatment of Irregular Migrants

A number of early EU soft-law measures make reference to detection of irregular migrants within Member States' territory and restrictions upon their status,[390] while the relevant International Labour Organization Convention and the UN Convention on the status of migrant workers instead set out requirements for a minimum level of social and legal protection for irregular migrants within the territory.[391] The principal binding EU measures in this area, which will be considered in turn, concern sanctions against employers for employment of irregular migrants and the legal status of victims of trafficking in persons. It should also be recalled that Member States may opt to check the fingerprints of an irregular migrant against the Eurodac database to see whether he or she has applied for asylum in any Member State,[392] and check those fingerprints in the Visa Information System for the purpose of verifying the identity of a possible irregular migrant or of identifying an irregular migrant.[393] The planned entry-exit system, if it is agreed and becomes operational, will also impact upon those irregular migrants who have overstayed on the territory.[394] Finally, the Returns Directive contains a number of important provisions concerning the treatment of irregular migrants pending expulsion; it is considered separately further below.[395]

7.6.1 Sanctions against employers of irregular migrants

The purpose of adopting legislation addressing employment of irregular migrants was threefold: to reduce the 'pull' factor attracting migrants to the EU; to reduce distortions of competition between companies in Member States that employed irregular migrants and those that did not; and to ensure that labour standards were not undercut by employment of irregular migrants. An early suggestion to adopt legislation on this issue as an internal market matter in the 1970s did not find favour.[396]

Over thirty years later, Directive 2009/52 was adopted by the EP and the Council in May 2009.[397] Member States had to apply the Directive by 20 July 2011,[398] and the Commission's report on the implementation of the Directive indicated that all had done so by 2014.[399] The Directive broke new ground as the first EC measure not related to environmental law to require Member States to impose criminal sanctions to enforce it.[400]

---

[388] Amended Art 6.

[389] Reg 1168/2011 ([2011] OJ L 304/1), replacing Art 14 of the Frontex Reg (Reg 2007/2004, [2004] OJ L 349/1).

[390] See I:7.2.1 above.   [391] See I:7.3.3 above.   [392] See I:5.8.3 above.

[393] Arts 19 and 20, Reg 767/2008 ([2008] OJ L 218/60). On this system, see I:4.8 above.

[394] See I:3.6.2 above.

[395] Dir 2008/115 ([2008] OJ L 348/98), in particular Arts 14 as regards, inter alia, education and health care and Arts 15–18 as regards detention; see I:7.7.1 below.

[396] Proposed Directive in [1976] OJ C 277/2, revised in [1978] OJ C 97/9.   [397] [2009] OJ L 168/24.

[398] Art 17(1). All references in this sub-section are to Dir 2009/52 unless otherwise indicated.

[399] COM (2014) 286, 22 May 2014 (the '2014 report').   [400] See further I:7.2.4 and II:5.2.4.

The purpose of the Directive is to prohibit the employment of irregular migrants 'in order to fight illegal immigration', and therefore 'to lay down minimum common standards on sanctions and measures' against employers who breach this prohibition.[401] Member States may set higher standards as regards employees' rights to receive back pay and as regards facilitation of employees' complaints, 'provided that such provisions are compatible with' the Directive,[402] and may also establish 'more stringent' rules relating to the liability of sub-contractors.[403] While it might be inferred from this that *other* provisions of the Directive fully harmonize national law, nonetheless the preamble to the Directive and its title suggest that it sets only 'minimum' standards throughout.[404] In light of this, the best interpretation is that the entire Directive sets minimum standards as regards enforcement, except for the specific provision which permits higher standards as regards employees' rights. In any event, it should be noted that the Directive explicitly provides for a number of options for Member States.[405]

It should be noted that the Directive does not apply to *legal* migrants who take up employment which is unauthorized, regardless of whether those migrants are prohibited from taking up any work or from taking up the particular work they have been employed to carry out.[406] In fact, the Directive could not apply to those groups of persons, due to the different decision-making procedures applying to the legal base for 'legal migration' at the time of the adoption of the Directive.[407] Furthermore, obviously the Directive does not apply either to self-employment by irregular migrants, or to the unauthorized self-employment of legal migrants.[408] Also, the Directive does not apply to those third-country nationals who enjoy the EU right of free movement.[409] Although the Directive fails to give express priority to any treaties concluded by the EU and/or the Member States, any treaties binding the EU nonetheless take priority over any EU secondary legislation.[410] Therefore employer sanctions cannot be imposed where a Turkish worker derives employment rights from the EU-Turkey association agreement.[411]

In the case of victims of trafficking in persons, other EU legislation provides for access to employment where a Member State gives them a residence permit;[412] it must

---

[401] Art 1.   [402] Art 15. On the meaning of the requirement of 'compatibility', see I:7.2.4 above.

[403] Art 8(4). This clause is not subject to the requirement of 'compatibility' with the Directive.

[404] Recital 4 in the preamble. Again, there is no reference to 'compatibility' with the Directive here.

[405] Arts 3(3), 4(2), 5(2)(b), 5(3), 6(2), 7(2), 10(2), and 12. For more on these various options, see below. Moreover, the Directive refers to 'national law' (or similar phrases) in Arts 2(c), 2(g), 2(h), 3(3), 6(1), 6(2), 6(5), 8(1), 8(3), 8(4), 9(1), 10(2), 13(1), 13(2), and 13(4).

[406] Recital 5 in the preamble states that the Dir is 'without prejudice' to national law dealing with this issue. The 2014 report states that twelve Member States have chosen to apply the Directive to this category of persons.

[407] See I:7.2.4 above. After the entry into force of the Treaty of Lisbon, this point is purely historic.

[408] There is no definition of 'self-employment' in the Directive, but see the definition of 'employment' in Art 2(b).

[409] See the definition of 'third-country national' in Art 2(a). Furthermore, recital 5 of the preamble states that the Directive does not apply to third-country nationals who have been posted by their employer between Member States in order to provide services. See also recital 32 in the preamble, and generally I:7.4 above.

[410] See Case C-228/06 *Soysal* [2009] ECR I-1031. However, this leaves open the question of priority as between the Dir and treaties concluded only by *Member States*.

[411] See Case C-65/98 *Eyup* [2000] ECR I-4747.

[412] Art 11 of Dir 2004/81 ([2004] OJ L 261/19). On this Dir, see I:7.6.2 below.

be assumed that such persons are not 'illegally staying' as long as the permit is valid, and therefore their position falls outside the scope of the prohibition in Directive 2009/52. Equally, any employment carried out pursuant to other EU legislation which provides for access to employment in connection with a residence permit must also fall outside the scope of this prohibition, since such persons are not 'illegally staying' either.[413] Also, the case law on the Returns Directive has confirmed that asylum seekers are not illegally staying,[414] and indeed the EU's reception conditions Directive requires the Member States to authorize their employment if they have been waiting a sufficient time for a decision on their asylum application.[415]

The basic obligation in Directive 2009/52 is that Member States have to prohibit the employment of irregular migrants,[416] with the Directive specifying the sanctions and other measures which apply to enforce this prohibition.[417] However, Member States have an option not to apply the prohibition 'to illegally staying third-country nationals whose removal has been postponed and who are allowed to work in accordance with national law'.[418] Returning again to the situation of victims of trafficking, a separate Directive provides for a mandatory postponement of removal during a period of reflection which may be granted pursuant to that Directive;[419] arguably this should entail an option for a Member State to permit the victim to work during this period.

To enforce the prohibition of employment of irregular migrants, employers have three obligations regarding each third-country national employee:[420] to ensure that each employee 'hold and present to the employer his/her valid residence permit or other authorisation for his or her stay' before starting employment;[421] to keep copies of such documents at least for the duration of the employment, for 'possible inspection' by the national authorities; and to notify those authorities of the start of employment of each third-country national by the time laid down by each Member State. The Directive does not expressly address what happens when a fixed-term contract is renewed or made permanent.

Member States may optionally *simplify* the notification requirement 'where the employers are natural persons and the employment is for their private purposes' (hereinafter 'household employers'),[422] but Member States do not have the option to *waive*

---

[413] See I:5.5, I:5.6, and I:6.5 to I:6.7 above.   [414] See I:7.7.1 below.

[415] Dir 2003/9 ([2003] OJ L 31/18), Art 11; Directive 2013/33 ([2013] OJ L 180/96), Art 15. See I:5.9 above.

[416] Art 3(1). 'Employment' and 'illegally staying' are defined in Art 2(b) and (c).

[417] Art 3(2).

[418] Art 3(3). See, for instance, Case C-192/89 *Sevince* [1990] ECR I-3461. On the definition of 'postponement' of expulsion in light of the Returns Directive, see I:7.7.1 below. It should also be noted that some EU measures on legal migration do not apply to persons whose expulsion is suspended as a matter of fact and law (see I:6.5 above). The 2014 report states that seven Member States apply this optional exception.

[419] Art 6(2) of Dir 2004/81, n 412 above.

[420] Art 4(1). For the definition of 'employer', see Art 2(e). An 'employer' includes a 'temporary work agency'; for a definition of the latter concept, see Art 2(h).

[421] According to recital 9 in the preamble, this provision should apply to third-country national workers posted by EU companies; this contradicts recital 5, which excludes such persons entirely from the scope of the Directive. Recital 12 in the preamble states that 'Member States should use their best endeavours to handle requests for renewal of residence permits in a timely manner'; this does not as such exempt employers from their obligations in cases where an employee is still awaiting a decision on an application for a renewal of his or her recently-expired residence permit when he or she starts work.

[422] Art 4(2), first sub-paragraph. According to the 2014 report, only three Member States apply this exception.

the notification requirement for this category of employers. Nor do Member States have any option, as regards household employers, to simplify *or* waive the requirements to check or keep copies of the relevant documents. Of course, in some circumstances it might be possible to argue that the persons concerned should be regarded as self-employed, in which case the obligations in the Directive would not apply.[423]

A wider optional exception applies to long-term residents as defined by EU law.[424] Member States are permitted to waive the notification requirement entirely as regards such employees.[425] Again, the obligation to check and keep copies of documents cannot be waived.

The consequence of employers fulfilling all their obligations is that they cannot be held liable for breach of the prohibition on hiring irregular migrants 'unless the employers knew that the document presented as a valid residence permit or another authorisation for stay was a forgery'.[426] This is clearly a subjective test (*mens rea*) only, but if the Directive must be interpreted as setting only minimum standards as regards enforcement (see above), it therefore remains an option for Member States to apply strict criminal liability for the employers of irregular migrants.[427] There is no express rule on what happens if the employee loses the right to work after employment begins, but arguably the basic rule applies *mutatis mutandis*.

The Directive then specifies the consequences if employers have infringed the prohibition on *employing* irregular migrants.[428] This is a distinct issue from the employers' obligations to check and keep documents and to notify the authorities when hiring third-country nationals, since it is conceivable that an employer that has breached one or more of these latter obligations has nonetheless employed a person who is *not* an irregular migrant. It follows that it is up to each Member State to determine whether and to what extent the penalties set out in the Directive, alternative penalties, or any penalties at all, must be applied to employers who breach the separate obligations to check and keep documents and to notify the authorities when hiring third-country nationals. For example, prima facie it is open to Member States to exempt household employers, or those employers who have breached the requirements only as regards a few employees, from any penalty. Against this, it might be argued that the EU law principle of effectiveness requires that Member States impose some penalty on employers who have breached such requirements, but on the other hand the same principle must mean that such penalties cannot apply where EU law itself permits the employment of such third-country nationals.[429]

Where employers have breached the key prohibition on employing irregular migrants, they must generally be made subject to 'effective, proportionate and dissuasive sanctions'.[430] These sanctions must include 'financial sanctions which shall increase in

---

[423] However, Member States are free, as a matter of national law, to extend some or all of these requirements to persons contracting with self-employed third-country nationals.

[424] Dir 2003/109 ([2004] OJ L 16/44). See I:6.7 above. Again, only three Member States use this exception, according to the 2014 report.

[425] Art 4(2), second sub-paragraph.   [426] Art 4(3).

[427] On principles of criminal liability in EU criminal law, see II:5.5.3.   [428] Art 5.

[429] For example, see *Eyup*, n 411 above.   [430] Art 5(1).

amount according to the number of illegally employed third-country nationals',[431] 'and' the payment of the costs of return, if return is carried out.[432] But Member States can instead 'decide to reflect at least the average costs of return in the financial sanctions' which they must impose. Member States also have an option to reduce the 'financial sanctions' applicable to household employers, if 'no particularly exploitative working conditions are involved'.[433] Again, this is only an option to *reduce* penalties for this category of employees, not to waive them altogether.

Next, employers which have breached the prohibition on employing irregular migrants are liable to pay any outstanding remuneration for the employee(s),[434] any taxes or social security contributions which would have been paid in the event of legal employment,[435] and any cost arising from sending the back payments to the country which the employee has returned to.[436] As for the amount of the pay and related taxes and social security contributions, Member States must presume a period of three months' prior employment unless either the employer or employee (or 'others') can prove differently.[437] Presumably this time period is calculated backward from the date on which the employment actually ceased.

Similarly, the level of pay 'shall be presumed to have been at least as high as the wage provided for by the applicable laws on minimum wages, by collective agreements or in accordance with established practice in the relevant occupational branches', again unless the employee or employer can prove otherwise, subject to the relevant mandatory national laws on wages.[438] There is also a definition of remuneration—'the wage or salary and any other consideration, whether in cash or in kind, which a worker receives directly or indirectly in respect of his employment from his employer and which is equivalent to that which would have been enjoyed by comparable workers in a legal employment relationship'.[439] The Directive does not specify any presumption concerning the working time of the employee concerned (ie how many hours per week the employee must be presumed to have worked during the reference period, which could be relevant for the calculation of salary), as regards holiday pay,[440] or as regards other labour law issues regulated by EU or national law. Presumably at least all issues related

---

[431] Art 5(2)(a). The precise application of this requirement (ie the exact numbers which will entail higher penalties) is implicitly left to Member States' law. The word 'include' in Art 5(2) must mean that the list of two measures mentioned in points (a) and (b) is not exhaustive. On Member States' practice, see the Annex to the 2014 report.

[432] Art 5(2)(b). See the more precise obligations regarding costs set out in the carrier sanctions Directive (Dir 2001/51, [2001] OJ L 187/45), discussed in I:7.5.1 above.

[433] Art 5(3). The definition of 'particularly exploitative working conditions' is set out in Art 2(i); note that prima facie it appears that even *legal* working conditions could be covered by this definition. According to the 2014 report, only five Member States use this option.

[434] Art 6(1)(a).

[435] Art 6(1)(b). This includes 'penalty payments for delays and relevant administrative fines'.

[436] Art 6(1)(c).   [437] Art 6(3). Three Member States fail to do this (see the 2014 report).

[438] Art 6(1)(a).

[439] Art 2(j). The relationship between this definition and the wording of Art 6(1)(a) is not entirely clear.

[440] Four weeks' paid holiday or pro rata periods of holiday pay is guaranteed by Art 7 of Dir 2003/88 on working time ([2003] OJ L 299/9). A payment in lieu must be made upon termination of employment (Art 7(2), Dir 2003/88); presumably this also applies when employment terminates due to the irregular migration status of the employee. Recital 20 in the preamble refers to both holiday funds and social funds as part of back pay.

to pay must be subject to the Directive, *mutatis mutandis*.[441] The Directive does not specifically address what happened if the employer can prove that *some* back pay was paid to the employee; presumably that amount should be offset against the remaining amount due, in accordance with the principle of proportionality. It is also not clear how to address the situation where the employee was in fact paid in full by the employer, but the pay rate agreed between them was less than the relevant minimum wage (or the level required by a generally applicable collective agreement). In that case, it should follow from the EU law principle of effectiveness that the employer must top up the employee's pay to the level which was legally required by national law.

The level of any tax and social security payments due implicitly must also be calculated in relation to the pay.[442] There is no provision for interest to be charged on back payments or on taxes or social security contributions; arguably Member States are under an obligation to ensure that interest is payable in order to ensure the effectiveness of the Directive.[443]

While the Directive does not expressly require Member States to impose a time limit for employers to pay the amounts due to employees and the authorities, presumably Member States have the power and even the obligation to set a time limit to pay, enforceable by further penalties, in order to ensure the effectiveness of EU law. But conversely, there is no provision for a limit to be placed on the amount of back pay which an employee could receive.[444] It should be recalled that this provision of the Directive only sets minimum standards, with Member States free to set more favourable standards 'compatible' with the Directive for the benefit of the third-country nationals concerned.[445] So Member States could establish a presumption of six months' back pay,[446] or arguably provide that the presumption relating to periods of back pay cannot be rebutted by the *employer*.[447]

While the Directive is silent on the application of labour law rules other than pay to irregular migrants, to the extent that labour law has been harmonized by EU law then it follows from CJEU case law (discussed in Chapter 6) that irregular migrants are covered by the relevant EU legislation.[448]

It is obviously also necessary to ensure that there are effective mechanisms for irregular migrants to recover the back pay which they are due.[449] To this end, the Directive requires Member States to 'enact mechanisms to ensure that' the migrants can either

---

[441] This includes sick pay, maternity pay, and pay (or arguably other forms of financial compensation) due from a prior employer due to redundancy, unfair dismissal, or insolvency. Some of these issues are addressed by EU legislation (for instance, back pay due following insolvency: see Dir 2008/94 ([2008] OJ L 283/36)).

[442] This is explicit as regards the presumption of three months' back payments (Art 6(3)).

[443] Case C-271/91 *Marshall II* [1993] ECR I-4367; but see Case C-66/95 *Sutton* [1997] ECR I-2163.

[444] A time limit for *bringing* a claim can be applied in accordance with Art 6(2)(a), discussed below.

[445] Art 15.

[446] One Member State provides for a six-month presumption (see the 2014 report).

[447] It must always be possible to permit the *employee* to rebut the presumed period, because preventing an employee from doing this would not constitute a more favourable rule for the third-country nationals concerned.

[448] See I:6.4.5.

[449] Art 6(2). Recital 16 in the preamble states that 'Member States should not be obliged to involve their missions or representations in third countries in those mechanisms.'

introduce a claim on their own behalf to obtain back pay, subject to time limits imposed by Member States, and then 'enforce a judgment' to this end,[450] *or* can 'call on' a national authority to collect this claim on their behalf, 'when provided for by national legislation'.[451] It must follow that when national legislation does not foresee the latter remedy, then the former remedy must be provided for, otherwise the provisions on back pay would be rendered ineffective. While the Directive refers to these remedies as alternatives, it must be open for Member States to provide for *both* measures if they wish, since the Article in question sets only minimum standards in respect of third-country nationals' rights. Member States must inform irregular migrants about these rights, and the rights concerning facilitation of complaints, before the enforcement of any return decision.[452] However, the 2014 report indicates that Member States have not implemented the law effectively in this area, with only a few of them expressly transposing these rules.

The individual remedy for the applicant is necessarily a judicial remedy, as evidenced by the words 'claim' and (most obviously) 'judgment'. It must follow that the EU rules on jurisdiction and conflict of law would apply.[453] Where a proceeding to reclaim back pay can only be brought through national authorities, the same principle must mean that the national authorities must act quickly when 'called on', and that if necessary a legal action or at least an effective complaints procedure must be in place for the employee where the authorities fail to act swiftly and competently. While there is no reference to costs, it should follow from the principle of effectiveness of EU law that the winning party in a judicial action should not have to pay costs,[454] and where national authorities act to reclaim back pay, at least that the costs charged to the employee are proportionate. For the avoidance of any doubt, the Directive provides that Member States must ensure that the employees are able to obtain the back pay concerned, whichever procedure is in place.[455]

Next, Member States are obliged to take four further measures, 'if appropriate', against employers who breach the prohibition against employing irregular migrants: exclusion from various forms of public aid, including EU funds, for up to five years; a claw-back of such aid given in the twelve months before the irregular employment was detected; exclusion from public procurement as defined by EU law for up to five years; and closure of the establishments used or withdrawal of licences to conduct the relevant activity.[456] Moreover, Member States can optionally exempt household employers from these

---

[450] Art 6(2)(a). According to the EU principle of effectiveness, such time limits cannot render the right impossible, and must be equivalent to those applying to comparable claims under national law. See, for instance, Case C-432/05 *Unibet* [2007] ECR I-2271.

[451] Art 6(2)(b). However, the preamble states that if employees are not able to regain back pay from their employer, the State is not therefore liable to pay it (recital 14).

[452] Arts 6(2) and 13. Due to the identical terms used, these provisions must surely be interpreted consistently with the Returns Directive, to the extent that the two Dirs overlap.

[453] On the substance of those rules, see II:8.5. If the rules on conflict of law in contracts do not apply, because an employment contract with an irregular migrant is considered void, then arguably the rules on conflict of laws concerning non-contractual liability should apply instead. It also seems obvious that an employer/employee dispute regarding pay is a civil claim, so Art 6 ECHR would apply, as would the right to a fair trial pursuant to the general principles of EU law.

[454] According to the Court of Justice, costs rules in EU law actions should follow the national rules on costs which apply in comparable cases: Case C-472/99 *Clean Car II* [2001] ECR I-9687.

[455] Art 6(4).   [456] Art 7(1).

measures,[457] although there is no option to exempt such employers from the core requirement to pay back pay, taxes, and social security contributions, or to reduce such obligations for such employers.

Where the employer is a sub-contractor,[458] Member States are obliged to ensure joint and several liability with the employer as regards back pay and financial penalties.[459] The same applies where there is a main sub-contractor and an intermediate subcontractor.[460] Sub-contractors shall be exempt if they have 'undertaken due diligence obligations as defined in national law',[461] but as noted at the outset, all of the rules on sub-contractors' liability are minimum standards, in that Member States may set more stringent liability rules under national law.[462]

Next, Member States are obliged to criminalize the employment of irregular migrants in five cases of intentional conduct 'as defined by national law':[463] a continued or 'persistently repeated' breach; the 'simultaneous employment of a significant number' of irregular migrants; there are 'particularly exploitative working conditions';[464] the employer was aware that the employees had been trafficked, pursuant to the EU legislation on trafficking in persons (even in the absence of a charge or conviction for a trafficking offence);[465] or the employee was a minor.[466] Member States must also criminalize inciting and aiding or abetting such offences.[467] There is no exemption as such for household employment. As compared to EU criminal law measures, there is no provision on jurisdiction.[468]

The penalties for this criminal offence are not harmonized, because the EC at the time of adoption of the Directive had no competence to harmonize criminal sanctions.[469] Rather, Member States must simply apply 'effective, proportionate and dissuasive criminal penalties' to natural persons.[470] It is notable that most of the EU's measures concerning mutual recognition in criminal law do not abolish the dual criminality requirement as regards the offence of employing irregular migrants,[471] although the obvious consequence of implementing the Directive must be that (for the participating Member States) the dual criminality requirement will be relatively easy to satisfy.[472] Member States may also apply 'other sanctions or measures of a non-criminal nature',

---

[457] Art 7(2). This is clearly an option to *exempt* such employers entirely, not merely to *reduce* the relevant sanctions.

[458] See the definition in Art 2(f).

[459] Art 8(1). The 2014 report indicates that two Member States have failed to comply with this rule.

[460] Art 8(2).   [461] Art 8(3).   [462] Art 8(4).

[463] Art 9(1). National law will necessarily have to define these offences more precisely, otherwise it will infringe the obligation to define criminal obligations sufficiently clearly as set out in Art 7 ECHR (see II:5.3.1).

[464] For the definition of this phrase, see Art 2(i).

[465] [2002] OJ L 203/1; see I:7.5.4 above. This only applies where the employer was not itself charged or convicted as regards trafficking in persons.

[466] 'Minor' is not defined in the Directive.   [467] Art 9(2).

[468] On criminal jurisdiction and EC/EU law, see further II:6.5.

[469] See C-440/05 *Commission v Council* [2007] ECR I-9097, and further I:7.2.4 and II:5.2.4.

[470] Art 10(1).

[471] See for instance, Art 2(2) of the Framework Decision establishing the European Arrest Warrant ([2002] OJ L 190/1). The exception is Art 5(1) of the Framework Decision on the mutual recognition of financial penalties ([2005] OJ L 76/16), which abolishes dual criminality as regards offences applied by a Member State in order to implement 'obligations arising from instruments adopted under the EC Treaty'.

[472] See generally ch 3 of volume 2.

unless this is 'prohibited by general principles of law', and may also publish the judgments relating to the case.[473] For legal persons, in common with other EU measures, Member States must ensure they are liable, without an obligation to apply criminal penalties as such,[474] although Member States must apply some form of penalty to legal persons, which may entail application of the 'other measures' referred to in the Directive (exclusion or repayment of state aid, ban from participation in public procurement, etc.).[475] Obviously legal persons will also be subject to the obligation to pay back pay and tax and social security contributions.

Member States must facilitate complaints by employees against employers as regards the obligations in the Directive, either directly or through third parties such as trade unions.[476] They must also ensure that third parties meeting 'the criteria laid down in their national law' can act on behalf or in support of employees in administrative or civil proceedings to ensure compliance with the Directive.[477] Providing assistance to third-country nationals to lodge complaints shall not be regarded as the facilitation of irregular migration within the scope of separate legislation prohibiting the facilitation of irregular migration.[478] Where there is a criminal offence involving 'particularly exploitative working conditions' or a minor, Member States 'shall define in national law the conditions under which they may grant, on a case-by-case basis, permits of limited duration, linked to the length of the relevant national proceedings' in a manner 'comparable' to the protection of the victims of trafficking in persons who cooperate with the prosecution authorities as set out in the separate Directive on the protection of the victims of such trafficking.[479] Furthermore, Member States 'shall define under national law the conditions under which the duration of these permits may be extended until the third country national has received any back payment' due under the Directive.[480]

There must be regular inspections of employers to enforce the Directive, based on a 'risk assessment' by national authorities,[481] which shall also 'regularly identify the sectors of activity in which the employment of illegally staying third-country nationals is concentrated on their territory'. Member States shall then inform the Commission annually of the numbers of inspections and their results.[482] According to the 2014 report, these reports were submitted late to the Commission, and were inconsistent and incomplete. In the Commission's view, 'the number of inspections carried out in some Member States is unlikely to dissuade an employer from hiring irregular migrants'.

This Directive takes as a given the objective of decreasing the attraction of the EU as a destination for irregular migrants, even though the Commission's impact assessment concerning its original proposal for this Directive states that there are economic

---

[473] Art 10(2).   [474] Art 11. On the issue of corporate criminal liability, see further II:5.5.2.1.
[475] Art 12, referring to Art 7.
[476] Art 13(1). As noted above, all of the obligations in Art 13 are minimum standards only (see Art 15).
[477] Art 13(2). According to the 2014 report, three Member States have failed to do this.
[478] Art 13(3), referring to Dir 2002/90 ([2002] OJ L 328/17). On that Dir, see I:7.5.3 above.
[479] Art 13(4), referring to Dir 2004/81 ([2004] OJ L 261/19). On that Dir, see I:7.6.2 below. The 2014 report indicates that only ten Member States have complied with this rule.
[480] Art 6(5); on the implementation in practice, see ibid. More generally, recital 15 in the preamble states that irregular migrants should not be able to derive a right to stay from the employment or back pay, etc.
[481] Art 14(1).   [482] Art 14(2). See Annex 3 of the 2014 report.

benefits to such employment.[483] The alternative route of legalizing it was not considered at all by the Commission. According to the impact assessment, almost all Member States had employer sanctions regarding employment of irregular migrants already in 2007, and moreover most Member States imposed criminal sanctions; the crucial issue was the *enforcement* of these obligations.[484] As to the reasons for the absence of enforcement, these stemmed from various inadequacies in the organization and financing of national administrations;[485] the EU could only add value in the form of supporting the costs of inspections or assisting coordination between different national administrations, but Directive 2009/52 did neither.

The Commission argument for EU action was to 'level the playing field' between employers in different Member States, along with the 'publicity effect' of adopting an EU-wide measure. But the first objective could only be accomplished if enforcement were actually stepped up. While the Commission's original proposal would have increased the rate of inspections from 2% to 10% of all employers annually,[486] and therefore could well prima facie have increased the level of enforcement, the final text of the Directive only requires Member States to carry out general and sectoral risk assessments. The impact assessment report had made little reference to the issue of risk assessment, but presumably national authorities were already aware that there are likely to be more irregular migrants cleaning hotel toilets than teaching EU law.

The 2014 report on implementation has now shown that indeed some Member States still place a low priority on monitoring of irregular migrants. Moreover, unlike some other legislation, there will not be much enforcement triggered by the persons concerned by the rules: irregular migrants are obviously in a weak position and the 2014 report shows that many Member States have not implemented the parts of the Directive which aim to ensure effective protection of migrants' rights. The Commission's 2015 migration agenda states an intention to prioritize infringement actions for breaches of this Directive,[487] and its 2015 Action Plan against migrant smuggling announced an intention to agree with Member States on targets for more effective inspections.[488] It is not clear how either of these intentions will be carried out, and so it remains to be seen whether the Directive will ever have much success in attaining its objective in practice.

7.6.2 Victims of trafficking or smuggling in persons

Due to public concern about the fate of victims of trafficking in persons and the apparent difficulties in prosecuting the perpetrators of trafficking crimes, since the victims who could testify against them were usually irregular migrants subject in principle to expulsion, the Council considered it necessary to adopt Directive 2004/81 in April 2004, addressing the issue of the immigration status of these victims.[489] Member States

---

[483] SEC (2007) 603, 16 May 2007.   [484] p 9 of the report.

[485] p 10 of the report. Some of these issues are referred to briefly in recital 30 of the preamble to the Directive (adequate powers to inspect, collection and processing of information, sufficient staff).

[486] COM (2007) 249, 15 May 2007, Art 15.   [487] COM (2015) 240, 13 May 2015.

[488] COM (2015) 285, 27 May 2015.

[489] [2004] OJ L 261/19. On the legal base of the Dir, see I:7.2.4 above. On the underlying issues, see D Haynes, 'Used, Abused, Arrested and Deported: Extending Immigration Benefits to Protect the Victims of

had to implement the Directive by 6 August 2006.[490] The Commission brought two infringement actions against Member States that did not apply this Directive by the deadline.[491] A subsequent Directive also provides that Member States shall define in national law the conditions under which they may apply comparable arrangements to Directive 2004/81, where there are criminal proceedings relating to the illegal employment of a minor or a third-country national has been illegally employed and also subject to 'particularly exploitative working conditions'.[492] The Commission has twice reported on the application of the Directive.[493]

The purpose of Directive 2004/81 is to define the conditions for issuing a limited residence permit, linked to the length of the judicial proceedings, to third-country nationals who cooperate in the fight against trafficking or the facilitation of illegal immigration.[494] The Directive defines trafficking and the facilitation of illegal immigration by reference to the EU acts concerning these issues, but the definition in the EU acts is not exhaustive.[495] It should be noted that the status of the victims as regards criminal procedure is regulated by separate EU measures.[496]

Member States are obliged to apply the Directive to victims of trafficking in persons, including those who did not enter legally.[497] They have an option to apply it to persons who have been 'the subject of an action to facilitate illegal migration'.[498] Its application to minors is also optional.[499] The preamble sets out a safeguard clause on protection for refugees, persons with subsidiary protection, and asylum seekers, along with human rights treaties, and also includes a non-discrimination clause.[500] On this point, it is conceivable that some victims might have a valid claim for international protection, if non-state persecutors (ie the criminal organizations which trafficked those victims) pose a sufficient risk of inflicting serious harm or persecution as defined by the EU Directive on qualification for refugee status or subsidiary protection.[501] Member States

---

Trafficking and to Secure the Prosecution of Traffickers' (2004) 26 HRQ 221 and H Askola, *Legal Responses to Trafficking in Women for Sexual Exploitation in the European Union* (Hart, 2007).

[490] Art 17, Dir 2004/81. All references in this sub-section are to Dir 2004/81 unless otherwise indicated.

[491] Cases: C-209/08 *Commission v Luxembourg* (withdrawn) and Case C-266/08 *Commission v Spain* (judgment of 14 May 2009, unreported).

[492] Art 13(4) of Dir 2009/52 ([2009] OJ L 168/24), referring to Arts 9(1)(c) and (e) of that Dir; for the relevant definitions, see Art 2(b), (d) and (i) of that Dir. On Dir 2009/52, see further I:7.6.1 above.

[493] COM (2010) 635, 17 Oct 2010 and COM (2014) 493, 15 Oct 2014. See the discussion of these reports at the end of this sub-section.

[494] Art 1. Note that the EU's criminal law measures against trafficking are not limited in scope to third-country nationals. This limitation of the personal scope of Directive 2004/81 makes sense because EU citizens who are victims of trafficking enjoy free movement rights, so will not need to rely upon any special rules as regards immigration status.

[495] Art 2(b) and (c), referring to acts 'such as' those defined in the other EU legislation. See the Framework Decision and Directive on facilitation of illegal entry and residence (I:7.5.3 above) and the Directive on trafficking in persons (I:7.5.4 above). The definition of a 'measure to enforce an expulsion order' (Art 2(d)) presumably must be understood in light of the definitions in Art 3(4) and (5) of the Returns Directive (Dir 2008/115, [2008] OJ L 348/98), to the extent that the victims fall within the scope of that Directive (see I:7.7.1 below).

[496] The Directive on trafficking in persons (n 495 above) as well as the Framework Decision (and soon the Directive) on crime victims (see II:4.7).

[497] Art 3(1).   [498] Art 3(2).

[499] Art 3(3). The Directive defines 'minors' by reference to national law. There is no such exception in the Council of Europe Convention.

[500] Recitals 4 and 7 in the preamble of the Directive.   [501] On that Directive, see I:5.5 above.

are free to provide for more extensive protection for persons covered by the Directive, without a requirement that such measures be 'compatible' with the Directive.[502]

Member States' authorities will usually trigger the application of the Directive by informing persons whom they believe could fall within its scope, although Member States have an option to decide if NGOs or associations specifically appointed by the Member State concerned can also trigger the process.[503] There is no specific requirement to identify victims; this is a failing as compared to other international instruments,[504] although it is arguable that such an obligation is nonetheless implicit in the EU law principle of effectiveness. After the victims are informed, they have a reflection period to decide if they wish to cooperate with the authorities; the starting point and length of this period are determined by national law.[505] During this period, expulsion orders cannot be enforced,[506] and the person concerned is entitled to minimum standards of treatment as regards subsistence, emergency medical treatment, translation and interpretation, and legal aid.[507] The reflection period does not create a right to subsequent residence,[508] and a Member State may end the period if the person concerned 'actively, voluntarily and on his/her own initiative' renews contact with the perpetrators, or on grounds of public policy or national security.[509]

Following (or possibly before) the end of the reflection period, the national authorities 'shall consider' the 'opportunity presented by' the continued stay of the victim, his/her intention to cooperate and whether he or she has severed relations with the perpetrators,[510] before issuing a residence permit.[511] While the Directive does not appear to create a right to a permit if the conditions are met, the words 'shall consider' suggest at least a procedural obligation for Member States.[512] The permit must be valid for at least

---

[502] Art 4. On the 'compatibility' issue, see I:7.2.4 above.   [503] Art 5.

[504] See the ECtHR judgment in *Rantsev v Russia* and Article 10 of the Council of Europe Convention on trafficking in persons.

[505] Art 6(1). Compare to the more favourable rules in Arts 12 and 13 of the trafficking Convention (n 504 above).

[506] Art 6(2). Although the Returns Directive (I:7.7.1 below) sets out a prima facie obligation to expel irregular migrants, Member States have a broad discretion to refrain from issuing or to withdraw or suspend a return decision, or to postpone removal (Arts 6(4) and 9(2), Dir 2008/115). In any event, the entire Returns Directive is subject to more favourable provisions in other EU immigration and asylum law (Art 4(2), Dir 2008/115). This provision in Dir 2004/81 is obviously one example of a more favourable provision. Also, the obligation to postpone removal in Art 6(2) of Dir 2004/81 entitles a Member State to permit the person concerned to work (see Art 3(3), Dir 2009/52, n 492 above).

[507] Arts 6(2) and 7. If removal of the victim has been postponed, this will overlap with Art 14 of the Returns Directive (see I:7.7.1 below). Again, compare to the more favourable rules in Arts 12 and 13 of the trafficking Convention.

[508] Art 6(3).

[509] Art 6(4). In light of the *Zh and O* ruling on the Returns Directive, the 'public policy' rule must arguably be interpreted by analogy with EU free movement law (see I.7.7.1 below). In the absence of indications to the contrary, the list of grounds for ending the period is exhaustive.

[510] Art 8(1). There is another 'public policy' exception in Art 8(2); again free movement law should apply by analogy (see I.7.7.1). In the absence of any indication to the contrary, the list of conditions for issuing the permit is exhaustive: see by analogy the case law on students' residence permits (I:6.5.3.2 above).

[511] The issue of the residence permit logically takes the victims outside the scope of other EU legislation on irregular migrants, for as long as the permit is valid. See, for instance, Art 2(b) and (d) of Dir 2009/52 (n 492 above).

[512] See by analogy Case C-83/11 *Rahman*, ECLI:EU:C:2012:519. Compare to the much stronger rule in Art 14(1) of the Council of Europe Convention.

six months, and 'shall' be renewed if these conditions are still met,[513] but there is no express reference to using the EU's uniform residence permit.[514] Member States are encouraged to consider authorizing the stay of the victim's family members on other grounds.[515]

The Directive also sets out rules on the treatment of the victims after the special permit is issued. Member States must continue to extend minimum standards regarding subsistence, emergency medical treatment, translation and interpretation, and (optionally) legal aid to victims, and must also give necessary medical or other assistance to victims with special needs and without sufficient resources.[516] If Member States apply the Directive to minors, they must take account of the best interests of the child, give access to education on the same basis as nationals (although this may be limited to the public education system), and establish the identity and nationality of, trace the family members of, and ensure legal representation for unaccompanied minors in accordance with national law.[517] Member States must define the rules for victims' access to the labour market, vocational training, and education during the period of the residence permit; this does not appear to grant them discretion over whether to allow such access, but only discretion as regards the extent of and procedures for exercising such access.[518]

Victims must be given access to schemes designed to assist them to develop a normal social life, if such schemes exist, including courses to improve professional skills or to prepare for assisted return to their country of origin. Member States may also provide for special schemes designed for the persons concerned, and may make the residence permit conditional on participation in either the general or special schemes.[519] Moreover, the subsequent Returns Directive provides that an 'entry ban' as defined by that Directive shall not be issued to victims of trafficking, although this is 'without prejudice' to the obligation to issue an entry ban if an obligation to return has not been complied with, and also subject to a derogation on grounds of 'public policy, public security or national security'.[520]

The permit 'shall' not be renewed if the proceedings are over or if the conditions for its issue cease to be satisfied.[521] After this point, normal immigration law applies,[522] but the preamble to the Directive states that Member States 'should consider the fact that' the person concerned already has a residence permit issued on the basis of this

---

[513] Art 8(3).   [514] See further I:6.9.1 above.   [515] Recital 15 in the preamble.
[516] Art 9.   [517] Art 10. Art 2(f) defines 'unaccompanied minors'.
[518] Art 11. See by analogy the case law on the students' Directive (I:6.5.3 above).   [519] Art 12.
[520] Art 11(3), Dir 2008/115 (n 506 above). This protection does not apply to victims of smuggling, or if a victim falls outside the personal scope of the Returns Directive (see further I:7.7.1 below). Presumably the protection will also expire with the residence permit. Note, however, that Member States have considerable discretion as to whether to issue or withdraw an entry ban in all such cases (Art 11(1) and (3), Dir 2008/115). Again, this 'public policy' exception should be interpreted consistently with EU free movement law (*Zh and O* judgment).
[521] Art 13(1), although Member States retain the power to apply more favourable provisions in Art 4. In the absence of any indication to the contrary, this is an exhaustive list of grounds for non-renewal of the permit.
[522] In particular, the Returns Directive then applies, if the victim concerned is within the scope of that Directive. This triggers a prima facie obligation to issue a return decision (Art 6(1) of that Dir), but Member States retain a broad discretion to grant an 'autonomous residence permit or other authorisation offering

Directive if that person applies to stay on another ground.[523] The permit 'may' be withdrawn 'if the conditions for issue are no longer satisfied'. This applies 'in particular' where: the victim 'actively, voluntarily and on his/her own initiative' renews contact with the suspected perpetrators; the authorities believe that there has been fraudulent cooperation or a fraudulent complaint by the person concerned; there is a public policy or national security risk; the victim ceases to cooperate; or proceedings are discontinued. The general ground for withdrawal of a permit is exhaustive, but the list of particular examples of when that rule applies is non-exhaustive ('in particular').[524] While there are no express procedural rights relating to the grant or removal of a reflection period or permit, arguably the general principles of EU law and Article 47 of the Charter nonetheless apply.[525]

How has this Directive been implemented? First of all, in 2008,[526] the Commission reported that the reflection period was not applied in practice in most Member States. Residence permits were available for periods of between forty days and one year, most often for six months. Victims have access to the labour market in accordance with the Directive in every Member State except Poland. The available figures from nine Member States indicated that 2,676 victims had received permits, but 80% of those were in Italy, which had a pre-existing very generous status for trafficking victims. The Commission concluded that 'at EU level the situation is still largely unsatisfactory', but also noted that 'in countries... which have a significant number of assisted victims, figures on criminal proceedings are also higher... [t]herefore, further regulation might be necessary in order to ensure more effective victim support mechanisms'.

Subsequently, the 2010 report on the implementation of the Directive stated first of all that in the Commission's view, there were some deficiencies in the definition of 'trafficking' by Member States. Two Member States used the option not to apply the Directive to minors, while nine Member States took up the option to extend the Directive to victims of smuggling. Some Member States did not sufficiently ensure that information was made available to trafficking victims, and in some other Member States there were problems in practice in applying this provision.

The length of the reflection period varied widely, although it was not clearly set out or mandatory in some Member States. One Member State did not prevent removals during the reflection period. Some Member States did not properly transpose the provision for possible termination of the reflection period, or required additional documentation or conditions before a residence permit could be obtained. Nine Member States additionally permitted trafficking victims to stay even if they were not cooperating with the authorities (reflecting the additional option set out in the Council of Europe Convention).

---

a right to stay for compassionate, humanitarian or other reasons' (Art 6(4) of that Dir). As noted already, the victim might have a claim for international protection (see I:5.5 above); asylum seekers are outside the scope of the Returns Directive (see I:7.7.1 below).

   [523] Recitals 15 and 18 in the preamble. Compare to Art 14(4) of the trafficking Convention, which has slightly stronger wording.

   [524] Art 14.

   [525] See by analogy the discussion of a right to a hearing in the context of the Returns Directive (I:7.7.1 below).

   [526] Communication on human trafficking (COM (2008) 657, 17 Oct 2008).

Two Member States did not comply with the Directive as regards the minimum period of validity of the residence permit, although all Member States provided for renewal of the permit.[527] In some cases, the rules on support for victims were not adequately applied, as regards subsistence in particular, although the majority of Member States provided legal aid, and some provided access to general medical care. The requirement to locate family members of unaccompanied minors was not fully applied in several Member States. Only one Member State prevented access to employment for victims, while another imposed a licence requirement. There was a wide variation in national rules regarding withdrawal of the permit, although five Member States provided for the possibility of remaining on other grounds after the proceedings were terminated.

As for the impact of the Directive in practice, five Member States gave out more than 100 permits a year, while five gave out fewer than 20; the other Member States provided no or insufficient information. This was a small fraction of the overall numbers who were trafficked in some Member States. The Commission threatened to bring infringement proceedings against Member States which were not applying the Directive correctly: overall, the report suggested that there were breaches in one or more Member States of the Directive's provisions as regards the definition of trafficking, information to victims, the length of and existence of the reflection period, conditions regarding the reflection period, the treatment of victims, the minimum period of validity of the permit, and tracing the family of unaccompanied minors. For the future, the Commission suggested that there might be need for amendments to the Directive, as regards 'the possibility of issuing a temporary residence permit based on the vulnerable situation of the victim and not necessarily in exchange for cooperation with competent authorities', having 'a specified length of reflection periods for victims', 'strengthening the framework of treatment, in particular for minors' and 'reinforcement of the obligation to inform victims of their rights'.

Four years passed with no infringement proceedings or proposal to amend the Directive. The Commission's second report, issued in 2014, indicated that about 1,000 permits per year were being granted—about half of the estimated number of victims. By this point, ten Member States extended the Directive to smuggling cases, while only one excluded children. There were still legal and practical problems with the identification of victims. Some Member States still provided for broader grounds for termination of the reflection period than the Directive provides for, and for an inadequate subsistence. In several Member States, there are additional conditions for obtaining the residence permit, and/or additional grounds to withdraw it. The minimum period of validity is not observed in all Member States.

The Commission concluded that the Directive was still 'under-utilised', and that the temporary residence permit valid only for criminal proceedings 'might not constitute an incentive strong enough for vulnerable individuals, who need time to recover from a traumatic experience before considering whether to embark on formal cooperation with law enforcement and judicial authorities'. There is also great uncertainty

---

[527] The report does not indicate whether, as Art 8(3) requires, the renewals have to be mandatory if the grounds in Art 8(1)—and only those grounds—are satisfied.

as to whether cooperation will lead to a permit, and the criteria used to issue one. The Commission suggests that issuing a permit not linked to criminal proceedings, or for a longer minimum period, 'could also contribute to assisting victims' recovery and thus fostering their cooperation'.

Having said this, though, the Commission declared that due to the links between this Directive and the criminal law Directive on human trafficking,[528] it would wait until it assesses the implementation of the latter Directive (planned for 2015), until it decides whether to propose amendments to the 2004 Directive, or issue guidelines concerning its application. In the meantime it will hold discussions with Member States about the correct application of the Directive. It also encouraged a series of practical measures, such as better identification, holding individual risk assessments, and granting reflection periods and residence permits more quickly. Subsequently, in its Action Plan on smuggling issued in 2015, the Commission announced that it would review the 2004 Directive and consider proposing amendments in 2016.[529]

This evidence of the two Commission reports suggests that the Directive, as it currently stands, was unable to avoid the inherent tension between trying to combat irregular immigration by encouraging victims of trafficking and smuggling to testify, and the risk that the incentives offered to the victims would either be abused or have the result that the victims would be able to stay in the 'host' Member State longer than that State would wish. The key changes to the text as initially proposed by the Commission made its application to smuggling cases optional and weakened the extent and precision of the obligations imposed upon Member States as regards victims.[530] These latter changes have made the scheme established by the Directive less attractive to victims, as evidenced by the higher numbers receiving permits under the more generous scheme in Italy. Moreover, the Directive contains more limited provisions on the status of victims than the UN Protocol or the Council of Europe Convention on trafficking in persons.[531] In particular, the Convention sets higher standards than the Directive as regards the identification of victims, the treatment of victims not taking part in criminal proceedings, the application of the Convention to minors, the minimum reflection period, the treatment of victims during and after the reflection period, and the obligation to issue a residence permit.

All but one Member State is a party to the Convention, but the Commission's implementation reports show implicitly that many Member States are not satisfying their Convention obligations either. So any action to enforce the Directive would necessarily raise the standard of Member States' compliance with the Convention as well. Indeed, it is clear that some proportion of the relative ineffectiveness of the Directive is the fault of the Commission, which has so far not brought infringement proceedings. Any notion that dialogue with Member States would be sufficient to address failures in implementation should be dispelled when comparing the implementation reports of 2010 and 2014, which show continued breaches in some Member States as regards

---

[528] On the criminal law measures and plans for further legislation on human smuggling, see I:7.5.4 above.
[529] COM (2015) 285, 27 May 2015.
[530] For the Commission's proposal, see COM (2002) 71, 11 Feb 2002.
[531] See Arts 6 and 7 of the Protocol ([2006] OJ L 262/51) and Arts 10–15 of the Convention (CETS 197).

core provisions of the Directive (victim identification, grounds for refusal of a permit, validity period of the permit). But the 2014 report simply recommits the Commission to the failed strategy of holding discussions with Member States on implementation.

Alongside ensuring correct implementation of the Directive, it would be useful to amend the Directive at an early stage, to enshrine within it the higher standards that exist in the Council of Europe Convention, to extend it to cover smuggling cases, and to make the prospect of testifying more attractive, perhaps by offering a form of temporary work and residence permit valid for one year. Quite apart from the abstract principle of upholding the rule of law, the victims of the worst cases of human trafficking have been violently abducted or coerced, then repeatedly raped. Ensuring the correct implementation of the Directive will not prevent or lead to successful prosecutions in all such cases, but even the smallest improvement in reducing or prosecuting these crimes is well worth the effort it would take to ensure it.

7.7 Expulsion

Of course, if persons who do not or no longer have authorization to stay on the territory of a Member State are detected, the primary response of Member States is to expel them from the territory,[532] but expulsions are necessarily subject to the protection afforded by human rights or refugee law and humanitarian concerns. Expulsion often involves cross-border elements, but there is an argument that a Member State should not assist another Member State to carry out an expulsion without guarantees that human rights standards will be upheld. The EU has become involved in expulsion issues, first of all in regulating cross-border aspects, and subsequently in adopting minimum standards to govern expulsions, in the form of the 'Returns Directive'.[533] Due to the importance of this Directive, it is considered in detail first, and then the earlier cross-border rules relating to mutual recognition of expulsion orders, expulsion for transit, and joint flights are considered in turn. The EU also contributes funds to assist with expulsions.[534]

The initial source of rules on this issue was the Schengen Convention, Article 23 of which provided that persons who do not, or no longer, fulfil the requirements of entry within a Member State for a short stay 'shall normally be required to leave' all the Member States immediately.[535] Where the persons concerned held 'valid residence permits or provisional residence permits' issued by another Member State, they were 'required to go to' that Member State immediately.[536] If they had not left voluntarily,

---

[532] This book generally uses the word 'expulsion' throughout, although in recent years the EU institutions have preferred the term 'return'. The word 'return' is used in this section to the extent that it is a specific legal term with a meaning defined in legislation.

[533] See also, as regards voluntary return, a Maastricht-era Decision ([1997] OJ L 147/3) and Council conclusions of 2005 (text in press release of JHA Council, 12 Oct 2005).

[534] See I:7.8 below.

[535] Art 23(1) of the Convention ([2000] OJ L 239). This sub-section refers to the Schengen Convention, except where otherwise indicated. On the allocation of Arts 23 and 24 following the entry into force of the Treaty of Amsterdam, see I:7.2.2.2 above.

[536] Art 23(2).

or it could be assumed that they would not, or where 'their immediate departure' was 'required for reasons of national security or public policy', they had to be expelled immediately from the Member State where they were apprehended, 'in accordance with' the relevant national law; but if that national law did not allow for expulsion, the person concerned could be allowed to stay on the territory.[537] They could be expelled either to their country of origin or to any State where they could have been admitted, in accordance with Member States' readmission agreements.[538] But the latter rule did 'preclude the application of' the Geneva Convention on asylum, national rules on asylum, or the Convention provision concerning the requirement to go to another Member State.[539]

Where the expulsion could be charged to the third-country national, Article 24 of the Schengen Convention provided that Member States had to reimburse to each other the costs of such expulsions, subject to the Schengen Executive Committee's determination of the costs and practical arrangements. In fact, the Executive Committee never adopted the relevant rules.

The Court of Justice ruled that Article 23 of the Convention applied to all persons who did not or no longer met the legal requirements for a short stay on the territory.[540] But it did not impose a strict obligation to expel such a person, on the grounds that it 'favour[ed] the voluntary departure' of the persons concerned.[541] Even where the Convention did create an obligation to expel, this 'is subordinate to the conditions laid down in the national law of the Member State concerned'.[542] Therefore it was up to 'the national law of each Member State to adopt, particularly with regard to the conditions under which expulsion may take place, the means for applying the basic rules established in Article 23 of the' Convention.[543] As we will see, this flexibility for Member States was subsequently tightened by the Returns Directive.

7.7.1 Returns Directive

The controversial 'Returns Directive' was adopted in December 2008 after a lengthy and difficult negotiation between the EP and the Council (and also within each institution).[544] Member States had to apply the Directive by Christmas Eve 2010, with a further delay of one year to apply the provisions on legal aid.[545] The Directive replaced the provisions

---

[537] Art 23(3).   [538] Art 23(4). On readmission treaties, see I:7.9.1 below.

[539] Art 23(5). On asylum, see generally ch 5 of this volume.

[540] Joined Cases C-261/08 *Zurita Garcia* and C-348/08 *Choque Cabrera* [2009] ECR I-10143. Implicitly the Court did not limit the scope of Art 23 to persons who had moved between Member States, despite the overall context of Art 23, which appeared in the Convention provisions concerning freedom to travel between Member States (see generally I:4.9 above).

[541] Ibid, para 61 of the judgment, as regards Art 23(1); see equally para 62, as regards Art 23(2).

[542] Para 63 of the judgment, concerning Art 23(3).   [543] Para 64 of the judgment.

[544] Dir 2008/115 ([2008] OJ L 348/98). On the Directive, see: A Baldaccini, 'The Return and Removal of Irregular Migrants under EU Law: An Analysis of the Returns Directive' (2009) 11 EJML 1; D Acosta, 'The Good, the Bad, and the Ugly in EU Migration Law' (2009) 11 EJML 19; the Statewatch analysis of June 2008: <http://www.statewatch.org/news/2008/jun/eu-analysis-returns-directive-june-2008-final.pdf>.; and the analysis by Acosta in S Peers et al., *EU Immigration and Asylum Law: Text and Commentary*, 2nd edn, vol 2 (Martinus Nijhoff, 2012), ch 17.

[545] Art 20(1), Dir 2008/115. All the references in this sub-section are to this Dir, unless otherwise indicated.

of Articles 23 and 24 of the Schengen Convention, which were summarized above.[546] The CJEU has delivered over a dozen judgments on the Directive,[547] and a further case is pending.[548] Furthermore, the Commission has reported on the implementation of the Directive by the Member States, and produced a Handbook to guide Member States applying the Directive.[549]

The Directive applies to third-country nationals whose legal status was still an open issue as of the deadline to implement, for instance as regards the time limits for detention (*Kadzoev*) and the time limits placed on entry bans (*Filev and Osmani*). As for its personal scope, the Directive applies to all third-country nationals 'staying illegally' in a Member State,[550] except that Member States may decide (optionally) not to apply it to persons who: i) were refused entry in accordance with the Schengen Borders Code, or who were 'apprehended or intercepted in connection with' irregular crossing of an external border and who were not later allowed to stay in that Member State; or ii) 'are subject to a return as a criminal law sanction or as a consequence of a criminal law sanction, according to national law, or who are the subject of extradition procedures.'[551] However, as regards persons who were refused entry or stopped in connection with irregular entry, Member States are nevertheless required to apply certain rules in the Directive,[552] as well as the principle of non-refoulement (on this principle, see the discussion below). Furthermore, the Directive does not apply to persons with EU free movement rights.[553]

The CJEU has ruled several times on the exception relating to criminal law, in the context of the criminalization of irregular entry. First of all, in *El Dridl*, it ruled that the removal order had been issued separately from the criminal offence of irregular

---

[546] Art 21.

[547] Cases: C-357/09 PPU *Kadzoev* [2009] ECR I-11189; C-61/11 PPU *El Dridl* [2011] ECR I-3015; C-329/11 *Achughbabian* [2011] ECR I-12695; C-430/11 *Sagor*, ECLI:EU:C:2012:777; C-522/11 *Mbaye*, ECLI:EU:C:2013:190; C-534/11 *Arslan*, ECLI:EU:C:2013:343; C-383/13 PPU *G and R*, ECLI:EU:C:2013:533; C-297/12 *Filev and Osmani*, ECLI:EU:C:2013:569; C-146/14 PPU *Mahdi*, ECLI:EU:C:2014:1320; C-189/13 *Da Silva*, ECLI:EU:C:2014:2043; C-473/13 and C-514/13 *Bouzalmate* and *Bero*, ECLI:EU:C:2014:2095; C-474/13 *Pham*, ECLI:EU:C:2014:2096; C-166/13 *Mukarubega*, ECLI:EU:C:2014:2336; C-249/13 *Boudjlida*, ECLI:EU:C:2014:2431; C-562/13 *Abdida*, ECLI:EU:C:2014:2453; C-38/14 *Zaizoune*, ECLI:EU:C:2015:260; and C-554/13 *Zh and O*, ECLI:EU:C:2015:377; and C-290/14 *Celaj*, ECLI:EU:C:2015:640.

[548] Case C-47/15 *Affum*.

[549] Respectively COM (2014) 199, 28 Mar 2014 and <http://ec.europa.eu/dgs/home-affairs/what-we-do/policies/european-agenda-migration/proposal-implementation-package/docs/return_handbook_en.pdf>.

[550] Art 2(1). According to the definition in Art 3(2), this is a person who *either* 'does not fulfil, or no longer fulfils the conditions of entry as set out in Article 5 of the Schengen Borders Code' *or* who does not or no longer fulfils 'other conditions for entry, stay or residence in that Member State'. Presumably the 'other' conditions referred to here could be established by either EU or national law. The Schengen Borders Code is set out in Reg 562/2006 ([2006] OJ L 105/1); on the code, see I:3.6.1 above. Note that the first category of persons covered matches the scope of Art 23(1) of the Schengen Convention, but the second category of persons concerned is wider. Equally the Directive only builds on the Schengen *acquis* as regards the first category of persons, not the latter (paras 25 to 30 in the preamble); this has implications for the territorial scope of the Dir (see further I:7.2.5 above).

[551] Art 2(2), referring in part to Art 13 of the Borders Code (n 550 above). The 2014 report states that the majority of Member States apply the exclusions.

[552] Art 4(4). The provisions concerned are 'Article 8(4) and (5) (limitations on use of coercive measures), Article 9(2)(a) (postponement of removal), Article 14(1) (b) and (d) (emergency health care and taking into account needs of vulnerable persons), and Articles 16 and 17 (detention conditions).'

[553] Art 2(3). See also the definition of 'third-country national' in Art 3(1). On the relationship between irregular migration and free movement law, see I:7.4.1 above.

entry, and so the criminal law exception from the scope of the Directive did not apply. Secondly, and more broadly, it ruled in *Achughbabian* that the criminal law exclusion did not apply to any cases where a criminal penalty was imposed only for irregular entry.[554] Logically this reasoning equally applies to cases where a criminal penalty is imposed for irregular stay or breach of an entry ban, and the CJEU implicitly confirmed this interpretation in *Celaj*.[555] The Court also ruled in *Filev and Osmani* that if a Member State did not apply this exception as of the deadline date to implement the Directive, it could not then apply it retroactively to worsen the position of the person concerned. That judgment concerns entry bans, but logically by analogy it also has general application to other issues regulated by the Directive (and to other exceptions).

As for the other express exclusions from the scope of the Directive, the exclusion relating to refusal of entry pursuant to the Borders Code is clear enough, but the exclusion relating to irregular border crossing is less clear.[556] Since there is no reference to national law as regards this exclusion (as compared to the criminal law exclusion), and the EU law rules on borders to which it implicitly refers are subject to a high degree of harmonization, this exclusion should have an autonomous EU law meaning.[557] Quite clearly, the drafters of the Directive did not intend that Member States should have *carte blanche* to exclude all cases of clandestine entry from the scope of the Directive, otherwise the Directive could simply have provided for an optional exclusion regarding all persons 'who have illegally entered the territory of a Member State'—which in fact it provides for separately in relation to one specific issue.[558] This suggests a strong argument for an *a contrario* interpretation of the more general optional exclusion. Moreover, the preamble to the Directive simply states without qualification that the Directive should apply to 'all' third-country nationals who do not or no longer meet the conditions for entry, stay, or residence;[559] this necessarily means that any exclusions from the scope of the Directive as regards third-country nationals must be interpreted narrowly. In this light, the optional exclusion for irregular border crossing should only apply where a person was stopped at or near the border, in principle by border guards carrying out border surveillance as part of their border control obligations,[560] and *not* when a clandestine entrant was later detected on the territory.

There is no express exclusion from the Directive for asylum seekers, but the Court's case law confirms that they cannot be regarded as irregular migrants in the first place. Indeed, the preamble to the Directive states that in accordance with the EU's asylum procedures Directive,[561] a third-country national asylum seeker 'should not be regarded

---

[554] This was reaffirmed in the order in *Mbaye*.   [555] N 547 above.

[556] The CJEU decided that it was not necessary to answer the questions in *Da Silva*, although they may have been relevant to this issue.

[557] See by analogy Case C-578/08 *Chakroun* [2010] ECR I-1839.   [558] Art 12(3).

[559] Recital 5. There is no mention in the preamble of any of the exclusions from the Directive's scope. On this basis of this recital, it can surely be concluded that the list of exceptions set out in Art 2(2) is exhaustive.

[560] See the definitions of 'border guard' and 'border surveillance' in Art 2(11) and (13) of the Borders Code, as well as the specific provision on border surveillance in Art 12 of the Code. The definition of 'border control' in Art 2(9) of the Code should also be used to define the scope of the exclusion in the Dir: an 'activity carried out at the border in accordance with and for the purposes of [the Code] in response exclusively to an intention to cross or the act of crossing that border'.

[561] Art 7 of Dir 2005/85, [2005] OJ L 326/13; Art 9 of Dir 2013/32, [2013] OJ L 180/60. On this Dir generally, see I:5.7 above.

as staying illegally on the territory of that Member State until a negative decision on the application, or a decision ending his or her right of stay as asylum seeker has entered into force'.[562] The Court of Justice ruled on this point first of all in *Kadzoev*, stating that asylum seekers were outside the scope of the Returns Directive due to the provision in the preamble and the *lex specialis* rules on detention in other EU asylum legislation. Subsequently, the Court elaborated in *Arslan* that the same rule applied even if the migrant applied for asylum while already detained, given that the EU's asylum procedures Directive had special rules dealing with asylum applicants in that position.[563]

More favourable provisions for the persons concerned can be set out either in agreements between the EU and/or the Member States with third countries, or in other EU legislation, or in national legislation. In the case of national legislation (but not otherwise), this possibility is subject to the proviso that the more favourable rules are 'compatible' with the Returns Directive.[564] The limits which this rule places upon Member States were clarified in *Zaizoune*, where the Court ruled that a national practice of fining irregular migrants in some cases, rather than expelling them, went beyond Member States' power of discretion, since it contradicted the basic objective of securing removal, contradicted the rules in the Directive obliging Member States to issue a return order and carry out a removal, and would 'thwart' common standards and 'delay' return. The Court emphasized that none of the exceptions to the basic rule requiring removal (discussed below) applied in this case. Since the main focus of the Court's judgment in *Zaizoune* (consistently with much of the other case law on the Directive, for instance as regards custodial penalties delaying removal) concerns the effective issue and enforcement of a return order, presumably the 'compatibility' rule applies only in that particular context, not to the other aspects of the Directive.[565]

The EU legislation which sets more favourable standards includes Directive 2004/81 on the rights of victims of trafficking,[566] which entails at the very least an obligatory postponement of expulsion during the reflection period set out in that Directive,[567] and might also mean suspension or withdrawal of a return decision for that period. If a residence permit is granted under the 2004 Directive it must follow that the person concerned is, for the time being, outside the scope of the Returns Directive entirely, so either a return decision cannot be issued or any such decision must be rescinded or withdrawn,[568] and the postponement (or, by implication, the rescinding) of removal necessarily follows. Victims also have more rights to health care, employment, and social assistance during the reflection period and while residing on the basis

---

[562] Recital 9 in the preamble. It should be recalled that the first-phase asylum procedures Directive, unlike the Returns Directive, also applies to the UK and Ireland, whereas the Returns Directive (in part), but not the asylum procedures Directive, applies to Schengen associates.

[563] The Court also referred to the plans to adopt more detailed rules on detention in the second-phase asylum legislation, which has since been adopted (for instance, Arts 8–11, Directive 2013/33, [2013] OJ L 180/96): see I:5.7 to I:5.9 above. Note that the EU's Dir on temporary protection does not have specific rules on this issue, and so arguably any persons who obtain temporary protection status but who are not also asylum seekers *would* be covered by the detention rules in the Returns Directive (see I:5.6 above).

[564] Art 4. On such requirements of 'compatibility' in EU immigration and asylum law, see I:5.2.4 above.

[565] The possible specific implications of the *Zaizoune* ruling are discussed further throughout this sub-section.

[566] Dir 2004/81 ([2004] OJ L 261/19), discussed in I:7.6.2 above.   [567] Art 9.   [568] Art 6(4).

of a residence permit than they would have under the Returns Directive.[569] It is arguable that the previous option (rather than an obligation) to expel a person pursuant to
the Schengen Borders Code is also still in place; if so, it also constitutes a more favourable rule.[570]

When implementing the Returns Directive, Member States 'shall take due account
of' the best interests of the child, family life, and the state of health of the persons concerned, and respect the principle of non-refoulement.[571] In *Abdida*, the CJEU confirmed that at least the non-refoulement clause prevented the enforcement of a return
decision. Moreover, the Court interpreted this provision of the Directive consistently
with Article 19(2) of the EU Charter, and in turn interpreted the Charter provision in
line with the case law of the European Court of Human Rights. That line of jurisprudence, interpreting the ban on torture or other inhuman or degrading treatment set out
in Article 3 ECHR, does not permit migrants to stay in a country to obtain social or
medical assistance as a general rule. But as the CJEU points out, the other Court's case
law provides that 'a decision to remove a foreign national suffering from a serious physical or mental illness to a country where the facilities for the treatment of the illness are
inferior to those available in that State may raise an issue under Article 3 ECHR in very
exceptional cases, where the humanitarian grounds against removal are compelling'. It
should be noted that this rule covers people who are not entitled to international protection (refugee or subsidiary protection status) under EU asylum legislation.[572]

It remains to be seen how the CJEU will interpret the other grounds which Member
States must take account of (best interests of the child, family life, and state of health),
although the case law on the effect of similar general provisions in the EU's family
reunion Directive suggests prima facie that these provisions of the Returns Directive
should have a comparable strong legal impact.[573] These are the only express substantive
grounds for objecting to an expulsion set out in the Directive. However, it should not be
forgotten that any substantive grounds for resisting expulsion set out in other EU legislation, national legislation, or international treaties will take priority over the Returns
Directive anyway.[574] Finally, it should be noted that the CJEU ruled in *Boudjlida* that
the right to a hearing on the expulsion decision (discussed further below) encompasses
an obligation to consider all of the arguments that the migrant might, as regards the
various considerations that Member States, have to take into account.

---

[569] Compare Arts 7 and 9–12 of Dir 2004/81 to Art 14, Returns Dir. It should also be noted that Dir 2004/
81 does not include an option to exclude persons refused entry or stopped in connection with illegal entry,
whereas the Returns Dir does.

[570] Art 11 of the Code (n 550 above), as interpreted by the Court of Justice in *Zurita Garcia* and *Choque
Cabrera* (n 540 above), was later amended in 2013 (see I:3.6.1 above). But it still says that an irregular
migrant 'may' be expelled, suggesting more flexibility than the Returns Directive.

[571] Art 5.

[572] In its parallel judgment in Case C-542/13 *M'Bodj* (ECLI:EU:C:2014:2452) the CJEU ruled that granting refugee or subsidiary protection status exceeded Member States' discretion to establish more favourable
standards pursuant to EU asylum legislation. See further I:5.5 above; and for more on the concept of non-
refoulement, see I:5.3.1 above.

[573] Case C-540/03 *EP v Council* [2006] ECR I-5759; see further I:6.6 above.

[574] Art 4(1) to (3). As discussed above, any higher national standards must be 'compatible' with the
Directive. In light of *Zaizoune*, therefore, it may be questionable whether Member States have any general
discretion to allow irregular migrants to stay on grounds not mentioned in Art 5, unless they invoke one of
the exceptions set out in Art 6.

Chapter II of the Directive contains six Articles concerning the 'termination of illegal stay'. First of all, there are basic rules regarding 'return decisions'.[575] Member States must issue a return decision to every third-country national staying illegally on their territory,[576] although decisions on return have to be decided on a case-by-case basis, not automatically for the sole reason that a person is not legally resident.[577] Furthermore, the general rule is 'without prejudice' to a number of exceptions. First of all, a third-country national who holds a residence permit or other authorization to stay in a second Member State 'shall be required to go' back there instead; he or she would only be subject to a return decision in cases of non-compliance with the obligation to return to the second Member State or for reasons of 'public policy or national security'.[578] Next, a third-country national 'may' instead be sent to another Member State pursuant to a pre-existing bilateral deal, but in that case the second Member State 'shall' then issue a return decision to the person concerned.[579] Presumably, where the person concerned has a residence permit or other authorization to stay in another Member State, the first exception takes precedence over the second one.

Next, Member States have a very wide discretion to regularize stays of irregular migrants, 'at any moment ... for compassionate, humanitarian or other reasons'.[580] In that case, no return decision shall be issued, but if a return decision has already been issued, Member States have the option of merely suspending the decision, rather than withdrawing it, for the duration of the authorized stay. The Directive is silent on the question of regularizing large numbers of persons, so in the absence of any other EU rules regulating this issue, Member States retain competence to regularize the stay of large numbers of irregular migrants collectively if they wish.[581] But equally there is no *right* to regularization as a matter of EU law,[582] or any harmonized procedural or substantive rules at EU level applicable to regularizations. It is open to Member States to limit regularization to particular categories of persons, or to regularize stay only for a limited time, at least initially, in light of the circumstances in the country of origin.[583]

---

[575] Art 6. For the definition of 'return decision', see Art 3(4).

[576] Art 6(1). The definition of 'return' is set out in Art 3(3): 'return' can be either to a country of origin or transit, or to another third country which the person concerned chooses to return to and in which that person will be admitted. There is no definition of 'third countries'. It is not clear whether a Member State (or a non-EU Schengen state) might be considered a 'third country', and furthermore if there is any distinction between the participating and non-participating Member States in this regard.

[577] Recital 6 in the preamble to the Directive.

[578] Art 6(2). On the interpretation of the public policy rule, see the analysis of Art 7 below.

[579] Art 6(3). The agreements in question had to exist already when the Directive entered into force (this was 13 Jan 2009: see Art 22). The implication is that no further such agreements can be made after this date.

[580] Art 6(4); the 2014 report states that all Member States provide for this possibility. Presumably this discretion also exists where an irregular migrant has been sent to another Member State pursuant to Art 6(3), because the second Member State in that case has taken over the entire return procedure (including any exceptions which may apply).

[581] See by comparison Art 7(2), which provides for extension of the required period to return in individual cases. The ruling in *Zaizoune* does not prevent Member States from doing this, since it expressly only sets limits on more favourable standards in cases where none of the exceptions in Art 6 apply.

[582] Leaving aside the possibility of becoming a family member of an EU citizen: see I:7.4.1 above. See also the discussion of 'limbo' cases below.

[583] If, however, some of the persons concerned wished to pursue asylum applications, the EU's asylum legislation would be applicable (see generally ch 5 of this volume).

Member States are not limited as regards the grounds for regularization in individual cases, which are clearly non-exhaustive ('or other reasons'),[584] or the timing of regularization, which expressly can take place at any time—presumably even after a removal has actually taken place. They do not have to report to the EU institutions on individual regularizations, although they might have obligations to report on large-scale regularizations pursuant to the Decision on the exchange of immigration information,[585] and the Schengen Convention imposes an obligation to consult another Member State which has issued a SIS alert on an individual before issuing that person with a residence permit or a long-stay visa.[586] Furthermore, Member States 'shall consider refraining from issuing a return decision' to persons whose applications for renewal of a permit to stay are pending, until that pending procedure is finished.[587]

As for the procedure of issuing return decisions, a return decision can be issued as a single act along with a decision terminating legal stay, a removal decision, or an entry ban, subject to the relevant safeguards in the Directive and other EU and national rules.[588] The Directive does not specify whether Member States must refrain from issuing, withdraw, or suspend removal orders and entry bans in the event that they refrain from issuing, withdraw, or suspend return decisions, but logically the former must be considered as a necessary corollary of the latter.

The Directive does not otherwise specifically regulate the process of taking a return decision. However, the CJEU case law (notably *Mukarubega* and *Boudjlida*) has developed a number of key principles of administrative procedural law which govern that process.[589] In particular, the Court ruled that the general principles of EU law guarantee a right to be heard before national administrations considering whether to issue a return decision, even where EU legislation (as in this case) does not regulate that issue in detail. They entail a right for the migrant to make his or her views known before the adoption of a decision, to correct an error or to submit information related to the decision. The administration must pay attention to those observations, subjecting them to a careful and impartial examination, giving a detailed statement of the reasons for its decision, which are specific, concrete, and understandable. However, the right to be heard can be incorporated into another process of determining immigration status, combining a return decision with a decision that the migrant's stay is illegal. This ensures, in the Court's view, a balance between human rights protection

---

[584] For that reason it does not matter that the grounds of exception from the obligation to expel irregular migrants set out in Art 6(2) to 6(5) are arguably exhaustive, since Art 6(4) is itself not subject to any limitations.

[585] See I:7.8 below.   [586] Art 25 of the Convention; on this provision, see further I:4.9 above.

[587] Art 6(5). Compare with the position of Turkish workers and their family members pursuant to the EU-Turkey association agreement (I:7.4.2 above). Arguably the words 'shall consider' at least constitute a procedural obligation to consider the possibility of refraining from a ban and to give reasons for not doing so: see by analogy Case C-83/11 *Rahman*, ECLI:EU:C:2012:519.

[588] Art 6(6); see also Art 8(3). For the definition of 'removal' and 'entry ban', see Art 3(5) and (6). The 2014 report states that the majority of Member States have a one-step process; only nine have a two-step process.

[589] See also *G and R*, discussed below, which concerns the right to be heard in the context of immigration detention. This case law may also mean that EU law implicitly includes principles relating to the process of apprehension—even though, as the 2014 report points out, the Directive does not expressly harmonize that process.

and the effectiveness of the returns process. In the *Mukarubega* case, the initial asylum decision, coupled with a police interview leading up to a second return decision, was adequate in the circumstances, since the police considered the situation 'beyond the mere fact of illegal stay' and the obligation to leave the territory was clearly set out in national law.

In *Boudjlida*, the Court elaborated on these principles, stating that the right to be heard must allow the migrant to submit observations on the legality of his or her stay, the applicability of any exceptions to the obligation to issue a return decision, the factors (such as non-refoulement and the rights of the child) that Member States had to consider when making return decisions, and the 'detailed arrangements' for return, such as the deadline to leave and whether departure could be voluntary.[590] Presumably this encompasses the question of whether removal should be postponed (see discussion below), although this question might arise at a later date. The right should also, by analogy, apply to the question of whether an entry ban ought to be issued and if so, for how long, in particular since an entry ban (according to the Directive) might be issued at the same time as the original return decision. If an entry ban is issued separately, there would arguably be a separate right to a hearing on that point.

Yet having ruled that the right to be heard in return proceedings has a wide scope, the Court then divested that right of much substantive content. It does not entail a right to disclosure of the evidence against the migrant, or a reflection period, or free legal assistance—although the migrant can obtain such assistance at his or her own expense. As an 'exception', though, there might be a stronger right to be heard if the migrant could not reasonably anticipate the evidence which would be used against him or her, or if he or she could only respond to that evidence by taking further steps, such as obtaining other documents. In general, there was no obligation to warn the migrant that a return decision might be taken, and the migrant must cooperate and provide all relevant information.[591] On the facts of this case, a thirty-minute police interview was sufficiently compliant with all these safeguards, even though (unlike *Mukarubega*) there had been no full asylum procedure beforehand as well.

Next, the Directive addresses voluntary departure. The basic principle is that a return decision must allow for a possible voluntary departure within a period of between seven and thirty days, although the persons concerned are free to leave earlier.[592] Also, this rule is subject to exceptions. On the one hand, Member States 'shall, where necessary, extend the period for voluntary departure for an appropriate period' in 'individual case[s]', on grounds 'such as' family and social links, the length of stay, or children's school attendance.[593] On the other hand, if there is a risk of

---

[590] In *Zh and O*, the Court made clear that the assessment of whether voluntary departure could be granted did not have to be the subject of a separate hearing, but could be considered when the initial return decision was being considered.

[591] Compare to the obligations to cooperate with the refugee determination process, discussed in I:5.5 above.

[592] Art 7(1). Member States may decide that this period applies only after application by the person concerned, although in that case they must inform the eligible persons about the possibility of applying. Only three Member States use this option, according to the 2014 report.

[593] Art 7(2). Implicitly Member States have no power to set a longer period for voluntary departure for all irregular migrants, or for a large group of collective migrants without consideration of individual

absconding,[594] if an application for legal stay has been dismissed as 'manifestly unfounded' or fraudulent,[595] or if 'the person concerned poses a risk to public policy, public security or national security', Member States may refrain from permitting voluntary departure or grant a period shorter than seven days.[596] They may also impose obligations upon individuals during the period allowed for voluntary departure, to avoid the risk of absconding.[597] The wording of the Directive suggests that the grounds for extension of the period for voluntary departure are non-exhaustive ('such as'), whereas the Court has confirmed that the grounds for refusing such an opportunity, limiting the period, or imposing obligations during that period are exhaustive.[598] Overall, the 2014 report indicates that the inclusion of these rules has had a positive effect, with a number of Member States providing for a voluntary departure period for the first time in their national law.[599]

The grant of a voluntary departure period is a crucial issue as regards the application of much of the Directive. It implicitly determines whether the migrant will be detained, and necessarily determines whether his or her removal will be coerced. If no voluntary departure is granted, then in principle the migrant must be subject to an entry ban,[600] and does not have access to minimum standards of treatment. In this context, the CJEU has made clear that the Directive provides for a 'gradation' of measures to be applied against a migrant, beginning with voluntary departure and progressing toward detention (*El Dridi*). Moreover, the purpose of the voluntary departure period is to secure the fundamental rights of the migrant (*Zh and O*). It follows that the exceptions from the rule have to be interpreted strictly (*Zh and O*). Two of these exceptions have been clarified by the CJEU: the risk of absconding (in *Mahdi*)[601] and the public policy exception (in *Zh and O*). In *Mahdi*, the Court ruled that any assessment of the risk of absconding has to be decided on a case-by-case basis, based on objective criteria. It breaches the Directive to detain someone on that basis purely because they do not have identity documents, without considering whether a less coercive measure could be applied.

As for the public policy exception, the CJEU ruled in *Zh and O* that it should be interpreted 'by analogy' with the similar provisions of EU free movement law.[602] It is up

---

circumstances, but arguably such a measure could fall within the scope of Member States' power to set higher standards pursuant to Art 4(3), although the counter-argument is that (in light of *Zaizoune*) this would be incompatible with the Directive. In any event, Member States which wished to refrain from expelling a large group of persons could regularize their stay for a limited period, pursuant to Art 6(4).

[594] The definition of 'risk of absconding' is set out in Art 3(7): the 'existence of reasons in an individual case which are based on objective criteria defined by law to believe that a third-country national who is the subject of return procedures may abscond'.

[595] It might be questioned whether the concept of a 'manifestly unfounded' application corresponds, at least for failed asylum seekers, to the equivalent concept in the asylum procedures Directive. See I:5.7 above.

[596] Art 7(4). If national law is not consistent with these provisions, a national court must disapply it (*Sagor*, para 48).

[597] Art 7(3).   [598] *El Dridi*, para 37, confirmed in *Zh and O*.

[599] The report states that in 2012, about 44% of removals took place after a voluntary departure. It is not known how these figures have changed over time.

[600] See discussion of Art 11 below.

[601] Paras 65–73 of that judgment. *Mahdi* concerned the grounds for detention in Art 15, but there is no reason to assume that 'risk of absconding' has a different meaning for the purposes of Art 7.

[602] See I:7.4.1 above.

to the Member State to 'prove' the risk to public policy, and while Member States 'retain the freedom' to decide on the concept of public policy, they do not have full latitude to determine the concept without any control by the Court. The exception has to be applied on a 'case-by-case basis', to decide if the 'personal conduct' of the migrant 'poses a genuine and present risk to public policy'. This means that the suspicion of committing a criminal act, or even a criminal conviction, cannot by itself justify the conclusion that a 'public policy' risk exists.

However, it is possible that the 'public policy' exception could still apply where an appeal against a criminal conviction has not yet been decided, or where there is no conviction, as long as 'other factors' justified the use of that exception. Those other factors include the 'nature and seriousness' of the act and 'the time which has elapsed since it was committed'. So the national court had to consider that in one case, the migrant was actually not trying to stay in the Netherlands without authorization, but was on his way out (travelling to Canada) when he was stopped. In the other case, the migrant had been accused of domestic abuse, but it was relevant that there was nothing to substantiate that accusation.

Member States are required in principle to remove a person once the period for voluntary departure has expired, or if no such period has been granted.[603] A removal cannot be carried out while the period for voluntary departure has not yet expired, unless that period has been curtailed pursuant to the Directive.[604] Any coercive measures must be used as a 'last resort', and must be 'proportional', 'not exceed reasonable force', and be in accordance with human rights and the dignity and physical integrity of the person concerned.[605] When removing persons by air, Member States 'shall take into account' the common guidelines on security provisions for joint removals, attached to the 2004 Decision on joint flights.[606] In all cases, Member States 'shall provide for an effective forced-return monitoring system'.[607] The 2014 report indicated that a large number of Member States introduced such a system as a 'direct result of the Directive'.

Member States are obliged to postpone removal where it would violate the principle of non-refoulement (see the discussion of this principle above), or where a suspensive effect of removal has been granted by a court (see below).[608] Member States *may* postpone removal in other specific cases,[609] and 'shall in particular take into account' the health of the person concerned or technical difficulties. These grounds are non-exhaustive ('in particular'). As we saw above, the CJEU accepted in the *Abdida* judgment that the state of health of a person could in exceptional cases constitute a non-refoulement issue.

It is odd that the Directive only refers to postponement of removal, rather than the possibility of cancellation of the return decision or the removal order, particularly as

---

[603] Art 8(1). On the definition of 'removal', see Art 3(5). Member States' power to set more favourable standards (Art 4(3)) is limited in this context (see the discussion of *Zaizoune* above).

[604] Art 8(2).   [605] Art 8(4).

[606] Art 8(5), referring to [2004] OJ L 261/28. On this Decision, see I:7.7.4 below.

[607] Art 8(6).

[608] Art 9(1); see the discussion of Art 5 and the *Abdida* judgment.

[609] Art 9(2). The definition of individual cases here is the same as set out in Art 7(2), although the examples of cases are different, and it is clear that while Art 9(2) is a discretionary exception, Art 7(2) is mandatory ('shall').

regards the non-refoulement principle,[610] but presumably the power to cancel a removal order entirely is implicit in Member States' power to grant authorized residence 'at any moment'.[611] As discussed further below, where removal has been postponed, there are provisions in this Directive and in the Directive on prohibition of employment of irregular migrants on the status of the person concerned in the meantime; but there is no obligation in the Returns Directive to end this 'state of limbo' at any particular point.

There are specific safeguards concerning the return or removal of unaccompanied minors.[612] Before a return decision is issued to such persons, there must be assistance from bodies other than the return authorities, 'with due consideration being given to the best interests of the child'.[613] Furthermore, before removal of an unaccompanied minor, the national authorities 'shall be satisfied that he or she will be returned to a member of his or her family, a nominated guardian or adequate reception facilities in the State of return'.[614]

Next, the rules on entry bans were among the most controversial provisions of the Directive.[615] An entry ban *must* be issued where a return decision was issued without a period for voluntary departure being granted, or where an obligation for return was not complied with.[616] In other cases, an entry ban *may* be issued.[617] The length of the entry ban must be based on 'all relevant circumstances of the individual case' and 'shall not in principle exceed five years', although longer bans are possible in cases of 'serious threat to public policy, public health or national security'.[618] According to the CJEU, the length of an entry ban *must* be limited by the Member State; such a limitation cannot depend upon an application by the third-country national concerned.[619] It should also be noted that the procedural rights in the Directive (discussed below) also apply to entry bans, and it is arguable that the right to be heard (discussed above) applies to any decision to issue one.

Member States 'shall consider withdrawing or suspending' an entry ban if the person concerned can demonstrate that he or she in fact left in compliance with a return decision.[620] They must not apply an entry ban to victims of trafficking in persons who have been granted a residence permit pursuant to Directive 2004/81, which concerns

---

[610] While protection status is subject to the possibility of 'cessation' if circumstances change (see I:5.5 above), it may be years before circumstances have changed sufficiently—or they might never change much at all.

[611] Art 6(4), discussed above. In particular, as suggested above, the suspension or withdrawal of a return decision must logically entail the suspension or withdrawal of a removal order in parallel. The general power to set higher standards pursuant to Art 4(3) must also entail a power to rescind removal orders entirely.

[612] There is no definition of 'unaccompanied minors' (or 'minors') in the Directive. For the definition in other measures, see, for instance, Art 2(f) of the family reunion Dir (Dir 2003/86, [2003] OJ L 251/12). See also the action plan on unaccompanied minors (COM (2010) 213, 6 May 2010) and the follow-up to that plan (COM (2012) 554, 28 Sep 2012).

[613] Art 10(1). See the discussion of this concept above.   [614] Art 10(2).

[615] Art 3(6) defines an 'entry ban' as a decision which applies to *all* the participating Member States. See also recital 18 in the preamble.

[616] Art 11(1). This matches the circumstances in which a removal decision must be carried out (Art 8(1)).

[617] N 616 above. This implies that an entry ban may be issued even if a period for voluntary departure has been granted (compare to Art 8(2), prohibits a removal order in those circumstances), and even if a voluntary departure obligation has been complied with (but see Art 11(3), discussed below).

[618] Art 11(2). This is an exhaustive list of cases where there can be a longer entry ban: see *Filev and Osmani*, para 32 ('except if').

[619] *Filev and Osmani*.   [620] Art 11(3), first sub-paragraph.

the immigration status of such victims,[621] but this is 'without prejudice' to the obligation to issue an entry ban where an obligation to return was not complied with, and also subject to an exception on grounds of public policy, public security, or national security.[622] Member States may refrain from issuing, or withdraw or suspend, an entry ban 'in individual cases for humanitarian reasons', and 'may withdraw or suspend' a ban 'in individual cases or certain categories of cases for other reasons'.[623] According to the 2014 report, the Directive resulted in an increased number of entry bans in some Member States, but a reduced maximum length of the ban in others.

The Directive also provides that if a Member State intends to issue a residence permit to a person who is subject to an entry ban issued by another Member State, the first Member State should first of all consult with the Member State that issued the entry ban according to the rules set out in the Schengen Convention.[624] The Convention rules previously applied only where an alert for the purpose of refusing entry had been entered into the SIS,[625] but the Directive appears to extend these rules to cases in which an entry ban has not been entered onto the SIS. But it is hard to see how Member States will be aware of other Member State's entry bans in any case unless those bans have been entered as SIS alerts. A Commission statement issued when the Directive was adopted indicates that when the operation of the second-generation Schengen Information System (SIS II) is reviewed, that will be 'an opportunity to propose an obligation to register in the SIS entry bans issued under this Directive', although of course Member States might choose to register those entry bans in the SIS even before they are obliged to do so.[626] In its recent anti-smuggling action plan, the Commission reiterated its intention to address this issue, and also suggested that 'return decisions' should also be included in the SIS.[627]

Chapter III of the Directive concerns procedural safeguards. This is distinct from the right to a hearing, as discussed above, and the specific rules on challenging detention, discussed below. Return decisions, removal decisions, and decisions on entry bans must be issued in writing and contain reasons in fact and law as well as information on remedies, although the obligation to give factual reasons can be limited by national law, 'in particular in order to safeguard national security, defence, public security and for the prevention, investigation, detection and prosecution of criminal offences'.[628]

---

[621] [2004] OJ L 261/19. On this Dir, see I:7.6.2 above.

[622] Art 11(3), second sub-paragraph. Presumably this exception (which also appears in Art 11(2)) must be interpreted the same way as Art 7(4) of the Directive (see the discussion of *Zh and O* above).

[623] Art 11(3), third and fourth sub-paragraphs. Note that in the latter case, there is no capacity to refrain from issuing bans, but then again Member States retain a power to set more favourable standards compatible with the Dir (Art 4(3)). Arguably the 'compatibility' clause in the Directive does not limit a more liberal approach to issuing entry bans, since the issue is not at the core of the Directive, ie removal of persons (see discussion of Art 4 and the *Zaizoune* judgment above).

[624] Art 11(4), referring to Art 25 of the Convention. On this provision of the Convention, see I:4.9 above.

[625] On these alerts, see I:3.7 above.

[626] Summary of Council acts for Dec 2008 (Council doc 7478/08, 11 Mar 2009). For a detailed discussion of the relationship between the Returns Directive and the SIS II Regulation, see I:3.7 above. The review is due in April 2016.

[627] COM (2015) 285, 27 May 2015.

[628] Art 12(1). The list of possible grounds for restricting information appears to be non-exhaustive. At least in part the exception should arguably be interpreted consistently with the *Zh and O* judgment, concerning Art 7. For the Court's interpretation of a similar exception in light of Art 47 of the Charter, see Case C-300/11 ZZ, ECLI:EU:C:2013:363.

The main elements of the decision must be translated upon request, including information on the available legal remedies, in a language which the person concerns understands or can be presumed to understand.[629] Member States have an option not to provide a translation where persons have entered irregularly and have not subsequently obtained authorization to stay; but in that case Member States must supply information by means of a standard form set out in national law, and must provide explanations of this form in at least five languages which are most frequently used or understood by irregular migrants who enter that Member State.[630] The 2014 report indicates that there are some concerns in practice about the lack of detail and reasoning in national decisions, as well as the translation of the main elements of the decisions.

The persons concerned must have an 'effective remedy' to appeal or review all types of decisions related to return before some sort of independent and impartial body, which could be (but need not be) a judicial or administrative body.[631] This entity must have the power to review the decisions related to return, including the power to suspend those decisions temporarily, unless such a power already exists in national law (ie because the legal challenge automatically suspends application of the decision concerned).[632] The person concerned must also be able to obtain 'legal advice, representation and, where necessary, linguistic assistance'.[633] As for legal aid, this must be available subject to the same limitations provided for in the asylum procedures directive.[634] According to the CJEU, in cases of refoulement, challenges to removal orders must have automatic suspensive effect.[635] The 2014 report indicated that there were problems in practice as regards legal aid and translation, and in some Member States appeals are uncommon.

The Returns Directive provides for safeguards pending return, in the case of voluntary departure or postponement of a removal decision.[636] The persons concerned must be given written confirmation of their position, and Member States must 'ensure that the following principles are taken into account as far as possible', except where persons are in detention: family unity; emergency health care and essential treatment of illness; minors' access to basic education; and 'special needs of vulnerable persons are taken into account'.[637] There is no express mention of social welfare, and according to the preamble, the 'basic conditions of subsistence' should be defined according to national law.[638]

These provisions were strengthened in the *Abdida* judgment. The Court ruled that Member States are 'required to provide' the safeguards to a third-country national whose return was suspended due to a very serious illness. This is a stronger obligation than a requirement that a 'principle' must be 'taken into account as far as possible', although it

---

[629] Art 12(2).   [630] Art 12(3).   [631] Art 13(1).

[632] Art 13(2). The 2014 report states that only a minority of Member States (nine) provide for automatic suspensive effect.

[633] Art 13(3).

[634] Art 13(4), referring to Art 15(3) to (6) of Dir 2005/85 (n 561 above). This now refers to Art 21 of the revised asylum procedures Directive (Dir 2013/32, idem; see Art 53 of that Directive). On the substance of these rules, see I:5.7 above.

[635] *Abdida*, paras 50–3.   [636] Art 14.

[637] The definition of 'vulnerable persons' is set out in Art 3(9).

[638] Point 12 in the preamble.

is not clear whether the stronger obligation would only apply in such exceptional cases, or more broadly to all those whose removals were postponed. Furthermore, the Court ruled that in such cases, Member States must provide for the 'basic needs' of the third-country national who could not provide for them him or herself, otherwise access to health care would be 'rendered meaningless'. In other words, there is little point discussing health care for a person who has no food or shelter. Arguably, again this ruling only applies to exceptional cases like *Abdida*; but then the same point would be true for any irregular migrant.

To what extent could irregular migrants provide for themselves in this situation? The most obvious possibility would be to obtain employment. In principle this is ruled out by a subsequent Directive, which prohibits the employment of irregular migrants; but nevertheless that Directive gives Member States an option to exempt the employment of persons 'whose removal has been postponed' from this prohibition.[639] Arguably this only applies to the specific rules in the Returns Directive on the obligation or possibility of postponing removal,[640] but the alternative interpretation is that any national decision under the Returns Directive which amounts *de facto* to a postponement of removal (ie because of the absence, withdrawal, or suspension of a return decision, even if the immigration status of the person concerned is *de jure* irregular), also triggers the option for Member States to authorize employment under the employer sanctions Directive. In any event, it should be recalled that the employer sanctions Directive has a wider personal scope than the Returns Directive, because there are no options to exclude cases relating to border crossing or criminal law from the scope of the employer sanctions Directive.[641]

The Returns Directive has the general objective of ending situations where irregular migrants remain on the territory in 'limbo', neither returning to their countries of origin nor gaining a formal legal status on the territory. Indeed, the Court's ruling in *Zaizoune* can be seen in this context: the Member State should either adopt and enforce a return decision or officially regularize the irregular migrant's position. However, even assuming that Member States full comply with this obligation, 'limbo' situations might still exist, where it proves impractical to enforce a return decision for a long period and irregular migrants therefore remain on the territory while their removal is postponed. The numbers involved are significant, since the 2014 report indicates that around 300,000 people a year are issued with return decisions that are not enforced in practice. Indeed, the majority of return decisions are not enforced.

Irregular migrants in 'limbo' cases are covered by the limited safeguards pending removal, and the option to permit them to work, but is there an implied obligation to do anything else to alleviate their position? According to the CJEU, there is not. In the *Mahdi* judgment, it ruled that there was no obligation to regularize the position of an

---

[639] Art 3(3) of Dir 2009/52 ([2009] OJ L 168/24), discussed in I:7.6.1 above. However, the EU rules on legal migration will not generally apply in such cases, as they do not apply where expulsion has been suspended for reasons of fact and law (see I:6.5 above). EU employment law will apply however (I:6.4 above).

[640] Art 9, discussed further above.

[641] It should be recalled, however, that persons subject to the optional 'border crossing' exclusion from the scope of the Returns Directive (but not the 'criminal law' exclusion) can rely on *parts* of Art 9 (see Art 4(4)).

irregular migrant who had been released from immigration detention on the grounds that there was no reasonable prospect of removal. More broadly, it ruled that the Returns Directive did not aim to regulate the access to legal immigration status of any irregular migrants. So there is no prospect of using the Directive to end 'limbo' for anyone (although it does not stand in the way of Member States' doing so). Furthermore, *Mahdi* raises the question of whether there might be two classes of irregular migrants in 'limbo': those whose removal has been formally postponed (and who therefore have the right to the safeguards in the Directive), and those whose removal has not been formally postponed, but who will nevertheless not in practice be removed for the foreseeable future. The latter category (like the former category) has the right to receive written confirmation of their position, but only on the basis of the preamble to the Directive. In fact, the Court was not asked as such in *Mahdi* whether two such categories exist, and so perhaps was not intending to create such a distinction. But it ought to clarify in future that there are not two such categories, and an informal postponement also entitles an irregular migrant to the safeguards in the Directive for those pending removal. Otherwise Member States could undercut the effectiveness of the Directive, denying even those modest safeguards to irregular migrants pending removal by not formally postponing it.

The Directive next addresses the controversial issue of immigration detention.[642] Persons subject to return procedures 'may only' be detained 'in order to prepare return and/or to carry out the removal process, "in particular" when' there is a risk of absconding or if the person concerned 'avoids or hampers' the return or removal process. Detention is only justified while removal arrangements 'are in process and executed with due diligence'. It can be ordered by administrative or judicial authorities, and must be 'ordered in writing with reasons in fact and law'. If the detention was ordered by administrative authorities, there must be some form of 'speedy' judicial review. There must be regular reviews of detention, either automatically or at the request of the person concerned. If there is no 'reasonable prospect of removal' or the conditions for detention no longer exist, the person concerned must be released immediately. Conversely, detention shall been maintained as long as the conditions exist, 'if necessary to ensure successful removal'. Detention shall not exceed six months, except where national law permits a further period of up to one extra year because the removal operation is likely to last longer due to lack of cooperation by the person concerned or delays in obtaining documentation, regardless of all 'reasonable efforts' by the State.

According to the 2014 report, the Directive has had the impact of harmonizing maximum time limits for immigration detention across Member States: several Member States reduced their time limit to the eighteen-month maximum, while others increased the limit. There is a wide variation of rules on the timing of subsequent reviews of detention, but a broad movement towards offering alternatives to detention.[643]

---

[642] Art 15; see also Arts 16–18 on detention standards, discussed further below. The CJEU has ruled that Arts 15 and 16 have direct effect: *El Dridi*, para 47, confirmed in *Mahdi*, para 54.

[643] See the study by the European Migration Network, at: <http://ec.europa.eu/dgs/home-affairs/what-we-do/networks/european_migration_network/reports/docs/emn-studies/emn_study_detention_alternatives_to_detention_synthesis_report_en.pdf>.

These provisions have been interpreted in a number of CJEU rulings. According to *Mahdi*, as noted above, the question of the irregular migrant's 'risk of absconding' has to be decided on a case-by-case basis, based on objective criteria; an irregular migrant cannot be detained purely because he or she does not have identity documents, without considering whether a less coercive measure could be applied. The Court's judgment in this case appears to limit the grounds for detention to cases of a risk of absconding or hampering the return process, despite the apparently non-exhaustive wording ('in particular').[644] Similarly, in *El Dridl*, the Court ruled that detention could 'only' be applied where the removal 'risks being compromised by the conduct' of the irregular migrant.[645]

As for the time limits on detention, first of all, in *Kadzoev*, the Court ruled that the relevant time limits for detention must take into account also time served already before the application of the Directive. The Court did not, however, explain how to address the situation where the detention was interrupted, either by periods which do not count because the person concerned applied for asylum, or for some other reason.[646] It would obviously be problematic if the Member States could evade the time limits in the Directive by releasing a person for one day at the end of the applicable time limit, and then re-arresting that person the next day to start a fresh lengthy period of detention. In order to avoid undercutting the effectiveness of the Directive's rules on detention time limits, it must follow that once the time limits have expired, the irregular migrant cannot be detained again unless it can be shown that he or she has left the Member State and later returned to begin an entirely separate period of irregular migration.

Next, the Court ruled that the period of detention spent while the removal decision was subject to judicial review could not be deducted from the relevant time limits, but had to count towards them.

When is there a 'reasonable prospect of removal'? In *Kadzoev*, the Court ruled that this criterion for releasing the person concerned is irrelevant where the time limits on detention have in any event expired. Where the criterion does apply, it means that a 'real prospect exists that the removal can be carried out successfully, having regard to' the relevant time limits, and that this prospect 'does not exist where it appears unlikely that the person concerned will be admitted to a third country, having regard to' those time limits. According to the *Mahdi* judgment, when reviewing whether there was such a reasonable prospect, authorities also had to review whether the original grounds for detention (whether other sufficient but less coercive measures can be applied; whether there is a risk of absconding; whether the irregular migrant is complicating the return or the process) were still satisfied. Member States cannot keep irregular migrants in detention, once the relevant time limit has expired, merely because they do not possess valid documents, their conduct is aggressive, and they have no financial support or accommodation (*Kadzoev*).

---

[644] *Mahdi* judgment, para 61.   [645] *El Dridl* judgment, para 39.
[646] However, the CJEU did state, in the *Arslan* judgment, that an application for asylum by a detainee would not automatically lead to release. See further I:5.9 above.

In deciding whether there was a 'lack of cooperation' by the irregular migrant (one of the grounds for extending detention beyond six months), the CJEU ruled in *Mahdi* that the key questions were whether the migrant had cooperated in ensuring the removal, and whether the implementation of removal was delayed for a longer period than anticipated because of that conduct. If the removal is taking longer than anticipated due to some other reason, then there was no causal link between the migrant and the delay, and there was therefore no lack of cooperation. The Court did not rule on what happens if a delay in removal has multiple causes, some of which are due to the irregular migrant's conduct and some of which are not. It did clarify that the State's obligation to take 'reasonable efforts' to ensure removal meant that the State must have tried, and still be actively trying, to obtain identity documents for the irregular migrant. The CJEU left it to the national court to decide whether there was sufficient cooperation in this case, where the irregular migrant had cooperated to some extent but withdrawn a statement regarding voluntary return.

As for judicial reviews of extension of detention, the CJEU ruled in *Mahdi* that the obligation to adopt a decision on detention in writing 'necessarily' applied to all decisions on extension of detention, because this was similar in nature to the original decision to detain. In either case the irregular migrant ought to know the reasons for the decision being taken, in order to consider a possible legal challenge and to defend his or her rights effectively, and to ensure proper judicial review of the legality of the decision. Otherwise the right to an effective remedy would be undermined. Oddly, though, the Court stated that this did not entail an obligation to state the 'factual and legal reasons' for the detention each time it was reviewed (although Member States are free to provide for this). But there must be a 'written reasoned decision' if detention was extended beyond six months, subject to judicial review even if the administration has already reviewed the issue, and even if the court was not expressly requested to carry out this review. When a court was asked to assess whether there was still a 'reasonable prospect of removal' as regards continuing detention, or otherwise regarding extension of detention, it had to be able to substitute its own decision for that of the administration (or the court which previously ordered detention). Moreover, it could not be limited to considering the evidence submitted by the administration: the observations of the irregular migrant, and 'any other relevant element', had to be considered too.

Although the Directive does not expressly provide for it, there is also a right for irregular migrants to be heard by the administration before it takes a decision extending their period of detention, according to the *G and R* judgment. It is not clear whether, in this context, this entails all of the aspects of that right which the Court later elaborated upon in *Mukarubega* and *Boudjlida* (discussed above). Nor is it clear if there is also such a right as regards the initial decision to detain; or whether that right can possibly be 'incorporated' into the initial process of deciding to issue a return decision. However, it is clear that the right to be heard is similarly weak in the detention context, in particular as regards remedies: the CJEU ruled that there was no obligation to release the person concerned due to breach of the right to be heard, unless that breach altered the substance of the decision on extended detention to the detriment of the irregular migrant. There is no mention of an alternative remedy, such as compensation, in such cases. The Court stressed the need to ensure the effectiveness of the returns process, but its judgment undercuts the effectiveness of the right to be heard.

Next, the Directive's rules on detention conditions address in turn: the place of detention (special facilities 'as a rule', separation from ordinary prisoners if detained in prison); the right to contact legal representatives, family members and consular authorities; the situation of vulnerable persons; the possibility for independent bodies to visit detention facilities; and information to be given to the persons concerned.[647] There are more detailed rules on the detention of minors and families.[648] The 2014 report indicates that there are problems applying these provisions in practice.

Member States may derogate from the rules concerning speedy judicial review, specialized facilities, separate detention from prisoners, and family privacy in 'exceptional' situations, where there is an 'exceptionally large number' of migrants placing an 'unforeseen heavy burden' on capacity of detention facilities or administrative or judicial staff.[649] Member States must inform the Commission in such cases.[650]

The CJEU has interpreted some of these provisions,[651] ruling that a Member State has an 'obligation' to detain irregular migrants in specialized facilities; the exception to that rule must be interpreted 'strictly'. So a Member State which did not have specialized facilities in each of its federal States would have to make arrangements to transfer irregular migrants across regional boundaries. Nor was it possible for irregular migrants to waive their right to separate detention from prisoners. While the Commission has recently encouraged Member States to use the derogations from the Directive in order to deal with an increased number of migrants,[652] it is clear that any use of the derogations is subject to very strict requirements, including the procedural requirement to inform the Commission.[653]

Comparing the detention rules with human rights standards,[654] the Directive includes the 'necessity' principle set out in the ICCPR jurisprudence on immigration detention,[655] along with a number of principles derived from ECHR case law such as due diligence in pursuing expulsion and the requirement to end detention if removal efforts are no longer underway. The time limits in the Directive regarding detention improve upon ECHR standards, given that there is no fixed time limit on immigration detention set out in the ECHR, and the rules on judicial review reflect the ECHR and relevant case law as well. Indeed, the CJEU's case law (particularly *El Dridl*) states that the Directive aims to implement the ECHR, including case law of the European Court of Human Rights, along with soft law deriving from the Council of Europe ('Twenty Guidelines on Forced Return'). While it is understandable that asylum seekers are generally excluded from the Directive because they should not be regarded as illegally present, it is unfortunate that separate rules in EU asylum legislation do not set a time limit for their detention.[656]

---

[647] Art 16. As noted above, the CJEU ruled in *El Dridl* that this Article has direct effect.

[648] Art 17.   [649] Art 18(1).   [650] Art 18(2).

[651] Judgments in *Bouzalmate and Bero*, and *Pham*.   [652] Council doc 10170/15, 22 June 2015.

[653] See by analogy Case C-571/10 *Kamberaj*, ECLI:EU:C:2012:233.

[654] See I:7.3 above, and particularly I:7.3.2 as regards detention.   [655] Art 15(5).

[656] See I:5.9 above, although note that there is a time limit for detention in the specific context of the Dublin rules on allocation of responsibility for asylum seekers (I:5.8 above).

Finally, an important strand of CJEU rulings on the Directive significantly limits the impact of Member States' criminalization of irregular migration. As noted above, the Court ruled that such criminalization does not take irregular migrants outside the scope of the Directive. But the case law goes even further, largely abolishing the possibility for Member States to impose custodial penalties as a criminal sanction for irregular migration.

According to the *El Dridl* judgment, imposing a custodial penalty for a criminal offence of breaching immigration law undermines the effectiveness of the Directive, since it delays in practice the execution of the removal of the individual concerned. In the Court's view, the Directive establishes a system of gradually increasing sanctions upon the individuals concerned, giving them first an opportunity for voluntary departure in principle (as discussed above) with immigration detention only as a last resort. A custodial penalty for a criminal offence would delay that process. However, the subsequent *Achughbabian* judgment clarified that irregular migrants could be detained for a brief period when initially questioned by the police, and possibly subjected to a form of custodial sentence for irregular migration if the expulsion process did not work out. More precisely, the Directive 'does not preclude penal sanctions being imposed, following national rules of criminal procedure, on third-country nationals to whom the return procedure established by [the] directive has been applied and who are illegally staying in the territory of a Member State without there being any justified ground for non-return'. The Court clarified in *Sagor* that criminal sanctions for irregular migration can be imposed in the form of fines, but not (following the logic of the prior judgments) home detention, since that would delay the implementation of the process of removal. Moreover, in *Filev and Osmani*, the Court ruled that a Member State could not impose a criminal penalty of *any* sort for breach of an entry ban, if that entry ban was imposed illegally. On the other hand, in *Celaj* the Court ruled that a custodial penalty *could* be imposed for a breach of a legal entry ban, unconvincingly distinguishing the *El Dridl* line of case law where the Court had objected to the delay in carrying out enforcement of an expulsion which would result from this.

So custodial penalties (or home detention) for irregular migration before or instead of the immigration detention provided for by that Directive are ruled out. Such penalties are only admitted where the irregular migrant has breached a legal entry ban, or after the return process has been applied, if there is no 'justified ground for non-return'. The latter concept has not yet been clarified by the Court, but it suggests that if there is a justified ground for postponement of the return, as set out in the Directive, custodial penalties still cannot be applied. While the overall thrust of the Directive remains, according to this case law, the guarantee of removal of the individual concerned, the rulings make it less likely that the irregular migrant will be detained at all (due to the preference for voluntary departure) and ensure that he or she will not normally be kept in prisons, along with other key detention standards.

How should this controversial Directive be assessed? Due to the case law of the CJEU, it is less restrictive than it initially appeared, in particular in light of the case law restricting the grounds for detention, limiting Member States' custodial penalties for irregular migration as a criminal offence, enhancing voluntary departure, prohibiting removal in non-refoulement cases (along with ensuring effective remedies and minimum welfare support in such cases), and widening the scope of the Directive (while clarifying that asylum seekers are not irregular migrants). Some of the Court's rulings are fairly modest, however: the right to a hearing has no effective content or remedies to enforce it. Moreover, the purpose of restricting Member States' custodial sentences in the criminal law context is to ensure a quicker return of the irregular migrants, and the Court has limited Member States' power to grant more favourable standards for the same reason. The idea that the Directive requires Member States to 'regularize or expel' is not manifested in practice, since irregular migrants can still often end up in 'limbo' with very limited status in the meantime. Since there would likely be concern that any attempt to amend the Directive would likely lead to lower standards, it seems probable that the main developments in this area will be driven by the case law of the CJEU for some time to come.

7.7.2 Mutual recognition of expulsion measures

In order to address the issue of persons subject to expulsion who travel between Member States, the Council adopted Directive 2001/40 on the mutual recognition of expulsion orders in May 2001.[657] This Directive had to be implemented by the Member States by 2 December 2002.[658] Several Member States were the subject of infringement proceedings brought by the Commission after they failed to implement the Directive on time.[659]

The Directive 'make[s] possible the enforcement of an expulsion order' issued by one Member State in another Member State, against a third-country national of any age.[660] The wording of the Directive suggests that this is only an option for the second Member State, not an obligation. While the subsequent Returns Directive refers to an obligation for a second Member State to apply the rules in that Directive to an irregular migrant who it has taken back pursuant to a bilateral agreement with a Member State where the irregular migrant was present on an irregular basis, this obligation will probably fall outside the scope of the 2001 Directive (since, in this scenario, the first Member State need not issue a return decision at all).[661]

The expulsion decision pursuant to Directive 2001/40 shall be enforced according to the national law of the enforcing state.[662] This should in principle be understood as a reference to the enforcing State's application of the Returns Directive, because the latter Directive does not exclude mutual recognition of expulsion decisions from its scope.[663]

---

[657] [2001] OJ L 149/34. All references in this sub-section are to Dir 2001/40 unless otherwise indicated.

[658] Art 8(1).

[659] Two Member States were condemned by the Court of Justice for failure to implement the Directive: Cases C-462/04 *Commission v Italy* and C-448/04 *Commission v Luxembourg*, judgments of 8 Sep 2005, unreported. Two other cases were withdrawn, presumably following late implementation of the Directive: Cases C-474/04 *Commission v Greece* and C-450/04 *Commission v France*.

[660] Art 1.   [661] Art 6(3), Dir 2008/115 ([2008] OJ L 348/98). See further I:7.7.1 above.

[662] Art 1(2).

[663] See Art 2(2) of the Returns Dir (n 661 above). It is possible, however, that either the issuing or the executing State has invoked an exclusion from the scope of that Dir, pursuant to its Art 2(2). This raises the awkward question of what happens if the criteria for exclusion from the scope of the Returns Dir are satisfied in one or the other of the two Member States, but not both.

But the definitions in the 2001 Directive do not entirely match those in the Returns Directive.[664] To the extent that the 2001 Directive sets higher standards than the Returns Directive, it should prevail over the latter.[665] However, the 2001 Directive does not provide that national law, other EU measures, or international treaties can set higher standards.[666] Questions arise as to whether the rules in the Returns Directive on postponement of removal, entry bans, detention, forced returns, voluntary returns, safeguards pending expulsion, procedural safeguards, and exceptions from the obligation to issue a return decision are applicable within the context of Directive 2001/40. Logically, in the absence of an exception for mutual recognition cases in the Returns Directive, the rules in that Directive are fully applicable in both States when Directive 2001/40 is applied. If this is correct, the purpose of the Directive is merely to avoid having to send an irregular migrant back to the Member State which initially issued the expulsion decision.

As for its scope, the 2001 Directive does not apply to family members of an EU citizen who has exercised his or her right to free movement,[667] and is 'without prejudice' to Articles 23 and 96 of the Schengen Convention (which respectively concern return decisions and the criteria for listing persons to be denied entry into the Schengen area) and to the Dublin Convention.[668]

Expulsions are enforceable under the Directive if a third-country national has received an expulsion decision on either a 'public policy and national security' ground (as further defined in the Directive) or the ground of 'failure to comply with national regulations on the entry or residence' of foreigners.[669] These criteria are taken from Article 96 of the Schengen Convention.[670]

The Directive must be applied with 'due respect for human rights and fundamental freedoms', but the specific implications of this are not set out.[671] Also, the expellee is entitled to a remedy against the expulsion order in the enforcing State, under that State's national law.[672] Again, it makes sense to assume that the Returns Directive governs these issues in the enforcing State, unless the situation falls within the scope of an exclusion from that Directive which is validly invoked by the enforcing State. The

---

[664] Compare the definition of 'expulsion decision' in Art 2(b) with the definition of 'return decision' in Art 3(4) of the Returns Dir, and the definition of 'enforcement measure' in Art 2(c) with the definition of 'removal' in Art 3(5) of the Returns Dir. Also, there are no exclusions from the scope of Dir 2001/40 as regards refusals of entry, border interceptions, or criminal law.

[665] See Art 4(2), Returns Dir.

[666] Compare to Art 4(1) to (3), Returns Dir. As the Court of Justice has pointed out, international treaties concluded by the EU nevertheless take precedence over secondary EU law: Case C-228/06 *Soysal* [2009] ECR I-1031. However, this leaves open the question of priority as between the Dir and treaties concluded only by *Member States*.

[667] Art 1(3); see I:7.4.1 above.

[668] Arts 1(1) and 3(3). On Art 23 of the Convention ([2000] OJ L 239), see the introduction to I:7.1 above; this Art was replaced by the Returns Dir when that Dir became applicable (Art 21, Returns Dir). Art 96 of the Convention was replaced when the SIS II rules became applicable (I:3.7 above). Presumably the reference to the Dublin Convention must now be taken to be a reference to the replacement Dublin III Regulation, and previously the Dublin II Reg (see I:5.8 above).

[669] Art 3(1).

[670] The replacement rules in the SIS II Regulation are only slightly different: see I:3.7 above.

[671] Art 3(2).   [672] Arts 4.

2001 Directive also includes data protection safeguards and provisions on cooperation between the issuing and enforcing Member States.[673]

The issue of compensation of those Member States which enforce other Member States' expulsion orders pursuant to the Directive, where expulsion cannot be charged to the expellee, was left subject to the adoption of a subsequent measure, which 'shall' also apply to Article 24 of the Schengen Convention.[674] The latter provision of the Convention has now also been replaced by the Returns Directive.[675] A Council Decision on this issue was subsequently adopted in February 2004;[676] it is unclear whether this Decision should be understood to apply to the Returns Directive. Given that this legislation does not *oblige* Member States to collect the costs of return from migrants, while other EU rules oblige Member States to collect the costs of return from employers or carriers,[677] it might be argued that there is an implied hierarchy: Member States must first attempt to collect the costs of return from employers or carriers, then (if that fails) from the migrant, and then (if that fails) from another Member State, if (in the latter case) Directive 2001/40 is applicable.

As for its substance, the 2004 Decision specifies that Member States issuing expulsion orders must compensate Member States enforcing expulsion orders for: transport costs, administrative costs, mission allowances for two escorts, and accommodation and emergency medical costs for the escorts and the expellee.[678] It also sets out the procedural requirements for submitting a valid claim for reimbursement.[679] Member States' contact points must inform the Commission of the total number of requests for reimbursement and refusals to reimburse.[680]

While there are no formal statistics or information on the use of Directive 2001/40, the Commission admitted in its 2004 report on EU policy on irregular migration that the Directive had little impact in practice.[681] The adoption of the Decision on the financial aspects of the Directive might have had the intended effect of encouraging Member States to use the mechanism in the Directive more frequently. It may also have the broader importance of serving as a template for other measures which require costs to be allocated.[682] However, as the Commission has pointed out, the Directive is likely to be little used as long as there is no exchange of data on national expulsion decisions.[683] This will only be fully achieved once there are clear links between the Returns Directive and the SIS II Regulation, in particular when and if the plans to include returns decisions in the SIS come to fruition.[684]

---

[673] Arts 5 and 6. There are no parallel provisions in the Returns Dir.

[674] Art 7. On Art 24 of the Convention, see the introduction to I:7.7 above.

[675] Art 21, Returns Dir.   [676] [2004] OJ L 60/55; in force 28 Feb 2004.

[677] Art 5(2), Dir 2009/52 ([2009] OJ L 168/24); Art 26 of the Schengen Convention ([2000] OJ L 239) and Arts 2 and 3, Dir 2001/51 ([2001] OJ L 187/45). See respectively I:7.6.1 and I:7.5.1 above.

[678] Art 2.   [679] Art 3.   [680] Art 4.

[681] Communication on policy regarding irregular migration (SEC (2004) 1349, 25 Oct 2004), page 10: 'So far, the impact, ie cases of formal recognition, was almost inexistent' [*sic*]. There was no mention of the Dir in the 2006 or 2009 reports on irregular migration policy (SEC (2006) 1010, 17 July 2006 and SEC (2009) 320, 9 Mar 2009).

[682] See Conclusions on transit for expulsion via land or sea (I:7.7.3.2 below).

[683] See the impact assessment for the Returns Directive (SEC (2005) 1057, 1 Sep 2005), pp 6–7.

[684] See the discussion of this issue in I:3.7.2 and I:7.7.1 above.

The ineffectiveness of Directive 2001/40 should be welcomed, because the Directive is highly problematic. It purportedly extends to persons with rights under international agreements agreed by the EU,[685] it inappropriately extends the principles of Article 96 of the Schengen Convention (and now the SIS II rules) to persons who are already present on the territory, and it does not sufficiently guarantee that expulsions carried out within its scope meet applicable human rights standards. Questions arise about the relationship between this Directive (and the 2004 Decision on costs) and the Returns Directive, due to the different wording and scope of the two measures. From a technical point of view, the 2001 Directive needs to be amended for consistency with the Returns Directive, and to confirm that both Member States need to apply all the safeguards set out in that Directive, since the expulsion of a person engages its jurisdiction and therefore the human rights obligations of each State.[686]

7.7.3 Transit for expulsion

7.7.3.1 Expulsion via air

Following early EU soft-law measures and a Schengen Executive Committee Decision on the issue of assistance in expulsion by air,[687] the Council adopted Directive 2003/110 on this issue in November 2003.[688] Member States had to implement the Directive by 6 December 2005.[689] The Commission brought an unusually high number of infringement actions against Member States for failure to apply this legislation on time.[690]

This Directive specifies that if a Member State wishes to request another to assist it with an expulsion (a 'requesting State'), it should first give priority to direct flights to the country of origin and should 'in principle' not request assistance if this involves transfer between different airports within another Member State.[691] A requested Member State may refuse to assist with expulsion if criminal charges would be brought against the person concerned in the requested State or if the person concerned 'is wanted for the carrying out of a sentence'; if transit to or admission into the State of destination is not feasible; if a change of airport in the requested State would be required; if the assistance is temporarily not available for 'practical reasons'; or if the person concerned 'will be a threat to public policy, public security, public health or to the international

---

[685] Although, as noted above, the EU's international agreements take priority over its secondary law, a failure to point this out expressly in the legislation concerned could lead to a failure to apply this rule by the national administrations which implement the legislation.

[686] If there were no second full procedure, the question would arise of what to do if it were alleged that the first Member State had not complied with the Directive when issuing its return decision or removal order.

[687] See respectively I:7.2.1 above and Sch/Com-ex (98) 10, 21 Apr 1998 ([2000] OJ L 239/193).

[688] [2003] OJ L 321/26. Art 11 of the Dir repealed the Schengen Executive Committee Decision (n 687 above). All references in this sub-section are to Dir 2003/110 unless otherwise indicated.

[689] Art 10(2).

[690] Cases: C-3/07 *Commission v Belgium* (judgment largely against Belgium, 8 Nov 2007, unreported); C-4/07 *Commission v Portugal* (judgment against Portugal, 27 Sep 2007, unreported); C-29/07 *Commission v Greece* (withdrawn); C-51/07 *Commission v Luxembourg* (withdrawn); C-58/07 *Commission v Spain* (judgment against Spain, 14 Feb 2008, unreported); C-79/07 *Commission v Malta* (withdrawn); C-86/07 *Commission v Italy* (withdrawn); and C-216/07 *Commission v Germany* (withdrawn).

[691] Art 3(2).

relations' of the requested Member State.[692] A transit authorization, once given, may also be revoked on the same grounds.[693] The requested Member State must give reasons to the requesting Member State in the event of refusal or revocation on these specified grounds 'or of any other reason why the transit is not possible';[694] this suggests strongly that the listed grounds for refusal or revocation are non-exhaustive. The preamble to the Directive states that transit by air 'should be neither requested nor granted if in the third country of destination or transit faces the threat of inhuman or humiliating treatment, torture or the death penalty' for the person concerned, or if his life or liberty would be at risk by reason of 'his race, religion, nationality, membership of a particular social group or political conviction.'

The Directive also describes the procedure for making and replying to requests and the specific obligations of requested Member States, makes clear that the requested Member State's law has responsibility for organizing such measures, sets out the status of escorts from the requesting Member States and allocates the cost of various aspects of the expulsion between the requesting and requested Member States.[695]

There are readmission obligations for the requesting Member State in the event that: transit was refused or revoked on the grounds listed in the Directive; the expulsion was unsuccessful; or the person concerned tried to enter the requested Member State without authorization; or 'transit by air is not possible for another reason'.[696] Again this wording suggests that the grounds for refusing or revoking assistance listed in the Directive are not exhaustive. Escorts sent by the requesting State may act in 'self-defence' and use 'reasonable and proportionate action' to prevent risks posed by third-country nationals, but may not carry weapons, must wear civilian clothes, and must comply with the requested State's legislation.[697]

There is a 'savings clause' specifying that the Directive is 'without prejudice to' the Geneva Convention on the status of refugees, international human rights treaties or international extradition treaties.[698] An Annex sets out a standard form for use in requesting cooperation under the Directive and for replying to those requests; the Commission is empowered to amend this Annex via use of a 'comitology' procedure.[699]

The fundamental problem with this Directive, as with Directive 2001/40,[700] is the principle of mutual recognition of expulsion decisions. In the absence of a binding obligation in the Directive to refrain from requesting or to refuse to assist with transit, or to revoke the request or agreement to assist, in case of a threat of human rights breach to the person concerned in another country, or even an obligation for the requesting State's authorities to certify when they fill out the Annex that no such grounds exist, the Directive contains insufficiently clear protection for human rights. The reference to human rights treaties in the savings clause is too vague to make up for this, because there are no detailed rules on how to ensure respect for the Geneva Convention or human rights treaties. In the absence of an express provision to require a full examination of any asylum claim and effective procedural remedies in the case of any appeal before applying this Directive, the 'savings clause' is simply window-dressing.

---

[692] Art 3(3).   [693] Art 3(5).   [694] Art 3(6).   [695] Arts 4 and 5.
[696] Art 6.   [697] Art 7.   [698] Art 8.   [699] Art 9.   [700] See I:7.7.2 above.

In any event, how is the requested Member State to determine whether there is such a human rights breach? The only information available to it is the brief information included on the standard request form, and as noted above, the form does not even contain a box to tick to indicate that, in the view of the requesting Member State, there is no human rights problem with expulsion. Clearly this does not supply enough information for the requested Member State to come to its own conclusion on that subject. The requesting Member State is not obliged to limit requests to certain situations, or to consider human rights issues before deciding to expel and requesting assistance of another Member State.

Compared with Directive 2001/40, which already sets a weak standard as regards human rights protection,[701] there is no obligation in the Directive for requested Member States to ensure that there are no human rights risks before they carry out an expulsion order at another Member State's request. Also, there is no comparable requirement upon the requested Member State to permit migrants to challenge its decision to enforce expulsion decisions. Directive 2001/40 only applies to expulsion where certain substantive criteria are met, and the family members of EU nationals are exempt from it. There are express data protection rights in the earlier Directive, and the main text of that Directive explicitly requires Member States to apply the Directive 'with due regard for human rights and fundamental freedoms'. All these essential limits and safeguards are missing from Directive 2003/110, which merely refers to human rights protection in the preamble and vaguely in the safeguard clause. So even the weak standards agreed in 2001 do not apply in the context of the 2003 Directive. Since the requested Member State will clearly be exercising jurisdiction over the person concerned if it agrees to cooperate in carrying out the expulsion, there are no grounds for a lower level of protection due to that State's more limited contact with the individual concerned.

It might be argued that following the application of the Returns Directive, these problems have been addressed sufficiently and Member States must extend mutual trust that each of them will comply with the standards in the Returns Directive. However, there is still a risk that the requesting State has failed to comply with the Returns Directive in a particular case.[702] So the 2003 Directive runs a risk of violating fundamental human rights when applied to particular cases.

7.7.3.2 *Expulsion via land or sea*

Following the agreement in principle on Directive 2003/110, Italy proposed a Directive on transit for expulsion via land (and apparently sea), which would have applied rules very similar to those governing transit for expulsion via air.[703] But due to misgivings among some Member States about this proposal, the Council adopted conclusions on the topic instead, in December 2003.[704]

These conclusions are much less specific than Directive 2003/110. First of all, the conclusions set out their scope, making it clear that they apply to transit expulsion both by land and sea. Such expulsions should only be requested when a direct or transit flight

---

[701] See ibid.   [702] See the critique in I:7.7.1 above.   [703] [2003] OJ C 223/5.
[704] For the text of these conclusions, see the press release of the environment Council, 22 Dec 2003.

is impossible or more difficult. But such expulsions could be particularly useful where they are used to send a person to the airport or seaport of another Member State which will carry out an expulsion, if they enable avoidance of complications which would result from having to transit through a non-EU State or where the requested Member State has a bilateral readmission agreement which it could use to effect expulsion.

Next, the conclusions set out basic principles to govern expulsions by land or sea. Such expulsions should take place with the consent of the requested State, and the accompaniment of that State's escorts in all cases. The requesting State has a duty to send the relevant information to the requested State, and is responsible for the expellee until reaching the requested State's territory. From that point, the requesting State's escorts should comply with the requested State's law. The costs of the operations should be compensated on the basis of 'appropriate financial arrangements, which may consider, in particular, the criteria defined in the Community legislation in the area of return [sic] of third-country nationals'. There is also a safeguard clause corresponding to the provision in Directive 2003/110.

These conclusions obviously share the fundamental defects of Directive 2003/110. In fact, their non-binding status exacerbates the problem, as it means that the safeguard provision is not binding either. Nor are any grounds for refusal set out. But on the other hand, it cannot be argued that a Member State is bound to accept any request to assist with such transit for expulsion, still less that there is only an exhaustive list of circumstances in which it may refuse to accept such a request.

7.7.4 Joint expulsion flights

A Decision on joint expulsion flights was adopted by the JHA Council in April 2004.[705] The Council subsequently adopted conclusions with a view to encouraging Member States to organize joint expulsion flights in practice,[706] and the EU's border agency (Frontex) also has a role in this area.[707] The joint flights are now supported by the EU's Return Fund.[708]

The Decision provides that Member States have to appoint national authorities responsible for organizing joint flights.[709] A Member State organizing a joint flight must first of all inform the other Member States, and has detailed obligations to make sure that the flight is organized properly.[710] If a Member State wishes to participate in the joint flight, it must inform the organizing Member State of the numbers of expellees it will be removing and provide a sufficient number of escorts.[711] The organizing and participating Member States have the common task of ensuring that the expellees and escorts have the necessary documentation and that their diplomatic and consular staff in the countries of transit and destination are informed of the expulsion flight, so that they can offer the necessary assistance.[712] When carrying out the joint expulsions,

---

[705] [2004] OJ L 261/28, in force 7 Aug 2004.

[706] See the press release of the General Affairs Council, 12–13 July 2004 and the JHA Council, 27–8 Apr 2006.

[707] See Art 9(1) of Reg 2007/2004 ([2004] OJ L 349/1), as amended in 2011. On the agency generally, see I:3.10.1 above.

[708] See I:7.8 below.   [709] Art 3.   [710] Art 4.   [711] Art 5.   [712] Art 6.

the Member States should 'take account' of detailed security guidelines set out in an Annex.[713]

As with the Directive and conclusions on transit for expulsion,[714] this Decision indicates that Member States are willing to adopt EU legislation concerning operational measures on expulsion without first having ensured that EU law guarantees sufficiently high minimum standards on human rights and other matters. Although some provisions in the Annex to the Decision do provide for protection for individuals during the flights,[715] this Annex is non-binding and in any event does not address the question of whether the initial expulsion decision met minimum standards. Moreover, the organization of such joint flights could run the risk of encouraging Member States (individually or collectively) to engage in collective expulsions, which are prohibited by international human rights law.[716]

If the joint operations are coordinated by Frontex, they are now covered by the rules in the revised Frontex Regulation that requires the application of a forced-return monitoring system. Otherwise they are covered by the less specific provisions of the Returns Directive (since it contains no exclusion for joint operations), which does not expressly require monitoring of every return operation. There is a potential problem applying those rules in the context of this Decision, because monitoring is subject to the approval of all participating Member States.[717] The Annex does make provision for mission reports to be drawn up, but '[a]ll mission reports are strictly confidential and for internal use only', even though the reports 'shall include statements on incidents, coercive and medical measures, if any have taken place'.[718] There is no reference to the requirement imposed by the ECHR to investigate the circumstances of any death or torture or inhuman or degrading treatment caused by the actions of public authorities. In light of the tragic deaths and injuries that have resulted during some expulsions from Europe in recent years, the Decision is wholly insufficient and should be modified to ensure effective forced-return monitoring in all cases.

7.8 Administrative Cooperation and EU Funding

The EC's funding programme, 'ARGO', which ran from 2002 to 2006, provided for spending for administrative cooperation on irregular migration.[719] Subsequently, the Commission also established a preparatory programme beginning in 2005 for a 'European Return Fund', upon which the Council adopted conclusions in June 2004.[720] The Return Fund was formalized in 2007 by a Decision establishing it officially.[721] For

---

[713] Art 7 and Annex.

[714] I:7.7.3 above. In fact, Point 4 of the Annex to the Decision indicates that Directive 2003/110 will be applicable if air transit takes place through Member States.

[715] See particularly point 3 of the Annex.

[716] See I:7.3.1 above, and particularly the judgment of the European Court of Human Rights in *Sultani v France*, 20 Sep 2007, which establishes the standards for such joint flights.

[717] Point 3.4.1 of the Annex.   [718] Point 3.4.2 of the Annex.

[719] Decision 2002/463 ([2002] OJ L 161/11); see particularly Art 7(d) to (f). On JHA funding in general, see I:2.6 above.

[720] For the text of the conclusions, see press release of JHA Council, 8 June 2004.

[721] [2005] OJ L 144/45.

2014–20, funding on these issues is provided for as part of the Asylum and Migration Fund.[722]

Aside from EU funding measures, operational cooperation between national administrations was first established as far back as 1992 when Member States' immigration ministers established CIREFI, a system for sharing information on irregular immigration trends and methods, including legislation and statistics.[723] From July 2010, CIREFI was abolished and replaced by Frontex, the EU's border control agency.[724]

CIREFI's role was augmented by the adoption of a Council resolution establishing an 'early warning' system for information concerning irregular migration flows, adopted in 1999.[725] A later Council decision of 2005 established a web-based information and coordination network (Iconet) for Member States' migration management services.[726] This Decision conferred competence on the Commission to manage a secure system of information exchange which would include 'at least' the early warning system, the network of immigration liaison officers;[727] visas, borders, and travel documents relating to irregular immigration, and expulsion-related issues.[728] This system is now managed by Frontex.[729]

As for statistics, the Council agreed in 1998 that the Commission's statistics body, Eurostat, would take over the role of compiling official statistics on immigration and asylum, while 'non-statistical confidential information' would 'continue to be processed in the context of CIREFI . . . on the basis of preparatory work carried out by the General Secretariat of the Council'.[730] In 2001, the Council agreed that statistics on immigration and asylum issues would be available to the public, in the form of annual reports and (to some extent) monthly and quarterly data, subject to possible restrictions on security grounds.[731] The Commission subsequently decided that information on irregular migration (detailing the numbers refused, apprehended, and removed) should be made public on an annual basis, with delayed publication of monthly or quarterly data.[732]

The collection and publication of such statistics was later formalized with the adoption of EU legislation concerning asylum and migration statistics.[733] This legislation requires Member States to forward information concerning third-country nationals found to be illegally present, who are subject to return decisions, and who have in fact left, and to disaggregate this data by citizenship (which they did before), as well as by age and sex (as regards persons who are irregularly present). In principle this information should assist with assessment of the effectiveness of EU policy in this area,[734]

---

[722] Reg 516/2014 ([2014] OJ L 150/168). See also Reg 514/2014 setting out general provisions on the various funds ([2014] OJ L 150/112).

[723] See T Bunyan, ed., *Key Texts on Justice and Home Affairs in the European Union* (1997) (n 9 above), and also Council conclusions of 30 Nov 2004 ([1996] OJ C 274/50).

[724] Council doc 17653/09, 16 Dec 2009. [725] Council doc 7965/99, 11 May 1999.

[726] [2005] OJ L 83/48, in force 21 Apr 2005. [727] See I:7.5.5 above. [728] Art 2.

[729] See I:3.10.1 above.

[730] Press release of the JHA Council, 19 Mar 1998. For more on EU immigration statistics, see I:6.11 above.

[731] Press release of the JHA Council, 28–9 May 2001.

[732] Commission Action Plan on immigration and asylum statistics (COM (2003) 179, 15 Apr 2003).

[733] Reg 862/2007, [2007] OJ L 199/23; see particularly Arts 5(1)(b), 7, and 8(1)(d) and (f).

[734] Ie, the definitions of illegal presence and return decisions in the Reg (Arts 2(1)(r) and 7(1)(a)) match the definitions in the Returns Dir (Art 3(2) and (4), Dir 2008/115 ([2008] OJ L 348/98)).

although it would also be useful to know how many return decisions are withdrawn and why (ie decisions to regularize, or to grant international protection), how many people leave voluntarily and how many by force, how many persons are in immigration detention and for how long, and what happens to persons after expulsion (particularly in the context of readmission agreements). Also, it is important to ensure that the statistics Regulation is applied consistently with the relevant legislation, otherwise the statistics will be misleading.[735] It can only be hoped that the official publication of such statistics will make a contribution to an informed public debate on the scale of irregular migration—keeping in mind that the number of irregular residents who are not apprehended can only ever be estimated.[736]

Other relevant measures in this field are a Decision on the exchange of information as regards national asylum and immigration law, the EU's Migration Network, a Joint Action on false documents, and a third-pillar Decision on counterfeit documents.[737]

7.9 External Relations

The EU's main mechanism for ensuring that persons its Member States wish to expel are removed from the territory is to insist that non-EU States sign readmission agreements with the EU, its Member States, or both. EU policy toward readmission agreements has evolved over time as the EU has gained new internal powers (and thus external powers) over migration law and as it has decided to place greater priority on securing readmission commitments from non-EU States, in the form of both specific stand-alone agreements and as part of association or cooperation agreements with the EU. Readmission also forms part of a broader policy integrating migration into the EU's overall external relations objectives. The EU also has external competence pursuant to its internal powers over irregular migration and related issues to ratify treaties concerning the issue of visas and readmission for Chinese tourists, and the Protocols to the UN organized crime convention concerning trafficking and smuggling of persons.[738]

7.9.1 Readmission agreements

Before the Treaty of Amsterdam entered into force, the EC (as it then was) lacked competence to agree readmission treaties. [739] However, in 1995 the Council agreed a standard clause to be considered for inclusion into 'mixed' agreements (treaties which have

---

[735] ie, the data relating to irregular migration should not include any asylum seekers, in light of the Court of Justice's interpretation of the Returns Directive: see I.7.7.1 above.

[736] See I:6.11 above.

[737] Respectively: [2006] OJ L 283/40; [2008] OJ L 131/7; [1998] OJ L 333/4; and [2000] OJ L 81/1. For details and comments on the first two measures, see I:6.11 above.

[738] See respectively [2004] OJ L 83/12 and I:7.5.3 and I:7.5.4 above.

[739] See also: N Coleman, *European Readmission Policy: Third Country Interests and Refugee Rights* (Martinus Nijhoff, 2009); N Albuquerque Abell, 'The Compatibility of Readmission Agreements With the 1951 Convention Relating to the Status of Refugees' (1999) 11 IJRL 60; D Bouteillet-Paquet, 'Passing the Buck: A Critical Analysis of the Readmission Policy Implemented by the European Union and its Member States' (2003) 5 EJML 359; and E Guild, 'Readmission Agreements' in S Peers et al., *EU Immigration and Asylum Law: Text and Commentary*, 2nd edn, vol 2, (Martinus Nijhoff, 2012), ch 20.

to be ratified by the EC and the Member States).[740] Also, in order to ensure that read-mission agreements signed by non-EU States with different Member States would be comparable, the Council had already agreed a Recommendation on a standard read-mission agreement between a Member State and a third country in 1994,[741] along with a Recommendation in 1995 on a standard Protocol on means of proof to be attached to such agreements.[742] It had also agreed in 1994 on a Recommendation on a standard travel document to be used for expulsion proceedings.[743]

Next, with the entry into force of the Treaty of Amsterdam, the EC gained external powers to sign and ratify readmission treaties in its own name. Not long after the entry into force of the Treaty of Amsterdam, the Tampere European Council endorsed the Community's involvement in readmission from two perspectives, asserting that: '[t]he Amsterdam Treaty conferred powers on the Community in the field of readmission' and inviting the Council 'to conclude readmission agreements or to include stand-ard clauses in other agreements between the European Community and relevant third countries or groups of countries'.

To implement the first part of the conclusions, the Council decided which states should be targeted for agreements with the Community and what negotiating posi-tion the Community wished to take. It approved in September 2000 a mandate for the Commission to negotiate readmission treaties with Russia, Pakistan, Sri Lanka, and Morocco. Subsequently, in conjunction with the decision to drop visa requirements for persons with legal status granted by Hong Kong or Macao, the Council decided that these entities should in return agree readmission agreements with the Community 'as soon as possible',[744] and so it granted a negotiating mandate to the Commission for such treaties in May 2001. Next, the Commission sought a mandate to negotiate a read-mission treaty with Ukraine, which the JHA Council granted in 2002. The Council then agreed criteria for which States to 'target' for future readmission agreements and applied those criteria to select four new target States (Algeria, Albania, China, and Turkey), which the Commission received a mandate to negotiate with in autumn 2002.[745] The criteria are: migration pressure upon the EU; States which have signed an association or cooperation agreement (excepting States negotiating accession); adjacent States; States where a readmission agreement would 'add value' to Member States' bilateral agreements; and 'geographical balance'. There is no explanation of how the criteria were applied to the individual cases; in fact, none of the four States which were 'targeted' meet the second criterion.[746] Also, as an implicit trade-off for the abolition of the visa

---

[740] Council doc 12509/95. See Press Releases of JHA Council, 23 Nov 1995 (agreement on the text) and Environment Council, 4 Apr 1996 (formal adoption of the text).

[741] [1996] OJ C 274/21. For analysis of this Recommendation, see E Guild and J Niessen, *The Developing Immigration and Asylum Policies of the European Union: Adopted Conventions, Resolutions, Recommendations, Decisions and Conclusions* (Kluwer, 1996).

[742] [1996] OJ C 274/25.

[743] [1996] OJ C 274/20. For further details, see and Coleman and Guild (n 739 above). The Commission has proposed a Regulation establishing a uniform format for this document: COM (2015) 677, 15 Dec 2015.

[744] See JHA Council Conclusions, 30 Nov/1 Dec 2000.

[745] Council doc 7990/02, 15 Apr 2002, approved by the JHA Council, 25/26 Apr 2002.

[746] The EU association agreement with Algeria ([2005] OJ L 265) contains a readmission clause, but that agreement had not been signed in Apr 2002, when the Council adopted and applied these criteria.

requirement for their nationals to enter the EU, Romania and Bulgaria were expected to make a number of changes to national immigration law going beyond readmission obligations, but this did not take the form of a formal treaty with the Community.[747] In 2006, the EC decided that it also wished to negotiate readmission agreements with most of the remaining States in the Western Balkans (plus Moldova), in conjunction with negotiating visa facilitation treaties; such a linkage had already been made as regards Russia and Ukraine.[748] Next, between 2008 and 2011, the Commission was granted further mandates to negotiate readmission treaties (again alongside visa facilitation treaties) with Belarus,[749] Georgia, Armenia, Azerbaijan, and Cape Verde. In 2013, it received a mandate to negotiate a visa facilitation treaty with Morocco, to encourage that State to sign the long-planned readmission treaty, while it received a mandate to negotiate parallel agreements with Tunisia in 2014.[750]

In the meantime, in 2011 the Commission issued an evaluation of the EU's readmission policy.[751] Its analysis began by noting the limited statistics available on Member States' use of the readmission treaties,[752] and calling for Member States to use them for all returns to the relevant States. In the Commission's view, the agreements were preventing irregular migration, since the share of readmission requests to the relevant countries had dropped. They were also an effective means of ensuring return: although the countries which had signed an EU readmission agreement accounted for 20% of return decisions, they amounted to 40% of actual returns carried out. In practice, the possibility of using EU readmission treaties to remove nationals of non-contracting parties was largely only relevant to Ukraine. Indeed, the inclusion of such clauses slowed down negotiations greatly, and the Commission suggested that the Council should not always insist upon them.

In order to negotiate readmission treaties more successfully, the Commission urged that the Council make more use of incentives, such as visa facilitation treaties (which had not led to an increase in irregular migration in practice) or financial support.[753] The EU should also include more detailed clauses relating to readmission in its general cooperation agreements (see discussion below) and impose sanctions on non-cooperative countries. Also, the EU side should be more flexible about the time limit which the non-Member State had to reply to a request for readmission, rather than insisting upon the shortest possible time period for immigration detention in any Member State. Also, the Commission had suggestions to address human rights concerns: greater monitoring of the situation in the country of origin; the inclusion of rules on asylum application at the border in the EU's Borders Handbook and the revised asylum procedures Directive; the possibility of suspending readmission treaties on human rights grounds; and the participation of NGOs in the Joint Committees that administer readmission treaties.

---

[747] See COM (2001) 61, 2 Feb 2002 and COM (2001) 361, 29 June 2001; see further I:4.5 above.
[748] On visa facilitation treaties, see I:4.11.2 above.   [749] Council doc 6424/1/11, 24 Feb 2011.
[750] Council doc 15141/14, 5 Dec 2014.   [751] COM (2011) 76, 23 Feb 2011.
[752] The information available (SEC (2011) 210, 23 Feb 2011) shows that around 19,000 people were subject to readmission requests under the relevant treaties from 2006 to 2009. But this data only covers requests from 21 Member States to nine non-EU States.
[753] On these treaties, see I:4.11.2 above.

The response from the Council was notably unenthusiastic.[754] It did not want to remove the inclusion of 'third-country transit' clauses in most cases, and referred reluctantly to the notion of offering further incentives to sign deals. Nonetheless, it wanted the EU to sign more treaties with countries of origin—willing the end without providing the means.

Most recently, responding to the large increases in migration, the Commission announced, in its 2015 Anti-Smuggling Action Plan, an intention to propose negotiation of readmission treaties with the main countries of origin in sub-Saharan Africa.[755] The June 2015 European Council then elaborated upon that with a call for greater incentives to agree such treaties (financial support and the admission of service providers), finally reacting to the Commission's argument on incentives after four years.

Seventeen EU readmission treaties have been concluded to date. First, a treaty with Hong Kong became the first EU readmission agreement to enter into force, on 1 March 2004.[756] Subsequently, an EU-Macao treaty entered into force on 1 June 2004;[757] an EU-Sri Lanka treaty entered into force on 1 May 2005;[758] a treaty with Albania entered into force on 1 May 2006;[759] a treaty with Russia entered into force on 1 June 2007, in parallel with an agreement on visa facilitation;[760] and treaties with Ukraine, Serbia, Montenegro, Bosnia-Herzegovina, the Former Yugoslav Republic of Macedonia, and Moldova entered into force on 1 January 2008, also in parallel with visa facilitation treaties.[761] An agreement with Pakistan entered into force on 1 December 2010.[762] The three countries in the Caucasus followed (Georgia on 1 March 2011; Armenia on 1 January 2014; and Azerbaijan on 1 September 2014).[763] Finally, the treaty with Cape Verde entered into force on 1 December 2014,[764] and the treaty with Turkey on 1 October 2014.[765] Negotiations with Belarus, Morocco, and Tunisia are ongoing,[766] while negotiations with Algeria and China never got started.[767]

Although there are minor differences between the agreements negotiated and published to date, all are essentially identical. The contracting parties have reciprocal obligations to take back their own nationals (or, in the case of Hong Kong and Macao, permanent residents) who have entered or stayed illegally in the other party.[768] They must also readmit nationals of non-contracting parties or stateless persons who have illegally entered or stayed on their territory, subject to certain conditions.[769]

---

[754] Council conclusions on readmission (Council doc 11260/11, 8 June 2011).

[755] COM (2015) 285, 27 May 2015.   [756] [2004] OJ L 64/38.   [757] [2004] OJ L 143/97.

[758] [2005] OJ L 124/43.

[759] [2005] OJ L 124/22; see Council Decision on conclusion ([2005] OJ L 304/14).

[760] [2007] OJ L 129; see note on entry into force ([2007] OJ L 156/37).

[761] [2007] OJ L 332 and L 334.   [762] [2010] OJ L 287/50.

[763] [2011] L 52/45; [2013] L 289/12; and [2014] L 128/17.   [764] [2013] OJ L 282/15.

[765] [2014] OJ L 134/3.

[766] See: <http://www.statewatch.org/news/2015/feb/eu-comm-readmission-and-agreemrents.pdf>.

[767] See the anti-smuggling action plan (n 755 above).

[768] The treaties with Georgia, Armenia, Azerbaijan, Turkey, and Cape Verde also apply this rule to nationals' spouses and children who are nationals of non-contracting parties.

[769] In particular, some treaties provide for delayed application of these rules (a two-year delay for Albania and Ukraine, and a three-year delay for Russia and Turkey). The treaties with the other Western Balkan States and Moldova allow for the relevant provisions to be suspended on grounds of 'security, protection of public order or public health'. The treaty with Pakistan limits the application of these rules to persons who entered the territory after the treaty's entry into force, and the treaty with Turkey waives the readmission

Furthermore, they must also permit transit of persons back to a non-contracting party if necessary. There are detailed rules on the procedure for handing back persons, including the types of documents which constitute proof or prima facie evidence that a person is a national or was on the territory. The agreements also require use of the EU's standard travel document in certain circumstances.[770] There are detailed provisions on data protection, although these omit to require the non-EU parties to apply basic principles concerning the effective collective or individual enforcement of data protection rules. Each agreement specifies that it is 'without prejudice to the rights, obligations and responsibilities' of the parties arising from 'International Law', but there is no specific reference to human rights or refugee law in the treaties with Hong Kong, Macao, Sri Lanka, Ukraine, and Pakistan. On the other hand, the treaties with Armenia and Azerbaijan provide for a stronger human rights clause, with reference to a preference for voluntary departure. A readmission committee is established by each agreement to perform specified technical tasks. Finally, each agreement provides that Member States can draw up special implementing protocols with the non-EU party, but conversely that the agreement takes precedence over any incompatible bilateral agreement between a Member State and the other contracting party. All the treaties provide for denunciation (none have ever been denounced), but there is no provision for settling disputes that might arise between the parties.

The second part of the Tampere conclusions concerned the insertion of readmission clauses into broader EU external agreements. This continued the pre-Amsterdam policy discussed above, although now with the imprimatur of the backing of the European Council. However, the Council decided it should adapt the standard clauses for such agreements, because of the EC's competence over readmission treaties following the Treaty of Amsterdam. It quickly adopted a Decision adapting the standard clause in December 1999,[771] apparently hurrying to ensure that the negotiating mandate for the 'Cotonou agreement' with African, Caribbean, and Pacific (ACP) States could be amended in time before those negotiations concluded. Moreover, the new position of the Council was that such clauses should *always* be included in EC agreements, not just considered for inclusion on a case-by-case basis, because the EC had enjoyed only mixed success encouraging countries to sign up to the 'first generation' readmission clause of 1995. Agreements signed with a number of countries before 1999 contain variations on the 1995 standard clause; all agreements signed afterward include the 1999 standard clause.[772] The CJEU has ruled that provisions such as these fall within the scope of the EU's development policy powers (or presumably, in other cases its powers regarding on association with third States),

---

obligations after the third-country national has been out of the requested State for five years. In Nov 2015, the EU and Turkey agreed to bring forward the date of application of these rules, in return for the EU fast-tracking the visa waiver process for Turkey.

[770] [1996] OJ C 274/20.   [771] Press Release of JHA Council, 2 Dec 1999.

[772] For details of the provisions in each agreement, see Coleman (n 739 above) and S Peers, 'Irregular Immigration and EU External Relations' in B Bogusz, et al., eds., *Irregular Migration and Human Rights* (Martinus Nijhoff, 2004), 193.

because they do not regulate readmission in sufficient detail to fall within the scope of EU immigration policy.[773]

Shortly after the entry into force of the Treaty of Amsterdam, the Commission and the Council disputed whether the EC's competence over readmission agreements is exclusive, or rather shared with Member States. In practice, it has been assumed that the power is shared, with Member States continuing to sign readmission agreements in their own name since 1999. It is submitted that this practice is correct, since the Community (now Union) has not acquired exclusive competence pursuant to sufficient harmonization of the relevant internal law; nor can it be argued that it is absolutely essential for the EU to exercise external competence in order for it to adopt internal legislation.[774]

7.9.2 Irregular migration and external relations policy

The external aspects of migration policy have been on the EU agenda for some time. The issue was addressed in an early Commission communication on immigration, prepared in the run up to the Maastricht Treaty,[775] and the Edinburgh European Council (summit meeting) of 1992 adopted a detailed statement of principles governing external aspects of migration policy. This Declaration recognized in detail the factors that would reduce migration, referred to coordination of EU action and the effective use of development aid, and set out principles to guide EU and Member States' policies.

However, this policy was for some time only implemented in a piecemeal fashion. In late 1998, the EU Council created a 'High-Level Working Group' on asylum and immigration, in which officials from home affairs, trade, development, and foreign affairs ministries had to work together in order to develop an external immigration policy.[776] The Group was tasked with identifying a list of third States which should be subject to unilateral high-profile 'Action Plans' relating to migration policy, and then elaborating the detail of each plan. Each plan would include an analysis of 'the cause of the influx', based on the 'political and human rights situation' in the relevant country; possible 'strengthening economic cooperation' between the EU and the relevant country; 'identification of the needs for humanitarian aid', and concrete proposals for sending such aid; proposed further 'political/diplomatic consultations' with the relevant State or nearby States; an assessment of the possibility or state of play regarding a readmission agreement or readmission clauses in a mixed agreement; the possibility of temporary reception of persons in the region; and the likelihood of safe return or internal flight alternatives within a country of origin.

In 2001–02, the EU's policy on irregular migration and external relations became more operational. In addition to agreeing new criteria and targets for readmission agreements (see above), the mandate of the High-Level Working Group was expanded

---

[773] Case C-377/12 *Commission v Council*, ECLI:EU:C:2014:1903.
[774] See further the detailed analysis of the issue in Coleman and Guild (n 739 above).
[775] SEC (91) 1855, 23 Oct 1991, points 48 and 49.
[776] See the first edition of this book, pp 102–03. The mandate of the group can be found in the press release of the General Affairs Council, 5/6 Dec 1998.

beyond the development and implementation of Action Plans, to examine the links between migration and other EU external policies, conduct dialogue on migration issues in certain cases with third states, intergovernmental organizations, and non-governmental organizations. Its mandate no longer referred expressly to facilitating trade with the relevant countries and the Action Plans were now to cover such new issues as joint measures on migration control policy and examination of voluntary repatriation.[777]

The Seville European Council of June 2002, which focused on immigration and asylum issues, developed a formal process and criteria regarding the external aspects of irregular migration. In its conclusions on this issue,[778] the summit first of all decided that each future EU association or cooperation agreement should include a clause on 'joint management of migration flows and compulsory readmission in the event of illegal immigration', having observed that trade expansion, economic cooperation, conflict prevention, and development assistance could all reduce the root causes of migration flows. Secondly, the EU declared its willingness to offer financial assistance to third States to assist with readmission of their own and other countries' nationals and broader joint migration management. Third, inadequate cooperation by a third State could hamper further development of relations with the EU, following a systematic assessment of relations with that country. Finally, if a non-EU state has demonstrated 'an unjustified lack of cooperation in joint management of migration flows', according to the Council following a unanimous vote, then the Council, after 'full use of existing Community mechanisms', could take 'measures or positions' as part of the EU's foreign policy or other policies, 'while honouring the Union's contractual commitments and not jeopardising development cooperation objectives'. This is an apparent threat to *reduce* the existing level of EU relations with a third state, but there is great political and legal ambiguity in the conclusions as regards what measures might be taken, the legal base for deciding on whether a State has failed to cooperate and the substantive grounds for concluding that there has been such a failure. In this area, the process and the criteria were still unclear.

EU policy then began to focus on means to ensure that the 'target' countries for readmission agreements would prove willing to agree them, given the EU's very limited willingness to lift visa requirements for most of its targets.[779] Next, the General Affairs Council on 18 November 2002 agreed to implement the Seville external relations conclusions in more detail, agreeing criteria for the application of the 'sanctions' policy and applying them.[780] The criteria for deciding which States to target were the extent of migration flows towards the EU, geography, the need to build capacity, the framework for cooperation and the attitude of that State regarding cooperation on migration issues. On this basis, the Council decided that the EU should intensify relations with Albania, China, Yugoslavia, Morocco, Russia, Tunisia, Ukraine, and Turkey, and to start

---

[777] Council doc 9433/02, 30 May 2002.

[778] For comments on all aspects of the Seville conclusions on immigration and asylum, see S Peers, 'EU Immigration and Asylum Law after Seville' (2002) 16 IANL Journal 176.

[779] See discussion in the Green Paper on Return [expulsion] Policy (COM (2002) 175, 10 Apr 2002) and the follow-up communication (COM (2002) 564, 14 Oct 2002).

[780] Council doc 13894/02, 13 Nov 2002.

cooperation with Libya as regards cooperation on migration issues, although the exact form such cooperation should take was not specified in detail. Also, the Council spelled out in detail the text of the future 'migration cooperation' clause to be included in all cooperation and association agreements with the Community (as it then was). This clause entails a dialogue on migration, a commitment to examine root causes, a joint examination of illegal immigration issues, the standard readmission clause (already, of course, part of EU policy before Seville), and 'cooperation regarding migratory flows to promote a fair treatment' of legal residents 'through an integration policy favouring non-discrimination and the fight against racism and xenophobia'.[781] In summer 2003, the Commission reported that this policy had been implemented in detail, comprising meetings with all the 'target' states except the former Yugoslavia.[782] As a result, Morocco agreed to negotiate the proposed readmission agreement, Turkey was aligning itself more fully with EU legislation, and there was progress in readmission talks with Ukraine.

A parallel development was a Commission paper from December 2002 covering two issues: the link between migration and development and the EU financial resources available for implementing internal and external migration policies.[783] Despite a decade of increasing EU interest in the external relations aspect of migration policy, this was the first detailed examination of the topic as regards developing countries—or indeed any other countries. The Commission set out the push and pull factors leading to migration from developing States and surveyed some recent literature. It concluded that poverty reduction should stay the main focus of EU development policy, and surveyed other policies that might reduce migration demand: liberalized trade and market access; more liberal rules on short-term movement of people (for the first time); conflict prevention; good governance; and rural development. But as for implementing these policies, it held out little hope for quick results, again pointing to the limited leverage of the Community and now also to the limits imposed by the World Trade Organization (WTO) on trade preferences for only selected developing countries, as well as the limits upon the Community budget. However, in the second part of the communication, the Commission stated an intention to expand the funds available for migration projects in non-EU countries dramatically.

The Council adopted conclusions on the Commission's paper in May 2003, stating that it did not intend to reduce current levels of funding for poverty eradication.[784] As regards dialogue to be conducted with developing countries, the EU would consider further proposals for policies on work permits, virtual returns, voluntary return programmes, management of remittances, integration of third-country nationals in the EU, problems that may arise from recruitment of highly-skilled labour from developing states, and a review of the policy of placing EU expatriates in jobs that could go to skilled local staff.

---

[781] These criteria took account of the criteria agreed by the JHA Council in Apr 2002 to decide which countries to negotiate Community readmission agreements with: see discussion above.
[782] SEC (2003) 815, 9 July 2003.   [783] COM (2002) 703, 3 Dec 2002.
[784] Council doc 8927/03, 5 May 2003.

The Thessaloniki European Council subsequently agreed in June 2003 to establish an 'evaluation mechanism' for third countries, taking account of the following criteria: participation in the international instruments relevant to this matter (eg, Conventions on Human Rights, the Geneva Convention of 28 July 1951 relating to the status of refugees as amended by the New York Protocol of 31 January 1967, etc.); cooperation of third countries in readmission/return of their nationals and of third-country nationals; efforts in border control and interception of illegal immigrants; combating of trafficking in human beings, including taking legislative and other measures; cooperation on visa policy and possible adaptation of visa systems; and creation of asylum systems, with specific reference to access to effective protection, and efforts in redocumentation of nationals. The policy will be assessed by an annual report from the Commission, which could make recommendations.[785] In November 2003, the Council approved more detailed guidelines for the functioning of this mechanism.[786] The guidelines concern particularly the Commission's annual report, with more detail on the application of the criteria, and a requirement of partnership 'where possible' with the relevant third countries, based on existing agreements between those countries and the EC. In a 'pilot phase', the mechanism would focus on selected countries in the Commission's first report. This first report indicated that cooperation with the EU was generally acceptable, and made recommendations for development of cooperation with the relevant States and for further development of the reporting mechanism, including the addition of more third States.[787] The Council broadly welcomed the report.[788]

In 2004, the EU established a funding programme on the external aspects of asylum and migration, since integrated into the EU's main external relations funding programmes.[789] Shortly afterward, the Commission released in 2005 a communication on the links between migration and development, addressing in detail the issues of remittances to countries of origin, the development role of diasporas, circular migration (migration back and forth to and from the EU and the country of origin), and 'brain drain', indicating its intention to address these issues through dialogue and possibly legislation.[790]

Soon afterwards, in response to a call from the informal European Council (or summit meeting) held at Hampton Court in autumn 2005, the Commission suggested an action plan regarding the external aspects of migration, which the European Council largely endorsed shortly afterwards, in the form of a 'Global Approach to Migration'. The plan included action by Frontex to support enhanced external border controls and further dialogue and cooperation with African and Mediterranean countries.[791]

---

[785] Paras 19–21, Thessaloniki European Council conclusions.
[786] Council doc 15292/03, 25 Nov 2003.   [787] COM (2005) 352, 28 July 2005.
[788] See Council conclusions on external relations and migration issues (Council doc 14769/05, 21 Nov 2005), point 7.
[789] Reg 491/2004 ([2004] OJ L 80/1), integrated into Art 16 of Reg 1905/2006 ([2006] OJ L 378/41). For more detail, see the second edition of this book, pp 295–6.
[790] COM (2005) 390, 1 Sep 2005. See Council conclusions on policy coherence for development, Council doc 15806/09, 12 Nov 2009.
[791] COM (2005) 621, 30 Nov 2005; Annex I to the European Council conclusions, 15/16 Dec 2005. See earlier Council conclusions on EU-Libya migration cooperation (press release of JHA Council, 2–3 June 2005).

The 'global approach' was then further developed subsequently as part of the EU's 'common immigration policy',[792] in particular being extended to develop the principle of 'circular migration' and to include the new concept of 'mobility partnerships'— informal agreements between the EU, its Member States and certain third countries which bundle together a number of promised actions by the EU and its Member States on the one hand and the partner country on the other.[793] After concluding mobility partnerships with an initial batch of countries,[794] the Commission relaunched the policy in 2011, redubbing it the 'Global Approach to Migration and *Mobility*' (GAMM).[795] The objective was to expand the strategy to include the EU's external visa policy,[796] and to link it more closely to other EU external polices (trade, development, foreign policy). The GAMM would now be based on four pillars: legal migration; irregular migration; international protection; and development. It would take the form of various regional and bilateral dialogues, with two levels of commitment: Mobility Partnerships, which would involve visa facilitation and readmission agreements; and a Common Agenda on Migration and Mobility, which would be a less developed package of commitments. The policy would be based on the EU's internal legislation, supplemented by pledges specific to each agreement.

Implementing the GAMM,[797] the EU has agreed more Mobility Partnerships with Morocco, Azerbaijan, Tunisia, and Jordan,[798] and is negotiating Common Agendas on Migration and Mobility with Nigeria, India, Ethiopia, and Brazil.[799]

The risk is ever-present that the EU's external migration policies will exacerbate human rights violations in countries of transit which will not want the burden of an increased migrant population, that insufficient attention is paid to the EU's other external objectives (relating to foreign policy, development, and trade), with the result that migration pressures actually increase, and that the root causes of migration within the EU's control (in particular the Common Agricultural Policy) are not addressed. Through harsh experience the EU learned that despite the demands of its interior ministers, few States are willing to offer it something in return for nothing. This has resulted in a more balanced policy of offering visa facilitation agreements and financial

---

[792] See the European Council conclusions of Dec 2006 and the follow-up Commission communications: COM (2006) 735, 30 Nov 2006; COM (2007) 780 and SEC (2007) 1632, 5 Dec 2007; COM (2008) 359, 17 June 2008; COM (2008) 611, 8 Oct 2008; and the Council conclusions in Council docs 9604/08, 20 May 2008 and 16041/08, 20 Nov 2008. See also COM (2007) 247, 16 May 2007, on extending the global approach to the areas to the eastern and south-eastern neighbours of the EU, and COM (2011) 292, 24 May 2011, on extending the global approach to the Southern Mediterranean following the 'Arab Spring'.

[793] See COM (2007) 248, 16 May 2007 and SEC (2009) 1240, 18 Sep 2009, and the Council conclusions in Council docs 16283/07, 7 Dec 2007, and 15811/09, 12 Nov 2009.

[794] Moldova, Cape Verde, Georgia, Armenia (respectively Council docs: 9460/08 add 1, 21 May 2008; 9460/08 add 1, 21 May 2008; 16396/09 add 1, 20 Nov 2009; 14963/11 add 1, 6 Oct 2011).

[795] COM (2011) 743, 18 Nov 2011. See the subsequent Council conclusions (Council doc 9417/12, 3 May 2012).

[796] See I:4.11 above.

[797] See also the Commission report on implementation of the GAMM in 2012–13 (COM (2014) 96, 21 Feb 2014) and the Council conclusions on the same topic (Council doc 8443/13, 2 April 2014). The Annexes to the report list the countries which the EU is interested in negotiating the two forms of agreement with.

[798] Respectively Council docs: 6139/13 add 1, 8 April 2013; 13477/13, 20 Sep 2013; 16371/13, 25 Nov 2013; and 10055/3/14, 20 Sep 2014. An agreement with Belarus is under negotiation.

[799] See COM (2014) 96, 21 Feb 2014.

assistance in return for readmission agreements, and linking together different aspects of EU external migration policy, in particular in the form of mobility partnerships.

7.10 Conclusions

The overall legal framework in this area remains fragmented at EU level, certainly as compared to the codification of the legislation on visas and borders. Nevertheless, EU policy on irregular migration addresses many key aspects of this issue, in particular in the form of the Returns Directive and the Directive on the employment of irregular migrants. However, the latter measure does not address the central issue of enforcement and despite some positive case law of the CJEU, the Returns Directive sets too low a standard from the point of view of human rights, in particular as regards detention. The recent attempts by the Commission to encourage Member States to derogate from the standards of that Directive are disturbing, and it is likely that the tension between an effective system for the return of irregular migrants and the humane treatment of those migrants will continue.

Ratification of Treaties

(as of 10 Dec 2015)

* An asterisk indicates that the treaty is not yet in force

Council of Europe

ETS 25	*European Agreement on Regulations Governing the Movement of Persons between Member States of the Council of Europe (1957)*
Ratified by:	12 Member States: Austria, Belgium, France, Germany, Greece, Italy, Luxembourg, the Netherlands, Portugal, Spain, Malta, and Slovenia.
Signed by:	1 Member State: Cyprus
ETS 31	*European Agreement on the Abolition of Visas for Refugees (1959)*
Ratified by:	17 Member States: Belgium, Czech Republic, Denmark, Finland, Germany, Ireland, Italy, Luxembourg, Malta, Netherlands, Portugal, Spain, Sweden, Poland, Slovakia, Hungary, and Romania; not ratified by Croatia
Signed by:	1 Member State: Cyprus
Denounced by:	2 Member States: France, UK
ETS 46	*Fourth Protocol to the ECHR (1963)*
Ratified by:	26 Member States: all except Greece and United Kingdom
Signed by:	1 Member State: United Kingdom
ETS 117	*Seventh Protocol to the ECHR (1984)*
Ratified by:	25 Member States: all except Germany, Netherlands, and United Kingdom
Signed by:	2 Member States: Germany and Netherlands
ETS 187	*Protocol 13 to the ECHR (2002)*
Ratified by:	All Member States
CETS 197	*Convention on trafficking in persons (2005)*
Ratified by:	27 Member States: all except Czech Republic

United Nations

	Convention on transnational organized crime
Ratified by:	All Member States
	Protocol on smuggling, Convention on transnational organized crime
Ratified by:	27 Member States: all except Ireland
Signed by:	1 Member State: Ireland
	Protocol on trafficking in persons, Convention on transnational organized crime
Ratified by:	All Member States

Schengen *Acquis* on Immigration and Asylum

Article 1

– still in force

Articles 2–8

– repealed by Schengen Borders Code ([2006] OJ L 105/1)

Articles 9–17

– repealed by Schengen Visa Code ([2009] OJ L 243/1)

Article 18

– amended by Reg 1091/2001 ([2001] OJ L 150/4), then again by Reg 265/2010 ([2010] OJ L 85/1) and Reg 610/2013

Articles 19–22

– Reg 265/2010 ([2010] OJ L 85/1) amended Article 21; Reg 610/2013 amended Arts 20, 21 and 22

Articles 23–24

– repealed by Returns Directive 2008/115 ([2008] OJ L 348/98), as from 24 Dec 2010

Article 25

– amended by Reg 265/2010 ([2010] OJ L 85/1)

Article 26

– supplemented by carrier sanctions Directive 2001/51, ([2001] OJ L 187/45)

Article 27

– repealed by Directive 2002/90 and Framework Decision on facilitation ([2002] OJ L 190/1)

Articles 82, 91

– still in force

Article 136

– Article 136(3) amended by Reg 1931/2006 on border traffic rules ([2006] OJ L 405); all of Article 136 repealed by Reg 610/2013

Executive Committee Decisions

SCH/Com-ex (93) 21 - 14.12.1993—Extending the uniform visa Article 62(2)(b) TEC

– *repealed by Schengen Visa Code*

SCH/Com-ex (93) 22 Rev - 14.12.1993—Confidential nature of certain documents

– *repealed by 2003 Council Decision ([2003] OJ L 5/78)*

SCH/Com-ex (93) 24 - 14.12.1993—Common procedures for cancelling, rescinding, or shortening the length of validity of the uniform visa

– *repealed by Schengen Visa Code*

SCH/Com-ex (94) 1 Rev 2 - 26.4.1994—Adjustment measures aiming to remove the obstacles and restrictions on traffic flows at road border crossing points at internal borders

– *repealed by Schengen Borders Code*

SCH/Com-ex (94) 2 - 26.4.1994—Issuing uniform visas at the borders

- *repealed by Reg 415/2003*

SCH/Com-ex (94) 15 Rev - 21.11.1994—Introducing a computerized procedure for consulting the central authorities provided for in Article 17(2) of the implementing Convention

- *repealed once VIS fully operational (Nov 2015)*

SCH/Com-ex (94) 16 Rev - 21.11.1994—Acquisition of common entry and exit stamps

- *still in force; proposed repeal by 'smart borders' legislation*

SCH/Com-ex (94) 17 Rev 4 - 22.12.1994—Introducing and applying the Schengen system in airports and aerodromes

  - *repealed by Schengen Borders Code*

SCH/Com-ex (94) 25 - 22.12.1994—Exchanges of statistical information on the issue of visas

  - *repealed by Schengen Visa Code*

SCH/Com-ex (94) 29 Rev 2 - 22.12.1994—Bringing into force the Convention implementing the Schengen Agreement of 19 June 1990

  - *still in force*

SCH/Com-ex (95) PV 1 Rev (Point No 8)—Common visa policy

  - *still in force; the Commission has proposed its repeal (COM (2014) 713)*

SCH/Com-ex (95) 20 Rev 2 - 20.12.1995—Approval of document SCH/I (95) 40 Rev 6 on the procedure for applying Article 2(2) of the Convention implementing the Schengen Agreement

  - *repealed by Schengen Borders Code*

SCH/Com-ex (95) 21 - 20.12.1995—Swift exchange between the Schengen States of statistical and tangible data on possible malfunctions at the external borders

  - *still in force; the Commission has proposed its repeal (COM (2014) 713)*

SCH/Com-ex (96) 13 Rev - 27.6.1996—Principles for issuing Schengen visas in accordance with Article 30(1)(a) of the Convention implementing the Schengen Agreement

  - *still in force; the Commission has proposed its repeal (COM (2014) 713)*

SCH/Com-ex (96) 27 - 19.12.1996—Issuing visas at borders to seamen in transit

  - *repealed by Reg 415/2003*

SCH/Com-ex (97) 29 Rev 2 - 7.10.1997—Bringing into force the Convention implementing the Schengen Agreement in Greece

  - *still in force*

SCH/Com-ex (97) 32 - 15.12.1997—Harmonization of visa policy

  - *repealed by Reg 539/2001, Art 7(3)*

SCH/Com-ex (97) 34 Rev - 15.12.1997—Implementation of the Joint Action on a uniform format for residence permits

  - *still in force*

SCH/Com-ex (97) 39 Rev - 15.12.1997—Guiding Principles for means of proof and indicative evidence within the framework of readmission agreements between Schengen States

  - *still in force; the Commission has proposed its repeal (COM (2014) 713)*

SCH/Com-ex (98) 1, 2 Rev - 21.4.1998—Report on the activities of the task force

  - *still in force; the Commission has proposed its repeal (COM (2014) 713)*

SCH/Com-ex (98) 10 - 21.4.1998—Cooperation between the Contracting Parties in returning aliens by air

  - *repealed by Directive 2003/110*

SCH/Com-ex (98) 12 - 21.4.1998—Exchange at local level of statistics on visas
  – *repealed by Schengen Visa Code*

SCH/Com-ex (98) 17 - 23.6.1998—Confidential nature of certain documents
  – *repealed by 2003 Council Decision ([2003] OJ L 5/78)*

SCH/Com-ex (98) 18 Rev - 23.6.1998—Measures to be taken in respect of countries posing problems with regard to the issue of documents required to remove their nationals from Schengen territory
  – *still in force; the Commission has proposed its repeal (COM (2014) 713)*

SCH/Com-ex (98) 19 - 23.6.1998—Monaco
  – *still in force*

SCH/Com-ex (98) 21 - 23.6.1998 - Stamping of passports of visa applicants
– *still in force; the Commission has proposed its repeal (COM (2014) 713)*

SCH/Com-ex (98) 26 def - 16.9.1998—Setting up of the Schengen implementing Convention Standing Committee
– *repealed by Reg 1053/2013*

SCH/Com-ex (98) 35 Rev 2 - 16.9.1998—Forwarding the Common Manual to EU applicant States
– *still in force*

SCH/Com-ex (98) 37 def 2 - 16.9.1998—Action plan to combat illegal immigration
– *still in force; the Commission has proposed its repeal (COM (2014) 713)*

SCH/Com-ex (98) 43 Rev - 16.12.1998—Ad hoc Committee for Greece Article 2 in conjunction with Annex to Schengen Protocol
– *still in force*

SCH/Com-ex (98) 49 Rev 3 - 16.12.1998—Bringing the Convention implementing the Schengen Agreement into force in Greece
– *still in force*

SCH/Com-ex (98) 53 Rev 2 - 16.12.1998—Harmonization of visa policy
– *repealed by Reg 539/2001*

SCH/Com-ex (98) 56 - 16.12.1998—Manual of documents to which a visa may be affixed
– *repealed by Decision ([2011] OJ L 287/9)*

SCH/Com-ex (98) 57 - 16.12.1998—Introduction of a harmonized form for invitations, proof of accommodation, and the acceptance of obligations of maintenance support
– *repealed by Schengen Visa Code*

SCH/Com-ex (98) 59 Rev - 16.12.1998—Coordinated deployment of document advisers
– *still in force; the Commission has proposed its repeal (COM (2014) 713)*

SCH/Com-ex (99) 13 - 28.4.1999—Withdrawal of old versions of the Common Manual and the Common Consular Instructions and Adoption of new versions
– *Common Manual repealed by Schengen Borders Code; CCI repealed by Visas Code*

SCH/Com-ex (99) 14 - 28.4.1999 - Manual of documents on which a visa may be affixed
– *repealed by Decision ([2011] OJ L 287/9)*

Decisions of the Central Group
SCH/C (98) 117 - 27.10.1998—Action plan to combat illegal immigration
– *still in force; the Commission has proposed to repeal this (COM (2014) 713)*

Bibliography

Acosta D, 'The Good, the Bad, and the Ugly in EU Migration Law' (2009) 11 EJML 19

Acosta D, *The Long-Term Residence Status as a Subsidiary Form of EU Citizenship* (Brill, 2011)

Albuquerque Abell N, 'The Compatibility of Readmission Agreements with the 1951 Convention Relating to the Status of Refugees' (1999) 11 IJRL 60

Allain J, 'The *jus cogens* Nature of *non-refoulement*' (2002) 4 IJRL 533

Andenas M and Turk V, eds., *Delegated Legislation and the Role of Committees in the EU* (Kluwer, 2000)

Askola H, *Legal Responses to Trafficking in Women for Sexual Exploitation in the European Union* (Hart, 2007)

Baldaccini A, *Asylum Support: A Practitioners' Guide to the EU Reception Directive* (Justice, 2005)

Baldaccini A, 'The Return and Removal of Irregular Migrants under EU Law: An Analysis of the Returns Directive' (2009) 11 EJML 1

Barrett G, 'Creation's Final Laws: The Impact of the Treaty of Lisbon on the "Final Provisions" of Earlier Treaties' (2008) 27 YEL 3

Battjes H, *European Asylum Law and International Law* (Martinus Nijhoff, 2006)

Bigo D and Carrera S, et al. (2012) 'Evaluating current and forthcoming proposals on JHA databases and a smart borders system at EU external borders', Study for the European Parliament

Boeles P, 'Schengen and the Rule of Law' in Meijers H, et al., eds., *Schengen: Internationalisation of Central Chapters of the Law on Aliens, Refugees, Privacy, Security and the Police*, 2nd edn (Stichting NJCM-Boekerij, 1992), 133

Boeles P, et al., *A New Immigration Law for Europe: The 1992 London and 1993 Copenhagen Rules on Immigration* (Standing Committee of Experts on Immigration, 1994)

Bouteillet-Paquet D, 'Passing the Buck: A Critical Analysis of the Readmission Policy Implemented by the European Union and its Member States' (2003) 5 EJML 359

Brinkmann G, 'Family Reunion, Third-Country Nationals and the Community's New Powers' in Guild E and Harlow C, eds., *Implementing Amsterdam: Immigration and Asylum Rights in EC Law* (Hart, 2001), 241

Brouwer E, 'Eurodac: Its Temptations and Limitations' (2002) 4 EJML 231

Bunyan T, ed., *Key Texts on Justice and Home Affairs in the European Union* (Statewatch, 1997)

Byrne R, 'Remedies of Limited Effect: Appeals under the Forthcoming Directive on EU Minimum Standards on Procedures' (2005) 7 EJML 71

Cholewinski R, 'The Protection of the Right of Economic Migrants to Family Reunion in Europe' (1994) 43 ICLQ 568

Cholewinski R, *Migrant Workers in International Human Rights Law* (OUP, 1997)

Cholewinski R, *Borders and Discrimination in the European Union* (ILPA/MPG, 2002)

Cholewinski R, 'Family Reunification and Conditions Placed on Family Members: Dismantling a Fundamental Human Right' (2002) 4 EJML 271

Cholewinski R, 'No Right of Entry: The Legal Regime on Crossing the EU External Border' in Guild E, Minderhoud P, and Groenendijk K, eds., *In Search of Europe's Borders* (Kluwer, 2003), 105

Cholewinski R, 'European Union Policy on Irregular Migration: Human Rights Lost?' in Bogusz B, et al., eds., *Irregular Migration and Human Rights* (Martinus Nijhoff, 2004), 159

Coleman N, '*Non-Refoulement* Revised. Renewed Review of the Status of *Non-refoulement* as Customary International Law' (2003) 5 EJML 23

Coleman N, *European Readmission Policy: Third Country Interests and Refugee Rights* (Martinus Nijhoff, 2009)

Costello C, 'The Asylum Procedures Directive and the Proliferation of Safe Third Countries Practices: Deterrence, Deflection and the Dismantling of International Protection?' (2005) 7 EJML 35

Costello C, 'The Asylum Procedures Directive in Legal Context: Equivocal Standards Meet General Principles' in Baldaccini A, Guild E, and Toner H, eds., *Whose Freedom, Security and Justice? EU Immigration and Asylum Law and Policy* (Hart, 2007), 151

Cremona M, 'The Completion of the Internal Market and the Incomplete Commercial Policy of the European Community' (1990) 15 ELRev 283

Curtin D, 'The Constitutional Structure of the Union: A Europe of Bits and Pieces' (1993) 30 CMLRev 17

Da Lomba S, *The Right to Seek Refugee Status in the European Union* (Intersentia, 2004)

de Witte B, 'Past and Future Role of the European Court of Justice in the Protection of Human Rights' in Alston P, ed., *The EU and Human Rights* (OUP, 1999), 859

Denza E, *The Intergovernmental Pillars of the European Union* (OUP, 2002)

Doerfel J, 'The Convention Against Torture and the Protection of Refugees' (2005) 24 RSQ 2:83

Donner J, 'Abolition of Border Controls' in Schermers H, et al., eds., *Free Movement of Persons in Europe: Legal Problems and Experiences* (Martinus Nijhoff, 1993), 55

ECRE, 'The EC Directive on the Reception of Asylum Seekers: Are Asylum Seekers in Europe Receiving Material Support and Access to Employment in Accordance with European Legislation?' November 2005

Eeckhout P, *EU External Relations Law*, 2nd edn (OUP, 2011)

Eicke T, 'Paradise Lost? Exclusion and Expulsion from the EU' in Guild E, Minderhoud P, and Groenendijk K, eds., *In Search of Europe's Borders* (Kluwer, 2003), 105 at 115–27

ELENA/ECRE, *The impact of the EU Qualification Directive on International Protection*, Oct 2008 (http://www.ecre.org/files/ECRE_QD_study_full.pdf)

Feller E, Turk V, and Nicholson F, eds., *Refugee Protection in International Law: UNHCR's Global Consultations on Refugee Protection* (CUP, 2003)

Gil-Bazo MT, 'Refugee Status and Subsidiary Protection under EC Law: The Qualification Directive and the Right to Be Granted Asylum' in Baldaccini A, Guild E, and, Toner H, eds., *Whose Freedom, Security and Justice? EU Immigration and Asylum Law and Policy* (Hart, 2007), 229

Goodwin-Gill G, 'Article 31 of the 1951 Convention Relating to the Status of Refugees: Non-Penalization, Detention and Protection' in Feller E, Turk V, and Nicholson F, eds., *Refugee Protection in International Law: UNHCR's Global Consultations on Refugee Protection* (CUP, 2003), 185

Goodwin-Gill G and McAdam J, *The Refugee in International Law*, 3rd edn (OUP, 2007)

Gortazar C, 'Abolishing Border Controls: Individual Rights and Common Control of EU External Borders' in Guild E and Harlow C, eds., *Implementing Amsterdam* (Hart, 2001), 121

Groenendijk K, 'New Borders Behind Old Ones: Post Schengen Controls Behind the Internal Borders—Inside the Netherlands and Germany' in Guild E, Minderhoud P, and Groenendijk K, eds., *In Search of Europe's Borders* (Kluwer, 2003), 131

Groenendijk K, 'Reinstatement of Controls at the Internal Borders of Europe: Why and Against Whom?' (2004) 10 ELJ 150

Guild E and Niessen J, *The Emerging Immigration and Asylum Law of the European Union* (Kluwer, 1996)

Guild E, *European Community Law from a Migrant's Perspective* (Kluwer, 2001)

Guild E, 'The Border Abroad—Visas and Border Controls' in Guild E, Minderhoud P, and Groenendijk K, eds., *In Search of Europe's Borders* (Kluwer, 2003), 87

Guild E, 'Who is an Irregular Migrant?' in Bogusz B, Cholewinski R, Cygan A, and Szyszczak E, eds., *Irregular Migration and Human Rights* (Martinus Nijhoff, 2004), 9

Guild E and Peers S, 'Out of the Ghetto? The Personal Scope of EU Law' in Peers S and Rogers N, eds., *EU Immigration and Asylum Law: Text and Commentary*, 1st edn (Martinus Nijhoff, 2006)

Guild E, Peers S, and Tomkin J, *The EU Citizenship Directive: A Commentary* (OUP, 2014), 81

Hailbronner K, 'Visa Regulations and Third-Country Nationals in EC Law' (1994) 31 CMLRev 969–95

Hailbronner K, 'Migration Law and Policy Within the Third Pillar of the European Union' in Bieber R and Monar J, eds., *Justice and Home Affairs in the European Union* (European University Press, 1995), 231

Hailbronner K, 'European Immigration and Asylum Law after the Amsterdam Treaty' (1998) 35 CMLRev 1047

Hailbronner K and Thiery C, 'Schengen II and Dublin: Responsibility for Asylum Applications in Europe' (1997) 34 CMLRev 957

Handoll J, 'Directive 2003/9 on Recepton Conditions of Asylum Seekers: Ensuring "Mere Subsistence" or a "Dignified Standard of Living"?' in Baldaccini A, Guild E, and Toner H, eds., *Whose Freedom, Security and Justice? EU Immigration and Asylum Law and Policy* (Hart, 2007), 195

Harvey C, 'Promoting Insecurity: Public Order, Expulsion and the European Convention on Human Rights' in Guild E and Minderhoud P, eds., *Security of Residence and Expulsion: Protection of Aliens in Europe* (Kluwer, 2001), 41

Hathaway J, *The Rights of Refugees under International Law* (CUP, 2005)

Hayes B and Vermeulen M, 'Borderline: Assessing the Costs and Fundamental Rights Implications of Eurosur and the Smart Borders' proposals, online at: <http://www.statewatch.org/news/2012/jun/borderline.pdf>

Haynes D, 'Used, Abused, Arrested and Deported: Extending Immigration Benefits to Protect the Victims of Trafficking and to Secure the Prosecution of Traffickers' (2004) 26 HRQ 221

Hedemann-Robinson M, 'Third-Country Nationals, European Union Citizenship and Free Movement of Persons: A Time for Bridges rather than Divisions?' (1996) 16 YEL 321

Hedemann-Robinson M, 'From Object to Subject? Non-EC Nationals and the Draft Proposal of the Commission for a Council Act Establishing the Rules for Admission of Third-Country Nationals to the Member States' (1998) 18 YEL 289

Hughes J and Liebaut F, eds., *Detention of Asylum-Seekers in Europe: Analysis and Perspectives* (Martinus Nijhoff, 1998)

Hurwitz A, 'The 1990 Dublin Convention: A Comprehensive Assessment' (1999) IJRL 646

Ingelse C, *The UN Committee Against Torture: An Assessment* (Kluwer, 2001)

Jileva E, 'Insiders and Outsiders in Central and Eastern Europe: The Case of Bulgaria' in Guild E, Minderhoud P, and Groenendijk K, eds., *In Search of Europe's Borders* (Kluwer, 2003), 273

Joerges C and Vos E, eds., *EU Committees: Social Regulation, Law and Politics* (Hart, 1999)

Joseph S, Schultz J, and Castan M, *The International Covenant on Civil and Political Rights: Cases, Materials and Commentary*, 2nd edn (OUP, 2004)

Justice Report, *The Schengen Information System: A Human Rights Audit* (Justice, 2000)

Kerber K, 'The Temporary Protection Directive' (2002) 4 EJML 193

Klabbers J, *Treaty Conflict and the European Union* (CUP, 2009)

Lambert H, 'The European Court of Human Rights and the Right of Refugees and Other Persons in Need of Protection to Family Reunion' (1999) 11 IJRL 427

Lambert H, 'Protection Against Refoulement from Europe: Human Rights Law comes to the Rescue' (1999) 48 ICLQ 515

Lambert H, 'The European Convention on Human Rights and the Protection of Refugees: Limits and Opportunities' (2005) 24:2 RSQ 39

Lauterpacht E and Bethlehem D, 'The Scope and Content of the Principle of *Non-Refoulement*: An Opinion' in Feller E, Turk V, and Nicholson F, eds., *Refugee Protection in International Law: UNHCR's Global Consultations on Refugee Protection* (CUP, 2003), 87

Legomsky S, 'Secondary Refugee Movements and the Return of Asylum Seekers to Third Countries: The Meaning of Effective Protection' (2003) 15 IJRL 567 at 673

Lenaerts K and Verhoeven J, 'Towards a Legal Framework for Executive Rule-Making in the EU? The Contribution of the New Comitology Decision' (2000) 37 CMLRev 645

McAdam J, 'The European Union Qualification Directive: The Creation of a Subsidiary Protection Regime' (2005) 17 IJRL 461

McMahon R, 'Maastricht's Third Pillar: Load-Bearing or Purely Decorative?' (1995) 22 LIEI 1:51

Marin J and O'Connell J, 'The European Convention and the Relative Rights of Resident Aliens' (1999) 5 ELJ 4

Marinho C, ed., *The Dublin Convention on Asylum* (EIPA, 2000)

Martenczuk B and van Thiel S, eds., *Justice, Liberty, Security: New Challenges for EU External Relations* (VUB Press, 2008)

Monar J, 'Justice and Home Affairs in the Treaty of Amsterdam: Reform at the Price of Fragmentation' (1998) 23 ELRev 320

Moreno-Lax V, 'Dismantling the Dublin System: *M.S.S. v Belgium and Greece*' (2012) 14 EJML 1

Muller-Graff P, 'The Legal Bases of the Third Pillar and its Position in the Framework of the Union Treaty' (1994) 29 CMLRev 493

Nicol A, 'From Dublin Convention to Dublin Regulation: A Progressive Move?' in Baldaccini A, Guild E, and Toner H, eds., *Whose Freedom, Security and Justice? EU Immigration and Asylum Law and Policy* (Hart, 2007), 265

Noll G, 'Visions of the Exceptional: Legal and Theoretical Issues Raised by Transit Processing Centers and Reception Zones' (2003) 5 EJML 303

O'Keeffe D, 'The Schengen Convention: A Suitable Model for European Integration?' (1991) 11 YEL 185

Papagianni G, *Institutional and Policy Dynamics of EU Migration Law* (Martinus Nijhoff, 2006)

Peers S, 'Equality, Free Movement and Social Security' (1997) 22 ELRev 342

Peers S, 'Border in Channel: Continent Cut Off' (1998) 19 JSWFL 108

Peers S, 'Building Fortress Europe: The Development of EU Migration Law' (1998) 35 CMLRev 1235

Peers S, 'Raising Minimum Standards or Racing to the Bottom? The Commission's Proposed Migration Convention' in Guild E, ed., *The Legal Framework and Social Consequences of Free Movement of Persons in the European Union* (Kluwer, 1999), 149

Peers S, 'Social Security Equality for Turkish Nationals' (1999) 24 EL Rev 627

Peers S, '*Caveat Emptor*? Integrating the Schengen *Acquis* into the European Union Legal Order' (2000) 2 CYELS 87

Peers S, 'The EC-Switzerland Agreement on Free Movement of Persons: Overview and Analysis' (2000) 2 EJML 127

Peers S, 'The New Regulation on Access to Documents: A Critical Analysis' (2001–02) 21 YEL 385

Peers S, 'EU Immigration and Asylum Law after Seville' (2002) 16 IANL Journal 176

Peers S, Case Note on Joined Cases C-95/99 to 98/99 *Khalil and others* and C-180/99 *Addou* [2001] ECR I-7413, (2002) 39 CMLRev 1395

Peers S, 'EU Borders and Globalisation' in Guild E, Minderhoud P, and Groenendijk K, eds., *In Search of Europe's Borders* (Kluwer, 2003), 45

Peers S, 'The European Court of Justice and the European Court of Human Rights: Comparative Approaches' in Orucu E, ed., *Judicial Comparativism in Human Rights Cases* (UKNCCL, 2003), 107

Peers S, 'EU Immigration and Asylum Law: Internal Market Model or Human Rights Model?' in Tridimas T and Nebbia P, eds., *EU Law for the Twenty-First Century: Rethinking the New Legal Order*, vol. 1 (Hart, 2004), 345

Peers S, 'Family Reunion and Community Law' in Walker N, ed., *Towards an Area of Freedom, Security and Justice* (OUP, 2004), 143

Peers S, 'Irregular Immigration and EU External Relations' in Bogusz B, et al., eds., *Irregular Migration and Human Rights* (Martinus Nijhoff, 2004), 193

Peers S, 'Civil and Political Rights: The Role of an EU Human Rights Agency' in Alston P and De Schutter O, eds., *Monitoring Fundamental Rights in the EU: The Contribution of the Fundamental Rights Agency* (Hart, 2005), 111

Peers S, 'EC Law on Family Members of Persons Seeking or Receiving International Protection' in Shah P, ed., *The Challenge of Asylum to Legal Systems* (Cavendish, 2005), 83

Peers S, 'Human Rights, Asylum and European Community Law' (2005) 24 RSQ 2:24

Peers S, 'EU Immigration and Asylum Competence and Decision-Making in the Treaty of Lisbon' (2008) 10 EJML 219

Peers S, 'EU Migration Law and Association Agreements' in Martenczuk B and van Thiel S, eds., *Justice, Liberty, Security: New Challenges for EU External Relations* (VUBPress, 2008), 53

Peers S, 'In a World of Their Own? Justice and Home Affairs Opt-Outs and the Treaty of Lisbon' (2008–09) 10 CYELS 383

Peers S, 'EC Immigration Law and EC Association Agreements: Fragmentation or Integration?' (2009) 34 ELRev 628

Peers S, 'Transfer of International Protection and European Union Law' (2012) 24 IJRL 527

Peers S, 'The EU's Accession to the ECHR: The Dream Becomes a Nightmare' (2015)16 GLJ 213–22

Peers S, Hervey T, Kenner J, and Ward A, eds., *Commentary on the EU Charter of Fundamental Rights* (Hart, 2014)

Peers S, Moreno Lax V, Garlick M, Guild E, Acosta D, Groenendijk K, and Tomkin J, *EU Immigration and Asylum Law: Text and Commentary*, 2nd edn (Brill, 3 vols: 2012, 2015)

Peers S and Rogers N, *EU Immigration and Asylum Law: Text and Commentary*, 1st edn (Martinus Nijhoff, 2006)

Piotrowicz R and van Eck C, 'Subsidiary Protection and Primary Rights' (2004) 53 ICLQ 107

Rosas A, 'The European Union and International Human Rights Instruments' in Kronenberger V, ed., *The EU and the International Legal Order: Discord or Harmony?* (Asser Press, 2001), 277

Schutte J, 'Schengen: Its Meaning for the Free Movement of Persons in Europe' (1991) 28 CMLRev 549

Steenbergen J, 'Schengen and the Movement of Persons' in Meijers H, et al., *Schengen: Internationalisation of Central Chapters of the Law on Aliens, Refugees, Privacy, Security and the Police*, 2nd edn (Stichting NJCM-Boekerij, 1992), 87

Storey H, 'The Right to Family Life and Immigration Case Law at Strasbourg' (1990) 39 ICLQ 329

Thym D, 'Schengen Law: A Challenge for Legal Accountability in the European Union' (2002) 8 ELJ 218

Timmermans C, 'Free Movement of Persons and the Division of Powers Between the Community and its Member States: Why do it the Intergovernmental Way?' in Schermers H, et al., eds., *Free Movement of Persons in Europe: Legal Problems and Experiences* (Martinus Nijhoff, 1993), 352

Tridimas T, *The General Principles of EU Law*, 2nd edn (OUP, 2006)

UNHCR, *Asylum in the European Union, A study on the implementation of the Qualification Directive*, Nov 2007 (http://www.unhcr.org/cgi-bin/texis/vtx/refworld/rwmain?docid=4730506 32&page=search)

UNHCR, *Improving Asylum Procedures: Comparative Analysis and Recommendations for Law and Practice* (UNHCR, 2010)

van Dijk J, 'Protection of "Integrated" Aliens against Expulsion under the European Convention on Human Rights' in Guild E and Minderhoud P, eds., *Security of Residence and Expulsion: Protection of Aliens in Europe* (Kluwer, 2001), 23

Vanheule D, van Selm J, and Boswell C (2011), *The Implications of Article 80 TFEU on the principle of solidarity and fair sharing of responsibility, including its financial implications, between the Member States in the field of border checks, asylum and immigration*, Study for the European Parliament's Committee on Civil Liberties, Justice and Home Affairs

Verschueren H, 'EC Social Security Coordination Excluding Third-Country Nationals: Still in Line with Fundamental Rights After the *Gaygusuz* Judgment?' (1997) 24 CMLRev 991

Wilsher D, 'Detention of Asylum-Seekers and Refugees and International Human Rights Law' in Shah P, ed., *The Challenge of Asylum to Legal Systems* (Cavendish, 2005), 145

Zwaan K, ed., *The Qualification Directive: Central Themes, Problem Issues, and Implementation in Selected Member States* (Wolf Legal Publishers, 2007)

Zwaan K, ed., *The Asylum Procedures Directive: Central Themes, Problem Issues, and Implementation in Selected Member States* (Wolf Legal Publishers, 2008)

Index